The Poetry and Prose of William Blake

THE POETRY AND PROSE OF

William Blake

EDITED BY

David V. Erdman

COMMENTARY BY

Harold Bloom

DOUBLEDAY & COMPANY, INC., GARDEN CITY, NEW YORK

Fourth Printing, with Revisions, 1970

CREDITS ON ILLUSTRATIONS

1. *America,* Plate 10, from the Rosenwald Collection
2. The Last Judgment, from the Petworth Collection
3. The Laocoön. Reproduced from an impression in
   the collection of Sir Geoffrey Keynes
4. Blake's Autograph, from the album of William Upcott
   in the Berg Collection, The New York Public Library

LIBRARY OF CONGRESS CATALOG CARD NUMBER 65–19918
COPYRIGHT © 1965 BY DAVID V. ERDMAN AND HAROLD BLOOM
ALL RIGHTS RESERVED
PRINTED IN THE UNITED STATES OF AMERICA

Acknowledgments

This new text of Blake's writings is in large part an outgrowth of six years of labor over perfecting a text for the Cornell University *Concordance to the Poetry and Prose of William Blake*, which may appear almost simultaneously with the present work. The editor is particularly indebted to his collaborators in this project, G. E. Bentley, Jr., Palmer Brown, Robert F. Gleckner, George M. Harper, Karl Kiralis, Martin K. Nurmi, Richard J. Wolfe, and Paul M. Zall, to the general editor of the concordance series, Stephen M. Parrish, and to the presiding spirit over all Blake textual study, Geoffrey Keynes.

For generous help and encouragement both of us are grateful to Ruth Aldrich, F. W. Bateson, John Beer, Morchard Bishop, Anthony Blunt, Edward E. Bostetter, Fredson Bowers, Martin Butlin, S. Foster Damon, Robert Carl Elliott, William Elton, Martha Winburn England, Wendy Erdman, Alvin Feinman, the late Peter F. Fisher, John Fleming, Anne Freedgood, Northrop Frye, George Goyder, John E. Grant, Jean Hagstrum, Geoffrey Hartman, Robert Hewetson, Désirée Hirst, John Hollander, Arthur Hudd, Anne T. Kostelanetz, Margot Kriel, Lewis and Heidi Lichterman, Paul Miner, Kerrison Preston, Martin Price, David H. Stam, W. H. Stevenson, Irene Tayler, Craig Thompson, Michael J. Tolley, Willis Van Devanter, and Lucyle Werkmeister; also to Marcia Allentuck, Margaret Manners, Ellie Thompson, Marvin Sadick, and William Coakley.

For their co-operation and courtesy in allowing original manuscripts or illuminated works to be consulted and photographed we are greatly obliged to the owners and curators indicated in the notes on sources, in particular Frederick B. Adams, Jr., Lady Cunliffe and the late Lord Rolf Cunliffe, David Foxon, John D. Gordan, Esther Harvey, the late William A. Jackson, Geoffrey Keynes, William H. McCarthy, Paul Mellon, Kerrison Preston, Landon K. Thorne, Charles J. Rosenbloom, Lessing J. Rosenwald, Lord Rothschild, T. C. Skeat, Lewis M. Stark, Willis Van Devanter, and Marjorie Wynne.

Contents

CONTENTS

CONTENTS

CONTENTS

CONTENTS

Illustrations

Preface

This edition of William Blake seeks to supply a sounder and more uncluttered text for reading than has been heretofore available, with a full apparatus of variant and deleted passages for study. Many of these deleted passages are printed here for the first time and allow us a comprehensive view of Blake as a reviser of his own poetry. Readers and students of Blake, with this text before them, confront an accurate and well-nigh complete collection—some erasures continue to defy transcription—of the writings of one of the greatest of English poets, and certainly one of the most original, and most relevant to us now.

The writings Blake issued in etched Illuminated Printing are given first, as the major canon of his Songs, Prophecies, and Tractates. The unpublished long poems follow, and then the lesser works, predominantly in verse, from *Poetical Sketches* to *The Everlasting Gospel.* Lyrics that were omitted from the illuminated canon are brought together as "Songs and Ballads," with a further group of "Satiric Verses and Epigrams." The late prose treatises are followed by the marginalia, other miscellaneous prose, and a selection of the twenty-three most important letters. Verses occurring in the Reynolds marginalia and in the letters have not been disturbed.

Within these groups a rough chronology is observed, but only when thematic or generic relations fail to offer more meaningful groupings. A definitive chronological sequence of Blake's writings is impossible from present knowledge.

Lines in the longer poems are here numbered by relatively small units, usually page or plate, since no standard numbering that suits a diplomatic text has been established. The numbering of plates for *Jerusalem,* which varies in Chapter II, is that of the British Museum, Rinder, and Morgan copies. Night VIIa of *The Four Zoas* is taken as a replacement of the earlier VIIb, which is printed as an appendix following Night IX.

The Textual Notes at the end of the book are exhaustive for the poetry, and the designation of first, second, and later readings will permit reconstruction of first and subsequent drafts. For the prose, however, deletions and insertions of any substance have been retained in the body of the text, distinguished by appropriate bracketing; trivial deletions and mendings have been ignored.

Sources of the text are indicated at the head of each group or subdivision of the notes, and problems of dating are discussed. For a more detailed account of editorial aims and procedures, see the introductory section of the Textual Notes.

The critical Commentary following these is an attempt to aid the student and reader of Blake in overcoming the initial difficulties that Blake's poetical canon frequently presents. The Commentary covers all Blake's most important works in Illuminated Printing, with the single exception of *Songs of Innocence and Experience* for which a wealth of criticism is available elsewhere. In addition it covers the early printed volume, *Poetical Sketches*, and two of the poems left in manuscript, *Tiriel* and *The Four Zoas*, as well as *The French Revolution*, preserved in proof sheet. Except in regard to the lyrics, the Commentary therefore aims at being a comprehensive and detailed guide to the reading of Blake's poetry. Only what are judged to be the most crucial of Blake's literary allusions and historical references are noted. The emphasis throughout, particularly in the notes to Blake's epics—*The Four Zoas, Milton,* and *Jerusalem*—is on the resolution of apparent problems in continuity and poetic unity.

SYMBOLS

Superior letters call attention to textual notes ᵗ or commentary ᵉ. Italics within square brackets [*thus*] indicate words or letters deleted or erased or written over. Matter in Roman type within square brackets [thus] is supplied by the editor. Angle brackets <thus> enclose words or letters written to replace deletions, or as additions, not including words written immediately following and in the same ink or pencil as deleted matter. For the poetry, however, all these details are relegated to the Textual Notes except for the few emendations necessary to avoid lacunae.

CHANGES IN THE FOURTH PRINTING

Some misprints have been corrected, on pages 408, 453, 499, and in J5:27 and J37:29. Blake's own corrections of punctuation in *Poetical Sketches* have been supplied on pages 413–415 and 434, thanks to M. C. Phillips. The "Shepherd" songs have been brought into conformity with the ms. The apparatus of variants has been amplified on pages 716 and 736. And after another look at the ms of *The Four Zoas* I have corrected the transcript of its 4th page (297–298) and corrected "binding" to "bending" in 90:30 and "Sons" to "Son" in 104:24.

Emendations have been made, duly bracketed, in J42:47, J43:28, J55:20, and FZ 42:18, at suggestions by W. H. Stevenson and Joanne Witke. Robert Kolker noted that "Dryden" should replace "Pope" on page 630. Donald Moore, reinterpreting the ms evidence, has led me to revise my account of the variants and offshoots of "Infant Sorrow" on Notebook pages 113, 111, 106 (see 720–721, 769, 770). With critical help from G. E. Bentley, Jr., I have corrected and tightened the dating of Blake's script (see my notes and his in the *Blake Newsletter*, June and Sept., 1969). I had misread the evidence for an idiosyncratic "g" in June 1805; it is now clear that its last use was ca November 1802 and that a return to the conventional "g" occurred by March 1804 (see pages 714, 722, 726, 730, 734, 738).

I have removed speculation from the caption of Plate 1, now convinced (by John E. Grant) that the picture more immediately illustrates the text of *America* (Orc mocking Urizen) than the concluding lines of *Europe*. And, returning to what I once knew but had forgotten, I have corrected the sequence of states of "Our End is Come" (page 660).   (D.V.E.)

The Poetry and Prose of William Blake

I

THERE is NO Natural Religion   t,c

The Author & Printer W Blake   t

[a]

The Argument.   Man has no notion of moral fitness but from Education. Naturally he is only a natural organ subject to Sense.

I   Man cannot naturally Percieve. but through his natural or bodily organs.

II   Man by his reasoning power. can only compare & judge of what he has already perciev'd.

III   From a perception of only 3 senses or 3 elements none could deduce a fourth or fifth

IV   None could have other than natural or organic thoughts if he had none but organic perceptions

V   Mans desires are limited by his perceptions. none can desire what he has not perciev'd

VI   The desires & perceptions of man untaught by any thing but organs of sense, must be limited to objects of sense.

Conclusion.   If it were not for the Poetic or Prophetic character the Philosophic & Experimental would soon be at the ratio of all things, & stand still unable to do other than repeat the same dull round over again

❧

THERE is NO Natural Religion

t,c

[b]

I Mans perceptions are not bounded by organs of perception. he percieves more than sense (tho' ever so acute) can discover.

II Reason or the ratio of all we have already known. is not the same that it shall be when we know more.

[III lacking]

IV The bounded is loathed by its possessor. The same dull round even of a univer[s]e would soon become a mill with complicated wheels

V If the many become the same as the few when possess'd, More! More! is the cry of a mistaken soul, less than All cannot satisfy Man.

VI If any could desire what he is incapable of possessing, despair must be his eternal lot.

VII The desire of Man being Infinite the possession is Infinite & himself Infinite

Application.   He who sees the Infinite in all things sees God. He who sees the Ratio only sees himself only.

Therefore God becomes as we are, that we may be as he is

❧

ALL RELIGIONS are ONE

t,c

The Voice of one crying in the Wilderness

The Argument.   As the true method of knowledge is experiment the true faculty of knowing must be the faculty which experiences. This faculty I treat of.

PRINCIPLE 1st That the Poetic Genius is the true Man. and that the body or outward form of Man is derived from the Poetic Genius. Likewise that the forms of all things are derived from their Genius. which by the Ancients was call'd an Angel & Spirit & Demon.

PRINCIPLE 2d As all men are alike in outward form, So (and with the same infinite variety) all are alike in the Poetic Genius

PRINCIPLE 3d No man can think write or speak from his heart, but he must intend truth. Thus all sects of Philosophy are from the Poetic Genius adapted to the weaknesses of every individual

PRINCIPLE 4. As none by travelling over known lands can find out the unknown. So from already acquired knowledge Man could not acquire more. therefore an universal Poetic Genius exists

PRINCIPLE. 5. The Religeons of all Nations are derived from each Nation's different reception of the Poetic Genius which is every where call'd the Spirit of Prophecy.

PRINCIPLE 6 The Jewish & Christian Testaments are An original derivation from the confined nature of
bodily sensation
PRINCIPLE 7th As all men are alike (tho' infinitely various) So all Religions & as all similars have one source.
The true Man is the source he being the Poetic Genius

 ~

THE BOOK of THEL

t,c

The Author & Printer Willm Blake, 1789.

PLATE i

THEL'S Motto,

c

Does the Eagle know what is in the pit?
Or wilt thou go ask the Mole:
Can Wisdom be put in a silver rod?
Or Love in a golden bowl?

PLATE I

THEL

I

The daughters of Mne Seraphim led round their sunny flocks,   t,c
All but the youngest. she in paleness sought the secret air.
To fade away like morning beauty from her mortal day:
Down by the river of Adona her soft voice is heard:
And thus her gentle lamentation falls like morning dew.   5

O life of this our spring! why fades the lotus of the water?
Why fade these children of the spring? born but to smile & fall.
Ah! Thel is like a watry bow, and like a parting cloud,
Like a reflection in a glass. like shadows in the water.
Like dreams of infants. like a smile upon an infants face,   10
Like the doves voice, like transient day, like music in the air;
Ah! gentle may I lay me down, and gentle rest my head.
And gentle sleep the sleep of death. and gentle hear the voice
Of him that walketh in the garden in the evening time.   c

The Lilly of the valley breathing in the humble grass   15
Answer'd the lovely maid and said; I am a watry weed,
And I am very small, and love to dwell in lowly vales;
So weak, the gilded butterfly scarce perches on my head
Yet I am visited from heaven and he that smiles on all.

Walks in the valley. and each morn over me spreads his hand   20
Saying, rejoice thou humble grass, thou new-born lilly flower,
Thou gentle maid of silent valleys. and of modest brooks;
For thou shalt be clothed in light, and fed with morning manna:
Till summers heat melts thee beside the fountains and the springs
To flourish in eternal vales: then why should Thel complain,   25
PLATE 2
Why should the mistress of the vales of Har, utter a sigh.

She ceasd & smild in tears, then sat down in her silver shrine.

Thel answerd. O thou little virgin of the peaceful valley.
Giving to those that cannot crave, the voiceless, the o'ertired.
Thy breath doth nourish the innocent lamb, he smells thy milky
    garments,   5
He crops thy flowers. while thou sittest smiling in his face,
Wiping his mild and meekin mouth from all contagious taints.
Thy wine doth purify the golden honey, thy perfume,
Which thou dost scatter on every little blade of grass that springs
Revives the milked cow, & tames the fire-breathing steed.   10
But Thel is like a faint cloud kindled at the rising sun:
I vanish from my pearly throne, and who shall find my place.

Queen of the vales the Lilly answerd, ask the tender cloud,
And it shall tell thee why it glitters in the morning sky,
And why it scatters its bright beauty thro' the humid air.   15
Descend O little cloud & hover before the eyes of Thel.

The Cloud descended, and the Lilly bowd her modest head:
And went to mind her numerous charge among the verdant grass.

PLATE 3

II

O little Cloud the virgin said, I charge thee tell to me,
Why thou complainest not when in one hour thou fade away:
Then we shall seek thee but not find; ah Thel is like to Thee.
I pass away. yet I complain, and no one hears my voice.

The Cloud then shew'd his golden head & his bright form emerg'd,   5
Hovering and glittering on the air before the face of Thel.

O virgin know'st thou not. our steeds drink of the golden springs
Where Luvah doth renew his horses: look'st thou on my youth,   e
And fearest thou because I vanish and am seen no more.
Nothing remains; O maid I tell thee, when I pass away,   10
It is to tenfold life, to love, to peace, and raptures holy:
Unseen descending, weigh my light wings upon balmy flowers;
And court the fair eyed dew. to take me to her shining tent;
The weeping virgin, trembling kneels before the risen sun,
Till we arise link'd in a golden band, and never part;   15
But walk united, bearing food to all our tender flowers

Dost thou O little Cloud? I fear that I am not like thee;
For I walk through the vales of Har. and smell the sweetest flowers;
But I feed not the little flowers: I hear the warbling birds,
But I feed not the warbling birds. they fly and seek their food;   20
But Thel delights in these no more because I fade away,
And all shall say, without a use this shining woman liv'd,
Or did she only live. to be at death the food of worms.

The Cloud reclind upon his airy throne and answer'd thus.

Then if thou art the food of worms. O virgin of the skies,   25
How great thy use. how great thy blessing; every thing that lives,
Lives not alone, nor for itself: fear not and I will call
The weak worm from its lowly bed, and thou shalt hear its voice.
Come forth worm of the silent valley, to thy pensive queen.

The helpless worm arose, and sat upon the Lillys leaf,   30
And the bright Cloud saild on, to find his partner in the vale.

PLATE 4
III.

Then Thel astonish'd view'd the Worm upon its dewy bed.   c

Art thou a Worm? image of weakness. art thou but a Worm?
I see thee like an infant wrapped in the Lillys leaf:
Ah weep not little voice, thou can'st not speak. but thou can'st weep;
Is this a Worm? I see thee lay helpless & naked: weeping,   5
And none to answer, none to cherish thee with mothers smiles.

The Clod of Clay heard the Worms voice, & raisd her pitying head;
She bow'd over the weeping infant, and her life exhal'd
In milky fondness, then on Thel she fix'd her humble eyes.

O beauty of the vales of Har. we live not for ourselves,   10
Thou seest me the meanest thing, and so I am indeed;
My bosom of itself is cold. and of itself is dark,
PLATE 5
But he that loves the lowly, pours his oil upon my head.
And kisses me, and binds his nuptial bands around my breast,
And says; Thou mother of my children, I have loved thee.
And I have given thee a crown that none can take away
But how this is sweet maid, I know not, and I cannot know,   5
I ponder, and I cannot ponder; yet I live and love.

The daughter of beauty wip'd her pitying tears with her white veil,
And said. Alas! I knew not this, and therefore did I weep:
That God would love a Worm I knew, and punish the evil foot
That wilful, bruis'd its helpless form: but that he cherish'd it   10
With milk and oil. I never knew; and therefore did I weep,
And I complaind in the mild air, because I fade away,
And lay me down in thy cold bed, and leave my shining lot.

Queen of the vales, the matron Clay answerd; I heard thy sighs.   e
And all thy moans flew o'er my roof. but I have call'd them down: 15
Wilt thou O Queen enter my house. 'tis given thee to enter,
And to return; fear nothing. enter with thy virgin feet.

PLATE 6

IV.   e

The eternal gates terrific porter lifted the northern bar:
Thel enter'd in & saw the secrets of the land unknown;
She saw the couches of the dead, & where the fibrous roots
Of every heart on earth infixes deep its restless twists:
A land of sorrows & of tears where never smile was seen.   5

She wanderd in the land of clouds thro' valleys dark, listning
Dolours & lamentations: waiting oft beside a dewy grave
She stood in silence. listning to the voices of the ground,
Till to her own grave plot she came, & there she sat down.
And heard this voice of sorrow breathed from the hollow pit.   10

Why cannot the Ear be closed to its own destruction?
Or the glistning Eye to the poison of a smile!
Why are Eyelids stord with arrows ready drawn,
Where a thousand fighting men in ambush lie?
Or an Eye of gifts & graces, show'ring fruits & coined gold!   15
Why a Tongue impress'd with honey from every wind?
Why an Ear, a whirlpool fierce to draw creations in?
Why a Nostril wide inhaling terror trembling & affright
Why a tender curb upon the youthful burning boy!   t
Why a little curtain of flesh on the bed of our desire?   20

The Virgin started from her seat, & with a shriek.
Fled back unhinderd till she came into the vales of Har

The End

❧

SONGS Of *INNOCENCE* and Of *EXPERIENCE*

Shewing the Two Contrary States of the Human Soul   t

SONGS of INNOCENCE
1789
The Author & Printer   W Blake

Introduction

Piping down the valleys wild
Piping songs of pleasant glee
On a cloud I saw a child.
And he laughing said to me.

Pipe a song about a Lamb;   5
So I piped with merry chear,
Piper pipe that song again—
So I piped, he wept to hear.

Drop thy pipe thy happy pipe
Sing thy songs of happy chear,   10
So I sung the same again
While he wept with joy to hear

Piper sit thee down and write
In a book that all may read—
So he vanish'd from my sight.   15
And I pluck'd a hollow reed.

And I made a rural pen,
And I stain'd the water clear,
And I wrote my happy songs
Every child may joy to hear   20

The Shepherd.

How sweet is the Shepherds sweet lot,
From the morn to the evening he strays:
He shall follow his sheep all the day
And his tongue shall be filled with praise.

For he hears the lambs innocent call,   5
And he hears the ewes tender reply,
He is watchful while they are in peace,
For they know when their Shepherd is nigh.

The Ecchoing Green

The Sun does arise,
And make happy the skies.
The merry bells ring
To welcome the Spring.
The sky-lark and thrush,   *5*
The birds of the bush,
Sing louder around,
To the bells chearful sound.
While our sports shall be seen
On the Ecchoing Green.   *10*

Old John with white hair
Does laugh away care,
Sitting under the oak,
Among the old folk,
They laugh at our play,   *15*
And soon they all say.
Such such were the joys.
When we all girls & boys,
In our youth-time were seen,
On the Ecchoing Green.   *20*

Till the little ones weary
No more can be merry
The sun does descend,
And our sports have an end:
Round the laps of their mothers,   *25*
Many sisters and brothers,
Like birds in their nest,
Are ready for rest;
And sport no more seen,
On the darkening Green.   *30*

The Lamb

Little Lamb who made thee
Dost thou know who made thee
Gave thee life & bid thee feed.
By the stream & o'er the mead;
Gave thee clothing of delight,   *5*
Softest clothing wooly bright;
Gave thee such a tender voice,
Making all the vales rejoice!
Little Lamb who made thee
Dost thou know who made thee   *10*

Little Lamb I'll tell thee,
Little Lamb I'll tell thee!
He is called by thy name,
For he calls himself a Lamb:
He is meek & he is mild,   15
He became a little child:
I a child & thou a lamb,
We are called by his name.
   Little Lamb God bless thee.
   Little Lamb God bless thee.   20

The Little Black Boy.

My mother bore me in the southern wild,
And I am black, but O! my soul is white;
White as an angel is the English child:
But I am black as if bereav'd of light.

My mother taught me underneath a tree   5
And sitting down before the heat of day,
She took me on her lap and kissed me,
And pointing to the east began to say.

Look on the rising sun: there God does live
And gives his light, and gives his heat away.   10
And flowers and trees and beasts and men recieve
Comfort in morning joy in the noon day.

And we are put on earth a little space,
That we may learn to bear the beams of love,
And these black bodies and this sun-burnt face   15
Is but a cloud, and like a shady grove.

For when our souls have learn'd the heat to bear
The cloud will vanish we shall hear his voice.
Saying: come out from the grove my love & care,
And round my golden tent like lambs rejoice.   20

Thus did my mother say and kissed me,
And thus I say to little English boy.
When I from black and he from white cloud free,
And round the tent of God like lambs we joy:

Ill shade him from the heat till he can bear,   25
To lean in joy upon our fathers knee.
And then I'll stand and stroke his silver hair,
And be like him and he will then love me.

The Blossom.

Merry Merry Sparrow
Under leaves so green
A happy Blossom
Sees you swift as arrow
Seek your cradle narrow   5
Near my Bosom.

Pretty Pretty Robin
Under leaves so green
A happy Blossom
Hears you sobbing sobbing   10
Pretty Pretty Robin
Near my Bosom.

The Chimney Sweeper

When my mother died I was very young,
And my father sold me while yet my tongue,
Could scarcely cry weep weep weep weep.   t
So your chimneys I sweep & in soot I sleep.

Theres little Tom Dacre, who cried when his head   5
That curl'd like a lambs back, was shav'd, so I said.
Hush Tom never mind it, for when your head's bare,
You know that the soot cannot spoil your white hair.

And so he was quiet, & that very night,
As Tom was a sleeping he had such a sight,   10
That thousands of sweepers Dick, Joe Ned & Jack
Were all of them lock'd up in coffins of black

And by came an Angel who had a bright key,
And he open'd the coffins & set them all free.
Then down a green plain leaping laughing they run   15
And wash in a river and shine in the Sun.

Then naked & white, all their bags left behind,
They rise upon clouds, and sport in the wind.
And the Angel told Tom if he'd be a good boy,
He'd have God for his father & never want joy.   20

And so Tom awoke and we rose in the dark
And got with our bags & our brushes to work.
Tho' the morning was cold, Tom was happy & warm,
So if all do their duty, they need not fear harm.

The Little Boy lost

Father, father, where are you going
O do not walk so fast.
Speak father, speak to your little boy
Or else I shall be lost,

The night was dark no father was there   5
The child was wet with dew.
The mire was deep, & the child did weep
And away the vapour flew.

The Little Boy Found

The little boy lost in the lonely fen,
Led by the wand'ring light,
Began to cry, but God ever nigh,
Appeard like his father in white.

He kissed the child & by the hand led   5
And to his mother brought,
Who in sorrow pale, thro' the lonely dale
Her little boy weeping sought.

Laughing Song,

When the green woods laugh, with the voice of joy
And the dimpling stream runs laughing by,
When the air does laugh with our merry wit,
And the green hill laughs with the noise of it.

When the meadows laugh with lively green   5
And the grasshopper laughs in the merry scene,
When Mary and Susan and Emily,
With their sweet round mouths sing Ha, Ha, He.

When the painted birds laugh in the shade
Where our table with cherries and nuts is spread   10
Come live & be merry and join with me,
To sing the sweet chorus of Ha, Ha, He.

A CRADLE SONG

Sweet dreams form a shade,
O'er my lovely infants head.
Sweet dreams of pleasant streams,
By happy silent moony beams.

Sweet sleep with soft down,
Weave thy brows an infant crown.
Sweet sleep Angel mild,
Hover o'er my happy child.

Sweet smiles in the night,
Hover over my delight.
Sweet smiles Mothers smiles
All the livelong night beguiles.

Sweet moans, dovelike sighs,
Chase not slumber from thy eyes.
Sweet moans, sweeter smiles,
All the dovelike moans beguiles.

Sleep sleep happy child.
All creation slept and smil'd.
Sleep sleep, happy sleep,
While o'er thee thy mother weep.

Sweet babe in thy face,
Holy image I can trace.
Sweet babe once like thee,
Thy maker lay and wept for me

Wept for me for thee for all,
When he was an infant small.
Thou his image ever see,
Heavenly face that smiles on thee.

Smiles on thee on me on all,
Who became an infant small,
Infant smiles are his own smiles.
Heaven & earth to peace beguiles.

The Divine Image.

To Mercy Pity Peace and Love,
All pray in their distress:
And to these virtues of delight
Return their thankfulness.

For Mercy Pity Peace and Love,
Is God our father dear:
And Mercy Pity Peace and Love,
Is Man his child and care.

For Mercy has a human heart
Pity, a human face:
And Love, the human form divine,
And Peace, the human dress.

Then every man of every clime,
That prays in his distress,
Prays to the human form divine   15
Love Mercy Pity Peace.

And all must love the human form,
In heathen, turk or jew.
Where Mercy, Love & Pity dwell
There God is dwelling too.   20

HOLY THURSDAY

Twas on a Holy Thursday their innocent faces clean
The children walking two & two in red & blue & green
Grey headed beadles walkd before with wands as white as snow
Till into the high dome of Pauls they like Thames waters flow

O what a multitude they seemd these flowers of London town   5
Seated in companies they sit with radiance all their own
The hum of multitudes was there but multitudes of lambs
Thousands of little boys & girls raising their innocent hands

Now like a mighty wind they raise to heaven the voice of song
Or like harmonious thunderings the seats of heaven among   10
Beneath them sit the aged men wise guardians of the poor
Then cherish pity, lest you drive an angel from your door

Night.

The sun descending in the west
The evening star does shine.
The birds are silent in their nest,
And I must seek for mine,
The moon like a flower,   5
In heavens high bower;
With silent delight,
Sits and smiles on the night.

Farewell green fields and happy groves,
Where flocks have took delight;   10
Where lambs have nibbled, silent moves
The feet of angels bright;
Unseen they pour blessing,
And joy without ceasing,
On each bud and blossom,   15
And each sleeping bosom.

They look in every thoughtless nest,
Where birds are coverd warm;
They visit caves of every beast,
To keep them all from harm;   20
If they see any weeping,
That should have been sleeping
They pour sleep on their head
And sit down by their bed.

When wolves and tygers howl for prey   25
They pitying stand and weep;
Seeking to drive their thirst away,
And keep them from the sheep.
But if they rush dreadful;
The angels most heedful,   30
Recieve each mild spirit,
New worlds to inherit.

And there the lions ruddy eyes,
Shall flow with tears of gold:
And pitying the tender cries,   35
And walking round the fold:
Saying: wrath by his meekness
And by his health, sickness,
Is driven away,
From our immortal day.   40

And now beside thee bleating lamb,
I can lie down and sleep;
Or think on him who bore thy name,
Grase after thee and weep.   t
For wash'd in lifes river,   45
My bright mane for ever,
Shall shine like the gold,
As I guard o'er the fold.

Spring

Sound the Flute!
Now it's mute.
Birds delight
Day and Night.
Nightingale   5

In the dale
Lark in Sky
Merrily
Merrily Merrily to welcome in the Year

Little Boy   10
Full of joy.
Little Girl
Sweet and small,
Cock does crow
So do you.   15
Merry voice
Infant noise
Merrily Merrily to welcome in the Year

Little Lamb
Here I am,   20
Come and lick
My white neck.
Let me pull
Your soft Wool.
Let me kiss   25
Your soft face.
Merrily Merrily we welcome in the Year

Nurse's Song   t

When the voices of children are heard on the green   t
And laughing is heard on the hill,   t
My heart is at rest within my breast
And every thing else is still

Then come home my children, the sun is gone down   5
And the dews of night arise
Come come leave off play, and let us away
Till the morning appears in the skies

No no let us play, for it is yet day
And we cannot go to sleep   t 10
Besides in the sky, the little birds fly   t
And the hills are all coverd with sheep

Well well go & play till the light fades away
And then go home to bed
The little ones leaped & shouted & laugh'd   15
And all the hills ecchoed

Infant Joy

I have no name
I am but two days old.—
What shall I call thee?
I happy am
Joy is my name,—   5
Sweet joy befall thee!

Pretty joy!
Sweet joy but two days old.
Sweet joy I call thee:
Thou dost smile.   10
I sing the while
Sweet joy befall thee.

A Dream

Once a dream did weave a shade,
O'er my Angel-guarded bed,
That an Emmet lost it's way
Where on grass methought I lay.

Troubled wilderd and folorn   5
Dark benighted travel-worn,
Over many a tangled spray
All heart-broke I heard her say.

O my children! do they cry
Do they hear their father sigh.   10
Now they look abroad to see,
Now return and weep for me.

Pitying I drop'd a tear:
But I saw a glow-worm near:
Who replied. What wailing wight   15
Calls the watchman of the night.

I am set to light the ground,
While the beetle goes his round:
Follow now the beetles hum,
Little wanderer hie thee home.   20

On Anothers Sorrow

Can I see anothers woe,
And not be in sorrow too.
Can I see anothers grief,
And not seek for kind relief.

Can I see a falling tear,   5
And not feel my sorrows share,
Can a father see his child,
Weep, nor be with sorrow fill'd.

Can a mother sit and hear,
An infant groan an infant fear—   10
No no never can it be.
Never never can it be.

And can he who smiles on all
Hear the wren with sorrows small,
Hear the small birds grief & care   15
Hear the woes that infants bear—

And not sit beside the nest
Pouring pity in their breast,
And not sit the cradle near
Weeping tear on infants tear.   20

And not sit both night & day,
Wiping all our tears away.
O! no never can it be.
Never never can it be.

He doth give his joy to all.   25
He becomes an infant small.
He becomes a man of woe
He doth feel the sorrow too.

Think not, thou canst sigh a sigh,
And thy maker is not by.   30
Think not, thou canst weep a tear,
And thy maker is not near.

O! he gives to us his joy,
That our grief he may destroy
Till our grief is fled & gone   35
He doth sit by us and moan

SONGS of Experience

1794

The Author & Printer W Blake

t

Introduction.

Hear the voice of the Bard!
Who Present, Past, & Future sees
Whose ears have heard,
The Holy Word,
That walk'd among the ancient trees.⠀⠀⠀⠀*5*

Calling the lapsed Soul
And weeping in the evening dew;
That might controll,
The starry pole;
And fallen fallen light renew!⠀⠀⠀⠀*10*

O Earth O Earth return!
Arise from out the dewy grass;
Night is worn,
And the morn
Rises from the slumberous mass.⠀⠀⠀⠀*15*

Turn away no more:
Why wilt thou turn away
The starry floor
The watry shore
Is giv'n thee till the break of day.⠀⠀⠀⠀20

EARTH'S Answer

t

Earth rais'd up her head,
From the darkness dread & drear.
Her light fled:⠀⠀⠀⠀⠀⠀⠀⠀⠀⠀t
Stony dread!
And her locks cover'd with grey despair.⠀⠀⠀⠀*5*

Prison'd on watry shore
Starry Jealousy does keep my den⠀⠀⠀⠀⠀t
Cold and hoar
Weeping o'er
I hear the Father of the ancient men⠀⠀⠀⠀t *10*

Selfish father of men⠀⠀⠀⠀⠀⠀⠀⠀⠀⠀t
Cruel jealous selfish fear⠀⠀⠀⠀⠀⠀⠀t
Can delight

Chain'd in night   t
The virgins of youth and morning bear.   15

Does spring hide its joy   t
When buds and blossoms grow?
Does the sower?   t
Sow by night?
Or the plowman in darkness plow?   20

Break this heavy chain,
That does freeze my bones around   t
Selfish! vain,
Eternal bane!   t
That free Love with bondage bound.   25

The CLOD & the PEBBLE   t

Love seeketh not Itself to please,
Nor for itself hath any care;
But for another gives its ease,
And builds a Heaven in Hells despair.

     So sang a little Clod of Clay,   t 5
     Trodden with the cattles feet:
     But a Pebble of the brook,
     Warbled out these metres meet.

Love seeketh only Self to please,
To bind another to its delight;   10
Joys in anothers loss of ease,
And builds a Hell in Heavens despite.

HOLY THURSDAY   t

Is this a holy thing to see,
In a rich and fruitful land,
Babes reducd to misery,
Fed with cold and usurous hand?

Is that trembling cry a song?   5
Can it be a song of joy?
And so many children poor?   t
It is a land of poverty!   t

And their sun does never shine.
And their fields are bleak & bare.   10
And their ways are fill'd with thorns.
It is eternal winter there.   t

For where-e'er the sun does shine,   t
And where-e'er the rain does fall: t
Babe can never hunger there,   15
Nor poverty the mind appall.

The Little Girl Lost   t

In futurity
I prophetic see,
That the earth from sleep,
(Grave the sentence deep)

Shall arise and seek   5
For her maker meek:
And the desart wild
Become a garden mild.

In the southern clime,
Where the summers prime,   10
Never fades away;
Lovely Lyca lay.

Seven summers old
Lovely Lyca told,
She had wanderd long,   15
Hearing wild birds song.

Sweet sleep come to me
Underneath this tree;
Do father, mother weep.—
"Where can Lyca sleep".   20

Lost in desart wild
Is your little child.
How can Lyca sleep,
If her mother weep.

If her heart does ake,   25
Then let Lyca wake;
If my mother sleep,
Lyca shall not weep.

Frowning frowning night,
O'er this desart bright,   30
Let thy moon arise,
While I close my eyes.

Sleeping Lyca lay;
While the beasts of prey,

Come from caverns deep,   35
View'd the maid asleep

The kingly lion stood
And the virgin view'd,
Then he gambold round
O'er the hallowd ground: 40

Leopards, tygers play,
Round her as she lay;
While the lion old,
Bow'd his mane of gold.

And her bosom lick,   45
And upon her neck,
From his eyes of flame,
Ruby tears there came;

While the lioness,
Loos'd her slender dress,   50
And naked they convey'd
To caves the sleeping maid.

The Little Girl Found

All the night in woe
Lyca's parents go:
Over vallies deep,
While the desarts weep.

Tired and woe-begone,   5
Hoarse with making moan:
Arm in arm seven days,
They trac'd the desart ways.

Seven nights they sleep,
Among shadows deep: 10
And dream they see their child
Starv'd in desert wild.

Pale thro pathless ways
The fancied image strays,
Famish'd, weeping, weak   15
With hollow piteous shriek

Rising from unrest,
The trembling woman prest,
With feet of weary woe;
She could no further go.   20

In his arms he bore,
Her arm'd with sorrow sore;
Till before their way,
A couching lion lay.

Turning back was vain,   25
Soon his heavy mane,
Bore them to the ground;
Then he stalk'd around,

Smelling to his prey.
But their fears allay,   30
When he licks their hands;
And silent by them stands.

They look upon his eyes
Fill'd with deep surprise:
And wondering behold,   35
A spirit arm'd in gold.

On his head a crown
On his shoulders down,
Flow'd his golden hair.
Gone was all their care.   40

Follow me he said,
Weep not for the maid;
In my palace deep,
Lyca lies asleep.

Then they followed,   45
Where the vision led:
And saw their sleeping child,
Among tygers wild.

To this day they dwell
In a lonely dell   50
Nor fear the wolvish howl,
Nor the lions growl.

THE Chimney Sweeper   t

A little black thing among the snow:
Crying weep, weep, in notes of woe!   t
Where are thy father & mother? say?
They are both gone up to the church to pray.

Because I was happy upon the heath,   5
And smil'd among the winters snow: t

— 22 —

They clothed me in the clothes of death,
And taught me to sing the notes of woe.

And because I am happy, & dance & sing,
They think they have done me no injury: 10
And are gone to praise God & his Priest & King   t
Who make up a heaven of our misery.

NURSES Song   t

When the voices of children, are heard on the green
And whisprings are in the dale:
The days of my youth rise fresh in my mind,   t
My face turns green and pale.

Then come home my children, the sun is gone down   5
And the dews of night arise
Your spring & your day, are wasted in play
And your winter and night in disguise.

The SICK ROSE   t

O Rose thou art sick.
The invisible worm,
That flies in the night
In the howling storm:

Has found out thy bed   t 5
Of crimson joy: t
And his dark secret love   t
Does thy life destroy.

THE FLY.   t

Little Fly
Thy summers play,   t
My thoughtless hand   t
Has brush'd away.   t

Am not I   5
A fly like thee?
Or art not thou
A man like me?

For I dance
And drink & sing;   10
Till some blind hand
Shall brush my wing.

If thought is life   t
And strength & breath;
And the want   t 15
Of thought is death;

Then am I
A happy fly,
If I live,
Or if I die.   20

The Angel   t

I Dreamt a Dream! what can it mean?
And that I was a maiden Queen:
Guarded by an Angel mild;
Witless woe, was ne'er beguil'd!

And I wept both night and day   5
And he wip'd my tears away
And I wept both day and night
And hid from him my hearts delight

So he took his wings and fled:
Then the morn blush'd rosy red: 10
I dried my tears & armd my fears,
With ten thousand shields and spears.

Soon my Angel came again:
I was arm'd, he came in vain:
For the time of youth was fled   t 15
And grey hairs were on my head.

The Tyger   t

Tyger Tyger, burning bright,
In the forests of the night;
What immortal hand or eye,   t
Could frame thy fearful symmetry?   t

In what distant deeps or skies   t 5
Burnt the fire of thine eyes!   t
On what wings dare he aspire?   t
What the hand, dare sieze the fire?

And what shoulder, & what art,
Could twist the sinews of thy heart? 10
And when thy heart began to beat,
What dread hand? & what dread feet?   t

What the hammer? what the chain,
In what furnace was thy brain?
What the anvil? what dread grasp, ^t 15
Dare its deadly terrors clasp?

When the stars threw down their spears
And water'd heaven with their tears:
Did he smile his work to see?
Did he who made the Lamb make thee? ^t 20

Tyger, Tyger burning bright,
In the forests of the night:
What immortal hand or eye,
Dare frame thy fearful symmetry?

My Pretty ROSE TREE

A flower was offerd to me;
Such a flower as May never bore.
But I said I've a Pretty Rose-tree,
And I passed the sweet flower o'er.

Then I went to my Pretty Rose-tree; 5
To tend her by day and by night.
But my Rose turnd away with jealousy:
And her thorns were my only delight.

AH! SUN-FLOWER

Ah Sun-flower! weary of time,
Who countest the steps of the Sun:
Seeking after that sweet golden clime
Where the travellers journey is done.

Where the Youth pined away with desire, 5
And the pale Virgin shrouded in snow:
Arise from their graves and aspire,
Where my Sun-flower wishes to go.

THE LILLY

The modest Rose puts forth a thorn:
The humble Sheep, a threatning horn:
While the Lilly white, shall in Love delight,
Nor a thorn nor a threat stain her beauty bright

—25—

The GARDEN of LOVE   t

I went to the Garden of Love,
And saw what I never had seen: t
A Chapel was built in the midst,   t
Where I used to play on the green.

And the gates of this Chapel were shut,   t 5
And Thou shalt not. writ over the door;
So I turn'd to the Garden of Love,
That so many sweet flowers bore,

And I saw it was filled with graves,
And tomb-stones where flowers should be: 10
And Priests in black gowns, were walking their rounds,
And binding with briars, my joys & desires.

The Little Vagabond   t

Dear Mother, dear Mother, the Church is cold.
But the Ale-house is healthy & pleasant & warm;
Besides I can tell where I am use'd well,   t
Such usage in heaven will never do well.   t

But if at the Church they would give us some Ale.   5
And a pleasant fire, our souls to regale;
We'd sing and we'd pray, all the live-long day;
Nor ever once wish from the Church to stray,

Then the Parson might preach & drink & sing.
And we'd be as happy as birds in the spring: 10
And modest dame Lurch, who is always at Church,
Wou'ld not have bandy children nor fasting nor birch.

And God like a father rejoicing to see,   t
His children as pleasant and happy as he:
Would have no more quarrel with the Devil or the Barrel   15
But kiss him & give him both drink and apparel.   t

LONDON   t

I wander thro' each charter'd street,   t
Near where the charter'd Thames does flow.   t
And mark in every face I meet   t
Marks of weakness, marks of woe.

In every cry of every Man,   5
In every Infants cry of fear,   t
In every voice: in every ban,   t
The mind-forg'd manacles I hear   t

How the Chimney-sweepers cry   t
Every blackning Church appalls,   t 10
And the hapless Soldiers sigh,
Runs in blood down Palace walls

But most thro' midnight streets I hear   t
How the youthful Harlots curse
Blasts the new-born Infants tear   15
And blights with plagues the Marriage hearse

The Human Abstract.   t

Pity would be no more,   t
If we did not make somebody Poor: t
And Mercy no more could be,
If all were as happy as we;

And mutual fear brings peace;   5
Till the selfish loves increase.
Then Cruelty knits a snare,
And spreads his baits with care.   t

He sits down with holy fears,
And waters the ground with tears: 10
Then Humility takes its root
Underneath his foot.

Soon spreads the dismal shade
Of Mystery over his head;
And the Catterpiller and Fly,   15
Feed on the Mystery.

And it bears the fruit of Deceit,
Ruddy and sweet to eat;
And the Raven his nest has made
In its thickest shade.   20

The Gods of the earth and sea,
Sought thro' Nature to find this Tree
But their search was all in vain:
There grows one in the Human Brain   t

INFANT SORROW

My mother groand! my father wept.
Into the dangerous world I leapt:
Helpless, naked, piping loud;
Like a fiend hid in a cloud.

Struggling in my fathers hands: 5
Striving against my swadling bands:
Bound and weary I thought best
To sulk upon my mothers breast.

A POISON TREE.

I was angry with my friend;
I told my wrath, my wrath did end.
I was angry with my foe:
I told it not, my wrath did grow.

And I waterd it in fears,   5
Night & morning with my tears:
And I sunned it with smiles,
And with soft deceitful wiles.

And it grew both day and night.
Till it bore an apple bright.   10
And my foe beheld it shine.
And he knew that it was mine.

And into my garden stole,
When the night had veild the pole;
In the morning glad I see;   15
My foe outstretchd beneath the tree.

A Little BOY Lost

Nought loves another as itself
Nor venerates another so.
Nor is it possible to Thought
A greater than itself to know:

And Father, how can I love you,   5
Or any of my brothers more?
I love you like the little bird
That picks up crumbs around the door.

The Priest sat by and heard the child.
In trembling zeal he siez'd his hair: 10
He led him by his little coat:
And all admir'd the Priestly care.

-28-

And standing on the altar high,   t
Lo what a fiend is here! said he:
One who sets reason up for judge   15
Of our most holy Mystery.

The weeping child could not be heard.
The weeping parents wept in vain:
They strip'd him to his little shirt.   t
And bound him in an iron chain.   t 20

And burn'd him in a holy place,   t
Where many had been burn'd before:
The weeping parents wept in vain.
Are such things done on Albions shore.   t

A Little GIRL Lost

Children of the future Age,
Reading this indignant page:
Know that in a former time,
Love! sweet Love! was thought a crime.

In the Age of Gold,   5
Free from winters cold:
Youth and maiden bright,
To the holy light,
Naked in the sunny beams delight.

Once a youthful pair   10
Fill'd with softest care:
Met in garden bright,
Where the holy light,
Had just removd the curtains of the night.

There in rising day,   15
On the grass they play:
Parents were afar:
Strangers came not near:
And the maiden soon forgot her fear.

Tired with kisses sweet   20
They agree to meet,
When the silent sleep
Waves o'er heavens deep;
And the weary tired wanderers weep.

To her father white   25
Came the maiden bright:
But his loving look,
Like the holy book,
All her tender limbs with terror shook.

Ona! pale and weak!
To thy father speak:
O the trembling fear!
O the dismal care!
That shakes the blossoms of my hoary hair

To Tirzah

Whate'er is Born of Mortal Birth,
Must be consumed with the Earth
To rise from Generation free;
Then what have I to do with thee?

The Sexes sprung from Shame & Pride
Blow'd in the morn: in evening died
But Mercy changd Death into Sleep;
The Sexes rose to work & weep.

Thou Mother of my Mortal part
With cruelty didst mould my Heart,
And with false self-decieving tears,
Didst bind my Nostrils Eyes & Ears.

Didst close my Tongue in senseless clay
And me to Mortal Life betray:
The Death of Jesus set me free,
Then what have I to do with thee?

The School Boy   t

I love to rise in a summer morn,
When the birds sing on every tree;
The distant huntsman winds his horn,
And the sky-lark sings with me.
O! what sweet company.   5

But to go to school in a summer morn
O! it drives all joy away;
Under a cruel eye outworn,
The little ones spend the day,
In sighing and dismay.   10

Ah! then at times I drooping sit,
And spend many an anxious hour.
Nor in my book can I take delight,
Nor sit in learnings bower,
Worn thro' with the dreary shower   15

How can the bird that is born for joy,
Sit in a cage and sing.
How can a child when fears annoy,
But droop his tender wing,
And forget his youthful spring.   20

O! father & mother, if buds are nip'd,
And blossoms blown away,
And if the tender plants are strip'd
Of their joy in the springing day,
By sorrow and cares dismay,   25

How shall the summer arise in joy
Or the summer fruits appear
Or how shall we gather what griefs destroy
Or bless the mellowing year,
When the blasts of winter appear.   30

The Voice of the Ancient Bard.   t

Youth of delight come hither:
And see the opening morn,
Image of truth new born
Doubt is fled & clouds of reason
Dark disputes & artful teazing.   5
Folly is an endless maze,
Tangled roots perplex her ways,

How many have fallen there!
They stumble all night over bones of the dead;
And feel they know not what but care;   *10*
And wish to lead others when they should be led.

A DIVINE IMAGE   t

[A rejected Song of Experience]

Cruelty has a Human Heart
And Jealousy a Human Face
Terror, the Human Form Divine
And Secrecy, the Human Dress

The Human Dress, is forged Iron   *5*
The Human Form, a fiery Forge.
The Human Face, a Furnace seal'd
The Human Heart, its hungry Gorge.

FOR CHILDREN
THE GATES of PARADISE   t

1793

Published by W Blake N⁰ 13 Hercules Buildings Lambeth
and J. Johnson Sᵗ Pauls' Church Yard

Frontispiece   What is Man!
1   I found him beneath a Tree   t
2   Water   t
3   Earth   t
4   Air   t
5   Fire   t
6   At length for hatching ripe he breaks the shell.   t
7   Alas!   t
8   My Son! my Son!   t
9   I want! I want!   t
10 Help! Help!   t
11 Aged Ignorance   t

12 Does thy God O Priest take such vengeance as this?   t
13 Fear & Hope are—Vision   t
14 The Traveller hasteth in the Evening   t
15 Death's Door   t
16 I have said to the Worm, Thou art my mother & my sister   t

[The Emblems accompanying these legends are reproduced with the later version, *For the Sexes The Gates of Paradise*, page 256.]

❧

THE *MARRIAGE* of HEAVEN and HELL   ^{t,c}

PLATE 2

The Argument.   c

Rintrah roars & shakes his fires in the burdend air;
Hungry clouds swag on the deep

Once meek, and in a perilous path,
The just man kept his course along
The vale of death.   5
Roses are planted where thorns grow.
And on the barren heath
Sing the honey bees.

Then the perilous path was planted:
And a river, and a spring   10
On every cliff and tomb;
And on the bleached bones
Red clay brought forth.

Till the villain left the paths of ease,
To walk in perilous paths, and drive   15
The just man into barren climes.

Now the sneaking serpent walks
In mild humility.
And the just man rages in the wilds
Where lions roam.   20

Rintrah roars & shakes his fires in the burdend air;
Hungry clouds swag on the deep.

PLATE 3

As a new heaven is begun, and it is now thirty-three years since its   t,c
advent: the Eternal Hell revives. And lo! Swedenborg is the Angel sitting at the tomb; his writings are the linen clothes folded up. Now is the
dominion of Edom, & the return of Adam into Paradise; see Isaiah
xxxiv & XXXV Chap:

Without Contraries is no progression. Attraction and Repulsion,
Reason and Energy, Love and Hate, are necessary to Human existence.

From these contraries spring what the religious call Good & Evil. Good
is the passive that obeys Reason[.] Evil is the active springing from
Energy.

Good is Heaven. Evil is Hell.

PLATE 4

The voice of the Devil   c

All Bibles or sacred codes. have been the causes of the following Errors.

1. That Man has two real existing principles Viz: a Body & a Soul.
2. That Energy. calld Evil. is alone from the Body. & that Reason.
calld Good. is alone from the Soul.
3. That God will torment Man in Eternity for following his Energies.

But the following Contraries to these are True

1 Man has no Body distinct from his Soul for that calld Body is a
portion of Soul discernd by the five Senses, the chief inlets of Soul in
this age

2 Energy is the only life and is from the Body and Reason is the
bound or outward circumference of Energy.

3 Energy is Eternal Delight

PLATE 5   c

Those who restrain desire, do so because theirs is weak enough to be
restrained; and the restrainer or reason usurps its place & governs the unwilling.

And being restraind it by degrees becomes passive till it is only the
shadow of desire.

The history of this is written in Paradise Lost. & the Governor or Reason is call'd Messiah.

And the original Archangel or possessor of the command of the heavenly host, is calld the Devil or Satan and his children are call'd Sin &
Death

But in the Book of Job Miltons Messiah is call'd Satan.

For this history has been adopted by both parties

It indeed appear'd to Reason as if Desire was cast out, but the Devils
account is, that the Messi[PL 6]ah fell. & formed a heaven of what he
stole from the Abyss

This is shewn in the Gospel, where he prays to the Father to send the comforter or Desire that Reason may have Ideas to build on, the Jehovah of the Bible being no other than he, who dwells in flaming fire. Know that after Christs death, he became Jehovah.

But in Milton; the Father is Destiny, the Son, a Ratio of the five senses. & the Holy-ghost, Vacuum!

Note. The reason Milton wrote in fetters when he wrote of Angels & God, and at liberty when of Devils & Hell, is because he was a true Poet and of the Devils party without knowing it

A Memorable Fancy.

As I was walking among the fires of hell, delighted with the enjoyments of Genius; which to Angels look like torment and insanity. I collected some of their Proverbs: thinking that as the sayings used in a nation, mark its character, so the Proverbs of Hell, shew the nature of Infernal wisdom better than any description of buildings or garments.

When I came home; on the abyss of the five senses, where a flat sided steep frowns over the present world. I saw a mighty Devil folded in black clouds, hovering on the sides of the rock, with cor[PL 7]roding fires he wrote the following sentence now percieved by the minds of men, & read by them on earth.

> How do you know but ev'ry Bird that cuts the airy way,
> Is an immense world of delight, clos'd by your senses five?

Proverbs of Hell.

In seed time learn, in harvest teach, in winter enjoy.
Drive your cart and your plow over the bones of the dead.
The road of excess leads to the palace of wisdom.
Prudence is a rich ugly old maid courted by Incapacity.
He who desires but acts not, breeds pestilence.
The cut worm forgives the plow.
Dip him in the river who loves water.
A fool sees not the same tree that a wise man sees.
He whose face gives no light, shall never become a star.
Eternity is in love with the productions of time.
The busy bee has no time for sorrow.
The hours of folly are measur'd by the clock, but of wisdom: no clock can measure.
All wholsom food is caught without a net or a trap.
Bring out number weight & measure in a year of dearth.
No bird soars too high. if he soars with his own wings.
A dead body. revenges not injuries.
The most sublime act is to set another before you.

If the fool would persist in his folly he would become wise
Folly is the cloke of knavery.
Shame is Prides cloke.   20

PLATE 8
Prisons are built with stones of Law, Brothels with bricks of Religion.
The pride of the peacock is the glory of God.
The lust of the goat is the bounty of God.
The wrath of the lion is the wisdom of God.
The nakedness of woman is the work of God.   25
Excess of sorrow laughs. Excess of joy weeps.
The roaring of lions, the howling of wolves, the raging of the stormy
     sea, and the destructive sword. are portions of eternity too great for
     the eye of man.
The fox condemns the trap, not himself.
Joys impregnate. Sorrows bring forth.
Let man wear the fell of the lion. woman the fleece of the sheep.   30
The bird a nest, the spider a web, man friendship.
The selfish smiling fool. & the sullen frowning fool. shall be both
     thought wise. that they may be a rod.
What is now proved was once, only imagin'd.
The rat, the mouse, the fox, the rabbet; watch the roots, the lion, the
     tyger, the horse, the elephant, watch the fruits.
The cistern contains: the fountain overflows   35
One thought. fills immensity.
Always be ready to speak your mind, and a base man will avoid you.
Every thing possible to be believ'd is an image of truth.
The eagle never lost so much time. as when he submitted to learn of
     the crow.

PLATE 9
The fox provides for himself. but God provides for the lion.   40
Think in the morning, Act in the noon, Eat in the evening, Sleep in the
     night.
He who has sufferd you to impose on him knows you.
As the plow follows words, so God rewards prayers.
The tygers of wrath are wiser than the horses of instruction
Expect poison from the standing water.   45
You never know what is enough unless you know what is more than
     enough.
Listen to the fools reproach! it is a kingly title!
The eyes of fire, the nostrils of air, the mouth of water, the beard of
     earth.
The weak in courage is strong in cunning.
The apple tree never asks the beech how he shall grow, nor the lion. the   50
     horse, how he shall take his prey.
The thankful reciever bears a plentiful harvest.
If others had not been foolish, we should be so.
The soul of sweet delight, can never be defil'd,   c

When thou seest an Eagle, thou seest a portion of Genius. lift up thy
  head!
As the catterpiller chooses the fairest leaves to lay her eggs on, so the   55
  priest lays his curse on the fairest joys.
To create a little flower is the labour of ages.
Damn. braces: Bless relaxes.
The best wine is the oldest. the best water the newest.
Prayers plow not! Praises reap not!
Joys laugh not! Sorrows weep not!   60

PLATE 10

The head Sublime, the heart Pathos, the genitals Beauty, the hands &
  feet Proportion.
As the air to a bird or the sea to a fish, so is contempt to the contempt-
  ible.
The crow wish'd every thing was black, the owl, that every thing was
  white.
Exuberance is Beauty.
If the lion was advise'd by the fox. he would be cunning.   65
Improve[me]nt makes strait roads, but the crooked roads without
  Improvement, are roads of Genius.
Sooner murder an infant in its cradle than nurse unacted desires
Where man is not nature is barren.
Truth can never be told so as to be understood, and not be believ'd.
              Enough! or Too much   70

PLATE 11   c

  The ancient Poets animated all sensible objects with Gods or Ge-
niuses, calling them by the names and adorning them with the properties of woods, rivers, mountains, lakes, cities, nations, and whatever
their enlarged & numerous senses could percieve.
  And particularly they studied the genius of each city & country. placing it under its mental deity.
  Till a system was formed, which some took advantage of & enslav'd
the vulgar by attempting to realize or abstract the mental deities from
their objects; thus began Priesthood.
  Choosing forms of worship from poetic tales.
  And at length they pronouncd that the Gods had orderd such things.
  Thus men forgot that All deities reside in the human breast.

PLATE 12   c

A Memorable Fancy.

  The Prophets Isaiah and Ezekiel dined with me, and I asked them
how they dared so roundly to assert. that God spake to them; and
whether they did not think at the time, that they would be misunderstood, & so be the cause of imposition.

Isaiah answer'd. I saw no God, nor heard any, in a finite organical perception; but my senses discover'd the infinite in every thing, and as I was then perswaded, & remain confirm'd; that the voice of honest indignation is the voice of God, I cared not for consequences but wrote.

Then I asked: does a firm perswasion that a thing is so, make it so?

He replied. All poets believe that it does, & in ages of imagination this firm perswasion removed mountains; but many are not capable of a firm perswasion of any thing.

Then Ezekiel said. The philosophy of the east taught the first principles of human perception some nations held one principle for the origin & some another, we of Israel taught that the Poetic Genius (as you now call it) was the first principle and all the others merely derivative, which was the cause of our despising the Priests & Philosophers of other countries, and prophecying that all Gods [PL 13] would at last be proved to originate in ours & to be the tributaries of the Poetic Genius, it was this. that our great poet King David desired so fervently & invokes so patheticly, saying by this he conquers enemies & governs kingdoms; and we so loved our God. that we cursed in his name all the deities of surrounding nations, and asserted that they had rebelled; from these opinions the vulgar came to think that all nations would at last be subject to the jews.

This said he, like all firm perswasions, is come to pass, for all nations believe the jews code and worship the jews god, and what greater subjection can be

I heard this with some wonder, & must confess my own conviction. After dinner I ask'd Isaiah to favour the world with his lost works, he said none of equal value was lost. Ezekiel said the same of his.

I also asked Isaiah what made him go naked and barefoot three years? he answerd, the same that made our friend Diogenes the Grecian.

I then asked Ezekiel. why he eat dung, & lay so long on his right & left side? he answerd. the desire of raising other men into a perception of the infinite this the North American tribes practise. & is he honest who resists his genius or conscience. only for the sake of present ease or gratification?

PLATE 14

The ancient tradition that the world will be consumed in fire at the c
end of six thousand years is true. as I have heard from Hell.

For the cherub with his flaming sword is hereby commanded to leave his guard at tree of life, and when he does, the whole creation will be consumed, and appear infinite. and holy whereas it now appears finite & corrupt.

This will come to pass by an improvement of sensual enjoyment.

But first the notion that man has a body distinct from his soul, is to be expunged; this I shall do, by printing in the infernal method, by corrosives, which in Hell are salutary and medicinal, melting apparent surfaces away, and displaying the infinite which was hid.

If the doors of perception were cleansed every thing would appear to man as it is, infinite.

For man has closed himself up, till he sees all things thro' narrow chinks of his cavern.

PLATE 15

A Memorable Fancy

I was in a Printing house in Hell & saw the method in which knowledge is transmitted from generation to generation.

In the first chamber was a Dragon-Man, clearing away the rubbish from a caves mouth; within, a number of Dragons were hollowing the cave,

In the second chamber was a Viper folding round the rock & the cave, and others adorning it with gold silver and precious stones.

In the third chamber was an Eagle with wings and feathers of air, he caused the inside of the cave to be infinite, around were numbers of Eagle like men, who built palaces in the immense cliffs.

In the fourth chamber were Lions of flaming fire raging around & melting the metals into living fluids.

In the fifth chamber were Unnam'd forms, which cast the metals into the expanse.

There they were reciev'd by Men who occupied the sixth chamber, and took the forms of books & were arranged in libraries.

PLATE 16

The Giants who formed this world into its sensual existence and now seem to live in it in chains, are in truth. the causes of its life & the sources of all activity, but the chains are, the cunning of weak and tame minds. which have power to resist energy, according to the proverb, the weak in courage is strong in cunning.

Thus one portion of being, is the Prolific. the other, the Devouring: to the devourer it seems as if the producer was in his chains, but it is not so, he only takes portions of existence and fancies that the whole.

But the Prolific would cease to be Prolific unless the Devourer as a sea recieved the excess of his delights.

Some will say, Is not God alone the Prolific? I answer, God only Acts & Is, in existing beings or Men.

These two classes of men are always upon earth, & they should be enemies; whoever tries [PL 17] to reconcile them seeks to destroy existence.

Religion is an endeavour to reconcile the two.

Note. Jesus Christ did not wish to unite but to seperate them, as in the Parable of sheep and goats! & he says I came not to send Peace but a Sword.

Messiah or Satan or Tempter was formerly thought to be one of the Antediluvians who are our Energies.

A Memorable Fancy

c

An Angel came to me and said O pitiable foolish young man! O horrible! O dreadful state! consider the hot burning dungeon thou art preparing for thyself to all eternity, to which thou art going in such career.

I said, perhaps you will be willing to shew me my eternal lot & we will contemplate together upon it and see whether your lot or mine is most desirable

So he took me thro' a stable & thro' a church & down into the church vault at the end of which was a mill: thro' the mill we went, and came to a cave. down the winding cavern we groped our tedious way till a void boundless as a nether sky appeard beneath us. & we held by the roots of trees and hung over this immensity, but I said, if you please we will commit ourselves to this void, and see whether providence is here also, if you will not I will? but he answerd, do not presume O young-man but as we here remain behold thy lot which will soon appear when the darkness passes away

So I remaind with him sitting in the twisted [PL 18] root of an oak. he was suspended in a fungus which hung with the head downward into the deep;

By degrees we beheld the infinite Abyss, fiery as the smoke of a burn-ing city; beneath us at an immense distance was the sun, black but shin-ing[;] round it were fiery tracks on which revolv'd vast spiders, crawl-ing after their prey; which flew or rather swum in the infinite deep, in the most terrific shapes of animals sprung from corruption. & the air was full of them, & seemd composed of them; these are Devils. and are called Powers of the air, I now asked my companion which was my eternal lot? he said, between the black & white spiders

But now, from between the black & white spiders a cloud and fire burst and rolled thro the deep blackning all beneath, so that the nether deep grew black as a sea & rolled with a terrible noise: beneath us was nothing now to be seen but a black tempest, till looking east be-tween the clouds & the waves, we saw a cataract of blood mixed with fire and not many stones throw from us appeard and sunk again the scaly fold of a monstrous serpent[.] at last to the east, distant about three degrees appeard a fiery crest above the waves[.] slowly it reared like a ridge of golden rocks till we discoverd two globes of crimson fire, from which the sea fled away in clouds of smoke, and now we saw, it was the head of Leviathan, his forehead was divided into streaks of green & purple like those on a tygers forehead: soon we saw his mouth & red gills hang just above the raging foam tinging the black deep with beams of blood, advancing toward [PL 19] us with all the fury of a spiritual existence.

My friend the Angel climb'd up from his station into the mill; I remain'd alone, & then this appearance was no more, but I found myself sitting on a pleasant bank beside a river by moon light hearing a harper who sung to the harp, & his theme was, The man who never alters his opinion is like standing water, & breeds reptiles of the mind.

But I arose, and sought for the mill, & there I found my Angel, who surprised asked me, how I escaped?

I answerd. All that we saw was owing to your metaphysics: for when you ran away, I found myself on a bank by moonlight hearing a harper, But now we have seen my eternal lot, shall I shew you yours? he laughd at my proposal; but I by force suddenly caught him in my arms, & flew westerly thro' the night, till we were elevated above the earths shadow: then I flung myself with him directly into the body of the sun, here I clothed myself in white, & taking in my hand Swedenborgs volumes sunk from the glorious clime, and passed all the planets till we came to saturn, here I staid to rest & then leap'd into the void, between saturn & the fixed stars.

Here said I! is your lot, in this space, if space it may be calld, Soon we saw the stable and the church, & I took him to the altar and open'd the Bible, and lo! it was a deep pit, into which I descended driving the Angel before me, soon we saw seven houses of brick, one we enterd; in it were a [PL 20] number of monkeys, baboons, & all of that species chaind by the middle, grinning and snatching at one another, but witheld by the shortness of their chains: however I saw that they sometimes grew numerous, and then the weak were caught by the strong and with a grinning aspect, first coupled with & then devourd, by plucking off first one limb and then another till the body was left a helpless trunk. this after grinning & kissing it with seeming fondness they devourd too; and here & there I saw one savourily picking the flesh off of his own tail; as the stench terribly annoyd us both we went into the mill, & I in my hand brought the skeleton of a body, which in the mill was Aristotles Analytics.

So the Angel said: thy phantasy has imposed upon me & thou oughtest to be ashamed.

I answerd: we impose on one another, & it is but lost time to converse with you whose works are only Analytics

Opposition is true Friendship.

PLATE 21

I have always found that Angels have the vanity to speak of themselves as the only wise; this they do with a confident insolence sprouting from systematic reasoning;

Thus Swedenborg boasts that what he writes is new; tho' it is only the Contents or Index of already publish'd books

A man carried a monkey about for a shew, & because he was a little wiser than the monkey, grew vain, and conciev'd himself as much wiser than seven men. It is so with Swedenborg; he shews the folly of churches & exposes hypocrites, till he imagines that all are religious. & himself the single [PL 22] one on earth that ever broke a net.

Now hear a plain fact: Swedenborg has not written one new truth: Now hear another: he has written all the old falshoods.

And now hear the reason. He conversed with Angels who are all religious, & conversed not with Devils who all hate religion, for he was incapable thro' his conceited notions.

Thus Swedenborgs writings are a recapitulation of all superficial opinions, and an analysis of the more sublime, but no further.

Have now another plain fact: Any man of mechanical talents may from the writings of Paracelsus or Jacob Behmen, produce ten thousand volumes of equal value with Swedenborg's. and from those of Dante or Shakespear, an infinite number.

But when he has done this, let him not say that he knows better than his master, for he only holds a candle in sunshine.

A Memorable Fancy

Once I saw a Devil in a flame of fire. who arose before an Angel that sat on a cloud. and the Devil utterd these words.

The worship of God is. Honouring his gifts in other men each according to his genius. and loving the [PL 23] greatest men best, those who envy or calumniate great men hate God, for there is no other God.

The Angel hearing this became almost blue but mastering himself he grew yellow, & at last white pink & smiling, and then replied,

Thou Idolater, is not God One? & is not he visible in Jesus Christ? and has not Jesus Christ given his sanction to the law of ten commandments and are not all other men fools, sinners, & nothings?

The Devil answer'd; bray a fool in a morter with wheat. yet shall not his folly be beaten out of him: if Jesus Christ is the greatest man, you ought to love him in the greatest degree; now hear how he has given his sanction to the law of ten commandments: did he not mock at the sabbath, and so mock the sabbaths God? murder those who were murderd because of him? turn away the law from the woman taken in adultery? steal the labor of others to support him? bear false witness when he omitted making a defence before Pilate? covet when he pray'd for his disciples, and when he bid them shake off the dust of their feet against such as refused to lodge them? I tell you, no virtue can exist without breaking these ten commandments.˙. Jesus was all virtue, and acted from im[PL 24]pulse. not from rules.

When he had so spoken: I beheld the Angel who stretched out his arms embracing the flame of fire & he was consumed and arose as Elijah.

Note. This Angel, who is now become a Devil, is my particular friend: we often read the Bible together in its infernal or diabolical sense which the world shall have if they behave well

I have also: The Bible of Hell: which the world shall have whether they will or no.

One Law for the Lion & Ox is Oppression

PLATE 25

A Song of Liberty

1. The Eternal Female groand! it was heard over all the Earth:
2. Albions coast is sick silent; the American meadows faint!
3 Shadows of Prophecy shiver along by the lakes and the rivers and mutter across the ocean? France rend down thy dungeon;
4. Golden Spain burst the barriers of old Rome;
5. Cast thy keys O Rome into the deep down falling, even to eternity down falling,
6. And weep
7. In her trembling hands she took the new born terror howling:
8. On those infinite mountains of light now barr'd out by the atlantic sea, the new born fire stood before the starry king!
9. Flag'd with grey brow'd snows and thunderous visages the jealous wings wav'd over the deep.
10. The speary hand burned aloft, unbuckled was the shield, forth went the hand of jealousy among the flaming hair, and [PL 26] hurl'd the new born wonder thro' the starry night.
11. The fire, the fire, is falling!
12. Look up! look up! O citizen of London. enlarge thy countenance; O Jew, leave counting gold! return to thy oil and wine; O African! black African! (go. winged thought widen his forehead.)
13. The fiery limbs, the flaming hair, shot like the sinking sun into the western sea.
14. Wak'd from his eternal sleep, the hoary element roaring fled away:
15. Down rushd beating his wings in vain the jealous king; his grey brow'd councellors, thunderous warriors, curl'd veterans, among helms, and shields, and chariots[,] horses, elephants: banners, castles, slings and rocks,
16. Falling, rushing, ruining! buried in the ruins, on Urthona's dens.
17. All night beneath the ruins, then their sullen flames faded emerge round the gloomy king,
18. With thunder and fire: leading his starry hosts thro' the waste wilderness [PL 27] he promulgates his ten commands, glancing his beamy eyelids over the deep in dark dismay,

19. Where the son of fire in his eastern cloud, while the morning plumes her golden breast,
20. Spurning the clouds written with curses, stamps the stony law to dust, loosing the eternal horses from the dens of night, crying

    Empire is no more! and now the lion & wolf shall cease.

Chorus

Let the Priests of the Raven of dawn, no longer in deadly black. with hoarse note curse the sons of joy. Nor his accepted brethren whom, tyrant, he calls free: lay the bound or build the roof. Nor pale religious letchery call that virginity, that wishes but acts not!

For every thing that lives is Holy

VISIONS of the Daughters of Albion   ^{t,c}

The Eye sees more than the Heart knows.   ^c

Printed by Will:ᵐ Blake: 1793.

PLATE iii

The Argument   ^c

I loved Theotormon
And I was not ashamed
I trembled in my virgin fears
And I hid in Leutha's vale!

I plucked Leutha's flower,   5
And I rose up from the vale;
But the terrible thunders tore
My virgin mantle in twain.

PLATE I

Visions   ^c

ENSLAV'D, the Daughters of Albion weep: a trembling lamentation
Upon their mountains; in their valleys. sighs toward America.

For the soft soul of America, Oothoon wanderd in woe,
Along the vales of Leutha seeking flowers to comfort her;
And thus she spoke to the bright Marygold of Leutha's vale   5

Art thou a flower! art thou a nymph! I see thee now a flower;
Now a nymph! I dare not pluck thee from thy dewy bed?

The Golden nymph replied; pluck thou my flower Oothoon the
    mild
Another flower shall spring, because the soul of sweet delight
Can never pass away. she ceas'd & closd her golden shrine.   *10*

Then Oothoon pluck'd the flower saying, I pluck thee from thy bed
Sweet flower. and put thee here to glow between my breasts
And thus I turn my face to where my whole soul seeks.

Over the waves she went in wing'd exulting swift delight;
And over Theotormons reign, took her impetuous course.   *15*

Bromion rent her with his thunders. on his stormy bed
Lay the faint maid, and soon her woes appalld his thunders hoarse

Bromion spoke. behold this harlot here on Bromions bed,
And let the jealous dolphins sport around the lovely maid;
Thy soft American plains are mine, and mine thy north & south: *20*
Stampt with my signet are the swarthy children of the sun:
They are obedient, they resist not, they obey the scourge:
Their daughters worship terrors and obey the violent:
PLATE 2
Now thou maist marry Bromions harlot, and protect the child
Of Bromions rage, that Oothoon shall put forth in nine moons time

Then storms rent Theotormons limbs; he rolld his waves around.
And folded his black jealous waters round the adulterate pair
Bound back to back in Bromions caves terror & meekness dwell   *5*

At entrance Theotormon sits wearing the threshold hard
With secret tears; beneath him sound like waves on a desart shore
The voice of slaves beneath the sun, and children bought with money.
That shiver in religious caves beneath the burning fires
Of lust, that belch incessant from the summits of the earth   *10*

Oothoon weeps not: she cannot weep! her tears are locked up;   e
But she can howl incessant writhing her soft snowy limbs.
And calling Theotormons Eagles to prey upon her flesh.

I call with holy voice! kings of the sounding air,
Rend away this defiled bosom that I may reflect.   *15*
The image of Theotormon on my pure transparent breast.

The Eagles at her call descend & rend their bleeding prey;
Theotormon severely smiles. her soul reflects the smile;   e
As the clear spring mudded with feet of beasts grows pure & smiles.

The Daughters of Albion hear her woes. & eccho back her sighs.   *20*

Why does my Theotormon sit weeping upon the threshold;
And Oothoon hovers by his side, perswading him in vain:
I cry arise O Theotormon for the village dog
Barks at the breaking day. the nightingale has done lamenting.
The lark does rustle in the ripe corn, and the Eagle returns   25
From nightly prey, and lifts his golden beak to the pure east;
Shaking the dust from his immortal pinions to awake
The sun that sleeps too long. Arise my Theotormon I am pure.
Because the night is gone that clos'd me in its deadly black.
They told me that the night & day were all that I could see;   30
They told me that I had five senses to inclose me up.
And they inclos'd my infinite brain into a narrow circle.
And sunk my heart into the Abyss, a red round globe hot burning
Till all from life I was obliterated and erased.
Instead of morn arises a bright shadow, like an eye   35
In the eastern cloud: instead of night a sickly charnel house;
That Theotormon hears me not! to him the night and morn
Are both alike: a night of sighs, a morning of fresh tears;
PLATE 3
And none but Bromion can hear my lamentations.

With what sense is it that the chicken shuns the ravenous hawk?
With what sense does the tame pigeon measure out the expanse?
With what sense does the bee form cells? have not the mouse & frog
Eyes and ears and sense of touch? yet are their habitations.   5
And their pursuits, as different as their forms and as their joys:
Ask the wild ass why he refuses burdens: and the meek camel
Why he loves man: is it because of eye ear mouth or skin
Or breathing nostrils? No. for these the wolf and tyger have.
Ask the blind worm the secrets of the grave, and why her spires   10
Love to curl round the bones of death; and ask the rav'nous snake
Where she gets poison: & the wing'd eagle why he loves the sun
And then tell me the thoughts of man, that have been hid of old.

Silent I hover all the night, and all day could be silent.
If Theotormon once would turn his loved eyes upon me;   15
How can I be defild when I reflect thy image pure?
Sweetest the fruit that the worm feeds on. & the soul prey'd on by woe
The new wash'd lamb ting'd with the village smoke & the bright swan
By the red earth of our immortal river: I bathe my wings.
And I am white and pure to hover round Theotormons breast.   20

Then Theotormon broke his silence. and he answered.

Tell me what is the night or day to one o'erflowd with woe?
Tell me what is a thought? & of what substance is it made?
Tell me what is a joy? & in what gardens do joys grow?
And in what rivers swim the sorrows? and upon what mountains   25

PLATE 4

Wave shadows of discontent? and in what houses dwell the wretched
Drunken with woe forgotten. and shut up from cold despair.

Tell me where dwell the thoughts forgotten till thou call them forth
Tell me where dwell the joys of old! & where the ancient loves?
And when will they renew again & the night of oblivion past?   5
That I might traverse times & spaces far remote and bring
Comforts into a present sorrow and a night of pain
Where goest thou O thought? to what remote land is thy flight?
If thou returnest to the present moment of affliction
Wilt thou bring comforts on thy wings. and dews and honey and balm;   10
Or poison from the desart wilds, from the eyes of the envier.

Then Bromion said: and shook the cavern with his lamentation

Thou knowest that the ancient trees seen by thine eyes have fruit;   c
But knowest thou that trees and fruits flourish upon the earth
To gratify senses unknown? trees beasts and birds unknown: 15
Unknown, not unpercievd, spread in the infinite microscope,
In places yet unvisited by the voyager. and in worlds
Over another kind of seas, and in atmospheres unknown:
Ah! are there other wars, beside the wars of sword and fire!
And are there other sorrows, beside the sorrows of poverty!   20
And are there other joys, beside the joys of riches and ease?
And is there not one law for both the lion and the ox?   c
And is there not eternal fire, and eternal chains?
To bind the phantoms of existence from eternal life?

Then Oothoon waited silent all the day. and all the night,   25
PLATE 5
But when the morn arose, her lamentation renewd,
The Daughters of Albion hear her woes, & eccho back her sighs.

O Urizen! Creator of men! mistaken Demon of heaven: c
Thy joys are tears! thy labour vain, to form men to thine image.
How can one joy absorb another? are not different joys   5
Holy, eternal, infinite! and each joy is a Love.

Does not the great mouth laugh at a gift? & the narrow eyelids mock
At the labour that is above payment, and wilt thou take the ape   c
For thy councellor? or the dog, for a schoolmaster to thy children?
Does he who contemns poverty, and he who turns with abhorrence   10
From usury: feel the same passion or are they moved alike?
How can the giver of gifts experience the delights of the merchant?
How the industrious citizen the pains of the husbandman.
How different far the fat fed hireling with hollow drum;
Who buys whole corn fields into wastes, and sings upon the heath: 15
How different their eye and ear! how different the world to them!
With what sense does the parson claim the labour of the farmer?

–47–

What are his nets & gins & traps. & how does he surround him
With cold floods of abstraction, and with forests of solitude,
To build him castles and high spires. where kings & priests may dwell.   20
Till she who burns with youth. and knows no fixed lot; is bound
In spells of law to one she loaths: and must she drag the chain
Of life, in weary lust! must chilling murderous thoughts. obscure
The clear heaven of her eternal spring? to bear the wintry rage
Of a harsh terror driv'n to madness, bound to hold a rod   25
Over her shrinking shoulders all the day; & all the night
To turn the wheel of false desire: and longings that wake her womb
To the abhorred birth of cherubs in the human form
That live a pestilence & die a meteor & are no more.
Till the child dwell with one he hates. and do the deed he loaths   30
And the impure scourge force his seed into its unripe birth
E'er yet his eyelids can behold the arrows of the day.

Does the whale worship at thy footsteps as the hungry dog?
Or does he scent the mountain prey, because his nostrils wide
Draw in the ocean? does his eye discern the flying cloud   35
As the ravens eye? or does he measure the expanse like the vulture?
Does the still spider view the cliffs where eagles hide their young?
Or does the fly rejoice. because the harvest is brought in?
Does not the eagle scorn the earth & despise the treasures beneath?   c
But the mole knoweth what is there, & the worm shall tell it thee.   40
Does not the worm erect a pillar in the mouldering church yard?
PLATE 6
And a palace of eternity in the jaws of the hungry grave
Over his porch these words are written. Take thy bliss O Man!
And sweet shall be thy taste & sweet thy infant joys renew!

Infancy, fearless, lustful, happy! nestling for delight
In laps of pleasure; Innocence! honest, open, seeking   5
The vigorous joys of morning light; open to virgin bliss,
Who taught thee modesty, subtil modesty! child of night & sleep
When thou awakest. wilt thou dissemble all thy secret joys
Or wert thou not, awake when all this mystery was disclos'd!
Then com'st thou forth a modest virgin knowing to dissemble   10
With nets found under thy night pillow, to catch virgin joy,
And brand it with the name of whore; & sell it in the night,
In silence. ev'n without a whisper, and in seeming sleep:
Religious dreams and holy vespers, light thy smoky fires:
Once were thy fires lighted by the eyes of honest morn   15
And does my Theotormon seek this hypocrite modesty!
This knowing, artful, secret, fearful, cautious, trembling hypocrite.
Then is Oothoon a whore indeed! and all the virgin joys
Of life are harlots: and Theotormon is a sick mans dream
And Oothoon is the crafty slave of selfish holiness.   20

But Oothoon is not so, a virgin fill'd with virgin fancies
Open to joy and to delight where ever beauty appears
If in the morning sun I find it: there my eyes are fix'd
PLATE 7
In happy copulation; if in evening mild. wearied with work;
Sit on a bank and draw the pleasures of this free born joy.

The moment of desire! the moment of desire! The virgin
That pines for man; shall awaken her womb to enormous joys
In the secret shadows of her chamber; the youth shut up from   5
The lustful joy. shall forget to generate. & create an amorous image
In the shadows of his curtains and in the folds of his silent pillow.
Are not these the places of religion? the rewards of continence?
The self enjoyings of self denial? Why dost thou seek religion?
Is it because acts are not lovely, that thou seekest solitude,   10
Where the horrible darkness is impressed with reflections of desire.

Father of Jealousy. be thou accursed from the earth!
Why hast thou taught my Theotormon this accursed thing?
Till beauty fades from off my shoulders darken'd and cast out,
A solitary shadow wailing on the margin of non-entity.   15

I cry, Love! Love! Love! happy happy Love! free as the mountain wind!
Can that be Love, that drinks another as a sponge drinks water?
That clouds with jealousy his nights, with weepings all the day:
To spin a web of age around him. grey and hoary! dark!
Till his eyes sicken at the fruit that hangs before his sight.   20
Such is self-love that envies all! a creeping skeleton
With lamplike eyes watching around the frozen marriage bed.

But silken nets and traps of adamant will Oothoon spread,
And catch for thee girls of mild silver, or of furious gold;
I'll lie beside thee on a bank & view their wanton play   25
In lovely copulation bliss on bliss with Theotormon:
Red as the rosy morning, lustful as the first born beam,
Oothoon shall view his dear delight, nor e'er with jealous cloud
Come in the heaven of generous love; nor selfish blightings bring.

Does the sun walk in glorious raiment. on the secret floor   30
PLATE 8
Where the cold miser spreads his gold? or does the bright cloud drop
On his stone threshold? does his eye behold the beam that brings
Expansion to the eye of pity? or will he bind himself
Beside the ox to thy hard furrow? does not that mild beam blot
The bat, the owl, the glowing tyger, and the king of night.   5
The sea fowl takes the wintry blast. for a cov'ring to her limbs:
And the wild snake, the pestilence to adorn him with gems & gold.
And trees. & birds. & beasts. & men. behold their eternal joy.

Arise you little glancing wings, and sing your infant joy!

Arise and drink your bliss, for every thing that lives is holy!　　10

Thus every morning wails Oothoon. but Theotormon sits

Upon the margind ocean conversing with shadows dire.

The Daughters of Albion hear her woes, & eccho back her sighs.

The End

~∿~

AMERICA *a* PROPHECY

LAMBETH

Printed by William Blake in the year 1793

PLATE 1

PRELUDIUM

The shadowy daughter of Urthona stood before red Orc.

When fourteen suns had faintly journey'd o'er his dark abode;

His food she brought in iron baskets, his drink in cups of iron;

Crown'd with a helmet & dark hair the nameless female stood;

A quiver with its burning stores, a bow like that of night,　　5

When pestilence is shot from heaven; no other arms she need:

Invulnerable tho' naked, save where clouds roll round her loins,

Their awful folds in the dark air; silent she stood as night;

For never from her iron tongue could voice or sound arise;

But dumb till that dread day when Orc assay'd his fierce embrace.　10

Dark virgin; said the hairy youth, thy father stern abhorr'd;

Rivets my tenfold chains while still on high my spirit soars;

Sometimes an eagle screaming in the sky, sometimes a lion,

Stalking upon the mountains, & sometimes a whale I lash

The raging fathomless abyss, anon a serpent folding　　15

Around the pillars of Urthona, and round thy dark limbs,

On the Canadian wilds I fold, feeble my spirit folds.

For chaind beneath I rend these caverns; when thou bringest food

I howl my joy! and my red eyes seek to behold thy face

In vain! these clouds roll to & fro, & hide thee from my sight.　20

PLATE 2

Silent as despairing love, and strong as jealousy,

The hairy shoulders rend the links, free are the wrists of fire;

Round the terrific loins he siez'd the panting struggling womb;

It joy'd: she put aside her clouds & smiled her first-born smile;
As when a black cloud shews its light'nings to the silent deep.　　5

Soon as she saw the terrible boy then burst the virgin cry.

I know thee, I have found thee, & I will not let thee go;
Thou art the image of God who dwells in darkness of Africa;
And thou art fall'n to give me life in regions of dark death.
On my American plains I feel the struggling afflictions　　10
Endur'd by roots that writhe their arms into the nether deep:
I see a serpent in Canada, who courts me to his love;
In Mexico an Eagle, and a Lion in Peru;
I see a Whale in the South-sea, drinking my soul away.
O what limb rending pains I feel. thy fire & my frost　　15
Mingle in howling pains, in furrows by thy lightnings rent;
This is eternal death; and this the torment long foretold.

The stern Bard ceas'd, asham'd of his own song; enrag'd he　　t,e
　　swung
His harp aloft sounding, then dash'd its shining frame against
A ruin'd pillar in glittring fragments; silent he turn'd away,　　20
And wander'd down the vales of Kent in sick & drear lamentings.

PLATE 3

A PROPHECY

The Guardian Prince of Albion burns in his nightly tent,　　e
Sullen fires across the Atlantic glow to America's shore:
Piercing the souls of warlike men, who rise in silent night,
Washington, Franklin, Paine & Warren, Gates, Hancock & Green;　　t
Meet on the coast glowing with blood from Albions fiery Prince.　　5

Washington spoke; Friends of America look over the Atlantic sea;
A bended bow is lifted in heaven, & a heavy iron chain
Descends link by link from Albions cliffs across the sea to bind
Brothers & sons of America, till our faces pale and yellow;
Heads deprest, voices weak, eyes downcast, hands work-bruis'd,　　t 10
Feet bleeding on the sultry sands, and the furrows of the whip　　t
Descend to generations that in future times forget.——

The strong voice ceas'd; for a terrible blast swept over the heaving sea;
The eastern cloud rent; on his cliffs stood Albions wrathful Prince　　t,e
A dragon form clashing his scales at midnight he arose,　　15
And flam'd red meteors round the land of Albion beneath[.]　　t
His voice, his locks, his awful shoulders, and his glowing eyes,
PLATE 4
Appear to the Americans upon the cloudy night.

Solemn heave the Atlantic waves between the gloomy nations,
Swelling, belching from its deeps red clouds & raging Fires!

Albion is sick! America faints! enrag'd the Zenith grew.
As human blood shooting its veins all round the orbed heaven   5
Red rose the clouds from the Atlantic in vast wheels of blood
And in the red clouds rose a Wonder o'er the Atlantic sea;   e
Intense! naked! a Human fire fierce glowing, as the wedge
Of iron heated in the furnace; his terrible limbs were fire
With myriads of cloudy terrors banners dark & towers   10
Surrounded; heat but not light went thro' the murky atmosphere

The King of England looking westward trembles at the vision

PLATE 5
Albions Angel stood beside the Stone of night, and saw   e
The terror like a comet, or more like the planet red
That once inclos'd the terrible wandering comets in its sphere.
Then Mars thou wast our center, & the planets three flew round
Thy crimson disk; so e'er the Sun was rent from thy red sphere;   5
The Spectre glowd his horrid length staining the temple long
With beams of blood; & thus a voice came forth, and shook the temple

PLATE 6
The morning comes, the night decays, the watchmen leave their stations;   e
The grave is burst, the spices shed, the linen wrapped up;
The bones of death, the cov'ring clay, the sinews shrunk & dry'd.
Reviving shake, inspiring move, breathing! awakening!
Spring like redeemed captives when their bonds & bars are burst;   5
Let the slave grinding at the mill, run out into the field:
Let him look up into the heavens & laugh in the bright air;
Let the inchained soul shut up in darkness and in sighing,
Whose face has never seen a smile in thirty weary years;
Rise and look out, his chains are loose, his dungeon doors are open.   10
And let his wife and children return from the opressors scourge;
They look behind at every step & believe it is a dream.
Singing. The Sun has left his blackness, & has found a fresher morning
And the fair Moon rejoices in the clear & cloudless night;
For Empire is no more, and now the Lion & Wolf shall cease.   15

PLATE 7
In thunders ends the voice. Then Albions Angel wrathful burnt   e
Beside the Stone of Night; and like the Eternal Lions howl
In famine & war, reply'd. Art thou not Orc; who serpent-form'd
Stands at the gate of Enitharmon to devour her children;
Blasphemous Demon, Antichrist, hater of Dignities;   5
Lover of wild rebellion, and transgresser of Gods Law;
Why dost thou come to Angels eyes in this terrific form?

PLATE 8
The terror answerd: I am Orc, wreath'd round the accursed tree: e
The times are ended; shadows pass the morning gins to break;

The fiery joy, that Urizen perverted to ten commands,
What night he led the starry hosts thro' the wide wilderness:
That stony law I stamp to dust: and scatter religion abroad   5
To the four winds as a torn book, & none shall gather the leaves;
But they shall rot on desart sands, & consume in bottomless deeps;
To make the desarts blossom, & the deeps shrink to their fountains,
And to renew the fiery joy, and burst the stony roof.
That pale religious letchery, seeking Virginity,   10
May find it in a harlot, and in coarse-clad honesty
The undefil'd tho' ravish'd in her cradle night and morn:
For every thing that lives is holy, life delights in life;
Because the soul of sweet delight can never be defil'd.
Fires inwrap the earthly globe, yet man is not consumd;   15
Amidst the lustful fires he walks: his feet become like brass,
His knees and thighs like silver, & his breast and head like gold.

PLATE 9   c
Sound! sound! my loud war-trumpets & alarm my Thirteen Angels!
Loud howls the eternal Wolf! the eternal Lion lashes his tail!
America is darkned; and my punishing Demons terrified
Crouch howling before their caverns deep like skins dry'd in the wind.
They cannot smite the wheat, nor quench the fatness of the earth.   5
They cannot smite with sorrows, nor subdue the plow and spade.
They cannot wall the city, nor moat round the castle of princes.
They cannot bring the stubbed oak to overgrow the hills.
For terrible men stand on the shores, & in their robes I see
Children take shelter from the lightnings, there stands Washington   10
And Paine and Warren with their foreheads reard toward the east
But clouds obscure my aged sight. A vision from afar!
Sound! sound! my loud war-trumpets & alarm my thirteen Angels:
Ah vision from afar! Ah rebel form that rent the ancient
Heavens; Eternal Viper self-renew'd, rolling in clouds   15
I see thee in thick clouds and darkness on America's shore.
Writhing in pangs of abhorred birth; red flames the crest rebellious
And eyes of death; the harlot womb oft opened in vain
Heaves in enormous circles, now the times are return'd upon thee,
Devourer of thy parent, now thy unutterable torment renews.   20
Sound! sound! my loud war trumpets & alarm my thirteen Angels!
Ah terrible birth! a young one bursting! where is the weeping mouth?
And where the mothers milk? instead those ever-hissing jaws
And parched lips drop with fresh gore; now roll thou in the clouds
Thy mother lays her length outstretch'd upon the shore beneath.   25
Sound! sound! my loud war-trumpets & alarm my thirteen Angels!
Loud howls the eternal Wolf: the eternal Lion lashes his tail!

PLATE 10
Thus wept the Angel voice & as he wept the terrible blasts   c
Of trumpets, blew a loud alarm across the Atlantic deep.

No trumpets answer; no reply of clarions or of fifes,
Silent the Colonies remain and refuse the loud alarm.

On those vast shady hills between America & Albions shore;   5
Now barr'd out by the Atlantic sea: call'd Atlantean hills:
Because from their bright summits you may pass to the Golden world
An ancient palace, archetype of mighty Emperies,
Rears its immortal pinnacles, built in the forest of God
By Ariston the king of beauty for his stolen bride,   10

Here on their magic seats the thirteen Angels sat perturb'd
For clouds from the Atlantic hover o'er the solemn roof.

PLATE 11
Fiery the Angels rose, & as they rose deep thunder roll'd   e
Around their shores: indignant burning with the fires of Orc
And Bostons Angel cried aloud as they flew thro' the dark night.

He cried: Why trembles honesty and like a murderer,
Why seeks he refuge from the frowns of his immortal station!   5
Must the generous tremble & leave his joy, to the idle: to the
    pestilence!
That mock him? who commanded this? what God? what Angel!
To keep the gen'rous from experience till the ungenerous
Are unrestraind performers of the energies of nature;
Till pity is become a trade, and generosity a science,   10
That men get rich by, & the sandy desert is giv'n to the strong
What God is he, writes laws of peace, & clothes him in a tempest
What pitying Angel lusts for tears, and fans himself with sighs
What crawling villain preaches abstinence & wraps himself
In fat of lambs? no more I follow, no more obedience pay.   15

PLATE 12
So cried he, rending off his robe & throwing down his scepter.
In sight of Albions Guardian, and all the thirteen Angels
Rent off their robes to the hungry wind, & threw their golden scepters
Down on the land of America. indignant they descended
Headlong from out their heav'nly heights, descending swift as fires   5
Over the land; naked & flaming are their lineaments seen
In the deep gloom, by Washington & Paine & Warren they stood
And the flame folded roaring fierce within the pitchy night
Before the Demon red, who burnt towards America,
In black smoke thunders and loud winds rejoicing in its terror   10
Breaking in smoky wreaths from the wild deep, & gath'ring thick
In flames as of a furnace on the land from North to South
PLATE 13
What time the thirteen Governors that England sent convene
In Bernards house; the flames coverd the land, they rouze they cry
Shaking their mental chains they rush in fury to the sea
To quench their anguish; at the feet of Washington down fall'n

They grovel on the sand and writhing lie, while all   5
The British soldiers thro' the thirteen states sent up a howl
Of anguish: threw their swords & muskets to the earth & ran
From their encampments and dark castles seeking where to hide
From the grim flames; and from the visions of Orc: in sight
Of Albions Angel; who enrag'd his secret clouds open'd   10
From north to south, and burnt outstretchd on wings of wrath cov'ring
The eastern sky, spreading his awful wings across the heavens;
Beneath him roll'd his num'rous hosts, all Albions Angels camp'd
Darkend the Atlantic mountains & their trumpets shook the valleys
Arm'd with diseases of the earth to cast upon the Abyss,   15
Their numbers forty millions, must'ring in the eastern sky.

PLATE 14
In the flames stood & view'd the armies drawn out in the sky
Washington Franklin Paine & Warren Allen Gates & Lee:
And heard the voice of Albions Angel give the thunderous command:
His plagues obedient to his voice flew forth out of their clouds
Falling upon America, as a storm to cut them off   5
As a blight cuts the tender corn when it begins to appear.
Dark is the heaven above, & cold & hard the earth beneath;
And as a plague wind fill'd with insects cuts off man & beast;
And as a sea o'erwhelms a land in the day of an earthquake:

Fury! rage! madness! in a wind swept through America   10
And the red flames of Orc that folded roaring fierce around
The angry shores, and the fierce rushing of th'inhabitants together:
The citizens of New-York close their books & lock their chests;
The mariners of Boston drop their anchors and unlade;
The scribe of Pensylvania casts his pen upon the earth;   15
The builder of Virginia throws his hammer down in fear.

Then had America been lost, o'erwhelm'd by the Atlantic,   e
And Earth had lost another portion of the infinite,
But all rush together in the night in wrath and raging fire
The red fires rag'd! the plagues recoil'd! then rolld they back with fury   20
PLATE 15
On Albions Angels; then the Pestilence began in streaks of red
Across the limbs of Albions Guardian, the spotted plague smote Bristols
And the Leprosy Londons Spirit, sickening all their bands:
The millions sent up a howl of anguish and threw off their hammerd
    mail,
And cast their swords & spears to earth, & stood a naked multitude.   5
Albions Guardian writhed in torment on the eastern sky
Pale quivring toward the brain his glimmering eyes, teeth chattering
Howling & shuddering his legs quivering; convuls'd each muscle &
    sinew
Sick'ning lay Londons Guardian, and the ancient miter'd York
Their heads on snowy hills, their ensigns sick'ning in the sky   10

The plagues creep on the burning winds driven by flames of Orc,
And by the fierce Americans rushing together in the night
Driven o'er the Guardians of Ireland and Scotland and Wales
They spotted with plagues forsook the frontiers & their banners seard
With fires of hell, deform their ancient heavens with shame & woe.   15
Hid in his caves the Bard of Albion felt the enormous plagues.
And a cowl of flesh grew o'er his head & scales on his back & ribs;
And rough with black scales all his Angels fright their ancient
    heavens
The doors of marriage are open, and the Priests in rustling scales
Rush into reptile coverts, hiding from the fires of Orc,   20
That play around the golden roofs in wreaths of fierce desire,
Leaving the females naked and glowing with the lusts of youth

For the female spirits of the dead pining in bonds of religion;
Run from their fetters reddening, & in long drawn arches sitting:
They feel the nerves of youth renew, and desires of ancient times,   25
Over their pale limbs as a vine when the tender grape appears

PLATE 16

Over the hills, the vales, the cities, rage the red flames fierce;
The Heavens melted from north to south; and Urizen who sat
Above all heavens in thunders wrap'd, emerg'd his leprous head
From out his holy shrine, his tears in deluge piteous
Falling into the deep sublime! flag'd with grey-brow'd snows   5
And thunderous visages, his jealous wings wav'd over the deep;
Weeping in dismal howling woe he dark descended howling
Around the smitten bands, clothed in tears & trembling shudd'ring cold.
His stored snows he poured forth, and his icy magazines
He open'd on the deep, and on the Atlantic sea white shiv'ring.   10
Leprous his limbs, all over white, and hoary was his visage.
Weeping in dismal howlings before the stern Americans
Hiding the Demon red with clouds & cold mists from the earth;
Till Angels & weak men twelve years should govern o'er the strong:
And then their end should come, when France reciev'd the Demons   15
    light.

Stiff shudderings shook the heav'nly thrones! France Spain & Italy,
In terror view'd the bands of Albion, and the ancient Guardians
Fainting upon the elements, smitten with their own plagues
They slow advance to shut the five gates of their law-built heaven
Filled with blasting fancies and with mildews of despair   20
With fierce disease and lust, unable to stem the fires of Orc;
But the five gates were consum'd, & their bolts and hinges melted
And the fierce flames burnt round the heavens, & round the abodes of
    men

FINIS   t

[Canceled Plates]

t

PLATE b
Reveal the dragon thro' the human; coursing swift as fire
To the close hall of counsel, where his Angel form renews.

In a sweet vale shelter'd with cedars, that eternal stretch
Their unmov'd branches, stood the hall; built when the moon shot
    forth,
In that dread night when Urizen call'd the stars round his feet;   5
Then burst the center from its orb, and found a place beneath;
And Earth conglob'd, in narrow room, roll'd round its sulphur Sun.

To this deep valley situated by the flowing Thames;
Where George the third holds council. & his Lords & Commons meet:
Shut out from mortal sight the Angel came; the vale was dark   10
With clouds of smoke from the Atlantic, that in volumes roll'd
Between the mountains, dismal visions mope around the house.

On chairs of iron, canopied with mystic ornaments
Of life by magic power condens'd; infernal forms art-bound
The council sat; all rose before the aged apparition;   15
His snowy beard that streams like lambent flames down his wide breast
Wetting with tears, & his white garments cast a wintry light.

Then as arm'd clouds arise terrific round the northern drum;
The world is silent at the flapping of the folding banners;
So still terrors rent the house: as when the solemn globe   20
Launch'd to the unknown shore, while Sotha held the northern helm,
Till to that void it came & fell; so the dark house was rent,
The valley mov'd beneath; its shining pillars split in twain,
And its roofs crack across down falling on th'Angelic seats.

PLATE c (as revised)
[*Then Albions Angel rose*] resolv'd to the cove of armoury: t
His shield that bound twelve demons & their cities in its orb,   t
He took down from its trembling pillar; from its cavern deep,
His helm was brought by Londons Guardian, & his thirsty spear
By the wise spirit of Londons river: silent stood the King breathing damp   t5
    mists:
And on his aged limbs they clasp'd the armour of terrible gold.   t
Infinite Londons awful spires cast a dreadful cold   t
Even on rational things beneath, and from the palace walls   t
Around Saint James's chill & heavy, even to the city gate.   t

On the vast stone whose name is Truth he stood, his cloudy shield   10
Smote with his scepter, the scale bound orb loud howld; th' ancie[nt]   t
    pillar
Trembling sunk, an earthquake roll'd along the mossy pile.

In glittring armour, swift as winds; intelligent as clouds;   t
Four winged heralds mount the furious blasts & blow their trumps
Gold, silver, brass & iron clangors clamoring rend the shores.   15
Like white clouds rising from the deeps, his fifty-two armies
From the four cliffs of Albion rise, mustering around their Prince;   t
Angels of cities and of parishes and villages and families,
In armour as the nerves of wisdom, each his station holds.   t

In opposition dire, a warlike cloud the myriads stood   20
In the red air before the Demon; [*seen even by mortal men:*   t
Who call it Fancy, or shut the gates of sense & in their chambers,
Sleep like the dead.] But like a constellation ris'n and blazing
Over the rugged ocean; so the Angels of Albion hung
a frowning shadow, like an aged King in arms of gold,   t 25
Who wept over a den, in which his only son outstretch'd
By rebels hands was slain; his white beard wav'd in the wild wind.   t

On mountains & cliffs of snow the awful apparition hover'd;
And like the voices of religious dead, heard in the mountains:
When holy zeal scents the sweet valleys of ripe virgin bliss;   30
Such was the hollow voice that o'er America lamented.   t

[Fragment]

[d]

As when a dream of Thiralatha flies the midnight hour: t
In vain the dreamer grasps the joyful images, they fly
Seen in obscured traces in the Vale of Leutha, So
The British Colonies beneath the woful Princes fade.

And so the Princes fade from earth, scarce seen by souls of men   5
But tho' obscur'd, this is the form of the Angelic land.

❧

EUROPE   t,c
a PROPHECY

LAMBETH Printed by Will: Blake 1794

PLATE iii   c

Five windows light the cavern'd Man; thro' one he breathes the air;
Thro' one, hears music of the spheres; thro' one, the eternal vine
Flourishes, that he may recieve the grapes; thro' one can look.
And see small portions of the eternal world that ever groweth;

Thro' one, himself pass out what time he please, but he will not;   5
For stolen joys are sweet, & bread eaten in secret pleasant.

So sang a Fairy mocking as he sat on a streak'd Tulip,
Thinking none saw him: when he ceas'd I started from the trees!
And caught him in my hat as boys knock down a butterfly
How know you this said I small Sir? where did you learn this song   10
Seeing himself in my possession thus he answered me:
My master, I am yours. command me, for I must obey.

Then tell me, what is the material world, and is it dead?
He laughing answer'd: I will write a book on leaves of flowers,
If you will feed me on love-thoughts, & give me now and then   15
A cup of sparkling poetic fancies; so when I am tipsie,
I'll sing to you to this soft lute; and shew you all alive
The world, when every particle of dust breathes forth its joy.

I took him home in my warm bosom: as we went along
Wild flowers I gatherd; & he shew'd me each eternal flower: 20
He laugh'd aloud to see them whimper because they were pluck'd.
They hover'd round me like a cloud of incense: when I came
Into my parlour and sat down, and took my pen to write:
My Fairy sat upon the table, and dictated EUROPE.

PLATE 1

PRELUDIUM

The nameless shadowy female rose from out the breast of Orc:
Her snaky hair brandishing in the winds of Enitharmon;
And thus her voice arose.

O mother Enitharmon wilt thou bring forth other sons?
To cause my name to vanish, that my place may not be found.   5
For I am faint with travel!   t
Like the dark cloud disburdend in the day of dismal thunder.

My roots are brandish'd in the heavens. my fruits in earth beneath
Surge, foam, and labour into life, first born & first consum'd!
Consumed and consuming!   10
Then why shouldst thou accursed mother bring me into life?

I wrap my turban of thick clouds around my lab'ring head;
And fold the sheety waters as a mantle round my limbs.
Yet the red sun and moon,
And all the overflowing stars rain down prolific pains.   15

PLATE 2

Unwilling I look up to heaven! unwilling count the stars!
Sitting in fathomless abyss of my immortal shrine.
I sieze their burning power
And bring forth howling terrors, all devouring fiery kings.

Devouring & devoured roaming on dark and desolate mountains 5
In forests of eternal death, shrieking in hollow trees.
Ah mother Enitharmon!
Stamp not with solid form this vig'rous progeny of fires.

I bring forth from my teeming bosom myriads of flames.
And thou dost stamp them with a signet, then they roam abroad 10
And leave me void as death:
Ah! I am drown'd in shady woe, and visionary joy.

And who shall bind the infinite with an eternal band?
To compass it with swaddling bands? and who shall cherish it
With milk and honey? 15
I see it smile & I roll inward & my voice is past.

    She ceast & rolld her shady clouds
     Into the secret place.

PLATE 3

A PROPHECY

    The deep of winter came; e
    What time the secret child,
Descended thro' the orient gates of the eternal day:
War ceas'd, & all the troops like shadows fled to their abodes.

Then Enitharmon saw her sons & daughters rise around. 5
Like pearly clouds they meet together in the crystal house:
And Los, possessor of the moon, joy'd in the peaceful night:
Thus speaking while his num'rous sons shook their bright fiery wings

Again the night is come t
That strong Urthona takes his rest, 10
And Urizen unloos'd from chains e
Glows like a meteor in the distant north
Stretch forth your hands and strike the elemental strings!
Awake the thunders of the deep,

PLATE 4

The shrill winds wake! t,e
Till all the sons of Urizen look out and envy Los:
Sieze all the spirits of life and bind
Their warbling joys to our loud strings
Bind all the nourishing sweets of earth 5
To give us bliss, that we may drink the sparkling wine of Los
And let us laugh at war,
Despising toil and care,
Because the days and nights of joy, in lucky hours renew.

Arise O Orc from thy deep den, 10
First born of Enitharmon rise!

And we will crown thy head with garlands of the ruddy vine;
For now thou art bound;
And I may see thee in the hour of bliss, my eldest born.

The horrent Demon rose, surrounded with red stars of fire,   15
Whirling about in furious circles round the immortal fiend.

Then Enitharmon down descended into his red light,
And thus her voice rose to her children, the distant heavens reply:

PLATE 6
Now comes the night of Enitharmons joy!   c
Who shall I call? Who shall I send?
That Woman, lovely Woman! may have dominion?
Arise O Rintrah thee I call! & Palamabron thee!
Go! tell the Human race that Womans love is Sin!   5
That an Eternal life awaits the worms of sixty winters
In an allegorical abode where existence hath never come:
Forbid all Joy, & from her childhood shall the little female
Spread nets in every secret path.

My weary eyelids draw towards the evening, my bliss is yet but new. 10

PLATE 8
Arise O Rintrah eldest born: second to none but Orc:
O lion Rintrah raise thy fury from thy forests black:
Bring Palamabron horned priest, skipping upon the mountains:
And silent Elynittria the silver bowed queen:
Rintrah where hast thou hid thy bride!   5
Weeps she in desert shades?
Alas my Rintrah! bring the lovely jealous Ocalythron.

Arise my son! bring all thy brethren O thou king of fire.
Prince of the sun I see thee with thy innumerable race:
Thick as the summer stars: 10
But each ramping his golden mane shakes,
And thine eyes rejoice because of strength O Rintrah furious king

PLATE 9
Enitharmon slept,   c
Eighteen hundred years: Man was a Dream!
The night of Nature and their harps unstrung:
She slept in middle of her nightly song,
Eighteen hundred years, a female dream!   5

Shadows of men in fleeting bands upon the winds: t,c
Divide the heavens of Europe:
Till Albions Angel smitten with his own plagues fled with his bands
The cloud bears hard on Albions shore:
Fill'd with immortal demons of futurity: 10

In council gather the smitten Angels of Albion
The cloud bears hard upon the council house; down rushing
On the heads of Albions Angels.

One hour they lay buried beneath the ruins of that hall;
But as the stars rise from the salt lake they arise in pain, 15
In troubled mists o'erclouded by the terrors of strugling times.
PLATE 10
In thoughts perturb'd, they rose from the bright ruins silent following c
The fiery King, who sought his ancient temple serpent-form'd
That stretches out its shady length along the Island white.
Round him roll'd his clouds of war; silent the Angel went,
Along the infinite shores of Thames to golden Verulam. 5
There stand the venerable porches that high-towering rear
Their oak-surrounded pillars, form'd of massy stones, uncut
With tool; stones precious; such eternal in the heavens,
Of colours twelve, few known on earth, give light in the opake,
Plac'd in the order of the stars, when the five senses whelm'd 10
In deluge o'er the earth-born man; then turn'd the fluxile eyes
Into two stationary orbs, concentrating all things.
The ever-varying spiral ascents to the heavens of heavens
Were bended downward; and the nostrils golden gates shut
Turn'd outward, barr'd and petrify'd against the infinite. 15

Thought chang'd the infinite to a serpent; that which pitieth: c
To a devouring flame; and man fled from its face and hid
In forests of night; then all the eternal forests were divided
Into earths rolling in circles of space, that like an ocean rush'd
And overwhelmed all except this finite wall of flesh. 20
Then was the serpent temple form'd, image of infinite
Shut up in finite revolutions, and man became an Angel;
Heaven a mighty circle turning; God a tyrant crown'd.

Now arriv'd the ancient Guardian at the southern porch, c
That planted thick with trees of blackest leaf, & in a vale 25
Obscure, inclos'd the Stone of Night; oblique it stood, o'erhung
With purple flowers and berries red; image of that sweet south,
Once open to the heavens and elevated on the human neck,
Now overgrown with hair and coverd with a stony roof,
Downward 'tis sunk beneath th' attractive north, that round the feet 30
A raging whirlpool draws the dizzy enquirer to his grave:
PLATE 11

> Albions Angel rose upon the Stone of Night. c
> He saw Urizen on the Atlantic;
> And his brazen Book,
> That Kings & Priests had copied on Earth
> Expanded from North to South. 5

PLATE 12

And the clouds & fires pale rolld round in the night of Enitharmon   ^c
Round Albions cliffs & Londons walls; still Enitharmon slept!
Rolling volumes of grey mist involve Churches, Palaces, Towers:
For Urizen unclaspd his Book! feeding his soul with pity
The youth of England hid in gloom curse the paind heavens; compell'd   5
Into the deadly night to see the form of Albions Angel
Their parents brought them forth & aged ignorance preaches canting,
On a vast rock, percievd by those senses that are clos'd from thought:
Bleak, dark, abrupt, it stands & overshadows London city
They saw his boney feet on the rock, the flesh consum'd in flames: 10
They saw the Serpent temple lifted above, shadowing the Island white:
They heard the voice of Albions Angel howling in flames of Orc,
Seeking the trump of the last doom

Above the rest the howl was heard from Westminster louder & louder:
The Guardian of the secret codes forsook his ancient mansion,   15
Driven out by the flames of Orc; his furr'd robes & false locks
Adhered and grew one with his flesh, and nerves & veins shot thro' them
With dismal torment sick, hanging upon the wind: he fled
Groveling along Great George Street thro' the Park gate; all the soldiers
Fled from his sight: he drag'd his torments to the wilderness.   20

Thus was the howl thro Europe!   ^c
For Orc rejoic'd to hear the howling shadows
But Palamabron shot his lightnings trenching down his wide back
And Rintrah hung with all his legions in the nether deep

Enitharmon laugh'd in her sleep to see (O womans triumph)   25
Every house a den, every man bound; the shadows are filld
With spectres, and the windows wove over with curses of iron:
Over the doors Thou shalt not; & over the chimneys Fear is written:
With bands of iron round their necks fasten'd into the walls
The citizens: in leaden gyves the inhabitants of suburbs   30
Walk heavy: soft and bent are the bones of villagers

Between the clouds of Urizen the flames of Orc roll heavy   ^c
Around the limbs of Albions Guardian, his flesh consuming.
Howlings & hissings, shrieks & groans, & voices of despair
Arise around him in the cloudy   ^t35
Heavens of Albion, Furious

PLATE 13

The red limb'd Angel siez'd, in horror and torment;
The Trump of the last doom; but he could not blow the iron tube!
Thrice he assay'd presumptuous to awake the dead to Judgment.

A mighty Spirit leap'd from the land of Albion,
Nam'd Newton; he siez'd the Trump, & blow'd the enormous blast!   5

–63–

Yellow as leaves of Autumn the myriads of Angelic hosts,
Fell thro' the wintry skies seeking their graves;
Rattling their hollow bones in howling and lamentation.

Then Enitharmon woke, nor knew that she had slept   t,e
And eighteen hundred years were fled   10
As if they had not been
She calld her sons & daughters
To the sports of night,
Within her crystal house;
And thus her song proceeds.   15

Arise Ethinthus! tho' the earth-worm call;
Let him call in vain;
Till the night of holy shadows
And human solitude is past!
PLATE 14
Ethinthus queen of waters, how thou shinest in the sky:
My daughter how do I rejoice! for thy children flock around
Like the gay fishes on the wave, when the cold moon drinks the dew.
Ethinthus! thou art sweet as comforts to my fainting soul:
For now thy waters warble round the feet of Enitharmon.   5

Manathu-Vorcyon! I behold thee flaming in my halls,
Light of thy mothers soul! I see thy lovely eagles round;
Thy golden wings are my delight, & thy flames of soft delusion.

Where is my lureing bird of Eden! Leutha silent love!
Leutha, the many coulourd bow delights upon thy wings: 10
Soft soul of flowers Leutha!
Sweet smiling pestilence! I see thy blushing light:
Thy daughters many changing,
Revolve like sweet perfumes ascending O Leutha silken queen!

Where is the youthful Antamon. prince of the pearly dew,   15
O Antamon, why wilt thou leave thy mother Enitharmon?
Alone I see thee crystal form,
Floting upon the bosomd air:
With lineaments of gratified desire.
My Antamon the seven churches of Leutha seek thy love.   20

I hear the soft Oothoon in Enitharmons tents:
Why wilt thou give up womans secrecy my melancholy child?
Between two moments bliss is ripe:
O Theotormon robb'd of joy, I see thy salt tears flow
Down the steps of my crystal house.   25

Sotha & Thiralatha, secret dwellers of dreamful caves,
Arise and please the horrent fiend with your melodious songs.

Still all your thunders golden hoofd, & bind your horses black.
Orc! smile upon my children!
Smile son of my afflictions.
Arise O Orc and give our mountains joy of thy red light.   30

She ceas'd, for All were forth at sport beneath the solemn moon   t
Waking the stars of Urizen with their immortal songs,
That nature felt thro' all her pores the enormous revelry,
Till morning ope'd the eastern gate.   t 35
Then every one fled to his station, & Enitharmon wept.

But terrible Orc, when he beheld the morning in the east,   c
PLATE 15
Shot from the heights of Enitharmon;   t
And in the vineyards of red France appear'd the light of his fury.

The sun glow'd fiery red!
The furious terrors flew around!
On golden chariots raging, with red wheels dropping with blood;   5
The Lions lash their wrathful tails!
The Tigers couch upon the prey & suck the ruddy tide:
And Enitharmon groans & cries in anguish and dismay.

Then Los arose his head he reard in snaky thunders clad:
And with a cry that shook all nature to the utmost pole,   10
Call'd all his sons to the strife of blood.

FINIS

❧

THE SONG of LOS   t,c

LAMBETH Printed by W Blake 1795

PLATE 3

AFRICA

I will sing you a song of Los. the Eternal Prophet:
He sung it to four harps at the tables of Eternity.   c
In heart-formed Africa.
Urizen faded! Ariston shudderd!
And thus the Song began   5

Adam stood in the garden of Eden:
And Noah on the mountains of Ararat;
They saw Urizen give his Laws to the Nations
By the hands of the children of Los.

– 65 –

Adam shudderd! Noah faded! black grew the sunny African   10
When Rintrah gave Abstract Philosophy to Brama in the East: e
(Night spoke to the Cloud!
Lo these Human form'd spirits in smiling hipocrisy War
Against one another; so let them War on; slaves to the eternal Elements)
Noah shrunk, beneath the waters;   15
Abram fled in fires from Chaldea;
Moses beheld upon Mount Sinai forms of dark delusion:

To Trismegistus. Palamabron gave an abstract Law: e
To Pythagoras Socrates & Plato.

Times rolled on o'er all the sons of Har, time after time   e 20
Orc on Mount Atlas howld, chain'd down with the Chain of Jealousy
Then Oothoon hoverd over Judah & Jerusalem   e
And Jesus heard her voice (a man of sorrows) he recievd
A Gospel from wretched Theotormon.

The human race began to wither, for the healthy built   25
Secluded places, fearing the joys of Love
And the disease'd only propagated:
So Antamon call'd up Leutha from her valleys of delight: e
And to Mahomet a loose Bible gave.
But in the North, to Odin, Sotha gave a Code of War,   30
Because of Diralada thinking to reclaim his joy.

PLATE 4
These were the Churches: Hospitals: Castles: Palaces: e
Like nets & gins & traps to catch the joys of Eternity
     And all the rest a desart;
Till like a dream Eternity was obliterated & erased.

Since that dread day when Har and Heva fled.   5
Because their brethren & sisters liv'd in War & Lust;
And as they fled they shrunk
Into two narrow doleful forms:
Creeping in reptile flesh upon
The bosom of the ground: 10
And all the vast of Nature shrunk
Before their shrunken eyes.

Thus the terrible race of Los & Enitharmon gave
Laws & Religions to the sons of Har binding them more
And more to Earth: closing and restraining: 15
Till a Philosophy of Five Senses was complete
Urizen wept & gave it into the hands of Newton & Locke

Clouds roll heavy upon the Alps round Rousseau & Voltaire:
And on the mountains of Lebanon round the deceased Gods
Of Asia; & on the desarts of Africa round the Fallen Angels   20
The Guardian Prince of Albion burns in his nightly tent

PLATE 6

ASIA

    The Kings of Asia heard   c
    The howl rise up from Europe!
    And each ran out from his Web;
    From his ancient woven Den;
    For the darkness of Asia was startled   5
    At the thick-flaming, thought-creating fires of Orc.

    And the Kings of Asia stood
    And cried in bitterness of soul.

    Shall not the King call for Famine from the heath?
    Nor the Priest, for Pestilence from the fen?   10
    To restrain! to dismay! to thin!
    The inhabitants of mountain and plain;
    In the day, of full-feeding prosperity;
    And the night of delicious songs.

    Shall not the Councellor throw his curb   15
    Of Poverty on the laborious?
    To fix the price of labour;
    To invent allegoric riches:

    And the privy admonishers of men
    Call for fires in the City   20
    For heaps of smoking ruins,
    In the night of prosperity & wantonness

    To turn man from his path,
    To restrain the child from the womb,

PLATE 7

    To cut off the bread from the city,
    That the remnant may learn to obey,

    That the pride of the heart may fail;
    That the lust of the eyes, may be quench'd:
    That the delicate ear in its infancy   5
    May be dull'd; and the nostrils clos'd up;

To teach mortal worms the path
That leads from the gates of the Grave.

Urizen heard them cry!
And his shudd'ring waving wings   10
Went enormous above the red flames
Drawing clouds of despair thro' the heavens
Of Europe as he went:
And his Books of brass iron & gold
Melted over the land as he flew,   15
Heavy-waving, howling, weeping.

And he stood over Judea:
And stay'd in his ancient place:
And stretch'd his clouds over Jerusalem;

For Adam, a mouldering skeleton
Lay bleach'd on the garden of Eden;   20
And Noah as white as snow
On the mountains of Ararat.

Then the thunders of Urizen bellow'd aloud
From his woven darkness above.   25

Orc, raging in European darkness
Arose like a pillar of fire above the Alps
Like a serpent of fiery flame!
    The sullen Earth
    Shrunk!   30

Forth from the dead dust rattling bones to bones
Join: shaking convuls'd the shivring clay breathes
And all flesh naked stands: Fathers and Friends;
Mothers & Infants; Kings & Warriors:

The Grave shrieks with delight, & shakes   35
Her hollow womb, & clasps the solid stem:
Her bosom swells with wild desire:
And milk & blood & glandous wine
In rivers rush & shout & dance,
On mountain, dale and plain.   40

    The SONG of LOS is Ended.
    Urizen Wept.

THE [*FIRST*] BOOK of URIZEN

t,c

LAMBETH. Printed by Will Blake 1794

PLATE 2

PRELUDIUM TO THE [*FIRST*] BOOK OF URIZEN

t,c

Of the primeval Priests assum'd power,
When Eternals spurn'd back his religion;
And gave him a place in the north,
Obscure, shadowy, void, solitary.

c

Eternals I hear your call gladly,   5
Dictate swift winged words, & fear not
To unfold your dark visions of torment.

PLATE 3

Chap: I

1. Lo, a shadow of horror is risen
In Eternity! Unknown, unprolific!
Self-closd, all-repelling: what Demon
Hath form'd this abominable void
This soul-shudd'ring vacuum?—Some said   5
"It is Urizen", But unknown, abstracted
Brooding secret, the dark power hid.

2. Times on times he divided, & measur'd
Space by space in his ninefold darkness
Unseen, unknown! changes appeard   10
In his desolate mountains rifted furious   t
By the black winds of perturbation

3. For he strove in battles dire   c
In unseen conflictions with shapes
Bred from his forsaken wilderness,   15
Of beast, bird, fish, serpent & element
Combustion, blast, vapour and cloud.

4. Dark revolving in silent activity:
Unseen in tormenting passions;
An activity unknown and horrible;   20
A self-contemplating shadow,
In enormous labours occupied

5. But Eternals beheld his vast forests
Age on ages he lay, clos'd, unknown,
Brooding shut in the deep; all avoid   25
The petrific abominable chaos

6. His cold horrors silent, dark Urizen   c
Prepar'd: his ten thousands of thunders
Rang'd in gloom'd array stretch out across
The dread world, & the rolling of wheels   30
As of swelling seas, sound in his clouds
In his hills of stor'd snows, in his mountains
Of hail & ice; voices of terror,
Are heard, like thunders of autumn,
When the cloud blazes over the harvests   35

Chap: II.   t

1. Earth was not: nor globes of attraction   c
The will of the Immortal expanded
Or contracted his all flexible senses.
Death was not, but eternal life sprung

2. The sound of a trumpet the heavens   40
Awoke & vast clouds of blood roll'd
Round the dim rocks of Urizen, so nam'd
That solitary one in Immensity

3. Shrill the trumpet: & myriads of Eternity,   t
                                                               t
Muster around the bleak desarts
Now fill'd with clouds, darkness & waters
That roll'd perplex'd labring & utter'd
Words articulate, bursting in thunders
That roll'd on the tops of his mountains   5

4: From the depths of dark solitude. From
The eternal abode in my holiness,   c
Hidden set apart in my stern counsels
Reserv'd for the days of futurity,   c
I have sought for a joy without pain,   c 10
For a solid without fluctuation
Why will you die O Eternals?
Why live in unquenchable burnings?

5 First I fought with the fire; consum'd
Inwards, into a deep world within: 15
A void immense, wild dark & deep,   c
Where nothing was; Natures wide womb[.]

-70-

And self balanc'd stretch'd o'er the void
I alone, even I! the winds merciless
Bound; but condensing, in torrents   20
They fall & fall; strong I repell'd
The vast waves, & arose on the waters
A wide world of solid obstruction

6. Here alone I in books formd of metals   e
Have written the secrets of wisdom   25
The secrets of dark contemplation
By fightings and conflicts dire,
With terrible monsters Sin-bred:
Which the bosoms of all inhabit;
Seven deadly Sins of the soul.   t 30

7. Lo! I unfold my darkness: and on
This rock, place with strong hand the Book
Of eternal brass, written in my solitude.

8. Laws of peace, of love, of unity:
Of pity, compassion, forgiveness.   35
Let each chuse one habitation:
His ancient infinite mansion:
One command, one joy, one desire,
One curse, one weight, one measure
One King, one God, one Law.   40

Chap: III.   t

1. The voice ended, they saw his pale visage   e
Emerge from the darkness; his hand
On the rock of eternity unclasping
The Book of brass. Rage siez'd the strong

2. Rage, fury, intense indignation   45
In cataracts of fire blood & gall
In whirlwinds of sulphurous smoke:
And enormous forms of energy;
All the seven deadly sins of the soul   t

PLATE 5
In living creations appear'd   t
In the flames of eternal fury.   t

3. Sund'ring, dark'ning, thund'ring!
Rent away with a terrible crash
Eternity roll'd wide apart   5
Wide asunder rolling

Mountainous all around
Departing; departing; departing:
Leaving ruinous fragments of life
Hanging frowning cliffs & all between   10
An ocean of voidness unfathomable.

4. The roaring fires ran o'er the heav'ns
In whirlwinds & cataracts of blood
And o'er the dark desarts of Urizen
Fires pour thro' the void on all sides   15
On Urizens self-begotten armies.   t

5. But no light from the fires. all was darkness
In the flames of Eternal fury

6. In fierce anguish & quenchless flames   e
To the desarts and rocks He ran raging   t 20
To hide, but He could not: combining   t
He dug mountains & hills in vast strength,   t
He piled them in incessant labour,   t
In howlings & pangs & fierce madness
Long periods in burning fires labouring   25
Till hoary, and age-broke, and aged,
In despair and the shadows of death.

7. And a roof, vast petrific around,
On all sides He fram'd: like a womb;   t
Where thousands of rivers in veins   30
Of blood pour down the mountains to cool
The eternal fires beating without
From Eternals; & like a black globe
View'd by sons of Eternity, standing
On the shore of the infinite ocean   35
Like a human heart strugling & beating
The vast world of Urizen appear'd.

8. And Los round the dark globe of Urizen,   e
Kept watch for Eternals to confine,
The obscure separation alone;   40
For Eternity stood wide apart,

PLATE 6

As the stars are apart from the earth

9. Los wept howling around the dark Demon:
And cursing his lot; for in anguish,
Urizen was rent from his side;
And a fathomless void for his feet;   5
And intense fires for his dwelling.

10. But Urizen laid in a stony sleep
Unorganiz'd, rent from Eternity   t

11. The Eternals said: What is this? Death[.]
Urizen is a clod of clay.   10

PLATE 7   t

12: Los howld in a dismal stupor,
Groaning! gnashing! groaning!
Till the wrenching apart was healed

13: But the wrenching of Urizen heal'd not
Cold, featureless, flesh or clay,   5
Rifted with direful changes
He lay in a dreamless night

14: Till Los rouz'd his fires, affrighted   t
At the formless unmeasurable death.

PLATE 8   t

Chap: IV:[a]

1: Los smitten with astonishment
Frightend at the hurtling bones

2: And at the surging sulphureous
Perturbed Immortal mad raging

3: In whirlwinds & pitch & nitre   5
Round the furious limbs of Los

4: And Los formed nets & gins
And threw the nets round about

5: He watch'd in shuddring fear
The dark changes & bound every change   10
With rivets of iron & brass;

6. And these were the changes of Urizen.

PLATE 10

Chap: IV.[b]

1. Ages on ages roll'd over him!   e
In stony sleep ages roll'd over him!
Like a dark waste stretching chang'able
By earthquakes riv'n, belching sullen fires
On ages roll'd ages in ghastly   5
Sick torment; around him in whirlwinds
Of darkness the eternal Prophet howl'd

Beating still on his rivets of iron
Pouring sodor of iron; dividing
The horrible night into watches.   10

2. And Urizen (so his eternal name)
His prolific delight obscurd more & more
In dark secresy hiding in surgeing
Sulphureous fluid his phantasies.
The Eternal Prophet heavd the dark bellows,   15
And turn'd restless the tongs; and the hammer
Incessant beat; forging chains new & new
Numb'ring with links. hours, days & years

3 The eternal mind bounded began to roll
Eddies of wrath ceaseless round & round,   20
And the sulphureous foam surgeing thick
Settled, a lake, bright, & shining clear:
White as the snow on the mountains cold.

4. Forgetfulness, dumbness, necessity!
In chains of the mind locked up,   25
Like fetters of ice shrinking together
Disorganiz'd, rent from Eternity,
Los beat on his fetters of iron;
And heated his furnaces & pour'd
Iron sodor and sodor of brass   30

5. Restless turnd the immortal inchain'd
Heaving dolorous! anguish'd! unbearable
Till a roof shaggy wild inclos'd
In an orb, his fountain of thought.

6. In a horrible dreamful slumber;   35
Like the linked infernal chain;
A vast Spine writh'd in torment
Upon the winds; shooting pain'd
Ribs, like a bending cavern
And bones of solidness, froze   40
Over all his nerves of joy.
And a first Age passed over,   t
And a state of dismal woe.   t

PLATE II

7 From the caverns of his jointed Spine,
Down sunk with fright a red
Round globe hot burning deep
Deep down into the Abyss:
Panting: Conglobing, Trembling   5
Shooting out ten thousand branches

Around his solid bones.
And a second Age passed over,
And a state of dismal woe.

8. In harrowing fear rolling round;   10
His nervous brain shot branches
Round the branches of his heart.
On high into two little orbs
And fixed in two little caves
Hiding carefully from the wind,   15
His Eyes beheld the deep,
And a third Age passed over:
And a state of dismal woe.

9. The pangs of hope began,
In heavy pain striving, struggling.   20
Two Ears in close volutions.
From beneath his orbs of vision
Shot spiring out and petrified
As they grew. And a fourth Age passed
And a state of dismal woe.   25

10. In ghastly torment sick;
Hanging upon the wind;

PLATE 13

Two Nostrils bent down to the deep.
And a fifth Age passed over;
And a state of dismal woe.

11. In ghastly torment sick;
Within his ribs bloated round,   5
A craving Hungry Cavern;
Thence arose his channeld Throat,
And like a red flame a Tongue.
Of thirst & of hunger appeard.
And a sixth Age passed over: 10
And a state of dismal woe.

12. Enraged & stifled with torment
He threw his right Arm to the north
His left Arm to the south
Shooting out in anguish deep,   15
And his Feet stampd the nether Abyss
In trembling & howling & dismay.
And a seventh Age passed over:
And a state of dismal woe.

Chap: V.

1. In terrors Los shrunk from his task:
His great hammer fell from his hand:
His fires beheld, and sickening,
Hid their strong limbs in smoke.
For with noises ruinous loud;
With hurtlings & clashings & groans   25
The Immortal endur'd his chains,
Tho' bound in a deadly sleep.

2. All the myriads of Eternity:
All the wisdom & joy of life:
Roll like a sea around him,   30
Except what his little orbs
Of sight by degrees unfold.

3. And now his eternal life
Like a dream was obliterated

4. Shudd'ring, the Eternal Prophet smote   35
With a stroke, from his north to south region
The bellows & hammer are silent now
A nerveless silence, his prophetic voice
Siez'd; a cold solitude & dark void
The Eternal Prophet & Urizen clos'd   40

5. Ages on ages rolld over them
Cut off from life & light frozen
Into horrible forms of deformity
Los suffer'd his fires to decay
Then he look'd back with anxious desire   45
But the space undivided by existence
Struck horror into his soul.

6. Los wept obscur'd with mourning:
His bosom earthquak'd with sighs;
He saw Urizen deadly black,   50
In his chains bound, & Pity began,

7. In anguish dividing & dividing
For pity divides the soul
In pangs eternity on eternity
Life in cataracts pourd down his cliffs   55
The void shrunk the lymph into Nerves
Wand'ring wide on the bosom of night
And left a round globe of blood
Trembling upon the Void

PLATE 15

Thus the Eternal Prophet was divided
Before the death-image of Urizen
For in changeable clouds and darkness
In a winterly night beneath,
The Abyss of Los stretch'd immense: 5
And now seen now obscur'd, to the eyes
Of Eternals the visions remote
Of the dark seperation appear'd.
As glasses discover Worlds
In the endless Abyss of space,   10
So the expanding eyes of Immortals
Beheld the dark visions of Los,
And the globe of life blood trembling.

PLATE 18

8. The globe of life blood trembled
Branching out into roots;
Fibrous, writhing upon the winds;
Fibres of blood, milk and tears;
In pangs, eternity on eternity.   5
At length in tears & cries imbodied
A female form trembling and pale
Waves before his deathy face

9. All Eternity shudderd at sight
Of the first female now separate   10
Pale as a cloud of snow
Waving before the face of Los

10. Wonder, awe, fear, astonishment,
Petrify the eternal myriads;
At the first female form now separate   15

PLATE 19

They call'd her Pity, and fled

11. "Spread a Tent, with strong curtains around them
"Let cords & stakes bind in the Void
That Eternals may no more behold them"

12. They began to weave curtains of darkness   5
They erected large pillars round the Void
With golden hooks fastend in the pillars
With infinite labour the Eternals
A woof wove, and called it Science

Chap: VI.

1. But Los saw the Female & pitied   10
He embrac'd her, she wept, she refus'd
In perverse and cruel delight
She fled from his arms, yet he followd

2. Eternity shudder'd when they saw,
Man begetting his likeness,   15
On his own divided image.

3. A time passed over, the Eternals
Began to erect the tent;
When Enitharmon, sick,
Felt a Worm within her womb.   20

4. Yet helpless it lay like a Worm
In the trembling womb
To be moulded into existence

5. All day the worm lay on her bosom
All night within her womb   25
The worm lay till it grew to a serpent
With dolorous hissings & poisons
Round Enitharmons loins folding,

6. Coild within Enitharmons womb
The serpent grew casting its scales,   30
With sharp pangs the hissings began
To change to a grating cry,
Many sorrows and dismal throes
Many forms of fish, bird & beast,
Brought forth an Infant form   35
Where was a worm before.

7. The Eternals their tent finished
Alarm'd with these gloomy visions
When Enitharmon groaning
Produc'd a man Child to the light.   40

8. A shriek ran thro' Eternity:
And a paralytic stroke;
At the birth of the Human shadow.

9. Delving earth in his resistless way;
Howling, the Child with fierce flames   45
Issu'd from Enitharmon.

10. The Eternals, closed the tent:
They beat down the stakes the cords

PLATE 20

Stretch'd for a work of eternity;
No more Los beheld Eternity.

11. In his hands he siez'd the infant
He bathed him in springs of sorrow
He gave him to Enitharmon.   5

Chap. VII.

1. They named the child Orc, he grew
Fed with milk of Enitharmon

2. Los awoke her; O sorrow & pain!
A tight'ning girdle grew,
Around his bosom. In sobbings   10
He burst the girdle in twain,
But still another girdle
Oppressd his bosom, In sobbings
Again he burst it. Again
Another girdle succeeds   15
The girdle was form'd by day;
By night was burst in twain.

3. These falling down on the rock
Into an iron Chain
In each other link by link lock'd   20

4. They took Orc to the top of a mountain.
O how Enitharmon wept!
They chain'd his young limbs to the rock
With the Chain of Jealousy
Beneath Urizens deathful shadow   25

5. The dead heard the voice of the child
And began to awake from sleep
All things. heard the voice of the child
And began to awake to life.

6. And Urizen craving with hunger   30
Stung with the odours of Nature
Explor'd his dens around

7. He form'd a line & a plummet
To divide the Abyss beneath.
He form'd a dividing rule: 35

8. He formed scales to weigh;
He formed massy weights;
He formed a brazen quadrant;

He formed golden compasses
And began to explore the Abyss   40
And he planted a garden of fruits

9. But Los encircled Enitharmon
With fires of Prophecy
From the sight of Urizen & Orc.

10. And she bore an enormous race   45

Chap. VIII.

1. Urizen explor'd his dens
Mountain, moor, & wilderness,
With a globe of fire lighting his journey
A fearful journey, annoy'd
By cruel enormities: forms   50

PLATE 23

Of life on his forsaken mountains

2. And his world teemd vast enormities
Frightning; faithless; fawning
Portions of life; similitudes
Of a foot, or a hand, or a head   5
Or a heart, or an eye, they swam mischevous
Dread terrors! delighting in blood

3. Most Urizen sicken'd to see
His eternal creations appear
Sons & daughters of sorrow on mountains   10
Weeping! wailing! first Thiriel appear'd
Astonish'd at his own existence
Like a man from a cloud born, & Utha
From the waters emerging, laments!
Grodna rent the deep earth howling   15
Amaz'd! his heavens immense cracks
Like the ground parch'd with heat; then Fuzon
Flam'd out! first begotten, last born.
All his eternal sons in like manner
His daughters from green herbs & cattle   20
From monsters, & worms of the pit.

4. He in darkness clos'd, view'd all his race
And his soul sicken'd! he curs'd
Both sons & daughters; for he saw
That no flesh nor spirit could keep   25
His iron laws one moment.

5. For he saw that life liv'd upon death

PLATE 25

The Ox in the slaughter house moans
The Dog at the wintry door
And he wept, & he called it Pity
And his tears flowed down on the winds

6. Cold he wander'd on high, over their cities   5
In weeping & pain & woe!
And where-ever he wanderd in sorrows
Upon the aged heavens
A cold shadow follow'd behind him
Like a spiders web, moist, cold, & dim   10
Drawing out from his sorrowing soul
The dungeon-like heaven dividing
Where ever the footsteps of Urizen
Walk'd over the cities in sorrow.

7. Till a Web dark & cold, throughout all   15
The tormented element stretch'd
From the sorrows of Urizens soul
And the Web is a Female in embrio.   t
None could break the Web, no wings of fire.

8. So twisted the cords, & so knotted   20
The meshes: twisted like to the human brain

9. And all calld it, The Net of Religion.

Chap: IX

1. Then the Inhabitants of those Cities: e
Felt their Nerves change into Marrow
And hardening Bones began   25
In swift diseases and torments,
In throbbings & shootings & grindings
Thro' all the coasts; till weaken'd
The Senses inward rush'd shrinking,
Beneath the dark net of infection.   30

2. Till the shrunken eyes clouded over
Discernd not the woven hipocrisy
But the streaky slime in their heavens
Brought together by narrowing perceptions
Appeard transparent air; for their eyes   35
Grew small like the eyes of a man
And in reptile forms shrinking together
Of seven feet stature they remaind

3. Six days they. shrunk up from existence
And on the seventh day they rested   40
And they bless'd the seventh day, in sick hope:
And forgot their eternal life

4. And their thirty cities divided
In form of a human heart
No more could they rise at will   45
In the infinite void, but bound down
To earth by their narrowing perceptions

PLATE 28

They lived a period of years
Then left a noisom body
To the jaws of devouring darkness

5. And their children wept, & built
Tombs in the desolate places,   5
And form'd laws of prudence, and call'd them
The eternal laws of God

6. And the thirty cities remain
Surrounded by salt floods, now call'd
Africa: its name was then Egypt.   10

7. The remaining sons of Urizen
Beheld their brethren shrink together
Beneath the Net of Urizen;
Perswasion was in vain;
For the ears of the inhabitants   15
Were wither'd, & deafen'd, & cold.
And their eyes could not discern,
Their brethren of other cities.

8. So Fuzon call'd all together
The remaining children of Urizen: 20
And they left the pendulous earth:
They called it Egypt, & left it.

9. And the salt ocean rolled englob'd

The End of the [first] book of Urizen

❧

−82−

THE BOOK of AHANIA

LAMBETH Printed by W Blake 1795

t, e

PLATE 2

AHANIA

Chap: Ist

1: Fuzon, on a chariot iron-wing'd   e
On spiked flames rose; his hot visage
Flam'd furious! sparkles his hair & beard
Shot down his wide bosom and shoulders.
On clouds of smoke rages his chariot   5
And his right hand burns red in its cloud
Moulding into a vast globe, his wrath
As the thunder-stone is moulded.
Son of Urizens silent burnings

2: Shall we worship this Demon of smoke,   10
Said Fuzon, this abstract non-entity
This cloudy God seated on waters
Now seen, now obscur'd; King of sorrow?

3: So he spoke, in a fiery flame,
On Urizen frowning indignant,   15
The Globe of wrath shaking on high
Roaring with fury, he threw
The howling Globe: burning it flew
Lengthning into a hungry beam. Swiftly

4: Oppos'd to the exulting flam'd beam   20
The broad Disk of Urizen upheav'd
Across the Void many a mile.

5: It was forg'd in mills where the winter
Beats incessant; ten winters the disk
Unremitting endur'd the cold hammer.   25

6: But the strong arm that sent it, remember'd
The sounding beam; laughing it tore through
That beaten mass: keeping its direction
The cold loins of Urizen dividing.

7: Dire shriek'd his invisible Lust   e 30
Deep groan'd Urizen! stretching his awful hand
Ahania (so name his parted soul)
He siez'd on his mountains of Jealousy.
He groand anguishd & called her Sin,

Kissing her and weeping over her;   35
Then hid her in darkness in silence;
Jealous tho' she was invisible.

8: She fell down a faint shadow wandring
In chaos and circling dark Urizen,
As the moon anguishd circles the earth;   40
Hopeless! abhorrd! a death-shadow,
Unseen, unbodied, unknown,
The mother of Pestilence.

9: But the fiery beam of Fuzon
Was a pillar of fire to Egypt   45
Five hundred years wandring on earth
Till Los siezd it and beat in a mass
With the body of the sun.

PLATE 3

Chap: II^d

1: But the forehead of Urizen gathering,
And his eyes pale with anguish, his lips
Blue & changing; in tears and bitter
Contrition he prepar'd his Bow,

2: Form'd of Ribs: that in his dark solitude   5
When obscur'd in his forests fell monsters,
Arose. For his dire Contemplations
Rush'd down like floods from his mountains
In torrents of mud settling thick
With Eggs of unnatural production   10
Forthwith hatching; some howl'd on his hills
Some in vales; some aloft flew in air

3: Of these: an enormous dread Serpent
Scaled and poisonous horned
Approach'd Urizen even to his knees   15
As he sat on his dark rooted Oak.

4: With his horns he push'd furious.
Great the conflict & great the jealousy
In cold poisons: but Urizen smote him

5: First he poison'd the rocks with his blood   20
Then polish'd his ribs, and his sinews
Dried; laid them apart till winter;
Then a Bow black prepar'd: on this Bow,
A poisoned rock plac'd in silence:
He utter'd these words to the Bow: 25

6: O Bow of the clouds of secresy!
O nerve of that lust form'd monster!
Send this rock swift, invisible thro'
The black clouds, on the bosom of Fuzon

7: So saying, In torment of his wounds,   30
He bent the enormous ribs slowly;
A circle of darkness! then fixed
The sinew in its rest: then the Rock
Poisonous source! plac'd with art, lifting difficult
Its weighty bulk: silent the rock lay.   35

8: While Fuzon his tygers unloosing
Thought Urizen slain by his wrath.
I am God. said he, eldest of things!

9: Sudden sings the rock, swift & invisible
On Fuzon flew, enter'd his bosom;   40
His beautiful visage, his tresses,
That gave light to the mornings of heaven
Were smitten with darkness, deform'd
And outstretch'd on the edge of the forest

10: But the rock fell upon the Earth,   45
Mount Sinai, in Arabia.

Chap: III:

1: The Globe shook; and Urizen seated   c
On black clouds his sore wound anointed
The ointment flow'd down on the void
Mix'd with blood; here the snake gets her poison[.]   50

2: With difficulty & great pain; Urizen
Lifted on high the dead corse:
On his shoulders he bore it to where
A Tree hung over the Immensity

3: For when Urizen shrunk away   55
From Eternals, he sat on a rock
Barren; a rock which himself
From redounding fancies had petrified[.]
Many tears fell on the rock,
Many sparks of vegetation;   60
Soon shot the pained root
Of Mystery, under his heel:
It grew a thick tree; he wrote
In silence his book of iron:

Till the horrid plant bending its boughs 65
Grew to roots when it felt the earth
And again sprung to many a tree.

4: Amaz'd started Urizen! when
He beheld himself compassed round
And high roofed over with trees 70
He arose but the stems stood so thick
He with difficulty and great pain
Brought his Books, all but the Book

PLATE 4

Of iron, from the dismal shade

5: The Tree still grows over the Void
Enrooting itself all around
An endless labyrinth of woe!

6: The corse of his first begotten 5
On the accursed Tree of MYSTERY:
On the topmost stem of this Tree
Urizen nail'd Fuzon's corse.

Chap: IV:

1: Forth flew the arrows of pestilence
Round the pale living Corse on the tree 10

2: For in Urizens slumbers of abstraction
In the infinite ages of Eternity:
When his Nerves of Joy melted & flow'd
A white Lake on the dark blue air
In perturb'd pain and dismal torment 15
Now stretching out, now swift conglobing.

3: Effluvia vapor'd above
In noxious clouds; these hover'd thick
Over the disorganiz'd Immortal,
Till petrific pain scurfd o'er the Lakes 20
As the bones of man, solid & dark

4: The clouds of disease hover'd wide
Around the Immortal in torment
Perching around the hurtling bones
Disease on disease, shape on shape, 25
Winged screaming in blood & torment.

5: The Eternal Prophet beat on his anvils
Enrag'd in the desolate darkness
He forg'd nets of iron around
And Los threw them around the bones 30

6: The shapes screaming flutter'd vain
Some combin'd into muscles & glands
Some organs for craving and lust
Most remain'd on the tormented void: 35
Urizens army of horrors.

7: Round the pale living Corse on the Tree
Forty years flew the arrows of pestilence

8: Wailing and terror and woe
Ran thro' all his dismal world:
Forty years all his sons & daughters   40
Felt their skulls harden; then Asia
Arose in the pendulous deep.

9: They reptilize upon the Earth.

10: Fuzon groand on the Tree.

Chap: V

1: The lamenting voice of Ahania   ᶜ 45
Weeping upon the void.
And round the Tree of Fuzon:
Distant in solitary night
Her voice was heard, but no form
Had she: but her tears from clouds   50
Eternal fell round the Tree

2: And the voice cried: Ah Urizen! Love!
Flower of morning! I weep on the verge
Of Non-entity; how wide the Abyss
Between Ahania and thee!   55

3: I lie on the verge of the deep.
I see thy dark clouds ascend,
I see thy black forests and floods,
A horrible waste to my eyes!

4: Weeping I walk over rocks   60
Over dens & thro' valleys of death
Why didst thou despise Ahania
To cast me from thy bright presence
Into the World of Loneness

5: I cannot touch his hand: 65
Nor weep on his knees, nor hear
His voice & bow, nor see his eyes
And joy, nor hear his footsteps, and

My heart leap at the lovely sound!
I cannot kiss the place   70
Whereon his bright feet have trod,

PLATE 5

But I wander on the rocks
With hard necessity.

6: Where is my golden palace
Where my ivory bed
Where the joy of my morning hour   5
Where the sons of eternity, singing

7: To awake bright Urizen, my king!
To arise to the mountain sport,
To the bliss of eternal valleys:

8: To awake my king in the morn!   10
To embrace Ahanias joy
On the bredth of his open bosom:
From my soft cloud of dew to fall
In showers of life on his harvests.

9: When he gave my happy soul   15
To the sons of eternal joy:
When he took the daughters of life.
Into my chambers of love:

10: When I found babes of bliss on my beds.
And bosoms of milk in my chambers   20
Fill'd with eternal seed
O! eternal births sung round Ahania,
In interchange sweet of their joys.

11: Swell'd with ripeness & fat with fatness
Bursting on winds my odors,   25
My ripe figs and rich pomegranates
In infant joy at thy feet
O Urizen, sported and sang;

12: Then thou with thy lap full of seed
With thy hand full of generous fire   30
Walked forth from the clouds of morning
On the virgins of springing joy,
On the human soul to cast
The seed of eternal science.

13: The sweat poured down thy temples   35
To Ahania return'd in evening

-88-

The moisture awoke to birth
My mothers-joys, sleeping in bliss.

14: But now alone over rocks, mountains
Cast out from thy lovely bosom: 40
Cruel jealousy! selfish fear!
Self-destroying: how can delight,
Renew in these chains of darkness
Where bones of beasts are strown
On the bleak and snowy mountains   45
Where bones from the birth are buried
Before they see the light.

FINIS

❧

THE BOOK of LOS

t,e

LAMBETH Printed by W Blake 1795

PLATE 3

LOS

Chap. I

1: Eno aged Mother,   e
Who the chariot of Leutha guides,
Since the day of thunders in old time

2: Sitting beneath the eternal Oak
Trembled and shook the stedfast Earth   5
And thus her speech broke forth.

3: O Times remote!
When Love & Joy were adoration:
And none impure were deem'd.
Not Eyeless Covet   10
Nor Thin-lip'd Envy
Nor Bristled Wrath
Nor Curled Wantonness

4: But Covet was poured full:
Envy fed with fat of lambs: 15
Wrath with lions gore:
Wantonness lulld to sleep
With the virgins lute,
Or sated with her love.

-89-

5: Till Covet broke his locks & bars,   20
And slept with open doors:
Envy sung at the rich mans feast:
Wrath was follow'd up and down
By a little ewe lamb
And Wantonness on his own true love   25
Begot a giant race:

6: Raging furious the flames of desire   c
Ran thro' heaven & earth, living flames
Intelligent, organiz'd: arm'd
With destruction & plagues. In the midst   30
The Eternal Prophet bound in a chain
Compell'd to watch Urizens shadow

7: Rag'd with curses & sparkles of fury
Round the flames roll as Los hurls his chains
Mounting up from his fury, condens'd   35
Rolling round & round, mounting on high
Into vacuum: into non-entity.
Where nothing was! dash'd wide apart
His feet stamp the eternal fierce-raging
Rivers of wide flame; they roll round   40
And round on all sides making their way
Into darkness and shadowy obscurity

8: Wide apart stood the fires: Los remain'd   c
In the void between fire and fire[.]
In trembling and horror they beheld him   45
They stood wide apart, driv'n by his hands
And his feet which the nether abyss
Stamp'd in fury and hot indignation

9: But no light from the fires all was

PLATE 4

Darkness round Los: heat was not; for bound up
Into fiery spheres from his fury
The gigantic flames trembled and hid

10: Coldness, darkness, obstruction, a Solid
Without fluctuation, hard as adamant   5
Black as marble of Egypt; impenetrable
Bound in the fierce raging Immortal.
And the seperated fires froze in
A vast solid without fluctuation,
Bound in his expanding clear senses   10

Chap: II

1: The Immortal stood frozen amidst
The vast rock of eternity; times
And times; a night of vast durance:
Impatient, stifled, stiffend, hardned.

2: Till impatience no longer could bear   15
The hard bondage, rent: rent, the vast solid
With a crash from immense to immense

3: Crack'd across into numberless fragments[.]
The Prophetic wrath, strug'ling for vent
Hurls apart, stamping furious to dust   20
And crumbling with bursting sobs; heaves
The black marble on high into fragments

4: Hurl'd apart on all sides, as a falling
Rock: the innumerable fragments away
Fell asunder; and horrible vacuum   25
Beneath him & on all sides round.

5: Falling, falling! Los fell & fell
Sunk precipitant heavy down down
Times on times, night on night, day on day
Truth has bounds. Error none: falling, falling: 30
Years on years, and ages on ages
Still he fell thro' the void, still a void
Found for falling day & night without end.
For tho' day or night was not; their spaces
Were measurd by his incessant whirls   35
In the horrid vacuity bottomless.

6: The Immortal revolving; indignant
First in wrath threw his limbs, like the babe
New born into our world: wrath subsided
And contemplative thoughts first arose   40
Then aloft his head rear'd in the Abyss
And his downward-borne fall chang'd oblique

7: Many ages of groans: till there grew   e
Branchy forms: organizing the Human
Into finite inflexible organs.   45

8: Till in process from falling he bore
Sidelong on the purple air, wafting
The weak breeze in efforts oerwearied

9: Incessant the falling Mind labour'd
Organizing itself: till the Vacuum   50
Became element, pliant to rise,
Or to fall, or to swim, or to fly:
With ease searching the dire vacuity

Chap: III

1: The Lungs heave incessant, dull and heavy
For as yet were all other parts formless   55
Shiv'ring: clinging around like a cloud
Dim & glutinous as the white Polypus
Driv'n by waves & englob'd on the tide.

2: And the unformed part crav'd repose
Sleep began: the Lungs heave on the wave   60
Weary overweigh'd, sinking beneath
In a stifling black fluid he woke

3: He arose on the waters, but soon
Heavy falling his organs like roots
Shooting out from the seed, shot beneath,   65
And a vast world of waters around him
In furious torrents began.

4: Then he sunk, & around his spent Lungs
Began intricate pipes that drew in
The spawn of the waters. Outbranching   70

PLATE 5

An immense Fibrous form, stretching out   t
Thro' the bottoms of immensity raging.

5: He rose on the floods: then he smote
The wild deep with his terrible wrath,
Seperating the heavy and thin.   5

6: Down the heavy sunk; cleaving around
To the fragments of solid: up rose
The thin, flowing round the fierce fires
That glow'd furious in the expanse.

Chap: IV:

1: Then Light first began; from the fires   10
Beams, conducted by fluid so pure
Flow'd around the Immense: Los beheld
Forthwith, writhing upon the dark void

The Back bone of Urizen appear
Hurtling upon the wind   15
Like a serpent! like an iron chain
Whirling about in the Deep.

2: Upfolding his Fibres together
To a Form of impregnable strength
Los astonish'd and terrified, built   20
Furnaces; he formed an Anvil
A Hammer of adamant then began
The binding of Urizen day and night

3: Circling round the dark Demon, with howlings
Dismay & sharp blightings; the Prophet   25
Of Eternity beat on his iron links.

4: And first from those infinite fires
The light that flow'd down on the winds
He siez'd; beating incessant, condensing
The subtil particles in an Orb.   30

5: Roaring indignant the bright sparks
Endur'd the vast Hammer; but unwearied
Los beat on the Anvil; till glorious
An immense Orb of fire he fram'd

6: Oft he quench'd it beneath in the Deeps   35
Then survey'd the all-bright mass. Again
Siezing fires from the terrific Orbs
He heated the round Globe, then beat[,]
While roaring his Furnaces endur'd
The chaind Orb in their infinite wombs   40

7: Nine ages completed their circles
When Los heated the glowing mass, casting
It down into the Deeps: the Deeps fled
Away in redounding smoke; the Sun
Stood self-balanc'd. And Los smild with joy.   45
He the vast Spine of Urizen siez'd
And bound down to the glowing illusion

8: But no light, for the Deep fled away
On all sides, and left an unform'd
Dark vacuity: here Urizen lay   50
In fierce torments on his glowing bed

9: Till his Brain in a rock, & his Heart
In a fleshy slough formed four rivers
Obscuring the immense Orb of fire
Flowing down into night: till a Form   55
Was completed, a Human Illusion
In darkness and deep clouds involvd.   e

The End of the
Book of LOS ·

❦

MILTON

a Poem in 2 Books   t,e

The Author & Printer W Blake 1804

To Justify the Ways of God to Men   e

PLATE I

Preface.   e

The Stolen and Perverted Writings of Homer & Ovid: of Plato & Cicero.
which all Men ought to contemn: are set up by artifice against the Sublime
of the Bible. but when the New Age is at leisure to Pronounce: all will be
set right: & those Grand Works of the more ancient & consciously & pro-
fessedly Inspired Men, will hold their proper rank, & the Daughters of Memory shall become the Daughters of Inspiration. Shakspeare & Milton were
both curbd by the general malady & infection from the silly Greek & Latin
slaves of the Sword.

Rouze up O Young Men of the New Age! set your foreheads against the
ignorant Hirelings! For we have Hirelings in the Camp, the Court & the
University: who would if they could, for ever depress Mental & prolong
Corporeal War. Painters! on you I call! Sculptors! Architects! Suffer not the
fash[i]onable Fools to depress your powers by the prices they pretend to
give for contemptible works or the expensive advertizing boasts that they
make of such works; believe Christ & his Apostles that there is a Class of
Men whose whole delight is in Destroying. We do not want either Greek or
Roman Models if we are but just & true to our own Imaginations, those
Worlds of Eternity in which we shall live for ever; in Jesus our Lord.

And did those feet in ancient time.   e
Walk upon Englands mountains green:

And was the holy Lamb of God,
On Englands pleasant pastures seen!

And did the Countenance Divine,　　　　　　　5
Shine forth upon our clouded hills?
And was Jerusalem builded here,
Among these dark Satanic Mills?

Bring me my Bow of burning gold:
Bring me my Arrows of desire:　　　　　　　10
Bring me my Spear: O clouds unfold!
Bring me my Chariot of fire!

I will not cease from Mental Fight,
Nor shall my Sword sleep in my hand:
Till we have built Jerusalem,　　　　　　　15
In Englands green & pleasant Land.

Would to God that all the Lords people were Prophets.　　c
　　　　　　　　　　　　Numbers XI. ch 29 v.

PLATE 2

MILTON

Book the First　　　　　　　c

Daughters of Beulah! Muses who inspire the Poets Song　　c
Record the journey of immortal Milton thro' your Realms
Of terror & mild moony lustre, in soft sexual delusions
Of varied beauty, to delight the wanderer and repose
His burning thirst & freezing hunger! Come into my hand　　5
By your mild power; descending down the Nerves of my right arm
From out the Portals of my Brain, where by your ministry
The Eternal Great Humanity Divine. planted his Paradise,
And in it caus'd the Spectres of the Dead to take sweet forms
In likeness of himself. Tell also of the False Tongue! vegetated　　10
Beneath your land of shadows: of its sacrifices. and
Its offerings; even till Jesus, the image of the Invisible God
Became its prey; a curse, an offering. and an atonement,
For Death Eternal in the heavens of Albion, & before the Gates
Of Jerusalem his Emanation, in the heavens beneath Beulah　　15

Say first! what mov'd Milton, who walkd about in Eternity　　c
One hundred years, pondring the intricate mazes of Providence
Unhappy tho in heav'n, he obey'd, he murmur'd not. he was silent
Viewing his Sixfold Emanation scatter'd thro' the deep
In torment! To go into the deep her to redeem & himself perish?　　20
What cause at length mov'd Milton to this unexampled deed?　　t
A Bards prophetic Song! for sitting at eternal tables,

Terrific among the Sons of Albion in chorus solemn & loud
A Bard broke forth! all sat attentive to the awful man.

Mark well my words! they are of your eternal salvation: 25

Three Classes are Created by the Hammer of Los, & Woven   t,c
PLATE 3   t
By Enitharmons Looms when Albion was slain upon his Mountains
And in his Tent, thro envy of Living Form, even of the Divine Vision
And of the sports of Wisdom in the Human Imagination
Which is the Divine Body of the Lord Jesus. blessed for ever.
Mark well my words. they are of your eternal salvation!   5

Urizen lay in darkness & solitude, in chains of the mind lock'd up   c
Los siezd his Hammer & Tongs; he labourd at his resolute Anvil
Among indefinite Druid rocks & snows of doubt & reasoning.

Refusing all Definite Form, the Abstract Horror roofd. stony hard
And a first Age passed over & a State of dismal woe!   10

Down sunk with fright a red round Globe hot burning. deep
Deep down into the Abyss. panting: conglobing: trembling
And a second Age passed over & a State of dismal woe.

Rolling round into two little Orbs & closed in two little Caves
The Eyes beheld the Abyss: lest bones of solidness freeze over all   15
And a third Age passed over & a State of dismal woe.

From beneath his Orbs of Vision, Two Ears in close volutions
Shot spiring out in the deep darkness & petrified as they grew
And a fourth Age passed over & a State of dismal woe.

Hanging upon the wind, Two Nostrils bent down into the Deep   20
And a fifth Age passed over & a State of dismal woe.

In ghastly torment sick, a Tongue of hunger & thirst flamed out
And a sixth Age passed over & a State of dismal woe.

Enraged & stifled without & within: in terror & woe, he threw his
Right Arm to the north, his left Arm to the south, & his Feet   25
Stampd the nether Abyss in trembling & howling & dismay
And a seventh Age passed over & a State of dismal woe

Terrified Los stood in the Abyss & his immortal limbs
Grew deadly pale; he became what he beheld: for a red
Round Globe sunk down from his Bosom into the Deep in pangs   30
He hoverd over it trembling & weeping. suspended it shook
The nether Abyss in tremblings. he wept over it, he cherish'd it
In deadly sickening pain: till separated into a Female pale
As the cloud that brings the snow: all the while from his Back
A blue fluid exuded in Sinews hardening in the Abyss   35
Till it separated into a Male Form howling in Jealousy

Within labouring. beholding Without: from Particulars to Generals
Subduing his Spectre, they Builded the Looms of Generation
They Builded Great Golgonooza Times on Times Ages on Ages
First Orc was Born then the Shadowy Female: then All Los's Family   40
At last Enitharmon brought forth Satan Refusing Form, in vain   c
The Miller of Eternity made subservient to the Great Harvest
That he may go to his own Place Prince of the Starry Wheels

PLATE 4   t
Beneath the Plow of Rintrah & the Harrow of the Almighty
In the hands of Palamabron. Where the Starry Mills of Satan
Are built beneath the Earth & Waters of the Mundane Shell
Here the Three Classes of Men take their Sexual texture[.] Woven
The Sexual is Threefold: the Human is Fourfold.   5

If you account it Wisdom when you are angry to be silent, and   c
Not to shew it: I do not account that Wisdom but Folly.
Every Mans Wisdom is peculiar to his own Individ[u]ality
O Satan my youngest born, art thou not Prince of the Starry Hosts
And of the Wheels of Heaven, to turn the Mills day & night?   10
Art thou not Newtons Pantocrator weaving the Woof of Locke[?]
To Mortals thy Mills seem every thing & the Harrow of Shaddai
A scheme of Human conduct invisible & incomprehensible[.]
Get to thy Labours at the Mills & leave me to my wrath.

Satan was going to reply, but Los roll'd his loud thunders.   15

Anger me not! thou canst not drive the Harrow in pitys paths.
Thy Work is Eternal Death, with Mills & Ovens & Cauldrons.
Trouble me no more. thou canst not have Eternal Life

So Los spoke! Satan trembling obeyd weeping along the way.
Mark well my words, they are of your eternal Salvation   20

Between South Molton Street & Stratford Place: Calvarys foot   c
Where the Victims were preparing for Sacrifice their Cherubim
Around their loins pourd forth their arrows & their bosoms beam
With all colours of precious stones, & their inmost palaces
Resounded with preparation of animals wild & tame   25
(Mark well my words! Corporeal Friends are Spiritual Enemies)   c
Mocking Druidical Mathematical Proportion of Length Bredth Highth   c
Displaying Naked Beauty! with Flute & Harp & Song

PLATE 5   t
Palamabron with the fiery Harrow in morning returning   c
From breathing fields. Satan fainted beneath the artillery
Christ took on Sin in the Virgins Womb, & put it off on the Cross

All pitied the piteous & was wrath with the wrathful & Los heard it.

And this is the manner of the Daughters of Albion in their beauty   c 5
Every one is threefold in Head & Heart & Reins, & every one

Has three Gates into the Three Heavens of Beulah which shine
Translucent in their Foreheads & their Bosoms & their Loins
Surrounded with fires unapproachable: but whom they please
They take up into their Heavens in intoxicating delight   10
For the Elect cannot be Redeemd, but Created continually
By Offering & Atonement in the crue[l]ties of Moral Law
Hence the three Classes of Men take their fix'd destinations
They are the Two Contraries & the Reasoning Negative.

While the Females prepare the Victims. the Males at Furnaces   c 15
And Anvils dance the dance of tears & pain: loud lightnings
Lash on their limbs as they turn the whirlwinds loose upon
The Furnaces, lamenting around the Anvils & this their Song[:]

Ah weak & wide astray! Ah shut in narrow doleful form
Creeping in reptile flesh upon the bosom of the ground   20
The Eye of Man a little narrow orb closd up & dark
Scarcely beholding the great light conversing with the Void
The Ear, a little shell in small volutions shutting out
All melodies & comprehending only Discord and Harmony
The Tongue a little moisture fills, a little food it cloys   25
A little sound it utters & its cries are faintly heard
Then brings forth Moral Virtue the cruel Virgin Babylon

Can such an Eye judge of the stars? & looking thro its tubes
Measure the sunny rays that point their spears on Udanadan
Can such an Ear filld with the vapours of the yawning pit.   30
Judge of the pure melodious harp struck by a hand divine?
Can such closed Nostrils feel a joy? or tell of autumn fruits
When grapes & figs burst their covering to the joyful air
Can such a Tongue boast of the living waters? or take in
Ought but the Vegetable Ratio & loathe the faint delight   35
Can such gross Lips percieve? alas! folded within themselves
They touch not ought but pallid turn & tremble at every wind

Thus they sing Creating the Three Classes among Druid Rocks   c
Charles calls on Milton for Atonement. Cromwell is ready
James calls for fires in Golgonooza. for heaps of smoking ruins   40
In the night of prosperity and wantonness which he himself Created
Among the Daughters of Albion among the Rocks of the Druids
When Satan fainted beneath the arrows of Elynittria
And Mathematic Proportion was subdued by Living Proportion

PLATE 6
From Golgonooza the spiritual Four-fold London eternal
In immense labours & sorrows, ever building, ever falling,
Thro Albions four Forests which overspread all the Earth,
From London Stone to Blackheath east: to Hounslow west:
To Finchley north: to Norwood south: and the weights   5

Of Enitharmons Loom play lulling cadences on the winds of Albion
From Caithness in the north, to Lizard-point & Dover in the south

Loud sounds the Hammer of Los, & loud his Bellows is heard
Before London to Hampsteads breadths & Highgates heights To
Stratford & old Bow: & across to the Gardens of Kensington   10
On Tyburns Brook: loud groans Thames beneath the iron Forge
Of Rintrah & Palamabron of Theotorm[on] & Bromion, to forge the   t
     instruments
Of Harvest: the Plow & Harrow to pass over the Nations

The Surrey hills glow like the clinkers of the furnace: Lambeths Vale
Where Jerusalems foundations began; where they were laid in ruins   15
Where they were laid in ruins from every Nation & Oak Groves
     rooted
Dark gleams before the Furnace-mouth a heap of burning ashes
When shall Jerusalem return & overspread all the Nations
Return: return to Lambeths Vale O building of human souls
Thence stony Druid Temples overspread the Island white   20
And thence from Jerusalems ruins.. from her walls of salvation
And praise: thro the whole Earth were reard from Ireland
To Mexico & Peru west, & east to China & Japan; till Babel
The Spectre of Albion frownd over the Nations in glory & war
All things begin & end in Albions ancient Druid rocky shore   25
But now the Starry Heavens are fled from the mighty limbs of Albion

Loud sounds the Hammer of Los, loud turn the Wheels of
     Enitharmon
Her Looms vibrate with soft affections, weaving the Web of Life
Out from the ashes of the Dead; Los lifts his iron Ladles
With molten ore: he heaves the iron cliffs in his rattling chains   30
From Hyde Park to the Alms-houses of Mile-end & old Bow
Here the Three Classes of Mortal Men take their fixd destinations
And hence they overspread the Nations of the whole Earth & hence
The Web of Life is woven: & the tender sinews of life created
And the Three Classes of Men regulated by Los's Hammer.   t 35
PLATE 7
The first, The Elect from before the foundation of the World: t
The second, The Redeem'd. The Third, The Reprobate & form'd
To destruction from the mothers womb: follow with me my plow!   t

Of the first class was Satan: with incomparable mildness;   e
His primitive tyrannical attempts on Los: with most endearing love   5
He soft intreated Los to give to him Palamabrons station;
For Palamabron returnd with labour wearied every evening
Palamabron oft refus'd; and as often Satan offer'd
His service till by repeated offers and repeated intreaties
Los gave to him the Harrow of the Almighty; alas blamable   10
Palamabron. fear'd to be angry lest Satan should accuse him of

Ingratitude, & Los believe the accusation thro Satans extreme
Mildness. Satan labour'd all day. it was a thousand years
In the evening returning terrified overlabourd & astonish'd
Embrac'd soft with a brothers tears Palamabron, who also wept   15

Mark well my words! they are of your eternal salvation

Next morning Palamabron rose: the horses of the Harrow
Were maddend with tormenting fury, & the servants of the Harrow
The Gnomes, accus'd Satan, with indignation fury and fire.
Then Palamabron reddening like the Moon in an eclipse,   20
Spoke saying, You know Satans mildness and his self-imposition,
Seeming a brother, being a tyrant, even thinking himself a brother
While he is murdering the just; prophetic I behold
His future course thro' darkness and despair to eternal death
But we must not be tyrants also! he hath assum'd my place   25
For one whole day, under pretence of pity and love to me:
My horses hath he maddend! and my fellow servants injur'd:
How should he[,] he[,] know the duties of another? O foolish   t
          forbearance
Would I had told Los, all my heart! but patience O my friends,
All may be well: silent remain, while I call Los and Satan.   30

Loud as the wind of Beulah that unroots the rocks & hills   e
Palamabron call'd! and Los & Satan came before him
And Palamabron shew'd the horses & the servants. Satan wept,
And mildly cursing Palamabron, him accus'd of crimes
Himself had wrought. Los trembled; Satans blandishments almost   35
Perswaded the Prophet of Eternity that Palamabron
Was Satans enemy, & that the Gnomes being Palamabron's friends
Were leagued together against Satan thro' ancient enmity.
What could Los do? how could he judge, when Satans self, believ'd
That he had not oppres'd the horses of the Harrow, nor the servants. 40

So Los said, Henceforth Palamabron, let each his own station   e
Keep: nor in pity false, nor in officious brotherhood, where
None needs, be active. Mean time Palamabrons horses.
Rag'd with thick flames redundant, & the Harrow maddend with fury.
Trembling Palamabron stood, the strongest of Demons trembled: 45
Curbing his living creatures; many of the strongest Gnomes,
They bit in their wild fury, who also madden'd like wildest beasts

Mark well my words; they are of your eternal salvation

PLATE 8
Mean while wept Satan before Los, accusing Palamabron;   e
Himself exculpating with mildest speech. for himself believ'd
That he had not opress'd nor injur'd the refractory servants.

But Satan returning to his Mills (for Palamabron had serv'd
The Mills of Satan as the easier task) found all confusion   5
And back return'd to Los, not fill'd with vengeance but with tears,
Himself convinc'd of Palamabrons turpitude. Los beheld
The servants of the Mills drunken with wine and dancing wild
With shouts and Palamabrons songs, rending the forests green
With ecchoing confusion, tho' the Sun was risen on high.   10

Then Los took off his left sandal placing it on his head,
Signal of solemn mourning: when the servants of the Mills
Beheld the signal they in silence stood, tho' drunk with wine.
Los wept! But Rintrah also came, and Enitharmon on
His arm lean'd tremblingly observing all these things   15

And Los said. Ye Genii of the Mills! the Sun is on high
Your labours call you! Palamabron is also in sad dilemma.
His horses are mad! his Harrow confounded! his companions enrag'd.
Mine is the fault! I should have remember'd that pity divides the soul
And man, unmans: follow with me my Plow. this mournful day   20
Must be a blank in Nature: follow with me, and tomorrow again
Resume your labours, & this day shall be a mournful day

Wildly they follow'd Los and Rintrah, & the Mills were silent   e
They mourn'd all day, this mournful day of Satan & Palamabron:
And all the Elect & all the Redeem'd mourn'd one toward another   25
Upon the mountains of Albion among the cliffs of the Dead.

They Plow'd in tears! incessant pourd Jehovahs rain, & Molechs
Thick fires contending with the rain, thunder'd above rolling
Terrible over their heads; Satan wept over Palamabron
Theotormon & Bromion contended on the side of Satan   30
Pitying his youth and beauty; trembling at eternal death:
Michael contended against Satan in the rolling thunder
Thulloh the friend of Satan also reprovd him; faint their reproof.

But Rintrah who is of the reprobate: of those form'd to destruction
In indignation. for Satans soft dissimulation of friendship!   35
Flam'd above all the plowed furrows, angry red and furious,
Till Michael sat down in the furrow weary dissolv'd in tears[.]
Satan who drave the team beside him, stood angry & red
He smote Thulloh & slew him, & he stood terrible over Michael
Urging him to arise: he wept! Enitharmon saw his tears   40
But Los hid Thulloh from her sight, lest she should die of grief
She wept: she trembled! she kissed Satan; she wept over Michael
She form'd a Space for Satan & Michael & for the poor infected[.]
Trembling she wept over the Space, & clos'd it with a tender Moon

Los secret buried Thulloh, weeping disconsolate over the moony Space   45

But Palamabron called down a Great Solemn Assembly,   e
That he who will not defend Truth, may be compelled to
Defend a Lie, that he may be snared & caught & taken

PLATE 9
And all Eden descended into Palamabrons tent
Among Albions Druids & Bards, in the caves beneath Albions
Death Couch, in the caverns of death, in the corner of the Atlantic.
And in the midst of the Great Assembly Palamabron pray'd:
O God, protect me from my friends, that they have not power over me   5
Thou hast giv'n me power to protect myself from my bitterest enemies.

Mark well my words, they are of your eternal salvation

Then rose the Two Witnesses, Rintrah & Palamabron:
And Palamabron appeal'd to all Eden, and recievd
Judgment: and Lo! it fell on Rintrah and his rage: 10
Which now flam'd high & furious in Satan against Palamabron
Till it became a proverb in Eden. Satan is among the Reprobate.

Los in his wrath curs'd heaven & earth, he rent up Nations,   e
Standing on Albions rocks among high-reard Druid temples
Which reach the stars of heaven & stretch from pole to pole.   15
He displacd continents, the oceans fled before his face
He alter'd the poles of the world, east, west & north & south
But he clos'd up Enitharmon from the sight of all these things

For Satan flaming with Rintrahs fury hidden beneath his own
    mildness
Accus'd Palamabron before the Assembly of ingratitude! of malice: 20
He created Seven deadly Sins drawing out his infernal scroll,
Of Moral laws and cruel punishments upon the clouds of Jehovah
To pervert the Divine voice in its entrance to the earth
With thunder of war & trumpets sound, with armies of disease
Punishments & deaths musterd & number'd; Saying I am God alone   25
There is no other! let all obey my principles of moral individuality
I have brought them from the uppermost innermost recesses
Of my Eternal Mind, transgressors I will rend off for ever,
As now I rend this accursed Family from my covering.

Thus Satan rag'd amidst the Assembly! and his bosom grew   30
Opake against the Divine Vision: the paved terraces of
His bosom inwards shone with fires, but the stones becoming opake!
Hid him from sight, in an extreme blackness and darkness,
And there a World of deeper Ulro was open'd, in the midst
Of the Assembly. In Satans bosom a vast unfathomable Abyss.   35

Astonishment held the Assembly in an awful silence: and tears   e
Fell down as dews of night, & a loud solemn universal groan
Was utter'd from the east & from the west & from the south

And from the north; and Satan stood opake immeasurable
Covering the east with solid blackness, round his hidden heart,   40
With thunders utterd from his hidden wheels: accusing loud
The Divine Mercy, for protecting Palamabron in his tent.

Rintrah rear'd up walls of rocks and pourd rivers & moats
Of fire round the walls: columns of fire guard around
Between Satan and Palamabron in the terrible darkness.   45

And Satan not having the Science of Wrath, but only of Pity:
Rent them asunder, and wrath was left to wrath, & pity to pity.
He sunk down a dreadful Death, unlike the slumbers of Beulah

The Separation was terrible: the Dead was repos'd on his Couch
Beneath the Couch of Albion, on the seven mou[n]tains of Rome   50
In the whole place of the Covering Cherub, Rome Babylon & Tyre.
His Spectre raging furious descended into its Space

PLATE 10   t
Then Los & Enitharmon knew that Satan is Urizen   t,c
Drawn down by Orc & the Shadowy Female into Generation
Oft Enitharmon enterd weeping into the Space, there appearing
An aged Woman raving along the Streets (the Space is named
Canaan) then she returnd to Los weary frighted as from dreams   5

The nature of a Female Space is this: it shrinks the Organs
Of Life till they become Finite & Itself seems Infinite   t
And Satan vibrated in the immensity of the Space! Limited
To those without but Infinite to those within: it fell down and
Became Canaan: closing Los from Eternity in Albions Cliffs   10
A mighty Fiend against the Divine Humanity mustring to War

Satan! Ah me! is gone to his own place, said Los! their God
I will not worship in their Churches, nor King in their Theatres
Elynittria! whence is this Jealousy running along the mountains
British Women were not Jealous when Greek & Roman were Jealous   15
Every thing in Eternity shines by its own Internal light: but thou
Darkenest every Internal light with the arrows of thy quiver
Bound up in the horns of Jealousy to a deadly fading Moon
And Ocalythron binds the Sun into a Jealous Globe
That every thing is fixd Opake without Internal light   20

So Los lamented over Satan, who triumphant divided the Nations

PLATE 11
He set his face against Jerusalem to destroy the Eon of Albion   e

But Los hid Enitharmon from the sight of all these things,
Upon the Thames whose lulling harmony repos'd her soul:
Where Beulah lovely terminates in rocky Albion:
Terminating in Hyde Park, on Tyburns awful brook.   5

And the Mills of Satan were separated into a moony Space
Among the rocks of Albions Temples, and Satans Druid sons
Offer the Human Victims throughout all the Earth, and Albions
Dread Tomb immortal on his Rock, overshadowd the whole Earth:
Where Satan making to himself Laws from his own identity.   10
Compell'd others to serve him in moral gratitude & submission
Being call'd God: setting himself above all that is called God.
And all the Spectres of the Dead calling themselves Sons of God
In his Synagogues worship Satan under the Unutterable Name

And it was enquir'd: Why in a Great Solemn Assembly   ᶜ 15
The Innocent should be condemn'd for the Guilty? Then an Eternal
    rose

Saying. If the Guilty should be condemn'd, he must be an Eternal
    Death
And one must die for another throughout all Eternity.
Satan is fall'n from his station & never can be redeem'd
But must be new Created continually moment by moment   20
And therefore the Class of Satan shall be calld the Elect, & those
Of Rintrah. the Reprobate, & those of Palamabron the Redeem'd
For he is redeem'd from Satans Law, the wrath falling on Rintrah,
And therefore Palamabron dared not to call a solemn Assembly
Till Satan had assum'd Rintrahs wrath in the day of mourning   25
In a feminine delusion of false pride self-deciev'd.

So spake the Eternal and confirm'd it with a thunderous oath.

But when Leutha (a Daughter of Beulah) beheld Satans condemnation   ᶜ
She down descended into the midst of the Great Solemn Assembly
Offering herself a Ransom for Satan, taking on her, his Sin.   30

Mark well my words. they are of your eternal salvation!

And Leutha stood glowing with varying colours immortal, heart-piercing
And lovely: & her moth-like elegance shone over the Assembly

At length standing upon the golden floor of Palamabron
She spake: I am the Author of this Sin! by my suggestion   35
My Parent power Satan has committed this transgression.
I loved Palamabron & I sought to approach his Tent,
But beautiful Elynittria with her silver arrows repelld me.
PLATE 12
For her light is terrible to me. I fade before her immortal beauty.
O wherefore doth a Dragon-form forth issue from my limbs
To sieze her new born son? Ah me! the wretched Leutha!
This to prevent, entering the doors of Satans brain night after night
Like sweet perfumes I stupified the masculine perceptions   5
And kept only the feminine awake. hence rose his soft

Delusory love to Palamabron: admiration join'd with envy
Cupidity unconquerable! my fault, when at noon of day
The Horses of Palamabron call'd for rest and pleasant death:
I sprang out of the breast of Satan, over the Harrow beaming   10
In all my beauty! that I might unloose the flaming steeds
As Elynittria use'd to do; but too well those living creatures
Knew that I was not Elynittria, and they brake the traces[.]
But me, the servants of the Harrow saw not: but as a bow
Of varying colours on the hills; terribly rag'd the horses.   15
Satan astonishd, and with power above his own controll
Compell'd the Gnomes to curb the horses, & to throw banks of sand
Around the fiery flaming Harrow in labyrinthine forms.
And brooks between to intersect the meadows in their course.
The Harrow cast thick flames: Jehovah thunderd above: 20
Chaos & ancient night fled from beneath the fiery Harrow:
The Harrow cast thick flames & orb'd us round in concave fires
A Hell of our own making. see, its flames still gird me round[.]
Jehovah thunder'd above! Satan in pride of heart
Drove the fierce Harrow among the constellations of Jehovah   25
Drawing a third part in the fires as stubble north & south
To devour Albion and Jerusalem the Emanation of Albion
Driving the Harrow in Pitys paths. 'twas then, with our dark fires
Which now gird round us (O eternal torment) I form'd the Serpent
Of precious stones & gold turn'd poisons on the sultry wastes   30
The Gnomes in all that day spar'd not; they curs'd Satan bitterly.
To do unkind things in kindness! with power armd, to say
The most irritating things in the midst of tears and love
These are the stings of the Serpent! thus did we by them; till thus
They in return retaliated, and the Living Creatures maddend.   35
The Gnomes labourd. I weeping hid in Satans inmost brain;
But when the Gnomes refus'd to labour more, with blandishments
I came forth from the head of Satan! back the Gnomes recoil'd.
And call'd me Sin, and for a sign portentous held me. Soon
Day sunk and Palamabron return'd, trembling I hid myself   40
In Satans inmost Palace of his nervous fine wrought Brain:
For Elynittria met Satan with all her singing women.
Terrific in their joy & pouring wine of wildest power
They gave Satan their wine: indignant at the burning wrath.
Wild with prophetic fury his former life became like a dream   45
Cloth'd in the Serpents folds, in selfish holiness demanding purity
Being most impure, self-condemn'd to eternal tears, he drove
Me from his inmost Brain & the doors clos'd with thunders sound
O Divine Vision who didst create the Female: to repose
The Sleepers of Beulah: pity the repentant Leutha. My   50
PLATE 13
Sick Couch bears the dark shades of Eternal Death infolding
The Spectre of Satan. he furious refuses to repose in sleep.

I humbly bow in all my Sin before the Throne Divine.
Not so the Sick-one; Alas what shall be done him to restore?
Who calls the Individual Law, Holy: and despises the Saviour.   5
Glorying to involve Albions Body in fires of eternal War—

Now Leutha ceas'd: tears flow'd: but the Divine Pity supported her.   c

All is my fault! We are the Spectre of Luvah the murderer
Of Albion: O Vala! O Luvah! O Albion! O lovely Jerusalem
The Sin was begun in Eternity, and will not rest to Eternity   10
Till two Eternitys meet together, Ah! lost! lost! lost! for ever!

So Leutha spoke. But when she saw that Enitharmon had
Created a New Space to protect Satan from punishment;
She fled to Enitharmons Tent & hid herself. Loud raging
Thunderd the Assembly dark & clouded, and they ratify'd   15
The kind decision of Enitharmon & gave a Time to the Space,
Even Six Thousand years; and sent Lucifer for its Guard.
But Lucifer refus'd to die & in pride he forsook his charge
And they elected Molech, and when Molech was impatient
The Divine hand found the Two Limits: first of Opacity, then of   20
    Contraction
Opacity was named Satan, Contraction was named Adam.
Triple Elohim came: Elohim wearied fainted: they elected Shaddai.
Shaddai angry, Pahad descended: Pahad terrified, they sent Jehovah
And Jehovah was leprous; loud he call'd, stretching his hand to Eternity
For then the Body of Death was perfected in hypocritic holiness,   25
Around the Lamb, a Female Tabernacle woven in Cathedrons Looms
He died as a Reprobate. he was Punish'd as a Transgressor!
Glory! Glory! Glory! to the Holy Lamb of God
I touch the heavens as an instrument to glorify the Lord!

The Elect shall meet the Redeem'd. on Albions rocks they shall meet   30
Astonish'd at the Transgressor, in him beholding the Saviour.
And the Elect shall say to the Redeemd. We behold it is of Divine
Mercy alone! of Free Gift and Election that we live.
Our Virtues & Cruel Goodnesses, have deserv'd Eternal Death.
Thus they weep upon the fatal Brook of Albions River.   35

But Elynittria met Leutha in the place where she was hidden.
And threw aside her arrows, and laid down her sounding Bow;
She sooth'd her with soft words & brought her to Palamabrons bed
In moments new created for delusion, interwoven round about,
In dreams she bore the shadowy Spectre of Sleep, & namd him Death.   40
In dreams she bore Rahab the mother of Tirzah & her sisters
In Lambeths vales; in Cambridge & in Oxford, places of Thought
Intricate labyrinths of Times and Spaces unknown, that Leutha lived
In Palamabrons Tent, and Oothoon was her charming guard.

The Bard ceas'd. All consider'd and a loud resounding murmur ᶜ45
Continu'd round the Halls; and much they questiond the immortal
Loud voicd Bard. and many condemn'd the high tone'd Song
Saying Pity and Love are too venerable for the imputation
Of Guilt. Others said. If it is true! if the acts have been perform'd
Let the Bard himself witness. Where hadst thou this terrible Song 50

The Bard replied. I am Inspired! I know it is Truth! for I Sing
PLATE 14
According to the inspiration of the Poetic Genius
Who is the eternal all-protecting Divine Humanity
To whom be Glory & Power & Dominion Evermore Amen

Then there was great murmuring in the Heavens of Albion
Concerning Generation & the Vegetative power & concerning 5
The Lamb the Saviour: Albion trembled to Italy Greece & Egypt
To Tartary & Hindostan & China & to Great America
Shaking the roots & fast foundations of the Earth in doubtfulness
The loud voic'd Bard terrify'd took refuge in Miltons bosom

Then Milton rose up from the heavens of Albion ardorous! ᶜ10
The whole Assembly wept prophetic, seeing in Miltons face
And in his lineaments divine the shades of Death & Ulro
He took off the robe of the promise, & ungirded himself from the oath
of God

And Milton said, I go to Eternal Death! The Nations still
Follow after the detestable Gods of Priam; in pomp 15
Of warlike selfhood, contradicting and blaspheming.
When will the Resurrection come; to deliver the sleeping body
From corruptibility: O when Lord Jesus wilt thou come?
Tarry no longer; for my soul lies at the gates of death.
I will arise and look forth for the morning of the grave. 20
I will go down to the sepulcher to see if morning breaks!
I will go down to self annihilation and eternal death,
Lest the Last Judgment come & find me unannihilate
And I be siez'd & giv'n into the hands of my own Selfhood.
The Lamb of God is seen thro' mists & shadows, hov'ring 25
Over the sepulchers in clouds of Jehovah & winds of Elohim
A disk of blood, distant; & heav'ns & earth's roll dark between
What do I here before the Judgment? without my Emanation?
With the daughters of memory, & not with the daughters of
inspiration[?]
I in my Selfhood am that Satan: I am that Evil One! 30
He is my Spectre! in my obedience to loose him from my Hells
To claim the Hells, my Furnaces, I go to Eternal Death.

And Milton said. I go to Eternal Death! Eternity shudder'd   e
For he took the outside course, among the graves of the dead
A mournful shade. Eternity shudderd at the image of eternal death   35

Then on the verge of Beulah he beheld his own Shadow;
A mournful form double; hermaphroditic: male & female
In one wonderful body. and he enterd into it
In direful pain for the dread shadow, twenty-seven-fold
Reachd to the depths of direst Hell, & thence to Albions land: 40
Which is this earth of vegetation on which now I write.

The Seven Angels of the Presence wept over Miltons Shadow!

PLATE 15
As when a man dreams, he reflects not that his body sleeps,   e
Else he would wake; so seem'd he entering his Shadow: but
With him the Spirits of the Seven Angels of the Presence
Entering; they gave him still perceptions of his Sleeping Body;
Which now arose and walk'd with them in Eden, as an Eighth   5
Image Divine tho' darken'd; and tho walking as one walks
In sleep; and the Seven comforted and supported him.

Like as a Polypus that vegetates beneath the deep!
They saw his Shadow vegetated underneath the Couch
Of death: for when he enterd into his Shadow: Himself: 10
His real and immortal Self: was as appeard to those
Who dwell in immortality, as One sleeping on a couch
Of gold; and those in immortality gave forth their Emanations
Like Females of sweet beauty, to guard round him & to feed
His lips with food of Eden in his cold and dim repose!   15
But to himself he seemd a wanderer lost in dreary night.

Onwards his Shadow kept its course among the Spectres; call'd
Satan, but swift as lightning passing them, startled the shades
Of Hell beheld him in a trail of light as of a comet
That travels into Chaos: so Milton went guarded within.   20

The nature of infinity is this: That every thing has its   e
Own Vortex; and when once a traveller thro' Eternity
Has passd that Vortex, he percieves it roll backward behind
His path, into a globe itself infolding; like a sun:
Or like a moon, or like a universe of starry majesty,   25
While he keeps onwards in his wondrous journey on the earth
Or like a human form, a friend with whom he livd benevolent.
As the eye of man views both the east & west encompassing
Its vortex; and the north & south, with all their starry host;
Also the rising sun & setting moon he views surrounding   30
His corn-fields and his valleys of five hundred acres square.
Thus is the earth one infinite plane, and not as apparent

To the weak traveller confin'd beneath the moony shade.
Thus is the heaven a vortex passd already, and the earth
A vortex not yet pass'd by the traveller thro' Eternity.   35

First Milton saw Albion upon the Rock of Ages,   e
Deadly pale outstretchd and snowy cold, storm coverd;
A Giant form of perfect beauty outstretchd on the rock
In solemn death: the Sea of Time & Space thunderd aloud
Against the rock, which was inwrapped with the weeds of death   40
Hovering over the cold bosom, in its vortex Milton bent down
To the bosom of death, what was underneath soon seemd above.
A cloudy heaven mingled with stormy seas in loudest ruin;
But as a wintry globe descends precipitant thro' Beulah bursting,
With thunders loud, and terrible: so Miltons shadow fell,   45
Precipitant loud thundring into the Sea of Time & Space.

Then first I saw him in the Zenith as a falling star,   e
Descending perpendicular, swift as the swallow or swift;
And on my left foot falling on the tarsus, enterd there;
But from my left foot a black cloud redounding spread over Europe.   50

Then Milton knew that the Three Heavens of Beulah were beheld   e
By him on earth in his bright pilgrimage of sixty years
PLATE 16
[Full-page design. For caption see Textual Note.]
PLATE 17
In those three females whom his Wives, & those three whom his
     Daughters
Had represented and contain'd, that they might be resum'd
By giving up of Selfhood: & they distant view'd his journey
In their eternal spheres, now Human, tho' their Bodies remain clos'd
In the dark Ulro till the Judgment: also Milton knew: they and   5
Himself was Human, tho' now wandering thro Death's Vale
In conflict with those Female forms, which in blood & jealousy
Surrounded him, dividing & uniting without end or number.

He saw the Cruelties of Ulro, and he wrote them down   e
In iron tablets: and his Wives & Daughters names were these   10
Rahab and Tirzah, & Milcah & Malah & Noah & Hoglah.
They sat rang'd round him as the rocks of Horeb round the land
Of Canaan: and they wrote in thunder smoke and fire
His dictate; and his body was the Rock Sinai; that body,
Which was on earth born to corruption: & the six Females   15
Are Hor & Peor & Bashan & Abarim & Lebanon & Hermon
Seven rocky masses terrible in the Desarts of Midian.

But Miltons Human Shadow continu'd journeying above
The rocky masses of The Mundane Shell; in the Lands
Of Edom & Aram & Moab & Midian & Amalek.   20

The Mundane Shell, is a vast Concave Earth: an immense
Hardend shadow of all things upon our Vegetated Earth
Enlarg'd into dimension & deform'd into indefinite space,
In Twenty-seven Heavens and all their Hells; with Chaos
And Ancient Night; & Purgatory. It is a cavernous Earth   25
Of labyrinthine intricacy, twenty-seven folds of opakeness
And finishes where the lark mounts; here Milton journeyed
In that Region call'd Midian, among the Rocks of Horeb[.]
For travellers from Eternity. pass outward to Satan's seat,
But travellers to Eternity. pass inward to Golgonooza.   30

Los the Vehicular terror beheld him, & divine Enitharmon   e
Call'd all her daughters, Saying. Surely to unloose my bond
Is this Man come! Satan shall be unloosd upon Albion

Los heard in terror Enitharmons words: in fibrous strength
His limbs shot forth like roots of trees against the forward path   35
Of Miltons journey. Urizen beheld the immortal Man,
PLATE 18   t
And Tharmas Demon of the Waters, & Orc, who is Luvah

The Shadowy Female seeing Milton, howl'd in her lamentation
Over the Deeps outstretching her Twenty seven Heavens over Albion

And thus the Shadowy Female howls in articulate howlings

I will lament over Milton in the lamentations of the afflicted   5
My Garments shall be woven of sighs & heart broken lamentations
The misery of unhappy Families shall be drawn out into its border
Wrought with the needle with dire sufferings poverty pain & woe
Along the rocky Island & thence throughout the whole Earth
There shall be the sick Father & his starving Family! there   10
The Prisoner in the stone Dungeon & the Slave at the Mill
I will have Writings written all over it in Human Words
That every Infant that is born upon the Earth shall read
And get by rote as a hard task of a life of sixty years
I will have Kings inwoven upon it & Councellors & Mighty Men   15
The Famine shall clasp it together with buckles & Clasps
And the Pestilence shall be its fringe & the War its girdle
To divide into Rahab & Tirzah that Milton may come to our tents
For I will put on the Human Form & take the Image of God
Even Pity & Humanity but my Clothing shall be Cruelty   20
And I will put on Holiness as a breastplate & as a helmet
And all my ornaments shall be of the gold of broken hearts
And the precious stones of anxiety & care & desperation & death
And repentance for sin & sorrow & punishment & fear
To defend me from thy terrors O Orc! my only beloved!   25

Orc answerd. Take not the Human Form O loveliest. Take not
Terror upon thee! Behold how I am & tremble lest thou also
Consume in my Consummation; but thou maist take a Form
Female & lovely, that cannot consume in Mans consummation
Wherefore dost thou Create & Weave this Satan for a Covering[?]   30
When thou attemptest to put on the Human Form, my wrath
Burns to the top of heaven against thee in Jealousy & Fear.
Then I rend thee asunder, then I howl over thy clay & ashes
When wilt thou put on the Female Form as in times of old
With a Garment of Pity & Compassion like the Garment of God   35
His garments are long sufferings for the Children of Men
Jerusalem is his Garment & not thy Covering Cherub O lovely
Shadow of my delight who wanderest seeking for the prey.

So spoke Orc when Oothoon & Leutha hoverd over his Couch
Of fire in interchange of Beauty & Perfection in the darkness   40
Opening interiorly into Jerusalem & Babylon shining glorious
In the Shadowy Females bosom. Jealous her darkness grew:
Howlings filld all the desolate places in accusations of Sin
In Female beauty shining in the unformd void & Orc in vain
Stretch'd out his hands of fire, & wooed: they triumph in his pain   45

Thus darkend the Shadowy Female tenfold & Orc tenfold
Glowd on his rocky Couch against the darkness: loud thunders
Told of the enormous conflict[.] Earthquake beneath: around;
Rent the Immortal Females, limb from limb & joint from joint
And moved the fast foundations of the Earth to wake the Dead   50

Urizen emerged from his Rocky Form & from his Snows,   e
PLATE 19
And he also darkend his brows: freezing dark rocks between
The footsteps. and infixing deep the feet in marble beds:
That Milton labourd with his journey, & his feet bled sore
Upon the clay now changd to marble; also Urizen rose,
And met him on the shores of Arnon; & by the streams of the brooks   5

Silent they met, and silent strove among the streams, of Arnon
Even to Mahanaim, when with cold hand Urizen stoop'd down
And took up water from the river Jordan: pouring on
To Miltons brain the icy fluid from his broad cold palm.
But Milton took of the red clay of Succoth, moulding it with care   10
Between his palms; and filling up the furrows of many years
Beginning at the feet of Urizen, and on the bones
Creating new flesh on the Demon cold, and building him,
As with new clay a Human form in the Valley of Beth Peor.

Four Universes round the Mundane Egg remain Chaotic   e 15
One to the North, named Urthona: One to the South, named Urizen:
One to the East, named Luvah: One to the West, named Tharmas

They are the Four Zoa's that stood around the Throne Divine!
But when Luvah assum'd the World of Urizen to the South:
And Albion was slain upon his mountains, & in his tent;   20
All fell towards the Center in dire ruin, sinking down.
And in the South remains a burning fire; in the East a void.
In the West, a world of raging waters; in the North a solid,
Unfathomable! without end. But in the midst of these,
Is built eternally the Universe of Los and Enitharmon: 25
Towards which Milton went, but Urizen oppos'd his path.

The Man and Demon strove many periods. Rahab beheld   c
Standing on Carmel; Rahab and Tirzah trembled to behold
The enormous strife. one giving life, the other giving death
To his adversary. and they sent forth all their sons & daughters   30
In all their beauty to entice Milton across the river,

The Twofold form Hermaphroditic: and the Double-sexed;
The Female-male & the Male-female, self-dividing stood
Before him in their beauty, & in cruelties of holiness!
Shining in darkness, glorious upon the deeps of Entuthon.   35

Saying. Come thou to Ephraim! behold the Kings of Canaan!
The beautiful Amalekites, behold the fires of youth
Bound with the Chain of Jealousy by Los & Enitharmon;
The banks of Cam: cold learnings streams: Londons dark-frowning
     towers,
Lament upon the winds of Europe in Rephaims Vale.   40
Because Ahania rent apart into a desolate night,
Laments! & Enion wanders like a weeping inarticulate voice
And Vala labours for her bread & water among the Furnaces
Therefore bright Tirzah triumphs: putting on all beauty.
And all perfection, in her cruel sports among the Victims,   45
Come bring with thee Jerusalem with songs on the Grecian Lyre!
In Natural Religion! in experiments on Men,
Let her be Offerd up to Holiness! Tirzah numbers her;
She numbers with her fingers every fibre ere it grow;
Where is the Lamb of God? where is the promise of his coming?   50
Her shadowy Sisters form the bones, even the bones of Horeb:
Around the marrow! and the orbed scull around the brain!
His Images are born for War! for Sacrifice to Tirzah!
To Natural Religion! to Tirzah the Daughter of Rahab the Holy!
She ties the knot of nervous fibres, into a white brain!   55
She ties the knot of bloody veins, into a red hot heart!
Within her bosom Albion lies embalmd, never to awake
Hand is become a rock! Sinai & Horeb, is Hyle & Coban: t
Scofield is bound in iron armour before Reubens Gate!
She ties the knot of milky seed into two lovely Heavens   60

PLATE 20

Two yet but one: each in the other sweet reflected! these
Are our Three Heavens beneath the shades of Beulah, land of rest!
Come then to Ephraim & Manasseh O beloved-one!
Come to my ivory palaces O beloved of thy mother!
And let us bind thee in the bands of War & be thou King 5
Of Canaan and reign in Hazor where the Twelve Tribes meet.

So spoke they as in one voice! Silent Milton stood before   c
The darkend Urizen; as the sculptor silent stands before
His forming image; he walks round it patient labouring.
Thus Milton stood forming bright Urizen, while his Mortal part   10
Sat frozen in the rock of Horeb: and his Redeemed portion,
Thus form'd the Clay of Urizen; but within that portion
His real Human walkd above in power and majesty
Tho darkend; and the Seven Angels of the Presence attended him.

O how can I with my gross tongue that cleaveth to the dust,   c 15
Tell of the Four-fold Man, in starry numbers fitly orderd
Or how can I with my cold hand of clay! But thou O Lord
Do with me as thou wilt! for I am nothing, and vanity.
If thou chuse to elect a worm, it shall remove the mountains.
For that portion namd the Elect: the Spectrous body of Milton: 20
Redounding from my left foot into Los's Mundane space,
Brooded over his Body in Horeb against the Resurrection
Preparing it for the Great Consummation; red the Cherub on Sinai
Glow'd; but in terrors folded round his clouds of blood.

Now Albions sleeping Humanity began to turn upon his Couch;   c 25
Feeling the electric flame of Miltons awful precipitate descent.
Seest thou the little winged fly, smaller than a grain of sand?
It has a heart like thee; a brain open to heaven & hell,
Withinside wondrous & expansive; its gates are not clos'd,
I hope thine are not: hence it clothes itself in rich array;   30
Hence thou art cloth'd with human beauty O thou mortal man.
Seek not thy heavenly father then beyond the skies:
There Chaos dwells & ancient Night & Og & Anak old:
For every human heart has gates of brass & bars of adamant,
Which few dare unbar because dread Og & Anak guard the gates   35
Terrific! and each mortal brain is walld and moated round
Within: and Og & Anak watch here; here is the Seat
Of Satan in its Webs; for in brain and heart and loins
Gates open behind Satans Seat to the City of Golgonooza
Which is the spiritual fourfold London, in the loins of Albion.   40

Thus Milton fell thro Albions heart, travelling outside of Humanity
Beyond the Stars in Chaos in Caverns of the Mundane Shell.

But many of the Eternals rose up from eternal tables   e
Drunk with the Spirit, burning round the Couch of death they stood
Looking down into Beulah: wrathful, fill'd with rage!   45
They rend the heavens round the Watchers in a fiery circle:
And round the Shadowy Eighth: the Eight close up the Couch
Into a tabernacle, and flee with cries down to the Deeps:
Where Los opens his three wide gates, surrounded by raging fires!
They soon find their own place & join the Watchers of the Ulro.   50

Los saw them and a cold pale horror coverd o'er his limbs
Pondering he knew that Rintrah & Palamabron might depart:
Even as Reuben & as Gad; gave up himself to tears.
He sat down on his anvil-stock; and leand upon the trough.
Looking into the black water, mingling it with tears.   55

At last when desperation almost tore his heart in twain
He recollected an old Prophecy in Eden recorded,
And often sung to the loud harp at the immortal feasts
That Milton of the Land of Albion should up ascend
Forwards from Ulro from the Vale of Felpham; and set free   60
Orc from his Chain of Jealousy, he started at the thought
PLATE 21
And down descended into Udan-Adan; it was night:
And Satan sat sleeping upon his Couch in Udan-Adan:
His Spectre slept, his Shadow woke; when one sleeps th'other wakes.

But Milton entering my Foot; I saw in the nether   e
Regions of the Imagination; also all men on Earth,   5
And all in Heaven, saw in the nether regions of the Imagination
In Ulro beneath Beulah, the vast breach of Miltons descent.
But I knew not that it was Milton, for man cannot know
What passes in his members till periods of Space & Time
Reveal the secrets of Eternity: for more extensive   10
Than any other earthly things, are Mans earthly lineaments.

And all this Vegetable World appeard on my left Foot,
As a bright sandal formd immortal of precious stones & gold:
I stooped down & bound it on to walk forward thro' Eternity.

There is in Eden a sweet River, of milk & liquid pearl.   e 15
Namd Ololon; on whose mild banks dwelt those who Milton drove
Down into Ulro: and they wept in long resounding song
For seven days of eternity, and the rivers living banks
The mountains wail'd! & every plant that grew, in solemn sighs
    lamented.

When Luvahs bulls each morning drag the sulphur Sun out of the   20
    Deep
Harnessd with starry harness black & shining kept by black slaves
That work all night at the starry harness, Strong and vigorous

-114-

They drag the unwilling Orb: at this time all the Family
Of Eden heard the lamentation, and Providence began.
But when the clarions of day sounded they drownd the lamentations   25
And when night came all was silent in Ololon: & all refusd to lament
In the still night fearing lest they should others molest.

Seven mornings Los heard them, as the poor bird within the shell
Hears its impatient parent bird; and Enitharmon heard them:
But saw them not, for the blue Mundane Shell inclos'd them in.   30

And they lamented that they had in wrath & fury & fire
Driven Milton into the Ulro; for now they knew too late
That it was Milton the Awakener: they had not heard the Bard,
Whose song calld Milton to the attempt; and Los heard these laments.
He heard them call in prayer all the Divine Family;   35
And he beheld the Cloud of Milton stretching over Europe.

But all the Family Divine collected as Four Suns
In the Four Points of heaven East, West & North & South,
Enlarging and enlarging till their Disks approachd each other;
And when they touch'd closed together Southward in One Sun   40
Over Ololon: and as One Man, who weeps over his brother,
In a dark tomb, so all the Family Divine. wept over Ololon.

Saying. Milton goes to Eternal Death! so saying, they groan'd in spirit
And were troubled! and again the Divine Family groaned in spirit!

And Ololon said, Let us descend also, and let us give   45
Ourselves to death in Ulro among the Transgressors.
Is Virtue a Punisher? O no! how is this wondrous thing:
This World beneath, unseen before: this refuge from the wars
Of Great Eternity! unnatural refuge! unknown by us till now!
Or are these the pangs of repentance? let us enter into them   50

Then the Divine Family said. Six Thousand Years are now
Accomplish'd in this World of Sorrow; Miltons Angel knew
The Universal Dictate; and you also feel this Dictate.
And now you know this World of Sorrow, and feel Pity. Obey
The Dictate! Watch over this World, and with your brooding wings,   55
Renew it to Eternal Life: Lo! I am with you alway
But you cannot renew Milton he goes to Eternal Death

So spake the Family Divine as One Man even Jesus
Uniting in One with Ololon & the appearance of One Man.
Jesus the Saviour appeard coming in the Clouds of Ololon!   60
PLATE 22
Tho driven away with the Seven Starry Ones into the Ulro
Yet the Divine Vision remains Every-where For-ever. Amen.
And Ololon lamented for Milton with a great lamentation.

While Los heard indistinct in fear, what time I bound my sandals   e
On; to walk forward thro' Eternity, Los descended to me: 5
And Los behind me stood; a terrible flaming Sun: just close
Behind my back; I turned round in terror, and behold.
Los stood in that fierce glowing fire; & he also stoop'd down
And bound my sandals on in Udan-Adan; trembling I stood
Exceedingly with fear & terror, standing in the Vale   10
Of Lambeth: but he kissed me, and wishd me health.
And I became One Man with him arising in my strength:
Twas too late now to recede. Los had enterd into my soul:
His terrors now posses'd me whole! I arose in fury & strength.

I am that Shadowy Prophet who Six Thousand Years ago   15
Fell from my station in the Eternal bosom. Six Thousand Years
Are finishd. I return! both Time & Space obey my will.
I in Six Thousand Years walk up and down: for not one Moment
Of Time is lost, nor one Event of Space unpermanent.
But all remain: every fabric of Six Thousand Years   20
Remains permanent: tho' on the Earth where Satan
Fell, and was cut off all things vanish & are seen no more
They vanish not from me & mine, we guard them first & last[.]
The generations of men run on in the tide of Time
But leave their destind lineaments permanent for ever & ever.   25

So spoke Los as we went along to his supreme abode   e

Rintrah and Palamabron met us at the Gate of Golgonooza
Clouded with discontent. & brooding in their minds terrible things

They said. O Father most beloved! O merciful Parent!
Pitying and permitting evil, tho strong & mighty to destroy.   30
Whence is this Shadow terrible? wherefore dost thou refuse
To throw him into the Furnaces! knowest thou not that he
Will unchain Orc? & let loose Satan, Og, Sihon & Anak,
Upon the Body of Albion? for this he is come! behold it written
Upon his fibrous left Foot black! most dismal to our eyes   t 35
The Shadowy Female shudders thro' heaven in torment inexpressible!
And all the Daughters of Los prophetic wail: yet in deceit,
They weave a new Religion from new Jealousy of Theotormon!
Miltons Religion is the cause: there is no end to destruction!
Seeing the Churches at their Period in terror & despair: 40
Rahab created Voltaire; Tirzah created Rousseau;
Asserting the Self-righteousness against the Universal Saviour,
Mocking the Confessors & Martyrs, claiming Self-righteousness;
With cruel Virtue: making War upon the Lambs Redeemed;
To perpetuate War & Glory. to perpetuate the Laws of Sin: 45
They perverted Swedenborgs Visions in Beulah & in Ulro;
To destroy Jerusalem as a Harlot & her Sons as Reprobates;
To raise up Mystery the Virgin Harlot Mother of War,

Babylon the Great, the Abomination of Desolation!
O Swedenborg! strongest of men, the Samson shorn by the Churches! 50
Shewing the Transgresors in Hell, the proud Warriors in Heaven:
Heaven as a Punisher & Hell as One under Punishment:
With Laws from Plato & his Greeks to renew the Trojan Gods,
In Albion; & to deny the value of the Saviours blood.
But then I rais'd up Whitefield, Palamabron raisd up Westley, 55
And these are the cries of the Churches before the two Witnesses['] t
Faith in God the dear Saviour who took on the likeness of men:
Becoming obedient to death, even the death of the Cross
The Witnesses lie dead in the Street of the Great City
No Faith is in all the Earth: the Book of God is trodden under Foot: 60
He sent his two Servants Whitefield & Westley; were they Prophets
Or were they Idiots or Madmen? shew us Miracles!

PLATE 23

Can you have greater Miracles than these? Men who devote
Their lifes whole comfort to intire scorn & injury & death
Awake thou sleeper on the Rock of Eternity Albion awake
The trumpet of Judgment hath twice sounded: all Nations are awake
But thou art still heavy and dull: Awake Albion awake! t 5
Lo Orc arises on the Atlantic. Lo his blood and fire
Glow on Americas shore: Albion turns upon his Couch
He listens to the sounds of War, astonishd and confounded:
He weeps into the Atlantic deep, yet still in dismal dreams
Unwakend! and the Covering Cherub advances from the East: 10
How long shall we lay dead in the Street of the great City
How long beneath the Covering Cherub give our Emanations
Milton will utterly consume us & thee our beloved Father[.]
He hath enterd into the Covering Cherub, becoming one with
Albions dread Sons, Hand, Hyle & Coban surround him as 15
A girdle; Gwendolen & Conwenna as a garment woven
Of War & Religion; let us descend & bring him chained
To Bowlahoola O father most beloved! O mild Parent!
Cruel in thy mildness, pitying and permitting evil
Tho strong and mighty to destroy, O Los our beloved Father! 20

Like the black storm, coming out of Chaos, beyond the stars:
It issues thro the dark & intricate caves of the Mundane Shell
Passing the planetary visions, & the well adorned Firmament
The Sun rolls into Chaos & the stars into the Desarts;
And then the storms become visible, audible & terrible, 25
Covering the light of day, & rolling down upon the mountains,
Deluge all the country round. Such is a vision of Los;
When Rintrah & Palamabron spoke; and such his stormy face
Appeard, as does the face of heaven, when coverd with thick storms
Pitying and loving tho in frowns of terrible perturbation 30

But Los dispersd the clouds even as the strong winds of Jehovah.   c
And Los thus spoke. O noble Sons, be patient yet a little[.]
I have embracd the falling Death, he is become One with me
O Sons we live not by wrath. by mercy alone we live!
I recollect an old Prophecy in Eden recorded in gold; and oft   35
Sung to the harp: That Milton of the land of Albion
Should up ascend forward from Felphams Vale & break the Chain
Of Jealousy from all its roots; be patient therefore O my Sons
These lovely Females form sweet night and silence and secret
Obscurities to hide from Satans Watch-Fiends. Human loves   40
And graces; lest they write them in their Books, & in the Scroll
Of mortal life, to condemn the accused: who at Satans Bar
Tremble in Spectrous Bodies continually day and night
While on the Earth they live in sorrowful Vegetations
O when shall we tread our Wine-presses in heaven; and Reap   45
Our wheat with shoutings of joy, and leave the Earth in peace
Remember how Calvin and Luther in fury premature
Sow'd War and stern division between Papists & Protestants
Let it not be so now! O go not forth in Martyrdoms & Wars
We were plac'd here by the Universal Brotherhood & Mercy   50
With powers fitted to circumscribe this dark Satanic death
And that the Seven Eyes of God may have space for Redemption.
But how this is as yet we know not, and we cannot know;
Till Albion is arisen; then patient wait a little while,
Six Thousand years are passd away the end approaches fast;   55
This mighty one is come from Eden, he is of the Elect,
Who died from Earth & he is returnd before the Judgment. This thing
Was never known that one of the holy dead should willing return
Then patient wait a little while till the Last Vintage is over:
Till we have quenchd the Sun of Salah in the Lake of Udan Adan   60
O my dear Sons! leave not your Father, as your brethren left me[.]
Twelve Sons successive fled away in that thousand years of sorrow
PLATE 24
Of Palamabrons Harrow, & of Rintrahs wrath & fury:
Reuben & Manazzoth & Gad & Simeon & Levi,
And Ephraim & Judah were Generated, because
They left me, wandering with Tirzah: Enitharmon wept
One thousand years, and all the Earth was in a watry deluge   5
We calld him Menassheh because of the Generations of Tirzah
Because of Satan: & the Seven Eyes of God continually
Guard round them, but I the Fourth Zoa am also set
The Watchman of Eternity, the Three are not! & I am preserved
Still my four mighty ones are left to me in Golgonooza   10
Still Rintrah fierce, and Palamabron mild & piteous
Theotormon filld with care, Bromion loving Science
You O my Sons still guard round Los. O wander not & leave me
Rintrah, thou well rememberest when Amalek & Canaan

Fled with their Sister Moab into that abhorred Void   15
They became Nations in our sight beneath the hands of Tirzah.
And Palamabron thou rememberest when Joseph an infant;
Stolen from his nurses cradle wrapd in needle-work
Of emblematic texture, was sold to the Amalekite,
Who carried him down into Egypt where Ephraim & Menassheh   20
Gatherd my Sons together in the Sands of Midian
And if you also flee away and leave your Fathers side,
Following Milton into Ulro, altho your power is great
Surely you also shall become poor mortal vegetations
Beneath the Moon of Ulro: pity then your Fathers tears[.]   25
When Jesus raisd Lazarus from the Grave I stood & saw
Lazarus who is the Vehicular Body of Albion the Redeemd
Arise into the Covering Cherub who is the Spectre of Albion
By martyrdoms to suffer: to watch over the Sleeping Body.
Upon his Rock beneath his Tomb. I saw the Covering Cherub   30
Divide Four-fold into Four Churches when Lazarus arose
Paul, Constantine, Charlemaine, Luther; behold they stand before us
Stretchd over Europe & Asia. come O Sons, come, come away
Arise O Sons give all your strength against Eternal Death
Lest we are vegetated, for Cathedrons Looms weave only Death   35
A Web of Death: & were it not for Bowlahoola & Allamanda
No Human Form but only a Fibrous Vegetation
A Polypus of soft affections without Thought or Vision
Must tremble in the Heavens & Earths thro all the Ulro space[.]
Throw all the Vegetated Mortals into Bowlahoola   40
But as to this Elected Form who is returnd again
He is the Signal that the Last Vintage now approaches
Nor Vegetation may go on till all the Earth is reapd

So Los spoke. Furious they descended to Bowlahoola & Allamanda   e
Indignant. unconvincd by Los's arguments & thun[d]ers rolling   45
They saw that wrath now swayd and now pity absorbd him
As it was, so it remaind & no hope of an end.

Bowlahoola is namd Law. by mortals, Tharmas founded it:
Because of Satan, before Luban in the City of Golgonooza.
But Golgonooza is namd Art & Manufacture by mortal men.   50

In Bowlahoola Los's Anvils stand & his Furnaces rage;
Thundering the Hammers beat & the Bellows blow loud
Living self moving mourning lamenting & howling incessantly
Bowlahoola thro all its porches feels tho' too fast founded
Its pillars & porticoes to tremble at the force   55
Of mortal or immortal arm: and softly lilling flutes   t
Accordant with the horrid labours make sweet melody

The Bellows are the Animal Lungs: the Hammers the Animal Heart
The Furnaces the Stomach for digestion. terrible their fury

Thousands & thousands labour. thousands play on instruments 60
Stringed or fluted to ameliorate the sorrows of slavery
Loud sport the dancers in the dance of death, rejoicing in carnage
The hard dentant Hammers are lulld by the flutes lula lula
The bellowing Furnaces['] blare by the long sounding clarion t
The double drum drowns howls & groans, the shrill fife. shrieks & cries: 65
The crooked horn mellows the hoarse raving serpent, terrible but
    harmonious
Bowlahoola is the Stomach in every individual man.

Los is by mortals nam'd Time Enitharmon is nam'd Space e
But they depict him bald & aged who is in eternal youth
All powerful and his locks flourish like the brows of morning 70
He is the Spirit of Prophecy the ever apparent Elias
Time is the mercy of Eternity; without Times swiftness
Which is the swiftest of all things: all were eternal torment:
All the Gods of the Kingdoms of Earth labour in Los's Halls.
Every one is a fallen Son of the Spirit of Prophecy 75
He is the Fourth Zoa, that stood arou[n]d the Throne Divine.

PLATE 25
Loud shout the Sons of Luvah, at the Wine-presses as Los descended e
With Rintrah & Palamabron in his fires of resistless fury.

The Wine-press on the Rhine groans loud, but all its central beams
Act more terrific in the central Cities of the Nations
Where Human Thought is crushd beneath the iron hand of Power. 5
There Los puts all into the Press, the Opressor & the Opressed
Together, ripe for the Harvest & Vintage & ready for the Loom.

They sang at the Vintage. This is the Last Vintage! & Seed
Shall no more be sown upon Earth, till all the Vintage is over
And all gatherd in, till the Plow has passd over the Nations 10
And the Harrow & heavy thundering Roller upon the mountains

And loud the Souls howl round the Porches of Golgonooza
Crying O God deliver us to the Heavens or to the Earths,
That we may preach righteousness & punish the sinner with death.
But Los refused, till all the Vintage of Earth was gatherd in. 15

And Los stood & cried to the Labourers of the Vintage in voice of awe.

Fellow Labourers! The Great Vintage & Harvest is now upon Earth
The whole extent of the Globe is explored: Every scatterd Atom
Of Human Intellect now is flocking to the sound of the Trumpet
All the Wisdom which was hidden in caves & dens, from ancient 20
Time; is now sought out from Animal & Vegetable & Mineral
The Awakener is come. outstretchd over Europe! the Vision of God is
    fulfilled
The Ancient Man upon the Rock of Albion Awakes,

He listens to the sounds of War astonishd & ashamed;
He sees his Children mock at Faith and deny Providence   25
Therefore you must bind the Sheaves not by Nations or Families
You shall bind them in Three Classes; according to their Classes
So shall you bind them.. Separating What has been Mixed
Since Men began to be Wove into Nations by Rahab & Tirzah
Since Albions Death & Satans Cutting-off from our awful Fields;   30
When under pretence to benevolence the Elect Subdud All
From the Foundation of the World. The Elect is one Class: You
Shall bind them separate: they cannot Believe in Eternal Life
Except by Miracle & a New Birth. The other two Classes;
The Reprobate who never cease to Believe, and the Redeemd,   35
Who live in doubts & fears perpetually tormented by the Elect
These you shall bind in a twin-bundle for the Consummation—
But the Elect must be saved [from] fires of Eternal Death,
To be formed into the Churches of Beulah that they destroy not the
     Earth
For in every Nation & every Family the Three Classes are born   40
And in every Species of Earth, Metal, Tree, Fish, Bird & Beast.
We form the Mundane Egg, that Spectres coming by fury or amity,
All is the same, & every one remains in his own energy[.]
Go forth Reapers with rejoicing. you sowed in tears
But the time of your refreshing cometh, only a little moment   45
Still abstain from pleasure & rest in the labours of eternity
And you shall Reap the whole Earth from Pole to Pole! from Sea to Sea
Begin[n]ing at Jerusalems Inner Court, Lambeth ruin'd and given
To the detestable Gods of Priam, to Apollo: and at the Asylum
Given to Hercules, who labour in Tirzahs Looms for bread   50
Who set Pleasure against Duty: who Create Olympic crowns
To make Learning a burden & the Work of the Holy Spirit: Strife.
T[o] Thor & cruel Odin who first reard the Polar Caves   t
Lambeth mourns calling Jerusalem. she weeps & looks abroad
For the Lords coming, that Jerusalem may overspread all Nations[.]   55
Crave not for the mortal & perishing delights, but leave them
To the weak, and pity the weak as your infant care; Break not
Forth in your wrath lest you also are vegetated by Tirzah
Wait till the Judgement is past, till the Creation is consumed
And then rush forward with me into the glorious spiritual   60
Vegetation; the Supper of the Lamb & his Bride; and the
Awaking of Albion our friend and ancient companion.

So Los spoke. But lightnings of discontent broke on all sides round
And murmurs of thunder rolling heavy long & loud over the mountains
While Los calld his Sons around him to the Harvest & the Vintage.   65

Thou seest the Constellations in the deep & wondrous Night   c
They rise in order and continue their immortal courses
Upon the mountains & in vales with harp & heavenly song

With flute & clarion; with cups & measures filld with foaming wine.
Glittring the streams reflect the Vision of beatitude, 70
And the calm Ocean joys beneath & smooths his awful waves!
PLATE 26
These are the Sons of Los, & these the Labourers of the Vintage
Thou seest the gorgeous clothed Flies that dance & sport in summer
Upon the sunny brooks & meadows: every one the dance t
Knows in its intricate mazes of delight artful to weave:
Each one to sound his instruments of music in the dance, 5
To touch each other & recede; to cross & change & return
These are the Children of Los; thou seest the Trees on mountains
The wind blows heavy, loud they thunder thro' the darksom sky
Uttering prophecies & speaking instructive words to the sons
Of men: These are the Sons of Los! These the Visions of Eternity 10
But we see only as it were the hem of their garments
When with our vegetable eyes we view these wond'rous Visions

There are Two Gates thro which all Souls descend. One Southward c
From Dover Cliff to Lizard Point. the other toward the North
Caithness & rocky Durness, Pentland & John Groats House. 15

The Souls descending to the Body, wail on the right hand
Of Los; & those deliverd from the Body, on the left hand
For Los against the east his force continually bends
Along the Valleys of Middlesex from Hounslow to Blackheath
Lest those Three Heavens of Beulah should the Creation destroy 20
And lest they should descend before the north & south Gates
Groaning with pity, he among the wailing Souls laments.

And these the Labours of the Sons of Los in Allamanda: c
And in the City of Golgonooza: & in Luban: & around
The Lake of Udan-Adan, in the Forests of Entuthon Benython 25
Where Souls incessant wail, being piteous Passions & Desires
With neither lineament nor form but like to watry clouds
The Passions & Desires descend upon the hungry winds
For such alone Sleepers remain meer passion & appetite;
The Sons of Los clothe them & feed & provide houses & fields 30

And every Generated Body in its inward form,
Is a garden of delight & a building of magnificence,
Built by the Sons of Los in Bowlahoola & Allamanda
And the herbs & flowers & furniture & beds & chambers
Continually woven in the Looms of Enitharmons Daughters 35
In bright Cathedrons golden Dome with care & love & tears[.]
For the various Classes of Men are all markd out determinate
In Bowlahoola; & as the Spectres choose their affinities
So they are born on Earth, & every Class is determinate
But not by Natural but by Spiritual power alone. Because 40
The Natural power continually seeks & tends to Destruction

Ending in Death: which would of itself be Eternal Death
And all are Class'd by Spiritual, & not by Natural power.

And every Natural Effect has a Spiritual Cause, and Not
A Natural: for a Natural Cause only seems, it is a Delusion   45
Of Ulro: & a ratio of the perishing Vegetable Memory.

PLATE 27   t
But the Wine-press of Los is eastward of Golgonooza, before the Seat e
Of Satan. Luvah laid the foundation & Urizen finish'd it in howling
     woe.
How red the sons & daughters of Luvah! here they tread the grapes.   t
Laughing & shouting drunk with odours many fall oerwearied
Drownd in the wine is many a youth & maiden: those around   5
Lay them on skins of Tygers & of the spotted Leopard & the Wild Ass
Till they revive, or bury them in cool grots, making lamentation.

This Wine-press is call'd War on Earth, it is the Printing-Press
Of Los; and here he lays his words in order above the mortal brain
As cogs are formd in a wheel to turn the cogs of the adverse wheel.   10

Timbrels & violins sport round the Wine-presses; the little Seed;
The sportive Root, the Earth-worm, the gold Beetle; the wise Emmet;
Dance round the Wine-presses of Luvah: the Centipede is there:
The ground Spider with many eyes: the Mole clothed in velvet
The ambitious Spider in his sullen web; the lucky golden Spinner;   15
The Earwig armd: the tender Maggot emblem of immortality:
The Flea: Louse: Bug: the Tape-Worm: all the Armies of Disease:
Visible or invisible to the slothful vegetating Man.
The slow Slug: the Grasshopper that sings & laughs & drinks:
Winter comes, he folds his slender bones without a murmur.   20
The cruel Scorpion is there: the Gnat: Wasp: Hornet & the Honey
     Bee:
The Toad & venomous Newt; the Serpent clothd in gems & gold:
They throw off their gorgeous raiment: they rejoice with loud jubilee
Around the Wine-presses of Luvah, naked & drunk with wine.

There is the Nettle that stings with soft down; and there   25
The indignant Thistle: whose bitterness is bred in his milk:
Who feeds on contempt of his neighbour: there all the idle Weeds
That creep around the obscure places, shew their various limbs.
Naked in all their beauty dancing round the Wine-presses.

But in the Wine-presses the Human grapes sing not, nor dance   30
They howl & writhe in shoals of torment; in fierce flames consuming,
In chains of iron & in dungeons circled with ceaseless fires.
In pits & dens & shades of death: in shapes of torment & woe.
The plates & screws & wracks & saws & cords & fires & cisterns
The cruel joys of Luvahs Daughters lacerating with knives   35
And whips their Victims & the deadly sport of Luvahs Sons.

They dance around the dying, & they drink the howl & groan
They catch the shrieks in cups of gold, they hand them to one another:
These are the sports of love, & these the sweet delights of amorous play
Tears of the grape, the death sweat of the cluster the last sigh   40
Of the mild youth who listens to the lureing songs of Luvah

But Allamanda calld on Earth Commerce, is the Cultivated land   c
Around the City of Golgonooza in the Forests of Entuthon:
Here the Sons of Los labour against Death Eternal; through all
The Twenty-seven Heavens of Beulah in Ulro, Seat of Satan,   45
Which is the False Tongue beneath Beulah: it is the Sense of Touch:
The Plow goes forth in tempests & lightnings & the Harrow cruel
In blights of the east; the heavy Roller follows in howlings of woe.

Urizens sons here labour also; & here are seen the Mills
Of Theotormon, on the verge of the Lake of Udan-Adan: 50
These are the starry voids of night & the depths & caverns of earth
These Mills are oceans, clouds & waters ungovernable in their fury
Here are the stars created & the seeds of all things planted
And here the Sun & Moon recieve their fixed destinations

But in Eternity the Four Arts: Poetry, Painting, Music,   55
And Architecture which is Science: are the Four Faces of Man.
Not so in Time & Space: there Three are shut out, and only
Science remains thro Mercy: & by means of Science, the Three
Become apparent in Time & Space, in the Three Professions
Poetry in Religion: Music, Law: Painting, in Physic & Surgery: t 60
That Man may live upon Earth till the time of his awaking,
And from these Three, Science derives every Occupation of Men.
And Science is divided into Bowlahoola & Allamanda.

PLATE 28
Some Sons of Los surround the Passions with porches of iron & silver   c
Creating form & beauty around the dark regions of sorrow,
Giving to airy nothing a name and a habitation
Delightful! with bounds to the Infinite putting off the Indefinite
Into most holy forms of Thought: (such is the power of inspiration)   5
They labour incessant; with many tears & afflictions:
Creating the beautiful House for the piteous sufferer.

Others; Cabinets richly fabricate of gold & ivory;
For Doubts & fears unform'd & wretched & melancholy   t
The little weeping Spectre stands on the threshold of Death   10
Eternal; and sometimes two Spectres like lamps quivering
And often malignant they combat (heart-breaking sorrowful & piteous)
Antamon takes them into his beautiful flexible hands,
As the Sower takes the seed, or as the Artist his clay
Or fine wax, to mould artful a model for golden ornaments.   15
The soft hands of Antamon draw the indelible line:

Form immortal with golden pen; such as the Spectre admiring
Puts on the sweet form; then smiles Antamon bright thro his windows
The Daughters of beauty look up from their Loom & prepare.
The integument soft for its clothing with joy & delight.   20

But Theotormon & Sotha stand in the Gate of Luban anxious
Their numbers are seven million & seven thousand & seven hundred
They contend with the weak Spectres, they fabricate soothing forms
The Spectre refuses. he seeks cruelty. they create the crested Cock
Terrified the Spectre screams & rushes in fear into their Net   25
Of kindness & compassion & is born a weeping terror.
Or they create the Lion & Tyger in compassionate thunderings[.]
Howling the Spectres flee: they take refuge in Human lineaments.

The Sons of Ozoth within the Optic Nerve stand fiery glowing
And the number of his Sons is eight millions & eight.   30
They give delights to the man unknown; artificial riches
They give to scorn, & their posessors to trouble & sorrow & care,
Shutting the sun. & moon. & stars. & trees. & clouds. & waters.
And hills. out from the Optic Nerve & hardening it into a bone
Opake. and like the black pebble on the enraged beach.   35
While the poor indigent is like the diamond which tho cloth'd
In rugged covering in the mine, is open all within
And in his hallowd center holds the heavens of bright eternity
Ozoth here builds walls of rocks against the surging sea
And timbers crampt with iron cramps bar in the joys of life   40
From fell destruction in the Spectrous cunning or rage. He Creates
The speckled Newt, the Spider & Beetle, the Rat & Mouse,
The Badger & Fox: they worship before his feet in trembling fear.

But others of the Sons of Los build Moments & Minutes & Hours   e
And Days & Months & Years & Ages & Periods; wondrous buildings   45
And every Moment has a Couch of gold for soft repose,
(A Moment equals a pulsation of the artery)
And between every two Moments stands a Daughter of Beulah
To feed the Sleepers on their Couches with maternal care.
And every Minute has an azure Tent with silken Veils.   50
And every Hour has a bright golden Gate carved with skill.
And every Day & Night, has Walls of brass & Gates of adamant,
Shining like precious stones & ornamented with appropriate signs:
And every Month, a silver paved Terrace builded high:
And every Year, invulnerable Barriers with high Towers.   55
And every Age is Moated deep with Bridges of silver & gold:
And every Seven Ages is Incircled with a Flaming Fire.
Now Seven Ages is amounting to Two Hundred Years
Each has its Guard. each Moment Minute Hour Day Month & Year.
All are the work of Fairy hands of the Four Elements   60
The Guard are Angels of Providence on duty evermore

Every Time less than a pulsation of the artery
Is equal in its period & value to Six Thousand Years.
PLATE 29
For in this Period the Poets Work is Done: and all the Great
Events of Time start forth & are concievd in such a Period
Within a Moment: a Pulsation of the Artery.

The Sky is an immortal Tent built by the Sons of Los   c
And every Space that a Man views around his dwelling-place: 5
Standing on his own roof, or in his garden on a mount
Of twenty-five cubits in height, such space is his Universe;
And on its verge the Sun rises & sets. the Clouds bow
To meet the flat Earth & the Sea in such an orderd Space:
The Starry heavens reach no further but here bend and set   10
On all sides & the two Poles turn on their valves of gold:
And if he move his dwelling-place, his heavens also move.
Wher'eer he goes & all his neighbourhood bewail his loss:
Such are the Spaces called Earth & such its dimension:
As to that false appearance which appears to the reasoner,   15
As of a Globe rolling thro Voidness, it is a delusion of Ulro
The Microscope knows not of this nor the Telescope. they alter
The ratio of the Spectators Organs but leave Objects untouchd
For every Space larger than a red Globule of Mans blood.
Is visionary: and is created by the Hammer of Los   20
And every Space smaller than a Globule of Mans blood. opens
Into Eternity of which this vegetable Earth is but a shadow:
The red Globule is the unwearied Sun by Los created
To measure Time and Space to mortal Men. every morning.
Bowlahoola & Allamanda are placed on each side   25
Of that Pulsation & that Globule, terrible their power.

But Rintrah & Palamabron govern over Day & Night   c
In Allamanda & Entuthon Benython where Souls wail:
Where Orc incessant howls burning in fires of Eternal Youth,
Within the vegetated mortal Nerves; for every Man born is joined   30
Within into One mighty Polypus, and this Polypus is Orc.

But in the Optic vegetative Nerves Sleep was transformed
To Death in old time by Satan the father of Sin & Death
And Satan is the Spectre of Orc & Orc is the generate Luvah

But in the Nerves of the Nostrils, Accident being formed   35
Into Substance & Principle, by the cruelties of Demonstration
It became Opake & Indefinite; but the Divine Saviour,
Formed it into a Solid by Los's Mathematic power.
He named the Opake Satan: he named the Solid Adam

And in the Nerves of the Ear, (for the Nerves of the Tongue are closed)   40
On Albions Rock Los stands creating the glorious Sun each morning

And when unwearied in the evening he creates the Moon
Death to delude, who all in terror at their splendor leaves
His prey while Los appoints, & Rintrah & Palamabron guide
The Souls clear from the Rock of Death, that Death himself may wake   45
In his appointed season when the ends of heaven meet.

Then Los conducts the Spirits to be Vegetated, into
Great Golgonooza, free from the four iron pillars of Satans Throne
(Temperance, Prudence, Justice, Fortitude, the four pillars of tyranny)
That Satans Watch-Fiends touch them not before they Vegetate.   50

But Enitharmon and her Daughters take the pleasant charge.
To give them to their lovely heavens till the Great Judgment Day
Such is their lovely charge. But Rahab & Tirzah pervert
Their mild influences, therefore the Seven Eyes of God walk round
The Three Heavens of Ulro, where Tirzah & her Sisters   55
Weave the black Woof of Death upon Entuthon Benython
In the Vale of Surrey where Horeb terminates in Rephaim
The stamping feet of Zelophehads Daughters are coverd with Human
    gore
Upon the treddles of the Loom: they sing to the winged shuttle:
The River rises above his banks to wash the Woof: 60
He takes it in his arms: he passes it in strength thro his current
The veil of human miseries is woven over the Ocean
From the Atlantic to the Great South Sea, the Erythrean.

Such is the World of Los the labour of six thousand years.
Thus Nature is a Vision of the Science of the Elohim.   65

End of the First Book.

PLATE 30

There is a place where Contrarieties are equally True
This place is called Beulah, It is a pleasant lovely Shadow
Where no dispute can come. Because of those who Sleep.
Into this place the Sons & Daughters of Ololon descended
With solemn mourning, into Beulahs moony shades & hills   5
Weeping for Milton: mute wonder held the Daughters of Beulah
Enrapturd with affection sweet and mild benevolence

Beulah is evermore Created around Eternity; appearing
To the Inhabitants of Eden, around them on all sides.
But Beulah to its Inhabitants appears within each district   10
As the beloved infant in his mothers bosom round incircled
With arms of love & pity & sweet compassion. But to
The Sons of Eden the moony habitations of Beulah,
Are from Great Eternity a mild & pleasant Rest.

And it is thus Created. Lo the Eternal Great Humanity   15
To whom be Glory & Dominion Evermore Amen
Walks among all his awful Family seen in every face
As the breath of the Almighty. such are the words of man to man
In the great Wars of Eternity, in fury of Poetic Inspiration,
To build the Universe stupendous: Mental forms Creating   20

But the Emanations trembled exceedingly, nor could they
Live, because the life of Man was too exceeding unbounded
His joy became terrible to them, they trembled & wept
Crying with one voice. Give us a habitation & a place
In which we may be hidden under the shadow of wings   25
For if we who are but for a time, & who pass away in winter
Behold these wonders of Eternity we shall consume

But you O our Fathers & Brothers, remain in Eternity
But grant us a Temporal Habitation. do you speak
To us; we will obey your words as you obey Jesus   30
The Eternal who is blessed for ever & ever. Amen

So spake the lovely Emanations; & there appeard a pleasant
Mild Shadow above: beneath: & on all sides round,
PLATE 31
Into this pleasant Shadow all the weak & weary
Like Women & Children were taken away as on wings
Of dovelike softness, & shadowy habitations prepared for them
But every Man returnd & went still going forward thro'
The Bosom of the Father in Eternity on Eternity   5
Neither did any lack or fall into Error without
A Shadow to repose in all the Days of happy Eternity

Into this pleasant Shadow Beulah, all Ololon descended   e
And when the Daughters of Beulah heard the lamentation
All Beulah wept, for they saw the Lord coming in the Clouds.   10
And the Shadows of Beulah terminate in rocky Albion.

And all Nations wept in affliction Family by Family
Germany wept towards France & Italy: England wept & trembled
Towards America: India rose up from his golden bed:
As one awakend in the night: they saw the Lord coming   15
In the Clouds of Ololon with Power & Great Glory!

And all the Living Creatures of the Four Elements, wail'd
With bitter wailing: these in the aggregate are named Satan
And Rahab: they know not of Regeneration, but only of Generation
The Fairies, Nymphs, Gnomes & Genii of the Four Elements   20
Unforgiving & unalterable: these cannot be Regenerated
But must be Created, for they know only of Generation
These are the Gods of the Kingdoms of the Earth: in contrarious
And cruel opposition: Element against Element, opposed in War
Not Mental, as the Wars of Eternity, but a Corporeal Strife   25
In Los's Halls continual labouring in the Furnaces of Golgonooza
Orc howls on the Atlantic: Enitharmon trembles: All Beulah weeps

Thou hearest the Nightingale begin the Song of Spring;   e
The Lark sitting upon his earthy bed: just as the morn
Appears; listens silent; then springing from the waving Corn-field! loud   30
He leads the Choir of Day! trill, trill, trill, trill,
Mounting upon the wings of light into the Great Expanse:
Reecchoing against the lovely blue & shining heavenly Shell:
His little throat labours with inspiration; every feather
On throat & breast & wings vibrates with the effluence Divine   35
All Nature listens silent to him & the awful Sun
Stands still upon the Mountain looking on this little Bird

With eyes of soft humility, & wonder love & awe.
Then loud from their green covert all the Birds begin their Song
The Thrush, the Linnet & the Goldfinch, Robin & the Wren   40
Awake the Sun from his sweet reverie upon the Mountain:
The Nightingale again assays his song, & thro the day,
And thro the night warbles luxuriant; every Bird of Song
Attending his loud harmony with admiration & love.
This is a Vision of the lamentation of Beulah over Ololon!   45

Thou percievest the Flowers put forth their precious Odours!
And none can tell how from so small a center comes such sweets
Forgetting that within that Center Eternity expands
Its ever during doors, that Og & Anak fiercely guard[.]
First eer the morning breaks joy opens in the flowery bosoms   50
Joy even to tears, which the Sun rising dries; first the Wild Thyme
And Meadow-sweet downy & soft waving among the reeds.
Light springing on the air lead the sweet Dance: they wake
The Honeysuckle sleeping on the Oak: the flaunting beauty
Revels along upon the wind; the White-thorn lovely May   55
Opens her many lovely eyes: listening the Rose still sleeps   t
None dare to wake her. soon she bursts her crimson curtaind bed
And comes forth in the majesty of beauty; every Flower:
The Pink, the Jessamine, the Wall-flower, the Carnation
The Jonquil, the mild Lilly opes her heavens! every Tree,   60
And Flower & Herb soon fill the air with an innumerable Dance
Yet all in order sweet & lovely, Men are sick with Love!
Such is a Vision of the lamentation of Beulah over Ololon

PLATE 32   t
And Milton oft sat up on the Couch of Death & oft conversed   e
In vision & dream beatific with the Seven Angels of the Presence

I have turned my back upon these Heavens builded on cruelty
My Spectre still wandering thro' them follows my Emanation
He hunts her footsteps thro' the snow & the wintry hail & rain   5
The idiot Reasoner laughs at the Man of Imagination
And from laughter proceeds to murder by undervaluing calumny

Then Hillel who is Lucifer replied over the Couch of Death   e
And thus the Seven Angels instructed him & thus they converse.

We are not Individuals but States: Combinations of Individuals   e 10
We were Angels of the Divine Presence: & were Druids in Annandale
Compelld to combine into Form by Satan, the Spectre of Albion,
Who made himself a God &, destroyed the Human Form Divine.
But the Divine Humanity & Mercy gave us a Human   כרבים
        Form   as multitudes
Because we were combined in Freedom & holy   Vox Populi   15
        Brotherhood

While those combind by Satans Tyranny first in the blood of War
And Sacrifice &, next, in Chains of imprisonment: are Shapeless Rocks
Retaining only Satans Mathematic Holiness, Length: Bredth & Highth
Calling the Human Imagination: which is the Divine Vision & Fruition
In which Man liveth eternally: madness & blasphemy, against   20
Its own Qualities, which are Servants of Humanity, not Gods or
    Lords[.]
Distinguish therefore States from Individuals in those States.
States Change: but Individual Identities never change nor cease:
You cannot go to Eternal Death in that which can never Die.
Satan & Adam are States Created into Twenty-seven Churches   25
And thou O Milton art a State about to be Created
Called Eternal Annihilation that none but the Living shall
Dare to enter: & they shall enter triumphant over Death
And Hell & the Grave: States that are not, but ah! Seem to be.

Judge then of thy Own Self: thy Eternal Lineaments explore   30
What is Eternal & what Changeable? & what Annihilable!
The Imagination is not a State: it is the Human Existence itself
Affection or Love becomes a State, when divided from Imagination
The Memory is a State always, & the Reason is a State
Created to be Annihilated & a new Ratio Created   35
Whatever can be Created can be Annihilated Forms cannot
The Oak is cut down by the Ax, the Lamb falls by the Knife
But their Forms Eternal Exist, For-ever. Amen Halle[l]ujah

Thus they converse with the Dead watching round the Couch of
    Death.
For God himself enters Death's Door always with those that enter   40
And lays down in the Grave with them, in Visions of Eternity
Till they awake & see Jesus & the Linen Clothes lying
That the Females had Woven for them, & the Gates of their Fathers
    House

PLATE 33
And the Divine Voice was heard in the Songs of Beulah Saying   c

When I first Married you, I gave you all my whole Soul
I thought that you would love my loves & joy in my delights
Seeking for pleasures in my pleasures O Daughter of Babylon
Then thou wast lovely, mild & gentle. now thou art terrible   5
In jealousy & unlovely in my sight, because thou hast cruelly
Cut off my loves in fury till I have no love left for thee
Thy love depends on him thou lovest & on his dear loves
Depend thy pleasures which thou hast cut off by jealousy
Therefore I shew my Jealousy & set before you Death.   10
Behold Milton descended to Redeem the Female Shade
From Death Eternal; such your lot, to be continually Redeem'd
By death & misery of those you love & by Annihilation

When the Sixfold Female percieves that Milton annihilates
Himself: that seeing all his loves by her cut off: he leaves   15
Her also: intirely abstracting himself from Female loves
She shall relent in fear of death: She shall begin to give
Her maidens to her husband: delighting in his delight
And then & then alone begins the happy Female joy
As it is done in Beulah, & thou O Virgin Babylon Mother of   20
        Whoredoms
Shalt bring Jerusalem in thine arms in the night watches; and
No longer turning her a wandering Harlot in the streets
Shalt give her into the arms of God your Lord & Husband.

Such are the Songs of Beulah in the Lamentations of Ololon

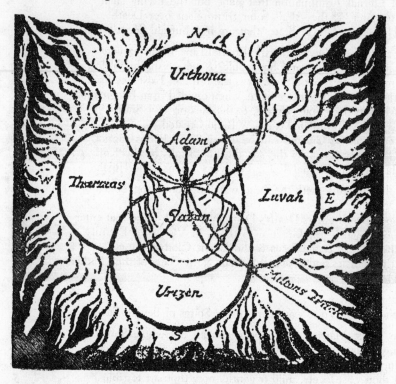

PLATE 34   t
And all the Songs of Beulah sounded comfortable notes   c
To comfort Ololons lamentation, for they said[:]
Are you the Fiery Circle that late drove in fury & fire
The Eight Immortal Starry-Ones down into Ulro dark
Rending the Heavens of Beulah with your thunders & lightnings   5
And can you thus lament & can you pity & forgive?
Is terror changd to pity O wonder of Eternity!

And the Four States of Humanity in its Repose,
Were shewed them. First of Beulah a most pleasant Sleep
On Couches soft, with mild music, tended by Flowers of Beulah   10
Sweet Female forms, winged or floating in the air spontaneous
The Second State is Alla & the third State Al-Ulro;
But the Fourth State is dreadful; it is named Or-Ulro:
The First State is in the Head, the Second is in the Heart:
The Third in the Loins & Seminal Vessels & the Fourth   15
In the Stomach & Intestines terrible, deadly, unutterable
And he whose Gates are opend in those Regions of his Body
Can from those Gates view all these wondrous Imaginations

But Ololon sought the Or-Ulro & its fiery Gates
And the Couches of the Martyrs: & many Daughters of Beulah   20
Accompany them down to the Ulro with soft melodious tears
A long journey & dark thro Chaos in the track of Miltons course
To where the Contraries of Beulah War beneath Negations Banner

Then view'd from Miltons Track they see the Ulro: a vast Polypus   c
Of living fibres down into the Sea of Time & Space growing   25
A self-devouring monstrous Human Death Twenty-seven fold[.]
Within it sit Five Females & the nameless Shadowy Mother
Spinning it from their bowels with songs of amorous delight
And melting cadences that lure the Sleepers of Beulah down
The River Storge (which is Arnon) into the Dead Sea: 30
Around this Polypus Los continual builds the Mundane Shell

Four Universes round the Universe of Los remain Chaotic
Four intersecting Globes, & the Egg form'd World of Los
In midst; stretching from Zenith to Nadir, in midst of Chaos[.]
One of these Ruind Universes is to the North named Urthona   35
One to the South this was the glorious World of Urizen
One to the East, of Luvah: One to the West; of Tharmas.
But when Luvah assumed the World of Urizen in the South
All fell towards the Center sinking downward in dire Ruin

Here in these Chaoses the Sons of Ololon took their abode   40
In Chasms of the Mundane Shell which open on all sides round!
Southward & by the East within the Breach of Miltons descent
To watch the time, pitying & gentle to awaken Urizen
They stood in a dark land of death of fiery corroding waters
Where lie in evil death the Four Immortals pale and cold   45
And the Eternal Man, even Albion, upon the Rock of Ages[.]
Seeing Miltons Shadow, some Daughters of Beulah trembling
Returnd, but Ololon remaind before the Gates of the Dead

And Ololon looked down into the Heavens of Ulro in fear
They said. How are the Wars of man which in Great Eternity   50
Appear around, in the External Spheres of Visionary Life

Here renderd Deadly within the Life & Interior Vision
How are the Beasts & Birds & Fishes, & Plants & Minerals
Here fixd into a frozen bulk subject to decay & death[?]
Those Visions of Human Life & Shadows of Wisdom & Knowledge   55
PLATE 35
Are here frozen to unexpansive deadly destroying terrors[.]
And War & Hunting: the Two Fountains of the River of Life
Are become Fountains of bitter Death & of corroding Hell
Till Brotherhood is changd into a Curse & a Flattery
By Differences between Ideas, that Ideas themselves, (which are   5
The Divine Members) may be slain in offerings for sin
O dreadful Loom of Death! O piteous Female forms compelld
To weave the Woof of Death, On Camberwell Tirzahs Courts
Malahs on Blackheath, Rahab & Noah. dwell on Windsors heights
Where once the Cherubs of Jerusalem spread to Lambeths Vale   10
Milcahs Pillars shine from Harrow to Hampstead where Hoglah
On Highgates heights magnificent Weaves over trembling Thames
To Shooters Hill and thence to Blackheath the dark Woof! Loud
Loud roll the Weights & Spindles over the whole Earth let down
On all sides round to the Four Quarters of the World, eastward on   15
Europe to Euphrates & Hindu, to Nile & back in Clouds
Of Death across the Atlantic to America North & South

So spake Ololon in reminiscence astonishd, but they
Could not behold Golgonooza without passing the Polypus
A wondrous journey not passable by Immortal feet, & none   20
But the Divine Saviour can pass it without annihilation.
For Golgonooza cannot be seen till having passd the Polypus
It is viewed on all sides round by a Four-fold Vision
Or till you become Mortal & Vegetable in Sexuality
Then you behold its mighty Spires & Domes of ivory & gold   25

And Ololon examined all the Couches of the Dead.
Even of Los & Enitharmon & all the Sons of Albion
And his Four Zoas terrified & on the verge of Death
In midst of these was Miltons Couch, & when they saw Eight
Immortal Starry-Ones, guarding the Couch in flaming fires   30
They thunderous utterd all a universal groan falling down
Prostrate before the Starry Eight asking with tears forgiveness
Confessing their crime with humiliation and sorrow.

O how the Starry Eight rejoic'd to see Ololon descended!   e
And now that a wide road was open to Eternity,   35
By Ololons descent thro Beulah to Los & Enitharmon.

For mighty were the multitudes of Ololon, vast the extent
Of their great sway, reaching from Ulro to Eternity
Surrounding the Mundane Shell outside in its Caverns

And through Beulah. and all silent forbore to contend   40
With Ololon for they saw the Lord in the Clouds of Ololon

There is a Moment in each Day that Satan cannot find   c
Nor can his Watch Fiends find it, but the Industrious find
This Moment & it multiply. & when it once is found
It renovates every Moment of the Day if rightly placed[.]   45
In this Moment Ololon descended to Los & Enitharmon
Unseen beyond the Mundane Shell Southward in Miltons track

Just in this Moment when the morning odours rise abroad
And first from the Wild Thyme, stands a Fountain in a rock
Of crystal flowing into two Streams, one flows thro Golgonooza   50
And thro Beulah to Eden beneath Los's western Wall
The other flows thro the Aerial Void & all the Churches
Meeting again in Golgonooza beyond Satans Seat

The Wild Thyme is Los's Messenger to Eden, a mighty Demon
Terrible deadly & poisonous his presence in Ulro dark   55
Therefore he appears only a small Root creeping in grass
Covering over the Rock of Odours his bright purple mantle
Beside the Fount above the Larks nest in Golgonooza
Luvah slept here in death & here is Luvahs empty Tomb
Ololon sat beside this Fountain on the Rock of Odours.   60

Just at the place to where the Lark mounts, is a Crystal Gate
It is the enterance of the First Heaven named Luther: for
The Lark is Los's Messenger thro the Twenty-seven Churches
That the Seven Eyes of God who walk even to Satans Seat
Thro all the Twenty-seven Heavens may not slumber nor sleep   65
But the Larks Nest is at the Gate of Los, at the eastern
Gate of wide Golgonooza & the Lark is Los's Messenger
PLATE 36
When on the highest lift of his light pinions he arrives
At that bright Gate, another Lark meets him & back to back
They touch their pinions tip tip: and each descend
To their respective Earths & there all night consult with Angels
Of Providence & with the Eyes of God all night in slumbers   5
Inspired: & at the dawn of day send out another Lark
Into another Heaven to carry news upon his wings
Thus are the Messengers dispatchd till they reach the Earth again
In the East Gate of Golgonooza, & the Twenty-eighth bright
Lark. met the Female Ololon descending into my Garden   10
Thus it appears to Mortal eyes & those of the Ulro Heavens
But not thus to Immortals, the Lark is a mighty Angel.

For Ololon step'd into the Polypus within the Mundane Shell   c
They could not step into Vegetable Worlds without becoming
The enemies of Humanity except in a Female Form   15

And as One Female, Ololon and all its mighty Hosts
Appear'd: a Virgin of twelve years nor time nor space was
To the perception of the Virgin Ololon but as the
Flash of lightning but more quick the Virgin in my Garden
Before my Cottage stood, for the Satanic Space is delusion   20

For when Los joind with me he took me in his firy whirlwind
My Vegetated portion was hurried from Lambeths shades
He set me down in Felphams Vale & prepard a beautiful
Cottage for me that in three years I might write all these Visions
To display Natures cruel holiness: the deceits of Natural Religion[.]   25
Walking in my Cottage Garden, sudden I beheld
The Virgin Ololon & address'd her as a Daughter of Beulah

Virgin of Providence fear not to enter into my Cottage
What is thy message to thy friend? What am I now to do
Is it again to plunge into deeper affliction? behold me   30
Ready to obey, but pity thou my Shadow of Delight
Enter my Cottage, comfort her, for she is sick with fatigue   t

PLATE 37
The Virgin answerd. Knowest thou of Milton who descended
Driven from Eternity; him I seek! terrified at my Act
In Great Eternity which thou knowest! I come him to seek

So Ololon utterd in words distinct the anxious thought   c
Mild was the voice, but more distinct than any earthly   5
That Miltons Shadow heard & condensing all his Fibres
Into a strength impregnable of majesty & beauty infinite
I saw he was the Covering Cherub & within him Satan
And Raha[b], in an outside which is fallacious! within   t
Beyond the outline of Identity, in the Selfhood deadly   10
And he appeard the Wicker Man of Scandinavia in whom
Jerusalems children consume in flames among the Stars

Descending down into my Garden, a Human Wonder of God
Reaching from heaven to earth a Cloud & Human Form
I beheld Milton with astonishment & in him beheld   15
The Monstrous Churches of Beulah, the Gods of Ulro dark
Twelve monstrous dishumanizd terrors Synagogues of Satan.
A Double Twelve & Thrice Nine: such their divisions.

And these their Names & their Places within the Mundane Shell

In Tyre & Sidon I saw Baal & Ashtaroth. In Moab Chemosh   c 20
In Ammon, Molech: loud his Furnaces rage among the Wheels
Of Og, & pealing loud the cries of the Victims of Fire!
And pale his Priestesses infolded in Veils of Pestilence, border'd
With War; Woven in Looms of Tyre & Sidon by beautiful Ashtaroth.
In Palestine Dagon, Sea Monster! worshipd o'er the Sea.   25

Thammuz in Lebanon & Rimmon in Damascus curtaind
Osiris: Isis: Orus: in Egypt: dark their Tabernacles on Nile
Floating with solemn songs, & on the Lakes of Egypt nightly
With pomp, even till morning break & Osiris appear in the sky
But Belial of Sodom & Gomorrha, obscure Demon of Bribes   30
And secret Assasinations, not worshipd nor adord; but   t
With the finger on the lips & the back turnd to the light
And Saturn Jove & Rhea of the Isles of the Sea remote
These Twelve Gods. are the Twelve Spectre Sons of the Druid Albion

And these the names of the Twenty-seven Heavens & their Churches   e 35
Adam, Seth, Enos, Cainan, Mahalaleel, Jared, Enoch,
Methuselah, Lamech: these are Giants mighty Hermaphroditic
Noah, Shem, Arphaxad, Cainan the second, Salah, Heber,
Peleg, Reu, Serug, Nahor, Terah, these are the Female-Males
A Male within a Female hid as in an Ark & Curtains,   40
Abraham, Moses, Solomon, Paul, Constantine, Charlemaine
Luther, these seven are the Male-Females, the Dragon Forms
Religion hid in War, a Dragon red & hidden Harlot

All these are seen in Miltons Shadow who is the Covering Cherub   e
The Spectre of Albion in which the Spectre of Luvah inhabits   45
In the Newtonian Voids between the Substances of Creation

For the Chaotic Voids outside of the Stars are measured by
The Stars, which are the boundaries of Kingdoms, Provinces
And Empires of Chaos invisible to the Vegetable Man
The Kingdom of Og. is in Orion: Sihon is in Ophiucus   50
Og has Twenty-seven Districts; Sihons Districts Twenty-one
From Star to Star, Mountains & Valleys, terrible dimension
Stretchd out, compose the Mundane Shell, a mighty Incrustation
Of Forty-eight deformed Human Wonders of the Almighty
With Caverns whose remotest bottoms meet again beyond   e 55
The Mundane Shell in Golgonooza, but the Fires of Los, rage
In the remotest bottoms of the Caves, that none can pass
Into Eternity that way, but all descend to Los
To Bowlahoola & Allamanda & to Entuthon Benython

The Heavens are the Cherub, the Twelve Gods are Satan   60
PLATE 38
And the Forty-eight Starry Regions are Cities of the Levites
The Heads of the Great Polypus, Four-fold twelve enormity
In mighty & mysterious comingling enemy with enemy
Woven by Urizen into Sexes from his mantle of years[.]
And Milton collecting all his fibres into impregnable strength   5
Descended down a Paved work of all kinds of precious stones
Out from the eastern sky; descending down into my Cottage
Garden: clothed in black, severe & silent he descended.

The Spectre of Satan stood upon the roaring sea & beheld   **e**
Milton within his sleeping Humanity! trembling & shuddring   10
He stood upon the waves a Twenty-seven-fold mighty Demon
Gorgeous & beautiful: loud roll his thunders against Milton
Loud Satan thunderd, loud & dark upon mild Felpham shore
Not daring to touch one fibre he howld round upon the Sea.

I also stood in Satans bosom & beheld its desolations!   15
A ruind Man: a ruind building of God not made with hands;
Its plains of burning sand, its mountains of marble terrible:
Its pits & declivities flowing with molten ore & fountains
Of pitch & nitre: its ruind palaces & cities & mighty works;
Its furnaces of affliction in which his Angels & Emanations   20
Labour with blackend visages among its stupendous ruins
Arches & pyramids & porches colonades & domes:
In which dwells Mystery Babylon, here is her secret place
From hence she comes forth on the Churches in delight
Here is her Cup filld with its poisons, in these horrid vales   25
And here her scarlet Veil woven in pestilence & war:
Here is Jerusalem bound in chains, in the Dens of Babylon

In the Eastern porch of Satans Universe Milton stood & said   **e**

Satan! my Spectre! I know my power thee to annihilate
And be a greater in thy place, & be thy Tabernacle   30
A covering for thee to do thy will, till one greater comes
And smites me as I smote thee & becomes my covering.
Such are the Laws of thy false Heavns! but Laws of Eternity
Are not such: know thou: I come to Self Annihilation
Such are the Laws of Eternity that each shall mutually   35
Annihilate himself for others good, as I for thee[.]
Thy purpose & the purpose of thy Priests & of thy Churches
Is to impress on men the fear of death; to teach
Trembling & fear, terror, constriction; abject selfishness
Mine is to teach Men to despise death & to go on   40
In fearless majesty annihilating Self, laughing to scorn
Thy Laws & terrors, shaking down thy Synagogues as webs
I come to discover before Heavn & Hell the Self righteousness
In all its Hypocritic turpitude, opening to every eye
These wonders of Satans holiness shewing to the Earth   45
The Idol Virtues of the Natural Heart, & Satans Seat
Explore in all its Selfish Natural Virtue & put off
In Self annihilation all that is not of God alone:
To put off Self & all I have ever & ever Amen

Satan heard! Coming in a cloud, with trumpets & flaming fire,   50
Saying I am God the judge of all, the living & the dead
Fall therefore down & worship me. submit thy supreme
Dictate, to my eternal Will & to my dictate bow
I hold the Balances of Right & Just & mine the Sword

Seven Angels bear my Name & in those Seven I appear   55
But I alone am God & I alone in Heavn & Earth
Of all that live dare utter this, others tremble & bow
PLATE 39
Till All Things become One Great Satan, in Holiness
Oppos'd to Mercy, and the Divine Delusion Jesus be no more

Suddenly around Milton on my Path, the Starry Seven   e
Burnd terrible! my Path became a solid fire, as bright
As the clear Sun & Milton silent came down on my Path.   5
And there went forth from the Starry limbs of the Seven: Forms
Human; with Trumpets innumerable, sounding articulate
As the Seven spake; and they stood in a mighty Column of Fire
Surrounding Felphams Vale, reaching to the Mundane Shell, Saying

Awake Albion awake! reclaim thy Reasoning Spectre. Subdue   10
Him to the Divine Mercy, Cast him down into the Lake
Of Los, that ever burneth with fire, ever & ever Amen!
Let the Four Zoa's awake from Slumbers of Six Thousand Years

Then loud the Furnaces of Los were heard! & seen as Seven Heavens
Stretching from south to north over the mountains of Albion   15

Satan heard; trembling round his Body, he incircled it
He trembled with exceeding great trembling & astonishment
Howling in his Spectre round his Body hungring to devour
But fearing for the pain for if he touches a Vital,
His torment is unendurable: therefore he cannot devour: 20
But howls round it as a lion round his prey continually.
Loud Satan thunderd, loud & dark upon mild Felphams Shore
Coming in a Cloud with Trumpets & with Fiery Flame
An awful Form eastward from midst of a bright Paved-work
Of precious stones by Cherubim surrounded: so permitted   25
(Lest he should fall apart in his Eternal Death) to imitate
The Eternal Great Humanity Divine surrounded by
His Cherubim & Seraphim in ever happy Eternity
Beneath sat Chaos: Sin on his right hand Death on his left
And Ancient Night spread over all the heavn his Mantle of Laws   30
He trembled with exceeding great trembling & astonishment

Then Albion rose up in the Night of Beulah on his Couch   e
Of dread repose seen by the visionary eye; his face is toward
The east, toward Jerusalems Gates: groaning he sat above
His rocks. London & Bath & Legions & Edinburgh   35
Are the four pillars of his Throne; his left foot near London
Covers the shades of Tyburn: his instep from Windsor
To Primrose Hill stretching to Highgate & Holloway
London is between his knees: its basements fourfold
His right foot stretches to the sea on Dover cliffs, his heel   40
On Canterburys ruins; his right hand covers lofty Wales

His left Scotland; his bosom girt with gold involves
York, Edinburgh, Durham & Carlisle & on the front
Bath, Oxford, Cambridge Norwich; his right elbow
Leans on the Rocks of Erins Land, Ireland ancient nation[.]   45
His head bends over London: he sees his embodied Spectre
Trembling before him with exceeding great trembling & fear
He views Jerusalem & Babylon, his tears flow down
He movd his right foot to Cornwall, his left to the Rocks of Bognor
He strove to rise to walk into the Deep. but strength failing   50
Forbad & down with dreadful groans he sunk upon his Couch
In moony Beulah. Los his strong Guard walks round beneath the Moon

Urizen faints in terror striving among the Brooks of Arnon
With Miltons Spirit: as the Plowman or Artificer or Shepherd
While in the labours of his Calling sends his Thought abroad   t 55
To labour in the ocean or in the starry heaven. So Milton
Labourd in Chasms of the Mundane Shell, tho here before
My Cottage midst the Starry Seven, where the Virgin Ololon
Stood trembling in the Porch: loud Satan thunder'd on the stormy Sea
Circling Albions Cliffs in which the Four-fold World resides   60
Tho seen in fallacy outside: a fallacy of Satans Churches

PLATE 40
Before Ololon Milton stood & percievd the Eternal Form   e
Of that mild Vision; wondrous were their acts by me unknown
Except remotely; and I heard Ololon say to Milton

I see thee strive upon the Brooks of Arnon. there a dread
And awful Man I see, oercoverd with the mantle of years.   5
I behold Los & Urizen. I behold Orc & Tharmas;
The Four Zoa's of Albion & thy Spirit with them striving
In Self annihilation giving thy life to thy enemies
Are those who contemn Religion & seek to annihilate it
Become in their Femin[in]e portions the causes & promoters   10
Of these Religions, how is this thing? this Newtonian Phantasm
This Voltaire & Rousseau: this Hume & Gibbon & Bolingbroke
This Natural Religion! this impossible absurdity
Is Ololon the cause of this? O where shall I hide my face
These tears fall for the little-ones: the Children of Jerusalem   15
Lest they be annihilated in thy annihilation.

No sooner she had spoke but Rahab Babylon appeard
Eastward upon the Paved work across Europe & Asia
Glorious as the midday Sun in Satans bosom glowing
A Female hidden in a Male, Religion hidden in War   20
Namd Moral Virtue; cruel two-fold Monster shining bright
A Dragon red & hidden Harlot which John in Patmos saw

And all beneath the Nations innumerable of Ulro
Appeard, the Seven Kingdoms of Canaan & Five Baalim

Of Philistea. into Twelve divided, calld after the Names   25
Of Israel: as they are in Eden. Mountain. River & Plain
City & sandy Desert intermingled beyond mortal ken

But turning toward Ololon in terrible majesty Milton   c
Replied. Obey thou the Words of the Inspired Man
All that can be annihilated must be annihilated   t 30
That the Children of Jerusalem may be saved from slavery
There is a Negation, & there is a Contrary
The Negation must be destroyd to redeem the Contraries
The Negation is the Spectre; the Reasoning Power in Man
This is a false Body: an Incrustation over my Immortal   35
Spirit; a Selfhood, which must be put off & annihilated alway
To cleanse the Face of my Spirit by Self-examination.

PLATE 41

To bathe in the Waters of Life; to wash off the Not Human
I come in Self-annihilation & the grandeur of Inspiration
To cast off Rational Demonstration by Faith in the Saviour
To cast off the rotten rags of Memory by Inspiration
To cast off Bacon, Locke & Newton from Albions covering   5
To take off his filthy garments, & clothe him with Imagination
To cast aside from Poetry, all that is not Inspiration
That it no longer shall dare to mock with the aspersion of Madness
Cast on the Inspired, by the tame high finisher of paltry Blots,
Indefinite, or paltry Rhymes; or paltry Harmonies.   10
Who creeps into State Government like a catterpiller to destroy
To cast off the idiot Questioner who is always questioning,
But never capable of answering; who sits with a sly grin
Silent plotting when to question, like a thief in a cave;
Who publishes doubt & calls it knowledge; whose Science is Despair,   15
Whose pretence to knowledge is Envy, whose whole Science is
To destroy the wisdom of ages to gratify ravenous Envy;
That rages round him like a Wolf day & night without rest
He smiles with condescension; he talks of Benevolence & Virtue
And those who act with Benevolence & Virtue, they murder time on   20
    time
These are the destroyers of Jerusalem, these are the murderers
Of Jesus, who deny the Faith & mock at Eternal Life!
Who pretend to Poetry that they may destroy Imagination;
By imitation of Natures Images drawn from Remembrance
These are the Sexual Garments, the Abomination of Desolation   c 25
Hiding the Human Lineaments as with an Ark & Curtains
Which Jesus rent: & now shall wholly purge away with Fire
Till Generation is swallowd up in Regeneration.

Then trembled the Virgin Ololon & replyd in clouds of despair   e

Is this our Femin[in]e Portion the Six-fold Miltonic Female   30
Terribly this Portion trembles before thee O awful Man

Altho' our Human Power can sustain the severe contentions
Of Friendship, our Sexual cannot: but flies into the Ulro.
Hence arose all our terrors in Eternity! & now remembrance
Returns upon us! are we Contraries O Milton, Thou & I   35
O Immortal! how were we led to War the Wars of Death
Is this the Void Outside of Existence, which if enter'd into
PLATE 42   t
Becomes a Womb? & is this the Death Couch of Albion
Thou goest to Eternal Death & all must go with thee

So saying, the Virgin divided Six-fold & with a shriek
Dolorous that ran thro all Creation a Double Six-fold Wonder!
Away from Ololon she divided & fled into the depths   5
Of Miltons Shadow as a Dove upon the stormy Sea.

Then as a Moony Ark Ololon descended to Felphams Vale
In clouds of blood, in streams of gore, with dreadful thunderings
Into the Fires of Intellect that rejoic'd in Felphams Vale
Around the Starry Eight: with one accord the Starry Eight became   10
One Man Jesus the Saviour. wonderful! round his limbs
The Clouds of Ololon folded as a Garment dipped in blood
Written within & without in woven letters: & the Writing
Is the Divine Revelation in the Litteral expression:
A Garment of War, I heard it namd the Woof of Six Thousand Years   15

And I beheld the Twenty-four Cities of Albion   e
Arise upon their Thrones to Judge the Nations of the Earth
And the Immortal Four in whom the Twenty-four appear Four-fold
Arose around Albions body: Jesus wept & walked forth
From Felphams Vale clothed in Clouds of blood, to enter into   20
Albions Bosom, the bosom of death & the Four surrounded him
In the Column of Fire in Felphams Vale; then to their mouths the Four
Applied their Four Trumpets & them sounded to the Four winds

Terror struck in the Vale I stood at that immortal sound
My bones trembled. I fell outstretchd upon the path   25
A moment, & my Soul returnd into its mortal state
To Resurrection & Judgment in the Vegetable Body
And my sweet Shadow of Delight stood trembling by my side

Immediately the Lark mounted with a loud trill from Felphams Vale
And the Wild Thyme from Wimbletons green & impurpled Hills   30
And Los & Enitharmon rose over the Hills of Surrey
Their clouds roll over London with a south wind, soft Oothoon
Pants in the Vales of Lambeth weeping oer her Human Harvest
Los listens to the Cry of the Poor Man: his Cloud
Over London in volume terrific, low bended in anger.   35

Rintrah & Palamabron view the Human Harvest beneath
Their Wine-presses & Barns stand open; the Ovens are prepar'd

The Waggons ready: terrific Lions & Tygers sport & play
All Animals upon the Earth, are prepard in all their strength
PLATE 43
To go forth to the Great Harvest & Vintage of the Nations

Finis

❧

JERUSALEM
The Emanation of The Giant Albion
1804 Printed by W. Blake Sth Molton S^t.
t
t

PLATE I

[Frontispiece]   t

[Above the archway:]

There is a Void, outside of Existence, which if enterd into   c
Englobes itself & becomes a Womb, such was Albions Couch
A pleasant Shadow of Repose calld Albions lovely Land

His Sublime & Pathos become Two Rocks fixd in the Earth
His Reason, his Spectrous Power, covers them above[.]   5
Jerusalem his Emanation is a Stone laying beneath[.]
O [*Albion behold Pitying*] behold the Vision of Albion   t

[On right side of archway:]

Half Friendship is the bitterest Enmity said Los
As he enterd the Door of Death for Albions sake Inspired
The long sufferings of God are not for ever there is a Judgment   10

[On left side, in reversed writing:]

Every Thing has its Vermin O Spectre of the Sleeping Dead!

PLATE 3

SHEEP   GOATS   t
To the Public

After my three years slumber on the banks of the Ocean, I again
display my Giant forms to the Public: My former Giants & Fairies having reciev'd the highest reward possible: the [*love*] and [*friendship*]
of those with whom to be connected, is to be [*blessed:*] I cannot doubt
that this more consolidated & extended Work, will be as kindly recieved

The Enthusiasm of the following Poem, the Author hopes [*no Reader will think presumptuousness or arroganc*[*e*] *when he is reminded that the Ancients entrusted their love to their Writing, to the full as Enthusiastically as I have who Acknowledge mine for my Saviour and Lord, for they were wholly absorb'd in their Gods.*] I also hope the Reader will be with me, wholly One in Jesus our Lord, who is the God [*of Fire*] and Lord [*of Love*] to whom the Ancients look'd and saw his day afar off, with trembling & amazement.

The Spirit of Jesus is continual forgiveness of Sin: he who waits to be righteous before he enters into the Saviours kingdom, the Divine Body; will never enter there. I am perhaps the most sinful of men! I pretend not to holiness! yet I pretend to love, to see, to converse with daily, as man with man, & the more to have an interest in the Friend of Sinners. Therefore [*Dear*] Reader, [*forgive*] what you do not approve, & [*love*] me for this energetic exertion of my talent.

> Reader! [*lover*] of books! [*lover*] of heaven,
> And of that God from whom [*all books are given,*]
> Who in mysterious Sinais awful cave
> To Man the wond'rous art of writing gave,
> Again he speaks in thunder and in fire!   5
> Thunder of Thought, & flames of fierce desire:
> Even from the depths of Hell his voice I hear,
> Within the unfathomd caverns of my Ear.
> Therefore I print; nor vain my types shall be:
> Heaven, Earth & Hell, henceforth shall live in harmony   10

> Of the Measure, in which
> the following Poem is written

We who dwell on Earth can do nothing of ourselves, every thing is conducted by Spirits, no less than Digestion or Sleep. [*to Note the last words of Jesus*, Εδοθη μοι πασα εξουσια εν ουρανω και επι γης]

When this Verse was first dictated to me I consider'd a Monotonous Cadence like that used by Milton & Shakspeare & all writers of English Blank Verse, derived from the modern bondage of Rhyming; to be a necessary and indispensible part of Verse. But I soon found that in the mouth of a true Orator such monotony was not only awkward, but as much a bondage as rhyme itself. I therefore have produced a variety in every line, both of cadences & number of syllables. Every word and every letter is studied and put into its fit place: the terrific numbers are reserved for the terrific parts—the mild & gentle, for the mild & gentle parts, and the prosaic, for inferior parts: all are necessary to each other. Poetry Fetter'd, Fetters the Human Race! Nations are Destroy'd, or Flourish, in proportion as Their Poetry Painting and Music, are Destroy'd or Flourish! The Primeval State of Man, was Wisdom, Art, and Science.

PLATE 4

Μονος ὁ Ιεσους

Jerusalem

Chap: 1

Of the Sleep of Ulro! and of the passage through
Eternal Death! and of the awaking to Eternal Life.

This theme calls me in sleep night after night, & ev'ry morn   e
Awakes me at sun-rise, then I see the Saviour over me
Spreading his beams of love, & dictating the words of this mild song.   5

Awake! awake O sleeper of the land of shadows, wake! expand!
I am in you and you in me, mutual in love divine:
Fibres of love from man to man thro Albions pleasant land.
In all the dark Atlantic vale down from the hills of Surrey
A black water accumulates, return Albion! return!   10
Thy brethren call thee, and thy fathers, and thy sons,
Thy nurses and thy mothers, thy sisters and thy daughters
Weep at thy souls disease, and the Divine Vision is darkend:
Thy Emanation that was wont to play before thy face,
Beaming forth with her daughters into the Divine bosom [*Where!!*]   15
Where hast thou hidden thy Emanation lovely Jerusalem
From the vision and fruition of the Holy-one?
I am not a God afar off, I am a brother and friend;
Within your bosoms I reside, and you reside in me:
Lo! we are One; forgiving all Evil; Not seeking recompense!   20
Ye are my members O ye sleepers of Beulah, land of shades!

But the perturbed Man away turns down the valleys dark;
[*Saying. We are not One: we are Many, thou most simulative*]
Phantom of the over heated brain! shadow of immortality!
Seeking to keep my soul a victim to thy Love! which binds   25
Man the enemy of man into deceitful friendships:
Jerusalem is not! her daughters are indefinite:
By demonstration, man alone can live, and not by faith.
My mountains are my own, and I will keep them to myself:
The Malvern and the Cheviot, the Wolds Plinlimmon & Snowdon   30
Are mine. here will I build my Laws of Moral Virtue!
Humanity shall be no more: but war & princedom & victory!

So spoke Albion in jealous fears, hiding his Emanation   e
Upon the Thames and Medway, rivers of Beulah: dissembling
His jealousy before the throne divine, darkening, cold!   35

PLATE 5

The banks of the Thames are clouded! the ancient porches of Albion
    are
Darken'd! they are drawn thro' unbounded space, scatter'd upon
The Void in incoherent despair! Cambridge & Oxford & London,
Are driven among the starry Wheels, rent away and dissipated,
In Chasms & Abysses of sorrow, enlarg'd without dimension, terrible[.]   5
Albions mountains run with blood, the cries of war & of tumult
Resound into the unbounded night, every Human perfection
Of mountain & river & city, are small & wither'd & darken'd
Cam is a little stream! Ely is almost swallowd up!
Lincoln & Norwich stand trembling on the brink of Udan-Adan!   10
Wales and Scotland shrink themselves to the west and to the north!
Mourning for fear of the warriors in the Vale of Entuthon-Benython
Jerusalem is scatterd abroad like a cloud of smoke thro' non-entity:
Moab & Ammon & Amalek & Canaan & Egypt & Aram
Recieve her little-ones for sacrifices and the delights of cruelty   15

Trembling I sit day and night, my friends are astonish'd at me.
Yet they forgive my wanderings, I rest not from my great task!
To open the Eternal Worlds, to open the immortal Eyes
Of Man inwards into the Worlds of Thought: into Eternity
Ever expanding in the Bosom of God. the Human Imagination   20
O Saviour pour upon me thy Spirit of meekness & love:
Annihilate the Selfhood in me, be thou all my life!
Guide thou my hand which trembles exceedingly upon the rock of ages,
While I write of the building of Golgonooza, & of the terrors of
    Entuthon:
Of Hand & Hyle & Coban, of Kwantok, Peachey, Brereton, Slayd &   c 25
    Hutton:
Of the terrible sons & daughters of Albion. and their Generations.

Scofield! Kox, Kotope and Bowen, revolve most mightily upon
The Furnace of Los: before the eastern gate bending their fury.
They war, to destroy the Furnaces, to desolate Golgonooza:
And to devour the Sleeping Humanity of Albion in rage & hunger.   30
They revolve into the Furnaces Southward & are driven forth
    Northward
Divided into Male and Female forms time after time.
From these Twelve all the Families of England spread abroad.

The Male is a Furnace of beryll; the Female is a golden Loom;
I behold them and their rushing fires overwhelm my Soul,   35
In Londons darkness; and my tears fall day and night,
Upon the Emanations of Albions Sons! the Daughters of Albion
Names anciently rememberd, but now contemn'd as fictions!
Although in every bosom they controll our Vegetative powers.

These are united into Tirzah and her Sisters, on Mount Gilead,   ᶜ 40
Cambel & Gwendolen & Conwenna & Cordella & Ignoge.
And these united into Rahab in the Covering Cherub on Euphrates
Gwiniverra & Gwinefred, & Gonorill & Sabrina beautiful,
Estrild, Mehetabel & Ragan, lovely Daughters of Albion,
They are the beautiful Emanations of the Twelve Sons of Albion   45

The Starry Wheels revolv'd heavily over the Furnaces;
Drawing Jerusalem in anguish of maternal love,
Eastward a pillar of a cloud with Vala upon the mountains
Howling in pain, redounding from the arms of Beulahs Daughters,
Out from the Furnaces of Los above the head of Los.   50
A pillar of smoke writhing afar into Non-Entity, redounding
Till the cloud reaches afar outstretch'd among the Starry Wheels
Which revolve heavily in the mighty Void above the Furnaces

O what avail the loves & tears of Beulahs lovely Daughters
They hold the Immortal Form in gentle bands & tender tears   55
But all within is open'd into the deeps of Entuthon Benython
A dark and unknown night, indefinite, unmeasurable, without end.
Abstract Philosophy warring in enmity against Imagination
(Which is the Divine Body of the Lord Jesus. blessed for ever).
And there Jerusalem wanders with Vala upon the mountains,   60
Attracted by the revolutions of those Wheels the Cloud of smoke
Immense, and Jerusalem & Vala weeping in the Cloud
Wander away into the Chaotic Void, lamenting with her Shadow
Among the Daughters of Albion, among the Starry Wheels;
Lamenting for her children, for the sons & daughters of Albion   65

Los heard her lamentations in the deeps afar! his tears fall   ᶜ
Incessant before the Furnaces, and his Emanation divided in pain,
Eastward toward the Starry Wheels. But Westward, a black Horror,
PLATE 6
His spectre driv'n by the Starry Wheels of Albions sons, black and
Opake divided from his back; he labours and he mourns!

For as his Emanation divided, his Spectre also divided
In terror of those starry wheels: and the Spectre stood over Los
Howling in pain: a blackning Shadow, blackning dark & opake   5
Cursing the terrible Los: bitterly cursing him for his friendship   ᶜ
To Albion, suggesting murderous thoughts against Albion.

Los rag'd and stamp'd the earth in his might & terrible wrath!   ᶜ
He stood and stampd the earth! then he threw down his hammer in
     rage &
In fury: then he sat down and wept, terrified! Then arose   10
And chaunted his song, labouring with the tongs and hammer:
But still the Spectre divided, and still his pain increas'd!

In pain the Spectre divided: in pain of hunger and thirst:
To devour Los's Human Perfection, but when he saw that Los
PLATE 7
Was living: panting like a frighted wolf, and howling
He stood over the Immortal, in the solitude and darkness:
Upon the darkning Thames, across the whole Island westward.
A horrible Shadow of Death, among the Furnaces: beneath
The pillar of folding smoke; and he sought by other means,   5
To lure Los: by tears, by arguments of science & by terrors:
Terrors in every Nerve, by spasms & extended pains:
While Los answer'd unterrified to the opake blackening Fiend   c

And thus the Spectre spoke: Wilt thou still go on to destruction?
Till thy life is all taken away by this deceitful Friendship?   10
He drinks thee up like water! like wine he pours thee
Into his tuns: thy Daughters are trodden in his vintage
He makes thy Sons the trampling of his bulls, they are plow'd
And harrowd for his profit, lo! thy stolen Emanation
Is his garden of pleasure! all the Spectres of his Sons mock thee   15
Look how they scorn thy once admired palaces! now in ruins
Because of Albion! because of deceit and friendship! For Lo!
Hand has peopled Babel & Nineveh: Hyle, Ashur & Aram:
Cobans son is Nimrod: his son Cush is adjoind to Aram,
By the Daughter of Babel, in a woven mantle of pestilence & war.   20
They put forth their spectrous cloudy sails; which drive their immense
Constellations over the deadly deeps of indefinite Udan-Adan[.]
Kox is the Father of Shem & Ham & Japheth, he is the Noah
Of the Flood of Udan-Adan. Hut'n is the Father of the Seven
From Enoch to Adam; Schofield is Adam who was New-   25
Created in Edom. I saw it indignant, & thou art not moved!
This has divided thee in sunder: and wilt thou still forgive?
O! thou seest not what I see! what is done in the Furnaces.
Listen, I will tell thee what is done in moments to thee unknown:
Luvah was cast into the Furnaces of affliction and sealed,   30
And Vala fed in cruel delight, the Furnaces with fire:
Stern Urizen beheld; urgd by necessity to keep
The evil day afar, and if perchance with iron power
He might avert his own despair: in woe & fear he saw
Vala incircle round the Furnaces where Luvah was clos'd: 35
With joy she heard his howlings, & forgot he was her Luvah,
With whom she liv'd in bliss in times of innocence & youth!
Vala comes from the Furnace in a cloud, but wretched Luvah
Is howling in the Furnaces, in flames among Albions Spectres,
To prepare the Spectre of Albion to reign over thee O Los,   40
Forming the Spectres of Albion according to his rage:
To prepare the Spectre sons of Adam, who is Scofield: the Ninth
Of Albions sons, & the father of all his brethren in the Shadowy

Generation. Cambel & Gwendolen wove webs of war & of
Religion, to involve all Albions sons, and when they had   45
Involv'd Eight; their webs roll'd outwards into darkness
And Scofield the Ninth remain on the outside of the Eight
And Kox, Kotope, & Bowen, One in him, a Fourfold Wonder
Involv'd the Eight: Such are the Generations of the Giant Albion,
To separate a Law of Sin, to punish thee in thy members.   50

Los answer'd. Altho' I know not this! I know far worse than this: e
I know that Albion hath divided me, and that thou O my Spectre,
Hast just cause to be irritated: but look stedfastly upon me:
Comfort thyself in my strength the time will arrive,
When all Albions injuries shall cease, and when we shall   55
Embrace him tenfold bright, rising from his tomb in immortality.
They have divided themselves by Wrath. they must be united by
Pity: let us therefore take example & warning O my Spectre,
O that I could abstain from wrath! O that the Lamb
Of God would look upon me and pity me in my fury.   60
In anguish of regeneration! in terrors of self annihilation:
Pity must join together those whom wrath has torn in sunder,
And the Religion of Generation which was meant for the destruction
Of Jerusalem, become her covering, till the time of the End.
O holy Generation [Image] of regeneration!   ᵗ65
O point of mutual forgiveness between Enemies!
Birthplace of the Lamb of God incomprehensible!
The Dead despise & scorn thee, & cast thee out as accursed:
Seeing the Lamb of God in thy gardens & thy palaces:
Where they desire to place the Abomination of Desolation.   70
Hand sits before his furnace: scorn of others & furious pride!   e
Freeze round him to bars of steel & to iron rocks beneath
His feet: indignant self-righteousness like whirlwinds of the north!
PLATE 8
Rose up against me thundering from the Brook of Albions River
From Ranelagh & Strumbolo, from Cromwells gardens & Chelsea
The place of wounded Soldiers. but when he saw my Mace
Whirld round from heaven to earth, trembling he sat: his cold
Poisons rose up: & his sweet deceits coverd them all over   5
With a tender cloud. As thou art now; such was he O Spectre
I know thy deceit & thy revenges, and unless thou desist
I will certainly create an eternal Hell for thee. Listen!
Be attentive! be obedient! Lo the Furnaces are ready to recieve thee.
I will break thee into shivers! & melt thee in the furnaces of death; 10
I will cast thee into forms of abhorrence & torment if thou
Desist not from thine own will, & obey not my stern command!
I am closd up from my children: my Emanation is dividing
And thou my Spectre art divided against me. But mark
I will compell thee to assist me in my terrible labours. To beat   15

These hypocritic Selfhoods on the Anvils of bitter Death
I am inspired: I act not for myself: for Albions sake
I now am what I am: a horror and an astonishment
Shuddring the heavens to look upon me: Behold what cruelties
Are practised in Babel & Shinar, & have approachd to Zions Hill   20

While Los spoke, the terrible Spectre fell shuddring before him   c
Watching his time with glowing eyes to leap upon his prey[.]
Los opend the Furnaces in fear. the Spectre saw to Babel & Shinar
Across all Europe & Asia. he saw the tortures of the Victims.
He saw now from the ou[t]side what he before saw & felt from   25
     within
He saw that Los was the sole, uncontrolld Lord of the Furnaces
Groaning he kneeld before Los's iron-shod feet on London Stone,
Hungring & thirsting for Los's life yet pretending obedience.
While Los pursud his speech in threat'nings loud & fierce.

Thou art my Pride & Self-righteousness: I have found thee out: c 30
Thou art reveald before me in all thy magnitude & power
Thy Uncircumcised pretences to Chastity must be cut in sunder!
Thy holy wrath & deep deceit cannot avail against me
Nor shalt thou ever assume the triple-form of Albions Spectre
For I am one of the living: dare not to mock my inspired fury   35
If thou wast cast forth from my life! if I was dead upon the mountains
Thou mightest be pitied & lovd: but now I am living; unless
Thou abstain ravening I will create an eternal Hell for thee.
Take thou this Hammer & in patience heave the thundering Bellows
Take thou these Tongs: strike thou alternate with me: labour   t 40
     obedient[.]
Hand & Hyle & Koban: Skofeld, Kox & Kotope, labour mightily[.]
In the Wars of Babel & Shinar, all their Emanations were
Condensd. Hand has absorbd all his Brethren in his might
All the infant Loves & Graces were lost, for the mighty Hand

PLATE 9

Condens'd his Emanations into hard opake substances;
And his infant thoughts & desires, into cold, dark, cliffs of death.
His hammer of gold he siezd; and his anvil of adamant.
He siez'd the bars of condens'd thoughts, to forge them:
Into the sword of war: into the bow and arrow: 5
Into the thundering cannon and into the murdering gun[.]
I saw the limbs form'd for exercise, contemn'd: & the beauty of
Eternity, look'd upon as deformity & loveliness as a dry tree:
I saw disease forming a Body of Death around the Lamb
Of God, to destroy Jerusalem, & to devour the body of Albion   10
By war and stratagem to win the labour of the husbandman:
Awkwardness arm'd in steel: folly in a helmet of gold:
Weakness with horns & talons: ignorance with a rav'ning beak!
Every Emanative joy forbidden as a Crime:

And the Emanations buried alive in the earth with pomp of religion: 15
Inspiration deny'd; Genius forbidden by laws of punishment!
I saw terrified; I took the sighs & tears, & bitter groans:
I lifted them into my Furnaces; to form the spiritual sword.
That lays open the hidden heart: I drew forth the pang
Of sorrow red hot: I workd it on my resolute anvil: 20
I heated it in the flames of Hand, & Hyle, & Coban
Nine times; Gwendolen & Cambel & Gwineverra
Are melted into the gold, the silver, the liquid ruby,
The crysolite, the topaz, the jacinth, & every precious stone.
Loud roar my Furnaces and loud my hammer is heard: 25
I labour day and night, I behold the soft affections
Condense beneath my hammer into forms of cruelty
But still I labour in hope, tho' still my tears flow down.
That he who will not defend Truth, may be compelld to defend
A Lie: that he may be snared and caught and snared and taken   30
That Enthusiasm and Life may not cease: arise Spectre arise!

Thus they contended among the Furnaces with groans & tears;   e
Groaning the Spectre heavd the bellows, obeying Los's frowns;
Till the Spaces of Erin were perfected in the furnaces
Of affliction, and Los drew them forth, compelling the harsh Spectre. 35

PLATE 10   t
Into the Furnaces & into the valleys of the Anvils of Death
And into the mountains of the Anvils & of the heavy Hammers
Till he should bring the Sons & Daughters of Jerusalem to be
The Sons & Daughters of Los that he might protect them from
Albions dread Spectres; storming, loud, thunderous & mighty   5
The Bellows & the Hammers move compell'd by Los's hand.

And this is the manner of the Sons of Albion in their strength   e
They take the Two Contraries which are calld Qualities, with which
Every Substance is clothed, they name them Good & Evil
From them they make an Abstract, which is a Negation   10
Not only of the Substance from which it is derived
A murderer of its own Body: but also a murderer
Of every Divine Member: it is the Reasoning Power
An Abstract objecting power, that Negatives every thing
This is the Spectre of Man: the Holy Reasoning Power   15
And in its Holiness is closed the Abomination of Desolation

Therefore Los stands in London building Golgonooza
Compelling his Spectre to labours mighty; trembling in fear
The Spectre weeps, but Los unmovd by tears or threats remains

I must Create a System, or be enslav'd by another Mans   20
I will not Reason & Compare: my business is to Create

So Los, in fury & strength: in indignation & burning wrath   e
Shuddring the Spectre howls. his howlings terrify the night
He stamps around the Anvil, beating blows of stern despair
He curses Heaven & Earth, Day & Night & Sun & Moon   25
He curses Forest Spring & River, Desart & sandy Waste
Cities & Nations, Families & Peoples, Tongues & Laws
Driven to desperation by Los's terrors & threatning fears

Los cries, Obey my voice & never deviate from my will
And I will be merciful to thee: be thou invisible to all   30
To whom I make thee invisible, but chief to my own Children
O Spectre of Urthona: Reason not against their dear approach
Nor them obstruct with thy temptations of doubt & despair[.]
O Shame O strong & mighty Shame I break thy brazen fetters
If thou refuse, thy present torments will seem southern breezes   35
To what thou shalt endure if thou obey not my great will.

The Spectre answer'd. Art thou not ashamd of those thy Sins
That thou callest thy Children? lo the Law of God commands
That they be offered upon his Altar: O cruelty & torment
For thine are also mine! I have kept silent hitherto,   40
Concerning my chief delight: but thou hast broken silence
Now I will speak my mind! Where is my lovely Enitharmon
O thou my enemy, where is my Great Sin? She is also thine
I said: now is my grief at worst: incapable of being
Surpassed: but every moment it accumulates more & more   45
It continues accumulating to eternity! the joys of God advance
For he is Righteous: he is not a Being of Pity & Compassion   t
He cannot feel Distress: he feeds on Sacrifice & Offering:
Delighting in cries & tears & clothed in holiness & solitude
But my griefs advance also, for ever & ever without end   50
O that I could cease to be! Despair! I am Despair
Created to be the great example of horror & agony: also my
Prayer is vain I called for compassion: compassion mockd[,]
Mercy & pity threw the grave stone over me & with lead
And iron, bound it over me for ever: Life lives on my   55
Consuming: & the Almighty hath made me his Contrary
To be all evil, all reversed & for ever dead: knowing
And seeing life, yet living not; how can I then behold
And not tremble; how can I be beheld & not abhorrd

So spoke the Spectre shuddring, & dark tears ran down his shadowy   60
    face
Which Los wiped off, but comfort none could give! or beam of hope
Yet ceasd he not from labouring at the roarings of his Forge
With iron & brass Building Golgonooza in great contendings
Till his Sons & Daughters came forth from the Furnaces
At the sublime Labours for Los. compelld the invisible Spectre   65

PLATE 11

To labours mighty, with vast strength, with his mighty chains,
In pulsations of time, & extensions of space, like Urns of Beulah
With great labour upon his anvils[;] & in his ladles the Ore t
He lifted, pouring it into the clay ground prepar'd with art;
Striving with Systems to deliver Individuals from those Systems; 5
That whenever any Spectre began to devour the Dead,
He might feel the pain as if a man gnawd his own tender nerves.

Then Erin came forth from the Furnaces, & all the Daughters of e
 Beulah
Came from the Furnaces, by Los's mighty power for Jerusalems
Sake: walking up and down among the Spaces of Erin: 10
And the Sons and Daughters of Los came forth in perfection lovely!
And the Spaces of Erin reach'd from the starry heighth, to the starry
 depth.

Los wept with exceeding joy & all wept with joy together!
They feard they never more should see their Father, who
Was built in from Eternity, in the Cliffs of Albion. 15

But when the joy of meeting was exhausted in loving embrace;
Again they lament. O what shall we do for lovely Jerusalem?
To protect the Emanations of Albions mighty ones from cruelty?
Sabrina & Ignoge begin to sharpen their beamy spears
Of light and love: their little children stand with arrows of gold: 20
Ragan is wholly cruel Scofield is bound in iron armour!
He is like a mandrake in the earth before Reubens gate:
He shoots beneath Jerusalems walls to undermine her foundations!
Vala is but thy Shadow, O thou loveliest among women!
A shadow animated by thy tears O mournful Jerusalem! 25

PLATE 12

Why wilt thou give to her a Body whose life is but a Shade?
Her joy and love, a shade: a shade of sweet repose:
But animated and vegetated, she is a devouring worm:
What shall we do for thee O lovely mild Jerusalem?

And Los said. I behold the finger of God in terrors! 5
Albion is dead! his Emanation is divided from him!
But I am living! yet I feel my Emanation also dividing
Such thing was never known! O pity me, thou all-piteous-one!
What shall I do! or how exist, divided from Enitharmon?
Yet why despair! I saw the finger of God go forth 10
Upon my Furnaces, from within the Wheels of Albions Sons:
Fixing their Systems, permanent: by mathematic power
Giving a body to Falshood that it may be cast off for ever.
With Demonstrative Science piercing Apollyon with his own bow!
God is within, & without! he is even in the depths of Hell! 15

Such were the lamentations of the Labourers in the Furnaces!

And they appeard within & without incircling on both sides
The Starry Wheels of Albions Sons, with Spaces for Jerusalem:
And for Vala the shadow of Jerusalem: the ever mourning shade:
On both sides, within & without beaming gloriously!   20

Terrified at the sublime Wonder, Los stood before his Furnaces.
And they stood around, terrified with admiration at Erins Spaces
For the Spaces reachd from the starry heighth, to the starry depth;
And they builded Golgonooza: terrible eternal labour!

What are those golden builders doing? where was the burying-place   ᶜ 25
Of soft Ethinthus? near Tyburns fatal Tree? is that
Mild Zions hills most ancient promontory; near mournful
Ever weeping Paddington? is that Calvary and Golgotha?
Becoming a building of pity and compassion? Lo!
The stones are pity, and the bricks, well wrought affections: 30
Enameld with love & kindness, & the tiles engraven gold
Labour of merciful hands: the beams & rafters are forgiveness:
The mortar & cement of the work, tears of honesty: the nails,
And the screws & iron braces, are well wrought blandishments,
And well contrived words, firm fixing, never forgotten,   35
Always comforting the remembrance: the floors, humility,
The cielings, devotion: the hearths, thanksgiving:
Prepare the furniture O Lambeth in thy pitying looms!
The curtains, woven tears & sighs, wrought into lovely forms
For comfort. there the secret furniture of Jerusalems chamber   40
Is wrought: Lambeth! the Bride the Lambs Wife loveth thee:
Thou art one with her & knowest not of self in thy supreme joy.
Go on, builders in hope: tho Jerusalem wanders far away,
Without the gate of Los: among the dark Satanic wheels.

Fourfold the Sons of Los in their divisions: and fourfold,   ᶜ 45
The great City of Golgonooza: fourfold toward the north
And toward the south fourfold, & fourfold toward the east & west
Each within other toward the four points: that toward
Eden, and that toward the World of Generation,
And that toward Beulah, and that toward Ulro: 50
Ulro is the space of the terrible starry wheels of Albions sons:
But that toward Eden is walled up, till time of renovation:
Yet it is perfect in its building, ornaments & perfection.

And the Four Points are thus beheld in Great Eternity
West, the Circumference: South, the Zenith: North,   55
The Nadir: East, the Center, unapproachable for ever.
These are the four Faces towards the Four Worlds of Humanity
In every Man. Ezekiel saw them by Chebars flood.
And the Eyes are the South, and the Nostrils are the East.
And the Tongue is the West, and the Ear is the North.   60

And the North Gate of Golgonooza toward Generation;
Has four sculpturd Bulls terrible before the Gate of iron.
And iron, the Bulls: and that which looks toward Ulro,
Clay bak'd & enamel'd, eternal glowing as four furnaces:
Turning upon the Wheels of Albions sons with enormous power.   65
And that toward Beulah four, gold, silver, brass, & iron:
PLATE 13
And that toward Eden, four, form'd of gold, silver, brass, & iron.

The South, a golden Gate, has four Lions terrible, living!
That toward Generation, four, of iron carv'd wondrous:
That toward Ulro, four, clay bak'd, laborious workmanship
That toward Eden, four; immortal gold, silver, brass & iron.   5

The Western Gate fourfold, is closd: having four Cherubim
Its guards, living, the work of elemental hands, laborious task!
Like Men, hermaphroditic, each winged with eight wings
That towards Generation, iron; that toward Beulah, stone;
That toward Ulro, clay: that toward Eden, metals.   10
But all clos'd up till the last day, when the graves shall yield their dead

The Eastern Gate, fourfold: terrible & deadly its ornaments:
Taking their forms from the Wheels of Albions sons; as cogs
Are formd in a wheel, to fit the cogs of the adverse wheel.

That toward Eden, eternal ice, frozen in seven folds   15
Of forms of death: and that toward Beulah, stone:
The seven diseases of the earth are carved terrible.
And that toward Ulro, forms of war: seven enormities:
And that toward Generation, seven generative forms.

And every part of the City is fourfold; & every inhabitant, fourfold.   20
And every pot & vessel & garment & utensil of the houses,
And every house, fourfold; but the third Gate in every one
Is closd as with a threefold curtain of ivory & fine linen & ermine.
And Luban stands in middle of the City. a moat of fire,
Surrounds Luban, Los's Palace & the golden Looms of Cathedron.   25

And sixty-four thousand Genii, guard the Eastern Gate:
And sixty-four thousand Gnomes, guard the Northern Gate:
And sixty-four thousand Nymphs, guard the Western Gate:
And sixty-four thousand Fairies, guard the Southern Gate:

Around Golgonooza lies the land of death eternal; a Land   c 30
Of pain and misery and despair and ever brooding melancholy:
In all the Twenty-seven Heavens, numberd from Adam to Luther;
From the blue Mundane Shell, reaching to the Vegetative Earth.

The Vegetative Universe, opens like a flower from the Earths center:
In which is Eternity. It expands in Stars to the Mundane Shell   35

-155-

And there it meets Eternity again, both within and without,
And the abstract Voids between the Stars are the Satanic Wheels.

There is the Cave; the Rock; the Tree; the Lake of Udan Adan;
The Forest, and the Marsh, and the Pits of bitumen deadly:
The Rocks of solid fire: the Ice valleys: the Plains   40
Of burning sand: the rivers, cataract & Lakes of Fire:
The Islands of the fiery Lakes: the Trees of Malice: Revenge:
And black Anxiety; and the Cities of the Salamandrine men:
(But whatever is visible to the Generated Man,
Is a Creation of mercy & love, from the Satanic Void.)   45
The land of darkness flamed but no light, & no repose:
The land of snows of trembling, & of iron hail incessant:
The land of earthquakes: and the land of woven labyrinths:
The land of snares & traps & wheels & pit-falls & dire mills:
The Voids, the Solids, & the land of clouds & regions of waters: 50
With their inhabitants: in the Twenty-seven Heavens beneath Beulah:
Self-righteousnesses conglomerating against the Divine Vision:
A Concave Earth wondrous, Chasmal, Abyssal, Incoherent!
Forming the Mundane Shell: above; beneath: on all sides surrounding
Golgonooza: Los walks round the walls night and day.   55

He views the City of Golgonooza, & its smaller Cities:
The Looms & Mills & Prisons & Work-houses of Og & Anak:
The Amalekite: the Canaanite: the Moabite: the Egyptian:
And all that has existed in the space of six thousand years:
Permanent, & not lost not lost nor vanishd, & every little act,   60
Word, work, & wish, that has existed, all remaining still
In those Churches ever consuming & ever building by the Spectres
Of all the inhabitants of Earth wailing to be Created:
Shadowy to those who dwell not in them, meer possibilities:
But to those who enter into them they seem the only substances   65
For every thing exists & not one sigh nor smile nor tear,

PLATE 14
One hair nor particle of dust, not one can pass away.

He views the Cherub at the Tree of Life, also the Serpent,
Orc the first born coild in the south: the Dragon Urizen:
Tharmas the Vegetated Tongue even the Devouring Tongue:
A threefold region, a false brain: a false heart: 5
And false bowels: altogether composing the False Tongue,
Beneath Beulah: as a watry flame revolving every way
And as dark roots and stems: a Forest of affliction, growing
In seas of sorrow. Los also views the Four Females:
Ahania, and Enion, and Vala, and Enitharmon lovely.   10
And from them all the lovely beaming Daughters of Albion,
Ahania & Enion & Vala, are three evanescent shades:

Enitharmon is a vegetated mortal Wife of Los:
His Emanation, yet his Wife till the sleep of Death is past.

Such are the Buildings of Los! & such are the Woofs of Enitharmon!　　15

And Los beheld his Sons, and he beheld his Daughters:　　　　　　　c
Every one a translucent Wonder: a Universe within,
Increasing inwards, into length and breadth, and heighth:
Starry & glorious: and they every one in their bright loins:
Have a beautiful golden gate which opens into the vegetative world:　　20
And every one a gate of rubies & all sorts of precious stones
In their translucent hearts, which opens into the vegetative world:
And every one a gate of iron dreadful and wonderful,
In their translucent heads, which opens into the vegetative world
And every one has the three regions Childhood: Manhood: & Age:　　25
But the gate of the tongue: the western gate in them is clos'd,
Having a wall builded against it: and thereby the gates
Eastward & Southward & Northward, are incircled with flaming fires.
And the North is Breadth, the South is Heighth & Depth:
The East is Inwards: & the West is Outwards every way.　　　　　　30

And Los beheld the mild Emanation Jerusalem eastward bending
Her revolutions toward the Starry Wheels in maternal anguish
Like a pale cloud arising from the arms of Beulahs Daughters:
In Entuthon Benythons deep Vales beneath Golgonooza.　　　　　　t

PLATE 15
And Hand & Hyle rooted into Jerusalem by a fibre　　　　　　　　c
Of strong revenge & Skofeld Vegetated by Reubens Gate
In every Nation of the Earth till the Twelve Sons of Albion
Enrooted into every Nation: a mighty Polypus growing
From Albion over the whole Earth: such is my awful Vision.　　　　　5

I see the Four-fold Man. The Humanity in deadly sleep
And its fallen Emanation. The Spectre & its cruel Shadow.
I see the Past, Present & Future, existing all at once
Before me; O Divine Spirit sustain me on thy wings!
That I may awake Albion from his long & cold repose.　　　　　　　10
For Bacon & Newton sheathd in dismal steel, their terrors hang
Like iron scourges over Albion, Reasonings like vast Serpents
Infold around my limbs, bruising my minute articulations

I turn my eyes to the Schools & Universities of Europe
And there behold the Loom of Locke whose Woof rages dire　　　　　15
Washd by the Water-wheels of Newton. black the cloth
In heavy wreathes folds over every Nation; cruel Works
Of many Wheels I view, wheel without wheel, with cogs tyrannic
Moving by compulsion each other: not as those in Eden: which
Wheel within Wheel in freedom revolve in harmony & peace.　　　　　20

I see in deadly fear in London Los raging round his Anvil
Of death: forming an Ax of gold: the Four Sons of Los
Stand round him cutting the Fibres from Albions hills
That Albions Sons may roll apart over the Nations
While Reuben enroots his brethren in the narrow Canaanite   25
From the Limit Noah to the Limit Abram in whose Loins
Reuben in his Twelve-fold majesty & beauty shall take refuge
As Abraham flees from Chaldea shaking his goary locks
But first Albion must sleep, divided from the Nations

I see Albion sitting upon his Rock in the first Winter   30
And thence I see the Chaos of Satan & the World of Adam
When the Divine Hand went forth on Albion in the mid Winter
And at the place of Death when Albion sat in Eternal Death
Among the Furnaces of Los in the Valley of the Son of Hinnom

PLATE 16
Hampstead Highgate Finchley Hendon Muswell hill: rage loud
Before Bromions iron Tongs & glowing Poker reddening fierce
Hertfordshire glows with fierce Vegetation! in the Forests
The Oak frowns terrible, the Beech & Ash & Elm enroot
Among the Spiritual fires; loud the Corn fields thunder along   5
The Soldiers fife; the Harlots shriek; the Virgins dismal groan
The Parents fear: the Brothers jealousy: the Sisters curse
Beneath the Storms of Theotormon[;] & the thundring Bellows
Heaves in the hand of Palamabron who in Londons darkness
Before the Anvil, watches the bellowing flames: thundering   10
The Hammer loud rages in Rintrahs strong grasp swinging loud
Round from heaven to earth down falling with heavy blow
Dead on the Anvil, where the red hot wedge groans in pain
He quenches it in the black trough of his Forge: Londons River
Feeds the dread Forge, trembling & shuddering along the Valleys   15

Humber & Trent roll dreadful before the Seventh Furnace
And Tweed & Tyne anxious give up their Souls for Albions sake
Lincolnshire Derbyshire Nottinghamshire Leicestershire
From Oxfordshire to Norfolk on the Lake of Udan Adan
Labour within the Furnaces, walking among the Fires   20
With Ladles huge & iron Pokers over the Island white.

Scotland pours out his Sons to labour at the Furnaces
Wales gives his Daughters to the Looms; England: nursing Mothers
Gives to the Children of Albion & to the Children of Jerusalem.
From the blue Mundane Shell even to the Earth of Vegetation   25
Throughout the whole Creation which groans to be deliverd
Albion groans in the deep slumbers of Death upon his Rock.

Here Los fixd down the Fifty-two Counties of England & Wales   e
The Thirty-six of Scotland, & the Thirty-four of Ireland

With mighty power, when they fled out at Jerusalems Gates   30
Away from the Conflict of Luvah & Urizen, fixing the Gates
In the Twelve Counties of Wales & thence Gates looking every way
To the Four Points: conduct to England & Scotland & Ireland
And thence to all the Kingdoms & Nations & Families of the Earth[.]
The Gate of Reuben in Carmarthenshire: the Gate of Simeon in   35
    Cardiganshire: & the Gate of Levi in Montgomeryshire
The Gate of Judah Merionethshire: the Gate of Dan Flintshire
The Gate of Napthali, Radnorshire: the Gate of Gad Pembrokeshire
The Gate of Asher, Carnarvonshire the Gate of Issachar Brecknokshire
The Gate of Zebulun, in Anglesea & Sodor. so is Wales divided.   40
The Gate of Joseph, Denbighshire: the Gate of Benjamin
    Glamorganshire
For the protection of the Twelve Emanations of Albions Sons

And the Forty Counties of England are thus divided in the Gates
Of Reuben Norfolk, Suffolk, Essex. Simeon Lincoln, York Lancashire
Levi. Middlesex Kent Surrey. Judah Somerset Glouster Wiltshire.   45
Dan. Cornwal Devon Dorset, Napthali., Warwick Leicester Worcester
Gad. Oxford Bucks Harford. Asher, Sussex Hampshire Berkshire
Issachar, Northampton Rutland Nottgham. Zebulun Bedford Huntgn
    Camb
Joseph Stafford Shrops Heref. Benjamin, Derby Cheshire Monmouth;
And Cumberland Northumberland Westmoreland & Durham are   50
Divided in the Gates of Reuben, Judah Dan & Joseph

And the Thirty-six Counties of Scotland, divided in the Gates
Of Reuben Kincard Haddntn Forfar, Simeon Ayr Argyll Banff
Levi Edinburh Roxbro Ross. Judah, Abrdeen Berwik Dumfries
Dan Bute Caitnes Clakmanan. Napthali Nairn Invernes Linlithgo   55
Gad Peebles Perth Renfru. Asher Sutherlan Sterling Wigtoun
Issachar Selkirk Dumbartn Glasgo. Zebulun Orkney Shetland Skye
Joseph Elgin Lanerk Kinros. Benjamin Kromarty Murra Kirkubriht
Governing all by the sweet delights of secret amorous glances
In Enitharmons Halls builded by Los & his mighty Children   60

All things acted on Earth are seen in the bright Sculptures of   e
Los's Halls & every Age renews its powers from these Works
With every pathetic story possible to happen from Hate or
Wayward Love & every sorrow & distress is carved here
Every Affinity of Parents Marriages & Friendships are here   65
In all their various combinations wrought with wondrous Art
All that can happen to Man in his pilgrimage of seventy years
Such is the Divine Written Law of Horeb & Sinai:
And such the Holy Gospel of Mount Olivet & Calvary:

PLATE 17
His Spectre divides & Los in fury compels it to divide: e
To labour in the fire, in the water, in the earth, in the air,

-159-

To follow the Daughters of Albion as the hound follows the scent
Of the wild inhabitant of the forest, to drive them from his own:
To make a way for the Children of Los to come from the Furnaces   5
But Los himself against Albions Sons his fury bends, for he
Dare not approach the Daughters openly lest he be consumed
In the fires of their beauty & perfection & be Vegetated beneath
Their Looms, in a Generation of death & resurrection to forgetfulness
They wooe Los continually to subdue his strength: he continually   10
Shews them his Spectre: sending him abroad over the four points of
      heaven
In the fierce desires of beauty & in the tortures of repulse! He is
The Spectre of the Living pursuing the Emanations of the Dead.
Shuddring they flee: they hide in the Druid Temples in cold chastity:
Subdued by the Spectre of the Living & terrified by undisguisd desire.   15

For Los said: Tho my Spectre is divided: as I am a Living Man
I must compell him to obey me wholly: that Enitharmon may not
Be lost: & lest he should devour Enitharmon: Ah me!
Piteous image of my soft desires & loves: O Enitharmon!
I will compell my Spectre to obey: I will restore to thee thy Children.   20
No one bruises or starves himself to make himself fit for labour!

Tormented with sweet desire for these beauties of Albion
They would never love my power if they did not seek to destroy
Enitharmon: Vala would never have sought & loved Albion
If she had not sought to destroy Jerusalem; such is that false   25
And Generating Love: a pretence of love to destroy love:
Cruel hipocrisy unlike the lovely delusions of Beulah:
And cruel forms, unlike the merciful forms of Beulahs Night

They know not why they love nor wherefore they sicken & die
Calling that Holy Love: which is Envy Revenge & Cruelty   30
Which separated the stars from the mountains: the mountains from
      Man
And left Man, a little grovelling Root, outside of Himself.
Negations are not Contraries: Contraries mutually Exist:
But Negations Exist Not: Exceptions & Objections & Unbeliefs
Exist not: nor shall they ever be Organized for ever & ever: 35
If thou separate from me, thou art a Negation: a meer
Reasoning & Derogation from me, an Objecting & cruel Spite
And Malice & Envy: but my Emanation, Alas! will become
My Contrary: O thou Negation, I will continually compell
Thee to be invisible to any but whom I please, & when   40
And where & how I please, and never! never! shalt thou be Organized
But as a distorted & reversed Reflexion in the Darkness
And in the Non Entity: nor shall that which is above
Ever descend into thee: but thou shalt be a Non Entity for ever
And if any enter into thee, thou shalt be an Unquenchable Fire   45

And he shall be a never dying Worm, mutually tormented by
Those that thou tormentest, a Hell & Despair for ever & ever.

So Los in secret with himself communed & Enitharmon heard   ^c
In her darkness & was comforted: yet still she divided away
In gnawing pain from Los's bosom in the deadly Night;   50
First as a red Globe of blood trembling beneath his bosom[.]
Suspended over her he hung: he infolded her in his garments
Of wool: he hid her from the Spectre, in shame & confusion of
Face; in terrors & pains of Hell & Eternal Death, the
Trembling Globe shot forth Self-living & Los howld over it: 55
Feeding it with his groans & tears day & night without ceasing:
And the Spectrous Darkness from his back divided in temptations,
And in grinding agonies in threats! stiflings! & direful strugglings.

Go thou to Skofield: ask him if he is Bath or if he is Canterbury
Tell him to be no more dubious: demand explicit words   60
Tell him: I will dash him into shivers, where & at what time
I please: tell Hand & Skofield they are my ministers of evil
To those I hate: for I can hate also as well as they!

PLATE 18
From every-one of the Four Regions of Human Majesty,   ^c
There is an Outside spread Without, & an Outside spread Within
Beyond the Outline of Identity both ways, which meet in One:
An orbed Void of doubt, despair, hunger, & thirst & sorrow.
Here the Twelve Sons of Albion, join'd in dark Assembly,   5
Jealous of Jerusalems children, asham'd of her little-ones
(For Vala produc'd the Bodies. Jerusalem gave the Souls)
Became as Three Immense Wheels, turning upon one-another
Into Non-Entity, and their thunders hoarse appall the Dead
To murder their own Souls, to build a Kingdom among the Dead[:]   10

Cast! Cast ye Jerusalem forth! The Shadow of delusions!   ^c
The Harlot daughter! Mother of pity and dishonourable forgiveness
Our Father Albions sin and shame! But father now no more!
Nor sons! nor hateful peace & love, nor soft complacencies
With transgressors meeting in brotherhood around the table,   15
Or in the porch or garden. No more the sinful delights
Of age and youth and boy and girl and animal and herb,
And river and mountain, and city & village, and house & family.
Beneath the Oak & Palm, beneath the Vine and Fig-tree.
In self-denial!—But War and deadly contention, Between   20
Father and Son, and light and love! All bold asperities
Of Haters met in deadly strife, rending the house & garden
The unforgiving porches, the tables of enmity, and beds
And chambers of trembling & suspition, hatreds of age & youth
And boy & girl, & animal & herb, & river & mountain   25

And city & village, and house & family. That the Perfect,
May live in glory, redeem'd by Sacrifice of the Lamb
And of his children, before sinful Jerusalem. To build
Babylon the City of Vala, the Goddess Virgin-Mother.
She is our Mother! Nature! Jerusalem is our Harlot-Sister   30
Return'd with Children of pollution, to defile our House,
With Sin and Shame. Cast! Cast her into the Potters field.
Her little-ones, She must slay upon our Altars: and her aged
Parents must be carried into captivity, to redeem her Soul
To be for a Shame & a Curse, and to be our Slaves for ever   35

So cry Hand & Hyle the eldest of the fathers of Albions
Little-ones; to destroy the Divine Saviour; the Friend of Sinners,
Building Castles in desolated places, and strong Fortifications.
Soon Hand mightily devour'd & absorb'd Albions Twelve Sons.
Out from his bosom a mighty Polypus, vegetating in darkness,   40
And Hyle & Coban were his two chosen ones, for Emissaries
In War: forth from his bosom they went and return'd.
Like Wheels from a great Wheel reflected in the Deep.
Hoarse turn'd the Starry Wheels, rending a way in Albions Loins   e
Beyond the Night of Beulah. In a dark & unknown Night,   45
Outstretch'd his Giant beauty on the ground in pain & tears:

PLATE 19
His Children exil'd from his breast pass to and fro before him
His birds are silent on his hills, flocks die beneath his branches
His tents are fall'n! his trumpets, and the sweet sound of his harp
Are silent on his clouded hills, that belch forth storms & fire.
His milk of Cows, & honey of Bees, & fruit of golden harvest,   5
Is gather'd in the scorching heat, & in the driving rain:
Where once he sat he weary walks in misery and pain:
His Giant beauty and perfection fallen into dust:
Till from within his witherd breast grown narrow with his woes:
The corn is turn'd to thistles & the apples into poison: 10
The birds of song to murderous crows, his joys to bitter groans!
The voices of children in his tents, to cries of helpless infants!
And self-exiled from the face of light & shine of morning,
In the dark world a narrow house! he wanders up and down,
Seeking for rest and finding none! and hidden far within,   15
His Eon weeping in the cold and desolated Earth.

All his Affections now appear withoutside: all his Sons,
Hand, Hyle & Coban, Guantok, Peachey, Brereton, Slayd & Hutton,
Scofeld, Kox, Kotope & Bowen; his Twelve Sons: Satanic Mill!
Who are the Spectres of the Twentyfour, each Double-form'd: 20
Revolve upon his mountains groaning in pain: beneath
The dark incessant sky, seeking for rest and finding none:
Raging against their Human natures, ravning to gormandize

The Human majesty and beauty of the Twentyfour.
Condensing them into solid rocks with cruelty and abhorrence   25
Suspition & revenge, & the seven diseases of the Soul
Settled around Albion and around Luvah in his secret cloud[.]
Willing the Friends endur'd, for Albions sake, and for
Jerusalem his Emanation shut within his bosom;
Which hardend against them more and more; as he builded onwards   30
On the Gulph of Death in self-righteousness, that roll'd
Before his awful feet, in pride of virtue for victory:
And Los was roofd in from Eternity in Albions Cliffs
Which stand upon the ends of Beulah, and withoutside, all
Appear'd a rocky form against the Divine Humanity.   35

Albions Circumference was clos'd: his Center began darkning
Into the Night of Beulah, and the Moon of Beulah rose
Clouded with storms: Los his strong Guard walkd round beneath the
    Moon
And Albion fled inward among the currents of his rivers.

He found Jerusalem upon the River of his City soft repos'd   c 40
In the arms of Vala, assimilating in one with Vala
The Lilly of Havilah: and they sang soft thro' Lambeths vales,
In a sweet moony night & silence that they had created
With a blue sky spread over with wings and a mild moon,
Dividing & uniting into many female forms: Jerusalem   45
Trembling! then in one comingling in eternal tears,
Sighing to melt his Giant beauty, on the moony river.

PLATE 20
But when they saw Albion fall'n upon mild Lambeths vale: c
Astonish'd! Terrified! they hover'd over his Giant limbs.
Then thus Jerusalem spoke, while Vala wove the veil of tears:
Weeping in pleadings of Love, in the web of despair.

Wherefore hast thou shut me into the winter of human life   5
And clos'd up the sweet regions of youth and virgin innocence:
Where we live, forgetting error, not pondering on evil:
Among my lambs & brooks of water, among my warbling birds:
Where we delight in innocence before the face of the Lamb:
Going in and out before him in his love and sweet affection.   10

Vala replied weeping & trembling, hiding in her veil.

When winter rends the hungry family and the snow falls:
Upon the ways of men hiding the paths of man and beast,
Then mourns the wanderer: then he repents his wanderings & eyes
The distant forest; then the slave groans in the dungeon of stone.   15
The captive in the mill of the stranger, sold for scanty hire.
They view their former life: they number moments over and over;

Stringing them on their remembrance as on a thread of sorrow.
Thou art my sister and my daughter! thy shame is mine also!
Ask me not of my griefs! thou knowest all my griefs.   20

Jerusalem answer'd with soft tears over the valleys.

O Vala what is Sin? that thou shudderest and weepest
At sight of thy once lov'd Jerusalem! What is Sin but a little
Error & fault that is soon forgiven; but mercy is not a Sin
Nor pity nor love nor kind forgiveness! O! if I have Sinned   25
Forgive & pity me! O! unfold thy Veil in mercy & love!
Slay not my little ones, beloved Virgin daughter of Babylon
Slay not my infant loves & graces, beautiful daughter of Moab
I cannot put off the human form I strive but strive in vain
When Albion rent thy beautiful net of gold and silver twine;   30
Thou hadst woven it with art, thou hadst caught me in the bands
Of love; thou refusedst to let me go: Albion beheld thy beauty
Beautiful thro' our Love's comeliness, beautiful thro' pity.
The Veil shone with thy brightness in the eyes of Albion,
Because it inclosd pity & love; because we lov'd one-another!   35
Albion lov'd thee! he rent thy Veil! he embrac'd thee! he lov'd thee!
Astonish'd at his beauty & perfection, thou forgavest his furious love:
I redounded from Albions bosom in my virgin loveliness.
The Lamb of God reciev'd me in his arms he smil'd upon us:
He made me his Bride & Wife: he gave thee to Albion.   40
Then was a time of love: O why is it passed away!

Then Albion broke silence and with groans reply'd

PLATE 21
O Vala! O Jerusalem! do you delight in my groans
You O lovely forms, you have prepared my death-cup:
The disease of Shame covers me from head to feet: I have no hope
Every boil upon my body is a separate & deadly Sin.
Doubt first assaild me, then Shame took possession of me   5
Shame divides Families. Shame hath divided Albion in sunder!
First fled my Sons, & then my Daughters, then my Wild Animations
My Cattle next, last ev'n the Dog of my Gate. the Forests fled
The Corn-fields, & the breathing Gardens outside separated
The Sea; the Stars: the Sun: the Moon: drivn forth by my disease   10
All is Eternal Death unless you can weave a chaste
Body over an unchaste Mind! Vala! O that thou wert pure!
That the deep wound of Sin might be clos'd up with the Needle,
And with the Loom: to cover Gwendolen & Ragan with costly Robes
Of Natural Virtue[,] for their Spiritual forms without a Veil   15
Wither in Luvahs Sepulcher. I thrust him from my presence
And all my Children followd his loud howlings into the Deep.
Jerusalem! dissembler Jerusalem! I look into thy bosom:
I discover thy secret places: Cordella! I behold

Thee whom I thought pure as the heavens in innocence & fear: 20
Thy Tabernacle taken down, thy secret Cherubim disclosed
Art thou broken? Ah me Sabrina, running by my side:
In childhood what wert thou? unutterable anguish! Conwenna
Thy cradled infancy is most piteous. O hide, O hide!
Their secret gardens were made paths to the traveller: 25
I knew not of their secret loves with those I hated most,
Nor that their every thought was Sin & secret appetite[.]
Hyle sees in fear, he howls in fury over them, Hand sees
In jealous fear: in stern accusation with cruel stripes
He drives them thro' the Streets of Babylon before my face: 30
Because they taught Luvah to rise into my clouded heavens
Battersea and Chelsea mourn for Cambel & Gwendolen!
Hackney and Holloway sicken for Estrild & Ignoge!
Because the Peak, Malvern & Cheviot Reason in Cruelty
Penmaenmawr & Dhinas-bran Demonstrate in Unbelief 35
Manchester & Liverpool are in tortures of Doubt & Despair
Malden & Colchester Demonstrate: I hear my Childrens voices t
I see their piteous faces gleam out upon the cruel winds
From Lincoln & Norwich, from Edinburgh & Monmouth:
I see them distant from my bosom scourgd along the roads 40
Then lost in clouds; I hear their tender voices! clouds divide
I see them die beneath the whips of the Captains! they are taken
In solemn pomp into Chaldea across the bredths of Europe
Six months they lie embalmd in silent death: worshipped
Carried in Arks of Oak before the armies in the spring 45
Bursting their Arks they rise again to life: they play before
The Armies: I hear their loud cymbals & their deadly cries
Are the Dead cruel? are those who are infolded in moral Law
Revengeful? O that Death & Annihilation were the same!

Then Vala answerd spreading her scarlet Veil over Albion 50

PLATE 22
Albion thy fear has made me tremble; thy terrors have surrounded me c
Thy Sons have naild me on the Gates piercing my hands & feet:
Till Skofields Nimrod the mighty Huntsman Jehovah came,
With Cush his Son & took me down. He in a golden Ark,
Bears me before his Armies tho my shadow hovers here 5
The flesh of multitudes fed & nourisd me in my childhood
My morn & evening food were prepard in Battles of Men
Great is the cry of the Hounds of Nimrod along the Valley
Of Vision, they scent the odor of War in the Valley of Vision.
All Love is lost! terror succeeds & Hatred instead of Love t 10
And stern demands of Right & Duty instead of Liberty
Once thou wast to me the loveliest Son of heaven; but now
Where shall I hide from thy dread countenance & searching eyes

I have looked into the secret Soul of him I loved
And in the dark recesses found Sin & can never return.   15

Albion again utterd his voice beneath the silent Moon

I brought Love into light of day to pride in chaste beauty
I brought Love into light & fancied Innocence is no more

Then spoke Jerusalem O Albion! my Father Albion
Why wilt thou number every little fibre of my Soul   20
Spreading them out before the Sun like stalks of flax to dry?
The Infant Joy is beautiful, but its anatomy
Horrible ghast & deadly! nought shalt thou find in it
But dark despair & everlasting brooding melancholy!

Then Albion turnd his face toward Jerusalem & spoke   25

Hide thou Jerusalem in impalpable voidness, not to be
Touchd by the hand nor seen with the eye: O Jerusalem
Would thou wert not & that thy place might never be found
But come O Vala with knife & cup: drain my blood
To the last drop! then hide me in thy Scarlet Tabernacle   30
For I see Luvah whom I slew. I behold him in my Spectre
As I behold Jerusalem in thee O Vala dark and cold

Jerusalem then stretchd her hand toward the Moon & spoke

Why should Punishment Weave the Veil with Iron Wheels of War
When Forgiveness might it Weave with Wings of Cherubim   35

Loud groand Albion from mountain to mountain & replied

PLATE 23
Jerusalem! Jerusalem! deluding shadow of Albion!
Daughter of my phantasy! unlawful pleasure! Albions curse!
I came here with intention to annihilate thee! But
My soul is melted away, inwoven within the Veil
Hast thou again knitted the Veil of Vala, which I for thee   5
Pitying rent in ancient times. I see it whole and more
Perfect, and shining with beauty! But thou! O wretched Father!   t

Jerusalem reply'd, like a voice heard from a sepulcher:
Father! once piteous! Is Pity a Sin? Embalm'd in Vala's bosom
In an Eternal Death for Albions sake, our best beloved.   10
Thou art my Father & my Brother: Why hast thou hidden me,
Remote from the divine Vision: my Lord and Saviour.

Trembling stood Albion at her words in jealous dark despair:
He felt that Love and Pity are the same; a soft repose!
Inward complacency of Soul: a Self-annihilation!   15

I have erred! I am ashamed! and will never return more:
I have taught my children sacrifices of cruelty: what shall I answer?
I will hide it from Eternals! I will give myself for my Children!
Which way soever I turn, I behold Humanity and Pity!

He recoil'd: he rush'd outwards; he bore the Veil whole away   20
His fires redound from his Dragon Altars in Errors returning.
He drew the Veil of Moral Virtue, woven for Cruel Laws,
And cast it into the Atlantic Deep, to catch the Souls of the Dead.
He stood between the Palm tree & the Oak of weeping   e
Which stand upon the edge of Beulah; and there Albion sunk   25
Down in sick pallid languor! These were his last words, relapsing!
Hoarse from his rocks, from caverns of Derbyshire & Wales
And Scotland, utter'd from the Circumference into Eternity.

Blasphemous Sons of Feminine delusion! God in the dreary Void
Dwells from Eternity, wide separated from the Human Soul   30
But thou deluding Image by whom imbu'd the Veil I rent
Lo here is Valas Veil whole, for a Law, a Terror & a Curse!
And therefore God takes vengeance on me: from my clay-cold bosom
My children wander trembling victims of his Moral Justice.
His snows fall on me and cover me, while in the Veil I fold   35
My dying limbs. Therefore O Manhood, if thou art aught
But a meer Phantasy, hear dying Albions Curse!
May God who dwells in this dark Ulro & voidness, vengeance take,
And draw thee down into this Abyss of sorrow and torture,
Like me thy Victim. O that Death & Annihilation were the same! 40

PLATE 24
What have I said? What have I done? O all-powerful Human Words!
You recoil back upon me in the blood of the Lamb slain in his Children.
Two bleeding Contraries equally true, are his Witnesses against me
We reared mighty Stones: we danced naked around them:
Thinking to bring Love into light of day, to Jerusalems shame: 5
Displaying our Giant limbs to all the winds of heaven! Sudden
Shame siezd us, we could not look on one-another for abhorrence: the
     Blue
Of our immortal Veins & all their Hosts fled from our Limbs,
And wanderd distant in a dismal Night clouded & dark:
The Sun fled from the Britons forehead: the Moon from his mighty 10
     loins:
Scandinavia fled with all his mountains filld with groans.

O what is Life & what is Man. O what is Death? Wherefore
Are you my Children, natives in the Grave to where I go
Or are you born to feed the hungry ravenings of Destruction
To be the sport of Accident! to waste in Wrath & Love, a weary 15
Life, in brooding cares & anxious labours, that prove but chaff.
O Jerusalem Jerusalem I have forsaken thy Courts

Thy Pillars of ivory & gold: thy Curtains of silk & fine
Linen: thy Pavements of precious stones: thy Walls of pearl
And gold, thy Gates of Thanksgiving thy Windows of Praise: 20
Thy Clouds of Blessing; thy Cherubims of Tender-mercy
Stretching their Wings sublime over the Little-ones of Albion[.]
O Human Imagination O Divine Body I have Crucified
I have turned my back upon thee into the Wastes of Moral Law:
There Babylon is builded in the Waste, founded in Human   25
    desolation.
O Babylon thy Watchman stands over thee in the night
Thy severe Judge all the day long proves thee O Babylon
With provings of destruction, with giving thee thy hearts desire.
But Albion is cast forth to the Potter his Children to the Builders
To build Babylon because they have forsaken Jerusalem   30
The Walls of Babylon are Souls of Men: her Gates the Groans
Of Nations: her Towers are the Miseries of once happy Families.
Her Streets are paved with Destruction, her Houses built with Death
Her Palaces with Hell & the Grave; her Synagogues with Torments
Of ever-hardening Despair squard & polishd with cruel skill   35
Yet thou wast lovely as the summer cloud upon my hills
When Jerusalem was thy hearts desire in times of youth & love.
Thy Sons came to Jerusalem with gifts, she sent them away
With blessings on their hands & on their feet, blessings of gold,
And pearl & diamond: thy Daughters sang in her Courts: 40
They came up to Jerusalem; they walked before Albion
In the Exchanges of London every Nation walkd
And London walkd in every Nation mutual in love & harmony
Albion coverd the whole Earth, England encompassd the Nations,
Mutual each within others bosom in Visions of Regeneration;   45
Jerusalem coverd the Atlantic Mountains & the Erythrean,
From bright Japan & China to Hesperia France & England.
Mount Zion lifted his head in every Nation under heaven:
And the Mount of Olives was beheld over the whole Earth:
The footsteps of the Lamb of God were there: but now no more   50
No more shall I behold him, he is closd in Luvahs Sepulcher.
Yet why these smitings of Luvah, the gentlest mildest Zoa?
If God was Merciful this could not be: O Lamb of God
Thou art a delusion and Jerusalem is my Sin! O my Children
I have educated you in the crucifying cruelties of Demonstration   55
Till you have assum'd the Providence of God & slain your Father
Dost thou appear before me who liest dead in Luvahs Sepulcher
Dost thou forgive me! thou who wast Dead & art Alive?   t
Look not so merciful upon me O thou Slain Lamb of God
I die! I die in thy arms tho Hope is banishd from me.   t60

Thundring the Veil rushes from his hand Vegetating Knot by   c
Knot, Day by Day, Night by Night; loud roll the indignant Atlantic
Waves & the Erythrean, turning up the bottoms of the Deeps
PLATE 25
And there was heard a great lamenting in Beulah: all the Regions
Of Beulah were moved as the tender bowels are moved: & they said:

Why did you take Vengeance O ye Sons of the mighty Albion?
Planting these Oaken Groves: Erecting these Dragon Temples
Injury the Lord heals but Vengeance cannot be healed: 5
As the Sons of Albion have done to Luvah: so they have in him
Done to the Divine Lord & Saviour, who suffers with those that suffer:
For not one sparrow can suffer, & the whole Universe not suffer also,
In all its Regions, & its Father & Saviour not pity and weep.
But Vengeance is the destroyer of Grace & Repentance in the bosom   10
Of the Injurer: in which the Divine Lamb is cruelly slain:
Descend O Lamb of God & take away the imputation of Sin
By the Creation of States & the deliverance of Individuals Evermore
    Amen

Thus wept they in Beulah over the Four Regions of Albion
But many doubted & despaird & imputed Sin & Righteousness   15
To Individuals & not to States, and these Slept in Ulro.

PLATE 26   t

SUCH VISIONS HAVE APPEARD TO ME
AS I MY ORDERD RACE HAVE RUN
JERUSALEM IS NAMED LIBERTY
AMONG THE SONS OF ALBION

PLATE 27   c

To the JEWS.

    Jerusalem the Emanation of the Giant Albion! Can it be? Is it a
Truth that the Learned have explored? Was Britain the Primitive Seat
of the Patriarchal Religion? If it is true: my title-page is also True, that
Jerusalem was & is the Emanation of the Giant Albion. It is True, and
cannot be controverted. Ye are united O ye Inhabitants of Earth in One
Religion. The Religion of Jesus: the most Ancient, the Eternal: & the
Everlasting Gospel—The Wicked will turn it to Wickedness, the Righ-
teous to Righteousness. Amen! Huzza! Selah!
    "All things Begin & End in Albions Ancient Druid Rocky Shore."

Your Ancestors derived their origin from Abraham, Heber, Shem,
and Noah, who were Druids: as the Druid Temples (which are the
Patriarchal Pillars & Oak Groves) over the whole Earth witness to this
day.

You have a tradition, that Man anciently contain'd in his mighty limbs all things in Heaven & Earth: this you recieved from the Druids. "But now the Starry Heavens are fled from the mighty limbs of Albion"

Albion was the Parent of the Druids; & in his Chaotic State of Sleep[,] Satan & Adam & the whole World was Created by the Elohim.

The fields from Islington to Marybone,   e
To Primrose Hill and Saint Johns Wood:
 Were builded over with pillars of gold,
And there Jerusalems pillars stood.

Her Little-ones ran on the fields   5
The Lamb of God among them seen
 And fair Jerusalem his Bride:
Among the little meadows green.

Pancrass & Kentish-town repose
Among her golden pillars high: 10
 Among her golden arches which
Shine upon the starry sky.

The Jews-harp-house & the Green Man;
The Ponds where Boys to bathe delight:
 The fields of Cows by Willans farm: ^t15
Shine in Jerusalems pleasant sight.

She walks upon our meadows green:
The Lamb of God walks by her side:
 And every English Child is seen,
Children of Jesus & his Bride,   20

Forgiving trespasses and sins
Lest Babylon with cruel Og,
 With Moral & Self-righteous Law
Should Crucify in Satans Synagogue!

What are those golden Builders doing   25
Near mournful ever-weeping Paddington
 Standing above that mighty Ruin
Where Satan the first victory won.

Where Albion slept beneath the Fatal Tree
And the Druids golden Knife,   30
 Rioted in human gore,
In Offerings of Human Life

They groan'd aloud on London Stone
They groan'd aloud on Tyburns Brook
 Albion gave his deadly groan,   35
And all the Atlantic Mountains shook

Albions Spectre from his Loins
Tore forth in all the pomp of War!
   Satan his name: in flames of fire
He stretch'd his Druid Pillars far.   40

Jerusalem fell from Lambeth's Vale,
Down thro Poplar & Old Bow;
   Thro Malden & acros the Sea,
In War & howling death & woe.

The Rhine was red with human blood: e 45
The Danube rolld a purple tide:
   On the Euphrates Satan stood:
And over Asia stretch'd his pride.

He witherd up sweet Zions Hill,
From every Nation of the Earth: 50
   He witherd up Jerusalems Gates,
And in a dark Land gave her birth.

He witherd up the Human Form,
By laws of sacrifice for sin:
   Till it became a Mortal Worm: 55
But O! translucent all within.

The Divine Vision still was seen
Still was the Human Form, Divine
   Weeping in weak & mortal clay
O Jesus still the Form was thine.   60

And thine the Human Face & thine
The Human Hands & Feet & Breath
   Entering thro' the Gates of Birth
And passing thro' the Gates of Death

And O thou Lamb of God, whom I   65
Slew in my dark self-righteous pride:
   Art thou return'd to Albions Land!
And is Jerusalem thy Bride?

Come to my arms & never more
Depart; but dwell for ever here: 70
   Create my Spirit to thy Love:
Subdue my Spectre to thy Fear.

Spectre of Albion! warlike Fiend!
In clouds of blood & ruin roll'd:
   I here reclaim thee as my own   75
My Selfhood! Satan! armd in gold.

Is this thy soft Family-Love
Thy cruel Patriarchal pride
   Planting thy Family alone,
Destroying all the World beside.   80

A mans worst enemies are those
Of his own house & family;
   And he who makes his law a curse,
By his own law shall surely die.

In my Exchanges every Land   85
Shall walk, & mine in every Land,
   Mutual shall build Jerusalem:
Both heart in heart & hand in hand.

If Humility is Christianity; you O Jews are the true Christians; If
your tradition that Man contained in his Limbs, all Animals, is True &
they were separated from him by cruel Sacrifices: and when compulsory
cruel Sacrifices had brought Humanity into a Feminine Tabernacle, in
the loins of Abraham & David: the Lamb of God, the Saviour became
apparent on Earth as the Prophets had foretold? The Return of Israel is
a Return to Mental Sacrifice & War. Take up the Cross O Israel & follow Jesus.

PLATE 28   t

Jerusalem.

Chap: 2.

Every ornament of perfection, and every labour of love,   c
In all the Garden of Eden, & in all the golden mountains
Was become an envied horror, and a remembrance of jealousy:
And every Act a Crime, and Albion the punisher & judge.

And Albion spoke from his secret seat and said   5

All these ornaments are crimes, they are made by the labours
Of loves: of unnatural consanguinities and friendships
Horrid to think of when enquired deeply into; and all
These hills & valleys are accursed witnesses of Sin
I therefore condense them into solid rocks, stedfast!   10
A foundation and certainty and demonstrative truth:
That Man be separate from Man, & here I plant my seat.

Cold snows drifted around him: ice coverd his loins around
He sat by Tyburns brook, and underneath his heel, shot up!
A deadly Tree, he nam'd it Moral Virtue, and the Law   15
Of God who dwells in Chaos hidden from the human sight.

The Tree spread over him its cold shadows, (Albion groand)
They bent down, they felt the earth and again enrooting
Shot into many a Tree! an endless labyrinth of woe!

From willing sacrifice of Self, to sacrifice of (miscall'd) Enemies   20
For Atonement: Albion began to erect twelve Altars,
Of rough unhewn rocks, before the Potters Furnace
He nam'd them Justice, and Truth. And Albions Sons
Must have become the first Victims, being the first transgressors
But they fled to the mountains to seek ransom: building A Strong   25
Fortification against the Divine Humanity and Mercy,
In Shame & Jealousy to annihilate Jerusalem!

PLATE 29 [33]   t
Turning his back to the Divine Vision, his Spectrous   c
Chaos before his face appeard: an Unformed Memory.

Then spoke the Spectrous Chaos to Albion darkning cold
From the back & loins where dwell the Spectrous Dead

I am your Rational Power O Albion & that Human Form   5
You call Divine, is but a Worm seventy inches long
That creeps forth in a night & is dried in the morning sun
In fortuitous concourse of memorys accumulated & lost
It plows the Earth in its own conceit, it overwhelms the Hills
Beneath its winding labyrinths, till a stone of the brook   10
Stops it in midst of its pride among its hills & rivers[.]
Battersea & Chelsea mourn, London & Canterbury tremble
Their place shall not be found as the wind passes over[.]
The ancient Cities of the Earth remove as a traveller
And shall Albions Cities remain when I pass over them   15
With my deluge of forgotten remembrances over the tablet

So spoke the Spectre to Albion. he is the Great Selfhood
Satan: Worshipd as God by the Mighty Ones of the Earth
Having a white Dot calld a Center from which branches out
A Circle in continual gyrations. this became a Heart   20
From which sprang numerous branches varying their motions
Producing many Heads three or seven or ten, & hands & feet
Innumerable at will of the unfortunate contemplator
Who becomes his food[:] such is the way of the Devouring Power

And this is the cause of the appearance in the frowning Chaos[.]   25
Albions Emanation which he had hidden in Jealousy   c
Appeard now in the frowning Chaos prolific upon the Chaos
Reflecting back to Albion in Sexual Reasoning Hermaphroditic

Albion spoke. Who art thou that appearest in gloomy pomp
Involving the Divine Vision in colours of autumn ripeness   30
I never saw thee till this time, nor beheld life abstracted

Nor darkness immingled with light on my furrowd field
Whence camest thou! who art thou O loveliest? the Divine Vision
Is as nothing before thee, faded is all life and joy

Vala replied in clouds of tears Albions garment embracing   ^c35

I was a City & a Temple built by Albions Children.
I was a Garden planted with beauty I allured on hill & valley
The River of Life to flow against my walls & among my trees
Vala was Albions Bride & Wife in great Eternity
The loveliest of the daughters of Eternity when in day-break   40
I emanated from Luvah over the Towers of Jerusalem
And in her Courts among her little Children offering up
The Sacrifice of fanatic love! why loved I Jerusalem!
Why was I one with her embracing in the Vision of Jesus
Wherefore did I loving create love, which never yet   45
Immingled God & Man, when thou & I, hid the Divine Vision
In cloud of secret gloom which behold involve me round about   t
Know me now Albion: look upon me I alone am Beauty
The Imaginative Human Form is but a breathing of Vala
I breathe him forth into the Heaven from my secret Cave   50
Born of the Woman to obey the Woman O Albion the mighty
For the Divine appearance is Brotherhood, but I am Love
PLATE 30 [34]
Elevate into the Region of Brotherhood with my red fires

Art thou Vala? replied Albion, image of my repose
O how I tremble! how my members pour down milky fear!
A dewy garment covers me all over, all manhood is gone!
At thy word & at thy look death enrobes me about   5
From head to feet, a garment of death & eternal fear
Is not that Sun thy husband & that Moon thy glimmering Veil?
Are not the Stars of heaven thy Children! art thou not Babylon?
Art thou Nature Mother of all! is Jerusalem thy Daughter
Why have thou elevate inward: O dweller of outward chambers   10
From grot & cave beneath the Moon dim region of death
Where I laid my Plow in the hot noon, where my hot team fed
Where implements of War are forged, the Plow to go over the Nations
In pain girding me round like a rib of iron in heaven! O Vala
In Eternity they neither marry nor are given in marriage   15
Albion the high Cliff of the Atlantic is become a barren Land

Los stood at his Anvil: he heard the contentions of Vala—   c
He heavd his thundring Bellows upon the valleys of Middlesex
He opend his Furnaces before Vala, then Albion frownd in anger
On his Rock: ere yet the Starry Heavens were fled away   20
From his awful Members, and thus Los cried aloud
To the Sons of Albion & to Hand the eldest Son of Albion

I hear the screech of Childbirth loud pealing, & the groans
Of Death, in Albions clouds dreadful utterd over all the Earth
What may Man be? who can tell! but what may Woman be? 25
To have power over Man from Cradle to corruptible Grave.
There is a Throne in every Man, it is the Throne of God
This Woman has claimd as her own & Man is no more!
Albion is the Tabernacle of Vala & her Temple
And not the Tabernacle & Temple of the Most High 30
O Albion why wilt thou Create a Female Will?
To hide the most evident God in a hidden covert, even
In the shadows of a Woman & a secluded Holy Place
That we may pry after him as after a stolen treasure
Hidden among the Dead & mured up from the paths of life 35
Hand! art thou not Reuben enrooting thyself into Bashan
Till thou remainest a vaporous Shadow in a Void! O Merlin!
Unknown among the Dead where never before Existence came
Is this the Female Will O ye lovely Daughters of Albion. To
Converse concerning Weight & Distance in the Wilds of Newton & 40
    Locke

So Los spoke standing on Mam-Tor looking over Europe & Asia
The Graves thunder beneath his feet from Ireland to Japan

Reuben slept in Bashan like one dead in the valley ᵉ
Cut off from Albions mountains & from all the Earths summits
Between Succoth & Zaretan beside the Stone of Bohan 45
While the Daughters of Albion divided Luvah into three Bodies
Los bended his Nostrils down to the Earth, then sent him over
Jordan to the Land of the Hittite: every-one that saw him
Fled! they fled at his horrible Form: they hid in caves
And dens, they looked on one-another & became what they beheld 50

Reuben return'd to Bashan, in despair he slept on the Stone.
Then Gwendolen divided into Rahab & Tirza in Twelve Portions[.]
Los rolled, his Eyes into two narrow circles, then sent him
Over Jordan; all terrified fled: they became what they beheld.

If Perceptive Organs vary: Objects of Perception seem to vary: 55
If the Perceptive Organs close: their Objects seem to close also:
Consider this O mortal Man! O worm of sixty winters said Los
Consider Sexual Organization & hide thee in the dust.

PLATE 31 [35]
Then the Divine hand found the Two Limits, Satan and Adam,
In Albions bosom: for in every Human bosom those Limits stand.
And the Divine voice came from the Furnaces, as multitudes without
Number! the voices of the innumerable multitudes of Eternity.
And the appearance of a Man was seen in the Furnaces; ᵉ5

Saving those who have sinned from the punishment of the Law,
(In pity of the punisher whose state is eternal death,)
And keeping them from Sin by the mild counsels of his love.

Albion goes to Eternal Death: In Me all Eternity.
Must pass thro' condemnation, and awake beyond the Grave!   10
No individual can keep these Laws, for they are death
To every energy of man, and forbid the springs of life;
Albion hath enterd the State Satan! Be permanent O State!
And be thou for ever accursed! that Albion may arise again:
And be thou created into a State! I go forth to Create   15
States: to deliver Individuals evermore! Amen.

So spoke the voice from the Furnaces, descending into Non-Entity
[*To Govern the Evil by Good: and States abolish Systems.*]   t

PLATE 32 [36]
Reuben return'd to his place, in vain he sought beautiful Tirzah
For his Eyelids were narrowd, & his Nostrils scented the ground
And Sixty Winters Los raged in the Divisions of Reuben:
Building the Moon of Ulro, plank by plank & rib by rib
Reuben slept in the Cave of Adam, and Los folded his Tongue   5
Between Lips of mire & clay, then sent him forth over Jordan
In the love of Tirzah he said Doubt is my food day & night—
All that beheld him fled howling and gnawed their tongues
For pain: they became what they beheld. In reasonings Reuben returned
To Heshbon. disconsolate he walkd thro Moab & he stood   10
Before the Furnaces of Los in a horrible dreamful slumber,
On Mount Gilead looking toward Gilgal: and Los bended
His Ear in a spiral circle outward; then sent him over Jordan.

The Seven Nations fled before him they became what they beheld
Hand, Hyle & Coban fled: they became what they beheld   15
Gwantock & Peachy hid in Damascus beneath Mount Lebanon
Brereton & Slade in Egypt. Hutton & Skofeld & Kox
Fled over Chaldea in terror in pains in every nerve
Kotope & Bowen became what they beheld, fleeing over the Earth
And the Twelve Female Emanations fled with them agonizing.   20

Jerusalem trembled seeing her Children drivn by Los's Hammer
In the visions of the dreams of Beulah on the edge of Non-Entity[.]
Hand stood between Reuben & Merlin, as the Reasoning Spectre
Stands between the Vegetative Man & his Immortal Imagination

And the Four Zoa's clouded rage East & West & North & South   c 25
They change their situations, in the Universal Man.
Albion groans, he sees the Elements divide before his face!
And England who is Brittannia divided into Jersualem & Vala
And Urizen assumes the East, Luvah assumes the South
In his dark Spectre ravening from his open Sepulcher   30

And the Four Zoa's who are the Four Eternal Senses of Man
Became Four Elements separating from the Limbs of Albion
These are their names in the Vegetative Generation
[*West Weighing East & North dividing Generation South* [ ]*ing*]   t
And Accident & Chance were found hidden in Length Bredth & Highth   35
And they divided into Four ravening deathlike Forms
Fairies & Genii & Nymphs & Gnomes of the Elements.
These are States Permanently Fixed by the Divine Power[.]
The Atlantic Continent sunk round Albions cliffy shore
And the Sea poured in amain upon the Giants of Albion   40
As Los bended the Senses of Reuben Reuben is Merlin
Exploring the Three States of Ulro; Creation; Redemption. & Judgment

And many of the Eternal Ones laughed after their manner   e

Have you known the Judgment that is arisen among the
Zoa's of Albion? where a Man dare hardly to embrace   45
His own Wife, for the terrors of Chastity that they call
By the name of Morality. their Daughters govern all
In hidden deceit! they are Vegetable only fit for burning:
Art & Science cannot exist but by Naked Beauty displayd

Then those in Great Eternity who contemplate on Death   50
Said thus. What seems to Be: Is: To those to whom
It seems to Be, & is productive of the most dreadful
Consequences to those to whom it seems to Be: even of
Torments, Despair, Eternal Death; but the Divine Mercy
Steps beyond and Redeems Man in the Body of Jesus Amen   55
And Length Bredth Highth again Obey the Divine Vision Hallelujah

PLATE 33 [37]
And One stood forth from the Divine family & said   t, e

I feel my Spectre rising upon me! Albion! arouze thyself!
Why dost thou thunder with frozen Spectrous wrath against us?
The Spectre is, in Giant Man; insane, and most deform'd.
Thou wilt certainly provoke my Spectre against thine in fury!   5
He has a Sepulcher hewn out of a Rock ready for thee:
And a Death of Eight thousand years, forg'd by thyself, upon   e
The point of his Spear! if thou persistest to forbid with Laws
Our Emanations, and to attack our secret supreme delights

So Los spoke: But when he saw blue death in Albions feet,   t 10
Again he join'd the Divine Body, following merciful;
While Albion fled more indignant! revengeful covering
PLATE 34 [38]
His face and bosom with petrific hardness, and his hands
And feet, lest any should enter his bosom & embrace
His hidden heart; his Emanation wept & trembled within him:
Uttering not his jealousy, but hiding it as with

Iron and steel, dark and opake, with clouds & tempests brooding: 5
His strong limbs shudderd upon his mountains high and dark.

Turning from Universal Love petrific as he went,
His cold against the warmth of Eden rag'd with loud
Thunders of deadly war (the fever of the human soul)
Fires and clouds of rolling smoke! but mild the Saviour follow'd him, 10
Displaying the Eternal Vision! the Divine Similitude!
In loves and tears of brothers, sisters, sons, fathers, and friends
Which if Man ceases to behold, he ceases to exist:

Saying. Albion! Our wars are wars of life, & wounds of love,
With intellectual spears, & long winged arrows of thought: 15
Mutual in one anothers love and wrath all renewing
We live as One Man; for contracting our infinite senses
We behold multitude; or expanding: we behold as one,
As One Man all the Universal Family; and that One Man
We call Jesus the Christ: and he in us, and we in him, 20
Live in perfect harmony in Eden the land of life,
Giving, recieving, and forgiving each others trespasses.
He is the Good shepherd, he is the Lord and master:
He is the Shepherd of Albion, he is all in all,
In Eden: in the garden of God: and in heavenly Jerusalem. 25
If we have offended, forgive us, take not vengeance against us.

Thus speaking; the Divine Family follow Albion:
I see them in the Vision of God upon my pleasant valleys.

I behold London; a Human awful wonder of God!
He says: Return, Albion, return! I give myself for thee: 30
My Streets are my, Ideas of Imagination.
Awake Albion, awake! and let us awake up together.
My Houses are Thoughts: my Inhabitants; Affections,
The children of my thoughts, walking within my blood-vessels,
Shut from my nervous form which sleeps upon the verge of Beulah 35
In dreams of darkness, while my vegetating blood in veiny pipes,
Rolls dreadful thro' the Furnaces of Los, and the Mills of Satan.
For Albions sake, and for Jerusalem thy Emanation
I give myself, and these my brethren give themselves for Albion.

So spoke London, immortal Guardian! I heard in Lambeths shades: 40
In Felpham I heard and saw the Visions of Albion
I write in South Molton Street, what I both see and hear
In regions of Humanity, in Londons opening streets.

I see thee awful Parent Land in light, behold I see!
Verulam! Canterbury! venerable parent of men, 45
Generous immortal Guardian golden clad! for Cities
Are Men, fathers of multitudes, and Rivers & Mountains
Are also Men; every thing is Human, mighty! sublime!

In every bosom a Universe expands, as wings
Let down at will around, and call'd the Universal Tent. 50
York, crown'd with loving kindness. Edinburgh, cloth'd
With fortitude as with a garment of immortal texture
Woven in looms of Eden, in spiritual deaths of mighty men
Who give themselves, in Golgotha, Victims to Justice; where
There is in Albion a Gate of Precious stones and gold 55
Seen only by Emanations, by vegetations viewless,
Bending across the road of Oxford Street; it from Hyde Park
To Tyburns deathful shades, admits the wandering souls
Of multitudes who die from Earth: this Gate cannot be found
PLATE 35 [39]
By Satans Watch-fiends tho' they search numbering every grain
Of sand on Earth every night, they never find this Gate.
It is the Gate of Los. Withoutside is the Mill, intricate, dreadful
And fill'd with cruel tortures; but no mortal man can find the Mill
Of Satan, in his mortal pilgrimage of seventy years 5

For Human beauty knows it not: nor can Mercy find it! But t
In the Fourth region of Humanity, Urthona namd[,]
Mortality begins to roll the billows of Eternal Death
Before the Gate of Los. Urthona here is named Los.
And here begins the System of Moral Virtue, named Rahab. t 10

Albion fled thro' the Gate of Los, and he stood in the Gate.

Los was the friend of Albion who most lov'd him. In Cambridgeshire
His eternal station, he is the twenty-eighth, & is four-fold.
Seeing Albion had turn'd his back against the Divine Vision,
Los said to Albion. Whither fleest thou? Albion reply'd. 15

I die! I go to Eternal Death! the shades of death
Hover within me & beneath, and spreading themselves outside
Like rocky clouds, build me a gloomy monument of woe:
Will none accompany me in my death? or be a Ransom for me
In that dark Valley? I have girded round my cloke, and on my feet 20
Bound these black shoes of death, & on my hands, deaths iron gloves:
God hath forsaken me, & my friends are become a burden e
A weariness to me, & the human footstep is a terror to me.

Los answerd, troubled: and his soul was rent in twain: e
Must the Wise die for an Atonement? does Mercy endure Atonement? 25
No! It is Moral Severity, & destroys Mercy in its Victim.
So speaking, not yet infected with the Error & Illusion,
PLATE 36 [40]
Los shudder'd at beholding Albion, for his disease
Arose upon him pale and ghastly: and he call'd around
The Friends of Albion: trembling at the sight of Eternal Death
The four appear'd with their Emanations in fiery

Chariots: black their fires roll beholding Albions House of Eternity   *5*
Damp couch the flames beneath and silent, sick, stand shuddering
Before the Porch of sixteen pillars: weeping every one
Descended and fell down upon their knees round Albions knees,
Swearing the Oath of God! with awful voice of thunders round
Upon the hills & valleys, and the cloudy Oath roll'd far and wide   *10*

Albion is sick! said every Valley, every mournful Hill
And every River: our brother Albion is sick to death.
He hath leagued himself with robbers! he hath studied the arts
Of unbelief! Envy hovers over him! his Friends are his abhorrence!
Those who give their lives for him are despised!   *15*
Those who devour his soul, are taken into his bosom!
To destroy his Emanation is their intention:
Arise! awake O Friends of the Giant Albion
They have perswaded him of horrible falshoods!
They have sown errors over all his fruitful fields!   *20*

The Twenty-four heard! they came trembling on watry chariots.
Borne by the Living Creatures of the third procession
Of Human Majesty, the Living Creatures wept aloud as they
Went along Albions roads, till they arriv'd at Albions House.

O! how the torments of Eternal Death, waited on Man: *25*
And the loud-rending bars of the Creation ready to burst:
That the wide world might fly from its hinges, & the immortal mansion
Of Man, for ever be possessd by monsters of the deeps:
And Man himself become a Fiend, wrap'd in an endless curse,
Consuming and consum'd for-ever in flames of Moral Justice.   *30*

For had the Body of Albion fall'n down, and from its dreadful ruins
Let loose the enormous Spectre on the darkness of the deep,
At enmity with the Merciful & fill'd with devouring fire,
A nether-world must have recievd the foul enormous spirit,
Under pretence of Moral Virtue, fill'd with Revenge and Law.   *35*
There to eternity chain'd down, and issuing in red flames
And curses, with his mighty arms brandish'd against the heavens
Breathing cruelty blood & vengeance, gnashing his teeth with pain
Torn with black storms, & ceaseless torrents of his own consuming fire:
Within his breast his mighty Sons chaind down & fill'd with cursings: *40*
And his dark Eon, that once fair crystal form divinely clear:
Within his ribs producing serpents whose souls are flames of fire.
But, glory to the Merciful-One, for he is of tender mercies!
And the Divine Family wept over him as One Man.

And these the Twenty-four in whom the Divine Family   *ᵉ45*
Appeard; and they were One in Him. A Human Vision!
Human Divine, Jesus the Saviour, blessed for ever and ever.

Selsey, true friend! who afterwards submitted to be devourd
By the waves of Despair, whose Emanation rose above

The flood, and was nam'd Chichester, lovely mild & gentle! Lo!   50
Her lambs bleat to the sea-fowls cry, lamenting still for Albion.
Submitting to be call'd the son of Los the terrible vision:
Winchester stood devoting himself for Albion: his tents
Outspread with abundant riches, and his Emanations
Submitting to be call'd Enitharmons daughters, and be born   55
In vegetable mould: created by the Hammer and Loom
In Bowlahoola & Allamanda where the Dead wail night & day.

(I call them by their English names: English, the rough basement.
Los built the stubborn structure of the Language, acting against
Albions melancholy, who must else have been a Dumb despair.)   60

Gloucester and Exeter and Salisbury and Bristol: and benevolent Bath
PLATE 37 [41]
Bath who is Legions: he is the Seventh, the physician and   e
The poisoner: the best and worst in Heaven and Hell:
Whose Spectre first assimilated with Luvah in Albions mountains
A triple octave he took, to reduce Jerusalem to twelve
To cast Jerusalem forth upon the wilds to Poplar & Bow: 5
To Malden & Canterbury in the delights of cruelty:
The Shuttles of death sing in the sky to Islington & Pancrass
Round Marybone to Tyburns River, weaving black melancholy as a net,
And despair as meshes closely wove over the west of London,
Where mild Jerusalem sought to repose in death & be no more.   10
She fled to Lambeths mild Vale and hid herself beneath
The Surrey Hills where Rephaim terminates: her Sons are siez'd
For victims of sacrifice; but Jerusalem cannot be found! Hid
By the Daughters of Beulah: gently snatch'd away: and hid in Beulah

There is a Grain of Sand in Lambeth that Satan cannot find   15
Nor can his Watch Fiends find it: tis translucent & has many Angles
But he who finds it will find Oothoons palace, for within
Opening into Beulah every angle is a lovely heaven
But should the Watch Fiends find it, they would call it Sin
And lay its Heavens & their inhabitants in blood of punishment   20
Here Jerusalem & Vala were hid in soft slumberous repose
Hid from the terrible East, shut up in the South & West.

The Twenty-eight trembled in Deaths dark caves, in cold despair   e
They kneeld around the Couch of Death in deep humiliation
And tortures of self condemnation while their Spectres ragd within.   25
The Four Zoa's in terrible combustion clouded rage
Drinking the shuddering fears & loves of Albions Families
Destroying by selfish affections the things that they most admire
Drinking & eating, & pitying & weeping, as at a trajic scene.
The soul drinks murder & revenge, & applauds its own holiness   30

They saw Albion endeavouring to destroy their Emanations.   t

PLATE 38 [43]

They saw their Wheels rising up poisonous against Albion
Urizen, cold & scientific: Luvah, pitying & weeping
Tharmas, indolent & sullen: Urthona, doubting & despairing
Victims to one another & dreadfully plotting against each other
To prevent Albion walking about in the Four Complexions.   5

They saw America clos'd out by the Oaks of the western shore;   e
And Tharmas dash'd on the Rocks of the Altars of Victims in Mexico.
If we are wrathful Albion will destroy Jerusalem with rooty Groves
If we are merciful, ourselves must suffer destruction on his Oaks!
Why should we enter into our Spectres, to behold our own   10
    corruptions
O God of Albion descend! deliver Jerusalem from the Oaken Groves!

Then Los grew furious raging: Why stand we here trembling around   e
Calling on God for help; and not ourselves in whom God dwells
Stretching a hand to save the falling Man: are we not Four
Beholding Albion upon the Precipice ready to fall into Non-Entity: 15
Seeing these Heavens & Hells conglobing in the Void. Heavens over
    Hells
Brooding in holy hypocritic lust, drinking the cries of pain

From howling victims of Law: building Heavens Twenty-seven-fold.
Swelld & bloated General Forms, repugnant to the Divine-
Humanity, who is the Only General and Universal Form   20
To which all Lineaments tend & seek with love & sympathy
All broad & general principles belong to benevolence
Who protects minute particulars, every one in their own identity.
But here the affectionate touch of the tongue is closd in by deadly teeth
And the soft smile of friendship & the open dawn of benevolence   25
Become a net & a trap, & every energy renderd cruel,
Till the existence of friendship & benevolence is denied:
The wine of the Spirit & the vineyards of the Holy-One.
Here: turn into poisonous stupor & deadly intoxication:
That they may be condemnd by Law & the Lamb of God be slain!   30
And the two Sources of Life in Eternity[,] Hunting and War,
Are become the Sources of dark & bitter Death & of corroding Hell:
The open heart is shut up in integuments of frozen silence
That the spear that lights it forth may shatter the ribs & bosom
A pretence of Art, to destroy Art: a pretence of Liberty   35
To destroy Liberty. a pretence of Religion to destroy Religion
Oshea and Caleb fight: they contend in the valleys of Peor
In the terrible Family Contentions of those who love each other:
The Armies of Balaam weep—no women come to the field
Dead corses lay before them, & not as in Wars of old.   40
For the Soldier who fights for Truth, calls his enemy his brother:
They fight & contend for life, & not for eternal death!
But here the Soldier strikes, & a dead corse falls at his feet
Nor Daughter nor Sister nor Mother come forth to embosom the Slain!
But Death! Eternal Death! remains in the Valleys of Peor.   45
The English are scatterd over the face of the Nations: are these
Jerusalems children? Hark! hear the Giants of Albion cry at night
We smell the blood of the English! we delight in their blood on our
        Altars!
The living & the dead shall be ground in our rumbling Mills
For bread of the Sons of Albion: of the Giants Hand & Scofield   50
Scofeld & Kox are let loose upon my Saxons! they accumulate
A World in which Man is by his Nature the Enemy of Man,
In pride of Selfhood unwieldy stretching out into Non Entity
Generalizing Art & Science till Art & Science is lost.
Bristol & Bath, listen to my words, & ye Seventeen: give ear!   55
It is easy to acknowledge a man to be great & good while we
Derogate from him in the trifles & small articles of that goodness:
Those alone are his friends, who admire his minutest powers[.]
Instead of Albions lovely mountains & the curtains of Jerusalem
I see a Cave, a Rock, a Tree deadly and poisonous, unimaginative: 60
Instead of the Mutual Forgivenesses, the Minute Particulars, I see
Pits of bitumen ever burning: artificial Riches of the Canaanite
Like Lakes of liquid lead: instead of heavenly Chapels, built

By our dear Lord: I see Worlds crusted with snows & ice;
I see a Wicker Idol woven round Jerusalems children. I see   65
The Canaanite, the Amalekite, the Moabite, the Egyptian:
By Demonstrations the cruel Sons of Quality & Negation.
Driven on the Void in incoherent despair into Non Entity
I see America closd apart, & Jerusalem driven in terror
Away from Albions mountains, far away from Londons spires!   70
I will not endure this thing! I alone withstand to death,
This outrage! Ah me! how sick & pale you all stand round me!
Ah me! pitiable ones! do you also go to deaths vale?
All you my Friends & Brothers! all you my beloved Companions!
Have you also caught the infection of Sin & stern Repentance?   75
I see Disease arise upon you! yet speak to me and give
Me some comfort: why do you all stand silent? I alone
Remain in permanent strength. Or is all this goodness & pity, only
That you may take the greater vengeance in your Sepulcher.

So Los spoke. Pale they stood around the House of Death: ᶜ 80
In the midst of temptations & despair: among the rooted Oaks:
Among reared Rocks of Albions Sons, at length they rose
PLATE 39 [44]
With one accord in love sublime, & as on Cherubs wings
They Albion surround with kindest violence to bear him back
Against his will thro Los's Gate to Eden: Four-fold; loud!
Their Wings waving over the bottomless Immense: to bear
Their awful charge back to his native home: but Albion dark,   5
Repugnant; rolld his Wheels backward into Non-Entity
Loud roll the Starry Wheels of Albion into the World of Death
And all the Gate of Los, clouded with clouds redounding from
Albions dread Wheels, stretching out spaces immense between
That every little particle of light & air, became Opake   10
Black & immense, a Rock of difficulty & a Cliff
Of black despair; that the immortal Wings labourd against
Cliff after cliff, & over Valleys of despair & death:
The narrow Sea between Albion & the Atlantic Continent:
Its waves of pearl became a boundless Ocean bottomless,   15
Of grey obscurity, filld with clouds & rocks & whirling waters
And Albions Sons ascending & descending in the horrid Void.

But as the Will must not be bended but in the day of Divine
Power: silent calm & motionless, in the mid-air sublime,
The Family Divine hover around the darkend Albion.   20

Such is the nature of the Ulro: that whatever enters: ᶜ
Becomes Sexual, & is Created, and Vegetated, and Born.
From Hyde Park spread their vegetating roots beneath Albion
In dreadful pain the Spectrous Uncircumcised Vegetation.—

Forming a Sexual Machine: an Aged Virgin Form.   25
In Erins Land toward the north, joint after joint & burning
In love & jealousy immingled & calling it Religion
And feeling the damps of death they with one accord delegated Los
Conjuring him by the Highest that he should Watch over them
Till Jesus shall appear: & they gave their power to Los   30
Naming him the Spirit of Prophecy, calling him Elijah

Strucken with Albions disease they become what they behold;
They assimilate with Albion in pity & compassion;
Their Emanations return not: their Spectres rage in the Deep
The Slumbers of Death came over them around the Couch of Death   35
Before the Gate of Los & in the depths of Non Entity
Among the Furnaces of Los: among the Oaks of Albion.

Man is adjoind to Man by his Emanative portion:
Who is Jerusalem in every individual Man: and her
Shadow is Vala, builded by the Reasoning power in Man   40
O search & see: turn your eyes inward: open O thou World
Of Love & Harmony in Man: expand thy ever lovely Gates.

They wept into the deeps a little space at length was heard
The voice of Bath, faint as the voice of the Dead in the House of Death
PLATE 40 [45]
Bath, healing City! whose wisdom in midst of Poetic   c
Fervor: mild spoke thro' the Western Porch, in soft gentle tears

O Albion mildest Son of Eden! clos'd is thy Western Gate
Brothers of Eternity! this Man whose great example
We all admir'd & lov'd, whose all benevolent countenance, seen   5
In Eden, in lovely Jerusalem, drew even from envy
The tear: and the confession of honesty, open & undisguis'd
From mistrust and suspition. The Man is himself become
A piteous example of oblivion. To teach the Sons
Of Eden, that however great and glorious; however loving   10
And merciful the Individuality; however high
Our palaces and cities, and however fruitful are our fields
In Selfhood, we are nothing: but fade away in mornings breath.
Our mildness is nothing: the greatest mildness we can use
Is incapable and nothing! none but the Lamb of God can heal   15
This dread disease: none but Jesus! O Lord descend and save!
Albions Western Gate is clos'd: his death is coming apace!
Jesus alone can save him; for alas we none can know
How soon his lot may be our own. When Africa in sleep
Rose in the night of Beulah, and bound down the Sun & Moon   20
His friends cut his strong chains, & overwhelm'd his dark
Machines in fury & destruction, and the Man reviving repented
He wept before his wrathful brethren, thankful & considerate

-185-

For their well timed wrath. But Albions sleep is not
Like Africa's: and his machines are woven with his life   25
Nothing but mercy can save him! nothing but mercy interposing
Lest he should slay Jerusalem in his fearful jealousy
O God descend! gather our brethren, deliver Jerusalem[.]
But that we may omit no office of the friendly spirit
Oxford take thou these leaves of the Tree of Life: with eloquence   30
That thy immortal tongue inspires; present them to Albion:
Perhaps he may recieve them, offerd from thy loved hands.

So spoke, unhear'd by Albion. the merciful Son of Heaven
To those whose Western Gates were open, as they stood weeping
Around Albion: but Albion heard him not; obdurate! hard!   35
He frown'd on all his Friends, counting them enemies in his sorrow

And the Seventeen conjoining with Bath, the Seventh:
In whom the other Ten shone manifest, a Divine Vision!
Assimilated and embrac'd Eternal Death for Albions sake.

And these the names of the Eighteen combining with those Ten   t 40

PLATE 41 [46]
Bath, mild Physician of Eternity, mysterious power
Whose springs are unsearchable & knowledge infinite.
Hereford, ancient Guardian of Wales, whose hands
Builded the mountain palaces of Eden, stupendous works!
Lincoln, Durham & Carlisle, Councellors of Los.   5
And Ely, Scribe of Los, whose pen no other hand
Dare touch! Oxford, immortal Bard! with eloquence
Divine, he wept over Albion: speaking the words of God
In mild perswasion: bringing leaves of the Tree of Life.

Thou art in Error Albion, the Land of Ulro: e 10
One Error not remov'd, will destroy a human Soul
Repose in Beulahs night, till the Error is remov'd
Reason not on both sides. Repose upon our bosoms
Till the Plow of Jehovah, and the Harrow of Shaddai
Have passed over the Dead, to awake the Dead to Judgment.   15
But Albion turn'd away refusing comfort.

Oxford trembled while he spoke, then fainted in the arms
Of Norwich, Peterboro, Rochester, Chester awful, Worcester,
Litchfield, Saint Davids, Landaff, Asaph, Bangor, Sodor,
Bowing their heads devoted: and the Furnaces of Los   20
Began to rage, thundering loud the storms began to roar
Upon the Furnaces, and loud the Furnaces rebellow beneath

And these the Four in whom the twenty-four appear'd four-fold:
Verulam, London, York, Edinburgh, mourning one towards another
Alas!—The time will come, when a mans worst enemies   25

Shall be those of his own house and family: in a Religion
Of Generation, to destroy by Sin and Atonement, happy Jerusalem,
The Bride and Wife of the Lamb. O God thou art Not an Avenger!

PLATE 42

Thus Albion sat, studious of others in his pale disease: c
Brooding on evil: but when Los opend the Furnaces before him:
He saw that the accursed things were his own affections,
And his own beloveds: then he turn'd sick! his soul died within him
Also Los sick & terrified beheld the Furnaces of Death   5
And must have died, but the Divine Saviour descended
Among the infant loves & affections, and the Divine Vision wept
Like evening dew on every herb upon the breathing ground

Albion spoke in his dismal dreams: O thou deceitful friend
Worshipping mercy & beholding thy friend in such affliction: 10
Los! thou now discoverest thy turpitude to the heavens.
I demand righteousness & justice. O thou ingratitude!
Give me my Emanations back[,] food for my dying soul!
My daughters are harlots! my sons are accursed before me.
Enitharmon is my daughter: accursed with a fathers curse!   15
O! I have utterly been wasted! I have given my daughters to devils

So spoke Albion in gloomy majesty, and deepest night
Of Ulro rolld round his skirts from Dover to Cornwall.

Los answerd. Righteousness & justice I give thee in return
For thy righteousness! but I add mercy also, and bind   20
Thee from destroying these little ones: am I to be only
Merciful to thee and cruel to all that thou hatest[?]
Thou wast the Image of God surrounded by the Four Zoa's
Three thou hast slain! I am the Fourth: thou canst not destroy me.
Thou art in Error; trouble me not with thy righteousness.   25
I have innocence to defend and ignorance to instruct:
I have no time for seeming; and little arts of compliment,
In morality and virtue: in self-glorying and pride.
There is a limit of Opakeness, and a limit of Contraction;
In every Individual Man, and the limit of Opakeness,   30
Is named Satan: and the limit of Contraction is named Adam.
But when Man sleeps in Beulah, the Saviour in mercy takes
Contractions Limit, and of the Limit he forms Woman: That
Himself may in process of time be born Man to redeem
But there is no Limit of Expansion! there is no Limit of Translucence. 35
In the bosom of Man for ever from eternity to eternity.
Therefore I break thy bonds of righteousness; I crush thy messengers!
That they may not crush me and mine: do thou be righteous,
And I will return it; otherwise I defy thy worst revenge:

– 187 –

Consider me as thine enemy: on me turn all thy fury   40
But destroy not these little ones, nor mock the Lords anointed:
Destroy not by Moral Virtue, the little ones whom he hath chosen!
The little ones whom he hath chosen in preference to thee.
He hath cast thee off for ever; the little ones he hath anointed!
Thy Selfhood is for ever accursed from the Divine presence   45

So Los spoke: then turn'd his face & wept for Albion.

Albion replied. Go! Hand & Hyle! sieze the abhorred [fiend]:   t
As you Have siezd the Twenty-four rebellious ingratitudes;
To atone for you, for spiritual death! Man lives by deaths of Men
Bring him to justice before heaven here upon London stone,   50
Between Blackheath & Hounslow, between Norwood & Finchley
All that they have is mine: from my free genrous gift,
They now hold all they have: ingratitude to me!
To me their benefactor calls aloud for vengeance deep.

Los stood before his Furnaces awaiting the fury of the Dead: 55
And the Divine hand was upon him, strengthening him mightily.

The Spectres of the Dead cry out from the deeps beneath
Upon the hills of Albion; Oxford groans in his iron furnace
Winchester in his den & cavern; they lament against
Albion: they curse their human kindness & affection   60
They rage like wild beasts in the forests of affliction
In the dreams of Ulro they repent of their human kindness.

Come up, build Babylon, Rahab is ours & all her multitudes
With her in pomp and glory of victory. Depart
Ye twenty-four into the deeps! let us depart to glory!   65

Their Human majestic forms sit up upon their Couches
Of death: they curb their Spectres as with iron curbs
They enquire after Jerusalem in the regions of the dead,
With the voices of dead men, low, scarcely articulate,
And with tears cold on their cheeks they weary repose.   70

O when shall the morning of the grave appear, and when
Shall our salvation come? we sleep upon our watch
We cannot awake! and our Spectres rage in the forests
O God of Albion where art thou! pity the watchers!

Thus mourn they. Loud the Furnaces of Los thunder upon   75
The clouds of Europe & Asia, among the Serpent Temples!

And Los drew his Seven Furnaces around Albions Altars
And as Albion built his frozen Altars, Los built the Mundane Shell,
In the Four Regions of Humanity East & West & North & South,

Till Norwood & Finchley & Blackheath & Hounslow, coverd the whole   80
    Earth.
This is the Net & Veil of Vala, among the Souls of the Dead.

PLATE 43 [29]
Then the Divine Vision like a silent Sun appeard above   c
Albions dark rocks: setting behind the Gardens of Kensington
On Tyburns River, in clouds of blood: where was mild Zion Hills
Most ancient promontory, and in the Sun, a Human Form appeard
And thus the Voice Divine went forth upon the rocks of Albion   5

I elected Albion for my glory; I gave to him the Nations,
Of the whole Earth. He was the Angel of my Presence: and all
The Sons of God were Albions Sons: and Jerusalem was my joy.
The Reactor hath hid himself thro envy. I behold him.
But you cannot behold him till he be reveald in his System   10
Albions Reactor must have a Place prepard: Albion must Sleep
The Sleep of Death, till the Man of Sin & Repentance be reveald.
Hidden in Albions Forests he lurks: he admits of no Reply
From Albion: but hath founded his Reaction into a Law
Of Action, for Obedience to destroy the Contraries of Man[.]   15
He hath compelld Albion to become a Punisher & hath possessd
Himself of Albions Forests & Wilds! and Jerusalem is taken!
The City of the Woods in the Forest of Ephratah is taken!
London is a stone of her ruins; Oxford is the dust of her walls!
Sussex & Kent are her scatterd garments: Ireland her holy place: 20
And the murderd bodies of her little ones are Scotland and Wales[.]
The Cities of the Nations are the smoke of her consummation
The Nations are her dust! ground by the chariot wheels
Of her lordly conquerors, her palaces levelld with the dust.
I come that I may find a way for my banished ones to return   25
Fear not O little Flock I come! Albion shall rise again.

So saying, the mild Sun inclosd the Human Family.

Forthwith from Albions darkning [r]ocks came two Immortal forms   t
Saying We alone are escaped. O merciful Lord and Saviour,
We flee from the interiors of Albions hills and mountains!   30
From his Valleys Eastward: from Amalek Canaan & Moab:
Beneath his vast ranges of hills surrounding Jerusalem.

Albion walkd on the steps of fire before his Halls
And Vala walkd with him in dreams of soft deluding slumber.
He looked up & saw the Prince of Light with splendor faded   35
Then Albion ascended mourning into the porches of his Palace
Above him rose a Shadow from his wearied intellect:
Of living gold, pure, perfect, holy: in white linen pure he hoverd
A sweet entrancing self-delusion a watry vision of Albion
Soft exulting in existence; all the Man absorbing!   40

Albion fell upon his face prostrate before the watry Shadow
Saying O Lord whence is this change! thou knowest I am nothing!
And Vala trembled & coverd her face! & her locks were spread on the
    pavement

We heard astonishd at the Vision & our hearts trembled within us:
We heard the voice of slumberous Albion, and thus he spake.   45
Idolatrous to his own Shadow words of eternity uttering:

O I am nothing when I enter into judgment with thee!
If thou withdraw thy breath I die & vanish into Hades
If thou dost lay thine hand upon me behold I am silent:
If thou withhold thine hand; I perish like a fallen leaf: 50
O I am nothing: and to nothing must return again:
If thou withdraw thy breath. Behold I am oblivion.

He ceasd: the shadowy voice was silent: but the cloud hoverd over their
    heads
In golden wreathes, the sorrow of Man; & the balmy drops fell down.
And lo! that son of Man that Shadowy Spirit of mild Albion: 55
Luvah descended from the cloud; in terror Albion rose:
Indignant rose the awful Man, & turnd his back on Vala.

We heard the voice of Albion starting from his sleep:

Whence is this voice crying Enion! that soundeth in my ears?
O cruel pity! O dark deceit! can love seek for dominion?   60

And Luvah strove to gain dominion over Albion
They strove together above the Body where Vala was inclosd
And the dark Body of Albion left prostrate upon the crystal pavement,
Coverd with boils from head to foot: the terrible smitings of Luvah.

Then frownd the fallen Man and put forth Luvah from his presence   65
Saying. Go and Die the Death of Man, for Vala the sweet wanderer.
I will turn the volutions of your ears outward, and bend your nostrils
Downward, and your fluxile eyes englob'd roll round in fear:
Your withring lips and tongue shrink up into a narrow circle,
Till into narrow forms you creep: go take your fiery way: 70
And learn what tis to absorb the Man you Spirits of Pity & Love.

They heard the voice and fled swift as the winters setting sun.
And now the human blood foamd high, the Spirits Luvah & Vala
Went down the Human Heart where Paradise & its joys abounded,
In jealous fears & fury & rage, & flames roll round their fervid feet: 75
And the vast form of Nature like a serpent playd before them
And as they fled in folding fires & thunders of the deep:
Vala shrunk in like the dark sea that leaves its slimy banks.
And from her bosom Luvah fell far as the east and west.

And the vast form of Nature like a serpent rolld between,   80
Whether of Jerusalems or Valas ruins congenerated, we know not:
All is confusion: all is tumult, & we alone are escaped.

So spoke the fugitives; they joind the Divine Family, trembling   t
PLATE 44 [30]
And the Two that escaped; were the Emanation of Los & his   e
Spectre: for whereever the Emanation goes, the Spectre
Attends her as her Guard, & Los's Emanation is named
Enitharmon, & his Spectre is named Urthona: they knew
Not where to flee: they had been on a visit to Albions Children   5
And they strove to weave a Shadow of the Emanation
To hide themselves: weeping & lamenting for the Vegetation
Of Albions Children: fleeing thro Albions vales in streams of gore.

Being not irritated by insult bearing insulting benevolences
They percieved that corporeal friends are spiritual enemies   10
They saw the Sexual Religion in its embryon Uncircumcision
And the Divine hand was upon them bearing them thro darkness
Back safe to their Humanity as doves to their windows:
Therefore the Sons of Eden praise Urthonas Spectre in Songs
Because he kept the Divine Vision in time of trouble.   15

They wept & trembled: & Los put forth his hand & took them in
Into his Bosom: from which Albion shrunk in dismal pain;
Rending the fibres of Brotherhood & in Feminine Allegories
Inclosing Los: but the Divine Vision appeard with Los
Following Albion into his Central Void among his Oaks.   20

And Los prayed and said. O Divine Saviour arise
Upon the Mountains of Albion as in ancient time. Behold!
The Cities of Albion seek thy face, London groans in pain
From Hill to Hill & the Thames laments along the Valleys
The little Villages of Middlesex & Surrey hunger & thirst   25
The Twenty-eight Cities of Albion stretch their hands to thee:
Because of the Opressors of Albion in every City & Village:
They mock at the Labourers limbs! they mock at his starvd Children!
They buy his Daughters that they may have power to sell his Sons:
They compell the Poor to live upon a crust of bread by soft mild arts: 30
They reduce the Man to want: then give with pomp & ceremony.
The praise of Jehovah is chaunted from lips of hunger & thirst!

Humanity knows not of Sex: wherefore are Sexes in Beulah?
In Beulah the Female lets down her beautiful Tabernacle;
Which the Male enters magnificent between her Cherubim: 35
And becomes One with her mingling condensing in Self-love
The Rocky Law of Condemnation & double Generation, & Death.
Albion hath enterd the Loins the place of the Last Judgment:

-191-

And Luvah hath drawn the Curtains around Albion in Vala's bosom
The Dead awake to Generation! Arise O Lord, & rend the Veil!   40

So Los in lamentations followd Albion. Albion coverd,
PLATE 45 [31]
His western heaven with rocky clouds of death & despair.

Fearing that Albion should turn his back against the Divine Vision   c
Los took his globe of fire to search the interiors of Albions
Bosom, in all the terrors of friendship, entering the caves
Of despair & death, to search the tempters out, walking among   5
Albions rocks & precipices! caves of solitude & dark despair,
And saw every Minute Particular of Albion degraded & murderd
But saw not by whom; they were hidden within in the minute
    particulars
Of which they had possessd themselves; and there they take up
The articulations of a mans soul, and laughing throw it down   10
Into the frame, then knock it out upon the plank, & souls are bak'd
In bricks to build the pyramids of Heber & Terah. But Los
Searchd in vain: closd from the minutia he walkd, difficult.
He came down from Highgate thro Hackney & Holloway towards
    London
Till he came to old Stratford & thence to Stepney & the Isle   15
Of Leuthas Dogs, thence thro the narrows of the Rivers side
And saw every minute particular, the jewels of Albion, running down
The kennels of the streets & lanes as if they were abhorrd.
Every Universal Form, was become barren mountains of Moral
Virtue: and every Minute Particular hardend into grains of sand: 20
And all the tendernesses of the soul cast forth as filth & mire,
Among the winding places of deep contemplation intricate
To where the Tower of London frownd dreadful over Jerusalem:
A building of Luvah builded in Jerusalems eastern gate to be
His secluded Court: thence to Bethlehem where was builded   25
Dens of despair in the house of bread: enquiring in vain
Of stones and rocks he took his way, for human form was none:
And thus he spoke, looking on Albions City with many tears

What shall I do! what could I do, if I could find these Criminals
I could not dare to take vengeance; for all things are so constructed   30
And builded by the Divine hand, that the sinner shall always escape,
And he who takes vengeance alone is the criminal of Providence;
If I should dare to lay my finger on a grain of sand
In way of vengeance; I punish the already punishd: O whom
Should I pity if I pity not the sinner who is gone astray!   35
O Albion, if thou takest vengeance; if thou revengest thy wrongs
Thou art for ever lost! What can I do to hinder the Sons
Of Albion from taking vengeance? or how shall I them perswade.

So spoke Los, travelling thro darkness & horrid solitude: c
And he beheld Jerusalem in Westminster & Marybone,   40
Among the ruins of the Temple: and Vala who is her Shadow,
Jerusalems Shadow bent northward over the Island white.
At length he sat on London Stone, & heard Jerusalems voice.

Albion I cannot be thy Wife. thine own Minute Particulars,
Belong to God alone. and all thy little ones are holy   45
They are of Faith & not of Demonstration: wherefore is Vala
Clothd in black mourning upon my rivers currents, Vala awake!
I hear thy shuttles sing in the sky, and round my limbs
I feel the iron threads of love & jealousy & despair.

Vala replyd. Albion is mine! Luvah gave me to Albion   50
And now recieves reproach & hate. Was it not said of old
Set your Son before a man & he shall take you & your sons
For slaves: but set your Daughter before a man & She
Shall make him & his sons & daughters your slaves for ever!
And is this Faith? Behold the strife of Albion & Luvah   55
Is great in the east, their spears of blood rage in the eastern heaven
Urizen is the champion of Albion, they will slay my Luvah:
And thou O harlot daughter! daughter of despair art all
This cause of these shakings of my towers on Euphrates.
Here is the House of Albion, & here is thy secluded place   60
And here we have found thy sins: & hence we turn thee forth,
For all to avoid thee: to be astonishd at thee for thy sins:
Because thou art the impurity & the harlot: & thy children!
Children of whoredoms: born for Sacrifice: for the meat & drink
Offering: to sustain the glorious combat & the battle & war   65
That Man may be purified by the death of thy delusions.

So saying she her dark threads cast over the trembling River:
And over the valleys; from the hills of Hertfordshire to the hills
Of Surrey across Middlesex. & across Albions House
Of Eternity! pale stood Albion at his eastern gate,   70
PLATE 46 [32]
Leaning against the pillars, & his disease rose from his skirts[.]
Upon the Precipice he stood! ready to fall into Non-Entity.

Los was all astonishment & terror: he trembled sitting on the Stone   c
Of London: but the interiors of Albions fibres & nerves were hidden
From Los; astonishd he beheld only the petrified surfaces: 5
And saw his Furnaces in ruins, for Los is the Demon of the Furnaces;
He saw also the Four Points of Albion reversd inwards
He siezd his Hammer & Tongs, his iron Poker & his Bellows,
Upon the valleys of Middlesex, Shouting loud for aid Divine.

In stern defiance came from Albions bosom Hand, Hyle, Koban,   10
Gwantok, Peachy, Brertun, Slaid, Huttn, Skofeld, Kock, Kotope

Bowen: Albions Sons: they bore him a golden couch into the porch
And on the Couch reposd his limbs, trembling from the bloody field.
Rearing their Druid Patriarchal rocky Temples around his limbs.
(All things begin & end, in Albions Ancient Druid Rocky Shore.)   15

PLATE 47
[*When Albion utterd his last words Hope is banishd from me*]   t
From Camberwell to Highgate where the mighty Thames shudders
    along,
Where Los's Furnaces stand, where Jerusalem & Vala howl:
Luvah tore forth from Albions Loins, in fibrous veins, in rivers
Of blood over Europe: a Vegetating Root in grinding pain.   5
Animating the Dragon Temples, soon to become that Holy Fiend
The Wicker Man of Scandinavia in which cruelly consumed
The Captives reard to heaven howl in flames among the stars
Loud the cries of War on the Rhine & Danube, with Albions Sons,
Away from Beulahs hills & vales break forth the Souls of the Dead,   10
With cymbal, trumpet, clarion; & the scythed chariots of Britain.

And the Veil of Vala, is composed of the Spectres of the Dead

Hark! the mingling cries of Luvah with the Sons of Albion
Hark! & Record the terrible wonder! that the Punisher
Mingles with his Victims Spectre, enslaved and tormented   15
To him whom he has murderd, bound in vengeance & enmity
Shudder not, but Write, & the hand of God will assist you!
Therefore I write Albions last words. Hope is banish'd from me.

PLATE 48
These were his last words, and the merciful Saviour in his arms
Reciev'd him, in the arms of tender mercy and repos'd
The pale limbs of his Eternal Individuality
Upon the Rock of Ages. Then, surrounded with a Cloud:
In silence the Divine Lord builded with immortal labour,   5
Of gold & jewels a sublime Ornament, a Couch of repose,
With Sixteen pillars: canopied with emblems & written verse.
Spiritual Verse, order'd & measur'd, from whence, time shall reveal.
The Five books of the Decalogue, the books of Joshua & Judges,
Samuel, a double book & Kings, a double book, the Psalms & Prophets   10
The Four-fold Gospel, and the Revelations everlasting
Eternity groan'd & was troubled, at the image of Eternal Death!

Beneath the bottoms of the Graves, which is Earths central joint,   e
There is a place where Contrarieties are equally true:
(To protect from the Giant blows in the sports of intellect,   15
Thunder in the midst of kindness, & love that kills its beloved:
Because Death is for a period, and they renew tenfold.)
From this sweet Place Maternal Love awoke Jerusalem
With pangs she forsook Beulahs pleasant lovely shadowy Universe
Where no dispute can come; created for those who Sleep.   20

Weeping was in all Beulah, and all the Daughters of Beulah
Wept for their Sister the Daughter of Albion, Jerusalem:
When out of Beulah the Emanation of the Sleeper descended
With solemn mourning out of Beulahs moony shades and hills:
Within the Human Heart, whose Gates closed with solemn sound. 25

And this the manner of the terrible Separation
The Emanations of the grievously afflicted Friends of Albion
Concenter in one Female form an Aged pensive Woman.
Astonish'd! lovely! embracing the sublime shade: the Daughters of
 Beulah
Beheld her with wonder! With awful hands she took 30
A Moment of Time, drawing it out with many tears & afflictions
And many sorrows: oblique across the Atlantic Vale
Which is the Vale of Rephaim dreadful from East to West,
Where the Human Harvest waves abundant in the beams of Eden
Into a Rainbow of jewels and gold, a mild Reflection from 35
Albions dread Tomb. Eight thousand and five hundred years
In its extension. Every two hundred years has a door to Eden
She also took an Atom of Space, with dire pain opening it a Center
Into Beulah: trembling the Daughters of Beulah dried
Her tears. she ardent embrac'd her sorrows. occupied in labours 40
Of sublime mercy in Rephaims Vale. Perusing Albions Tomb
She sat: she walk'd among the ornaments solemn mourning.
The Daughters attended her shudderings, wiping the death sweat
Los also saw her in his seventh Furnace, he also terrified
Saw the finger of God go forth upon his seventh Furnace: 45
Away from the Starry Wheels to prepare Jerusalem a place.
When with a dreadful groan the Emanation mild of Albion
Burst from his bosom in the Tomb like a pale snowy cloud,
Female and lovely, struggling to put off the Human form
Writhing in pain. The Daughters of Beulah in kind arms reciev'd 50
Jerusalem: weeping over her among the Spaces of Erin,
In the Ends of Beulah, where the Dead wail night & day.

And thus Erin spoke to the Daughters of Beulah, in soft tears e

Albion the Vortex of the Dead! Albion the Generous!
Albion the mildest son of Heaven! The Place of Holy Sacrifice! 55
Where Friends Die for each other: will become the Place,
Of Murder, & Unforgiving, Never-awaking Sacrifice of Enemies[.]
The Children must be sacrific'd! (a horror never known
Till now in Beulah.) unless a Refuge can be found
To hide them from the wrath of Albions Law that freezes sore 60
Upon his Sons & Daughters, self-exiled from his bosom
Draw ye Jerusalem away from Albions Mountains
To give a Place for Redemption, let Sihon and Og
Remove Eastward to Bashan and Gilead, and leave

PLATE 49

The secret coverts of Albion & the hidden places of America
Jerusalem Jerusalem! why wilt thou turn away
Come ye O Daughters of Beulah, lament for Og & Sihon
Upon the Lakes of Ireland from Rathlin to Baltimore:
Stand ye upon the Dargle from Wicklow to Drogheda   5
Come & mourn over Albion the White Cliff of the Atlantic
The Mountain of Giants: all the Giants of Albion are become
Weak! witherd! darkend! & Jerusalem is cast forth from Albion.
They deny that they ever knew Jerusalem, or ever dwelt in Shiloh[.]
The Gigantic roots & twigs of the vegetating Sons of Albion   10
Filld with the little-ones are consumed in the Fires of their Altars
The vegetating Cities are burned & consumed from the Earth:
And the Bodies in which all Animals & Vegetations, the Earth &
    Heaven
Were contain in the All Glorious Imagination are witherd & darkend;
The golden Gate of Havilah, and all the Garden of God,   15
Was caught up with the Sun in one day of fury and war:
The Lungs, the Heart, the Liver, shrunk away far distant from Man
And left a little slimy substance floating upon the tides.
In one night the Atlantic Continent was caught up with the Moon,
And became an Opake Globe far distant clad with moony beams.   20
The Visions of Eternity, by reason of narrowed perceptions,
Are become weak Visions of Time & Space, fix'd into furrows of death;
Till deep dissimulation is the only defence an honest man has left[.]
O Polypus of Death O Spectre over Europe and Asia
Withering the Human Form by Laws of Sacrifice for Sin   25
By Laws of Chastity & Abhorrence I am witherd up.
Striving to Create a Heaven in which all shall be pure & holy
In their Own Selfhoods, in Natural Selfish Chastity to banish Pity
And dear Mutual Forgiveness; & to become One Great Satan
Inslavd to the most powerful Selfhood: to murder the Divine Humanity 30
In whose sight all are as the dust & who chargeth his Angels with folly!
Ah! weak & wide astray! Ah shut in narrow doleful form!
Creeping in reptile flesh upon the bosom of the ground!
The Eye of Man, a little narrow orb, closd up & dark,
Scarcely beholding the Great Light; conversing with the [Void]:   35
The Ear, a little shell, in small volutions shutting out
True Harmonies, & comprehending great, as very small:
The Nostrils, bent down to the earth & clos'd with senseless flesh.
That odours cannot them expand, nor joy on them exult:
The Tongue, a little moisture fills, a little food it cloys,   40
A little sound it utters, & its cries are faintly heard.
Therefore they are removed: therefore they have taken root
In Egypt & Philistea: in Moab & Edom & Aram:
In the Erythrean Sea their Uncircu[m]cision in Heart & Loins
Be lost for ever & ever. then they shall arise from Self   45

By Self Annihilation into Jerusalems Courts & into Shiloh
Shiloh the Masculine Emanation among the Flowers of Beulah
Lo Shiloh dwells over France, as Jerusalem dwells over Albion
Build & prepare a Wall & Curtain for Americas shore!
Rush on: Rush on! Rush on! ye vegetating Sons of Albion   50
The Sun shall go before you in Day: the Moon shall go
Before you in Night. Come on! Come on! Come on! The Lord
Jehovah is before, behind, above, beneath, around
He has builded the arches of Albions Tomb binding the Stars
In merciful Order, bending the Laws of Cruelty to Peace.   55
He hath placed Og & Anak, the Giants of Albion for their Guards:
Building the Body of Moses in the Valley of Peor: the Body
Of Divine Analogy; and Og & Sihon in the tears of Balaam
The Son of Beor, have given their power to Joshua & Caleb.
Remove from Albion, far remove these terrible surfaces.   60
They are beginning to form Heavens & Hells in immense
Circles: the Hells for food to the Heavens: food of torment,
Food of despair: they drink the condemnd Soul & rejoice
In cruel holiness, in their Heavens of Chastity & Uncircumcision
Yet they are blameless & Iniquity must be imputed only   65
To the State they are enterd into that they may be deliverd:
Satan is the State of Death, & not a Human existence:
But Luvah is named Satan, because he has enterd that State.
A World where Man is by Nature the enemy of Man
Because the Evil is Created into a State. that Men   70
May be deliverd time after time evermore. Amen.
Learn therefore O Sisters to distinguish the Eternal Human
That walks about among the stones of fire in bliss & woe
Alternate! from those States or Worlds in which the Spirit travels:
This is the only means to Forgiveness of Enemies   75
Therefore remove from Albion these terrible Surfaces
And let wild seas & rocks close up Jerusalem away from

PLATE 50
The Atlantic Mountains where Giants dwelt in Intellect;
Now given to stony Druids, and Allegoric Generation
To the Twelve Gods of Asia, the Spectres of those who Sleep:
Sway'd by a Providence oppos'd to the Divine Lord Jesus:
A murderous Providence! A Creation that groans, living on Death. 5
Where Fish & Bird & Beast & Man & Tree & Metal & Stone
Live by Devouring, going into Eternal Death continually:
Albion is now possess'd by the War of Blood! the Sacrifice
Of envy Albion is become, and his Emanation cast out:
Come Lord Jesus, Lamb of God descend! for if; O Lord!   10
If thou hadst been here, our brother Albion had not died.
Arise sisters! Go ye & meet the Lord, while I remain—
Behold the foggy mornings of the Dead on Albions cliffs!

Ye know that if the Emanation remains in them:
She will become an Eternal Death, an Avenger of Sin   15
A Self-righteousness: the proud Virgin-Harlot! Mother of War!
And we also & all Beulah, consume beneath Albions curse.

So Erin spoke to the Daughters of Beulah. Shuddering
With their wings they sat in the Furnace, in a night
Of stars, for all the Sons of Albion appeard distant stars,   20
Ascending and descending into Albions sea of death.
And Erins lovely Bow enclos'd the Wheels of Albions Sons.

Expanding on wing, the Daughters of Beulah replied in sweet response

Come O thou Lamb of God and take away the remembrance of Sin
To Sin & to hide the Sin in sweet deceit. is lovely!!   25
To Sin in the open face of day is cruel & pitiless! But
To record the Sin for a reproach: to let the Sun go down
In a remembrance of the Sin: is a Woe & a Horror!
A brooder of an Evil Day, and a Sun rising in blood
Come then O Lamb of God and take away the remembrance of Sin   30

End of Chap. 2^d.

PLATE 52

Rahab is an } To the Deists. { The Spiritual States of
Eternal State   the Soul are all Eternal
            Distinguish between the
            Man, & his present State

   He never can be a Friend to the Human Race who is the Preacher of
Natural Morality or Natural Religion. he is a flatterer who means to betray, to perpetuate Tyrant Pride & the Laws of that Babylon which
he forsees shall shortly be destroyed, with the Spiritual and not the Natural Sword: He is in the State named Rahab: which State must be put
off before he can be the Friend of Man.
   You O Deists profess yourselves the Enemies of Christianity: and you
are so: you are also the Enemies of the Human Race & of Universal
Nature. Man is born a Spectre or Satan & is altogether an Evil, & requires a New Selfhood continually & must continually be changed into
his direct Contrary. But your Greek Philosophy (which is a remnant of
Druidism) teaches that Man is Righteous in his Vegetated Spectre: an
Opinion of fatal & accursed consequence to Man, as the Ancients saw
plainly by Revelation to the intire abrogation of Experimental Theory.
and many believed what they saw, and Prophecied of Jesus.
   Man must & will have Some Religion; if he has not the Religion of
Jesus, he will have the Religion of Satan, & will erect the Synagogue of
Satan. calling the Prince of this World, God; and destroying all who do
not worship Satan under the Name of God. Will any one say: Where

are those who worship Satan under the Name of God! Where are they? Listen! Every Religion that Preaches Vengeance for Sin is the Religion of the Enemy & Avenger; and not of the Forgiver of Sin, and their God is Satan, Named by the Divine Name. Your Religion O Deists: Deism, is the Worship of the God of this World by the means of what you call Natural Religion and Natural Philosophy, and of Natural Morality or Self-Righteousness, the Selfish Virtues of the Natural Heart. This was the Religion of the Pharisees who murderd Jesus. Deism is the same & ends in the same.

Voltaire Rousseau Gibbon Hume. charge the Spiritually Religious with Hypocrisy! but how a Monk or a Methodist either, can be a Hypocrite: I cannot concieve. We are Men of like passions with others & pretend not to be holier than others: therefore, when a Religious Man falls into Sin, he ought not to be calld a Hypocrite: this title is more properly to be given to a Player who falls into Sin; whose profession is Virtue & Morality & the making Men Self-Righteous. Foote in calling Whitefield, Hypocrite: was himself one: for Whitefield pretended not to be holier than others: but confessed his Sins before all the World; Voltaire! Rousseau! You cannot escape my charge that you are Pharisees & Hypocrites, for you are constantly talking of the Virtues of the Human Heart, and particularly of your own, that you may accuse others & especially the Religious, whose errors, you by this display of pretended Virtue, chiefly design to expose. Rousseau thought Men Good by Nature; he found them Evil & found no friend. Friendship cannot exist without Forgiveness of Sins continually. The Book written by Rousseau calld his Confessions is an apology & cloke for his sin & not a confession.

But you also charge the poor Monks & Religious with being the causes of War: while you acquit & flatter the Alexanders & Caesars, the Lewis's & Fredericks: who alone are its causes & its actors. But the Religion of Jesus, Forgiveness of Sin, can never be the cause of a War nor of a single Martyrdom.

Those who Martyr others or who cause War are Deists, but never can be Forgivers of Sin. The Glory of Christianity is, To Conquer by Forgiveness. All the Destruction therefore, in Christian Europe has arisen from Deism, which is Natural Religion.

> I saw a Monk of Charlemaine   t
> Arise before my sight
>   I talkd with the Grey Monk as we stood   t
>   In beams of infernal light
>
> Gibbon arose with a lash of steel   t 5
> And Voltaire with a wracking wheel
>   The Schools in clouds of learning rolld   t
>   Arose with War in iron & gold.

-199-

Thou lazy Monk they sound afar
In vain condemning glorious War
And in your Cell you shall ever dwell
Rise War & bind him in his Cell.

t
t 10
t

The blood. red ran from the Grey Monks side
His hands & feet were wounded wide
His body bent, his arms & knees
Like to the roots of ancient trees

15

When Satan first the black bow bent
And the Moral Law from the Gospel rent
He forgd the Law into a Sword
And spilld the blood of mercys Lord.

t

20

Titus! Constantine! Charlemaine!
O Voltaire! Rousseau! Gibbon! Vain
Your Grecian Mocks & Roman Sword
Against this image of his Lord!

t

t

For a Tear is an Intellectual thing;
And a Sigh is the Sword of an Angel King
And the bitter groan of a Martyrs woe
Is an Arrow from the Almighties Bow!

t 25

t

PLATE 53

Jerusalem

Chap 3.

But Los, who is the Vehicular Form of strong Urthona
Wept vehemently over Albion where Thames currents spring
From the rivers of Beulah; pleasant river! soft, mild, parent stream
And the roots of Albions Tree enterd the Soul of Los
As he sat before his Furnaces clothed in sackcloth of hair
In gnawing pain dividing him from his Emanation;
Inclosing all the children of Los time after time.

c

5

Their Giant forms condensing into Nations & Peoples & Tongues
Translucent the Furnaces, of Beryll & Emerald immortal:
And Seven-fold each within other: incomprehensible
To the Vegetated Mortal Eye's perverted & single vision
The Bellows are the Animal Lungs. the Hammers, the Animal Heart
The Furnaces, the Stomach for Digestion; terrible their fury
Like seven burning heavens rang'd from South to North

t

10

Here on the banks of the Thames, Los builded Golgonooza,
Outside of the Gates of the Human Heart, beneath Beulah
In the midst of the rocks of the Altars of Albion. In fears
He builded it, in rage & in fury. It is the Spiritual Fourfold

15

London: continually building & continually decaying desolate!
In eternal labours: loud the Furnaces & loud the Anvils   20
Of Death thunder incessant around the flaming Couches of
The Twentyfour Friends of Albion and round the awful Four
For the protection of the Twelve Emanations of Albions Sons
The Mystic Union of the Emanation in the Lord; Because   t
Man divided from his Emanation is a dark Spectre   25
His Emanation is an ever-weeping melancholy Shadow
But she is made receptive of Generation thro' mercy
In the Potters Furnace, among the Funeral Urns of Beulah
From Surrey hills, thro' Italy and Greece, to Hinnoms vale.

PLATE 54
In Great Eternity, every particular Form gives forth or Emanates   c
Its own peculiar Light, & the Form is the Divine Vision
And the Light is his Garment. This is Jerusalem in every Man
A Tent & Tabernacle of Mutual Forgiveness Male & Female Clothings.
And Jerusalem is called Liberty among the Children of Albion   5

But Albion fell down a Rocky fragment from Eternity hurld
By his own Spectre, who is the Reasoning Power in every Man
Into his own Chaos which is the Memory between Man & Man

The silent broodings of deadly revenge springing from the
All powerful parental affection, fills Albion from head to foot   10
Seeing his Sons assimilate with Luvah, bound in the bonds
Of spiritual Hate, from which springs Sexual Love as iron chains:
He tosses like a cloud outstretchd among Jerusalems Ruins
Which overspread all the Earth, he groans among his ruind porches

But the Spectre like a hoar frost & a Mildew rose over Albion   15
Saying, I am God O Sons of Men! I am your Rational Power!
Am I not Bacon & Newton & Locke who teach Humility to Man!
Who teach Doubt & Experiment & my two Wings Voltaire: Rousseau.
Where is that Friend of Sinners! that Rebel against my Laws!
Who teaches Belief to the Nations, & an unknown Eternal Life   20
Come hither into the Desart & turn these stones to bread.
Vain foolish Man! wilt thou believe without Experiment?

And build a World of Phantasy upon my Great Abyss!
A World of Shapes in craving lust & devouring appetite

So spoke the hard cold constrictive Spectre he is named Arthur 25
Constricting into Druid Rocks round Canaan Agag & Aram & Pharoh

Then Albion drew England into his bosom in groans & tears
But she stretchd out her starry Night in Spaces against him. like
A long Serpent, in the Abyss of the Spectre which augmented
The Night with Dragon wings coverd with stars & in the Wings 30
Jerusalem & Vala appeard: & above between the Wings magnificent
The Divine Vision dimly appeard in clouds of blood weeping.

PLATE 55
When those who disregard all Mortal Things, saw a Mighty-One
Among the Flowers of Beulah still retain his awful strength
They wonderd; checking their wild flames & Many gathering
Together into an Assembly; they said, let us go down
And see these changes! Others said, If you do so prepare 5
For being driven from our fields, what have we to do with the Dead?
To be their inferiors or superiors we equally abhor;
Superior, none we know: inferior none: all equal share
Divine Benevolence & joy, for the Eternal Man
Walketh among us, calling us his Brothers & his Friends: 10
Forbidding us that Veil which Satan puts between Eve & Adam
By which the Princes of the Dead enslave their Votaries
Teaching them to form the Serpent of precious stones & gold
To sieze the Sons of Jerusalem & plant them in One Mans Loins
To make One Family of Contraries: that Joseph may be sold 15
Into Egypt: for Negation; a Veil the Saviour born & dying rends.

But others said: Let us to him who only Is, & who
Walketh among us, give decision. bring forth all your fires!

So saying, an eternal deed was done: in fiery flames
The Universal Conc[l]ave raged, such thunderous sounds as never 20
Were sounded from a mortal cloud, nor on Mount Sinai old
Nor in Havilah where the Cherub rolld his redounding flame.

Loud! loud! the Mountains lifted up their voices, loud the Forests
Rivers thunderd against their banks, loud Winds furious fought
Cities & Nations contended in fires & clouds & tempests. 25
The Seas raisd up their voices & lifted their hands on high
The Stars in their courses fought. the Sun! Moon! Heaven: Earth.
Contending for Albion & for Jerusalem his Emanation
And for Shiloh, the Emanation of France & for lovely Vala.

Then far the greatest number were about to make a Separation 30
And they Elected Seven, calld the Seven Eyes of God;
Lucifer, Molech, Elohim, Shaddai, Pahad, Jehovah, Jesus.
They namd the Eighth. he came not, he hid in Albions Forests

But first they said: (& their Words stood in Chariots in array
Curbing their Tygers with golden bits & bridles of silver & ivory)   35

Let the Human Organs be kept in their perfect Integrity   c
At will Contracting into Worms, or Expanding into Gods
And then behold! what are these Ulro Visions of Chastity[?]
Then as the moss upon the tree: or dust upon the plow:
Or as the sweat upon the labouring shoulder: or as the chaff   40
Of the wheat-floor or as the dregs of the sweet wine-press
Such are these Ulro Visions, for tho we sit down within
The plowed furrow. listning to the weeping clods till we
Contract or Expand Space at will: or if we raise ourselves
Upon the chariots of the morning. Contracting or Expanding Time!   45
Every one knows, we are One Family: One Man blessed for ever

Silence remaind & every one resumd his Human Majesty
And many conversed on these things as they labourd at the furrow
Saying: It is better to prevent misery, than to release from misery
It is better to prevent error, than to forgive the criminal: 50
Labour well the Minute Particulars, attend to the Little-ones:
And those who are in misery cannot remain so long
If we do but our duty: labour well the teeming Earth.

They Plow'd in tears, the trumpets sounded before the golden Plow
And the voices of the Living Creatures were heard in the clouds of   55
     heaven
Crying: Compell the Reasoner to Demonstrate with unhewn
     Demonstrations
Let the Indefinite be explored. and let every Man be Judged
By his own Works, Let all Indefinites be thrown into Demonstrations
To be pounded to dust & melted in the Furnaces of Affliction:
He who would do good to another, must do it in Minute Particulars   c 60
General Good is the plea of the scoundrel hypocrite & flatterer:
For Art & Science cannot exist but in minutely organized Particulars
And not in generalizing Demonstrations of the Rational Power.
The Infinite alone resides in Definite & Determinate Identity
Establishment of Truth depends on destruction of Falshood continually   65
On Circumcision: not on Virginity, O Reasoners of Albion

So cried they at the Plow. Albions Rock frowned above
And the Great Voice of Eternity rolled above terrible in clouds
Saying Who will go forth for us! & Who shall we send before our face?

PLATE 56
Then Los heaved his thund'ring Bellows on the Valley of Middlesex   c
And thus he chaunted his Song: the Daughters of Albion reply.

What may Man be? who can tell! But what may Woman be?   c
To have power over Man from Cradle to corruptible Grave.
He who is an Infant, and whose Cradle is a Manger   5

Knoweth the Infant sorrow: whence it came, and where it goeth:
And who weave it a Cradle of the grass that withereth away.
This World is all a Cradle for the erred wandering Phantom:
Rock'd by Year, Month, Day & Hour; and every two Moments
Between, dwells a Daughter of Beulah, to feed the Human Vegetable   10
Entune: Daughters of Albion. your hymning Chorus mildly!
Cord of affection thrilling extatic on the iron Reel:
To the golden Loom of Love! to the moth-labourd Woof
A Garment and Cradle weaving for the infantine Terror:
For fear; at entering the gate into our World of cruel   15
Lamentation: it flee back & hide in Non-Entitys dark wild
Where dwells the Spectre of Albion: destroyer of Definite Form.
The Sun shall be a Scythed Chariot of Britain: the Moon; a Ship
In the British Ocean! Created by Los's Hammer; measured out
Into Days & Nights & Years & Months. to travel with my feet   20
Over these desolate rocks of Albion: O daughters of despair!
Rock the Cradle, and in mild melodies tell me where found
What you have enwoven with so much tears & care? so much
Tender artifice: to laugh: to weep: to learn: to know;
Remember! recollect! what dark befel in wintry days   25

O it was lost for ever! and we found it not: it came
And wept at our wintry Door: Look! look! behold! Gwendolen
Is become a Clod of Clay! Merlin is a Worm of the Valley!

Then Los uttered with Hammer & Anvil: Chaunt! revoice!
I mind not your laugh: and your frown I not fear! and   30
You must my dictate obey from your gold-beam'd Looms; trill
Gentle to Albions Watchman, on Albions mountains; reeccho
And rock the Cradle while! Ah me! Of that Eternal Man
And of the cradled Infancy in his bowels of compassion:
Who fell beneath his instruments of husbandry & became   35
Subservient to the clods of the furrow! the cattle and even
The emmet and earth-Worms are his superiors & his lords.

Then the response came warbling from trilling Looms in Albion

We Women tremble at the light therefore: hiding fearful
The Divine Vision with Curtain & Veil & fleshly Tabernacle   40

Los utter'd: swift as the rattling thunder upon the mountains[:]
Look back into the Church Paul! Look! Three Women around
The Cross! O Albion why didst thou a Female Will Create?

PLATE 57
And the voices of Bath & Canterbury & York & Edinburgh. Cry
Over the Plow of Nations in the strong hand of Albion thundering
    along
Among the Fires of the Druid & the deep black rethundering Waters
Of the Atlantic which poured in impetuous loud loud. louder & louder.

And the Great Voice of the Atlantic howled over the Druid Altars: 5
Weeping over his Children in Stone-henge in Malden & Colchester.
Round the Rocky Peak of Derbyshire London Stone & Rosamonds
   Bower

What is a Wife & what is a Harlot? What is a Church? & What
Is a Theatre? are they Two & not One? can they Exist Separate?
Are not Religion & Politics the Same Thing? Brotherhood is Religion   10
O Demonstrations of Reason Dividing Families in Cruelty & Pride!

But Albion fled from the Divine Vision, with the Plow of Nations
   enflaming
The Living Creatures maddend and Albion fell into the Furrow, and
The Plow went over him & the Living was Plowed in among the Dead
But his Spectre rose over the starry Plow. Albion fled beneath the Plow   15
Till he came to the Rock of Ages. & he took his Seat upon the Rock.

Wonder siezd all in Eternity! to behold the Divine Vision. open
The Center into an Expanse, & the Center rolled out into an Expanse.

PLATE 58
In beauty the Daughters of Albion divide & unite at will   c
Naked & drunk with blood Gwendolen dancing to the timbrel
Of War: reeling up the Street of London she divides in twain   t
Among the Inhabitants of Albion. the People fall around[.]
The Daughters of Albion. divide & unite in jealousy & cruelty   5
The Inhabitants of Albion at the Harvest & the Vintage
Feel their Brain cut round beneath the temples shrieking
Bonifying into a Scull, the Marrow exuding in dismal pain.
They flee over the rocks bonifying: Horses: Oxen: feel the knife.
And while the Sons of Albion by severe War & Judgment, bonify[,]   10
The Hermaphroditic Condensations are divided by the Knife
The obdurate Forms are cut asunder by Jealousy & Pity.

Rational Philosophy and Mathematic Demonstration
Is divided in the intoxications of pleasure & affection
Two Contraries War against each other in fury & blood,   15
And Los fixes them on his Anvil, incessant his blows:
He fixes them with strong blows. placing the stones & timbers.
To Create a World of Generation from the World of Death:
Dividing the Masculine & Feminine: for the comingling
Of Albions & Luvahs Spectres was Hermaphroditic   20

Urizen wrathful strode above directing the awful Building:
As a Mighty Temple; delivering Form out of confusion[.]
Jordan sprang beneath its threshold bubbling from beneath
Its pillars: Euphrates ran under its arches: white sails
And silver oars reflect on its pillars, & sound on its ecchoing   25
Pavements: where walk the Sons of Jerusalem who remain Ungenerate

But the revolving Sun and Moon pass thro its porticoes,
Day & night, in sublime majesty & silence they revolve
And shine glorious within! Hand & Koban archd over the Sun
In the hot noon, as he traveld thro his journey; Hyle & Skofield   30
Archd over the Moon at midnight & Los Fixd them there,
With his thunderous Hammer; terrified the Spectres rage & flee!
Canaan is his portico; Jordan is a fountain in his porch;
A fountain of milk & wine to relieve the traveller:
Egypt is the eight steps within. Ethiopia supports his pillars;   35
Lybia & the Lands unknown. are the ascent without;
Within is Asia & Greece, ornamented with exquisite art:
Persia & Media are his halls: his inmost hall is Great Tartary.
China & India & Siberia are his temples for entertainment
Poland & Russia & Sweden, his soft retired chambers[.]   40
France & Spain & Italy & Denmark & Holland & Germany
Are the temples among his pillars. Britain is Los's Forge;
America North & South are his baths of living waters.

Such is the Ancient World of Urizen in the Satanic Void
Created from the Valley of Middlesex by Londons River   45
From Stone-henge and from London Stone, from Cornwall to Cathnes
The Four Zoa's rush around on all sides in dire ruin
Furious in pride of Selfhood the terrible Spectres of Albion
Rear their dark Rocks among the Stars of God: stupendous
Works! A World of Generation continually Creating; out of   50
The Hermaphroditic Satanic World of rocky destiny.

PLATE 59
And formed into Four precious stones. for enterance from Beulah

For the Veil of Vala which Albion cast into the Atlantic Deep
To catch the Souls of the Dead: began to Vegetate & Petrify
Around the Earth of Albion. among the Roots of his Tree
This Los formed into the Gates & mighty Wall, between the Oak   5
Of Weeping & the Palm of Suffering beneath Albions Tomb.
Thus in process of time it became the beautiful Mundane Shell,
The Habitation of the Spectres of the Dead & the Place
Of Redemption & of awaking again into Eternity

For Four Universes round the Mundane Egg remain Chaotic   c 10
One to the North; Urthona: One to the South; Urizen:
One to the East: Luvah: One to the West, Tharmas;
They are the Four Zoas that stood around the Throne Divine.
Verulam: London: York & Edinburgh: their English names
But when Luvah assumed the World of Urizen Southward   15
And Albion was slain upon his Mountains & in his Tent.
All fell towards the Center, sinking downwards in dire ruin,
In the South remains a burning Fire: in the East. a Void
In the West, a World of raging Waters: in the North; solid Darkness

Unfathomable without end: but in the midst of these   20
Is Built eternally the sublime Universe of Los & Enitharmon

And in the North Gate, in the West of the North. toward Beulah
Cathedrons Looms are builded. and Los's Furnaces in the South[.]
A wondrous golden Building immense with ornaments sublime
Is bright Cathedrons golden Hall, its Courts Towers & Pinnacles   25

And one Daughter of Los sat at the fiery Reel & another
Sat at the shining Loom with her Sisters attending round
Terrible their distress & their sorrow cannot be utterd
And another Daughter of Los sat at the Spinning Wheel
Endless their labour, with bitter food. void of sleep,   30
Tho hungry they labour: they rouze themselves anxious
Hour after hour labouring at the whirling Wheel
Many Wheels & as many lovely Daughters sit weeping

Yet the intoxicating delight that they take in their work
Obliterates every other evil; none pities their tears   35
Yet they regard not pity & they expect no one to pity
For they labour for life & love, regardless of any one
But the poor Spectres that they work for, always incessantly

They are mockd, by every one that passes by. they regard not
They labour; & when their Wheels are broken by scorn & malice   40
They mend them sorrowing with many tears & afflictions.

Other Daughters Weave on the Cushion & Pillow, Network fine
That Rahab & Tirzah may exist & live & breathe & love
Ah, that it could be as the Daughters of Beulah wish!

Other Daughters of Los, labouring at Looms less fine   45
Create the Silk-worm & the Spider & the Catterpiller
To assist in their most grievous work of pity & compassion[.]
And others Create the wooly Lamb & the downy Fowl
To assist in the work: the Lamb bleats: the Sea-fowl cries
Men understand not the distress & the labour & sorrow   50
That in the Interior Worlds is carried on in fear & trembling
Weaving the shuddring fears & loves of Albions Families
Thunderous rage the Spindles of iron. & the iron Distaff
Maddens in the fury of their hands, weaving in bitter tears
The Veil of Goats-hair & Purple & Scarlet & fine twined Linen   55

PLATE 60
The clouds of Albions Druid Temples rage in the eastern heaven   e
While Los sat terrified beholding Albions Spectre who is Luvah
Spreading in bloody veins in torments over Europe & Asia;
Not yet formed but a wretched torment unformed & abyssal
In flaming fire; within the Furnaces the Divine Vision appeard   5
On Albions hills: often walking from the Furnaces in clouds

And flames among the Druid Temples & the Starry Wheels
Gatherd Jerusalems Children in his arms & bore them like
A Shepherd in the night of Albion which overspread all the Earth

I gave thee liberty and life O lovely Jerusalem   ᶜ 10
And thou hast bound me down upon the Stems of Vegetation
I gave thee Sheep-walks upon the Spanish Mountains Jerusalem
I gave thee Priams City and the Isles of Grecia lovely!
I gave thee Hand & Scofield & the Counties of Albion:
They spread forth like a lovely root into the Garden of God: 15
They were as Adam before me: united into One Man,
They stood in innocence & their skiey tent reachd over Asia
To Nimrods Tower to Ham & Canaan walking with Mizraim
Upon the Egyptian Nile, with solemn songs to Grecia
And sweet Hesperia even to Great Chaldea & Tesshina   20
Following thee as a Shepherd by the Four Rivers of Eden
Why wilt thou rend thyself apart, Jerusalem?
And build this Babylon & sacrifice in secret Groves,
Among the Gods of Asia: among the fountains of pitch & nitre

Therefore thy Mountains are become barren Jerusalem!   25
Thy Valleys, Plains of burning sand. thy Rivers: waters of death[.]
Thy Villages die of the Famine and thy Cities
Beg bread from house to house, lovely Jerusalem
Why wilt thou deface thy beauty & the beauty of thy little-ones
To please thy Idols, in the pretended chastities of Uncircumcision[?]   30
Thy Sons are lovelier than Egypt or Assyria; wherefore
Dost thou blacken their beauty by a Secluded place of rest.
And a peculiar Tabernacle, to cut the integuments of beauty
Into veils of tears and sorrows O lovely Jerusalem!
They have perswaded thee to this, therefore their end shall come   35
And I will lead thee thro the Wilderness in shadow of my cloud
And in my love I will lead thee, lovely Shadow of Sleeping Albion.

This is the Song of the Lamb, sung by Slaves in evening time.

But Jerusalem faintly saw him, closd in the Dungeons of Babylon
Her Form was held by Beulahs Daughters. but all within unseen   40
She sat at the Mills, her hair unbound her feet naked
Cut with the flints: her tears run down, her reason grows like
The Wheel of Hand. incessant turning day & night without rest
Insane she raves upon the winds hoarse, inarticulate:
All night Vala hears. she triumphs in pride of holiness   45
To see Jerusalem deface her lineaments with bitter blows
Of despair. while the Satanic Holiness triumphd in Vala
In a Religion of Chastity & Uncircumcised Selfishness
Both of the Head & Heart & Loins, closd up in Moral Pride.

But the Divine Lamb stood beside Jerusalem. oft she saw   50
The lineaments Divine & oft the Voice heard, & oft she said:

O Lord & Saviour, have the Gods of the Heathen pierced thee?
Or hast thou been pierced in the House of thy Friends?
Art thou alive! & livest thou for-evermore? or art thou
Not: but a delusive shadow, a thought that liveth not.   ^t55
Babel mocks saying, there is no God nor Son of God
That thou O Human Imagination, O Divine Body art all
A delusion. but I know thee O Lord when thou arisest upon
My weary eyes even in this dungeon & this iron mill.
The Stars of Albion cruel rise; thou bindest to sweet influences: 60
For thou also sufferest with me altho I behold thee not;
And altho I sin & blaspheme thy holy name, thou pitiest me;
Because thou knowest I am deluded by the turning mills.
And by these visions of pity & love because of Albions death.

Thus spake Jerusalem, & thus the Divine Voice replied.   65

Mild Shade of Man, pitiest thou these Visions of terror & woe!
Give forth thy pity & love. fear not! lo I am with thee always.
Only believe in me that I have power to raise from death
Thy Brother who Sleepeth in Albion: fear not trembling Shade
PLATE 61
Behold: in the Visions of Elohim Jehovah. behold Joseph & Mary   e
And be comforted O Jerusalem in the Visions of Jehovah Elohim

She looked & saw Joseph the Carpenter in Nazareth & Mary
His espoused Wife. And Mary said, If thou put me away from thee
Dost thou not murder me? Joseph spoke in anger & fury. Should I   5
Marry a Harlot & an Adulteress? Mary answerd, Art thou more pure
Than thy Maker who forgiveth Sins & calls again Her that is Lost
Tho She hates. he calls her again in love. I love my dear Joseph
But he driveth me away from his presence. yet I hear the voice of God
In the voice of my Husband. tho he is angry for a moment, he will not   10
Utterly cast me away. if I were pure, never could I taste the sweets
Of the Forgive[ne]ss of Sins! if I were holy! I never could behold the
   tears
Of love! of him who loves me in the midst of his anger in furnace of
   fire.

Ah my Mary: said Joseph: weeping over & embracing her closely in
His arms: Doth he forgive Jerusalem & not exact Purity from her who   15
   is
Polluted. I heard his voice in my sleep & his Angel in my dream:

Saying, Doth Jehovah Forgive a Debt only on condition that it shall
Be Payed? Doth he Forgive Pollution only on conditions of Purity
That Debt is not Forgiven! That Pollution is not Forgiven
Such is the Forgiveness of the Gods, the Moral Virtues of the   20

Heathen, whose tender Mercies are Cruelty. But Jehovahs Salvation
Is without Money & without Price, in the Continual Forgiveness of
    Sins
In the Perpetual Mutual Sacrifice in Great Eternity! for behold!
There is none that liveth & Sinneth not! And this is the Covenant
Of Jehovah: If you Forgive one-another, so shall Jehovah Forgive You: 25
That He Himself may Dwell among You. Fear not then to take
To thee Mary thy Wife, for she is with Child by the Holy Ghost

Then Mary burst forth into a Song! she flowed like a River of
Many Streams in the arms of Joseph & gave forth her tears of joy
Like many waters, and Emanating into gardens & palaces upon   30
Euphrates & to forests & floods & animals wild & tame from
Gihon to Hiddekel, & to corn fields & villages & inhabitants
Upon Pison & Arnon & Jordan. And I heard the voice among   e
The Reapers Saying, Am I Jerusalem the lost Adulteress? or am I
Babylon come up to Jerusalem? And another voice answerd Saying   35

Does the voice of my Lord call me again? am I pure thro his Mercy
And Pity. Am I become lovely as a Virgin in his sight who am
Indeed a Harlot drunken with the Sacrifice of Idols does he
Call her pure as he did in the days of her Infancy when She
Was cast out to the loathing of her person. The Chaldean took   40
Me from my Cradle. The Amalekite stole me away upon his Camels
Before I had ever beheld with love the Face of Jehovah; or known
That there was a God of Mercy: O Mercy O Divine Humanity!
O Forgiveness & Pity & Compassion! If I were Pure I should never
Have known Thee; If I were Unpolluted I should never have   45
Glorified thy Holiness, or rejoiced in thy great Salvation.

Mary leaned her side against Jerusalem, Jerusalem recieved
The Infant into her hands in the Visions of Jehovah. Times passed on
Jerusalem fainted over the Cross & Sepulcher She heard the voice
Wilt thou make Rome thy Patriarch Druid & the Kings of Europe his   50
Horsemen? Man in the Resurrection changes his Sexual Garments at
    will
Every Harlot was once a Virgin: every Criminal an Infant Love!   e
PLATE 62
Repose on me till the morning of the Grave. I am thy life.

Jerusalem replied. I am an outcast: Albion is dead!   e
I am left to the trampling foot & the spurning heel!
A Harlot I am calld. I am sold from street to street!
I am defaced with blows & with the dirt of the Prison!   5
And wilt thou become my Husband O my Lord & Saviour?
Shall Vala bring thee forth! shall the Chaste be ashamed also?
I see the Maternal Line, I behold the Seed of the Woman!
Cainah, & Ada & Zillah & Naamah Wife of Noah.
Shuahs daughter & Tamar & Rahab the Canaanites: 10

Ruth the Moabite & Bathsheba of the daughters of Heth
Naamah the Ammonite, Zibeah the Philistine, & Mary
These are the Daughters of Vala, Mother of the Body of death
But I thy Magdalen behold thy Spiritual Risen Body   c
Shall Albion arise? I know he shall arise at the Last Day!   15
I know that in my flesh I shall see God: but Emanations
Are weak. they know not whence they are, nor whither tend.

Jesus replied. I am the Resurrection & the Life.   c
I Die & pass the limits of possibility, as it appears
To individual perception. Luvah must be Created   20
And Vala; for I cannot leave them in the gnawing Grave.
But will prepare a way for my banished-ones to return
Come now with me into the villages. walk thro all the cities.
Tho thou art taken to prison & judgment, starved in the streets
I will command the cloud to give thee food & the hard rock   25
To flow with milk & wine, tho thou seest me not a season
Even a long season & a hard journey & a howling wilderness!
Tho Valas cloud hide thee & Luvahs fires follow thee!   c
Only believe & trust in me, Lo. I am always with thee!

So spoke the Lamb of God while Luvahs Cloud reddening above   30
Burst forth in streams of blood upon the heavens & dark night
Involvd Jerusalem. & the Wheels of Albions Sons turnd hoarse
Over the Mountains & the fires blaz'd on Druid Altars
And the Sun set in Tyburns Brook where Victims howl & cry.

But Los beheld the Divine Vision among the flames of the Furnaces   35
Therefore he lived & breathed in hope. but his tears fell incessant
Because his Children were closd from him apart: & Enitharmon
Dividing in fierce pain: also the Vision of God was closd in clouds
Of Albions Spectres, that Los in despair oft sat, & often ponderd
On Death Eternal in fierce shudders upon the mountains of Albion   40
Walking: & in the vales in howlings fierce, then to his Anvils
Turning, anew began his labours, tho in terrible pains!

PLATE 63
Jehovah stood among the Druids in the Valley of Annandale   c
When the Four Zoas of Albion, the Four Living Creatures, the
   Cherubim
Of Albion tremble before the Spectre, in the starry Harness of the Plow
Of Nations. And their Names are Urizen & Luvah & Tharmas &
   Urthona

Luvah slew Tharmas the Angel of the Tongue & Albion brought him   5
To Justice in his own City of Paris, denying the Resurrection
Then Vala the Wife of Albion, who is the Daughter of Luvah
Took vengeance Twelve-fold among the Chaotic Rocks of the Druids
Where the Human Victims howl to the Moon & Thor & Friga

Dance the dance of death contending with Jehovah among the   10
    Cherubim.
The Chariot Wheels filled with Eyes rage along the howling Valley
In the Dividing of Reuben & Benjamin bleeding from Chesters River

The Giants & the Witches & the Ghosts of Albion dance with
Thor & Friga, & the Fairies lead the Moon along the Valley of
    Cherubim
Bleeding in torrents from Mountain to Mountain, a lovely Victim   15
And Jehovah stood in the Gates of the Victim, & he appeared
A weeping Infant in the Gates of Birth in the midst of Heaven

The Cities & Villages of Albion became Rock & Sand Unhumanized
The Druid Sons of Albion & the Heavens a Void around unfathomable
No Human Form but Sexual & a little weeping Infant pale reflected   20
Multitudinous in the Looking Glass of Enitharmon, on all sides
Around in the clouds of the Female, on Albions Cliffs of the Dead

Such the appearance in Cheviot: in the Divisions of Reuben
When the Cherubim hid their heads under their wings in deep
    slumbers
When the Druids demanded Chastity from Woman & all was lost.   25

How can the Female be Chaste O thou stupid Druid Cried Los
Without the Forgiveness of Sins in the merciful clouds of Jehovah
And without the Baptism of Repentance to wash away Calumnies. and
The Accusations of Sin that each may be Pure in their Neighbours
    sight
O when shall Jehovah give us Victims from his Flocks & Herds   30
Instead of Human Victims by the Daughters of Albion & Canaan

Then laugh'd Gwendolen & her laughter shook the Nations & Familys
    of
The Dead beneath Beulah from Tyburn to Golgotha, and from
Ireland to Japan. furious her Lions & Tygers & Wolves sport before
Los on the Thames & Medway. London & Canterbury groan in pain   35

Los knew not yet what was done: he thought it was all in Vision
In Visions of the Dreams of Beulah among the Daughters of Albion
Therefore the Murder was put apart in the Looking-Glass of
    Enitharmon

He saw in Vala's hand the Druid Knife of Revenge & the Poison Cup
Of Jealousy, and thought it a Poetic Vision of the Atmospheres   40
Till Canaan rolld apart from Albion across the Rhine: along the
    Danube

And all the Land of Canaan suspended over the Valley of Cheviot
From Bashan to Tyre & from Troy to Gaza of the Amalekite
And Reuben fled with his head downwards among the Caverns

PLATE 64

Of the Mundane Shell which froze on all sides round Canaan on
The vast Expanse: where the Daughters of Albion Weave the Web
Of Ages & Generations, folding & unfolding it, like a Veil of
    Cherubim
And sometimes it touches the Earths summits, & sometimes spreads
Abroad into the Indefinite Spectre, who is the Rational Power.   5

Then All the Daughters of Albion became One before Los: even Vala!   e
And she put forth her hand upon the Looms in dreadful howlings
Till she vegetated into a hungry Stomach & a devouring Tongue.
Her Hand is a Court of Justice, her Feet: two Armies in Battle
Storms & Pestilence: in her Locks: & in her Loins Earthquake.   10
And Fire. & the Ruin of Cities & Nations & Families & Tongues

She cries: The Human is but a Worm, & thou O Male: Thou art
Thyself Female, a Male: a breeder of Seed: a Son & Husband: & Lo.
The Human Divine is Womans Shadow, a Vapor in the summers heat
Go assume Papal dignity thou Spectre, thou Male Harlot! Arthur   15
Divide into the Kings of Europe in times remote O Woman-born
And Woman-nourishd & Woman-educated & Woman-scorn'd!

Wherefore art thou living? said Los, & Man cannot live in thy presence
Art thou Vala the Wife of Albion O thou lovely Daughter of Luvah
All Quarrels arise from Reasoning. the secret Murder, and   20
The violent Man-slaughter. these are the Spectres double Cave
The Sexual Death living on accusation of Sin & Judgment
To freeze Love & Innocence into the gold & silver of the Merchant
Without Forgiveness of Sin Love is Itself Eternal Death.

Then the Spectre drew Vala into his bosom magnificent terrific   25
Glittering with precious stones & gold, with Garments of blood & fire[.]
He wept in deadly wrath of the Spectre, in self-contradicting agony
Crimson with Wrath & green with Jealousy dazling with Love
And Jealousy immingled & the purple of the violet darkend deep
Over the Plow of Nations thundring in the hand of Albions Spectre   30

A dark Hermaphrodite they stood frowning upon Londons River
And the Distaff & Spindle in the hands of Vala with the Flax of
Human Miseries turnd fierce with the Lives of Men along the Valley
As Reuben fled before the Daughters of Albion Taxing the Nations

Derby Peak yawnd a horrid Chasm at the Cries of Gwendolen, & at   35
The stamping feet of Ragan upon the flaming Treddles of her Loom
That drop with crimson gore with the Loves of Albion & Canaan
Opening along the Valley of Rephaim, weaving over the Caves of   e
    Machpelah

PLATE 65

To decide Two Worlds with a great decision: a World of Mercy, and
A World of Justice: the World of Mercy for Salvation
To cast Luvah into the Wrath, and Albion into the Pity
In the Two Contraries of Humanity & in the Four Regions.

For in the depths of Albions bosom in the eastern heaven,   5
They sound the clarions strong! they chain the howling Captives!   c
They cast the lots into the helmet: they give the oath of blood in Lam-
   beth
They vote the death of Luvah, & they naild him to Albions Tree in
   Bath:
They staind him with poisonous blue, they inwove him in cruel roots
To die a death of Six thousand years bound round with vegetation   10
The sun was black & the moon rolld a useless globe thro Britain!

Then left the Sons of Urizen the plow & harrow, the loom
The hammer & the chisel, & the rule & compasses; from London fleeing
They forg'd the sword on Cheviot, the chariot of war & the battle-ax,
The trumpet fitted to mortal battle, & the flute of summer in   15
   Annandale
And all the Arts of Life. they changd into the Arts of Death in Albion.
The hour-glass contemnd because its simple workmanship.
Was like the workmanship of the plowman, & the water wheel,
That raises water into cisterns: broken & burnd with fire:
Because its workmanship. was like the workmanship of the shepherd.   20
And in their stead, intricate wheels invented, wheel without wheel:
To perplex youth in their outgoings, & to bind to labours in Albion
Of day & night the myriads of eternity that they may grind
And polish brass & iron hour after hour laborious task!
Kept ignorant of its use, that they might spend the days of wisdom   25
In sorrowful drudgery, to obtain a scanty pittance of bread:
In ignorance to view a small portion & think that All,
And call it Demonstration: blind to all the simple rules of life.

Now: now the battle rages round thy tender limbs O Vala,
Now smile among thy bitter tears: now put on all thy beauty   30
Is not the wound of the sword sweet! & the broken bone delightful?
Wilt thou now smile among the scythes when the wounded groan in
   the field[?]
We were carried away in thousands from London; & in tens
Of thousands from Westminster & Marybone in ships closd up:
Chaind hand & foot, compelld to fight under the iron whips   35
Of our captains; fearing our officers more than the enemy.
Lift up thy blue eyes Vala & put on thy sapphire shoes:
O melancholy Magdalen behold the morning over Malden break;
Gird on thy flaming zone, descend into the sepulcher of Canterbury.
Scatter the blood from thy golden brow, the tears from thy silver locks: 40

Shake off the waters from thy wings! & the dust from thy white
    garments
Remember all thy feigned terrors on the secret couch of Lambeths Vale
When the sun rose in glowing morn, with arms of mighty hosts
Marching to battle who was wont to rise with Urizens harps
Girt as a sower with his seed to scatter life abroad over Albion: 45
Arise O Vala! bring the bow of Urizen: bring the swift arrows of light.
How rag'd the golden horses of Urizen, compelld to the chariot of love!
Compelld to leave the plow to the ox, to snuff up the winds of
    desolation
To trample the corn fields in boastful neighings: this is no gentle harp
This is no warbling brook, nor shadow of a mirtle tree: 50
But blood and wounds and dismal cries, and shadows of the oak:
And hearts laid open to the light, by the broad grizly sword:
And bowels hid in hammerd steel rip'd quivering on the ground.
Call forth thy smiles of soft deceit: call forth thy cloudy tears:
We hear thy sighs in trumpets shrill when morn shall blood renew.   55

So sang the Spectre Sons of Albion round Luvahs Stone of Trial:
Mocking and deriding at the writhings of their Victim on Salisbury:
Drinking his Emanation in intoxicating bliss rejoicing in Giant dance;
For a Spectre has no Emanation but what he imbibes from decieving
A Victim! Then he becomes her Priest & she his Tabernacle.   60
And his Oak Grove, till the Victim rend the woven Veil.
In the end of his sleep when Jesus calls him from his grave

Howling the Victims on the Druid Altars yield their souls
To the stern Warriors: lovely sport the Daughters round their Victims;
Drinking their lives in sweet intoxication. hence arose from Bath   65
Soft deluding odours, in spiral volutions intricately winding
Over Albions mountains, a feminine indefinite cruel delusion.
Astonishd: terrified & in pain & torment. Sudden they behold
Their own Parent the Emanation of their murderd Enemy
Become their Emanation and their Temple and Tabernacle   70
They knew not. this Vala was their beloved Mother Vala Albions Wife.

Terrified at the sight of the Victim: at his distorted sinews!   c
The tremblings of Vala vibrate thro' the limbs of Albions Sons:
While they rejoice over Luvah in mockery & bitter scorn:
Sudden they become like what they behold in howlings & deadly pain. 75
Spasms smite their features, sinews & limbs: pale they look on one
    another.
They turn, contorted: their iron necks bend unwilling towards
Luvah: their lips tremble: their muscular fibres are crampd & smitten
They become like what they behold! Yet immense in strength & power,
PLATE 66
In awful pomp & gold, in all the precious unhewn stones of Eden

They build a stupendous Building on the Plain of Salisbury; with
    chains
Of rocks round London Stone: of Reasonings: of unhewn
    Demonstrations
In labyrinthine arches. (Mighty Urizen the Architect.) thro which
The Heavens might revolve & Eternity be bound in their chain.   5
Labour unparallelld! a wondrous rocky World of cruel destiny
Rocks piled on rocks reaching the stars: stretching from pole to pole.
The Building is Natural Religion & its Altars Natural Morality
A building of eternal death: whose proportions are eternal despair
Here Vala stood turning the iron Spindle of destruction   10
From heaven to earth: howling! invisible! but not invisible
Her Two Covering Cherubs afterwards named Voltaire & Rousseau:
Two frowning Rocks: on each side of the Cove & Stone of Torture:
Frozen Sons of the feminine Tabernacle of Bacon, Newton & Locke.
For Luvah is France: the Victim of the Spectres of Albion.   15

Los beheld in terror: he pour'd his loud storms on the Furnaces: c
The Daughters of Albion clothed in garments of needle work
Strip them off from their shoulders and bosoms, they lay aside
Their garments; they sit naked upon the Stone of trial.
The Knife of flint passes over the howling Victim: his blood   20
Gushes & stains the fair side of the fair Daug[h]ters of Albion.
They put aside his curls; they divide his seven locks upon
His forehead: they bind his forehead with thorns of iron
They put into his hand a reed, they mock: Saying: Behold
The King of Canaan whose are seven hundred chariots of iron!   25
They take off his vesture whole with their Knives of flint:

But they cut asunder his inner garments: searching with
Their cruel fingers for his heart, & there they enter in pomp,
In many tears; & there they erect a temple & an altar:
They pour cold water on his brain in front, to cause   30
Lids to grow over his eyes in veils of tears: and caverns
To freeze over his nostrils, while they feed his tongue from cups
And dishes of painted clay. Glowing with beauty & cruelty:
They obscure the sun & the moon; no eye can look upon them.

Ah! alas! at the sight of the Victim, & at sight of those who are smitten,   35
All who see. become what they behold. their eyes are coverd
With veils of tears and their nostrils & tongues shrunk up
Their ear bent outwards. as their Victim, so are they in the pangs
Of unconquerable fear! amidst delights of revenge Earth-shaking!
And as their eye & ear shrunk, the heavens shrunk away   40
The Divine Vision became First a burning flame, then a column
Of fire, then an awful fiery wheel surrounding earth & heaven:
And then a globe of blood wandering distant in an unknown night:
Afar into the unknown night the mountains fled away:

Six months of mortality; a summer: & six months of mortality; a winter: 45
The Human form began to be alterd by the Daughters of Albion
And the perceptions to be dissipated into the Indefinite. Becoming
A mighty Polypus nam'd Albions Tree: they tie the Veins
And Nerves into two knots: & the Seed into a double knot:
They look forth: the Sun is shrunk: the Heavens are shrunk 50
Away into the far remote: and the Trees & Mountains witherd
Into indefinite cloudy shadows in darkness & separation.
By Invisible Hatreds adjoind, they seem remote and separate
From each other; and yet are a Mighty Polypus in the Deep!
As the Mistletoe grows on the Oak, so Albions Tree on Eternity: Lo! 55
He who will not comingle in Love, must be adjoind by Hate

They look forth from Stone-henge! from the Cove round London Stone
They look on one another: the mountain calls out to the mountain:
Plinlimmon shrunk away: Snowdon trembled: the mountains
Of Wales & Scotland beheld the descending War: the routed flying: 60
Red run the streams of Albion: Thames is drunk with blood:
As Gwendolen cast the shuttle of war: as Cambel returnd the beam.
The Humber & the Severn: are drunk with the blood of the slain:
London feels his brain cut round: Edinburghs heart is circumscribed!
York & Lincoln hide among the flocks, because of the griding Knife. 65
Worcester & Hereford: Oxford & Cambridge reel & stagger,
Overwearied with howling: Wales & Scotland alone sustain the fight!
The inhabitants are sick to death: they labour to divide into Days
And Nights, the uncertain Periods. and into Weeks & Months. In vain
They send the Dove & Raven: & in vain the Serpent over the 70
    mountains.
And in vain the Eagle & Lion over the four-fold wilderness.
They return not: but generate in rocky places desolate.
They return not; but build a habitation separate from Man.
The Sun forgets his course like a drunken man; he hesitates,
Upon the Cheselden hills, thinking to sleep on the Severn 75
In vain: he is hurried afar into an unknown Night
He bleeds in torrents of blood as he rolls thro heaven above
He chokes up the paths of the sky; the Moon is leprous as snow:
Trembling & descending down seeking to rest upon high Mona:
Scattering her leprous snows in flakes of disease over Albion. 80
The Stars flee remote: the heaven is iron, the earth is sulphur,
And all the mountains & hills shrink up like a withering gourd,
As the Senses of Men shrink together under the Knife of flint,
In the hands of Albions Daughters, among the Druid Temples.
PLATE 67
By those who drink their blood & the blood of their Covenant

And the Twelve Daughters of Albion united in Rahab & Tirzah   e
A Double Female: and they drew out from the Rocky Stones
Fibres of Life to Weave for every Female is a Golden Loom

The Rocks are opake hardnesses covering all Vegetated things.   5
And as they Wove & Cut from the Looms in various divisions
Stretching over Europe & Asia from Ireland to Japan
They divided into many lovely Daughters to be counterparts
To those they Wove, for when they Wove a Male, they divided
Into a Female to the Woven Male. in opake hardness   10
They cut the Fibres from the Rocks groaning in pain they Weave;
Calling the Rocks Atomic Origins of Existence; denying Eternity
By the Atheistical Epicurean Philosophy of Albions Tree
Such are the Feminine & Masculine when separated from Man
They call the Rocks Parents of Men, & adore the frowning Chaos   15
Dancing around in howling pain clothed in the bloody Veil.
Hiding Albions Sons within the Veil, closing Jerusalems
Sons without; to feed with their Souls the Spectres of Albion
Ashamed to give Love openly to the piteous & merciful Man
Counting him an imbecile mockery: but the Warrior   20
They adore: & his revenge cherish with the blood of the Innocent
They drink up Dan & Gad, to feed with milk Skofeld & Kotope
They strip off Josephs Coat & dip it in the blood of battle

Tirzah sits weeping to hear the shrieks of the dying: her Knife
Of flint is in her hand: she passes it over the howling Victim[.]   25
The Daughters Weave their Work in loud cries over the Rock
Of Horeb! still eyeing Albions Cliffs eagerly siezing & twisting
The threads of Vala & Jerusalem running from mountain to mountain
Over the whole Earth: loud the Warriors rage in Beth Peor
Beneath the iron whips of their Captains & consecrated banners   30
Loud the Sun & Moon rage in the conflict: loud the Stars
Shout in the night of battle & their spears grow to their hands
With blood, weaving the deaths of the Mighty into a Tabernacle
For Rahab & Tirzah; till the Great Polypus of Generation covered the
     Earth.

In Verulam the Polypus's Head, winding around his bulk   35
Thro Rochester, and Chichester, & Exeter & Salisbury,
To Bristol: & his Heart beat strong on Salisbury Plain
Shooting out Fibres round the Earth, thro Gaul & Italy
And Greece, & along the Sea of Rephaim into Judea
To Sodom & Gomorrha: thence to India, China & Japan   40

The Twelve Daughters in Rahab & Tirzah have circumscribd the Brain
Beneath & pierced it thro the midst with a golden pin.
Blood hath staind her fair side beneath her bosom.

O thou poor Human Form! said she. O thou poor child of woe!   c
Why wilt thou wander away from Tirzah: why me compel to bind   45
     thee?
If thou dost go away from me I shall consume upon these Rocks[.]
These fibres of thine eyes that used to beam in distant heavens

Away from me: I have bound down with a hot iron.
These nostrils that expanded with delight in morning skies
I have bent downward with lead melted in my roaring furnaces   50
Of affliction; of love; of sweet despair; of torment unendurable
My soul is seven furnaces, incessant roars the bellows
Upon my terribly flaming heart, the molten metal runs
In channels thro my fiery limbs: O love! O pity! O fear!
O pain! O the pangs, the bitter pangs of love forsaken   55
Ephraim was a wilderness of joy where all my wild beasts ran
The River Kanah wanderd by my sweet Manassehs side
To see the boy spring into heavens sounding from my sight!
Go Noah fetch the girdle of strong brass, heat it red-hot:
Press it around the loins of this ever expanding cruelty   60
Shriek not so my only love! I refuse thy joys: I drink
Thy shrieks because Hand & Hyle are cruel & obdurate to me

PLATE 68
O Skofield why art thou cruel? Lo Joseph is thine! to make
You One: to weave you both in the same mantle of skin
Bind him down Sisters bind him down on Ebal. Mount of cursing:
Malah come forth from Lebanon: & Hoglah from Mount Sinai:
Come circumscribe this tongue of sweets & with a screw of iron   5
Fasten this ear into the rock! Milcah the task is thine
Weep not so Sisters! weep not so! our life depends on this
Or mercy & truth are fled away from Shechem & Mount Gilead
Unless my beloved is bound upon the Stems of Vegetation

And thus the Warriors cry, in the hot day of Victory, in Songs.   ᶜ 10

Look: the beautiful Daughter of Albion sits naked upon the Stone
Her panting Victim beside her: her heart is drunk with blood
Tho her brain is not drunk with wine: she goes forth from Albion
In pride of beauty: in cruelty of holiness: in the brightness
Of her tabernacle, & her ark & secret place, the beautiful Daughter   15
Of Albion, delights the eyes of the Kings. their hearts & the
Hearts of their Warriors glow hot before Thor & Friga. O Molech!
O Chemosh! O Bacchus! O Venus! O Double God of Generation
The Heavens are cut like a mantle around from the Cliffs of Albion
Across Europe; across Africa; in howlings & deadly War   20
A sheet & veil & curtain of blood is let down from Heaven
Across the hills of Ephraim & down Mount Olivet to
The Valley of the Jebusite: Molech rejoices in heaven
He sees the Twelve Daughters naked upon the Twelve Stones
Themselves condensing to rocks & into the Ribs of a Man   25
Lo they shoot forth in tender Nerves across Europe & Asia
Lo they rest upon the Tribes, where their panting Victims lie[.]
Molech rushes into the Kings in love to the beautiful Daughters
But they frown & delight in cruelty, refusing all other joy

Bring your Offerings, your first begotten: pamperd with milk & blood 30
Your first born of seven years old: be they Males or Females:
To the beautiful Daughters of Albion! they sport before the Kings
Clothed in the skin of the Victim! blood! human blood! is the life
And delightful food of the Warrior: the well fed Warriors flesh
Of him who is slain in War: fills the Valleys of Ephraim with 35
Breeding Women walking in pride & bringing forth under green trees
With pleasure, without pain, for their food is. blood of the Captive
Molech rejoices thro the Land from Havilah to Shur: he rejoices
In moral law & its severe penalties: loud Shaddai & Jehovah
Thunder above: when they see the Twelve panting Victims 40
On the Twelve Stones of Power, & the beautiful Daughters of Albion
If you dare rend their Veil with your Spear; you are healed of Love!
From the Hills of Camberwell & Wimbledon: from the Valleys
Of Walton & Esher: from Stone-henge & from Maldens Cove
Jerusalems Pillars fall in the rendings of fierce War 45
Over France & Germany: upon the Rhine & Danube
Reuben & Benjamin flee; they hide in the Valley of Rephaim
Why trembles the Warriors limbs when he beholds thy beauty
Spotted with Victims blood? by the fires of thy secret tabernacle
And thy ark & holy place: at thy frowns: at thy dire revenge 50
Smitten as Uzzah of old: his armour is softend; his spear   c
And sword faint in his hand, from Albion across Great Tartary
O beautiful Daughter of Albion: cruelty is thy delight
O Virgin of terrible eyes, who dwellest by Valleys of springs
Beneath the Mountains of Lebanon, in the City of Rehob in Hamath   c 55
Taught to touch the harp: to dance in the Circle of Warriors
Before the Kings of Canaan: to cut the flesh from the Victim
To roast the flesh in fire: to examine the Infants limbs
In cruelties of holiness: to refuse the joys of love: to bring
The Spies from Egypt, to raise jealousy in the bosoms of the Twelve 60
Kings of Canaan: then to let the Spies depart to Meribah Kadesh   c
To the place of the Amalekite; I am drunk with unsatiated love
I must rush again to War: for the Virgin has frownd & refusd   c
Sometimes I curse & sometimes bless thy fascinating beauty
Once Man was occupied in intellectual pleasures & energies 65
But now my soul is harrowd with grief & fear & love & desire
And now I hate & now I love & Intellect is no more:
There is no time for any thing but the torments of love & desire
The Feminine & Masculine Shadows soft, mild & ever varying
In beauty: are Shadows now no more, but Rocks in Horeb 70

PLATE 69
Then all the Males combined into One Male & every one   t,c
Became a ravening eating Cancer growing in the Female
A Polypus of Roots of Reasoning Doubt Despair & Death.

Going forth & returning from Albions Rocks to Canaan:
Devouring Jerusalem from every Nation of the Earth.   5

Envying stood the enormous Form at variance with Itself
In all its Members: in eternal torment of love & jealousy:
Drivn forth by Los time after time from Albions cliffy shore,
Drawing the free loves of Jerusalem into infernal bondage;
That they might be born in contentions of Chastity & in   10
Deadly Hate between Leah & Rachel, Daughters of Deceit & Fraud
Bearing the Images of various Species of Contention
And Jealousy & Abhorrence & Revenge & deadly Murder.
Till they refuse liberty to the Male; & not like Beulah
Where every Female delights to give her maiden to her husband   15
The Female searches sea & land for gratifications to the
Male Genius: who in return clothes her in gems & gold
And feeds her with the food of Eden. hence all her beauty beams
She Creates at her will a little moony night & silence
With Spaces of sweet gardens & a tent of elegant beauty: 20
Closed in by a sandy desart & a night of stars shining.
And a little tender moon & hovering angels on the wing.
And the Male gives a Time & Revolution to her Space
Till the time of love is passed in ever varying delights
For All Things Exist in the Human Imagination   25
And thence in Beulah they are stolen by secret amorous theft,
Till they have had Punishment enough to make them commit Crimes[.]
Hence rose the Tabernacle in the Wilderness & all its Offerings,
From Male & Female Loves in Beulah & their Jealousies
But no one can consummate Female bliss in Los's World without   30
Becoming a Generated Mortal, a Vegetating Death

And now the Spectres of the Dead awake in Beulah: all
The Jealousies become Murderous: uniting together in Rahab
A Religion of Chastity, forming a Commerce to sell Loves,
With Moral Law, an Equal Balance, not going down with decision   35
Therefore the Male severe & cruel filld with stern Revenge:
Mutual Hate returns & mutual Deceit & mutual Fear.

Hence the Infernal Veil grows in the disobedient Female: e
Which Jesus rends & the whole Druid Law removes away
From the Inner Sanctuary: a False Holiness hid within the Center,   40
For the Sanctuary of Eden. is in the Camp: in the Outline,
In the Circumference: & every Minute Particular is Holy:
Embraces are Cominglings: from the Head even to the Feet;
And not a pompous High Priest entering by a Secret Place.

Jerusalem pined in her inmost soul over Wandering Reuben   e 45
As she slept in Beulahs Night hid by the Daughters of Beulah

PLATE 70

And this the form of mighty Hand sitting on Albions cliffs
Before the face of Albion, a mighty threatning Form.

His bosom wide & shoulders huge overspreading wondrous
Bear Three strong sinewy Necks & Three awful & terrible Heads
Three Brains in contradictory council brooding incessantly.   5
Neither daring to put in act its councils, fearing each-other,
Therefore rejecting Ideas as nothing & holding all Wisdom
To consist. in the agreements & disagree[me]nts of Ideas.
Plotting to devour Albions Body of Humanity & Love.

Such Form the aggregate of the Twelve Sons of Albion took; & such   10
Their appearance when combind: but often by birth-pangs & loud groans
They divide to Twelve: the key-bones & the chest dividing in pain
Disclose a hideous orifice; thence issuing the Giant-brood
Arise as the smoke of the furnace, shaking the rocks from sea to sea.
And there they combine into Three Forms, named Bacon & Newton &   15
    Locke,
In the Oak Groves of Albion which overspread all the Earth.

Imputing Sin & Righteousness to Individuals; Rahab   c
Sat deep within him hid: his Feminine Power unreveal'd
Brooding Abstract Philosophy. to destroy Imagination, the Divine-
-Humanity A Three-fold Wonder: feminine: most beautiful: Three-   20
    fold
Each within other. On her white marble & even Neck, her Heart
Inorb'd and bonified: with locks of shadowing modesty, shining
Over her beautiful Female features, soft flourishing in beauty
Beams mild, all love and all perfection, that when the lips
Recieve a kiss from Gods or Men, a threefold kiss returns   25
From the pressd loveliness: so her whole immortal form three-fold
Three-fold embrace returns: consuming lives of Gods & Men
In fires of beauty melting them as gold & silver in the furnace[.]
Her Brain enlabyrinths the whole heaven of her bosom & loins
To put in act what her Heart wills; O who can withstand her power   30
Her name is Vala in Eternity: in Time her name is Rahab

The Starry Heavens all were fled from the mighty limbs of Albion   c
PLATE 71
And above Albions Land was seen the Heavenly Canaan
As the Substance is to the Shadow: and above Albions Twelve Sons
Were seen Jerusalems Sons: and all the Twelve Tribes spreading
Over Albion. As the Soul is to the Body, so Jerusalems Sons,
Are to the Sons of Albion: and Jerusalem is Albions Emanation   5

What is Above is Within, for every-thing in Eternity is translucent:
The Circumference is Within: Without, is formed the Selfish Center

And the Circumference still expands going forward to Eternity.
And the Center has Eternal States! these States we now explore.

And these the Names of Albions Twelve Sons, & of his Twelve   10
    Daughters
With their Districts. Hand dwelt in Selsey & had Sussex & Surrey
And Kent & Middlesex: all their Rivers & their Hills, of flocks & herds:
Their Villages Towns Cities Sea-Ports Temples sublime Cathedrals;
All were his Friends & their Sons & Daughters intermarry in Beulah
For all are Men in Eternity. Rivers Mountains Cities Villages,   15
All are Human & when you enter into their Bosoms you walk
In Heavens & Earths; as in your own Bosom you bear your Heaven
And Earth, & all you behold, tho it appears Without it is Within
In your Imagination of which this World of Mortality is but a Shadow.

Hyle dwelt in Winchester comprehending Hants Dorset Devon   20
    Cornwall.
Their Villages Cities SeaPorts, their Corn fields & Gardens spacious
Palaces, Rivers & Mountains, and between Hand & Hyle arose
Gwendolen & Cambel who is Boadicea: they go abroad & return
Like lovely beams of light from the mingled affections of the Brothers
The Inhabitants of the whole Earth rejoice in their beautiful light.   25

Coban dwelt in Bath. Somerset Wiltshire Gloucestershire,
Obeyd his awful voice Ignoge is his lovely Emanation;
She adjoind with Gwantokes Children, soon lovely Cordella arose.
Gwantoke forgave & joyd over South Wales & all its Mountains.

Peachey had North Wales Shropshire Cheshire & the Isle of Man.   30
His Emanation is Mehetabel terrible & lovely upon the Mountains

Brertun had Yorkshire Durham Westmoreland & his Emanation
Is Ragan, she adjoind to Slade, & produced Gonorill far beaming.

Slade had Lincoln Stafford Derby Nottingham & his lovely
Emanation Gonorill rejoices over hills & rocks & woods & rivers.   35

Huttn had Warwick Northampton Bedford Buckingham
Leicester & Berkshire: & his Emanation is Gwinefred beautiful

Skofeld had Ely Rutland Cambridge Huntingdon Norfolk
Suffolk Hartford & Essex: & his Emanation is Gwinevera
Beautiful, she beams towards the east, all kinds of precious stones   40
And pearl, with instruments of music in holy Jerusalem

Kox had Oxford Warwick Wilts: his Emanation is Estrild:
Joind with Cordella she shines southward over the Atlantic.

Kotope had Hereford Stafford Worcester, & his Emanation
Is Sabrina joind with Mehetabel she shines west over America   45

Bowen had all Scotland, the Isles, Northumberland & Cumberland
His Emanation is Conwenna, she shines a triple form
Over the north with pearly beams gorgeous & terrible
Jerusalem & Vala rejoice in Bowen & Conwenna.

But the Four Sons of Jerusalem that never were Generated 50
Are Rintrah and Palamabron and Theotormon and Bromion. They
Dwell over the Four Provinces of Ireland in heavenly light
The Four Universities of Scotland, & in Oxford & Cambridge &
    Winchester

But now Albion is darkened & Jerusalem lies in ruins:
Above the Mountains of Albion, above the head of Los. 55

And Los shouted with ceaseless shoutings & his tears poured down e
His immortal cheeks, rearing his hands to heaven for aid Divine!
But he spoke not to Albion: fearing lest Albion should turn his Back
Against the Divine Vision: & fall over the Precipice of Eternal Death.
But he receded before Albion & before Vala weaving the Veil 60
With the iron shuttle of War among the rooted Oaks of Albion;
Weeping & shouting to the Lord day & night; and his Children
Wept round him as a flock silent Seven Days of Eternity

PLATE 72
And the Thirty-two Counties of the Four Provinces of Ireland e
Are thus divided: The Four Counties are in the Four Camps
Munster South in Reubens Gate, Connaut West in Josephs Gate
Ulster North in Dans Gate, Leinster East in Judahs Gate

For Albion in Eternity has Sixteen Gates among his Pillars 5
But the Four towards the West were Walled up & the Twelve
That front the Four other Points were turned Four Square
By Los for Jerusalems sake & called the Gates of Jerusalem
Because Twelve Sons of Jerusalem fled successive thro the Gates
But the Four Sons of Jerusalem who fled not but remaind 10
Are Rintrah & Palamabron & Theotormon & Bromion
The Four that remain with Los to guard the Western Wall
And these Four remain to guard the Four Walls of Jerusalem
Whose foundations remain in the Thirty-two Counties of Ireland
And in Twelve Counties of Wales, & in the Forty Counties 15
Of England & in the Thirty-six Counties of Scotland

And the names of the Thirty-two Counties of Ireland are these
Under Judah & Issachar & Zebulun are Lowth Longford
Eastmeath Westmeath Dublin Kildare Kings County
Queens County Wicklow Catherloh Wexford Kilkenny 20
And those under Reuben & Simeon & Levi are these
Waterford Tipperary Cork Limerick Kerry Clare
And those under Ephraim Manasseh & Benjamin are these
Galway Roscommon Mayo Sligo Leitrim

And those under Dan Asher & Napthali are these   25
Donnegal Antrim Tyrone Fermanagh Armagh Londonderry
Down Managhan Cavan. These are the Land of Erin

All these Center in London & in Golgonooza. from whence
They are Created continually East & West & North & South
And from them are Created all the Nations of the Earth   30
Europe & Asia & Africa & America, in fury Fourfold!

And Thirty-two the Nations: to dwell in Jerusalems Gates
O Come ye Nations Come ye People Come up to Jerusalem
Return Jerusalem & dwell together as of old! Return
Return! O Albion let Jerusalem overspread all Nations   35
As in the times of old! O Albion awake! Reuben wanders
The Nations wait for Jerusalem, they look up for the Bride

France Spain Italy Germany Poland Russia Sweden Turkey
Arabia Palestine Persia Hindostan China Tartary Siberia
Egypt Lybia Ethiopia Guinea Caffraria Negroland Morocco   40
Congo Zaara Canada Greenland Carolina Mexico
Peru Patagonia Amazonia Brazil. Thirty-two Nations
And under these Thirty-two Classes of Islands in the Ocean
All the Nations Peoples & Tongues throughout all the Earth

And the Four Gates of Los surround the Universe Within and   45
Without; & whatever is visible in the Vegetable Earth, the same
Is visible in the Mundane Shell; reversd in mountain & vale
And a Son of Eden was set over each Daughter of Beulah to guard
In Albions Tomb the wondrous Creation: & the Four-fold Gate
Towards Beulah is to the South[.] Fenelon, Guion, Teresa,   50
Whitefield & Hervey, guard that Gate; with all the gentle Souls
Who guide the great Wine-press of Love; Four precious Stones that
    Gate:

                                    t

PLATE 73

Such are Cathedrons golden Halls: in the City of Golgonooza   c

And Los's Furnaces howl loud; living: self-moving: lamenting
With fury & despair, & they stretch from South to North
Thro all the Four Points: Lo! the Labourers at the Furnaces
Rintrah & Palamabron, Theotormon & Bromion, loud labring   5
With the innumerable multitudes of Golgonooza, round the Anvils
Of Death. But how they came forth from the Furnaces & how long
Vast & severe the anguish eer they knew their Father; were
Long to tell & of the iron rollers, golden axle-trees & yokes
Of brass, iron chains & braces & the gold, silver & brass   10
Mingled or separate: for swords; arrows; cannons; mortars
The terrible ball: the wedge: the loud sounding hammer of destruction
The sounding flail to thresh: the winnow: to winnow kingdoms
The water wheel & mill of many innumerable wheels resistless
Over the Four fold Monarchy from Earth to the Mundane Shell.   15

Perusing Albions Tomb in the starry characters of Og & Anak:
To Create the lion & wolf the bear: the tyger & ounce:
To Create the wooly lamb & downy fowl & scaly serpent
The summer & winter: day & night: the sun & moon & stars
The tree: the plant: the flower: the rock: the stone: the metal: 20
Of Vegetative Nature: by their hard restricting condensations.

Where Luvahs World of Opakeness grew to a period: It
Became a Limit, a Rocky hardness without form & void
Accumulating without end: here Los who is of the Elohim
Opens the Furnaces of affliction in the Emanation   25
Fixing the Sexual into an ever-prolific Generation
Naming the Limit of Opakeness Satan & the Limit of Contraction
Adam, who is Peleg & Joktan: & Esau & Jacob: & Saul & David   c

Voltaire insinuates that these Limits are the cruel work of God
Mocking the Remover of Limits & the Resurrection of the Dead   30
Setting up Kings in wrath: in holiness of Natural Religion
Which Los with his mighty Hammer demolishes time on time
In miracles & wonders in the Four-fold Desart of Albion
Permanently Creating to be in Time Reveald & Demolishd
Satan Cain Tubal Nimrod Pharoh Priam Bladud Belin   35
Arthur Alfred the Norman Conqueror Richard John
[Edward Henry Elizabeth James Charles William George]   t
And all the Kings & Nobles of the Earth & all their Glories
These are Created by Rahab & Tirzah in Ulro: but around
These, to preserve them from Eternal Death Los Creates   40
Adam Noah Abraham Moses Samuel David Ezekiel
[Pythagoras Socrates Euripedes Virgil Dante Milton]   t
Dissipating the rocky forms of Death, by his thunderous Hammer[.]

As the Pilgrim passes while the Country permanent remains
So Men pass on: but States remain permanent for ever   45

The Spectres of the Dead howl round the porches of Los   c
In the terrible Family feuds of Albions cities & villages
To devour the Body of Albion, hungring & thirsting & ravning
The Sons of Los clothe them & feed, & provide houses & gardens[.]
And every Human Vegetated Form in its inward recesses   50
Is a house of ple[as]antness & a garden of delight Built by the
Sons & Daughters of Los in Bowlahoola & in Cathedron

From London to York & Edinburgh the Furnaces rage terrible
Primrose Hill is the mouth of the Furnace & the Iron Door;
PLATE 74
The Four Zoa's clouded rage; Urizen stood by Albion
With Rintrah and Palamabron and Theotormon and Bromion
These Four are Verulam & London & York & Edinburgh
And the Four Zoa's are Urizen & Luvah & Tharmas & Urthona
In opposition deadly, and their Wheels in poisonous   5
And deadly stupor turn'd against each other loud & fierce
Entering into the Reasoning Power, forsaking Imagination
They became Spectres; & their Human Bodies were reposed
In Beulah, by the Daughters of Beulah with tears & lamentations

The Spectre is the Reasoning Power in Man; & when separated   10
From Imagination, and closing itself as in steel, in a Ratio
Of the Things of Memory. It thence frames Laws & Moralities
To destroy Imagination! the Divine Body, by Martyrdoms & Wars

Teach me O Holy Spirit the Testimony of Jesus! let me
Comprehend wonderous things out of the Divine Law[.]   15
I behold Babylon in the opening Streets of London, I behold
Jerusalem in ruins wandering about from house to house
This I behold the shudderings of death attend my steps
I walk up and down in Six Thousand Years: their Events are present
     before me
To tell how Los in grief & anger, whirling round his Hammer on high   20
Drave the Sons & Daughters of Albion from their ancient mountains
They became the Twelve Gods of Asia Opposing the Divine Vision

The Sons of Albion are Twelve: the Sons of Jerusalem Sixteen
I tell how Albions Sons by Harmonies of Concords & Discords   c
Opposed to Melody, and by Lights & Shades, opposed to Outline   25
And by Abstraction opposed to the Visions of Imagination
By cruel Laws divided Sixteen into Twelve Divisions
How Hyle roofd Los in Albions Cliffs by the Affections rent
Asunder & opposed to Thought, to draw Jerusalems Sons
Into the Vortex of his Wheels. therefore Hyle is called Gog   30
Age after age drawing them away towards Babylon

Babylon, the Rational Morality deluding to death the little ones
In strong temptations of stolen beauty; I tell how Reuben slept
On London Stone & the Daughters of Albion ran around admiring
His awful beauty: with Moral Virtue the fair deciever; offspring   35
Of Good & Evil, they divided him in love upon the Thames & sent
Him over Europe in streams of gore out of Cathedrons Looms
How Los drave them from Albion & they became Daughters of Canaan
Hence Albion was calld the Canaanite & all his Giant Sons.
Hence is my Theme. O Lord my Saviour, open thou the Gates   40
And I will lead forth thy Words, telling how the Daughters
Cut the Fibres of Reuben, how he rolld apart & took Root
In Bashan, terror-struck Albions Sons look toward Bashan
They have divided Simeon he also rolld apart in blood
Over the Nations till he took Root beneath the shining Looms   45
Of Albions Daughters in Philistea by the side of Amalek
They have divided Levi: he hath shot out into Forty eight Roots
Over the Land of Canaan: they have divided Judah
He hath took Root in Hebron, in the Land of Hand & Hyle
Dan: Napthali: Gad: Asher: Issachar: Zebulun: roll apart   50
From all the Nations of the Earth to dissipate into Non Entity

I see a Feminine Form arise from the Four terrible Zoas
Beautiful but terrible struggling to take a form of beauty
Rooted in Shechem: this is Dinah, the youthful form of Erin
The Wound I see in South Molton S[t]reet & Stratford place   55
Whence Joseph & Benjamin rolld apart away from the Nations
In vain they rolld apart; they are fixd into the Land of Cabul

PLATE 75
And Rahab Babylon the Great hath destroyed Jerusalem   c

Bath stood upon the Severn with Merlin & Bladud & Arthur
The Cup of Rahab in his hand: her Poisons Twenty-seven-fold

And all her Twenty-seven Heavens now hid & now reveal'd
Appear in strong delusive light of Time & Space drawn out   5
In shadowy pomp by the Eternal Prophet created evermore

For Los in Six Thousand Years walks up & down continually
That not one Moment of Time be lost & every revolution
Of Space he makes permanent in Bowlahoola & Cathedron.

And these the names of the Twenty-seven Heavens & their Churches   10
Adam, Seth, Enos, Cainan, Mahalaleel, Jared, Enoch,
Methuselah, Lamech; these are the Giants mighty, Hermaphroditic
Noah, Shem, Arphaxad, Cainan the Second, Salah, Heber,
Peleg, Reu, Serug, Nahor, Terah: these are the Female Males:
A Male within a Female hid as in an Ark & Curtains.   15
Abraham, Moses, Solomon, Paul, Constantine, Charlemaine,
Luther. these Seven are the Male Females: the Dragon Forms

The Female hid within a Male: thus Rahab is reveald
Mystery Babylon the Great: the Abomination of Desolation
Religion hid in War: a Dragon red, & hidden Harlot   20
But Jesus breaking thro' the Central Zones of Death & Hell
Opens Eternity in Time & Space; triumphant in Mercy

Thus are the Heavens formd by Los within the Mundane Shell
And where Luther ends Adam begins again in Eternal Circle
To awake the Prisoners of Death; to bring Albion again   25
With Luvah into light eternal, in his eternal day.

But now the Starry Heavens are fled from the mighty limbs of Albion

PLATE 77   t,c

To the Christians.

Devils are	I give you the end of a golden string, t
False Religions	Only wind it into a ball:
"Saul Saul"	It will lead you in at Heavens gate,
"Why persecutest thou me."	Built in Jerusalems wall.

We are told to abstain from fleshly desires that we may lose no time
from the Work of the Lord. Every moment lost, is a moment that cannot be redeemed   every pleasure that intermingles with the duty of our
station is a folly unredeemable & is planted like the seed of a wild flower
among our wheat. All the tortures of repentance. are tortures of self-re-
proach on account of our leaving the Divine Harvest to the Enemy,
the struggles of intanglement with incoherent roots. I know of no other
Christianity and of no other Gospel than the liberty both of body &
mind to exercise the Divine Arts of Imagination   Imagination the real
& eternal World of which this Vegetable Universe is but a faint shadow
& in which we shall live in our Eternal or Imaginative Bodies, when
these Vegetable Mortal Bodies are no more. The Apostles knew of no
other Gospel. What were all their spiritual gifts? What is the Divine
Spirit? is the Holy Ghost any other than an Intellectual Fountain?
What is the Harvest of the Gospel & its Labours? What is that Talent
which it is a curse to hide? What are the Treasures of Heaven which
we are to lay up for ourselves, are they any other than Mental Studies &
Performances? What are all the Gifts of the Gospel, are they not all
Mental Gifts? Is God a Spirit who must be worshipped in Spirit & in
Truth and are not the Gifts of the Spirit Every-thing to Man? O ye
Religious discountenance every one among you who shall pretend to de-
spise Art & Science! I call upon you in the Name of Jesus! What is the
Life of Man but Art & Science? is it Meat & Drink? is not the Body
more than Raiment? What is Mortality but the things relating to the
Body, which Dies? What is Immortality but the things relating to the
Spirit, which Lives Eternally! What is the Joy of Heaven but Improve-
ment in the things of the Spirit? What are the Pains of Hell but Igno-

rance, Bodily Lust, Idleness & devastation of the things of the Spirit[?]
Answer this to yourselves, & expel from among you those who pretend
to despise the labours of Art & Science, which alone are the labours of
the Gospel: Is not this plain & manifest to the thought? Can you think
at all & not pronounce heartily! That to Labour in Knowledge. is to
Build up Jerusalem: and to Despise Knowledge, is to Despise Jerusalem
& her Builders. And remember: He who despises & mocks a Mental
Gift in another; calling it pride & selfishness & sin; mocks Jesus the
giver of every Mental Gift, which always appear to the ignorance-loving
Hypocrite, as Sins. but that which is a Sin in the sight of cruel Man, is
not so in the sight of our kind God.

Let every Christian as much as in him lies engage himself openly &
publicly before all the World in some Mental pursuit for the Building
up of Jerusalem

I stood among my valleys of the south
And saw a flame of fire, even as a Wheel
Of fire surrounding all the heavens: it went
From west to east against the current of
Creation and devourd all things in its loud   5
Fury & thundering course round heaven & earth
By it the Sun was rolld into an orb:
By it the Moon faded into a globe,
Travelling thro the night: for from its dire
And restless fury, Man himself shrunk up   10
Into a little root a fathom long.
And I asked a Watcher & a Holy-One
Its Name? he answerd. It is the Wheel of Religion
I wept & said. Is this the law of Jesus
This terrible devouring sword turning every way   15
He answerd; Jesus died because he strove
Against the current of this Wheel: its Name
Is Caiaphas, the dark Preacher of Death
Of sin, of sorrow, & of punishment;
Opposing Nature! It is Natural Religion   20
But Jesus is the bright Preacher of Life
Creating Nature from this fiery Law,
By self-denial & forgiveness of Sin.
Go therefore, cast out devils in Christs name
Heal thou the sick of spiritual disease   25
Pity the evil, for thou art not sent
To smite with terror & with punishments
Those that are sick, like to the Pharisees
Crucifying & encompassing sea & land
For proselytes to tyranny & wrath.   30
But to the Publicans & Harlots go!

Teach them True Happiness, but let no curse
Go forth out of thy mouth to blight their peace
For Hell is opend to Heaven; thine eyes beheld
The dungeons burst & the Prisoners set free.   35

England! awake! awake! awake!
Jerusalem thy Sister calls!
Why wilt thou sleep the sleep of death?
And close her from thy ancient walls.

     Thy hills & valleys felt her feet,   5
      Gently upon their bosoms move:
     Thy gates beheld sweet Zions ways;
      Then was a time of joy and love.

   And now the time returns again:
    Our souls exult & Londons towers,   10
   Receive the Lamb of God to dwell
    In Englands green & pleasant bowers.

PLATE 78

Jerusalem. C 4

The Spectres of Albions Twelve Sons revolve mightily   c
Over the Tomb & over the Body: ravning to devour
The Sleeping Humanity. Los with his mace of iron
Walks round: loud his threats, loud his blows fall   c
On the rocky Spectres, as the Potter breaks the potsherds;   5
Dashing in pieces Self-righteousnesses: driving them from Albions
Cliffs: dividing them into Male & Female forms in his Furnaces
And on his Anvils: lest they destroy the Feminine Affections
They are broken. Loud howl the Spectres in his iron Furnace

While Los laments at his dire labours, viewing Jerusalem,   10
Sitting before his Furnaces clothed in sackcloth of hair;
Albions Twelve Sons surround the Forty-two Gates of Erin,
In terrible armour, raging against the Lamb & against Jerusalem,
Surrounding them with armies to destroy the Lamb of God.
They took their Mother Vala, and they crown'd her with gold: 15
They namd her Rahab, & gave her power over the Earth
The Concave Earth round Golgonooza in Entuthon Benython,
Even to the stars exalting her Throne, to build beyond the Throne
Of God and the Lamb, to destroy the Lamb & usurp the Throne of God
Drawing their Ulro Voidness round the Four-fold Humanity   20

Naked Jerusalem lay before the Gates upon Mount Zion
The Hill of Giants, all her foundations levelld with the dust!

Her Twelve Gates thrown down: her children carried into captivity
Herself in chains: this from within was seen in a dismal night
Outside, unknown before in Beulah, & the twelve gates were fill'd   25
With blood; from Japan eastward to the Giants causway, west
In Erins Continent: and Jerusalem wept upon Euphrates banks
Disorganizd; an evanescent shade, scarce seen or heard among
Her childrens Druid Temples dropping with blood wanderd weeping!
And thus her voice went forth in the darkness of Philisthea.   30

My brother & my father are no more! God hath forsaken me
The arrows of the Almighty pour upon me & my children
I have sinned and am an outcast from the Divine Presence!

PLATE 79

My tents are fall'n! my pillars are in ruins! my children dashd
Upon Egypts iron floors, & the marble pavements of Assyria;
I melt my soul in reasonings among the towers of Heshbon;   c
Mount Zion is become a cruel rock & no more dew
Nor rain: no more the spring of the rock appears: but cold   5
Hard & obdurate are the furrows of the mountain of wine & oil:
The mountain of blessing is itself a curse & an astonishment:
The hills of Judea are fallen with me into the deepest hell
Away from the Nations of the Earth, & from the Cities of the Nations;
I walk to Ephraim. I seek for Shiloh: I walk like a lost sheep   10
Among precipices of despair: in Goshen I seek for light
In vain: and in Gilead for a physician and a comforter.
Goshen hath followd Philistea: Gilead hath joind with Og!
They are become narrow places in a little and dark land:
How distant far from Albion! his hills & his valleys no more   15
Recieve the feet of Jerusalem: they have cast me quite away:
And Albion is himself shrunk to a narrow rock in the midst of the sea!
The plains of Sussex & Surrey, their hills of flocks & herds
No more seek to Jerusalem nor to the sound of my Holy-ones.
The Fifty-two Counties of England are hardend against me   20
As if I was not their Mother, they despise me & cast me out
London coverd the whole Earth. England encompassd the Nations:
And all the Nations of the Earth were seen in the Cities of Albion:
My pillars reachd from sea to sea: London beheld me come
From my east & from my west; he blessed me and gave   25
His children to my breasts, his sons & daughters to my knees
His aged parents sought me out in every city & village:
They discernd my countenance with joy! they shewd me to their sons
Saying Lo Jerusalem is here! she sitteth in our secret chambers
Levi and Judah & Issachar: Ephra[i]m, Manasseh, Gad and Dan   30
Are seen in our hills & valleys: they keep our flocks & herds:
They watch them in the night: and the Lamb of God appears among
        us!

The river Severn stayd his course at my command:
Thames poured his waters into my basons and baths:
Medway mingled with Kishon: Thames recievd the heavenly Jordan   35
Albion gave me to the whole Earth to walk up & down; to pour
Joy upon every mountain; to teach songs to the shepherd & plowman
I taught the ships of the Sea to sing the songs of Zion.
Italy saw me, in sublime astonishment: France was wholly mine:
As my garden & as my secret bath; Spain was my heavenly couch:
I slept in his golden hills: the Lamb of God met me there.   40
There we walked as in our secret chamber among our little ones
They looked upon our loves with joy: they beheld our secret joys:
With holy raptures of adoration rapd sublime in the Visions of God:
Germany; Poland & the North wooed my footsteps they found   45
My gates in all their mountains & my curtains in all their vales
The furniture of their houses was the furniture of my chamber
Turkey & Grecia saw my instr[u]ments of music, they arose
They siezd the harp: the flute: the mellow horn of Jerusalems joy
They sounded thanksgivings in my courts: Egypt & Lybia heard   50
The swarthy sons of Ethiopia stood round the Lamb of God
Enquiring for Jerusalem: he led them up my steps to my altar:
And thou America! I once beheld thee but now behold no more
Thy golden mountains where my Cherubim & Seraphim rejoicd
Together among my little-ones. But now, my Altars run with blood!   55
My fires are corrupt! my incense is a cloudy pestilence
Of seven diseases! Once a continual cloud of salvation. rose
From all my myriads; once the Four-fold World rejoicd among
The pillars of Jerusalem, between my winged Cherubim:
But now I am closd out from them in the narrow passages   60
Of the valleys of destruction, into a dark land of pitch & bitumen.
From Albions Tomb afar and from the four-fold wonders of God
Shrunk to a narrow doleful form in the dark land of Cabul;
There is Reuben & Gad & Joseph & Judah & Levi, closd up
In narrow vales: I walk & count the bones of my beloveds   65
Along the Valley of Destruction, among these Druid Temples
Which overspread all the Earth in patriarchal pomp & cruel pride
Tell me O Vala thy purposes; tell me wherefore thy shuttles
Drop with the gore of the slain; why Euphrates is red with blood
Wherefore in dreadful majesty & beauty outside appears   70
Thy Masculine from thy Feminine hardening against the heavens
To devour the Human! Why dost thou weep upon the wind among
These cruel Druid Temples: O Vala! Humanity is far above
Sexual organization; & the Visions of the Night of Beulah
Where Sexes wander in dreams of bliss among the Emanations   75
Where the Masculine & Feminine are nurs'd into Youth & Maiden
By the tears & smiles of Beulahs Daughters till the time of Sleep is past.
Wherefore then do you realize these nets of beauty & delusion

In open day to draw the souls of the Dead into the light.
Till Albion is shut out from every Nation under Heaven.   80
PLATE 80
Encompassd by the frozen Net and by the rooted Tree
I walk weeping in pangs of a Mothers torment for her Children:
I walk in affliction: I am a worm, and no living soul!
A worm going to eternal torment! raisd up in a night
To an eternal night of pain, lost! lost! lost! for ever!   ᵉ5

Beside her Vala howld upon the winds in pride of beauty
Lamenting among the timbrels of the Warriors: among the Captives
In cruel holiness, and her lamenting songs were from Arnon
And Jordan to Euphrates. Jerusalem followd trembling
Her children in captivity. listening to Valas lamentation   10
In the thick cloud & darkness. & the voice went forth from
The cloud. O rent in sunder from Jerusalem the Harlot daughter!
In an eternal condemnation in fierce burning flames
Of torment unendurable! and if once a Delusion be found
Woman must perish & the Heavens of Heavens remain no more   15

My Father gave to me command to murder Albion
In unreviving Death; my Love, my Luvah orderd me in night
To murder Albion the King of Men. he fought in battles fierce
He conquerd Luvah my beloved: he took me and my Father
He slew them: I revived them to life in my warm bosom   20
He saw them issue from my bosom, dark in Jealousy
He burnd before me: Luvah framd the Knife & Luvah gave
The Knife into his daughters hand! such thing was never known
Before in Albions land, that one should die a death never to be reviv'd!
For in our battles we the Slain men view with pity and love: 25
We soon revive them in the secret of our tabernacles
But I Vala, Luvahs daughter, keep his body embalmd in moral laws
With spices of sweet odours of lovely jealous stupefaction:
Within my bosom, lest he arise to life & slay my Luvah
Pity me then O Lamb of God! O Jesus pity me!   30
Come into Luvahs Tents, and seek not to revive the Dead!

So sang she: and the Spindle turnd furious as she sang: ᵉ
The Children of Jerusalem the Souls of those who sleep
Were caught into the flax of her Distaff, & in her Cloud
To weave Jerusalem a body according to her will   35
A Dragon form on Zion Hills most ancient promontory

The Spindle turnd in blood & fire: loud sound the trumpets
Of war: the cymbals play loud before the Captains
With Cambel & Gwendolen in dance and solemn song
The Cloud of Rahab vibrating with the Daughters of Albion   40
Los saw terrified, melted with pity & divided in wrath
He sent them over the narrow seas in pity and love

Among the Four Forests of Albion which overspread all the Earth
They go forth & return swift as a flash of lightning.
Among the tribes of warriors: among the Stones of power!   45
Against Jerusalem they rage thro all the Nations of Europe
Thro Italy & Grecia, to Lebanon & Persia & India.

The Serpent Temples thro the Earth, from the wide Plain of Salisbury
Resound with cries of Victims, shouts & songs & dying groans
And flames of dusky fire, to Amalek, Canaan and Moab[.]   50
And Rahab like a dismal and indefinite hovering Cloud
Refusd to take a definite form. she hoverd over all the Earth
Calling the definite, sin: defacing every definite form;
Invisible, or Visible, stretchd out in length or spread in breadth:
Over the Temples drinking groans of victims weeping in pity,   55
And joying in the pity, howling over Jerusalems walls.

Hand slept on Skiddaws top: drawn by the love of beautiful
Cambel: his bright, beaming Counterpart, divided from him
And her delusive light beamd fierce above the Mountain,
Soft: invisible: drinking his sighs in sweet intoxication: 60
Drawing out fibre by fibre: returning to Albions Tree
At night: and in the morning to Skiddaw; she sent him over
Mountainous Wales into the Loom of Cathedron fibre by fibre:
He ran in tender nerves across Europe to Jerusalems Shade,
To weave Jerusalem a Body repugnant to the Lamb.   65

Hyle on East Moor in rocky Derbyshire, rav'd to the Moon
For Gwendolen: she took up in bitter tears his anguishd heart,
That apparent to all in Eternity, glows like the Sun in the breast:
She hid it in his ribs & back: she hid his tongue with teeth
In terrible convulsions pitying & gratified drunk with pity   70
Glowing with loveliness before him, becoming apparent
According to his changes: she roll'd his kidneys round
Into two irregular forms: and looking on Albions dread Tree,
She wove two vessels of seed, beautiful as Skiddaws snow;

Giving them bends of self interest & selfish natural virtue: 75
She hid them in his loins; raving he ran among the rocks,
Compelld into a shape of Moral Virtue against the Lamb.
The invisible lovely one giving him a form according to
His Law a form against the Lamb of God opposd to Mercy
And playing in the thunderous Loom in sweet intoxication   80
Filling cups of silver & crystal with shrieks & cries, with groans
And dolorous sobs: the wine of lovers in the Wine-press of Luvah

O sister Cambel said Gwendolen, as their long beaming light   c
Mingled above the Mountain[:] what shall we do to keep
These awful forms in our soft bands: distracted with trembling   85

-235-

PLATE 81

I have mockd those who refused cruelty & I have admired
The cruel Warrior. I have refused to give love to Merlin the piteous.
He brings to me the Images of his Love & I reject in chastity
And turn them out into the streets for Harlots to be food
To the stern Warrior. I am become perfect in beauty over my Warrior   5
For Men are caught by Love: Woman is caught by Pride
That Love may only be obtaind in the passages of Death.
Let us look! let us examine! is the Cruel become an Infant
Or is he still a cruel Warrior? look Sisters, look! O piteous
I have destroyd Wandring Reuben who strove to bind my Will   10
I have stripd off Josephs beautiful integument for my Beloved,
The Cruel-one of Albion: to clothe him in gems of my Zone
I have named him Jehovah of Hosts. Humanity is become
A weeping Infant in ruind lovely Jerusalems folding Cloud:

In Heaven Love begets Love! but Fear is the Parent of Earthly Love!   t 15
And he who will not bend to Love must be subdud by Fear,

PLATE 82

I have heard Jerusalems groans; from Vala's cries & lamentations
I gather our eternal fate: Outcasts from life and love:
Unless we find a way to bind these awful Forms to our
Embrace we shall perish annihilate, discoverd our Delusions.
Look I have wrought without delusion: Look! I have wept!   5
And given soft milk mingled together with the spirits of flocks
Of lambs and doves, mingled together in cups and dishes
Of painted clay; the mighty Hyle is become a weeping infant;
Soon shall the Spectres of the Dead follow my weaving threads.

The Twelve Daughters of Albion attentive listen in secret shades   10
On Cambridge and Oxford beaming soft uniting with Rahabs cloud
While Gwendolen spoke to Cambel turning soft the spinning reel:
Or throwing the wingd shuttle; or drawing the cords with softest songs
The golden cords of the Looms animate beneath their touches soft,
Along the Island white, among the Druid Temples, while Gwendolen   15
Spoke to the Daughters of Albion standing on Skiddaws top.

So saying she took a Falshood & hid it in her left hand:
To entice her Sisters away to Babylon on Euphrates.
And thus she closed her left hand and utterd her Falshood:
Forgetting that Falshood is prophetic, she hid her hand behind her,   20
Upon her back behind her loins & thus utterd her Deceit.

I heard Enitharmon say to Los! Let the Daughters of Albion
Be scatterd abroad and let the name of Albion be forgotten!
Divide them into three! name them Amalek Canaan & Moab:
Let Albion remain a desolation without an inhabitant: 25
And let the Looms of Enitharmon & the Furnaces of Los
Create Jerusalem, & Babylon & Egypt & Moab & Amalek,
And Helle & Hesperia & Hindostan & China & Japan.
But hide America, for a Curse an Altar of Victims & a Holy Place.
See Sisters Canaan is pleasant, Egypt is as the Garden of Eden: 30
Babylon is our chief desire, Moab our bath in summer:
Let us lead the stems of this Tree let us plant it before Jerusalem
To judge the Friend of Sinners to death without the Veil:
To cut her off from America, to close up her secret Ark:
And the fury of Man exhaust in War! Woman permanent remain   35
See how the fires of our loins point eastward to Babylon
Look. Hyle is become an infant Love: look! behold! see him lie!
Upon my bosom. look! here is the lovely wayward form
That gave me sweet delight by his torments beneath my Veil;
By the fruit of Albions Tree I have fed him with sweet milk   40
By contentions of the mighty for Sacrifice of Captives;
Humanity the Great Delusion: is changd to War & Sacrifice:
I have naild his hands on Beth Rabbim & his [feet] on Heshbons Wall: t
O that I could live in his sight: O that I could bind him to my arm.

So saying: She drew aside her Veil from Mam-Tor to Dovedale   45
Discovering her own perfect beauty to the Daughters of Albion
And Hyle a winding Worm beneath [*her Loom upon the scales.*
Hyle was become a winding Worm:] & not a weeping Infant.
Trembling & pitying she screamd & fled upon the wind:
Hyle was a winding Worm and herself perfect in beauty: 50
The desarts tremble at his wrath: they shrink themselves in fear.

Cambel trembled with jealousy: she trembled! she envied!
The envy ran thro Cathedrons Looms into the Heart
Of mild Jerusalem, to destroy the Lamb of God. Jerusalem
Languishd upon Mount Olivet, East of mild Zions Hill.   55

Los saw the envious blight above his Seventh Furnace
On Londons Tower on the Thames: he drew Cambel in wrath,
Into his thundering Bellows, heaving it for a loud blast!
And with the blast of his Furnace upon fishy Billingsgate,
Beneath Albions fatal Tree, before the Gate of Los: 60
Shewd her the fibres of her beloved to ameliorate
The envy; loud she labourd in the Furnace of fire,
To form the mighty form of Hand according to her will.
In the Furnaces of Los & in the Wine-press treading day & night

Naked among the human clusters: bringing wine of anguish   65
To feed the afflicted in the Furnaces: she minded not
The raging flames, tho she returnd [*consumd day after day*
A redning skeleton in howling woe:] instead of beauty
Defo[r]mity: she gave her beauty to another: bearing abroad
Her struggling torment in her iron arms: and like a chain,   70
Binding his wrists & ankles with the iron arms of love.

Gwendolen saw the Infant in her siste[r]s arms; she howld
Over the forests with bitter tears, and over the winding Worm
Repentant: and she also in the eddying wind of Los's Bellows
Began her dolorous task of love in the Wine-press of Luvah   75
To form the Worm into a form of love by tears & pain.
The Sisters saw! trembling ran thro their Looms! soften[in]g mild
Towards London: then they saw the Furna[c]es opend, & in tears
Began to give their souls away in the Furna[c]es of affliction.

Los saw & was comforted at his Furnaces uttering thus his voice.   ᵉ 80

I know I am Urthona keeper of the Gates of Heaven,
And that I can at will expatiate in the Gardens of bliss;
But pangs of love draw me down to my loins which are
Become a fountain of veiny pipes: O Albion! my brother!
PLATE 83
Corrup[t]ability appears upon thy limbs, and never more   ᵉ
Can I arise and leave thy side, but labour here incessant
Till thy awaking! yet alas I shall forget Eternity!

Against the Patriarchal pomp and cruelty, labouring incessant
I shall become an Infant horror. Enion! Tharmas! friends   5
Absorb me not in such dire grief: O Albion, my brother!
Jerusalem hungers in the desart! affection to her children!
The scorn'd and contemnd youthful girl, where shall she fly?
Sussex shuts up her Villages. Hants, Devon & Wilts
Surrounded with masses of stone in orderd forms, determine then   10
A form for Vala and a form for Luvah, here on the Thames
Where the Victim nightly howls beneath the Druids knife:
A Form of Vegetation, nail them down on the stems of Mystery:
O when shall the Saxon return with the English his redeemed brother!
O when shall the Lamb of God descend among the Reprobate!   15
I woo to Amalek to protect my fugitives[.] Amalek trembles:
I call to Canaan & Moab in my night watches, they mourn:
They listen not to my cry, they rejo[i]ce among their warriors
Woden and Thor and Friga wholly consume my Saxons
On their enormous Altars built in the terrible north: 20
From Irelands rocks to Scandinavia Persia and Tartary:
From the Atlantic Sea to the universal Erythrean.
Found ye London! enormous City! weeps thy River?
Upon his parent bosom lay thy little ones O Land
Forsaken. Surrey and Sussex are Enitharmons Chamber.   25
Where I will build her a Couch of repose & my pillars
Shall surround her in beautiful labyrinths: Oothoon?
Where hides my child? in Oxford hidest thou with Antamon?
In graceful hidings of error: in merciful deceit
Lest Hand the terrible destroy his Affection. thou hidest her: t30
In chaste appearances for sweet deceits of love & modesty
Immingled, interwoven, glistening to the sickening sight.
Let Cambel and her Sisters sit within the Mundane Shell:
Forming the fluctuating Globe according to their will.
According as they weave the little embryon nerves & veins   35
The Eye, the little Nostrils, & the delicate Tongue & Ears
Of labyrinthine intricacy: so shall they fold the World
That whatever is seen upon the Mundane Shell, the same
Be seen upon the Fluctuating Earth woven by the Sisters.
And sometimes the Earth shall roll in the Abyss & sometimes   40
Stand in the Center & sometimes stretch flat in the Expanse,
According to the will of the lovely Daughters of Albion.
Sometimes it shall assimilate with mighty Golgonooza:
Touching its summits: & sometimes divided roll apart.
As a beautiful Veil so these Females shall fold & unfold   45
According to their will the outside surface of the Earth
An outside shadowy Surface superadded to the real Surface;
Which is unchangeable for ever & ever Amen: so be it!
Separate Albions Sons gently from their Emanations,
Weaving bowers of delight on the current of infant Thames   50

Where the old Parent still retains his youth as I alas!
Retain my youth eight thousand and five hundred years.
The labourer of ages in the Valleys of Despair!   c
The land is markd for desolation & unless we plant
The seeds of Cities & of Villages in the Human bosom   55
Albion must be a rock of blood: mark ye the points
Where Cities shall remain & where Villages[;] for the rest!
It must lie in confusion till Albions time of awaking.
Place the Tribes of Llewellyn in America for a hiding place!
Till sweet Jerusalem emanates again into Eternity   60
The night falls thick: I go upon my watch: be attentive:
The Sons of Albion go forth; I follow from my Furnaces:
That they return no more: that a place be prepard on Euphrates
Listen to your Watchmans voice: sleep not before the Furnaces
Eternal Death stands at the door. O God pity our labours.   65

So Los spoke. to the Daughters of Beulah while his Emanation
Like a faint rainbow waved before him in the awful gloom
Of London City on the Thames from Surrey Hills to Highgate:
Swift turn the silver spindles, & the golden weights play soft
And lulling harmonies beneath the Looms, from Caithness in the north   70
To Lizard-point & Dover in the south: his Emanation
Joy'd in the many weaving threads in bright Cathedrons Dome
Weaving the Web of life for Jerusalem. the Web of life
Down flowing into Entuthons Vales glistens with soft affections.

While Los arose upon his Watch, and down from Golgonooza   75
Putting on his golden sandals to walk from mountain to mountain,
He takes his way, girding himself with gold & in his hand
Holding his iron mace: The Spectre remains attentive
Alternate they watch in night: alternate labour in day
Before the Furnaces labouring, while Los all night watches   80
The stars rising & setting, & the meteors & terrors of night!
With him went down the Dogs of Leutha, at his feet   c
They lap the water of the trembling Thames then follow swift
And thus he heard the voice of Albions daughters on Euphrates,

Our Father Albions land: O it was a lovely land! & the Daughters of   c 85
    Beulah
Walked up and down in its green mountains: but Hand is fled
Away: & mighty Hyle: & after them Jerusalem is gone: Awake   t
PLATE 84
Highgates heights & Hampsteads, to Poplar Hackney & Bow:
To Islington & Paddington & the Brook of Albions River
We builded Jerusalem as a City & a Temple; from Lambeth
We began our Foundations; lovely Lambeth! O lovely Hills
Of Camberwell, we shall behold you no more in glory & pride   5
For Jerusalem lies in ruins & the Furnaces of Los are builded there

You are now shrunk up to a narrow Rock in the midst of the Sea
But here we build Babylon on Euphrates, compelld to build
And to inhabit, our Little-ones to clothe in armour of the gold
Of Jerusalems Cherubims & to forge them swords of her Altars   10
I see London blind & age-bent begging thro the Streets
Of Babylon, led by a child. his tears run down his beard
The voice of Wandering Reuben ecchoes from street to street
In all the Cities of the Nations Paris Madrid Amsterdam

The Corner of Broad Street weeps; Poland Street languishes   15
To Great Queen Street & Lincolns Inn, all is distress & woe.
            [*three lines* gouged out irrecoverably]
The night falls thick Hand comes from Albion in his strength   20
He combines into a Mighty-one the Double Molech & Chemosh
Marching thro Egypt in his fury the East is pale at his course
The Nations of India, the Wild Tartar that never knew Man
Starts from his lofty places & casts down his tents & flees away
But we woo him all the night in songs, O Los come forth O Los   25
Divide us from these terrors & give us power them to subdue
Arise upon thy Watches let us see thy Globe of fire
On Albions Rocks & let thy voice be heard upon Euphrates.

Thus sang the Daughters in lamentation, uniting into One
With Rahab as she turnd the iron Spindle of destruction.   30

Terrified at the Sons of Albion they took the Falshood which   e
Gwendolen hid in her left hand. it grew & grew till it
PLATE 85
Became a Space & an Allegory around the Winding Worm[.]
They namd it Canaan & built for it a tender Moon
Los smild with joy thinking on Enitharmon & he brought
Reuben from his twelvefold wandrings & led him into it
Planting the Seeds of the Twelve Tribes & Moses & David   5
And gave a Time & Revolution to the Space Six Thousand Years
He calld it Divine Analogy, for in Beulah the Feminine
Emanations Create Space. the Masculine Create Time, & plant
The Seeds of beauty in the Space: listning to their lamentation
Los walks upon his ancient Mountains in the deadly darkness   10
Among his Furnaces directing his laborious Myriads watchful   t
Looking to the East: & his voice is heard over the whole Earth
As he watches the Furnaces by night, & directs the labourers

And thus Los replies upon his Watch: the Valleys listen silent: e
The Stars stand still to hear: Jerusalem & Vala cease to mourn: 15
His voice is heard from Albion: the Alps & Appenines
Listen: Hermon & Lebanon bow their crowned heads
Babel & Shinar look toward the Western Gate, they sit down
Silent at his voice: they view the red Globe of fire in Los's hand

As he walks from Furnace to Furnace directing the Labourers   20
And this is the Song of Los, the Song that he sings on his Watch

O lovely mild Jerusalem! O Shiloh of Mount Ephraim!   c
I see thy Gates of precious stones: thy Walls of gold & silver:
Thou art the soft reflected Image of the Sleeping Man
Who stretchd on Albions rocks reposes amidst his Twenty-eight   25
Cities: where Beulah lovely terminates, in the hills & valleys of Albion
Cities not yet embodied in Time and Space: plant ye
The Seeds O Sisters in the bosom of Time & Spaces womb
To spring up for Jerusalem: lovely Shadow of Sleeping Albion
Why wilt thou rend thyself apart & build an Earthly Kingdom   30
To reign in pride & to opress & to mix the Cup of Delusion
O thou that dwellest with Babylon! Come forth O lovely-one
PLATE 86
I see thy Form O lovely mild Jerusalem, Wingd with Six Wings
In the opacous Bosom of the Sleeper, lovely Three-fold
In Head & Heart & Reins three Universes of love & beauty
Thy forehead bright: Holiness to the Lord, with Gates of pearl
Reflects Eternity beneath thy azure wings of feathery down   5
Ribbd delicate & clothd with featherd gold & azure & purple
From thy white shoulders shadowing, purity in holiness!
Thence featherd with soft crimson of the ruby bright as fire
Spreading into the azure Wings which like a canopy
Bends over thy immortal Head in which Eternity dwells   10
Albion beloved Land; I see thy mountains & thy hills
And valleys & thy pleasant Cities Holiness to the Lord
I see the Spectres of thy Dead O Emanation of Albion.

Thy Bosom white, translucent coverd with immortal gems
A sublime ornament not obscuring the outlines of beauty   15
Terrible to behold for thy extreme beauty & perfection
Twelve-fold here all the Tribes of Israel I behold
Upon the Holy Land: I see the River of Life & Tree of Life
I see the New Jerusalem descending out of Heaven
Between thy Wings of gold & silver featherd immortal   20
Clear as the rainbow, as the cloud of the Suns tabernacle

Thy Reins coverd with Wings translucent sometimes covering
And sometimes spread abroad reveal the flames of holiness
Which like a robe covers: & like a Veil of Seraphim
In flaming fire unceasing burns from Eternity to Eternity   25
Twelvefold I there behold Israel in her Tents
A Pillar of a Cloud by day: a Pillar of fire by night
Guides them: there I behold Moab & Ammon & Amalek
There Bells of silver round thy knees living articulate
Comforting sounds of love & harmony & on thy feet   30
Sandals of gold & pearl, & Egypt & Assyria before me
The Isles of Javan, Philistea, Tyre and Lebanon

Thus Los sings upon his Watch walking from Furnace to Furnace.   e
He siezes his Hammer every hour, flames surround him as
He beats: seas roll beneath his feet, tempests muster   35
Arou[n]d his head. the thick hail stones stand ready to obey
His voice in the black cloud, his Sons labour in thunders
At his Furnaces; his Daughters at their Looms sing woes[.]
His Emanation separates in milky fibres agonizing
Among the golden Looms of Cathedron sending fibres of love   40
From Golgonooza with sweet visions for Jerusalem, wanderer.

Nor can any consummate bliss without being Generated
On Earth; of those whose Emanations weave the loves
Of Beulah for Jerusalem & Shiloh, in immortal Golgonooza
Concentering in the majestic form of Erin in eternal tears   45
Viewing the Winding Worm on the Desarts of Great Tartary
Viewing Los in his shudderings, pouring balm on his sorrows
So dread is Los's fury, that none dare him to approach
Without becoming his Children in the Furnaces of affliction

And Enitharmon like a faint rainbow waved before him   50
Filling with Fibres from his loins which reddend with desire
Into a Globe of blood beneath his bosom trembling in darkness
Of Albions clouds. he fed it, with his tears & bitter groans
Hiding his Spectre in invisibility from the timorous Shade
Till it became a separated cloud of beauty grace & love   55
Among the darkness of his Furnaces dividing asunder till
She separated stood before him a lovely Female weeping
Even Enitharmon separated outside, & his Loins closed
And heal'd after the separation: his pains he soon forgot:
Lured by her beauty outside of himself in shadowy grief.   60
Two Wills they had; Two Intellects: & not as in times of old.

Silent they wanderd hand in hand like two Infants wandring
From Enion in the desarts, terrified at each others beauty
Envying each other yet desiring, in all devouring Love,
PLATE 87
Repelling weeping Enion blind & age-bent into the fourfold
Desarts. Los first broke silence & began to utter his love

O lovely Enitharmon: I behold thy graceful forms
Moving beside me till intoxicated with the woven labyrinth
Of beauty & perfection my wild fibres shoot in veins   5
Of blood thro all my nervous limbs. soon overgrown in roots

I shall be closed from thy sight. sieze therefore in thy hand
The small fibres as they shoot around me draw out in pity
And let them run on the winds of thy bosom: I will fix them
With pulsations. we will divide them into Sons & Daughters   10
To live in thy Bosoms translucence as in an eternal morning

Enitharmon answerd. No! I will sieze thy Fibres & weave
Them: not as thou wilt but as I will, for I will Create
A round Womb beneath my bosom lest I also be overwoven
With Love; be thou assured I never will be thy slave   15
Let Mans delight be Love; but Womans delight be Pride[.]
In Eden our loves were the same here they are opposite
I have Loves of my own I will weave them in Albions Spectre
Cast thou in Jerusalems shadows thy Loves! silk of liquid
Rubies Jacinths Crysolites: issuing from thy Furnaces. While   20
Jerusalem divides thy care: while thou carest for Jerusalem
Know that I never will be thine: also thou hidest Vala
From her these fibres shoot to shut me in a Grave.
You are Albions Victim, he has set his Daughter in your path

PLATE 88
Los answerd sighing like the Bellows of his Furnaces

I care not! the swing of my Hammer shall measure the starry round[.]
When in Eternity Man converses with Man they enter
Into each others Bosom (which are Universes of delight)
In mutual interchange. and first their Emanations meet   5
Surrounded by their Children. if they embrace & comingle
The Human Four-fold Forms mingle also in thunders of Intellect
But if the Emanations mingle not; with storms & agitations
Of earthquakes & consuming fires they roll apart in fear
For Man cannot unite with Man but by their Emanations   10
Which stand both Male & Female at the Gates of each Humanity
How then can I ever again be united as Man with Man
While thou my Emanation refusest my Fibres of dominion?
When Souls mingle & join thro all the Fibres of Brotherhood
Can there be any secret joy on Earth greater than this?   15

Enitharmon answerd: This is Womans World, nor need she any
Spectre to defend her from Man. I will Create secret places
And the masculine names of the places Merlin & Arthur.
A triple Female Tabernacle for Moral Law I weave
That he who loves Jesus may loathe terrified Female love   20
Till God himself become a Male subservient to the Female.

She spoke in scorn & jealousy, alternate torments; and
So speaking she sat down on Sussex shore singing lulling
Cadences, & playing in sweet intoxication among the glistening
Fibres of Los: sending them over the Ocean eastward into   25
The realms of dark death; O perverse to thyself, contrarious
To thy own purposes; for when she began to weave
Shooting out in sweet pleasure her bosom in milky Love
Flowd into the aching fibres of Los. yet contending against him
In pride sending his Fibres over to her objects of jealousy   30
In the little lovely Allegoric Night of Albions Daughters

Which stretchd abroad, expanding east & west & north & south
Thro' all the World of Erin & of Los & all their Children

A sullen smile broke from the Spectre in mockery & scorn   e
Knowing himself the author of their divisions & shrinkings, gratified   35
At their contentions, he wiped his tears he washd his visage.

The Man who respects Woman shall be despised by Woman
And deadly cunning & mean abjectness only, shall enjoy them
For I will make their places of joy & love, excrementitious[.]
Continually building, continually destroying in Family feuds   40
While you are under the dominion of a jealous Female
Unpermanent for ever because of love & jealousy.
You shall want all the Minute Particulars of Life

Thus joyd the Spectre in the dusky fires of Los's Forge, eyeing
Enitharmon who at her shining Looms sings lulling cadences   45
While Los stood at his Anvil in wrath the victim of their love
And hate; dividing the Space of Love with brazen Compasses
In Golgonooza & in Udan-Adan & in Entuthon of Urizen.

The blow of his Hammer is Justice. the swing of his Hammer: Mercy.   e
The force of Los's Hammer is eternal Forgiveness; but   50
His rage or his mildness were vain, she scatterd his love on the wind
Eastward into her own Center, creating the Female Womb
In mild Jerusalem around the Lamb of God. Loud howl
The Furnaces of Los! loud roll the Wheels of Enitharmon
The Four Zoa's in all their faded majesty burst out in fury   55
And fire. Jerusalem took the Cup which foamd in Vala's hand   e
Like the red Sun upon the mountains in the bloody day
Upon the Hermaphroditic Wine-presses of Love & Wrath.

PLATE 89
Tho divided by the Cross & Nails & Thorns & Spear   e
In cruelties of Rahab & Tirzah[,] permanent endure   t
A terrible indefinite Hermaphroditic form
A Wine-press of Love & Wrath double Hermaph[r]oditic
Twelvefold in Allegoric pomp in selfish holiness   5
The Pharisaion, the Grammateis, the Presbuterion,
The Archiereus, the Iereus, the Saddusaion, double
Each withoutside of the other, covering eastern heaven

Thus was the Covering Cherub reveald majestic image
Of Selfhood, Body put off, the Antichrist accursed   10
Coverd with precious stones, a Human Dragon terrible
And bright, stretchd over Europe & Asia gorgeous
In three nights he devourd the rejected corse of death   e

His Head dark, deadly, in its Brain incloses a reflexion
Of Eden all perverted: Egypt on the Gihon many tongued   15

-245-

And many mouthd: Ethiopia, Lybia, the Sea of Rephaim
Minute Particulars in slavery I behold among the brick-kilns
Disorganiz'd, & there is Pharoh in his iron Court:
And the Dragon of the River & the Furnaces of iron.
Outwoven from Thames & Tweed & Severn awful streams   20
Twelve ridges of Stone frown over all the Earth in tyrant pride
Frown over each River stupendous Works of Albions Druid Sons
And Albions Forests of Oaks coverd the Earth from Pole to Pole

His Bosom wide reflects Moab & Ammon, on the River
Pison, since calld Arnon, there is Heshbon beautiful   25
The Rocks of Rabbath on the Arnon & the Fish-pools of Heshbon
Whose currents flow into the Dead Sea by Sodom & Gomorra
Above his Head high arching Wings black filld with Eyes
Spring upon iron sinews from the Scapulæ & Os Humeri.
There Israel in bondage to his Generalizing Gods   30
Molech & Chemosh, & in his left breast is Philistea
In Druid Temples over the whole Earth with Victims Sacrifice,
From Gaza to Damascus Tyre & Sidon & the Gods
Of Javan thro the Isles of Grecia & all Europes Kings
Where Hiddekel pursues his course among the rocks   35
Two Wings spring from his ribs of brass, starry, black as night
But translucent their blackness as the dazling of gems

His Loins inclose Babylon on Euphrates beautiful
And Rome in sweet Hesperia. there Israel scatterd abroad
In martyrdoms & slavery I behold: ah vision of sorrow!   40
Inclosed by eyeless Wings, glowing with fire as the iron
Heated in the Smiths forge, but cold the wind of their dread fury

But in the midst of a devouring Stomach, Jerusalem
Hidden within the Covering Cherub as in a Tabernacle
Of threefold workmanship in allegoric delusion & woe[.]   45
There the Seven Kings of Canaan & Five Baalim of Philistea
Sihon & Og the Anakim & Emim, Nephilim & Gibborim
From Babylon to Rome & the Wings spread from Japan
Where the Red Sea terminates the World of Generation & Death
To Irelands farthest rocks where Giants builded their Causeway 50
Into the Sea of Rephaim, but the Sea oerwhelmd them all.

A Double Female now appeard within the Tabernacle,
Religion hid in War, a Dragon red & hidden Harlot
Each within other, but without a Warlike Mighty-one
Of dreadful power, sitting upon Horeb pondering dire   55
And mighty preparations mustering multitudes innumerable
Of warlike sons among the sands of Midian & Aram[.]
For multitudes of those who sleep in Alla descend
Lured by his warlike symphonies of tabret pipe & harp
Burst the bottoms of the Graves & Funeral Arks of Beulah[;] 60

Wandering in that unknown Night beyond the silent Grave
They become One with the Antichrist & are absorbd in him   e

PLATE 90
The Feminine separates from the Masculine & both from Man,   e
Ceasing to be His Emanations, Life to Themselves assuming!
And while they circumscribe his Brain, & while they circumscribe
His Heart, & while they circumscribe his Loins! a Veil & Net
Of Veins of red Blood grows around them like a scarlet robe.   5
Covering them from the sight of Man like the woven Veil of Sleep
Such as the Flowers of Beulah weave to be their Funeral Mantles
But dark! opake! tender to touch, & painful! & agonizing
To the embrace of love, & to the mingling of soft fibres
Of tender affection. that no more the Masculine mingles   10
With the Feminine. but the Sublime is shut out from the Pathos
In howling torment, to build stone walls of separation, compelling
The Pathos, to weave curtains of hiding secresy from the torment.

Bowen & Conwenna stood on Skiddaw cutting the Fibres
Of Benjamin from Chesters River: loud the River; loud the Mersey   15
And the Ribble. thunder into the Irish sea, as the Twelve Sons
Of Albion drank & imbibed the Life & eternal Form of Luvah
Cheshire & Lancashire & Westmoreland groan in anguish
As they cut the fibres from the Rivers he sears them with hot
Iron of his Forge & fixes them into Bones of chalk & Rock   20
Conwenna sat above: with solemn cadences she drew
Fibres of life out from the Bones into her golden Loom
Hand had his Furnace on Highgates heights & it reachd
To Brockley Hills across the Thames: he with double Boadicea
In cruel pride cut Reuben apart from the Hills of Surrey   25
Comingling with Luvah & with the Sepulcher of Luvah
For the Male is a Furnace of beryll: the Female is a golden Loom

Los cries: No Individual ought to appropriate to Himself
Or to his Emanation, any of the Universal Characteristics
Of David or of Eve, of the Woman, or of the Lord.   30
Of Reuben or of Benjamin, of Joseph or Judah or Levi[.]
Those who dare appropriate to themselves Universal Attributes
Are the Blasphemous Selfhoods & must be broken asunder[.]
A Vegetated Christ & a Virgin Eve, are the Hermaphroditic
Blasphemy, by his Maternal Birth he is that Evil-One   35
And his Maternal Humanity must be put off Eternally
Lest the Sexual Generation swallow up Regeneration
Come Lord Jesus take on thee the Satanic Body of Holiness

So Los cried in the Valleys of Middlesex in the Spirit of Prophecy
While in Selfhood Hand & Hyle & Bowen & Skofeld appropriate   40
The Divine Names: seeking to Vegetate the Divine Vision
In a corporeal & ever dying Vegetation & Corruption
Mingling with Luvah in One. they become One Great Satan

Loud scream the Daughters of Albion beneath the Tongs & Hammer
Dolorous are their lamentations in the burning Forge   45
They drink Reuben & Benjamin as the iron drinks the fire
They are red hot with cruelty: raving along the Banks of Thames
And on Tyburns Brook among the howling Victims in loveliness
While Hand & Hyle condense the Little-ones & erect them into
A mighty Temple even to the stars: but they Vegetate 50
Beneath Los's Hammer, that Life may not be blotted out.

For Los said: When the Individual appropriates Universality
He divides into Male & Female: & when the Male & Female,
Appropriate Individuality, they become an Eternal Death.
Hermaphroditic worshippers of a God of cruelty & law! 55
Your Slaves & Captives; you compel to worship a God of Mercy.
These are the Demonstrations of Los, & the blows of my mighty
  Hammer

So Los spoke. And the Giants of Albion terrified & ashamed t,e
With Los's thunderous Words, began to build trembling rocking Stones
For his Words roll in thunders & lightnings among the Temples 60
Terrified rocking to & fro upon the earth, & sometimes
Resting in a Circle in Malden or in Strathness or Dura.
Plotting to devour Albion & Los the friend of Albion
Denying in private: mocking God & Eternal Life: & in Public
Collusion, calling themselves Deists, Worshipping the Maternal 65
Humanity; calling it Nature, and Natural Religion

But still the thunder of Los peals loud & thus the thunder's cry t

These beautiful Witchcrafts of Albion are gratifyd by Cruelty
PLATE 91   t
It is easier to forgive an Enemy than to forgive a Friend: e
The man who permits you to injure him, deserves your vengeance:
He also will recieve it; go Spectre! obey my most secret desire:
Which thou knowest without my speaking: Go to these Fiends of
  Righteousness
Tell them to obey their Humanities, & not pretend Holiness; 5
When they are murderers: as far as my Hammer & Anvil permit
Go, tell them that the Worship of God, is honouring his gifts e
In other men: & loving the greatest men best, each according
To his Genius: which is the Holy Ghost in Man; there is no other e
God, than that God who is the intellectual fountain of Humanity; 10
He who envies or calumniates: which is murder & cruelty, e
Murders the Holy-one: Go tell them this & overthrow their cup,
Their bread, their altar-table, their incense & their oath:
Their marriage & their baptism, their burial & consecration:
I have tried to make friends by corporeal gifts but have only 15
Made enemies: I never made friends but by spiritual gifts;
By severe contentions of friendship & the burning fire of thought. e

He who would see the Divinity must see him in his Children
One first, in friendship & love; then a Divine Family, & in the midst
Jesus will appear; so he who wishes to see a Vision; a perfect Whole   20
Must see it in its Minute Particulars; Organized & not as thou
O Fiend of Righteousness pretendest; thine is a Disorganized
And snowy cloud: brooder of tempests & destructive War.
You smile with pomp & rigor: you talk of benevolence & virtue!
I act with benevolence & Virtue & get murderd time after time: 25
You accumulate Particulars, & murder by analyzing, that you
May take the aggregate; & you call the aggregate Moral Law:
And you call that Swelld & bloated Form; a Minute Particular.
But General Forms have their vitality in Particulars: & every
Particular is a Man; a Divine Member of the Divine Jesus.   30

So Los cried at his Anvil in the horrible darkness weeping!

The Spectre builded stupendous Works, taking the Starry Heavens   c
Like to a curtain & folding them according to his will
Repeating the Smaragdine Table of Hermes to draw Los down
Into the Indefinite, refusing to believe without demonstration[.]   35
Los reads the Stars of Albion! the Spectre reads the Voids
Between the Stars; among the arches of Albions Tomb sublime
Rolling the Sea in rocky paths: forming Leviathan
And Behemoth: the War by Sea enormous & the War
By Land astounding: erecting pillars in the deepest Hell,   40
To reach the heavenly arches; Los beheld undaunted furious
His heavd Hammer; he swung it round & at one blow,
In unpitying ruin driving down the pyramids of pride
Smiting the Spectre on his Anvil & the integuments of his Eye
And Ear unbinding in dire pain, with many blows,   45
Of strict severity self-subduing, & with many tears labouring.

Then he sent forth the Spectre all his pyramids were grains
Of sand & his pillars: dust on the flys wing: & his starry
Heavens; a moth of gold & silver mocking his anxious grasp
Thus Los alterd his Spectre & every Ratio of his Reason   50
He alterd time after time, with dire pain & many tears
Till he had completely divided him into a separate space.

Terrified Los sat to behold trembling & weeping & howling
I care not whether a Man is Good or Evil; all that I care
Is whether he is a Wise Man or a Fool. Go! put off Holiness   55
And put on Intellect: or my thundrous Hammer shall drive thee
To wrath which thou condemnest: till thou obey my voice

So Los terrified cries: trembling & weeping & howling! Beholding

PLATE 92   t
What do I see? The Briton Saxon Roman Norman amalgamating   c
In my Furnaces into One Nation the English: & taking refuge

In the Loins of Albion. The Canaanite united with the fugitive
Hebrew, whom she divided into Twelve, & sold into Egypt
Then scatterd the Egyptian & Hebrew to the four Winds!   5
This sinful Nation Created in our Furnaces & Looms is Albion

So Los spoke. Enitharmon answerd in great terror in Lambeths Vale   c

The Poets Song draws to its period & Enitharmon is no more.
For if he be that Albion I can never weave him in my Looms
But when he touches the first fibrous thread, like filmy dew   10
My Looms will be no more & I annihilate vanish for ever
Then thou wilt Create another Female according to thy Will.

Los answerd swift as the shuttle of gold. Sexes must vanish & cease
To be, when Albion arises from his dread repose O lovely Enitharmon:
When all their Crimes, their Punishments their Accusations of Sin: 15
All their Jealousies Revenges. Murders. hidings of Cruelty in Deceit
Appear only in the Outward Spheres of Visionary Space and Time.
In the shadows of Possibility by Mutual Forgiveness forevermore
And in the Vision & in the Prophecy, that we may Foresee & Avoid
The terrors of Creation & Redemption & Judgment. Beholding them   20
Displayd in the Emanative Visions of Canaan in Jerusalem & in Shiloh
And in the Shadows of Remembrance, & in the Chaos of the Spectre
Amalek, Edom, Egypt, Moab, Ammon, Ashur, Philistea, around
    Jerusalem
Where the Druids reard their Rocky Circles to make permanent
    Remembrance
Of Sin. & the Tree of Good & Evil sprang from the Rocky Circle &   25
    Snake
Of the Druid, along the Valley of Rephaim from Camberwell to
    Golgotha
And framed the Mundane Shell Cavernous in Length Bredth & Highth

PLATE 93

Enitharmon heard. She raisd her head like the mild Moon   c

-250-

O Rintrah! O Palamabron! What are your dire & awful purposes
Enitharmons name is nothing before you: you forget all my Love!
The Mothers love of obedience is forgotten & you seek a Love
Of the pride of dominion, that will Divorce Ocalythron & Elynittria 5
Upon East Moor in Derbyshire & along the Valleys of Cheviot
Could you Love me Rintrah, if you Pride not in my Love
As Reuben found Mandrakes in the field & gave them to his Mother e
Pride meets with Pride upon the Mountains in the stormy day
In that terrible Day of Rintrahs Plow & of Satans driving the Team. 10
Ah! then I heard my little ones weeping along the Valley!
Ah! then I saw my beloved ones fleeing from my Tent
Merlin was like thee Rintrah among the Giants of Albion
Judah was like Palamabron: O Simeon! O Levi! ye fled away
How can I hear my little ones weeping along the Valley 15
Or how upon the distant Hills see my beloveds Tents.

Then Los again took up his speech as Enitharmon ceast

Fear not my Sons this Waking Death. he is become One with me e
Behold him here! We shall not Die! we shall be united in Jesus.
Will you suffer this Satan this Body of Doubt that Seems but Is Not 20
To occupy the very threshold of Eternal Life. if Bacon, Newton,
    Locke,
Deny a Conscience in Man & the Communion of Saints & Angels
Contemning the Divine Vision & Fruition, Worshiping the Deus
Of the Heathen, The God of This World, & the Goddess Nature
Mystery Babylon the Great, The Druid Dragon & hidden Harlot[,] 25
Is it not that Signal of the Morning which was told us in the Beginning

Thus they converse upon Mam-Tor. the Graves thunder under their
    feet
PLATE 94
Albion cold lays on his Rock: storms & snows beat round him. e
Beneath the Furnaces & the starry Wheels & the Immortal Tomb
Howling winds cover him: roaring seas dash furious against him
In the deep darkness broad lightnings glare long thunders roll

The weeds of Death inwrap his hands & feet blown incessant 5
And washd incessant by the for-ever restless sea-waves foaming abroad
Upon the white Rock. England a Female Shadow as deadly damps
Of the Mines of Cornwall & Derbyshire lays upon his bosom heavy
Moved by the wind in volumes of thick cloud returning folding round
His loins & bosom unremovable by swelling storms & loud rending 10
Of enraged thunders. Around them the Starry Wheels of their Giant
    Sons
Revolve: & over them the Furnaces of Los & the Immortal Tomb
    around

Erin sitting in the Tomb, to watch them unceasing night and day
And the Body of Albion was closed apart from all Nations.

Over them the famishd Eagle screams on boney Wings and around   15
Them howls the Wolf of famine deep heaves the Ocean black
    thundering!
Around the wormy Garments of Albion: then pausing in deathlike
    silence

Time was Finished! The Breath Divine Breathed over Albion
Beneath the Furnaces & starry Wheels and in the Immortal Tomb
And England who is Brittannia awoke, from Death on Albions bosom   20
She awoke pale & cold she fainted seven times on the Body of Albion

O pitious Sleep O pitious Dream! O God O God awake I have slain
In Dreams of Chastity & Moral Law I have Murdered Albion! Ah!
In Stone-henge & on London Stone & in the Oak Groves of Malden
I have Slain him in my Sleep with the Knife of the Druid O England   25
O all ye Nations of the Earth behold ye the Jealous Wife
The Eagle & the Wolf & Monkey & Owl & the King & Priest were   t
    there

PLATE 95
Her voice pierc'd Albions clay cold ear. he moved upon the Rock.
The Breath Divine went forth upon the morning hills, Albion mov'd
Upon the Rock, he opend his eyelids in pain; in pain he mov'd
His stony members, he saw England. Ah! shall the Dead live again

The Breath Divine went forth over the morning hills Albion rose   5
In anger: the wrath of God breaking bright flaming on all sides around
His awful limbs: into the Heavens he walked clothed in flames
Loud thundring, with broad flashes of flaming lightning & pillars
Of fire, speaking the Words of Eternity in Human Forms, in direful
Revolutions of Action & Passion, thro the Four Elements on all sides   10
Surrounding his awful Members. Thou seest the Sun in heavy clouds
Struggling to rise above the Mountains. in his burning hand
He takes his Bow, then chooses out his arrows of flaming gold
Murmuring the Bowstring breathes with ardor! clouds roll round the
Horns of the wide Bow, loud sounding winds sport on the mountain   15
    brows
Compelling Urizen to his Furrow; & Tharmas to his Sheepfold;
And Luvah to his Loom: Urthona he beheld mighty labouring at
His Anvil, in the Great Spectre Los unwearied labouring & weeping
Therefore the Sons of Eden praise Urthonas Spectre in songs   e
Because he kept the Divine Vision in time of trouble.   20

As the Sun & Moon lead forward the Visions of Heaven & Earth   e
England who is Brittannia enterd Albions bosom rejoicing,
Rejoicing in his indignation! adoring his wrathful rebuke.
She who adores not your frowns will only loathe your smiles

PLATE 96

As the Sun & Moon lead forward the Visions of Heaven & Earth
England who is Brittannia entered Albions bosom rejoicing

Then Jesus appeared standing by Albion as the Good Shepherd
By the lost Sheep that he hath found & Albion knew that it
Was the Lord the Universal Humanity, & Albion saw his Form   5
A Man. & they conversed as Man with Man, in Ages of Eternity
And the Divine Appearance was the likeness & similitude of Los

Albion said. O Lord what can I do! my Selfhood cruel
Marches against thee deceitful from Sinai & from Edom
Into the Wilderness of Judah to meet thee in his pride   10
I behold the Visions of my deadly Sleep of Six Thousand Years
Dazling around thy skirts like a Serpent of precious stones & gold
I know it is my Self: O my Divine Creator & Redeemer

Jesus replied Fear not Albion unless I die thou canst not live
But if I die I shall arise again & thou with me   15
This is Friendship & Brotherhood without it Man Is Not

So Jesus spoke: the Covering Cherub coming on in darkness
Overshadowd them & Jesus said Thus do Men in Eternity
One for another to put off by forgiveness, every sin

Albion replyd. Cannot Man exist without Mysterious   20
Offering of Self for Another, is this Friendship & Brotherhood
I see thee in the likeness & similitude of Los my Friend

Jesus said. Wouldest thou love one who never died
For thee or ever die for one who had not died for thee
And if God dieth not for Man & giveth not himself   25
Eternally for Man Man could not exist! for Man is Love:
As God is Love: every kindness to another is a little Death
In the Divine Image nor can Man exist but by Brotherhood

So saying the Cloud overshadowing divided them asunder
Albion stood in terror: not for himself but for his Friend   30
Divine, & Self was lost in the contemplation of faith
And wonder at the Divine Mercy & at Los's sublime honour

Do I sleep amidst danger to Friends! O my Cities & Counties
Do you sleep! rouze up. rouze up. Eternal Death is abroad

So Albion spoke & threw himself into the Furnaces of affliction   35
All was a Vision, all a Dream: the Furnaces became
Fountains of Living Waters flowing from the Humanity Divine
And all the Cities of Albion rose from their Slumbers, and All
The Sons & Daughters of Albion on soft clouds Waking from Sleep
Soon all around remote the Heavens burnt with flaming fires   40
And Urizen & Luvah & Tharmas & Urthona arose into

Albions Bosom: Then Albion stood before Jesus in the Clouds
Of Heaven Fourfold among the Visions of God in Eternity

PLATE 97

Awake! Awake Jerusalem! O lovely Emanation of Albion   c
Awake and overspread all Nations as in Ancient Time
For lo! the Night of Death is past and the Eternal Day
Appears upon our Hills: Awake Jerusalem, and come away

So spake the Vision of Albion & in him so spake in my hearing   5
The Universal Father. Then Albion stretchd his hand into Infinitude.
And took his Bow. Fourfold the Vision for bright beaming Urizen
Layd his hand on the South & took a breathing Bow of carved Gold
Luvah his hand stretch'd to the East & bore a Silver Bow bright shining
Tharmas Westward a Bow of Brass pure flaming richly wrought   10
Urthona Northward in thick storms a Bow of Iron terrible thundering.

And the Bow is a Male & Female & the Quiver of the Arrows of Love,
Are the Children of this Bow: a Bow of Mercy & Loving-kindness:
   laying
Open the hidden Heart in Wars of mutual Benevolence Wars of Love
And the Hand of Man grasps firm between the Male & Female Loves   15
And he Clothed himself in Bow & Arrows in awful state Fourfold
In the midst of his Twenty-eight Cities each with his Bow breathing

PLATE 98

Then each an Arrow flaming from his Quiver fitted carefully
They drew fourfold the unreprovable String, bending thro the wide
   Heavens
The horned Bow Fourfold, loud sounding flew the flaming Arrow
   fourfold

Murmuring the Bow-string breathes with ardor. Clouds roll round the
   horns
Of the wide Bow, loud sounding Winds sport on the Mountains brows: 5
The Druid Spectre was Annihilate loud thundring rejoicing terrific
   vanishing
Fourfold Annihilation & at the clangor of the Arrows of Intellect
The innumerable Chariots of the Almighty appeard in Heaven
And Bacon & Newton & Locke, & Milton & Shakspear & Chaucer
A Sun of blood red wrath surrounding heaven on all sides around   10
Glorious incompreh[en]sible by Mortal Man & each Chariot was   t
   Sexual Threefold

And every Man stood Fourfold. each Four Faces had. One to the West
One toward the East One to the South One to the North. the Horses
   Fourfold
And the dim Chaos brightend beneath, above, around! Eyed as the
   Peacock

According to the Human Nerves of Sensation, the Four Rivers of the   15
    Water of Life

South stood the Nerves of the Eye. East in Rivers of bliss the Nerves
    of the
Expansive Nostrils West, flowd the Parent Sense the Tongue. North
    stood
The labyrinthine Ear. Circumscribing & Circumcising the
    excrementitious
Husk & Covering into Vacuum evaporating revealing the lineaments of
    Man
Driving outward the Body of Death in an Eternal Death & Resurrection   20
Awaking it to Life among the Flowers of Beulah rejoicing in Unity
In the Four Senses in the Outline the Circumference & Form, for ever
In Forgiveness of Sins which is Self Annihilation. it is the Covenant
    of Jehovah

The Four Living Creatures Chariots of Humanity Divine
    Incomprehensible
In beautiful Paradises expand These are the Four Rivers of Paradise   25
And the Four Faces of Humanity fronting the Four Cardinal Points
Of Heaven going forward forward irresistible from Eternity to Eternity

And they conversed together in Visionary forms dramatic which bright   e
Redounded from their Tongues in thunderous majesty, in Visions
In new Expanses, creating exemplars of Memory and of Intellect   30
Creating Space, Creating Time according to the wonders Divine
Of Human Imagination, throughout all the Three Regions immense
Of Childhood, Manhood & Old Age[;] & the all tremendous
    unfathomable Non Ens
Of Death was seen in regenerations terrific or complacent varying   t
According to the subject of discourse & every Word & Every Character   35
Was Human according to the Expansion or Contraction, the
    Translucence or
Opakeness of Nervous fibres such was the variation of Time & Space
Which vary according as the Organs of Perception vary & they walked
To & fro in Eternity as One Man reflecting each in each & clearly seen
And seeing: according to fitness & order. And I heard Jehovah speak   40
Terrific from his Holy Place & saw the Words of the Mutual
    Covenant Divine
On Chariots of gold & jewels with Living Creatures starry & flaming
With every Colour, Lion, Tyger, Horse, Elephant, Eagle Dove, Fly,
    Worm,
And the all wondrous Serpent clothed in gems & rich array Humanize
In the Forgiveness of Sins according to the Covenant of Jehovah. They   45
    Cry

Where is the Covenant of Priam, the Moral Virtues of the Heathen   e
Where is the Tree of Good & Evil that rooted beneath the cruel heel
Of Albions Spectre the Patriarch Druid! where are all his Human   t
    Sacrifices
For Sin in War & in the Druid Temples of the Accuser of Sin: beneath
The Oak Groves of Albion that coverd the whole Earth beneath his   50
    Spectre
Where are the Kingdoms of the World & all their glory that grew on
    Desolation
The Fruit of Albions Poverty Tree when the Triple Headed
    Gog-Magog Giant
Of Albion Taxed the Nations into Desolation & then gave the Spectrous
    Oath

Such is the Cry from all the Earth from the Living Creatures of the
    Earth
And from the great City of Golgonooza in the Shadowy Generation   55
And from the Thirty-two Nations of the Earth among the Living
    Creatures

PLATE 99   t
All Human Forms identified even Tree Metal Earth & Stone. all   e
Human Forms identified, living going forth & returning wearied
Into the Planetary lives of Years Months Days & Hours reposing
And then Awaking into his Bosom in the Life of Immortality.

And I heard the Name of their Emnations they are named Jerusalem   5

The End of The Song
of Jerusalem

❧

FOR THE SEXES
THE GATES of PARADISE

[Prologue]

Mutual Forgiveness of each Vice
Such are the Gates of Paradise
Against the Accusers chief desire
Who walkd among the Stones of Fire
Jehovahs Finger Wrote the Law   t 5
Then Wept! then rose in Zeal & Awe
And the Dead Corpse from Sinais heat   t
Buried beneath his Mercy Seat   t
O Christians Christians! tell me Why
You rear it on your Altars high   10

Frontispiece

What is Man!

<The Suns Light when he unfolds it
Depends on the Organ that beholds it.>

I
I found him beneath a Tree

2
Water
<Thou Waterest him with Tears>

3
Earth
<He struggles into Life>

4
Air
<On Cloudy Doubts & Reasoning Cares>

5
Fire
<That end in endless Strife>

6

At length for hatching ripe
he breaks the shell

7

<What are these?> ALAS! <the Female Martyr
Is She also the Divine Image?>

8

My Son! my Son!

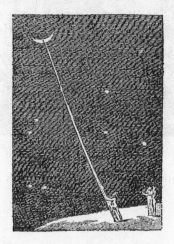

9

I want! I want!

10
Help! Help!

11
Aged Ignorance
<Perceptive Organs closed their Objects close>

12

Does thy God O Priest take such vengeance as this?

13

Fear & Hope are—Vision

14
The Traveller hasteth in the Evening

15
Death's Door

16

I have said to the Worm: Thou art my mother & my sister

The Keys

The Catterpiller on the Leaf
Reminds thee of thy Mothers Grief

of the Gates

1 My Eternal Man set in Repose
The Female from his darkness rose
And She found me beneath a Tree   5
A Mandrake & in her Veil hid me
Serpent Reasonings us entice
Of Good & Evil: Virtue & Vice
2 Doubt Self Jealous Watry folly
3 Struggling thro Earths Melancholy   10
4 Naked in Air in Shame & Fear
5 Blind in Fire with shield & spear
Two Horn'd Reasoning Cloven Fiction
In Doubt which is Self contradiction
A dark Hermaphrodite We stood   t 15
Rational Truth Root of Evil & Good
Round me flew the Flaming Sword
Round her snowy Whirlwinds roard
Freezing her Veil the Mundane Shell
6 I rent the Veil where the Dead dwell   20

When weary Man enters his Cave
He meets his Saviour in the Grave
Some find a Female Garment there

And some a Male, woven with care
Lest the Sexual Garments sweet   25
Should grow a devouring Winding sheet

7 One Dies! Alas! the Living & Dead
   One is slain & One is fled

8 In Vain-glory hatcht & nurst
   By double Spectres Self Accurst   30
   My Son! my Son! thou treatest me
   But as I have instructed thee

9 On the shadows of the Moon
   Climbing thro Nights highest noon

10 In Times Ocean falling drownd   35
   In Aged Ignorance profound

11 Holy & cold I clipd the Wings
   Of all Sublunary Things

12 And in depths of my Dungeons
   Closed the Father & the Sons   40

13 But when once I did descry
   The Immortal Man that cannot Die

14 Thro evening shades I haste away
   To close the Labours of my Day

15 The Door of Death I open found   45
   And the Worm Weaving in the Ground

16 Thou'rt my Mother from the Womb
   Wife, Sister, Daughter to the Tomb
   Weaving to Dreams the Sexual strife
   And weeping over the Web of Life   50

[Epilogue]

To The Accuser who is
The God of This World

Truly My Satan thou art but a Dunce
And dost not know the Garment from the Man
Every Harlot was a Virgin once
Nor canst thou ever change Kate into Nan

Tho thou art Worshipd by the Names Divine   5
Of Jesus & Jehovah: thou art still
The Son of Morn in weary Nights decline
The lost Travellers Dream under the Hill

⚯

ON HOMERS POETRY

Every Poem must necessarily be a perfect Unity, but why Homers is pecu-
liarly so, I cannot tell: he has told the story of Bellerophon & omitted the
Judgment of Paris which is not only a part, but a principal part of Homers
subject

But when a Work has Unity it is as much in a Part as in the Whole. the
Torso is as much a Unity as the Laocoon

As Unity is the cloke of folly so Goodness is the cloke of knavery Those
who will have Unity exclusively in Homer come out with a Moral like a
sting in the tail: Aristotle says Characters are either Good or Bad: now Goodness or Badness has nothing to do with Character. an Apple tree a Pear tree
a Horse a Lion, are Characters but a Good Apple tree or a Bad, is an Apple
tree still: a Horse is not more a Lion for being a Bad Horse. that is its Character: its Goodness or Badness is another consideration.

It is the same with the Moral of a whole Poem as with the Moral Goodness of its parts Unity & Morality, are secondary considerations & belong to
Philosophy & not to Poetry, to Exception & not to Rule, to Accident & not
to Substance. the Ancients calld it eating of the tree of good & evil.

The Classics, it is the Classics! & not Goths nor Monks, that Desolate
Europe with Wars.

❧

ON VIRGIL

Sacred Truth has pronounced that Greece & Rome as Babylon & Egypt:
so far from being parents of Arts & Sciences as they pretend: were destroyers of all Art. Homer Virgil & Ovid confirm this opinion & make us reverence
The Word of God, the only light of antiquity that remains unperverted by
War. Virgil in the Eneid Book VI. line 848 says Let others study Art: Rome
has somewhat better to do, namely War & Dominion

Rome & Greece swept Art into their maw & destroyd it   a Warlike State
never can produce Art. It will Rob & Plunder & accumulate into one place, &
Translate & Copy & Buy & Sell & Criticise, but not Make. Grecian is Mathematic Form   Gothic is Living Form   Mathematic Form is Eternal in
the Reasoning Memory. Living Form is Eternal Existence.

❧

THE GHOST of ABEL

A Revelation In the Visions of Jehovah
Seen by William Blake

PLATE I

To LORD BYRON in the Wilderness

                              What doest thou here Elijah?
Can a Poet doubt the Visions of Jehovah? Nature has no Outline:
but Imagination has. Nature has no Tune: but Imagination has!
Nature has no Supernatural & dissolves: Imagination is Eternity

*Scene. A rocky Country. Eve fainted over the dead body
of Abel which lays near a Grave. Adam kneels by her Jehovah
stands above*

Jehovah—	Adam!
Adam—	I will not hear thee more thou Spiritual Voice
	Is this Death?
Jehovah—	Adam!
Adam—	It is in vain: I will not hear thee
	Henceforth! Is this thy Promise that the Womans Seed
	Should bruise the Serpents head: Is this the Serpent? Ah!
	Seven times, O Eve thou hast fainted over the Dead. Ah! Ah! 5

Eve revives

Eve—	Is this the Promise of Jehovah! O it is all a vain delusion
	This Death & this Life & this Jehovah!
Jehovah—	Woman: lift thine eyes

A Voice is heard coming on

Voice—	O Earth cover not thou my Blood! cover not thou my Blood

Enter the Ghost of Abel

Eve—	Thou Visionary Phantasm thou art not the real Abel.
Abel—	Among the Elohim a Human Victim I wander I am their 10
	House
	Prince of the Air & our dimensions compass Zenith & Nadir
	Vain is thy Covenant O Jehovah I am the Accuser &
	Avenger
	Of Blood O Earth Cover not thou the Blood of Abel
Jehovah—	What Vengeance dost thou require
Abel—	Life for Life! Life for Life!
Jehovah—	He who shall take Cains life must also Die O Abel 15
	And who is he? Adam wilt thou, or Eve thou do this
Adam—	It is all a Vain delusion of the all creative Imagination

Eve come away & let us not believe these vain delusions
Abel is dead & Cain slew him! We shall also Die a Death
And then! what then? be as poor Abel a Thought: or as   20
This! O what shall I call thee Form Divine! Father of
    Mercies
That appearest to my Spiritual Vision: Eve seest thou also.

Eve—   I see him plainly with my Minds Eye. I see also Abel living:
Tho terribly afflicted as We also are, yet Jehovah sees him

PLATE 2

Alive & not Dead: were it not better to believe Vision
With all our might & strength tho we are fallen & lost

Adam—   Eve thou hast spoken truly. let us kneel before his feet.

They Kneel before Jehovah

Abel—   Are these the Sacrifices of Eternity O Jehovah, a Broken
    Spirit
And a Contrite Heart. O I cannot Forgive! the Accuser hath   5
Enterd into Me as into his House & I loathe thy Tabernacles
As thou hast said so is it come to pass: My desire is unto
    Cain
And He doth rule over Me: therefore My Soul in fumes
    of Blood
Cries for Vengeance: Sacrifice on Sacrifice Blood on Blood

Jehovah— Lo I have given you a Lamb for an Atonement instead   10
Of the Transgres[s]or, or no Flesh or Spirit could ever Live

Abel—   Compelled I cry O Earth cover not the Blood of Abel

Abel sinks down into the Grave from which arises Satan
Armed in glittering scales with a Crown & a Spear

Satan—   I will have Human Blood & not the blood of Bulls or
    Goats
And no Atonement O Jehovah the Elohim live on Sacrifice
Of Men: hence I am God of Men: Thou Human O   15
    Jehovah.
By the Rock & Oak of the Druid creeping Mistletoe &
    Thorn
Cains City built with Human Blood, not Blood of Bulls &
    Goats
Thou shalt Thyself be Sacrificed to Me thy God on Calvary

Jehovah— Such is My Will.   *Thunders*
           that Thou Thyself go to Eternal Death
In Self Annihilation even till Satan Self-subdud Put off   20
    Satan
Into the Bottomless Abyss whose torment arises for ever &
    ever.

On each side a Chorus of Angels entering Sing the following

The Elohim of the Heathen Swore Vengeance for Sin! Then Thou
    stoodst
Forth O Elohim Jehovah! in the midst of the darkness of the Oath! All
    Clothed
In Thy Covenant of the Forgiveness of Sins: Death O Holy! Is this
    Brotherhood
The Elohim saw their Oath Eternal Fire; they rolled apart trembling   25
    over The
Mercy Seat: each in his station fixt in the Firmament by Peace
    Brotherhood and Love.

The Curtain falls

The Voice of Abels Blood   t

1822 W Blakes Original Stereotype was 1788   t

❧

[The Laocoön]

[See plate, following page 454]

Drawn & Engraved by William Blake

ית[Jah, for Jehovah] & his two Sons Satan & Adam as they were copied
    from the Cherubim of Solomons Temple by three Rhodians & applied
    to Natural Fact or. History of Ilium

[Above the father's head:]

The Angel of the Divine Presence
מלאך יהוה [Angel of Jehovah]
οφιουχος [Serpent-holder]
He repented that he had made Adam
(of the Female, the Adamah)
& it grieved him at his heart

[About the serpent and figure (? Satan) to the right:]

Good
לילית [Lilith]
Santans Wife The Goddess Nature is War & Misery & Heroism a Miser

[About the serpent and figure (? Adam) to the left:]

Evil
Good & Evil are

-270-

Riches & Poverty a Tree of Misery
propagating Generation & Death

[Remaining aphorisms, reading outward in thematic order:]

What can be Created Can be Destroyed
Adam is only The Natural Man & not the Soul or Imagination

The Eternal Body of Man is The IMAGINATION.

that is
God himself
The Divine Body
} יש[ו]ע [Yeshua] JESUS we are his Members

It manifests itself in his Works of Art (In Eternity All is Vision)
All that we See is VISION from Generated Organs gone as soon as come
Permanent in The Imagination; considered as Nothing by the NATURAL
    MAN

HEBREW ART is called SIN by the Deist SCIENCE

The whole Business of Man Is The Arts & All Things Common

Christianity is Art & not Money
Money is its Curse

The Old & New Testaments are the Great Code of Art

Jesus & his Apostles & Disciples were all Artists
Their Works were destroyd by the Seven Angels of the Seven
    Churches in Asia. Antichrist Science

SCIENCE is the Tree of DEATH
ART is the Tree of LIFE GOD is JESUS

The Gods of Priam are the Cherubim of Moses & Solomon The Hosts
    of Heaven

The Gods of Greece & Egypt were Mathematical Diagrams See Plato's
    Works
There are States in which all Visionary Men are accounted Mad
    Men   such are Greece & Rome   Such is Empire or Tax
    See Luke Ch 2 v 1

Art Degraded Imagination Denied War Governed the Nations

Divine Union Deriding And Denying Immediate Communion with
    God
The Spoilers say Where are his Works That he did in the Wilderness
Lo what are these Whence came they These are not the Works
Of Egypt nor Babylon Whose Gods are the Powers of this World.
    Goddess, Nature.

Who first spoil & then destroy Imaginative Art For their Glory is
  War and Dominion

Empire against Art   See Virgils Eneid. Lib. VI. v 848

Spiritual War

Israel deliverd from Egypt is Art deliverd from Nature & Imitation
What we call Antique Gems are the Gems of Aarons Breast Plate
Prayer is the Study of Art
Praise is the Practise of Art
Fasting &c. all relate to Art
The outward Ceremony is Antichrist
Without Unceasing Practise nothing can be done

A Poet a Painter a Musician an Architect: the Man
Or Woman who is not one of these is not a Christian
You must leave Fathers & Mothers & Houses & Lands
  if they stand in the way of ART

The unproductive Man is not a Christian much less the Destroyer

Practise is Art   If you leave off you are Lost

The True Christian Charity not dependent on Money (the lifes blood
  of Poor Families) that is on Caesar or Empire or Natural Religion

For Every Pleasure Money Is Useless

Money, which is The Great Satan or Reason the Root of Good & Evil
  In The Accusation of Sin

Where any view of Money exists Art cannot be carried on, but War
  only (Read Matthew C X. 9 & 10 v) by pretences to the Two Impossibilities Chastity & Abstinence Gods of the Heathen

Is not every Vice possible to Man described in the Bible openly

All is not Sin that Satan calls so   all the Loves & Graces of Eternity.

If Morality was Christianity Socrates was the Saviour

Art can never exist without Naked Beauty displayed

No Secresy in Art

II

[PROPHETIC WORKS, UNENGRAVED]

TIRIEL
t,c

I
c

And Aged Tiriel. stood before the Gates of his beautiful palace t
With Myratana. once the Queen of all the western plains
But now his eyes were darkned. & his wife fading in death
They stood before their once delightful palace. & thus the Voice
Of aged Tiriel. arose. that his sons might hear in their gates 5

Accursed race of Tiriel. behold your father t
Come forth & look on her that bore you. come you accursed sons.
In my weak arms. I here have borne your dying mother t
Come forth sons of the Curse come forth. see the death of Myratana c

His sons ran from their gates. & saw their aged parents stand 10
And thus the eldest son of Tiriel raisd his mighty voice

Old man unworthy to be calld. the father of Tiriels race
For evry one of those thy wrinkles. each of those grey hairs
Are cruel as death. & as obdurate as the devouring pit
Why should thy sons care for thy curses thou accursed man 15
Were we not slaves till we rebeld. Who cares for Tiriels curse
His blessing was a cruel curse. His curse may be a blessing

He ceast the aged man raisd up his right hand to the heavens
His left supported Myratana shrinking in pangs of death t
The orbs of his large eyes he opend. & thus his voice went forth 20

Serpents not sons. wreathing around the bones of Tiriel
Ye worms of death feasting upon your aged parents flesh
Listen & hear your mothers groans. No more accursed Sons
She bears. she groans not at the birth of Heuxos or Yuva
These are the groans of death ye serpents These are the groans of 25
    death

Nourishd with milk ye serpents. nourishd with mothers tears & cares
Look at my eyes blind as the orbless scull among the stones
Look at my bald head. Hark listen ye serpents listen
What Myratana. What my wife. O Soul O Spirit O fire   c
What Myratana. art thou dead. Look here ye serpents look   30
The serpents sprung from her own bowels have draind her dry as this
Curse on your ruthless heads. for I will bury her even here

So saying he began to dig a grave with his aged hands
But Heuxos calld a son of Zazel. to dig their mother a grave

Old cruelty desist & let us dig a grave for thee   35
Thou hast refusd our charity thou hast refusd our food
Thou hast refusd our clothes our beds our houses for thy dwelling
Chusing to wander like a Son of Zazel in the rocks
Why dost thou curse. is not the curse now come upon your head
Was it not you enslavd the sons of Zazel. & they have cursd   40
And now you feel it. Dig a grave & let us bury our mother

There take the body. cursed sons. & may the heavens rain wrath
As thick as northern fogs. around your gates. to choke you up
That you may lie as now your mother lies. like dogs. cast out
The stink. of your dead carcases. annoying man & beast   45
Till your white bones are bleachd with age for a memorial.
No your remembrance shall perish. for when your carcases
Lie stinking on the earth. the buriers shall arise from the east
And. not a bone of all the sons of Tiriel remain
Bury your mother but you cannot bury the curse of Tiriel   50

He ceast & darkling oer the mountains sought his pathless way

2   c

He wanderd day & night to him both day & night were dark
The sun he felt but the bright moon was now a useless globe
Oer mountains & thro vales of woe. the blind & aged man
Wanderd till he that leadeth all. led him to the vales of Har

And Har & Heva like two children sat beneath the Oak   5
Mnetha now aged waited on them. & brought them food & clothing
But they were as the shadow of Har. & as the years forgotten
Playing with flowers. & running after birds they spent the day
And in the night like infants slept delighted with infant dreams

Soon as the blind wanderer enterd the pleasant gardens of Har   t 10
They ran weeping like frighted infants for refuge in Mnethas arms
The blind man felt his way & cried peace to these open doors
Let no one fear for poor blind Tiriel hurts none but himself
Tell me O friends where am I now. & in what pleasant place

This is the valley of Har said Mnetha & this the tent of Har   15
Who art thou poor blind man. that takest the name of Tiriel on thee
Tiriel is king of all the west. who art thou I am Mnetha
And this is Har & Heva. trembling like infants by my side

I know Tiriel is king of the west & there he lives in joy
No matter who I am O Mnetha. if thou hast any food   20
Give it me. for I cannot stay my journey is far from hence

Then Har said O my mother Mnetha venture not so near him
For he is the king of rotten wood & of the bones of death
He wanders. without eyes. & passes thro thick walls & doors
Thou shalt not smite my mother Mnetha O thou eyeless man   ᵗ25

A wanderer. I beg for food. you see I cannot weep   ᵗ
I cast away my staff the kind companion of my travel
And I kneel down that you may see I am a harmless man

He kneeled down & Mnetha said Come Har & Heva rise
He is an innocent old man & hungry with his travel   30

Then Har arose & laid his hand upon old Tiriels head

God bless thy poor bald pate. God bless. thy hollow winking eyes
God bless thy shriveld beard. God. bless. thy many wrinkled forehead
Thou hast no teeth old man & thus I kiss thy sleek bald head
Heva come kiss his bald head for he will not hurt us Heva   35

Then Heva came & took old Tiriel in her mothers arms

Bless thy poor eyes old man. & bless the old father of Tiriel
Thou art my Tiriels old father. I know thee thro thy wrinkles
Because thou smellest. like the figtree. thou smellest like ripe figs
How didst thou lose thy eyes old Tiriel. bless thy wrinkled face   ᵗ40

Mnetha said come in aged wanderer tell us of thy name
Why shouldest thou conceal thyself from those of thine own flesh

I am not of this region. said Tiriel dissemblingly   ᵗ
I am an aged wanderer once father of a race
Far in the north. but they were wicked & were all destroyd   45
And I their father sent an outcast. I have told you all
Ask me no more I pray for grief hath seald my precious sight

O Lord said Mnetha how I tremble are there then more people
More human creatures on this earth beside the sons of Har

No more said Tiriel but I remain on all this globe   50
And I remain an outcast. hast thou any thing to drink

Then Mnetha gave him milk & fruits. & they sat down together

3

They sat & eat & Har & Heva smild on Tiriel

Thou art a very old old man but I am older than thou
How came thine hair to leave thy forehead how came thy face so brown
My hair is very long my beard. doth cover all my breast
God bless thy piteous face. to count the wrinkles in thy face   5
Would puzzle Mnetha. bless thy face for thou art Tiriel   t

Tiriel I never saw but once I sat with him & eat
He was as chearful as a prince & gave me entertainment
But long I staid not at his palace for I am forcd to wander

What wilt thou leave us too said Heva thou shalt not leave us too   10
For we have many sports to shew thee & many songs to sing
And after dinner we will walk into the cage of Har
And thou shalt help us to catch birds. & gather them ripe cherries
Then let thy name be Tiriel & never leave us more

If thou dost go said Har I wish thine eyes may see thy folly   15
My sons have left me did thine leave thee O twas very cruel

No venerable man said Tiriel ask me not such things
For thou dost make my heart to bleed my sons were not like thine
But worse O never ask me more or I must flee away

Thou shalt not go said Heva till thou hast seen our singing birds   20
And heard Har sing in the great cage & slept upon our fleeces
Go not for thou art so like Tiriel. that I love thine head
Tho it is wrinkled like the earth parchd with the summer heat

Then Tiriel rose up from the seat & said god bless these tents   t
My Journey is oer rocks & mountains. not in pleasant vales   25
I must not sleep nor rest because of madness & dismay   t

And Mnetha said Thou must not go to wander dark. alone
But dwell with us & let us be to thee instead of eyes
And I will bring thee food old man. till death shall call thee hence

Then Tiriel frownd & answerd. Did I not command you saying   30
Madness & deep dismay posses[s] the heart of the blind man
The wanderer who seeks the woods leaning upon his staff   t

Then Mnetha trembling at his frowns led him to the tent door
And gave to him his staff & blest him. he went on his way

But Har & Heva stood & watchd him till he enterd the wood   35
And then they went & wept to Mnetha. but they soon forgot their tears

Over the weary hills the blind man took his lonely way
To him the day & night alike was dark & desolate
But far he had not gone when Ijim from his woods come down
Met him at entrance of the forest in a dark & lonely way

Who art thou Eyeless wretch that thus obstructst the lions path   5
Ijim shall rend thy feeble joints thou tempter of dark Ijim
Thou hast the form of Tiriel but I know thee well enough
Stand from my path foul fiend is this the last of thy deceits
To be a hypocrite & stand in shape of a blind beggar

The blind man heard his brothers voice & kneeld down on his knee   10

O brother Ijim if it is thy voice that speaks to me
Smite not thy brother Tiriel tho weary of his life
My sons have smitten me already. and if thou smitest me
The curse that rolls over their heads will rest itself on thine
Tis now seven years Since in my palace I beheld thy face   15

Come thou dark fiend I dare thy cunning know that Ijim scorns
To smite the[e] in the form of helpless age & eyeless policy
Rise up for I discern thee & I dare thy eloquent tongue
Come I will lead thee on thy way & use thee as a scoff

O Brother Ijim thou beholdest wretched Tiriel   20
Kiss me my brother & then leave me to wander desolate

No artful fiend. but I will lead thee dost thou want to go
Reply not lest I bind thee with the green flags of the brook
Ay now thou art discoverd I will use thee like a slave

When Tiriel heard the words of Ijim he sought not to reply   25
He knew twas vain for Ijims words were as the voice of Fate

And they went on together over hills thro woody dales
Blind to the pleasures of the sight & deaf to warbling birds
All day they walkd & all the night beneath the pleasant Moon
Westwardly journeying till Tiriel grew weary with his travel   30

O Ijim I am faint & weary for my knees forbid
To bear me further. urge me not lest I should die with travel
A little rest I crave a little water from a brook
Or I shall soon discover that I am a mortal man
And you will lose your once lovd Tiriel alas how faint I am   35

Impudent fiend said Ijim hold thy glib & eloquent tongue
Tiriel is a king. & thou the tempter of dark Ijim
Drink of this running brook. & I will bear thee on my shoulders

He drank & Ijim raisd him up & bore him on his shoulders
All day he bore him & when evening drew her solemn curtain   40
Enterd the gates of Tiriels palace. & stood & calld aloud

Heuxos come forth I here have brought the fiend that troubles Ijim
Look knowst thou aught of this grey beard. or of these blinded eyes

Heuxos & Lotho ran forth at the sound of Ijims voice
And saw their aged father borne upon his mighty shoulders   45
Their eloquent tongues were dumb & sweat stood on their trembling
     limbs
They knew twas vain to strive with Ijim they bowd & silent stood

What Heuxos call thy father for I mean to sport to night
This is the hypocrite that sometimes roars a dreadful lion
Then I have rent his limbs & left him rotting in the forest   50
For birds to eat but I have scarce departed from the place
But like a tyger he would come & so I rent him too
Then like a river he would seek to drown me in his waves
But soon I buffetted the torrent anon like to a cloud
Fraught with the swords of lightning. but I bravd the vengeance too 55
Then he would creep like a bright serpent till around my neck
While I was Sleeping he would twine I squeezd his poisnous soul
Then like a toad or like a newt. would whisper in my ears
Or like a rock stood in my way. or like a poisnous shrub
At last I caught him in the form of Tiriel blind & old   60
And so Ill keep him fetch your father fetch forth Myratana

They stood confounded. and Thus Tiriel raisd his silver voice

Serpents not sons why do you stand fetch hither Tiriel   t
Fetch hither Myratana & delight yourselves with scoffs
For poor blind Tiriel is returnd & this much injurd head   65
Is ready for your bitter taunts. come forth sons of the curse

Mean time the other sons of Tiriel ran around their father
Confounded at the terrible strength of Ijim they knew twas vain
Both spear & shield were useless & the coat of iron mail
When Ijim stretchd his mighty arm. the arrow from his limbs   70
Rebounded & the piercing sword broke on his naked flesh   t

Then is it true Heuxos that thou hast turnd thy aged parent
To be the sport of wintry winds. (said Ijim) is this true
It is a lie & I am like the tree torn by the wind
Thou eyeless fiend. & you dissemblers. Is this Tiriels house   75
It is as false [as] Matha. & as dark as vacant Orcus   t,c
Escape ye fiends for Ijim will not lift his hand against ye

So saying. Ijim gloomy turnd his back & silent sought
The secret forests & all night wanderd in desolate ways

–278–

5

And aged Tiriel stood & said where does the thunder sleep
Where doth he hide his terrible head & his swift & fiery daughters
Where do they shroud their fiery wings & the terrors of their hair
Earth thus I stamp thy bosom rouse the earthquake from his den
To raise his dark & burning visage thro the cleaving ground   t 5
To thrust these towers with his shoulders. let his fiery dogs
Rise from the center belching flames & roarings. dark smoke
Where art thou Pestilence that bathest in fogs & standing lakes
Rise up thy sluggish limbs. & let the loathsomest of poisons
Drop from thy garments as thou walkest. wrapt in yellow clouds   10
Here take thy seat. in this wide court. let it be strown with dead
And sit & smile upon these cursed sons of Tiriel
Thunder & fire & pestilence. here you not Tiriels curse

He ceast the heavy clouds confusd rolld round the lofty towers
Discharging their enormous voices. at the fathers curse   15
The earth trembled fires belched from the yawning clefts
And when the shaking ceast a fog possest the accursed clime

The cry was great in Tiriels palace his five daughters ran
And caught him by the garments weeping with cries of bitter woe

Aye now you feel the curse you cry. but may all ears be deaf   20
As Tiriels & all eyes as blind as Tiriels to your woes
May never stars shine on your roofs may never sun nor moon   t
Visit you but eternal fogs hover around your walls
Hela my youngest daughter you shall lead me from this place   t
And let the curse fall on the rest & wrap them up together   25

He ceast & Hela led her father from the noisom place
In haste they fled while all the sons & daughters of Tiriel
Chaind in thick darkness utterd cries of mourning all the night
And in the morning Lo an hundred men in ghastly death
The four daughters stretchd on the marble pavement silent all   t 30
falln by the pestilence the rest moped round in guilty fears   t
And all the children in their beds were cut off in one night
Thirty of Tiriels sons remaind. to wither in the palace
Desolate. Loathed. Dumb Astonishd waiting for black death

6

And Hela led her father thro the silent of the night
Astonishd silent. till the morning beams began to spring

Now Hela I can go with pleasure & dwell with Har & Heva
Now that the curse shall clean devour all those guilty sons
This is the right & ready way I know it by the sound   5

That our feet make. Remember Hela I have savd thee from death
Then be obedient to thy father for the curse is taken off thee
I dwelt with Myratana five years in the desolate rock
And all that time we waited for the fire to fall from heaven
Or for the torrents of the sea to overwhelm you all   10
But now my wife is dead & all the time of grace is past
You see the parents curse. Now lead me where I have commanded

O Leagued with evil spirits thou accursed man of sin
True I was born thy slave who askd thee to save me from death—   t
Twas for thy self thou cruel man because thou wantest eyes   15

True Hela this is the desert of all those cruel ones
Is Tiriel cruel look. his daughter & his youngest daughter
Laughs at affection glories in rebellion. scoffs at Love:—
I have not eat these two days lead me to Har & Hevas tent
Or I will wrap the[e] up in such a terrible fathers curse   20
That thou shalt feel worms in thy marrow creeping thro thy bones
Yet thou shalt lead me. Lead me I command to Har & Heva

O cruel O destroyer O consumer. O avenger
To Har & Heva I will lead thee then would that they would curse
Then would they curse as thou hast cursed but they are not like thee   25
O they are holy. & forgiving filld with loving mercy
Forgetting the offences of their most rebellious children
Or else thou wouldest not have livd to curse thy helpless children

Look on my eyes Hela & see for thou hast eyes to see
The tears swell from my stony fountains. wherefore do I weep   30
Wherefore from my blind orbs art thou not siezd with poisnous stings
Laugh serpent youngest venomous reptile of the flesh of Tiriel
Laugh. for thy father Tiriel shall give the[e] cause to laugh
Unless thou lead me to the tent of Har child of the curse

Silence thy evil tongue thou murderer of thy helpless children   35
I lead thee to the tent of Har not that I mind thy curse
But that I feel they will curse thee & hang upon thy bones
Fell shaking agonies. & in each wrinkle of that face
Plant worms of death to feast upon the tongue of terrible curses

Hela my daughter listen. thou art the daughter of Tiriel   40
Thy father calls. Thy father lifts his hand unto the heavens   t
For thou hast laughed at my tears. & curst thy aged father
Let snakes rise from thy bedded locks & laugh among thy curls

He ceast her dark hair upright stood while snakes infolded round
Her madding brows. her shrieks apalld the soul of Tiriel   45

What have I done Hela my daughter fearst thou now the curse
Or wherefore dost thou cry Ah wretch to curse thy aged father
Lead me to Har & Heva & the curse of Tiriel
Shall fail. If thou refuse howl in the desolate mountains

7

She howling led him over mountains & thro frighted vales
Till to the caves of Zazel they approachd at even tide

Forth from their caves old Zazel & his sons ran. when they saw
Their tyrant prince blind & his daughter howling & leading him

They laughd & mocked some threw dirt & stones as they passd by   5
But when Tiriel turnd around & raisd his awful voice
Some fled away but Zazel stood still & thus began   t

Bald tyrant. wrinkled cunning listen to Zazels chains   t
Twas thou that chaind thy brother Zazel where are now thine eyes
Shout beautiful daughter of Tiriel. thou singest a sweet song   10
Where are you going. come & eat some roots & drink some water
Thy crown is bald old man. the sun will dry thy brains away
And thou wilt be as foolish as thy foolish brother Zazel

The blind man heard. & smote his breast & trembling passed on
They threw dirt after them. till to the covert of a wood   15
The howling maiden led her father where wild beasts resort
Hoping to end her woes. but from her cries the tygers fled   t
All night they wanderd thro the wood & when the sun arose
They enterd on the mountains of Har at Noon the happy tents
Were frighted by the dismal cries of Hela on the mountains   20

But Har & Heva slept fearless as babes. on loving breasts
Mnetha awoke she ran & stood at the tent door & saw
The aged wanderer led towards the tents she took her bow
And chose her arrows then advancd to meet the terrible pair

8   c

And Mnetha hasted & met them at the gate of the lower garden

Stand still or from my bow recieve a sharp & winged death

Then Tiriel stood. saying what soft voice threatens such bitter things
Lead me to Har & Heva I am Tiriel King of the west   t

And Mnetha led them to the tent of Har. and Har & Heva   5
Ran to the door. when Tiriel felt the ankles of aged Har
He said. O weak mistaken father of a lawless race
Thy laws O Har & Tiriels wisdom end together in a curse   t
Why is one law given to the lion & the patient Ox   t,c
And why men bound beneath the heavens in a reptile form   t 10
A worm of sixty winters creeping on the dusky ground
The child springs from the womb. the father ready stands to form
The infant head while the mother idle plays with her dog on her couch
The young bosom is cold for lack of mothers nourishment & milk

-281-

Is cut off from the weeping mouth with difficulty & pain   *15*
The little lids are lifted & the little nostrils opend
The father forms a whip to rouze the sluggish senses to act
And scourges off all youthful fancies from the new-born man
Then walks the weak infant in sorrow compelld to number footsteps t
Upon the sand. &c   *20*
And when the drone has reachd his crawling length
Black berries appear that poison all around him. Such was Tiriel t
Compelld to pray repugnant & to humble the immortal spirit
Till I am subtil as a serpent in a paradise
Consuming all both flowers & fruits insects & warbling birds   *25*
And now my paradise is falln & a drear sandy plain
Returns my thirsty hissings in a curse on thee O Har
Mistaken father of a lawless race my voice is past

He ceast outstretchd at Har & Hevas feet in awful death

❧

THE
FRENCH REVOLUTION.
A POEM,
IN SEVEN BOOKS.

t,c

BOOK THE FIRST.

LONDON: Printed for J. Johnson, Nº 72,
St Paul's Church-yard. MDCCXCI.
{Price One Shilling.}

PAGE [iii]

ADVERTISEMENT.

The remaining Books of this Poem are finished, and will be
published in their Order.

PAGE [1]

THE FRENCH REVOLUTION

Book the First.

The dead brood over Europe, the cloud and vision descends over
    chearful France;
O cloud well appointed! Sick, sick: the Prince on his couch, wreath'd
    in dim
And appalling mist; his strong hand outstretch'd, from his shoulder
    down the bone

Runs aching cold into the scepter too heavy for mortal grasp. No more
To be swayed by visible hand, nor in cruelty bruise the mild 5
    flourishing mountains.

Sick the mountains, and all their vineyards weep, in the eyes of the
    kingly mourner;
Pale is the morning cloud in his visage. Rise, Necker: the ancient
    dawn calls us
To awake from slumbers of five thousand years. I awake, but my soul
    is in dreams;
From my window I see the old mountains of France, like aged men,
    fading away.

PAGE 2

Troubled, leaning on Necker, descends the King, to his chamber of 10
    council; shady mountains
In fear, utter voices of thunder; the woods of France embosom the
    sound;
Clouds of wisdom prophetic reply, and roll over the palace roof heavy.
Forty men: each conversing with woes in the infinite shadows of his
    soul,
Like our ancient fathers in regions of twilight, walk, gathering round
    the King;
Again the loud voice of France cries to the morning, the morning 15
    prophecies to its clouds.

For the Commons convene in the Hall of the Nation. France shakes!
    And the heavens of France
Perplex'd vibrate round each careful countenance! Darkness of old
    times around them
Utters loud despair, shadowing Paris; her grey towers groan, and the
    Bastile trembles.
In its terrible towers the Governor stood, in dark fogs list'ning the
    horror;
A thousand his soldiers, old veterans of France, breathing red clouds of 20
    power and dominion,
Sudden seiz'd with howlings, despair, and black night, he stalk'd like
    a lion from tower
To tower, his howlings were heard in the Louvre; from court to court
    restless he dragg'd
His strong limbs; from court to court curs'd the fierce torment
    unquell'd,
Howling and giving the dark command; in his soul stood the purple
    plague,
Tugging his iron manacles, and piercing through the seven towers 25
    dark and sickly,
Panting over the prisoners like a wolf gorg'd; and the den nam'd
    Horror held a man

Chain'd hand and foot, round his neck an iron band, bound to the
impregnable wall.

In his soul was the serpent coil'd round in his heart, hid from the
light, as in a cleft rock;

And the man was confin'd for a writing prophetic: in the tower nam'd
Darkness, was a man

Pinion'd down to the stone floor, his strong bones scarce cover'd   30
with sinews; the iron rings

Were forg'd smaller as the flesh decay'd, a mask of iron on his face hid
the lineaments

PAGE 3

Of ancient Kings, and the frown of the eternal lion was hid from the
oppressed earth.

In the tower named Bloody, a skeleton yellow remained in its chains
on its couch

Of stone, once a man who refus'd to sign papers of abhorrence; the
eternal worm

Crept in the skeleton. In the den nam'd Religion, a loathsome sick   35
woman, bound down

To a bed of straw; the seven diseases of earth, like birds of prey, stood
on the couch,

And fed on the body. She refus'd to be whore to the Minister, and
with a knife smote him.

In the tower nam'd Order, an old man, whose white beard cover'd the
stone floor like weeds

On margin of the sea, shrivel'd up by heat of day and cold of night;
his den was short

And narrow as a grave dug for a child, with spiders webs wove, and   40
with slime

Of ancient horrors cover'd, for snakes and scorpions are his
companions; harmless they breathe

His sorrowful breath: he, by conscience urg'd, in the city of Paris
rais'd a pulpit,

And taught wonders to darken'd souls. In the den nam'd Destiny a
strong man sat,

His feet and hands cut off, and his eyes blinded; round his middle a
chain and a band

Fasten'd into the wall; fancy gave him to see an image of despair in   45
his den,

Eternally rushing round, like a man on his hands and knees, day and
night without rest:

He was friend to the favourite. In the seventh tower, nam'd the tower
of God, was a man

Mad, with chains loose, which he dragg'd up and down; fed with
hopes year by year, he pined

For liberty; vain hopes: his reason decay'd, and the world of attraction
in his bosom

Center'd, and the rushing of chaos overwhelm'd his dark soul. He was 50
    confin'd

For a letter of advice to a King, and his ravings in winds are heard over
    Versailles.

But the dens shook and trembled, the prisoners look up and assay to
    shout; they listen,

Then laugh in the dismal den, then are silent, and a light walks round
    the dark towers.

PAGE 4

For the Commons convene in the Hall of the Nation; like spirits of
    fire in the beautiful

Porches of the Sun, to plant beauty in the desart craving abyss, they 55
    gleam

On the anxious city; all children new-born first behold them; tears are
    fled,

And they nestle in earth-breathing bosoms. So the city of Paris, their
    wives and children,

Look up to the morning Senate, and visions of sorrow leave pensive
    streets.

But heavy brow'd jealousies lower o'er the Louvre, and terrors of
    ancient Kings

Descend from the gloom and wander thro' the palace, and weep   60
    round the King and his Nobles.

While loud thunders roll, troubling the dead, Kings are sick
    throughout all the earth,

The voice ceas'd: the Nation sat: And the triple forg'd fetters of
    times were unloos'd.

The voice ceas'd: the Nation sat: but ancient darkness and trembling
    wander thro' the palace.

As in day of havock and routed battle, among thick shades of
    discontent,

On the soul-skirting mountains of sorrow cold waving: the Nobles 65
    fold round the King,

Each stern visage lock'd up as with strong bands of iron, each strong
    limb bound down as with marble,

In flames of red wrath burning, bound in astonishment a quarter of
    an hour.

Then the King glow'd: his Nobles fold round, like the sun of old
    time quench'd in clouds;

In their darkness the King stood, his heart flam'd, and utter'd a
    with'ring heat, and these words burst forth:

"The nerves of five thousand years ancestry tremble, shaking the 70
    heavens of France;

"Throbs of anguish beat on brazen war foreheads, they descend and
    look into their graves.

PAGE 5

"I see thro' darkness, thro' clouds rolling round me, the spirits of
    ancient Kings

"Shivering over their bleached bones; round them their counsellors look
    up from the dust,

"Crying: 'Hide from the living! Our b[a]nds and our prisoners shout in   t
    the open field,

"'Hide in the nether earth! Hide in the bones! Sit obscured in the   75
    hollow scull.

"'Our flesh is corrupted, and we [wear] away. We are not numbered   t
    among the living. Let us hide

"'In stones, among roots of trees. The prisoners have burst their dens,

"'Let us hide; let us hide in the dust; and plague and wrath and tempest
    shall cease.'"

He ceas'd, silent pond'ring, his brows folded heavy, his forehead was
    in affliction,

Like the central fire: from the window he saw his vast armies spread   80
    over the hills,

Breathing red fires from man to man, and from horse to horse; then
    his bosom

Expanded like starry heaven, he sat down: his Nobles took their
    ancient seats.

Then the ancientest Peer, Duke of Burgundy, rose from the
    Monarch's right hand, red as wines

From his mountains, an odor of war, like a ripe vineyard, rose from
    his garments,

And the chamber became as a clouded sky; o'er the council he   85
    stretch'd his red limbs,

Cloth'd in flames of crimson, as a ripe vineyard stretches over sheaves
    of corn,

The fierce Duke hung over the council; around him croud, weeping
    in his burning robe,

A bright cloud of infant souls; his words fall like purple autumn on
    the sheaves.

"Shall this marble built heaven become a clay cottage, this earth an
    oak stool, and these mowers

"From the Atlantic mountains, mow down all this great starry harvest   90
    of six thousand years?

"And shall Necker, the hind of Geneva, stretch out his crook'd sickle
    o'er fertile France,

PAGE 6

"Till our purple and crimson is faded to russet, and the kingdoms of
    earth bound in sheaves,

"And the ancient forests of chivalry hewn, and the joys of the combat
    burnt for fuel;
"Till the power and dominion is rent from the pole, sword and scepter
    from sun and moon,
"The law and gospel from fire and air, and eternal reason and science   95
"From the deep and the solid, and man lay his faded head down on
    the rock
"Of eternity, where the eternal lion and eagle remain to devour?
"This to prevent, urg'd by cries in day, and prophetic dreams hovering
    in night,
"To enrich the lean earth that craves, furrow'd with plows; whose seed
    is departing from her;
"Thy Nobles have gather'd thy starry hosts round this rebellious city   100
"To rouze up the ancient forests of Europe, with clarions of [loud]
    breathing war;
"To hear the horse neigh to the drum and trumpet, and the trumpet
    and war shout reply;
"Stretch the hand that beckons the eagles of heaven; they cry over
    Paris, and wait
"Till Fayette point his finger to Versailles; the eagles of heaven must
    have their prey."

The King lean'd on his mountains, then lifted his head and look'd   105
    on his armies, that shone
Through heaven, tinging morning with beams of blood, then turning
    to Burgundy troubled:

PAGE 7

"Burgundy, thou wast born a lion! My soul is o'ergrown with distress
"For the Nobles of France, and dark mists roll round me and blot the
    writing of God
"Written in my bosom. Necker rise, leave the kingdom, thy life is
    surrounded with snares;
"We have call'd an Assembly, but not to destroy; we have given gifts,   110
    not to the weak;
"I hear rushing of muskets, and bright'ning of swords, and visages
    redd'ning with war,
"Frowning and looking up from brooding villages and every dark'ning
    city;
"Ancient wonders frown over the kingdom, and cries of women and
    babes are heard,
"And tempests of doubt roll around me, and fierce sorrows, because
    of the Nobles of France;
"Depart, answer not, for the tempest must fall, as in years that are   115
    passed away."

He ceas'd, and burn'd silent, red clouds roll round Necker, a weeping
    is heard o'er the palace;

Like a dark cloud Necker paus'd, and like thunder on the just man's
    burial day he paus'd;
Silent sit the winds, silent the meadows, while the husbandman and
    woman of weakness
And bright children look after him into the grave, and water his clay
    with love,
Then turn towards pensive fields; so Necker paus'd, and his visage   ^t *120*
    was cover'd with clouds.

Dropping a tear the old man his place left, and when he was gone out
He set his face toward Geneva to flee, and the women and children
    of the city
Kneel'd round him and kissed his garments and wept; he stood a short
    space in the street,
Then fled; and the whole city knew he was fled to Geneva, and the
    Senate heard it.

But the Nobles burn'd wrathful at Necker's departure, and wreath'd   *125*
    their clouds and waters
In dismal volumes; as risen from beneath the Archbishop of Paris
    arose,
In the rushing of scales and hissing of flames and rolling of sulphurous
    smoke.

"Hearken, Monarch of France, to the terrors of heaven, and let thy
    soul drink of my counsel;
"Sleeping at midnight in my golden tower, the repose of the labours
    of men
"Wav'd its solemn cloud over my head. I awoke; a cold hand passed   *130*
    over my limbs, and behold
"An aged form, white as snow, hov'ring in mist, weeping in the
    uncertain light,
PAGE 8
"Dim the form almost faded, tears fell down the shady cheeks; at his
    feet many cloth'd
"In white robes, strewn in air censers and harps, silent they lay
    prostrated;
"Beneath, in the awful void, myriads descending and weeping thro'
    dismal winds,
"Endless the shady train shiv'ring descended, from the gloom where   *135*
    the aged form wept.
"At length, trembling, the vision sighing, in a low voice, like the voice
    of the grasshopper whisper'd:
"'My groaning is heard in the abbeys, and God, so long worshipp'd,
    departs as a lamp
"'Without oil; for a curse is heard hoarse thro' the land, from a godless
    race

"'Descending to beasts; they look downward and labour and forget my holy law;

"'The sound of prayer fails from lips of flesh, and the holy hymn from 140 thicken'd tongues:

"'For the bars of Chaos are burst; her millions prepare their fiery way

"'Thro' the orbed abode of the holy dead, to root up and pull down and remove,

"'And Nobles and Clergy shall fail from before me, and my cloud and vision be no more;

"'The mitre become black, the crown vanish, and the scepter and ivory staff

"'Of the ruler wither among bones of death; they shall consume from 145 the thistly field,

"'And the sound of the bell, and voice of the sabbath, and singing of the holy choir,

"'Is turn'd into songs of the harlot in day, and cries of the virgin in night.

"'They shall drop at the plow and faint at the harrow, unredeem'd, unconfess'd, unpardon'd;

"'The priest rot in his surplice by the lawless lover, the holy beside the accursed,

"'The King, frowning in purple, beside the grey plowman, and their 150 worms embrace together.'

"The voice ceas'd, a groan shook my chamber; I slept, for the cloud of repose returned,

"But morning dawn'd heavy upon me. I rose to bring my Prince heaven utter'd counsel.

"Hear my counsel, O King, and send forth thy Generals, the command of Heaven is upon thee;

"Then do thou command, O King, to shut up this Assembly in their final home;

PAGE 9

"Let thy soldiers possess this city of rebels, that threaten to bathe their 155 feet

"In the blood of Nobility; trampling the heart and the head; let the Bastile devour

"These rebellious seditious; seal them up, O Anointed, in everlasting chains."

He sat down, a damp cold pervaded the Nobles, and monsters of worlds unknown

Swam round them, watching to be delivered; When Aumont, whose chaos-born soul

Eternally wand'ring a Comet and swift-falling fire, pale enter'd the 160 chamber;

Before the red Council he stood, like a man that returns from hollow graves.

"Awe surrounded, alone thro' the army a fear and a with'ring blight
blown by the north;

"The Abbe de S[i]eyes from the Nation's Assembly. O Princes and
Generals of France,

"Unquestioned, unhindered, awe-struck are the soldiers; a dark
shadowy man in the form

"Of King Henry the Fourth walks before him in fires, the captains   165
like men bound in chains

"Stood still as he pass'd, he is come to the Louvre, O King, with a
message to thee;

"The strong soldiers tremble, the horses their manes bow, and the
guards of thy palace are fled."

Up rose awful in his majestic beams Bourbon's strong Duke; his proud
sword from his thigh

Drawn, he threw on the Earth! the Duke of Bretagne and the Earl
of Borgogne

Rose inflam'd, to and fro in the chamber, like thunder-clouds ready   170
to burst.

"What, damp all our fires, O spectre of Henry," said Bourbon; "and
rend the flames

"From the head of our King! Rise, Monarch of France; command me,
and I will lead

"This army of superstition at large, that the ardor of noble souls
quenchless,

"May yet burn in France, nor our shoulders be plow'd with the furrows
of poverty."

PAGE 10

Then Orleans generous as mountains arose, and unfolded his robe,   175
and put forth

His benevolent hand, looking on the Archbishop, who changed as pale
as lead;

Would have risen but could not, his voice issued harsh grating; instead
of words harsh hissings

Shook the chamber; he ceas'd abash'd. Then Orleans spoke, all was
silent,

He breath'd on them, and said, "O princes of fire, whose flames are
for growth not consuming,

"Fear not dreams, fear not visions, nor be you dismay'd with sorrows   180
which flee at the morning;

"Can the fires of Nobility ever be quench'd, or the stars by a stormy
night?

"Is the body diseas'd when the members are healthful? can the man be
bound in sorrow

"Whose ev'ry function is fill'd with its fiery desire? can the soul whose
brain and heart

"Cast their rivers in equal tides thro' the great Paradise, languish because the feet

"Hands, head, bosom, and parts of love, follow their high breathing joy? *185*

"And can Nobles be bound when the people are free, or God weep when his children are happy?

"Have you never seen Fayette's forehead, or Mirabeau's eyes, or the shoulders of Target,

"Or Bailly the strong foot of France, or Clermont the terrible voice, and your robes

"Still retain their own crimson? mine never yet faded, for fire delights in its form.

"But go, merciless man! enter into the infinite labyrinth of another's *190*
brain

"Ere thou measure the circle that he shall run. Go, thou cold recluse, into the fires

"Of another's high flaming rich bosom, and return unconsum'd, and write laws.

"If thou canst not do this, doubt thy theories, learn to consider all men as thy equals,

"Thy brethren, and not as thy foot or thy hand, unless thou first fearest to hurt them."

The Monarch stood up, the strong Duke his sword to its golden *195*
scabbard return'd,

The Nobles sat round like clouds on the mountains, when the storm is passing away.

PAGE II

"Let the Nation's Ambassador come among Nobles, like incense of the valley."

Aumont went out and stood in the hollow porch, his ivory wand in his hand;

A cold orb of disdain revolv'd round him, and covered his soul with snows eternal.

Great Henry's soul shuddered, a whirlwind and fire tore furious *200*
from his angry bosom;

He indignant departed on horses of heav'n. Then the Abbe de S[i]eyes rais'd his feet

On the steps of the Louvre, like a voice of God following a storm, the Abbe follow'd

The pale fires of Aumont into the chamber, as a father that bows to his son;

Whose rich fields inheriting spread their old glory, so the voice of the people bowed

Before the ancient seat of the kingdom and mountains to be renewed. *205*

"Hear, O Heavens of France, the voice of the people, arising from valley and hill,

"O'erclouded with power. Hear the voice of vallies, the voice of meek cities,

"Mourning oppressed on village and field, till the village and field is a waste.

"For the husbandman weeps at blights of the fife, and blasting of trumpets consume

"The souls of mild France; the pale mother nourishes her child to the deadly slaughter.   210

"When the heavens were seal'd with a stone, and the terrible sun clos'd in an orb, and the moon

"Rent from the nations, and each star appointed for watchers of night,

"The millions of spirits immortal were bound in the ruins of sulphur heaven

"To wander inslav'd; black, deprest in dark ignorance, kept in awe with the whip,

"To worship terrors, bred from the blood of revenge and breath of desire,   215

"In beastial forms; or more terrible men, till the dawn of our peaceful morning,

"Till dawn, till morning, till the breaking of clouds, and swelling of winds, and the universal voice,

PAGE 12

"Till man raise his darken'd limbs out of the caves of night, his eyes and his heart

"Expand: where is space! where O Sun is thy dwelling! where thy tent, O faint slumb'rous Moon.

"Then the valleys of France shall cry to the soldier, 'throw down thy sword and musket,   220

"'And run and embrace the meek peasant.' Her Nobles shall hear and shall weep, and put off

"The red robe of terror, the crown of oppression, the shoes of contempt, and unbuckle

"The girdle of war from the desolate earth; then the Priest in his thund'rous cloud

"Shall weep, bending to earth embracing the valleys, and putting his hand to the plow,

"Shall say, 'No more I curse thee; but now I will bless thee: No more in deadly black   225

"'Devour thy labour; nor lift up a cloud in thy heavens, O laborious plow,

"'That the wild raging millions, that wander in forests, and howl in law blasted wastes,

"'Strength madden'd with slavery, honesty, bound in the dens of superstition,

"'May sing in the village, and shout in the harvest, and woo in pleasant gardens,

" 'Their once savage loves, now beaming with knowledge, with gentle   230
      awe adorned;

" 'And the saw, and the hammer, the chisel, the pencil, the pen, and the
      instruments

" 'Of heavenly song sound in the wilds once forbidden, to teach the
      laborious plowman

" 'And shepherd deliver'd from clouds of war, from pestilence, from
      night-fear, from murder,

" 'From falling, from stifling, from hunger, from cold, from slander,
      discontent and sloth;

" 'That walk in beasts and birds of night, driven back by the sandy   235
      desert

" 'Like pestilent fogs round cities of men: and the happy earth sing in
      its course,

" 'The mild peaceable nations be opened to heav'n, and men walk with
      their fathers in bliss.'

"Then hear the first voice of the morning: 'Depart, O clouds of night,
      and no more

" 'Return; be withdrawn cloudy war, troops of warriors depart, nor
      around our peaceable city

" 'Breathe fires, but ten miles from Paris, let all be peace, nor a soldier   240
      be seen!' "

PAGE 13

He ended; the wind of contention arose and the clouds cast their
      shadows, the Princes

Like the mountains of France, whose aged trees utter an awful voice,
      and their branches

Are shatter'd, till gradual a murmur is heard descending into the
      valley,

Like a voice in the vineyards of Burgundy, when grapes are shaken
      on grass;

Like the low voice of the labouring man, instead of the shout of joy;   245

And the palace appear'd like a cloud driven abroad; blood ran down
      the ancient pillars,

Thro' the cloud a deep thunder, the Duke of Burgundy, delivers the
      King's command.

"Seest thou yonder dark castle, that moated around, keeps this city of
      Paris in awe.

"Go command yonder tower, saying, 'Bastile depart, and take thy
      shadowy course.

" 'Overstep the dark river, thou terrible tower, and get thee up into the   250
      country ten miles.

" 'And thou black southern prison, move along the dusky road to
      Versailles; there

" 'Frown on the gardens', and if it obey and depart, then the King will
      disband

"This war-breathing army; but if it refuse, let the Nation's Assembly
   thence learn,
"That this army of terrors, that prison of horrors, are the bands of the
   murmuring kingdom."

Like the morning star arising above the black waves, when a   255
   shipwreck'd soul sighs for morning,
Thro' the ranks, silent, walk'd the Ambassador back to the Nation's
   Assembly, and told
The unwelcome message; silent they heard; then a thunder roll'd
   round loud and louder,
Like pillars of ancient halls, and ruins of times remote they sat.
Like a voice from the dim pillars Mirabeau rose; the thunders
   subsided away;

PAGE 14

A rushing of wings around him was heard as he brighten'd, and cried   260
   out aloud,
"Where is the General of the Nation?" the walls re-echo'd: "Where is
   the General of the Nation?"

Sudden as the bullet wrapp'd in his fire, when brazen cannons rage
   in the field,
Fayette sprung from his seat saying, Ready! then bowing like clouds,
   man toward man, the Assembly
Like a council of ardors seated in clouds, bending over the cities of
   men,
And over the armies of strife, where their children are marshall'd   265
   together to battle;
They murmuring divide, while the wind sleeps beneath, and the
   numbers are counted in silence,
While they vote the removal of War, and the pestilence weighs his
   red wings in the sky.

So Fayette stood silent among the Assembly, and the votes were given
   and the numbers numb'red;
And the vote was, that Fayette should order the army to remove ten
   miles from Paris.

The aged sun rises appall'd from dark mountains, and gleams a dusky   270
   beam
On Fayette, but on the whole army a shadow, for a cloud on the
   eastern hills
Hover'd, and stretch'd across the city and across the army, and across
   the Louvre,
Like a flame of fire he stood before dark ranks, and before expecting
   captains
On pestilent vapours around him flow frequent spectres of religious
   men weeping
In winds driven out of the abbeys, their naked souls shiver in keen   275
   open air,

Driven out by the fiery cloud of Voltaire, and thund'rous rocks of
Rousseau,
They dash like foam against the ridges of the army, uttering a faint
feeble cry.

PAGE 15

Gleams of fire streak the heavens, and of sulphur the earth, from
Fayette as he lifted his hand;
But silent he stood, till all the officers rush round him like waves
Round the shore of France, in day of the British flag, when heavy   280
cannons
Affright the coasts, and the peasant looks over the sea and wipes a
tear;
Over his head the soul of Voltaire shone fiery, and over the army
Rousseau his white cloud
Unfolded, on souls of war-living terrors silent list'ning toward
Fayette,
His voice loud inspir'd by liberty, and by spirits of the dead, thus
thunder'd.

"The Nation's Assembly command, that the Army remove ten miles   285
from Paris;
"Nor a soldier be seen in road or in field, till the Nation command
return."

Rushing along iron ranks glittering the officers each to his station
Depart, and the stern captain strokes his proud steed, and in front of
his solid ranks
Waits the sound of trumpet; captains of foot stand each by his cloudy
drum;
Then the drum beats, and the steely ranks move, and trumpets   290
rejoice in the sky.
Dark cavalry like clouds fraught with thunder ascend on the hills,
and bright infantry, rank
Behind rank, to the soul shaking drum and shrill fife along the roads
glitter like fire.

The noise of trampling, the wind of trumpets, smote the palace walls
with a blast.
Pale and cold sat the King in midst of his peers, and his noble heart
sunk, and his pulses
Suspended their motion, a darkness crept over his eye-lids, and chill   295
cold sweat
Sat round his brows faded in faint death, his peers pale like
mountains of the dead,
Cover'd with dews of night, groaning, shaking forests and floods. The
cold newt

PAGE 16

And snake, and damp toad, on the kingly foot crawl, or croak on the
awful knee,

Shedding their slime, in folds of the robe the crown'd adder builds
    and hisses
From stony brows; shaken the forests of France, sick the kings of   300
    the nations,
And the bottoms of the world were open'd, and the graves of
    arch-angels unseal'd;
The enormous dead, lift up their pale fires and look over the rocky
    cliffs.

A faint heat from their fires reviv'd the cold Louvre; the frozen blood
    reflow'd.
Awful up rose the king, him the peers follow'd, they saw the courts
    of the Palace
Forsaken, and Paris without a soldier, silent, for the noise was gone   305
    up
And follow'd the army, and the Senate in peace, sat beneath morning's
    beam.

END of the FIRST BOOK.

[No further books are extant.]

❦

THE FOUR ZOAS
The torments of Love & Jealousy in
The Death and Judgement
of Albion the Ancient Man
by William Blake 1797

PAGE 2

Rest before Labour

PAGE 3

Οτι ουκ εστιν ημιν η παλη προς αιμα και ϛαρκα, αλλα
προς τας αρχας, προς τας εξουϛιας, προς τους
κοϛμοκρατορας του ϛκοτους του αιωνος τουτου, προς
τα πνευματικα της πονηριας εν τοις επουρανιοις.
                Εφες: VI κεφ. 12 ver.

[For we wrestle not against flesh and blood, but
    against principalities, against powers, against the
    rulers of the darkness of this world, against
    spiritual wickedness in high places. (King James version)]

VALA

Night the First

The Song of the Aged Mother which shook the heavens with wrath   ^{t,c}

Hearing the march of long resounding strong heroic Verse
Marshalld in order for the day of Intellectual Battle

Four Mighty Ones are in every Man;
     a Perfect Unity   John XVII c. 21 & 22 & 23 v
Cannot Exist. but from the Universal   5
     Brotherhood of Eden   John I c. 14 v
The Universal Man. To Whom be
     Glory Evermore Amen   και· εσκηνωσεν εν· ημιν

[What] are the Natures of those Living Creatures the Heavenly
     Father only
[Knoweth] no Individual [Knoweth nor] Can know in all Eternity   ^t

Los was the fourth immortal starry one, & in the Earth   ^c
Of a bright Universe Empery attended day & night   10
Days & nights of revolving joy, Urthona was his name   ^c
                                                          ^t
PAGE 4
In Eden; in the Auricular Nerves of Human life
Which is the Earth of Eden, he his Emanations propagated
Fairies of Albion afterwards Gods of the Heathen, Daughter of Beulah   ^c
     Sing
His fall into Division & his Resurrection to Unity
His fall into the Generation of Decay & Death & his Regeneration   ^t5
     by the Resurrection from the dead

Begin with Tharmas Parent power. darkning in the West   ^c

Lost! Lost! Lost! are my Emanations   Enion O Enion   ^t
We are become a Victim to the Living We hide in secret   ^t
I have hidden Jerusalem in Silent Contrition   O Pity Me   ^t
I will build thee a Labyrinth also O pity me   O Enion   ^t10
Why hast thou taken sweet Jerusalem from my inmost Soul   ^t
Let her Lay secret in the Soft recess of darkness & silence
It is not Love I bear to Enitharmon It is Pity
She hath taken refuge in my bosom & I cannot cast her out.

The Men have recieved their death wounds & their Emanations are fled   15
To me for refuge & I cannot turn them out for Pitys sake

Enion said—Thy fear has made me tremble thy terrors have surrounded   ^t
     me
All Love is lost Terror succeeds & Hatred instead of Love
And stern demands of Right & Duty instead of Liberty.

Once thou wast to Me the loveliest son of heaven—But now 20
Why art thou Terrible and yet I love thee in thy terror till
I am almost Extinct & soon shall be a Shadow in Oblivion
Unless some way can be found that I may look upon thee & live
Hide me some Shadowy semblance. secret whispring in my Ear
In secret of soft wings. in mazes of delusive beauty 25
I have lookd into the secret soul of him I lovd
And in the Dark recesses found Sin & cannot return

Trembling & pale sat Tharmas weeping in his clouds

Why wilt thou Examine every little fibre of my soul
Spreading them out before the Sun like Stalks of flax to dry 30
The infant joy is beautiful but its anatomy
Horrible Ghast & Deadly nought shalt thou find in it
But Death Despair & Everlasting brooding Melancholy

Thou wilt go mad with horror if thou dost Examine thus
Every moment of my secret hours Yea I know 35
That I have sinnd & that my Emanations are become harlots
I am already distracted at their deeds & if I look
Upon them more Despair will bring self murder on my soul
O Enion thou art thyself a root growing in hell
Tho thus heavenly beautiful to draw me to destruction 40

Sometimes I think thou art a flower expanding
Sometimes I think thou art fruit breaking from its bud
In dreadful dolor & pain & I am like an atom
A Nothing left in darkness yet I am an identity
I wish & feel & weep & groan Ah terrible terrible 45

PAGE 5

In Eden Females sleep the winter in soft silken veils t
Woven by their own hands to hide them in the darksom grave
But Males immortal live renewd by female deaths. in soft
Delight they die & they revive in spring with music & songs
Enion said Farewell I die I hide from thy searching eyes 5

So saying—From her bosom weaving soft in Sinewy threads
A tabernacle for Jerusalem she sat among the Rocks t
Singing her lamentation. Tharmas groand among his Clouds
Weeping, then bending from his Clouds he stoopd his innocent head t
And stretching out his holy hand in the vast Deep sublime 10
Turnd round the circle of Destiny with tears & bitter sighs
And said. Return O Wanderer when the Day of Clouds is oer

So saying he sunk down into the sea a pale white corse
In torment he sunk down & flowd among her filmy Woof
His Spectre issuing from his feet in flames of fire c 15
In gnawing pain drawn out by her lovd fingers every nerve t

She counted. every vein & lacteal threading them among
Her woof of terror. Terrified & drinking tears of woe
Shuddring she wove—nine days & nights Sleepless her food was tears
Wondring she saw her woof begin to animate. & not   20
As Garments woven subservient to her hands but having a will
Of its own perverse & wayward Enion lovd & wept

Nine days she labourd at her work. & nine dark sleepless nights
But on the tenth trembling morn the Circle of Destiny Complete   t
Round rolld the Sea Englobing in a watry Globe self balancd   25
A Frowning Continent appeard Where Enion in the Desert
Terrified in her own Creation   viewing her woven shadow   c
Sat in a dread intoxication of Repentance & Contrition   t

There is from Great Eternity a mild & pleasant rest   c
Namd Beulah a Soft Moony Universe feminine lovely   30
Pure mild & Gentle given in Mercy to those who sleep
Eternally. Created by the Lamb of God around
On all sides within & without the Universal Man
The Daughters of Beulah follow sleepers in all their Dreams   t
Creating Spaces lest they fall into Eternal Death   35
The Circle of Destiny complete they gave to it a Space
And namd the Space Ulro & brooded over it in care & love

They said The Spectre is in every man insane & most
Deformd Thro the three heavens descending in fury & fire
We meet it with our Songs & loving blandishments & give   40
To it a form of vegetation But this Spectre of Tharmas
Is Eternal Death What shall we do O God pity & help   t
So spoke they & closd the Gate of the Tongue in trembling fear   t

PAGE 6
She drew the Spectre forth from Tharmas in her shining loom   t
Of Vegetation weeping in wayward infancy & sullen youth
Listning to her soft lamentations soon his tongue began
To Lisp out words & soon in masculine strength augmenting he
Reard up a form of gold & stood upon the glittering rock   5
A shadowy human form winged   & in his depths
The dazzlings as of gems shone clear, rapturous in fury   t
Glorying in his own eyes   Exalted in terrific Pride   t
PAGE 7 (& 143)
Opening his rifted rocks mingling together they join in burning anguish t
Mingling his horrible darkness with her tender limbs then high she
    soard
Shrieking above the ocean: a bright wonder that nature shudderd at   t
Half Woman & half beast all his darkly waving colours mix   t
With her fair crystal clearness in her lips & cheeks his metals rose t 5
In blushes like the morning & his rocky features softning   t

A wonder lovely in the heavens or wandring on the earth   t
With female voice warbling upon the hollow vales   t
Beauty all blushing with desire a self enjoying wonder

For Enion brooded groaning loud the rough seas vegetate.   t 10
Golden rocks rise from the [vortex] vast
And thus her voice. Glory, delight: & sweet enjoyment born
To mild Eternity shut in a threefold shape delightful
To wander in sweet solitude enrapturd at every wind   t

PAGE 8
Till with fierce pain she brought forth on the rocks her sorrow & woe   c
Behold two little Infants wept upon the desolate wind.   t

The first state weeping they began & helpless as a wave
Beaten along its sightless way growing enormous in its motion to
Its utmost goal, till strength from Enion like richest summer shining   t 5
Raisd the bright boy & girl with glories from their heads out beaming   t
Drawing forth drooping mothers pity drooping mothers sorrow   t

They sulk upon her breast her hair became like snow on mountains
Weaker & weaker, weeping woful, wearier and wearier
Faded & her bright Eyes decayd melted with pity & love   10

PAGE 9
And then they wanderd far away she sought for them in vain   t
In weeping blindness stumbling she followd them oer rocks & mountains
Rehumanizing from the Spectre in pangs of maternal love
Ingrate they wanderd scorning her drawing her Spectrous Life   t
Repelling her away & away by a dread repulsive power   5
Into Non Entity revolving round in dark despair.
And drawing in the Spectrous life in pride and haughty joy   t
Thus Enion gave them all her spectrous life   t

Then Eno a daughter of Beulah took a Moment of Time   t,c
And drew it out to Seven thousand years with much care & affliction   t 10
And many tears & in Every year made windows into Eden   t
She also took an atom of space & opend its center
Into Infinitude & ornamented it with wondrous art
Astonishd sat her Sisters of Beulah to see her soft affections
To Enion & her children & they ponderd these things wondring   15
And they Alternate kept watch over the Youthful terrors
They saw not yet the Hand Divine for it was not yet reveald
But they went on in Silent Hope & Feminine repose

But Los & Enitharmon delighted in the Moony spaces of Eno   t
Nine Times they livd among the forests, feeding on sweet fruits   20
And nine bright Spaces wanderd weaving mazes of delight
Snaring the wild Goats for their milk they eat the flesh of Lambs
A male & female naked & ruddy as the pride of summer

Alternate Love & Hate his breast; hers Scorn & Jealousy
In embryon passions. they kiss'd not nor embrac'd for shame & fear   t 25
His head beamd light & in his vigorous voice was prophecy
He could controll the times & seasons, & the days & years
She could controll the spaces, regions, desart, flood & forest
But had no power to weave a Veil of covering for her Sins
She drave the Females all away from Los   30
And Los drave all the Males from her away
They wanderd long, till they sat down upon the margind sea.
Conversing with the visions of Beulah in dark slumberous bliss   t

But the two youthful wonders wanderd in the world of Tharmas   t
Thy name is Enitharmon; said the fierce prophetic boy   t 35
While thy mild voice fills all these Caverns with sweet harmony
O how our Parents sit & mourn in their silent secret bowers   t

PAGE 10
But Enitharmon answerd with a dropping tear & frowning   t
Dark as a dewy morning when the crimson light appears   t
To make us happy let them weary their immortal powers   t
While we draw in their sweet delights while we return them scorn
On scorn to feed our discontent; for if we grateful prove   5
They will withhold sweet love, whose food is thorns & bitter roots.
We hear the warlike clarions we view the turning spheres
Yet Thou in indolence reposest holding me in bonds
Hear! I will sing a Song of Death! it is a Song of Vala!   t,e
The Fallen Man takes his repose: Urizen sleeps in the porch   t 10
Luvah and Vala woke & flew up from the Human Heart   t
Into the Brain; from thence upon the pillow Vala slumber'd.
And Luvah siez'd the Horses of Light, & rose into the Chariot of Day
Sweet laughter siezd me in my sleep! silent & close I laughd   t
For in the visions of Vala I walkd with the mighty Fallen One   t 15
I heard his voice among the branches, & among sweet flowers.

Why is the light of Enitharmon darken'd in dewy morn   t
Why is the silence of Enitharmon a terror & her smile a whirlwind   t
Uttering this darkness in my halls, in the pillars of my Holy-ones
Why dost thou weep as Vala? & wet thy veil with dewy tears,   t 20
In slumbers of my night-repose, infusing a false morning?
Driving the Female Emanations all away from Los
I have refusd to look upon the Universal Vision   t
And wilt thou slay with death him who devotes himself to thee   t
Once born for the sport & amusement of Man now born to drink up   25
    all his Powers
PAGE 11
I heard the sounding sea; I heard the voice weaker and weaker;
The voice came & went like a dream, I awoke in my sweet bliss.

-301-

Then Los smote her upon the Earth twas long eer she revivd
He answer'd, darkning more with indignation hid in smiles   t

I die not Enitharmon tho thou singst thy Song of Death   t 5
Nor shalt thou me torment For I behold the Fallen Man   t
Seeking to comfort Vala,   she will not be comforted
She rises from his throne and seeks the shadows of her garden
Weeping for Luvah lost, in the bloody beams of your false morning
Sickning lies the Fallen Man his head sick his heart faint   t 10
Mighty atchievement of your power! Beware the punishment
I see, invisible descend into the Gardens of Vala
Luvah walking on the winds, I see the invisible knife
I see the shower of blood: I see the swords & spears of futurity
Tho in the Brain of Man we live, & in his circling Nerves.   15
Tho' this bright world of all our joy is in the Human Brain.
Where Urizen & all his Hosts hang their immortal lamps
Thou neer shalt leave this cold expanse where watry Tharmas mourns

So spoke Los. Scorn & Indignation rose upon Enitharmon
Then Enitharmon reddning fierce stretchd her immortal hands   t,c 20

Descend O Urizen descend with horse & chariots
Threaten not me O visionary thine the punishment
The Human Nature shall no more remain nor Human acts
Form the rebellious Spirits of Heaven. but War & Princedom & Victory   t
     & Blood

PAGE 12   t
Night darkend as she spoke! a shuddring ran from East to West
A Groan was heard on high. The warlike clarions ceast. the Spirits   t
Of Luvah & Vala shudderd in their Orb: an orb of blood!   t

Eternity groand & was troubled at the Image of Eternal Death
The Wandering Man bow'd his faint head and Urizen descended   5
And the one must have murderd the other if he had not descended   t
Indignant muttering low thunders; Urizen descended
Gloomy sounding, Now I am God from Eternity to Eternity

Sullen sat Los plotting Revenge. Silent he eye'd the Prince   t
Of Light. Silent the prince of Light viewd Los. at length a brooded   t 10
Smile broke from Urizen for Enitharmon brightend more & more
Sullen he lowerd on Enitharmon but he smild on Los

Saying Thou art the Lord of Luvah into thine hands I give
The prince of Love the murderer his soul is in thine hands
Pity not Vala for she pitied not the Eternal Man   15
Nor pity thou the cries of Luvah. Lo these starry hosts
They are thy servants if thou wilt obey my awful Law   t

Los answerd furious art thou one of those who when most complacent
Mean mischief most. If you are such Lo! I am also such

– 302 –

One must be master. try thy Arts I also will try mine   20
For I percieve Thou hast Abundance which I claim as mine

Urizen startled stood but not Long soon he cried
Obey my voice young Demon I am God from Eternity to Eternity

Thus Urizen spoke collected in himself in awful pride

Art thou a visionary of Jesus the soft delusion of Eternity   25
Lo I am God the terrible destroyer & not the Saviour
Why should the Divine Vision compell the sons of Eden
to forego each his own delight to war against his Spectre   t
The Spectre is the Man the rest is only delusion & fancy

So spoke the Prince of Light & sat beside the Seat of Los   30
Upon the sandy shore rested his chariot of fire

Ten thousand thousand were his hosts of spirits on the wind:
Ten thousand thousand glittering Chariots shining in the sky:
They pour upon the golden shore beside the silent ocean.
Rejoicing in the Victory & the heavens were filld with blood   t 35
                                                                      c
The Earth spread forth her table wide. the Night a silver cup
Fill'd with the wine of anguish waited at the golden feast
But the bright Sun was not as yet; he filling all the expanse
Slept as a bird in the blue shell that soon shall burst away

Los saw the wound of his blow he saw he pitied he wept   40
Los now repented that he had smitten Enitharmon he felt love
Arise in all his Veins he threw his arms around her loins
To heal the wound of his smiting

They eat the fleshly bread, they drank the nervous wine   t
PAGE 13
They listend to the Elemental Harps & Sphery Song
They view'd the dancing Hours, quick sporting thro' the sky
With winged radiance scattering joys thro the ever changing light

But Luvah & Vala standing in the bloody sky   t
On high remaind alone forsaken in fierce jealousy   5
They stood above the heavens forsaken desolate suspended in blood
Descend they could not. nor from Each other avert their eyes
Eternity appeard above them as One Man infolded   c
In Luvah[s] robes of blood & bearing all his afflictions   t
As the sun shines down on the misty earth Such was the Vision   10

But purple night and crimson morning & golden day descending   t
Thro' the clear changing atmosphere display'd green fields among
The varying clouds, like paradises stretch'd in the expanse
With towns & villages and temples, tents sheep-folds and pastures
Where dwell the children of the elemental worlds in harmony.   15
Not long in harmony they dwell, their life is drawn away   t

And wintry woes succeed; successive driven into the Void
Where Enion craves: successive drawn into the golden feast

And Los & Enitharmon sat in discontent & scorn   t
The Nuptial Song arose from all the thousand thousand spirits   t 20
Over the joyful Earth & Sea, and ascended into the Heavens
For Elemental Gods their thunderous Organs blew; creating
Delicious Viands. Demons of Waves their watry Eccho's woke!
Bright Souls of vegetative life, budding and blossoming   t

PAGE 14
Stretch their immortal hands to smite the gold & silver Wires
And with immortal Voice soft warbling fill all Earth & Heaven.
With doubling Voices & loud Horns wound round sounding
Cavernous dwellers fill'd the enormous Revelry, Responsing!
And Spirits of Flaming fire on high, govern'd the mighty Song.   5

And This the Song! sung at The Feast of Los & Enitharmon

Ephraim calld out to Zion: Awake O Brother Mountain   t
Let us refuse the Plow & Spade, the heavy Roller & spiked
Harrow. burn all these Corn fields. throw down all these fences
Fattend on Human blood & drunk with wine of life is better far   10

Than all these labours of the harvest & the vintage. See the river
Red with the blood of Men. swells lustful round my rocky knees
My clouds are not the clouds of verdant fields & groves of fruit
But Clouds of Human Souls. my nostrils drink the lives of Men   t

The Villages Lament. they faint outstretchd upon the plain   15
Wailing runs round the Valleys from the Mill & from the Barn   t
But most the polishd Palaces dark silent bow with dread   t
Hiding their books & pictures. underneath the dens of Earth

The Cities send to one another saying My sons are Mad
With wine of cruelty. Let us plat a scourge O Sister City   t 20
Children are nourishd for the Slaughter; once the Child was fed
With Milk; but wherefore now are Children fed with blood   t

PAGE 15
The Horse is of more value than the Man. The Tyger fierce
Laughs at the Human form. the Lion mocks & thirsts for blood
They cry O Spider spread thy web! Enlarge thy bones & fill'd
With marrow. sinews & flesh Exalt thyself attain a voice

Call to thy dark armd hosts, for all the sons of Men muster together   5
To desolate their cities! Man shall be no more! Awake O Hosts
The bow string sang upon the hills! Luvah & Vala ride
Triumphant in the bloody sky. & the Human form is no more   t

The listning Stars heard, & the first beam of the morning started back
He cried out to his Father, depart! depart! but sudden Siez'd   t 10
And clad in steel. & his Horse proudly neighd; he smelt the battle   t
Afar off, Rushing back, reddning with rage the Mighty Father   t

Siezd his bright Sheephook studded with gems & gold, he Swung it
    round
His head shrill sounding in the sky, down rushd the Sun with noise
Of war. The Mountains fled away they sought a place beneath   15
Vala remaind in desarts of dark solitude. nor Sun nor Moon

By night nor day to comfort her, she labourd in thick smoke   t
Tharmas endurd not, he fled howling. then a barren waste sunk down
Conglobing in the dark confusion, Mean time Los was born
And Thou O Enitharmon! Hark I hear the hammers of Los   t 20

PAGE 16
They melt the bones of Vala, & the bones of Luvah into wedges
The innumerable sons & daughters of Luvah closd in furnaces
Melt into furrows. winter blows his bellows: Ice & Snow
Tend the dire anvils. Mountains mourn & Rivers faint & fail

There is no City nor Corn-field nor Orchard! all is Rock & Sand   5
There is no Sun nor Moon nor Star. but rugged wintry rocks
Justling together in the void suspended by inward fires
Impatience now no longer can endure. Distracted Luvah

Bursting forth from the loins of Enitharmon, Thou fierce Terror   e
Go howl in vain, Smite Smite his fetters Smite O wintry hammers   10
Smite Spectre of Urthona, mock the fiend who drew us down   e
From heavens of joy into this Deep. Now rage but rage in vain

Thus Sang the Demons of the Deep. the Clarions of War blew loud
The Feast redounds & Crownd with roses & the circling vine
The Enormous Bride & Bridegroom sat, beside them Urizen   15
With faded radiance sighd, forgetful of the flowing wine
And of Ahania his Pure Bride but She was distant far

But Los & Enitharmon sat in discontent & scorn
Craving the more the more enjoying, drawing out sweet bliss
From all the turning wheels of heaven & the chariots of the Slain   20

At distance Far in Night repelld. in direful hunger craving   e
Summers & Winters round revolving in the frightful deep.

PAGE 17
Enion blind & age-bent wept upon the desolate wind   t

Why does the Raven cry aloud and no eye pities her?
Why fall the Sparrow & the Robin in the foodless winter?
Faint! shivering they sit on leafless bush, or frozen stone   t

Wearied with seeking food across the snowy waste; the little   5
Heart, cold; and the little tongue consum'd, that once in thoughtless joy
Gave songs of gratitude to waving corn fields round their nest.   t

Why howl the Lion & the Wolf? why do they roam abroad?   t
Deluded by summers heat they sport in enormous love   t
And cast their young out to the hungry wilds & sandy desarts   10

PAGE 18
Why is the Sheep given to the knife? the Lamb plays in the Sun
He starts! he hears the foot of Man! he says, Take thou my wool
But spare my life, but he knows not that winter cometh fast.   t

The Spider sits in his labourd Web, eager watching for the Fly
Presently comes a famishd Bird & takes away the Spider   5
His Web is left all desolate, that his little anxious heart
So careful wove; & spread it out with sighs and weariness.

This was the Lamentation of Enion round the golden Feast
Eternity groand and was troubled at the image of Eternal Death
Without the body of Man an Exudation from his sickning limbs   10

Now Man was come to the Palm tree & to the Oak of Weeping   c
Which stand upon the Edge of Beulah & he sunk down
From the Supporting arms of the Eternal Saviour; who disposd
The pale limbs of his Eternal Individuality
Upon The Rock of Ages. Watching over him with Love & Care   t 15

PAGE 21
Then those in Great Eternity met in the Council of God   c
As one Man for contracting their Exalted Senses
They behold Multitude or Expanding they behold as one
As One Man all the Universal family & that one Man   t
They call Jesus the Christ & they in him & he in them   5
Live in Perfect harmony in Eden the land of life
Consulting as One Man above the Mountain of Snowdon Sublime   t,c

For messengers from Beulah come in tears & darkning clouds
Saying Shiloh is in ruins our brother is sick Albion He   t
Whom thou lovest is sick he wanders from his house of Eternity   10
The daughters of Beulah terrified have closd the Gate of the Tongue
Luvah & Urizen contend in war around the holy tent

So spoke the Ambassadors from Beulah & with solemn mourning   t
They were introducd to the divine presence & they kneeled down
In Conways Vale thus recounting the Wars of Death Eternal   t,c 15

The Eternal Man wept in the holy tent Our Brother in Eternity
Even Albion whom thou lovest wept in pain his family
Slept round on hills & valleys in the regions of his love
But Urizen awoke & Luvah woke & thus conferrd

Thou Luvah said the Prince of Light behold our sons & daughters   20
Reposd on beds. let them sleep on. do thou alone depart
Into thy wished Kingdom where in Majesty & Power
We may erect a throne. deep in the North I place my lot   c
Thou in the South listen attentive. In silent of this night
I will infold the Eternal tent in clouds opake while thou   25
Siezing the chariots of the morning. Go outfleeting ride
Afar into the Zenith high bending thy furious course
Southward with half the tents of men inclosd in clouds
Of Tharmas & Urthona. I remaining in porches of the brain
Will lay my scepter on Jerusalem the Emanation   30
On all her sons & on thy sons O Luvah & on mine   t
Till dawn was wont to wake them then my trumpet sounding loud
Ravishd away in night my strong command shall be obeyd
For I have placd my centinels in stations each tenth man
Is bought & sold & in dim night my Word shall be their law   35

PAGE 22
Luvah replied Dictate to thy Equals. am not I
The Prince of all the hosts of Men nor Equal know in Heaven
If I arise into the Zenith leaving thee to watch
The Emanation & her Sons the Satan & the Anak   c
Sihon and Og. wilt thou not rebel to my laws remain   5
In darkness building thy strong throne & in my ancient night
Daring my power wilt arm my sons against me in the Atlantic   t
My deep   My night which thou assuming hast assumd my Crown
I will remain as well as thou & here with hands of blood
Smite this dark sleeper in his tent then try my strength with thee 10

While thus he spoke his fires reddend oer the holy tent   t
Urizen cast deep darkness round him silent brooding death
Eternal death to Luvah. raging Luvah pourd
The Lances of Urizen from chariots. round the holy tent
Discord began & yells & cries shook the wide firmament   15

Beside his anvil stood Urthona dark. a mass of iron
Glowd furious on the anvil prepard for spades & coulters   All
His sons fled from his side to join the conflict pale he heard
The Eternal voice he stood the sweat chilld on his mighty limbs
He dropd his hammer. dividing from his aking bosom fled   20
A portion of his life shrieking upon the wind she fled
And Tharmas took her in pitying Then Enion in jealous fear
Murderd her & hid her in her bosom embalming her for fear
She should arise again to life   Embalmd in Enions bosom
Enitharmon remains a corse such thing was never known   25
In Eden that one died a death never to be revivd
Urthona stood in terror but not long his spectre fled

To Enion & his body fell. Tharmas beheld him fall
Endlong a raging serpent rolling round the holy tent
The sons of war astonishd at the Glittring monster drove 30
Him far into the world of Tharmas into a cavernd rock

But Urizen with darkness overspreading all the armies
Sent round his heralds   secretly commanding to depart
Into the north Sudden with thunders sound his multitudes
Retreat from the fierce conflict all the sons of Urizen at once 35
Mustring together in thick clouds leaving the rage of Luvah
To pour its fury on himself & on the Eternal Man

Sudden down fell they all together into an unknown Space
Deep horrible without End. Separated from Beulah far beneath
The Mans exteriors are become indefinite opend to pain 40
In a fierce hungring void & none can visit his regions

PAGE 19
Jerusalem his Emanation is become a ruin t
Her little ones are slain on the top of every street t
And she herself le[d] captive & scatterd into the indefinite t
Gird on thy sword O thou most mighty in glory & majesty
Destroy these opressors of Jerusalem & those who ruin Shiloh 5

So spoke the Messengers of Beulah. Silently removing
The Family Divine drew up the Universal tent
Above High Snowdon & closd the Messengers in clouds around t
Till the time of the End. Then they Elected Seven. called the Seven c
Eyes of God & the Seven lamps of the Almighty 10
The Seven are one within the other the Seventh is named Jesus
The Lamb of God blessed for ever & he followd the Man
Who wanderd in mount Ephraim seeking a Sepulcher c
His inward eyes closing from the Divine vision & all
His children wandering outside from his bosom fleeing away t 15

PAGE 20 t
The Daughters of Beulah beheld the Emanation they pitied c
They wept before the Inner gates of Enitharmons bosom
And of her fine wrought brain & of her bowels within her loins
Three gates within Glorious & bright open into Beulah t
From Enitharmons inward parts but the bright female terror 5
Refusd to open the bright gates she closd and barrd them fast
Lest Los should enter into Beulah thro her beautiful gates

The Emanation stood before the Gates of Enitharmon t
Weeping. the Daughters of Beulah silent in the Porches
Spread her a couch unknown to Enitharmon here reposd 10
Jerusalem in slumbers soft lulld into silent rest

Terrific ragd the Eternal Wheels of intellect terrific ragd
The living creatures of the wheels in the Wars of Eternal life
But perverse rolld the wheels of Urizen & Luvah back reversd
Downwards & outwards consuming in the wars of Eternal Death   t 15

PAGE 23

VALA

Night the [Second]   t,c

Rising upon his Couch of Death Albion beheld his Sons   c
Turning his Eyes outward to Self. losing the Divine Vision
Albion calld Urizen & said. Behold these sickning Spheres   t,c
Whence is this Voice of Enion that soundeth in my Porches   t
Take thou possession! take this Scepter! go forth in my might   5
For I am weary, & must sleep in the dark sleep of Death   t
Thy brother Luvah hath smitten me but pity thou his youth   t
Tho thou hast not pitid my Age   O Urizen Prince of Light

Urizen rose from the bright Feast like a star thro' the evening sky   c
Exulting at the voice that calld him from the Feast of envy   t 10
First he beheld the body of Man pale, cold, the horrors of death
Beneath his feet shot thro' him as he stood in the Human Brain
And all its golden porches grew pale with his sickening light
No more Exulting for he saw Eternal Death beneath
Pale he beheld futurity; pale he beheld the Abyss   c 15
Where Enion blind & age bent wept in direful hunger craving
All rav'ning like the hungry worm, & like the silent grave
PAGE 24
Mighty was the draught of Voidness to draw Existence in

Terrific Urizen strode above, in fear & pale dismay
He saw the indefinite space beneath & his soul shrunk with horror
His feet upon the verge of Non Existence; his voice went forth   t

Luvah & Vala trembling & shrinking, beheld the great Work master   t,c 5
And heard his Word! Divide ye bands influence by influence
Build we a Bower for heavens darling in the grizly deep
Build we the Mundane Shell around the Rock of Albion

The Bands of Heaven flew thro the air singing & shouting to Urizen   c
Some fix'd the anvil, some the loom erected, some the plow   10
And harrow formd & framd the harness of silver & ivory
The golden compasses, the quadrant & the rule & balance   c
They erected the furnaces, they formd the anvils of gold beaten in mills
Where winter beats incessant, fixing them firm on their base
The bellows began to blow & the Lions of Urizen stood round the   15
    anvil

PAGE 25

And the leopards coverd with skins of beasts tended the roaring fires
Sublime distinct their lineaments divine of human beauty   t
The tygers of wrath called the horses of instruction from their mangers   e
They unloos'd them & put on the harness of gold & silver & ivory
In human forms distinct they stood round Urizen prince of Light   5
Petrifying all the Human Imagination into rock & sand   t,e
Groans ran along Tyburns brook and along the River of Oxford   e
Among the Druid Temples. Albion groand on Tyburns brook
Albion gave his loud death groan The Atlantic Mountains trembled   e
Aloft the Moon fled with a cry the Sun with streams of blood   10
From Albions Loins fled all Peoples and Nations of the Earth   t
Fled with the noise of Slaughter & the stars of heaven Fled
Jerusalem came down in a dire ruin over all the Earth
She fell cold from Lambeths Vales in groans & Dewy death   e
The dew of anxious souls the death-sweat of the dying   15
In every pillard hall & arched roof of Albions skies
The brother & the brother bathe in blood upon the Severn   e
The Maiden weeping by. The father & the mother with
The Maidens father & her mother fainting over the body
And the Young Man the Murderer fleeing over the mountains   20

Reuben slept on Penmaenmawr & Levi slept on Snowdon   e
Their eyes their ears nostrils & tongues roll outward   they behold
What is within now seen without they are raw to the hungry wind
They become Nations far remote in a little & dark Land
The Daughters of Albion girded around their garments of Needlework   25
Stripping Jerusalems curtains from mild demons of the hills
Across Europe & Asia to China & Japan like lightenings
They go forth & return to Albion on his rocky couch
Gwendolen Ragan Sabrina Gonorill Mehetabel Cordella
Boadicea Conwenna Estrild Gwinefrid Ignoge Cambel   30
Binding Jerusalems Children in the dungeons of Babylon
They play before the Armies before the hounds of Nimrod
While The Prince of Light on Salisbury plain among the druid stones   t,e

Rattling the adamantine chains & hooks heave up the ore
In mountainous masses, plung'd in furnaces, & they shut & seald   t 35
The furnaces a time & times; all the while blew the North
His cloudy bellows & the South & East & dismal West
And all the while the plow of iron cut the dreadful furrows
In Ulro beneath Beulah where the Dead wail Night & Day

Luvah was cast into the Furnaces of affliction & sealed   e 40
And Vala fed in cruel delight, the furnaces with fire
Stern Urizen beheld urg'd by necessity to keep
The evil day afar, & if perchance with iron power
He might avert his own despair; in woe & fear he saw

PAGE 26

Vala incircle round the furnaces where Luvah was clos'd
In joy she heard his howlings, & forgot he was her Luvah
With whom she walkd in bliss, in times of innocence & youth

Hear ye the voice of Luvah from the furnaces of Urizen   e

If I indeed am Valas King & ye O sons of Men   t 5
The workmanship of Luvahs hands; in times of Everlasting
When I calld forth the Earth-worm from the cold & dark obscure
I nurturd her I fed her with my rains & dews, she grew
A scaled Serpent, yet I fed her tho' she hated me
Day after day she fed upon the mountains in Luvahs sight   10
I brought her thro' the Wilderness, a dry & thirsty land
And I commanded springs to rise for her in the black desert
[Till] she became a Dragon winged bright & poisonous   t
I opend all the floodgates of the heavens to quench her thirst

PAGE 27

And I commanded the Great deep to hide her in his hand
Till she became a little weeping Infant a span long
I carried her in my bosom as a man carries a lamb
I loved her I gave her all my soul & my delight
I hid her in soft gardens & in secret bowers of Summer   5
Weaving mazes of delight along the sunny Paradise
Inextricable labyrinths, She bore me sons & daughters
And they have taken her away & hid her from my sight
They have surrounded me with walls of iron & brass, O Lamb   t
Of God clothed in Luvahs garments little knowest thou   t 10
Of death Eternal that we all go to Eternal Death
To our Primeval Chaos in fortuitous concourse of incoherent
Discordant principles of Love & Hate I suffer affliction
Because I love. for I was love but hatred awakes in me   t
And Urizen who was Faith & Certainty is changd to Doubt   15
The hand of Urizen is upon me because I blotted out
That Human delusion to deliver all the sons of God   t
From bondage of the Human form, O first born Son of Light
O Urizen my enemy I weep for thy stern ambition
But weep in vain   O when will you return Vala the Wanderer   20

PAGE 28

These were the words of Luvah patient in afflictions
Reasoning from the loins in the unreal forms of Ulros night   t,e

And when Luvah age after age was quite melted with woe   e
The fires of Vala faded like a shadow cold & pale
An evanescent shadow. last she fell a heap of Ashes   5
Beneath the furnaces a woful heap in living death

Then were the furnaces unseald with spades & pickaxes
Roaring let out the fluid, the molten metal ran in channels
Cut by the plow of ages held in Urizens strong hand
In many a valley, for the Bulls of Luvah dragd the Plow   ᶜ 10

With trembling horror pale aghast the Children of Man   t,c
Stood on the infinite Earth & saw these visions in the air
In waters & in Earth beneath they cried to one another
What are we terrors to one another. Come O brethren wherefore
Was this wide Earth spread all abroad. not for wild beasts to roam   15
But many stood silent & busied in their families
And many said We see no Visions in the darksom air
Measure the course of that sulphur orb that lights the darksom day   t
Set stations on this breeding Earth & let us buy & sell
Others arose & schools Erected forming Instruments   20
To measure out the course of heaven. Stern Urizen beheld
In woe his brethren & his Sons in darkning woe lamenting   c
Upon the winds in clouds involvd Uttering his voice in thunders
Commanding all the work with care & power & severity

Then siezd the Lions of Urizen their work, & heated in the forge   ᶜ 25
Roar the bright masses, thund'ring beat the hammers, many a pyramid   t,c
Is form'd & thrown down thund'ring into the deeps of Non Entity
Heated red hot they hizzing rend their way down many a league
Till resting. each his [center] finds; suspended there they stand   t
Casting their sparkles dire abroad into the dismal deep   30
For measurd out in orderd spaces the Sons of Urizen   t
With compasses divide the deep; they the strong scales erect   c
PAGE 29
That Luvah rent from the faint Heart of the Fallen Man   t
And weigh the massy Cubes, then fix them in their awful stations   t

And all the time in Caverns shut, the golden Looms erected
First spun, then wove the Atmospheres, there the Spider & Worm   c
Plied the wingd shuttle piping shrill thro' all the list'ning threads   5
Beneath the Caverns roll the weights of lead & spindles of iron
The enormous warp & woof rage direful in the affrighted deep

While far into the vast unknown, the strong wing'd Eagles bend
Their venturous flight, in Human forms distinct; thro darkness deep
They bear the woven draperies; on golden hooks they hang abroad   10
The universal curtains & spread out from Sun to Sun
The vehicles of light, they separate the furious particles
Into mild currents as the water mingles with the wine.

While thus the Spirits of strongest wing enlighten the dark deep
The threads are spun & the cords twisted & drawn out; then the weak   15
Begin their work; & many a net is netted; many a net   c

PAGE 30

Spread & many a Spirit caught, innumerable the nets
Innumerable the gins & traps; & many a soothing flute
Is form'd & many a corded lyre, outspread over the immense
In cruel delight they trap the listeners, & in cruel delight
Bind them, condensing the strong energies into little compass   t 5
Some became seed of every plant that shall be planted; some
The bulbous roots, thrown up together into barns & garners

Then rose the Builders; First the Architect divine his plan
Unfolds, The wondrous scaffold reard all round the infinite
Quadrangular the building rose the heavens squared by a line.   e 10
Trigon & cubes divide the elements in finite bonds
Multitudes without number work incessant: the hewn stone
Is placd in beds of mortar mingled with the ashes of Vala   e
Severe the labour, female slaves the mortar trod oppressed

Twelve halls after the names of his twelve sons composd   15
The wondrous building & three Central Domes after the Names   t
Of his three daughters were encompassd by the twelve bright halls
Every hall surrounded by bright Paradises of Delight
In which are towns & Cities Nations Seas Mountains & Rivers   t
Each Dome opend toward four halls & the Three Domes Encompassd   20
The Golden Hall of Urizen whose western side glowd bright
With ever streaming fires beaming from his awful limbs

His Shadowy Feminine Semblance here reposd on a White Couch   t,e
Or hoverd oer his Starry head & when he smild she brightend
Like a bright Cloud in harvest. but when Urizen frownd She wept   25
In mists over his carved throne & when he turnd his back
Upon his Golden hall & sought the Labyrinthine porches
Of his wide heaven Trembling, cold in paling fears she sat
A Shadow of Despair therefore toward the West Urizen formd
A recess in the wall for fires to glow upon the pale   30
Females limbs in his absence & her Daughters oft upon
A Golden Altar burnt perfumes with Art Celestial formd
Foursquare sculpturd & sweetly Engravd to please their shadowy   t
    mother
Ascending into her misty garments the blue smoke rolld to revive   t
Her cold limbs in the absence of her Lord. Also her sons   35
With lives of Victims sacrificed upon an altar of brass
On the East side. Revivd her Soul with lives of beasts & birds
Slain on the Altar up ascending into her cloudy bosom
Of terrible workmanship the Altar labour of ten thousand Slaves
One thousand Men of wondrous power spent their lives in its   40
    formation
It stood on twelve steps namd after the names of her twelve sons
And was Erected at the chief entrance of Urizens hall

When Urizen returnd from his immense labours & travels   t
Descending She reposd beside him folding him around
In her bright skirts. Astonishd & Confounded he beheld   45
Her shadowy form now Separate he shudderd & was silent
Till her caresses & her tears revivd him to life & joy
Two wills they had two intellects & not as in times of old
This Urizen percievd & silent brooded in darkning Clouds
To him his Labour was but Sorrow & his Kingdom was Repentance   50
He drave the Male Spirits all away from Ahania
And she drave all the Females from him away

Los joyd & Enitharmon laughd, saying   Let us go down
And see this labour & sorrow; They went down to see the woes
Of Vala & the woes of Luvah, to draw in their delights   55

And Vala like a shadow oft appeard to Urizen
PAGE 31
The King of Light beheld her mourning among the Brick kilns
     compelld
To labour night & day among the fires, her lamenting voice
Is heard when silent night returns & the labourers take their rest

O Lord wilt thou not look upon our sore afflictions
Among these flames incessant labouring, our hard masters laugh   5
At all our sorrow. We are made to turn the wheel for water
To carry the heavy basket on our scorched shoulders, to sift
The sand & ashes, & to mix the clay with tears & repentance
I see not Luvah as of old I only see his feet   t
Like pillars of fire travelling thro darkness & non entity   10
The times are now returnd upon us, we have given ourselves
To scorn and now are scorned by the slaves of our enemies
Our beauty is coverd over with clay & ashes, & our backs
Furrowd with whips, & our flesh bruised with the heavy basket
Forgive us O thou piteous one whom we have offended, forgive   15
The weak remaining shadow of Vala that returns in sorrow to thee.

Thus she lamented day & night, compelld to labour & sorrow
Luvah in vain her lamentations heard; in vain his love
Brought him in various forms before her still she knew him not
PAGE 32
Still she despisd him, calling on his name & knowing him not
Still hating still professing love, still labouring in the smoke

And Los & Enitharmon joyd, they drank in tenfold joy   t
From all the sorrow of Luvah & the labour of Urizen
And Enitharmon joyd Plotting to rend the secret cloud   5
To plant divisions in the Soul of Urizen & Ahania

But infinitely beautiful the wondrous work arose   t
In sorrow & care. a Golden World whose porches round the heavens   t
And pillard halls & rooms recievd the eternal wandering stars
A wondrous golden Building; many a window many a door   10
And many a division let in & out into the vast unknown
[Cubed] in [window square] immoveable, within its walls & cielings   t
The heavens were closd and spirits mournd their bondage night and day
And the Divine Vision appeard in Luvahs robes of blood   t

Thus was the Mundane shell builded by Urizens strong power   15

Sorrowing went the Planters forth to plant, the Sowers to sow   t
They dug the channels for the rivers & they pourd abroad

PAGE 33
The seas & lakes, they reard the mountains & the rocks & hills
On broad pavilions, on pillard roofs & porches & high towers
In beauteous order, thence arose soft clouds & exhalations
Wandering even to the sunny Cubes of light & heat   t
For many a window ornamented with sweet ornaments   5
Lookd out into the World of Tharmas, where in ceaseless torrents   t
His billows roll where monsters wander in the foamy paths

On clouds the Sons of Urizen beheld Heaven walled round   t
They weighd & orderd all & Urizen comforted saw   t
The wondrous work flow forth like visible out of the invisible   10
For the Divine Lamb Even Jesus who is the Divine Vision   t
Permitted all lest Man should fall into Eternal Death
For when Luvah sunk down himself put on the robes of blood
Lest the state calld Luvah should cease. & the Divine Vision
Walked in robes of blood till he who slept should awake   15

Thus were the stars of heaven created like a golden chain   e
To bind the Body of Man to heaven from falling into the Abyss   t
Each took his station, & his course began with sorrow & care   t

In sevens & tens & fifties, hundreds, thousands, numberd all   t
According to their various powers. Subordinate to Urizen   20
And to his sons in their degrees & to his beauteous daughters

Travelling in silent majesty along their orderd ways   t
In right lined paths outmeasurd by proportions of number weight   t
And measure. mathematic motion wondrous. along the deep
In fiery pyramid. or Cube. or unornamented pillar   t 25
Of fire far shining. travelling along even to its destind end
Then falling down. a terrible space recovring in winter dire
Its wasted strength. it back returns upon a nether course   t
Till fired with ardour fresh recruited in its humble season   t
It rises up on high all summer till its wearied course   30
Turns into autumn. such the period of many worlds
Others triangular right angled course maintain. others obtuse   t

-315-

Acute Scalene, in simple paths. but others move   t
In intricate ways biquadrate. Trapeziums Rhombs Rhomboids
Paralellograms. triple & quadruple. polygonic   35
In their amazing hard subdued course in the vast deep   t

PAGE 34
And Los & Enitharmon were drawn down by their desires
Descending sweet upon the wind among soft harps & voices
To plant divisions in the Soul of Urizen & Ahania   t
To conduct the Voice of Enion to Ahanias midnight pillow

Urizen saw & envied & his imagination was filled   5
Repining he contemplated the past in his bright sphere   t
Terrified with his heart & spirit at the visions of futurity
That his dread fancy formd before him in the unformd void

For Los & Enitharmon walkd forth on the dewy Earth   t
Contracting or expanding their all flexible senses   10
At will to murmur in the flowers small as the honey bee
At will to stretch across the heavens & step from star to star
Or standing on the Earth erect, or on the stormy waves
Driving the storms before them or delighting in sunny beams
While round their heads the Elemental Gods kept harmony   t 15

And Los said. Lo the Lilly pale & the rose reddning fierce
Reproach thee & the beamy gardens sicken at thy beauty
I grasp thy vest in my strong hand in vain. like water springs
In the bright sands of Los. evading my embrace. then I alone
Wander among the virgins of the summer Look they cry   20
The poor forsaken Los mockd by the worm the shelly snail
The Emmet & the beetle hark they laugh & mock at Los

Enitharmon answerd Secure now from the smitings of thy Power
Demon of fury If the God enrapturd me infolds   t
In clouds of sweet obscurity my beauteous form dissolving   25
Howl thou over the body of death tis thine But if among the virgins
Of summer I have seen thee sleep & turn thy cheek delighted
Upon the rose or lilly pale. or on a bank where sleep   t
The beamy daughters of the light starting they rise they flee
From thy fierce love for tho I am dissolvd in the bright God   30
My spirit still pursues thy false love over rocks & valleys

Los answerd Therefore fade I thus dissolvd in rapturd trance
Thou canst repose on clouds of secrecy while oer my limbs
Cold dews & hoary frost creeps tho I lie on banks of summer
Among the beauties of the World Cold & repining Los   35
Still dies for Enitharmon nor a spirit springs from my dead corse
Then I am dead till thou revivest me with thy sweet song
Now taking on Ahanias form & now the form of Enion
I know thee not as once I knew thee in those blessed fields
Where memory wishes to repose among the flocks of Tharmas   40

Enitharmon answerd Wherefore didst thou throw thine arms around
Ahanias Image I decievd thee & will still decieve
Urizen saw thy sin & hid his beams in darkning Clouds
I still keep watch altho I tremble & wither across the heavens
In strong vibrations of fierce jealousy for thou art mine   45
Created for my will my slave tho strong tho I am weak
Farewell the God calls me away   I depart in my sweet bliss

She fled vanishing on the wind And left a dead cold corse
In Los's arms howlings began over the body of death
Los spoke. Thy God in vain shall call thee if by my strong power   50
I can infuse my dear revenge into his glowing breast
Then jealousy shall shadow all his mountains & Ahania
Curse thee thou plague of woful Los & seek revenge on thee

So saying in deep sobs he languishd till dead he also fell
Night passd & Enitharmon eer the dawn returnd in bliss   55
She sang Oer Los. reviving him to Life his groans were terrible
But thus she sang   I sieze the sphery harp I strike the strings   c

At the first Sound the Golden sun arises from the Deep
And shakes his awful hair
The Eccho wakes the moon to unbind her silver locks   60
The golden sun bears on my song
And nine bright spheres of harmony rise round the fiery King

The joy of woman is the Death of her most best beloved
Who dies for Love of her
In torments of fierce jealousy & pangs of adoration.   65
The Lovers night bears on my song
And the nine Spheres rejoice beneath my powerful controll

They sing unceasing to the notes of my immortal hand
The solemn silent moon
Reverberates the living harmony upon my limbs   70
The birds & beasts rejoice & play
And every one seeks for his mate to prove his inmost joy

Furious & terrible they sport & rend the nether deeps
The deep lifts up his rugged head
And lost in infinite hum[m]ing wings vanishes with a cry   75
The fading cry is ever dying
The living voice is ever living in its inmost joy

Arise you little glancing wings & sing your infant joy
Arise & drink your bliss
For every thing that lives is holy for the source of life   80
Descends to be a weeping babe
For the Earthworm renews the moisture of the sandy plain

Now my left hand I stretch to earth beneath
And strike the terrible string
I wake sweet joy in dens of sorrow & I plant a smile   85
In forests of affliction
And wake the bubbling springs of life in regions of dark death

O I am weary lay thine hand upon me or I faint
I faint beneath these beams of thine
For thou hast touchd my five senses & they answerd thee   90
Now I am nothing & I sink
And on the bed of silence sleep till thou awakest me

Thus sang the Lovely one in Rapturous delusive trance
Los heard reviving he siezd her in his arms delusive hopes   t
Kindling She led him into Shadows & thence fled outstretchd   95
Upon the immense like a bright rainbow weeping & smiling & fading

Thus livd Los driving Enion far into the deathful infinite   t
That he may also draw Ahania's spirit into her Vortex
Ah happy blindness Enion sees not the terrors of the uncertain   t
Thus Enion wails from the dark deep, the golden heavens tremble   t 100

PAGE 35
I am made to sow the thistle for wheat; the nettle for a nourishing   c
    dainty
I have planted a false oath in the earth, it has brought forth a poison
    tree
I have chosen the serpent for a councellor & the dog
For a schoolmaster to my children
I have blotted out from light & living the dove & nightingale   5
And I have caused the earth worm to beg from door to door
I have taught the thief a secret path into the house of the just
I have taught pale artifice to spread his nets upon the morning
My heavens are brass my earth is iron my moon a clod of clay
My sun a pestilence burning at noon & a vapour of death in night   10

What is the price of Experience do men buy it for a song   c
Or wisdom for a dance in the street? No it is bought with the price
Of all that a man hath his house his wife his children
Wisdom is sold in the desolate market where none come to buy
And in the witherd field where the farmer plows for bread in vain   15

It is an easy thing to triumph in the summers sun
And in the vintage & to sing on the waggon loaded with corn
It is an easy thing to talk of patience to the afflicted
To speak the laws of prudence to the houseless wanderer
PAGE 36
To listen to the hungry ravens cry in wintry season
When the red blood is filld with wine & with the marrow of lambs

It is an easy thing to laugh at wrathful elements
To hear the dog howl at the wintry door, the ox in the slaughter house
   moan
To see a god on every wind & a blessing on every blast   5
To hear sounds of love in the thunder storm that destroys our enemies
   house
To rejoice in the blight that covers his field, & the sickness that cuts off
   his children
While our olive & vine sing & laugh round our door & our children
   bring fruits & flowers

Then the groan & the dolor are quite forgotten & the slave grinding at
   the mill
And the captive in chains & the poor in the prison, & the soldier in the   10
   field
When the shatterd bone hath laid him groaning among the happier
   dead

It is an easy thing to rejoice in the tents of prosperity
Thus could I sing & thus rejoice, but it is not so with me!

Ahania heard the Lamentation & a swift Vibration
Spread thro her Golden frame. She rose up eer the dawn of day   ᵗ 15
When Urizen slept on his couch. drawn thro unbounded space
Onto the margin of Non Entity the bright Female came
There she beheld the Spectrous form of Enion in the Void   ᵗ
And never from that moment could she rest upon her pillow

End of the Second Night

PAGE 37

VALA

Night the Third

    t,c

Now sat the King of Light on high upon his starry throne
And bright Ahania bow'd herself before his splendid feet

O Urizen look on Me. like a mournful stream   ᵗ
I Embrace round thy knees & wet My bright hair with my tears: ᵗ
Why sighs my Lord! are not the morning stars thy obedient Sons   5
Do they not bow their bright heads at thy voice? at thy command
Do they not fly into their stations & return their light to thee
The immortal Atmospheres are thine, there thou art seen in glory
Surrounded by the ever changing Daughters of the Light
Why wilt thou look upon futurity darkning present joy   ᵗ 10

She ceas'd the Prince his light obscurd & the splendors of his crown
PAGE 38
Infolded in thick clouds, from whence his mighty voice burst forth
O bright [Ahania] a Boy is born of the dark Ocean   ᵗ

Whom Urizen doth serve, with Light replenishing his darkness
I am set here a King of trouble commanded here to serve
And do my ministry to those who eat of my wide table   5
All this is mine yet I must serve & that Prophetic boy
Must grow up to command his Prince but hear my determind Decree   t
Vala shall become a Worm in Enitharmons Womb   t
Laying her seed upon the fibres soon to issue forth
And Luvah in the loins of Los a dark & furious death   10
Alas for me! what will become of me at that dread time?

Ahania bow'd her head & wept seven days before the King
And on the eighth day when his clouds unfolded from his throne
She rais'd her bright head sweet perfumd & thus with heavenly voice

O Prince the Eternal One hath set thee leader of his hosts   15
PAGE 39
Leave all futurity to him Resume thy fields of Light   t
Why didst thou listen to the voice of Luvah that dread morn
To give the immortal steeds of light to his deceitful hands
No longer now obedient to thy will thou art compell'd
To forge the curbs of iron & brass to build the iron mangers   5
To feed them with intoxication from the wine presses of Luvah   e
Till the Divine Vision & Fruition is quite obliterated
They call thy lions to the fields of blood, they rowze thy tygers
Out of the halls of justice, till these dens thy wisdom framd
Golden & beautiful but O how unlike those sweet fields of bliss   10
Where liberty was justice & eternal science was mercy
Then O my dear lord listen to Ahania, listen to the vision
The vision of Ahania in the slumbers of Urizen
When Urizen slept in the porch & the Ancient Man was smitten   t

The Darkning Man walkd on the steps of fire before his halls   t,e 15
And Vala walkd with him in dreams of soft deluding slumber
He looked up & saw thee Prince of Light thy splendor faded   t
[But saw not Los nor Enitharmon for Luvah hid them in shadow]   t
PAGE 40
[In a soft cloud Outstretch'd across, & Luvah dwelt in the cloud]   t

Then Man ascended mourning into the splendors of his palace   t
Above him rose a Shadow from his wearied intellect   t
Of living gold, pure, perfect, holy; in white linen pure he hover'd
A sweet entrancing self delusion, a watry vision of Man   5
Soft exulting in existence all the Man absorbing

Man fell upon his face prostrate before the watry shadow
Saying O Lord whence is this change thou knowest I am nothing
And Vala trembled & coverd her face, & her locks. were spread on the
    pavement
I heard astonishd at the Vision & my heart trembled within me   t 10
I heard the voice of the Slumberous Man & thus he spoke   t

Idolatrous to his own Shadow words of Eternity uttering   t
O I am nothing when I enter into judgment with thee
If thou withdraw thy breath I die & vanish into Hades
If thou dost lay thine hand upon me behold I am silent   15
If thou withhold thine hand I perish like a fallen leaf
O I am nothing & to nothing must return again
If thou withdraw thy breath, behold I am oblivion

He ceasd: the shadowy voice was silent; but the cloud hoverd over their
     heads

PAGE 41

In golden wreathes, the sorrow of Man & the balmy drops fell down
And Lo that Son of Man, that shadowy Spirit of the Fallen One   t
Luvah, descended from the cloud; In terror Albion rose   t
Indignant rose the Awful Man & turnd his back on Vala   t

Why roll thy clouds in sick'ning mists. I can no longer hide   t 5
The dismal vision of mine Eyes, O love & life & light!   t
Prophetic dreads urge me to speak. futurity is before me
Like a dark lamp. Eternal death haunts all my expectation
Rent from Eternal Brotherhood we die & are no more

[I] heard the Voice of Albion starting from his sleep   t 10

Whence is this voice crying Enion that soundeth in my ears
O cruel pity! O dark deceit! can Love seek for dominion   t

And Luvah strove to gain dominion over the mighty Albion   t,e
They strove together above the Body where Vala was inclos'd
And the dark Body of Albion left prostrate upon the crystal pavement   t 15
Coverd with boils from head to foot. the terrible smitings of Luvah

Then frownd the Fallen Man & put forth Luvah from his presence   t
(I heard him: frown not Urizen: but listen to my Vision)   t

PAGE 42

Saying, Go & die the Death of Man for Vala the sweet wanderer
I will turn the volutions of your Ears outward; & bend your Nostrils
Downward; & your fluxile Eyes englob'd, roll round in fear
Your withring Lips & Tongue shrink up into a narrow circle
Till into narrow forms you creep. Go take your fiery way   5
And learn what 'tis to absorb the Man you Spirits of Pity & Love

O Urizen why art thou pale at the visions of Ahania   t
Listen to her who loves thee lest we also are driven away.

They heard the Voice & fled swift as the winters setting sun   t
And now the Human Blood foamd high, I saw that Luvah & Vala   t 10
Went down the Human Heart where Paradise & its joys abounded   t
In jealous fears in fury & rage, & flames roll'd round their fervid feet
And the vast form of Nature like a Serpent play'd before them   e

And as they went in folding fires & thunders of the deep
Vala shrunk in like the dark sea that leaves its slimy banks   15
And from her bosom Luvah fell far as the east & west
And the vast form of Nature like a Serpent roll'd between.   t,c

She ended. [From] his wrathful throne burst forth the black hail storm   t

Am I not God   said Urizen. Who is Equal to me   c
Do I not stretch the heavens abroad or fold them up like a garment   20

He spoke mustering his heavy clouds around him black opake
PAGE 43
Then thunders rolld around & lightnings darted to & fro
His visage changd to darkness & his strong right hand came forth
To cast Ahania to the Earth he siezd her by the hair
And threw her from the steps of ice that froze around his throne

Saying Art thou also become like Vala. thus I cast thee out   5
Shall the feminine indolent bliss. the indulgent self of weariness
The passive idle sleep the enormous night & darkness of Death
Set herself up to give her laws to the active masculine virtue
Thou little diminutive portion that darst be a counterpart
Thy passivity thy laws of obedience & insincerity   10
Are my abhorrence. Wherefore hast thou taken that fair form
Whence is this power given to thee! once thou wast in my breast
A sluggish current of dim waters. on whose verdant margin
A cavern shaggd with horrid shades. dark cool & deadly. where
I laid my head in the hot noon after the broken clods   15
Had wearied me. there I laid my plow & there my horses fed
And thou hast risen with thy moist locks into a watry image
Reflecting all my indolence my weakness & my death
To weigh me down beneath the grave into non Entity
Where Luvah strives scorned by Vala age after age wandering   20
Shrinking & shrinking from her Lord & calling him the Tempter
And art thou also become like Vala thus I cast thee out.

So loud in thunders spoke the King folded in dark despair
And threw Ahania from his bosom obdurate   She fell like lightning
Then fled the sons of Urizen from his thunderous throne petrific   25
They fled to East & West & left the North & South of Heaven
A crash ran thro the immense The bounds of Destiny were broken
The bounds of Destiny crashd direful & the swelling Sea
Burst from its bonds in whirlpools fierce roaring with Human voice
Triumphing even to the Stars at bright Ahanias fall   30

Down from the dismal North the Prince in thunders & thick clouds
PAGE 44
As when the thunderbolt down falleth on the appointed place
Fell down down rushing ruining thundering shuddering   t
Into the Caverns of the Grave & places of Human Seed

Where the impressions of Despair & Hope enroot forever
A world of Darkness. Ahania fell far into Non Entity   5

She Continued falling. Loud the Crash continud loud & Hoarse
From the Crash roared a flame of blue sulphureous fire from the flame   t
A dolorous groan that struck with dumbness all confusion
Swallowing up the horrible din in agony on agony
Thro the Confusion like a crack across from immense to immense   10
Loud strong a universal groan of death louder
Than all the wracking elements deafend & rended worse
Than Urizen & all his hosts in curst despair down rushing
But from the Dolorous Groan one like a shadow of smoke appeard
And human bones rattling together in the smoke & stamping   15
The nether Abyss & gnasshing in fierce despair. panting in sobs
Thick short incessant bursting sobbing. deep despairing stamping
    struggling
Struggling to utter the voice of Man struggling to take the features of
    Man. Struggling   t
To take the limbs of Man at length emerging from the smoke   c
Of Urizen dashed in pieces from his precipitant fall   20
Tharmas reard up his hands & stood on the affrighted Ocean
The dead reard up his Voice & stood on the resounding shore

Crying. Fury in my limbs. destruction in my bones & marrow
My skull riven into filaments. my eyes into sea jellies
Floating upon the tide wander bubbling & bubbling   25
Uttering my lamentations & begetting little monsters
Who sit mocking upon the little pebbles of the tide
In all my rivers & on dried shells that the fish

PAGE 45
Have quite forsaken. O fool fool to lose my sweetest bliss
Where art thou Enion ah too near to cunning too far off
And yet too near. Dashd down I send thee into distant darkness
Far as my strength can hurl thee wander there & laugh & play
Among the frozen arrows they will tear thy tender flesh   5
Fall off afar from Tharmas come not too near my strong fury
Scream & fall off & laugh at Tharmas lovely summer beauty
Till winter rends thee into Shivers as thou hast rended me

So Tharmas bellowd oer the ocean thundring sobbing bursting
The bounds of Destiny were broken & hatred now began   10
Instead of love to Enion. Enion blind & age bent
Plungd into the cold billows living a life in midst of waters
In terrors she witherd away to Entuthon Benithon   c
A world of deep darkness where all things in horrors are rooted

These are the words of Enion heard from the cold waves of despair 15

O Tharmas I had lost thee. & when I hoped I had found thee
O Tharmas do not thou destroy me quite but let
A little shadow. but a little showery form of Enion
Be near thee loved Terror. let me still remain & then do thou
Thy righteous doom upon me. only let me hear thy voice   20
Driven by thy rage I wander like a cloud into the deep
Where never yet Existence came, there losing all my life
I back return weaker & weaker, consume me not away
In thy great wrath. tho I have sinned. tho I have rebelld
Make me not like the things forgotten as they had not been   25
Make not the thing that loveth thee. a tear wiped away

Tharmas replied riding on storms his voice of Thunder rolld   t

Image of grief thy fading lineaments make my eyelids fail
What have I done! both rage & mercy are alike to me
Looking upon thee Image of faint waters. I recoil   30
From my fierce rage into thy semblance. Enion return
Why does thy piteous face Evanish like a rainy cloud
PAGE 46
Melting. a shower of falling tears. nothing but tears! Enion:
Substanceless. voiceless, weeping. vanishd. nothing but tears! Enion
Art thou for ever vanishd from the watry eyes of Tharmas
Rage Rage shall never from my bosom. winds & waters of woe
Consuming all to the end consuming Love and Hope are ended   t 5

For now no more remaind of Enion in the dismal air
Only a voice eternal wailing in the Elements

Where Enion, blind & age bent wanderd Ahania wanders now
She wanders in Eternal fear of falling into the indefinite
For her bright eyes behold the Abyss. Sometimes a little sleep   10
Weighs down her eyelids then she falls then starting wakes in fears
Sleepless to wander round repelld on the margin of Non Entity

The End of the Third Night

PAGE 47

VALA

Night The Fourth   c

But Tharmas rode on the dark Abyss. the voice of Tharmas rolld
Over the heaving deluge. he saw Los & Enitharmon Emerge   c
In strength & brightness from the Abyss his bowels yearnd over them
They rose in strength above the heaving deluge. in mighty scorn
Red as the Sun in the hot morning of the bloody day   5
Tharmas beheld them his bowels yearnd over them

And he said Wherefore do I feel such love & pity
Ah Enion Ah Enion Ah lovely lovely Enion
How is this All my hope is gone for ever fled
Like a famishd Eagle Eyeless raging in the vast expanse   10
Incessant tears are now my food. incessant rage & tears
Deathless for ever now I wander seeking oblivion
In torrents of despair in vain. for if I plunge beneath
Stifling I live. If dashd in pieces from a rocky height
I reunite in endless torment. would I had never risen   15
From deaths cold sleep beneath the bottom of the raging Ocean
And cannot those who once have lovd. ever forget their Love?
Are love & rage the same passion? they are the same in me
Are those who love. like those who died. risen again from death
Immortal. in immortal torment. never to be deliverd   20
Is it not possible that one risen again from Death
Can die! When dark despair comes over can I not
Flow down into the sea & slumber in oblivion. Ah Enion

PAGE 48

Deformd I see these lineaments of ungratified Desire
The all powerful curse of an honest man be upon Urizen & Luvah
But thou My Son Glorious in brightness comforter of Tharmas
Go forth Rebuild this Universe beneath my indignant power
A Universe of Death & Decay. Let Enitharmons hands   5
Weave soft delusive forms of Man above my watry world
Renew these ruind souls of Men thro Earth Sea Air & Fire
To waste in endless corruption. renew thou I will destroy
Perhaps Enion may resume some little semblance
To ease my pangs of heart & to restore some peace to Tharmas   10

Los answerd in his furious pride sparks issuing from his hair
Hitherto shalt thou come. no further. here thy proud waves cease
We have drunk up the Eternal Man by our unbounded power
Beware lest we also drink up thee rough demon of the waters
Our God is Urizen the King. King of the Heavenly hosts   15
We have no other God but he thou father of worms & clay
And he is falln into the Deep rough Demon of the waters
And Los remains God over all. weak father of worms & clay
I know I was Urthona keeper of the gates of heaven
But now I am all powerful Los & Urthona is but my shadow   20

Doubting stood Tharmas in the solemn darkness. his dim Eyes
Swam in red tears. he reard his waves above the head of Los
In wrath. but pitying back withdrew with many a sigh
Now he resolvd to destroy Los & now his tears flowd down

In scorn stood Los red sparks of blighting from his furious head   25
Flew over the waves of Tharmas. pitying Tharmas stayd his Waves

For Enitharmon shriekd amain crying O my sweet world
Built by the Architect divine whose love to Los & Enitharmon   e
Thou rash abhorred Demon in thy fury hast oerthrown

PAGE 49
What Sovereign Architect said Tharmas dare my will controll
For if I will I urge these waters. If I will they sleep
In peace beneath my awful frown my will shall be my Law

So Saying in a Wave he rap'd bright Enitharmon far
Apart from Los. but coverd her with softest brooding care   5
On a broad wave in the warm west. balming her bleeding wound

O how Los howld at the rending asunder all the fibres rent
Where Enitharmon joind to his left side in griding pain   t
He falling on the rocks bellowd his Dolor. till the blood
Stanch'd, then in ululation waild his woes upon the wind   10

And Tharmas calld to the Dark Spectre who upon the Shores   e
With dislocated Limbs had falln. The Spectre rose in pain
A Shadow blue obscure & dismal. like a statue of lead
Bent by its fall from a high tower the dolorous shadow rose

Go forth said Tharmas works of joy are thine   obey & live   15
So shall the spungy marrow issuing from thy splinterd bones
Bonify. & thou shalt have rest when this thy labour is done
Go forth bear Enitharmon back to the Eternal Prophet
Build her a bower in the midst of all my dashing waves
Make first a resting place for Los & Enitharmon. then   20
Thou shalt have rest. If thou refusest dashd abroad on all
My waves. thy limbs shall separate in stench & rotting & thou
Become a prey to all my demons of despair & hope

The Spectre of Urthona seeing Enitharmon writhd   t
His cloudy form in jealous fear & muttering thunders hoarse   25
And casting round thick glooms. thus utterd his fierce pangs of heart

Tharmas I know thee. how are we alterd our beauty decayd   e
But still I know thee tho in this horrible ruin whelmd
Thou once the mildest son of heaven art now become a Rage
A terror to all living things. think not that I am ignorant   30
That thou art risen from the dead or that my power forgot
PAGE 50
I slumber here in weak repose. I well remember the Day
The day of terror & abhorrence   t
When fleeing from the battle thou fleeting like the raven
Of dawn outstretching an expanse where neer expanse had been
Drewst all the Sons of Beulah into thy dread vortex following   t 5
Thy Eddying spirit down the hills of Beulah. All my sons
Stood round me at the anvil where new heated the wedge

Of iron glowd furious prepard for spades & mattocks
Hearing the symphonies of war loud sounding   All my sons
Fled from my side then pangs smote me unknown before. I saw 10
My loins begin to break forth into veiny pipes & writhe t
Before me in the wind englobing trembling with strong vibrations
The bloody mass began to animate. I bending over
Wept bitter tears incessant. Still beholding how the piteous form
Dividing & dividing from my loins a weak & piteous 15
Soft cloud of snow a female pale & weak I soft embracd
My counter part & calld it Love   I named her Enitharmon
But found myself & her together issuing down the tide
Which now our rivers were become delving thro caverns huge
Of goary blood strugg[l]ing to be deliverd from our bonds 20
She strove in vain not so Urthona strove for breaking forth,
A shadow blue obscure & dismal from the breathing Nostrils
Of Enion I issued into the air divided from Enitharmon
I howld in sorrow   I beheld thee rotting upon the Rocks
I pitying hoverd over thee I protected thy ghastly corse 25
From Vultures of the deep then wherefore shouldst thou rage
Against me who thee guarded in the night of death from harm

Tharmas replied. Art thou Urthona My friend my old companion,
With whom I livd in happiness before that deadly night
When Urizen gave the horses of Light into the hands of Luvah 30
Thou knowest not what Tharmas knows. O I could tell thee tales
That would enrage thee as it has Enraged me even
From Death in wrath & fury. But now come bear back
Thy loved Enitharmon. For thou hast her here before thine Eyes
PAGE 51
But my sweet Enion is vanishd & I never more
Shall see her unless thou O Shadow. wilt protect this Son
Of Enion & him assist. to bind the fallen King
Lest he should rise again from death in all his dreary power t
Bind him, take Enitharmon for thy sweet reward while I 5
In vain am driven on false hope. hope sister of despair

Groaning the terror rose & drave his solid rocks before e
Upon the tide till underneath the feet of Los a World
Dark dreadful rose & Enitharmon lay at Los's feet
The dolorous shadow joyd. weak hope appeard around his head 10

Tharmas before Los stood & thus the Voice of Tharmas rolld

Now all comes into the power of Tharmas. Urizen is falln
And Luvah hidden in the Elemental forms of Life & Death
Urthona is My Son   O Los thou art Urthona & Tharmas
Is God. The Eternal Man is seald never to be deliverd 15
I roll my floods over his body my billows & waves pass over him
The Sea encompasses him & monsters of the deep are his companions

-327-

Dreamer of furious oceans cold sleeper of weeds & shells
Thy Eternal form shall never renew my uncertain prevails against thee
Yet tho I rage God over all. A portion of my Life   20
That in Eternal fields in comfort wanderd with my flocks
At noon & laid her head upon my wearied bosom at night
She is divided   She is vanishd even like Luvah & Vala   t
O why did foul ambition sieze thee Urizen Prince of Light   t
And thee O Luvah prince of Love till Tharmas was divided   25
And I what can I now behold but an Eternal Death
Before my Eyes & an Eternal weary work to strive
Against the monstrous forms that breed among my silent waves   e
Is this to be A God far rather would I be a Man
To know sweet Science & to do with simple companions   30
Sitting beneath a tent & viewing sheepfolds & soft pastures
Take thou the hammer of Urthona rebuild these furnaces
Dost thou refuse   mind I the sparks that issue from thy hair

PAGE 52

I will compell thee to rebuild by these my furious waves
Death choose or life thou strugglest in my waters, now choose life
And all the Elements shall serve thee to their soothing flutes
Their sweet inspiriting lyres thy labours shall administer
And they to thee only remit not faint not thou my son   5
Now thou dost know what tis to strive against the God of waters

So saying Tharmas on his furious chariots of the Deep
Departed far into the Unknown & left a wondrous void
Round Los. afar his waters bore on all sides round. with noise
Of wheels & horses hoofs & Trumpets Horns & Clarions   t 10

Terrified Los beheld the ruins of Urizen beneath
A horrible Chaos to his eyes. a formless unmeasurable Death
Whirling up broken rocks on high into the dismal air
And fluctuating all beneath in Eddies of molten fluid

Then Los with terrible hands siezd on the Ruind Furnaces   15
Of Urizen. Enormous work: he builded them anew
Labour of Ages in the Darkness & the war of Tharmas
And Los formd Anvils of Iron petrific. for his blows
Petrify with incessant beating many a rock. many a planet

But Urizen slept in a stoned stupor in the nether Abyss   20
A dreamful horrible State in tossings on his icy bed
Freezing to solid all beneath, his grey oblivious form
Stretchd over the immense heaves in strong shudders. silent his voice
In brooding contemplation stretching out from North to South
In mighty power. Round him Los rolld furious   25
His thunderous wheels from furnace to furnace. tending diligent
The contemplative terror. frightend in his scornful sphere

Frightend with cold infectious madness. in his hand the thundering
Hammer of Urthona. forming under his heavy hand the hours

PAGE 53

The days & years. in chains of iron round the limbs of Urizen
Linkd hour to hour & day to night & night to day & year to year
In periods of pulsative furor. mills he formd & works
Of many wheels resistless in the power of dark Urthona

But Enitharmon wrapd in clouds waild loud. for as Los beat   5
The anvils of Urthona link by link the chains of sorrow
Warping upon the winds & whirling round in the dark deep
Lashd on the limbs of Enitharmon & the sulphur fires
Belchd from the furnaces wreathd round her. chaind in ceaseless fire
The lovely female howld & Urizen beneath deep groand   10
Deadly between the hammers beating grateful to the Ears
Of Los. absorbd in dire revenge he drank with joy the cries
Of Enitharmon & the groans of Urizen fuel for his wrath
And for his pity secret feeding on thoughts of cruelty

The Spectre wept at his dire labours when from Ladles huge   t 15
He pourd the molten iron round the limbs of Enitharmon
But when he pourd it round the bones of Urizen he laughd
Hollow upon the hollow wind. his shadowy form obeying
The voice of Los compelld he labourd round the Furnaces

And thus began the binding of Urizen day & night in fear   20
Circling round the dark Demon with howlings dismay & sharp
     blightings
The Prophet of Eternity beat on his iron links & links of brass
And as he beat round the hurtling Demon. terrified at the Shapes
Enslavd humanity put on he became what he beheld
Raging against Tharmas his God & uttering   25
Ambiguous words blasphemous filld with envy firm resolvd
On hate Eternal in his vast disdain he labourd beating
The Links of fate link after link an endless chain of sorrows

PAGE 54

The Eternal Mind bounded began to roll eddies of wrath ceaseless   e
Round & round & the sulphureous foam surging thick
Settled a Lake bright & shining clear. White as the snow

Forgetfulness dumbness necessity in chains of the mind lockd up
In fetters of ice shrinking. disorganizd rent from Eternity   5
Los beat on his fetters & heated his furnaces   t
And pourd iron sodor & sodor of brass

Restless the immortal inchaind heaving dolorous
Anguished unbearable till a roof shaggy wild inclosd
In an orb his fountain of thought   10

–329–

In a horrible dreamful slumber like the linked chain
A vast spine writhd in torment upon the wind
Shooting paind. ribbs like a bending Cavern
And bones of solidness froze over all his nerves of joy
A first age passed. a state of dismal woe   15

From the Caverns of his jointed spine down sunk with fright
A red round globe. hot burning. deep deep down into the Abyss
Panting Conglobing trembling Shooting out ten thousand branches
Around his solid bones & a Second Age passed over

In harrowing fear rolling his nervous brain shot branches   t 20
On high into two little orbs hiding in two little caves
Hiding carefully from the wind his eyes beheld the deep
And a third age passed a State of dismal woe

The pangs of hope began in heavy pain striving struggling
Two Ears in close volutions from beneath his orbs of vision   25
Shot spiring out & petrified as they grew. And a Fourth
Age passed over & a State of dismal woe

In ghastly torment sick hanging upon the wind
Two nostrils bent down to the deeps—

PAGE 55 (FIRST PORTION)
And a fifth age passed & a state of dismal woe

In ghastly torment sick. within his ribs bloated round
A craving hungry cavern. Thence arose his channeld
Throat. then like a red flame a tongue of hunger
And thirst appeard and a sixth age passed of dismal woe   5

Enraged & stifled with torment he threw his right arm to the north
His left arm to the south shooting out in anguish deep
And his feet stampd the nether abyss in trembling howling & dismay
And a seventh age passed over & a state of dismal woe

The Council of God on high watching over the Body   t 10
Of Man clothd in Luvahs robes of blood saw & wept
Descending over Beulahs mild moon coverd regions
The daughters of Beulah saw the Divine Vision they were comforted
And as a Double female form loveliness & perfection of beauty
They bowd the head & worshippd & with mild voice spoke these 15
    words

PAGE 56
Lord. Saviour if thou hadst been here our brother had not died   c
And now we know that whatsoever thou wilt ask of God
He will give it thee for we are weak women & dare not lift
Our eyes to the Divine pavilions. therefore in mercy thou
Appearest clothd in Luvahs garments that we may behold thee   5
And live. Behold Eternal Death is in Beulah Behold

We perish & shall not be found unless thou grant a place
In which we may be hidden under the Shadow of wings   e
For if we who are but for a time & who pass away in winter
Behold these wonders of Eternity we shall consume   10

Such were the words of Beulah of the Feminine Emanation   t
The Empyrean groand throughout All Eden was darkend
The Corse of Albion lay on the Rock the sea of Time & Space   t
Beat round the Rock in mighty waves & as a Polypus   e
That vegetates beneath the Sea the limbs of Man vegetated   15
In monstrous forms of Death a Human polypus of Death

The Saviour mild & gentle bent over the corse of Death
Saying If ye will Believe your Brother shall rise again   e
And first he found the Limit of Opacity & namd it Satan
In Albions bosom for in every human bosom these limits stand   20
And next he found the Limit of Contraction & namd it Adam
While yet those beings were not born nor knew of good or Evil

Then wondrously the Starry Wheels felt the divine hand. Limit   t,e
Was put to Eternal Death Los felt the Limit & saw
The Finger of God touch the Seventh furnace in terror   25
And Los beheld the hand of God over his furnaces
Beneath the Deeps in dismal Darkness beneath immensity   t

PAGE 55 (SECOND PORTION)

In terrors Los shrunk from his task. his great hammer   16
Fell from his hand his fires hid their strong limbs in smoke
For with noises ruinous   hurtlings & clashings & groans   t
The immortal endur'd. tho bound in a deadly sleep
Pale terror siezd the Eyes of Los as he beat round   20
The hurtling Demon. terrifd at the shapes
Enslavd humanity put on he became what he beheld
He became what he was doing he was himself transformd   t

Bring in here the Globe of Blood as in the B of Urizen

Spasms siezd his muscular fibres writhing to & fro his pallid lips   t
Unwilling movd as Urizen howld his loins wavd like the sea   25
At Enitharmons shriek his knees each other smote & then he lookd
With stony Eyes on Urizen & then swift writhd his neck
Involuntary to the Couch where Enitharmon lay
The bones of Urizen hurtle on the wind the bones of Los
Twinge & his iron sinews bend like lead & fold   30
Into unusual forms dancing & howling stamping the Abyss

PAGE 56 (SECOND PORTION)

End of the Fourth Night   t

Vala

Night The Fifth

t,e

Infected Mad he dancd on his mountains high & dark as heaven   e
Now fixd into one stedfast bulk his features stonify
From his mouth curses & from his eyes sparks of blighting
Beside the anvil cold he dancd with the hammer of Urthona
Terrific pale. Enitharmon stretchd on the dreary Earth   t 5
Felt her immortal limbs freeze stiffning pale inflexible
His feet shr[u]nk withring from the deep shrinking & withering   t
And Enitharmon shrunk up all their fibres withring beneath
As plants witherd by winter leaves & stems & roots decaying
Melt into thin air while the seed drivn by the furious wind   10
Rests on the distant Mountains top. So Los & Enitharmon
Shrunk into fixed space stood trembling on a Rocky cliff
Yet mighty bulk & majesty & beauty remaind but unexpansive
As far as highest Zenith from the lowest Nadir. so far shrunk   t
Los from the furnaces a Space immense & left the cold   15
Prince of Light bound in chains of intellect among the furnaces
But all the furnaces were out & the bellows had ceast to blow

He stood trembling & Enitharmon clung around his knees   e
Their senses unexpansive in one stedfast bulk remain
The night blew cold & Enitharmon shriekd on the dismal wind   20
PAGE 58
Her pale hands cling around her husband & over her weak head
Shadows of Eternal Death sit in the leaden air

But the soft pipe the flute the viol organ harp & cymbal
And the sweet sound of silver voices calm the weary couch
Of Enitharmon but her groans drown the immortal harps   5
Loud & more loud the living music floats upon the air
Faint & more faint the daylight wanes. The wheels of turning
    darkness
Began in solemn revolutions. Earth convulsd with rending pangs
Rockd to & fro & cried sore at the groans of Enitharmon
Still the faint harps & silver voices calm the weary couch   t
But from the caves of deepest night ascending in clouds of mist   10
The winter spread his wide black wings across from pole to pole
Grim frost beneath & terrible snow linkd in a marriage chain
Began a dismal dance. The winds around on pointed rocks
Settled like bats innumerable ready to fly abroad
The groans of Enitharmon shake the skies the labring Earth   15
Till from her heart rending his way a terrible Child sprang forth
In thunder smoke & sullen flames & howlings & fury & blood

Soon as his burning Eyes were opend on the Abyss
The horrid trumpets of the deep bellowd with bitter blasts   20
The Enormous Demons woke & howld around the new born king   t
Crying Luvah King of Love thou art the King of rage & death
Urizen cast deep darkness round him raging Luvah pourd   t
The spears of Urizen from Chariots round the Eternal tent
Discord began then yells & cries shook the wide firma[m]ent   t 25

PAGE 59
Where is Sweet Vala gloomy prophet where the lovely form
That drew the body of Man from heaven into this dark Abyss
Soft tears & sighs where are you come forth shout on bloody fields
Shew thy soul Vala shew thy bow & quiver of secret fires

Draw thy bow Vala from the depths of hell thy black bow draw   t,c 5
And twang the bow string to our howlings let thine arrows black
Sing in the Sky as once they sang upon the hills of Light
When dark Urthona wept in torment of the secret pain

He wept & he divided & he laid his gloomy head
Down on the Rock of Eternity on darkness of the deep   10
Torn by black storms & ceaseless torrents of consuming fire   c
Within his breast his fiery sons chaind down & filld with cursings

And breathing terrible blood & vengeance gnashing his teeth with pain
Let loose the Enormous Spirit in the darkness of the deep
And his dark wife that once fair crystal form divinely clear   15
Within his ribs producing serpents whose souls are flames of fire

But now the times return upon thee Enitharmons womb
Now holds thee soon to issue forth. Sound Clarions of war
Call Vala from her close recess in all her dark deceit
Then rage on rage shall fierce redound out of her crystal quiver   20

So sung the Demons round red Orc & round faint Enitharmon   t,c
Sweat & blood stood on the limbs of Los in globes. his fiery Eyelids
Faded. he rouzd he siezd the wonder in his hands & went
Shuddring & weeping thro the Gloom & down into the deeps

Enitharmon nursd her fiery child in the dark deeps   25
Sitting in darkness. over her Los mournd in anguish fierce
Coverd with gloom. the fiery boy grew fed by the milk
Of Enitharmon. Los around her builded pillars of iron
PAGE 60
And brass & silver & gold fourfold in dark prophetic fear
For now he feard Eternal Death & uttermost Extinction   t
He builded Golgonooza on the Lake of Udan Adan   c
Upon the Limit of Translucence then he builded Luban
Tharmas laid the Foundations & Los finishd it in howling woe   5

But when fourteen summers & winters had revolved over
Their solemn habitation Los beheld the ruddy boy
Embracing his bright mother & beheld malignant fires
In his young eyes discerning plain that Orc plotted his death
Grief rose upon his ruddy brows. a tightening girdle grew   10
Around his bosom like a bloody cord. in secret sobs
He burst it, but next morn another girdle succeeds
Around his bosom. Every day he viewd the fiery youth
With silent fear & his immortal cheeks grew deadly pale
Till many a morn & many a night passd over in dire woe   15
Forming a girdle in the day & bursting it at night
The girdle was formd by day by night was burst in twain
Falling down on the rock an iron chain link by link lockd

Enitharmon beheld the bloody chain of nights & days
Depending from the bosom of Los & how with griding pain   t 20
He went each morning to his labours with the spectre dark
Calld it the chain of Jealousy. Now Los began to speak
His woes aloud to Enitharmon. since he could not hide
His uncouth plague. He siezd the boy in his immortal hands
While Enitharmon followd him weeping in dismal woe   25
Up to the iron mountains top & there the Jealous chain
Fell from his bosom on the mountain. The Spectre dark
Held the fierce boy Los naild him down binding around his limbs
The accursed chain O how bright Enitharmon howld & cried   t
Over her son. Obdurate Los bound down her loved Joy   30

PAGE 61
The hammer of Urthona smote the rivets in terror. of brass
Tenfold. the Demons rage flamd tenfold forth rending
Roaring redounding. Loud Loud Louder & Louder & fird
The darkness warring with the waves of Tharmas & Snows of Urizen
Crackling the flames went up with fury from the immortal demon   5
Surrounded with flames the Demon grew loud howling in his fires
Los folded Enitharmon in a cold white cloud in fear
Then led her down into the deeps & into his labyrinth
Giving the Spectre sternest charge over the howling fiend

Concenterd into Love of Parent Storgous Appetite Craving   c 10
His limbs bound down mock at his chains for over them a flame
Of circling fire unceasing plays to feed them with life & bring
The virtues of the Eternal worlds ten thousand thousand spirits
Of life lament around the Demon going forth & returning   t
At his enormous call they flee into the heavens of heavens   15
And back return with wine & food. Or dive into the deeps
To bring the thrilling joys of sense to quell his ceaseless rage
His eyes the lights of his large soul contract or else expand
Contracted they behold the secrets of the infinite mountains

The veins of gold & silver & the hidden things of Vala   20
Whatever grows from its pure bud or breathes a fragrant soul
Expanded they behold the terrors of the Sun & Moon
The Elemental Planets & the orbs of eccentric fire
His nostrils breathe a fiery flame. his locks are like the forests   t
Of wild beasts there the lion glares the tyger & wolf howl there   25
And there the Eagle hides her young in cliffs & precipices
His bosom is like starry heaven expanded all the stars
Sing round. there waves the harvest & the vintage rejoices. the Springs
Flow into rivers of delight. there the spontaneous flowers
Drink laugh & sing. the grasshopper the Emmet & the Fly   30
The golden Moth builds there a house & spreads her silken bed
PAGE 62
His loins inwove with silken fires are like a furnace fierce
As the strong Bull in summer time when bees sing round the heath
Where the herds low after the shadow & after the water spring
The numrous flocks cover the mountain & shine along the valley
His knees are rocks of adamant & rubie & emerald   5
Spirits of strength in Palaces rejoice in golden armour   t
Armed with spear & shield they drink & rejoice over the slain
Such is the Demon such his terror in the nether deep

But when returnd to Golgonooza Los & Enitharmon
Felt all the sorrow Parents feel. they wept toward one another   10
And Los repented that he had chaind Orc upon the mountain
And Enitharmons tears prevaild   parental love returnd
Tho terrible his dread of that infernal chain   They rose
At midnight hasting to their much beloved care
Nine days they traveld thro the Gloom of Entuthon Benithon   15
Los taking Enitharmon by the hand led her along
The dismal vales & up to the iron mountains top where Orc
Howld in the furious wind he thought to give to Enitharmon
Her son in tenfold joy & to compensate for her tears
Even if his own death resulted so much pity him paind   20

But when they came to the dark rock & to the spectrous cave
Lo the young limbs had strucken root into the rock & strong
Fibres had from the Chain of Jealousy inwove themselves
In a swift vegetation round the rock & round the Cave
And over the immortal limbs of the terrible fiery boy   25
In vain they strove now to unchain. In vain with bitter tears
To melt the chain of Jealousy. not Enitharmons death
Nor the Consummation of Los could ever melt the chain
Nor unroot the infernal fibres from their rocky bed
Nor all Urthonas strength nor all the power of Luvahs Bulls   30
Tho they each morning drag the unwilling Sun out of the deep
Could uproot the infernal chain. for it had taken root

PAGE 63

Into the iron rock & grew a chain beneath the Earth
Even to the Center wrapping round the Center & the limbs
Of Orc entering with fibres. became one with him a living Chain
Sustained by the Demons life. Despair & Terror & Woe & Rage
Inwrap the Parents in cold clouds as they bend howling over   5
The terrible boy till fainting by his side the Parents fell

Not long they lay Urthonas spectre found herbs of the pit
Rubbing their temples he reviv'd them. all their lamentations
I write not here but all their after life was lamentation

When satiated with grief they returnd back to Golgonooza   t 10
Enitharmon on the road of Dranthon felt the inmost gate   c
Of her bright heart burst open & again close with a deadly pain   t
Within her heart Vala began to reanimate in bursting sobs
And when the Gate was open she beheld that dreary Deep   t
Where bright Ahania wept. She also saw the infernal roots   15
Of the chain of Jealousy & felt the rendings of fierce howling Orc

Rending the Caverns like a mighty wind pent in the Earth
Tho wide apart as furthest north is from the furthest south   t
Urizen trembled where he lay to hear the howling terror
The rocks shook the Eternal bars tuggd to & fro were rifted   20
Outstretchd upon the stones of ice the ruins of his throne
Urizen shuddring heard his trembling limbs shook the strong caves

The Woes of Urizen shut up in the deep dens of Urthona

Ah how shall Urizen the King submit to this dark mansion   c
Ah how is this! Once on the heights I stretchd my throne sublime   25
The mountains of Urizen once of silver where the sons of wisdom
     dwelt
And on whose tops the Virgins sang are rocks of Desolation

My fountains once the haunt of Swans now breed the scaly tortoise
The houses of my harpers are become a haunt of crows
The gardens of wisdom are become a field of horrid graves   30
And on the bones I drop my tears & water them in vain

PAGE 64

Once how I walked from my palace in gardens of delight
The sons of wisdom stood around the harpers followd with harps
Nine virgins clothd in light composd the song to their immortal voices
And at my banquets of new wine my head was crownd with joy

Then in my ivory pavilions I slumberd in the noon   t 5
And walked in the silent night among sweet smelling flowers
Till on my silver bed I slept & sweet dreams round me hoverd
But now my land is darkend & my wise men are departed

My songs are turned to cries of Lamentation
Heard on my Mountains & deep sighs under my palace roofs   10
Because the Steeds of Urizen once swifter than the light
Were kept back from my Lord & from his chariot of mercies

O did I keep the horses of the day in silver pastures
O I refusd the Lord of day the horses of his prince
O did I close my treasuries with roofs of solid stone   15
And darken all my Palace walls with envyings & hate

O Fool to think that I could hide from his all piercing eyes
The gold & silver & costly stones his holy workmanship
O Fool could I forget the light that filled my bright spheres
Was a reflection of his face who calld me from the deep   20

I well remember for I heard the mild & holy voice
Saying O light spring up & shine & I sprang up from the deep
He gave to me a silver scepter & crownd me with a golden crown
& said Go forth & guide my Son who wanders on the ocean

I went not forth. I hid myself in black clouds of my wrath   25
I calld the stars around my feet in the night of councils dark
The stars threw down their spears & fled naked away
We fell. I siezd thee dark Urthona In my left hand falling

I siezd thee beauteous Luvah thou art faded like a flower
And like a lilly is thy wife Vala witherd by winds   30
When thou didst bear the golden cup at the immortal tables
Thy children smote their fiery wings crownd with the gold of heaven

PAGE 65
Thy pure feet stepd on the steps divine. too pure for other feet
And thy fair locks shadowd thine eyes from the divine effulgence
Then thou didst keep with Strong Urthona the living gates of heaven
But now thou art bound down with him even to the gates of hell

Because thou gavest Urizen the wine of the Almighty   5
For steeds of Light that they might run in thy golden chariot of pride
I gave to thee the Steeds I pourd the stolen wine
And drunken with the immortal draught fell from my throne sublime

I will arise Explore these dens & find that deep pulsation
That shakes my caverns with strong shudders. perhaps this is the night   10
Of Prophecy & Luvah hath burst his way from Enitharmon
When Thought is closd in Caves. Then love shall shew its root in
      deepest Hell

End of the Fifth Night

VALA

Night the Sixth

So Urizen arose & leaning on his Spear explord his dens
He threw his flight thro the dark air to where a river flowd
And taking off his silver helmet filled it & drank
But when unsatiated his thirst he assayd to gather more
Lo three terrific women at the verge of the bright flood e 5
Who would not suffer him to approach. but drove him back with storms

Urizen knew them not & thus addressd the spirits of darkness

Who art thou Eldest Woman sitting in thy clouds
What is that name written on thy forehead? what art thou?
And wherefore dost thou pour this water forth in sighs & care 10

She answerd not but filld her urn & pourd it forth abroad

Answerest thou not said Urizen. then thou maist answer me
Thou terrible woman clad in blue, whose strong attractive power
Draws all into a fountain at the rock of thy attraction
With frowning brow thou sittest mistress of these mighty waters 15

She answerd not but stretchd her arms & threw her limbs abroad

Or wilt thou answer youngest Woman clad in shining green t
With labour & care thou dost divide the current into four t
Queen of these dreadful rivers speak & let me hear thy voice

They reard up a wall of rocks and Urizen raisd his spear. t
They gave a scream, they knew their father Urizen knew his daughters
They shrunk into their channels. dry the rocky strand beneath his feet
Hiding themselves in rocky forms from the Eyes of Urizen

Then Urizen wept & thus his lamentation poured forth e 5

O horrible O dreadful state! those whom I loved best
On whom I pourd the beauties of my light adorning them
With jewels & precious ornament labourd with art divine
Vests of the radiant colours of heaven & crowns of golden fire
I gave sweet lillies to their breasts & roses to their hair 10
I taught them songs of sweet delight. I gave their tender voices
Into the blue expanse & I invented with laborious art
Sweet instruments of sound. in pride encompassing my Knees
They pourd their radiance above all. the daughters of Luvah Envied
At their exceeding brightness & the sons of eternity sent them gifts 15
Now will I pour my fury on them & I will reverse
The precious benediction. for their colours of loveliness

-338-

I will give blackness for jewels hoary frost for ornament deformity
For crowns wreathd Serpents for sweet odors stinking corruptibility
For voices of delight hoarse croakings inarticulate thro frost   20
For labourd fatherly care & sweet instruction. I will give
Chains of dark ignorance & cords of twisted self conceit
And whips of stern repentance & food of stubborn obstinacy
That they may curse Tharmas their God & Los his adopted son
That they may curse & worship the obscure Demon of destruction   25
That they may worship terrors & obey the violent
Go forth sons of my curse   Go forth daughters of my abhorrence

Tharmas heard the deadly scream across his watry world   c
And Urizens loud sounding voice lamenting on the wind
And he came riding in his fury. froze to solid were his waves   30
PAGE 69
Silent in ridges he beheld them stand round Urizen
A dreary waste of solid waters for the King of Light
Darkend his brows with his cold helmet & his gloomy spear
Darkend before him. Silent on the ridgy waves he took
His gloomy way before him Tharmas fled & flying fought   5

Crying. What & who art thou Cold Demon. art thou Urizen
Art thou like me risen again from death or art thou deathless
If thou art he my desperate purpose hear & give me death
For death to me is better far than life. death my desire
That I in vain in various paths have sought but still I live   10
The Body of Man is given to me I seek in vain to destroy
For still it surges forth in fish & monsters of the deeps
And in these monstrous forms I Live in an Eternal woe   t
And thou O Urizen art falln never to be deliverd
Withhold thy light from me for ever & I will withhold   15
From thee thy food so shall we cease to be & all our sorrows
End & the Eternal Man no more renew beneath our power   t
If thou refusest in eternal flight thy beams in vain
Shall pursue Tharmas & in vain shalt crave for food I will
Pour down my flight thro dark immensity Eternal falling   20
Thou shalt pursue me but in vain till starvd upon the void
Thou hangst a dried skin shrunk up weak wailing in the wind

So Tharmas spoke but Urizen replied not. On his way   c
He took. high bounding over hills & desarts floods & horrible chasms
Infinite was his labour without end his travel   he strove   25
In vain for hideous monsters of the deeps annoyd him sore
Scaled & finnd with iron & brass they devour the path before him
Incessant was the conflict. On he bent his weary steps
Making a path toward the dark world of Urthona. he rose
With pain upon the dreary mountains & with pain descended   t 30
And saw their grizly fears & his eyes sickend at the sight

−339−

The howlings gnashings groanings shriekings shudderings sobbings
    burstings
Mingle together to create a world for Los. In cruel delight
PAGE 70 (FIRST PORTION)
Los brooded on the darkness. nor saw Urizen with a Globe of fire
Lighting his dismal journey thro the pathless world of death
Writing in bitter tears & groans in books of iron & brass
The enormous wonders of the Abysses once his brightest joy

For Urizen beheld the terrors of the Abyss wandring among   5
The ruind spirits once his children & the children of Luvah
Scard at the sound of their own sigh that seems to shake the immense
They wander Moping in their heart a Sun a Dreary moon
A Universe of fiery constellations in their brain
An Earth of wintry woe beneath their feet & round their loins   t 10
Waters or winds or clouds or brooding lightnings & pestilential plagues
Beyond the bounds of their own self their senses cannot penetrate
As the tree knows not what is outside of its leaves & bark
And yet it drinks the summer joy & fears the winter sorrow
So in the regions of the grave none knows his dark compeer   15
Tho he partakes of his dire woes & mutual returns the pang
The throb the dolor the convulsion in soul sickening woes   t

The horrid shapes & sights of torment in burning dungeons & in
Fetters of red hot iron some with crowns of serpents & some
With monsters girding round their bosoms. Some lying on beds of   20
    sulphur
On racks & wheels he beheld women marching oer burning wastes
Of Sand in bands of hundreds & of fifties & of thousands strucken with
Lightnings which blazed after them upon their shoulders in their march
In successive vollies with loud thunders swift flew the King of Light
Over the burning desarts   Then the desarts passd. involvd in clouds   25
Of smoke with myriads moping in the stifling vapours. Swift
Flew the King tho flagd his powers labring. till over rocks
And Mountains faint weary he wanderd. where multitudes were shut
Up in the solid mountains & in rocks which heaved with their torments
Then came he among fiery cities & castles built of burning steel   30
Then he beheld the forms of tygers & of Lions dishumanizd men
Many in serpents & in worms stretchd out enormous length
Over the sullen mould & slimy tracks obstruct his way
Drawn out from deep to deep woven by ribbd
And scaled monsters or armd in iron shell or shell of brass   35
Or gold a glittering torment shining & hissing in eternal pain
Some [as] columns of fire or of water sometimes stretchd out in heighth   t
Sometimes in length sometimes englobing wandering in vain seeking   t
    for ease
His voice to them was but an inarticulate thunder for their Ears

Were heavy & dull & their eyes & nostrils closed up   40
Oft he stood by a howling victim Questioning in words
Soothing or Furious no one answerd every one wrapd up
In his own sorrow howld regardless of his words, nor voice
Of sweet response could he obtain tho oft assayd with tears
He knew they were his Children ruind in his ruind world   ᵗ45

PAGE 71 (FIRST PORTION)

Oft would he stand & question a fierce scorpion glowing with gold
In vain the terror heard not. then a lion he would Sieze
By the fierce mane staying his howling course in vain the voice   ᵗ
Of Urizen in vain the Eloquent tongue. A Rock a Cloud a Mountain
Were now not Vocal as in Climes of happy Eternity   5
Where the lamb replies to the infant voice & the lion to the man of years
Giving them sweet instructions Where the Cloud the River & the Field
Talk with the husbandman & shepherd. But these attackd him sore
Siezing upon his feet & rending the Sinews that in Caves
He hid to recure his obstructed powers with rest & oblivion   10

PAGE 70 (SECOND PORTION)

Here he had time enough to repent of his rashly threatend curse   46
He saw them cursd beyond his Curse his soul melted with fear

PAGE 71 (SECOND PORTION)

He could not take their fetters off for they grew from the soul
Nor could he quench the fires for they flamd out from the heart
Nor could he calm the Elements because himself was Subject
So he threw his flight in terror & pain & in repentant tears

When he had passd these southern terrors he approachd the East   ᵉ15
Void pathless beaten with iron sleet & eternal hail & rain   ᵗ
No form was there no living thing & yet his way lay thro
This dismal world. he stood a while & lookd back oer his former
Terrific voyage. Hills & Vales of torment & despair
Sighing & wiping a fresh tear. then turning round he threw   20
Himself into the dismal void. falling he fell & fell
Whirling in unresistible revolutions down & down
In the horrid bottomless vacuity falling falling falling
Into the Eastern vacuity the empty world of Luvah

The ever pitying one who seeth all things saw his fall   25
And in the dark vacuity created a bosom of clay   ᵗ
When wearied dead he fell his limbs reposd in the bosom of slime
As the seed falls from the sowers hand so Urizen fell & death
Shut up his powers in oblivion. then as the seed shoots forth
In pain & sorrow. So the slimy bed his limbs renewd   30
At first an infant weakness. periods passd he gatherd strength
But still in solitude he sat then rising threw his flight
Onward tho falling thro the waste of night & ending in death

And in another resurrection to sorrow & weary travel
But still his books he bore in his strong hands & his iron pen   ᶜ35
For when he died they lay beside his grave & when he rose   ᵗ
He siezd them with a gloomy smile for wrapd in his death clothes   ᵗ
He hid them when he slept in death when he revivd the clothes
Were rotted by the winds the books remaind still unconsumd
Still to be written & interleavd with brass & iron & gold   40
Time after time for such a journey none but iron pens
Can write And adamantine leaves recieve nor can the man who goes
PAGE 72
The journey obstinate refuse to write time after time

Endless had been his travel but the Divine hand him led   ᵗ
For infinite the distance & obscurd by Combustions dire
By rocky masses frowning in the abysses revolving erratic
Round Lakes of fire in the dark deep the ruins of Urizens world   5
Oft would he sit in a dark rift & regulate his books
Or sleep such sleep as spirits eternal wearied in his dark
Tearful & sorrowful state. then rise look out & ponder
His dismal voyage eyeing the next sphere tho far remote
Then darting into the Abyss of night his venturous limbs   10
Thro lightnings thunders earthquakes & concussions fires & floods
Stemming his downward fall labouring up against futurity
Creating many a Vortex fixing many a Science in the deep   ᵉ
And thence throwing his venturous limbs into the Vast unknown
Swift Swift from Chaos to chaos from void to void a road immense   15

For when he came to where a Vortex ceasd to operate
Nor down nor up remaind then if he turnd & lookd back
From whence he came twas upward all. & if he turnd and viewd
The unpassd void upward was still his mighty wandring
The midst between an Equilibrium grey of air serene   20
Where he might live in peace & where his life might meet repose

But Urizen said Can I not leave this world of Cumbrous wheels   ᵉ
Circle oer Circle nor on high attain a void
Where self sustaining I may view all things beneath my feet
Or sinking thro these Elemental wonders swift to fall   25
I thought perhaps to find an End a world beneath of voidness
Whence I might travel round the outside of this Dark confusion
When I bend downward bending my head downward into the deep   ᵉ
Tis upward all which way soever I my course begin
But when A Vortex formd on high by labour & sorrow & care   30
And weariness begins on all my limbs then sleep revives
My wearied spirits waking then tis downward all which way
So ever I my spirits turn no end I find of all
O what a world is here unlike those climes of bliss
Where my sons gatherd round my knees   O thou poor ruind world   35

Thou horrible ruin once like me thou wast all glorious
And now like me partaking desolate thy masters lot
Art thou O ruin the once glorious heaven are these thy rocks
Where joy sang in the trees & pleasure sported on the rivers
PAGE 73
And laughter sat beneath the Oaks & innocence sported round
Upon the green plains & sweet friendship met in palaces
And books & instruments of song & pictures of delight
Where are they whelmd beneath these ruins in horrible destruction   t
And if Eternal falling I repose on the dark bosom   5
Of winds & waters or thence fall into a Void where air
Is not down falling thro immensity ever & ever
I lose my powers weakend every revolution till a death
Shuts up my powers then a seed in the vast womb of darkness
I dwell in dim oblivion. brooding over me the Enormous worlds   10
Reorganize me shooting forth in bones & flesh & blood
I am regenerated to fall or rise at will or to remain
A labourer of ages a dire discontent a living woe
Wandring in vain. Here will I fix my foot & here rebuild   c
Here Mountains of Brass promise much riches in their dreadful bosoms   t 15

So he began to dig form[ing] of gold silver & iron   t
And brass vast instruments to measure out the immense & fix
The whole into another world better suited to obey
His will where none should dare oppose his will himself being King
Of All & all futurity be bound in his vast chain   20

And the Sciences were fixd & the Vortexes began to operate
On all the sons of men & every human soul terrified
At the turning wheels of heaven shrunk away inward withring away
Gaining a New Dominion over all his sons & Daughters
& over the Sons & daughters of Luvah in the horrible Abyss   25
For Urizen lamented over them in a selfish lamentation
Till a white woof coverd his cold limbs from head to feet   t
Hair white as snow coverd him in flaky locks terrific
Overspreading his limbs. in pride he wanderd weeping
Clothed in aged venerableness obstinately resolvd   30
Travelling thro darkness & whereever he traveld a dire Web   c
Followd behind him as the Web of a Spider dusky & cold
Shivering across from Vortex to Vortex drawn out from his mantle of
    years
A living Mantle adjoind to his life & growing from his Soul

And the Web of Urizen stre[t]chd direful shivring in clouds   35
And uttering such woes such bursts such thunderings   t
The eyelids expansive as morning & the Ears
As a golden ascent winding round to the heavens of heavens
Within the dark horrors of the Abysses lion or tyger or scorpion

PAGE 74

For every one opend within into Eternity at will
But they refusd because their outward forms were in the Abyss
And the wing like tent of the Universe beautiful surrounding all
Or drawn up or let down at the will of the immortal man
Vibrated in such anguish the eyelids quiverd   5
Weak & Weaker their expansive orbs began shrinking
Pangs smote thro the brain & a universal shriek
Ran thro the Abysses rending the web torment on torment

Thus Urizen in sorrows wanderd many a dreary way
Warring with monsters of the Deeps in his most hideous pilgrimage   10
Till his bright hair scatterd in snows his skin barkd oer with wrinkles
Four Caverns rooting downwards their foundations thrusting forth   c
The metal rock & stone in ever painful throes of vegetation
The Cave of Orc stood to the South a furnace of dire flames
Quenchless unceasing. In the west the Cave of Urizen   15
For Urizen fell as the Midday sun falls down into the West
North stood Urthonas stedfast throne a World of Solid darkness
Shut up in stifling obstruction rooted in dumb despair
The East was Void. But Tharmas rolld his billows in ceaseless eddies
Void pathless beat with Snows eternal & iron hail & rain   t 20
All thro the caverns of fire & air & Earth. Seeking
For Enions limbs nought finding but the black sea weed & sickning
      slime
Flying away from Urizen that he might not give him food
Above beneath on all sides round in the vast deep of immensity
That he might starve the sons & daughters of Urizen on the winds   25
Making between horrible chasms into the vast unknown
All these around the world of Los cast forth their monstrous births
But in Eternal times the Seat of Urizen is in the South   t
Urthona in the North Luvah in East Tharmas in West

And now he came into the Abhorred world of Dark Urthona   c 30
By Providence divine conducted not bent from his own will
Lest death Eternal should be the result for the Will cannot be violated
Into the doleful vales where no tree grew nor river flowd   c
Nor man nor beast nor creeping thing nor sun nor cloud nor star
Still he with his globe of fire immense in his venturous hand   35
Bore on thro the Affrighted vales ascending & descending
Oerwearied or in cumbrous flight he venturd oer dark rifts
Or down dark precipices or climbd with pain and labour huge
Till he beheld the world of Los from the Peaked rock of Urthona
And heard the howling of red Orc distincter & distincter   40

PAGE 75

Redoubling his immortal efforts thro the narrow vales   c
With difficulty down descending guided by his Ear

And by his globe of fire he went down the Vale of Urthona   t
Between the enormous iron walls built by the Spectre dark
Dark grew his globe reddning with mists & full before his path   5
Striding across the narrow vale the Shadow of Urthona   t
A spectre Vast appeard whose feet & legs with iron scaled
Stampd the hard rocks expectant of the unknown wanderer
Whom he had seen wandring his nether world when distant far
And watchd his swift approach collected dark the Spectre stood   10
Beside hi[m] Tharmas stayd his flight & stood in stern defiance   t
Communing with the Spectre who rejoicd along the vale
Round his loins a girdle glowd with many colourd fires
In his hand a knotted Club whose knots like mountains frownd
Desart among the Stars them withering with its ridges cold   15
Black scales of iron arm the dread visage iron spikes instead
Of hair shoot from his orbed scull. his glowing eyes
Burn like two furnaces. he calld with Voice of Thunder

Four winged heralds mount the furious blasts & blow their trumps   c
Gold Silver Brass & iron clangors clamoring rend the shores   t 20
Like white clouds rising from the Vales his fifty two armies
From the four Cliffs of Urthona rise glowing around the Spectre
Four sons of Urizen the Squadrons of Urthona led in arms
Of gold & silver brass & iron he knew his mighty sons

Then Urizen arose upon the wind back many a mile   c 25
Retiring into his dire Web scattering fleecy snows
As he ascended howling loud the Web vibrated strong
From heaven to heaven from globe to globe. In vast excentric paths
Compulsive rolld the Comets at his dread command the dreary way
Falling with wheel impetuous down among Urthonas vales   30
And round red Orc returning back to Urizen gorgd with blood   t
Slow roll the massy Globes at his command & slow oerwheel
The dismal squadrons of Urthona. weaving the dire Web
In their progressions & preparing Urizens path before him

End of The Sixth Night

PAGE 77

Vala

Night the Seventh [a]

[Written later than and presumably to replace Night Seven [b]]

Then Urizen arose The Spectre fled & Tharmas fled   c
The darkning Spectre of Urthona hid beneath a rock
Tharmas threw his impetuous flight thro the deeps of immensity
Revolving round in whirlpools fierce all round the cavernd worlds

But Urizen silent descended to the Caves of Orc & saw   ^{t,e} 5
A Cavernd Universe of flaming fire the horses of Urizen
Here bound to fiery mangers furious dash their golden hoofs
Striking fierce sparkles from their brazen fetters. fierce his lions   ^t
Howl in the burning dens his tygers roam in the redounding smoke
In forests of affliction. the adamantine scales of justice   10
Consuming in the raging lamps of mercy pourd in rivers
The holy oil rages thro all the cavernd rocks fierce flames
Dance on the rivers & the rocks howling & drunk with fury
The plow of ages & the golden harrow wade thro fields
Of goary blood the immortal seed is nourishd for the slaughter   15
The bulls of Luvah breathing fire bellow on burning pastures
Round howling Orc whose awful limbs cast forth red smoke & fire
That Urizen approachd not near but took his seat on a rock
And rangd his books around him brooding Envious over Orc   ^t

Howling & rending his dark caves the awful Demon lay   ^e20
Pulse after pulse beat on his fetters pulse after pulse his spirit
Darted & darted higher & higher to the shrine of Enitharmon
As when the thunder folds himself in thickest clouds
The watry nations couch & hide in the profoundest deeps
Then bursting from his troubled head with terrible visages & flaming   25
    hair
His swift wingd daughters sweep across the vast black ocean

Los felt the Envy in his limbs like to a blighted tree
PAGE 78
For Urizen fixd in Envy sat brooding & coverd with snow   ^e
His book of iron on his knees he tracd the dreadful letters
While his snows fell & his storms beat to cool the flames of Orc
Age after Age till underneath his heel a deadly root
Struck thro the rock the root of Mystery accursed shooting up   5
Branches into the heaven of Los they pipe formd bending down
Take root again whereever they touch again branching forth
In intricate labyrinths oerspreading many a grizly deep

Amazd started Urizen when he found himself compassd round
And high roofed over with trees. he arose but the stems   10
Stood so thick he with difficulty & great pain brought
His books out of the dismal shade. all but the book of iron
Again he took his seat & rangd his Books around   ^t
On a rock of iron frowning over the foaming fires of Orc

And Urizen hung over Orc & viewd his terrible wrath   15
Sitting upon an iron Crag at length his words broke forth   ^t

Image of dread whence art thou whence is this most woful place   ^e
Whence these fierce fires but from thyself No other living thing
In all this Chasm I behold. No other living thing

Dare thy most terrible wrath abide   Bound here to waste in pain   20
Thy vital substance in these fires that issue new & new
Around thee sometimes like a flood & sometimes like a rock
Of living pangs thy horrible bed glowing with ceaseless fires
Beneath thee & around Above a Shower of fire now beats
Moulded to globes & arrowy wedges rending thy bleeding limbs   25
And now a whirling pillar of burning sands to overwhelm thee
Steeping thy wounds in salts infernal & in bitter anguish
And now a rock moves on the surface of this lake of fire
To bear thee down beneath the waves in stifling despair
Pity for thee movd me to break my dark & long repose   30
And to reveal myself before thee in a form of wisdom
Yet thou dost laugh at all these tortures & this horrible place
Yet throw thy limbs these fires abroad that back return upon thee
While thou reposest throwing rage on rage feeding thyself
With visions of sweet bliss far other than this burning clime   35
Sure thou art bathd in rivers of delight on verdant fields
Walking in joy in bright Expanses sleeping on bright clouds
With visions of delight so lovely that they urge thy rage
Tenfold with fierce desire to rend thy chain & howl in fury
And dim oblivion of all woe & desperate repose   40
Or is thy joy founded on torment which others bear for thee

Orc answer'd Curse thy hoary brows. What dost thou in this deep
Thy Pity I contemn scatter thy snows elsewhere
PAGE 79
I rage in the deep for Lo my feet & hands are naild to the burning rock
Yet my fierce fires are better than thy snows   Shuddring thou sittest
Thou art not chaind Why shouldst thou sit cold grovelling demon of
      woe
In tortures of dire coldness now a Lake of waters deep
Sweeps over thee freezing to solid still thou sitst closd up   5
In that transparent rock as if in joy of thy bright prison
Till overburdend with its own weight drawn out thro immensity
With a crash breaking across the horrible mass comes down
Thundring & hail & frozen iron haild from the Element
Rends thy white hair   yet thou dost fixd obdurate brooding sit   10
Writing thy books. Anon a cloud filld with a waste of snows
Covers thee still obdurate still resolvd & writing still
Tho rocks roll oer thee tho floods pour tho winds black as the Sea
Cut thee in gashes tho the blood pours down around thy ankles
Freezing thy feet to the hard rock still thy pen obdurate   15
Traces the wonders of Futurity in horrible fear of the future
I rage furious in the deep for lo my feet & hands are naild
To the hard rock or thou shouldst feel my enmity & hate
In all the diseases of man falling upon thy grey accursed front

– 347 –

Urizen answerd Read my books explore my Constellations 20
Enquire of my Sons & they shall teach thee how to War
Enquire of my Daughters who accursd in the dark depths
Knead bread of Sorrow by my stern command for I am God
Of all this dreadful ruin Rise O daughters at my Stern command

Rending the Rocks Eleth & Uveth rose & Ona rose c 25
Terrific with their iron vessels driving them across
In the dim air they took the book of iron & placd above
On clouds of death & sang their songs Kneading the bread of Orc
Orc listend to the song compelld hungring on the cold wind
That swaggd heavy with the accursed dough. the hoar frost ragd 30
Thro Onas sieve the torrent rain pourd from the iron pail
Of Eleth & the icy hands of Uveth kneaded the bread
The heavens bow with terror underneath their iron hands
Singing at their dire work the words of Urizens book of iron
While the enormous scrolls rolld dreadful in the heavens above 35
And still the burden of their song in tears was poured forth
The bread is Kneaded let us rest O cruel father of children

But Urizen remitted not their labours upon his rock
PAGE 80
And Urizen Read in his book of brass in sounding tones t,c

Listen O Daughters to my voice Listen to the Words of Wisdom
So shall [you] govern over all let Moral Duty tune your tongue t
But be your hearts harder than the nether millstone
To bring the shadow of Enitharmon beneath our wondrous tree 5
That Los may Evaporate like smoke & be no more
Draw down Enitharmon to the Spectre of Urthona
And let him have dominion over Los the terrible shade

Compell the poor to live upon a Crust of bread by soft mild arts
Smile when they frown frown when they smile & when a man looks 10
    pale
With labour & abstinence say he looks healthy & happy
And when his children sicken let them die there are enough
Born even too many & our Earth will be overrun
Without these arts If you would make the poor live with temper
With pomp give every crust of bread you give with gracious cunning 15
Magnify small gifts reduce the man to want a gift & then give with
    pomp
Say he smiles if you hear him sigh If pale say he is ruddy
Preach temperance say he is overgorgd & drowns his wit
In strong drink tho you know that bread & water are all
He can afford Flatter his wife pity his children till we can 20
Reduce all to our will as spaniels are taught with art
Lo how the heart & brain are formed in the breeding womb
Of Enitharmon how it buds with life & forms the bones

-348-

The little heart the liver & the red blood in its labyrinths
By gratified desire by strong devouring appetite she fills   25
Los with ambitious fury that his race shall all devour

Then Orc cried Curse thy Cold hypocrisy. already round thy Tree   t,e
In scales that shine with gold & rubies thou beginnest to weaken
My divided Spirit Like a worm I rise in peace unbound
From wrath Now When I rage my fetters bind me more   30
O torment O torment A Worm compelld. Am I a worm
Is it in strong deceit that man is born. In strong deceit
Thou dost restrain my fury that the worm may fold the tree
Avaunt Cold hypocrite I am chaind or thou couldst not use me thus
The Man shall rage bound with this Chain the worm in silence creep 35
Thou wilt not cease from rage Grey Demon silence all thy storms
Give me example of thy mildness King of furious hail storms
Art thou the cold attractive power that holds me in this chain
I well remember how I stole thy light & it became fire
Consuming. Thou Knowst me now O Urizen Prince of Light   40
And I know thee is this the triumph this the Godlike State
That lies beyond the bounds of Science in the Grey obscure

Terrified Urizen heard Orc now certain that he was Luvah
And Orc began to Organize a Serpent body   t
Despising Urizens light & turning it into flaming fire   45
Recieving as a poisond Cup Recieves the heavenly wine   e
And turning affection into fury & thought into abstraction   t
A Self consuming dark devourer rising into the heavens

Urizen envious brooding sat & saw the secret terror
Flame high in pride & laugh to scorn the source of his deceit   50
Nor knew the source of his own but thought himself the Sole author
PAGE 81
Of all his wandering Experiments in the horrible Abyss
He knew that weakness stretches out in breadth & length he knew
That wisdom reaches high & deep & therefore he made Orc
In Serpent form compelld stretch out & up the mysterious tree
He sufferd him to Climb that he might draw all human forms   5
Into submission to his will nor knew the dread result

Los sat in showers of Urizen watching cold Enitharmon   t
His broodings rush down to his feet producing Eggs that hatching
Burst forth upon the winds above the tree of Mystery
Enitharmon lay on his knees. Urizen tracd his Verses   10
In the dark deep the dark tree grew. her shadow was drawn down
Down to the roots it wept over Orc. the Shadow of Enitharmon

Los saw her stretchd the image of death upon his witherd valleys
Her Shadow went forth & returnd Now she was pale as Snow

When the mountains & hills are coverd over & the paths of Men   ^t 15
   shut up
But when her spirit returnd as ruddy as a morning when
The ripe fruit blushes into joy in heavens eternal halls   ^t
Sorrow shot thro him from his feet it shot up to his head
Like a cold night that nips the roots & shatters off the leaves
Silent he stood oer Enitharmon watching her pale face   20
He spoke not he was Silent till he felt the cold disease
Then Los mournd on the dismal wind in his jealous lamentation

Why can I not Enjoy thy beauty   Lovely Enitharmon   ^c
When I return from clouds of Grief in the wandring Elements
Where thou in thrilling joy in beaming summer loveliness   25
Delectable reposest ruddy in my absence flaming with beauty
Cold pale in sorrow at my approach trembling at my terrific
Forehead & eyes thy lips decay like roses in the spring   ^t
How art thou Shrunk thy grapes that burst in summers vast Excess
Shut up in little purple covering faintly bud & die   30
Thy olive trees that pourd down oil upon a thousand hills
Sickly look forth & scarcely stretch their branches to the plain
Thy roses that expanded in the face of glowing morn

PAGE 82

Hid in a little silken veil scarce breathe & faintly shine
Thy lilies that gave light what time the morning looked forth
Hid in the Vales faintly lament & no one hears their voice
All things beside the woful Los enjoy the delights of beauty
Once how I sang & calld the beasts & birds to their delights   5
Nor knew that I alone exempted from the joys of love
Must war with secret monsters of the animating worlds
O that I had not seen the day then should I be at rest
Nor felt the stingings of desire nor longings after life
For life is Sweet to Los the wretched to his winged woes   10
Is given a craving cry that they may sit at night on barren rocks
And whet their beaks & snuff the air & watch the opening dawn
And Shriek till at the smells of blood they stretch their boney wings
And cut the winds like arrows shot by troops of Destiny

Thus Los lamented in the night unheard by Enitharmon   ^c 15
For the Shadow of Enitharmon descended down the tree of Mystery
The Spectre saw the Shade Shivering over his gloomy rocks
Beneath the tree of Mystery which in the dismal Abyss
Began to blossom in fierce pain shooting its writhing buds
In throes of birth & now the blossoms falling shining fruit   20
Appeard of many colours & of various poisonous qualities
Of Plagues hidden in shining globes that grew on the living tree

The Spectre of Urthona saw the Shadow of Enitharmon
Beneath the Tree of Mystery among the leaves & fruit   ^t

Reddning the Demon strong prepard the poison of sweet Love 25
He turnd from side to side in tears he wept & he embracd t
The fleeting image & in whispers mild wood the faint shade

Loveliest delight of Men. Enitharmon shady hiding
In secret places where no eye can trace thy watry way
Have I found thee have I found thee tremblest thou in fear 30
Because of Orc because he rent his discordant way
From thy sweet loins of bliss. red flowd thy blood
Pale grew thy face lightnings playd around thee thunders hoverd t
Over thee, & the terrible Orc rent his discordant way t
But the next joy of thine shall be in sweet delusion 35
And its birth in fainting & sleep & Sweet delusions of Vala t

The Shadow of Enitharmon answerd Art thou terrible Shade
Set over this sweet boy of mine to guard him lest he rend
PAGE 83
His mother to the winds of heaven Intoxicated with
The fruit of this delightful tree. I cannot flee away
From thy embrace else be assurd so horrible a form
Should never in my arms repose. now listen I will tell
Thee Secrets of Eternity which neer before unlockd 5
My golden lips nor took the bar from Enitharmons breast
Among the Flowers of Beulah walkd the Eternal Man & Saw
Vala the lilly of the desert. melting in high noon
Upon her bosom in sweet bliss he fainted Wonder siezd
All heaven they saw him dark. they built a golden wall 10
Round Beulah There he reveld in delight among the Flowers
Vala was pregnant & brought forth Urizen Prince of Light
First born of Generation. Then behold a wonder to the Eyes
Of the now fallen Man a double form Vala appeard. A Male
And female shuddring pale the Fallen Man recoild 15
From the Enormity & calld them Luvah & Vala. turning down
The vales to find his way back into Heaven but found none
For his frail eyes were faded & his ears heavy & dull

Urizen grew up in the plains of Beulah Many Sons
And many daughters flourishd round the holy Tent of Man 20
Till he forgot Eternity delighted in his sweet joy
Among his family his flocks & herds & tents & pastures

But Luvah close conferrd with Urizen in darksom night
To bind the father & enslave the brethren Nought he knew
Of sweet Eternity the blood flowd round the holy tent & rivn 25
From its hinges uttering its final groan all Beulah fell
In dark confusion mean time Los was born & Enitharmon
But how I know not then forgetfulness quite wrapd me up
A period nor do I more remember till I stood
Beside Los in the Cavern dark enslavd to vegetative forms 30

According to the Will of Luvah who assumd the Place
Of the Eternal Man & smote him. But thou Spectre dark
Maist find a way to punish Vala in thy fiery South
To bring her down subjected to the rage of my fierce boy

PAGE 84

The Spectre said. Thou lovely Vision this delightful Tree   c
Is given us for a Shelter from the tempests of Void & Solid
Till once again the morn of ages shall renew upon us
To reunite in those mild fields of happy Eternity
Where thou & I in undivided Essence walkd about   5
Imbodied. thou my garden of delight & I the spirit in the garden
Mutual there we dwelt in one anothers joy revolving
Days of Eternity with Tharmas mild & Luvah sweet melodious
Upon our waters. This thou well rememberest listen I will tell
What thou forgettest. They in us & we in them alternate Livd   10
Drinking the joys of Universal Manhood. One dread morn
Listen O vision of Delight One dread morn of goary blood
The manhood was divided for the gentle passions making way   t
Thro the infinite labyrinths of the heart & thro the nostrils issuing
In odorous stupefaction stood before the Eyes of Man   15
A female bright. I stood beside my anvil dark a mass
Of iron glowd bright prepard for spades & plowshares. sudden down
I sunk with cries of blood issuing downward in the veins
Which now my rivers were become rolling in tubelike forms
Shut up within themselves descending down I sunk along   20
The goary tide even to the place of seed & there dividing
I was divided in darkness & oblivion thou an infant woe
And I an infant terror in the womb of Enion
My masculine spirit scorning the frail body issud forth
From Enions brain In this deformed form leaving thee there   25
Till times passd over thee but still my spirit returning hoverd
And formd a Male to be a counterpart to thee O Love
Darkend & Lost In due time issuing forth from Enions womb
Thou & that demon Los wert born Ah jealousy & woe
Ah poor divided dark Urthona now a Spectre wandering   30
The deeps of Los the Slave of that Creation I created
I labour night & day for Los but listen thou my vision
I view futurity in thee I will bring down soft Vala
To the embraces of this terror & I will destroy
That body I created then shall we unite again in bliss   35

Thou knowest that the Spectre is in Every Man insane brutish   t
Deformd that I am thus a ravening devouring lust continually
Craving & devouring but my Eyes are always upon thee O lovely
Delusion & I cannot crave for any thing but thee not so   t
The spectres of the Dead for I am as the Spectre of the Living   40

For till these terrors planted round the Gates of Eternal life
Are driven away & annihilated we never can repass the Gates

PAGE 85
Astonishd filld with tears the spirit of Enitharmon beheld
And heard the Spectre bitterly she wept Embracing fervent   t
Her once lovd Lord now but a Shade herself also a shade
Conferring times on times among the branches of that Tree

Thus they conferrd among the intoxicating fumes of Mystery   5
Till Enitharmons shadow pregnant in the deeps beneath
Brought forth a wonder horrible. While Enitharmon shriekd   e
And trembled thro the Worlds above Los wept his fierce soul was terrifid

At the shrieks of Enitharmon at her tossings nor could his eyes percieve
The cause of her dire anguish for she lay the image of Death   10
Movd by strong shudders till her shadow was deliverd then she ran
Raving about the upper Elements in maddning fury

She burst the Gates of Enitharmons heart with direful Crash
Nor could they ever be closd again the golden hinges were broken
And the gates broke in sunder & their ornaments defacd   t 15
Beneath the tree of Mystery for the immortal shadow shuddering
Brought forth this wonder horrible a Cloud she grew & grew
Till many of the dead burst forth from the bottoms of their tombs
In male forms without female counterparts or Emanations   t
Cruel and ravening with Enmity & Hatred & War   20
In dreams of Ulro dark delusive drawn by the lovely shadow   t

The Spectre terrified gave her Charge over the howling Orc   t
Then took the tree of Mystery root in the World of Los
Its topmost boughs shooting a fibre beneath Enitharmons couch   t
The double rooted Labyrinth soon wavd around their heads   25

But then the Spectre enterd Los's bosom Every sigh & groan   t,e
Of Enitharmon bore Urthonas Spectre on its wings
Obdurate Los felt Pity Enitharmon told the tale
Of Urthona. Los embracd the Spectre first as a brother
Then as another Self; astonishd humanizing & in tears   30
In Self abasement Giving up his Domineering lust

Thou never canst embrace sweet Enitharmon terrible Demon. Till
Thou art united with thy Spectre Consummating by pains & labours   t
That mortal body & by Self annihilation back returning   t
To Life Eternal be assurd I am thy real Self   35
Tho thus divided from thee & the Slave of Every passion
Of thy fierce Soul Unbar the Gates of Memory look upon me
Not as another but as thy real Self I am thy Spectre
Tho horrible & Ghastly to thine Eyes tho buried beneath
The ruins of the Universe. hear what inspird I speak & be silent   40
Thou didst subdue me in old times by thy Immortal Strength   t

-353-

When I was a ravning hungring & thirsting cruel lust & murder
If we unite in one[,] another better world will be   t
Opend within your heart & loins & wondrous brain
Threefold as it was in Eternity & this the fourth Universe   45
Will be Renewd by the three & consummated in Mental fires
But if thou dost refuse Another body will be prepared

PAGE 86

For me & thou annihilate evaporate & be no more
For thou art but a form & organ of life & of thyself
Art nothing being Created Continually by Mercy & Love divine

Los furious answerd. Spectre horrible thy words astound my Ear
With irresistible conviction I feel I am not one of those   5
Who when convincd can still persist tho furious controllable
By Reasons power. Even I already feel a World within
Opening its gates & in it all the real substances
Of which these in the outward World are shadows which pass away
Come then into my Bosom & in thy shadowy arms bring with thee   10
My lovely Enitharmon. I will quell my fury & teach
Peace to the Soul of dark revenge & repentance to Cruelty

So spoke Los & Embracing Enitharmon & the Spectre
Clouds would have folded round in Extacy & Love uniting

PAGE 87

But Enitharmon trembling fled & hid beneath Urizens tree
But mingling together with his Spectre the Spectre of Urthona   t
Wondering beheld the Center opend by Divine Mercy inspired   t
He in his turn Gave Tasks to Los Enormous to destroy   t
That body he created but in vain for Los performd   5
Wonders of labour
They Builded Golgonooza Los labouring builded pillars high   t
And Domes terrific in the nether heavens for beneath
Was opend new heavens & a new Earth beneath & within
Threefold within the brain within the heart within the loins   10
A Threefold Atmosphere Sublime continuous from Urthonas world   t
But yet having a Limit Twofold named Satan & Adam

But Los stood on the Limit of Translucence weeping & trembling   e
Filled with doubts in self accusation beheld the fruit   t
Of Urizens Mysterious tree For Enitharmon thus spake   e 15

When In the Deeps beneath I gatherd of this ruddy fruit
It was by that I knew that I had Sinnd & then I knew
That without a ransom I could not be savd from Eternal death
That Life lives upon Death & by devouring appetite
All things subsist on one another thenceforth in Despair   20
I spend my glowing time but thou art strong & mighty
To bear this Self conviction take then Eat thou also of
The fruit & give me proof of life Eternal or I die

Then Los plucked the fruit & Eat & sat down in Despair
And must have given himself to death Eternal But   25
Urthonas spectre in part mingling with him comforted him
Being a medium between him & Enitharmon   But This Union
Was not to be Effected without Cares & Sorrows & Troubles
Of six thousand Years of self denial and of bitter Contrition   t

Urthonas Spectre terrified beheld the Spectres of the Dead   c 30
Each Male formd without a counterpart without a concentering vision
The Spectre of Urthona wept before Los Saying I am the cause
That this dire state commences I began the dreadful state
Of Separation & on my dark head the curse & punishment
Must fall unless a way be found to Ransom & Redeem   t 35

But I have thee my [*Counterpart Vegetating*] miraculous   t
These Spectres have no [*Counter*(parts)] therefore they ravin
Without the food of life Let us Create them Coun[terparts]
For without a Created body the Spectre is Eternal Death

Los trembling answerd Now I feel the weight of stern repentance   c 40
Tremble not so my Enitharmon at the awful gates
Of thy poor broken Heart I see thee like a shadow withering
As on the outside of Existence but look! behold! take comfort!
Turn inwardly thine Eyes & there behold the Lamb of God
Clothed in Luvahs robes of blood descending to redeem   45
O Spectre of Urthona take comfort O Enitharmon
Couldst thou but cease from terror & trembling & affright
When I appear before thee in forgiveness of ancient injuries   t
Why shouldst thou remember & be afraid. I surely have died in pain
Often enough to convince thy jealousy & fear & terror   50
Come hither be patient let us converse together because
I also tremble at myself & at all my former life

Enitharmon answerd I behold the Lamb of God descending
To Meet these Spectres of the Dead I therefore fear that he
Will give us to Eternal Death fit punishment for such   55
Hideous offenders Uttermost extinction in eternal pain
An ever dying life of stifling & obstruction shut out
Of existence to be a sign & terror to all who behold
Lest any should in futurity do as we have done in heaven
Such is our state nor will the Son of God redeem us but destroy   60

PAGE 90   t
So Enitharmon spoke trembling & in torrents of tears   c

Los sat in Golgonooza in the Gate of Luban where   t
He had erected many porches where branchd the Mysterious Tree   t
Where the Spectrous dead wail & sighing thus he spoke to Enitharmon

Lovely delight of Men Enitharmon shady refuge from furious war   ^t5
Thy bosom translucent is a soft repose for the weeping souls
Of those piteous victims of battle there they sleep in happy obscurity
They feed upon our life we are their victims. Stern desire
I feel to fabricate embodied semblances in which the dead
May live before us in our palaces & in our gardens of labour   ^t10
Which now opend within the Center we behold spread abroad
To form a world of Sacrifice of brothers & sons & daughters   ^t
To comfort Orc in his dire sufferings look my fires enlume afresh   ^e
Before my face ascending with delight as in ancient times

Enitharmon spread her beaming locks upon the wind & said   ^e15
O Lovely terrible Los wonder of Eternity O Los my defence & guide   ^t
Thy works are all my joy. & in thy fires my soul delights
If mild they burn in just proportion & in secret night
And silence build their day in shadow of soft clouds & dews
Then I can sigh forth on the winds of Golgonooza piteous forms   20
That vanish again into my bosom but if thou my Los
Wilt in sweet moderated fury. fabricate forms sublime   ^t
Such as the piteous spectres may assimilate themselves into
They shall be ransoms for our Souls that we may live

So Enitharmon spoke & Los his hands divine inspired began   ^{t,e}25
To modulate his fires studious the loud roaring flames
He vanquishd with the strength of Art bending their iron points
And drawing them forth delighted upon the winds of Golgonooza   ^t
From out the ranks of Urizens war & from the fiery lake
Of Orc bending down as the binder of the Sheaves follows   30
The reaper in both arms embracing the furious raging flames
Los drew them forth out of the deeps planting his right foot firm   ^e
Upon the Iron crag of Urizen thence springing up aloft
Into the heavens of Enitharmon in a mighty circle

And first he drew a line upon the walls of shining heaven   ^e35
And Enitharmon tincturd it with beams of blushing love
It remaind permanent a lovely form inspird divinely human
Dividing into just proportions Los unwearied labourd
The immortal lines upon the heavens till with sighs of love
Sweet Enitharmon mild Entrancd breathd forth upon the wind   40
The spectrous dead Weeping the Spectres viewd the immortal works
Of Los Assimilating to those forms Embodied & Lovely
In youth & beauty in the arms of Enitharmon mild reposing

First Rintrah & then Palamabron drawn from out the ranks of war
In infant innocence reposd on Enitharmons bosom   45
Orc was comforted in the deeps his soul revivd in them
As the Eldest brother is the fathers image So Orc became   ^t
As Los a father to his brethren & he joyd in the dark lake
Tho bound with chains of Jealousy & in scales of iron & brass

But Los loved them & refusd to Sacrifice their infant limbs 50
And Enitharmons smiles & tears prevaild over self protection
They rather chose to meet Eternal death than to destroy
The offspring of their Care & Pity Urthonas spectre was comforted
But Tharmas most rejoicd in hope of Enions return
For he beheld new Female forms born forth upon the air 55
Who wove soft silken veils of covering in sweet rapturd trance
Mortal & not as Enitharmon without a covering veil

First his immortal spirit drew Urizen[s] Shadow away t
From out the ranks of war separating him in sunder
Leaving his Spectrous form which could not be drawn away e 60
Then he divided Thiriel the Eldest of Urizens sons
Urizen became Rintrah Thiriel became Palamabron
Thus dividing the powers of Every Warrior
Startled was Los he found his Enemy Urizen now
In his hands. he wonderd that he felt love & not hate 65
His whole soul loved him he beheld him an infant
Lovely breathd from Enitharmon he trembled within himself

PAGE 99

VALA

Night the Eighth c

Then All in Great Eternity Met in the Council of God t,c
as one Man Even Jesus upon Gilead & Hermon t
Upon the Limit of Contraction to create the fallen Man
The Fallen Man stretchd like a Corse upon the oozy Rock t
Washd with the tides Pale overgrown with weeds 5
That movd with horrible dreams hovring high over his head
Two winged immortal shapes one standing at his feet
Toward the East one standing at his head toward the west
Their wings joind in the Zenith over head t
Such is a Vision of All Beulah hovring over the Sleeper 10

The limit of Contraction now was fixd & Man began c
To wake upon the Couch of Death he sneezed seven times
A tear of blood dropped from either eye again he reposd
In the saviours arms, in the arms of tender mercy & loving kindness

Then Los said I behold the Divine Vision thro the broken Gates t,c 15
Of thy poor broken heart astonishd melted into Compassion & Love
And Enitharmon said I see the Lamb of God upon Mount Zion t
Wondring with love & Awe they felt the divine hand upon them t

For nothing could restrain the dead in Beulah from descending
Unto Ulros night tempted by the Shadowy females sweet 20
Delusive cruelty they descend away from the Daughters of Beulah

And Enter Urizens temple Enitharmon pitying & her heart
Gates broken down. they descend thro the Gate of Pity
The broken heart Gate of Enitharmon She sighs them forth upon   t
    the wind
Of Golgonooza Los stood recieving them   t 25
For Los could enter into Enitharmons bosom & explore
Its intricate Labyrinths now the Obdurate heart was broken

PAGE 100 (FIRST PORTION)

From out the War of Urizen & Tharmas recieving them   t
Into his hands. Then Enitharmon erected Looms in Lubans Gate
And calld the Looms Cathedron in these Looms She wove the Spectres
Bodies of Vegetation Singing lulling Cadences to drive away
Despair from the poor wandering spectres and Los loved them   5
With a parental love for the Divine hand was upon him
And upon Enitharmon & the Divine Countenance shone
In Golgonooza Looking down the Daughters of Beulah saw
With joy the bright Light & in it a Human form
And knew he was the Saviour Even Jesus & they worshipped   10

Astonishd Comforted Delighted in notes of Rapturous Extacy   t
All Beulah stood astonishd Looking down to Eternal Death
They saw the Saviour beyond the Pit of death & destruction
For whether they lookd upward they saw the Divine Vision
Or whether they lookd downward still they saw the Divine Vision   15
Surrounding them on all sides beyond sin & death & hell

Enitharmon wove in tears singing Songs of Lamentation
And pitying comfort as she sighd forth on the wind the Spectres
Also the Vegetated bodies which Enitharmon wove
Opend within their hearts & in their loins & in their brain   20
To Beulah & the Dead in Ulro descended from the War
Of Urizen & Tharmas & from the Shadowy females clouds
And some were woven single & some two fold & some three fold   t
In Head or Heart or Reins according to the fittest order
Of most merciful pity & compassion to the Spectrous dead   t 25

PAGE 101 (FIRST PORTION)

When Urizen saw the Lamb of God clothed in Luvahs robes   e
Perplexd & terrifid he Stood tho well he knew that Orc
Was Luvah But he now beheld a new Luvah. Or One
Who assumd Luvahs form & stood before him opposite
But he saw Orc a Serpent form augmenting times on times   5
In the fierce battle & he saw the Lamb of God & the World of Los
Surrounded by his dark machines for Orc augmented swift
In fury a Serpent wondrous among the Constellations of Urizen
A crest of fire rose on his forehead red as the carbuncle
Beneath down to his eyelids scales of pearl then gold & silver   10
Immingled with the ruby overspread his Visage down

His furious neck writ[h]ing contortive in dire budding pains
The scaly armour shot out. Stubborn down his back & bosom
The Emerald Onyx Sapphire jasper beryl amethyst
Strove in terrific emulation which should gain a place   15
Upon the mighty Fiend the fruit of the mysterious tree   t
Kneaded in Uveths kneading trough. Still Orc devourd the food
In raging hunger Still the pestilential food in gems & gold
Exuded round his awful limbs Stretching to serpent length
His human bulk While the dark shadowy female brooding over   t 20
Measurd his food morning & evening in cups & baskets of iron

With tears of sorrow incessant she labourd the food of Orc
Compelld by the iron hearted sisters Daughters of Urizen
Gathring the fruit of that mysterious tree circling its root
She spread herself thro all the branches in the power of Orc   25

Thus Urizen in self deceit his warlike preparations fabricated
And when all things were finishd sudden wavd among the Stars   t
His hurtling hand gave the dire signal thunderous Clarions blow
And all the hollow deep rebellowd with the wonderous war   t
PAGE 100 (SECOND PORTION)
But Urizen his mighty rage let loose in the mid deep   t
Sparkles of Dire affliction issud round his frozen limbs   t
Horrible hooks & nets he formd twisting the cords of iron
And brass & molten metals cast in hollow globes & bor'd
Tubes in petrific steel & rammd combustibles & wheels   30
And chains & pullies fabricated all round the heavens of Los
Communing with the Serpent of Orc in dark dissimulation
And with the Synagogue of Satan in dark Sanhedrim
To undermine the World of Los & tear bright Enitharmon
PAGE 101 (SECOND PORTION)
To the four winds hopeless of future. All futurity   30
Seems teeming with Endless destruction never to be repelld   t
Desperate remorse swallows the present in a quenchless rage

Terrified & astonishd Urizen beheld the battle take a form   t
Which he intended not a Shadowy hermaphrodite black & opake   t
The Soldiers namd it Satan but he was yet unformd & vast   35
Hermaphroditic it at length became hiding the Male
Within as in a Tabernacle Abominable Deadly

The battle howls the terrors fird rage in the work of death
Enormous Works Los Contemplated inspird by the holy Spirit   e
Los builds the Walls of Golgonooza against the stirring battle   40
That only thro the Gates of Death they can enter to Enitharmon
Raging they take the human visage & the human form

Feeling the hand of Los in Golgonooza & the force
Attractive of his hammers beating & the Silver looms

-359-

Of Enitharmon singing lulling cadences on the wind   45
They humanize in the fierce battle where in direful pain
Troop by troop the beastial droves rend one another sounding loud
The instruments of sound & troop by troop in human forms they urge

PAGE 102

The dire confusion till the battle faints those that remain
Return in pangs & horrible convulsions to their beastial state
For the monsters of the Elements Lions or Tygers or Wolves
Sound loud the howling music Inspird by Los & Enitharmon Sounding
     loud terrific men
They seem to one another laughing terrible among the banners   5
And when the revolution of their day of battles over
Relapsing in dire torment they return to forms of woe   t
To moping visages returning inanimate tho furious
No more erect tho strong drawn out in length they ravin
For senseless gratification & their visages thrust forth   10
Flatten above & beneath & stretch out into beastial length
Weakend they stretch beyond their power in dire droves till war begins
Or Secret religion in their temples before secret shrines

And Urizen gave life & sense by his immortal power   c
To all his Engines of deceit that linked chains might run   15
Thro ranks of war spontaneous & that hooks & boring screws
Might act according to their forms by innate cruelty
He formed also harsh instruments of sound
To grate the soul into destruction or to inflame with fury
The spirits of life to pervert all the faculties of sense   20
Into their own destruction if perhaps he might avert   t
His own despair even at the cost of every thing that breathes

Thus in the temple of the Sun his books of iron & brass
And silver & gold he consecrated reading incessantly
To myriads of perturbed spirits thro the universe   25
They propagated the deadly words the Shadowy Female absorbing   t
The enormous Sciences of Urizen ages after ages exploring
The fell destruction. And she said O Urizen Prince of Light
What words of Dread pierce my faint Ear what fal[l]ing snows around
My feeble limbs infold my destind misery   30
I alone dare the lash abide to sit beneath the blast
Unhurt & dare the inclement forehead of the King of Light
From dark abysses of the times remote fated to be

PAGE 103

The sorrower of Eternity in love with tears Submiss I rear
My Eyes to thy Pavilions hear my prayer for Luvahs Sake
I see the murderer of my Luvah clothd in robes of blood   c
He who assumd my Luvahs throne in times of Everlasting
Where hast thou hid him whom I love in what remote Abyss   5

Resides that God of my delight O might my eyes behold
My Luvah then could I deliver all the sons of God
From Bondage of these terrors & with influences sweet   t
As once in those eternal fields in brotherhood & Love
United we should live in bliss as those who sinned not   10
The Eternal Man is seald by thee never to be deliverd
We are all servants to thy will O King of Light relent
Thy furious power be our father & our loved King
But if my Luvah is no more If thou hast smitten him   t
And laid him in the Sepulcher Or if thou wilt revenge   t 15
His murder on another Silent I bow with dread

But happiness can never [come] to thee O King nor me
For he was source of every joy that this mysterious tree
Unfolds in Allegoric fruit. When shall the dead revive
Can that which has existed cease or can love & life Expire   20

Urizen heard the Voice & saw the Shadow. underneath
His woven darkness & in laws & deceitful religions
Beginning at the tree of Mystery circling its root
She spread herself thro all the branches in the power of Orc
A shapeless & indefinite cloud in tears of sorrow incessant   25
Steeping the Direful Web of Religion swagging heavy it fell
From heaven to heavn thro all its meshes altering the Vortexes
Misplacing every Center hungry desire & lust began
Gathering the fruit of that Mysterious tree till Urizen
Sitting within his temple furious felt the num[m]ing stupor   30
Himself tangled in his own net in sorrow lust repentance

Enitharmon wove in tears Singing Songs of Lamentations   e
And pitying comfort as she sighd forth on the wind the spectres
And wove them bodies calling them her belovd sons & daughters
Employing the daughters in her looms & Los employd the Sons   35
In Golgonoozas Furnaces among the Anvils of time & space
Thus forming a Vast family wondrous in beauty & love
And they appeard a Universal female form created
From those who were dead in Ulro from the Spectres of the dead

PAGE 104 (FIRST PORTION)
And Enitharmon namd the Female Jerusa[le]m the holy
Wondring she saw the Lamb of God within Jerusalems Veil
The divine Vision seen within the inmost deep recess
Of fair Jerusalems bosom in a gently beaming fire

Then sang the Sons of Eden round the Lamb of God & said   5
Glory Glory Glory to the holy Lamb of God
Who now beginneth to put off the dark Satanic body
Now we behold redemption Now we know that life Eternal

Depends alone upon the Universal hand & not in us
Is aught but death In individual weakness sorrow & pain   t 10
PAGE 113 (FIRST PORTION)
We behold with wonder Enitharmons Looms & Los's Forges   t,c
And the Spindles of Tirzah & Rahab and the Mills of Satan &   t
     Beelzeboul
In Golgonooza Los's anvils stand & his Furnaces rage   t
Ten thousand demons labour at the forges Creating Continually
The times & spaces of Mortal Life the Sun the Moon the Stars   5
In periods of Pulsative furor beating into wedges & bars   t
Then drawing into wires the terrific Passions & Affections
Of Spectrous dead. Thence to the Looms of Cathedron conveyd
The Daughters of Enitharmon weave the ovarium & the integument
In soft silk drawn from their own bowels in lascivious delight   10
With songs of sweetest cadence to the turning spindle & reel
Lulling the weeping spectres of the dead. Clothing their limbs
With gifts & gold of Eden. Astonishd stupified with delight
The terrors put on their sweet clothing on the banks of Arnon   t
Whence they plunge into the river of space for a period till   15
The dread Sleep of Ulro is past. But Satan Og & Sihon   t
Build Mills of resistless wheels to unwind the soft threads & reveal
Naked of their clothing the poor spectres before the accusing heavens
While Rahab & Tirzah far different mantles prepare webs of torture
Mantles of despair girdles of bitter compunction shoes of indolence   20
Veils of ignorance covering from head to feet with a cold web

We look down into Ulro we behold the Wonders of the Grave
Eastward of Golgonooza stands the Lake of Udan Adan In
Entuthon Benithon a Lake not of Waters but of Spaces   t
Perturbd black & deadly in its Islands & its Margins   t 25
The Mills of Satan and Beelzeboul stand round the roots of Urizens
     tree
For this Lake is formd from the tears & sighs & death sweat of the
     Victims
Of Urizens laws. to irrigate the roots of the tree of Mystery
They unweave the soft threads then they weave them anew in the forms
Of dark death & despair & none from Eternity to Eternity could   t 30
     Escape
But thou O Universal Humanity who is One Man blessed for Ever   t
Recievest the Integuments woven Rahab beholds the Lamb of God
She smites with her knife of flint She destroys her own work
Times upon times thinking to destroy the Lamb blessed for Ever
He puts off the clothing of blood he redeems the spectres from their   35
     bonds
He awakes the sleepers in Ulro the Daughters of Beulah praise him
They anoint his feet with ointment they wipe them with the hair of
     their head

PAGE 104 (SECOND PORTION)
We now behold the Ends of Beulah & we now behold
Where Death Eternal is put off Eternally
Assume the dark Satanic body in the Virgins womb
O Lamb divin[e] it cannot thee annoy O pitying one
Thy pity is from the foundation of the World & thy Redemption   15
Begun Already in Eternity   Come then O Lamb of God   t
Come Lord Jesus come quickly

So sang they in Eternity looking down into Beulah.

The war roard round Jerusalems Gates it took a hideous form
Seen in the aggregate a Vast Hermaphroditic form   20
Heavd like an Earthquake labring with convulsive groans   t
Intolerable at length an awful wonder burst
From the Hermaphroditic bosom Satan he was namd
Son of Perdition terrible his form dishumanizd monstrous   t
A male without a female counterpart a howling fiend   25
Fo[r]lorn of Eden & repugnant to the forms of life
Yet hiding the shadowy female Vala as in an ark & Curtains
Abhorrd accursed ever dying an Eternal death

Being multitudes of tyrant Men in union blasphemous
Against the divine image. Congregated Assemblies of wicked men   30

Los said to Enitharmon Pitying I saw
Pitying the Lamb of God Descended thro Jerusalems gates
To put off Mystery time after time & as a Man
Is born on Earth so was he born of Fair Jerusalem
In mysterys woven mantle & in the Robes of Luvah   35

He stood in fair Jerusalem to awake up into Eden
The fallen Man but first to Give his vegetated body   t
To be cut off & separated that the Spiritual body may be Reveald

PAGE 105
The Lamb of God stood before Satan opposite   t,c
In Entuthon Benithon in the shadows of torments & woe   t
Upon the heights of Amalek taking refuge in his arms   t
The Victims fled from punishment for all his words were peace   t

Urizen calld together the Synagogue of Satan in dire Sanhedrim   t 5
To Judge the Lamb of God to Death as a murderer & robber
As it is written he was numberd among the transgressors   c

Cold dark opake the Assembly met twelvefold in Amalek
Twelve rocky unshapd forms terrific forms of torture & woe
Such seemd the Synagogue to distant view amidst them beamd   t 10
A False Feminine Counterpart Lovely of Delusive Beauty   t

Dividing & Uniting at will in the Cruelties of Holiness
Vala drawn down into a Vegetated body now triumphant   c
The Synagogue of Satan Clothed her with Scarlet robes & Gems
And on her forehead was her name written in blood   Mystery   15
When viewd remote She is One when viewd near she divides
To multitude as it is in Eden so permitted because
It was the best possible in the State called Satan to Save
From Death Eternal & to put off Satan Eternally

The Synagogue Created her from Fruit of Urizens tree   20
By devilish arts abominable unlawful unutterable
Perpetually vegetating in detestable births
Of Female forms beautiful thro poisons hidden in secret
Which give a tincture to false beauty there was hidden within   t
The bosom of Satan The false Female as in an ark & veil   25
Which christ must rend & her reveal Her Daughters are Calld
Tirzah She is namd Rahab their various divisions are calld   t
The Daughters of Amalek Canaan & Moab binding on the Stones   t
Their victims & with knives tormenting them singing with tears
Over their victims Hear ye the song of the Females of Amalek   30

O thou poor human form O thou poor child of woe   c
Why dost thou wander away from Tirzah why me compell to bind thee
If thou dost go away from me I shall consume upon the rocks
These fibres of thine eyes that used to wander in distant heavens
Away from me I have bound down with a hot iron   t 35
These nostrils that Expanded with delight in morning skies
I have bent downward with lead molten in my roaring furnaces
My soul is seven furnaces incessant roars the bellows
Upon my terribly flaming heart the molten metal runs
In channels thro my fiery limbs O love O pity O pain   40
O the pangs the bitter pangs of love forsaken
Ephraim was a wilderness of joy where all my wild beasts ran
The river Kanah wanderd by my sweet Manassehs side   t
Go Noah fetch the girdle of strong brass heat it red hot   t
Press it around the loins of this expanding cruelty   45
Shriek not so my only love
Bind him down Sisters bind him down on Ebal mount of Cursing
Malah come forth from Lebanon & Hoglah from Mount sinai
Come circumscribe this tongue of sweets & with a Screw of iron
Fasten this Ear into the Rock Milcah the task is thine   t 50
Weep not so sisters weep not so our life depends on this
Or mercy & truth are fled away from Shechem & Mount Gilead   c
Unless my beloved is bound upon the Stems of Vegetation

Such are the songs of Tirzah such the loves of Amalek
The Lamb of God descended thro the twelve portions of Luvah   c 55
Bearing his sorrows & rec[iev]ing all his cruel wounds

PAGE 106 (FIRST PORTION)
Thus was the Lamb of God condemnd to Death   t
They naild him upon the tree of Mystery weeping over him
And then mocking & then worshipping calling him Lord & King
Sometimes as twelve daughters lovely & sometimes as five
They stood in beaming beauty & sometimes as one even Rahab   t 5
Who is Mystery Babylon the Great the Mother of Harlots   t

Jerusalem saw the Body dead upon the Cross She fled away   t
Saying Is this Eternal Death   Where shall I hide from Death
Pity me Los pity me Urizen & let us build   t
A Sepulcher & worship Death in fear while yet we live   10
Death! God of All from whom we rise to whom we all return
And Let all Nations of the Earth worship at the Sepulcher   t
With Gifts & Spices with lamps rich embossd jewels & gold

Los took the Body from the Cross Jerusalem weeping over   c
They bore it to the Sepulcher which Los had hewn in the rock   15
Of Eternity for himself he hewd it despairing of Life Eternal   t
PAGE 113 (SECOND PORTION)
But when Rahab had cut off the Mantle of Luvah from   t
The Lamb of God it rolld apart, revealing to all in heaven
And all on Earth the Temple & the Synagogue of Satan & Mystery   40
Even Rahab in all her turpitude Rahab divided herself
She stood before Los in her Pride among the Furnaces   t
Dividing & uniting in Delusive feminine pomp questioning him

He answerd her with tenderness & love not uninspird
Los sat upon his anvil stock they sat beside the forge   c 45
Los wipd the sweat from his red brow & thus began
To the delusive female forms shining among his furnaces

I am that shadowy Prophet who six thousand years ago
Fell from my station in the Eternal bosom. I divided
To multitude & my multitudes are children of Care & Labour   50
O Rahab I behold thee I was once like thee a Son
Of Pride and I also have piercd the Lamb of God in pride & wrath
Hear me repeat my Generations that thou mayst also repent
PAGE 115
And these are the Sons of Los & Enitharmon Rintrah Palamabron   t,c
Theotormon Bromion Antamon Ananton Ozoth Ohana
Sotha Mydon Ellayol Natho Gon Harhath Satan
Har Ochim Ijim Adam Reuben Simeon Levi Judah Dan Naphtali
Gad Asher Issachar Zebulun Joseph Benjamin David Solomon   5
Paul Constantine Charlemaine Luther Milton
These are our daughters Ocalythron Elynittria Oothoon Leutha   t
Elythiria Enanto Manathu Vorcyon Ethinthus Moab Midian
Adah Zillah Caina Naamah Tamar Rahab Tirzah Mary
And myriads more of Sons & Daughters to whom our love increasd   t 10

To each according to the multiplication of their multitudes
But Satan accusd Palamabron before his brethren also he maddend   t
The horses of palambrons harrow wherefor Rintrah & Palamabron
Cut him off from Golgonooza. But Enitharmon in tears
Wept over him Created him a Space closd with a tender moon   15
And he rolld down beneath the fires of Orc a Globe immense
Crusted with snow in a dim void. here by the Arts of Urizen
He tempted many of the Sons & Daughters of Los to flee
Away from Me first Reuben fled then Simeon then Levi then Judah   t
Then Dan then Naphtali then Gad then Asher then Issachar   20
Then Zebulun then Joseph then Benjamin twelve sons of Los
And this is the manner in which Satan became the Tempter

There is a State namd Satan learn distinct to know O Rahab   t
The Difference between States & Individuals of those States
The State namd Satan never can be redeemd in all Eternity   25
But when Luvah in Orc became a Serpent he des[c]ended into
That State calld Satan Enitharmon breathd forth on the Winds
Of Golgonooza her well beloved knowing he was Orc's human remains
She tenderly lovd him above all his brethren he grew up
In mothers tenderness The Enormous worlds rolling in Urizens   30
   power
Must have given Satan by these mild arts Dominion over all
Wherefore Palamabron being accusd by Satan to Los   t
Calld down a Great Solemn assembly Rintrah in fury & fire
Defended Palamabron & rage filld the Universal Tent

Because Palamabron was good naturd Satan suppos'd he feard him   35
And Satan not having the Science of Wrath but only of Pity
Was soon condemnd & wrath was left to wrath & Pity to Pity
Rintrah & Palamabron Cut sheer off from Golgonooza
Enitharmons Moony space & in it Satan & his companions
They rolld down a dim world Crusted with Snow deadly & dark   40

Jerusalem pitying them wove them mantles of life & death
Times after times And those in Eden sent Lucifer for their Guard   e
Lucifer refusd to die for Satan & in pride he forsook his charge
Then they sent Molech Molech was impatient They sent
Molech impatient They Sent Elohim who created Adam   45
To die for Satan Adam refusd but was compelld to die
By Satans arts. Then the Eternals Sent Shaddai
Shaddai was angry Pachad descended Pachad was terrified
And then they Sent Jehovah who leprous stretchd his hand to
   Eternity
Then Jesus Came & Died willing beneath Tirzah & Rahab   50
Thou art that Rahab Lo the Tomb what can we purpose more
PAGE 116
Lo Enitharmon terrible & beautiful in Eternal youth
Bow down before her you her children & set Jerusalem free

Rahab burning with pride & revenge departed from Los
Los dropd a tear at her departure but he wipd it away in hope
She went to Urizen in pride the Prince of Light beheld   5
Reveald before the face of heaven his secret holiness   t

PAGE 106 (SECOND PORTION)
Darkness & sorrow coverd all flesh Eternity was darkend

Urizen sitting in his web of dece[i]tful Religion   t,c
felt the female death a dull & numming stupor such as neer   t
Before assaulted the bright human form he felt his pores   20
Drink in the deadly dull delusion horrors of Eternal death
Shot thro him Urizen sat Stonied upon his rock
Forgetful of his own Laws pitying he began to Embrace
The Shadowy Female since life cannot be quenchd Life exuded
His eyes shot outwards then his breathing nostrils drawn forth 25
Scales coverd over a cold forehead & a neck outstretchd
Into the deep to sieze the shadow scales his neck & bosom
Coverd & scales his hands & feet upon his belly falling
Outstretchd thro the immense his mouth wide opening tongueless t
His teeth a triple row he strove to sieze the shadow in vain   30
And his immense tail lashd the Abyss his human form a Stone
A form of Senseless Stone remaind in terrors on the rock
Abominable to the eyes of mortals who explore his books
His wisdom still remaind & all his memory stord with woe

And still his stony form remaind in the Abyss immense   35
Like the pale visage in its sheet of lead that cannot follow
Incessant stern disdain his scaly form gnaws inwardly
With deep repentance for the loss of that fair form of Man
With Envy he saw Los with Envy Tharmas & the Spectre   t
With Envy & in vain he swam around his stony form   40

No longer now Erect the King of Light outstretchd in fury
Lashes his tail in the wild deep his Eyelids like the Sun   t
Arising in his pride enlighten all the Grizly deeps
His scales transparent give forth light like windows of the morning
His neck flames with wrath & majesty he lashes the Abyss   45
Beating the Desarts & the rocks the desarts feel his power
They shake their slumbers off. They wave in awful fear
Calling the Lion & the Tyger the horse & the wild Stag
PAGE 107
The Elephant the wolf the Bear the Lamia the Satyr
His Eyelids give their light around his folding tail aspires
Among the stars the Earth & all the Abysses feel h[i]s fury   t
When as the snow covers the mountain oft petrific hardness
Covers the deeps at his vast fury mo[a]ning in his rock   t 5
Hardens the Lion & the Bear trembling in the Solid mountain
They view the light & wonder crying out in terrible existence
Up bound the wild stag & the horse behold the King of Pride

Oft doth his Eye emerge from the Abyss into the realms
Of his Eternal day & memory strives to augment his ruthfulness   10
Then weeping he descends in wrath drawing all things in his fury
Into obedience to his will & now he finds in vain
That not of his own power he bore the human form erect
Nor of his own will gave his Laws in times of Everlasting
For now fierce Orc in wrath & fury rises into the heavens   *t* 15
A King of wrath & fury a dark enraged horror
And Urizen repentant forgets his wisdom in the abyss   t
In forms of priesthood in the dark delusions of repentance
Repining in his heart & spirit that Orc reignd over all
And that his wisdom servd but to augment the indefinite lust   20

Then Tharmas & Urthona felt the stony stupor rise   c
Into their limbs Urthona shot forth a Vast Fibrous form
Tharmas like a pillar of sand rolld round by the whirlwind
An animated Pillar rolling round & round in incessant rage

Los felt the stony stupor & his head rolld down beneath   25
Into the Abysses of his bosom the vessels of his blood
Dart forth upon the wind in pipes writhing about in the Abyss
And Enitharmon pale & cold in milky juices flowd
Into a form of Vegetation living having a voice
Moving in rootlike fibres trembling in fear upon the Earth   30

And Tharmas gave his Power to Los Urthona gave his strength   c
Into the youthful prophet for the Love of Enitharmon
And of the nameless Shadowy female in the nether deep
And for the dread of the dark terrors of Orc & Urizen

Thus in a living Death the nameless shadow all things bound   35
All mortal things made permanent that they may be put off
Time after time by the Divine Lamb who died for all
And all in him died. & he put off all mortality

PAGE 108
Tharmas on high rode furious thro the afflicted worlds   *t,c*
Pursuing the Vain Shadow of Hope fleeing from identity
In abstract false Expanses that he may not hear the Voice
Of Ahania wailing on the winds in vain he flies for still
The voice incessant calls on all the children of Men   5
For she spoke of all in heaven & all upon the Earth
Saw not as yet the Divine vision her Eyes are Toward Urizen
And thus Ahania cries aloud to the Caverns of the Grave

Will you keep a flock of wolves & lead them will you take the wintry
    blast
For a covering to your limbs or the summer pestilence for a tent to   10
    abide in
Will you erect a lasting habitation in the mouldering Church yard

Or a pillar & palace of Eternity in the jaws of the hungry grave
Will you seek pleasure from the festering wound or marry for a Wife
The ancient Leprosy that the King & Priest may still feast on your
    decay
And the grave mock & laugh at the plowd field saying   15
I am the nourisher thou the destroyer in my bosom is milk & wine
And a fountain from my breasts to me come all multitudes
To my breath they obey they worship me I am a goddess & queen
But listen to Ahania O ye sons of the Murderd one
Listen to her whose memory beholds your ancient days   20
Listen to her whose eyes behold the dark body of corruptible death
Looking for Urizen in vain. in vain I seek for morning
The Eternal Man sleeps in the Earth nor feels the vigrous sun
Nor silent moon nor all the hosts of heaven move in his body
His fiery halls are dark & round his limbs the Serpent Orc   25
Fold without fold encompasses him And his corrupting members

Vomit out the Scaly monsters of the restless deep
They come up in the rivers & annoy the nether parts
Of Man who lays upon the shores leaning his faded head
Upon the Oozy rock inwrapped with the weeds of death   30
His eyes sink hollow in his head his flesh coverd with slime
And shrunk up to the bones alas that Man should come to this
His strong bones beat with snows & hid within the caves of night
Marrowless bloodless falling into dust driven by the winds
O how the horrors of Eternal Death take hold on Man   35
His faint groans shake the caves & issue thro the desolate rocks
PAGE 109
And the Strong Eagle now with num[m]ing cold blighted of feathers
Once like the pride of the sun now flagging in cold night
Hovers with blasted wings aloft watching with Eager Eye
Till Man shall leave a corruptible body he famishd hears him groan
And now he fixes his strong talons in the pointed rock   5
And now he beats the heavy air with his enormous wings
Beside him lies the Lion dead & in his belly worms
Feast on his death till universal death devours all
And the pale horse seeks for the pool to lie him down & die
But finds the pools filled with serpents devouring one another   10
He droops his head & trembling stands & his bright eyes decay
These are the Visions of My Eyes the Visions of Ahania

Thus cries Ahania Enion replies from the Caverns of the Grave

Fear not O poor forsaken one O land of briars & thorns
Where once the Olive flourishd & the Cedar spread his wings   15
Once I waild desolate like thee my fallow fields in fear
Cried to the Churchyards & the Earthworm came in dismal state
I found him in my bosom & I said the time of Love

Appears upon the rocks & hills in silent shades but   soon
A voice came in the night a midnight cry upon the mountains   20
Awake the bridegroom cometh I awoke to sleep no more   c
But an Eternal Consummation is dark Enion
The watry Grave. O thou Corn field O thou Vegetater happy
More happy is the dark consumer hope drowns all my torment
For I am now surrounded by a shadowy vortex drawing   25
The Spectre quite away from Enion that I die a death
Of bitter hope altho I consume in these raging waters
The furrowd field replies to the grave I hear her reply to me
Behold the time approaches fast that thou shalt be as a thing
Forgotten when one speaks of thee he will not be believd   30
When the man gently fades away in his immortality
When the mortal disappears in improved knowledge cast away
The former things so shall the Mortal gently fade away
And so become invisible to those who still remain
Listen I will tell thee what is done in the caverns of the grave 35
PAGE 110 (FIRST PORTION)
The Lamb of God has rent the Veil of Mystery soon to return
In Clouds & Fires around the rock & the Mysterious tree
As the seed waits Eagerly watching for its flower & fruit
Anxious its little soul looks out into the clear expanse
To see if hungry winds are abroad with their invisible army   5
So Man looks out in tree & herb & fish & bird & beast
Collecting up the scatterd portions of his immortal body
Into the Elemental forms of every thing that grows
He tries the sullen north wind riding on its angry furrows
The sultry south when the sun rises & the angry east   10
When the sun sets when the clods harden & the cattle stand
Drooping & the birds hide in their silent nests. he stores his thoughts
As in a store house in his memory he regulates the forms
Of all beneath & all above & in the gentle West
Reposes where the Suns heat dwells he rises to the Sun   15
And to the Planets of the Night & to the stars that gild
The Zodiac & the stars that sullen stand to north & south
He touches the remotest pole & in the Center weeps
That Man should Labour & sorrow & learn & forget & return
To the dark valley whence he came to begin his labours anew   20
In pain he sighs in pain he labours in his universe
Screaming in birds over the deep & howling in the Wolf
Over the slain & moaning in the cattle & in the winds
And weeping over Orc & Urizen in clouds & flaming fires   t
And in the cries of birth & in the groans of death his voice   25
Is heard throughout the Universe whereever a grass grows
Or a leaf buds The Eternal Man is seen is heard is felt
And all his Sorrows till he reassumes his ancient bliss

Such are the words of Ahania & Enion. Los hears & weeps   t
And Los & Enitharmon took the Body of the Lamb   30
Down from the Cross & placd it in a Sepulcher which Los had hewn
For himself in the Rock of Eternity trembling & in despair   t
Jerusalem wept over the Sepulcher two thousand Years

PAGE III

Rahab triumphs over all she took Jerusalem   e
Captive A Willing Captive by delusive arts impelld
To worship Urizens Dragon form to offer her own Children
Upon the bloody Altar. John Saw these things Reveald in Heaven
On Patmos Isle & heard the Souls cry out to be deliverd   5
He saw the Harlot of the Kings of Earth & saw her Cup
Of fornication food of Orc & Satan pressd from the fruit of Mystery
But when she saw the form of Ahania weeping on the Void
And heard Enions voice sound from the caverns of the Grave
No more spirit remain in her She secretly left the Synagogue of   10
    Satan
She commund with Orc in secret She hid him with the flax
That Enitharmon had numberd away from the Heavens   t
She gatherd it together to consume her Harlot Robes
In bitterest Contrition sometimes Self condemning repentant
And Sometimes kissing her Robes & Jewels & weeping over them   15
Sometimes returning to the Synagogue of Satan in Pride
And Sometimes weeping before Orc in humility & trembling
The Synagogue of Satan therefore uniting against Mystery
Satan divided against Satan resolvd in open Sanhedrim
To burn Mystery with fire & form another from her ashes   20
For God put it into their heart to fulfill all his will

The Ashes of Mystery began to animate they calld it Deism
And Natural Religion as of old so now anew began
Babylon again in Infancy Calld Natural Religion

PAGE 110 (SECOND PORTION)

[End of the Eighth Night]

PAGE 117

VALA

Night the Ninth

Being The Last Judgment

And Los & Enitharmon builded Jerusalem weeping   t,e
Over the Sepulcher & over the Crucified body
Which to their Phantom Eyes appear'd still in the Sepulcher
But Jesus stood beside them in the Spirit Separating
Their Spirit from their body. Terrified at Non Existence   5

For such they deemd the death of the body. Los his vegetable hands
Outstretchd his right hand branching out in fibrous Strength   e
Siezd the Sun. His left hand like dark roots coverd the Moon
And tore them down cracking the heavens across from immense to
    immense
Then fell the fires of Eternity with loud & shrill   10
Sound of Loud Trumpet thundering along from heaven to heaven
A mighty sound articulate Awake ye dead & come
To Judgment from the four winds Awake & Come away
Folding like scrolls of the Enormous volume of Heaven & Earth   e
With thunderous noise & dreadful shakings rocking to & fro   15
The heavens are shaken & the Earth removed from its place
The foundations of the Eternal hills discoverd
The thrones of Kings are shaken they have lost their robes & crowns
The poor smite their opressors they awake up to the harvest   e
The naked warriors rush together down to the sea shore   20
Trembling before the multitudes of slaves now set at liberty
They are become like wintry flocks like forests stripd of leaves
The opressed pursue like the wind there is no room for escape
The Spectre of Enitharmon let loose on the troubled deep   e
Waild shrill in the confusion & the Spectre of Urthona   25
PAGE 118
Recievd her in the darkning South their bodies lost they stood
Trembling & weak a faint embrace a fierce desire as when
Two shadows mingle on a wall they wail & shadowy tears
Fell down & shadowy forms of joy mixd with despair & grief
Their bodies buried in the ruins of the Universe   5
Mingled with the confusion. Who shall call them from the Grave

Rahab & Tirzah wail aloud in the wild flames they give up themselves
    to Consummation

The books of Urizen unroll with dreadful noise the folding Serpent
Of Orc began to Consume in fierce raving fire his fierce flames
Issud on all sides gathring strength in animating volumes   10
Roaming abroad on all the winds raging intense reddening
Into resistless pillars of fire rolling round & round gathering
Strength from the Earths consumd & heavens & all hidden abysses
Wherever the Eagle has Explord or Lion or Tyger trod
Or where the Comets of the night or stars of asterial day   t 15
Have shot their arrows or long beamed spears in wrath & fury

And all the while the trumpet sounds from the clotted gore & from the   t
    hollow den
Start forth the trembling millions into flames of mental fire
Bathing their limbs in the bright visions of Eternity

Then like the doves from pillars of Smoke the trembling families   20
Of women & children throughout every nation under heaven
Cling round the men in bands of twenties & of fifties pale

As snow that falls around a leafless tree upon the green
Their opressors are falln they have Stricken them they awake to life
Yet pale the just man stands erect & looking up to heavn   25
Trembling & strucken by the Universal stroke the trees unroot
The rocks groan horrible & run about. The mountains &
Their rivers cry with a dismal cry   the cattle gather together
Lowing they kneel before the heavens. the wild beasts of the forests
Tremble the Lion shuddering asks the Leopard. Feelest thou   30
The dread I feel unknown before My voice refuses to roar
And in weak moans I speak to thee This night
Before the mornings dawn the Eagle calld the Vulture
The Raven calld the hawk I heard them from my forests black
Saying Let us go up far for soon I smell upon the wind   35
A terror coming from the South. The Eagle & Hawk fled away
At dawn & Eer the sun arose the raven & Vulture followd
Let us flee also to the north. They fled. The Sons of Men
Saw them depart in dismal droves. The trumpet sounded loud
And all the Sons of Eternity Descended into Beulah   40

PAGE 119
In the fierce flames the limbs of Mystery lay consuming with howling   t
And deep despair. Rattling go up the flames around the Synagogue
Of Satan   Loud the Serpent Orc ragd thro his twenty Seven
Folds. The tree of Mystery went up in folding flames
Blood issud out in mighty volumes pouring in whirlpools fierce   5
From out the flood gates of the Sky The Gates are burst down pour
The torrents black upon the Earth the blood pours down incessant
Kings in their palaces lie drownd Shepherds their flocks their tents
Roll down the mountains in black torrents Cities Villages
High spires & Castles drownd in the black deluge Shoal on Shoal   10
Float the dead carcases of Men & Beasts driven to & fro on waves
Of foaming blood beneath the black incessant Sky till all
Mysterys tyrants are cut off & not one left on Earth

And when all Tyranny was cut off from the face of Earth
Around the Dragon form of Urizen & round his stony form   15
The flames rolling intense thro the wide Universe   c
Began to Enter the Holy City   Entring the dismal clouds   t,c
In furrowd lightnings break their way the wild flames whirring up   t
The Bloody Deluge living flames winged with intellect
And Reason round the Earth they march in order flame by flame   20
From the clotted gore & from the hollow den
Start forth the trembling millions into flames of mental fire
Bathing their Limbs in the bright visions of Eternity

Beyond this Universal Confusion beyond the remotest Pole   t
Where their vortexes begin to operate there stands   25
A Horrible rock far in the South   it was forsaken when   c
Urizen gave the horses of Light into the hands of Luvah

On this rock lay the faded head of the Eternal Man
Enwrapped round with weeds of death pale cold in sorrow & woe
He lifts the blue lamps of his Eyes & cries with heavenly voice   30
Bowing his head over the consuming Universe he cried

O weakness & O weariness   O war within my members
My sons exiled from my breast pass to & fro before me   c
My birds are silent on my hills flocks die beneath my branches
My tents are fallen my trumpets & the sweet sounds of my harp   35
Is silent on my clouded hills that belch forth storms & fires
My milk of cows & honey of bees & fruit of golden harvest
Are gatherd in the scorching heat & in the driving rain
My robe is turned to confusion & my bright gold to stones
Where once I sat   I weary walk in misery & pain   40
For from within my witherd breast grown narrow with my woes   t
The Corn is turnd to thistles & the apples into poison
The birds of song to murderous crows My joys to bitter groans
PAGE 120
The voices of children in my tents to cries of helpless infants
And all exiled from the face of light & shine of morning
In this dark world a narrow house I wander up & down
I hear Mystery howling in these flames of Consummation
When shall the Man of future times become as in days of old   5
O weary life why sit I here & give up all my powers
To indolence to the night of death when indolence & mourning
Sit hovring over my dark threshold. tho I arise look out
And scorn the war within my members yet my heart is weak
And my head faint Yet will I look again unto the morning   10
Whence is this sound of rage of Men drinking each others blood
Drunk with the smoking gore & red but not with nourishing wine

The Eternal Man sat on the Rocks & cried with awful voice

O Prince of Light where art thou   I behold thee not as once
In those Eternal fields in clouds of morning stepping forth   15
With harps & songs where bright Ahania sang before thy face
And all thy sons & daughters gatherd round my ample table
See you not all this wracking furious confusion
Come forth from slumbers of thy cold abstraction come forth
Arise to Eternal births shake off thy cold repose   20
Schoolmaster of souls great opposer of change arise
That the Eternal worlds may see thy face in peace & joy
That thou dread form of Certainty maist sit in town & village
While little children play around thy feet in gentle awe
Fearing thy frown loving thy smile O Urizen Prince of light   25

He calld the deep buried his voice & answer none returnd

Then wrath burst round the Eternal Man was wrath again he cried

Arise O stony form of death O dragon of the Deeps   c
Lie down before my feet O Dragon let Urizen arise
O how couldst thou deform those beautiful proportions   t 30
Of life & person for as the Person so is his life proportiond
Let Luvah rage in the dark deep even to Consummation
For if thou feedest not his rage it will subside in peace
But if thou darest obstinate refuse my stern behest
Thy crown & scepter I will sieze & regulate all my members   35
In stern severity & cast thee out into the indefinite
Where nothing lives, there to wander. & if thou returnst weary
Weeping at the threshold of Existence I will steel my heart
Against thee to Eternity & never recieve thee more
Thy self destroying beast formd Science shall be thy eternal lot   40
My anger against thee is greater than against this Luvah
For war is energy Enslavd but thy religion   t
The first author of this war & the distracting of honest minds
Into confused perturbation & strife & honour & pride
Is a deceit so detestable that I will cast thee out   45
If thou repentest not & leave thee as a rotten branch to be burnd
With Mystery the Harlot & with Satan for Ever & Ever
Error can never be redeemd in all Eternity
But Sin Even Rahab is redeemd in blood & fury & jealousy   c
That line of blood that stretchd across the windows of the morning   c 50
Redeemd from Errors power. Wake thou dragon of the Deeps

PAGE 121

Urizen wept in the dark deep anxious his Scaly form
To reassume the human & he wept in the dark deep

Saying O that I had never drank the wine nor eat the bread
Of dark mortality nor cast my view into futurity nor turnd   t
My back darkning the present clouding with a cloud   5
And building arches high & cities turrets & towers & domes   t
Whose smoke destroyd the pleasant gardens & whose running Kennels   t
Chokd the bright rivers burdning with my Ships the angry deep
Thro Chaos seeking for delight & in spaces remote
Seeking the Eternal which is always present to the wise   10
Seeking for pleasure which unsought falls round the infants path
And on the fleeces of mild flocks who neither care nor labour
But I the labourer of ages whose unwearied hands
Are thus deformd with hardness with the sword & with the spear   t
And with the Chisel & the mallet I whose labours vast   15
Order the nations separating family by family
Alone enjoy not   I alone in misery supreme
Ungratified give all my joy unto this Luvah & Vala   t
Then Go O dark futurity I will cast thee forth from these   t
Heavens of my brain nor will I look upon futurity more   t 20
I cast futurity away & turn my back upon that void   t

Which I have made for lo futurity is in this moment   t
Let Orc consume let Tharmas rage let dark Urthona give
All strength to Los & Enitharmon & let Los self cursd
Rend down this fabric as a wall ruind & family extinct   25
Rage Orc Rage Tharmas Urizen no longer curbs your rage

So Urizen spoke he shook his snows from off his Shoulders & arose
As on a Pyramid of mist his white robes scattering
The fleecy white renewd he shook his aged mantles off
Into the fires Then glorious bright Exulting in his joy   30
He sounding rose into the heavens in naked majesty
In radiant Youth. when Lo like garlands in the Eastern sky
When vocal may comes dancing from the East Ahania came   c
Exulting in her flight as when a bubble rises up
On to the surface of a lake. Ahania rose in joy   35
Excess of Joy is worse than grief—her heart beat high her blood
Burst its bright Vessels She fell down dead at the feet of Urizen
Outstretchd a Smiling corse they buried her in a silent cave
Urizen dropt a tear the Eternal Man Darkend with sorrow

The three daughters of Urizen guard Ahanias Death couch   40
Rising from the confusion in tears & howlings & despair
Calling upon their fathers Name upon their Rivers dark

And the Eternal Man Said Hear my words O Prince of Light   t
PAGE 122
Behold Jerusalem in whose bosom the Lamb of God
Is seen tho slain before her Gates he self renewd remains
Eternal & I thro him awake from deaths dark vale
The times revolve the time is coming when all these delights
Shall be renewd & all these Elements that now consume   5
Shall reflourish. Then bright Ahania shall awake from death
A glorious Vision to thine Eyes a Self renewing Vision   t
The spring. the summer to be thine then sleep the wintry days
In silken garments spun by her own hands against her funeral
The winter thou shalt plow & lay thy stores into thy barns   10
Expecting to recieve Ahania in the spring with joy
Immortal thou. Regenerate She & all the lovely Sex   c
From her shall learn obedience & prepare for a wintry grave
That spring may see them rise in tenfold joy & sweet delight
Thus shall the male & female live the life of Eternity   15
Because the Lamb of God Creates himself a bride & wife
That we his Children evermore may live in Jerusalem
Which now descendeth out of heaven a City yet a Woman   c
Mother of myriads redeemd & born in her spiritual palaces
By a New Spiritual birth Regenerated from Death   20

Urizen said. I have Erred & my Error remains with me
What Chain encompasses in what Lock is the river of light confind

That issues forth in the morning by measure & the evening by
    carefulness
Where shall we take our stand to view the infinite & unbounded
Or where are human feet for Lo our eyes are in the heavens   25

He ceasd for rivn link from link the bursting Universe explodes
All things reversd flew from their centers rattling bones
To bones Join, shaking convulsd the shivering clay breathes
Each speck of dust to the Earths center nestles round & round
In pangs of an Eternal Birth in torment & awe & fear   30
All spirits deceasd let loose from reptile prisons come in shoals
Wild furies from the tygers brain & from the lions Eyes   t
And from the ox & ass come moping terrors. from the Eagle
And raven numerous as the leaves of autumn every species
Flock to the trumpet muttring over the sides of the grave & crying   35
In the fierce wind round heaving rocks & mountains filld with groans
On rifted rocks suspended in the air by inward fires
Many a woful company & many on clouds & waters
Fathers & friends Mothers & Infants Kings & Warriors
Priests & chaind Captives met together in a horrible fear   40
And every one of the dead appears as he had livd before
PAGE 123
And all the marks remain of the slaves scourge & tyrants Crown
And of the Priests oergorged Abdomen & of the merchants thin
Sinewy deception & of the warriors ou[t]braving & thoughtlessness
In lineaments too extended & in bones too strait & long

They shew their wounds they accuse they sieze the opressor howlings   5
    began
On the golden palace Songs & joy on the desart the Cold babe
Stands in the furious air he cries the children of six thousand years
Who died in infancy rage furious a mighty multitude rage furious
Naked & pale standing on the expecting air to be deliverd
Rend limb from limb the Warrior & the tyrant reuniting in pain   10
The furious wind still rends around they flee in sluggish effort

They beg they intreat in vain now they Listend not to intreaty
They view the flames red rolling on thro the wide universe
From the dark jaws of death beneath & desolate shores remote   t
These covering Vaults of heaven & these trembling globes of Earth   15
One Planet calls to another & one star enquires of another   t
What flames are these coming from the South what noise what dreadful
    rout
As of a battle in the heavens hark heard you not the trumpet
As of fierce battle While they spoke the flames come on intense roaring

They see him whom they have piercd they wail because of him   c 20
They magnify themselves no more against Jerusalem Nor
Against her little ones the innocent accused before the Judges

Shines with immortal Glory trembling the Judge springs from his throne
Hiding his face in the dust beneath the prisoners feet & saying
Brother of Jesus what have I done intreat thy lord for me   25
Perhaps I may be forgiven While he speaks the flames roll on

And after the flames appears the Cloud of the Son of Man   c
Descending from Jerusalem with power and great Glory
All nations look up to the Cloud & behold him who was Crucified

The Prisoner answers you scourgd my father to death before my face   30
While I stood bound with cords & heavy chains. your hipocrisy
Shall now avail you nought. So speaking he dashd him with his foot

The Cloud is Blood dazling upon the heavens & in the cloud
Above upon its volumes is beheld a throne & a pavement   t,c
Of precious stones. surrounded by twenty four venerable patriarchs   35
And these again surrounded by four Wonders of the Almighty   t
Incomprehensible. pervading all amidst & round about
Fourfold each in the other reflected they are named Life's in Eternity   c
Four Starry Universes going forward from Eternity to Eternity
And the Falln Man who was arisen upon the Rock of Ages   40
PAGE 124
Beheld the Vision of God & he arose up from the Rock   c
And Urizen arose up with him walking thro the flames
To meet the Lord coming to Judgment but the flames repelld them
Still to the Rock in vain they strove to Enter the Consummation
Together for the Redeemd Man could not enter the Consummation   t 5

Then siezd the Sons of Urizen the Plow they polishd it   c
From rust of ages all its ornaments of Gold & silver & ivory
Reshone across the field immense where all the nations
Darkend like Mould in the divided fallows where the weed
Triumphs in its own destruction they took down the harness   10
From the blue walls of heaven starry jingling ornamented
With beautiful art the study of angels the workmanship of Demons
When Heaven & Hell in Emulation strove in sports of Glory

The noise of rural work resounded thro the heavens of heavens
The horse[s] neigh from the battle the wild bulls from the sultry   15
    waste
The tygers from the forests & the lions from the sandy desarts
They Sing they sieze the instruments of harmony they throw away   c
The spear the bow the gun the mortar they level the fortifications
They beat the iron engines of destruction into wedges
They give them to Urthonas Sons ringing the hammers sound   20
In dens of death to forge the spade the mattock & the ax   c
The heavy roller to break the clods to pass over the nations

The Sons of Urizen Shout Their father rose The Eternal horses
Harnessd They calld to Urizen the heavens moved at their call

The limbs of Urizen shone with ardor. He laid his ha[n]d on the   ^t25
    Plow
Thro dismal darkness drave the Plow of ages over Cities
And all their Villages over Mountains & all their Vallies
Over the graves & caverns of the dead   Over the Planets
And over the void Spaces over Sun & moon & star & constellation

Then Urizen commanded & they brought the Seed of Men   ^c30
The trembling souls of All the Dead stood before Urizen
Weak wailing in the troubled air East west & north & south
PAGE 125
He turnd the horses loose & laid his Plow in the northern corner
Of the wide Universal field. then Stepd forth into the immense   ^t

Then he began to sow the seed he girded round his loins
With a bright girdle & his skirt filld with immortal souls
Howling & Wailing fly the souls from Urizens strong hand   5

For from the hand of Urizen the myriads fall like stars
Into their own appointed places driven back by the winds
The naked warriors rush together down to the sea shores
They are become like wintry flocks like forests stripd of leaves
The Kings & Princes of the Earth cry with a feeble cry   10
Driven on the unproducing sands & on the hardend rocks
And all the while the flames of Orc follow the ventrous feet
Of Urizen & all the while the Trump of Tharmas sounds
Weeping & wailing fly the souls from Urizens strong hand
The daughters of Urizen stand with Cups & measures of foaming   15
    wine
Immense upon the heavens with bread & delicate repasts

Then follows the golden harrow in the midst of Mental fires
To ravishing melody of flutes & harps & softest voice
The seed is harrowd in while flames heat the black mould & cause
The human harvest to begin Towards the south first sprang   20
The myriads & in silent fear they look out from their graves

Then Urizen sits down to rest & all his wearied Sons   ^c
Take their repose on beds they drink they sing they view the flames
Of Orc in joy they view the human harvest springing up
A time they give to sweet repose till all the harvest is ripe   ^c25

And Lo like the harvest Moon Ahania cast off her death clothes   ^c
She folded them up in care in silence & her brightning limbs
Bathd in the clear spring of the rock then from her darksom cave
Issud in majesty divine   Urizen rose up from his couch
On wings of tenfold joy clapping his hands his feet his radiant   30
    wings
In the immense as when the Sun dances upon the mountains
A shout of jubilee in lovely notes responding from daughter to daughter

From son to Son as if the Stars beaming innumerable
Thro night should sing soft warbling filling Earth & heaven
And bright Ahania took her seat by Urizen in songs & joy   35

The Eternal Man also sat down upon the Couches of Beulah   e
Sorrowful that he could not put off his new risen body
In mental flames the flames refusd they drove him back to Beulah
His body was redeemd to be permanent thro the Mercy Divine

PAGE 126
And now fierce Orc had quite consumd himself in Mental flames   e
Expending all his energy against the fuel of fire
The Regenerate Man stoopd his head over the Universe & in   t
His holy hands recievd the flaming Demon & Demoness of Smoke
And gave them to Urizens hands the Immortal frownd Saying   5

Luvah & Vala henceforth you are Servants obey & live
You shall forget your former state return O Love in peace   t
Into your place the place of seed not in the brain or heart
If Gods combine against Man Setting their Dominion above   e
The Human form Divine. Thrown down from their high Station   10
In the Eternal heavens of Human Imagination: buried beneath   t
In dark oblivion with incessant pangs ages on ages
In Enmity & war first weakend then in stern repentance
They must renew their brightness & their disorganizd functions
Again reorganize till they resume the image of the human   15
Cooperating in the bliss of Man obeying his Will
Servants to the infinite & Eternal of the Human form

Luvah & Vala descended & enterd the Gates of Dark Urthona   e
And walkd from the hands of Urizen in the shadows of Valas Garden
Where the impressions of Despair & Hope for ever vegetate   20
In flowers in fruits in fishes birds & beasts & clouds & waters
The land of doubts & shadows sweet delusions unformd hopes
They saw no more the terrible confusion of the wracking universe
They heard not saw not felt not all the terrible confusion
For in their orbed senses within closd up they wanderd at will   25
And those upon the Couches viewd them in the dreams of Beulah
As they reposd from the terrible wide universal harvest
Invisible Luvah in bright clouds hoverd over Valas head
And thus their ancient golden age renewd for Luvah spoke
With voice mild from his golden Cloud upon the breath of morning   30

Come forth O Vala from the grass & from the silent Dew
Rise from the dews of death for the Eternal Man is Risen

She rises among flowers & looks toward the Eastern clearness
She walks yea runs her feet are wingd on the tops of the bending   e
        grass
Her garments rejoice in the vocal wind & her hair glistens with dew   35

She answerd thus Whose voice is this in the voice of the nourishing air
In the spirit of the morning awaking the Soul from its grassy bed
PAGE 127
Where dost thou dwell for it is thee I seek & but for thee
I must have slept Eternally nor have felt the dew of thy morning
Look how the opening dawn advances with vocal harmony
Look how the beams foreshew the rising of some glorious power
The sun is thine he goeth forth in his majestic brightness   5
O thou creating voice that callest & who shall answer thee

Where dost thou flee O fair one where dost thou seek thy happy place   e

To yonder brightness there I haste for sure I came from thence
Or I must have slept eternally nor have felt the dew of morning

Eternally thou must have slept nor have felt the morning dew   10
But for yon nourishing sun tis that by which thou art arisen
The birds adore the sun the beasts rise up & play in his beams
And every flower & every leaf rejoices in his light
Then O thou fair one sit thee down for thou art as the grass
Thou risest in the dew of morning & at night art folded up   15

Alas am I but as a flower then will I sit me down
Then will I weep then Ill complain & sigh for immortality
And chide my maker thee O Sun that raisedst me to fall

So saying she sat down & wept beneath the apple trees

O be thou blotted out thou Sun that raisedst me to trouble   20
That gavest me a heart to crave & raisedst me thy phantom
To feel thy heat & see thy light & wander here alone
Hopeless if I am like the grass & so shall pass away

Rise sluggish Soul why sitst thou here why dost thou sit & weep
Yon Sun shall wax old & decay but thou shalt ever flourish   25
The fruit shall ripen & fall down & the flowers consume away
But thou shalt still survive arise O dry thy dewy tears

Hah! Shall I still survive whence came that sweet & comforting voice
And whence that voice of sorrow O sun thou art nothing now to me
Go on thy course rejoicing & let us both rejoice together   30
I walk among his flocks & hear the bleating of his lambs
O that I could behold his face & follow his pure feet
I walk by the footsteps of his flocks come hither tender flocks
Can you converse with a pure Soul that seeketh for her maker
You answer not then am I set your mistress in this garden   35
Ill watch you & attend your footsteps you are not like the birds
PAGE 128
That sing & fly in the bright air but you do lick my feet
And let me touch your wooly backs follow me as I sing
For in my bosom a new song arises to my Lord

-381-

Rise up O Sun most glorious minister & light of day   c
Flow on ye gentle airs & bear the voice of my rejoicing   5
Wave freshly clear waters flowing around the tender grass
And thou sweet smelling ground put forth thy life in fruits & flowers
Follow me O my flocks & hear me sing my rapturous Song
I will cause my voice to be heard on the clouds that glitter in the sun
I will call & who shall answer me   I will sing   who shall reply   10
For from my pleasant hills behold the living living springs
Running among my green pastures delighting among my trees
I am not here alone my flocks you are my brethren
And you birds that sing & adorn the sky you are my sisters
I sing & you reply to my Song   I rejoice & you are glad   15
Follow me O my flocks we will now descend into the valley
O how delicious are the grapes flourishing in the Sun
How clear the spring of the rock running among the golden sand
How cool the breezes of the vally & the arms of the branching trees
Cover us from the Sun come & let us sit in the Shade   20
My Luvah here hath placd me in a Sweet & pleasant Land
And given me fruits & pleasant waters & warm hills & cool valleys
Here will I build myself a house & here Ill call on his name
Here Ill return when I am weary & take my pleasant rest

So spoke the Sinless Soul & laid her head on the downy fleece   25
Of a curld Ram who stretchd himself in sleep beside his mistress
And soft sleep fell upon her eyelids in the silent noon of day

Then Luvah passed by & saw the sinless Soul
And said   Let a pleasant house arise to be the dwelling place
Of this immortal Spirit growing in lower Paradise   30

He spoke & pillars were builded & walls as white as ivory
The grass she slept upon was pavd with pavement as of pearl
Beneath her rose a downy bed & a cieling coverd all

Vala awoke. When in the pleasant gates of sleep I enterd
I saw my Luvah like a spirit stand in the bright air   35
Round him stood spirits like me who reard me a bright house
And here I see thee house remain in my most pleasant world
PAGE 129
My Luvah smild I kneeled down he laid his hand on my head
And when he laid his hand upon me from the gates of sleep I came
Into this bodily house to tend my flocks in my pleasant garden

So saying she arose & walked round her beautiful house
And then from her white door she lookd to see her bleating lambs   5
But her flocks were gone up from beneath the trees into the hills

I see the hand that leadeth me doth also lead my flocks
She went up to her flocks & turned oft to see her shining house
She stopd to drink of the clear spring & eat the grapes & apples

She bore the fruits in her lap she gatherd flowers for her bosom   10
She called to her flocks saying follow me o my flocks

They followd her to the silent vally beneath the spreading trees   c
And on the rivers margin she ungirded her golden girdle
She stood in the river & viewd herself within the watry glass
And her bright hair was wet with the waters She rose up from the river   15
And as she rose her Eyes were opend to the world of waters
She saw Tharmas sitting upon the rocks beside the wavy sea
He strokd the water from his beard & mournd faint thro the summer
    vales

And Vala stood on the rocks of Tharmas & heard his mournful voice

O Enion my weary head is in the bed of death   20
For weeds of death have wrapd around my limbs in the hoary deeps
I sit in the place of shells & mourn & thou art closd in clouds
When will the time of Clouds be past & the dismal night of Tharmas
Arise O Enion Arise & smile upon my head   t
As thou dost smile upon the barren mountains and they rejoice   25
When wilt thou smile on Tharmas O thou bringer of golden day
Arise O Enion arise for Lo I have calmd my seas

So saying his faint head he laid upon the Oozy rock
And darkness coverd all the deep the light of Enion faded
Like a fa[i]nt flame quivering upon the surface of the darkness   30

Then Vala lifted up her hands to heaven to call on Enion
She calld but none could answer her & the Eccho of her voice returnd

Where is the voice of God that calld me from the silent dew
Where is the Lord of Vala dost thou hide in clefts of the rock   c
Why shouldst thou hide thyself from Vala from the soul that wanders   35
    desolate

She ceas'd & light beamd round her like the glory of the morning
PAGE 130
And She arose out of the river & girded on her golden girdle

And now her feet step on the grassy bosom of the ground
Among her flocks & she turnd her eyes toward her pleasant house
And saw in the door way beneath the trees two little children playing   c
She drew near to her house & her flocks followd her footsteps   5
The Children clung around her knees she embracd them & wept over
    them

Thou little Boy art Tharmas & thou bright Girl Enion
How are ye thus renewd & brought into the Gardens of Vala

She embracd them in tears. till the sun descended the western hills
And then she enterd her bright house leading her mighty children   10
And when night came the flocks laid round the house beneath the trees

−383−

She laid the Children on the beds which she saw prepard in the house
Then last herself laid down & closd her Eyelids in soft slumbers

And in the morning when the Sun arose in the crystal sky
Vala awoke & calld the children from their gentle slumbers   *15*

Awake O Enion awake & let thine innocent Eyes
Enlighten all the Crystal house of Vala awake awake
Awake Tharmas awake awake thou child of dewy tears
Open the orbs of thy blue eyes & smile upon my gardens

The Children woke & smild on Vala. she kneeld by the golden couch   *20*
She presd them to her bosom & her pearly tears dropd down
O my sweet Children Enion let Tharmas kiss thy Cheek
Why dost thou turn thyself away from his sweet watry eyes
Tharmas henceforth in Valas bosom thou shalt find sweet peace
O bless the lovely eyes of Tharmas & the Eyes of Enion   *25*

They rose they went out wandring sometimes together sometimes alone
Why weepest thou Tharmas Child of tears in the bright house of joy
Doth Enion avoid the sight of thy blue heavenly Eyes
And dost thou wander with my lambs & wet their innocent faces   *t*
With thy bright tears because the steps of Enion are in the gardens   *30*
Arise sweet boy & let us follow the path of Enion

So saying they went down into the garden among the fruits
And Enion sang among the flowers that grew among the trees
And Vala said Go Tharmas weep not Go to Enion

PAGE 131
He said O Vala I am sick & all this garden of Pleasure
Swims like a dream before my eyes but the sweet smelling fruit
Revives me to new deaths I fade even like a water lilly
In the suns heat till in the night on the couch of Enion
I drink new life & feel the breath of sleeping Enion   *5*
But in the morning she arises to avoid my Eyes
Then my loins fade & in the house I sit me down & weep

Chear up thy Countenance bright boy & go to Enion
Tell her that Vala waits her in the shadows of her garden

He went with timid steps & Enion like the ruddy morn   *10*
When infant spring appears in swelling buds & opening flowers
Behind her Veil withdraws so Enion turnd her modest head

But Tharmas spoke Vala seeks thee sweet Enion in the shades
Follow the steps of Tharmas, O thou brightness of the gardens
He took her hand reluctant she followd in infant doubts   *15*

Thus in Eternal Childhood straying among Valas flocks
In infant sorrow & joy alternate Enion & Tharmas playd

Round Vala in the Gardens of Vala & by her rivers margin
They are the shadows of Tharmas & of Enion in Valas world

And the sleepers who rested from their harvest work beheld these   20
    visions
Thus were the sleepers entertaind upon the Couches of Beulah

When Luvah & Vala were closd up in their world of shadowy forms   e
Darkness was all beneath the heavens only a little light
Such as glows out from sleeping spirits appeard in the deeps beneath
As when the wind sweeps over a Corn field the noise of souls   25
Thro all the immense borne down by Clouds swagging in autumnal
    heat
Muttering along from heaven to heaven hoarse roll the human forms
Beneath thick clouds dreadful lightnings burst & thunders roll
Down pour the torrent Floods of heaven on all the human harvest
Then Urizen sitting at his repose on beds in the bright South   30
Cried Times are Ended he Exulted he arose in joy he exulted
He pourd his light & all his Sons & daughters pourd their light
To exhale the spirits of Luvah & Vala thro the atmosphere
And Luvah & Vala saw the Light their spirits were Exhald
In all their ancient innocence the floods depart the clouds   35
Dissipate or sink into the Seas of Tharmas   Luvah sat
Above on the bright heavens in peace. the Spirits of Men beneath
Cried out to be deliverd & the Spirit of Luvah wept
Over the human harvest & over Vala the sweet wanderer
In pain the human harvest wavd in horrible groans of woe   40
PAGE 132
The Universal Groan went up the Eternal Man was Darkend

Then Urizen arose & took his Sickle in his hand   e
There is a brazen sickle & a scythe of iron hid
Deep in the South guarded by a few solitary stars
This sickle Urizen took the scythe his sons embracd   5
And went forth & began to reap & all his joyful sons
Reapd the wide Universe & bound in Sheaves a wondrous harvest
They took them into the wide barns with loud rejoicings & triumph
Of flute & harp & drum & trumpet horn & clarion

The feast was spread in the bright South & the Regenerate Man   10
Sat at the feast rejoicing & the wine of Eternity
Was servd round by the flames of Luvah all Day & all the Night
And when Morning began to dawn upon the distant hills
a whirlwind rose up in the Center & in the Whirlwind a shriek   t
And in the Shriek a rattling of bones & in the rattling of bones   15
A dolorous groan & from the dolorous groan in tears
Rose Enion like a gentle light & Enion spoke saying

O Dreams of Death the human form dissolving companied   e
By beasts & worms & creeping things & darkness & despair   t

-385-

The clouds fall off from my wet brow the dust from my cold limbs   20
Into the Sea of Tharmas Soon renewd a Golden Moth   c
I shall cast off my death clothes & Embrace Tharmas again
For Lo the winter melted away upon the distant hills
And all the black mould sings. She speaks to her infant race her milk
Descends down on the sand. the thirsty sand drinks & rejoices   t 25
Wondering to behold the Emmet the Grasshopper the jointed worm
The roots shoot thick thro the solid rocks bursting their way
They cry out in joys of existence. the broad stems
Rear on the mountains stem after stem the scaly newt creeps
From the stone & the armed fly springs from the rocky crevice   30
The spider. The bat burst from the hardend slime crying
To one another What are we & whence is our joy & delight
Lo the little moss begins to spring & the tender weed
Creeps round our secret nest. Flocks brighten the Mountains
Herds throng up the Valley wild beasts fill the forests   35

Joy thrilld thro all the Furious form of Tharmas humanizing
Mild he Embracd her whom he sought he raisd her thro the heavens
Sounding his trumpet to awake the dead on high he soard
Over the ruind worlds the smoking tomb of the Eternal Prophet   c

PAGE 133
The Eternal Man arose He welcomd them to the Feast   c
The feast was spread in the bright South & the Eternal Man
Sat at the feast rejoicing & the wine of Eternity
Was servd round by the flames of Luvah all day & all the night

And Many Eternal Men sat at the golden feast to see   5
The female form now separate They shudderd at the horrible thing
Not born for the sport and amusement of Man but born to drink up all
    his powers
They wept to see their shadows they said to one another this is Sin t
This is the Generative world they rememberd the Days of old   t

And One of the Eternals spoke All was silent at the feast   10

Man is a Worm wearied with joy he seeks the caves of sleep
Among the Flowers of Beulah in his Selfish cold repose
Forsaking Brotherhood & Universal love in selfish clay
Folding the pure wings of his mind seeking the places dark
Abstracted from the roots of Science then inclosd around   t 15
In walls of Gold we cast him like a Seed into the Earth
Till times & spaces have passd over him duly every morn
We visit him covering with a Veil the immortal seed
With windows from the inclement sky we cover him & with walls
And hearths protect the Selfish terror till divided all   20
In families we see our shadows born. & thence we know   ) Ephesi-
That Man subsists by Brotherhood & Universal Love   } ans iii c.
We fall on one anothers necks more closely we embrace   ) 10 v

Not for ourselves but for the Eternal family we live
Man liveth not by Self alone but in his brothers face   25
Each shall behold the Eternal Father & love & joy abound

So spoke the Eternal at the Feast they embracd the New born Man
Calling him Brother image of the Eternal Father. they sat down
At the immortal tables sounding loud their instruments of joy
Calling the Morning into Beulah the Eternal Man rejoicd   ͨ 30

When Morning dawnd The Eternals rose to labour at the Vintage   ͨ
Beneath they saw their sons & daughters wondering inconceivable
At the dark myriads in Shadows in the worlds beneath

The morning dawnd Urizen rose & in his hand the Flail
Sounds on the Floor heard terrible by all beneath the heavens   35
Dismal loud redounding the nether floor shakes with the sound
PAGE 134
And all Nations were threshed out & the stars threshd from their husks   ͨ

Then Tharmas took the Winnowing fan the winnowing wind furious
Above veerd round by the violent whirlwind driven west & south
Tossed the Nations like Chaff into the seas of Tharmas

O Mystery Fierce Tharmas cries Behold thy end is come   5
Art thou she that made the nations drunk with the cup of Religion
Go down ye Kings & Councillors & Giant Warriors
Go down into the depths go down & hide yourselves beneath
Go down with horse & Chariots & Trumpets of hoarse war

Lo how the Pomp of Mystery goes down into the Caves   10
Her great men howl & throw the dust & rend their hoary hair
Her delicate women & children shriek upon the bitter wind
Spoild of their beauty their hair rent & their skin shriveld up
Lo darkness covers the long pomp of banners on the wind
And black horses & armed men & miserable bound captives   15
Where shall the graves recieve them all & where shall be their place
And who shall mourn for Mystery who never loosd her Captives

Let the slave grinding at the mill run out into the field   ͨ
Let him look up into the heavens & laugh in the bright air
Let the inchaind soul shut up in darkness & in sighing   20
Whose face has never seen a smile in thirty weary years
Rise & look out his chains are loose his dungeon doors are open
And let his wife & children return from the opressors scourge

They look behind at every step & believe it is a dream
Are these the Slaves that groand along the streets of Mystery   25
Where are your bonds & task masters are these the prisoners
Where are your chains where are your tears why do you look around
If you are thirsty there is the river go bathe your parched limbs
The good of all the Land is before you for Mystery is no more

Then All the Slaves from every Earth in the wide Universe   ^c 30
Sing a New Song drowning confusion in its happy notes   ^c
While the flail of Urizen sounded loud & the winnowing wind of
     Tharmas
So loud so clear in the wide heavens & the song that they sung was this
Composed by an African Black from the little Earth of Sotha

Aha Aha how came I here so soon in my sweet native land   35
How came I here Methinks I am as I was in my youth
PAGE 135
When in my fathers house I sat & heard his chearing voice
Methinks I see his flocks & herds & feel my limbs renewd
And Lo my Brethren in their tents & their little ones around them

The song arose to the Golden feast the Eternal Man rejoicd   ^c
Then the Eternal Man said Luvah the Vintage is ripe arise   5
The sons of Urizen shall gather the vintage with sharp hooks
And all thy sons O Luvah bear away the families of Earth
I hear the flail of Urizen his barns are full no roo[m]
Remains & in the Vineyards stand the abounding sheaves beneath
The falling Grapes that odorous burst upon the winds. Arise   10
My flocks & herds trample the Corn my cattle browze upon
The ripe Clusters The shepherds shout for Luvah prince of Love
Let the Bulls of Luvah tread the Corn & draw the loaded waggon
Into the Barn while children glean the Ears around the door
Then shall they lift their innocent hands & stroke his furious nose   15
And he shall lick the little girls white neck & on her head
Scatter the perfume of his breath while from his mountains high
The lion of terror shall come down & bending his bright mane
And couching at their side shall eat from the curld boys white lap
His golden food and in the evening sleep before the Door   20

Attempting to be more than Man We become less said Luvah
As he arose from the bright feast drunk with the wine of ages
His crown of thorns fell from his head he hung his living Lyre
Behind the seat of the Eternal Man & took his way
Sounding the Song of Los descending to the Vineyards bright   25
His sons arising from the feast with golden baskets follow
A fiery train as when the Sun sings in the ripe vineyards
Then Luvah stood before the wine press all his fiery sons
Brought up the loaded Waggons with shoutings ramping tygers play
In the jingling traces furious lions sound the song of joy   30
To the golden wheels circling upon the pavement of heaven & all
The Villages of Luvah ring the golden tiles of the villages
Reply to violins & tabors to the pipe flute lyre & cymbal
Then fell the Legions of Mystery in maddning confusion   ^c
Down Down thro the immense with outcry fury & despair   35
Into the wine presses of Luvah howling fell the Clusters

Of human families thro the deep. the wine presses were filld
The blood of life flowd plentiful Odors of life arose
All round the heavenly arches & the Odors rose singing this song   t

PAGE 136
O terrible wine presses of Luvah O caverns of the Grave
How lovely the delights of those risen again from death
O trembling joy excess of joy is like Excess of grief   c

So sang the Human Odors round the wine presses of Luvah

But in the Wine presses is wailing terror & despair   5
Forsaken of their Elements they vanish & are no more
No more but a desire of Being a distracted ravening desire
Desiring like the hungry worm & like the gaping grave   t
They plunge into the Elements the Elements cast them forth
Or else consume their shadowy semblance Yet they obstinate   10
Tho pained to distraction Cry O let us Exist for
This dreadful Non Existence is worse than pains of Eternal Birth   t
Eternal Death who can Endure. let us consume in fires
In waters stifling or in air corroding or in earth shut up
The Pangs of Eternal birth are better than the Pangs of Eternal Death   15

How red the sons & daughters of Luvah how they tread the Grapes
Laughing & shouting drunk with odors many fall oerwearied
Drownd in the wine is many a youth & maiden those around
Lay them on skins of tygers or the spotted Leopard or wild Ass
Till they revive or bury them in cool Grots making lamentation   20

But in the Wine Presses the Human Grapes Sing not nor dance
They howl & writhe in shoals of torment in fierce flames consuming   t
In chains of iron & in dungeons circled with ceaseless fires
In pits & dens & shades of death in shapes of torment & woe
The Plates the Screws and Racks & Saws & cords & fires & floods   t 25
The cruel joy of Luvahs daughters lacerating with knives
And whip[s] their Victims & the deadly sports of Luvahs sons   t

Timbrels & Violins sport round the Wine Presses The little Seed
The Sportive root the Earthworm the small beetle the wise Emmet
Dance round the Wine Presses of Luvah. the Centipede is there   30
The ground Spider with many Eyes the Mole clothed in Velvet
The Earwig armd the tender maggot emblem of Immortality
The Slow Slug the grasshopper that sings & laughs & drinks
The winter comes he folds his slender bones without a murmur
There is the Nettle that stings with soft down & there   t 35
The indignant Thistle whose bitterness is bred in his milk
And who lives on the contempt of his neighbour there all the idle weeds
That creep about the obscure places shew their various limbs
Naked in all their beauty dancing round the Wine Presses

-389-

They Dance around the Dying & they Drink the howl & groan 40
They catch the Shrieks in cups of gold they hand them to one another
These are the sports of love & these the sweet delights of amorous play
Tears of the grapes the death sweat of the Cluster the last sigh
Of the mild youth who listens to the luring songs of Luvah

The Eternal Man darkend with Sorrow & a wintry mantle ᵉ5
Coverd the Hills   He said O Tharmas rise & O Urthona

Then Tharmas & Urthona rose from the Golden feast satiated
With Mirth & Joy Urthona limping from his fall on Tharmas leand
In his right hand his hammer Tharmas held his Shepherds crook
Beset with gold gold were the ornaments formd by sons of Urizen 10

Then Enion & Ahania & Vala & the wife of Dark Urthona
Rose from the feast in joy ascending to their Golden Looms
There the wingd shuttle Sang the spindle & the distaff & the Reel
Rang sweet the praise of industry. Thro all the golden rooms
Heaven rang with winged Exultation   All beneath howld loud 15
With tenfold rout & desolation roard the Chasms beneath
Where the wide woof flowd down & where the Nations are gatherd
    together

Tharmas went down to the Wine presses & beheld the sons & daughters
Of Luvah quite exhausted with the Labour & quite filld
With new wine. that they began to torment one another and to tread 20
The weak. Luvah & Vala slept on the floor o'erwearied

Urthona calld his Sons around him Tharmas calld his sons
Numrous. they took the wine they separated the Lees
And Luvah was put for dung on the ground by the Sons of Tharmas &
    Urthona
They formed heavens of sweetest wo[o]d[s] of gold & silver & ivory 25
Of glass & precious stones They loaded all the waggons of heaven
And took away the wine of ages with solemn songs & joy

Luvah & Vala woke & all the sons & daughters of Luvah
Awoke they wept to one another & they reascended
To the Eternal Man in woe he cast them wailing into 30
The world of shadows thro the air till winter is over & gone

But the Human Wine stood wondering in all their delightful Expanses
The Elements subside the heavens rolld on with vocal harmony

Then Los who is Urthona rose in all his regenerate power ᵉ
The Sea that rolld & foamd with darkness & the shadows of death 35
Vomited out & gave up all the floods lift up their hands
Singing & shouting to the Man they bow their hoary heads
And murmuring in their channels flow & circle round his feet

PAGE 138
Then Dark Urthona took the Corn out of the Stores of Urizen
He ground it in his rumbling Mills Terrible the distress
Of all the Nations of Earth ground in the Mills of Urthona
In his hand Tharmas takes the Storms. he turns the whirlwind Loose
Upon the wheels the stormy seas howl at his dread command   5
And Eddying fierce rejoice in the fierce agitation of the wheels
Of Dark Urthona Thunders Earthquakes Fires Water floods
Rejoice to one another loud their voices shake the Abyss
Their dread forms tending the dire mills The grey hoar frost was there
And his pale wife the aged Snow they watch over the fires   10
They build the Ovens of Urthona Nature in darkness groans   e
And Men are bound to sullen contemplations in the night
Restless they turn on beds of sorrow. in their inmost brain
Feeling the crushing Wheels they rise they write the bitter words
Of Stern Philosophy & knead the bread of knowledge with tears &   15
    groans

Such are the works of Dark Urthona Tharmas sifted the corn
Urthona made the Bread of Ages & he placed it
In golden & in silver baskets in heavens of precious stone
And then took his repose in Winter in the night of Time   e

The Sun has left his blackness & has found a fresher morning   e 20
And the mild moon rejoices in the clear & cloudless night   t
And Man walks forth from midst of the fires the evil is all consumd
His eyes behold the Angelic spheres arising night & day
The stars consumd like a lamp blown out & in their stead behold
The Expanding Eyes of Man behold the depths of wondrous worlds   t 25

One Earth one sea beneath nor Erring Globes wander but Stars
Of fire rise up nightly from the Ocean & one Sun
Each morning like a New born Man issues with songs & Joy
Calling the Plowman to his Labour & the Shepherd to his rest
He walks upon the Eternal Mountains raising his heavenly voice   30
Conversing with the Animal forms of wisdom night & day
That risen from the Sea of fire renewd walk oer the Earth

For Tharmas brought his flocks upon the hills & in the Vales
Around the Eternal Mans bright tent the little Children play
Among the wooly flocks The hammer of Urthona sounds   35
In the deep caves beneath his limbs renewd his Lions roar
Around the Furnaces & in Evening sport upon the plains
They raise their faces from the Earth conversing with the Man

How is it we have walkd thro fires & yet are not consumd
How is it that all things are changd even as in ancient times   40

PAGE 139

The Sun arises from his dewy bed & the fresh airs
Play in his smiling beams giving the seeds of life to grow
And the fresh Earth beams forth ten thousand thousand springs of life
Urthona is arisen in his strength no longer now
Divided from Enitharmon no longer the Spectre Los   5
Where is the Spectre of Prophecy where the delusive Phantom
Departed & Urthona rises from the ruinous walls
In all his ancient strength to form the golden armour of science
For intellectual War The war of swords departed now
The dark Religions are departed & sweet Science reigns   10

End of The Dream

[Alternate Version of Night VII]

PAGE 91 (FIRST PORTION)

VALA

Night the Seventh [b]   t

PAGE 95 (SECOND PORTION)

But in the deeps beneath the Roots of Mystery in darkest night   t,c 15
Where Urizen sat on his rock the Shadow brooded   t
Urizen saw & triumphd & he cried to his warriors   t

The time of Prophecy is now revolvd & all
This Universal Ornament is mine & in my hands
The ends of heaven like a Garment will I fold them round me   c 20
Consuming what must be consumd then in power & majesty
I will walk forth thro those wide fields of endless Eternity
A God & not a Man a Conqueror in triumphant glory
And all the Sons of Everlasting shall bow down at my feet   t

First Trades & Commerce ships & armed vessels he builded laborious   25
To swim the deep & on the Land children are sold to trades
Of dire necessity still laboring day & night till all
Their life extinct they took the spectre form in dark despair
And slaves in myriads in ship loads burden the hoarse sounding deep
Rattling with clanking chains the Universal Empire groans   30

And he commanded his Sons found a Center in the Deep   c
And Urizen laid the first Stone & all his myriads
Builded a temple in the image of the human heart
PAGE 96
And in the inner part of the Temple wondrous workmanship
They formd the Secret place reversing all the order of delight
That whosoever enterd into the temple might not behold

The hidden wonders allegoric of the Generations
Of secret lust when hid in chambers dark the nightly harlot   5
Plays in Disguise in whisperd hymn & mumbling prayer The priests
He ordaind & Priestesses clothd in disguises beastial
Inspiring secrecy & lamps they bore intoxicating fumes
Roll round the Temple & they took the Sun that glowd oer Los
And with immense machines down rolling. the terrific orb   10
Compell'd. The Sun reddning like a fierce lion in his chains
Descended to the sound of instruments that drownd the noise
Of the hoarse wheels & the terrific howlings of wild beasts
That dragd the wheels of the Suns chariot & they put the Sun
Into the temple of Urizen to give light to the Abyss   15
To light the War by day to hide his secret beams by night
For he divided day & night in different orderd portions
The day for war the night for secret religion in his temple   t

Los reard his mighty stature on Earth stood his feet. Above   t,c
The moon his furious forehead circled with black bursting thunders   20
His naked limbs glittring upon the dark blue sky his knees
Bathed in bloody clouds. his loins in fires of war where spears
And swords rage where the Eagles cry & the Vultures laugh saying
Now comes the night of Carnage now the flesh of Kings & Princes
Pamperd in palaces for our food the blood of Captains nurturd   t 25
With lust & murder for our drink the drunken Raven shall wander
All night among the slain & mock the wounded that groan in the field

Tharmas laughd furious among the Banners clothd in blood   e
Crying As I will I rend the Nations all asunder rending
The People, vain their combinations I will scatter them   30
But thou O Son whom I have crowned and inthrond thee Strong
I will preserve tho Enemies arise around thee numberless
I will command my winds & they shall scatter them or call

PAGE 97

My Waters like a flood around thee fear not trust in me
And I will give thee all the ends of heaven for thy possession
In war shalt thou bear rule in blood shalt thou triumph for me
Because in times of Everlasting I was rent in sunder
And what I loved best was divided among my Enemies   5
My little daughters were made captives & I saw them beaten
With whips along the sultry sands. I heard those whom I lovd   t
Crying in secret tents at night & in the morn compelld
To labour & behold my heart sunk down beneath
In sighs & sobbings all dividing till I was divided   t 10
In twain & lo my Crystal form that lived in my bosom
Followd her daughters to the fields of blood they left me naked
Alone & they refusd to return from the fields of the mighty
Therefore I will reward them as they have rewarded me

I will divide them in my anger & thou O my King   15
Shalt gather them from out their graves & put thy fetter on them
And bind them to thee that my crystal form may come to me

So cried the Demon of the Waters in the Clouds of Los
Outstretchd upon the hills lay Enitharmon clouds & tempests
Beat round her head all night all day she riots in Excess   20
But night or day Los follows War & the dismal moon rolls over her   t
That when Los warrd upon the South reflected the fierce fires
Of his immortal head into the North upon faint Enitharmon
Red rage the furies of fierce Orc black thunders roll round Los
Flaming his head like the bright sun seen thro a mist that magnifies   25
His disk into a terrible vision to the Eyes of trembling mortals

And Enitharmon trembling & in fear utterd these words

I put not any trust in thee nor in thy glittering scales   c
Thy eyelids are a terror to me & the flaming of thy crest
The rushing of thy Scales confound me thy hoarse rushing scales   30
And if that Los had not built me a tower upon a rock
I must have died in the dark desert among noxious worms
How shall I flee how shall I flee into the tower of Los
My feet are turned backward & my footsteps slide in clay   c
And clouds are closd around my tower my arms labour in vain   35
Does not the God of waters in the wracking Elements
Love those who hate rewarding with hate the Loving Soul
PAGE 98
And must not I obey the God thou Shadow of Jealousy
I cry the watchman heareth not I pour my voice in roarings   c
Watchman the night is thick & darkness cheats my rayie sight
Lift up Lift up O Los awake my watchman for he sleepeth
Lift up Lift up Shine forth O Light watchman thy light is out   5
O Los unless thou keep my tower the Watchman will be slain

So Enitharmon cried upon her terrible Earthy bed   c
While the broad Oak wreathd his roots round her forcing his dark way
Thro caves of death into Existence The Beech long limbd advancd
Terrific into the paind heavens The fruit trees humanizing   10
Shewd their immortal energies in warlike desperation
Rending the heavens & earths & drinking blood in the hot battle
To feed their fruit to gratify their hidden sons & daughters
That far within the close recesses of their secret palaces
Viewd the vast war & joyd wishing to vegetate   15
Into the Worlds of Enitharmon Loud the roaring winds
Burdend with clouds howl round the Couch sullen the wooly sheep
Walks thro the battle Dark & fierce the Bull his rage
Propagates thro the warring Earth The Lion raging in flames   t
The Tyger in redounding smoke The Serpent of the woods   t 20
And of the waters & the scorpion of the desart irritate

With harsh songs every living soul. The Prester Serpent runs
Along the ranks crying Listen to the Priest of God ye warriors
This Cowl upon my head he placd in times of Everlasting
And said Go forth & guide my battles. like the jointed spine   25
Of Man I made thee when I blotted Man from life & light
Take thou the seven Diseases of Man store them for times to come
In store houses in secret places that I will tell the[e] of
To be my great & awful curses at the time appointed

The Prester Serpent ceasd the War song sounded loud & strong   30
Thro all the heavens Urizens Web vibrated torment on torment   t

PAGE 91 (SECOND PORTION)   c
Thus in the Caverns of the Grave & Places of human seed   t
The nameless shadowy Vortex stood before the face of Orc
The Shadow reard her dismal head over the flaming youth
With sighs & howling & deep sobs that he might lose his rage
And with it lose himself in meekness she embracd his fire   5
As when the Earthquake rouzes from his den his shoulders huge
Appear above the crumb[l]ing Mountain. Silence waits around him
A moment then astounding horror belches from the Center
The fiery dogs arise the shoulders huge appear
So Orc rolld round his clouds upon the deeps of dark Urthona   10
Knowing the arts of Urizen were Pity & Meek affection   t
And that by these arts the Serpent form exuded from his limbs
Silent as despairing love & strong as Jealousy
Jealous that she was Vala now become Urizens harlot   c
And the Harlot of Los & the deluded harlot of the Kings of Earth   15
His soul was gnawn in sunder
The hairy shoulders rend the links free are the wrists of fire
Red rage redounds he rouzd his lions from his forests black
They howl around the flaming youth rending the nameless shadow
And running their immortal course thro solid darkness borne   20

Loud sounds the war song round red Orc in his [*triumphant*] fury   t
And round the nameless shadowy Female in her howling terror
When all the Elemental Gods joind in the wondrous Song

Sound the War trumpet terrific Souls clad in attractive steel
Sound the shrill fife serpents of war. I hear the northern drum   25
Awake, I hear the flappings of the folding banners

The dragons of the North put on their armour
Upon the Eastern sea direct they take their course
The glittring of their horses trapping stains the vault of night

Stop we the rising of the glorious King. spur spur your clouds   t,c 30
PAGE 92
Of death O northern drum awake O hand of iron sound
The northern drum. Now give the charge! bravely obscurd!

–395–

With darts of wintry hail. Again the black bow draw
Again the Elemental Strings to your right breasts draw
And let the thundring drum speed on the arrows black 5

The arrows flew from cloudy bow all day. till blood
From east to west flowd like the human veins in rivers
Of life upon the plains of death & valleys of despair

Now sound the clarions of Victory now strip the slain
clothe yourselves in golden arms brothers of war ᵗ 10
They sound the clarions strong they chain the howling captives
they give the Oath of blood They cast the lots into the helmet, ᵗ'ᵉ
They vote the death of Luvah & they naild him to the tree
They piercd him with a spear & laid him in a sepulcher
To die a death of Six thousand years bound round with desolation 15
The sun was black & the moon rolld a useless globe thro heaven

Then left the Sons of Urizen the plow & harrow the loom
The hammer & the Chisel & the rule & compasses
They forgd the sword the chariot of war the battle ax
The trumpet fitted to the battle & the flute of summer 20
And all the arts of life they changd into the arts of death
The hour glass contemnd because its simple workmanship
Was as the workmanship of the plowman & the water wheel
That raises water into Cisterns broken & burnd in fire
Because its workmanship was like the workmanship of the Shepherd 25
And in their stead intricate wheels invented Wheel without wheel
To perplex youth in their outgoings & to bind to labours
Of day & night the myriads of Eternity. that they might file
And polish brass & iron hour after hour laborious workmanship
Kept ignorant of the use that they might spend the days of wisdom 30
In sorrowful drudgery to obtain a scanty pittance of bread
In ignorance to view a small portion & think that All
And call it Demonstration blind to all the simple rules of life

Now now the Battle rages round thy tender limbs O Vala
Now smile among thy bitter tears now put on all thy beauty 35
Is not the wound of the sword Sweet & the broken bone delightful
Wilt thou now smile among the slain when the wounded groan in the
        field

PAGE 93
Lift up thy blue eyes Vala & put on thy sapphire shoes
O Melancholy Magdalen behold the morning breaks
Gird on thy flaming Zone. descend into the Sepulcher
Scatter the blood from thy golden brow the tears from thy silver locks
Shake off the waters from thy wings & the dust from thy white 5
        garments

Remember all thy feigned terrors on the secret Couch
When the sun rose in glowing morn with arms of mighty hosts
Marching to battle who was wont to rise with Urizens harps
Girt as a Sower with his seed to scatter life abroad

Arise O Vala bring the bow of Urizen bring the swift arrows of light   10
How ragd the golden horses of Urizen bound to the chariot of Love
Compelld to leave the plow to the Ox to snuff up the winds of
    desolation
To trample the corn fields in boastful neighings. this is no gentle harp
This is no warbling brook nor Shadow of a Myrtle tree

But blood & wounds & dismal cries & clarions of war   15
And hearts laid open to the light by the broad grizly sword
And bowels hidden in hammerd steel rippd forth upon the Ground   t
Call forth thy Smiles of soft deceit call forth thy cloudy tears
We hear thy sighs in trumpets shrill when Morn shall blood renew   t

So sung the demons of the deep the Clarions of war blew loud   20
Orc rent her & his human form consumd in his own fires
Mingled with her dolorous members strewn thro the Abyss
She joyd in all the Conflict Gratified & drinking tears of woe   t
No more remaind of Orc but the Serpent round the tree of Mystery   c
The form of Orc was gone he reard his serpent bulk among   25
The stars of Urizen in Power rending the form of life   t
Into a formless indefinite & strewing her on the Abyss
Like clouds upon the winter sky broken with winds & thunders
This was to her Supreme delight The Warriors mournd disappointed
They go out to war with Strong Shouts & loud Clarions O Pity   30
They return with lamentations mourning & weeping

Invisible or visible drawn out in length or stretchd in breadth
The Shadowy Female varied in the War in her delight
Howling in discontent black & heavy uttering brute sounds
Wading thro fens among the slimy weeds making Lamentations   35
To decieve Tharmas in his rage to soothe his furious soul   c
To stay him in his flight that Urizen might live tho in pain
He said Art thou bright Enion is the Shadow of hope returnd

And She said Tharmas I am Vala bless thy innocent face
Doth Enion avoid the sight of thy blue watry eyes   40
Be not perswaded that the air knows this or the falling dew

Tharmas replid O Vala once I livd in a garden of delight
PAGE 94
I wakend Enion in the Morning & she turnd away
Among the apple trees & all the gardens of delight
Swam like a dream before my eyes I went to seek the steps
Of Enion in the gardens & the shadows compassd me
And closd me in a watry world of woe where Enion stood   5

Trembling before me like a shadow like a mist like air
And she is gone & here alone I war with darkness & death
I hear thy voice but not thy form see. thou & all delight
And life appear & vanish mocking me with shadows of false hope
Hast thou forgot that the air listens thro all its districts telling   10
The subtlest thoughts shut up from light in chambers of the Moon

Tharmas. The Moon has chambers where the babes of love lie hid
And whence they never can be brought in all Eternity
Unless exposd by their vain parents. Lo him whom I love
Is hidden from me & I never in all Eternity   15
Shall see him   Enitharmon & Ahania combind with Enion
Hid him in that Outrageous form of Orc which torments me for Sin   t
For all my Secret faults which he brings forth upon the light
Of day in jealousy & blood my Children are led to Urizens war
Before my eyes & for every one of these I am condemnd   20
To Eternal torment in these flames for tho I have the power
To rise on high Yet love here binds me down & never never
Will I arise till him I love is loosd from this dark chain

Tharmas replied Vala thy Sins have lost us heaven & bliss
Thou art our Curse and till I can bring love into the light   25
I never will depart from my great wrath

So Tharmas waild wrathful then rode upon the Stormy Deep   t
Cursing the Voice that mockd him with false hope in furious mood
Then She returns swift as a blight upon the infant bud
Howling in all the notes of woe to stay his furious rage   30
Stamping the hills wading or swimming flying furious or falling
Or like an Earthquake rumbling in the bowels of the earth
Or like a cloud beneath & like a fire flaming in high
Walking in pleasure of the hills or murmuring in the dales
Like to a rushing torrent beneath & a falling rock above   35
A thunder cloud in the south & a lulling voice heard in the north

And she went forth & saw the forms of Life & of delight   c
Walking on Mountains or flying in the open expanse of heaven
She heard sweet voices in the winds & in the voices of birds
That rose from waters for the waters were as the voice of Luvah   40
Not seen to her like waters or like this dark world of death
Tho all those fair perfections which men know only by name
In beautiful substantial forms appeard & served her
As food or drink or ornament or in delightful works
To build her bowers for the Elements brought forth abundantly   45
The living soul in glorious forms & every one came forth
Walking before her Shadowy face & bowing at her feet
But in vain delights were poured forth on the howling melancholy
For her delight the horse his proud neck bowd & his white mane
And the Strong Lion deignd in his mouth to wear the golden bit   50

While the far beaming Peacock waited on the fragrant wind
To bring her fruits of sweet delight from trees of richest wonders
And the strong piniond Eagle bore the fire of heaven in the night
   season
Wood & subdud into Eternal Death the Demon Lay
In rage against the dark despair. the howling Melancholy   t 55

PAGE 95 (FIRST PORTION)

For far & wide she stretchd thro all the worlds of Urizens journey
And was Ajoind to Beulah as the Polypus to the Rock
Mo[u]rning the daughters of Beulah saw nor could they have sustaind
The horrid sight of death & torment   But the Eternal Promise
They wrote on all their tombs & pillars & on every Urn   5
These words   If ye will believe your B[r]other shall rise again
In golden letters ornamented with sweet labours of Love
Waiting with Patience for the fulfilment of the Promise Divine   t

And all the Songs of Beulah sounded comfortable notes
Not suffring doubt to rise up from the Clouds of the Shadowy Female   10
Then myriads of the Dead burst thro the bottoms of their tombs
Descending on the shadowy females clouds in Spectrous terror
Beyond the Limit of Translucence on the Lake of Udan Adan
These they namd Satans & in the Aggregate they namd Them Satan

PAGE 98

End of The Seventh Night [b]

[For PAGES 141, 142, see textual notes]

III

POETICAL SKETCHES.

By W. B.

London: Printed in the Year MDCCLXXXIII.

MISCELLANEOUS POEMS.

TO SPRING.

    O thou, with dewy locks, who lookest down
Thro' the clear windows of the morning; turn
Thine angel eyes upon our western isle,
Which in full choir hails thy approach, O Spring!

    The hills tell each other, and the list'ning   5
Vallies hear; all our longing eyes are turned
Up to thy bright pavillions: issue forth,
And let thy holy feet visit our clime.

    Come o'er the eastern hills, and let our winds
Kiss thy perfumed garments; let us taste   10
Thy morn and evening breath; scatter thy pearls
Upon our love-sick land that mourns for thee.

    O deck her forth with thy fair fingers; pour
Thy soft kisses on her bosom; and put
Thy golden crown upon her languish'd head,   15
Whose modest tresses were bound up for thee!

TO SUMMER.

    O thou, who passest thro' our vallies in
Thy strength, curb thy fierce steeds, allay the heat
That flames from their large nostrils! thou, O Summer,
Oft pitched'st here thy golden tent, and oft
Beneath our oaks hast slept, while we beheld   5
With joy, thy ruddy limbs and flourishing hair.

Beneath our thickest shades we oft have heard
Thy voice, when noon upon his fervid car
Rode o'er the deep of heaven; beside our springs
Sit down, and in our mossy vallies, on   10
Some bank beside a river clear, throw thy
Silk draperies off, and rush into the stream:
Our vallies love the Summer in his pride.

Our bards are fam'd who strike the silver wire:
Our youth[s] are bolder than the southern swains: t 15
Our maidens fairer in the sprightly dance:
We lack not songs, nor instruments of joy,
Nor echoes sweet, nor waters clear as heaven,
Nor laurel wreaths against the sultry heat.

TO AUTUMN   c

O Autumn, laden with fruit, and stained
With the blood of the grape, pass not, but sit
Beneath my shady roof, there thou may'st rest,
And tune thy jolly voice to my fresh pipe;
And all the daughters of the year shall dance!   5
Sing now the lusty song of fruits and flowers.

"The narrow bud opens her beauties to
"The sun, and love runs in her thrilling veins;
"Blossoms hang round the brows of morning, and
"Flourish down the bright cheek of modest eve,   10
"Till clust'ring Summer breaks forth into singing,
"And feather'd clouds strew flowers round her head.

"The spirits of the air live on the smells
"Of fruit; and joy, with pinions light, roves round
"The gardens, or sits singing in the trees."   15
Thus sang the jolly Autumn as he sat,
Then rose, girded himself, and o'er the bleak
Hills fled from our sight; but left his golden load.

TO WINTER.   c

O Winter! bar thine adamantine doors:
The north is thine; there hast thou built thy dark
Deep-founded habitation. Shake not thy roofs,
Nor bend thy pillars with thine iron car.

He hears me not, but o'er the yawning deep   5
Rides heavy; his storms are unchain'd; sheathed
In ribbed steel, I dare not lift mine eyes;
For he hath rear'd his sceptre o'er the world.

Lo! now the direful monster, whose skin clings
To his strong bones, strides o'er the groaning rocks:
He withers all in silence, and his hand
Unclothes the earth, and freezes up frail life.

He takes his seat upon the cliffs, the mariner
Cries in vain. Poor little wretch! that deal'st
With storms; till heaven smiles, and the monster
Is driv'n yelling to his caves beneath mount Hecla.

TO THE
EVENING STAR

Thou fair-hair'd angel of the evening,
Now, while the sun rests on the mountains, light
Thy bright torch of love; thy radiant crown
Put on, and smile upon our evening bed!
Smile on our loves; and, while thou drawest the
Blue curtains of the sky, scatter thy silver dew
On every flower that shuts its sweet eyes
In timely sleep. Let thy west wind sleep on
The lake; speak si[l]ence with thy glimmering eyes,
And wash the dusk with silver. Soon, full soon,
Dost thou withdraw; then the wolf rages wide,
And the lion glares thro' the dun forest:
The fleeces of our flocks are cover'd with
Thy sacred dew: protect them with thine influence.

TO MORNING

O holy virgin! clad in purest white,
Unlock heav'n's golden gates, and issue forth;
Awake the dawn that sleeps in heaven; let light
Rise from the chambers of the east, and bring
The honied dew that cometh on waking day.
O radiant morning, salute the sun,
Rouz'd like a huntsman to the chace; and, with
Thy buskin'd feet, appear upon our hills.

FAIR ELENOR

The bell struck one, and shook the silent tower;
The graves give up their dead: fair Elenor
Walk'd by the castle gate, and looked in.
A hollow groan ran thro' the dreary vaults.

She shriek'd aloud, and sunk upon the steps 5
On the cold stone her pale cheek. Sickly smells t
Of death, issue as from a sepulchre,
And all is silent but the sighing vaults.

Chill death withdraws his hand, and she revives;
Amaz'd, she finds herself upon her feet, 10
And, like a ghost, thro' narrow passages
Walking, feeling the cold walls with her hands.

Fancy returns, and now she thinks of bones,
And grinning skulls, and corruptible death,
Wrap'd in his shroud; and now, fancies she hears 15
Deep sighs, and sees pale sickly ghosts gliding.

At length, no fancy, but reality
Distracts her. A rushing sound, and the feet
Of one that fled, approaches—Ellen stood,
Like a dumb statue, froze to stone with fear. 20

The wretch approaches, crying, "The deed is done;
"Take this, and send it by whom thou wilt send;
"It is my life—send it to Elenor:—
"He's dead, and howling after me for blood!

"Take this," he cry'd; and thrust into her arms 25
A wet napkin, wrap'd about; then rush'd
Past, howling: she receiv'd into her arms
Pale death, and follow'd on the wings of fear.

They pass'd swift thro' the outer gate; the wretch,
Howling, leap'd o'er the wall into the moat, 30
Stifling in mud. Fair Ellen pass'd the bridge,
And heard a gloomy voice cry, "Is it done?"

As the deer wounded Ellen flew over
The pathless plain; as the arrows that fly c
By night; destruction flies, and strikes in darkness, 35
She fled from fear, till at her house arriv'd.

Her maids await her; on her bed she falls,
That bed of joy, where erst her lord hath press'd:
"Ah, woman's fear!" she cry'd; "Ah, cursed duke!
"Ah, my dear lord! ah, wretched Elenor! 40

"My lord was like a flower upon the brows
"Of lusty May! Ah, life as frail as flower!
"O ghastly death! withdraw thy cruel hand,
"Seek'st thou that flow'r to deck thy horrid temples?

"My lord was like a star, in highest heav'n 45
"Drawn down to earth by spells and wickedness:
"My lord was like the opening eyes of day,
"When western winds creep softly o'er the flowers:

"But he is darken'd; like the summer's noon,
"Clouded; fall'n like the stately tree, cut down; 50
"The breath of heaven dwelt among his leaves.
"O Elenor, weak woman, fill'd with woe!"

Thus having spoke, she raised up her head,
And saw the bloody napkin by her side,
Which in her arms she brought; and now, tenfold 55
More terrified, saw it unfold itself.

Her eyes were fix'd; the bloody cloth unfolds,
Disclosing to her sight the murder'd head
Of her dear lord, all ghastly pale, clotted
With gory blood; it groan'd, and thus it spake: 60

"O Elenor, behold thy husband's head,   t
"Who, sleeping on the stones of yonder tower,
"Was 'reft of life by the accursed duke!
"A hired villain turn'd my sleep to death!

"O Elenor, beware the cursed duke, 65
"O give not him thy hand, now I am dead;
"He seeks thy love; who, coward, in the night,
"Hired a villain to bereave my life."

She sat with dead cold limbs, stiffen'd to stone;
She took the gory head up in her arms; 70
She kiss'd the pale lips; she had no tears to shed;
She hugg'd it to her breast, and groan'd her last.

SONG   c

How sweet I roam'd from field to field,
   And tasted all the summer's pride,
'Till I the prince of love beheld,
   Who in the sunny beams did glide!

He shew'd me lilies for my hair,
   And blushing roses for my brow; 5
He led me through his gardens fair,
   Where all his golden pleasures grow.

With sweet May dews my wings were wet,
   And Phoebus fir'd my vocal rage;
He caught me in his silken net, 10
   And shut me in his golden cage.

He loves to sit and hear me sing,
    Then, laughing, sports and plays with me;
Then stretches out my golden wing,   *15*
    And mocks my loss of liberty.

SONG

My silks and fine array,
    My smiles and languish'd air,
By love are driv'n away;
    And mournful lean Despair
Brings me yew to deck my grave: *5*
Such end true lovers have.

His face is fair as heav'n,
    When springing buds unfold;
O why to him was't giv'n,
    Whose heart is wintry cold?   *10*
His breast is love's all worship'd tomb,
Where all love's pilgrims come.

Bring me an axe and spade,
    Bring me a winding sheet;
When I my grave have made,   *15*
    Let winds and tempests beat:
Then down I'll lie, as cold as clay.
True love doth pass away!

SONG

Love and harmony combine,
And around our souls intwine,
While thy branches mix with mine,
And our roots together join.

Joys upon our branches sit,   *5*
Chirping loud, and singing sweet;
Like gentle streams beneath our feet
Innocence and virtue meet.

Thou the golden fruit dost bear,
I am clad in flowers fair;   *10*
Thy sweet boughs perfume the air,
And the turtle buildeth there.

There she sits and feeds her young,
Sweet I hear her mournful song;
And thy lovely leaves among,   *15*
There is love: I hear his tongue.   t

There his charming nest doth lay,
There he sleeps the night away;
There he sports along the day,
And doth among our branches play.   20

SONG

I love the jocund dance,
    The softly-breathing song,
Where innocent eyes do glance,
    And where lisps the maiden's tongue.

I love the laughing vale,   5
    I love the echoing hill,
Where mirth does never fail,
    And the jolly swain laughs his fill.

I love the pleasant cot,
    I love the innocent bow'r.   10
Where white and brown is our lot,
    Or fruit in the mid-day hour.

I love the oaken seat,
    Beneath the oaken tree,
Where all the old villagers meet,   15
    And laugh our sports to see.

I love our neighbours all,
    But, Kitty, I better love thee;
And love them I ever shall;
    But thou art all to me.   20

SONG

Memory, hither come,
    And tune your merry notes;
And, while upon the wind,
    Your music floats,
I'll pore upon the stream,   5
Where sighing lovers dream,
And fish for fancies as they pass
Within the watery glass.

I'll drink of the clear stream,
    And hear the linnet's song;   10
And there I'll lie and dream
    The day along:

And, when night comes, I'll go
  To places fit for woe;
Walking along the darken'd valley,   15
  With silent Melancholy.

MAD SONG

The wild winds weep,
  And the night is a-cold;
Come hither, Sleep,
  And my griefs infold:
But lo! the morning peeps   5
  Over the eastern steeps,
And the rustling birds of dawn
The earth do scorn.

Lo! to the vault
  Of paved heaven,   10
With sorrow fraught
  My notes are driven:
They strike the ear of night,
  Make weep the eyes of day;
They make mad the roaring winds,   15
  And with tempests play.

Like a fiend in a cloud
  With howling woe,
After night I do croud,
  And with night will go;   20
I turn my back to the east,
From whence comforts have increas'd;
For light doth seize my brain
With frantic pain.

SONG

Fresh from the dewy hill, the merry year
Smiles on my head, and mounts his flaming car;
Round my young brows the laurel wreathes a shade,
And rising glories beam around my head.

My feet are wing'd, while o'er the dewy lawn,   5
I meet my maiden, risen like the morn:
Oh bless those holy feet, like angels' feet;
Oh bless those limbs, beaming with heav'nly light!

Like as an angel glitt'ring in the sky,
In times of innocence, and holy joy;   10

The joyful shepherd stops his grateful song,
To hear the music of an angel's tongue.

So when she speaks, the voice of Heaven I hear
So when we walk, nothing impure comes near;
Each field seems Eden, and each calm retreat;   15
Each village seems the haunt of holy feet.

But that sweet village where my black-ey'd maid,
Closes her eyes in sleep beneath night's shade:
Whene'er I enter, more than mortal fire
Burns in my soul, and does my song inspire.   20

SONG

When early morn walks forth in sober grey;
Then to my black ey'd maid I haste away,
When evening sits beneath her dusky bow'r,
And gently sighs away the silent hour;
The village bell alarms, away I go;   5
And the vale darkens at my pensive woe.

To that sweet village, where my black ey'd maid
Doth drop a tear beneath the silent shade,
I turn my eyes; and, pensive as I go,
Curse my black stars, and bless my pleasing woe.   10

Oft when the summer sleeps among the trees,
Whisp'ring faint murmurs to the scanty breeze,
I walk the village round; if at her side
A youth doth walk in stolen joy and pride,
I curse my stars in bitter grief and woe,   15
That made my love so high, and me so low.

O should she e'er prove false, his limbs I'd tear,
And throw all pity on the burning air;
I'd curse bright fortune for my mixed lot,
And then I'd die in peace, and be forgot.   20

TO THE MUSES

Whether on Ida's shady brow,
    Or in the chambers of the East,
The chambers of the sun, that now
    From antient melody have ceas'd;

Whether in Heav'n ye wander fair,   5
    Or the green corners of the earth,
Or the blue regions of the air,
    Where the melodious winds have birth;

Whether on chrystal rocks ye rove,
   Beneath the bosom of the sea
Wand'ring in many a coral grove,
   Fair Nine, forsaking Poetry!   *10*

How have you left the antient love
   That bards of old enjoy'd in you!
The languid strings do scarcely move!   *15*
   The sound is forc'd, the notes are few!

GWIN, KING OF NORWAY   c

Come, Kings, and listen to my song,
   When Gwin, the son of Nore,
Over the nations of the North
   His cruel sceptre bore:

The Nobles of the land did feed   *5*
   Upon the hungry Poor;
They tear the poor man's lamb, and drive
   The needy from their door!

The land is desolate; our wives   t
   And children cry for bread;   *10*
Arise, and pull the tyrant down;
   Let Gwin be humbled.

Gordred the giant rous'd himself
   From sleeping in his cave;
He shook the hills, and in the clouds   *15*
   The troubl'd banners wave.

Beneath them roll'd, like tempests black,
   The num'rous sons of blood;
Like lions' whelps, roaring abroad,
   Seeking their nightly food.   *20*

Down Bleron's hills they dreadful rush,
   Their cry ascends the clouds;
The trampling horse, and clanging arms
   Like rushing mighty floods!

Their wives and children, weeping loud,   *25*
   Follow in wild array,
Howling like ghosts, furious as wolves
   In the bleak wintry day.

"Pull down the tyrant to the dust,
   "Let Gwin be humbled,"   *30*
They cry; "and let ten thousand lives
   "Pay for the tyrant's head."

From tow'r to tow'r the watchmen cry,
  "O Gwin, the son of Nore,
"Arouse thyself! the nations black,   35
  "Like clouds, come rolling o'er!"

Gwin rear'd his shield, his palace shakes,
  His chiefs come rushing round;
Each, like an awful thunder cloud,
  With voice of solemn sound.   40

Like reared stones around a grave
  They stand around the King;
Then suddenly each seiz'd his spear,
  And clashing steel does ring.

The husbandman does leave his plow,   45
  To wade thro' fields of gore;
The merchant binds his brows in steel,
  And leaves the trading shore:

The shepherd leaves his mellow pipe,
  And sounds the trumpet shrill;   50
The workman throws his hammer down
  To heave the bloody bill.

Like the tall ghost of Barraton,
  Who sports in stormy sky,
Gwin leads his host as black as night,   55
  When pestilence does fly.

With horses and with chariots—
  And all his spearmen bold,
March to the sound of mournful song,
  Like clouds around him roll'd.   60

Gwin lifts his hand—the nations halt;
  "Prepare for war," he cries——
Gordred appears!—his frowning brow   t
  Troubles our northern skies.

The armies stand, like balances   65
  Held in th' Almighty's hand;——
"Gwin, thou hast fill'd thy measure up,
  "Thou'rt swept from out the land."

And now the raging armies rush'd,
  Like warring mighty seas;   70
The Heav'ns are shook with roaring war,
  The dust ascends the skies!

Earth smokes with blood, and groans, and shakes,
  To drink her childrens' gore,
A sea of blood; nor can the eye
  See to the trembling shore!   75

And on the verge of this wild sea
  Famine and death doth cry;
The cries of women and of babes.
  Over the field doth fly.   80

The King is seen raging afar;
  With all his men of might;
Like blazing comets, scattering death
  Thro' the red fev'rous night.

Beneath his arm like sheep they die,   85
  And groan upon the plain;
The battle faints, and bloody men
  Fight upon hills of slain.

Now death is sick, and riven men
  Labour and toil for life;   90
Steed rolls on steed, and shield on shield,
  Sunk in this sea of strife!

The god of war is drunk with blood,
  The earth doth faint and fail;
The stench of blood makes sick the heav'ns;   95
  Ghosts glut the throat of hell!

O what have Kings to answer for,
  Before that awful throne!
When thousand deaths for vengeance cry,
  And ghosts accusing groan!   100

Like blazing comets in the sky,
  That shake the stars of light,
Which drop like fruit unto the earth,
  Thro' the fierce burning night;

Like these did Gwin and Gordred meet,   105
  And the first blow decides;
Down from the brow unto the breast
  Gordred his head divides!

Gwin fell; the Sons of Norway fled,
  All that remain'd alive;   110
The rest did fill the vale of death,
  For them the eagles strive.

The river Dorman roll'd their blood
  Into the northern sea;
Who mourn'd his sons, and overwhelm'd   *115*
  The pleasant south country.

AN

IMITATION of SPEN[S]ER.   t,c

Golden Apollo, that thro' heaven wide
  Scatter'st the rays of light, and truth's beams!
In lucent words my darkling verses dight,
  And wash my earthy mind in thy clear streams,
  That wisdom may descend in fairy dreams: *5*
All while the jocund hours in thy train
Scatter their fancies at thy poet's feet;
  And when thou yields to night thy wide domain,
Let rays of truth enlight his sleeping brain.

For brutish Pan in vain might thee assay   *10*
  With tinkling sounds to dash thy nervous verse,
Sound without sense; yet in his rude affray,
  (For ignorance is Folly's leesing nurse,   t
  And love of Folly needs none other curse;)   t
Midas the praise hath gain'd of lengthen'd eares,   *t 15*
  For which himself might deem him ne'er the worse
  To sit in council with his modern peers,
And judge of tinkling rhimes, and elegances terse.

And thou, Mercurius, that with winged brow
  Dost mount aloft into the yielding sky,   *20*
And thro' Heav'n's halls thy airy flight dost throw,
Entering with holy feet to where on high
Jove weighs the counsel of futurity;
  Then, laden with eternal fate, dost go
Down, like a falling star, from autumn sky,   *25*
And o'er the surface of the silent deep dost fly.

  If thou arrivest at the sandy shore,
Where nought but envious hissing adders dwell,
  Thy golden rod, thrown on the dusty floor,
Can charm to harmony with potent spell;   *30*
Such is sweet Eloquence, that does dispel
  Envy and Hate, that thirst for human gore:
And cause in sweet society to dwell
Vile savage minds that lurk in lonely cell.

  O Mercury, assist my lab'ring sense,   *35*
That round the circle of the world wou'd fly!

As the wing'd eagle scorns the tow'ry fence
Of Alpine hills round his high aery,
And searches thro' the corners of the sky,
  Sports in the clouds to hear the thunder's sound,   40
And see the winged lightnings as they fly,   t
  Then, bosom'd in an amber cloud, around
Plumes his wide wings, and seeks Sol's palace high.

  And thou, O warrior maid, invincible,   t
Arm'd with the terrors of Almighty Jove!   45
  Pallas, Minerva, maiden terrible,
Lov'st thou to walk the peaceful solemn grove,
  In solemn gloom of branches interwove?
Or bear'st thy Egis o'er the burning field,
  Where, like the sea, the waves of battle move?   50
Or have thy soft piteous eyes beheld
  The weary wanderer thro' the desert rove?
Or does th' afflicted man thy heav'nly bosom move?

BLIND-MAN'S BUFF

When silver Snow decks Susan's cloaths,
And jewel hangs at th' shepherd's nose,
The blushing bank is all my care,
With hearth so red, and walls so fair;
"Heap the sea-coal; come, heap it higher,   5
"The oaken log lay on the fire:"
The well-wash'd stools, a circling row,
With lad and lass, how fair the show!
The merry can of nut-brown ale,
The laughing jest, the love-sick tale,   10
'Till tir'd of chat, the game begins,
The lasses prick the lads with pins;
Roger from Dolly twitch'd the stool,
She falling, kiss'd the ground, poor fool!
She blush'd so red, with side-long glance   15
At hob-nail Dick, who griev'd the chance.
But now for Blind-man's Buff they call;
Of each incumbrance clear the hall—
Jenny her silken 'kerchief folds,
And blear-ey'd Will the black lot holds;   20
Now laughing, stops, with "Silence! hush!"
And Peggy Pout gives Sam a push.——
The Blind-man's arms, extended wide,
Sam slips between;—"O woe betide
Thee, clumsy Will!"—but titt'ring Kate   25
Is pen'd up in the corner strait!

And now Will's eyes beheld the play,
He thought his face was t'other way.——
"Now, Kitty, now; what chance hast thou,
"Roger so near thee, Trips; I vow!["]   30
She catches him—then Roger ties
His own head up—but not his eyes;
For thro' the slender cloth he sees,
And runs at Sam, who slips with ease
His clumsy hold; and, dodging round,   35
Sukey is tumbled on the ground!——
"See what it is to play unfair!
"Where cheating is, there's mischief there."
But Roger still pursues the chace,—
"He sees! he sees! cries softly Grace;   40
"O Roger, thou, unskill'd in art,
"Must, surer bound, go thro' thy part!"
Now Kitty, pert, repeats the rhymes,
And Roger turns him round three times;
Then pauses ere he starts——but Dick   45
Was mischief bent upon a trick:
Down on his hands and knees he lay,
Directly in the Blind-man's way—
Then cries out, "Hem!" Hodge heard, and ran
With hood-wink'd chance—sure of his man;   50
But down he came.—Alas, how frail
Our best of hopes, how soon they fail!
With crimson drops he stains the ground,
Confusion startles all around!
Poor piteous Dick supports his head,   55
And fain would cure the hurt he made;
But Kitty hasted with a key,
And down his back they strait convey
The cold relief—the blood is stay'd,
And Hodge again holds up his head.   60
Such are the fortunes of the game,
And those who play should stop the same
By wholesome laws; such as[—]all those
Who on the blinded man impose,   t
Stand in his stead; as long a-gone   65
When men were first a nation grown;
Lawless they liv'd—till wantonness
And liberty began t' increase;
And one man lay in another's way,
Then laws were made to keep fair play.   70

❧

KING EDWARD THE THIRD.   c

PERSONS.

King Edward.   Lord Audley.
The Black Prince.   Lord Percy.
Queen Philippa.   Bishop.
Duke of Clarence.   William, Dagworth's
Sir John Chandos.   Man.
Sir Thomas Dagworth.   Peter Blunt, a common
Sir Walter Manny.   Soldier.

SCENE [1], *The Coast of France, King Edward and Nobles.*   t
The Army.

King.

O thou, to whose fury the nations are
But as dust! maintain thy servant's right.
Without thine aid, the twisted mail, and spear,
And forged helm, and shield of seven times beaten brass,
Are idle trophies of the vanquisher.   5
When confusion rages, when the field is in a flame,
When the cries of blood tear horror from heav'n,
And yelling death runs up and down the ranks,
Let Liberty, the charter'd right of Englishmen,
Won by our fathers in many a glorious field,   10
Enerve my soldiers; let Liberty
Blaze in each countenance, and fire the battle.
The enemy fight in chains, invisible chains, but heavy;
Their minds are fetter'd; then how can they be free,
While, like the mounting flame,   15
We spring to battle o'er the floods of death?
And these fair youths, the flow'r of England,
Vent'ring their lives in my most righteous cause,
O sheathe their hearts with triple steel, that they
May emulate their fathers' virtues.   20
And thou, my son, be strong; thou fightest for a crown
That death can never ravish from thy brow,
A crown of glory: but from thy very dust
Shall beam a radiance, to fire the breasts
Of youth unborn! Our names are written equal   25
In fame's wide trophied hall; 'tis ours to gild
The letters, and to make them shine with gold
That never tarnishes: whether Third Edward,
Or the Prince of Wales, or Montacute, or Mortimer,

Or ev'n the least by birth, shall gain the brightest fame,   30
Is in his hand to whom all men are equal.
The world of men are like the num'rous stars,
That beam and twinkle in the depth of night,
Each clad in glory according to his sphere;—
But we, that wander from our native seats,   35
And beam forth lustre on a darkling world,
Grow larger as we advance! and some perhaps
The most obscure at home, that scarce were seen
To twinkle in their sphere, may so advance,
That the astonish'd world, with up-turn'd eyes,   40
Regardless of the moon, and those that once were bright,
Stand only for to gaze upon their splendor!

> [*He here knights the Prince, and other young Nobles.*

Now let us take a just revenge for those
Brave Lords, who fell beneath the bloody axe
At Paris. Thanks, noble Harcourt, for 'twas   45
By your advice we landed here in Brittany—
A country not yet sown with destruction,
And where the fiery whirlwind of swift war
Has not yet swept its desolating wing.——
Into three parties we divide by day,   50
And separate march, but join again at night:
Each knows his rank, and Heav'n marshal all. [*Exeunt.*

SCENE [2], *English Court; Lionel, Duke of Clarence;*
Queen Philippa, Lords, Bishop, &c.

Clarence.

My Lords, I have, by the advice of her
Whom I am doubly bound to obey, my Parent
And my Sovereign, call'd you together.
My task is great, my burden heavier than
My unfledg'd years;   5
Yet, with your kind assistance, Lords, I hope
England shall dwell in peace; that while my father
Toils in his wars, and turns his eyes on this
His native shore, and sees commerce fly round
With his white wings, and sees his golden London,   10
And her silver Thames, throng'd with shining spires
And corded ships; her merchants buzzing round
Like summer bees, and all the golden cities
In his land, overflowing with honey,
Glory may not be dimm'd with clouds of care.   15
Say, Lords, should not our thoughts be first to commerce?

My Lord Bishop, you would recommend us agriculture?

Bishop. Sweet Prince! the arts of peace are great,
And no less glorious than those of war,
Perhaps more glorious in the ph[i]losophic mind.   20
When I sit at my home, a private man,
My thoughts are on my gardens, and my fields,
How to employ the hand that lacketh bread.
If Industry is in my diocese,
Religion will flourish; each man's heart   25
Is cultivated, and will bring forth fruit:
This is my private duty and my pleasure.
But as I sit in council with my prince,
My thoughts take in the gen'ral good of the whole,
And England is the land favour'd by Commerce;   30
For Commerce, tho' the child of Agriculture,
Fosters his parent, who else must sweat and toil,
And gain but scanty fare. Then, my dear Lord,
Be England's trade our care; and we, as tradesmen,
Looking to the gain of this our native land.   35

Clar. O my good Lord, true wisdom drops like honey
From your tongue, as from a worship'd oak!
Forgive, my Lords, my talkative youth, that speaks
Not merely what my narrow observation has
Pick'd up, but what I have concluded from your lessons: 40
Now, by the Queen's advice, I ask your leave
To dine to-morrow with the Mayor of London:
If I obtain your leave, I have another boon
To ask, which is, the favour of your company;
I fear Lord Percy will not give me leave.   45

Percy. Dear Sir, a prince should always keep his state,
And grant his favours with a sparing hand,
Or they are never rightly valued.
These are my thoughts, yet it were best to go;
But keep a proper dignity, for now   50
You represent the sacred person of
Your father; 'tis with princes as 'tis with the sun,
If not sometimes o'er-clouded, we grow weary
Of his officious glory.

Clar. Then you will give me leave to shine sometimes,   55
My Lord?

Lord. Thou hast a gallant spirit, which I fear
Will be imposed on by the closer sort! [*Aside.*

Clar. Well, I'll endeavour to take
Lord Percy's advice; I have been used so much   60
To dignity, that I'm sick on't.

Queen Phil. Fie, Fie, Lord Clarence; you proceed not to business,
But speak of your own pleasures.

I hope their Lordships will excuse your giddiness.

Clar. My Lords, the French have fitted out many 65
Small ships of war, that, like to ravening wolves,
Infest our English seas, devouring all
Our burden'd vessels, spoiling our naval flocks.
The merchants do complain, and beg our aid.

Percy. The merchants are rich enough; 70
Can they not help themselves?

Bish. They can, and may; but how to gain their will,
Requires our countenance and help.

Percy. When that they find they must, my Lord, they will:
Let them but suffer awhile, and you shall see 75
They will bestir themselves.

Bish. Lord Percy cannot mean that we should suffer
This disgrace; if so, we are not sovereigns
Of the sea; our right, that Heaven gave
To England, when at the birth of nature 80
She was seated in the deep, the Ocean ceas'd
His mighty roar; and, fawning, play'd around
Her snowy feet, and own'd his awful Queen.
Lord Percy, if the heart is sick, the head
Must be aggriev'd; if but one member suffer, 85
The heart doth fail. You say, my Lord, the merchants
Can, if they will, defend themselves against
These rovers: this is a noble scheme,
Worthy the brave Lord Percy, and as worthy
His generous aid to put it into practice. 90

Percy. Lord Bishop, what was rash in me, is wise
In you; I dare not own the plan. 'Tis not
Mine. Yet will I, if you please,
Quickly to the Lord Mayor, and work him onward
To this most glorious voyage, on which cast 95
I'll set my whole estate.
But we will bring these Gallic rovers under.

Queen Phil. Thanks, brave Lord Percy; you have the thanks
Of England's Queen, and will, ere long, of England. [*Exeunt.*

SCENE [3], *At Cressey. Sir Thomas Dagworth and Lord Audley, meeting.*

Aud. Good morrow, brave Sir Thomas; the bright morn
Smiles on our army, and the gallant sun
Springs from the hills like a young hero
Into the battle, shaking his golden locks
Exultingly; this is a promising day. 5

Dagw. Why, my Lord Audley, I don't know.

Give me your hand, and now I'll tell you what
I think you do not know—Edward's afraid of Philip.

    Aud. Ha, Ha, Sir Thomas! you but joke;
Did you eer see him fear? At Blanchetaque,   **t** 10
When almost singly he drove six thousand
French from the ford, did he fear then?

    Dagw. Yes, fear; that made him fight so.

    Aud By the same reason I might say, 'tis fear
That makes you fight.   15

    Dagw. Mayhap you may; look upon Edward's face—
No one can say he fears. But when he turns
His back, then I will say it to his face,
He is afraid; he makes us all afraid.
I cannot bear the enemy at my back.   20
Now here we are at Cressy; where, to-morrow,
To-morrow we shall know. I say, Lord Audley,
That Edward runs away from Philip.

    Aud. Perhaps you think the Prince too is afraid?

    Dagw. No; God forbid! I'm sure he is not—   25
He is a young lion. O I have seen him fight,
And give command, and lightning has flashed
From his eyes across the field; I have seen him
Shake hands with death, and strike a bargain for
The enemy; he has danc'd in the field   30
Of battle, like the youth at morrice play.
I'm sure he's not afraid, nor Warwick, nor none,
None of us but me; and I am very much afraid.

    Aud. Are you afraid too, Sir Thomas?
I believe that as much as I believe   35
The King's afraid; but what are you afraid of?

    Dagw. Of having my back laid open; we turn
Our backs to the fire, till we shall burn our skirts.

    Aud. And this, Sir Thomas, you call fear? Your fear
Is of a different kind then from the King's;   40
He fears to turn his face, and you to turn your back.—
I do not think, Sir Thomas, you know what fear is.

    Enter Sir John Chandos.

    Chand. Good morrow, Generals; I give you joy:
Welcome to the fields of Cressy. Here we stop,
And wait for Philip.   45

    Dagw. I hope so.

    Aud. There, Sir Thomas; do you call that fear?

    Dagw. I don't know; perhaps he takes it by fits.
Why, noble Chandos, look you here—
One rotten sheep spoils the whole flock;   50
And if the bell-weather is tainted, I wish

The Prince may not catch the distemper too.
    Chand. Distemper, Sir Thomas! what distemper?
I have not heard.
    Dagw. Why, Chandos, you are a wise man,   55
I know you understand me; a distemper
The King caught here in France of running away.
    Aud. Sir Thomas, you say, you have caught it too.
    Dag. And so will the whole army; 'tis very catching,
For when the coward runs, the brave man totters.   60
Perhaps the air of the country is the cause.—
I feel it coming upon me, so I strive against it;
You yet are whole, but after a few more
Retreats, we all shall know how to retreat
Better than fight.—To be plain, I think retreating   65
Too often, takes away a soldier's courage.
    Chand. Here comes the King himself; tell him your thoughts
Plainly, Sir Thomas.
    Dagw. I've told him before, but his disorder
Makes him deaf.   70

Enter King Edward and Black Prince.

    King. Good morrow, Generals; when English courage fails,
Down goes our right to France;
But we are conquerors every where; nothing
Can stand our soldiers; each man is worthy
Of a triumph. Such an army of heroes   75
Ne'er shouted to the Heav'ns, nor shook the field.
Edward, my son, thou art
Most happy, having such command; the man
Were base who were not fir'd to deeds
Above heroic, having such examples.   80
    Prince. Sire! with respect and deference I look
Upon such noble souls, and wish myself
Worthy the high command that Heaven and you
Have given me. When I have seen the field glow,
And in each countenance the soul of war   85
Curb'd by the manliest reason, I have been wing'd
With certain victory; and 'tis my boast,
And shall be still my glory. I was inspir'd
By these brave troops.
    Dagw. Your Grace had better make   90
Them all Generals.
    King. Sir Thomas Dagworth, you must have your joke,
And shall, while you can fight as you did at
The Ford.
    Dagw. I have a small petition to your Majesty.   95

King. What can Sir Thomas Dagworth ask, that Edward
Can refuse?

Dagw. I hope your Majesty cannot refuse so great
A trifle; I've gilt your cause with my best blood,
And would again, were I not forbid   100
By him whom I am bound to obey: my hands
Are tied up, my courage shrunk and wither'd,
My sinews slacken'd, and my voice scarce heard;
Therefore I beg I may return to England.

King. I know not what you could have ask'd, Sir Thomas,   105
That I would not have sooner parted with
Than such a soldier as you have been, and such a friend;
Nay, I will know the most remote particulars
Of this your strange petition; that, if I can,
I still may keep you here.   110

Dagw. Here on the fields of Cressy we are settled,
'Till Philip springs the tim'rous covey again.
The Wolf is hunted down by causeless fear;
The Lion flees, and fear usurps his heart;
Startled, astonish'd at the clam'rous Cock;   115
The Eagle, that doth gaze upon the sun,
Fears the small fire that plays about the fen;
If, at this moment of their idle fear,
The Dog doth seize the Wolf, the Forester the Lion,
The Negro in the crevice of the rock,   120
Doth seize the soaring Eagle; undone by flight,
They tame submit: such the effect flight has
On noble souls. Now hear its opposite:
The tim'rous Stag starts from the thicket wild,
The fearful Crane springs from the splashy fen,   125
The shining Snake glides o'er the bending grass,
The Stag turns head! and bays the crying Hounds;
The Crane o'ertaken, sigheth with the Hawk;
The Snake doth turn, and bite the padding foot;
And, if your Majesty's afraid of Philip,   130
You are more like a Lion than a Crane:
Therefore I beg I may return to England.

King. Sir Thomas, now I understand your mirth,
Which often plays with Wisdom for its pastime,
And brings good counsel from the breast of laughter,   135
I hope you'll stay, and see us fight this battle,
And reap rich harvest in the fields of Cressy;
Then go to England, tell them how we fight,
And set all hearts on fire to be with us.
Philip is plum'd, and thinks we flee from him,   140
Else he would never dare to attack us. Now,
Now the quarry's set! and Death doth sport

In the bright sunshine of this fatal day.
   Dagw. Now my heart dances, and I am as light
As the young bridegroom going to be married.   *145*
Now must I to my soldiers, get them ready,
Furbish our armours bright, new plume our helms,
And we will sing, like the young housewives busied
In the dairy; my feet are wing'd, but not
For flight, an please your grace.   *150*
   King. If all my soldiers are as pleas'd as you,
'Twill be a gallant thing to fight or die;
Then I can never be afraid of Philip.
   Dagw. A raw-bon'd fellow t'other day pass'd by me;
I told him to put off his hungry looks—   *155*
He answer'd me, "I hunger for another battle."
I saw a little Welchman with a fiery face;
I told him he look'd like a candle half
Burn'd out; he answer'd, he was "pig enough
"To light another pattle." Last night, beneath   *160*
The moon I walk'd abroad, when all had pitch'd
Their tents, and all were still,
I heard a blooming youth singing a song
He had compos'd, and at each pause he wip'd
His dropping eyes. The ditty was, "if he   *165*
"Return'd victorious, he should wed a maiden
"Fairer than snow, and rich as midsummer."
Another wept, and wish'd health to his father.
I chid them both, but gave them noble hopes.
These are the minds that glory in the battle,   *170*
And leap and dance to hear the trumpet sound.
   King. Sir Thomas Dagworth, be thou near our person;
Thy heart is richer than the vales of France:
I will not part with such a man as thee.
If Philip came arm'd in the ribs of death,   *175*
And shook his mortal dart against my head,
Thoud'st laugh his fury into nerveless shame!
Go now, for thou art suited to the work,
Throughout the camp; enflame the timorous,
Blow up the sluggish into ardour, and   *180*
Confirm the strong with strength, the weak inspire,
And wing their brows with hope and expectation:
Then to our tent return, and meet to council. [*Exit Dagworth.*
   Chand. That man's a hero in his closet, and more
A hero to the servants of his house   *185*
Than to the gaping world; he carries windows
In that enlarged breast of his, that all
May see what's done within.
   Prince. He is a genuine Englishman, my Chandos,

And hath the spirit of Liberty within him.   *190*
Forgive my prejudice, Sir John; I think
My Englishmen the bravest people on
The face of the earth.
    Chand. Courage, my Lord, proceeds from self-dependence;
Teach man to think he's a free agent,   *195*
Give but a slave his liberty, he'll shake
Off sloth, and build himself a hut, and hedge
A spot of ground; this he'll defend; 'tis his
By right of nature: thus set in action,
He will still move onward to plan conveniences,   *200*
'Till glory fires his breast to enlarge his castle,
While the poor slave drudges all day, in hope
To rest at night.
    King. O Liberty, how glorious art thou!
I see thee hov'ring o'er my army, with   *205*
Thy wide-stretch'd plumes; I see thee
Lead them on to battle;
I see thee blow thy golden trumpet, while
Thy sons shout the strong shout of victory!
O noble Chandos! think thyself a gardener,   *210*
My son a vine, which I commit unto
Thy care; prune all extravagant shoots, and guide
Th' ambitious tendrils in the paths of wisdom;
Water him with thy advice, and Heav'n
Rain fresh'ning dew upon his branches. And,   *215*
O Edward, my dear son! learn to think lowly of
Thyself, as we may all each prefer other—
'Tis the best policy, and 'tis our duty. [*Exit King Edward.*   t
    Prince. And may our duty, Chandos, be our pleasure—
Now we are alone, Sir John, I will unburden,   *220*
And breathe my hopes into the burning air,
Where thousand deaths are posting up and down,
Commission'd to this fatal field of Cressy;
Methinks I see them arm my gallant soldiers,
And gird the sword upon each thigh, and fit   *225*
Each shining helm, and string each stubborn bow,
And dance to the neighing of our steeds.
Methinks the shout begins, the battle burns;
Methinks I see them perch on English crests,
And roar the wild flame of fierce war, upon   *230*
The thronged enemy! In truth, I am too full;
It is my sin to love the noise of war.
Chandos, thou seest my weakness; strong nature
Will bend or break us; my blood, like a springtide,
Does rise so high, to overflow all bounds   *235*
Of moderation; while Reason, in his   t

Frail bark, can see no shore or bound for vast
Ambition. Come, take the helm, my Chandos,
That my full-blown sails overset me not
In the wild tempest; condemn my 'ventrous youth,   240
That plays with danger, as the innocent child,
Unthinking, plays upon the viper's den:
I am a coward, in my reason, Chandos.

    Chand. You are a man, my prince, and a brave man,
If I can judge of actions; but your heat   245
Is the effect of youth, and want of use;
Use makes the armed field and noisy war
Pass over as a summer cloud, unregarded,
Or but expected as a thing of course.
Age is contemplative; each rolling year   250
Brings forth fruit to the mind's treasure-house;
While vacant youth doth crave and seek about
Within itself, and findeth discontent:
Then, tir'd of thought, impatient takes the wing,
Seizes the fruits of time, attacks experience,   255
Roams round vast Nature's forest, where no bounds
Are set, the swiftest may have room, the strongest
Find prey; till tir'd at length, sated and tired
With the changing sameness, old variety,
We sit us down, and view our former joys   260
With distaste and dislike.

    Prince. Then if we must tug for experience,
Let us not fear to beat round Nature's wilds,
And rouze the strongest prey; then if we fall,
We fall with glory; I know the wolf   265
Is dangerous to fight, not good for food,
Nor is the hide a comely vestment; so
We have our battle for our pains. I know
That youth has need of age to point fit prey,
And oft the stander-by shall steal the fruit   270
Of th' other's labour. This is philosophy;
These are the tricks of the world; but the pure soul
Shall mount on native wings, disdaining
Little sport, and cut a path into the heaven of glory,
Leaving a track of light for men to wonder at.   275
I'm glad my father does not hear me talk;
You can find friendly excuses for me, Chandos;
But do you not think, Sir John, that if it please
Th' Almighty to stretch out my span of life,
I shall with pleasure view a glorious action,   280
Which my youth master'd.

    Chand. Considerate age, my Lord, views motives,

And not acts; when neither warbling voice,
Nor trilling pipe is heard, nor pleasure sits
With trembling age; the voice of Conscience then,   285
Sweeter than music in a summer's eve,
Shall warble round the snowy head, and keep
Sweet symphony to feather'd angels, sitting
As guardians round your chair; then shall the pulse
Beat slow, and taste, and touch, and sight, and sound, and smell,   290
That sing and dance round Reason's fine-wrought throne,
Shall flee away, and leave him all forlorn;   t
Yet not forlorn if Conscience is his friend. [*Exeunt.*

SCENE [4] *in Sir Thomas Dagworth's Tent. Dag-*
worth and William his Man.

Dagw. Bring hither my armour, William;
Ambition is the growth of ev'ry clime.
Will. Does it grow in England, Sir?
Dagw. Aye, it grows most in lands most cultivated.
Will. Then it grows most in France; the vines here   5
Are finer than any we have in England.
Dagw. Aye, but the oaks are not.
Will. What is the tree you mentioned? I don't think
I ever saw it.
Dagw. Ambition.   10
Will. Is it a little creeping root that grows in ditches?
Dagw. Thou dost not understand me, William.
It is a root that grows in every breast;
Ambition is the desire or passion that one man
Has to get before another, in any pursuit after glory;   15
But I don't think you have any of it.
Will. Yes, I have; I have a great ambition to know every thing, Sir.
Dagw. But when our first ideas are wrong, what follows must all be
wrong of course; 'tis best to know a little, and to know that little
aright.   20
Will. Then, Sir, I should be glad to know if it was not ambition that
brought over our King to France to fight for his right?
Dagw. Tho' the knowledge of that will not profit thee much, yet I
will tell you that it was ambition.
Will. Then if ambition is a sin, we are all guilty in coming with   25
him, and in fighting for him.
Dagw. Now, William, thou dost thrust the question home; but I
must tell you, that guilt being an act of the mind, none are guilty
but those whose minds are prompted by that same ambition.
Will. Now I always thought, that a man might be guilty of doing   30
wrong, without knowing it was wrong.

-425-

Dagw. Thou art a natural philosopher, and knowest truth by instinct; while reason runs aground, as we have run our argument. Only
remember, William, all have it in their power to know the motives of
their own actions, and 'tis a sin to act without some reason.   35

Will. And whoever acts without reason, may do a great deal of harm
without knowing it.

Dagw. Thou art an endless moralist.

Will. Now there's a story come into my head, that I will tell your
honour, if you'll give me leave.   40

Dagw. No, William, save it till another time; this is no time for story-
telling; but here comes one who is as entertaining as a good story.

Enter Peter Blunt.

Peter. Yonder's a musician going to play before the King; it's a new
song about the French and English, and the Prince has made the   ᵗ45
minstrel a 'squire, and given him I don't know what, and I can't tell
whether he don't mention us all one by one; and he is to write another
about all us that are to die, that we may be remembered in Old En-   ᵗ
gland, for all our blood and bones are in France; and a great deal more
that we shall all hear by and by; and I came to tell your honour, be-   50
cause you love to hear war-songs.

Dagw. And who is this minstrel, Peter, do'st know?

Peter. O aye, I forgot to tell that; he has got the same name as Sir
John Chandos, that the prince is always with—the wise man, that
knows us all as well as your honour, only e'nt so good natur'd.   55

Dagw. I thank you, Peter, for your information, but not for your
compliment, which is not true; there's as much difference between him
and me, as between glittering sand and fruitful mold; or shining glass
and a wrought diamond, set in rich gold, and fitted to the finger of an
emperor: such is that worthy Chandos.   60

Peter. I know your honour does not think any thing of yourself, but
every body else does.

Dagw. Go, Peter, get you gone; flattery is delicious, even from the
lips of a babbler. [*Exit Peter.*

Will. I never flatter your honour.   65

Dagw. I don't know that.

Will. Why you know, Sir, when we were in England, at the tour-
nament at Windsor, and the Earl of Warwick was tumbled over, you
ask'd me if he did not look well when he fell? and I said, No, he look'd
very foolish; and you was very angry with me for not flattering you.   70

Dagw. You mean that I was angry with you for not flattering the
Earl of Warwick. [*Exeunt.*

SCENE [5], *Sir Thomas Dagworth's Tent. Sir Thomas Dagworth—to him.*

Enter Sir Walter Manny.

Sir Walter. Sir Thomas Dagworth, I have been weeping
Over the men that are to die to-day.
  Dagw. Why, brave Sir Walter, you or I may fall.
  Sir Walter. I know this breathing flesh must lie and rot,
Cover'd with silence and forgetfulness.—   5
Death wons in cities' smoke, and in still night,
When men sleep in their beds, walketh about!
How many in walled cities lie and groan,
Turning themselves upon their beds,
Talking with death, answering his hard demands!   10
How many walk in darkness, terrors are round
The curtains of their beds, destruction is
Ready at the door! How many sleep
In earth, cover'd with stones and deathy dust,
Resting in quietness, whose spirits walk   15
Upon the clouds of heaven, to die no more!
Yet death is terrible, tho' borne on angels' wings!
How terrible then is the field of death,
Where he doth rend the vault of heaven,
And shake the gates of hell!   20
O Dagworth, France is sick! the very sky,
Tho' sunshine light it, seems to me as pale
As the pale fainting man on his death-bed,
Whose face is shewn by light of sickly taper!
It makes me sad and sick at very heart,   25
Thousands must fall to-day!
  Dagw. Thousands of souls must leave this prison house,
To be exalted to those heavenly fields,
Where songs of triumph, palms of victory,
Where peace, and joy, and love, and calm content,   30
Sit singing in the azure clouds, and strew
Flowers of heaven's growth over the banquet-table:
Bind ardent Hope upon your feet like shoes,
Put on the robe of preparation,
The table is prepar'd in shining heaven,   35
The flowers of immortality are blown;
Let those that fight, fight in good stedfastness,
And those that fall shall rise in victory.
  Sir Walter. I've often seen the burning field of war,
And often heard the dismal clang of arms;   40
But never, till this fatal day of Cressy,

Has my soul fainted with these views of death!
I seem to be in one great charnel-house,
And seem to scent the rotten carcases!
I seem to hear the dismal yells of death,   45
While the black gore drops from his horrid jaws:
Yet I not fear the monster in his pride.——
But O the souls that are to die to-day!

   Dagw. Stop, brave Sir Walter; let me drop a tear,
Then let the clarion of war begin;   50
I'll fight and weep, 'tis in my country's cause;
I'll weep and shout for glorious liberty.
Grim war shall laugh and shout, decked in tears,
And blood shall flow like streams across the meadows,
That murmur down their pebbly channels, and   55
Spend their sweet lives to do their country service:
Then shall England's verdure shoot, her fields shall smile,
Her ships shall sing across the foaming sea,
Her mariners shall use the flute and viol,
And rattling guns, and black and dreary war,   60
Shall be no more.

   Sir Walter. Well; let the trumpet sound, and the drum beat;
Let war stain the blue heavens with bloody banners,
I'll draw my sword, nor ever sheath it up,
'Till England blow the trump of victory,   65
Or I lay stretch'd upon the field of death!

                          Exeunt.

SCENE [6], *in the Camp. Several of the Warriors
met at the King's Tent with a Minstrel, who sings
the following Song:*

O sons of Trojan Brutus, cloath'd in war,
Whose voices are the thunder of the field,
Rolling dark clouds o'er France, muffling the sun
In sickly darkness like a dim eclipse,
Threatening as the red brow of storms, as fire   5
Burning up nations in your wrath and fury!

Your ancestors came from the fires of Troy,
(Like lions rouz'd by light'ning from their dens,
Whose eyes do glare against the stormy fires)
Heated with war, fill'd with the blood of Greeks,   10
With helmets hewn, and shields covered with gore,
In navies black, broken with wind and tide!

They landed in firm array upon the rocks
Of Albion; they kiss'd the rocky shore;

"Be thou our mother, and our nurse," they said;   15
"Our children's mother, and thou shalt be our grave;
"The sepulchre of ancient Troy, from whence
"Shall rise cities, and thrones, and arms, and awful pow'rs.

Our fathers swarm from the ships. Giant voices
Are heard from the hills, the enormous sons   20
Of Ocean run from rocks and caves: wild men,
Naked and roaring like lions, hurling rocks,
And wielding knotty clubs, like oaks entangled
Thick as a forest, ready for the axe.

Our fathers move in firm array to battle,   25
The savage monsters rush like roaring fire;
Like as a forest roars with crackling flames,
When the red lightning, borne by furious storms,
Lights on some woody shore; the parched heavens
Rain fire into the molten raging sea!   30

The smoaking trees are strewn upon the shore,
Spoil'd of their verdure! O how oft have they
Defy'd the storm that howled o'er their heads!
Our fathers, sweating, lean on their spears, and view
The mighty dead: giant bodies, streaming blood,   35
Dread visages, frowning in silent death!

Then Brutus spoke, inspir'd; our fathers sit
Attentive on the melancholy shore:——
Hear ye the voice of Brutus—"The flowing waves
"Of time come rolling o'er my breast," he said;   40
"And my heart labours with futurity:
"Our sons shall rule the empire of the sea.

"Their mighty wings shall stretch from east to west,
"Their nest is in the sea; but they shall roam
"Like eagles for the prey; nor shall the young   45
"Crave or be heard; for plenty shall bring forth,
"Cities shall sing, and vales in rich array
"Shall laugh, whose fruitful laps bend down with fulness.

"Our sons shall rise from thrones in joy,
"Each one buckling on his armour; Morning   50
"Shall be prevented by their swords gleaming,
"And Evening hear their song of victory!
"Their towers shall be built upon the rocks,
"Their daughters shall sing, surrounded with shining spears!

"Liberty shall stand upon the cliffs of Albion,   55
"Casting her blue eyes over the green ocean;

"Or, tow'ring, stand upon the roaring waves,
"Stretching her mighty spear o'er distant lands;
"While, with her eagle wings, she covereth
"Fair Albion's shore, and all her families." 60

❧

PROLOGUE,
INTENDED FOR A DRAMATIC PIECE OF
KING EDWARD THE FOURTH. c

O For a voice like thunder, and a tongue
To drown the throat of war!—When the senses
Are shaken, and the soul is driven to madness,
Who can stand? When the souls of the oppressed
Fight in the troubled air that rages, who can stand? 5
When the whirlwind of fury comes from the
Throne of God, when the frowns of his countenance
Drive the nations together, who can stand?
When Sin claps his broad wings over the battle,
And sails rejoicing in the flood of Death; 10
When souls are torn to everlasting fire,
And fiends of Hell rejoice upon the slain,
O who can stand? O who hath caused this?
O who can answer at the throne of God?
The Kings and Nobles of the Land have done it! 15
Hear it not, Heaven, thy Ministers have done it!

PROLOGUE to KING JOHN. c

Justice hath heaved a sword to plunge in Albion's breast; for Albion's
sins are crimson dy'd, and the red scourge follows her desolate sons!
Then Patriot rose; full oft did Patriot rise, when Tyranny hath stain'd
fair Albion's breast with her own children's gore. Round his majestic
feet deep thunders roll; each heart does tremble, and each knee grows
slack. The stars of heaven tremble: the roaring voice of war, the trumpet, calls to battle! Brother in brother's blood must bathe, rivers of
death! O land, most hapless! O beauteous island, how forsaken! Weep
from thy silver fountains; weep from thy gentle rivers! The angel of
the island weeps! Thy widowed virgins weep beneath thy shades! Thy
aged fathers gird themselves for war! The sucking infant lives to die in
battle; the weeping mother feeds him for the slaughter! The husband-

Thus wept the Angel voice & as he wept the terrible blasts
Of trumpets, blew a loud alarm across the Atlantic deep.
No trumpets answer; no reply of clarions or of fifes,
Silent the Colonies remain and refuse the loud alarm.

On those vast shady hills between America & Albions shore;
Now barr'd out by the Atlantic sea: call'd Atlantean hills;
Because from their bright summits you may pass to the Golden world
An ancient palace, archetype of mighty Emperies,
Rears its immortal pinnacles, built in the forest of God
By Ariston the king of beauty for his stolen bride.

Here on their magic seats the thirteen Angels sat perturb'd
For clouds from the Atlantic hover oer the solemn roof.

1. Blake's Illuminated Printing. *America*, Plate 10

2. The Last Judgment

man doth leave his bending harvest! Blood cries afar! The land doth sow itself! The glittering youth of courts must gleam in arms! The aged senators their ancient swords assume! The trembling sinews of old age must work the work of death against their progeny; for Tyranny hath stretch'd his purple arm, and "blood," he cries; "the chariots and the horses, the noise of shout, and dreadful thunder of the battle heard afar!"—Beware, O Proud! thou shalt be humbled; thy cruel brow, thine iron heart is smitten, though lingering Fate is slow. O yet may Albion smile again, and stretch her peaceful arms, and raise her golden head, exultingly! Her citizens shall throng about her gates, her mariners shall sing upon the sea, and myriads shall to her temples crowd! Her sons shall joy as in the morning! Her daughters sing as to the rising year!

A WAR SONG
TO ENGLISHMEN.

t,e

Prepare, prepare, the iron helm of war,
Bring forth the lots, cast in the spacious orb;
Th' Angel of Fate turns them with mighty hands,
And casts them out upon the darken'd earth!
             Prepare, prepare.   5

Prepare your hearts for Death's cold hand! prepare
Your souls for flight, your bodies for the earth!
Prepare your arms for glorious victory!
Prepare your eyes to meet a holy God!
             Prepare, prepare.   10

Whose fatal scroll is that? Methinks 'tis mine!
Why sinks my heart, why faultereth my tongue?
Had I three lives, I'd die in such a cause,
And rise, with ghosts, over the well-fought field.
             Prepare, prepare.   15

The arrows of Almighty God are drawn!
Angels of Death stand in the low'ring heavens!
Thousands of souls must seek the realms of light,
And walk together on the clouds of heaven!
             Prepare, prepare.   20

Soldiers, prepare! Our cause is Heaven's cause;
Soldiers, prepare! Be worthy of our cause:
Prepare to meet our fathers in the sky:
Prepare, O troops, that are to fall to-day!
             Prepare, prepare.   25

Alfred shall smile, and make his harp rejoice;
The Norman William, and the learned Clerk,
And Lion Heart, and black-brow'd Edward, with
His loyal queen shall rise, and welcome us!

Prepare, prepare.   30

THE
COUCH OF DEATH.   c

The veiled Evening walked solitary down the western hills, and Silence reposed in the valley; the birds of day were heard in their nests, rustling in brakes and thickets; and the owl and bat flew round the darkening trees: all is silent when Nature takes her repose.—In former times, on such [a]n evening, when the cold clay breathed with life, and our ancestors, who now sleep in their graves, walked on the stedfast globe, the remains of a family of the tribes of Earth, a mother and a sister were gathered to the sick bed of a youth: Sorrow linked them together, leaning on one another's necks alternately—like lilies, dropping tears in each other's bosom, they stood by the bed like reeds bending over a lake, when the evening drops trickle down. His voice was low as the whisperings of the woods when the wind is asleep, and the visions of Heaven unfold their visitation. "Parting is hard, and death is terrible; I seem to walk through a deep valley, far from the light of day, alone and comfortless! The damps of death fall thick upon me! Horrors stare me in the face! I look behind, there is no returning; Death follows after me; I walk in regions of Death, where no tree is; without a lantern to direct my steps, without a staff to support me."—Thus he laments through the still evening, till the curtains of darkness were drawn! Like the sound of a broken pipe, the aged woman raised her voice. "O my son, my son, I know but little of the path thou goest! But lo, there is a God, who made the world; stretch out thy hand to Him." The youth replied, like a voice heard from a sepulchre, "My hand is feeble, how should I stretch it out? My ways are sinful, how should I raise mine eyes? My voice hath used deceit, how should I call on Him who is Truth? My breath is loathsome, how should he not be offended? If I lay my face in the dust, the grave opens its mouth for me; if I lift up my head, sin covers me as a cloak! O my dear friends, pray ye for me! Stretch forth your hands, that my helper may come! Through the void space I walk between the sinful world and eternity! Beneath me burns eternal fire! O for a hand to pluck me forth!" As the voice of an omen heard in the silent valley, when the few inhabitants cling trembling together; as the voice of the Angel of Death, when the thin beams of the moon give a faint light, such was this young man's voice to his friends! Like the bubbling waters of the brook in the dead of night, the aged woman raised her cry, and said, "O Voice, that dwellest in my breast, can I not cry, and lift my eyes to Heaven? Thinking of this, my spirit is turned within me into confusion! O my child, my child! is thy breath infected? So is mine. As the deer, wounded by the brooks of water, so the arrows of sin stick in my flesh; the poison hath entered into my marrow."—Like rolling waves, upon a desert shore, sighs succeeded sighs; they covered their faces, and wept! The youth lay silent—his mother's arm was under his head; he was like a cloud tossed by the winds, till the sun shine, and the drops of rain glisten, the yellow harvest breathes, and the thankful eyes of the villagers are turned up in smiles. The traveller that hath taken shelter under an oak, eyes the distant country with joy! Such smiles were seen upon the face of the youth! a visionary hand wiped away his tears, and a ray of light beamed around his head! All was still. The moon hung not out her lamp, and the stars faintly glimmered in the summer sky; the breath of night slept among the leaves of the forest; the bosom of the lofty hill drank in the silent dew, while on his majestic brow the voice of Angels is heard, and stringed sounds ride upon the wings of night. The sorrowful pair lift up their heads, hovering Angels are around them, voices of comfort are heard over the Couch of Death, and the youth breathes out his soul with joy into eternity.

CONTEMPLATION.

Who is this, that with unerring step dares tempt the wilds, where only Nature's foot hath trod? 'Tis Contemplation, daughter of the grey Morning! Majestical she steppeth, and with her pure quill on every flower writeth Wisdom's name. Now lowly bending, whispers in mine ear, "O man, how great, how little thou! O man, slave of each moment, lord of eternity! seest thou where Mirth sits on the painted cheek? doth it not seem ashamed of such a place, and grow immoderate to brave it out? O what an humble garb true Joy puts on! Those who want Happiness must stoop to find it; it is a flower that grows in every vale. Vain foolish man, that roams on lofty rocks! where, 'cause his garments are swoln with wind, he fancies he is grown into a giant! Lo then, Humility, take it, and wear it in thine heart; lord of thyself, thou then art lord of all. Clamour brawls along the streets, and destruction hovers in the city's smoak; but on these plains, and in these silent woods, true joys descend: here build thy nest; here fix thy staff; delights blossom around; numberless beauties blow; the green grass springs in joy, and the nimble air kisses the leaves; the brook stretches its arms along the velvet meadow, its silver inhabitants sport and play; the youthful sun joys like a hunter rouzed to the chace: he rushes up the sky, and lays hold on the immortal coursers of day; the sky glitters with the jingling trappings! Like a triumph, season follows season, while the airy music fills the world with joyful sounds." I answered, "Heavenly goddess! I am wrapped in mortality, my flesh is a prison, my bones the bars of death, Misery builds over our cottage roofs, and Discontent runs like a brook. Even in childhood, Sorrow slept with me in my cradle; he followed me up and down in the house; when I grew up he was my school-fellow: thus he was in my steps and in my play, till he became to me as my brother. I walked through dreary places with him, and in church-yards; and I oft found myself sitting by Sorrow on a tomb-stone!"

SAMSON.

c

Samson, the strongest of the children of men, I sing; how he was foiled by woman's arts, by a false wife brought to the gates of death! O Truth, that shinest with propitious beams, turning our earthly night to heavenly day, from presence of the Almighty Father! thou visitest our darkling world with blessed feet, bringing good news of Sin and Death destroyed! O white-robed Angel, guide my timorous hand to write as on a lofty rock with iron pens the words of truth, that all who pass may read.—Now Night, noon-tide of damned spirits, over the silent earth spreads her pavilion, while in dark council sat Philista's lords; and where strength failed, black thoughts in ambush lay. Their helmed youth and aged warriors in dust together ly, and Desolation spreads his wings over the land of Palestine; from side to side the land groans, her prowess lost, and seeks to hide her bruised head under the mists of night, breeding dark plots. For Dalila's fair arts have long been tried in vain; in vain she wept in many a treacherous tear. "Go on, fair traitress; do thy guileful work; ere once again the changing moon her circuit hath performed, thou shalt overcome, and conquer him by force unconquerable, and wrest his secret from him. Call thine alluring arts and honest-seeming brow, the holy kiss of love, and the transparent tear; put on fair linen, that with the lily vies, purple and silver; neglect thy hair, to seem more lovely in thy loose attire; put on thy country's pride, deceit; and eyes of love decked in mild sorrow, and sell thy Lord for gold."—For now, upon her sumptuous couch reclined, in gorgeous pride, she still intreats, and still she grasps his vigorous knees with her fair arms.— "Thou lov'st me not! thou'rt war, thou art not love! O foolish Dalila! O weak woman! it is death cloathed in flesh thou lovest, and thou hast been incircled in his arms!—Alas, my Lord, what am I calling thee? Thou art my God! To thee I pour my tears for sacrifice morning and evening: My days are covered with sorrow! Shut up; darkened: By night I am deceived! Who says that thou wast born of mortal kind? Destruction was thy father, a lioness suckled thee, thy young hands tore human limbs, and gorged human flesh! Come hither, Death; art thou not Samson's servant? 'Tis Dalila that calls; thy master's wife; no, stay, and let thy master do the deed: one blow of that strong arm would ease my pain; then should I lay at quiet, and have rest. Pity forsook thee at thy birth! O Dagon furious, and all ye gods of Palestine, withdraw your hand! I am but a weak woman. Alas, I am wedded to your enemy! I will go mad, and tear my crisped hair; I'll run about, and pierce the

ears o'th' gods! O Samson, hold me not; thou lovest me not! Look not
upon me with those deathful eyes! Thou wouldst my death, and death
approaches fast."—Thus, in false tears, she bath'd his feet, and thus she
day by day oppressed his soul: he seemed a mountain, his brow among
the clouds; [s]he seemed a silver stream, his feet embracing. Dark
thoughts rolled to and fro in his mind, like thunder clouds, troubling
the sky; his visage was troubled; his soul was distressed.—"Though I
should tell her all my heart, what can I fear? Though I should tell this
secret of my birth, the utmost may be warded off as well when told as
now." She saw him moved, and thus resumes her wiles.—"Samson, I'm
thine; do with me what thou wilt; my friends are enemies; my life is
death; I am a traitor to my nation, and despised; my joy is given into
the hands of him who hates me, using deceit to the wife of his bosom.
Thrice hast thou mocked me, and grieved my soul. Didst thou not tell
me with green with[e]s to bind thy nervous arms, and after that, when
I had found thy falshood, with new ropes to bind thee fast? I knew
thou didst but mock me. Alas, when in thy sleep I bound thee with
them to try thy truth, I cried, The Philistines be upon thee, Samson!
Then did suspicion wake thee; how didst thou rend the feeble ties!
Thou fearest nought, what shouldst thou fear? Thy power is more than
mortal, none can hurt thee; thy bones are brass, thy sinews are iron!
Ten thousand spears are like the summer grass; an army of mighty men
are as flocks in the vallies; what canst thou fear? I drink my tears like
water; I live upon sorrow! O worse than wolves and tygers, what canst
thou give when such a trifle is denied me? But O at last thou mockest
me to shame my over-fond inquiry! Thou toldest me to weave thee to
the beam by thy strong hair; I did even that to try thy truth: but when
I cried, The Philistines be upon thee, then didst thou leave me to bewail that Samson loved me not."—He sat, and inward griev'd, he saw
and lov'd the beauteous supplicant, nor could conceal aught that might
appease her; then, leaning on her bosom, thus he spoke: "Hear, O
Dalila! doubt no more of Samson's love; for that fair breast was made
the ivory palace of my inmost heart, where it shall lie at rest; for sorrow
is the lot of all of woman born: for care was I brought forth, and labour is my lot: nor matchless might, nor wisdom, nor every gift enjoyed, can from the heart of man hide sorrow.—Twice was my birth
foretold from heaven, and twice a sacred vow enjoined me that I should
drink no wine, nor eat of any unclean thing, for holy unto Israel's God
I am, a Nazarite even from my mother's womb. Twice was it told, that
it might not be broken. Grant me a son, kind Heaven, Manoa cried;
but Heaven refused! Childless he mourned, but thought his God knew
best. In solitude, though not obscure, in Israel he lived, till venerable
age came on: his flocks increased, and plenty crowned his board: beloved, revered of man! But God hath other joys in store. Is burdened
Israel his grief? The son of his old age shall set it free! The venerable
sweetner of his life receives the promise first from Heaven. She saw the
maidens play, and blessed their innocent mirth; she blessed each new-
joined pair; but from her the long-wished deliverer shall spring. Pen-

sive, alone she sat within the house, when busy day was fading, and calm evening, time for contemplation, rose from the forsaken east, and drew the curtains of heaven; pensive she sat,.and thought on Israel's grief, and silent prayed to Israel's God; when lo, an angel from the fields of light entered the house! His form was manhood in the prime, and from his spacious brow shot terrors through the evening shade! But mild he hailed her——Hail, highly favoured! said he; for lo, thou shalt conceive, and bear a son, and Israel's strength shall be upon his shoulders, and he shall be called Israel's Deliverer! Now therefore drink no wine, and eat not any unclean thing, for he shall be a Nazarite to God. —Then, as a neighbour when his evening tale is told, departs, his blessing leaving; so seemed he to depart: she wondered with exceeding joy, nor knew he was an angel. Manoa left his fields to sit in the house, and take his evening's rest from labour—the sweetest time that God has allotted mortal man. He sat, and heard with joy, and praised God who Israel still doth keep. The time rolled on, and Israel groaned oppressed. The sword was bright, while the plow-share rusted, till hope grew feeble, and was ready to give place to doubting: then prayed Manoa—O Lord, thy flock is scattered on the hills! The wolf teareth them, Oppression stretches his rod over our land, our country is plowed with swords, and reaped in blood! The echoes of slaughter reach from hill to hill! Instead of peaceful pipe, the shepherd bears a sword; the ox goad is turned into a spear! O when shall our Deliverer come? The Philistine riots on our stocks, our vintage is gathered by bands of enemies! Stretch forth thy hand, and save.——Thus prayed Manoa. The aged woman walked into the field, and lo, again the angel came! Clad as a traveller fresh risen on his journey, she ran and called her husband, who came and talked with him.——O man of God, said he, thou comest from far! Let us detain thee while I make ready a kid, that thou mayest sit and eat, and tell us of thy name and warfare; that when thy sayings come to pass, we may honour thee. The Angel answered, My name is wonderful; enquire not after it, seeing it is a secret: but, if thou wilt, offer an offering unto the Lord."

THE END.

[Further Sketches]

[In a Manuscript Fragment]

"then She bore Pale desire . . ." _t

PAGE I

then She bore Pale desire father of Curiosity a Virgin ever young. And   e
after. Leaden Sloth from whom came Ignorance. who brought forth
wonder. These are the Gods which Came from fear. for Gods like these.
nor male nor female are but Single Pregnate or if they list together
mingling bring forth mighty powrs[.] She knew them not yet they all   5
war with Shame and Strengthen her weak arm. But Pride awoke nor   t
knew that Joy was born. and taking Poisnous Seed from her own
Bowels. in the Monster Shame infusd. forth Came Ambition Crawling
like a toad Pride Bears it in her Bosom. and the Gods. all bow to it.
So Great its Power. that Pride inspird by it Prophetic Saw the King-   10
doms of the World & all their Glory. Giants of Mighty arm before the
flood. Cains City. built with Murder. Then Babel mighty Reard him to
the Skies. Babel with thousand tongues Confusion it was calld. and
Givn to Shame. this Pride observing inly Grievd. but knew not that.   t
the rest was Givn to Shame as well as this. Then Nineva & Babylon &   t 15
Costly tyre. And evn Jerusalem was Shewn. the holy City. Then Athens
Learning & the Pride of Greece. and further from [P 2] the Rising
Sun. was Rome Seated on Seven hills the mistress of the world. Emblem
of Pride She Saw the Arts their treasures Bring and luxury his bounte-
ous table Spread. but now a Cloud oercasts. and back to th'East. to Con-   20
stantines Great City Empire fled, Ere long to bleed & die a Sacrifice
done by a Priestly hand[.] So once the Sun his. Chariot drew. back. to
prolong a Good kings life.

    The Cloud oer past & Rome now Shone again Miterd & Crown'd
with triple crown. Then Pride was better Pleasd She Saw the World   25
fall down in Adoration[.] But now full to the Setting Sun a Sun arose   t
out of the Sea. it rose & shed Sweet Influence oer the Earth Pride
feared for her City, but not long. for looking Stedfastly She saw that
Pride Reignd here. Now Direful Pains accost her. and Still pregnant.
so Envy came & Hate. twin progeny Envy hath a Serpents head of fear-   30
ful bulk hissing with hundred tongues, her poisnous breath breeds
Satire foul Contagion from which none are free. oer whelmd by ever
During Thirst She Swalloweth her own Poison. which consumes her
nether Parts. from whence a River Springs. Most Black & loathsom
through the land it Runs Rolling with furious [P 3] Noise. but at the   35
last it Settles in a lake called Oblivion. tis at this Rivers fount where
evry mortals Cup is Mix't My Cup is fill'd with Envy's Rankest Draught   t
a miracle No less can set me Right. Desire Still pines but for one Cool-
ing Drop and tis Deny'd. while others in Contentments downy Nest do

sleep, it is the Cursed thorn wounding my breast that makes me sing.   *40*
however sweet tis Envy that Inspires my Song. prickt. by the fame of
others how I mourn and my complaints are Sweeter than their Joys but
O could I at Envy Shake my hands. my notes Should Rise to meet the
New born Day. Hate Meager hag Sets Envy on unable to Do ought
herself. but Worn away a Bloodless Daemon The Gods all Serve her at   *45*
her will so great her Power is[.] like. fabled hecate She doth bind them
to her law. Far in a Direful Cave She lives unseen Closd from the Eye
of Day. to the hard Rock transfixt by fate and here She works her witch-
eries that when She Groans She Shakes the Solid Ground Now Envy
She controlls with numming trance & Melancholy Sprung from her   *50*
dark womb There is a Melancholy, O how lovely tis whose heaven is in
the heavnly Mind for she from heaven came, and where She goes
heaven still doth follow her. She [P 4] brings true Joy once fled. & Contemplation is her Daughter. Sweet Contemplation. She brings humil-   *t*
ity to man take her She Says & wear her in thine heart lord of thy Self   *55*
thou then art lord of all. Tis Contemplation teacheth knowledge truly
how to know. and Reinstates him on his throne once lost how lost I'll
tell. But Stop the motley Song I'll Shew. how Conscience Came from
heaven. But O who listens to his Voice. T'was Conscience who brought
Melancholy down Conscience was sent a Guard to Reason. Reason once   *60*
fairer than the light till fould in Knowledges dark Prison house. For
knowledge drove sweet Innocence away. and Reason would have
followd but fate sufferd not. Then down Came Conscience with his
lovely band The Eager Song Goes on telling how Pride against her father Warrd & Overcame. Down his white Beard the Silver torrents   *65*
Roll. and Swelling Sighs burst forth his Children all in arms appear to
tear him from his throne Black was the deed. most Black. Shame in a
Mist Sat Round his troubled head. & filld him with Confusion. Fear as
a torrent wild Roard Round his throne the mighty pillars shake Now all
the Gods in blackning Ranks appear. like a tempestuous thunder Cloud   *70*
Pride leads. them on. Now they Surround the God. and bind him fast.
Pride bound him, then usurpd oer all the Gods. She Rode upon the
Swelling wind and Scatterd all who durst t'oppose. but Shame opposing
fierce and hovering. over her in the darkning Storm. She brought forth
Rage. Shame bore honour & made league with Pride. Mean while   *t 75*
Strife Mighty Prince was born Envy in direful Pains him bore. then
Envy brought forth Care. Care Sitteth in the wrinkled brow. Strife
Shapeless Sitteth under thrones of kings. like Smouldring fire. or in the
Buzz of Cities flies abroad Care brought forth Covet Eyeless & prone
to th' [P 5] Earth, and Strife brought forth Revenge. Hate brooding   *80*
in her Dismal den grew Pregnant & bore Scorn, & Slander. Scorn waits   *t*
on Pride. but Slander. flies around the World to do the Work of hate
her drudge & Elf. but Policy doth drudge for hate as well as Slander. &
oft makes use of her. Policy Son of Shame. Indeed hate Controlls all
the Gods. at will. Policy brought forth Guile & fraud. these Gods last   *85*

namd live in the Smoke of Cities. on Dusky wing breathing forth
Clamour & Destruction. alas in Cities wheres the man whose face is not
a mask unto his heart Pride made a Goddess. fair   or Image rather
till knowledge animated it. 'twas Calld Selflove. The Gods admiring
loaded her with Gifts as once Pandora She 'mongst men was Sent. and   90
worser ills attended her by far. She was a Goddess Powerful & bore Conceit[.] & Policy doth dwell with her by whom she [had] Mistrust &   t
Suspition. Then bore a Daughter called Emulation. who. married.
honour these follow her around the World[.] Go See the City friends
Joind Hand in Hand. Go See. the Natural tie of flesh & blood. Go See   95
more strong the ties of marriage love. thou Scarce Shall find but Self
love Stands Between

*

"Woe cried the muse . . ."

PAGE 6
Woe cried the muse tears Started at the Sound. Grief perch't upon   e
my brow and thought Embracd Her. What does this mean I cried. when
all around. Summer hath Spre'd her Plumes and tunes her Notes.   t
When Buxom Joy doth. fan his wings. & Golden Pleasures Beam
around my head. why. Grief dost thou accost me. The Muse then   5
Struck her Deepest string & Sympathy Came forth. She Spred her aw-   t
ful Wings. & gave me up. my Nerves with trembling Curdle all my
blood. & ev'ry piece of flesh doth Cry out Woe. how soon the Winds   t
Sing round the Darkning Storm ere while so fair. and now they fall &
beg the Skies will weep. a Day like this laid Elfrid in the Dust. Sweet   10
Elfrid fairer than the Beaming Sun O Soon cut off ith morning of her
days. twas the Rude thunder Stroke that Closd her Eyes. and laid her
lilied Beauties on the Green, The dance was broke the Circle just Begun the flower was Pluckd & yet it was not blown. But what are thou!
I could no more. till mute attention Struck my listning Ear. It Spoke   t 15
I come my friend to take my last farewell. Sunk by. the hand of Death
in Wat'ry tomb Oer yonder lake swift as the Nightly Blast that   t
Blights the Infant Bud The winds their Sad complainings bear. for.
Conrade lost untimely lost thy Conrade once. When living thee I lovd.
ev'n unto Death now Dead. Ill guard thee from approaching ill. fare-
well my time is gone, it Said no more. but vanished. ever from my
Sight

IV

[AN ISLAND IN THE MOON]

[In a Manuscript Fragment]

PAGE I

[Chapter 1]

In the Moon, is a certain Island near by a mighty continent, which
small island seems to have some affinity to England. & what is more extraordinary the people are so much alike & their language so much the
same that you would think you was among your friends. in this
Island dwells three Philosophers Suction, the Epicurean, Quid the
Cynic, & Sipsop, the Pythagorean I call them by the names of these
sects tho the sects are not ever mentiond there as being quite out of
date however the things still remain, and the vanities are the same.
the three Philosophers sat together thinking of nothing. in comes —
Etruscan Column the Antiquarian & after an abundance of En-
quiries to no purpose sat himself down & described something that
nobody listend to so they were employd when Mrs Gimblet came in
[? tipsy] the corners of her mouth seemd I dont know how, but very
odd as if she hoped you had not an ill opinion of her. to be sure we are
all poor creatures.   well she seated & [listened] seemd to listen with
great attention while the Antiquarian seemd to be talking of virtuous
cats, but it was not so. she was thinking of the shape of her eyes &
mouth & he was thinking, of his eternal fame the three Philosophers
at this time were each endeavouring to conceal his laughter, (not at
them but) at his own imaginations. this was the situation of this improving company, when in a great hurry, Inflammable Gass the Wind
finder enterd. they seemd to rise & salute each other

Etruscan Column & Inflammable Gass fixd their eyes on each
other, their tongues went in question & answer, but their thoughts
were otherwise employd

I dont like his eyes said Etruscan Column. he's a foolish puppy
said Inflammable Gass, smiling on him. the 3 Philosophers [<the>
? older] the Cynic smiling the Epicurean seeming [not] studying

-440-

the flame of the candle & the Pythagorean playing with the cat, listend
with open mouths to the edifying discourses.

Sir said the Antiquarian I have seen these works & I do affirm that
they are no such thing. they seem to me to be the most wretched
paltry flimsy Stuff that ever — What d'ye say What dye say said
Inflammable Gass, why why I wish I could see you write so. Sir said
the Antiquarian, according to my opinion the author is an errant blockhead.—Your reason Your reason said Inflammable Gass—why why I
think it very abominable to call a man a blockhead that you know
nothing of.—Reason Sir said the Antiquarian I'll give you an example
for your reason As I was walking along the street I saw a <vast>
number of swallows on the [*top of an house*] rails of an old Gothic
square they seemd to be going on their passage, as Pliny says as
I was looking up, a little outré fellow pulling me by the sleeve
cries pray Sir who do all they belong to. I turnd my self about with
great [P 2] contempt. Said I, Go along you fool.—Fool said he who do
you call fool I only askd you a civil question—[*here the*] I had a great
mind to have thrashd the fellow only he was bigger than I—here
Etruscan column left off—Inflammable Gass, recollecting himself Indeed I do not think the man was a fool for he seems to me to have been
desirous of enquiring into the works of nature—Ha Ha Ha said the
Pythagorean. it was reechod by Inflammable Gass to overthrow the
argument—Etruscan Column then star[t]ing up & clenching both his
fists was prepared to give a formal answer to the company But
Ob[t]use Angle, entering the room having made a gentle bow, proceeded to empty his pockets of a vast number of papers, turned about
& sat down wiped his [*head*] <face> with his pocket handkerchief
& shutting his eyes began to scratch his head—well gentlemen said he
what is the cause of strife the Cynic answerd. they are only quarreling about Voltaire—Yes said the Epicurean & having a bit of fun with
him. And said the Pythagorean endeavoring to incorporate their souls
with their bodies

Obtuse Angle giving a grin said Voltaire understood nothing of the
Mathematics and a man must be a fool ifaith not to understand the
Mathematics

Inflammable Gass turning round hastily in his chair said Mathematics he found out a number of Queries in Philosophy. Obtuse Angle
shutting his eyes & saying that he always understood better when he
shut his eyes <said> In the first place it is of no use for a man to
make Queries but to solve them, for a man may be a fool & make
Queries but a man must have good sound sense to solve them. a query
& an answer are as different as a strait line & a crooked one. secondly
I, I, I. aye Secondly, Voltaire's a fool, says the Epicurean—Pooh says
the Mathematician scratching his head with double violence, it is not
worth Quarreling about.—The Antiquarian here got up—& hemming
twice to shew the strength of his Lungs, said but my good Sir, Voltaire
was immersed in matter, & seems to have understood very little but

what he saw before his eyes, like the Animal upon the Pythagoreans lap always playing with its own tail. Ha Ha Ha said Inflammable Gass   he was the Glory of France—I have got a bottle of air that would spread a Plague. here the Antiquarian shruggd up his shoulders & was silent while Inflammable Gass talkd for half an hour

When Steelyard <the lawgiver> coming in stalking—with an act of parliament in his hand said that it was a shameful thing that acts of parliament should be in a free state, it had so engrossed his mind that he did not salute the company

Mrs Gimblet drew her mouth downwards

PAGE 3

Chap 2^d

Tilly Lally the Siptippidist Aradobo, the dean of Morocco, Miss Gittipin Mrs Nannicantipot, <Mrs Sigtagatist> Gibble Gabble the wife of Inflammable Gass—& Little Scopprell enterd the room

(If I have not presented you with every character in the piece call me ass—)

Chap 3^d

In the Moon as Phebus stood over his oriental Gardening O ay come Ill sing you a song said the Cynic. the trumpeter shit in his hat said the Epicurean & clapt it on his head said the Pythagorean
Ill begin again said the Cynic
    Little Phebus came strutting in
    With his fat belly & his round chin
    What is it you would please to have
    Ho Ho
    I wont let it go at only so & so
Mrs Gimblet lookd as if they meant her. Tilly Lally laught like a Cherry clapper. Aradobo askd who was Phebus Sir. Obtuse Angle answerd, quickly, He was the God of Physic, Painting Perspective Geometry Geography Astronomy, Cookery, Chymistry [*Conjunctives*] Mechanics, Tactics Pathology Phraseology Theolog[y] Mythology Astrology Osteology, Somatology in short every art & science adorn'd him as beads round his neck. here Aradobo lookd Astonishd & askd if he understood Engraving—Obtuse Angle Answerd indeed he did.—Well said the other he was as great as Chatterton. Tilly Lally turnd round to Obtuse Angle & askd who it was that was as great as Chatterton. Hay, how should I know Answerd Obtuse Angle who was It Aradobo. why sir said he the Gentleman that the song was about. Ah said Tilly Lally I did not hear it. what was it Obtuse Angle. Pooh said he Nonsense. Mhm said Tilly Lally—it was Phebus said the Epicurean Ah that was the Gentleman said Aradobo. Pray Sir said Tilly Lally who was

Phebus. Obtuse Angle answerd the heathens in the old ages usd to have Gods that they worshipd & they usd to sacrifice to them you have read about that in the bible. Ah said Aradobo I thought I had read of Phebus in the Bible.—Aradobo you should always think before you speak said Obtuse Angle—Ha Ha Ha he means Pharaoh said Tilly Lally—I am ashamd of you making [P 4] use of the names in the Bible said M^rs. Sigtagatist. Ill tell you what Mrs Sinagain I dont think theres any harm in it, said Tilly Lally—No said Inflammable Gass. I have got a camera obscura at home what was it you was talking about. Law said Tilly Lally what has that to do with Pharaoh—. Pho nonsense hang Pharoh & all his host said the Pythagorean sing away Quid—

Then the Cynic sung

> Honour & Genius is all I ask
> And I ask the Gods no more
>   No more No more) the three Philosophers
>   No more No more) bear Chorus

Here Aradobo suckd his under lip

Chap 4

Hang names said the Pythagorean whats Pharoh better than Phebus or Phebus than Pharoh. hang them both said the Cynic Dont be prophane said Mrs Sigtagatist. Why said Mrs Nannicantipot I dont think its prophane to say hang Pharoh. ah said Mrs Sinagain, I'm sure you ought to hold your tongue, for you never say any thing about the scriptures, & you hinder your husband from going to church—Ha Ha said Inflammable Gass what dont you like to go to church. no said Mrs Nannicantipot I think a person may be as good at home. If I had not a place of profit that forces me to go to church said Inflammable Gass Id see the parsons all hangd a parcel of lying—O said Mrs Sigtagatist if it was not for churches & chapels I should not have livd so long—there was I up in a Morning at four o clock when I was a Girl. I would run like the dickins till I was all in a heat. I would stand till I was ready to sink into the earth. ah Mr Huffcap would kick the bottom of the Pulpit out, with Passion, would tear off the sleeve of his Gown, & set his wig on fire & throw it at the people hed cry & stamp & kick & sweat and all for the good of their souls.—Im sure he must be a wicked villain said Mrs Nannicantipot a passionate wretch. If I was a man Id wait at the bottom of the pulpit stairs & knock him down & run away.— You would You Ignorant jade I wish I could see you hit any of the ministers. you deserve to have your ears boxed you do.—Im sure this is not religion answers the [P 5] other—Then Mr Inflammable Gass ran & shovd his head into the fire & set his [head] hair all in a flame & ran about the room—No No he did not I was only making a fool of you

Chap 5

Obtuse Angle Scopprell Aradobo & Tilly Lally are all met in Obtuse Angles study—

Pray said Aradobo is Chatterton a Mathematician. No said Obtuse Angle how can you be so foolish as to think he was. Oh I did not think he was I only askd said Aradobo. How could you think he was not, & ask if he was said Obtuse Angle.—Oh no Sir I did think he was before you told me but afterwards I thought he was not

Obtuse Angle said in the first place you thought he was & then afterwards when I said he was not you thought he was not. why I know that—Oh no sir I thought that he was not but I askd to know whether he was.—How can that be said Obtuse Angle how could you ask & think that he was not—why said he. It came into my head that he was not—Why then said Obtuse Angle you said that he was. Did I say so Law I did not think I said that—Did not he said Obtuse Angle   Yes said Scopprell. But I meant said Aradobo I I I cant think Law Sir I wish youd tell me, how it is

Then Obtuse Angle put his chin in his hand & said whenever you think you must always think for yourself—How Sir said Aradobo, whenever I think I must think myself I think I do—In the first place said he with a grin—Poo Poo said Obtuse Angle dont be a fool—

Then Tilly Lally took up a Quadrant & askd. [*what is this gim crank for*]. Is not this a sun dial. Yes said Scopprell but its broke—at this moment the three Philosophers enterd and lowring darkness hoverd oer th assembly.

Come said the Epicurean lets have some rum & water & hang the mathematics come Aradobo say some thing then Aradobo began In the first place I think I think in the first place that Chatterton was clever at Fissic Follogy, Pistinology, Aridology, Arography, Transmography Phizography, Hogamy HAtomy, & hall that but in the first place he eat wery little wickly that is he slept very little which he brought into a consumsion, & what was that that he took Fissic or somethink & so died

So all the people in the book enterd into the room & they could not talk any more to the present purpose

PAGE 6

Chap 6

Then all went home & left the Philosophers. then Suction Askd if Pindar was not a better Poet than Ghiotto was a Painter

Plutarch has not the life of Ghiotto said Sipsop   no said Quid to be sure he was an Italian. well said Suction that is not any proof. Plutarch was a nasty ignorant puppy said Quid I hate your sneaking rascals. theres Aradobo in [*twen*[ty]] ten or twelve years will be a far superior genius. Ah, said the Pythagorean Aradobo will make a very clever fellow. why said Quid I think that [a] <any> natural fool would make a clever fellow if he was properly brought up—Ah hang your reasoning said the Epicurean I hate reasoning I do every thing by my feelings—

Ah said Sipsop, I only wish Jack [Hunter] Tearguts had had the cutting of Plutarch he understands anatomy better than any of the Ancients hell plunge his knife up to the hilt in a single drive and thrust his fist in, and all in the space of a Quarter of an hour. he does not mind their crying—tho they cry ever so hell Swear at them & keep them down with his fist & tell them that hell scrape their bones if they dont lay still & be quiet—What the devil should the people in the hospital that have it done for nothing, make such a piece of work for

Hang that said Suction let us have a Song

Then [Sipsop sang] the Cynic sang

> When old corruption first begun
> Adornd in yellow vest
> He committed on flesh a whoredom
> O what a wicked beast
>
> 2
> From them a callow babe did spring   5
> And old corruption smild
> To think his race should never end
> For now he had a child
>
> 3
> He calld him Surgery & fed
> The babe with his own milk   10
> For flesh & he could neer agree
> She would not let him suck

PAGE 7

> 4
> And this he always kept in mind
> And formd a crooked knife
> And ran about with bloody hands   15
> To seek his mothers life
>
> 5
> And as he ran to seek his mother
> He met with a dead woman
> He fell in love & married her
> A deed which is not common   20
>
> 6
> She soon grew pregnant & brought forth
> Scurvy & spotted fever
> The father grind & skipt about
> And said I'm made for ever

7

For now I have procurd these imps   25
Ill try experiments
With that he tied poor scurvy down
& stopt up all its vents

8

And when the child began to swell
He shouted out aloud   30
Ive found the dropsy out & soon
Shall do the world more good

9

He took up fever by the neck
And cut out all its spots
And thro the holes which he had made   35
He first discoverd guts

Ah said Sipsop you think we are rascals & we think you are rascals. I
do as I chuse   what is it to any body what I do   I am always unhappy
too. when I think of Surgery—I dont know   I do it because I like it.
My father does what he likes & so do I. I think some how Ill leave it
off   there was a woman having her cancer cut & she shriekd so, that
I was quite sick

Chap 7

Good night said Sipsop, Good night said the other two then Quid &
Suction were left alone. then said Quid I think that Homer is bombast
& Shakespeare is too wild & Milton has no feelings they might be easily
outdone   Chatterton never writ those poems. a parcel of fools going to
Bristol—if I was to go Id find it out in a minute. but Ive found it out
already—If I dont knock them all up next year in the Exhibition Ill be
hangd said Suction. hang Philosophy   I would not give a farthing for it
do all by your feelings and never think at all about it. Im hangd if I
dont get up to morrow morning by four o clock & work Sir Joshua—Before ten years are at an end said Quid how I will work these poor milk
[p 8] sop devils, an ignorant pack of wretches
So they went to bed

Chap 8

Steelyard the Lawgiver, sitting at his table taking extracts from Her-
veys Meditations among the tombs & Youngs Night thoughts. [*This is
unfair* . . .] He is not able to hurt me (said he) more than making me
Constable or taking away the parish business. Hah!

[*O what a scene is here what a disguise*]
My crop of corn is but a field of tares

−446−

Says Jerome happiness is not for us poor crawling reptiles of the earth   Talk of happiness & happiness its no such thing—every person has a something

> Hear then the pride & knowledge of a Sailor
> His sprit sail fore sail main sail & his mizen
> A poor frail man god wot I know none frailer
> I know no greater sinner than John Taylor

If I had only myself to care for I'd soon make Double Elephant look foolish, & Filligree work I hope shall live to see—

> The wreck of matter & the crush of worlds
>   as Younge says

Obtuse Angle enterd the Room. What news Mr Steelyard—I am Reading Theron & Aspasio, said he. Obtuse Angle took up the books one by one   I dont find it here said he. Oh no said the other it was the meditations. Obtuse Angle took up the book & read till the other was quite tir'd out

Then S[c]opprell & Miss Gittipin, coming in Scopprell took up a book & read the following passage.

An Easy of [*Human*] <Huming> Understanding by John Lookye Gent

John Locke said Obtuse Angle. O ay Lock said Scopprell.

Now here said Miss Gittipin I never saw such company in my life. you are always talking of your books I like to be where we talk.—you had better take a walk, that we may have some pleasure I am sure I never see any pleasure. theres Double Elephants Girls they have their own way, & theres Miss Filligree work she goes out in her coaches & her footman & her maids & Stormonts & Balloon hats & a pair of Gloves every day & the sorrows of Werter & Robinsons & the Queen of Frances Puss colour & my Cousin Gibble Gabble says that I am like nobody else   I might as well be in a nunnery There they go in Post chaises & Stages to Vauxhall & Ranelagh And I hardly know what a coach is, except when I go to [P 9] Mr Jacko's he knows what riding is & his wife is the most agreeable woman you hardly know she has a tongue in her head   and he is the funniest fellow, & I do believe he'll go in partnership with his master. & they have black servants lodge at their house   I never saw such a place in my life   he says he has Six & twenty rooms in his house, and I believe it & he is not such a liar as Quid thinks he is. [*but he is always Envying*] Poo Poo hold your tongue, said the Lawgiver. this quite provokd Miss Gittipin to interrupt her in her favourite topic & she proceeded to use every Provoking speech that ever she could, & he bore it <more> like a Saint than a Lawgiver and with great Solemnity he addressd the company in these words

They call women the weakest vessel but I think they are the strongest A girl has always more tongue than a boy   I have seen a little brat no

higher than a nettle & she had as much tongue as a city clark but a boy
would be such a fool not have any thing to say and if any body askd
him a question he would put his head into a hole & hide it. I am sure I
take but little pleasure you have as much pleasure as I have. there I
stand & bear every fools insult. if I had only myself to care for, I'd
wring off their noses

To this Scopprell answerd, I think the Ladies discourses Mr Steelyard are some of them more improving than any book. that is the way
I have got some of my knowledge

Then said Miss Gittipin, Mr Scopprell do you know the song of
Phebe and Jellicoe—no Miss said Scopprell—then she repeated these
verses while Steelyard walkd about the room

> Phebe drest like beauties Queen
> Jellicoe in faint peagreen
> Sitting all beneath a grot
> Where the little lambkins trot　　　　　　　　　　t
>
> Maidens dancing　loves a sporting　　　　　　　　5
> All the country folks a courting
> Susan Johnny Bet & Joe
> Lightly tripping on a row
>
> Happy people who can be
> In happiness compard with ye　　　　　　　　　　10
> The Pilgrim with his crook & hat
> Sees your happiness compleat

A charming Song indeed miss said Scopprell [*That was all for*] here
they recievd a summons for a merry making at the Philosophers house

PAGE 10

Chap 9

I say this evening [*we'd*] <we'll> all get drunk. I say dash, an Anthem　an Anthem, said Suction

> Lo the Bat with Leathern wing
> Winking & blinking
> Winking & blinking
> Winking & blinking
> Like Doctor Johnson　　　　　　　　　　　　　5
>
> Quid———O ho Said Doctor Johnson
> To Scipio Africanus
> If you dont own me a Philosopher
> Ill kick your Roman Anus

Suction—A ha To Doctor Johnson
    Said Scipio Africanus
    Lift up my Roman Petticoatt
    And kiss my Roman Anus

    And the Cellar goes down with a Step (Grand Chorus

Ho Ho Ho Ho Ho Ho Ho Hooooo my poooooor siiides I I should
die if I was to live here said Scopprell Ho Ho Ho Ho Ho

1ˢᵗ Vo	Want Matches
2ᵈ Vo	Yes Yes Yes
1 Vo	Want Matches
2ᵈ Vo	No————————

1ˢᵗ Vo	Want Matches
2ᵈ Vo	Yes Yes Yes
1ˢᵗ Vo	Want Matches
2ᵈ Vo	No————————

Here was Great confusion & disorder Aradobo said that the boys in
the street sing something very pritty & funny [*about London O no*]
about Matches Then Mʳˢ Nannicantipot sung

    I cry my matches as far as Guild hall
    God bless the duke & his aldermen all

Then sung Scopprell

    I ask the Gods no more
      no more no more

Then Said Suction come Mʳ Lawgiver your song and the Lawgiver
sung

    As I walkd forth one may morning
    To see the fields so pleasant & so gay
    O there did I spy a young maiden sweet

PAGE 11

    Among the Violets that smell so sweet
      Smell so sweet
      Smell so sweet
    Among the Violets that smell so sweet

Hang your Violets heres your Rum & water [*sweeter*] O ay said
Tilly Lally. Joe Bradley & I was going along one day in the Sugar
house Joe Bradley saw for he had but one eye saw a treacle
Jar So he goes of his blind side & dips his hand up to the shoulder in
treacle. here lick lick lick said he . Ha Ha Ha Ha Ha For he had
but one eye Ha Ha Ha Ho then sung Scopprell

And I ask the Gods no more
no more no more
no more no more

Miss Gittipin said he you sing like a harpsichord. let your bounty descend to our fair ears and favour us with a fine song
<then she sung>

This frog he would a wooing ride
Kitty alone   Kitty alone
This frog he would a wooing ride
Kitty alone & I
Sing cock I cary Kitty alone
Kitty alone   Kitty alone
Cock I cary Kitty alone
Kitty alone & I

Charming truly elegant said Scopprell

And I ask the gods no more

Hang your Serious Songs, said Sipsop   & he sung as follows

Fa ra so bo ro
Fa ra bo ra
Sa ba ra ra ba rare roro
Sa ra ra ra bo ro ro ro
Radara
Sarapodo no flo ro

Hang Italian songs   lets have English said Quid [*Sing a Mathematical Song Obtuse Angle then he sung*] <English Genius for ever   here I go>

Hail Matrimony made of Love
To thy wide gates how great a drove
On purpose to be yok'd do come
Widows & maids & Youths also
That lightly trip on beauty's toe
Or sit on beauty's bum

Hail fingerfooted lovely Creatures
The females of our human Natures
Formed to suckle all Mankind
Tis you that come in time of need
Without you we shoud never Breed
Or any Comfort find

For if a Damsel's blind or lame
Or Nature's hand has crooked her frame

Or if she's deaf or is wall eyed   *15*
Yet if her heart is well inclined
Some tender lover she shall find
That panteth for a Bride   t

The universal Poultice this
To cure whatever is amiss   20
In damsel or in Widow gay
It makes them smile it makes them skip
Like Birds just cured of the pip
They chirp & hop away

Then come ye Maidens come ye Swains   25
Come & be eased of all your pains
In Matrimony's Golden cage—

I [*None of*] Go & be hanged said Scopprel how can you have the
face to make game of Matrimony [*What you skipping flea how dare
ye? Ill dash you through your chair says the Cynic This Quid (cries
out Miss Gittipin) always spoils good company in this manner & its a
shame*]
    Then Quid calld upon Obtuse Angle for a Song & he wiping his
face & looking on the corner of the cieling Sang

To be or not to be
Of great capacity
Like Sir Isaac Newton
Or Locke or Doctor South
Or Sherlock upon death   5
Id rather be Sutton

For he did build a house
For aged men & youth
With walls of brick & stone
He furnishd it within   10
With whatever he could win
And all his own

He drew out of the Stocks
His money in a box
And sent his servant   15
To Green the Bricklayer
And to the Carpenter
He was so fervent

The chimneys were three score   t
The windows many more   t 20
And for convenience

He sinks & gutters made
And all the way he pavd
To hinder pestilence

Was not this a good man   25
Whose life was but a span
Whose name was Sutton

PAGE 13

As Locke or Doctor South
Or Sherlock upon Death
Or Sir Isaac Newton   30

The Lawgiver was very attentive & begd to have it sung over again &
again till the company were tired & insisted on the Lawgiver singing a
song himself which he readily complied with

This city & this country has brought forth many mayors
To sit in state & give forth laws out of their old oak chairs
With face as brown as any nut with drinking of strong ale
Good English hospitality O then it did not fail

With scarlet gowns & broad gold lace would make a yeoman sweat   5
With stockings rolld above their knees & shoes as black as jet   t
With eating beef & drinking beer O they were stout & hale
Good English hospitality O then it did not fail

Thus sitting at the table wide the Mayor & Aldermen
Were fit to give law to the city each eat as much as ten   10
The hungry poor enterd the hall to eat good beef & ale
Good English hospitality O then it did not fail

Here they gave a shout & the company broke up

Chap 10

Thus these happy Islanders spent their time but felicity does not
last long, for being met at the house of Inflammable Gass the wind-
finder, the following affairs happend.

Come Flammable said Gibble Gabble & lets enjoy ourselves bring
the Puppets. Hay Hay, said he, you sho, why ya ya, how can you be
so foolish.—Ha Ha Ha she calls the experiments puppets Then he
went up stairs & loaded the maid, with glasses, & brass tubes, & magic
pictures

Here ladies & gentlemen said he Ill shew you a louse [climing] or a
flea or a butterfly or a cock chafer the blade bone of a tittle back no
no heres a bottle of wind that I took up in the bog house. o dear o
dear the waters got into the sliders. look here Gibble Gabble—
lend me your handkerchief, Tilly Lally Tilly Lally took out his handkerchief which smeard the glass worse than ever. then he screwd it on

then he took the sliders & then he set up the glasses for the Ladies
to view the pictures   thus he was employd & quite out of breath
   While Tilly Lally & Scopprell were pumping at the air pump Smack
went the glass—. Hang said Tilly Lally. Inflammable Gass turnd short
round & threw down the table & Glasses & Pictures, & broke the bottles
of wind & let out the Pestilence   He saw the Pestilence fly out of the
bottle & cried out [P 14] while he ran out of the room, come out come
out   we are putrified, we are corrupted, our lungs are destroyd with
the Flogiston   this will spread a plague all thro' the Island   he was
down stairs the very first   on the back of him came all the others in a
heap
   So they need not bidding go

Chap 11

Another merry meeting at the house of Steelyard the Lawgiver
   After Supper Steelyard & Obtuse Angle had pumpd Inflammable
Gass quite dry. they playd at forfeits & tryd every method to get
good humour. said Miss Gittipin pray Mr Obtuse Angle sing us a
song   then he sung

Upon a holy thursday their innocent faces clean
The children walking two & two in grey & blue & green
Grey headed beadles walkd before with wands as white as snow
Till into the high dome of Pauls they like thames water flow

O what a multitude they seemd, these flowers of London town   5
Seated in companies they sit with radiance all their own
The hum of multitudes were there but multitudes of lambs
Thousands of little girls & boys raising their innocent hands   t

Then like a mighty wind they raise to heavn the voice of song   t
Or like harmonious thunderings the seats of heavn among   10
Beneath them sit the revrend men the guardians of the poor
Then cherish pity lest you drive an angel from your door

After this they all sat silent for a quarter of an hour [& *Mrs Sigta-*
gatist] <& Mrs Nannicantipot> said it puts me in Mind of my
[*grand*] mothers song

When the tongues of children are heard on the green   t
And laughing is heard on the hill   t
My heart is at rest within my breast
And every thing else is still

Then come home my children the sun is gone down   t5
And the dews of night arise
Come Come leave off play & let us away
Till the morning appears in the skies

PAGE 15

No No let us play for it is yet day
And we cannot go to sleep   t 10
Besides in the Sky the little birds fly   t
And the meadows are coverd with Sheep

Well Well go & play till the light fades away
And then go home to bed
The little ones leaped & shouted & laughd   15
And all the hills ecchoed

Then [*Miss Gittipin*] [*Tilly Lally sung*] [*Quid*] sung <Quid>

O father father where are you going   t
O do not walk so fast
O speak father speak to your little boy
Or else I shall be lost

The night it was dark & no father was there   5
And the child was wet with dew
The mire was deep & the child did weep
And away the vapour flew

Here nobody could sing any longer, till Tilly Lally pluckd up a
spirit & he sung.

                    O I say you Joe
                    Throw us the ball
                    Ive a good mind to go
                    And leave you all
                    I never saw saw such a bowler   5
                    To bowl the ball in a tansey   t
                    And to clean it with my handkercher
                    Without saying a word

                    That Bills a foolish fellow
                    He has given me a black eye   t 10
                    He does not know how to handle a bat
                    Any more than a dog or a cat   t
                    He has knockd down the wicket
                    And broke the stumps
                    And runs without shoes to save his pumps 15

Here a laugh began and Miss Gittipin sung

                    Leave O leave [me] to my sorrows
                    Here Ill sit & fade away
                    Till Im nothing but a spirit
                    And I lose this form of clay

3. The Laocoön

4. Blake's Autograph. From the album of William Upcott

    Then if chance along this forest   5
    Any walk in pathless ways
    Thro the gloom he'll see my shadow
    Hear my voice upon the Breeze

The Lawgiver all the while sat delighted to see them in such a
serious humour Mr Scopprell said he you must be acquainted with a
great many songs. O dear sir Ho Ho Ho I am no singer I must beg of
one of these tender hearted ladies to sing for me—they all declined & he
was forced to sing himself

    Theres Doctor Clash
    And Signior Falalasole
    O they sweep in the cash
    Into their purse hole
    Fa me la sol La me fa Sol   t5

    Great A little A
    Bouncing B
    Play away Play away
    Your out of the key
    Fa me la sol La me fa sol   10

    Musicians should have
    A pair of very good ears
    And Long fingers & thumbs
    And not like clumsy bears
    Fa me la sol La me fa sol   15

    Gentlemen Gentlemen
    Rap Rap Rap
    Fiddle Fiddle Fiddle
    Clap Clap Clap
    Fa me la sol La me fa sol   20

Hm said the Lawgiver, funny enough lets have handels waterpiece
then Sipsop sung

    A crowned king,
    On a white horse sitting
    With his trumpets sounding
    And Banners flying
    Thro the clouds of smoke he makes his way   5
And the shout of his thousands fills his heart with rejoicing & victory
And the shout of his thousands fills his heart with rejoicing & victory
Victory Victory—twas William the prince of Orange

[Here a leaf or more is missing]

PAGE X

them Illuminating the Manuscript—Ay said she that would be excellent. Then said he I would have all the writing Engraved instead of Printed & at every other leaf a high finishd print all in three Volumes folio, & sell them a hundred pounds a piece. they would Print off two thousand   then said she whoever will not have them will be ignorant fools & will not deserve to live   Dont you think I have something of the Goats face says he. Very like a Goats face—she answerd—I think your face said he is like that noble beast the Tyger—Oh I was at Mrs Sicknakens & I was speaking of my abilities but their nasty hearts poor devils are eat up with envy—they envy me my abilities & all the Women envy your abilities my dear they hate people who are of higher abil[it]ies than their nasty filthy [*Souls*] Selves but do you outface them & then Strangers will see you have an opinion—now I think we should do as much good as we can when we are at Mr Femality's   do yo[u] snap & take me up—and I will fall into such a passion Ill hollow and stamp & frighten all the People there & show them what truth is—at this Instant Obtuse Angle came in   Oh I am glad you are come said quid

V

[Written in a copy of *Poetical Sketches*]

SONG 1st BY A SHEPHERD

Welcome stranger to this place,
Where joy doth sit on every bough,
Paleness flies from every face,
We reap not what we do not sow.

Innocence doth like a Rose,   5
Bloom on every Maidens cheek;
Honor twines around her brows,
The jewel Health adorns her neck.

SONG 3ᵈ by an Old Shepherd

When silver snow decks Sylvio's cloaths
And jewel hangs at shepherd's nose,
We can abide life's pelting storm
That makes our limbs quake, if our hearts be warm.

Whilst Virtue is our walking staff,   5
And Truth a lantern to our path;
We can abide life's pelting storm
That makes our limbs quake, if our hearts be warm.

Blow boisterous Wind, stern Winter frown,
Innocence is a Winter's gown;   10
So clad, we'll abide life's pelting storm
That makes our limbs quake, if our hearts be warm.

[From Blake's Notebook]

t

[For early drafts of *Songs of Experience* see textual notes thereto]

t

Never pain to tell thy love
Love that never told can be
For the gentle wind does move
Silently invisibly

I told my love I told my love   5
I told her all my heart
Trembling cold in ghastly fears
Ah she doth depart

Soon as she was gone from me
A traveller came by   10
Silently invisibly
O was no deny

t

*

I feard the fury of my wind   t
Would blight all blossoms fair & true
And my sun it shind & shind
And my wind it never blew   t

But a blossom fair or true   5
Was not found on any tree
For all blossoms grew & grew
Fruitless false tho fair to see

*

I saw a chapel all of gold
That none did dare to enter in
And many weeping stood without
Weeping mourning worshipping

I saw a serpent rise between   5
The white pillars of the door
And he forcd & forcd & forcd
Down the golden hinges tore   t

And along the pavement sweet
Set with pearls & rubies bright   10
All his slimy length he drew
Till upon the altar white

Vomiting his poison out
On the bread & on the wine
So I turnd into a sty   15
And laid me down among the swine

*

I laid me down upon a bank
Where love lay sleeping
I heard among the rushes dank
Weeping Weeping

Then I went to the heath & the wild   5
To the thistles & thorns of the waste
And they told me how they were beguild
Driven out & compeld to be chaste

*

A cradle song   t

Sleep Sleep beauty bright
Dreaming oer the joys of night   t
Sleep Sleep: in thy sleep
Little sorrows sit & weep   t

Sweet Babe in thy face   t 5
Soft desires I can trace
Secret joys & secret smiles
Little pretty infant wiles   t

As thy softest limbs I feel   t
Smiles as of the morning steal   t 10
Oer thy cheek & oer thy breast
Where thy little heart does rest

O the cunning wiles that creep
In thy little heart asleep
When thy little heart does wake   15
Then the dreadful lightnings break

From thy cheek & from thy eye   t
Oer the youthful harvests nigh
Infant wiles & infant smiles   t
Heaven & Earth of peace beguiles   20

*

I askéd a thief to steal me a peach   t
He turned up his eyes   t
I ask'd a lithe lady to lie her down
Holy & meek she cries—   t

As soon as I went   5
An angel came.
He wink'd at the thief   t
And smild at the dame—   t

And without one word said   t
Had a peach from the tree   10
And still as a maid   t
Enjoy'd the lady.   t

*

in a mirtle shade   t

Why should I be bound to thee
O my lovely mirtle tree
Love free love cannot be bound
To any tree that grows on ground

O how sick & weary I   5
Underneath my mirtle lie
Like to dung upon the ground
Underneath my mirtle bound

Oft my mirtle sighd in vain
To behold my heavy chain   10
Oft my father saw us sigh   t
And laughd at our simplicity

So I smote him & his gore
Staind the roots my mirtle bore
But the time of youth is fled   15
And grey hairs are on my head

*

To my Mirtle   t

To a lovely mirtle bound
Blossoms showring all around
O how sick & weary I
Underneath my mirtle lie
Why should I be bound to thee   5
O my lovely mirtle tree

*

[To go] on 1 Plate   t

O lapwing thou fliest around the heath
Nor seest the net that is spread beneath
Why dost thou not fly among the corn fields
They cannot spread nets where a harvest yields

———

An answer to the parson

Why of the sheep do you not learn peace
Because I dont want you to shear my fleece

[Experiment]

Thou hast a lap full of seed
And this is a fine country
Why dost thou not cast thy seed
And live in it merrily

Shall I cast it on the sand ^{t}5
And turn it into fruitful land ^{t}
For on no other ground ^{t}
Can I sow my seed
Without tearing up ^{t}
Some stinking weed   10

Riches

The countless gold of a merry heart ^{t}
The rubies & pearls of a loving eye
The indolent never can bring to the mart ^{t}
Nor the secret hoard up in his treasury ^{t}

If you trap the moment before its ripe ^{t}
The tears of repentance youll certainly wipe
But if once you let the ripe moment go
You can never wipe off the tears of woe ^{t}

*

Eternity

He who binds to himself a joy ^{t}
Does the winged life destroy
But he who kisses the joy as it flies ^{t}
Lives in eternity's sun rise ^{t}

* ^{t}

I heard an Angel singing
When the day was springing
Mercy Pity Peace ^{t}
Is the worlds release

Thus he sung all day   5
Over the new mown hay
Till the sun went down
And haycocks looked brown

I heard a Devil curse
Over the heath & the furze   10
Mercy could be no more
If there was nobody poor

And pity no more could be
If all were as happy as we
At his curse the sun went down   t 15
And the heavens gave a frown

Down pourd the heavy rain   t
Over the new reapd grain
And Miseries increase   t
Is Mercy Pity Peace   20

*

Silent Silent Night
Quench the holy light
Of thy torches bright

For possessd of Day
Thousand spirits stray   5
That sweet joys betray

Why should joys be sweet
Used with deceit
Nor with sorrows meet

But an honest joy   10
Does itself destroy
For a harlot coy

*

To Nobodaddy   t

Why art thou silent & invisible
Father of Jealousy   t
Why dost thou hide thyself in clouds
From every searching Eye

Why darkness & obscurity   5
In all thy words & laws
That none dare eat the fruit but from

The wily serpents jaws
Or is it because Secrecy   t
gains females loud applause   t 10

＊   t

Are not the joys of morning sweeter
Than the joys of night
And are the vigrous joys of youth
Ashamed of the light

Let age & sickness silent rob   5
The vineyards in the night
But those who burn with vigrous youth
Pluck fruits before the light

＊   t

How came pride in Man
From Mary it began
How Contempt & Scorn

What a world is Man
His Earth   5

＊

[*How to know Love from Deceit*]   t

Love to faults is always blind
Always is to joy inclind
Lawless wingd & unconfind   t
And breaks all chains from every mind

Deceit to secresy confind   t 5
Lawful cautious & refind   t
To every thing but interest blind   t
And forges fetters for the mind   t

＊

The wild flowers song   t

As I wanderd the forest
The green leaves among
I heard a wild flower   t
Singing a song

I slept in the earth   t 5
In the silent night
I murmurd my fears
And I felt delight

In the morning I went
As rosy as morn
To seek for new Joy
But I met with scorn

10

*

Soft Snow

t

I walked abroad in a snowy day
I askd the soft snow with me to play
She playd & she melted in all her prime
And the winter calld it a dreadful crime

t

*

Merlins prophecy

The harvest shall flourish in wintry weather
When two virginities meet together

The King & the Priest must be tied in a tether
Before two virgins can meet together

*

t

Why should I care for the men of thames
Or the cheating waves of charterd streams
Or shrink at the little blasts of fear
That the hireling blows into my ear

Tho born on the cheating banks of Thames
Tho his waters bathed my infant limbs
The Ohio shall wash his stains from me
I was born a slave but I go to be free

5

t
t

*

Day

t

The Sun arises in the East
Clothd in robes of blood & gold
Swords & spears & wrath increast
All around his bosom rolld
Crownd with warlike fires & raging desires

t

t

t
5

*

The sword sung on the barren heath
The sickle in the fruitful field
The sword he sung a song of death
But could not make the sickle yield

-464-

*

Abstinence sows sand all over
The ruddy limbs & flaming hair
But Desire Gratified
Plants fruits of life & beauty there

*

In a wife I would desire
What in whores is always found
The lineaments of Gratified desire

*

Lacedemonian Instruction

Come hither my boy tell me what thou seest there
A fool tangled in a religious snare

*

An old maid early eer I knew
Ought but the love that on me grew
And now Im coverd oer & oer
And wish that I had been a Whore

O I cannot cannot find
The undaunted courage of a Virgin Mind
For Early I in love was crost
Before my flower of love was lost

*

Several Questions Answerd

He who binds to himself a joy
Doth the winged life destroy
But he who kisses the joy as it flies
Lives in Eternitys sun rise

———————

The look of love alarms
Because tis filld with fire
But the look of soft deceit
Shall Win the lovers hire

———————

Soft deceit & Idleness
These are Beautys sweetest dress   t *10*

What is it men in women do require   t
The lineaments of Gratified Desire
What is it women do in men require   t
The lineaments of Gratified Desire

An ancient Proverb

Remove away that blackning church   *15*
Remove away that marriage hearse
Remove away that———of blood   t
Youll quite remove the ancient curse   t

*

The Fairy   t

Come hither my sparrows
My little arrows
If a tear or a smile
Will a man beguile
If an amorous delay   *5*
Clouds a sunshiny day
If the step of a foot   t
Smites the heart to its root
Tis the marriage ring
Makes each fairy a king   *10*

So a fairy sung
From the leaves I sprung
He leapd from the spray
To flee away
But in my hat caught   t *15*
He soon shall be taught
Let him laugh let him cry
Hes my butterfly   t
For I've pulld out the Sting
Of the marriage ring   *20*

*

The Kid

Thou little Kid didst play
   &c   t

*   t

My Spectre around me night & day
Like a Wild beast guards my way
My Emanation far within   t
Weeps incessantly for my Sin

A Fathomless & boundless deep   5
There we wander there we weep
On the hungry craving wind
My Spectre follows thee behind

He scents thy footsteps in the snow
Wheresoever thou dost go   10
Thro the wintry hail & rain
When wilt thou return again

Dost thou not in Pride & Scorn   t
Fill with tempests all my morn
And with jealousies & fears   15
Fill my pleasant nights with tears

Seven of my sweet loves thy knife
Has bereaved of their life
Their marble tombs I built with tears   t
And with cold & shuddering fears   20

Seven more loves weep night & day
Round the tombs where my loves lay
And seven more loves attend each night   t
Around my couch with torches bright

And seven more Loves in my bed   25
Crown with wine my mournful head   t
Pitying & forgiving all
Thy transgressions great & small

When wilt thou return & view
My loves & them to life renew   30
When wilt thou return & live
When wilt thou pity as I forgive   t

Never Never I return   t
Still for Victory I burn
Living thee alone Ill have   35
And when dead Ill be thy Grave

Thro the Heaven & Earth & Hell
Thou shalt never never quell

I will fly & thou pursue
Night & Morn the flight renew 40

Till I turn from Female Love t
And root up the Infernal Grove t
I shall never worthy be t
To Step into Eternity

And to end thy cruel mocks t 45
Annihilate thee on the rocks
And another form create
To be subservient to my Fate

Let us agree to give up Love
And root up the infernal grove 50
Then shall we return & see
The worlds of happy Eternity

& Throughout all Eternity t
I forgive you you forgive me
As our Dear Redeemer said 55
This the Wine & this the Bread

[Postscript]

Oer my Sins Thou sit & moan t
Hast thou no sins of thy own t
Oer my Sins thou sit & weep t
And lull thy own Sins fast asleep t

What transgressions I commit 5
Are for thy Transgressions fit
They thy Harlots thou their Slave
And my Bed becomes their Grave

Poor pale pitiable form
That I follow in a Storm 10
Iron tears & groans of lead
Bind around my akeing head

And let us go to the highest downs
With many pleasing wiles
The Woman that does not love your Frowns 15
Will never embrace your smiles

*

Mock on Mock on Voltaire Rousseau
Mock on Mock on tis all in vain

You throw the sand against the wind
And the wind blows it back again

And every sand becomes a Gem   5
Reflected in the beams divine
Blown back they blind the mocking Eye   t
But still in Israels paths they shine

The Atoms of Democritus
And Newtons Particles of light   10
Are sands upon the Red sea shore
Where Israels tents do shine so bright

*

Morning

To find the Western path
Right thro the Gates of Wrath
I urge my way
Sweet Mercy leads me on
With soft repentant moan   5
I see the break of day

The war of swords & spears
Melted by dewy tears
Exhales on high
The Sun is freed from fears   10
And with soft grateful tears
Ascends the sky

*

Terror in the house does roar
But Pity stands before the door

*

The Birds

He. Where thou dwellest in what Grove
Tell me Fair one tell me love
Where thou thy charming Nest dost build
O thou pride of every field

She. Yonder stands a lonely tree   5
There I live & mourn for thee
Morning drinks my silent tear
And evening winds my sorrows bear

He.	O thou Summers harmony
	I have livd & mournd for thee	10
	Each day I mourn along the wood
	And night hath heard my sorrows loud

She.	Dost thou truly long for me
	And am I thus sweet to thee
	Sorrow now is at an End	15
	O my Lover & my Friend

He.	Come on wings of joy well fly
	To where my Bower hangs on high
	Come & make thy calm retreat
	Among green leaves & blossoms sweet	20

*

I will tell you what Joseph of Arimathea
Said to my Fairy was not it very queer
Pliny & Trajan what are You here
Come listen to Joseph of Arimathea
Listen patient & when Joseph has done	5
Twill make a fool laugh & a Fairy Fun

*

Why was Cupid a Boy
And why a boy was he
He should have been a Girl
For ought that I can see

For he shoots with his bow	5
And the Girl shoots with her Eye
And they both are merry & glad
And laugh when we do cry

And to make Cupid a Boy	t
Was the Cupid Girls mocking plan	t 10
For a boy cant interpret the thing	t
Till he is become a man

And then hes so piercd with care
And wounded with arrowy smarts
That the whole business of his life	15
Is to pick out the heads of the darts

Twas the Greeks love of war
Turnd Love into a Boy
And Woman into a Statue of Stone
And away fled every Joy	20

—470—

*

Now Art has lost its mental Charms   t
France shall subdue the World in Arms
So spoke an Angel at my birth
Then said Descend thou upon Earth
Renew the Arts on Britains Shore   5
And France shall fall down & adore
With works of Art their Armies meet
And War shall sink beneath thy feet   t
But if thy Nation Arts refuse
And if they scorn the immortal Muse   10
France shall the arts of Peace restore
And save thee from the Ungrateful shore   t

Spirit who lovst Brittannias Isle   t
Round which the Fiends of Commerce smile   t

[unfinished]

*

[Dedication to Blake's Illustrations to Blair's *Grave*, printed 1808]

TO THE QUEEN   t

The Door of Death is made of Gold,
That Mortal Eyes cannot behold;
But, when the Mortal Eyes are clos'd,
And cold and pale the Limbs repos'd,
The Soul awakes; and, wond'ring, sees   5
In her mild Hand the golden Keys
The Grave is Heaven's golden Gate,
And rich and poor around it wait;
O Shepherdess of England's Fold,
Behold this Gate of Pearl and Gold!   10

To dedicate to England's Queen
The Visions that my Soul has seen,
And, by Her Kind permission, bring
What I have borne on solemn Wing
From the vast regions of the Grave,   15
Before Her Throne my Wings I wave;
Bowing before my Sov'reign's Feet,
"The Grave produc'd these Blossoms sweet
"In mild repose from Earthly strife;
"The Blossoms of Eternal Life!"   20

WILLIAM BLAKE

*

[From Blake's Notebook]

The Caverns of the Grave Ive seen   t
And these I shewd to Englands Queen
But now the Caves of Hell I view   t
Who shall I dare to shew them to
What mighty Soul in Beautys form   t 5
Shall dauntless View the Infernal Storm   t
Egremonts Countess can controll   t
The flames of Hell that round me roll   t
If she refuse I still go on
Till the Heavens & Earth are gone   10
Still admird by Noble minds   t
Followd by Envy on the winds
Reengravd Time after Time
Ever in their youthful prime
My Designs unchangd remain   t 15
Time may rage but rage in vain
For above Times troubled Fountains
On the Great Atlantic Mountains
In my Golden House on high
There they Shine Eternally   20

*

I rose up at the dawn of day
Get thee away get thee away
Prayst thou for Riches away away
This is the Throne of Mammon grey

Said I this sure is very odd   5
I took it to be the Throne of God
For every Thing besides I have
It is only for Riches that I can crave

I have Mental Joy & Mental Health
And Mental Friends & Mental wealth   t 10
Ive a Wife I love & that loves me
Ive all But Riches Bodily

I am in Gods presence night & day   t
And he never turns his face away
The accuser of sins by my side does stand   15
And he holds my money bag in his hand

For my worldly things God makes him pay   t
And hed pay for more if to him I would pray

And so you may do the worst you can do
Be assurd Mr Devil I wont pray to you   20

Then If for Riches I must not Pray
God knows I little of Prayers need say
So as a Church is known by its Steeple   t
If I pray it must be for other People   t

He says if I do not worship him for a God   25
I shall eat coarser food & go worse shod
So as I dont value such things as these
You must do Mr Devil just as God please

*

[A Separate Manuscript]

A fairy skipd upon my knee   t
Singing & dancing merrily
I said Thou thing of patches rings
Pins Necklaces & such like things
Disguiser of the Female Form   5
Thou paltry gilded poisnous worm
Weeping he fell upon my thigh
And thus in tears did soft reply
Knowest thou not O Fairies Lord
How much by us Contemnd Abhorrd   10
Whatever hides the Female form
That cannot bear the Mental storm
Therefore in Pity still we give
Our lives to make the Female live
And what would turn into disease   15
We turn to what will joy & please

*

[With Blake's Illustrations to Gray's *Poems*]   t

Around the Springs of Gray my wild root weaves
Traveller repose & Dream among my leaves.

—WILL. BLAKE

*

To Mrs Ann Flaxman

A little Flower grew in a lonely Vale
Its form was lovely but its colours. pale
One standing in the Porches of the Sun
When his Meridian Glories were begun

Leapd from the steps of fire & on the grass   5
Alighted where this little flower was
With hands divine he movd the gentle Sod
And took the Flower up in its native Clod
Then planting it upon a Mountains brow
'Tis your own fault if you dont flourish now   10

WILLIAM BLAKE

～

[The Pickering Manuscript]   t

The Smile

There is a Smile of Love
And there is a Smile of Deceit
And there is a Smile of Smiles
In which these two Smiles meet

And there is a Frown of Hate   5
And there is a Frown of disdain
And there is a Frown of Frowns
Which you strive to forget in vain

For it sticks in the Hearts deep Core
And it sticks in the deep Back bone   10
And no Smile that ever was smild
But only one Smile alone

That betwixt the Cradle & Grave
It only once Smild can be
But when it once is Smild   15
Theres an end to all Misery

*

The Golden Net   t

Three Virgins at the break of day
Whither young Man whither away
Alas for woe! alas for woe!   t
They cry & tears for ever flow
The one was Clothd in flames of fire   t 5
The other Clothd in iron wire   t
The other Clothd in tears & sighs   t
Dazling bright before my Eyes
They bore a Net of Golden twine
To hang upon the Branches fine   10
Pitying I wept to see the woe   t

-474-

That Love & Beauty undergo
To be consumd in burning Fires
And in ungratified desires
And in tears clothd Night & day   15
Melted all my Soul away
When they saw my Tears a Smile
That did Heaven itself beguile
Bore the Golden Net aloft
As on downy Pinions soft   t 20
Over the Morning of my day   t
Underneath the Net I stray
Now intreating Burning Fire   t
Now intreating Iron Wire   t
Now intreating Tears & Sighs   25
O when will the morning rise   t

*

The Mental Traveller   t

I traveld thro' a Land of Men
A Land of Men & Women too
And heard & saw such dreadful things
As cold Earth wanderers never knew

For there the Babe is born in joy   5
That was begotten in dire woe
Just as we Reap in joy the fruit
Which we in bitter tears did sow

And if the Babe is born a Boy
He's given to a Woman Old   10
Who nails him down upon a rock
Catches his shrieks in cups of gold

She binds iron thorns around his head
She pierces both his hands & feet
She cuts his heart out at his side   15
To make it feel both cold & heat

Her fingers number every Nerve
Just as a Miser counts his gold
She lives upon his shrieks & cries
And she grows young as he grows old   20

Till he becomes a bleeding youth
And she becomes a Virgin bright
Then he rends up his Manacles
And binds her down for his delight

He plants himself in all her Nerves   25
Just as a Husbandman his mould
And she becomes his dwelling place
And Garden fruitful seventy fold

An aged Shadow soon he fades
Wandring round an Earthly Cot   30
Full filled all with gems & gold
Which he by industry had got

And these are the gems of the Human Soul
The rubies & pearls of a lovesick eye
The countless gold of the akeing heart   35
The martyrs groan & the lovers sigh

They are his meat they are his drink
He feeds the Beggar & the Poor
And the wayfaring Traveller
For ever open is his door   40

His grief is their eternal joy
They make the roofs & walls to ring
Till from the fire on the hearth
A little Female Babe does spring

And she is all of solid fire   45
And gems & gold that none his hand
Dares stretch to touch her Baby form
Or wrap her in his swaddling-band

But She comes to the Man she loves
If young or old or rich or poor   50
They soon drive out the aged Host
A Beggar at anothers door

He wanders weeping far away
Untill some other take him in
Oft blind & age-bent sore distrest   55
Untill he can a Maiden win

And to allay his freezing Age
The Poor Man takes her in his arms
The Cottage fades before his sight
The Garden & its lovely Charms   60

The Guests are scatterd thro' the land
For the Eye altering alters all
The Senses roll themselves in fear
And the flat Earth becomes a Ball

The Stars Sun Moon all shrink away   65
A desert vast without a bound
And nothing left to eat or drink
And a dark desert all around

The honey of her Infant lips
The bread & wine of her sweet smile   70
The wild game of her roving Eye
Does him to Infancy beguile

For as he eats & drinks he grows
Younger & younger every day
And on the desart wild they both   75
Wander in terror & dismay

Like the wild Stag she flees away
Her fear plants many a thicket wild
While he pursues her night & day
By various arts of Love beguild   80

By various arts of Love & Hate
Till the wide desert planted oer
With Labyrinths of wayward Love
Where roams the Lion Wolf & Boar   t

Till he becomes a wayward Babe   85
And she a weeping Woman Old
Then many a Lover wanders here
The Sun & Stars are nearer rolld

The trees bring forth sweet Extacy
To all who in the desert roam   90
Till many a City there is Built
And many a pleasant Shepherds home

But when they find the frowning Babe
Terror strikes thro the region wide
They cry the Babe the Babe is Born   95
And flee away on Every side   t

For who dare touch the frowning form
His arm is witherd to its root
Lions Boars Wolves all howling flee
And every Tree does shed its fruit   100

And none can touch that frowning form
Except it be a Woman Old
She nails him down upon the Rock
And all is done as I have told

*

The Land of Dreams

Awake awake my little Boy
Thou wast thy Mothers only joy
Why dost thou weep in thy gentle sleep
Awake thy Father does thee keep

O what Land is the Land of Dreams   5
What are its Mountains & what are its Streams
O Father I saw my Mother there
Among the Lillies by waters fair

Among the Lambs clothed in white
She walkd with her Thomas in sweet delight   10
I wept for joy like a dove I mourn
O when shall I again return

Dear Child I also by pleasant Streams
Have wanderd all Night in the Land of Dreams
But tho calm & warm the waters wide   15
I could not get to the other side

Father O Father what do we here
In this Land of unbelief & fear
The Land of Dreams is better far
Above the light of the Morning Star   20

*

Mary   t

Sweet Mary the first time she ever was there
Came into the Ball room among the Fair
The young Men & Maidens around her throng
And these are the words upon every tongue

An Angel is here from the heavenly Climes   5
Or again does return the Golden times   t
Her eyes outshine every brilliant ray
She opens her lips tis the Month of May

Mary moves in soft beauty & conscious delight
To augment with sweet smiles all the joys of the Night   10
Nor once blushes to own to the rest of the Fair
That sweet Love & Beauty are worthy our care

In the Morning the Villagers rose with delight
And repeated with pleasure the joys of the night
And Mary arose among Friends to be free   15
But no Friend from henceforward thou Mary shalt see

—478—

Some said she was proud some calld her a whore
And some when she passed by shut to the door
A damp cold came oer her her blushes all fled
Her lillies & roses are blighted & shed 20

O why was I born with a different Face
Why was I not born like this Envious Race t
Why did Heaven adorn me with bountiful hand
And then set me down in an envious Land

To be weak as a Lamb & smooth as a dove 25
And not to raise Envy is calld Christian Love
But if you raise Envy your Merits to blame
For planting such spite in the weak & the tame

I will humble my Beauty I will not dress fine
I will keep from the Ball & my Eyes shall not shine 30
And if any Girls Lover forsakes her for me
I'll refuse him my hand & from Envy be free

She went out in Morning attird plain & neat
Proud Marys gone Mad said the Child in the Street
She went out in Morning in plain neat attire 35
And came home in Evening bespatterd with mire

She trembled & wept sitting on the Bed side
She forgot it was Night & she trembled & cried
She forgot it was Night she forgot it was Morn
Her soft Memory imprinted with Faces of Scorn 40

With Faces of Scorn & with Eyes of disdain
Like foul Fiends inhabiting Marys mild Brain
She remembers no Face like the Human Divine
All Faces have Envy sweet Mary but thine

And thine is a Face of sweet Love in Despair 45
And thine is a Face of mild sorrow & care
And thine is a Face of wild terror & fear
That shall never be quiet till laid on its bier

*

The Crystal Cabinet

The Maiden caught me in the Wild
Where I was dancing merrily
She put me into her Cabinet
And Lockd me up with a golden Key

This Cabinet is formd of Gold 5
And Pearl & Crystal shining bright
And within it opens into a World
And a little lovely Moony Night t

Another England there I saw
Another London with its Tower   *10*
Another Thames & other Hills
And another pleasant Surrey Bower

Another Maiden like herself
Translucent lovely shining clear
Threefold each in the other closd   *15*
O what a pleasant trembling fear

O what a smile a threefold Smile
Filld me that like a flame I burnd
I bent to Kiss the lovely Maid
And found a Threefold Kiss returnd   20

I strove to sieze the inmost Form
With ardor fierce & hands of flame
But burst the Crystal Cabinet
And like a Weeping Babe became

A weeping Babe upon the wild   25
And Weeping Woman pale reclind
And in the outward air again
I filld with woes the passing Wind

*

The Grey Monk   t

I die I die the Mother said
My Children die for lack of Bread   t
What more has the merciless Tyrant said
The Monk sat down on the Stony Bed   t

The blood red ran from the Grey Monks side   5
His hands & feet were wounded wide
His Body bent his arms & knees
Like to the roots of ancient trees

His eye was dry no tear could flow
A hollow groan first spoke his woe   10
He trembled & shudderd upon the Bed   t
At length with a feeble cry he said

When God commanded this hand to write
In the studious hours of deep midnight
He told me the writing I wrote should prove   t 15
The Bane of all that on Earth I lovd   t

My Brother starvd between two Walls
His Childrens Cry my Soul appalls
I mockd at the wrack & griding chain   t
My bent body mocks their torturing pain   t 20

Thy Father drew his sword in the North
With his thousands strong he marched forth   t
Thy Brother has armd himself in Steel   t
To avenge the wrongs thy Children feel   t

But vain the Sword & vain the Bow   25
They never can work Wars overthrow
The Hermits Prayer & the Widows tear
Alone can free the World from fear

For a Tear is an Intellectual Thing   t
And a Sigh is the Sword of an Angel King   30
And the bitter groan of the Martyrs woe   t
Is an Arrow from the Almighties Bow

The hand of Vengeance found the Bed   t
To which the Purple Tyrant fled
The iron hand crushd the Tyrants head   35
And became a Tyrant in his stead   t

*

Auguries of Innocence   t

To see a World in a Grain of Sand
And a Heaven in a Wild Flower
Hold Infinity in the palm of your hand
And Eternity in an hour
A Robin Red breast in a Cage   5
Puts all Heaven in a Rage
A dove house filld with doves & Pigeons
Shudders Hell thro all its regions
A dog starvd at his Masters Gate
Predicts the ruin of the State   10
A Horse misusd upon the Road
Calls to Heaven for Human blood
Each outcry of the hunted Hare
A fibre from the Brain does tear
A Skylark wounded in the wing   15
A Cherubim does cease to sing
The Game Cock clipd & armd for fight
Does the Rising Sun affright
Every Wolfs & Lions howl
Raises from Hell a Human Soul   20
The wild deer wandring here & there
Keeps the Human Soul from Care
The Lamb misusd breeds Public strife
And yet forgives the Butchers Knife
The Bat that flits at close of Eve   25
Has left the Brain that wont Believe

The Owl that calls upon the Night
Speaks the Unbelievers fright
He who shall hurt the little Wren
Shall never be belovd by Men   30
He who the Ox to wrath has movd
Shall never be by Woman lovd
The wanton Boy that kills the Fly
Shall feel the Spiders enmity
He who torments the Chafers sprite   35
Weaves a Bower in endless Night
The Catterpiller on the Leaf
Repeats to thee thy Mothers grief
Kill not the Moth nor Butterfly
For the Last Judgment draweth nigh   40
He who shall train the Horse to War
Shall never pass the Polar Bar
The Beggers Dog & Widows Cat
Feed them & thou wilt grow fat
The Gnat that sings his Summers song   45
Poison gets from Slanders tongue
The poison of the Snake & Newt
Is the sweat of Envys Foot
The Poison of the Honey Bee
Is the Artists Jealousy   50
The Princes Robes & Beggars Rags
Are Toadstools on the Misers Bags
A truth thats told with bad intent
Beats all the Lies you can invent
It is right it should be so   55
Man was made for Joy & Woe
And when this we rightly know
Thro the World we safely go
Joy & Woe are woven fine
A Clothing for the Soul divine   60
Under every grief & pine
Runs a joy with silken twine
The Babe is more than swadling Bands
Throughout all these Human Lands
Tools were made & Born were hands   65
Every Farmer Understands
Every Tear from Every Eye
Becomes a Babe in Eternity
This is caught by Females bright
And returnd to its own delight   70
The Bleat the Bark Bellow & Roar
Are Waves that Beat on Heavens Shore

The Babe that weeps the Rod beneath
Writes Revenge in realms of death
The Beggars Rags fluttering in Air   75
Does to Rags the Heavens tear
The Soldier armd with Sword & Gun
Palsied strikes the Summers Sun
The poor Mans Farthing is worth more
Than all the Gold on Africs Shore   80
One Mite wrung from the Labrers hands
Shall buy & sell the Misers Lands
Or if protected from on high
Does that whole Nation sell & buy
He who mocks the Infants Faith   85
Shall be mock'd in Age & Death
He who shall teach the Child to Doubt
The rotting Grave shall neer get out
He who respects the Infants faith
Triumphs over Hell & Death   90
The Childs Toys & the Old Mans Reasons
Are the Fruits of the Two seasons
The Questioner who sits so sly
Shall never know how to Reply
He who replies to words of Doubt   95
Doth put the Light of Knowledge out
The Strongest Poison ever known
Came from Caesars Laurel Crown
Nought can deform the Human Race
Like to the Armours iron brace   100
When Gold & Gems adorn the Plow
To peaceful Arts shall Envy Bow
A Riddle or the Crickets Cry
Is to Doubt a fit Reply
The Emmets Inch & Eagles Mile   105
Make Lame Philosophy to smile
He who Doubts from what he sees
Will neer Believe do what you Please
If the Sun & Moon should doubt
Theyd immediately Go out   110
To be in a Passion you Good may do
But no Good if a Passion is in you
The Whore & Gambler by the State
Licencd build that Nations Fate
The Harlots cry from Street to Street   115
Shall weave Old Englands winding Sheet
The Winners Shout the Losers Curse

Dance before dead Englands Hearse
Every Night & every Morn
Some to Misery are Born   120
Every Morn & every Night
Some are Born to sweet delight
Some are Born to sweet delight
Some are Born to Endless Night
We are led to Believe a Lie   125
When we see not Thro the Eye   t
Which was Born in a Night to perish in a Night
When the Soul Slept in Beams of Light
God Appears & God is Light
To those poor Souls who dwell in Night   130
But does a Human Form Display
To those who Dwell in Realms of day

*

Auguries of Innocence

[An Editorial Arrangement]

To see a World in a Grain of Sand
And a Heaven in a Wild Flower
Hold Infinity in the palm of your hand
And Eternity in an hour

A Robin Red breast in a Cage   5
Puts all Heaven in a Rage
A dove house filld with doves & Pigeons
Shudders Hell thro all its regions
A dog starvd at his Masters Gate
Predicts the ruin of the State   10
A Horse misusd upon the Road
Calls to Heaven for Human blood
Each outcry of the hunted Hare
A fibre from the Brain does tear
A Skylark wounded in the wing   15
A Cherubim does cease to sing   16
The Game Cock clipd & armd for fight   17
Does the Rising Sun affright   18
The Lamb misusd breeds Public strife   23
And yet forgives the Butchers Knife   24
He who shall train the Horse to War   41
Shall never pass the Polar Bar   42
Every Wolfs & Lions howl   19
Raises from Hell a Human Soul   20
The Bleat the Bark Bellow & Roar   71
Are Waves that Beat on Heavens Shore   72

The wild deer wandring here & there   21
Keeps the Human Soul from Care   22
The Beggers Dog & Widows Cat   43
Feed them & thou wilt grow fat   44
He who shall hurt the little Wren   29
Shall never be belovd by Men   30
He who the Ox to wrath has movd   31
Shall never be by Woman lovd   32
He who torments the Chafers sprite   35
Weaves a Bower in endless Night   36
The wanton Boy that kills the Fly   33
Shall feel the Spiders enmity   34
The Catterpiller on the Leaf   37
Repeats to thee thy Mothers grief   38
Kill not the Moth nor Butterfly   39
For the Last Judgment draweth nigh   40
The Bat that flits at close of Eve   25
Has left the Brain that wont Believe   26
The Owl that calls upon the Night   27
Speaks the Unbelievers fright   28
The Gnat that sings his Summers song   45
Poison gets from Slanders tongue
The poison of the Snake & Newt
Is the sweat of Envys Foot
The Poison of the Honey Bee
Is the Artists Jealousy   50
A Riddle or the Crickets Cry   103
Is to Doubt a fit Reply   104
The Emmets Inch & Eagles Mile   105
Make Lame Philosophy to smile
He who Doubts from what he sees
Will neer Believe do what you Please
If the Sun & Moon should doubt
Theyd immediately Go out   110
He who mocks the Infants Faith   85
Shall be mock'd in Age & Death
He who shall teach the Child to Doubt
The rotting Grave shall neer get out
He who respects the Infants faith
Triumphs over Hell & Death   90
The Childs Toys & the Old Mans Reasons
Are the Fruits of the Two seasons
The Questioner who sits so sly
Shall never know how to Reply
He who replies to words of Doubt   95
Doth put the Light of Knowledge out   96
A truth thats told with bad intent   53

Beats all the Lies you can invent   54
Joy & Woe are woven fine   59
A Clothing for the Soul divine   60
Under every grief & pine   61
Runs a joy with silken twine   62
It is right it should be so   55
Man was made for Joy & Woe   56
And when this we rightly know   57
Thro the World we safely go   58
The Babe is more than swadling Bands   63
Throughout all these Human Lands   64
Tools were made & Born were hands   65
Every Farmer Understands
Every Tear from Every Eye
Becomes a Babe in Eternity
This is caught by Females bright
And returnd to its own delight   70
The Babe that weeps the Rod beneath   73
Writes Revenge in realms of death   74
The Princes Robes & Beggars Rags   51
Are Toadstools on the Misers Bags   52
The Beggars Rags fluttering in Air   75
Does to Rags the Heavens tear   76
The poor Mans Farthing is worth more   79
Than all the Gold on Africs Shore   80
One Mite wrung from the Labrers hands   81
Shall buy & sell the Misers Lands   82
Or if protected from on high   83
Does that whole Nation sell & buy   84
The Strongest Poison ever known   97
Came from Caesars Laurel Crown   98
Nought can deform the Human Race   99
Like to the Armours iron brace   100
The Soldier armd with Sword & Gun   77
Palsied strikes the Summers Sun   78
When Gold & Gems adorn the Plow   101
To peaceful Arts shall Envy Bow   102
To be in a Passion you Good may do   111
But no Good if a Passion is in you   112
The Whore & Gambler by the State   113
Licencd build that Nations Fate   114
The Harlots cry from Street to Street   115
Shall weave Old Englands winding Sheet
The Winners Shout the Losers Curse
Dance before dead Englands Hearse
Every Night & every Morn

Some to Misery are Born   120
Every Morn & every Night
Some are Born to sweet delight
Some are Born to sweet delight
Some are Born to Endless Night
We are led to Believe a Lie   125
When we see not Thro the Eye
Which was Born in a Night to perish in a Night
When the Soul Slept in Beams of Light
God Appears & God is Light
To those poor Souls who dwell in Night   130
But does a Human Form Display
To those who Dwell in Realms of day

*

Long John Brown & Little Mary Bell   t

Little Mary Bell had a Fairy in a Nut   t
Long John Brown had the Devil in his Gut
Long John Brown lovd Little Mary Bell
And the Fairy drew the Devil into the Nut-shell

Her Fairy skipd out & her Fairy skipd in   5
He laughd at the devil saying Love is a Sin
The devil he raged & the devil he was wroth
And the devil enterd into the Young Mans broth   t

He was soon in the Gut of the loving Young Swain
For John eat & drank to drive away Loves pain   10
But all he could do he grew thinner & thinner
Tho he eat & drank as much as ten Men for his dinner

Some said he had a Wolf in his stomach day & night
Some said he had the devil & they guessd right
The fairy skipd about in his glory Joy & Pride   15
And he laughd at the devil till poor John Brown died

Then the Fairy skipd out of the old Nut shell
And woe & alack for Pretty Mary Bell
For the Devil crept in when the Fairy skipd out
And there goes Miss Bell with her fusty old Nut   20

*

William Bond

I wonder whether the Girls are mad
And I wonder whether they mean to kill
And I wonder if William Bond will die
For assuredly he is very ill

He went to Church in a May morning   *5*
Attended by Fairies one two & three
But the Angels of Providence drove them away
And he returnd home in Misery

He went not out to the Field nor Fold
He went not out to the Village nor Town   *10*
But he came home in a black black cloud
And took to his Bed & there lay down

And an Angel of Providence at his Feet
And an Angel of Providence at his Head
And in the midst a Black Black Cloud   *15*
And in the midst the Sick Man on his Bed

And on his Right hand was Mary Green
And on his Left hand was his Sister Jane
And their tears fell thro the black black Cloud
To drive away the sick mans pain   20

O William if thou dost another Love
Dost another Love better than poor Mary
Go & take that other to be thy Wife
And Mary Green shall her Servant be

Yes Mary I do another Love   25
Another I Love far better than thee
And Another I will have for my Wife
Then what have I to do with thee

For thou art Melancholy Pale
And on thy Head is the cold Moons shine   30
But she is ruddy & bright as day
And the sun beams dazzle from her eyne

Mary trembled & Mary chilld
And Mary fell down on the right hand floor
That William Bond & his Sister Jane   35
Scarce could recover Mary more

When Mary woke & found her Laid
On the Right hand of her William dear
On the Right hand of his loved Bed
And saw her William Bond so near   40

The Fairies that fled from William Bond
Danced around her Shining Head
They danced over the Pillow white
And the Angels of Providence left the Bed

I thought Love livd in the hot sun shine   45
But O he lives in the Moony light
I thought to find Love in the heat of day
But sweet Love is the Comforter of Night

Seek Love in the Pity of others Woe
In the gentle relief of anothers care   50
In the darkness of night & the winters snow
In the naked & outcast Seek Love there

VI

[From Blake's Notebook]   t

Motto to the Songs of Innocence & of Experience

The Good are attracted by Mens perceptions
And Think not for themselves
   Till Experience teaches them to catch
And to cage the Fairies & Elves

And then the Knave begins to snarl   5
And the Hypocrite to howl
And all his good Friends shew their private ends
And the Eagle is known from the Owl

*   t

Let the Brothels of Paris be opened
With many an alluring dance
To awake the Physicians thro the city   t
Said the beautiful Queen of France

Then old Nobodaddy aloft   5
Farted & belchd & coughd
And said I love hanging & drawing & quartering
Every bit as well as war & slaughtering   t

Then he swore a great & solemn Oath   t
To kill the people I am loth   10
But If they rebel they must go to hell
They shall have a Priest & a passing bell

The King awoke on his couch of gold
As soon as he heard these tidings told
Arise & come both fife & drum   15
And the [Famine] shall eat both crust & crumb   t

The Queen of France just touchd this Globe
And the Pestilence darted from her robe   t
But our good Queen quite grows to the ground
And a great many suckers grow all around   t 20

                    t

*

                    t

Who will exchange his own fire side
For the stone of anothers door   t
Who will exchange his wheaten loaf
For the links of a dungeon floor

Fayette beheld the King & Queen   5
In curses & iron bound   t
But mute Fayette wept tear for tear
And guarded them around

O who would smile on the wintry seas
& Pity the stormy roar   t 10
Or who will exchange his new born child
For the dog at the wintry door

                    *   t

When Klopstock England defied
Uprose terrible Blake in his pride   t
For old Nobodaddy aloft
Farted & Belchd & coughd
Then swore a great oath that made heavn quake   5
And calld aloud to English Blake
Blake was giving his body ease
At Lambeth beneath the poplar trees
From his seat then started he
And turnd himself round three times three   t 10
The Moon at that sight blushd scarlet red
The stars threw down their cups & fled
And all the devils that were in hell   t
Answered with a ninefold yell
Klopstock felt the intripled turn   t 15
And all his bowels began to churn   t
And his bowels turned round three times three   t
And lockd in his soul with a ninefold key
That from his body it neer could be parted
Till to the last trumpet it was farted   20
Then again old Nobodaddy swore
He neer had seen such a thing before
Since Noah was shut in the ark
Since Eve first chose her hell fire spark

Since twas the fashion to go naked   25
Since the old anything was created
And so feeling he begd him to turn again
And ease poor Klopstocks nine fold pain
From pity then he redend round   t
And the Spell removed unwound   t 30
If Blake could do this when he rose up from shite
What might he not do if he sat down to write

*

On the Virginity of the Virgin
Mary & Johanna Southcott

Whateer is done to her she cannot know
And if youll ask her she will swear it so   t
Whether tis good or evil none's to blame
No one can take the pride no one the shame

*

You dont believe I wont attempt to make ye
You are asleep I wont attempt to wake ye
Sleep on Sleep on while in your pleasant dreams
Of Reason you may drink of Lifes clear streams
Reason and Newton they are quite two things   5
For so the Swallow & the Sparrow sings
Reason says Miracle. Newton says Doubt
Aye thats the way to make all Nature out   t
Doubt Doubt & dont believe without experiment
That is the very thing that Jesus meant   10
When he said Only Believe Believe & try   t
Try Try & never mind the Reason why

*

If it is True What the Prophets write
That the heathen Gods are all stocks & stones
Shall we for the sake of being Polite
Feed them with the juice of our marrow bones

And if Bezaleel & Aholiab drew   5
What the Finger of God pointed to their View
Shall we suffer the Roman & Grecian Rods
To compell us to worship them as Gods

They stole them from the Temple of the Lord
And Worshippd them that they might make Inspired Art   ^t10
  Abhorrd

The Wood & Stone were calld The Holy Things
And their Sublime Intent given to their Kings
All the Atonements of Jehovah spurnd
And Criminals to Sacrifices Turnd

*

I am no Homers Hero you all know
I profess not Generosity to a Foe
My Generosity is to my Friends
That for their Friendship I may make amends.
The Generous to Enemies promotes their Ends   5
And becomes the Enemy & Betrayer of his Friends

*

The Angel that presided oer my birth
Said Little creature formd of Joy & Mirth   t
Go love without the help of any King on Earth   t

*

Some Men created for destruction come
Into the World & make the World their home
Be they as Vile & Base as Eer they can   t
Theyll still be called The Worlds honest man   t

*

If I eer Grow to Mans Estate
O Give to me a Womans fate
May I govern all both great & small
Have the last word & take the wall

*

From Cratetos

Me Time has Crook'd. no good Workman
Is he. Infirm is all that he does

*

If Men will act like a maid smiling over a Churn
They ought not, when it comes to anothers turn

To grow sower at what a friend may utter
Knowing & feeling that we all have need of Butter

False Friends fie fie our Friendship you shant sever
In spite we will be greater friends than ever

*

Anger & Wrath my bosom rends
I thought them the Errors of friends
But all my limbs with warmth glow
I find them the Errors of the foe

*

An Epitaph

Come knock your heads against this stone
For sorrow that poor John Thompsons gone

*

Another

I was buried near this Dike
That my Friends may weep as much as they like

*

Another

Here lies John Trot the Friend of all mankind
He has not left one Enemy behind
Friends were quite hard to find old authors say
But now they stand in every bodies way

*

He is a Cock would
And would be a Cock if he could

*

And his legs carried it like a long fork
Reachd all the way from Chichester to York
From York all across Scotland to the Sea
This was a Man of Men as seems to me
Not only in his Mouth his own Soul lay
But my Soul also would he bear away
Like as a Pedlar bears his weary Pack
So Stewhards Soul he buckld to his Back

But once alas committing a Mistake
He bore the wretched Soul of William Blake   10
That he might turn it into Eggs of Gold
But neither Back nor mouth those Eggs could hold
His under jaw dropd as those Eggs he laid
And Stewhards Eggs are addled & decayd   t
The Examiner whose very name is Hunt   t 15
Calld Death a Madman trembling for the affront   t
Like trembling Hare sits on his weakly paper
On which he usd to dance & sport & caper
Yorkshire Jack Hemp & gentle blushing daw
Clapd Death into the corner of their jaw   20
And Felpham Billy rode out every morn
Horseback with Death over the fields of corn
Who with iron hand cuffd in the afternoon
The Ears of Billys Lawyer & Dragoon
And Cur my Lawyer & Dady Jack Hemps Parson   t 25
Both went to Law with Death to keep our Ears on
For how to starve Death we had laid a plot
Against his Price but Death was in the Pot
He made them pay his Price alack a day
He knew both Law & Gospel better than they   30
O that I neer ha[d] seen that William Blake
Or could from death Assassinetti wake
We thought Alas that such a thought should be
That Blake would Etch for him & draw for me
For twas a kind of Bargain Screwmuch made   35
That Blakes designs should be by us displayed
Because he makes designs so very cheap
Then Screwmuch at Blakes soul took a long leap
Twas not a Mouse twas Death in a disguise
And I alas live to weep out mine Eyes   40
And Death sits laughing on their Monuments   t
On which hes written Recievd the Contents   t
But I have writ so sorrowful my thought is   t
His Epitaph for my tears are aqua fortis

Come Artists knock your heads against this stone   45
For Sorrow that our friend Bob Screwmuchs gone   t
And now the Men upon me smile & Laugh
Ill also write my own dear Epitaph
And Ill be buried near a Dike
That my friends may weep as much as they like   50
Here lies Stewhard the Friend of All &c   t

*

Was I angry with Hayley who usd me so ill
Or can I be angry with Felphams old Mill   t
Or angry with Flaxman or Cromek or Stothard
Or poor Schiavonetti whom they to death botherd
Or angry with Macklin or Boydel or Bowyer   t 5
Because they did not say O what a Beau ye are   t
At a Friends Errors Anger shew
Mirth at the Errors of a Foe

*

Blakes apology for his Catalogue   t

Having given great offence by writing in Prose
Ill write in Verse as soft as Bartolloze   t
Some blush at what others can see no crime in
But nobody sees any harm in Rhyming
Dryden in Rhyme cries Milton only plannd   5
Every Fool shook his bells throughout the land
Tom Cooke cut Hogarth down with his clean graving
Thousands of Connoisseurs with joy ran raving   t
Thus Hayley on his Toilette seeing the sope
Cries Homer is very much improvd by Pope   t 10
Some say Ive given great Provision to my foes   t
And that now I lead my false friends by the nose   t
Flaxman & Stothard smelling a sweet savour
Cry Blakified drawing spoils painter & Engraver
While I looking up to my Umbrella   15
Resolvd to be a very contrary fellow
Cry looking quite from Skumference to Center   t
No one can finish so high as the original Inventor
Thus Poor Schiavonetti died of the Cromek
A thing thats tied around the Examiners neck   t 20
This is my sweet apology to my friends
That I may put them in mind of their latter Ends

*

Cosway Frazer & Baldwin of Egypts Lake
Fear to associate with Blake
This Life is a Warfare against Evils
They heal the sick he casts out devils
Hayley Flaxman & Stothard are also in doubt   5
Lest their Virtue should be put to the rout
One grins tother spits & in corners hides   t
And all the Virtuous have shewn their backsides   t

*

My title as [a] Genius thus is provd
Not Praisd by Hayley nor by Flaxman lovd

*

To H

You think Fuseli is not a Great Painter Im Glad
This is one of the best compliments he ever had

*

P—— loved me not as he lovd his Friends
For he lovd them for gain to serve his Ends
He loved me and for no Gain at all
But to rejoice & triumph in my fall

*

The Sussex Men are Noted Fools
And weak is their brain pan
I wonder if H—— the painter
Is not a Sussex Man

*

Of H s birth this was the happy lot
His Mother on his Father him begot

*

To forgive Enemies H—— does pretend
Who never in his Life forgave a friend

*

On H——ys Friendship

When H——y finds out what you cannot do
That is the very thing hell set you to
If you break not your Neck tis not his fault
But pecks of poison are not pecks of salt
And when he could not act upon my wife
Hired a Villain to bereave my Life

*

To H——

Thy Friendship oft has made my heart to ake
Do be my Enemy for Friendships sake

*

On H—— the Pick thank

I write the Rascal Thanks till he & I
With Thanks & Compliments are quite drawn dry

*

Imitation of Pope A Compliment to the Ladies

Wondrous the Gods more wondrous are the Men
More Wondrous Wondrous still the Cock & Hen
More Wondrous still the Table Stool & Chair
But Ah! More wondrous still the Charming Fair

*

William Cowper Esqre

For this is being a Friend just in the nick   t
Not when hes well but waiting till hes sick
He calls you to his help be you not movd   t
Untill by being Sick his wants are provd   t

You see him spend his Soul in Prophecy   5
Do you believe it a confounded lie
Till some Bookseller & the Public Fame
Proves there is truth in his extravagant claim

For tis atrocious in a Friend you love   t
To tell you any thing that he cant prove   10
And tis most wicked in a Christian Nation
For any Man to pretend to Inspiration

*

The only Man that eer I knew
Who did not make me almost spew
Was Fuseli he was both Turk & Jew
And so dear Christian Friends how do you do   t

*

Madman I have been calld Fool they call thee
I wonder which they Envy Thee or Me

*

To F——

I mock thee not tho I by thee am Mocked
Thou callst me Madman but I call thee Blockhead

*

Hes a Blockhead who wants a proof of what he Can't Percieve
And he's a Fool who tries to make such a Blockhead believe

*

To Nancy F——

How can I help thy Husbands copying Me
Should that make difference twixt me & Thee

To F——

You call me Mad tis Folly to do so
To seek to turn a Madman to a Foe
If you think as you speak you are an Ass
If you do not you are but what you was

*

S—— in Childhood on the Nursery floor
Was extreme Old & most extremely poor
He is grown old & rich & what he will
He is extreme old & extreme poor still

*

He has observd the Golden Rule
Till hes become the Golden Fool

*

To S   d

You all your Youth observd the Golden Rule
Till youre at last become the golden fool
I sport with Fortune Merry Blithe & Gay

Like to the Lion Sporting with his Prey
Take you the hide & horns which you may wear   5
Mine is the flesh the bones may be your Share

*

On S——

You say reserve & modesty he has
Whose heart is iron his head wood & his face brass
The Fox the Owl the Beetle & the Bat
By sweet reserve & modesty get Fat

*

old acquaintance well renew
Prospero had One Caliban & I have Two

*

On F—— & S——

I found them blind I taught them how to see
And now they know neither themselves nor me
Tis Excellent to turn a thorn to a pin
A Fool to a bolt a Knave to a glass of gin

*

Mr Stothard to Mr Cromek

For Fortunes favours you your riches bring
But Fortune says she gave you no such thing
Why should you be ungrateful to your friends
Sneaking & Backbiting & Odds & Ends

Mr Cromek to Mr Stothard

Fortune favours the Brave old Proverbs say
But not with Money. that is not the way
Turn back turn back you travel all in vain
Turn thro the iron gate down Sneaking lane

*

Cr—— loves artists as he loves his Meat
He loves the Art but tis the Art to Cheat

*

A Petty sneaking Knave I knew
O M^r Cr—— how do ye do

*

Cromek Speaks

I always take my judgment from a Fool
Because his judgment is so very Cool   t
Not prejudicd by feelings great or small
Amiable state he cannot feel at all   t

*

English Encouragement of Art   t

[First reading]

If you mean to Please Every body you will
Set to work both Ignorance & skill
For a great multitude are Ignorant   t
And skill to them seems raving & rant
Like putting oil & water into a lamp   5
Twill make a great splutter with smoke & damp
For there is no use as it seems to me
Of lighting a Lamp when you dont wish to see

[Final reading]

English Encouragement of Art

Cromeks opinions put into Rhyme

If you mean to Please Every body you will
Menny wouver both Bunglishness & skill   t
For a great Conquest are Bunglery
And Jenous looks to ham like mad Rantery   t
Like displaying oil & water into a lamp   5
Twill hold forth a huge splutter with smoke & damp
For its all sheer loss as it seems to me
Of displaying up a light when we want not to see

*

When you look at a picture you always can see
If a Man of Sense has Painted he
Then never flinch but keep up a Jaw
About freedom & Jenny suck awa'   t

And when it smells of the Lamp we can 5
Say all was owing to the Skilful Man
For the smell of water is but small
So een let Ignorance do it all

*

The Cunning sures & the Aim at yours

*

All Pictures thats Panted with Sense & with Thought t
Are Painted by Madmen as sure as a Groat
For the Greater the Fool in the Pencil more blest
And when they are drunk they always pant best
Thy never can Rafael it Fuseli it nor Blake it 5
If they cant see an outline pray how can they make it
When Men will draw outlines begin you to jaw them
Madmen see outlines & therefore they draw them

*

You say their Pictures well Painted be
And yet they are Blockheads you all agree
Thank God I never was sent to school
To be Flogd into following the Style of a Fool t

*

The Errors of a Wise Man make your Rule
Rather than the Perfections of a Fool

*

Great things are done when Men & Mountains meet
This is not done by Jostling in the Street

*

If you play a Game of Chance know before you begin
If you are benevolent you will never win

*

No real Style of Colouring ever appears
But advertising in the News Papers
Look there youll see Sr Joshuas Colouring
Look at his Pictures All has taken Wing t

*

Can there be any thing more mean
More Malice in disguise
Than Praise a Man for doing what   t
That Man does most despise
Reynolds Lectures Exactly so   t 5
When he praises Michael Angelo

*   t

Sir Joshua Praises Michael Angelo
Tis Christian Mildness when Knaves Praise a Foe
But Twould be Madness all the World would say   t
Should Michael Angelo praise Sir Joshua
Christ usd the Pharisees in a rougher way   5

*

Sir Jo[s]hua praised Rubens with a Smile
By Calling his the ornamental Style
And yet his praise of Flaxman was the smartest
When he calld him the Ornamental Artist
But sure such ornaments we well may spare   5
As Crooked limbs & louzy heads of hair   t

*

Florentine Ingratitude

Sir Joshua sent his own Portrait to
The birth Place of Michael Angelo
And in the hand of the simpering fool
He put a dirty paper scroll
And on the paper to be polite   5
Did Sketches by Michael Angelo write   t
The Florentines said Tis a Dutch English bore
Michael Angelos Name writ on Rembrandts door
The Florentines call it an English Fetch
For Michael Angelo did never Sketch   10
Every line of his has Meaning
And needs neither Suckling nor Weaning
Tis the trading English Venetian Cant   t
To speak Michael Angelo & Act Rembrandt
It will set his Dutch friends all in a roar   15
To write Mch Ang on Rembrandts Door
But You must not bring in your hand a Lie
If you mean that the Florentines should buy

Ghiottos Circle or Apelles Line
Were not the Work of Sketchers drunk with Wine   20
Nor of the City Clarks merry hearted Fashion
Nor of Sir Isaac Newtons Calculation
Nor of the City Clarks Idle Facilities
Which sprang from Sir Isaac Newtons great Abilities

These Verses were written by a very Envious Man   25
Who whatever likeness he may have to Michael Angelo
Never can have any to Sir Jehoshuan

*

A Pitiful Case   t

    The Villain at the Gallows tree
    When he is doomd to die
    To assuage his misery
    In Virtues praise does cry

    So Reynolds when he came to die   5
    To assuage his bitter woe:
    Thus aloud did howl & cry   t
    Michael Angelo Michael Angelo

*

To the Royal Academy

A strange Erratum in all the Editions
Of Sir Joshua Reynoldss Lectures
Shou[l]d be corrected by the Young Gentlemen
And the Royal Academys Directors

Instead of Michael Angelo   5
Read Rembrandt for it is fit   t
To make meer common honesty   t
In all that he has writ

*

The Cripple every step Drudges & labours
And says come learn to walk of me Good Neighbours
Sir Joshua in astonishment cries out
See what Great Labour Pain him & Modest Doubt   t
Newton & Bacon cry being badly Nurst   5
He is all Experiments from last to first
He walks & stumbles as if he crep
And how high labourd is every step

[For other verses on Joshua Reynolds see Marginalia, pages 630, 631, 645]

*

I Rubens am a Statesman & a Saint
Deceptions? O no—so I'll learn to Paint

*

To English Connoisseurs

You must agree that Rubens was a Fool
And yet you make him master of your School
And give more money for his slobberings
Than you will give for Rafaels finest Things
I understood Christ was a Carpenter   5
And not a Brewers Servant my good Sir

*

Swelld limbs, with no outline that you can descry
That Stink in the Nose of a Stander by
But all the Pulp washd painted finishd with labour
Of an hundred Journeymens how dye do Neighbour

*

A Pretty Epigram for the Entertainment of those who have Paid Great Sums in the Venetian & Flemish Ooze

Nature & Art in this together Suit
What is Most Grand is always most Minute
Rubens thinks Tables Chairs & Stools are Grand
But Rafael thinks A Head a foot a hand

*

These are the Idiots chiefest arts
To blend & not define the Parts
The Swallow sings in Courts of Kings
That Fools have their high finishings
And this the Princes golden rule   5
The Laborious stumble of a Fool
To make out the parts is the wise mans aim
But to lose them the Fool makes his foolish Game

*

Rafael Sublime Majestic Graceful Wise
His Executive Power must I despise
Rubens Low Vulgar Stupid Ignorant

—505—

His power of Execution I must grant
Learn the Laborious stumble of a Fool
And from an Idiots Actions form my rule
Go send your Children to the Slobbering School

*

On the Great Encouragement
Given by English Nobility & Gentry to Correggio Rubens
Rembrandt Reynolds Gainsborough Catalani
DuCrowe & Dilbury Doodle

As the Ignorant Savage will sell his own Wife
For a Sword or a Cutlass a dagger or Knife
So the Taught Savage Englishman spends his whole Fortune
On a smear or a squall to destroy Picture or Tune
And I call upon Colonel Wardle
To give these Rascals a dose of Cawdle

*

Give pensions to the Learned Pig
Or the Hare playing on a Tabor
Anglus can never see Perfection
But in the Journeymans Labour

*

When I see a Rubens Rembrant Correggio
I think of the Crippled Harry & Slobbering Joe
And then I question thus are artists rules
To be drawn from the works of two manifest fools
Then God defend us from the Arts I say
Send Battle Murder Sudden Death O pray
Rather than be such a blind Human Fool
Id be an Ass a Hog a Worm a Chair a Stool

*

Delicate Hands & Heads will never appear
While Titians &c as in the Book of Moonlight p 5

*

I askd my Dear Friend Orator Prigg
Whats the first part of Oratory he said a great wig
And what is the second then dancing a jig

And bowing profoundly he said a great wig
And what is the third then he snord like a pig   5
And puffing his cheeks he replied a Great wig   t

So if a Great Painter with Questions you push
Whats the first Part of Painting hell say a Paint Brush
And what is the second with most modest blush
Hell smile like a Cherub & say a paint Brush   t 10
And what is the third hell bow like a rush
With a lear in his Eye hell reply a Paint Brush

Perhaps this is all a Painter can want
But look yonder that house is the house of Rembrant

*

O dear Mother outline of knowledge most sage
Whats the First Part of Painting she said Patronage
And what is the second to Please & Engage   t
She frownd like a Fury & said Patronage
And what is the Thrid she put off Old Age   5
And smild like a Syren & said Patronage

*

To Venetian Artists

That God is colouring Newton does shew   t
And the devil is a Black outline all of us know
Perhaps this little Fable may make us merry
A dog went over the water without a wherry
A bone which he had stolen he had in his mouth   5
He cared not whether the wind was north or south
As he swam he saw the reflection of the bone
This is quite Perfection, one Generalizing Tone   t
Outline Theres no outline Theres no such thing   t
All is Chiaro Scuro Poco Pen its all colouring   10
Snap. Snap! he has lost shadow & substance too   t
He had them both before now how do ye do
A great deal better than I was before
Those who taste colouring love it more & more   t

*

Great Men & Fools do often me Inspire
But the Greater Fool the Greater Liar

Some people admire the work of a Fool
For its sure to keep your judgment cool
It does not reproach you with want of wit
It is not like a lawyer serving a writ

*

Her whole Life is an Epigram smack smooth & neatly pend
Platted quite neat to catch applause with a sliding noose at the end

*

When a Man has Married a Wife
he finds out whether
Her knees & elbows are only
glued together

*

Grown old in Love from Seven till Seven times Seven
I oft have wishd for Hell for Ease from Heaven

*

The Hebrew Nation did not write it
Avarice & Chastity did shite it

*

To God

If you have formd a Circle to go into
Go into it yourself & see how you would do

*

Since all the Riches of this World
May be gifts from the Devil & Earthly Kings
I should suspect that I worshipd the Devil
If I thankd my God for Worldly things

*

To Chloes breast young Cupid slily stole
But he crept in at Myras pocket hole

*

Nail his neck to the Cross nail it with a nail
Nail his neck to the Cross ye all have power over his tail

*

A Woman Scaly & a Man all Hairy
Is such a Match as he who dares
Will find the Womans Scales scrape off the Mans Hairs

*

The Washer Womans Song

I washd them out & washd them in
And they told me it was a great Sin

VII

THE EVERLASTING GOSPEL

PAGES 52–54

Was Jesus Humble or did he
Give any Proofs of Humility
Boast of high Things with Humble tone
And give with Charity a Stone
When but a Child he ran away   5
And left his Parents in dismay
When they had wanderd three days long
These were the words upon his tongue
No Earthly Parents I confess
I am doing my Fathers business   10
When the rich learned Pharisee
Came to consult him secretly
Upon his heart with Iron pen
He wrote Ye must be born again
He was too proud to take a bribe   15
He spoke with authority not like a Scribe
He says with most consummate Art
Follow me I am meek & lowly of heart
As that is the only way to escape
The Misers net & the Gluttons trap   20
What can be done with such desperate Fools
Who follow after the Heathen Schools
I was standing by when Jesus died
What I calld Humility they calld Pride
He who loves his Enemies betrays his Friends   25
This surely is not what Jesus intends
But the sneaking Pride of Heroic Schools
And the Scribes & Pharisees Virtuous Rules
For he acts with honest triumphant Pride
And this is the cause that Jesus died   30
He did not die with Christian Ease

Asking pardon of his Enemies
If he had Caiphas would forgive
Sneaking submission can always live
He had only to say that God was the devil   35
And the devil was God like a Christian Civil
Mild Christian regrets to the devil confess
For affronting him thrice in the Wilderness
He had soon been bloody Caesars Elf
And at last he would have been Caesar himself   40
Like d^r Priestly & Bacon & Newton   t
Poor Spiritual Knowledge is not worth a button
For thus the Gospel Sr Isaac confutes
God can only be known by his Attributes
And as for the Indwelling of the Holy Ghost   45
Or of Christ & his Father its all a boast
And Pride & Vanity of Imagination
That disdains to follow this Worlds Fashion
To teach doubt & Experiment
Certainly was not what Christ meant   50
What was he doing all that time
From twelve years old to manly prime
Was he then Idle or the Less
About his Fathers business
Or was his wisdom held in scorn   55
Before his wrath began to burn
In Miracles throughout the Land
That quite unnervd Lord Caiaphas hand   t
If he had been Antichrist Creeping Jesus   t
Hed have done any thing to please us   60
Gone sneaking into Synagogues
And not usd the Elders & Priests like dogs
But Humble as a Lamb or Ass
Obeyd himself to Caiaphas
God wants not Man to Humble himself   65
This is the trick of the ancient Elf
This is the Race that Jesus ran   t
Humble to God Haughty to Man
Cursing the Rulers before the People
Even to the temples highest Steeple   70
And when he Humbled himself to God
Then descended the Cruel Rod
If thou humblest thyself thou humblest me   t
Thou also dwellst in Eternity
Thou art a Man God is no more   75
Thy own humanity learn to adore
For that is my Spirit of Life
Awake arise to Spiritual Strife

And thy Revenge abroad display
In terrors at the Last Judgment day   80
Gods Mercy & Long Suffering
Is but the Sinner to Judgment to bring
Thou on the Cross for them shalt pray
And take Revenge at the Last Day   t
Jesus replied & thunders hurld   85
I never will Pray for the World
Once [I] did so when I prayd in the Garden   t
I wishd to take with me a Bodily Pardon
Can that which was of woman born
In the absence of the Morn   90
When the Soul fell into Sleep
And Archangels round it weep
Shooting out against the Light
Fibres of a deadly night
Reasoning upon its own dark Fiction   95
In doubt which is Self Contradiction
Humility is only doubt
And does the Sun & Moon blot out
Rooting over with thorns & stems
The buried Soul & all its Gems.   100
This Lifes dim Windows of the Soul
Distorts the Heavens from Pole to Pole
And leads you to Believe a Lie
When you see with not thro the Eye
That was born in a night to perish in a night   105
When the Soul slept in the beams of Light.

PAGES 48–52

Was Jesus Chaste or did he
Give any Lessons of Chastity
The morning blushd fiery red
Mary was found in Adulterous bed
Earth groand beneath & Heaven above   5
Trembled at discovery of Love
Jesus was sitting in Moses Chair
They brought the trembling Woman There
Moses commands she be stoned to death
What was the sound of Jesus breath   t 10
He laid His hand on Moses Law
The Ancient Heavens in Silent Awe
Writ with Curses from Pole to Pole
All away began to roll
The Earth trembling & Naked lay   15
In secret bed of Mortal Clay

On Sinai felt the hand Divine
Putting back the bloody shrine
And she heard the breath of God
As she heard by Edens flood   20
Good & Evil are no more
Sinais trumpets cease to roar
Cease finger of God to write
The Heavens are not clean in thy Sight
Thou art Good & thou Alone   25
Nor may the sinner cast one stone
To be Good only is to be
A Devil or else a Pharisee   t
Thou Angel of the Presence Divine
That didst create this Body of Mine   30
Wherefore has thou writ these Laws
And Created Hells dark jaws
My Presence I will take from thee
A Cold Leper thou shalt be
Tho thou wast so pure & bright   35
That Heaven was Impure in thy Sight
Tho thy Oath turnd Heaven Pale
Tho thy Covenant built Hells Jail
Tho thou didst all to Chaos roll
With the Serpent for its soul   40
Still the breath Divine does move
And the breath Divine is Love
Mary Fear Not Let me see
The Seven Devils that torment thee
Hide not from my Sight thy Sin   45
That forgiveness thou maist win
Has no Man Condemned thee
No Man Lord! then what is he
Who shall Accuse thee. Come Ye forth
Fallen Fiends of Heavnly birth   50
That have forgot your Ancient love
And driven away my trembling Dove
You shall bow before her feet
You shall lick the dust for Meat
And tho you cannot Love but Hate   55
Shall be beggars at Loves Gate
What was thy love Let me see it
Was it love or Dark Deceit
Love too long from Me has fled.
Twas dark deceit to Earn my bread   60
Twas Covet or twas Custom or
Some trifle not worth caring for
That they may call a shame & Sin   t

Loves temple that God dwelleth in
And hide in secret hidden Shrine   65
The Naked Human form divine
And render that a Lawless thing
On which the Soul Expands its wing
But this O Lord this was my Sin
When first I let these Devils in   70
In dark pretence to Chastity
Blaspheming Love blaspheming thee
Thence Rose Secret Adulteries
And thence did Covet also rise
My sin thou hast forgiven me   75
Canst thou forgive my Blasphemy
Canst thou return to this dark Hell
And in my burning bosom dwell
And canst thou die that I may live
And canst thou Pity & forgive   80
Then Rolld the shadowy Man away
From the Limbs of Jesus to make them his prey
An Ever devo[u]ring appetite
Glittering with festering Venoms bright
Crying Crucify this cause of distress   t85
Who dont keep the secrets of Holiness   t
All Mental Powers by Diseases we bind
But he heals the Deaf & the Dumb & the Blind
Whom God has afflicted for Secret Ends
He comforts & Heals & calls them Friends   90
But when Jesus was Crucified
Then was perfected his glittring pride   t
In three Nights he devourd his prey
And still he devours the Body of Clay
For dust & Clay is the Serpents meat   t95
Which never was made for Man to Eat

PAGES 100—101

Was Jesus gentle or did he
Give any marks of Gentility
When twelve years old he ran away
And left his Parents in dismay
When after three days sorrow found   5
Loud as Sinai's trumpet sound
No Earthly Parents I confess
My Heavenly Fathers business
Ye understand not what I say
And angry force me to obey   10
Obedience is a duty then
And favour gains with God & Men

John from the Wilderness loud cried
Satan gloried in his Pride
Come said Satan come away 15
Ill soon see if youll obey
John for disobedience bled
But you can turn the stones to bread
Gods high king & Gods high Priest
Shall Plant their Glories in your breast 20
If Caiaphas you will obey
If Herod you with bloody Prey
Feed with the Sacrifice & be
Obedient fall down worship me
Thunders & lightnings broke around 25
And Jesus voice in thunders sound
Thus I sieze the Spiritual Prey
Ye smiters with disease make way
I come Your King & God to sieze
Is God a Smiter with disease 30
The God of this World raged in vain
He bound Old Satan in his Chain
And bursting forth his furious ire
Became a Chariot of fire
Throughout the land he took his course 35
And traced diseases to their source
He cursd the Scribe & Pharisee
Trampling down Hipocrisy
Where eer his Chariot took its way
There Gates of Death let in the day 40
Broke down from every Chain & Bar
And Satan in his Spiritual War
Dragd at his Chariot wheels loud howld
The God of this World louder rolld
The Chariot Wheels & louder still 45
His voice was heard from Zions hill
And in his hand the Scourge shone bright
He scourgd the Merchant Canaanite
From out the Temple of his Mind
And in his Body tight does bind 50
Satan & all his Hellish Crew
And thus with wrath he did subdue
The Serpent Bulk of Natures dross
Till he had naild it to the Cross
He took on Sin in the Virgins Womb 55
And put it off on the Cross & Tomb t
To be Worshipd by the Church of Rome

The Vision of Christ that thou dost see
Is my Visions Greatest Enemy
Thine has a great hook nose like thine
Mine has a snub nose like to mine
Thine is the friend of All Mankind   5
Mine speaks in parables to the Blind
Thine loves the same world that mine hates
Thy Heaven doors are my Hell Gates
Socrates taught what Melitus
Loathd as a Nations bitterest Curse   10
And Caiphas was in his own Mind
A benefactor to Mankind
Both read the Bible day & night
But thou readst black where I read white

VIII

[Advertisement of the Exhibition]

Exhibition of *Paintings in Fresco,*
Poetical and Historical Inventions,

By. Wm. Blake.

PAGE I

THE ANCIENT BRITONS—Three Ancient Britons overthrowing the
Army of armed Romans; the Figures full as large as Life—From the
Welch Triades.

In the last Battle that Arthur fought, the most Beautiful was one
That return'd, and the most Strong another: with them also return'd
The most Ugly, and no other beside return'd from the bloody Field.

The most Beautiful, the Roman Warriors trembled before and worshipped:
The most Strong, they melted before him and dissolved in his presence:
The most Ugly they fled with outcries and contortion of their Limbs.

THE CANTERBURY PILGRIMS from *Chaucer*—a cabinet Picture in
Fresco—Thirty Figures on Horse-back, in a brilliant Morning Scene.

Two Pictures, representing grand Apotheoses of NELSON and PITT,
with variety of cabinet Pictures, unchangeable and permanent in
Fresco, and Drawings for Public Inspection and for Sale by Private
Contract, at

No. 28, Corner of BROAD STREET, Golden-Square.

"Fit audience find tho' few" MILTON.

Admittance 2s. 6d. each Person, a discriptive Catalogue included. <Containing Ample Illustrations on Art>

Watts & Co. Printers, Southmolton St.

PAGE 2

The Invention of a portable Fresco.

A Wall on Canvas or Wood, or any other portable thing, of dimensions ever so large, or ever so small, which may be removed with the same convenience as so many easel Pictures; is worthy the consideration of the Rich and those who have the direction of public Works. If the Frescos of APELLES, of PROTOGENES, of RAPHAEL, or MICHAEL ANGELO could have been removed, we might, perhaps, have them now in England. I could divide Westminster Hall, or the walls of any other great Building, into compartments and ornament them with Frescos, which would be removable at pleasure.

Oil will not drink or absorb Colour enough to stand the test of very little Time and of the Air; it grows yellow, and at length brown. It was never generally used till after VANDYKE's time. All the little old Pictures, called cabinet Pictures, are in Fresco, and not in Oil.

Fresco Painting is properly Miniature, or Enamel Painting; every thing in Fresco is as high finished as Miniature or Enamel, although in Works larger than Life. The Art has been lost: I have recovered it. How this was done, will be told, together with the whole Process, in a Work on Art, now in the Press. The ignorant Insults of Individuals will not hinder me from doing my duty to my Art. Fresco Painting, as it is now practised, is like most other things, the contrary of what it pretends to be.

The execution of my Designs, being all in Water-colours, (that is in Fresco) are regularly refused to be exhibited by the *Royal Academy*, and the *British Institution* has, this year, followed its example, and has effectually excluded me by this Resolution; I therefore invite those Noblemen and Gentlem[e]n, who are its Subscribers, to inspect what they have excluded: and those who have been told that my Works are but an unscientific and irregular Eccentricity, a Madman's Scrawls, I demand of them to do me the justice to examine before they decide.

There cannot be more than two or three great Painters or Poets in any Age or Country; and these, in a corrupt state of Society, are easily excluded, but not so easily obstructed. They have ex[c]luded Water-colours; it is therefore become necessary that I should exhibit to the Public, in an Exhibition of my own, my Designs, Painted in Water-colours. If Italy is enriched and made great by RAPHAEL, if MICHAEL ANGELO is its supreme glory, if Art is the glory of a Nation, if Genius and Inspiration are the great Origin and Bond of Society, the distinction

my Works have obtained from those who best understand such things, calls for my Exhibition as the greatest of Duties to my Country.
<May 15. 1809>

WILLIAM BLAKE.

❧

[Advertisement of the Catalogue]

A Descriptive Catalogue of Blake's Exhibition,

At No. 28, Corner of
BROAD-STREET
GOLDEN-SQUARE.

THE grand style of Art restored; in FRESCO, or Water-colour Painting, and England protected from the too just imputation of being the Seat and Protectress of bad (that is blotting and blurring) Art.

In this Exhibition will be seen real Art, as it was left us by *Raphael* and *Albert Durer, Michael Angelo,* and *Julio Romano;* stripped from the Ignorances of *Rubens* and *Rembrandt, Titian* and *Correggio;*

BY WILLIAM BLAKE.

The Descriptive Catalogue, Price 2s. 6d. containing Mr. B.'s Opinions and Determinations on Art, very necessary to be known by Artists and Connoisseurs of all Ranks. Every Purchaser of a Catalogue will be entitled, at the time of purchase, to view the Exhibition.

These Original Conceptions on Art, by an Original Artist, are sold only at the Corner of BROAD STREET.

Admittance to the Exhibition 1 Shilling; an Index to the Catalogue gratis.

Printed by Watts & Bridgewater, Southmolton-street.

❧

[The Catalogue]

A DESCRIPTIVE CATALOGUE OF PICTURES,

Poetical and Historical Inventions,

Painted by William Blake, in Water Colours, Being the Ancient Method of Fresco Painting Restored: and Drawings, For Public Inspection, and for Sale by Private Contract, <At N 28 Corner of Broad Street—Golden Square>

London; Printed by D. N. Shury, 7, Berwick-Street, Soho, for J. Blake, 28, Broad-Street, Golden-Square. 1809.

PAGE [ii]

CONDITIONS OF SALE.

I. One third of the price to be paid at the time of Purchase and remainder on Delivery.

II. The Pictures and Drawings to remain in the Exhibition till its close, which will be the 29th of September 1809; and the Picture of the Canterbury Pilgrims, which is to be engraved, will be Sold only on condition of its remaining in the Artist's hands twelve months, when it will be delivered to the Buyer.

PAGE [iii]

PREFACE.

THE eye that can prefer the Colouring of Titian and Rubens to that of Michael Angelo and Rafael, ought to be modest and to doubt its own powers. Connoisseurs talk as if Rafael and Michael Angelo had never seen the colouring of Titian or Correggio: They ought to know that Correggio was born two years before Michael Angelo, and Titian but four years after. Both Rafael and Michael Angelo knew the Venetian, and contemned and rejected all he did with the utmost disdain, as that which is fabricated for the purpose to destroy art.

Mr. B. appeals to the Public, from the judgment of those narrow blinking eyes, that have too long governed art in a dark corner. The eyes of stupid cunning never will be [P iv] pleased with the work any more than with the look of self-devoting genius. The quarrel of the Florentine with the Venetian is not because he does not understand Drawing, but because he does not understand Colouring. How should he? he who does not know how to draw a hand or a foot, know how to colour it.

Colouring does not depend on where the Colours are put, but on where the lights and darks are put, and all depends on Form or Outline. On where that is put; where that is wrong, the Colouring never can be right; and it is always wrong in Titian and Correggio, Rubens and Rembrandt. Till we get rid of Titian and Correggio, Rubens and Rembrandt, We never shall equal Rafael and Albert Durer, Michael Angelo, and Julio Romano.

PAGE 1

DESCRIPTIVE CATALOGUE, &C. &C.

NUMBER I.

The spiritual form of Nelson guiding Leviathan, in whose wreathings are infolded the Nations of the Earth.

CLEARNESS and precision have been the chief objects in painting these Pictures. Clear colours unmudded by oil, and firm and determinate lineaments unbroken by shadows, which ought to display and not to hide form, as is the practice of the latter Schools of Italy and Flanders.

PAGE 2

NUMBER II, ITS COMPANION

The spiritual form of Pitt, guiding Behemoth; he is that Angel who, pleased to perform the Almighty's orders, rides on the whirlwind, directing the storms of war: He is ordering the Reaper to reap the Vine of the Earth, and the Plowman to plow up the Cities and Towers.

THIS Picture also is a proof of the power of colours unsullied with oil or with any cloggy vehicle. Oil has falsely been supposed to give strength to colours: but a little consideration must shew the fallacy of this opinion. Oil will not drink or absorb colour enough to stand the test of very little time and of the air. It deadens every colour it is mixed with, at its first mixture, and in a little time becomes a yellow mask over all that it touches. Let the works of modern Artists since Rubens' time [P 3] witness the villany of some one at that time, who first brought oil Painting into general opinion and practice: since which we have never had a Picture painted, that could shew itself by the side of an earlier production. Whether Rubens or Vandyke, or both, were guilty of this villany, is to be enquired in another work on Painting, and who first forged the silly story and known falshood, about John of Bruges inventing oil colours: in the meantime let it be observed, that before Vandyke's time, and in his time all the genuine Pictures are on Plaster or Whiting grounds and none since.

The two Pictures of Nelson and Pitt are compositions of a mythological cast, similar to those Apotheoses of Persian, Hindoo, and Egyptian Antiquity, which are still preserved on rude monuments, being copies from some stupendous originals now lost or perhaps buried till some happier age. The Artist having been [P 4] taken in vision into the ancient republics, monarchies, and patriarchates of Asia, has seen those wonderful originals called in the Sacred Scriptures the Cherubim, which were sculptured and painted on walls of Temples, Towers, Cities, Palaces, and erected in the highly cultivated states of Egypt, Moab, Edom, Aram, among the Rivers of Paradise, being originals from which the Greeks and Hetrurians copied Hercules, Farnese, Venus of Medicis, Apollo Belvidere, and all the grand works of ancient art. They were executed in a very superior style to those justly admired copies, being with their accompaniments terrific and grand in the highest degree. The Artist has endeavoured to emulate the grandeur of those seen in his vision, and to apply it to modern Heroes, on a smaller scale.

No man can believe that either Homer's Mythology, or Ovid's, were the production of Greece, or of Latium; neither will any one [P 5] believe, that the Greek statues, as they are called, were the invention of Greek Artists; perhaps the Torso is the only original work remaining; all the rest are evidently copies, though fine ones, from greater works of the Asiatic Patriarchs. The Greek Muses are daughters of Mnemosyne, or Memory, and not of Inspiration or Imagination, therefore not authors of such sublime conceptions. Those wonderful originals seen in my visions, were some of them one hundred feet in height; some were painted as pictures, and some carved as basso relievos, and some as groupes of statues, all containing mythological and recondite meaning, where more is meant than meets the eye. The Artist wishes it was now the fashion to make such monuments, and then he should not doubt of having a national commission to execute these two Pictures on a scale that is suitable to the grandeur of the nation, who is the parent of his heroes, in high [P 6] finished fresco, where the colours would be as pure and as permanent as precious stones though the figures were one hundred feet in height.

All Frescos are as high finished as miniatures or enamels, and they are known to be unchangeable; but oil being a body itself, will drink or absorb very little colour, and changing yellow, and at length brown, destroys every colour it is mixed with, especially every delicate colour. It turns every permanent white to a yellow and brown putty, and has compelled the use of that destroyer of colour, white lead; which, when its protecting oil is evaporated, will become lead again. This is an awful thing to say to oil Painters; they may call it madness, but it is true. All the genuine old little Pictures, called Cabinet Pictures, are in fresco and not in oil. Oil was not used except by blundering ignorance, till after Vandyke's time, but the art of fresco painting [P 7] being lost, oil became a fetter to genius, and a dungeon to art. But one convincing proof among many others, that these assertions are true is, that real gold and silver cannot be used with oil, as they are in all the old pictures and in Mr. B.'s frescos.

NUMBER III.

Sir Jeffery Chaucer and the nine and twenty Pilgrims on their journey to Canterbury.

THE time chosen is early morning, before sunrise, when the jolly company are just quitting the Tabarde Inn. The Knight and Squire with the Squire's Yeoman lead the Procession, next follow the youthful Abbess, her nun and three priests; her greyhounds attend her.

> "Of small hounds had she that she fed
> "With roast flesh, milk and wastel bread."

Next follow the Friar and Monk; then the Tapiser, the Pardoner, and the Somner and Manciple. After these "Our Host," who oc[P 8]cupies the center of the cavalcade; directs them to the Knight as the person who would be likely to commence their task of each telling a tale in their order. After the Host follow the Shipman, the Haberdasher, the Dyer, the Franklin, the Physician, the Plowman, the Lawyer, the poor Parson, the Merchant, the Wife of Bath, the Miller, the Cook, the Oxford Scholar, Chaucer himself, and the Reeve comes as Chaucer has described:

> "And ever he rode hinderest of the rout."

These last are issuing from the gateway of the Inn; the Cook and the Wife of Bath are both taking their morning's draught of comfort. Spectators stand at the gateway of the Inn, and are composed of an old Man, a Woman and Children.

The Landscape is an eastward view of the country, from the Tabarde Inn, in Southwark, as it may be supposed to have appeared in [P 9] Chaucer's time; interspersed with cottages and villages; the first beams of the Sun are seen above the horizon; some buildings and spires indicate the situation of the great City; the Inn is a gothic building, which Thynne in his Glossary says was the lodging of the Abbot of Hyde, by Winchester. On the Inn is inscribed its title, and a proper advantage is taken of this circumstance to describe the subject of the Picture. The words written over the gateway of the Inn, are as follow: "The Tabarde Inn, by Henry Baillie, the lodgynge-house for Pilgrims, who journey to Saint Thomas's Shrine at Canterbury."

The characters of Chaucer's Pilgrims are the characters which compose all ages and nations: as one age falls, another rises, different to mortal sight, but to immortals only the same; for we see the same characters repeated again and again, in animals, vegetables, minerals, and in men; nothing new occurs in iden[P 10]tical existence; Accident ever varies, Substance can never suffer change nor decay.

Of Chaucer's characters, as described in his Canterbury Tales, some of the names or titles are altered by time, but the characters themselves for ever remain unaltered, and consequently they are the physiognomies or lineaments of universal human life, beyond which Nature never steps. Names alter, things never alter. I have known multitudes of those who would have been monks in the age of monkery, who in this deistical age are deists. As Newton numbered the stars, and as Linneus numbered the plants, so Chaucer numbered the classes of men.

The Painter has consequently varied the heads and forms of his personages into all Nature's varieties; the Horses he has also varied to accord to their Riders, the Costume is correct according to authentic monuments.

The Knight and Squire with the Squire's [P 11] Yeoman lead the procession, as Chaucer has also placed them first in his prologue. The Knight is a true Hero, a good, great, and wise man; his whole length portrait on horseback, as written by Chaucer, cannot be surpassed. He has spent his life in the field; has ever been a conqueror, and is that species of character which in every age stands as the guardian of man against the oppressor. His son is like him with the germ of perhaps greater perfection still, as he blends literature and the arts with his warlike studies. Their dress and their horses are of the first rate, without ostentation, and with all the true grandeur that unaffected simplicity when in high rank always displays. The Squire's Yeoman is also a great character, a man perfectly knowing in his profession:

"And in his hand he bare a mighty bow."

Chaucer describes here a mighty man; one who in war is the worthy attendant on noble heroes.

[PAGE 12] The Prioress follows these with her female chaplain.

"Another Nonne also with her had she,
"That was her Chaplaine and Priests three."

This Lady is described also as of the first rank; rich and honoured. She has certain peculiarities and little delicate affectations, not unbecoming in her, being accompanied with what is truly grand and really polite; her person and face, Chaucer has described with minuteness; it is very elegant, and was the beauty of our ancestors, till after Elizabeth's time, when voluptuousness and folly began to be accounted beautiful.

Her companion and her three priests were no doubt all perfectly delineated in those parts of Chaucer's work which are now lost; we ought to suppose them suitable attendants on rank and fashion.

[PAGE 13] The Monk follows these with the Friar. The Painter has also grouped with these, the Pardoner and the Sompnour and the Manciple, and has here also introduced one of the rich citizens of London. Characters likely to ride in company, all being above the common rank in life or attendants on those who were so.

For the Monk is described by Chaucer, as a man of the first rank in society, noble, rich, and expensively attended: he is a leader of the age, with certain humourous accompaniments in his character, that do not degrade, but render him an object of dignified mirth, but also with other accompaniments not so respectable.

The Friar is a character also of a mixed kind.

"A friar there was, a wanton and a merry."

[B]ut in his office he is said to be a "full solemn man:" eloquent, amorous, witty, and satyri[P 14]cal; young, handsome, and rich; he is a complete rogue; with constitutional gaiety enough to make him a master of all the pleasures of the world.

"His neck was white as the flour de lis,
Thereto strong he was as a champioun."

It is necessary here to speak of Chaucer's own character, that I may set certain mistaken critics right in their conception of the humour and fun that occurs on the journey. Chaucer is himself the great poetical observer of men, who in every age is born to record and eternize its acts. This he does as a master, as a father, and superior, who looks down on their little follies from the Emperor to the Miller; sometimes with severity, oftener with joke and sport.

Accordingly Chaucer has made his Monk a great tragedian, one who studied poetical art. [P 15] So much so, that the generous Knight is, in the compassionate dictates of his soul, compelled to cry out

"Ho quoth the Knyght, good Sir, no more of this,
That ye have said, is right ynough I wis;
And mokell more, for little heaviness,
Is right enough for much folk as I guesse.
I say for me, it is a great disease,
Whereas men have been in wealth and ease;
To heare of their sudden fall alas,
And the contrary is joy and solas."

The Monk's definition of tragedy in the proem to his tale is worth repeating:

"Tragedie is to tell a certain story,
As old books us maken memory;
Of hem that stood in great prosperity.
And be fallen out of high degree,
Into miserie and ended wretchedly."

[PAGE 16] Though a man of luxury, pride and pleasure, he is a master of art and learning, though affecting to despise it. Those who can think that the proud Huntsman, and noble Housekeeper, Chaucer's Monk, is intended for a buffoon or burlesque character, know little of Chaucer.

For the Host who follows this group, and holds the center of the cavalcade, is a first rate character, and his jokes are no trifles; they are always, though uttered with audacity, and equally free with the Lord and the Peasant, they are always substantially and weightily expressive of knowledge and experience; Henry Baillie, the keeper of the greatest Inn, of the greatest City; for such was the Tabarde Inn in Southwark, near London: our Host was also a leader of the age.

By way of illustration, I instance Shakspeare's Witches in Macbeth. Those who dress [P 17] them for the stage, consider them as wretched old women, and not as Shakspeare intended, the Goddesses of Destiny; this shews how Chaucer has been misunderstood in his sublime work. Shakspeare's Fairies also are the rulers of the vegetable world, and so are Chaucer's; let them be so considered, and then the poet will be understood, and not else.

But I have omitted to speak of a very prominent character, the Pardoner, the Age's Knave, who always commands and domineers over the high and low vulgar. This man is sent in every age for a rod and scourge, and for a blight, for a trial of men, to divide the classes of men, he is in the most holy sanctuary, and he is suffered by Providence for wise ends, and has also his great use, and his grand leading destiny.

His companion the Sompnour, is also a Devil of the first magnitude, grand, terrific, rich and honoured in the rank of which he holds [P 18] the destiny. The uses to society are perhaps equal of the Devil and of the Angel, their sublimity who can dispute.

> "In daunger had he at his own gise,
> The young girls of his diocese,
> And he knew well their counsel, &c."

The principal figure in the next groupe, is the Good Parson; an Apostle, a real Messenger of Heaven, sent in every age for its light and its warmth. This man is beloved and venerated by all, and neglected by all: He serves all, and is served by none; he is, according to Christ's definition, the greatest of his age. Yet he is a Poor Parson of a town. Read Chaucer's description of the Good Parson, and bow the head and the knee to him, who, in every age sends us such a burning and a shining light. Search O ye rich and powerful, for these men and obey their counsel, then [P 19] shall the golden age return: But alas! you will not easily distinguish him from the Friar or the Pardoner, they also are "full solemn men," and their counsel, you will continue to follow.

I have placed by his side, the Sergeant at Lawe, who appears delighted to ride in his company, and between him and his brother, the Plowman; as I wish men of Law would always ride with them, and take their counsel, especially in all difficult points. Chaucer's Lawyer is a character of great venerableness, a Judge, and a real master of the jurisprudence of his age.

The Doctor of Physic is in this groupe, and the Franklin, the voluptuous country gentleman, contrasted with the Physician, and on his other hand, with two Citizens of London. Chaucer's characters live age after age. Every age is a Canterbury Pilgrimage; we all pass on, each

sustaining one or other [P 20] of these characters; nor can a child be born, who is not one of these characters of Chaucer. The Doctor of Physic is described as the first of his profession; perfect, learned, completely Master and Doctor in his art. Thus the reader will observe, that Chaucer makes every one of his characters perfect in his kind, every one is an Antique Statue; the image of a class, and not of an imperfect individual.

This groupe also would furnish substantial matter, on which volumes might be written. The Franklin is one who keeps open table, who is the genius of eating and drinking, the Bacchus; as the Doctor of Physic is the Esculapius, the Host is the Silenus, the Squire is the Apollo, the Miller is the Hercules, &c. Chaucer's characters are a description of the eternal Principles that exist in all ages. The Franklin is voluptuousness itself most nobly pourtrayed:

PAGE 21

> "It snewed in his house of meat and drink."

The Plowman is simplicity itself, with wisdom and strength for its stamina. Chaucer has divided the ancient character of Hercules between his Miller and his Plowman. Benevolence is the plowman's great characteristic, he is thin with excessive labour, and not with old age, as some have supposed.

> "He would thresh and thereto dike and delve
> For Christe's sake, for every poore wight,
> Withouten hire, if it lay in his might."

Visions of these eternal principles or characters of human life appear to poets, in all ages; the Grecian gods were the ancient Cherubim of Phoenicia; but the Greeks, and since them the Moderns, have neglected to subdue the gods of Priam. These Gods are visions of the eternal attributes, or divine names, which, when [P 22] erected into gods, become destructive to humanity. They ought to be the servants, and not the masters of man, or of society. They ought to be made to sacrifice to Man, and not man compelled to sacrifice to them; for when separated from man or humanity, who is Jesus the Saviour, the vine of eternity, they are thieves and rebels, they are destroyers.

The Plowman of Chaucer is Hercules in his supreme eternal state, divested of his spectrous shadow; which is the Miller, a terrible fellow, such as exists in all times and places, for the trial of men, to astonish every neighbourhood, with brutal strength and courage, to get rich and powerful to curb the pride of Man.

The Reeve and the Manciple are two characters of the most consummate worldly wisdom. The Shipman, or Sailor, is a similar genius of Ulyssean art; but with the highest courage superadded.

The Citizens and their Cook are each leaders [P 23] of a class. Chaucer has been somehow made to number four citizens, which would make his whole company, himself included, thirty-one. But he says there was but nine and twenty in his company.

"Full nine and twenty in a company."

The Webbe, or Weaver, and the Tapiser, or Tapestry Weaver, apar to me to be the same person; but this is only an opinion, for full ne and twenty may signify one more or less. But I dare say that haucer wrote "A Webbe Dyer," that is a Cloth Dyer.

"A Webbe Dyer and a Tapiser."

The Merchant cannot be one of the Three Citizens, as his dress is lifferent, and his character is more marked, whereas Chaucer says of his rich citizens:

PAGE 24

"All were yclothed in o liverie."

The characters of Women Chaucer has divided into two classes, the Lady Prioress and the Wife of Bath. Are not these leaders of the ages of men? The lady prioress, in some ages, predominates; and in some the wife of Bath, in whose character Chaucer has been equally minute and exact; because she is also a scourge and a blight. I shall say no more of her, nor expose what Chaucer has left hidden; let the young reader study what he has said of her: it is useful as a scare-crow. There are of such characters born too many for the peace of the world.

I come at length to the Clerk of Oxenford. This character varies from that of Chaucer, as the contemplative philosopher varies from the poetical genius. There are always these two classes of learned sages, the poetical and the philosophical. The painter has put them side by side, as if the youthful clerk had put him[P 25]self under the tuition of the mature poet. Let the Philosopher always be the servant and scholar of inspiration and all will be happy.

Such are the characters that compose this Picture, which was painted in self-defence against the insolent and envious imputation of unfitness for finished and scientific art; and this imputation, most artfully and industriously endeavoured to be propagated among the public by ignorant hirelings. The painter courts comparison with his competitors, who, having received fourteen hundred guineas and more from the profits of his designs, in that well-known work, Designs for Blair's Grave, have left him to shift for himself, while others, more obedient to an employer's opinions and directions, are employed, at a great expence, to produce works, in succession to his, by which they acquired public patronage. This has hitherto been his lot—to get patronage for others and then to be left and neglected, and his work, which gained [P 26] that patronage, cried down as eccentricity and madness; as unfinished and neglected by the artist's violent temper, he is sure the works now exhibited, will give the lie to such aspersions.

Those who say that men are led by interest are knaves. A knavish character will often say, of what interest is it to me to do so and so? I answer, of none at all, but the contrary, as you well know. It is of

malice and envy that you have done this; hence I am aware of you, because I know that you act not from interest but from malice, even to your own destruction. It is therefore become a duty which Mr. B. owes to the Public, who have always recognized him, and patronized him, however hidden by artifices, that he should not suffer such things to be done or be hindered from the public Exhibition of his finished productions by any calumnies in future.

The character and expression in this picture could never have been produced with Ruben's [P 27] light and shadow, or with Rembrandt's, or any thing Venetian or Flemish. The Venetian and Flemish practice is broken lines, broken masses, and broken colours. Mr. B.'s practice is unbroken lines, unbroken masses, and unbroken colours. Their art is to lose form, his art is to find form, and to keep it. His arts are opposite to theirs in all things.

As there is a class of men, whose whole delight is the destruction of men, so there is a class of artists, whose whole art and science is fabricated for the purpose of destroying art. Who these are is soon known: "by their works ye shall know them." All who endeavour to raise up a style against Rafael, Mich. Angelo, and the Antique; those who separate Painting from Drawing; who look if a picture is well Drawn; and, if it is, immediately cry out, that it cannot be well Coloured—those are the men.

But to shew the stupidity of this class of [P 28] men, nothing need be done but to examine my rival's prospectus.

The two first characters in Chaucer, the Knight and the Squire, he has put among his rabble; and indeed his prospectus calls the Squire the fop of Chaucer's age. Now hear Chaucer.

> "Of his Stature, he was of even length,
> And wonderly deliver, and of great strength;
> And he had be sometime in Chivauchy,
> In Flanders, in Artois, and in Picardy,
> And borne him well as of so litele space."

Was this a fop?

> "Well could he sit a horse, and faire ride,
> He could songs make, and eke well indite
> Just, and eke dance, pourtray, and well write.

Was this a fop?

PAGE 29

> "Curteis he was, and meek, and serviceable;
> And kerft before his fader at the table."

Was this a fop?

It is the same with all his characters; he has done all by chance, or perhaps his fortune, money, money. According to his prospectus he has Three Monks; these he cannot find in Chaucer, who has only One

Monk, and that no vulgar character, as he has endeavoured to make him. When men cannot read they should not pretend to paint. To be sure Chaucer is a little difficult to him who has only blundered over novels and catchpenny trifles of booksellers. Yet a little pains ought to be taken even by the ignorant and weak. He has put The Reeve, a vulgar fellow, between his Knight and Squire, as if he was resolved to go contrary in every thing to Chaucer, who says of the Reeve:

PAGE 30

"And ever he rode hinderest of the rout."

In this manner he has jumbled his dumb dollies together, and is praised by his equals for it; for both himself and his friend are equally masters of Chaucer's language. They both think that the Wife of Bath is a young beautiful blooming damsel; and H[oppner] says, that she is the Fair Wife of Bath, and that the Spring appears in her Cheeks. Now hear what Chaucer has made her say of herself, who is no modest one,

> "But Lord when it remembereth me
> Upon my youth and on my jollity,
> It tickleth me about the heart root.
> Unto this day it doth my heart boot,
> That I have had my world as in my time;
> But age, alas, that all will envenime,
> Hath me bireft, my beauty and my pith
> Let go; farewell: the devil go therewith,

PAGE 31

> The flower is gone, there is no more to tell.
> The bran, as best, I can, I now mote sell;
> And yet, to be right merry, will I fond,
> Now forth to tell of my fourth husband."

She has had four husbands, a fit subject for this painter; yet the painter ought to be very much offended with his friend H——, who has called his "a common scene," "and very ordinary forms;" which is the truest part of all, for it is so, and very wretchedly so indeed. What merit can there be in a picture of which such words are spoken with truth.

But the prospectus says that the Painter has represented Chaucer himself as a knave, who thrusts himself among honest people, to make game of and laugh at them; though I must do justice to the painter, and say that he has made him look more like a fool than a knave. But it appears, in all the writings of Chaucer, and particularly in his Canterbury Tales, that [P 32] he was very devout, and paid respect to true enthusiastic superstition. He has laughed at his knaves and fools as I do now. But he has respected his True Pilgrims, who are a majority of his company, and are not thrown together in the random manner that Mr. S[tothard] has done. Chaucer has no where called the Plowman old, worn out with age and labour, as the prospectus has represented him, and says, that the picture has done so too. He is worn down with labour, but not with age. How spots of brown and yellow, smeared about at random, can be either young or old, I cannot see. It may be an old man; it may be a young one; it may be any thing that a prospectus pleases. But I know that where there are no lineaments there can be no character. And what connoisseurs call touch, I know by experience, must be the destruction of all character and expression, as it is of every lineament.

The scene of Mr. S——'s Picture is by [P 33] Dulwich Hills, which was not the way to Canterbury; but, perhaps the painter thought he would give them a ride round about, because they were a burlesque set of scare-crows, not worth any man's respect or care.

But the painter's thoughts being always upon gold, he has introduced a character that Chaucer has not; namely, a Goldsmith; for so the prospectus tells us. Why he has introduced a Goldsmith, and what is the wit of it, the prospectus does not explain. But it takes care to mention the reserve and modesty of the Painter; this makes a good epigram enough.

> "The fox, the owl, the spider, and the mole,
> By sweet reserve and modesty get fat."

But the prospectus tells us, that the painter has introduced a Sea Captain; Chaucer has a Ship-man, a Sailor, a Trading Master of a Ves-[P 34]sel, called by courtesy Captain, as every master of a boat is; but this does not make him a Sea Captain. Chaucer has purposely omitted such a personage, as it only exists in certain periods: it is the soldier by sea. He who would be a Soldier in inland nations is a sea captain in commercial nations.

All is misconceived, and its mis-execution is equal to its misconception. I have no objection to Rubens and Rembrandt being employed, or even to their living in a palace; but it shall not be at the expence of Rafael and Michael Angelo living in a cottage, and in contempt and derision. I have been scorned long enough by these fellows, who owe to me all that they have; it shall be so no longer.

> I found them blind, I taught them how to see;
> And, now, they know me not, nor yet themselves.

PAGE 35

NUMBER IV.
The Bard, from Gray.

> On a rock, whose haughty brow
> Frown'd o'er old Conway's foaming flood,
> Robed in the sable garb of woe,
> With haggard eyes the Poet stood,
> Loose his beard, and hoary hair
> Stream'd like a meteor to the troubled air.
>
> Weave the warp, and weave the woof,
> The winding sheet of Edward's race.

Weaving the winding sheet of Edward's race by means of sounds of spiritual music and its accompanying expressions of articulate speech is a bold, and daring, and most masterly conception, that the public have embraced and approved with avidity. Poetry consists in these conceptions; and shall Painting be confined to the sordid drudgery of fac-simile re[P 36]presentations of merely mortal and perishing substances, and not be as poetry and music are, elevated into its own proper sphere of invention and visionary conception? No, it shall not be so! Painting, as well as poetry and music, exists and exults in immortal thoughts. If Mr. B.'s Canterbury Pilgrims had been done by any other power than that of the poetic visionary, it would have been as dull as his adversary's.

The Spirits of the murdered bards assist in weaving the deadly woof.

> With me in dreadful harmony they join,
> And weave, with bloody hands, the tissue of thy line.

The connoisseurs and artists who have made objections to Mr. B.'s mode of representing spirits with real bodies, would do well to consider that the Venus, the Minerva, the Jupiter, the Apollo, which they admire in Greek sta[P 37]tues, are all of them representations of spiritual existences of God's immortal, to the mortal perishing organ of sight; and yet they are embodied and organized in solid marble. Mr. B. requires the same latitude and all is well. The Prophets describe what they saw in Vision as real and existing men whom they saw with their imaginative and immortal organs; the Apostles the same; the clearer the organ the more distinct the object. A Spirit and a Vision are not, as the modern philosophy supposes, a cloudy vapour or a nothing: they are organized and minutely articulated beyond all that the mortal and perishing nature can produce. He who does not imagine in stronger and better lineaments, and in stronger and better light than his perishing mortal eye can see does not imagine at all. The painter of this work asserts that all his imaginations appear to him infinitely more perfect and more minutely organized than any thing seen by his mortal eye. Spi[P 38]rits are organized men: Moderns wish to draw figures without lines, and with great and heavy shadows; are not shadows more unmeaning than lines, and more heavy? O who can doubt this!

King Edward and his Queen Elenor are prostrated, with their horses, at the foot of a rock on which the Bard stands; prostrated by the terrors of his harp on the margin of the river Conway, whose waves bear up a corse of a slaughtered bard at the foot of the rock. The armies of Edward are seen winding among the mountains.

> "He wound with toilsome march his long array."

Mortimer and Gloucester lie spell bound behind their king.
The execution of this picture is also in Water Colours, or Fresco.

NUMBER V.
The Ancient Britons.

In the last Battle of King Arthur only Three Britons escaped, these were the Strongest Man, the Beautifullest Man, and the Ugliest Man; these three marched through the field unsubdued, as Gods, and the Sun of Britain s[e]t, but shall arise again with tenfold splendor when Arthur shall awake from sleep, and resume his dominion over earth and ocean.

The three general classes of men who are represented by the most Beautiful, the most Strong, and the most Ugly, could not be represented by any historical facts but those of our own country, the Ancient Britons; without violating costume. The Britons (say historians) were naked civilized men, learned, studious, abstruse in thought and contemplation; naked, simple, plain, in their acts and manners; [P 40] wiser than after-ages. They were overwhelmed by brutal arms all but a small remnant; Strength, Beauty, and Ugliness escaped the wreck, and remain for ever unsubdued, age after age.

The British Antiquities are now in the Artist's hands; all his visionary contemplations, relating to his own country and its ancient glory, when it was as it again shall be, the source of learning and inspiration. Arthur was a name for the constellation Arcturus, or Bootes, the Keeper of the North Pole. And all the fables of Arthur and his round table; of the warlike naked Britons; of Merlin; of Arthur's conquest of the whole world; of his death, or sleep, and promise to return again; of the Druid monuments, or temples; of the pavement of Watling-street; of London stone; of the caverns in Cornwall, Wales, Derbyshire, and Scotland; of the Giants of Ireland and Britain; of the elemental beings, called [P 41] by us by the general name of Fairies; and of these three who escaped, namely, Beauty, Strength, and Ugliness. Mr. B. has in his hands poems of the highest antiquity. Adam was a Druid, and Noah; also Abraham was called to succeed the Druidical age, which began to turn allegoric and mental signification into corporeal command, whereby human sacrifice would have depopulated the earth. All these things are written in Eden. The artist is an inhabitant of that happy country; and if every thing goes on as it has begun, the world of vegetation and generation may expect to be opened again to Heaven, through Eden, as it was in the beginning.

The Strong man represents the human sublime. The Beautiful man represents the human pathetic, which was in the wars of Eden divided into male and female. The Ugly man represents the human reason. They were originally one man, who was fourfold; he was self-divided, and [P 42] his real humanity slain on the stems of generation, and the form of the fourth was like the Son of God. How he became divided is a subject of great sublimity and pathos. The Artist has written it under inspiration, and will, if God please, publish it; it is voluminous, and contains the ancient history of Britain, and the world of Satan and of Adam.

In the mean time he has painted this Picture, which supposes that in the reign of that British Prince, who lived in the fifth century, there were remains of those naked Heroes, in the Welch Mountains; they are there now, Gray saw them in the person of his bard on Snowdon; there they dwell in naked simplicity; happy is he who can see and converse with them above the shadows of generation and death. The giant Albion, was Patriarch of the Atlantic; he is the Atlas of the Greeks, one of those the Greeks called Titans. The stories of Arthur are the acts of Albion, ap[P 43]plied to a Prince of the fifth century, who conquered Europe, and held the Empire of the world in the dark age, which the Romans never again recovered. In this Picture, believing with Milton, the ancient British History, Mr. B. has done, as all the ancients did, and as all the moderns, who are worthy of fame, given the historical fact in its poetical vigour; so as it always happens, and not in that dull way that some Historians pretend, who being weakly organized themselves, cannot see either miracle or prodigy; all is to them a dull round of probabilities and possibilities; but the history of all times and places is nothing else but improbabilities and impossibilities; what we should say was impossible if we did not see it always before our eyes.

The antiquities of every Nation under Heaven, is no less sacred than that of the Jews. They are the same thing as Jacob Bryant, [P 44] and all antiquaries have proved. How other antiquities came to be neglected and disbelieved, while those of the Jews are collected and arranged, is an enquiry, worthy of both the Antiquarian and the Divine. All had originally one language, and one religion, this was the religion of Jesus, the everlasting Gospel. Antiquity preaches the Gospel of Jesus. The reasoning historian, turner and twister of causes and consequences, such as Hume, Gibbon and Voltaire; cannot with all their artifice, turn or twist one fact or disarrange self evident action and reality. Reasons and opinions concerning acts, are not history. Acts themselves alone are history, and these are neither the exclusive property of Hume, Gibbon nor Voltaire, Echard, Rapin, Plutarch, nor Herodotus. Tell me the Acts, O historian, and leave me to reason upon them as I please; away with your reasoning and your rubbish. All that is not action is not [P 45] worth reading. Tell me the What; I do not want you to tell me the Why, and the How; I can find that out myself, as well as you can, and I will not be fooled by you. into opinions, that you please to impose, to disbelieve what you think improbable or impossible. His opinions, who does not see spiritual agency, is not worth any man's reading; he who rejects a fact because it is improbable, must reject all History and retain doubts only.

It has been said to the Artist, take the Apollo for the model of your beautiful Man and the Hercules for your strong Man, and the Dancing Fawn for your Ugly Man. Now he comes to his trial. He knows that what he does is not inferior to the grandest Antiques. Superior they cannot be, for human power cannot go beyond either what he does, or what they have done, it is the gift of God, it is inspiration and vision. He had resolved to emulate those [P 46] precious remains of antiquity, he has done so and the result you behold; his ideas of strength and beauty have not been greatly different. Poetry as it exists now on earth, in the various remains of ancient authors, Music as it exists in old tunes or melodies, Painting and Sculpture as it exists in the remains of Antiquity and in the works of more modern genius, is Inspiration, and cannot be surpassed; it is perfect and eternal. Milton, Shakspeare, Michael Angelo, Rafael, the finest specimens of Ancient Sculpture and Painting, and Architecture, Gothic, Grecian, Hindoo and Egyptian, are the extent of the human mind. The human mind cannot go beyond the gift of God, the Holy Ghost. To suppose that Art can go beyond the finest specimens of Art that are now in the world, is not knowing what Art is; it is being blind to the gifts of the spirit.

[PAGE 47] It will be necessary for the Painter to say something concerning his ideas of Beauty, Strength and Ugliness.

The Beauty that is annexed and appended to folly, is a lamentable accident and error of the mortal and perishing life; it does but seldom happen; but with this unnatural mixture the sublime Artist can have nothing to do; it is fit for the burlesque. The Beauty proper for sublime art, is lineaments, or forms and features that are capable of being the receptacles of intellect; accordingly the Painter has given in his beautiful man, his own idea of intellectual Beauty. The face and limbs that deviates or alters least, from infancy to old age, is the face and limbs of greatest Beauty and perfection.

The Ugly likewise, when accompanied and annexed to imbecility and disease, is a subject for burlesque and not for historical grandeur; the Artist has imagined his Ugly man; one [P 48] approaching to the beast in features and form, his forehead small, without frontals; his jaws large; his nose high on the ridge, and narrow; his chest and the stamina of his make, comparatively little, and his joints and his extremities large; his eyes with scarce any whites, narrow and cunning, and every thing tending toward what is truly Ugly; the incapability of intellect.

The Artist has considered his strong Man as a receptacle of Wisdom, a sublime energizer; his features and limbs do not spindle out into length, without strength, nor are they too large and unwieldy for his brain and bosom. Strength consists in accumulation of power to the principal seat, and from thence a regular gradation and subordination; strength is compactness, not extent nor bulk.

The strong Man acts from conscious superiority, and marches on in fearless dependance on the divine decrees, raging with the inspira[P 49]tions of a prophetic mind. The Beautiful Man acts from duty, and anxious solicitude for the fates of those for whom he combats. The Ugly Man acts from love of carnage, and delight in the savage barbarities of war, rushing with sportive precipitation into the very teeth of the affrighted enemy.

The Roman Soldiers rolled together in a heap before them: "Like the rolling thing before the whirlwind;" each shew a different character, and a different expression of fear, or revenge, or envy, or blank horror, or amazement, or devout wonder and unresisting awe.

The dead and the dying, Britons naked, mingled with armed Romans, strew the field beneath. Among these, the last of the Bards who were capable of attending warlike deeds, is seen falling, outstretched among the dead and the dying; singing to his harp in the pains of death.

[PAGE 50] Distant among the mountains, are Druid Temples, similar to Stone Henge. The Sun sets behind the mountains, bloody with the day of battle.

The flush of health in flesh, exposed to the open air, nourished by the spirits of forests and floods, in that ancient happy period, which history has recorded, cannot be like the sickly daubs of Titian or Rubens. Where will the copier of nature, as it now is, find a civilized man, who has been accustomed to go naked. Imagination only, can furnish us with colouring appropriate, such as is found in the Frescos of Rafael and Michael Angelo: the disposition of forms always directs colouring in works of true art. As to a modern Man stripped from his load of cloathing, he is like a dead corpse. Hence Rubens, Titian, Correggio, and all of that class, are like leather and chalk; their men are like leather, and their women like chalk, for the disposition of their [P 51] forms will not admit of grand colouring; in Mr. B.'s Britons, the blood is seen to circulate in their limbs; he defies competition in colouring.

NUMBER VI.

A Spirit vaulting from a cloud to turn and wind a fiery Pegasus—Shakspeare. The Horse of Intellect is leaping from the cliffs of Memory and Reasoning; it is a barren Rock: it is also called the Barren Waste of Locke and Newton.

THIS Picture was done many years ago, and was one of the first Mr. B. ever did in Fresco; fortunately or rather providentially he left it unblotted and unblurred, although molested continually by blotting and blurring demons; but he was also compelled to leave it unfinished for reasons that will be shewn in the following.

PAGE 52

NUMBER VII.
The Goats, an experiment Picture.

THE subject is taken from the Missionary Voyage and varied from the literal fact, for the sake of picturesque scenery. The savage girls had dressed themselves with vine leaves, and some goats on board the missionary ship stripped them off presently. This Picture was painted at intervals, for experiment, with the colours, and is laboured to a super-abundant blackness; it has however that about it, which may be worthy the attention of the Artist and Connoisseur for reasons that follow.

NUMBER VIII.
The spiritual Preceptor, an experiment Picture.

THIS subject is taken from the visions of Emanuel Swedenborg. Universal Theology, [P 53] No. 623. The Learned, who strive to ascend into Heaven by means of learning, appear to Children like dead horses, when repelled by the celestial spheres. The works of this visionary are well worthy the attention of Painters and Poets; they are foundations for grand things; the reason they have not been more attended to, is, because corporeal demons have gained a predominance; who the leaders of these are, will be shewn below. Unworthy Men who gain fame among Men, continue to govern mankind after death, and in their spiritual bodies, oppose the spirits of those, who worthily are famous; and as Swedenborg observes, by entering into disease and excrement, drunkenness and concupiscence, they possess themselves of the bodies of mortal men, and shut the doors of mind and of thought, by placing Learning above Inspiration. O Artist! you may disbelieve all this, but it shall be at your own peril.

PAGE 54

NUMBER IX.
Satan calling up his Legions, from Milton's Paradise Lost; a composition for a more perfect Picture, afterward executed for a Lady of high rank. An experiment Picture.

THIS Picture was likewise painted at intervals, for experiment on colours, without any oily vehicle; it may be worthy of attention, not only on account of its composition, but of the great labour which has been bestowed on it, that is, three or four times as much as would have finished a more perfect Picture; the labour has destroyed the lineaments, it was with difficulty brought back again to a certain effect, which it had at first, when all the lineaments were perfect.

These Pictures, among numerous others painted for experiment, were the result of [P 55] temptations and perturbations, labouring to destroy Imaginative power, by means of that infernal machine, called Chiaro Oscuro, in the hands of Venetian and Flemish Demons; whose enmity to the Painter himself, and to all Artists who study in the Florentine and Roman Schools, may be removed by an exhibition and exposure of their vile tricks. They cause that every thing in art shall become a Machine. They cause that the execution shall be all blocked up with brown shadows. They put the original Artist in fear and doubt of his own original conception. The spirit of Titian was particularly active, in raising doubts concerning the possibility of executing without a model, and when once he had raised the doubt, it became easy for him to snatch away the vision time after time, for when the Artist took his pencil, to execute his ideas, his power of imagination weakened so much, and darkened, that memory of nature and of Pictures [P 56] of the various Schools possessed his mind, instead of appropriate execution, resulting from the inventions; like walking in another man's style, or speaking or looking in another man's style and manner, unappropriate and repugnant to your own individual character; tormenting the true Artist, till he leaves the Florentine, and adopts the Venetian practice, or does as Mr. B. has done, has the courage to suffer poverty and disgrace, till he ultimately conquers.

Rubens is a most outrageous demon, and by infusing the remembrances of his Pictures, and style of execution, hinders all power of individual thought: so that the man who is possessed by this demon, loses all admiration of any other Artist, but Rubens, and those who were his imitators and journeymen, he causes to the Florentine and Roman Artist fear to execute; and though the original conception was all fire and animation, he loads it with [P 57] hellish brownness, and blocks up all its gates of light, except one, and that one he closes with iron bars, till the victim is obliged to give up the Florentine and Roman practice, and adopt the Venetian and Flemish.

Correggio is a soft and effeminate and consequently a most cruel demon, whose whole delight is to cause endless labour to whoever suffers him to enter his mind. The story that is told in all Lives of the Painters about Correggio being poor and but badly paid for his Pictures, is altogether false; he was a petty Prince, in Italy, and employed numerous Journeymen in manufacturing (as Rubens and Titian did) the Pictures that go under his name. The manual labour in these Pictures of Correggio is immense, and was paid for originally at the immense prices that those who keep manufactories of art always charge to their employers, while they themselves pay their journeymen little enough. But though [P 58] Correggio was not poor, he will make any true artist so, who permits him to enter his mind, and take possession of his affections; he infuses a love of soft and even tints without boundaries, and of endless reflected lights, that confuse one another, and hinder all correct drawing from appearing to be correct; for if one of Rafael or Michael Angelo's figures was to be traced, and Correggio's reflections and refractions to be added to it, there would soon be an end of proportion and strength, and it would be weak, and pappy, and lumbering, and thick headed, like his own works; but then it would have softness and evenness, by a twelvemonth's labour, where a month would with judgment have finished it better and higher; and the poor wretch who executed it, would be the Correggio that the life writers have written of: a drudge and a miserable man, compelled to softness by poverty. I say again, O Artist, you may disbe[P 59]lieve all this, but it shall be at your own peril.

Note. These experiment Pictures have been bruized and knocked about, without mercy, to try all experiments.

NUMBER X.
The Bramins.—A Drawing.

The subject is, Mr. Wilkin, translating the Geeta; an ideal design, suggested by the first publication of that part of the Hindoo Scriptures, translated by Mr. Wilkin. I understand that my Costume is incorrect, but in this I plead the authority of the ancients, who often deviated from the Habits, to preserve the Manners, as in the instance of Laocoon, who, though a priest, is represented naked.

PAGE 60

NUMBER XI.

The body of Abel found by Adam and Eve; Cain, who was about to bury it, fleeing from the face of his Parents.—A Drawing.

NUMBER XII.
The Soldiers casting lots for Christ's Garment.—A Drawing.

NUMBER XIII.
Jacob's Ladder.—A Drawing.

NUMBER XIV.
The Angels hovering over the Body of Jesus in the Sepulchre.—A Drawing.

The above four drawings the Artist wishes were in Fresco, on an enlarged scale to ornament [P 61] the altars of churches, and to make England like Italy, respected by respectable men of other countries on account of Art. It is not the want of genius, that can hereafter be laid to our charge, the Artist who has done these Pictures and Drawings will take care of that; let those who govern the Nation, take care of the other. The times require that every one should speak out boldly; England expects that every man should do his duty, in Arts, as well as in Arms, or in the Senate.

NUMBER XV.
Ruth.—A Drawing.

THIS Design is taken from that most pathetic passage in the Book of Ruth, where Naomi having taken leave of her daughters in law, with intent to return to her own country; Ruth cannot leave her, but says, "Whither [P 62] thou goest I will go; and where thou lodgest I will lodge, thy people shall be my people, and thy God my God: where thou diest I will die, and there will I be buried; God do so to me and more also, if ought but death part thee and me."

The distinction that is made in modern times between a Painting and a Drawing proceeds from ignorance of art. The merit of a Picture is the same as the merit of a Drawing. The dawber dawbs his Drawings; he who draws his Drawings draws his Pictures. There is no difference between Rafael's Cartoons and his Frescos, or Pictures, except that the Frescos, or Pictures, are more finished. When Mr. B. formerly painted in oil colours his Pictures were shewn to certain painters and connoisseurs, who said that they were very admirable Drawings on canvass; but not Pictures: but they said the same of Rafael's Pictures. [P 63] Mr. B. thought this the greatest of compliments, though it was meant otherwise. If losing and obliterating the outline constitutes a Picture, Mr. B. will never be so foolish as to do one. Such art of losing the outlines is the art of Venice and Flanders; it loses all character, and leaves what some people call, expression: but this is a false notion of expression; expression cannot exist without character as its stamina; and neither character nor expression can exist without firm and determinate outline. Fresco Painting is susceptible of higher finishing than Drawing on Paper, or than any other method of Painting. But he must have a strange organization of sight who does not prefer a Drawing on Paper to a Dawbing in Oil by the same master, supposing both to be done with equal care.

The great and golden rule of art, as well as of life, is this: That the more distinct, sharp, [P 64] and wirey the bounding line, the more perfect the work of art; and the less keen and sharp, the greater is the evidence of weak imitation, plagiarism, and bungling. Great inventors, in all ages, knew this: Protogenes and Apelles knew each other by this line. Rafael and Michael Angelo, and Albert Durer, are known by this and this alone. The want of this determinate and bounding form evidences the want of idea in the artist's mind, and the pretence of the plagiary in all its branches. How do we distinguish the oak from the beech, the horse from the ox, but by the bounding outline? How do we distinguish one face or countenance from another, but by the bounding line and its infinite inflexions and movements? What is it that builds a house and plants a garden, but the definite and determinate? What is it that distinguishes honesty from knavery, but the hard and wirey line of rectitude and certainty [P 65] in the actions and intentions. Leave out this l[i]ne and you leave out life itself; all is chaos again, and the line of the almighty must be drawn out upon it before man or beast can exist. Talk no more then of Correggio, or Rembrandt, or any other of those plagiaries of Venice or Flanders. They were but the lame imitators of lines drawn by their predecessors, and their works prove themselves contemptible dis-arranged imitations and blundering misapplied copies.

t

NUMBER XVI.
The Penance of Jane Shore in St. Paul's Church.—A Drawing.

THIS Drawing was done above Thirty Years ago, and proves to the Author, and he thinks will prove to any discerning eye, that the productions of our youth and of our maturer age [P 66] are equal in all essential points. If a man is master of his profession, he cannot be ignorant that he is so; and if he is not employed by those who pretend to encourage art, he will employ himself, and laugh in secret at the pretences of the ignorant, while he has every night dropped into his shoe, as soon as he puts it off, and puts out the candle, and gets into bed, a reward for the labours of the day, such as the world cannot give, and patience and time await to give him all that the world can give.

FINIS.

D. N. SHURY, PRINTER, BERWICK-STREET, SOHO, LONDON.

PAGE 68

INDEX TO THE CATALOGUE.

IX

[DESCRIPTIONS OF THE LAST JUDGMENT]

[The Design of The Last Judgment]

To Ozias Humphry Esqre

The Design of The Last Judgment which I have completed by your
recommendation [*under a fortunate star*] for The Countess of Egre-
mont [*by a happy accident*] it is necessary to give some account of &
its various parts ought to be described for the accomodation of those
who give it the honor of attention

Christ seated on the Throne of Judgment [*The Heavens in Clouds
rolling before him & around him*] before his feet & around him the
heavens in clouds are rolling like a scroll ready to be consumed in the
fires of the Angels who descend [*before his feet*] with the[ir] Four
Trumpets sounding to the Four Winds

Beneath [*the*] Earth is convulsed with the labours of the Resurrection—in the Caverns of the Earth is the Dragon with Seven heads
& ten Horns chained by two Angels & above his Cavern[s] on the
Earths Surface is the Harlot siezed & bound by two Angels with chains
while her Palaces are falling [*in*] into ruins & her councellors & warriors
are descending into the Abyss in wailing & despair

Hell opens beneath the Harlots seat on the left hand into which the
Wicked are descending [*while others rise from their Graves on the
brink of the Pit*]

The right hand of the Design is appropriated to the Resurrection
of the Just the left hand of the Design is appropriated to the Resurrection & Fall of the Wicked

Immediately before the Throne of Christ is Adam & Eve kneeling in
humiliation as representatives of the whole Human Race Abraham &
Moses kneel on each side beneath them from the cloud on which Eve
kneels [*& beneath Moses & from the Tables of Stone which utter lightnings*] is seen Satan wound round by the Serpent & falling headlong
the Pharisees appear on the left hand pleading their own righteousness

before the Throne of Christ & before the Book of Death which is opend on clouds by two Angels & many groupes of Figures are falling from before the Throne & from before the Sea of Fire which flows before the steps of the Throne on which [are] is seen the seven Lamps of the Almighty burning before the Throne many Figures chained & bound together & in various attitudes of Despair & Horror fall thro the air & some are scourged by Spirits with flames of fire into the Abyss of Hell which opens [to recieve them] beneath on the left hand of the Harlots Seat where others are howling & [descending into the flames & in the act of] dragging each other into Hell & [of] in contending in fighting with each other on the [very] brink of Perdition

Before the Throne of Christ on the Right hand the Just in humiliation & in exultation rise thro the Air with their Children & Families some of whom are bowing before the Book of Life which is opend [by two Angels on Clouds] on clouds by two Angels many groupes arise [with] in [joy] exultation among them is a Figure crownd with Stars & the Moon beneath her feet with six infants around her She represents the Christian Church [The] Green hills appear beneath with the Graves of the Blessed which are seen bursting with their births of immortality Parents & Children Wives & Husbands embrace & arise together & in exulting attitudes of great joy tell each other that the New Jerusalem is ready to descend upon Earth they arise upon the Air rejoicing others newly awakend from the Grave stand upon the Earth embracing & shouting to the Lamb who cometh in the Clouds in Power & great Glory

The Whole upper part of the Design is a View of Heaven opened around the Throne of Christ in the Cloud which rolls away are the Four Living Creatures filled with Eyes attended by the Seven Angels with the Seven Vials of the Wrath of God & above these [there are] Seven Angels with the Seven Trumpets these compose [composing] the Cloud which by its rolling away displays the opening seats of the Blessed on the right & left of which are seen the Four & Twenty Elders seated on Thrones to Judge the Dead

Behind the Seat & Throne of Christ [appear] appears the Tabernacle with its Veil opened [&] the Candlestick on the right the Table with the Shew bread on the left [&] in [the] midst is the Cross in place of the Ark [with the two] Cherubim bowing over it

On the Right hand of the Throne of Christ is Baptism On [his] the left is the Lords Supper the two introducers into Eternal Life Women with Infants approach the Figure of an aged Apostle which represents Baptism & on the left hand the Lords Supper is administerd by Angels from the hands of another [aged] Apostle these kneel on each side of the Throne which is surrounded by a Glory [in the glory] many Infants appear in the Glory representing the Eternal Creation flowing from the Divine Humanity in Jesus who opens the Scroll of Judgment upon his knees before the Living & the Dead

Such is the Design which you my Dear Sir have been the cause of my producing & which but for you might have slept till the Last Judgment

WILLIAM BLAKE

[*18 January 1808*] Feby 1808

❧

[A Vision of The Last Judgment]   t

PAGE 70

For the Year 1810
Additions to Blakes Catalogue of Pictures &ᶜ

The Last Judgment when all those are Cast away who trouble Religion with Questions concerning Good & Evil or Eating of the Tree of those Knowledges or Reasonings which hinder the Vision of God turning all into a Consuming fire <When> Imaginative Art & Science & all Intellectual Gifts all the Gifts of the Holy Ghost are [*despisd*] lookd upon as of no use & only Contention remains to Man then the Last Judgment begins & its Vision is seen by the [*Imaginative Eye*] of Every one according to the situation he holds

[PAGE 68] The Last Judgment is not Fable or Allegory but Vision Fable or Allegory are a totally distinct & inferior kind of Poetry. Vision or Imagination is a Representation of what Eternally Exists. Really & Unchangeably. Fable or Allegory is Formd by the Daughters of Memory. Imagination is Surrounded by the daughters of Inspiration who in the aggregate are calld Jerusalem [P 69] <Fable is Allegory but what Critics call The Fable is Vision itself> [P 68] The Hebrew Bible & the Gospel of Jesus are not Allegory but Eternal Vision or Imagination of All that Exists <Note here that Fable or Allgory is Seldom without some Vision Pilgrims Progress is full of it the Greek Poets the same but [*Fable* [*al*] <&> *Allegory*] <Allegory & Vision> [<& *Visions of Imagination*>] ought to be known as Two Distinct Things & so calld for the Sake of Eternal Life Plato has made Socrates say that Poets & Prophets do not Know or Understand what they write or Utter this is a most Pernicious Falshood. If they do not pray is an inferior Kind to be calld Knowing Plato confutes himself>

The Last Judgment is one of these Stupendous Visions[.] I have represented it as I saw it[.] to different People it appears differently as [P 69] every thing else does for tho on Earth things seem Permanent they are less permanent than a Shadow as we all know too well

The Nature of Visionary Fancy or Imagination is very little Known & the Eternal nature & permanence of its ever Existent Images is con-

siderd as less permanent than the things of Vegetative & Generative
Nature yet the Oak dies as well as the Lettuce but Its Eternal Image &
Individuality never dies. but renews by its seed. just [as] <so> the
Imaginative Image returns [according to] <by> the seed of Contemplative Thought the Writings of the Prophets illustrate these conceptions of the Visionary Fancy by their various sublime & Divine Images
as seen in the Worlds of Vision

[PAGE 71 (TOP OF PAGE CUT AWAY)] The Learned m . . . [of]
<or> Heroes <this as n . . .> [it] ans . . . & not Spiritu . . . while
the Bibl . . . of Virtue & Vic . . . as they are Ex . . . is the Real
Di . . . Things The . . . when they Assert that Jupiter usurped the
Throne of his Father Saturn & brought on an Iron Age & Begat on
Mnemosyne or Memory The Greek Muses which are not Inspiration as
the Bible is. Reality was Forgot & the Vanities of Time & Space only
Rememberd & calld Reality Such is the Mighty difference between Al-
legoric Fable & Spiritual Mystery Let it. here be Noted that the Greek
Fables originated in Spiritual Mystery & Real Vision [P 72] and Real
Visions Which are lost & clouded in Fable & Alegory [which]
<while> the Hebrew Bible & the Greek Gospel are Genuine Preservd
by the Saviours Mercy The Nature of my Work is Visionary or Imaginative it is an Endeavour to Restore <what the Ancients calld> the
Golden Age

[PAGE 69] This world of Imagination is the World of Eternity it
is the Divine bosom into which we shall all go after the death of the
Vegetated body   This World <of Imagination> is Infinite & Eternal
whereas the world of Generation or Vegetation is Finite & [for a
small moment] Temporal   There Exist in that Eternal World the Permanent Realities of Every Thing which we see reflected in this Vegetable Glass of Nature

All Things are comprehended in their Eternal Forms in the Divine
[P 70] body of the Saviour the True Vine of Eternity The Human
Imagination who appeard to Me as Coming to Judgment. among his
Saints & throwing off the Temporal that the Eternal might be Estab-
lishd. around him were seen the Images of Existences according to [their
aggregate Imaginations] a certain order suited to my Imaginative Eye
[In the following order] <as follows>

Here follows the description of the Picture <Query the Above ought
to follow the description>

[PAGE 76] Jesus seated between the Two Pillars Jachin & Boaz with
the Word of <Divine> Revelation on his knees <& on each side the
four & twenty Elders sitting in judgment> the Heavens opening around
him by unfolding the clouds around his throne <The Old H[eaven]
& old Earth are passing away & the N[ew] H[eaven] & N[ew] Earth
descending> [as a Scroll]   The Just arise on his right & the wicked on
his Left hand <A Sea of fire Issues from before the throne> Adam &
Eve appear first before the [throne] <Judgment Seat> in humiliation
Abel surrounded by Innocents & Cain <with the flint in his hand with

which he slew his brother> falling with the head downward   From the
Cloud on which Eve stands Satan is seen falling headlong wound round
by the tail of the serpent whose bulk naild to the Cross round which
he wreathes is falling into the Abyss Sin is also represented as a female
bound in one of the Serpents folds surrounded by her fiends Death
is Chaind to the Cross & Time falls together with death dragged down
by [*an Angel*] a Demon crownd with Laurel another demon with a
Key has the charge of Sin & is dragging her down by the hair beside
them a figure is seen scaled with iron scales from head to feet precipitat-
ing himself into the Abyss with the Sword & Balances he is Og King
of Bashan—

<On the Right> Beneath the Cloud on which Abel kneels is Abra-
ham with Sarah & Isaac [&] also Hagar & Ishmael. <Abel kneels on a
bloody Cloud [p 80] descriptive of those Churches before the flood that
they were filld with blood & fire & vapour of smoke even till Abrahams
time the vapour & heat was not Extinguishd These States Exist now
Man Passes on but States remain for Ever he passes thro them like a
traveller who may as well suppose that the places he has passed thro
exist no more as a Man may suppose that the States he has passd
thro Exist no more Every Thing is Eternal>

[PAGE 79] In Eternity one Thing never Changes into another Thing
Each Identity is Eternal consequently Apuleius's Golden Ass & Ovids
Metamorphosis & others of the like kind are Fable yet they contain
Vision in a Sublime degree being derived from real Vision in More
Ancient Writings[.] Lots Wife being Changed into Pillar of Salt al-
ludes to the Mortal Body being renderd a Permanent Statue but not
Changed or Transformed into Another Identity while it retains its
own Individuality. A Man can never become Ass nor Horse some are
born with shapes of Men who may be both but Eternal Identity is one
thing & Corporeal Vegetation is another thing Changing Water into
Wine by Jesus & into Blood by Moses relates to Vegetable Nature also

[PAGE 76] [Beneath] <Ishmael is Mahomet> & <on the left> beneath the falling figure of Cain is Moses casting his tables of stone into
the deeps. it ought to be understood that the Persons Moses & Abraham
are not here meant but the States Signified by those Names the Individuals being representatives or Visions of those States as they were
reveald to Mortal Man in the Series of Divine Revelations. as they are
written in the Bible these various States I have seen in my Imagination
when distant they appear as One Man but as you approach they appear
Multitudes of Nations. Abraham hovers above his posterity which appear as Multitudes of Children ascending from the Earth surrounded by
Stars as it was said As the Stars of Heaven for Multitude Jacob & his
Twelve Sons hover beneath the feet of Abraham & recieve their children
from the Earth <I have seen when at a distance Multitudes of Men in
Harmony appear like a single Infant sometimes in the Arms of a Female [*they*] <this> represented the Church>

But to proceed with the description of those on the Left hand. be-

neath the Cloud on which Moses kneels is two figures a Male & Female
chaind [P 77] together by the feet[.] they represent those who perishd
by the flood[.] beneath them a multitude of their associates are seen
falling headlong[.] by the side of them is a Mighty fiend with a Book
in his hand which is Shut he represents the person namd in Isaiah
XXII.c & 20.v. Eliakim the Son of Hilkiah he drags Satan down
headlong he is crownd with oak [& has] by the side of the Scaled figure representing Og King of Bashan is a Figure with a Basket emptiing
out the vanities of Riches & Worldly Honours <he is Araunah the
Jebusite> <master of the threshing floor> above him are two figures
<elevated on a Cloud> representing the Pharisees who plead their
own Righteousness before the throne. they are weighed down by two
fiends[.] Beneath the Man with the Basket are three fiery fiends with
grey beards & scourges of fire they represent Cruel Laws they scourge
a groupe of figures down into the Deeps beneath them are various figures in attitudes of contention representing various States of Misery
which alas every one on Earth is liable to enter into & against which
we should all watch

The Ladies will be pleasd to see that I have represented the Furies
by Three Men & not by three Women It is not because I think the
Ancients wrong but they will be pleasd to remember that mine is Vision
& not Fable The Spectator may suppose them Clergymen in the Pulpit
Scourging Sin instead of Forgiving it

The Earth beneath these falling Groupes of figures is rocky & burning and seems as if convulsd by Earthquakes a Great City <on fire>
is seen in the distance <the Armies are fleeing upon the Mountains>
On the foreground hell is opened & many figures are descending into
it down stone steps & beside a Gate beneath a rock [howling & lament-
ing] <where Sin & Death are to be closed Eternally by that Fiend
who carries the Key in one hand & drags them down with the other>
On the rock & above the Gate a fiend with wings urges the wicked
onwards with fiery darts he [represents the Assyrian] <is Hazael
the Syrian> who drives abroad all those who rebell against their Saviour beneath the steps Babylon represented by a King crowned
Grasping his Sword & his Scepter he is just awakend out of his Grave
around him are other Kingdoms arising to Judgment. represented in
this Picture as Single Personages according to the descriptions in the
Prophets The Figure dragging up a Woman by her hair represents the
Inquisition as do those contending on the sides of the Pit & in Particular the Man Strangling two Women represents a Cruel Church

[PAGE 78] Two persons one in Purple the other in Scarlet are descending [into Hell] <down the Steps into the Pit> these are Caiphas
& Pilate Two States where all those reside who Calumniate & Murder
<under Pretence of Holiness & Justice> Caiphas has a Blue Flame like
a Miter on his head   Pilate has bloody hands that never can be cleansed
the Females behind them represent the Females belonging to such States
who are under perpetual terrors & vain dreams plots & secret deceit.

Those figures that descend into the Flames before Caiphas & Pilate are Judas & those of his Class Achitophel is also here with the cord in his hand

[PAGE 80] Between the Figures of Adam & Eve appears a fiery Gulph descending from the sea of fire Before the throne in this Cataract Four Angels descend headlong with four trumpets to awake the dead. beneath these is the Seat of the Harlot <namd> Mystery in the Revelations. She is [bound] siezed by Two Beings each with three heads they Represent Vegetative Existence. <as> it is written in Revelations they strip her naked & burn her with fire <it represents the Eternal Consummation of Vegetable Life & Death with its Lusts The wreathed Torches in their hands represents Eternal Fire which is the fire of Generation or Vegetation it is an Eternal Consummation Those who are blessed with Imaginative Vision see This Eternal Female & tremble at what others fear not while they <despise &> laugh at what others fear> <Her Kings & Councellors & Warriors descend in Flames Lamenting & looking upon her in astonishment & Terror. & Hell is opend beneath her Seat on the Left hand>. beneath her feet is a flaming Cavern in which is seen the Great Red Dragon with Seven heads & ten Horns [who] <he has Satans book of Accusations lying on the rock open before him> <he> is bound in chains by Two strong demons they are Gog & Magog <who have been compelld to subdue their Master Ezekiel> <XXXVIIIc 8v> <with their Hammer & Tongs about to new Create the Seven Headed Kingdoms>. The Graves beneath are opend & the dead awake & obey the call of the Trumpet those on the Right hand awake in joy those on the Left in Horror. beneath the Dragons Cavern a Skeleton begins to Animate starting into life at the Trumpets sound while the Wicked contend with each other on the brink of [P 81] perdition. <on the Right> a Youthful couple are awakd by their Children an Aged patriarch is awakd by his aged wife <He is Albion our Ancestor <patriarch of the Atlantic Continent> whose History Preceded that of the Hebrews <& in whose Sleep <or Chaos> Creation began, [his Emanation or Wife is Jerusalem < who is about to be recievd like the Bride of the>] at their head> <the Aged Woman is Brittannica the Wife of Albion Jerusalem is their daughter>> little Infants creep out of the [mould] [<ground>] flowery mould into the Green fields of the blessed who in various joyful companies embrace & ascend to meet Eternity

The Persons who ascend to Meet the Lord coming in the Clouds with power & great Glory. are representations of those States described in the Bible under the Names of the Fathers before & after the Flood Noah is seen in the Midst of these Canopied by a Rainbow. on his right hand Shem & on his Left Japhet these three Persons represent Poetry Painting & Music the three Powers <in Man> of conversing with Paradise which the flood did not Sweep away

Above Noah is the Church Universal represented by a Woman Surrounded by Infants There is such a State in Eternity it is composed of the Innocent <civilized> Heathen & the Uncivilized Savage who having not the Law do by Nature the things contain in the Law. This State appears like a Female crownd with Stars driven into the Wilderness She has the Moon under her feet

The Aged Figure with Wings having a writing tablet & taking account of the numbers who arise is That Angel of the Divine Presence mentiond in Exodus XIVc 19v & in other Places this Angel is frequently calld by the Name of Jehovah Elohim The I Am of the Oaks of Albion

Around Noah & beneath him are various figures Risen into the Air <among> these are Three Females representing those who are not of the dead but of those found Alive at the Last Judgment they appear to be innocently gay & thoughtless not <being> among the Condemnd because ignorant of crime in the midst of a corrupted Age <the Virgin Mary was of this Class>. A Mother Meets her <numerous> Family in the Arms of their Father these are representations of the Greek Learned & Wise as also of those of other Nations such as Egypt & Babylon in which were multitudes who shall meet the Lord coming in the Clouds

The Children of Abraham or Hebrew Church are represented as a Stream of [*Light*] <Figures> on which are seen Stars somewhat like the Milky way they ascend from the Earth where Figures kneel Embracing above the Graves & Represent Religion or Civilized Life such as it is in the Christian Church who are the Offspring of the Hebrew

[PAGE 82] Just above the graves & above the spot where the Infants creep out of the Ground Stand two a Man & Woman these are the Primitive Christians. The two Figures in <purifying> flames by the side of the Dragons cavern represents the Latter state of the Church when on the verge of Perdition yet protected by a Flaming Sword. Multitudes are seen ascending from the Green fields of the blessed in which a Gothic Church is representative of true Art Calld Gothic in All Ages <by those who follow <the> Fashion> <as that is calld which is without Shape or Fashion> <On the right hand of Noah a Woman with Children represents the State Calld Laban the Syrian it is the Remains of Civilization in the State from whence Abraham was taken> <Also> On the right hand of Noah A Female descends to meet her Lover or Husband representative of that Love calld Friendship which Looks for no other heaven than their Beloved & in him sees all reflected as in a Glass of Eternal Diamond

On the right hand of these rise the diffident & Humble & on their left a <solitary> Woman with her infant these are caught up by three aged Men who appear as suddenly emerging from the blue sky for their help. These three Aged Men represent Divine Providence as oppos'd to & distinct from divine vengeance represented by three Aged men on the side of the Picture among the Wicked with scourges of fire

If the Spectator could Enter into these Images in his Imagination approaching them on the Fiery Chariot of his Contemplative Thought if he could Enter into Noahs Rainbow or into his bosom or could make a Friend & Companion of one of these Images of wonder which always intreats him to leave mortal things as he must know then would he arise from his Grave then would he meet the Lord in the Air & then he would be happy General Knowledge is Remote Knowledge it is in Particulars that Wisdom consists & Happiness too. Both in Art & in Life General Masses are as Much Art as a Pasteboard Man is Human Every Man has Eyes Nose & Mouth this Every Idiot knows but he who enters into & discriminates most minutely the Manners & Intentions [P 83] the [Expression] Characters in all their branches is the alone Wise or Sensible Man & on this discrimination All Art is founded. I intreat then that the Spectator will attend to the Hands & Feet to the Lineaments of the Countenances they are all descriptive of Character & not a line is drawn without intention & that most discriminate & particular <as Poetry admits not a Letter that is Insignificant so Painting admits not a Grain of Sand or a Blade of Grass <Insignificant> much less an Insignificant Blur or Mark>

Above the Head of Noah is Seth this State calld Seth is Male & Female in a higher state of Happiness & wisdom than Noah being nearer the State of Innocence beneath the feet of Seth two figures represent the two Seasons of Spring & Autumn. while beneath the feet of Noah Four Seasons represent [our present changes of Extremes] the Changed State made by the flood.

By the side of Seth is Elijah he comprehends all the Prophetic Characters he is seen on his fiery Chariot bowing before the throne of the Saviour. in like manner The figures of Seth & his wife Comprehends the Fathers before the flood & their Generations when seen remote they appear as One Man. a little below Seth on his right are Two Figures a Male & Female with numerous Children these represent those who were not in the Line of the Church & yet were Saved from among the Antediluvians who Perished. between Seth & these a female figure [with the back turnd] represents the Solitary State of those who previous to the Flood walked with God

All these arise toward the opening Cloud before the Throne led onward by triumphant Groupes of Infants. <& the Morning Stars sang together>

Between Seth & Elijah three Female Figures crownd with Garlands Represent Learning & Science which accompanied Adam out of Eden

The Cloud that opens rolling apart before the throne & before the New Heaven & the New Earth is Composed of Various Groupes of Figures particularly the Four Living Creatures mentiond in Revelations as Surrounding the Throne these I suppose to have the chief agency in removing the [former] [P 84] old heavens & the old Earth to make way for the New Heaven & the New Earth to descend from the throne of God & of the Lamb. that Living Creature on the Left of the Throne

Gives to the Seven Angels the Seven Vials of the wrath of God <with> which they hovering over the Deeps beneath pour out upon the wicked their Plagues the Other Living Creatures are descending with a Shout & with the Sound of the Trumpet Directing the Combats in the upper Elements <in the two Corners of the Picture> on the Left hand Apollyon is foild before the Sword of Michael & on the Right the Two Witnesses <are> subduing their Enemies [*Around the Throne Heaven is Opened*] On the Cloud are opend the Books of Remembrance of Life & of Death before that of Life <on the Right> some figures bow in humiliation before that of Death <on the left> the Pharisees are pleading their own Righteousness the one Shines with beams of Light the other utters Lightnings & tempests

<A Last Judgment is Necessary because Fools flourish>

Nations Flourish under Wise Rulers & are depressd under foolish Rulers it is the same with Individuals as Nations works of Art can only be produced in Perfection where the Man is either in Affluence or is Above the Care of it Poverty is the Fools Rod which at last is turnd on his own back <this is A Last Judgment when Men of Real Art Govern & Pretenders Fall Some People & not a few Artists have asserted that the Painter of this Picture would not have done so well if he had been properly [*patr*[onized]] Encouragd Let those who think so reflect on the State of Nations under Poverty & their incapability of Art. tho Art is Above Either the Argument is better for Affluence than Poverty & tho he would not have been a greater Artist yet he would have produced Greater works of Art in proportion to [P 85] his means A Last Judgment is not for the purpose of making Bad Men better but for the Purpose of hindering them from opressing the Good with Poverty & Pain by means of Such Vile Arguments & Insinuations>

[PAGE 84] Around the Throne Heaven is opend & the Nature of Eternal Things Displayd All Springing from the Divine Humanity All beams from him [<Because> *as he himself has said All dwells in him*] He is the Bread & the Wine he is the Water of Life accordingly on Each Side of the opening Heaven appears an Apostle that on the Right Represents Baptism that on the Left Represents the Lords Supper All Life consists of these Two Throwing off Error <& Knaves from our company> continually & recieving Truth <or Wise Men into our Company> Continually. he who is out of the Church & opposes it is no less an Agent of Religion than he who is in it. to be an Error & to be Cast out is a part of Gods Design No man can Embrace True Art till he has Explord & Cast out False Art <such is the Nature of Mortal Things> or he will be himself Cast out by those who have Already Embraced True Art Thus My Picture is a History of Art & Science [& *its*] <the Foundation of Society> Which is Humanity itself. What are all the Gifts of the Spirit but Mental Gifts whenever any Individual Rejects Error & Embraces Truth a Last Judgment passes upon that Individual

[PAGE 85] Over the Head of the Saviour & Redeemer The Holy Spirit like a Dove is surrounded by a blue Heaven in which are the two Cherubim that bowd over the Ark for here the temple is opend in Heaven & the Ark of the Covenant is as a Dove of Peace The Curtains are drawn apart Christ having rent the Veil The Candlestick & the Table of Shew bread appear on Each side a Glorification of Angels with Harps surround the Dove

The Temple stands on the Mount of God from it flows on each side the River of Life on whose banks Grows the tree of Life among whose branches temples & Pinnacles tents & pavilions Gardens & Groves display Paradise with its Inhabitants walking up & down in Conversations concerning Mental Delights

[PAGE 90] Here they are no longer talking of what is Good & Evil or of what is Right or Wrong & puzzling themselves in Satans [Maze] Labyrinth But are Conversing with Eternal Realities as they Exist in the Human Imagination We are in a World of Generation & death & this world we must cast off if we would be Painters [P 91] Such as Rafa[e]ll Mich Angelo & the Ancient Sculptors. if we do not cast off this world we shall be only Venetian Painters who will be cast off & Lost from Art

[PAGE 85] Jesus is surrounded by Beams of Glory in which are seen all around him Infants emanating from him these represent the Eternal Births of Intellect from the divine Humanity A Rainbow surrounds the throne & the Glory in which youthful Nuptials recieve the infants in their hands <In Eternity Woman is the Emanation of Man she has No Will of her own There is no such thing in Eternity as a Female Will>

On the Side next Baptism are seen those calld in the Bible Nursing Fathers & Nursing Mothers [<they have Crowns the Spectator may suppose them to be the good Kings>] <& Queens [of England]> they represent Education On the Side next the Lords Supper. The Holy Family consisting of Mary Joseph John the Baptist Zacharias & Elizabeth recieving the Bread & Wine among other Spirits of <the> Just made perfect. beneath these a Cloud of Women & Children are taken up fleeing from the rolling Cloud which separates the Wicked from the Seats of Bliss. These represent those who tho willing were too weak to Reject Error without the Assistance & Countenance of those Already in the Truth for a Man Can only Reject Error by the Advice of a Friend or by the Immediate Inspiration of God it is for this Reason among many others that I have put the Lords Supper on the Left hand of the Throne for it appears so at the Last Judgment for a Protection

[PAGE 91] Many suppose that before [Adam] <the Creation> All was Solitude & Chaos This is the most pernicious Idea that can enter the Mind as it takes away all sublimity from the Bible & Limits All Existence to Creation & to Chaos To the Time & Space fixed by the Corporeal Vegetative Eye & leaves the Man who entertains such an Idea the habitation of Unbelieving Demons Eternity Exists and All

things in Eternity Independent of Creation which was an act of Mercy
I have [P 92] represented those who are in Eternity by some in a
Cloud within the Rainbow that surrounds the Throne they merely
appear as in a Cloud when any thing of Creation Redemption or
Judgment are the Subjects of Contemplation tho their Whole Contemplation is Concerning these things the Reason they so appear is The
Humiliation of <the Reasoning & doubting> Selfhood & the Giving
all up to Inspiration By this it will be seen that I do not consider
either the Just or the Wicked to be in a Supreme State but to be every
one of them States of the Sleep which the Soul may fall into in its
deadly dreams of Good & Evil when it leaves Paradise [with] <follow-
ing> the Serpent

[PAGE 91] <The Greeks represent Chronos or Time as a very Aged
Man this is Fable but the Real Vision of Time is in Eternal Youth I
have <however> somewhat accomodated my Figure of Time to
<the> Common opinion as I myself am also infected with it & my
Visions also infected & I see Time Aged alas too much so>

Allegories are things that Relate to Moral Virtues Moral Virtues do
not Exist they are Allegories & dissimulations <But Time & Space are
Real Beings a Male & a Female Time is a Man Space is a Woman &
her Masculine Portion is Death>

[PAGE 86] The Combats of Good & Evil <is Eating of the Tree of
Knowledge The Combats of Truth & Error is Eating of the Tree of
Life> [& of Truth & Error which are the same thing] <these> are
not only Universal but Particular. Each are Personified There is not an
Error but it has a Man for its [Actor] Agent that is it is a Man: There
is not a Truth but it has also a Man <Good & Evil are Qualities in
Every Man whether <a> Good or Evil Man> These are Enemies &
destroy one another by every Means in their power both of deceit & of
open Violence The Deist & the Christian are but the Results of these
Opposing Natures Many are Deists who would in certain Circumstances have been Christians in outward appearance Voltaire was one
of this number he was as intolerant as an Inquisitor Manners make
the Man not Habits. It is the same in Art by their Works ye [P 90]
shall know them the Knave who is Converted to Deism & the Knave
who is Converted to Christianity is still a Knave but he himself will
not know it tho Every body else does Christ comes as he came at first
to deliver those who were bound under the Knave not to deliver the
Knave He Comes to Deliver Man the [Forgiven] <Accused &> not
Satan the Accuser we do not find any where that Satan is Accused
of Sin he is only accused of Unbelief & thereby drawing Man into
Sin that he may accuse him. Such is the Last Judgment a Deliverance
from Satans Accusation Satan thinks that Sin is displeasing to God he
ought to know that Nothing is displeasing to God but Unbelief &
Eating of the Tree of Knowledge of Good & Evil

[PAGE 87] Men are admitted into Heaven not because they have
<curbed &> governd their Passions or have No Passions but because

they have Cultivated their Understandings. The Treasures of Heaven are not Negations of Passion but Realities of Intellect from which All the Passions Emanate <Uncurbed> in their Eternal Glory   The Fool shall not enter into Heaven let him be ever so Holy. Holiness is not The Price of Enterance into Heaven Those who are cast out Are All Those who having no Passions of their own because No Intellect. Have spent their lives in Curbing & Governing other Peoples by the Various arts of Poverty & Cruelty of all kinds   Wo Wo Wo to you Hypocrites   Even Murder the Courts of Justice <more merciful than the Church> are compelld to allow is not done in Passion but in Cool Blooded Design & Intention

The Modern Church Crucifies Christ with the Head Downwards

[PAGE 92] Many Persons such as Paine & Voltaire <with <some of> the Ancient Greeks> say we will not converse concerning Good & Evil we will live in Paradise & Liberty   You may do so in Spirit but not in the <Mortal> Body as you pretend till after the Last Judgment for in Paradise they have no Corporeal <& Mortal> Body that originated with the Fall & was calld Death & cannot be removed but by a Last Judgment while we are in the world of Mortality we Must Suffer   The Whole Creation Groans to be deliverd there will always be as many Hypocrites born as Honest Men & they will always have superior Power in Mortal Things   You cannot have Liberty in this World without <what you call> Moral Virtue & you cannot have Moral Virtue without the Slavery of that half of the Human Race who hate <what you call> Moral Virtue

The Nature of Hatred & Envy & of All the Mischiefs in the World are here depicted. No one Envies or Hates one of his Own Party even the devils love one another in their Way they torment one another for other reasons than Hate or Envy these are only employd against the Just. Neither can Seth Envy Noah or Elijah Envy Abraham but they may both of them Envy the Success [P 93] of Satan or of Og or Molech The Horse never Envies the Peacock nor the Sheep the Goat but they Envy a Rival in Life & Existence whose ways & means exceed their own let him be of what Class of Animals he will a Dog will envy a Cat who is pamperd at the expense of his comfort as I have often seen   The Bible never tells us that Devils torment one another thro Envy it is thro this that they torment the Just   but for what do they torment one another   I answer For the Coercive Laws of Hell Moral Hypocrisy. They torment a Hypocrite when he is discoverd they Punish a Failure in the tormentor who has sufferd the Subject of his torture to Escape   In Hell all is Self Righteousness there is no such thing there as Forgiveness of Sin he who does Forgive Sin is Crucified as an Abettor of Criminals. & he who performs Works of Mercy in Any shape whatever is punishd & if possible destroyd not thro Envy or Hatred or Malice but thro Self Righteousness that thinks it does God service which God is Satan <They do not Envy one another They contemn <& despise> one another>

Forgiveness of Sin is only at the Judgment Seat of Jesus the Saviour where the Accuser is cast out. not because he Sins but because he torments the Just & makes them do what he condemns as Sin & what he knows is opposite to their own Identity

It is not because Angels are Holier than Men or Devils that makes them Angels but because they do not Expect Holiness from one another but from God only

The Player is a liar when he Says Angels are happier than [p 94] Men because they are better   Angels are happier than Men <& Devils> because they are not always Prying after Good & Evil in one Another & eating the Tree of Knowledge for Satans Gratification

Thinking as I do that the Creator of this World is a very Cruel Being & being a Worshipper of Christ I cannot help saying the Son O how unlike the Father <First God Almighty comes with a Thump on the Head   Then Jesus Christ comes with a balm to heal it>

The Last Judgment is an Overwhelming of Bad Art & Science. Mental Things are alone Real what is Calld Corporeal Nobody Knows of its dwelling Place <it> is in Fallacy & its Existence an Imposture Where is the Existence Out of Mind or Thought Where is it but in the Mind of a Fool. Some People flatter themselves that there will be No Last Judgment & [p 95] that Bad Art will be adopted & mixed with Good Art That Error or Experiment will make a Part of Truth & they Boast that it is its Foundation these People flatter themselves   I will not Flatter them Error is Created Truth is Eternal   Error or Creation will be Burned Up & then & not till then Truth or Eternity will appear It is Burnt up the Moment Men cease to behold it I assert for My self that I do not behold the Outward Creation & that to me it is hindrance & not Action it is as the Dirt upon my feet No part of Me. What it will be Questiond When the Sun rises do you not see a round Disk of fire somewhat like a Guinea O no no I see an Innumerable company of the Heavenly host crying Holy Holy Holy is the Lord God Almighty I question not my Corporeal or Vegetative Eye any more than I would Question a Window concerning a Sight I look thro it & not with it.

X

[First Prospectus]

BLAKE'S CHAUCER,
THE CANTERBURY PILGRIMS.
THE FRESCO PICTURE,

Representing Chaucer's Characters painted by
WILLIAM BLAKE,
As it is now submitted to the Public,

The Designer proposes to Engrave, in a correct and finished Line manner of Engraving, similar to those original Copper Plates of Albert Durer, Lucas, Hisben, Aldegrave and the old original Engravers, who were great Masters in Painting and Designing, whose method, alone, can delineate Character as it is in this Picture, where all the Lineaments are distinct.

It is hoped that the Painter will be allowed by the Public (notwithstanding artfully dissemminated insinuations to the contrary) to be better able than any other to keep his own Characters and Expressions; having had sufficient evidence in the Works of our own Hogarth, that no other Artist can reach the original Spirit so well as the Painter himself, especially as Mr. B. is an old well-known and acknowledged Engraver.

The size of the Engraving will be 3-feet 1-inch long, by 1-foot high. —The Artist engages to deliver it, finished, in One Year from September next.—No Work of Art, can take longer than a Year: it may be worked backwards and forwards without end, and last a Man's whole Life; but he will, at length, only be forced to bring it back to what it was, and it will be worse than it was at the end of the first Twelve Months. The Value of this Artist's Year is the Criterion of Society: and as it is valued, so does Society flourish or decay.

The Price to Subscribers—Four Guineas, Two to be paid at the time of Subscribing, the other Two, on delivery of the Print.

Subscriptions received at No. 28, Corner of Broad-street, Golden-Square; where the Picture is now Exhibiting, among other Works, by the same Artist.

The Price will be considerably raised to Non-subscribers. May 15th, 1809.

Printed by Watts & Bridgewater, Southmolton-Street.

❧

[Second Prospectus, Composite Draft]   t

BLAKES CHAUCER

An Original Engraving by [*William Blake*] <him> from his Fresco Painting of [*Chaucers Canterbury Pilgrims*]

[*Mr B having from early Youth cultivated the two Arts Painting & Engraving & during a Period of Forty Years never suspended his Labours on Copper for a single Day Submits with Confidence to Public Patronage & requests the attention of the Amateur in a Large Stroke Engraving*] 3 feet 1 inch long by one foot high <Price Three Guineas> [*Containing Thirty original high finishd whole Length Portraits on Horseback Of Chaucers Characters, where every Character & every Expression, every Lineament of Head Hand & Foot. every particular of Dress or Costume. where every Horse is appropriate to his Rider & the Scene or Landscape with its Villages Cottages Churches & the Inn in Southwark is minutely labourd not by the hands of Journeymen but by the Original Artist himself even to the Stuffs & Embroidery of the Garments. the hair upon the Horses the Leaves upon the Trees. & the Stones & Gravel upon the road; the Great Strength of Colouring & depth of work peculiar to Mr B's Prints will be here found accompanied by a Precision not to be seen but in the work of an Original Artist*]

> Sir Jeffery Chaucer & the nine & twenty
> Pilgrims on their Journey to Canterbury

The time chosen is early morning before Sunrise. when the jolly Company are just quitting the Tabarde Inn. The Knight &. Squire with the Squires Yeoman lead the Procession: then the Youthful Abbess her Nun & three Priests. her Greyhounds attend her.

> "Of small Hounds had she that she fed
> With roast flesh milk & wastel bread"

Next follow the Friar & Monk. then the Tapiser the Pardoner. the Sompnour & the Manciple. After these "Our Host" who occupies the Center of the Cavalcade [(*the Fun afterwards exhibited on the road may be seen depicted in his jolly face*)] directs them to the Knight [(*whose solemn Gallantry no less fixes attention*)] as the person who will be likely to commense their Task of each telling a Tale in their order. After the Host, follow, the Shipman, the Haberdasher, the Dyer, the Franklin, the Physician the Plowman, the Lawyer, the [*Poor*] Parson, the Merchant, the Wife of Bath the Cook. the Oxford Scholar. Chaucer himself & the Reeve comes as Chaucer has described

"And ever he rode hinderest of the rout"

These last are issuing from the Gateway of the Inn the Cook & Wife of Bath are both taking their mornings draught of comfort. Spectators stand at the Gateway of the Inn & are composed of an old man a woman & children

<The Inn is yet extant under the name of the Talbot; and the Landlord, Robert Bristow, Esq. of Broxmore near Rumsey, has continued a Board over the Gateway, inscribed, "This is the Inn from which Sir Jeffrey Chaucer and his Pilgrims set out for Canterbury."

St. Thomas's Hospital which is situated near to it, is one of the most amiable features of the Christian Church; it belonged to the Monastery [o]f St. Mary Overies and was dedicated to Thomas a Becket. The Pilgrims, if sick or lame, on their Journey to and from his Shrine, were received at this House. Even at this day every friendless wretch who wants the succour of it, is considered as a Pilgrim travelling through this Journey of Life.>

The Landscape is an Eastward view of the Country from the Tabarde Inn in Southwark as it may be supposed to have appeard in Chaucers time. interspersed with Cottages & Villages, the first beams of the Sun, are seen above the Horizon. some buildings & spires indicate the situation of the Great City. The Inn is a Gothic Building which Thynne in his Glossary says was the Lodging of the Abbot of Hyde by Winchester. On the Inn is inscribed its title & a proper advantage is taken of this circumstance to describe the Subject of the Picture. the Words written in Gothic Letters over the Gateway are as follow "The Tabarde Inne by Henry Bailly the Lodgynge House for Pilgrims who Journey to Saint Thomass Shrine at Canterbury."

[*The Characters of Chaucers Pilgrims are the Characters that compose all Ages & Nations, as one Age falls another rises. different to Mortal Sight but to Immortals only the same, for we see the same Characters repeated again & again in Animals in Vegetables in Minerals & in Men. Nothing new occurs in Identical Existence ∴ Accident ever varies Substance can never suffer change nor decay*]

<Of Chaucer's Characters as described in his Canterbury Tales, some of the Names are altered by Time, but the Characters themselves for ever remain unaltered [a]nd consequently they are the Physiognomies or L[i]neaments of Universal Human Life beyond which Nature never steps. The Painter has consequently varied the heads and forms of his Personages into all Nature's varieties; the Horses he has varied

-558-

to accord to their riders, the Costume is correct according to authentic Monuments.

Subscriptions received at No. 28, Corner of Broad Street, Golden Square.

G. Smeeton, Printer, 17, St. Martin's Lane, London.>

XI

[PUBLIC ADDRESS]

PAGE 65

Chaucers Canterbury Pilgrims
Being a Complete Index of Human Characters
as they appear Age after Age

PAGE 51

[Engravd by William Blake tho Now Surrounded by Calumny & Envy]

PAGE 56

This Day is Publishd Advertisements to Blakes Canterbury
Pilgrims from Chaucer.
Containing Anecdotes of Artists. Price 6ᵈ

PAGE I

If Men of weak Capacities have alone the Power of Execution in
Art Mʳ B has now put to the test. If to Invent & to Draw well hinders
the Executive Power in Art & his Strokes are still to be Condemnd because they are unlike those of Artists who are Unacquainted with
Drawing is now to be Decided by The Public[.] Mʳ B s Inventive
Powers & his Scientific Knowledge of Drawing is on all hands ac-
knowledgd it only remains to be Certified whether Physiognomic
Strength & Power is to give Place to Imbecillity *[and whether an artist
who has carried on an unabated study & practise of forty Years [—]
for I devoted myself to Engraving in my Earliest Youth [—] are sufficient to elevate me above the Mediocrity to which I have hitherto been
the victim]* <In a work of Art it is not fine tints that are required but
Fine Forms, fine Tints without, are loathsom> <Fine Tints without
Fine Forms are always the Subterfuge of the Blockhead>

I account it a Public Duty respectfully to address myself to The
Chalcographic Society & to Express to them my opinion the result of
the incessant Practise & Experience of Many Years That Engraving
[is in a most wretched state of injury from an] <as an Art is Lost in

England owing to an artfully propagated> opinion that Drawing spoils an Engraver [*which opinion has been held out to me by such men as Flaxman Romney Stothard*] I request the Society to inspect my Print of which Drawing is the Foundation & indeed the Superstructure it is Drawing on Copper as Painting ought to be Drawing on Canvas or any other [*table*] <surface> & nothing Else[.] I request likewise that the Society will compare the Prints of Bartollouzzi Woolett Strange &c with the old English Portraits that is <Compare the Modern Art> with the Art as it Existed Previous to the Enterance of Vandyke & Rubens into this Country <since which English Engraving is Lost> & I am sure [*the*] Result <of this comparison> will be that the Society must be of my Opinion that Engraving by Losing drawing has Lost all Character & all Expression without which <The> Art is Lost.

PAGE 51

In this Plate M^r B has resumed the style with which he set out in life of which Heath & Stothard were the awkward imitators at that time it is the style of Alb Durers Histries & the old Engravers which cannot be imitated by any one who does not understand drawing & which according to Heath & Stothard Flaxman & even Romney. Spoils an Engraver for Each of these Men have repeatedly asserted this Absurdity to me in condemnation [P 52] of my Work & approbation of Heaths lame imitation Stothard being such a fool as to suppose that his blundering blurs can be made out & delineated by any Engraver who knows how to cut dots & lozenges equally well with those little prints which I engraved after him five & twenty years ago & by which he got his reputation as a draughtsman

The manner in which my Character <has been blasted these thirty years> both as an artist & a Man may be seen particularly in a Sunday Paper cald the Examiner Publishd in Beaufort Buildings. <(We all know that Editors of Newspapers trouble their heads very little about art & science & that they are always paid for what they put in upon these ungracious Subjects> & the manner in which I have routed out the nest of villains will be seen in a Poem concerning my Three years <Herculean> Labours at Felpham which I will soon Publish. Secret Calumny & open Professions of Friendship are common enough all the world over but have never been so good an occasion of Poetic Imagery[.] When a Base Man means to be your Enemy he always begins with being your Friend [P 53] Flaxman cannot deny that one of the very first Monuments he did I gratuitously designd for him <at the same time he was blasting my character as an Artist to Macklin my Employer as Macklin told me at the time> how much of his Homer & Dante he will allow to be mine I do not know as he went far enough off to Publish them even to Italy. but the Public will know & Posterity will know

Many People are so foolish to think that they can wound Mr Fuseli over my Shoulder they will find themselves mistaken they could not wound even Mr Barry so

A certain Portrait Painter said To me in a boasting way Since I have Practised Painting I have lost all idea of Drawing. Such a Man must know that I lookd upon him with contempt he did not care for this any more than West did who hesitated & equivocated with me upon the same subject at which time he asserted that Wooletts [P 55] Prints were superior to Basires because they had more Labour & Care now this is contrary to the truth[.] Woolett did not know how to put so much labour into a head or a foot as Basire did he did not know how to draw the Leaf of a tree all his study was clean strokes & mossy tints[.] how then should he be able to make use of either Labour or Care unless the Labour & Care of Imbecillity[?] The Lifes Labour of Mental Weakness scarcely Equals one Hour of the Labour of Ordinary Capacity like the full Gallop of the Gouty Man to the ordinary walk of youth & health I allow that there is such a thing as high finishd Ignorance as there may be a fool or a knave. in an Embroiderd Coat but I say that the Embroidery of the Ignorant finisher is not like a Coat made by another but is an Emanation from Ignorance itself & its finishing is like its master The Lifes Labour of Five Hundred Idiots for he never does the Work Himself

What is Calld the English Style of Engraving such as proceeded from the Toilettes of Woolett & Strange (for theirs were <Fribbles> Toilettes) can never produce Character & Expression. I knew the Men intimately from their Intimacy with Basire my Master & knew them both to be heavy lumps of Cunning & Ignorance as their works shew to all the Continent who Laugh at the Contemptible Pretences of Englishmen to Improve Art before they even know the first [lines] <Beginnings> of Art[.] I hope this Print will redeem my Country from this Coxcomb situation & shew that it is only some Englishmen [P 56] and not All who are thus ridiculous in their Pretences Advertizements in Newspapers are no proof of Popular approbation. but often the Contrary A Man who Pretends to Improve Fine Art does not know what Fine Art is Ye English Engravers must come down from your high flights ye must condescend to study Marc Antonio & Albert Durer[.] Ye must begin before you attempt to finish or improve & when you have begun you will know better than to think of improving what cannot be improvd It is very true what you have said [P 57] for these thirty two Years I am Mad or Else you are so both of us cannot be in our right senses Posterity will judge by our Works[.] Wooletts & Stranges works are like those of Titian & Correggio the Lifes Labour of Ignorant Journeymen Suited to the Purposes of Commerce no doubt for Commerce Cannot endure Individual Merit its insatiable Maw must be fed by What all can do Equally well at least it is so in England as I have found to my Cost these Forty Years

<Commerce is so far from being beneficial to Arts or to Empire that it is destructive of both <as all their History shews> for the above Rea-

son of Individual Merit being its Great hatred. Empires flourish till they become Commercial & then they are scatterd abroad to the four winds>

Wooletts best works were Etchd by Jack Brown Woolet Etchd very bad himself. Stranges Prints were when I knew him all done by Aliamet & his french journeymen whose names I forget.

The Cottagers & Jocund Peasants the Views in Kew Gardens Foots Cray & Diana & Acteon & in short all that are Calld Wooletts were Etched by Jack Browne & in Wooletts works the Etching is All tho even in these a single leaf of a tree is never correct

PAGE 56

Such Prints as Woolett & Strange producd will do for those who choose to purchase the Lifes labour of Ignorance & Imbecillity in Preference to the Inspired Moments of Genius & Animation

PAGE 60

I also knew something of Tom Cooke who Engraved after Hogarth Cooke wished to give to Hogarth what he could take from Rafael that is Outline & Mass & Colour but he could not [& *Hogarth with all his Merit never* g]

PAGE 57

I do not pretend to Paint better than Rafael or Mch Anglo <or Julio Romano or Alb Durer> but I do Pretend to Paint finer than Rubens or Remb^t or Correggio or Titian. I do not Pretend to Engrave finer than Alb Durer Goltzius Sadeler or Edelinck but I do pretend to Engrave finer than Strange Woolett Hall or Bartolozzi <& All> because I understand Drawing which they understand not

PAGE 58

In this manner the English Public have been imposed upon for many Years under the impression that Engraving & Painting are somewhat Else besides Drawing[.] Painting is Drawing on Canvas & Engraving is drawing on Copper & Nothing Else & he who pretends to be either Painter or Engraver without being a Master of Drawing is an Impostor. We may be Clever as Pugilists but as Artists we are & have long been the Contempt of the Continent [*Aliamet*] <Gravelot> once said to My Master Basire De English may be very clever in deir own opinions but dey do not draw De draw

Resentment for Personal Injuries has had some share in this Public Address But Love to My Art & Zeal for my Country a much Greater.

PAGE 59

Men think they can Copy Nature as Correctly as I copy Imagination this they will find Impossible. & all the Copies or Pretended Copiers of Nature from Rembrat to Reynolds Prove that Nature becomes [*tame*] to its Victim nothing but Blots & Blurs. Why are Copiers of Nature Incorrect while Copiers of Imagination are Correct this is manifest to all

PAGE 39

I do not condemn Rubens Rembrant or Titian because they did not understand Drawing but because they did not Understand Colouring how long shall I be forced to beat this into Mens Ears I do not condemn [*Bartolozzi*] <Strange> or Woolett because they did not understand Drawing but because they did not understand Graving I do not condemn Pope or Dryden because they did not understand Imagination but because they did not understand Verse[.] Their Colouring Graving & Verse can never be applied to Art <That is not either colouring Graving or Verse which is Unappropriate to the Subject> He who makes a design must know the Effect & Colouring Proper to be put to that design & will never take that of Rubens Rembrandt or Titian to [*put*] <turn> that which is Soul & Life into a Mill or Machine

PAGE 46

They say there is no Strait Line in Nature this Is a Lie like all that they say, For there is Every Line in Nature But I will tell them what is Not in Nature. An Even Tint is not in Nature it produces Heaviness. Natures Shadows <are> Ever varying. & a Ruled Sky that is quite Even never can Produce a Natural Sky the same with every Object in a Picture its Spots are its beauties[.] Now Gentlemen Critics how do you like this[?] You may rage but what I say I will prove by Such Practise & have already done so that you will rage to your own destruction[.] Woolett I knew very intimately by his intimacy with Basire & I knew him to be one of the most ignorant fellows that I ever knew. A Machine is not a Man nor a Work of Art it is destructive of Humanity & of Art the Word Machination [*seems*]

Woolett I know did not know how to Grind his Graver I know this he has often proved his Ignorance before me at Basires by laughing at Basires knife tools & [P 47] ridiculing the Forms of Basires other Gravers till Basire was quite dashd & out of Conceit with what he himself knew but his Impudence had a Contrary Effect on me[.] Englishmen have been so used to Journeymens undecided bungling that they cannot bear the firmness of a Masters Touch[.] Every Line is the Line of Beauty it is only fumble & Bungle which cannot draw a Line this only is Ugliness[.] That is not a Line which Doubts & Hesitates in the Midst of its Course

PAGE 38

There is just the same Science in Lebrun or Rubens or even Vanloo that there is in Rafael or Mich Angelo but not the same Genius[.] Science is soon got the other never can be acquired but must be Born

PAGE 60

The Originality of this Production makes it necessary to say a few words

While the Works [*of Translators*] of Pope & Dryden are looked upon as the Same Art with those of Milton & Shakespeare while the works of Strange & Woollett are lookd upon as the same Art with those of Rafael & Albert Durer there can be no Art in a Nation but such as is Subservient to the interest of the Monopolizing Trader [*who Manufactures Art by the Hands of Ignorant Journeymen till at length Christian Charity is held out as a Motive to encourage a Blockhead & he is Counted the Greatest Genius who can sell a Good for Nothing Commodity for a Great Price*[.] Obedience to the Will of the Monopolist is called Virtue [P 61] *and the really <Industrious> Virtuous & Independent Barry is driven out to make room for a pack of Idle Sycophants with whitlors on their fingers*] Englishmen rouze yourselves from the fatal Slumber into which Booksellers & Trading Dealers have thrown you Under the artfully propagated pretence that a Translation or a Copy of any kind can be as honourable to a Nation as An Original Be-lying the English Character in that well known Saying Englishmen Improve what others Invent[.] This Even Hogarths Works Prove [P 62] a detestable Falshood. No Man Can Improve An Original Invention. [*Since Hogarths time we have had very few Efforts of Originality*] <Nor can an Original Invention Exist without Execution Organized & minutely delineated & Articulated Either by God or Man[.] I do not mean smoothd up & Niggled & Poco Pend <and all the beauties pickd out & blurrd & blotted> but Drawn with a firm <and decided> hand at once [*with all its Spots & Blemishes which are beauties & not faults*] like Fuseli & Michael Angelo Shakespear & Milton>   t

PAGE 44

Let a Man who has made a Drawing go on & on & he will produce a Picture or Painting but if he chooses to leave off before he has spoild it he will Do a Better Thing

PAGE 62

I have heard many People say Give me the Ideas. It is no matter what Words you put them into & others say Give me the Design it is no matter for the Execution. These People know <Enough of Artifice but> Nothing Of Art. Ideas cannot be Given but in their minutely Appropriate Words nor Can a Design be made without its minutely Appropriate Execution[.] The unorganized Blots & Blurs of Rubens & Titian are not Art nor can their Method ever express Ideas or Imaginations any more than Popes Metaphysical Jargon of Rhyming[.] Unappropriate Execution is the Most nauseous <of all> affectation & foppery He who copies does not Execute he only Imitates what is already Executed Execution is only the result of Invention

PAGE 63

Whoever looks at any of the Great & Expensive Works <of Engraving> that have been Publishd by English Traders must feel a Loathing & disgust & accordingly most Englishmen have a Contempt for Art which is the Greatest Curse that can fall upon a Nation

He who could represent Christ uniformly like a Drayman must have

Queer Conceptions consequently his Executi[o]n must have been as Queer & those must be Queer fellows who give great sums for such nonsense & think it fine Art

The <Modern Chalcographic> Connoisseurs & Amateurs admire only the work of the journeyman Picking out of whites & blacks in what is calld Tints they despise drawing which despises them in return. They see only whether every thing is coverd down but one spot of light

M^r B submits to a more severe tribunal he invites the admirers of old English Portraits to look at his Print

PAGE 64

I do not know whether Homer is a Liar & that there is no such thing as Generous Contention[.] I know that all those with whom I have Contended in Art have strove not to Excell but to Starve me out by Calumny & the Arts of Trading Combination

PAGE 66

It is Nonsense for Noblemen & Gentlemen to offer Premiums for the Encouragement of Art when such Pictures as these can be done without Premiums let them Encourage what Exists Already & not endeavour to counteract by tricks[.] let it no more be said that Empires Encourage Arts for it is Arts that Encourage Empires Arts & Artists are Spiritual & laugh at Mortal Contingencies[.] It is in their Power to hinder Instruction but not to Instruct just as it is in their Power to Murder a Man but not to Make a Man

Let us teach Buonaparte & whomsoever else it may concern That it is not Arts that follow & attend upon Empire but Empire that attends upon & follows The Arts

PAGE 67

No Man of Sense can think that an Imitation of the Objects of Nature is The Art of Painting or that such Imitation which any one may easily perform is worthy of Notice much less that such an Art should be the Glory & Pride of a Nation The Italians laugh at English Connoisseurs who are <most of them> such silly Fellows as to believe this

A Man sets himself down with Colours & with all the Articles of Painting he puts a Model before him & he copies that so neat as to make it a Deception now let any Man of Sense ask himself one Question Is this Art. can it be worthy of admiration to any body of Understanding. Who could not do this what man who has eyes and an ordinary share of patience cannot do this neatly. Is this Art Or is it glorious to a Nation to produce such contemptible Copies Countrymen Countrymen do not suffer yourselves to be disgracd

PAGE 66

The English Artist may be assured that he is doing an injury & injustice to his Country while he studies & imitates the Effects of Nature.

England will never rival Italy while we servilely copy. what the Wise Italians Rafael & Michael Angelo scorned nay abhorred as Vasari tells us

> Call that the Public Voice which is their Error
> Like as a Monkey peeping in a Mirror
> Admires all his colours brown & warm
> And never once percieves his ugly form

What kind of Intellects must he have who sees only the Colours of things & not the Forms of Things

PAGE 71

A Jockey that is any thing of a Jockey will never buy a Horse by the Colour & a Man who has got any brains will never buy a Picture by the Colour

When I tell any Truth it is not for the sake of Convincing those who do not know it but for the sake of defending those who do

PAGE 76

No Man of Sense ever supposes that Copying from Nature is the Art of Painting if the Art is no more than this it is no better than any other[']s Manual Labour any body may do it & the fool often will do it best as it is a work of no Mind

PAGE 78

The Greatest part of what are calld in England Old Pictures are Oil Colour Copies from Fresco Originals the Comparison is Easily made & the Copy Detected Note I mean Fresco Easel or Cabinet Pictures on Canvas & Wood & Copper &c

PAGE 86

The Painter hopes that his Friends Anytus Melitus <& Lycon> will percieve that they are not now in Ancient Greece & tho they can use the Poison of Calumny the English Public will be convincd that such a Picture as this Could never be Painted by a Madman or by one in a State of Outrageous manners as these [Villains] <Bad Men> both Print & Publish by all the means in their Power. the Painter begs Public Protection & all will be well

PAGE 17

I wonder who can say Speak no Ill of the Dead when it is asserted in the Bible that the name of the Wicked shall Rot[.] It is Deistical Virtue I suppose but as I have none of this I will pour Aqua fortis on the Name of the Wicked & turn it into an Ornament & an Example to be Avoided by Some and Imitated by Others if they Please

Columbus discoverd America but Americus Vesputius finishd & smoothd it over like an English Engraver or Corregio or Titian

PAGE 18

What Man of Sense will lay out his Money upon the Lifes Labours of Imbecillity & Imbecillitys Journeymen or think to Educate a Fool how to build a Universe with Farthing Balls The Contemptible Idiots who have been calld Great Men of late Years ought to rouze the Public Indignation of Men of Sense in all Professions

There is not because there cannot be any difference of Effect in the Pictures of Rubens & Rembrandt when you have seen one of their Pictures you have seen All It is not so with Rafael Julio Romano Alb D Mich Ang Every Picture of theirs has a different & appropriate Effect

Yet I do not shrink from the Comparison in Either Relief or Strength of Colour with either Rembrandt or Rubens on the Contrary I court the Comparison & fear not the Result but not in a dark Corner[.] their Effects are in Every Picture the same Mine are in Every Picture different

I hope my Countrymen will Excuse me if I tell them a Wholesome truth Most Englishmen when they look at a Picture immediately set about searching for Points of Light <& clap the Picture into a dark corner [this in] <This when done by> Grand Works is like looking for Epigrams in Homer> A point of light is a Witticism many are destructive of all Art <One is an Epigram only> & no Grand Work can have them they Produce System & Monotony

Rafael Mich Ang Alb D Jul Rom are accounted ignorant of that Epigrammatic Wit in Art because they avoid it as a destructive Machine as it is

That Vulgar Epigram in Art Rembrandts Hundred Guelders has intirely put an End to all Genuine & Appropriate Effect all both Morning & Night is now a dark cavern [P 19] When you view a Collection of Pictures painted since Venetian Art was the Fashion or Go into a Modern Exhibition with a Very few Exceptions Every Picture has the same Effect. a Piece of Machinery or Points of Light to be put into a dark hole

PAGE 18

Mr B repeats that there is not one Character or Expression in this Print which could be Produced with the Execution of Titian Rubens Coreggio Rembrandt or any of that Class[.] Character & Expression can only be Expressed by those who Feel Them Even Hogarths Execution cannot be Copied or Improved. Gentlemen of Fortune who give Great Prices for Pictures should consider the following [P 19] Rubens s Luxembourg Gallery is Confessd on all hands to be the work of a Blockhead <it bears this Evidence in its face> how can its Execution be any other than the Work of a Blockhead. <Bloated Gods> Mercury Juno Venus & the rattle traps of Mythology & the lumber of an awkward French Palace are thrown together around <Clumsy & Ricketty> Princes & Princesses higgledy piggledy On the Contrary Julio Rom[ano's] <Palace of T at Mantua> is allowed on all hands to be <the Production of> a Man of the Most Profound sense & Genius & Yet his Execution is Pronouncd by English Connoisseurs & Reynolds their doll to be unfit for the Study of the Painter. Can I speak with too great Contempt of such Contemptible fellows. If all the Princes in Europe <like Louis XIV & Charles the first> were to Patronize such Blockheads I William Blake a Mental Prince should decollate & Hang their Souls as Guilty of Mental High Treason

Who that has Eyes cannot see that Rubens & Correggio must have been very weak & Vulgar fellows & we are to imitate their Execution. This is like what Sr Francis Bacon says that a healthy Child should be taught & compelld to walk like a Cripple while the Cripple must be taught to walk like healthy people O rare wisdom

PAGE 18

I am really sorry to see my Countrymen trouble themselves about Politics. If Men were Wise <the Most arbitrary> Princes could not hurt them If they are not Wise the Freest Government is compelld to be a Tyranny[.] Princes appear to me to be Fools Houses of Commons & Houses of Lords appear to me to be fools they seem to me to be something Else besides Human Life

PAGE 20

The wretched State of the Arts in this Country & in Europe originating in the wretched State of Political Science which is the Science of Sciences Demands a firm & determinate conduct on the part of Artists to Resist the Contemptible Counter Arts established by such contemptible Politicians as Louis XIV & originally set on foot by Venetian Picture traders Music traders & Rhime traders to the destruction of all true art as it is this Day. To recover Art has been the business of my life to the Florentine Original & if possible to go beyond that Original <this> I thought the only pursuit worthy of [an Englishman] <a Man>. To Imitate I abhore I obstinately adhere to the true Style of Art such as Michael Angelo Rafael Jul Rom Alb Durer left it [the Art of Invention not of Imitation. Imagination is My World this world of Dross is beneath my Notice & Beneath the Notice of the Public] I demand therefore of the Amateurs of [p 21] art the Encouragem^{ent} which is my due if they <continue to> refuse theirs is the loss not mine <& theirs is the Contempt of Posterity> I have Enough in the Approbation of fellow labourers this is my glory & exceeding great reward I go on & nothing can hinder my course

And in Melodious Accents I
Will sit me down & Cry. I. I.

PAGE 20

An Example of these Contrary Arts is given us in the Characters of Milton & Dryden as they are written in a Poem signed with the name of Nat Lee which perhaps he never wrote & perhaps he wrote in a

paroxysm of insanity In which it is said that Miltons Poem is a rough
Unfinishd Piece & Dryden has finishd it Now let Drydens Fall & Miltons Paradise be read & I will assert that every Body of Understanding
must cry out Shame on such Niggling & Poco Pen as Dryden has degraded Milton with But at the same time I will allow that Stupidity will
Prefer Dryden because it is in Rhyme <& Monotonous Sing Song Sing
Song> from beginning to end Such are Bartollozzi Woolett & Strange

PAGE 23

[*That Painted as well as Sculptured Monuments were common
among the Ancients is evident from the words of the Sævants who compared Those Sepulchures Painted on the outside with others only of
Stone. Their Beauty is Confessd even by the Lips of Pasch himself.*]
The Painters of England are unemployd in Public Works. while the
Sculptors have continual & superabundant employment Our Churches
& Abbeys are treasures of [*Spiritual riches*] their producing for ages
back While Painting is excluded Painting the Principal Art has no place
among our almost only public works. Yet it is more adapted to solemn
ornament that [*dead*] Marble can be as it is capable of being Placed in
any heighth & indeed would make a Noble finish <Placed> above the
Great Public Monuments in Westminster St Pauls & other Cathedrals.
To the Society for Encouragement of Arts I address myself with Re-
spectful duty requesting their Consideration of my Plan as a Great
Public [*deed*] means of advancing Fine Art in Protestant Communities
Monuments to the dead Painted by Historical & Poetical Artists like
Barry & Mortimer. I forbear to name living Artists tho equally worthy
I say Monuments so Painted must make England What Italy is an En-
vied Storehouse of Intellectual Riches

PAGE 24

It has been said of late years The English Public have no Taste for
Painting This is a Falshood The English are as Good Judges of Painting as of Poetry & they prove it in their Contempt for Great Collections
of all the Rubbish of the Continent brought here by Ignorant Picture
dealers An Englishman may well say I am no Judge of Painting when
he is shewn these Smears & Dawbs at an immense price & told that such
is the Art of Painting I say the English Public are true Encouragers of
real Art while they discourage & look with Contempt on False Art

PAGE 25

In a Commercial Nation Impostors are abroad in all Professions these
are the greatest Enemies of Genius [*Mr B thinks it his duty to Caution
the Public against a Certain Impostor who*]. In the Art of Painting
these Impostors sedulously propagate an Opinion that Great Inventors
Cannot Execute This Opinion is as destructive of the true Artists as it
is false by all Experience Even Hogarth cannot be either Copied or Improved <Can Anglus never Discern Perfection but in the Journeymans
Labour>

PAGE 24

I know my Execution is not like Any Body Else I do not intend it should be so <none but Blockheads copy one another> My Conception & Invention are on all hands allowd to be Superior My Execution will be found so too. To what is it that Gentlemen of the first Rank both in Genius & Fortune have subscribed their Names[—] To My Inventions. the Executive part they never disputed [P 25] the Lavish praise I have recieved from all Quarters for Invention & Drawing has Generally been accompanied by this he can concieve but he cannot Execute this Absurd assertion has done me & may still do me the greatest mischief I call for Public protection against these Villains I am like others Just Equal in Invention & in Execution as my works shew I in my own defence Challenge a Competition with the finest Engravings & defy the most critical judge to <make> the Comparison Honestly [P 24] asserting in my own Defence that This Print is the Finest that has been done or is likely to be done in England where drawing <its foundation> is Contemnd and absurd Nonsense about dots & Lozenges & Clean Strokes made to occupy the attention to the Neglect of all real Art I defy any Man to Cut Cleaner Strokes than I do or rougher when I please & assert that he who thinks he can Engrave or Paint either without being a Master of drawing is a Fool. Painting is Drawing on Canvas & Engraving is Drawing on Copper & nothing Else <Drawing is Execution & nothing Else> & he who Draws best must be the best Artist [&] to this I subscribe <my name as a Public Duty>

WILLIAM BLAKE

PAGE 25

P.S. I do not believe that this Absurd opinion ever was set on foot till in my Outset into life it was artfully publishd both in whispers & in print by Certain persons whose robberies from me made it necessary to them that I should be hid in a corner it never was supposed that a Copy could be better than an original or near so Good till a few Years ago it became the interest of certain envious Knaves

XII

[THE MARGINALIA]

Excerpts from the works marked and annotated by Blake are followed by Blake's remarks in larger type. Unbracketed *italics*, in the excerpts or in Blake's own notes, indicate underlining by Blake. Words printed in SOLID CAPITALS were in italics in the original texts; *ITALIC CAPITALS* are used to indicate original italics plus Blake's underlining.

Fuller titles of the volumes annotated are given in the textual notes.

Annotations to Lavater's *Aphorisms on Man*   t

London [1789]

TITLE PAGE

Willm Blake

[signed and underlined, beneath the printed "Lavater", the two names then being enclosed in an outline of a heart]

PAGE I

for the reason of these remarks see the last aphorism

[Blake is referring to 643: "If you mean to know yourself, interline such of these aphorisms as affected you agreeably in reading, and set a mark to such as left a sense of uneasiness with you; and then shew your copy to whom you please."

Blake's mark of uneasiness, a large rough X in the margin, is shown here by an X beside the number of the aphorism. His underlining of agreeable passages is represented by *italics*, and he occasionally supplements the underlining with a square dagger † of emphatic approval, as shown.]

1. Know, in the first place, that mankind agree in essence, as they do in their limbs and senses.
2. Mankind differ as much in essence as they do in form, limbs, and senses—and only so, and not more.

This is true Christian philosophy far above all abstraction

[written beside both aphorisms, with lines pointing to both]

-572-

3. As in *looking upward* each beholder *thinks himself the* centre *of the sky; so Nature formed her individuals, that each must see* himself *the centre of being.*

Let me refer here, to a remark on aphorism 533 & another on. 630

8. Who pursues means of enjoyment contradictory, irreconcilable, and self-destructive, is a fool, or what is called a sinner—*Sin and destruction of order are the same.*

a golden sentence

11. *The less* you *can enjoy, the poorer, the scantier* yourself—the more you *can enjoy,* the richer, the more *vigorous.*

You enjoy with wisdom or with folly, as the gratification of your appetites capacitates or unnerves your powers.

false for weak is the joy that is never wearied

(Written beside the second paragraph)

13. Joy and grief decide character. What exalts prosperity? what imbitters grief? what leaves us indifferent? what interests us? As the interest of *man, so his God—as his God, so he.*

All Gold

14. *What is a man's interest? what constitutes his God, the ultimate* of his wishes, his end of existence? Either that which on every occasion he communicates with the most unrestrained cordiality, or hides from every profane eye and ear with mysterious awe; to which he makes every other thing a mere appendix;—the vortex, the centre, the comparative point from which he sets out, on which he fixes, to which he irresistably returns;—that, at the loss of which you may safely think him inconsolable;—that which he rescues from the gripe of danger with equal anxiety and boldness.

The story of the painter and the prince is well known: to get at the best piece in the artist's collection, . . .

Pure gold

(After the underlined words, the rest of the passage is bracketed to this comment. The story continues, unmarked, and concludes:) . . . of thousands it may be decided what loss, what gain, would affect them most. And suppose we cannot pronounce on others, cannot we determine on ourselves? This the sage of Nazareth meant when he said, WHERE THY TREASURE IS, THERE WILL THY HEART BE ALSO—*The object of your love is your God.*

This should be written in gold letters on our temples

16. The greatest of characters, no doubt, was he, who, free of all trifling accidental helps, could see objects through one grand immutable medium, always at hand, and proof against illusion and time, reflected by every object, and invariably traced through all the fluctuation of things.

this was Christ

20. Distinguish with exactness, in thyself and others, between WISHES and WILL, in the strictest sense.

Who has many wishes has generally but little will. Who has energy of will has few diverging wishes. Whose will is bent with energy on ONE, MUST renounce the wishes for MANY things. Who cannot do this is not stamped with the majesty of human nature. *The energy of choice, the unison of various powers for one is only WILL, born under the agonies of self-denial and renounced desires.*

Regeneration

✗ 21. Calmness of will is a sign of grandeur. The vulgar, far from hiding their WILL, blab their wishes—a single spark of occasion discharges the child of passions into a thousand crackers of desire.

uneasy

See 384

23. Who in the same given time can produce more than many others, has VIGOUR; who can produce more and better, has TALENTS; *who can produce what none else can, has GENIUS.*

25. WISHES run over into loquacious impotence, WILL presses on with laconic energy. (Horizontal line in left margin)

28. *The glad gladdens—who gladdens not is not glad. Who is fatal* to others *is so to himself—to him,* heaven, earth, wisdom, folly, *virtue, vice, are equally* so—to such an one tell neither good nor bad of yourself.

✕ 32. Let the degree of egotism be the measure of confidence.
uneasy

✕ 36. Who begins with severity, in judging of another, ends commonly with falsehood.
false
Severity of judgment is a great virtue

✕ 37. The smiles that encourage severity of judgment, hide malice and insincerity.
false
Aphorisms should be universally true

✕ 39. Who, without pressing temptation, tells a lie, will, without pressing temptation, act ignobly and meanly.
uneasy
false
a man may lie for his own pleasure. but if any one is hurt by his lying will confess his lie see N 124

40. *Who, under pressing temptations to lie, adheres to truth, nor to the profane betrays aught of a sacred trust, is near the summit of wisdom and virtue.*
Excellent

43. *As the present character* of a man, *so his past, so his future. Who knows intuitively the history of the past, knows his destiny to come.*

44. You can depend on no man, on no friend, but him who can depend on himself. *He only* who acts consequentially *toward himself* will act so toward others, and VICE VERSA.
Man is for ever the same; the same under every form, in all situations and relations that admit of free and unrestrained exertion. The same regard which you have for *yourself, you* have for others, for *nature, for the* invisible NUMEN, *which you call God*—Who has *witnessed one free* and unconstrained act of yours, has witnessed all.

✕ 54. Frequent laughing has been long called a sign of a little mind—whist the scarcer smile of harmless quiet has been complimented as the mark of a noble heart—But to abstain from laughing, and exciting laughter, merely not to offend, or to risk giving offence, or not to debase the inward dignity of character—is a power unknown to many a vigorous mind.
I hate scarce smiles   I love laughing

59. *A sneer is often the sign* of *heartless malignity.*
damn sneerers

60. Who *courts the* intimacy of a *professed sneerer,* is a professed *knave.*

61. I know not which of these two I should wish to avoid most; the scoffer at virtue and religion, who, with heartless villany, butchers innocence and truth; *or the pietist, who crawls, groans, blubbers,* and *secretly says to gold, thou* art my hope! and to his belly, thou art my god!
I hate crawlers

62. All *moral dependence* on him, who *has been guilty of* ONE act of *positive cool villainy*, against an acknowledged, virtuous and noble character, is credulity, imbecility, or insanity.

is being like him rather

63. The most stormy ebullitions of passion, *from blasphemy* to murder, are *less terrific than* one single act of cool *villany: a still* RABIES *is more dangerous than the paroxisms of a fever—Fear* the boisterous *savage of passion less than the sedate grin of villany.*

bravo

66. *Can he love truth who* can take *a knave to his bosom?*

—No

67. There *are offences against individuals, to all appearance* trifling, which *are capital offences against* the *human race—fly him who can commit them.*

68. There ought to be a perpetual whisper in the ear of plain honesty—take heed not even to pronounce the name of a knave—he will make the very sound of his name a handle of mischief. And do you think a knave begins mischief to leave off? Know this—whether he overcome or be foiled, he will wrangle on.

therefore pronounce him a knave, why should honesty fear a knave

69. Humility and love, whatever obscurities may involve religious tenets, constitute the essence of true religion. *The humble is formed to adore; the loving to associate with eternal love.*

Sweet.

✗ 70. Have you ever seen a vulgar mind warm or humble? or a proud one that could love?—where pride begins, love ceases—as love, so humility—as both, so the still real power of man.

<pride may love>

(over a deletion)

✗ 71. Every thing may be mimicked by hypocrisy, but humility and love united. The humblest star twinkles most in the darkest night—the more rare humility and love united, the more radiant where they meet.

all this may be mimicked very well. this Aphorism certainly was an oversight for what are all crawlers but mimickers of humility & love

✗ 73. Modesty is silent when it would not be improper to speak: the humble, without being called upon, never recollects to say any thing of himself.

uneasy

78. *The wrath that on conviction subsides into mildness, is* the wrath *of a generous mind.*

80. Thousands are hated, *whilst none* are ever *loved, without a real cause. The amiable alone can be loved.*

81. He who is loved and commands love, *when he corrects or is the cause of uneasiness, must be loveliness itself; and*

82. He *who can love him, in the moment of correction, is* the most *amiable of mortals.*

83. He, *to whom you* may tell any thing, may *see every* thing, and will *betray nothing.*

✗ 86. The *freer you feel yourself* in the presence *of another,* the more free *is he: who is free* makes free.

rather uneasy

✕ 92. Who instantly does the best that can be done, what no other could have done, and what all must acknowledge to be the best, is a genius and a hero at once.
uneasy

93. The discovery of truth, by slow progressive meditation, is wisdom—*Intuition of truth, not* preceded by *perceptible meditation, is genius.*

94. The degree of genius is determined by its velocity, clearness, depth, simplicity, copiousness, extent of glance (COUP D'OEIL), and instantaneous intuition of the whole at once.
copiousness of glance

✕ 96. Dread more the blunderer's friendship than the calumniator's enmity.
I doubt this

✕ 97. He only, who can give durability to his exertions, has genuine power *and energy of mind.*
uneasy
Sterling

✕ 98. Before thou callest a man hero or genius, investigate whether his exertion has features of indelibility; for all that is celestial, all genius, *is the offspring of immortality.*
uneasy Sterling

99. Who *despises all that is despicable, is made to be impressed with all that is grand.*

107. Who takes from you, ought to give in his turn, or he is a thief; I distinguish taking and accepting, robbing and receiving: many give already by the mere wish to give; their still unequivocal wish of improvement and gratitude, whilst it draws *from us, opens treasures within us, that might have remained locked up, even* to ourselves.
Noble & Generous

114. Who *writes as he speaks*, speaks as he *writes, looks as he* speaks *and writes—is* honest.

115. A habit of sneering marks the egotist, or the fool, or the knave—or all three.
—all three

✕ 121. Who knows not how to wait with YES, will often be with shame reduced to say NO. Letting "I DARE NOT wait upon I WOULD."
uneasy

124. Who *has a daring eye, tells downright truths and downright lies.*
contrary to N 39 but *most True*

✕ 141. Many trifling inattentions, neglects, indiscretions—are so many unequivocal proofs of dull frigidity, hardness, or extreme egotism.
rather uneasy

✕ 150. As your enemies and your friends, so are you.
very uneasy

✕ 151. You may depend upon it that he is a good man whose intimate friends are all good, and whose enemies are characters decidedly bad.
uneasy
I fear I have not many enemies

157. Say not you *know another entirely, till you have divided* an *inheritance with him*
!!

✕ 163. Who, at the pressing solicitation of bold and noble confidence, hesitates one moment before he consents, proves himself at once inexorable.

uneasy

I do not believe it

✕ 164. Who, at the solicitations of cunning, self-interest, silliness, or impudence, hesitates one moment before he refuses, proves himself at once a silly giver.

uneasy

165. Examine carefully whether a man is fonder of exceptions than of rules; as he makes use of exceptions he is sagacious; as he applies them against the rule he is wrong-headed. I heard in one day a man, who thought himself wise, . . . sophist's character. . . .
(Vertical line in margin of passage from "rules" to "wise")

✕ 168. Whenever a man undergoes a considerable change, in consequence of being observed by others, whenever he assumes another gait, another language, than what he had before he thought himself observed, be advised to guard yourself against him.

rather uneasy

170. I am *prejudiced in favour of him who can solicit boldly, without impudence—he has faith in humanity—he* has faith in himself. No one, who is not accustomed to give grandly, can ask nobly and with boldness.

176. As a *man's salutation,* so the *total of his character: in* nothing *do we lay ourselves so* open as in *our manner of meeting* and *salutation.*

177. Be *afraid of him who meets* you with *friendly aspect,* and, in the *midst of a flattering* salutation, *avoids your direct open look.*

185. All finery is a sign of littleness.

not always

200. The more *honesty a man has, the less he affects the* air of a *saint—the affectation of sanctity is a blotch* on the face *of piety.*

bravo

201. There are more heroes than saints; (heroes I call rulers over the minds and destinies of men); more saints than humane characters. Him, who humanises all that is within and around himself, adore: I know but of one such by tradition.

Sweet

203. *Who seeks those that* are greater *than himself, their greatness* enjoys, *and forgets his greatest* qualities in *their greater ones, is* already *truly great.*

I hope I do not flatter my self that this is pleasant to me

219. †None love without being loved; *and none* beloved *is without loveliness.*

225. The friend of *order has made half his way to virtue.*

✕ 226. There is no mortal truly wise and restless at once—wisdom is the repose of minds.

rather uneasy

242. The connoisseur in painting discovers an original by some great line, though covered with dust, and disguised by daubing; so he who studies man discovers a valuable character by some original trait, though unnoticed, disguised, or debased—ravished at the discovery, he feels it his duty to restore it to its own genuine splendour. *Him who, in spite of contemptuous pretenders, has the boldness to do this, choose for your friend.*

244. Who writes what he should tell, and dares not tell what he writes, is either like a wolf in sheep's clothing, or like a sheep in a wolf's skin.

Some cannot tell what they can write tho they dare

248. Know that the great art to love your enemy consists in never losing sight of MAN in him: humanity has power over all that is human; the most inhuman man still remains man, and never CAN throw off all taste for what becomes a man—but you must learn to wait.

none can see the man in the enemy   if he is ignorantly so, he is not truly an enemy   if maliciously not a man

I cannot love my enemy for my enemy is not man but beast & devil if I have any. I can love him as a beast & wish to beat him

253. Who *welcomes the look of the good is good himself.*

254. I know deists, whose religiousness I venerate, and atheists, whose honesty and nobleness of mind I wish for; but I have not yet seen the man who could have tempted *me to think him honest who*[m] *I knew publicly acted the Christian whilst privately he was a positive deist.*

bravo

(Whom *corrected to* who, in accord with Errata list)

256. He who *laughed at you* till he got *to your door, flattered you as you opened it—felt the force* of your *argument* whilst he was with you—*applauded when he rose,* and, *after he went* away, blasts you—has the most indisputable *title to an* archdukedom in hell.

Such a one I can never forgive while he continues such a one

X 261. Ask not only, am I hated? but, by whom?—*am I loved?* but why?—*as the* GOOD *love* thee, *the* BAD *will hate thee.*

uneasy

272. Who can *act or perform* as if each work *or action were the first, the last, and only one in his life, is great [in his sphere.]*

(The last three words deleted by Blake)

X 276. We can do all by speech and silence. He, who understands the double art of speaking opportunely to the moment, and of saying not a syllable more or less than it demanded—and he who can wrap himself up in silence when every word would be in vain—will understand to connect energy with patience.

uneasy

278. Let the unhappiness you feel at *another's errors, and the* happiness you *enjoy in their perfections,* be *the measure of your* progress in *wisdom and virtue.*

Excellent

279. Who becomes every day more sagacious, in observing his own faults, and the perfections of another, without either envying him or despairing of himself, is ready to mount the ladder on which angels ascend and descend.

Noble

282. The *more there is of* mind in your *solitary employments,* the more *dignity there is* in your *character.*

285. He, *who can at all times* sacrifice *pleasure to duty,* approaches *sublimity.*

(Vertical line in margin; also underlined)

287. The most eloquent speaker, the most ingenious writer, and the most accomplished statesman, cannot effect so much as the mere presence of the man [*who tempers his wisdom and his vigour with humanity.*]

unsophisticated

289. Between the best and the worst, there are, you say, innumerable degrees—and you are right; but admit that I am right too, in saying that the best and the worst differ only in one thing—†*in the object of their love.*

†would to God that every one would consider this

290. What is it you love in him you love? what is it you hate in him you hate? Answer this closely to yourself, pronounce it loudly, and you will know yourself and him.

All Gold

292. If you see one cold and vehement at the same time, set him down for a fanatic.

i.e hypocrite

295. Who *can hide magnanimity,* stands *on the supreme* degree of *human nature, and is admired* by *the world of spirits.*

301. He has not a little of the devil in him who prays and bites.

there is no other devil, he who bites without praying is only a beast

302. He who, when called upon to speak a *disagreeable truth,* tells it boldly *and has done, is both bolder* and *milder than he who* nibbles in *a low voice,* and never ceases *nibbling.*

damn such

305. Be *not the fourth friend* of him who *had three before and* lost *them.*

an excellent rule

✕ 308. Want of friends argues either want of humility or courage, or both.

uneasy

309. He who, at a table of forty covers, thirty-nine of which are exquisite, and one indifferent, lays hold of that, and with a "damn your dinner" dashes it in the landlord's face, should be sent to Bethlem or to Bridewell—and whither he, who blasphemes a book, a work of art, or perhaps a man of nine-and-thirty good and but one bad quality, and calls those fools or flatterers who, engrossed by the superior number of good qualities, would fain forget the bad one<?>

(Question mark added by Blake)

to hell till he behaves better.   mark that I do not believe there is such a thing litterally.   but hell is the being shut up in the possession of corporeal desires which shortly weary the man. for *all life is holy*

328. Keep *him at least three paces distant who hates bread, music, and the laugh of a child.*

the best in the book

333. Between passion and lie there is not a finger's breadth.

Lie, is the contrary to Passion

334. Avoid, *like a serpent, him who writes impertinently, yet speaks politely.*

a dog   get a stick to him

✕ 338. Search carefully if one patiently finishes what he boldly began.

uneasy

339. Who comes from the kitchen smells of its smoke; *who adheres to a sect has something of its cant:* the college-air pursues the student, and dry inhumanity him who herds with literary pedants.

341. Call *him truly religious who* believes in *something higher,* more *powerful, more living, than* visible nature; *and who, clear* as his own *existence, feels his* conformity to *that superior being.*

342. [*Superstition*] <Hipocrisy> always inspires littleness, religion grandeur of mind: the [*superstitious*] <hypocrite> raises beings inferiour to himself to deities.

no man was ever truly superstitious who was not truly religious as far as he knew

True superstition is ignorant honesty & this is beloved of god & man

I do not allow that there is such a thing as Superstition taken in the strict sense of the word

A man must first decieve himself before he is <thus> Superstitious & so he is a hypocrite

Hipocrisy. is as distant from superstition. as the wolf from the lamb.

343. Who are the saints of humanity? those whom perpetual habits of goodness and of grandeur have made nearly unconscious that what they do is good or grand—†heroes *with infantine simplicity.*

†this is heavenly

345. The jealous is possessed by a "fine mad devil*" and a dull spirit at once.

*Shakspeare.

pity the jealous

352. He alone has *energy that cannot be deprived of it.*

353. Sneers are the blasts that precede quarrels.

hate the sneerer

354. Who loves will not be adored.

false

359. *No great character cavils.*

365. He can *love who can forget* all *and nothing.*

366. The *purest religion is the most refined Epicurism.* He, who in *the smallest given time can enjoy most of what he never shall repent,* and *what furnishes* enjoyments, still more unexhausted, still less changeable—is the most religious and the most voluptuous of men.

True Christian philosophy

370. The generous, who is always just—and the just, who is always generous—*may, unannounced, approach the throne of God.*

375. Let me once more, in other words, repeat it—he is the king of kings who longs for nothing, *and wills but ONE at once.*

376. Spare the lover without flattering his passion; to make the pangs of love the butt of ridicule, is unwise and harsh—soothing meekness and wisdom subdue in else unconquerable things.

and consider that *love is life*

377. There is none so bad to do the twentieth part of the evil he might, nor any so good as to do the tenth part of the good it is in his power to do. Judge of yourself by the good you might do and neglect—and of others by the evil they might do and omit—and your judgment will be poised between too much indulgence for yourself and too much severity on others.

Most Excellent

380. To him who is simple, and inexhaustible, *like nature, simple and inexhausted nature resigns her sway.*

383. How can he be pious who loves not the beautiful, whilst piety is nothing but the love of beauty? Beauty we call the MOST VARIED ONE, the MOST UNITED VARIETY. Could there be a man who should harmoniously unite each variety of knowledge and of powers —were he not the most beautiful? were he not your *god?*

this is our Lord

384. Incredible are his powers who DESIRES nothing that he CANNOT WILL.

See 20 & 21

✕ 385. The unloved cannot love.

doubtful

✕ 386. Let the object of love be careful to lose none of its loveliness.

✕ 389. We cannot be great, if we calculate how great we and how little others are, and calculate not how great others, how minute, how impotent ourselves.

uneasy

391. He loves unalterably who keeps within the bounds of love; who always shews somewhat less than what he is *possessed of*—nor ever utters a *syllable,* or gives a hint, of *more than* what in fact remains *behind*—is just and friendly in the same degree.

396. Who *kindles love loves* warmly.

400. There is a manner of forgiving so divine, that you are ready to embrace the offender for having called it forth.

this I cannot concieve

401. Expect the secret resentment of him whom your forgiveness has impressed with a sense of his inferiority; expect the resentment of the woman whose proffered love you have repulsed; yet surer still expect the unceasing rancour of envy against the progress of genius and merit—renounce the hopes of reconciling him: but know, what whilst you steer on, mindless of his grin, allruling destiny will either change his rage to awe, or blast his powers to their deepest root.

If you expect his resentment you do not forgive him *now.* tho you did once forgiveness of enemies can only come upon their repentance

407. Whatever is visible is the vessel or veil of the invisible past, present, future—as man penetrates to this more, or perceives it less, he raises or depresses his dignity of being.

A vision of the Eternal Now—

408. Let none turn over books, or roam the stars *in quest of God, who sees him not in man.*

409. He alone is good, who, though possessed of energy, prefers virtue, *with the appearance of* weakness, *to the invitation of* acting *brilliantly ill.*

Noble   But Mark   Active Evil is better than Passive Good

✕ 410. Clearness, rapidity, comprehension of look, glance (what the French call 'COUP D'OEIL'), is the greatest, simplest, most inexhausted gift a mortal can receive from heaven: who has that has all; and who has it not has little of what constitutes the good and great.

uneasy
doubtful

413. As the presentiment of the possible, deemed impossible, so genius, so heroism—
every genius, every hero, is a prophet.

✕ 414. He who goes one step beyond his real faith, or presentiment, is in danger of
deceiving himself and others.
uneasy

416. He, who to obtain much will suffer little or nothing, can never be called great; and
none ever little, who, to obtain one great object, will suffer much.
the man who does this is a Sectary therefore not great

419. You *beg as you question; you give as you answer.*
Excellent

424. Love sees what no eye sees; love *hears what no ear hears;* and *what never rose in
the heart of man love prepares for its* object.
Most Excellent

426. Him, who arrays malignity in good nature and treachery in familiarity, a miracle
of Omnipotence alone can make an honest man.
no Omnipotence can act against order

427. He, who sets fire to one part of a town to rob more safely in another, is, no doubt,
a villain: what will you call him, who, to avert suspicion from himself, accuses the
innocent of a crime he knows himself guilty of, and means to commit again?
damn him

432. The richer you are, the more calmly you bear the reproach of poverty: *the more
genius you have, the more easily you bear the imputation of mediocrity.*

435. There is no instance of a miser becoming a prodigal without losing his intellect;
but there are thousands of prodigals becoming misers; if, therefore, *your turn be pro-
fuse, nothing is so much to be avoided as avarice:* and, if you be a miser, procure a
physician who can cure an irremediable disorder.
Excellent

437. Avarice has sometimes been the flaw of great men, but never of great minds; great
men produce effects that cannot be produced by a thousand of the vulgar; but great
minds are stamped *with expanded benevolence,* unattainable by most.

✕ 440. He is much greater and more authentic, who produces one thing entire and
perfect, than he who does many by halves.
uneasy

✕ 444. Say what you please of your humanity, no wise man will ever believe a syllable while I and MINE are the two only gates at which you sally forth and enter, and
through which alone all must pass who seek admittance.
uneasy

447. Who hides love, to bless with unmixed happiness, is great, like the king of heaven.
I do not understand this or else I do not agree to it I know not what hiding
love means

✕ 449. Trust not him with your secrets, who, when left alone in your room, turns over
your papers.
uneasy yet I hope I should not do it

450. A woman whose ruling passion *is not vanity, is superior to any man of equal
faculties.*
Such a woman I adore

451. He who has but one way of seeing every thing, is as important for him who studies man as fatal to friendship.

this I do not understand

452. Who has written will write again, says the Frenchman; [*he who has written against you will write against you again*]: he who has begun certain things is under the [*curse*] <blessing> of leaving off no more.

(Text altered by Blake)

X 460. Nothing is more impartial than the stream-like public; always the same and never the same; of whom, sooner or later, each misrepresented character obtains justice, and each calumniated, honour: he who cannot wait for that, is either ignorant of human nature, or feels that he was not made for honour.

uneasy

462. The *obstinacy of the indolent* and *weak is less conquerable* than *that of the fiery and bold.*

463. Who, with calm wisdom alone, imperceptibly directs the obstinacy of others, will be the most eligible friend or the most dreadful enemy.

this must be a grand fellow

X 465. He is condemned to depend on no man's modesty and honour who dares not depend on his own.

uneasy

477. The frigid smiler, crawling, indiscreet, obtrusive, brazen-faced, is a scorpion-whip of destiny—avoid him!

& never forgive him till he mends

X 486. Distrust your heart and the durability of your fame, if from the stream of occasion you snatch a handful of foam; deny the stream, and give its name to the frothy bursting bubble.

uneasy
this I lament that I have done

487. If you ask me which is the real hereditary sin of human nature, do you imagine I shall answer pride? or luxury? or ambition? or egotism? no; I shall say indolence—who conquers indolence will conquer all the rest.

Pride fullness of bread & *abundance of Idleness* was the sin of Sodom. See Ezekiel Ch xvi. 49 ver

489. An entirely honest man, in the severe sense of the word, exists no more than an entirely dishonest knave: the best and the worst are only approximations of those qualities. Who are those that never contradict themselves? yet honesty never contradicts itself: who are those that always contradict themselves? yet knavery is mere self-contradiction. Thus the knowledge of man determines not the things themselves, but their proportions, the quantum of congruities and incongruities.

Man is a twofold being. one part capable of evil & the other capable of good that which is capable of good is not also capable of evil. but that which is capable of evil is also capable of good. this aphorism seems to consider man as simple & yet capable of evil. now both evil & good cannot exist in a simple being. for thus 2 contraries would. spring from one essence which is impossible. but if man is considerd as only evil. & god only good. how then is regeneration effected which turns the evil to good. by casting out the evil. by the good. See Matthew XII. Ch. 26. 27. 28. 29 &ᶜ

496. Sense seeks and finds the thought; the thought seeks and finds genius.

& vice. versa. genius finds thought without seek^g & thought thus producd finds sense

506. The poet, who composes not before the *moment of inspiration,* and as that *leaves him ceases—composes, and he alone, for all men, all classes, all ages.*

Most Excellent

507. He, *who has frequent* moments of *complete existence, is* a hero, though *not laurelled, is* crowned, and *without crowns, a king:* he *only who has enjoyed immortal moments can reproduce them.*

O that men would seek immortal moments   O that men would converse with God

508. *The greater that which you can HIDE, THE GREATER YOURSELF.* (The last words triply underlined by Blake)

Pleasant

X 514. He, who cannot forgive <a> trespass of malice to his enemy, has never yet tasted the most sublime enjoyment of love.

uneasy   this I know not

X 518. You may have hot enemies without having a warm friend; but not a fervid friend without a bitter enemy. The qualities of your friends will be those of your enemies: cold friends, cold enemies—half friends, half enemies—fervid enemies, warm friends.

very Uneasy indeed but *truth*

521. He, *who reforms himself,* has *done more toward reforming* the *public than a crowd* of noisy, *impotent patriots.*

Excellent

523. He will do great things who can avert his words and thoughts from past irremediable evils.

.not if evils are past sins. for these a man should never avert his thoughts from

X 526. He, who is ever intent on great ends, has an eagle-eye for great means, and scorns not the smallest.

Great ends never look at means but produce them spontaneously

532. Take from LUTHER his roughness and fiery courage; from CALVIN his hectic obstinacy; from ERASMUS his timid prudence; hypocrisy and fanaticism from CROMWELL; from HENRY IV. his sanguine character; mysticism from FENELON; from HUME his all-unhinging wit; love of paradox and brooding suspicion from ROUSSEAU; naiveté and elegance of knavery from VOLTAIRE; from MILTON the extravagance of his all-personifying fancy; from RAFFAELLE his dryness and nearly hard precision; and from RUBENS his supernatural luxury of colours:—deduct this oppressive EXUBERANCE from each; rectify them according to your own taste—what will be the result? your own correct, pretty, flat, useful—for me, to be sure, quite convenient vulgarity. And why this amongst maxims of humanity? that you may learn to know this EXUBERANCE, this LEVEN, of each great character, and its effects on contemporaries and posterity—that you may know where d, e, f, is, there must be a, b, c: he alone has knowledge of man, who knows the ferment that raises each character, and makes it that which it shall be, and something more or less than it shall be.

deduct from a rose its redness, from a lilly its whiteness from a diamond its hardness from a spunge its softness from an oak its heighth from a daisy its lowness & rectify every thing in Nature as the Philosophers do. & then we shall return to Chaos & God will be compelld to be Excentric if he Creates   O happy Philosopher

Variety does not necessarily suppose deformity. for a rose & a lilly. are various. & both beautiful

Beauty is exuberant but not of ugliness but of beauty & if ugliness is adjoind to beauty it is not the exuberance of beauty. so if Rafael is hard & dry it is not his genius but an accident acquired for how can Substance & Accident be predicated of the same Essence! I cannot concieve

But the substance gives tincture to the accident & makes it physiognomic

Aphorism 47. speaks of the heterogeneous, which all extravagance is. but exuberance not.

(47: Man has an inward sense of consequence—of all that is pertinent. This sense is the essence of humanity: this, developed and determined, characterises him—this, displayed, is his education. The more strict you are in observing what is pertinent and impertinent, (or heterogeneous) in character, actions, works of art and literature—the wiser, nobler, greater, the more humane yourself.)

533. I have often, too often, been tempted, at the daily relation of new knaveries, to despise human nature in every individual, till, on minute anatomy of each trick, I found that the knave was only an ENTHUSIAST or MOMENTARY FOOL. This discovery of momentary folly, symptoms of which assail the wisest and the best, has thrown a great consolatory light on my inquiries into man's moral nature: by this the theorist is enabled to assign to each class and each individual its own peculiar fit of vice or folly; and, by the same, he has it in his power to contrast the ludicrous or dismal catalogue with the more pleasing one of sentiment and virtue, more properly their own.

man is the ark of God the mercy seat is above upon the ark cherubims guard it on either side & in the midst is the holy law. man is either the ark of God or a phantom of the earth & of the water   if thou seekest by human policy to guide this ark. remember Uzzah   II Sam[1]. VI Ch:

knaveries are not human nature   knaveries are knaveries   See N 554 this aphorism seems to me to want discrimination

534. He, who is master of the fittest moment to crush his enemy, and magnanimously neglects it, is born to be a conqueror.

this was old George the second

539. A great woman not imperious, a fair woman not vain, a woman of common talents not jealous, an accomplished woman, who scorns to shine—are four wonders, just great enough to be divided among the four quarters of the globe.

let the men do their duty & the women will be such wonders, the female life lives from the light of the male. see a mans female dependants you know the man

543. Depend *not much upon your rectitude, if you are uneasy in the presence of the good;/*

[Line drawn by Blake]

easy

X nor trust to your humility if you are mortified when you are not noticed.

uneasy

549. He, who [hates] <loves> the wisest and best of men, [hates] <loves> the Father of men; for, where is *the Father of men to be seen but in the most perfect of his children?*

this is true worship

552. *He, who adores an impersonal God, has none; and, without guide or rudder, launches on an immense abyss that first absorbs his powers, and next himself.*

Most superlatively beautiful & Most affectionatly Holy & pure would to God that all men would consider it

554. The enemy of art is the enemy of nature; art is nothing but the highest sagacity and exertion of human nature; *and what nature will he honour who honours not the human?*

human nature is the image of God

556. Where there is much pretension, much has been borrowed—*nature never pretends.*

557. Do you think *him a common man who can make what is common exquisite?*

559. Whose *promise may* you depend upon? his *who dares refuse* what he knows *he cannot perform; who promises calmly, strictly, conditionally, and never excites a hope which he may disappoint.*

560. *You promise as you speak.*

562. Avoid him *who speaks softly, and writes sharply.*

Ah rogue I could be thy hangman

566. Neither *patience nor inspiration* can *give wings to a snail*—you waste your own force, you destroy what remained of energy in the indolent, by urging him to move beyond his rate of power.

573. *Your humility is equal to your desire of being unnoticed, unobserved in your acts of virtue.*

true humility

574. There are certain light characteristic momentary features of man, which, in spite of masks and all exterior mummery, represent him as he is and shall be. If once in an individual you have discovered one ennobling feature, let him debase it, *let it at times shrink from him, no matter; he will, in the end, prove superior to thousands of his* critics.

the wise man falleth 7 times in a day & riseth again &ᶜ

576. The man who has and uses but one scale for every thing, for himself and his enemy, the past and the future, the grand and the trifle, for truth and error, virtue and vice, religion, superstition, infidelity; for nature, art, and works of genius and art—is truly wise, just, great.

this is most true but how does this agree with 451

✕ 577. The infinitely little constitutes the infinite difference in works of art, and in the degrees of morals and religion; the greater the rapidity, precision, acuteness, with which this is observed and determined, the more authentic, the greater the observer.

uneasy

580. Range him high amongst your saints, who, with all-acknowledged powers, and his own stedfast scale for every thing, can, on the call of judgment or advice, submit to transpose *himself into another's situation, and to adopt* his point of sight.

582. *No communications and no gifts can exhaust genius, or impoverish charity.*
Most Excellent

585. Distrust yourself if you fear the eye of the sincere; *but be afraid of neither God or man, if you have no reason to distrust yourself.*

586. *Who comes as he goes, and is present as he came and went, is sincere.*

✕ 588. He loves grandly (I speak of friendship) who is not jealous when he has partners of love.
uneasy but I hope to mend

590. He *knows himself greatly who never opposes his genius.*
Most Excellent

596. "Love as if you could hate and might be hated;"—a maxim of detested prudence in real friendship, the bane of all tenderness, the death of all familiarity. Consider the *fool who follows it as nothing inferior to him who* at every *bit of bread trembles* at the thought *of its being poisoned.*
Excellent

597. "Hate as if you could love or should be loved;"—him who follows this maxim, if all the world were to declare an idiot and enthusiast, I shall esteem, of all men, the most eminently formed for friendship.
Better than Excellent

600. Distinguish with exactness, if you mean to know yourself and others, what is so often mistaken—the SINGULAR, the ORIGINAL, the EXTRAORDINARY, *the GREAT, and the SUBLIME man: the SUBLIME alone unites the singular, original, extraordinary, and great, with his own uniformity* and *simplicity: the GREAT, with many powers, and uniformity of ends, is destitute of that superior calmness* and inward harmony which soars above the atmosphere of praise: the EXTRAORDINARY is distinguished by copiousness, and a wide range of energy: *the ORIGINAL need not be very rich, only* that which he produces is unique, and has the exclusive stamp of individuality: the SINGULAR, as such, is placed between originality and whim, and often makes a trifle the medium of fame.

601. Forwardness nips affection in the bud.
the more is the pity

✕ 602. If you mean to be loved, give more than what is asked, but not more than what is wanted; [*and ask less than what is expected.*]
this is human policy as it is calld—this whole aphorism is an oversight

603. Whom smiles and [*tears*] <frowns> make equally lovely, [*all*] <only good> hearts [*may*] <can or dare> court.

604. Take here the grand secret—if not of pleasing all, yet of displeasing none—court mediocrity, avoid originality, and sacrifice to fashion.
& go to hell

605. He who pursues the glimmering steps of hope, with stedfast, not presumptuous, eye, may pass the gloomy rock, on either side of which [*superstition*] <hypocrisy> and incredulity their dark abysses spread.
Superstition has been long a bug bear by reason of its being united with hypocrisy. but let them be fairly seperated & then superstition will be honest feeling & God who loves all honest men. will lead the poor enthusiast in the paths of holiness

–587–

606. The public seldom forgive twice.

let us take their example

✕ 607. Him who is hurried on by the furies of immature, impetuous wishes, stern repentance shall drag, bound and reluctant, back to the place from which he sallied: where you hear the crackling of wishes expect intolerable vapours or repining grief.

uneasy

608. He submits to be seen through a microscope, who suffers himself to be caught in a fit of passion.

& such a one I dare love

609. Venerate four characters; the sanguine, who has checked volatility *and the rage for pleasure;* the choleric, *who has subdued passion* and *pride; the phlegmatic, emerged* from *indolence; and the* melancholy, *who has dismissed* avarice, *suspicion, and asperity.*

4 most holy men

610. All *great minds sympathize.*

612. Men carry their character not seldom in their pockets: you might decide on more than half of your acquaintance, had you will or right to turn their pockets inside out.

I seldom carry money in my pockets they are generally full of paper [*for* (6 or 7 words erased)]

615. Not *he who forces himself on opportunity, but he who watches its approach, and welcomes its arrival by immediate use, is wise.*

616. Love and hate are the genius of invention, the parents of virtue and of vice—*forbear to decide on yourself till you have had opportunities of warm attachment or deep dislike.*

True Experience

✕ 619. Each heart is a world of nations, classes, and individuals; full of friendships, enmeties, indifferences; . . . the number and character of your friends within bears an exact resemblance to your external ones; . . .

Be assured then, that to know yourself perfectly you have only to set down a true statement of those that ever loved or hated you.

uneasy because I cannot do this

623. Avoid connecting yourself with characters whose good and bad sides are unmixed, and have not fermented together; they resemble phials of vinegar and oil, or pallets set with colours: they are either excellent at home and intolerable abroad, or insufferable within doors and excellent in public: . . .

Most Excellent

✕ 624. The fool separates his object from all surrounding ones; all abstraction is temporary folly.

uneasy because I once thought otherwise but now know it is Truth

626. Let me repeat it—He only is great who has the habits of greatness; who, after performing what none in ten thousand could accomplish, *passes on, like Samson, and* "TELLS NEITHER FATHER NOR MOTHER OF IT."

This is Excellent

630. A GOD, an ANIMAL, a PLANT, are not companions of man; nor is the FAULTLESS—then judge with lenity of all; the coolest, wisest, best, all without exception, have their points, their moments of enthusiasm, fanaticism, absence of mind, faint-heartedness, stupidity—if you allow not for these, your criticisms on man will be a mass of accusations or caricatures.

It is the God in *all* that is our companion & friend, for our God himself says, you are my brother my sister & my mother; & St John. Whoso dwelleth in love dwelleth in God & God in him. & such an one cannot judge of any but in love. & his feelings will be attractions or repulses

See Aphorisms 549 & 554

God is in the lowest effects as well as in the highest causes for he is become a worm that he may nourish the weak

For let it be rememberd that creation is. God descending according to the weakness of man for our Lord is the word of God & every thing on earth is the word of God & in its essence is God

631. Genius *always gives its best at first, prudence at last.*

633. You think to meet with some additions here to your stock of moral knowledge—and not in vain, I hope: but know, a great many rules cannot be given by him who means not to offend, and many of mine have perhaps offended already;

Those who are offended with any thing in this book would be offended with the innocence of a child & for the same reason. because it reproaches him with the errors of acquired folly.

believe me, for him who has an open ear and eye, every minute teems with observations of precious import, yet scarcely communicable to the most faithful friend; so incredibly weak, so vulnerable in certain points, is man: forbear to meddle with these at your first setting out, and make amusement the minister of reflection: sacrifice all egotism—sacrifice ten points to one, if that one have the value of twenty; and if you are happy enough to impress your disciple with respect for himself, with probability of success in his exertions of growing better; and, above all, with the idea of your disinterestedness—you may perhaps succeed in making one proselyte to virtue.

—lovely.

635. Keep your heart from him who begins his acquaintance with you by indirect flattery of your favourite paradox or foible.

unless you find it to be his also. previous to your acquaintance

636. Receive no satisfaction for premeditated impertinence—forget it, forgive it—but keep him inexorably at a distance who offered it.

This is a paradox

✕ 638. Let the cold, who offers the nauseous mimickry of warm affection, meet with what he deserves—a repulse; but from that moment depend on his irreconcilable enmity.

uneasy because I do not know how to do this but I will try to do it the first opportunity

640. The moral enthusiast, who in the maze of his refinements loses or despises the plain paths of honesty and duty, is on the brink of crimes.

Most True

[P 224] End of Vol. 1.

I hope no one will call what I have written cavilling because he may think my remarks of small consequence   For I write from the warmth of my heart. & cannot resist the impulse I feel to rectify what I think false in a book I love so much. & approve so generally

[P 225, blank]

Man is bad or good. as he unites himself with bad or good spirits. tell me with whom you go & Ill tell you what you do

As we cannot experience pleasure but by means of others who experience either pleasure or pain thro us. And as all of us on earth are united in thought, for it is impossible to think without images of somewhat on earth— So it is impossible to know God or heavenly things without conjunction with those who know God & heavenly things. therefore, all who converse in the Spirit, converse with Spirits. [& *they converse with the spirit of God*]

For these reasons I say that this Book is written by consultation with Good Spirits because it is Good. & that the name Lavater. is the amulet of those who purify the heart of man.

[P 226, blank]

There is a strong objection to Lavaters principles (as I understand them) & that is He makes every thing originate in its accident he makes the vicious propensity <not only> a leading feature of the man but the Stamina on which all his virtues grow. But as I understand Vice it is a Negative—It does not signify what the laws of Kings & Priests have calld Vice we who are philosophers ought not to call the Staminal Virtues of Humanity by the same name that we call the omissions of intellect springing from poverty.

Every mans <leading> propensity ought to be calld his leading Virtue & his good Angel But the Philosophy of Causes & Consequences misled Lavater as it has all his cotemporaries. Each thing is its own cause & its own effect Accident is the omission of act in self & the hindering of act in another, This is Vice but all Act [<*from Individual propensity*>] is Virtue. To hinder another [P 227, blank] is not an act it is the contrary it is a restraint on action both in ourselves & in the person hinderd. for he who hinders another omits his own duty. at the time

Murder is Hindering Another

Theft is Hindering Another

Backbiting. Undermining C[i]rcumventing & whatever is Negative is Vice

But the or[i]gin of this mistake in Lavater & his cotemporaries, is, They suppose that Womans Love is Sin. in consequence all the Loves & Graces with them are Sin

---

Annotations to Swedenborg's *Heaven and Hell*
London, 1784

HALF-TITLE [inscribed in pencil in a hand not Blake's]

"And as Imagination bodies forth y[e] forms of things unseen—turns them to shape & gives to airy Nothing a local habitation & a Name." Sh.

[Blake's comment, in crayon]

Thus Fools quote Shakespeare The Above is Theseus's opinion Not Shakespeares You might as well quote Satans blasphemies from Milton & give them as Miltons Opinions

TITLE PAGE [signed in ink]
William Blake
[pencil note in another hand: "belonged to Blake the Artist"]

[P 206, paragraphs 333 and 334, scored in left margin by erased pencil or by finger-nail] 333. Little Children . . . appear in Heaven . . . in the province of the eyes . . . because the Lord appears to the Angels of the Spiritual Kingdom, fronting the left eye; and to the Angels of the Celestial Kingdom, fronting the right eye; see above, n. 118. Little Children being thus in the province of the eyes, denotes them to be under the immediate guardianship and protection of the Lord.
334. How Infants are educated in Heaven shall here briefly be told. They are first taught to speak by those that have the care of them: their first utterance is only a kind of affectionate sound, which, by degrees, grows more distinct, as their minds become furnished with ideas: for the ideas of the mind springing from the affectionate part, immediately give birth and form to the speech of the Angels, as mentioned above, n. 234 to 245. . . .

[P 339, PARAGRAPH 513, with Blake's dagger and note] 513. †The angels appointed for instructors are from several societies, but chiefly from such as are in the north and the south, as their understanding and wisdom more particularly consist in the distinct knowledges of good and truth. The places set apart for instructing are towards the north, . . .
†See N 73 Worlds in Universe. for account of Instructing Spirits ᵗ

[P 389, PARAGRAPH 588] . . . That the Hells are so many and various, appears from it's being given me to know, that under every mountain, hill, rock, plain, and valley, there were particular Hells of different extent in length, breadth, and depth. In a word, both Heaven and the World of Spirits may be considered as convexities, under which are arrangements of those infernal mansions. So much concerning the Plurality of Hells.
under every *Good* is a hell. i.e hell is the outward or external of heaven. & is of the body of the lord. for nothing is destroyd

⟡

Annotations to Swedenborg's
Divine Love and Divine Wisdom ᵗ
London, 1788

FLYLEAF ᵗ
There can be no Good-Will. Will is always Evil   It is pernicious to others or selfish   If God is any thing he is Understanding   He is the Influx from that into the Will This Good to others or benevolent Understanding can [?& ?does] Work [?harm] ignorantly but never can ?the Truth [be ?evil] because Man is only Evil [when he wills an untruth]
H[eaven] & Hell   Chapter 425
Understanding or Thought is not natural to Man it is acquired by means of Suffering & Distress i.e Experience. Will, Desire, Love, Rage, Envy, & all other Affections are Natural. but Understanding is Acquired   But Observe.

without these is to be less than Man. Man could ?never [have received] ?light from heaven ?without [aid of the] affections one woud be ?limited to the ?five [?heavens &] ?hells [& live] in different periods of time

Wisdom of Angels 10

[Numbers refer to sections, not pages]

1. . . . Doth it not happen that in Proportion as the Affection which is of Love groweth cold, the Thought, Speech and Action grow cold also? And that in Proportion as it is heated, they also are heated? But this a wise Man perceiveth, not from a Knowledge that Love is the Life of Man, but from Experience of this Fact.

They also percieve this from Knowledge but not with the natural part

2. No one knoweth what is the Life of Man, unless he knoweth that it is Love; if this be not known, . . .

This was known to me & thousands

7. That the Divine or God is not in Space . . . cannot be comprehended by any merely natural Idea, but it may by a spiritual Idea: The Reason why it cannot be comprehended by a natural Idea, is, because in that Idea there is Space; . . .

What a natural Idea is—

Nevertheless, Man may comprehend this by natural Thought, if he will only admit into such Thought somewhat of spiritual Light; . . . (bracketed by Blake)

Mark this

A spiritual Idea doth not derive any Thing from Space, but it derives every Thing appertaining to it from State: . . .

Poetic idea

8. Hence it may appear, that Man from a *merely natural* Idea cannot comprehend that the Divine is every where, and yet not in Space; and yet that Angels and Spirits clearly comprehend this; consequently *that Man also may,* if so be he will admit something of spiritual Light into his Thought;

Observe the distinction here between Natural & Spiritual as seen by Man

the Reason why Man may comprehend it is, because his Body doth not think, but his Spirit, therefore not his natural but his spiritual [Part]

Man may comprehend. but not the natural or external man

10. It hath been said, that in the spiritual World Spaces appear equally as in the natural World. . . . Hence it is that the Lord, although he is in the Heavens with the Angels every where, nevertheless appears high above them as a Sun: And whereas the Reception of Love and Wisdom constitutes Affinity with him, therefore those Heavens appear nearer to him where the Angels are in a nearer Affinity from Reception, than where they are in a more remote Affinity: . . .

He who Loves feels love descend into him & if he has wisdom may percieve it is from the Poetic Genius which is the Lord

11. In all the Heavens there is no other Idea of God than that of a Man: . . .

Man can have no idea of any thing greater than Man as a cup cannot contain more than its capaciousness But God is a man not because he is so percievd by man but because he is the creator of man

[Quotation from Swedenborg's *The Last Judgment*, No. 74] The Gentiles, particularly the Africans . . . entertain an Idea of God as of a Man, and say that no one can have any other Idea of God: When they hear that many form an Idea of God as existing in the Midst of a Cloud, they ask where such are; . . .

Think of a white cloud. as being holy you cannot love it but think of a holy man within the cloud love springs up in your thought. for to think of holiness distinct from man is impossible to the affections. Thought alone can make monsters, but the affections cannot

12. . . . they who are wiser than the common People pronounce God to be invisible, . . .

Worldly wisdom or demonstration by the senses is the cause of this

13. . . . The Negation of God constitutes Hell, and in the Christian World the Negation of the Lord's Divinity.

the Negation of the Poetic Genius

14. . . . when Love is in Wisdom then it existeth. These two are such a ONE, that they may be distinguished indeed in Thought, but not in Act.

Thought without affection makes a distinction between Love & Wisdom as it does between body & Spirit

27. What Person of Sound Reason doth not perceive, that the Divine is not divisible; . . . If another, who hath no Reason, should say that it is possible there may be several Infinities, Uncreates, Omnipotents and Gods, provided they have the same Essence, and that thereby there is one Infinite, Uncreate, Omnipotent and God—is not one and the same Essence but one and the same Identity?

Answer   Essence is not Identity but from Essence proceeds Identity & from one Essence may proceed many Identities as from one Affection may proceed. many thoughts   Surely this is an oversight

That there is but one Omnipotent Uncreate & God I agree but that there is but one Infinite I do not. for if all but God is not Infinite they shall come to an End which God forbid

If the Essence was the same *as the* Identity there could be but one Identity. which is false

Heaven would upon this plan be but a Clock but one & the same Essence is therefore Essence & not Identity

40. . . . Appearances are the first Things from which the human Mind forms it's Understanding, and . . . it cannot shake them off but by an Investigation of the Cause, and if the Cause lies very deep, it cannot investigate it, *without keeping the Understanding some Time in spiritual Light*, . . .

this Man can do while in the body—

41. . . . it cannot be demonstrated except by such Things as a Man can perceive by his bodily Senses, . . .

Demonstration is only by bodily Senses.

49. With Respect to God, it is not possible that he can love and be reciprocally beloved by others, in whom there is . . . any Thing Divine; for if there was . . . any Thing Divine in them, then it would not be beloved by others, but it would love itself; . . .

False   Take it so or the contrary it comes to the same for if a thing loves it is infinite   Perhaps we only differ in the meaning of the words Infinity & Eternal

68. . . . Man is only a Recipient of Life. From this Cause it is, that Man, from his own hereditary Evil, reacts against God; but so far as he believes that all his Life is from God, and every Good of Life from the Action of God, and every Evil of Life from the Reaction of Man, Reaction thus becomes correspondent with Action, and Man acts with God as from himself. [Bracketed by Blake]

Good & Evil are here both Good & the two contraries Married

69. . . . But he who knows how to elevate his Mind above the Ideas of Thought which are derived from Space and Time, such a Man passes from Darkness to Light, and becomes wise in Things spiritual and Divine . . . and then by Virtue of that Light he shakes off the Darkness of natural Light, and removes *its Fallacies* from the Center to the Circumference.

When the fallacies of darkness are in the circumference they cast a bound about the infinite

70. Now inasmuch as the Thoughts of the Angels derive nothing from Space and Time, but from States of Life, it is evident that they do not comprehend what is meant when it is said, that the Divine fills Space, for they do not know what Space is, but that they comprehend clearly, when it is said, without any Idea of Space, that the Divine fills all Things.

Excellent

PART THE SECOND

[Title heading Nos. 163–166] That without two Suns, the one living and the other dead, there can be no Creation.

False philosophy according to the letter. but true according to the spirit

164. . . . it follows that the one Sun is living and that the other Sun is dead, also that the dead Sun itself was created by the living Sun from the Lord.

how could Life create death

165. The reason why a dead Sun was created is to the End that in the Ultimates all Things may be fixed. . . . On this and no other Ground Creation is founded: The terraqueous Globe . . . is as it were the Basis and Firmament. . . .

they exist literally about the sun & not about the earth

166. That all Things were created from the Lord by the living Sun, *and nothing by the dead Sun*, may appear from this Consideration. . . .

the dead Sun is only a phantasy of evil Man

PART THE THIRD

181. . . . It is the same upon Earth with Men, but with this Difference, that the Angels feel that [spiritual] Heat, and see that [spiritual] Light, whereas Men do not. . . .

He speaks of Men as meer earthly Men not as receptacles of spirit, or else he contradicts N 257

Now forasmuch as Man, whilst he is in natural Heat and Light, knoweth nothing of spiritual Heat and Light in himself, and this cannot be known but by Experience from the spiritual World. . . .

This is certainly not to be understood according to the letter for it is false by all experience. Who does not or may not know of love & wisdom in himself

220. . . . From these Considerations a Conclusion was drawn, that the Whole of Charity and Faith is in Works, . . .

The Whole of the New Church is in the Active Life & not in Ceremonies at all

237. These three Degrees of Altitude are named Natural, Spiritual and Celestial. . . . Man, at his Birth, first comes into the natural Degree, and this increases in him by Continuity according to the Sciences, and according to the Understanding acquired by them, to the Summit of Understanding which is called Rational: . . .

Study Sciences till you are blind

Study intellectuals till you are cold

Yet Science cannot teach intellect

Much less can intellect teach Affection

How foolish then is it to assert that Man is born in only one degree when that one degree is reception of the 3 degrees. two of which he must destroy or close up or they will descend, if he closes up the two superior then he is not truly in the 3ᵈ but descends out of it into meer Nature or Hell

See N 239

Is it not also evident that one degree will not open the other & that science will not open intellect but that they are discrete & not continuous so as to explain each other except by correspondence which has nothing to do with demonstration for you cannot demonstrate one degree by the other for how can science be brought to demonstrate intellect, without making them continuous & not discrete

238. Man, so long as he lives in the World, does not know any Thing of the opening of these Degrees in himself. . . .

See N 239

239. . . . In every Man there is a natural, spiritual and celestial Will and Understanding, in Power from his Birth, and in Act whilst they are opening.

Mark this it explains N 238

In a Word, the Mind of Man . . . is of three Degrees, so that . . . a Man thereby may be elevated to Angelic Wisdom, and possess it, while he lives in the World, but nevertheless he does not come into it till after Death, if he becomes an Angel, *and then he speaks Things ineffable and incomprehensible to the natural Man.*

Not to a Man but to the natural Man

241. . . . Every one who consults his Reason, *whilst it is in the Light,* may see, that Man's Love is the End of all Things appertaining to him. . . .

244. . . . And hence it also follows, that the Understanding does not lead the Will, or that Wisdom does not produce Love, but that it only teaches and shows the Way, it teaches how a Man ought to live, and shows the Way in which he ought to walk. (Bracketed by Blake)

Mark this

256. . . . From this it is evident, that Man, so *long as he lives in the World, and is thereby in the natural Degree,* cannot be elevated into Wisdom itself, . . .

See Sect. 4 of the next Number

257. . . . IV. . . . But still Man, in whom the spiritual Degree is open, comes into that Wisdom when he dies, and may also come into it by laying asleep the Sensations of the Body, and by Influx from above at the same Time into the Spirituals of his Mind. (Bracketed by Blake)

this is while in the Body

This is to be understood as unusual in our time but common in ancient

V. The natural Mind of Man consists of spiritual Substances, and at the same Time of natural Substances; from its *spiritual Substances* Thought is produced, but not from its *natural Substances*; . . .

Many perversely understand him. as if man while in the body was only conversant with natural Substances. because themselves are mercenary & worldly & have no idea of any but worldly gain

267. . . . for the natural Man can elevate his Understanding to superior Light as far as he desires it, but he who is principled in Evils and thence in Things false, does not elevate it higher than to the superior Region of his natural Mind; . . .

Who shall dare to say after this that all elevation is of self & is Enthusiasm & Madness & is it not plain that self derived intelligence is worldly demonstration

PART THE FOURTH

294. Forasmuch as the Things, which constitute the Sun of the spiritual World, are from the Lord, and not the Lord, therefore they are not Life in itself, . . .

This assertion that the spiritual Sun is not Life explains how the natural Sun is dead

This is an Arcanum, which the Angels by their spiritual Ideas can see in Thought, and also express in Speech, but not Men by their *natural Ideas*; . . . (Double underlining by Blake)

How absurd then would it be to say that no man on earth has a spiritual idea after reading N 257

295. That there is such a Difference between the Thoughts of Angels and Men, was made known to me by this Experience: They were told to think of something spiritually, and afterwards to tell me what they thought of; when this was done and they would have told me, they could not, . . .

they could not tell him in natural ideas how absurd must men be to understand him as if he said the angels could not express themselves at all to him

304. . . . Forasmuch as there is such a Progression of the Fibres and Vessels in a Man from first Principles to Ultimates, therefore there is a similar Progression of their States; their States are the Sensations, Thoughts and Affections; these also from their first Principles *where they are in the Light,* pervade to their Ultimates, where they are in Obscurity; or from their first Principles, where they are in Heat, to their Ultimates where they are not *in Heat:* . . .

We see here that the cause of an ultimate is the absence from heat & light

315. It is to be observed, that the Heat, Light and Atmospheres of the natural World conduce nothing to this image of Creation, . . .

Therefore the Natural Earth & Atmosphere is a Phantasy.

The Heat, Light and Atmospheres of the natural World only open Seeds; . . . but this not by Powers derived from their own Sun, . . . [Bracketed by Blake]

Mark this

. . . but by Powers from the spiritual Sun, . . . *for the Image of Creation is spiritual,* nevertheless that it may appear, and furnish Use *in the natural World,* . . . it must be clothed in Matter, . . .

316. . . . it is evident, that as there is a Resemblance of Creation in the Forms of Vegetables, so there is also in the Forms of Animals, viz. that there is a Progression from first Principles to Ultimates, and from Ultimates to first Principles.

A going forth & returning

324. . . . there doth not exist any Thing in the created Universe, which hath not Correspondence with something of Man, not only with his Affections and his Thoughts thence derived, but also with the Organs and Viscera of his Body, not with them as Substances, but with them as Uses.

Uses & substances are so different as not to correspond

336. . . . The Reason why the Things which do Hurt to Man are called Uses, is, because they are of Use, to the Wicked to do Evil, and because they contribute to absorb Malignities, therefore also they contribute as Cures: Use is applied in both Senses, in like Manner as Love, for we speak of good Love and evil Love, and Love calls all that Use, which is done by itself. [Marked by a large cross in the right margin]

PART THE FIFTH

404. . . . *Thought indeed exists first, because it is of the natural Mind, but Thought from the Perception of Truth, which is from the Affection of Truth, exists last; this Thought is the Thought of Wisdom, but the other is Thought from the Memory by the Sight of the natural Mind.* [Bracketed as well as underlined]

Note this

410. . . . *From these Things it may be seen, that Love or the Will joins itself to Wisdom or the Understanding, and not that Wisdom or the Understanding joins itself to Love or the Will;* . . . (Bracketed and underlined; lower part of bracket shaped like a pointing finger)

Mark this

Thoughts, Perceptions, and Knowledge, thence derived, flow indeed from the spiritual World, *but still they are not received by the Understanding, but by the Love according to it's Affections in the Understanding.* [Bracketed and underlined]

Mark this

It appears also as if the Understanding joined itself to Love or the Will, *but this also is a Fallacy;* Love or the Will joins itself to the Understanding and causeth the Understanding to be reciprocally joined to it: . . . [Bracketed and underlined]

Mark this

. . . For the Life of Man is his Love, . . . that is, according as he has exalted his Affections by Truths, . . . [Bracketed]

Mark this

411. . . . From these Considerations it is also evident, *that Love joins itself to the Understanding, and not vice versa.* . . .

Mark this

412. . . . He who knows all the Fabric of the Lungs from Anatomy, if he compares them with the Understanding, may clearly see that the *Understanding does nothing from itself, that it does not perceive nor think from itself, but all from Affections which are of the Love,* which in the Understanding are called the Affection of knowing, understanding and of seeing it, which were treated of above: . . . [Bracketed]

Mark

From the Structure of the Lungs . . . *I was fully convinced that the Love by it's Affections joins itself to the Understanding, and that the Understanding does not join itself to any Affection of the Love,* . . . [Bracketed]

Mark this

413. XIII. THAT WISDOM OR THE UNDERSTANDING BY MEANS OF THE POWER GIVEN IT BY LOVE, CAN BE ELEVATED, AND RECEIVE THE THINGS WHICH ARE OF THE LIGHT FROM HEAVEN, AND PERCEIVE THEM. [Bracketed]

Mark this

414. . . . Love however, or the Will, is elevated into the Heat of Heaven, but the Understanding into the Light of Heaven, and if they are both elevated, a Marriage of them is effected there, which is called the celestial Marriage. . . .

Is it not false then, that love recieves influx thro the understand^g as was asserted in the society

419. . . . and moreover this Love became impure by Reason of the Separation of celestial Love from it in the Parents.

Therefore it was not created impure & is not naturally so.

. . . so far the Love is purged of its Uncleannesses, and purified, that is, so far it is elevated into the Heat of Heaven, and joined to the Light of Heaven, in which the Understanding is, and Marriage is effected, which is called the Marriage of Good and Truth, that is, of Law and Wisdom.

Therefore it does not recieve influx thro the understanding

421. XVII. THAT LOVE OR THE WILL IS DEFILED IN THE UNDERSTANDING, AND BY IT, IF THEY ARE NOT ELEVATED TOGETHER: . . . [Bracketed]

Mark this   they are elevated together

422. . . . *The Understanding is not made spiritual and celestial, but the Love is;* and when the Love is, it also maketh the Understanding it's Spouse spiritual and celestial. (Bracketed)

[Concluding Number, headed "What the Beginning or Rudiment of Man is from Conception."]

432. . . . Moreover it was shown in the Light of Heaven, . . . that the interior Compages of this little Brain was . . . in the Order and form of Heaven; and that it's exterior Compages was in Opposition to that Order and Form.

Heaven & Hell are born together.

∽

Annotations to Swedenborg's *Divine Providence* †
London, 1790

HALF-TITLE [signed]
William Blake

TRANSLATOR'S PREFACE

PAGE v Perhaps there never was a Period . . . which required a Vindication and Elucidation of the Divine Providence of the Lord, more than the present. . . .

For if we allow a GENERAL Providence, and yet deny a PARTICULAR one, or if we allow a PARTICULAR one, and yet deny a SINGULAR one, that is, one extending to Things and Circumstances most SINGULAR and minute, what is this but denying a GENERAL Providence?

Is not this Predestination?

PAGE xviii . . . Nothing doth IN GENERAL so contradict Man's natural and favourite Opinions as TRUTH, and . . . all the grandest and purest Truths of Heaven must needs seem obscure and perplexing to the natural Man at first View—

Lies & Priestcraft Truth is Nature

—*until his intellectual* [P xix] *Eye becomes accustomed to the Light, and can thereby behold it with Satisfaction.*

that is: till he agrees to the Priests interest

CHAPTER THREE

69. But the Man who doth not suffer himself to be led to, and enrolled in Heaven, is prepared for his Place in Hell; for Man from himself continually tends to the lowest Hell, but is continually with-held by the Lord;

What is Enrolling but Predestination

and he, who cannot be with-held, is prepared for a certain Place there, in which he is also enrolled immediately after his Departure out of the World; and this Place there is opposite to a certain Place in Heaven, for Hell is in Opposition to Heaven;

Query Does he also occupy that place in Heaven.—See N. 185 & 329 at the End See 277 & 307. & 203 where he says that a Place for Every Man is Foreseen & at the same time provided.

CHAPTER NINE

185. . . . after Death . . . the . . . great and rich . . . at first speak of God, and of the Divine Providence, as if they acknowledged them in their Hearts; But whereas they then manifestly see the Divine Providence, and from it their final Portion, which is that they are to be in Hell, they connect themselves with Devils there, . . .

What could Calvin Say more than is Said in this Number Final Portion is Predestination See N 69 & 329 at the End & 277 & 203 Where he says A Place for Each Man is Foreseen & at the same time Provided

CHAPTER TEN

201. If it should be alledged, that the Divine Providence is an universal Government, and that not any Thing is governed, but only kept in it's Connection, and the Things which relate to Government (illuquae Regiminis sunt) are disposed by others, can this be called an universal Government? No King hath such a Government as this; for if a King were to allow his Subjects to govern every Thing in his Kingdom, he would no

longer be a King, but would only be called a King, therefore would have only a nominal Dignity and no real Dignity: Such a King cannot be said to hold the Government, much less universal Government. [Cited in Blake's note on 220]

203. Since every Man therefore lives after Death to Eternity, and according to his Life here hath his Place assigned to him either in Heaven or in Hell, . . . it follows, that the Human Race throughout the whole World is under the Auspices of the Lord, and that everyone, from his Infancy even to the End of his Life, is led of Him in the most minute Particulars, and his *Place foreseen*, and at the same *Time provided*.

Devils & Angels are Predestinated.

CHAPTER ELEVEN

220. . . . when a Man . . . cannot but think . . . that the State was made for him, and not he for the State; he is like a King *who* thinks his Kingdom and all the Men in it are for him, *and not he for the* Kingdom and all the Men of which it consists. . . .

He says at N 201 No King hath such a Government as this for all Kings are Universal in their Government otherwise they are No Kings

CHAPTER THIRTEEN

274. That a Doubt may be inferred against *Divine Providence, because it was not known heretofore* [i.e. before Swedenborg's preaching], *that Man liveth after Death; and this* was not discovered till now. . . . *But yet all who have any Religion, have in them an inherent Knowledge, that Men live after Death; . . .* [Bracketed]

It was not known & yet All Know

CHAPTER FOURTEEN

277.2 . . . he who is in Evil in the World, the same is in Evil after he goes out of *the World; wherefore if Evil be not removed* in the *World, it cannot be removed afterwards;* where the Tree falls, there it lieth; so also it is with the Life of Man; as it was at his Death, such it remaineth; everyone also is judged according to his Actions, not that they are enumerated, but because he returns to them, and does the like again; for Death is a Continuation of Life; with this Difference, that then Man cannot be reformed.

Cursed Folly!

Predestination after this Life is more Abominable than Calvins & Swedenborg is Such a Spiritual Predestinarian—witness this Number & many others, In 69 & 185 & 329 & 307

CHAPTER FIFTEEN

307. . . . That the Wicked, who are in the World, are governed in Hell by the Lord; . . . because Man with Respect to his Spirit is in the spiritual World, . . . in an infernal Society if he is wicked, and in a celestial Society if good; . . . . wherefore according to his Life and the Changes thereof, he is translated by the Lord from one Society of Hell to another, [or] led out of Hell and introduced into Heaven, and there also . . . translated from one Society to another, and this until the Time of his Death, after which he is no longer carried from one Society to another, because he is then no longer in any State of Reformation, but remains in that in which he is according to his Life; wherefore when a Man dies, he is inscribed in his own Place. . . .

Predestination

CHAPTER SEVENTEEN

329. . . . there is not wanting to any Man a Knowledge of the Means whereby he may be saved, nor the Power of being saved if he will; from which it follows, that all are predestined or intended for Heaven, and none for Hell. But forasmuch as there prevails among some a Belief in Predestination to no Salvation, which is Predestination to Damnation, and such a Belief is hurtful, and cannot be dispelled, unless Reason also sees the Madness and Cruelty of it, therefore it shall be treated of in the following Series.

I. That any other Predestination, than Predestination to Heaven, is contrary to the Divine Love and it's Infinity. 2. That any other Predestination, than Predestination to Heaven, is contrary to the Divine Wisdom and it's Infinity. 3. That it is an insane Heresy, to suppose that they only are saved who are born within the Church. 4. That it is a cruel Heresy, to suppose that any of the human Race are predestined to be damned.

Read N 185 & There See how Swedenborg contradicts himself & N 69 See also 277 & 203 where he Says that a Place for Each Man is foreseen & at the same time provided

∾

Annotations to *An Apology for the Bible*   ᵗ
by R. Watson, Bishop of Landaff. London, 1797

BACK OF TITLE PAGE

Notes on the B[ishop] of L[andaff]'s Apology for the Bible by William Blake

[An asterisk marks a point from which Blake drew a line to his comment.]

To defend the Bible in this year 1798 would cost a man his life
The Beast & the Whore rule without control.

It is an easy matter for a Bishop to triumph over Paines attack but it is not so easy, for one who loves the Bible

The Perversions of Christs words & acts are attackd by Paine & also the perversions of the Bible; Who dare defend either the Acts of Christ or the Bible Unperverted?

But to him who sees this mortal pilgrimage in the light that I see it. Duty to [*my*] <his> country is the first consideration & safety the last

Read patiently take not up this Book in an idle hour the consideration of these things is the whole duty of man & the affairs of life & death trifles sports of time <But> these considerations business of Eternity

I have been commanded from Hell not to print this as it is what our Enemies wish

[BISHOP WATSON'S PREFACE]
PAGE [*iii*]
. . . the deistical writings of Mr. Paine are circulated . . . amongst the unlearned . . . especially in large manufacturing towns; . . . this Defence of Revealed Religion might . . . be efficacious in stopping that torrent of infidelity which endangers alike the future happiness of individuals, and the present safety of all *christian states*. . . .

Paine has not attacked Christianity. Watson has defended Antichrist.

PAGE [*iv*]
Read the XXIII Chap of Matthew & then condemn Paines hatred of Priests if you dare

[Books by Bishop Watson] 7. The Wisdom and Goodness of God, in having made both *Rich and Poor*: a Sermon. . . .

God made Man happy & Rich but the Subtil made the innocent Poor
This must be a most wicked & blasphemous book

LETTER I

PAGE [I]

If this first Letter is written without Railing & Illiberality I have never read one that is. To me it is all Daggers & Poison. the sting of the serpent is in every Sentence as well as the glittering Dissimulation. Achilles' wrath is blunt abuse Thersites' sly insinuation Such is the Bishops If such is the characteristic of a modern polite gentleman we may hope to see Christs discourses Expung'd

I have not the Charity for the Bishop that he pretends to have for Paine. I believe him to be a State trickster

THE AGE OF REASON, part the second, . . . Extraordinary . . . not from any novelty in the objections which *you have produced against revealed* religion, (for I *find little or no novelty in them,*) . . .

Dishonest Misrepresentation

. . . I give you credit for your sincerity, *how much soever I may question your wisdom,* . . .

Priestly Impudence

. . . I . . . lament, that these *talents have not been applied in a manner more useful to human kind, and more creditable to yourself.*

Contemptible Falshood & Detraction

I hope there is no want of charity in saying, that it would have been fortunate for the christian world, *had your life been terminated before you had fulfilled your intention.*

Presumptuous Murderer dost thou O Priest wish thy brothers death when God has preserved him

. . . you have unsettled the faith of thousands; . . . [introduced] a state of corrupted morals.

Mr Paine has not extinguishd & cannot Extinguish Moral rectitude. he has Extinguishd Superstition which took the Place of Moral Rectitude what has Moral Rectitude to do with Opinions concerning historical fact

[P 2] . . . absolution, as practised in the church of Rome, . . . I cannot, with you, attribute the guillotine-massacres* to that cause.

To what does the Bishop attribute the English Crusade against France. is it not to State Religion. blush for shame

Men's minds were . . . prepared . . . *by their not thoroughly believing even that religion. What may not society expect from those, who shall imbibe the principles of your book?*

Folly & Impudence! Does the thorough belief of Popery hinder crimes or can the man who writes the latter sentiment be in the good humour the bishop Pretends to be. If we are to expect crimes from Paine & his followers. are we to believe that Bishops do not Rail I should Expect that the man who wrote this sneaking sentence would be as good an inquisitor as any other Priest

What is conscience? . . . an internal monitor implanted in us by the *Supreme Being,* and dictating . . . what is *right or wrong? Or is it merely* our own judgment of the moral rectitude or turpitude of our own actions? I *take the word* (with Mr. Locke) in the latter, *as in the only intelligible sense.*

Conscience in those that have it is unequivocal, it is the voice of God
Our judgment of right & wrong is Reason   I believe that the Bishop laught
at the Bible in his slieve & so did Locke

. . . it can be no criterion of moral* rectitude, even when it is certain, . . .
If Conscience is not a Criterion of Moral Rectitude What is it?
He who thinks that Honesty is changeable knows nothing about it

because the certainty of an opinion is no proof. . . .
Virtue is not Opinion

[P 3] . . . [not] that he will, in obeying the dictates of his conscience,† *on all occasions
act right.*
†Always, or the Bible is false

. . . a thousand perpetrators of different crimes, may all follow *the dictates of conscience;* . . .
Contemptible Falshood & Wickedness

. . . their conscientious composure can be no proof to others of the rectitude of their
principles, . . .
Virtue & honesty or the dictates of Conscience are of no doubtful Signification to any one

Opinion is one Thing. Principle another. No Man can change his Principles Every Man changes his opinions.   He who supposes that his Principles
are to be changed is a Dissembler who Disguises his Principles & calls that
change

If you have made the best examination you can, and yet reject revealed religion. . . .
Paine is either a Devil or an Inspired man. Men who give themselves to
their Energetic Genius in the manner that Paine does are no [*modest
Enquirers*] <Examiners>. If they are not determinately wrong they must be
Right or the Bible [P 4] is false. as to [*modest Enquirers*] <Examiners
in these points> they will [*always be found to be neither cold nor hot & will*]
be spewed out. The Man who pretends to be a modest enquirer into the
truth of a self evident thing is a Knave   The truth & certainty of Virtue &
Honesty i.e Inspiration needs no one to prove it   it is Evident as the Sun &
Moon [*What doubt is virtuous even Honest that depends upon Examination*] He who stands doubting of what he intends whether it is Virtuous or
Vicious knows not what Virtue means. no man can do a Vicious action &
think it to be Virtuous. no man can take darkness for light. he may pretend
to do so & may pretend to be a modest Enquirer. but he is a Knave

[P 3]—I think that you are in error; but whether that error be to you a vincible or an invincible error, I presume not to determine.
Serpentine Dissimulation

[P 4] You hold it impossible that the Bible can be the Word of God, because it is therein
said, that the Israelites [P 5] destroyed the Canaanites by the express command of God:
and to believe the Bible to be true, we must, you affirm, unbelieve all our belief of the
moral justice of God; . . . I am astonished that so acute a reasoner should . . . bring
. . . forward this exploded . . . objection. . . . The Word of God is in perfect harmony with his work; crying or smiling infants are subjected to death in both.
[P 5] To me who believe the Bible & profess myself a Christian a de-

fence of the Wickedness of the Israelites in murdering so many thousands under pretence of a command from God is altogether Abominable & Blasphemous. Wherefore did Christ come was it not to abolish the Jewish Imposture Was not Christ murderd because he taught that God loved all Men & was their father & forbad all contention for Worldly prosperity in opposition to the Jewish Scriptures which are only an Example of the wickedness & deceit of the Jews & were written as an Example of the possibility of Human Beastliness in all its branches. Christ died as an Unbeliever. & if the Bishops had their will so would Paine. <see page 1> but he who speaks a word against the Son of man shall be forgiven let the Bishop prove that he has not spoken against [p 6] the Holy Ghost who in Paine strives with Christendom as in Christ he strove with the Jews

[p 6] . . . God not only primarily formed, but . . . hath through all ages executed, the laws of nature; . . . for the general happiness of his creatures, . . . you have no right, in fairness of reasoning, to urge any apparent deviation from moral justice, as an argument against revealed religion, because you do not urge an equally apparent deviation from it, as an argument against natural religion: . . .

The Bible says that God formed Nature perfect but that Man perverted the order of Nature since which time the Elements are filld with the Prince of Evil who has the power of the air

Natural Religion is the voice of God & not the result of reasoning on the Powers of Satan

[p 6] Now, I think, it will be impossible to prove, that it was a *proceeding contrary to God's moral justice*, to exterminate *so wicked a people.*

Horrible the Bishop is an Inquisitor God never makes one man murder another nor one nation

[p 7] There is a vast difference between an accident brought on by a mans own carelessness & a destruction from the designs of another. The Earthquakes at Lisbon &c were the Natural result of Sin. but the destruction of the Canaanites by Joshua was the Unnatural design of wicked men To Extirpate a nation by means of another nation is as wicked as to destroy an individual by means of another individual which God considers (in the Bible) as Murder & commands that it shall not be done

Therefore the Bishop has not answerd Paine

[p 7] Human kind, by long experience; . . . . is in a far more distinguished situation, as to the powers of the mind, than it was in the childhood of the world.

That mankind are in a less distinguishd situation with regard to mind than they were in the time of Homer Socrates Phidias. Glycon. Aristotle &c let all their works witness [*the Deists*] <Paine> say<s> that Christianity put a stop to improvement & the Bishop has not shewn the contrary

It appears incredible to many, that God Almighty [p 8] should have had colloquial intercourse with our first parents; . . .

That God does & always did converse with honest Men Paine never denies. he only denies that God conversd with Murderers & Revengers such as the Jews were. & of course he holds that the Jews conversed with their own [*self will*] <State Religion> which they calld God & so were liars as Christ says

[P 8] . . . that he should have . . . become the God and governor of one particular nation; . . .

That the Jews assumed a right <Exclusively> to the benefits of God. will be a lasting witness against them. & the same will it be against Christians

[P 8] . . . when I consider how nearly man, in *a savage state, approaches to the brute creation,* as to intellectual excellence;

Read the Edda of Iceland the Songs of Fingal the accounts of North American Savages (as they are calld) Likewise Read Homers Iliad. he was certainly a Savage. in the Bishops sense. He knew nothing of God. in the Bishops sense of the word & yet he was no fool

[P 9] . . . the jewish and christian dispensations mediums to convey to all men . . . that knowledge concerning himself, which he had vouchsafed to give immediately to the first.

The Bible or <Peculiar> Word of God, Exclusive of Conscience or the Word of God Universal, is that Abomination which like the Jewish ceremonies is for ever removed & henceforth every man may converse with God & be a King & Priest in his own house

I own it is strange, very strange, that he should have made an immediate manifestation of himself . . . but what is there that is not strange? It is strange that you and I are here— . . . that there is a sun, and moon, and stars— . . .

It is strange that God should speak to man formerly & not now. because it is not true but the Strangeness of Sun Moon or Stars is Strange on a contrary account

. . . the *plan of providence,* in my opinion, so obviously *wise and good,* . . .

The Bible tells me that the plan of Providence was Subverted at the Fall of Adam & that it was not restored till [*we in*] Christ [xxx xxxxxxxx]

I will . . . examine what you shall produce, with as much coolness and respect, as if you had given the priests no provocation; *as if you were a man of the most unblemished character,* . . .

Is not this Illiberal has not the Bishop given himself the lie in the moment the first words were out of his mouth Can any man who writes so pretend that he is in a good humour. Is not this the Bishops cloven foot. has he not spoild the hasty pudding

LETTER II

PAGE 10

The trifles which the Bishop has combated in the following Letters are such as do nothing against Paines Arguments none of which the Bishop has dared to Consider. One for instance, which is That the books of the Bible were never believd willingly by any nation & that none but designing Villains ever pretended to believe That the Bible is all a State Trick, thro which tho' the People at all times could see they never had. the power to throw off Another Argument is that all the Commentators on the Bible are Dishonest Designing Knaves who in hopes of a good living adopt the State religion this he has shewn with great force which calls upon His Opponent loudly for an answer. I could name an hundred such [p 11] If it be found that the books ascribed to Moses, Joshua, and Samuel, were not written by Moses, Joshua, and Samuel, . . . they may still contain a true account of real transactions, . . .

He who writes things for true which none could write. but the actor. such are most of the acts of Moses. must either be the actor or a fable writer or a liar. If Moses did not write the history of his acts. it takes away the authority altogether it ceases to be history & becomes a Poem of probable impossibilities fabricated for pleasure as moderns say but I say by Inspiration.

[p 11] Had, indeed, Moses said that he wrote the five first [p 12] books . . . and had it been found, that Moses . . . did not write these books; then, I grant, the authority of the whole would have been gone at once; . . . .

[p 12] If Paine means that a history tho true in itself is false When it is attributed to a wrong author. he's a fool. But he says that Moses being proved not the author of that history which is written in his name & in which he says I did so & so Undermines the veracity intirely the writer says he is Moses if this is proved false the history is false Deut xxxi v 24 But perhaps Moses is not the author & then the Bishop loses his Author

[p 12] . . . the evidence for the miracles recorded in the Bible is . . . so greatly superior to that for the prodigies mentioned by Livy, or the miracles related by Tacitus, as to justify us in giving credit to the one as the work of God, and in with-holding it from the other as the effect of superstition and imposture.

Jesus could not do miracles where unbelief hinderd hence we must conclude that the man who holds miracles to be ceased puts it out of his own power to ever witness one   The manner of a miracle being performd is in modern times considerd as an arbitrary command of the agent upon the patient but this is an impossibility not a miracle neither did Jesus ever do such a miracle. Is it a greater miracle to feed five thousand men with five loaves than to overthrow all [p 13] the armies of Europe with a small pamphlet. look over the events of your own life & if you do not find that you have both done such miracles & lived by such you do not see as I do   True I cannot do a miracle thro experiment & to domineer over & prove to others my superior power as neither could Christ   But I can & do work such as both astonish & comfort me & mine   How can Paine the worker of miracles ever doubt Christs in the above sense of the word miracle   But how can Watson ever believe the above sense of a miracle who considers it as an arbitrary act of the agent upon an unbelieving patient. whereas the Gospel says that Christ could not do a miracle because of Unbelief

[p 14] If Christ could not do miracles because of Unbelief the reason alledged by Priests for miracles is false for those who believe want not to be confounded by miracles. Christ & his Prophets & Apostles were not ambitious miracle mongers

[p 14] You esteem all prophets to be such lying rascals, that I dare not venture to predict the fate of your book.

Prophets in the modern sense of the word have never existed Jonah was no prophet in the modern sense for his prophecy of Nineveh failed   Every honest man is a Prophet he utters his opinion both of private & public matters Thus If you go on So the result is So He never says such a thing Shall happen let you do what you will. a Prophet is a Seer not an Arbitrary Dictator. It is mans fault if God is not able to do him good. for he gives to the just & to the unjust but the unjust reject his gift

[P 15] What if I should admit, that SAMUEL, or EZRA, or . . . composed these books, *from public* records, many years after the death of Moses? . . . every fact recorded *in them may be true,* . . .

Nothing can be more contemptible than to suppose Public RECORDS to be True   Read them & Judge. if you are not a Fool.

Of what consequence is it whether Moses wrote the Pentateuch or no.   If Paine trifles in some of his objections it is folly to confute him so seriously in them & leave his more material ones unanswered. PUBLIC RECORDS as If Public Records were True   Impossible for the facts are such as none but the actor could tell, if it is True Moses & none but he could write it unless we allow it to be Poetry & that poetry inspired

[P 16] If historical facts can be written by inspiration Miltons Paradise Lost is as true as Genesis. or Exodus. but the Evidence is nothing for how can he who writes what he has neither seen nor heard of. be an Evidence of The Truth of his history

[P 17] . . . kings and priests . . . never, I believe, did you any harm; but you have done them all the harm you could, . . .

Paine says that Kings & Priests have done him harm from his birth

LETTER III

[P 22] Having done with . . . the grammatical evidence . . . you come to your historical and chronological evidence; . . .

I cannot concieve the Divinity of the <books in the> Bible to consist either in who they were written by or at what time or in the historical evidence which may be all false in the eyes of one man & true in the eyes of another but in the Sentiments & Examples which whether true or Parabolic are Equally useful as Examples given to us of the perverseness of some & its consequent evil & the honesty of others & its consequent good This sense of the Bible is equally true to all & equally plain to all. none can doubt the impression which he recieves from a book of Examples. If he is good he will abhor wickedness in David or Abraham if he is wicked he will make their wickedness an excuse for his & so he would do by any other book

[P 25] . . . you may as reasonably attribute cruelty and murder to the judge of the land in condemning criminals to death, as butchery and massacre to Moses in executing the command of God.

All Penal Laws court Transgression & therefore are cruelty & Murder

The laws of the Jews were (both ceremonial & real) the basest & most oppressive of human codes. & being like all other codes given under pretence of divine command were what Christ pronouncd them The Abomination that maketh desolate. i.e State Religion which [P 26] is the Source of all Cruelty

LETTER IV

[P 29] [Suppose an unsigned contemporary] history of the reigns of George the first and second, . . . would any man, three or four hundreds or thousands of years hence, question the authority of that book, . . .

Hundreds or Thousands of Years   O very fine Records as if he Knew that there were Records the Ancients Knew Better

[P 29] If I am right in this reasoning, . . .

as if Reasoning was of any Consequence to a Question   Downright Plain   Truth is Something but Reasoning is Nothing

[P 31] . . . the gospel of St. Matthew . . . was written not many centuries, probably . . . not a quarter of one century after the death of Jesus; . . .

There are no Proofs that Matthew the Earliest of all the Writings of the New Testament was written within the First Century   See p 94 & 95

[P 33] . . . you do not perfectly comprehend what is meant by the expression—the Word of God—or the divine authority of the scriptures: . . . [P 34] God . . . has interposed his more immediate assistance. . . .

They seem to Forget that there is a God. of This World. A God Worshipd in this World as God & Set above all that is calld God

[P 35] You proceed to shew that these books were not written by Samuel, . . .

Who gave them the Name of Books of Samuel it is not of Consequence

[P 36] . . . what has been conjectured by men of judgment, . . . a passage from Dr. Hartley's Observations of Man.

Hartley a Man of Judgment then Judgment was a Fool what Nonsense

LETTER V

[P 48] [Solomon's] admirable sermon on the vanity of every thing but piety and virtue.

Piety & Virtue   is Seneca Classical   O Fine Bishop

[P 49] What shall be said of you, who, either designedly, or ignorantly, represent one of the most clear and important prophecies in the Bible [Isaiah 44–45], as an historical compliment, written above an hundred and fifty years after the death of the prophet?

The Bishop never saw the Everlasting Gospel any more than Tom Paine

LETTER IX

[P 95] Did you ever read the apology for the Christians, which Justin Martyr presented to the emperor . . . not fifty years after the death of St. John, . . .

A:D: 150

. . . *probably* the *gospels*, and certainly some of St. Paul's epistles, were known. . . . *yet I hold it to be a certain* fact, that *all the books*, . . . were written, . . . within a few years after his death.

This is No Certain Fact   Presumption is no Proof

LETTER X

[P 108] . . . The moral precepts of the gospel. . . .

The Gospel is Forgiveness of Sins & has No Moral Precepts these belong to Plato & Seneca & Nero

[P 109] Two precepts you particularize as inconsistent with the dignity and the nature of man—that of not resenting injuries, and that of loving enemies.

Well done Paine

Who but yourself ever interpreted literally. . . . Did Jesus himself turn the other *cheek when the officer of the high priest smote* him?

Yes I have no doubt he did

It is evident, that a patient acquiescence under *slight* personal injuries is here enjoined; . . .

O Fool Slight Hypocrite & Villain

[P 117] The importance of revelation . . . apparent . . . by the discordant sentiments of learned and good men (for I speak not of the *ignorant and immoral*) on this point.

O how Virtuous Christ came not to call the Virtuous

[P 118] . . . if we are to live again, we are interested in knowing—whether it be possible for us to do any thing whilst we live here, . . .

Do or Act to Do Good or to do Evil who Dare to Judge but God alone

These are tremendous truths to bad men; . . .

Who does the Bishop call Bad Men Are they the Publicans & Sinners that Christ loved to associate with Does God Love The Righteous according to the Gospel or does he not cast them off.

The generality of unbelievers . . . [P 119] have neither ability, inclination, nor leisure, to enter into critical disquisitions concerning the truth of christianity.

[P 119] For who is really Righteous It is all Pretension

[P 120, last page of book]

It appears to me Now that Tom Paine is a better Christian than the Bishop

I have read this Book with attention & find that the Bishop has only hurt Paines heel while Paine has broken his head the Bishop has not answerd one of Paines grand objections

Annotations to Bacon's *Essays Moral, Economical and Political*

London, 1798

HALF-TITLE

Is it True or is it False that the Wisdom of this World is Foolishness with God

This is Certain If what Bacon says Is True what Christ says Is False If Caesar is Right Christ is Wrong both in Politics & Religion since they will divide them in Two

TITLE PAGE

Good Advice for Satans Kingdom

EDITOR'S PREFACE

PAGE i

I am astonishd how such Contemptible Knavery & Folly as this Book contains can ever have been calld Wisdom by Men of Sense but perhaps this never was the Case & all Men of Sense have despised the Book as Much as I do

Per WILLIAM BLAKE   t

PAGE iv Editor's Preface

But these Essays, written at a period of better taste, and on subjects of immediate importance to the conduct of common life "such as come home to men's *business and bosoms,*" are still read with pleasure. . . .

Erratum   to Mens Pockets

PAGE xii, blank

Every Body Knows that this is Epi[c]urus and Lucretius & Yet Every Body Says that it is Christian Philosophy how is this Possible   Every Body must be a Liar & deciever but Every Body does not do this   But The Hirelings of Kings & Courts who make themselves Every Body & Knowingly propagate Falshood

It was a Common opinion in the Court of Queen Elizabeth that Knavery Is Wisdom: Cunning Plotters were considerd as wise Machiavels

OF TRUTH

PAGE 1

Self Evident Truth is one Thing and Truth the result of Reasoning is another Thing Rational Truth is not the Truth of Christ but of Pilate   It is the Tree of the Knowledge of Good & Evil

What is truth? said jesting Pilate, and would not stay for an answer. Certainly there be that delight in giddiness, and count it a bondage to fix a belief; affecting free-will in thinking, as well as in acting: and, though the sects of philosophers of that kind be gone, yet there remain certain discoursing wits which are of the same veins, though there be not so much blood in them as was in those of the ancients.

But more Nerve if by Ancients he means Heathen Authors

But it is not only the difficulty and labour which men take in finding out of truth; nor again, that, when it is found, it imposeth upon men's thoughts, that doth bring lies in favour; [PAGE 2] but a natural, though corrupt love of the lie itself. One of the later school of the Grecians examineth the matter, and is at a stand to think what should be in it, that men should love lies, where neither they make for pleasure, as with poets; nor for advantage, as with the merchant; but for the lie's sake. But I cannot tell: this same truth is a naked and open daylight, that doth not shew the masques, and mummeries, and triumphs of the world half so stately and daintily as candlelights.

What Bacon calls Lies is Truth itself

PAGE 3 But howsoever these things are thus in men's depraved judgments and affections, yet truth, which only doth judge itself, teacheth that the inquiry of truth, which is the love-making, or wooing of it; the knowledge of truth, which is the presence of it; and the belief of truth, which is the enjoying of it, is the sovereign good of human nature. The first creature of God, in the works of the days, was the light of the sense; the last was the light of reason; and his sabbath work, ever since, is the illumination of his Spirit.

Pretence to Religion to destroy Religion

PAGE 4 To pass from theological and philosophical truth to the truth of civil business, it will be acknowledged; even by those that practise it not, that clear and round dealing is the honour of man's nature, and that mixture of falsehood is like allay in coin of gold and silver. . . .

Christianity is Civil Business Only There is & can Be No Other to Man what Else Can Be Civil is Christianity or Religion or whatever is Humane

PAGE 5 Surely the wickedness of falsehood and breach of faith cannot possibly be so highly expressed as in that it shall be the last peal to call the judgments of God upon the generations of men: it being foretold, that when "Christ cometh," he shall not "find faith upon earth".

Bacon put an End to Faith

OF DEATH

PAGES 5–6 You shall read in some of the friars books of mortification, that a man should think with himself what the pain is, if we have but his finger's end pressed, or tortured, and thereby imagine what the pains of death are when the whole body is corrupted and dissolved; when many times death passeth with less pain than the torture of a limb; for the most vital parts are not the quickest of sense: and by him that spake only as a philosopher and natural man, it was well said, "Pompa mortis magis terret, quam mors ipsa".

Bacon supposes all Men alike

PAGE 6 Revenge triumphs over death; love [s]lights it; honour aspireth to it; grief flieth to it; fear pre-occupieth it; nay, we read, after Otho the emperor had slain himself, pity (which is the tenderest of affections) provoked many to die out of mere compassion to their sovereign, and as the truest sort of followers.

One Mans Revenge or Love is not the same as Anothers The tender Mercies of some Men are Cruel

OF UNITY IN RELIGION

PAGE 8 Religion being the chief band of human society, it is a happy thing when itself is well contained within the true band of unity. The quarrels and divisions about religion were evils *unknown to the heathen.*

False O Satan

The reason was, because the religion of the heathen consisted rather in rites and ceremonies, than in any constant belief: for you may imagine what kind of faith theirs was, when the chief doctors and fathers of their church were the *poets.*

Prophets

PAGE 9 The fruits of unity (next unto the well-pleasing of God, which is all in all) are two; the one towards those that are without the church; the other towards those that are within. For the former, it is certain, that heresies and schisms are of all others the greatest scandals; yea, more than corruption of manners: for as in the natural body a wound or solution of continuity is worse than a corrupt humour, so in the spiritual: . . .

False

PAGES 9–10 The doctor of the Gentiles (the propriety of whose vocation drew him to have a special care of those without) saith, "If an heathen come in, and hear you speak with several tongues, will he not say that you are mad?" and, certainly, it is little better: when atheists and profane persons do hear of so many discordant and contrary opinions in religion, it doth avert them from the church, and maketh them "to sit down in the chair of the scorners". It is but a light thing to be vouched in so serious a matter, but yet it expresseth well the deformity.

Trifling Nonsense

PAGES 11–12 Men ought to take heed of rending God's church by two kinds of controversies; the one is, when the matter of the point controverted is too small and light, not worth the heat and strife about it, kindled only by contradiction; for, as it is noted by one of the fathers, Christ's coat indeed had no seam, but the church's vesture was of divers colours; whereupon he saith, "in veste varietas sit, scissura non sit", they be two things, unity and uniformity: the other is when the matter of the point controverted is great, but it is driven to an over-great subtilty and obscurity, so that it becometh a thing rather ingenious than substantial.

Lame Reasoning upon Premises This Never can Happen

PAGE 14 It was great blasphemy when the devil said, "I will ascend and be like the Highest"; but it is greater blasphemy to personate God, and bring him in saying, "I will descend, and be like the prince of darkness."

Did not Jesus descend & become a Servant The Prince of darkness is a Gentleman & not a Man he is a Lord Chancellor

OF REVENGE

PAGE 17 This is certain, that a man that studieth revenge keeps his own wounds green, which otherwise would heal and do well. Public revenges are for the most part fortunate.

A Lie

OF SIMULATION AND DISSIMULATION

PAGE 22 In a few words, mysteries are due to secrecy. Besides (to say truth) nakedness is uncomely, as well in mind as in body.

This is Folly Itself

OF ENVY

PAGE 32 A man that hath no virtue in himself ever envieth virtue in others: for men's minds will either feed upon their own good, or upon others evil; and who wanteth the one will prey upon the other; and whoso is out of hope to attain to another's virtue, will seek to come at even hand by depressing another's fortune.

What do these Knaves mean by Virtue   Do they mean War & its horrors & its Heroic Villains

PAGE 37 Lastly, to conclude this part, as we said in the beginning that the act of envy had somewhat in it of witchcraft, so there is no other cure of envy but the cure of witchcraft; and that is, to remove the lot, (as they call it), and to lay it upon another; for which purpose, the wiser sort of great persons bring in ever upon the stage somebody upon whom to derive the envy that would come upon themselves.

Politic Foolery & most contemptible Villainy & Murder

Now to speak of public envy: there is yet some good in public envy, whereas in private there is none; for public envy is as an ostracism, that eclipseth men when they grow too great.

Foolish & tells into the hands of a Tyrant

PAGE 38 This public envy seemeth to beat [bear] chiefly upon principle officers or ministers, rather than upon kings and estates themselves.

A Lie   Every Body hates a King   Bacon was afraid to say that the Envy was upon a King but is This Envy   or Indignation

OF GREAT PLACE

PAGE 44 But power to do good is the true and lawful end of aspiring; for good thoughts (though God accept them), yet towards men are little better than good dreams, except they be put in act.

Thought is Act. Christs Acts were Nothing to Caesars if this is not so

PAGE 45 In the discharge of thy place set before thee the best examples; for imitation is a globe of precepts; and after a time set before thee thine own example; and examine thyself strictly whether thou didst not best at first.

Here is nothing of Thy own Original Genius but only Imitation what Folly

PAGE 48 Be not too sensible or too remembering of thy place in conversation and private answers to suitors, but let it rather be said, "When he sits in place he is another man."

A Flogging Magistrate I have seen many such fly blows of Bacon

OF GOODNESS AND GOODNESS OF NATURE

PAGE 54 And beware how in making the portrait thou breakest the pattern: for divinity maketh the love of ourselves the pattern; the love of our neighbours but the portraiture: "Sell all thou hast, and give it to the poor, and follow me:" but sell not all thou hast, except thou come and follow me; that is except thou have a vocation wherein thou mayest do as much good with little means as great.

Except is Christ You Lie Except did anyone <ever> do this & not follow Christ who Does by Nature

PAGE 55
[A drawing of] The devils arse [with a chain of excrement ending in] A King

OF A KING

PAGE 56 A king is a mortal god on earth, unto whom the living God hath lent his own name as a great honour.

O Contemptible & Abject Slave

PAGE 58 That king which is not feared is not loved; and he that is well seen in his craft must as well study to be feared as loved; yet not loved for fear, but feared for love.

Fear Cannot Love

PAGE 60 He then that honoureth him [the King] not is next an atheist, wanting the fear of God in his heart.

Blasphemy

OF NOBILITY

PAGE 60 We will speak of nobility first as a portion of an estate, then as a condition of particular persons.

Is Nobility a portion of a State i.e Republic

A monarchy, where there is no nobility at all, is ever a pure and absolute tyranny, as that of the Turks; for nobility attempers sovereignty, and draws the eyes of the people somewhat aside from the line royal: but for *democracies they need* it not; and they are *commonly more quiet, and less* subject to sedition, than where there are stirps of nobles.

Self Contradiction Knave & Fool

PAGE 62 Those that are first raised to nobility, are commonly more virtuous, but less innocent than their descendants; for there is rarely any rising but by a commixture of good and evil arts.

Virtuous I supposed to be Innocents was I Mistaken or is Bacon a Liar

On the other side, nobility extinguisheth the passive envy from others towards them, because they are in possession of honour. Certainly, kings that have able men of their nobility shall find ease in employing them, and a better slide into their business; but people naturally bend to them as born in some sort to command.

Nonsense

OF SEDITIONS AND TROUBLES

PAGE 63

This Section contradicts the Preceding

Shepherds of all people had need know the calendars of tempests in state, which are commonly greatest when things grow to *equality*.

What Shepherds does he mean Such as Christ describes by Ravening Wolves

PAGE 65 Also, when discords, and quarrels, and factions are carried openly and audaciously it is a sign the reverence of government is lost.

When the Reverence of Government is Lost it is better than when it is found Reverence is all For Reverence

PAGE 66 So when any of the four pillars of government are mainly shaken, or weakened, (which are religion, justice, counsel, and treasure,) men had need to pray for fair weather.

Four Pillars of different heights and Sizes

Concerning the materials of sedition, it is a thing well to be considered. . . . The matter of sedition is of two kinds, much poverty and much discontentment.

These are one Kind Only

PAGE 67 As for discontentments, they are in the politic body like to humours in the natural, which are apt to gather a preternatural heat and to enflame; and let no prince measure the danger of them by this, whether they be just or unjust.

A Tyrant is the Worst disease & the Cause of all others

. . . in great oppressions, the same things that provoke the patience, do withal mate the courage.

a lie

PAGES 68–69 The first remedy or prevention is to remove by all means possible that material cause of sedition whereof we speak, which is want and poverty in the estate; to which purpose serveth the opening and well balancing of trade; the cherishing of manufactures; the banishing of idleness; the repressing of waste and excess by sumptuary laws; the improvement and husbanding of the soil; the regulating of prices of things vendible; the moderating of taxes and tributes, and the like.

You cannot regulate the price of Necessaries without destruction All False

PAGES 69–70 It is likewise to be remembered, that forasmuch as the increase of any estate must be upon the foreigner, (for whatsoever is somewhere gotten is somewhere lost,) there be but three things which one nation selleth unto another: the commodity as nature yieldeth it; the manufacture; and the vecture or carriage: so that if these two [three] wheels go, wealth will flow as in a spring tide.

The Increase of a State as of a Man is from Internal Improvement or Intellectual Acquirement. Man is not Improved by the hurt of another States are not Improved at the Expense of Foreigners

Bacon has no notion of any thing but Mammon

PAGE 71 The poets feign that the rest of the gods would have bound Jupiter, which he hearing of by the counsel of Pallas, sent for Briareus with his hundred hands to come in to his aid: an emblem, no doubt, to shew how safe it is for monarchs to make sure of the good will of common people.

Good Advice for the Devil

PAGES 71–72 Certainly, the politic and artificial nourishing and entertaining of hopes, and carrying men from hopes to hopes is one of the best antidotes against the poison of discontentments.

Subterfuges

PAGE 74 Lastly, let princes against all events, not be without some great person, one or rather more, of military valour, near unto them, for the repression of seditions in their beginnings.

Contemptible Knave Let the People look to this

. . . but let such military persons be assured and well reputed of, rather than factious and popular.

Factious is Not Popular & never can be except Factious is Christianity

OF ATHEISM

PAGE 75 I had rather believe all the fables in the Legend, and the Talmud, and the Alcoran than that this universal frame is without a *mind*: and, therefore, God never wrought miracle to convince atheism, because his ordinary works convince it.

The Devil is the Mind of the Natural Frame

It is true that a little philosophy inclineth man's mind to atheism; but depth in philosophy bringeth men's minds about to religion; for while the mind of man looketh upon second causes scattered, it may sometimes rest in them and go no farther.

There is no Such Thing as a Second Cause nor as a Natural Cause for any Thing in any Way

PAGE 76

He who says there are Second Causes has already denied a First The Word Cause is a foolish Word

PAGE 77 The contemplative atheist is rare, a Diagoras, a Bion, a Lucian perhaps, and some others.

A Lie! Few believe it is a New Birth   Bacon was a Contemplative Atheist Evidently an Epicurean Lucian disbelievd Heathen Gods he did not perhaps disbelieve for all that   Bacon did

PAGES 77–78–79 The causes of atheism are, divisions in religion, if they be many; . . . another is, scandal of priests . . . : a third is, a custom of profane scoffing in holy matters . . . ; and, lastly, learned times, especially with peace and prosperity; for troubles and *adversities* do more bow men's minds to religion.

a Lie

They that deny a God destroy man's nobility; for certainly man is of kin to the beasts by his body; and, if he be not of kin to God by his spirit, he is a base and ignoble creature. [Bracketed by Blake]

an artifice

It destroys likewise magnanimity, and the raising of human nature; for take an example of a dog, and mark what a generosity and courage he will put on when he finds himself maintained by a man, who to him is instead of a God, or "melior natura"; which courage is manifestly such as that creature, without that confidence of a better nature than his own, could never attain;

Self Contradiction

. . . therefore, as atheism is in all respects hateful, so in this, that it depriveth human nature of the means to exalt itself above human frailty.

An Atheist pretending to talk against Atheism

OF SUPERSTITION

PAGE 79 It were better to have no opinion of God at all, than such an opinion as is unworthy of him.

Is this true   is it better

PAGE 80 . . . as the contumely is greater *towards God, so the danger* is greater towards men. Atheism *leaves* a man to sense, to philosophy, to natural *piety,* to laws, to reputation; all which may *be guides* to an outward moral virtue, though religion were not;

Praise of Atheism

but superstition dismounts all these, and erecteth an absolute monarchy in the minds of men: *therefore atheism* did *never perturb* states; for it makes men wary of themselves, as looking no farther, and we see the times inclined to atheism, (as the time of Augustus Caesar,) were civil times.

Atheism is thus the best of all Bacon fools us

The master of superstition is the people, and in all superstition wise men follow fools; and arguments are fitted to practise in a reversed order.

What must our Clergy be who Allow Bacon to be Either Wise or even of Common Capacity   I cannot

PAGE 82 There is a superstition in avoiding superstition, when men think to do best if they go farthest from the superstition formerly received; therefore care should be had that, (as it fareth in ill purgings,) the good be not taken away with the bad, which commonly is done when the *people* is the reformer.

Who is to be the Reformer Bacons [Reformer] Villain is a King or Who   t

OF TRAVEL

PAGE 83 The things to be seen and observed are the courts of princes, especially when they give audience to ambassadors; the courts of justice . . . the churches and monasteries . . . the walls and fortifications . . . and so the havens and harbours, antiquities and ruins, libraries, colleges, disputations, and lectures where any are; shipping and navies; houses and gardens of state and pleasure near great cities; armories, arsenals, magazines, exchanges, burses, warehouses, exercises of horsemanship, fencing, training of soldiers, and the like; comedies . . . treasures of jewels and robes; cabinets and rarieties; . . .

The Things worthy to be seen are all the Trumpery he could rake together

Nothing of Arts or Artists or Learned Men or of Agriculture or any Useful Thing His Business & Bosom was to be Lord Chancellor

PAGE 84 As for triumphs, masks, feasts, weddings, funerals, capital executions, and such shews, men need not to be put in mind of them; yet are they not to be neglected.

Bacon supposes that the Dragon Beast & Harlot are worthy of a Place in the New Jerusalem Excellent Traveller Go on & be damnd

If you will have a young man to put his travel into a little room, and in short time to gather much, this you must do . . . let him not stay long in one city or town, more or less as the place deserveth, but not long; nay, when he stayeth in one city or town, let him change his lodging from one end and part of the town to another, which is a great adamant of acquaintance;

Harum Scarum who can do this

let him sequester himself from the company of his countrymen and diet in such places where there is good company of the nation where he travelleth; let him upon his removes from one place to another procure recommendation to some person of *quality* residing in the place whither he removeth . . .

The Contrary is the best Advice

PAGE 85 As for the acquaintance which is to be sought in travel, that which is most of all profitable is acquaintance with the secretaries and employed men of ambassadors.

Acquaintance with Knaves

OF EMPIRE

PAGE 86 It is a miserable state of mind to have few things to desire, and many things to fear.

He who has few Things to desire cannot have many to fear

PAGE 87 . . . the mind of man is more cheered and refreshed by profiting in small things, than by standing at a stay in great.

A lie

OF COUNSEL

PAGE 98 For weakening of authority the fable sheweth the remedy: nay, the majesty of kings is rather exalted than diminished when they are in the chair of council; neither was there ever prince bereaved of his dependances by his council, except where there hath been either an over-greatness in one counsellor, or an overstrict combination in divers, which are things soon found and holpen. [Bracketed]

Did he mean to Ridicule a King & his Council

PAGE 101 In choice of committees for ripening business for the council, it is better to choose indifferent persons, than to make an indifferency by putting in those that are strong on both sides.

better choose Fools at once

OF CUNNING

PAGE 104 There be that can pack the cards, and yet cannot play well; so there are some that are good in canvasses and factions, that are otherwise weak men.

Nonsense

Again, it is one thing to understand persons, and another thing to understand matters; for many are perfect in men's humours that are not greatly capable of the real part of business, which is the constitution of one that hath studied men more than books.

Nonsense

Such men are fitter for practice than for counsel, and they are good but in their own ally.

How absurd

PAGE 105 If a man would cross a business that he doubts some other would handsomely and effectually move, let him pretend to wish it well, and move it himself in such sort as may soil it.

None but a Fool can act so

PAGES 106–107 I knew one that, when he wrote a letter, he would put that which was most material in the post-script, as if it had been a bye matter.

I knew another that, when he came to have speech, he would pass over that that he intended most; and go forth, and come back again, and speak of it as of a thing that he had almost forgot.

What Fools

PAGES 107–108 It is a point of cunning to let fall those words in a man's own name which he would have another man learn and use, and thereupon take advantage. I knew two that were competitors for the secretary's place in queen Elizabeth's time, . . . and the one of them said, that to be a secretary in the declination of a monarchy was a ticklish thing, and that he did not affect it: the other straight caught up those words, and discoursed with divers of his friends, that he had no reason to desire to be secretary in the declination of a monarchy. The first man took hold of it, and found means it was told the queen; who hearing of a declination of a monarchy took it so ill, as she would never after hear of the other's suit.

This is too stupid to have been True

OF INNOVATIONS

PAGE 113 As the births of living creatures at first are ill shapen, so are all innovations, which are the births of time.

What a Cursed Fool is this   Ill Shapen   are Infants or small Plants ill shapen because they are not yet come to their maturity   What a contemptible Fool is This Bacon

OF FRIENDSHIP

PAGES 123–124 L. Sylla, when he commanded Rome, raised Pompey . . . to that height, that Pompey vaunted himself for Sylla's over-match; . . . With Julius Caesar Decimus Brutus had obtained that interest as he set him down in his testament for heir in remainder after his nephew; . . . Augustus raised Agrippa, (though of mean birth,) to that height, as, when he consulted with Mecaenas about the marriage of his daughter Julia, Mecaenas took the liberty to tell him, that he must either marry his daughter to Agrippa, or take away his life.

The Friendship of these Roman Villains is a strange Example to alledge for our imitation & approval

OF EXPENSE

PAGE 133 Certainly, if a man will keep but of even hand, his ordinary expenses ought to be but to the half of his receipts; and if he think to wax rich, but to the third part.

If this is advice to the Poor, it is mocking them—If to the Rich, it is worse still it is The Miser If to the Middle Class it is the direct Contrary to Christs advice

PAGE 134 He that can look into his estate but seldom, it behoveth him to turn all to certainties.

Nonsense

OF THE TRUE GREATNESS OF KINGDOMS AND ESTATES

PAGE 135 The speech of Themistocles the Athenian, which was haughty and arrogant in taking so much to himself, had been a grave and wise observation and censure, applied at large to others. Desired at a feast to touch a lute, he said, "he could not fiddle, but yet he could make a small town a great city". These words, (holpen with a little metaphor,) may express two differing abilities in those that deal in business of estate.

a Lord Chancellor's opinions as different from Christ as those of Caiphas or Pilate or Herod   what such Men call Great is indeed detestable

PAGE 136 . . . let us speak of the work; that is, the true greatness of kingdoms and estates; and the means thereof. An argument fit for great and mighty *princes* to have in their hand; to the end, that neither by over-measuring their forces they lose themselves in vain enterprises . . .

Princes Powers
Powers of darkness

PAGE 137 The Kingdom of heaven is compared, not to any great Kernal or nut but, to a grain of mustard seed; which is one of the least grains, but hath in it a property and spirit hastily to get up and spread.

The Kingdom of Heaven is the direct Negation of Earthly domination

PAGES 137–138 Walled towns, stored arsenals and armories, goodly races of horse, chariots of war, elephants, ordnance, artillery, and the like; all this is but a sheep in lion's skin, except the breed and disposition of the people be stout and warlike. Nay, number (itself) in armies importeth not much, where the people is of weak courage. . . . The army of the Persians, in the plains of Arbela was such a vast sea of people as it did somewhat astonish the commanders in Alexander's army, who came to him therefore, and wished him to set upon them by night; but he answered, he would not pilfer the victory; and the defeat was easy.

Bacon knows the Wisdom of War   if it is Wisdom

PAGE 142 Never any state was, in this point, so open to receive strangers into their body as were the Romans; therefore it sorted with them accordingly, for they grew to the *greatest monarchy.*

Is this Great   Is this Christian   No

PAGES 143–144 It is certain, that sedentary and within-door arts, and delicate manufactures, (that require rather the finger than the arm,) have in their nature a contrariety to a military disposition; . . . therefore it was great advantage in the ancient states of Sparta, Athens, Rome, and others that they had the use of slaves, which commonly did rid those manufactures; but that is abolished, in greatest part, by the christian law. That which cometh nearest to it is, to leave those arts chiefly to strangers . . . and to contain the principal bulk of the vulgar natives within those three kinds, tillers of the ground, free servants, and handicraftmen of strong and manly arts; as smiths, masons, carpenters, &c. not reckoning professed soldiers.

Bacon calls Intellectual Arts Unmanly   Poetry Painting Music are in his opinion Useless & so they are for Kings & Wars & shall in the End Annihilate them

PAGE 147 No body can be healthful without exercise, neither natural body nor politic: and, certainly, to a kingdom or estate a just and honourable war is the true exercise.

Is not this the Greatest Folly

PAGE 149 There be now, for martial encouragement, some degrees and orders of chivalry, which, nevertheless, are conferred promiscuously upon soldiers and no soldiers, and some remembrance perhaps upon the escutcheon . . .

what can be worse than this or more foolish

OF REGIMEN OF HEALTH

PAGE 151 . . . strength of nature in youth passeth over many excesses which are owing a man till his age.

Excess in Youth is Necessary to Life

Beware of sudden change in any great point of diet, and if necessity enforce it, fit the rest to it;

Nonsense

for it is a secret both in nature and state, that it is safer to change many things than one.

False

PAGE 152 If you fly physic in health altogether, it will be too strange for your body when you shall need it.

Very Pernicious Advice

The work of a Fool to use Physic but for Necessity

PAGE 153 In sickness, respect health principally; and in health, action: for those that put their bodies to endure in health, may in most sicknesses which are not very sharp, be cured only with diet and tendering.

Those that put their Bodies To endure are Fools

Celsus could never have spoken it as a physician, had he not been a wise man withal, when he giveth it for one of the great precepts of health and lasting, that a man do vary and interchange contraries;

Celsus was a bad adviser

but with an inclination to the more benign extreme: use fasting and full eating, but rather full eating; watching and sleep, but rather sleep; sitting and exercise, but rather exercise, and the like: so shall nature be cherished, and yet taught masteries. [Bracketed]

Nature taught to Ostentation

OF SUSPICION

PAGE 154 Suspicions amongst thoughts are like bats amongst birds, they ever fly by twilight; certainly they are to be repressed, or, at the least, well guarded.

What is Suspition in one Man is Caution in Another & Truth or Discernment in Another & in Some it is Folly.

OF DISCOURSE

PAGE 156 Some in their discourse desire rather commendation of wit, in being able to hold all arguments, than of judgment, in discerning what is true; as if it were a praise to know what might be said, and not what should be thought.

Surely the Man who wrote this never talkd to any but Coxcombs

PAGE 158 Discretion of speech is more than eloquence; and to speak agreeably to him with whom we deal, is more than to speak in good words, or in good order.

Bacon hated Talents of all Kinds Eloquence is discret[io]n of Speech

OF RICHES

PAGE 169 Be not penny-wise; riches have wings, and sometimes they fly away of themselves, sometimes they must be set flying to bring in more.

Bacon was always a poor Devil if History says true   how should one so foolish know about Riches Except Pretence to be Rich   if that is it

OF NATURE IN MEN

PAGE 182 Neither is the ancient rule amiss, to bend nature as a wand to a contrary extreme, whereby to set it right; understanding it where the contrary extreme is no vice.

Very Foolish

OF FORTUNE

PAGE 187 It cannot be denied but outward accidents conduce much to fortune; favour, opportunity, death of others, occasion fitting virtue; but chiefly, the mould of a man's fortune is in his own hands.

What is Fortune but an outward Accident for a few years sixty at most & then gone

OF USURY

PAGE 190
Bacon was a Usurer

PAGE 191 The discommodities of usury are, first, that it makes fewer merchants; for were it not for this lazy trade of usury, money would not lie still, but would in great part be employed upon merchandizing.
A Lie it makes Merchants & nothing Else

PAGE 192 On the other side, the commodities of usury are first, that howsoever usury in some respect hindereth merchandizing, yet in some other it advanceth it.
Commodities of Usury can it Be

PAGE 193 I remember a cruel monied man in the country, that would say, "The devil take this usury, it keeps us from forfeitures of mortgages and bonds".
It is not True what a Cruel Man says

To speak now of the reformation and reglement of usury; how the discommodities of it may be best avoided, and the commodities retained.
Bacon is in his Element on Usury it is himself & his Philosophy

OF YOUTH AND AGE

PAGE 197 The errors of young men are the ruin of business; but the errors of aged men amount but to this, that more might have been done, or sooner.
Bacons Business is not Intellect or Art

PAGE 198 . . . and age doth profit rather in the powers of understanding, than in the virtues of the will and affections.
a Lie

PAGE 199 There be some have an over-early ripeness in their years, which fadeth betimes: these are, first, such as have brittle wits, the edge whereof is soon turned; such as was Hermogenes the rhetorician, whose books are exceeding subtile, who afterwards waxed stupid.
Such was Bacon Stupid Indeed

OF DEFORMITY

PAGE 202 Certainly there is a consent between the body and the mind, and where nature erreth in the one, she ventureth in the other.
False
Contemptible

Whosoever hath any thing fixed in his person that doth induce contempt, hath also a perpetual spur in himself to rescue and deliver himself from scorn; therefore all deformed persons are extreme bold.
Is not this Very Very Contemptible Contempt is the Element of the Contemptible

PAGE 203 Kings in ancient times (and at this present in some countries,) were wont to put great trust in eunuchs, because they that are envious towards all are more obnoxious and officious towards one.
because Kings do it is it Wisdom

OF BUILDING

PAGE 206 First, therefore, I say you cannot have a perfect *palace*, except you have two several sides; a side for the banquet, as is spoken of in the book of Esther, and a side for the household.

What Trifling Nonsense & Self Conceit

OF FACTION

PAGE 235 The even carriage between two factions proceedeth not always of moderation, but of a trueness to a man's self, with end to make use of both. Certainly, in Italy they hold it a little suspect in popes, when they have often in their mouth "Padre commune"; and take it to be a sign of one that meaneth to refer all to the greatness of his own house.

None but God is This

PAGES 235–236 Kings had need beware how they side themselves . . . The motions of factions under Kings, ought to be like the motions, (as the astronomers speak,) of the inferior orbs; which may have their proper motions, but yet still are quietly carried by the higher motion of "primum mobile".

King James was Bacons Primum Mobile

OF CEREMONIES AND RESPECTS

PAGE 236 . . . for the proverb is true, "That light gains make heavy purses"; for light gains come thick, whereas great come but now and then: so it is true, that *small matters* win great commendation, because they are continually in use and in note.

Small matters What are They   Caesar seems to me a Very Small Matter & so he seemd to Jesus   is the Devil Great Consider

OF PRAISE

PAGE 239 Praise is the reflection of virtue; but it is as the glass or body which giveth the reflection: if it be from the *common people,* it is commonly false and nought, and rather followeth vain persons, than virtuous.

Villain   did Christ Seek the Praise of the Rulers

Annotations to Boyd's *Historical Notes* on Dante ᵗ

Dublin, 1785

A COMPARATIVE VIEW OF THE INFERNO, WITH SOME OTHER POEMS RELATIVE TO THE ORIGINAL PRINCIPLES OF HUMAN NATURE

PAGE 35 [*But*] the most daring flights of fancy, the most accurate delineations of character, and the most artful conduct of fable, are [*not, even*] when combined together, sufficient of themselves to make a poem interesting. [Deletions by Blake]

PAGES 35–36 The discord of Achilles and Agamemnon may produce the most tragical consequences; but if we, who are cool and impartial in the affair . . . cannot enter warmly into the views of either party, the story, though adorned with all the genius of an Homer, will be read by us with some degree of nonchalance. The superstitions that led the Crusaders to rescue the Holy Land from the Infidels, instead of interesting us, appear frigid, if not ridiculous. We cannot be much concerned for the fate of such a crew of fanatics, notwithstanding the magic numbers of a Tasso . . . we cannot sympathise with Achilles for the loss of his Mistress, when we feel that he gained her by the massacre of her family.

nobody considers these things when they read Homer or Shakespear or Dante

PAGE 37 When a man, where no interest is concerned, no provocation given, lays a whole nation in blood merely for his glory; we, to whom his glory is indifferent, cannot enter into his resentment.

false All poetry gives the lie to this

PAGES 37–38 Such may be good poetical characters, of that mixt kind that Aristotle admits; but the most beautiful mixture of light and shade has no attraction unless it warms <or freezes> the heart. It must have something that engages the sympathy, something that appeals to the [moral sense] <passions & senses>; for nothing can thoroughly captivate the fancy, however artfully delineated, that does not awake the sympathy and interest the passions [that enlist on the side of Virtue] and appeal to our native notions of right and wrong. [Deletions and insertions by Blake]

PAGES 38–39 It is this that sets the Odyssey, in point of sentiment, so far above the Iliad. We feel the injuries of Ulysses; . . . we seem to feel the generous indignation of the young Telemachus, and we tremble at the dangers of the fair Penelope . . . we can go along with the resentment of Ulysses, because it is just, but our feelings must tell us that Achilles carries his resentment to a savage length, a length where we cannot follow him.

If Homers merit was only in these Historical combinations & Moral sentiments he would be no better than Clarissa

PAGES 39–40 ILIACOS EXTRA MUROS PECCATUR; ET INTRA. It is a contest between barbarians, equally guilty of injustice, rapine, and bloodshed; and we are not sorry to see the vengeance of Heaven equally inflicted on both parties.

Homer meant this

Aeneas indeed is a more amiable personage than Achilles; he seems meant for a perfect character. But compare his conduct with respect to Dido with the self-denial of Dryden's Cleomenes, or with the conduct of Titus in the Berenice of Racine, we will then see what is meant by making a character interesting.

Every body naturally hates a perfect character because they are all greater Villains than the imperfect as Eneas is here shewn a worse man than Achilles in leaving Dido

PAGES 45–46 Antecedent to and independent of all laws, a man may learn to argue on the nature of moral obligation, and the duty of universal benevolence, from Cumberland, Wollaston, Shaftesbury, Hutcheson; but would he feel what vice is in itself . . . let him enter into the passions of Lear, when he feels the ingratitude of his children; of Hamlet, when he learns the story of his father's murder; . . . and he will know the difference of right and wrong much more clearly than from all the moralists that ever wrote.

the grandest Poetry is Immoral the Grandest characters Wicked. Very Satan. Capanius Othello a murderer. Prometheus. Jupiter. Jehovah, Jesus a wine bibber

Cunning & Morality are not Poetry but Philosophy the Poet is Independent & Wicked the Philosopher is Dependent & Good

Poetry is to excuse Vice & shew its reason & necessary purgation

PAGE 49 The industrious knave cultivates the soil; the indolent good man leaves it uncultivated. Who ought to reap the harvest? . . . The natural course of things decides in favour of the villain; the natural sentiments of men in favour of the man of virtue.

false

PAGES 56–57 As to those who think the notion of a future Life arose from the descriptions and inventions of the Poets, they may just as well suppose that eating and drinking had the same original . . . The Poets indeed altered the genuine sentiments of nature, and tinged the Light of Reason by introducing the wild conceits of Fancy . . . But still the root was natural, though the fruit was wild. All that *nature teaches* is, that there is a future life, distinguished into different states of happiness and misery.

False

Nature Teaches nothing of Spiritual Life but only of Natural Life

HISTORICAL ESSAY OF THE STATE OF AFFAIRS
IN THE THIRTEENTH AND FOURTEENTH CENTURIES:
WITH RESPECT TO THE HISTORY OF FLORENCE

PAGE 118 . . . horrors of a civil war. †—Dante was at this time Prior of Florence and it was he who gave the advice, *ruinous to himself,* and *pernicious to his native country,* of calling in the heads of the two factions to Florence.

† Dante was a Fool or his Translator was Not   That is Dante was Hired or Tr was Not

It appears to Me that Men are hired to Run down Men of Genius under the Mask of Translators, but Dante gives too much Caesar he is not a Republican

Dante was an Emperors <a Caesars> Man   Luther also left the Priest & joind the Soldier

PAGES 129–130 The fervours of religion have often actuated the passions to deeds of the wildest fanaticism. The booted Apostles of Germany, and the Crusards of Florence, carried their zeal to a very guilty degree. But the passion for any thing laudable will hardly carry men to a proper pitch, unless it be so strong as sometimes to push them beyond the golden mean.

How very Foolish all this Is

PAGE 131 Such were the effects of intolerance even in the extreme. In a more moderate degree, every well-regulated government, both ancient and modern, were *so far intolerant,* as not to admit the pollutions of every superstition and *every pernicious opinion.* It was from a regard to the morals of the people, that the Roman Magistrates expelled the Priest of Bacchus, in the first and most virtuous ages of the republic. It was on this principle that the *Persians* destroyed the *temples of Greece wherever they came.*

If Well regulated Governments act so who can tell so well as the hireling Writer whose praise is contrary to what he Knows to be true

Persians destroy the Temples & are praised for it

PAGES 133–134 The Athenians and Romans kept a watchful eye, not only over the grosser superstitions, but over impiety . . . Polybius plainly attributes the fall of freedom in Greece to the prevalence of atheism . . . It was not till the republic was verging to its fall, that Caesar dared in open senate to laugh at the SPECULATIVE opinion of a future state. These were the times of universal toleration, when every pollution, from every clime, flowed to Rome, whence they had carefully been kept out before.

What is Liberty without Universal Toleration

PAGES 135–136 I leave it to these who are best acquainted with the spirit of antiquity, to determine whether a species of religion . . . had or had not a very principal share in raising those celebrated nations to the summit of their glory: their decline and fall, at least, may be fairly attributed to irreligion, and to the want of some general standard of morality, whose authority they all allowed and to which they all appealed. The want of this pole-star left them adrift in the boundless ocean of conjecture; the disputes of their philosophers were endless, and their opinions of the grounds of morality were as different as their conditions, their tastes and their pursuits.

Yet simple country Hinds are Moral Enthusiasts Indignant against Knavery without a Moral criterion other than Native Honesty untaught while other country Hinds are as indignant against honesty & Enthusiasts for Cunning & Artifice

PAGE 148 . . . but there are certain *bounds* even to *liberty.* . . .

If it is thus the extreme of black is white & of sweet sower & of good Evil & of Nothing Something

꙳

Annotations to *The Works of Sir Joshua Reynolds,* ᵗ
edited by Edmond Malone. London, 1798

TITLE PAGE

This Man was Hired to Depress Art   This is the opinion of Will Blake my Proofs of this Opinion are given in the following Notes

<Advice of the Popes who succeeded the Age of Rafael>
Degrade first the Arts if you'd Mankind degrade,
Hire Idiots to Paint with cold light & hot shade:
Give high Price for the worst, leave the best in disgrace,
And with Labours of Ignorance fill every place.

[BACK OF TITLE PAGE]

Having spent the Vigour of my Youth & Genius under the Opression of Sʳ Joshua & his Gang of Cunning Hired Knaves Without Employment & as much as could possibly be Without Bread, The Reader must Expect to Read in all my Remarks on these Books Nothing but Indignation & Resentment While Sʳ Joshua was rolling in Riches Barry was Poor & [*Independent*] <Unemployd except by his own Energy> Mortimer was [*despised & Mocked*] <calld a Madman> [*I now despise & Mock in turn although Suffring Neglect*] <& only Portrait Painting applauded & rewarded by the Rich & Great.> Reynolds & Gainsborough Blotted & Blurred one against the other & Divided all the English World between them   Fuseli Indignant <almost> hid himself—I [*was*] <am> hid

[CONTENTS PAGES]

The Arts & Sciences are the Destruction of Tyrannies or Bad Governments Why should A Good Government endeavour to Depress What is its Chief & only Support

The Foundation of Empire is Art & Science   Remove them or Degrade them & the Empire is No More—Empire follows Art & Not Vice Versa as Englishmen suppose

On peut dire que le Pape Léon Xme en encourageant les Études donna les armes contre lui-même. J'ai ouï dire à un Seigneur Anglais qu'il avait vu une Lettre du Seigneur Polus, ou de La Pole, depuis Cardinal, à ce Pape; dans laquelle, en le félicitant sur ce qu'il etendait le progrès de Science en Europe, il l'avertissait *qu'il était dangereux de rendre les hommes trop Savans*—

VOLTAIRE, Moeurs de[s] Nations, Tome 4

O Englishmen! why are you still of this foolish Cardinals opinion?

Much copying discountenanced

To learn the Language of Art Copy for Ever. is My Rule

[BLANK PAGE FACING DEDICATION]
Who will Dare to Say that [*Fine*] <Polite> Art is Encouraged, or Either Wished or Tolerated in a Nation where The Society for the Encouragement of Art. Sufferd Barry to Give them, his Labour for Nothing A Society Composed of the Flower of the English Nobility & Gentry—[*A Society*] Suffering an Artist to Starve while he Supported Really what They under pretence of Encouraging were Endeavouring to Depress.—Barry told me that while he Did that Work—he Lived on Bread & Apples

[P i]
O Society for Encouragement of Art—O King & Nobility of England! Where have you hid Fuseli's Milton Is Satan troubled at his Exposure

TO THE KING.

The regular progress of cultivated life is from necessaries to accommodations, from accommodations to ornaments.

The Bible says That Cultivated Life. Existed First—Uncultivated Life. comes afterwards from Satans Hirelings[.] Necessaries Accomodations & Ornaments [*are Lifes Wants*] <are the whole of Life> [*First were Created Wine & Happiness ?Good ?Looks & Fortune*] Satan took away Ornament First. <Next he took away Accomodations & Then he became Lord & Master of> Necessaries [*last*]

[P ii]
To give advice to those who are contending for royal liberality, . . .

Liberality! We want not Liberality We want a Fair Price & Proportionate Value <& a General Demand for Art>

<Let not that Nation where Less than Nobility is the Reward. Pretend that Art is Encouraged by that Nation: Art is the First in Intellectuals & Ought to be First in Nations>

[P iii]
<Invention depends Altogether upon Execution or Organization. as that is right or wrong so is the Invention perfect or imperfect. Whoever is set to Undermine the Execution of Art is set to Destroy Art   Michael Angelos Art Depends on Michael Angelos Execution Altogether>

[P viii, Malone on Reynolds' boyhood:] . . . Richardson's Treatise on Painting; the perusal of which so delighted and inflamed his mind, that Raffaelle appeared to him superior to the most illustrious . . .

Why then did he not follow Rafaels Track

[P ix, note 7, quoting Walpole on Thomas Hudson, Reynolds' first master] The better taste introduced by Sir Joshua Reynolds, put an end to Hudson's reign, . . .

Hudson Drew Correctly

[P xiv: the keeper of the Vatican informed Reynolds that "the works of Raffaelle" frequently made "little impression" on visitors.]

Men who have been Educated with Works of Venetian Artists. under their Eyes Cannot see Rafael unless they are born with Determinate Organs

[Reynolds quoted:] . . . I remember very well my own disappointment, when I first visited the Vatican; . . .

I am happy I cannot say that Rafael Ever was from my Earliest Childhood hidden from Me. I saw & I Knew immediately the difference between Rafael & Rubens

[P xv]

> <Some look. to see the sweet Outlines
> And beauteous Forms that Love does wear
> Some look. to find out Patches. Paint.
> Bracelets & Stays & Powderd Hair>

[Reynolds:] . . . though disappointed and mortified at not finding myself enraptured with the works of this great master, I did not for a moment conceive or suppose that the name of Raffaelle, and those admirable paintings in particular, owed their reputation to the ignorance and prejudice of mankind; . . .

Here are Mocks on those who Saw Rafael [*But not Sir Joshua*]

. . . I felt my ignorance, and stood abashed.

A Liar he never was Abashed in his Life & never felt his Ignorance

[P xvi] . . . I was convinced that I had originally formed a false opinion of the perfection of art, . . .

All this Concession is to prove that Genius is Acquired as follows in the Next page

[P xvii] . . . I am now clearly of opinion, that a relish for the higher excellencies of art is an acquired taste, which no man ever possessed without long cultivation, and great labour . . .

[*Fool*]

. . . as if . . . our minds, like tinder, should instantly catch fire from the divine spark of Raffaelle's genius.

A Mock

. . . the excellence of his style . . . lies deep; and at the first view is seen but mistily.

A Mock

It is the florid style, which strikes at once, and captivates the eye for a time, . . .

A Lie The Florid Style such as the Venetian & the Flemish. Never Struck Me at Once nor At-All.

[P xviii]

[*to good Artists*] The Style that Strikes the Eye is the True Style But A Fools Eye is Not to be. a Criterion

I consider *general copying* (he adds) *as a delusive kind of industry:* . . .

Here he Condemns Generalizing which he almost always Approves & Recommends

[P xix] How incapable of producing any thing of their own, those are, who have spent most of their time in making finished copies, . . .

Finishd. What does he Mean Niggling Without the Correct <& Definite> Outline If he means That Copying Correctly is a hindrance he is a Liar. for that is the only School to the Language of Art

[P xxix] It is the thoughts expressed in the works of Michael Angelo, Correggio, Raffaelle, Parmegiano, and perhaps some of the old Gothick masters, . . . which we seek after with avidity.

Here is an Acknowledgment of all that I could wish But if it is True. Why are we to be told that Masters who Could Think had not the Judgment to Perform the Inferior Parts of Art as Reynolds artfully calls them. But that we are to Learn to Think from Great Masters & to Learn to Perform from Underlings? Learn to Design from Rafael & to Execute from Rubens [line cut away]?

[P xxxi] Thus Bacon became a great thinker, by first entering into and making himself master of the thoughts of other men.

[*This is the Character of a Knave*]

[PP xxxiii–xxxiv, Burke on Reynolds] . . . He . . . owed his first disposition to generalize . . . to old Mr. Mudge . . . a learned and venerable old man . . . much conversant in the Platonick Philosophy, . . . originally a dissenting minister; . . .

Slang   Villainy

[To call generalizing "the Platonick Philosophy" was Slang; for a dissenting minister to preach it was Villainy.—D.V.E.]

[PP xli–xlv, note 28: Malone scotching rumors that the Discourses were written by Johnson or Burke.]

The Contradictions in Reynolds's Discourses are Strong Presumptions that they are the Work of Several Hands   But this is no Proof that Reynolds did not Write them   The Man Either Painter or Philosopher who Learns or Acquires all he Knows from Others. Must be full of Contradictions

[P xlvii, Reynolds' eulogy of George Moser as "the FATHER of the present race of Artists".]

I was once looking over the Prints from Rafael & Michael Angelo. in the Library of the Royal Academy   Moser came to me & said   You should not Study these old Hard Stiff & Dry Unfinishd Works of Art, Stay a little & I will shew you what you should Study. He then went & took down Le Bruns & Rubens's Galleries   How I did secretly Rage.   I also spoke my Mind [line cut away]

I said to Moser, These things that you call Finishd are not Even Begun how can they then, be Finishd? The Man who does not know The Beginning, never can know the End of Art

[P xlix, Reynolds on his own "merits and defects"] I consoled myself . . . by remarking that these ready inventors, are extremely apt to acquiese *in imperfection;* . . .

Villainy a Lie

[P l] . . . Metastasio . . . complained of the great difficulty he found in attaining correctness, in consequence of having been in his youth an IMPROVVISATORE.

I do not believe this Anecdote

[P liii, from Reynolds' 11th Discourse] . . . the general effect of the whole. . . . requires the painter's entire mind; whereas the PARTS may be finishing by nice touches, while his mind is engaged on other matters: . . . indolence, . . .

A Lie Working up Effect is more an operation of Indolence than the Making out of the Parts: as far as Greatest is more than Least I speak here of Rembrandts & Rubenss & Reynolds's Effect.—For Real Effect. is Making out the Parts & it is Nothing Else but That

[P lvii, note 34, Malone on Reynolds' efforts to recover the secrets of the Venetian colourists] Our great painter . . . had undoubtedly attained a part of the ancient process used in the Venetian School; and by various methods of his own invention produced a similar, though perhaps not quite so brilliant an effect of colour.

Oil Colours will not Do—

Why are we told that Reynolds is a Great Colourist & yet inferior to the Venetians

[P lx, note 36] A notion prevails . . . that in the MAJORITY of his works the colours have entirely faded . . . ; but [most] have preserved their original hue, . . .

I do not think that the Change is so much in the Pictures as in the Opinions of the Public

[P lxx, note 38, quoting Dr Johnson in 1761] Reynolds is without a rival, and continues to add thousands to thousands.

How much did Barry Get

[P lxxii, Malone, on the French plundering] . . . of the most celebrated works of the Flemish School in the Netherlands (for I will not gratify our English republicans by calling it BELGIUM). . . .

[*why then gratify Flemish Knaves & Fools*]

[P lxxii] . . . he . . . devoted several days to contemplating the productions of that great painter [Rubens].

If Reynolds had Really admired Mich Angelo he never would have followd Rubens

[P lxxxiii, note 48 on the Literary Club] The original members were, Sir Joshua Reynolds, Dr. Johnson, Mr. Burke, Dr. Nugent, Mr. Langton, Mr. Antony Chamier, Sir John Hawkins, the Hon. Topham Beauclerk, and Dr. Goldsmith.

[*Oliver Goldsmith ?never should have known such knaves*]

[P lxxxvi, Malone on Reynolds' sincerity] His ardent love of truth, . . . his strong antipathy to all false pretensions, . . .

[*O Shame False*]

[P lxxxvii, note 49] He had painted, as he once observed to me, two generations of the beauties of England.

[*God blasts Them As Though ?he ?were lost ?Eurydice*]

[P lxxxix, note 51, on Reynolds' deafness] When in company with only one person, he heard very well, . . .

A Sly Dog   So can Everybody; but bring Two People & the Hearing is Stopped

[P xc, note 53 quoting Goldsmith's epitaph on Reynolds]

Such Men as Goldsmith ought not to have been Acquainted with such Men as Reynolds

[P xci, Malone comparing Reynolds to Laelius]

[Why should Laelius be considered Sir Joshuas Counterpart]

[Who dares ?worship ?a ?man Whod have Driven you long Ago Insane]

[P xcvi, summing up: If Reynolds had been an orator, he would have resembled Laelius rather than Galba]

He certainly would have been more like a Fool than a Wise Man

[PP xcvii–xcviii, note 54, Burke on Reynolds] But this disposition to abstractions, to generalizing and classification, is the great glory of the human mind, . . .

To Generalize is to be an Idiot   To Particularize is the Alone Distinction of Merit—General Knowledges are those Knowledges that Idiots possess *[As do Fools that adore Things & ?ideas x x x of General Knowledge]*

[PP xcviii–xcix] . . . during the greater part of his life, laboured as hard with his pencil, as any mechanick. . . .

The Man who does not Labour more than the Hireling must be a poor Devil.

[P ciii] [Malone, praising Reynolds' endorsement of Burke's anti-revolutionary sagacity, applies Dryden—"They led their wild desires to woods and caves, / And thought that all but SAVAGES were slaves"—to those who would assimilate England "to the model of the FEROCIOUS and ENSLAVED Republick of France!"]

When France got free Europe 'twixt Fools & Knaves
Were Savage first to France, & after; Slaves

[P civ, Malone on Reynolds' good fortune to have escaped the present era of sedition] . . . England is at present in an unparalleled state of wealth and prosperity, . . . These FACTS ought to be sounded from one end of England to the other, . . . a complete answer to all the SEDITIOUS DECLAMATIONS. . . .

This Whole Book was Written to Serve Political Purposes *[?First to Serve Nobility & Fashionable Taste & S^r. Joshua]*

[P cix, on Reynolds' death Feb 23 1792, from "the inordinate growth" of his liver]

When Sr Joshua Reynolds died
   All Nature was degraded;
The King dropd a tear into the Queens Ear;
   And all his Pictures Faded.

[P cxi, the Dukes, Marquisses, and other noblemen at Reynolds' funeral]

A Mock

[P cxv]
To each of the gentlemen who attended . . . was presented a print engraved by Bartolozzi. . . .

[*Funeral granted to Sir Joshua for having destroyd Art However the (?gentlemen were rewarded) for standing Near*]

[P cxvi, note 65: Reynolds' wish to have St Paul's decorated by paintings prevented by the Bishop of London]
    [*The Rascals who ?See Painting want to Destroy Art & Learning*]

[P cxx, Burke on Reynolds] . . . one of the most memorable men of his time.†
    † Is not this a Manifest Lie
    Barry Painted a Picture for Burke equal to Rafael or Mich Ang or any of the Italians Burke used to shew this Picture to his friends & to say I gave Twenty Guineas for this horrible Dawb & if any one would give [line cut away] Such was Burkes Patronage of Art & Science

DISCOURSE I

[P 2, back of title]
    I consider Reynolds's Discourses to the Royal Academy as the Simulations of the Hypocrite who smiles particularly where he means to Betray. His Praise of Rafael is like the Hysteric Smile of Revenge His Softness & Candour. the hidden trap. & the poisoned feast, He praises Michael Angelo for Qualities which Michael Angelo Abhorrd; & He blames Rafael for the only Qualities which Rafael Valued, Whether Reynolds. knew what he was doing. is nothing to me; the Mischief is just the same, whether a Man does it Ignorantly or Knowingly: I always consider'd True Art & True Artists to be particularly Insulted & Degraded by the Reputation of these Discourses As much as they were Degraded by the Reputation of Reynolds's Paintings. & that Such Artists as Reynolds, are at all times Hired by the Satan's. for the Depression of Art A Pretence of Art: To Destroy Art [3 or 4 erased lines follow]

[P 3, beginning Reynolds' foreword "To The Members of The Royal Academy"]
    The Neglect of Fuselis Milton in a Country pretending to the Encouragement of Art is a Sufficient Apology for My Vigorous Indignation if indeed the Neglect of My own Powers had not been Ought not the <Artists &> Employers [*Imbecility*] of Fools to be Execrated in future Ages. They Will & Shall
    Foolish Men Your own real Greatness depends on your Encouragement of the Arts & your Fall will depend on [*your*] <their> Neglect & Depression
    What you Fear is your true Interest Leo X was advised not to Encourage the Arts he was too Wise to take this Advice

[P 4, misnumbered "[iv]", at end of foreword]
    The Rich Men of England form themselves into a Society. to Sell & Not to Buy Pictures The Artist who does not throw his Contempt on such Trading Exhibitions. does not know either his own Interest or his Duty. [*Are there Artists who live upon Assasinations of other Men*]
            <When Nations grow Old. The Arts grow Cold
            And Commerce settles on every Tree
            And the Poor & the Old can live upon Gold
            For all are Born Poor. Aged Sixty three>

Reynoldss Opinion was that Genius May be Taught & that all Pretence to Inspiration is a Lie & a Deceit to say the least of it [*If the Inspiration is Great why Call it Madness*] <For if it is a Deceit the Whole Bible is Madness> This Opinion originates in the Greeks Caling the Muses Daughters of Memory

An Academy, in which the Polite Arts may be regularly cultivated, . . .

<The Enquiry in England is not whether a Man has Talents. & Genius? But whether he is Passive & Polite & a Virtuous Ass: & obedient to Noblemens Opinions in Art & Science. If he is; he is a Good Man: If Not he must be Starved>

[P 7] . . . the wisdom and generosity of the Institution: . . .

3 Farthings

[P 9] Raffaelle . . . had not the advantage of studying in an Academy; but all Rome, and the works of Michael Angelo in particular, were to him an Academy.

I do not believe that Rafael taught Mich. Angelo or that Mich. Ang: taught Rafael., any more than I believe that the Rose teaches the Lilly how to grow or the Apple tree teaches the [*Pine tree to bear Fruit*] <Pear tree how to bear Fruit.> I do not believe the tales of Anecdote writers when they militate against Individual Character

. . . the minute accidental discriminations of particular . . . objects, . . .

Minute Discrimination is Not Accidental All Sublimity is founded on Minute Discrimination

[P 11] . . . models . . . for their imitation, not their criticism.

<Imitation is Criticism>

[P 13] A facility in composing,—a lively, and what is called a masterly, handling of the chalk or pencil, are, it must be confessed, captivating qualities to young minds, and become of course the objects of their ambition.

<I consider> The Following sentence is Supremely Insolent <for the following Reasons Why this Sentence should be begun by the Words A Facility in Composing I cannot tell unless it was to cast [*an Eye*] <a stigma> upon Real facility in Composition by Assimilating it with a Pretence to & Imitation of Facility in Execution or are we to understand him to mean that Facility in Composing. is a Frivolous pursuit. A Facility in Composing is the Greatest Power of Art & Belongs to None but the Greatest Artists i.e. the Most Minutely Discriminating & Determinate>

[P 14] . . . they have taken the shadow for the substance; and make the mechanical felicity the chief excellence of the art, . . .

<Mechanical Excellence is the Only Vehicle of Genius>

. . . pleased with this premature dexterity in their pupils, . . . praised their dispatch at the expence of their correctness.

<This is all False & Self-Contradictory>

. . . frivolous ambition of being thought masters of execution, . . .

<Execution is the Chariot of Genius>

[P 15] . . . youth . . . disgusted at the slow approaches. . . . labour is the only price of solid fame, . . . whatever their force of genius may be, . . .
   <This is All Self-Contradictory! Truth & Falshood Jumbled Together>

When we read the lives of the most eminent Painters, every page informs us, that no part of their time was spent in dissipation.
   The Lives of Painters say that Rafael died of Dissipation   Idleness is one Thing & Dissipation Another   He who has Nothing to Dissipate Cannot Dissipate the Weak Man may be Virtuous Enough but will Never be an Artist [?*What painters have only been dissipated without wildness*] <Painters are noted for being Dissipated & Wild.>

[P 16] . . . they then painted the picture, *and ofter all re-touched it from the life.*
   <This is False>

The Students, instead of vying with each other which shall have the readiest hand, should be taught to contend who shall have the purest and most correct out-line; . . .
   <Excellent>

[P 17] . . . a habit of drawing correctly what we see, will . . . give a proportionable power of drawing correctly what we imagine.
   <This is Admirably Said. Why does he not always allow as much>

[P 18] [Nice copying teaches] exactness and precision, . . .
   <Excellent>

DISCOURSE II

[P 22, back of title]
   <The Labourd Works of Journeymen employed by Correggio. Titian Veronese & all the Venetians ought not to be shewn to the Young Artist as the Works of original Conception any more than the Engravings of Strange Bartollozzi or Woollett. They are Works of Manual Labour>

[P 23] MUCH COPYING DISCOUNTENANCED . . . ARTISTS . . . SHOULD BE EMPLOYD IN LAYING UP MATERIALS. . . .
   <What is Laying up materials but Copying>

[P 25] . . . once enabled to express himself . . . he must . . . amass a stock of ideas, . . . he is now to consider the Art itself as his master.
   After having been a Fool a Student is to amass a Stock of Ideas & [*then to be insolent in his Foolery*] <knowing himself to be a Fool he is to assume the Right to put other Mens Ideas into his Foolery>

[P 26] . . . he must still be afraid of trusting his own judgment, and of deviating into any track where he cannot find the footsteps of some former master.
   Instead of Following One Great Master he is to follow a Great Many Fools

[P 28] A Student unacquainted with the attempts [p 29] of former adventurers, is always apt to over-rate his own abilities; to mistake . . . every coast new to him, for a new-found country.
   <Contemptible Mocks>

[P 29] The productions of such minds. . . . differ . . . from their predecessors . . . only in irregular sallies, and trifling conceits.
   <Thus Reynolds Depreciates the Efforts of Inventive Genius Trifling Conceits are better than Colouring without any meaning at all>

[P 30] On whom then can [the student] rely . . . ? . . . those great masters who have travelled the same road with success. . . .

[*This is Encouragement for Artists . . . (about 4 illegible words) . . . to those who are born for it*]

[P 32] How incapable those . . . who have spent much of their time in making finished copies, . . .

This is most False <for no one can ever Design till he has learnd the Language of Art by making many Finishd Copies both of Nature & Art & of whatever comes in his way from Earliest Childhood>

<The difference between a bad Artist & a Good One Is the Bad Artist Seems to Copy a Great Deal: The Good one Really Does Copy a Great Deal>

[P 33] The great use in copying, if it be at all useful, should seem to be in learning to colour; . . .

<Contemptible>

. . . yet even colouring will never be perfectly attained by servilely copying the model before you.

<Servile Copying is the Great Merit of Copying>

[P 34] . . . you cannot do better than have recourse to nature herself, who is always at hand, . . .

<Nonsense—Every Eye Sees differently   As the Eye—Such the Object>

[P 35] Labour to invent on their general principles. . . . how a Michael Angelo or a Raffaelle would have treated this subject: . . .

<General Principle(s) Again! Unless. You Consult. Particulars. You Cannot. even Know or See Mich: Ang.° or Rafael or any Thing Else>

But as mere enthusiasm will carry you but a little way, . . .

[*Damn The Fool*]

Meer Enthusiasm is the All in All!—Bacons Philosophy has Ruind England <Bacon is only Epicurus over again>

[P 36] . . . enter into a kind of competition, by . . . making a companion to any picture that you consider as a model. . . . and compare them. . . .

[*What but a Puppy will dare to do this*]

. . . a severe and mortifying task, . . .

[*?Why shoud ?comparing* (or *?copying*) *Great Masters* (be done) *Painfully*]

[P 37] [To compare one's work with a Great Master's] requires not only great resolution, but great humility.

[*Who will or Can ?endure ?such Humiliation (?either ?he ?is) dishonest ?or he is ?Insane*]

Few have been taught to any purpose, who have not been their own teachers.

True!

[P 38] . . . to choose . . . models, . . . take the world's opinion rather than your own.

[*Fools opinions & Endeavours destroy Invention!*]

[P 40] A facility . . . cannot be acquired but by an infinite number of acts.
 True

[P 41] . . . endeavour to draw the figure by memory. [And persevere] in this custom, . . .
 Good Advice

. . . remember, that the pencil [i.e. paint brush] is the instrument by which . . . to obtain eminence.
 <Nonsense>

[P 42] The Venetian and Flemish schools, which owe much of their fame to colouring, . . .
 <because they could not Draw>

[P 43] [Titian, Paul Veronese, Tintoret, the Bassans] Their sketches on paper are as rude as their pictures are excellent in . . . harmony of colouring.
 <All the Pictures said to be by these Men are the Laboured fabrication of Journey-work>

. . . finished drawings . . . sold under [their] names . . . are [copies]
 <They could not Draw>

[P 47] . . . he who would have you believe that he is waiting for the inspirations of Genius, is in reality at a loss how to begin; and is at last delivered of his monsters, with difficulty and pain.
 A Stroke at Mortimer

[P 48] [The well-grounded painter] is contented that all shall be as great as himself, who have undergone the same fatigue; . . .
 The Man who asserts that there is no Such Thing as Softness in Art & that every thing in Art is Definite & Determinate has not been told this by Practise but by Inspiration & Vision because Vision is Determinate & Perfect & he Copies That without Fatigue Every thing being Definite & determinate Softness is Produced Alone by Comparative Strength & Weakness in the Marking out of the Forms
 I say These Principles could never be found out by the Study of Nature without Con or Innate Science

DISCOURSE III
[P 50, back of title]
 <A Work of Genius is a Work "Not to be obtaind by the Invocation of Memory & her Syren Daughters. but by Devout prayer to that Eternal Spirit. who can enrich with all utterance & knowledge & sends out his Seraphim with the hallowed fire of his Altar to touch & purify the lips of whom he pleases." Milton
 The following [Letter] <Discourse> is particularly Interesting to Blockheads. as it Endeavours to prove That there is No such thing as Inspiration & that any Man of a plain Understanding may by Thieving from Others. become a Mich Angelo>

[P 52] . . . the genuine painter . . . instead of endeavouring to amuse mankind with the minute neatness of his imitations, . . . must endeavour to improve [P 53] them by the grandeur of his ideas; . . .

Without Minute Neatness of Execution. The. Sublime cannot Exist! Grandeur of Ideas is founded on Precision of Ideas

[P 54] The Moderns are not less convinced than the Ancients of this superior power [i.e. something beyond mere imitation] existing in the art; nor less sensible of its effects.

<I wish that this was True>

[P 55, an introductory remark by Blake:]

Now he begins to Degrade [&] to Deny [*destroy*] & <to> Mock

Such is the warmth with which both the Ancients and Moderns speak of this divine principle of the art; . . .

And such is the Coldness with which Reynolds speaks! And such is his Enmity

. . . enthusiastick admiration seldom promotes knowledge.

Enthusiastic Admiration is the first Principle of Knowledge & its last

He examines his own mind, and perceives there nothing of . . . divine inspiration, . . .

The Man who on Examining his own Mind finds nothing of Inspiration ought not to dare to be an Artist he is a Fool. & a Cunning Knave suited to the Purposes of Evil Demons

[P 56] [He never] travelled to heaven to gather new ideas; . . .

The Man who never in his Mind & Thoughts traveld to Heaven Is No Artist

. . . no other qualifications than what . . . a plain understanding can confer.

Artists who are above a plain Understanding are Mockd & Destroyd by this President of Fools

[P 56] . . . figurative declamation [makes art seem] out of the reach of human industry. But . . . we ought to distinguish how much is to be given to enthusiasm, and how much to reason. . . . not . . . vague admiration, . . .

It is Evident that Reynolds Wishd none but Fools to be in the Arts & in order to this, he calls all others Vague Enthusiasts or Madmen

<What has Reasoning to do with the Art of Painting?>

[P 57] Could we teach taste or genius by rules, they would be no longer taste and genius.

[*This must be how Liars Reason*]

. . . most people err . . . from not knowing what object to pursue.

The Man who does not know what Object to Pursue is an Idiot

This great ideal perfection and beauty are not to be sought in the heavens, but upon the earth.

A Lie

They are about us, and upon every side of us.

A Lie

But the power of discovering . . . can be acquired only by experience; . . .
A Lie

[p 58] . . . art [must] get above all singular forms, local customs, particularities, and details of every kind.
A Folly
Singular & Particular Detail is the Foundation of the Sublime

The most beautiful forms have something about them like weakness, minuteness, or imperfection.
Minuteness is their whole Beauty

[p 59] This idea [acquired by habit of observing] . . . which the Artist calls the Ideal Beauty, is the great leading principle. . . .
Knowledge of Ideal Beauty. is Not to be Acquired It is Born with us Innate Ideas. are in Every Man Born with him. they are <truly> Himself. The Man who says that we have No Innate Ideas must be a Fool & Knave. Having No Con-Science <or Innate Science>

[p 60] . . . an artist becomes possessed of the idea of that central form . . . from which every deviation is deformity.
One Central Form Composed of all other Forms being Granted it does not therefore follow that all other Forms are Deformity

. . . the ancient sculptors . . . being indefatigable in the school of nature, have left models of that perfect form. . . .
All Forms are Perfect in the Poets Mind. but these are not Abstracted nor Compounded from Nature <but are from Imagination>

[p 61] [Even the] great Bacon treats with ridicule the idea of confining proportion to rules, or of producing beauty by selection.
The Great Bacon he is Calld I call him the Little Bacon says that Every Thing must be done by Experiment his first princip[le] is Unbelief And Yet here he says that Art must be producd Without such Method. He is Like Sʳ Joshu[a] full of Self-Contradiction & Knavery

There is a rule, obtained out of general nature, . . .
What is General Nature is there Such a Thing
what is General Knowledge is there such a Thing [Strictly Speaking] All Knowledge is Particular

[p 62] . . . it may be objected, that in every particular species there are various central forms, . . .
Here he loses sight of A Central Form. & Gets into Many Central Forms

[p 63] . . . still none of them is the representation of an individual, but of a class.
Every Class is Individual

. . . in each of these classes. . . . childhood and age . . . there is a common form. . . .
There is no End to the Follies of this Man Childhood & Age are Equally belonging to Every Class

. . . that form which is taken from them all, and which partakes equally of the activity of the Gladiator, of the delicacy of the Apollo, and. . . .
Here he comes again to his Central Form

[P 64] There is . . . a kind of symmetry, or proportion, which may properly be said to belong to deformity. A figure lean or corpulent . . . though deviating from beauty, . . .

The Symmetry of Deformity is a Pretty Foolery

Can any Man who Thinks. [argue] <Talk> so? Leanness or Fatness is not Deformity. but Reynolds thought Character Itself Extravagance & Deformity

Age & Youth are not Classes but [Accidents] [<Situations>] <Properties> of Each Class so are Leanness & Fatness

[P 65] . . . when [the Artist] has reduced the variety of nature to the abstract idea; What Folly

his next task will be to become acquainted with the genuine habits of nature, as distinguished from those of fashion.

[Is Fashion the concern of Artists   The Knave Calls any thing found in Nature fit for Art]

[P 67] . . . [the painter] must divest himself of all prejudices . . . disregard all local and temporary ornaments, and look only on those general habits. . . .

Generalizing in Every thing the Man would soon be a Fool but a Cunning Fool

[P 71] . . . a wrong direction . . . without ever knowing there was a nobler to pursue. Albert Durer, as Vasari has justly remarked,

[Albert Durer would never have got his Manners from the Nobility]

would, probably, have been one of the first painters of his age, (and he lived in an era of great artists,) had he been initiated into those great principles. . . .

What does this mean "Would have been" one of the first Painters of his Age" Albert Durer Is! Not would have been! Besides. let them look at Gothic Figures & Gothic Buildings. & not talk of Dark Ages or of Any Age! Ages are All Equal. But Genius is Always Above The Age

[P 74] I [do not mean] to countenance a careless or indetermined manner of painting. For though the painter is to overlook the accidental discriminations of nature,

Here he is for Determinate & yet for Indeterminate

he is to exhibit [general forms] distinctly, and with precision, . . .

Distinct General Form Cannot Exist   Distinctness is Particular Not General

[P 75] A firm and determined outline is one of the characteristics of the great style in painting; and . . . he who possesses the knowledge of the exact form which every part of nature ought to have, will be fond of expressing that knowledge with correctness and precision in all his works.

A Noble Sentence

Here is a Sentence Which overthrows all his Book

. . . I have endeavoured to reduce the idea of beauty to general principles: . . . the only means of advancing science; of clearing the mind . . .

[Sir Joshua Proves that] Bacons Philosophy makes both Statesmen & Artists Fools & Knaves

DISCOURSE IV

[p 78, back of title]

The <Two> Following Discourse<s> [is] <are> Particularly Calcu-
lated for the Setting Ignorant & Vulgar Artists as Models of Execution in
Art. Let him who will. follow such advice I will not. I know that The Mans
Execution is as his Conception & No better

[p 79] The value and rank of every art is in proportion to the mental labour employed
in it, or the mental pleasure produced by it.

Why does he not always allow This

[p 80] [The principle of] leaving out particularities, and retaining only general ideas
. . . extends itself to every part of the Art. . . .

General Ideas <again>

Invention in Painting does not imply the invention of the subject; for that is commonly
supplied by the Poet or Historian.

All but Names of Persons & Places is Invention both in Poetry & Painting

[p 82] . . . the . . . most dangerous error is on the side of minuteness; . . .

<Here is Nonsense!>

[p 83] All smaller things, however perfect in their way, are to be sacrificed without
mercy to the greater.

<Sacrifice the Parts. What becomes of the Whole>

Even in portraits, the grace, and . . . the likeness, consists more in taking the general
air, than in observing the exact similitude of every feature.

How Ignorant

[p 86] A painter of portraits retains the individual likeness; a painter of history shews
the man by shewing his actions.

<If he does not shew the Man as well as the Action he is a poor Artist>

[p 87] . . . be well studied in the analysis of those circumstances, which constitute
dignity of appearance in real life.

Here he allows an Analysis of Circumstances

Those expressions alone should be given to the figures which their respective situations
generally produce.

[Nonsense]

[p 89] . . . the distinct blue, red, and yellow . . . in the draperies of the Roman and
Florentine schools . . . effect of grandeur. . . . Perhaps these distinct colours strike
the mind more forcibly, from there not being any great union between them; . . .

These are Fine & Just Notions Why does he not always allow as much

[p 90] . . . the historical Painter never enters into the detail of colours [nor] does he
debase his conceptions with minute attention to the discriminations of Drapery.

Excellent Remarks

Carlo Maratti [thought] that the disposition of drapery was a more difficult art than
even that of drawing the human figure; . . .

I do not believe that Carlo Maratti thought so or that any body can
think so. the Drapery is formed alone by the Shape of the Naked [next
word cut away in binding]

[P 92] . . . the Venetians . . . accomplished perfectly the thing they attempted. But as mere elegance is their principal object, . . .

They accomplishd Nothing <As to Elegance they have not a Spark>

[P 93] To this question [why Veronese had put his principal figure in shade—Reynolds answers that he was] an ornamental Painter [whose] intention was solely to produce an effect of light and shadow; . . .

This is not a Satisfactory Answer

To produce an Effect of True Light & Shadow [*Nothing must be sacrificd for Light & Shadow depends on Distinctness of Form*] <is Necessary to the Ornamental Style—which altogether depends on Distinctness of Form. The Venetian ought not to be calld the Ornamental Style>

[P 94] The language of Painting must indeed be allowed these masters [the Venetians]; . . .

The Language of Painters cannot be allowd them if Reynolds says right at p. 97 he there says that the Venetian Will Not Correspond with the Great Style

<The Greek Gems are in the Same Style as the Greek Statues>

[P 95] Such as suppose that the great style might happily be blended with the ornamental, that the simple, grave and majestick dignity of Raffaelle could unite with the glow and bustle of a Paolo, or Tintoret, are totally mistaken.

What can be better Said. on this Subject? but Reynolds contradicts what he says continually He makes little Concessions, that he may take Great Advantages

[P 97] And though in [colouring] the Venetians must be allowed extraordinary skill, yet even that skill, as they have employed it, will but ill correspond with the great style.

<Somebody Else wrote this page for Reynolds I think that Barry or Fuseli wrote it or [*said*] <dictated> it>

[P 98] . . . Michael Angelo [thought] that the principal attention of the Venetian painters [was to] the study of colours, to the neglect of the IDEAL BEAUTY OF FORM, . . .

Venetian Attention is to a Contempt & Neglect of Form Itself & to the Destruction of all Form or Outline <Purposely & Intentionally>

But if general censure was given to that school from the sight of a picture of Titian, . . .

As if Mich. Ang°. had seen but One Picture of Titians
Mich. Ang. Knew & Despised all that Titian could do

<On the Venetian Painter
He makes the Lame to walk we all agree
But then he strives to blind those who can see.>

[P 99]
<If the Venetians Outline was Right his Shadows would destroy it & deform its appearance

A Pair of Stays to mend the Shape
Of crooked Humpy Woman:
Put on O Venus! now thou art,
Quite a Venetian Roman.>

–640–

[P 100] . . . there is a sort of senatorial dignity about [Titian] . . .

<Titian as well as the other Venetians so far from Senatorial Dignity appears to me to give always the Characters of Vulgar Stupidity>

Why should Titian & The Venetians be Named in a discourse on Art Such Idiots are not Artists

<Venetian; all thy Colouring is no more
Than Boulsterd Plasters on a Crooked Whore.>

[P 101] The Venetian is indeed the most splendid of the schools of elegance; . . .

<Vulgarity & not Elegance—The Word Elegance ought to be applied to Forms. not to Colours>

[P 102] . . . elaborate harmony of colouring, a brilliancy of tints, a soft and gradual transition from one to another, . . .

Broken Colours & Broken Lines & Broken Masses are Equally Subversive of the Sublime

Such excellence . . . is weak . . . when the work aspires to grandeur and sublimity.

Well Said <Enough>

[P 103] But it must be allowed in favour of the Venetians, that [Rubens] was more gross than they. . . .

<How can that be calld the Ornamental Style of which Gross Vulgarity forms the Principal Excellence>

[P 104] Some inferior dexterity, some extraordinary mechanical power is apparently that from which [the Dutch school] seek distinction.

<The Words Mechanical Power should not be thus Prostituted>

[P 106] An History-painter paints man in general; a Portrait-painter, a particular man, . . .

A History Painter Paints The Hero, & not Man in General. but most minutely in Particular

[P 109] Thus . . . a portrait-painter. . . . leaves out all the minute breaks and peculiarities in the face. . . .

Folly! Of what consequence is it to the Arts what a Portrait Painter does

[P 110] . . . the composite style, . . . Correggio. . . . modern grace and elegance, . . .

There is No Such <a> Thing as A Composite Style

[P 111] The errors of genius, however, are pardonable. . . .

<Genius has no Error it is Ignorance that is Error>

[P 112] On the whole . . . one presiding principle. . . . The works . . . built upon general nature, live for ever; . . .

<All Equivocation & Self-Contradiction>

DISCOURSE V

[P 114, back of title]

Gainsborough told a Gentleman of Rank & Fortune that the Worst Painters always chose the Grandest Subjects. I desired the Gentleman to Set Gainsborough about one of Rafaels Grandest Subjects Namely Christ delivering the Keys to St Peter. & he would find that in Gainsboroughs hands it would be a Vulgar Subject of Poor Fishermen & a Journeyman Carpenter

The following Discourse is written with the same End in View. that Gainsborough had in making the Above assertion Namely To Represent Vulgar Artists as the Models of Executive Merit

[P 116] That which is most worthy of esteem in its allotted sphere, becomes an object ... of derision, when it is forced into a higher, to which it is not suited; ...
Concessions to Truth for the sake of Oversetting Truth

... keep your principal attention fixed upon the higher excellencies. ... you may be very imperfect; but still, you are an imperfect artist of the highest order.
[*Caesar said hed rather be the* (first in) *a Village* (than) *second in Rome was not Caesar* (a) *Dutch Painter*]

[P 117–118] ... to preserve the most perfect beauty IN ITS MOST PERFECT STATE, you cannot express the passions, all of which produce distortion and deformity, more or less, in the most beautiful faces.
[117] What Nonsense
[118] Passion & Expression is Beauty Itself—The Face that is Incapable of Passion & Expression is Deformity Itself Let it be Painted <& Patchd> & Praised & Advertised for Ever <it will only be admired by Fools>

[P 119] ... pictures of Raffaelle, where the Criticks have described their own imaginations; ...
If Reynolds could not see. variety of Character in Rafael Others Can

We can easily ... suppose a Jupiter to be possessed of all ... powers and perfections. ... Yet [in art the ancients] confined his character to majesty alone.
False
The Ancients were chiefly attentive to Complicated & Minute Discrimination of Character it is the Whole of Art

Pliny ... wrong when he speaks of ... [P 120] three different characters [in one statue]. ...
Reynolds cannot bear Expression

A statue in which you endeavour to unite ... dignity ... elegance ... valour, must surely possess none of these. ...
Why not? <O Poverty!>

The summit of excellence seems to be an assemblage of contrary qualities, ... such ... that no one part is found to counteract the other.
A Fine Jumble

[P 121] If any man shall be master of ... highest ... lowest, flights of art, ... he is fitter to give example than to receive instruction.
<Mocks>

[P 123] ... FRESCO, a mode of painting which excludes attention to minute elegancies: ...
This is False
Fresco Painting is the Most Minute
<Fresco Painting is Like Miniature Painting; a Wall is a Large Ivory>

[P 124] Raffaelle ... foremost [for] his excellence in the higher parts. ... His easel works ... lower ... never arrived at ... perfection. ...
Folly & Falshood. The Man who can say that Rafael knew not the

smaller beauties of the Art ought to be Contemnd & I. accordingly hold Reynolds in Contempt for this Sentence in particular

[P 125] When he painted in oil, his hand seemed to be so cramped and confined, . . .
Rafael did as he Pleased. He who does not admire Rafaels Execution does not Even See Rafael

I have no desire to degrade Raffaelle from the high rank. . . .
A Lie

[P 126] . . . Michael Angelo . . . did not possess so many excellencies as Raffaelle, but. . . .
According to Reynolds Mich Angelo was worse still & knew Nothing at all about Art as an object of Imitation
Can any Man be such a fool as to believe that Rafael & Michael Angelo were Incapable of the meer Language of Art & That Such Idiots as Rubens. Correggio & Titian Knew how to Execute what they could not Think or Invent

He never attempted those lesser elegancies and graces in the art.
Damnd Fool

If any man had a right to look down . . . it was certainly Michael Angelo; . . .
O. Yes!

[P 127] . . . together with these [graces and embellishments], which we wish he had more attended to, he has rejected all the false . . . ornaments, . . .
Here is another Contradiction   If. Mich Ang.° Neglected any thing. that <Titian or> Veronese did: He Rejected it. for Good Reasons. Sr Joshua in other Places owns that the Venetian Cannot Mix with the Roman or Florentine   What then does he Mean when he says that Mich. Ang.° & Rafael were not worthy of Imitation in the Lower parts of Art

[P 128] . . . Raffaelle had more Taste and Fancy, Michael Angelo more Genius and imagination.
<What Nonsense>

[P 129] [Michael Angelo] never needed . . . help. [Raffaelle had] propriety, beauty, and majesty . . . judicious contrivance . . . correctness of Drawing, purity of Taste, . . .
If all this is True Why does not Reynolds recommend The Study of Rafael & Mich: Angelos Execution   at page 97 he allows that the Venetian Style will Ill correspond with the Great Style

[P 131] Such is the great style, . . . [in it] search after novelty . . . has no place.
The Great Style is always Novel or New in all its Operations

But there is another style . . . inferior. . . . the original or characteristical style, . . .
Original & Characteristical are the Two Grand Merits of the Great Style   Why should these words be applied to such a Wretch as Salvator Rosa

[P 132] . . . Salvator Rosa. . . . a peculiar cast of nature . . . though void of all grace, . . .
Salvator Rosa was precisely what he Pretended Not to be. His Pictures. are high Labourd pretensions to Expeditious Workmanship. He was

the Quack Doctor of Painting His Roughnesses & Smoothnesses. are the Production of Labour & Trick. As to Imagination he was totally without Any.

[P 133] . . . yet . . . that sort of dignity which belongs to savage and uncultivated nature: . . .

Savages are [*Fribbles & Fops*] <Fops & Fribbles> more than any other Men

Every thing is of a piece: his Rocks, Trees, Sky, even to his *handling,* . . .

Handling is All that he has. & we all know this

Handling is Labour & Trick <Salvator Rosa employd Journeymen>

[P 134] . . . Rubens . . . a remarkable instance of the same mind being seen in all the various parts of the art. The whole is so much of a piece, . . .

All Rubens's Pictures are Painted by Journeymen & so far from being all of a Piece. are The most wretched Bungles

[P 135] His Colouring, in which he is eminently skilled, is . . . too much . . . tinted.

To My Eye Rubens's Colouring is most Contemptible His Shadows are of a Filthy Brown somewhat of the Colour of Excrement these are filld with tints & messes of yellow & red His lights are all the Colours of the Rainbow laid on Indiscriminately & broken one into another. Altogether his Colouring is Contrary to The Colouring. of Real Art & Science

Opposed to this . . . [is the] correct style of Poussin. . . .

<Opposed to Rubenss Colouring Sᵉ Joshua has placd Poussin but he ought to put All Men of Genius who ever Painted. Rubens & the Venetians are Opposite in every thing to True Art & they Meant to be so they were hired for this Purpose>

[P 137] [Poussin's later pictures] softer and richer, . . . [but not] at all comparable to many in his [early] dry manner which we have in England.

<True>

The favourite subjects of Poussin were Ancient Fables; and no painter was ever better qualified . . .

<True>

[P 138] Poussin seemed to think that the style and the language [should preserve] some relish of the old way of painting, . . .

<True>

[P 139] . . . if the Figures . . . had a modern air . . . how ridiculous would Apollo appear instead of the Sun; . . .

<These remarks on Poussin are Excellent>

[P 141] . . . the lowest style will be the most popular . . . ignorance . . .

<Well said>

[P 142] . . . our Exhibitions . . . a mischievous tendency, . . . seducing the Painter to an ambition of pleasing indiscriminately the mixed multitude. . . .

Why then does he talk in other places of pleasing Every body

DISCOURSE VI

[P 144, back of title]

When a Man talks of Acquiring Invention & of learning how to produce Original Conception he must expect to be calld a Fool <by Men of Understanding but such a Hired Knave cares not for the Few. His Eye is on the Many. or rather on the Money>

[P 147] Those who have [written of art as inspiration are better received] than he who attempts to examine, coldly, whether there are any means by which this art may be acquired. . . .

<Bacons Philosophy has Destroyd all Art & Science> The Man who says that the Genius is not Born. but Taught.—Is a Knave

It is very natural for those. . . . who have never observed the gradation by which art is acquired . . . to conclude . . . that it is not only inaccessible to themselves. . . .

<O Reader behold the Philosophers Grave.

He was born quite a Fool: but he died quite a Knave>

[P 149] It would be no wonder if a student . . . should . . . consider it as hopeless, to set about acquiring by the imitation of any human master, what he is taught to suppose is matter of inspiration from heaven.

How ridiculous it would be to see the Sheep Endeavouring to walk like the Dog. or the Ox striving to trot like the Horse just as Ridiculous it is to see One Man Striving to Imitate Another   Man varies from Man more than Animal from Animal of Different Species

[P 152] . . . DEGREE of excellence [of] GENIUS is different, in different times and different places;

<Never!>

and what shews it to be so is, that mankind have often changed their opinion upon this matter.

<Never!>

[P 153] . . . if genius is not taken for inspiration, but as the effect of close observation and experience.

<Damnd Fool>

[P 154] . . . as . . . art shall advance, its powers will be still more and more fixed by rules.

<If Art was Progressive We should have had Mich Angelo's & Rafaels to Succeed & to Improve upon each other But it is not so.   Genius dies with its Possessor & comes not again till Another is Born with It>

[155] . . . even works of Genius, like every other effect, . . . must have their cause, . . .

<Identities or Things are Neither Cause nor Effect   They are Eternal>

[P 157] . . . our minds should . . . continue a settled intercourse with all the true examples of grandeur.

<Reynolds Thinks that Man Learns all that he Knows I say on the Contrary That Man Brings All that he has or Can have Into the World with

him.   Man is Born Like a Garden ready Planted & Sown This World is too poor to produce one Seed>

The mind is but a barren soil; a soil which is soon exhausted, and will produce no crop, . . .
  <The Mind that could have produced this Sentence must have been a Pitiful a Pitiable Imbecillity.   I always thought that the Human Mind was the most Prolific of All Things & Inexhaustible <I certainly do Thank God that I am not like Reynolds>>

[p 158] . . . or only one, unless it be continually fertilized and enriched with foreign matter.
  Nonsense

[p 159] Nothing can come of nothing.
  <Is the Mind Nothing?>

. . . Michael Angelo, and Raffaelle, were . . . possessed of all the knowledge in the art . . . of their predecessors.
  If so. they knew all that Titian & Correggio knew Correggio was two Years older than Mich. Angelo
  Correggio born <1472> Mich Angelo [on] <born 1474>

[p 161] . . . any endeavour to copy the exact peculiar colour . . . of another man's mind . . . must always be . . . ridiculous. . . .
  <Why then Imitate at all?>

[p 163] Art in its perfection is not ostentatious; it lies hid, and works its effect, itself unseen.
  <This is a Very Clever Sentence who wrote it God knows>

[p 165] Peculiar marks . . . generally . . . defects; . . .
  Peculiar Marks are the Only Merit

Peculiarities . . . so many blemishes; which, however, both in real life and in painting, cease to appear deformities, . . .
  Infernal Falshood

[p 166] Even the great name of Michael Angelo may be used, to keep in countenance a deficiency . . . of colouring, and every [other ornamental part]
  No Man who can see Michael Angelo. can say that he wants either Colouring or Ornamental parts of Art. in the highest degree. for he has Every [perquisite] <Thing> of Both [O what Wisdom & Learning ?adorn his Superiority—]

[p 167] . . . these defects . . . have a right to our pardon, but not to our admiration.
  He who Admires Rafael Must admire Rafaels Execution
  He who does not admire Rafaels Execution Cannot Admire Rafael

[p 172] . . . a want which cannot be completely supplied; that is, want of strength of parts.
  A Confession

[p 176] . . . very finished artists in the inferior branches. . . .
  This Sentence is to Introduce another in Condemnation & Contempt of Alb. Durer

The works of Albert Durer . . . afford a rich mass of genuine materials, which wrought up and polished. . . .

A Polishd Villain <who Robs & Murders>

[P 177] Though Coypel wanted a simplicty of taste, . . .

[O Yes Coypel indeed]

[P 178] The greatest style . . . would receive an additional grace by . . . precision of pencil. . . .

What does Precision of Pencil mean? If it does not mean Outline it means Nothing

[P 179] [Jan Steen if taught by Michael Angelo and Raffaelle] would have ranged with the great. . . .

Jan Steen was a Boor & neither Rafael nor Mich Ang. could have made him any better

[P 180] Men who although . . . bound down by . . . early habits, have still exerted. . . .

He who Can be bound down is No Genius Genius cannot be Bound it may be Renderd Indignant & Outrageous

"Oppression makes the Wise Man Mad"

Solomon

DISCOURSE VII

[P 188, back of title]

<The Purpose of the following Discourse is to Prove That Taste & Genius are not of Heavenly Origin & that all who have Supposed that they Are so. Are to be Considerd as Weak headed Fanatics

The obligations Reynolds has laid on Bad Artists of all Classes will at all times make them his Admirers but most especially for this Discourse in which it is proved that the Stupid are born with Faculties Equal to other Men Only they have not Cultivated them because they thought it not worth the trouble>

[P 194] . . . obscurity . . . is one source of the sublime.

<Obscurity is Neither the Source of the Sublime nor of any Thing Else>

[That] liberty of imagination is cramped by . . . rules; . . . smothered . . . by too much judgment; . . . [are] notions not only groundless, but pernicious.

<The Ancients & the wisest of the Moderns were of the opinion that Reynolds Condemns & laughs at>

[P 195] . . . scarce a poet is to be found, . . . whose latter works are not as replete with . . . imagination, as those [of] his more youthful days.

<As Replete but Not More Replete>

To understand literally these metaphors . . . seems . . . absurd. . . .

<The Ancients did not mean to Impose when they affirmd their belief in Vision & Revelation Plato was in Earnest. Milton was in Earnest. They believd that God did Visit Man Really & Truly & not as Reynolds pretends

[P 196] [idea absurd that a winged genius] did really inform him in a whisper what he was to write; . . .

How very Anxious Reynolds is to Disprove & Contemn Spiritual Perception

[P 197] It is supposed that . . . under the name of genius great works are produced, . . . without our being under the least obligation to reason, precept, or experience.

<Who Ever said this>

. . . scarce state these opinions without exposing their absurdity; yet . . . constantly in the mouths of . . . artists.

<He states Absurdities in Company with Truths & calls both Absurd>

[P 198] . . . prevalent opinion . . . considers the principles of taste . . . as having less solid foundations, than . . . they really have. . . . [and imagines taste of too high origin] to submit to the authority of an earthly tribunal.

<The Artifice of the Epicurean Philosophers is to Call all other Opinions Unsolid & Unsubstantial than those which are Derived from Earth>

We often appear to differ in sentiments . . . merely from the inaccuracy of terms, . . .

It is not in Terms that Reynolds & I disagree Two Contrary Opinions can never by any Language be made alike. I say Taste & Genius are Not Teachable or Acquirable but are born with us Reynolds says the Contrary

[P 199] . . . take words as we find them; . . . distinguish the THINGS to which they are applied.

<This is False the Fault is not in Words. but in Things Lockes Opinions of Words & their Fallaciousness are Artful Opinions & Fallacious also>

[P 200] It is the very same taste which relishes a demonstration in geometry, that is pleased with the resemblance of a picture to an original, and touched with the harmony of musick.

Demonstration Similitude & Harmony are Objects of Reasoning Invention Identity & Melody are Objects of Intuition

[P 201] . . . as true as mathematical demonstration; . . .

<God forbid that Truth should be Confined to Mathematical Demonstration>

But beside real, there is also apparent truth, . . .

<He who does not Know Truth at Sight is unworthy of Her Notice>

. . . taste . . . approaches . . . a sort of resemblance to real science, even where opinions are . . . no better than prejudices.

<Here is a great deal to do to Prove that All Truth is Prejudice for All that is Valuable in Knowledge[s] is Superior to Demonstrative Science such as is Weighed or Measured>

[P 202] As these prejudices become more narrow, . . . this secondary taste becomes more and more fantastical; . . .

<And so he thinks he has proved that Genius & Inspiration are All a Hum>

. . . I shall [now] proceed with less method, . . .

<He calls the Above proceeding with Method>

We will take it for granted, that reason is something invariable . . .
<Reason or A Ratio of All We have Known is not the Same it shall be
when we know More. he therefore takes a Falshood for granted to set out
with>

[P 203] [Whatever of taste we can] fairly bring under the dominion of reason, must
be considered as equally exempt from change.
<Now this is Supreme Fooling>

The arts would lie open for ever to caprice . . . if those who . . . judge . . . had no
settled principles. . . .
<He may as well say that if Man does not. lay down settled Principles.
The Sun will not rise in a Morning>

[P 204] My notion of nature comprehends . . . also the . . . human mind and imagination.
<Here is a Plain Confession that he Thinks Mind & Imagination not to
be above the Mortal & Perishing Nature. Such is the End of Epicurean or
Newtonian Philosophy it is Atheism>

[P 208] [Poussin's Perseus and Medusa's head] . . . I remember turning from it with
disgust, . . .
<Reynolds's Eye. could not bear Characteristic Colouring or Light &
Shade>

A picture should please at first sight, . . .
Please! Whom? Some Men Cannot See a Picture except in a Dark Corner

[P 209] No one can deny, that violent passions will naturally emit harsh and disagre-
able tones: . . .
Violent Passions Emit the Real Good & Perfect Tones

[P 214] . . . Rubens . . . thinking it necessary to make his work so very
ornamental, . . .
<Here it is calld Ornamental that the Roman & Bolognian Schools may
be Insinuated not to be Ornamental>

[P 215] Nobody will dispute but some of the best of the Roman or Bolognian schools
would have produced a more learned and more noble work [than that of Rubens].
<Learned & Noble is Ornamental>

. . . weighing the value of the different classes of the art, . . .
<A Fools Balance is no Criterion because tho it goes down on the heaviest
side we ought to look what he puts into it.>

[P 228] Thus it is the ornaments, rather than the proportions of architecture, which
at the first glance distinguish the different orders from each other; the Dorick is known
by its triglyphs, the Ionick by its volutes, and the Corinthian by its acanthus.
[He could not tell Ionick from the Corinthian or Dorick or one column
from another.]

[P 232] [European meeting Cherokee Indian] . . . which ever first feels himself
provoked to laugh, is the barbarian.
<Excellent>

[p 242] [In the highest] flights of . . . imagination, reason ought to preside from first to last, . . .

    < If this is True it is a Devilish Foolish Thing to be An Artist >

DISCOURSE VIII

[p 244, back of title]

    < Burke's Treatise on the Sublime & Beautiful is founded on the Opinions of Newton & Locke on this Treatise Reynolds has grounded many of his assertions. in all his Discourses   I read Burkes Treatise when very Young at the same time I read Locke on Human Understanding & Bacons Advancement of Learning   on Every one of these Books I wrote my Opinions & on looking them over find that my Notes on Reynolds in this Book are exactly Similar. I felt the Same Contempt & Abhorrence then; that I do now.   They mock Inspiration & Vision   Inspiration & Vision was then & now is & I hope will always Remain my Element my Eternal Dwelling place. how can I then hear it Contemnd without returning Scorn for Scorn— >

[p 245] The Principles of Art . . . in their Excess Become Defects. . . .

    < Principles according to Sʳ Joshua become Defects >

. . . form an idea of perfection from the . . . various schools. . . .

    In another Discourse he says that we cannot Mix the Florentine & Venetian

[p 251] [Rembrandt] often . . . exhibits little more than one spot of light in the midst of a large quantity of shadow: . . . Poussin . . . has scarce any principal mass of light. . . .

    Rembrandt was a Generalizer Poussin was a Particularizer

    Poussin knew better than to make all his Pictures have the same light & shadow any fool may concentrate a light in the Middle

[p 256] . . . Titian, where dignity . . . has the appearance of an unalienable adjunct; . . .

    Dignity an Adjunct

[p 260] [Young artist made vain by] certain animating words, of Spirit, Dignity, Energy, Grace, greatness of Style, and brilliancy of Tints, . . .

    Mocks

[p 262] But this kind of barbarous simplicity, would be better named Penury, . . .

    Mocks

[The ancients'] simplicity was the offspring, not of choice, but necessity.

    A Lie

[Painters who] ran into the contrary extreme [should] deal out their abundance with a more sparing hand, . . .

    Abundance of Stupidity

[p 264] . . . the painter must add grace to strength, if he desires to secure the first impression in his favour.

    If you Endeavour to Please the Worst you will never Please the Best To please All Is Impossible

[P 266] [Raffaelle's St Paul preaching at Athens] . . . add contrast, and the whole energy and unaffected grace of the figure is destroyed.
Well Said

[P 267] It is given as a rule by Fresnoy, That the principle figure . . . must appear . . . under the principal light, . . .
What a Devil of a Rule

[P 272] . . . bad pictures will instruct as well as good.
Bad Pictures are always Sr Joshuas Friends

[Rules of colouring of the] Venetian painters, . . .
Colouring formed upon these Principles is destructive of All Art because it takes away the possibility of Variety & only promotes Harmony or Blending of Colours one into another

[P 274] . . . harmony of colouring was not [attended to by Poussin]
Such Harmony of Colouring is destructive of Art   One Species of General Hue over all is the Cursed Thing calld Harmony it is like the Smile of a Fool

[P 275] The illuminated parts of objects are in nature of a warmer tint than those that are in the shade: . . .
Shade is always Cold & never as in Rubens & the Colourists Hot & Yellowy Brown

[P 277] . . . fulness of manner . . . Correggio . . . Rembrandt. . . . by melting and losing the shadows in a ground still darker. . . .
All This is Destructive of Art

[P 279] . . . must depart from nature for a greater advantage. [Cannot paint moon as relatively bright as in nature.]
These are Excellent Remarks on Proportional Colour

[P 281] [Rembrandt made head too dark to preserve contrast with bright armour, but] it is necessary that the work should be seen, not only without difficulty . . . but with pleasure. . . .
If the Picture ought to be seen with Ease surely The Nobler parts of the Picture such as the Heads ought to be Principal but this Never is the Case except in the Roman & Florentine Schools
Note I Include the Germans in the Florentine School

[P 284] From a slight undetermined drawing . . . the imagination supplies more than the painter himself, probably, could produce; . . .
What Falshood

[P 285] . . . indispensable rule . . . that everything shall be carefully and distinctly expressed. . . . This is what with us is called Science, and Learning; . . .
Excellent & Contrary to his usual Opinions

[P 286] Falconet . . . thinks meanly of this trick of concealing, . . .
<I am of Falconets opinion>

Annotations to Spurzheim's *Observations on Insanity* [t]

London, 1817

[p 106] . . . In children . . . the disturbances of the organization appear merely as organic diseases, because the functions are entirely suppressed.

Corporeal disease. to which I readily agree. Diseases of the mind I pity him. Denies mental health and perfection Stick to this all is right. But see page 152

[p 152] As the functions depend on the organization, disturbed functions will derange the organization, and one deranged cerebral part, will have an influence on others, and so arises insanity. . . . Whatever occupies the mind too intensely or exclusively is hurtful to the brain, and induces a state favourable to insanity, in diminishing the influence of the will.

[p 154] Religion is another fertile cause of insanity. Mr. Haslam, though he declares it sinful to consider religion as a cause of insanity, adds, however, that he would be ungrateful, did he not avow his obligations to Methodism for its supply of numerous cases. Hence the primitive feelings of religion may be misled and produce insanity; that is what I would contend for, and in that sense religion often leads to insanity.

Methodism &ᵉ p. 154. Cowper came to me & said. O that I were insane always I will never rest. Can you not make me truly insane. I will never rest till I am so. O that in the bosom of God I was hid. You retain health & yet are as mad as any of us all—over us all—mad as a refuge from unbelief—from Bacon Newton & Locke

~

Annotations to Berkeley's *Siris* [t]

Dublin, 1744

[p 203] God knoweth all things, as pure mind or intellect, but nothing by sense, nor in nor through a sensory. Therefore to suppose a sensory of any kind, whether space or any other, in God would be very wrong, and lead us into false conceptions of his nature.

Imagination or the Human Eternal Body in Every Man

[p 204] But in respect of a perfect spirit, there is nothing hard or impenetrable: there is no resistance to the deity. Nor hath he any Body: Nor is the supreme being united to the world, as the soul of an animal is to its body, which necessarily implieth defect, both as an instrument and as a constant weight and impediment.

Imagination or the Divine Body in Every Man

[p 205] Natural phaenomena are only natural appearances. . . . They and the phantomes that result from those appearances, *the children of imagination* grafted upon sense, such for example as pure space, are thought by many the very first in existence and stability, and to embrace and comprehend all beings.

The All in Man The Divine Image or Imagination
The Four Senses are the Four Faces of Man & the Four Rivers of the
Water of Life

[P 212] Plato and Aristotle considered God as abstracted or distinct from the natural
world. But the Aegyptians considered God and nature as making one whole, or all things
together as making one universe.

They also considerd God as abstracted or distinct from the Imaginative
World but Jesus as also Abraham & David considerd God as a Man in the
Spiritual or Imaginative Vision

Jesus considerd Imagination to be the Real Man & says I will not leave
you Orphanned and I will manifest myself to you   he says also the Spiritual
Body or Angel as little Children always behold the Face of the Heavenly
Father

[P 213] The perceptions of sense are gross: but even in the senses there is a difference.
Though harmony and proportion are not objects of sense, yet the eye and the ear are
organs, which offer to the mind such materials, by means whereof she may apprehend
both the one and the other.

Harmony [and] Proportion are Qualities & Not Things The Harmony
& Proportion of a Horse are not the same with those of a Bull Every Thing
has its own Harmony & Proportion Two Inferior Qualities in it For its
Reality is Its Imaginative Form

[P 214] By experiments of sense we become acquainted with the lower faculties of the
soul; and from them, whether by a gradual evolution or ascent, we arrive at the highest.
These become subjects for fancy to work upon. Reason considers and judges of the
imaginations. And these acts of reason become new objects to the understanding.

Knowledge is not by deduction but Immediate by Perception or Sense at
once Christ addresses himself to the Man not to his Reason   Plato did not
bring Life & Immortality to Light Jesus only did this

[P 215] There is according to Plato properly no knowledge, but only opinion concerning things sensible and perishing, not because they are naturally abstruse and involved in darkness: but because their nature and existence is uncertain, ever fleeting and
changing.

Jesus supposes every Thing to be Evident to the Child & to the Poor &
Unlearned Such is the Gospel

The Whole Bible is filld with Imagination & Visions from End to End &
not with Moral Virtues   that is the business of Plato & the Greeks & all
Warriors The Moral Virtues are continual Accusers of Sin & promote Eternal
Wars & Dominency over others

[P 217] Aristotle maketh a threefold distinction of objects according to the three speculative sciences. Physics he supposeth to be conversant about such things as have a principle
of motion in themselves, mathematics about things permanent but not abstracted, and
theology about being abstracted and immoveable, which distinction may be seen in the
ninth book of his metaphysics.

God is not a Mathematical Diagram

[P 218] It is a maxim of the Platonic philosophy, that the soul of man was originally
furnished with native inbred notions, and stands in need of sensible occasions, not
absolutely for producing them, but only for awakening, rousing or exciting into act
what was already pre-existent, dormant, and latent in the soul.

The Natural Body is an Obstruction to the Soul or Spiritual Body

[P 219] . . . Whence, according to Themistius, . . . it may be inferred that all beings are in the soul. For, saith he, the forms are the beings. By the form every thing is what it is. And, he adds, it is the soul that imparteth forms to matter, . . .

This is my Opinion but Forms must be apprehended by Sense or the Eye of Imagination Man is All Imagination God is Man & exists in us & we in him

PAGE 241

What Jesus came to Remove was the Heathen or Platonic Philosophy which blinds the Eye of Imagination The Real Man

❧

Annotations to Wordsworth's *Poems*

London, 1815

Titles marked "X" in pencil in the table of Contents are: Lucy Gray, We Are Seven, The Blind Highland Boy, The Brothers, Strange Fits of Passion, I met Louisa, Ruth, Michael . . . , Laodamia, To the Daisy, To the small Celandine, To the Cuckoo, A Night Piece, Yew Trees, She was a Phantom, I wandered lonely, Reverie of Poor Susan, Yarrow Unvisited, Yarrow Visited, Resolution and Independence, The Thorn, Hart-leap Well, Tintern Abbey, Character of a Happy Warrior, Rob Roy's Grave, Ex-postulation and Reply, The Tables Turned, Ode to Duty, Miscellaneous Sonnets, Sonnets Dedicated to Liberty, The Old Cumberland Beggar, Ode—Intimations, &c.

PREFACE

[PAGE viii] The powers requisite for the production of poetry are, first, those of observation and description, . . . whether the things depicted be actually present to the senses, or have a place only in the memory. . . . 2ndly, Sensibility, . . .

One Power alone makes a Poet.—Imagination The Divine Vision

[PAGE 1] Poems Referring to the Period of Childhood

I see in Wordsworth the Natural Man rising up against the Spiritual Man Continually & then he is No Poet but a Heathen Philosopher at Enmity against all true Poetry or Inspiration

[PAGE 3]   And I could wish my days to be
                 Bound each to each by natural piety.

There is no such Thing as Natural Piety Because The Natural Man is at Enmity with God

[PAGE 43] To H.C. Six Years Old

This is all in the highest degree Imaginative & equal to any Poet but not Superior I cannot think that Real Poets have any competition None are greatest in the Kingdom of Heaven it is so in Poetry

[PAGE 44]

Influence of Natural Objects
In calling forth and strengthening the Imagination
in Boyhood and early Youth.

Natural Objects always did & now do Weaken deaden & obliterate Imagination in Me Wordsworth must know that what he Writes Valuable is Not to be found in Nature Read Michael Angelos Sonnet vol 2 p. 179

[PAGE 341] Essay, Supplementary to the Preface.

I do not know who wrote these Prefaces they are very mischievous & direct contrary to Wordsworths own Practise

[PAGE 364] From what I saw with my own eyes, I knew that the imagery was spurious. In nature everything is distinct, yet nothing defined into absolute independent singleness. In Macpherson's work, it is exactly the reverse; everything (that is not stolen) is in this manner defined, insulated, dislocated, deadened,—yet nothing distinct. It will always be so when words are substituted for things. . . . Yet, much as these pretended treasures of antiquity have been admired, . . .

I Believe both Macpherson & Chatterton, that what they say is Ancient, Is so

[PAGE 365] . . . no Author in the least distinguished, has ventured formally to imitate them—except the Boy, Chatterton, on their first appearance.

I own myself an admirer of Ossian equally with any other Poet whatever Rowley & Chatterton also

[PAGE 375, final paragraph] . . . if [the Writer] were not persuaded that the Contents of these Volumes . . . evinced something of the "Vision and the Faculty divine," . . . he would not, if a wish could do it, save them from immediate destruction.

It appears to me as if the last Paragraph beginning With "Is it the result" Was writ by another hand & mind from the rest of these Prefaces. Perhaps they are the opinions of a Portrait or Landscape Painter   Imagination is the Divine Vision not of The World nor of Man nor from Man as. he is a Natural Man but only as he is a Spiritual Man   Imagination has nothing to do with Memory

❧

Annotations to Wordsworth's Preface to
The Excursion, being a portion of
The Recluse, A Poem
London, 1814

Blake's notes are in the margins and at the end of a four-page transcript he made in 1826 of the last paragraph of Wordsworth's Preface and the 107 lines there quoted "from the Conclusion of the first Book of the Recluse".

We quote here, from Blake's transcript, only the lines of *The Recluse* upon which he made comment.

[LINES 31–35] All strength, all terror, single or in bands
That ever was put forth in personal Form
Jehovah—with his thunder & the choir
Of shouting Angels & the empyreal thrones—
I pass them unalarmd, . . .

[Blake, at end of ms]

Solomon when he Married Pharohs daughter & became a Convert to the
Heathen Mythology Talked exactly in this way of Jehovah as a Very inferior object of Mans Contemplations he also passed him by unalarmd & was
permitted. Jehovah dropped a tear & followd him by his Spirit into the
Abstract Void it is called the Divine Mercy Satan dwells in it but Mercy
does not dwell in him he knows not to Forgive

W Blake

[LINES 63–68] How exquisitely the individual Mind
(And the progressive powers perhaps no less
(Of the whole species) to the external World
Is fitted:—& how exquisitely too,   †
Theme this but little heard of among Men
The external World is fitted to the Mind.

You shall not bring me down to believe such fitting & fitted I know better
& Please your Lordship

[LINES 72–82] —Such grateful haunts forgoing. if I oft
Must turn elsewhere—to travel near the tribes
And fellowships of Men, & see ill sights
Of madding passions mutually inflamd
Must hear *Humanity in fields & groves*   ‡
Pipe solitary anguish; or must hang
Brooding above the fierce confederate storm
Of Sorrow barricadoed evermore
Within the walls of cities; may these sounds
Have their authentic comment—that even these
Hearing I be not downcast nor forlorn

does not this Fit & is it not Fitting most Exquisitely too but to what not
to Mind but to the Vile Body only & to its Laws of Good & Evil & its En-
mities against Mind

❧

Annotations to Thornton's
The Lord's Prayer, Newly Translated
London, 1827

Italics do not represent underlining by Blake.

[TITLE PAGE]

I look upon this as a Most Malignant & Artful attack upon the Kingdom
of Jesus By the Classical Learned thro the Instrumentality of Dr Thornton The Greek & Roman Classics is the Antichrist I say Is & not Are as
most expressive & correct too

[PAGE iii] DOCTOR JOHNSON *on the Bible.*
["]The BIBLE is the *most difficult* book in the world to *comprehend,* nor can it be understood at all by the *unlearned,* except through the aid of CRITICAL and EXPLANATORY *notes. . . ."*

Christ & his Apostles were Illiterate Men   Caiphas Pilate & Herod were Learned.

LORD BYRON *on the Ethics of* CHRIST.
". . . What made SOCRATES *the greatest of men?* His *moral truths—his ethics.* What *proved* JESUS CHRIST to be the SON OF GOD, HARDLY LESS *than his miracles did?* His *moral precepts. . . ."*

If Morality was Christianity Socrates was The Savior.

The Beauty of the Bible is that the most Ignorant & Simple Minds Understand it Best—Was Johnson hired to Pretend to Religious Terrors while he was an Infidel or how was it

[PAGE iv]   Reasons for a New Translation of the Whole Bible.
The only thing for Newtonian & Baconian Philosophers to Consider is this   Whether Jesus did not suffer himself to be Mockd by Caesars Soldiers Willingly & [*I hope they will*] <to> Consider this to all Eternity will be Comment Enough

[PAGE 1]
Such things as these depend on the Fashion of the Age
    In a book where all may Read & ⎫
    In a book which all may Read & ⎬ are Equally Right
    In a book that all may Read   ⎭
That Man who &ᵉ is equally so   The Man that & the Man which

THE LORD'S PRAYER,
(Translated from the Greek,) by Dr. Thornton.

[The Greek text after the second and third verses is supplied by Blake.]

Come let us *worship,* and *bow down,* and *kneel,* before the LORD, OUR MAKER. Psalm XCV.

O FATHER OF MANKIND, THOU, who dwellest in *the highest of the* HEAVENS, *Reverenc'd be* THY *Name!*
ΠΑΤΕΡ ἡμῶν ὁ ἐν τοῖς οὐρανοῖς, ἁγιασθήτω τὸ ονομα σου.

——————

May THY REIGN be, *every where, proclaim'd* so that THY *Will* may be *done* upon *the Earth,* as it is in the MANSIONS of HEAVEN:
——ἐλθέτω η βασιλεία σου γενηθήτω τὸ θέλημα σου.

——————

Grant unto *me,* and *the whole world, day* by *day,* an abundant supply of *spiritual* and *corporeal* Food:

——————

Forgive US OUR TRANSGRESSIONS against THEE, AS WE EXTEND OUR *Kindness,* and *Forgiveness,* TO ALL:

——————

O GOD! ABANDON us *not,* when surrounded, by TRIALS;

——————

But PRESERVE us from *the Dominion* of SATAN: For THINE only, IS THE SOVEREIGNTY, THE POWER, and THE GLORY, throughout ETERNITY!!!
                                          AMEN.

Men from their *childhood* have been so accustomed *to mouth* the LORD'S PRAYER, that they continue this *through life,* and call it *"Saying their Prayers."* . . .

It is the learned that Mouth & not the Vulgar

Lawful Bread Bought with Lawful Money & a Lawful Heaven seen thro a Lawful Telescope by means of Lawful Window Light The Holy Ghost [*who*] <& whatever> cannot be Taxed is Unlawful & Witchcraft.

Spirits are Lawful but not Ghosts especially Royal Gin is Lawful Spirit [*real*] No Smuggling <real> British Spirit & Truth

[PAGE 2] Critical and Explanatory Notes.

Give us the Bread that is our due & Right by taking away Money or a Price or Tax upon what is Common to all in thy Kingdom

[PAGE 3]

Jesus our Father who art in <thy> Heavns call'd by thy Name the Holy Ghost Thy Kingdom on Earth is Not nor thy Will done but [*Beelzebub*] <[*his*] <Satans> Will who is the God of this World> The Accuser [*Let his Judgment be Forgiveness that he may be cons[u]md in his own Shame*] <[*His Judgment*] <the Accusation> shall be Forgiveness that he may be consumd in his own Shame>

Give us This Eternal Day our [*Ghostly*] <own right> Bread & take away Money or Debt or Tax <a Value or Price> as we have all things common among us Every Thing has as much right to Eternal Life as God who is the Servant of Man

Leave us not in [*?Poverty ?and ?Want*] Parsimony <Satans Kingdom> [*but deliver*] <liberate> us from the Natural Man & want or Jobs Kingdom

For thine is the Kingdom & the Power & the Glory & not Caesars or Satans Amen.

(Many illegible erasures, partial restorations, and repetitions probably meant to replace one another have been omitted from this transcript.)

[PAGE 5] Dim at best are the conceptions we have of the SUPREME BEING, who, as it were, keeps the human race in suspense, neither discovering, nor hiding HIMSELF; . . .

a Female God

[PAGE 6] What is the WILL of GOD *we* are ordered to obey? . . . Let us consider whose WILL it is. . . . It is the WILL of our MAKER. . . . It is finally the WILL of HIM, who is *uncontrolably powerful;* . . .

So you See That God is just such a Tyrant as Augustus Caesar & is not this Good & Learned & Wise & Classical

[PAGE 12, blank]

This is Saying the Lords Prayer Backwards which they say Raises the Devil

Doctor Thorntons <Tory> Translation Translated out of its disguise in the <Classical &> Scotch language into [*plain*] <the vulgar> English

Our Father Augustus Caesar who art in these thy <Substantial Astronomical Telescopic> Heavens Holiness to thy Name <or Title & reverence to thy Shadow> Thy Kingship come upon Earth first & thence in Heaven Give us day by day our Real Taxed <Substantial Money bought> Bread [*& take*] <deliver from the Holy Ghost <so we call Nature> what-

ever cannot be Taxed> [*debt that was owing to him*] <for all is debts &
Taxes between Caesar & us & one another> lead us not to read the Bible
<but let our Bible be Virgil & Shakspeare> & deliver us from Poverty in
Jesus <that Evil One> For thine is the Kingship <or Allegoric Godship>
& the Power or War & the Glory or Law Ages after Ages in thy Descendents
<for God is only an Allegory of Kings & nothing Else> Amen

I swear that Basileia βασιλεια is not Kingdom but Kingship   I Nature
Hermaphrotitic Priest & King Live in Real Substantial Natural Born Man
& that Spirit is the Ghost of Matter or Nature & God is The Ghost of the
Priest & King who Exist whereas God exists not except from [*them*] <their
Effluvia>

Here is Signed Two Names which are too Holy to be Written

Thus we see that the Real God is the Goddess Nature & that God Creates
nothing but what can be Touchd & Weighed & Taxed & Measured   all
else is Heresy & Rebellion against Caesar Virgils Only God   See Eclogue
i   for all this we thank Dr Thornton

<hr>

Annotation to Cellini(?)   t

[Note said to be in Cennini's *Trattato della Pittura* (Roma, 1821) but probably in
Benvenuto Cellini's *Trattato dell' Oreficeria* (1568, 1731, [1795] or 1811)]

[Cellini's 8th chapter tells of a commission from Pope Paul III for a gift for Emperor
Charles V. Cellini suggested an allegorical group of "Faith, Hope, and Charity" up-
holding a crucifix of gold. The Pope was induced to order instead a breviary of the
Virgin bound in jeweled gold.]

The Pope supposes Nature and the Virgin Mary to be the same allegorical
personages, but the Protestant considers Nature as incapable of bearing a
child.

XIII

[INSCRIPTIONS AND NOTES
ON OR FOR PICTURES]

engraved
JOSEPH of Arimathea among The Rocks of Albion
Engraved by W Blake 1773 from an old Italian Drawing
This is One of the Gothic Artists who Built the Cathedrals in what we
call the Dark Ages Wandering about in sheep skins & goat skins. of whom
the World was not worthy   such were the Christians in all Ages
Michael Angelo Pinxit

ink [on a proof of the early state of the plate]
Engraved when I was a beginner at Basire's from a drawing by Salviati
after Michael Angelo

*

engraved
WB inv 1780.
Albion rose from where he labourd at the Mill with Slaves
Giving himself for the Nations he danc'd the dance of Eternal Death

*

engraved
[first state of plate]:
Our End is Come
Published June 5 1793 by W Blake Lambeth
[second state of plate]:
When the senses are shaken
And the Soul is driven to madness. Page 56
[third state of plate]:
The Accusers of Theft Adultery Murder
W Blake inv & sculp
A Scene in the Last Judgment
Satans' holy Trinity The Accuser The Judge & The Executioner

*

Notebook p 116, ink

[List of Subjects for The History of England]   t

1 Giants ancient inhabitants of England
2 The Landing of Brutus
3 Corineus throws Gogmagog the Giant into the sea
4 King Lear
[5] The Ancient Britons according to Caesar [<*The frontispiece*>]   t
6 The Druids
7 The Landing of Julius Caesar
8 Boadicea inspiring the Britons against the Romans
   <The Britons distress & depopulation
      Women fleeing from War
      Women in a Siege>
9 Alfred in the countrymans house
10 Edwin & Morcar stirring up the Londoners to resist W the Conq^r
11 W the Conq Crownd
12 King John & Mag Charta
   <A Famine occasiond by the Popish interdict>
13 Edward at Calais
14 Edward the Black Prince brings his Captives to his father
15 The Penance of Jane Shore
   <17 [*The Reformation*] by H VIII.>
      <18 [*Ch I beheaded*]>
[16] [<17>] <19> The Plague
[17] [<18>] <20> The fire of London
[18] <16> The Cruelties used by Kings & Priests [*whose arts*]
[19] <21> A prospect of Liberty
[20] <22> A Cloud

*

Notebook p 116, pencil

[List of Subjects from] Exodus VII   t

1 Aaron [ ]	8 Boils & Blains
2 Moses [ ]	9 Hail
3 River [ ] ?blood	10 Locusts
4 Frogs	11 Darkness
5 Lice	12 First born [ ]
6 [*Flies*] Swarms of Flies	13 Red Sea Egyptians Drownd
7 Murrain of Beasts	

*

[Legends in a Small Book of Designs]

[*Urizen*, title-page design]

Which is the Way
The Right or the Left

[*The Marriage of Heaven and Hell*, plate 11]

Death & Hell
Team with Life

[The same, plate 14]

a Flaming Sword
Revolving every way

[*Urizen*, plate 2]

Teach these Souls to Fly

[The same, plate 10]

Does the Soul labour thus
In Caverns of The Grave

[*Visions of the Daughters of Albion*, plate 7]

Wait Sisters
Tho all is Lost

[*Urizen*, plate 5]

The Book of my Remembrance

[The same, plate 9]

Eternally I labour on

[The same, plate 12]

I labour upwards into futurity

*

[Legend in a Large Book of Designs]

[*Urizen*, plate 22]

Frozen doors to mock
The World: while they within torments uplock

*

[On the back of *The Fall of Man*, watercolor drawing "1807 W Blake inv"]

ink

The Father indignant at the Fall—the SAVIOUR, while the Evil Angels
are driven, gently conducts our first Parents out of Eden through a guard of
Weeping Angels—SATAN now awakes Sin, Death, & Hell, to celebrate with
him the birth of War & Misery: while the Lion seizes the Bull, the Tiger the
Horse, the Vulture and the Eagle contend for the Lamb

engraved

Chaucers Canterbury Pilgrims

Painted in Fresco by William Blake & by him Engraved & Published October 8 1810. . . .

The use of Money & its Wars
An Allegory of Idolatry or Politics

*

etched

Chaining of Orc

Type by W Blake 1812

*

[Descriptions of Illustrations to Milton's *L'Allegro* and *Il Penseroso*]

Blake's manuscript notes accompanying his watercolors

Mirth. Allegro

1   Heart easing Mirth.
    Haste thee Nymph & bring with thee
    Jest & Youthful Jollity
    Quips & Cranks & Wanton Wiles
    Nods & Becks & wreathed smiles
    Sport that wrinkled Care derides
    And Laughter holding both his Sides
    Come & trip it as you go
    On the light phantastic toe
    And in thy right hand lead with thee
    The Mountain Nymph Sweet Liberty

These Personifications are all brought together in the First Design. Surrounding the Principal Figure which is Mirth herself

2   To hear the Lark begin his flight
    And singing startle the dull Night
    From his Watch Tower in the Skies
    Till the dappled Dawn does rise

The Lark is an Angel on the Wing Dull Night starts from his Watch Tower on a Cloud. The Dawn with her dappled Horses arises above the Earth The Earth beneath awakes at the Larks Voice

3   Sometime walking not unseen
    By hedgerow Elms on Hillocks green
    Right against the Eastern Gate
    When the Great Sun begins his state

Robed in Flames & amber Light
The Clouds in thousand Liveries dight
While the Plowman near at hand
Whistles o'er the Furrow'd Land
And the Milkmaid singeth blithe
And the Mower whets his Scythe
And every Shepherd tells his Tale
Under the Hawthorn in the Dale

The Great Sun is represented clothed in Flames Surrounded by the Clouds in their Liveries, in their various Offices at the Eastern Gate. beneath in Small Figures Milton walking by Elms on Hillocks green The Plowman. The Milkmaid   The Mower whetting his Scythe. & The Shepherd & his Lass under a Hawthorn in the Dale

4   Sometimes with secure delight
The upland Hamlets will invite
When the merry Bells ring round
And the jocund Rebecks Sound
To many a Youth & many a Maid
Dancing in the chequerd Shade
And Young & Old come forth to play
On a Sunshine Holiday

In this Design is Introduced

Mountains on whose barren breast
The Labring Clouds do often rest

Mountains Clouds Rivers Trees appear Humanized on the Sunshine Holiday. The Church Steeple with its merry bells The Clouds arise from the bosoms of Mountains While Two Angels sound their Trumpets in the Heavens to announce the Sunshine Holiday

5   Then to the Spicy Nut brown Ale
With Stories told of many a Treat
How Fairy Mab the junkets eat
She was pinchd & pulld she said
And he by Friars Lantern led
Tells how the drudging Goblin sweat
To earn his Cream Bowl duly set
When in one Night e'er glimpse of Morn
His shadowy Flail had threshd the Corn
That ten day labourers could not end
Then crop-full out of door he flings
E'er the first Cock his Matin rings

The Goblin crop full flings out of doors from his Laborious task dropping his Flail & Cream bowl. yawning & stretching vanishes into the Sky. in which is seen Queen Mab Eating the Junkets. The Sports of the Fairies are seen thro the Cottage where "She" lays in Bed "pinchd & pulld" by Fairies as they dance on the Bed the Cieling & the Floor & a Ghost pulls the Bed Clothes at her Feet. "He" is seen following the Friars Lantern towards the Convent

6   There let Hymen oft appear
In Saffron Robe with Taper clear
With Mask & Antique Pageantry
Such sights as Youthful Poets dream

On Summers Eve by haunted Stream
Then lo the well trod Stage anon
If Johnsons learned Sock be on
Or Sweetest Shakespeare Fancys Child
Warble his native wood notes wild

The youthful Poet sleeping on a bank by the Haunted Stream by Sun Set sees in his Dream the more bright Sun of Imagination. under the auspices of Shakespeare & Johnson. in which is Hymen at a Marriage & the Antique Pageantry attending it

Melancholy. Pensieroso

7 Come pensive Nun devout & pure
Sober stedfast & demure
All in Robe of darkest grain
Flowing with majestic train
Come but keep thy wonted state
With even step & musing gait
And looks commercing with the Skies
————
And join with thee calm Peace & Quiet
Spare Fast who oft with Gods doth diet
And hears the Muses in a ring
Ay. round about Joves altar sing
And add to these retired Leisure
Who in trim Gardens takes his pleasure
But first & Chiefest with thee bring
Him who yon soars on golden Wing
Guiding the Fiery wheeled Throne
The Cherub Contemplation
————
Less Philomel will deign a song
In her sweetest saddest plight
Smoothing the rugged Brow of Night
While Cynthia Checks her dragon yoke
Gently o'er the accustomd Oak

These Personifications are all brought together in this design surrounding the Principal Figure Who is Melancholy herself

8 To behold the wandring Moon
Riding near her highest Noon
Like one that has been led astray
Thro the heavens wide pathless way
And oft as if her head she bowd
Stooping thro' a fleecy Cloud
Oft on a plat of rising ground
I hear the far off Curfew sound
Over some wide waterd shore
Swinging slow with sullen roar

Milton in his Character of a Student at Cambridge. Sees the Moon terrified as one led astray in the midst of her path thro heaven. The distant Steeple seen across a wide water indicates the Sound of the Curfew Bell

9   Where I may oft outwatch the Bear
With thrice great Hermes or unsphear
The Spirit of Plato to unfold
What Worlds or what vast regions hold
The Immortal Mind that has forsook
Its Mansion in this Fleshly nook
And of those Spirits that are found
In Fire. Air. Flood. & Underground

The Spirit of Plato unfolds his Worlds to Milton in Contemplation. The Three destinies sit on the Circles of Platos Heavens weaving the Thread of Mortal Life thèse Heavens are Venus Jupiter & Mars. Hermes flies before as attending on the Heaven of Jupiter the Great Bear is seen in the Sky beneath Hermes & The Spirits of Fire. Air. Water & Earth Surround Miltons Chair

10   And when the Sun begins to fling
His flaring Beams me Goddess bring
To arched walks of twilight Groves
And Shadows brown that Sylvan Coves

Milton led by Melancholy into the Groves away from the Suns flaring Beams who is seen in the Heavens throwing his darts & flames of fire The Spirits of the Trees on each side are seen under the domination of Insects raised by the Suns heat

11   There in close Covert by some Brook
Where no profaner Eye may look
With such concert as they keep
Entice the dewy featherd Sleep
And let some strange mysterious Dream
Wave on his Wings in airy stream
Of liveliest Portraiture displayd
On my Sleeping eyelids laid
And as I wake sweet Music breathe
Above; about: or underneath:
Sent by some Spirit to Mortals good
Or the unseen Genius of the Wood

Milton sleeping on a Bank. Sleep descending with a Strange Mysterious Dream upon his Wings of Scrolls & Nets & Webs unfolded by Spirits in the Air & in the Brook around Milton are Six Spirits or Fairies hovering on the air with Instruments of Music

12   And may at last my weary Age
Find out the peaceful Hermitage
The hairy Gown the mossy Cell
Where I may sit & rightly spell
Of every Star that heavn doth shew
And every Herb that sips the dew
Till old Experience do attain
To somewhat like Prophetic strain

Milton in his Old Age sitting in his Mossy Cell Contemplating the Constellations. surrounded by the Spirits of the Herbs & Flowers. bursts forth into a rapturous Prophetic Strain

*

[Engraving of Mirth and Her Companions, illustrating Milton's *L'Allegro*]

[Late state, inscribed at bottom:]

Solomon says Vanity of Vanities all is Vanity & What can be Foolisher than this

*

[Note on a Pencil Drawing of Nine Grotesque Heads]

All Genius varies[.] Thus Devils are various Angels are all alike

*

Genesis

t

[Chapter Titles in Blake's Illustrated Manuscript. A Fragment]

Chapter I   The Creation of the Natural Man
Chapter II   The Natural Man divided into Male & Female & of the Tree of Life & of the Tree of Good & Evil
Chapter III   Of the Sexual Nature & its Fall into Generation & Death
Chapter IV   How Generation & Death took possession of the Natural Man & of the Forgiveness of Sins written upon the Murderers Forehead

*

[On Blake's Illustrations to Dante]

t

On design No 3, "Hell Canto 2"
[A Jehovah figure with outstretched human and cloven hands:]
The Angry God of This World & his ?Porch in Purgatory
[Lightning below his hands:]
The Thunder of Egypt
[Kneeling figure with symbols of empire:]
Caesar

On design No 7, "Hell Canto 4", Homer with sword and laurel crown, in center of diagram of celestial Universe
[Spheres from outer to inner] Vacuum   Starry Heaven   Saturn
Jupiter   Mars   Sun   Venus   Mercury   Moon   [all marked as:] Limbo of Weak Shadows [then:] Terrestrial Paradise   It is an Island in Limbo   Purgatory
Every thing in Dantes Comedia shews That for Tyrannical Purposes he

has made This World the Foundation of All & the Goddess Nature & not the Holy Ghost   as Poor Churchill said Nature thou art my Goddess

[Reading after insertions:] . . . & the Goddess Nature <Memory> <is his Inspirer> & not <Imagination> the Holy Ghost. . . .

Round Purgatory is Paradise & round Paradise is Vacuum or Limbo. so that Homer is the Center of All   I mean the Poetry of the Heathen Stolen & Perverted from the Bible not by Chance but by design by the Kings of Persia and their Generals   The Greek Heroes & lastly by The Romans

Swedenborg does the same in saying that in this World is the Ultimate of Heaven

This is the most damnable Falshood of Satan & his Antichrist

On design No 14, Plutus
[Coins in sack labeled:]
Money

On design No 15, "HELL Canto 7"
[Battle under water labeled:]
The Stygian Lake

On design No 16, "HELL Canto 7", [Goddess of Fortune in a pit]
The hole of a Shit house
The Goddess Fortune is the devils servant ready to Kiss any ones Arse
Celestial Globe   Terrestrial Globe

On design No 17, "HELL Canto 7"
Stygian Lake

On design No 72, "P-g Canto 2"
Cato

On design No 86, "P-g Canto 27"
Leah & Rachel ?Dantes ?Dream

On design No 99, [Mary and Beatrice on sunflower]
Saturn
Mary   Scepter   Looking Glass   Thrones   Dominion(s) chaind round
Bible chaind round   Homer   Aristotle

On design No 101, [a diagram of the 9 Circles of Hell]
This is Upside Down When viewd from Hells Gate But right When Viewd from Purgatory after they have passed the Center
In Equivocal Worlds Up & Down are Equivocal
Limbo
1 Charon
2 Minos
3 Cerberus
4 Plutus & Phlegyas
5 City of Dis   Queen of Endless Woe [   ] furies & [   ] Lesser Circle   Point of the Universe   Canto Eleventh line 68

6 Minotaur The City of Dis seems to occupy the Space between the Fifth & Sixth Circles or perhaps it occupies both Circles with its Environs
7 Centaurs Most likely Dante describes the 7 8 & 9 Circles in Canto XI v 18 3 Compartments Dante calls them Cerchietti
8 Geryon Malebolge Containing 10 Gulphs
9 Lucifer Containing 9 Rounds
It seems as if Dantes supreme Good was something Superior to the Father or Jesus [as] <for> if he gives his rain to the Evil & the Good & his Sun to the Just & the Unjust He could never have Builded Dantes Hell nor the Hell of the Bible neither in the way our Parsons explain it It must have been originally Formed by the Devil Him self & So I understand it to have been

Whatever Book is for Vengeance for Sin & whatever Book is Against the Forgiveness of Sins is not of the Father but of Satan the Accuser & Father of Hell

*

[On Blake's Epitome of Hervey's Meditations among the Tombs]   t

[Reading from left to right, bottom to top]
Widow   Father   Babe   Baptism   Hervey   Angel of Death
Virgin   Wife   Infancy   Old Age   Husband   Angel of Providence   Guardian Angel   Child   Angel of Death   Mother
Where is your Father   The Lost Child   Orphans   Sophronia died in Childbed   She died on the Wedding Day   Orphan   Moses
Elias   JESUS   David   Solomon   Protecting Angel   Aaron
Abraham believed God   These died for Love   Ministering Angels
Mother of Leah & Rachel   Mother of Rebecca   Recording Angels
Protecting Angel   NOAH   Enoch   Cain   Serpent   Abel
Eve   Adam   God out of Christ is a Consuming Fire   MERCY
WRATH

XIV

[Prospectus]

TO THE PUBLIC

October 10, 1793.

The Labours of the Artist, the Poet, the Musician, have been proverbially attended by poverty and obscurity; this was never the fault of the Public, but was owing to a neglect of means to propagate such works as have wholly absorbed the Man of Genius. Even Milton and Shakespeare could not publish their own works.

This difficulty has been obviated by the Author of the following productions now presented to the Public; who has invented a method of Printing both Letter-press and Engraving in a style more ornamental, uniform, and grand, than any before discovered, while it produces works at less than one fourth of the expense.

If a method of Printing which combines the Painter and the Poet is a phenomenon worthy of public attention, provided that it exceeds in elegance all former methods, the Author is sure of his reward.

Mr. Blake's powers of invention very early engaged the attention of many persons of eminence and fortune; by whose means he has been regularly enabled to bring before the Public works (he is not afraid to say) of equal magnitude and consequence with the productions of any age or country: among which are two large highly finished engravings (and two more are nearly ready) which will commence a Series of subjects from the Bible, and another from the History of England.

The following are the Subjects of the several Works now published and on Sale at Mr. Blake's, No. 13, Hercules Buildings, Lambeth.

1. Job, a Historical Engraving. Size 1 ft. 7½ in. by 1 ft. 2 in.: price 12s.
2. Edward and Elinor, a Historical Engraving. Size 1 ft. 6½ in. by 1 ft.: price 10s. 6d.
3. America, a Prophecy, in Illuminated Printing. Folio, with 18 designs: price 10s. 6d.

4. Visions of the Daughters of Albion, in Illuminated Printing. Folio, with 8 designs, price 7s. 6d.

5. The Book of Thel, a Poem in Illuminated Printing. Quarto, with 6 designs, price 3s.

6. The Marriage of Heaven and Hell, in Illuminated Printing. Quarto, with 14 designs, price 7s. 6d.

7. Songs of Innocence, in Illuminated Printing. Octavo, with 25 designs, price 5s.

8. Songs of Experience, in Illuminated Printing. Octavo, with 25 designs, price 5s.

9. The History of England, a small book of Engravings. Price 3s.

10. The Gates of Paradise, a small book of Engravings. Price 3s.

The Illuminated Books are Printed in Colours, and on the most beautiful wove paper that could be procured.

No Subscriptions for the numerous great works now in hand are asked, for none are wanted; but the Author will produce his works, and offer them to sale at a fair price.

*

[On the Back of a Drawing]

The Bible of Hell, in Nocturnal Visions collected Vol. I. Lambeth.

*

[On the drawings of Thomas Heath Malkin]

[Paragraph in *A Father's Memoirs of his Child*,
by Benjamin Heath Malkin. London, 1806, pp 33–35]

They are all firm, determinate outline, or identical form. Had the hand which executed these little ideas been that of a plagiary, who works only from the memory, we should have seen blots, called masses; blots without form, and therefore without meaning. These blots of light and dark, as being the result of labour, are always clumsy and indefinite; the effect of rubbing out and putting in, like the progress of a blind man, or of one in the dark, who feels his way, but does not see it. These are not so. Even the copy from Raphael's Cartoon of St. Paul preaching, is a firm, determinate outline, struck at once, as Protogenes struck his line, when he meant to make himself known to Apelles. The map of Allestone has the same character of the firm and determinate. All his efforts prove this little boy to have had that greatest of all blessings, a strong imagination, a clear idea, and a determinate vision of things in his own mind.

*

[Memoranda from the Notebook]

PAGE 14 (facing the first emblem drawing)
Ideas of Good & Evil

PAGE 4
I say I shant live five years
And if I live one it will be a
Wonder   June 1793

Tuesday Jan^{ry}. 20. 1807 between Two & Seven in the Evening—Despair

Memorandum

To Engrave on Pewter. Let there be first a drawing made correctly with black lead pencil, let nothing be to seek, then rub it off on the plate coverd with white wax. or perhaps pass it thro press. this will produce certain & determind forms on the plate & time will not be wasted in seeking them afterwards

Memorandum

To Woodcut on Pewter. lay a ground on the Plate & smoke it as for Etching, then trace you outline<s> [& *draw them in with a needle*]. and beginning with the spots of light on each object with an oval pointed needle scrape off the ground. [& *instead of etching the shadowy strokes*] as a direction for your graver then proceed to graving with the ground on the plate being as careful as possible not to hurt the ground because it being black will shew perfectly what is wanted [*?towards*]

Memorandum

To Woodcut on Copper Lay a Ground as for Etching. trace &^c. & instead of Etching the blacks Etch the whites & bite it in

PAGE 59

From Bells Weekly Messenger Augst 4. 1811.

Salisbury July 29
A Bill of Indictment was preferred against Peter Le Cave for Felony but returnd Ignoramus by the Grand Jury. It appeard that he was in extreme indigence but was an Artist of very superior Merit[.] while he was in Wilton [*Jail*] <Goal> he painted many pieces in the Style of

Morland some of which are stated to be even superior to the performances of that Artist. with whom Le Cave lived many years as a
Professional Assistant & he states that many Paintings of his were only
Varnished over by Morland & sold by that Artist as his own. Many
of the Principal Gentlemen of the County have visited Le Cave in
the Goal & declared his drawings & Paintings in many instances to
excel Morlands. The Writer of this Article has seen many of Le Caves
Works & tho he does not pretend to the knowledge of an artist yet he
considers them as Chaste delineations of Rural Objects.

Such is the Paragraph   It confirms the Suspition I entertaind
concerning those two [*Prints*] I Engraved From for J. R. Smith.   t
That Morland could not have Painted them as they were the works
of a Correct Mind & no Blurrer

*

PAGE 64

I always thought that Jesus Christ was a Snubby or I should not have
worshipd him if I had thought he had been one of those long spindle
nosed rascals

PAGE 67

23 May 1810 found the Word Golden

PAGE 72

Jesus does not treat [?all ?alike] because he makes a Wide Distinction between the Sheep & the Goats consequently he is Not Charitable

[Paper cut away]

PAGE 96

Who shall bind the Infinite

PAGE 92 REVERSED

Every thing which is in harmony with me I call In harmony—But there
may be things which are Not in harmony with Me & yet are in a More
perfect Harmony

PAGE 101 REVERSED   t

on 1 Plate ⎧ O Lapwing &c
           ⎪ An answer to the Parson
           ⎨ Experiment
           ⎪ Riches
           ⎩ If you trap &c

[Fortunes in Bysshe]

<South Molton Street>

Sunday August . 1807 My Wife was told by a Spirit to look for her
fortune by opening by chance a book which she had in her hand it was
Bysshes Art of Poetry. She opend the following

 I saw 'em kindle with desire
 While with soft sighs they blew the fire
 Saw the approaches of their joy
 He growing more fierce & she less coy
 Saw how they mingled melting rays
 Exchanging Love a thousand ways
 Kind was the force on every side)
 Her new desire she could not hide }
 Nor would the shepherd be denied)
 The blessed minute he pursud
 Till she transported in his arms
 Yields to the Conqueror all her charms
 His panting breast to hers now Joind
 They feast on raptures unconfind
 Vast & luxuriant such as prove
 The immortality of Love
 For who but a Divinity)
 Could mingle souls to that degree }
 And melt them into Extasy)
 Now like the Phoenix both expire)
 While from the ashes of their fire }
 Spring up a new & soft desire)
 Like charmers thrice they did invoke
 The God & thrice new Vigor took
       BEHN

I was so well pleased with her Luck that I thought I would try my Own
& opend the following

 As when the winds their airy quarrel try
 Justling from every quarter of the Sky
 This way & that the Mountain oak they bear
 His boughs they shatter & his branches tear

 With leaves & falling mast they spread the Ground
 The hollow Valleys Eccho [the] to the Sound
 Unmovd the royal plant their fury mocks
 Or shaken clings more closely to the rocks
 For as he shoots his lowring head on high
 So deep in earth his fixd foundations lie
       DRYDENS VIRGIL

[Blake's Autograph in the Album of William Upcott] ᵗ

WILLIAM BLAKE one who is very much delighted with being in good Company

Born 28 Novr 1757 in London
& has died several times since

January 16
1826

    The above was written & the drawing annexed by the desire of Mr Leigh how far it is an Autograph is a Question   I do not think an Artist can write an Autograph especially one who has Studied in the Florentine & Roman Schools as such an one will Consider what he is doing but an Autograph as I understand it, is Writ helter skelter like a hog upon a rope or a Man who walks without Considering whether he shall run against a Post or a House or a Horse or a Man & I am apt to believe that what is done without meaning is very different from that which a Man Does with his Thought & Mind & ought not to be Calld by the Same Name.

    I consider the Autograph of Mr Cruikshank which very justly stands first in the Book & that Beautiful Specimen of Writing by Mr Comfield & my own; as standing [in] the same Predicament they are in some measure Works of Art & not of Nature or Chance

Heaven born the Soul a Heavenward Course must hold
For what delights the Sense is False & Weak
Beyond the Visible World she soars to Seek
Ideal Form, The Universal Mold
Michael Angelo. Sonnet as Translated by Mr Wordsworth

XV

[To] Rev^d Dr Trusler, Englefield Green, Egham, Surrey

13 Hercules Buildings, Lambeth, August 23, 1799

Revd Sir

I really am sorry that you are falln out with the Spiritual World Especially if I should have to answer for it I feel very sorry that your Ideas & Mine on Moral Painting differ so much as to have made you angry with my method of Study. If I am wrong I am wrong in good company. I had hoped your plan comprehended All Species of this Art & Especially that you would not regret that Species which gives Existence to Every other. namely Visions of Eternity You say that I want somebody to Elucidate my Ideas. But you ought to know that What is Grand is necessarily obscure to Weak men. That which can be made Explicit to the Idiot is not worth my care. The wisest of the Ancients considerd what is not too Explicit as the fittest for Instruction because it rouzes the faculties to act. I name Moses Solomon Esop Homer Plato

But as you have favord me with your remarks on my Design permit me in return to defend it against a mistaken one, which is. That I have supposed Malevolence without a Cause.—Is not Merit in one a Cause of Envy in another & Serenity & Happiness & Beauty a Cause of Malevolence. But Want of Money & the Distress of A Thief can never be alledged as the Cause of his Thievery. for many honest people endure greater hard ships with Fortitude We must therefore seek the Cause elsewhere than in want of Money for that is the Misers passion, not the Thiefs

I have therefore proved your Reasonings Ill proportiond which you can never prove my figures to be. They are those of Michael Angelo Rafael & the Antique & of the best living Models. I percieve that your Eye[s] is perverted by Caricature Prints, which ought not to abound so much as they do. Fun I love but too much Fun is of all things the most loathsom. Mirth is better than Fun & Happiness is better than Mirth—I feel that a Man may be happy in This World. And I know that This World Is a World of

Imagination & Vision I see Every thing I paint In This World, but Every body does not see alike. To the Eyes of a Miser a Guinea is more beautiful than the Sun & a bag worn with the use of Money has more beautiful proportions than a Vine filled with Grapes. The tree which moves some to tears of joy is in the Eyes of others only a Green thing that stands in the way. Some See Nature all Ridicule & Deformity & by these I shall not regulate my proportions, & Some Scarce see Nature at all But to the Eyes of the Man of Imagination Nature is Imagination itself. As a man is So he Sees. As the Eye is formed such are its Powers You certainly Mistake when you say that the Visions of Fancy are not to be found in This World. To Me This World is all One continued Vision of Fancy or Imagination & I feel Flatterd when I am told So. What is it sets Homer Virgil & Milton in so high a rank of Art. Why is the Bible more Entertaining & Instructive than any other book. Is it not because they are addressed to the Imagination which is Spiritual Sensation & but mediately to the Understanding or Reason Such is True Painting and such <was> alone valued by the Greeks & the best modern Artists. Consider what Lord Bacon says "Sense sends over to Imagination before Reason have judged & Reason sends over to Imagination before the Decree can be acted." See Advancem^t of Learning Part 2 P 47 of first Edition

But I am happy to find a Great Majority of Fellow Mortals who can Elucidate My Visions & Particularly they have been Elucidated by Children who have taken a greater delight in contemplating my Pictures than I even hoped. Neither Youth nor Childhood is Folly or Incapacity Some Children are Fools & so are some Old Men. But There is a vast Majority on the side of Imagination or Spiritual Sensation

To Engrave after another Painter is infinitely more laborious than to Engrave ones own Inventions. And of the Size you require my price has been Thirty Guineas & I cannot afford to do it for less. I had Twelve for the Head I sent you as a Specimen, but after my own designs I could do at least Six times the quantity of labour in the same time which will account for the difference of price as also that Chalk Engraving is at least six times as laborious as Aqua tinta. I have no objection to Engraving after another Artist. Engraving is the profession I was apprenticed to, & should never have attempted to live by any thing else If orders had not come in for my Designs & Paintings, which I have the pleasure to tell you are Increasing Every Day. Thus If I am a Painter it is not to be attributed to Seeking after. But I am contented whether I live by Painting or Engraving

I am Revd Sir Your very obedient servant

WILLIAM BLAKE

[To] William Hayley Esq\u02b3, Eartham,
near Chichester, Sussex

Lambeth May 6, 1800

Dear Sir

I am very sorry for your immense loss, which is a repetition of what all feel in this valley of misery & happiness mixed. I send the Shadow of the departed Angel. hope the likeness is improved. The lip I have again lessened as you advised & done a good many other softenings to the whole. I know that our deceased friends are more really with us than when they were apparent to our mortal part. Thirteen years ago I lost a brother & with his spirit I converse daily & hourly in the Spirit & See him in my remembrance in the regions of my Imagination. I hear his advice & even now write from his Dictate. Forgive me for Expressing to you my Enthusiasm which I wish all to partake of Since it is to me a Source of Immortal Joy even in this world by it I am the companion of Angels. May you continue to be so more & more & to be more & more perswaded that every Mortal loss is an Immortal Gain. The Ruins of Time builds Mansions in Eternity.—I have also sent A Proof of Pericles for your Remarks thanking you for the kindness with which you Express them & feeling heartily your Grief with a brothers Sympathy

I remain Dear Sir Your humble Servant
WILLIAM BLAKE

[To] Mr [George] Cumberland, Bishopsgate,
Windsor Great Park

13 Hercules Buildings, Lambeth, 2 July 1800

Dear Cumberland

I have to congratulate you on your plan for a National Gallery being put into Execution. All your wishes shall in due time be fulfilled the immense flood of Grecian light & glory which is coming on Europe will more than realize our warmest wishes. Your honours will be unbounded when your plan shall be carried into Execution as it must be if England continues a Nation. I hear that it is now in the hands of Ministers That the King shews it great Countenance & Encouragement, that it will soon be up before Parliament & that it *must* be extended & enlarged to take in Originals both of Painting & Sculpture by considering Every valuable original that is brought into England or can be purchasd Abroad as its objects of Acquisition. Such is the Plan as I am told & such must be the plan if England wishes to continue at all worth notice as you have yourself observd only now we must possess Originals as well as France or be Nothing

Excuse I intreat you my not returning Thanks at the proper moment for your kind present. No perswasion could make my stupid head believe that it was proper for me to trouble you with a letter of meer Compliment & Expression of thanks. I begin to Emerge from a Deep pit of Melancholy, Melancholy without any real reason for it, a Disease which God keep you from & all good men. Our artists of all ranks praise your outlines & wish for more. Flaxman is very warm in your commendation & more and more of A Grecian. Mr Hayley has lately mentiond your Work on outline in Notes to [*Epistles on Sculpture*] an Essay on Sculpture in Six Epistles to John Flaxman I have been too little among friends which I fear they will not Excuse & I know not how to apologize for. Poor Fuseli sore from the lash of Envious tongues praises you & dispraises with the same breath he is not naturally good natured but he is artificially very ill natured yet even from him I learn the Estimation you are held in among artists & connoisseurs.

I am still Employd in making Designs & little Pictures with now & then an Engraving & find that in future to live will not be so difficult as it has been It is very Extraordinary that London in so few years from a City of meer Necessaries or at l[e]ast a commerce of the lowest order of luxuries should have become a City of Elegance in some degree & that its once stupid inhabitants should enter into an Emulation of Grecian manners. There are now I believe as many Booksellers as there are Butchers & as many Printshops as of any other trade We remember when a Print shop was a rare bird in London & I myself remember when I thought my pursuits of Art a kind of Criminal Dissipation & neglect of the main chance which I hid my face for not being able to abandon as a Passion which is forbidden by Law & Religion, but now it appears to be Law & Gospel too, at least I hear so from the few friends I have dared to visit in my stupid Melancholy. Excuse this communication of sentiments which I felt necessary to my repose at this time. I feel very strongly that I neglect my Duty to my Friends, but It is not want of Gratitude or Friendship but perhaps an Excess of both.

Let me hear of your welfare. Remember My & My Wifes Respectful Compliments to Mrs Cumberland & Family

& believe me to be for Ever

Yours

WILLIAM BLAKE

[To] Mr [John] Flaxman, Buckingham Street, Fitzroy Square

[Manuscript lost]

[Postmark: 12 o'clock 12 Sp. 1800]

My Dearest Friend,

It is to you I owe All my present Happiness. It is to you I owe perhaps the Principal Happiness of my life. I have presum'd on your friendship in staying so long away & not calling to know of your welfare, but hope now every thing is nearly completed for our removal to Felpham, that I shall see you on Sunday, as we have appointed Sunday afternoon to call on Mrs. Flaxman at Hampstead. I send you a few lines, which I hope you will Excuse. And As the time is arriv'd when Men shall again converse in Heaven & walk with Angels, I know you will be pleased with the Intention, & hope you will forgive the Poetry.

To My Dearest Friend, John Flaxman, these lines:

I bless thee, O Father of Heaven & Earth, that ever I saw Flaxman's face.
Angels stand round my Spirit in Heaven, the blessed of Heaven are my friends upon Earth.
When Flaxman was taken to Italy, Fuseli was given to me for a season,
And now Flaxman hath given me Hayley his friend to be mine, such my lot upon Earth.
Now my lot in the Heavens is this, Milton lov'd me in childhood &   5
shew'd me his face.
Ezra came with Isaiah the Prophet, but Shakespeare in riper years gave me his hand;
Paracelsus & Behmen appear'd to me, terrors appear'd in the Heavens above
And in Hell beneath, & a mighty & awful change threatened the Earth.
The American War began. All its dark horrors passed before my face
Across the Atlantic to France. Then the French Revolution commenc'd   10
in thick clouds,
And My Angels have told me that seeing such visions I could not subsist on the Earth,
But by my conjunction with Flaxman, who knows to forgive Nervous Fear.

I remain, for Ever Yours,
WILLIAM BLAKE

Be so kind as to Read & then seal the Inclosed & send it on its much beloved Mission.

To my dear Friend Mrs Anna Flaxman

H[ercules] B[uildings] Lambeth, 14 Sepr 1800

This Song to the flower of Flaxmans joy
To the blossom of hope for a sweet decoy
Do all that you can or all that you may
To entice him to Felpham & far away

Away to Sweet Felpham for Heaven is there   5
The Ladder of Angels descends thro the air

On the Turret its spiral does softly descend
Thro' the village then winds at My Cot i[t] does end

You stand in the village & look up to heaven
The precious stones glitter on flights seventy seven   10
And My Brother is there & My Friend & Thine
Descend & Ascend with the Bread & the Wine

The Bread of sweet Thought & the Wine of Delight
Feeds the Village of Felpham by day & by night
And at his own door the blessd Hermit does stand   15
Dispensing Unceasing to all the whole Land

W. Blake

[To William Hayley]

H[ercules] B[uildings] Lambeth Sept 16. 1800

Leader of My Angels

My Dear & too careful & over joyous Woman has Exhausted her strength
to such a degree with expectation & gladness added to labour in our removal that I fear it will be Thursday before we can get away from this――
City I shall not be able to avail myself of the assistance of Brunos fairies.
But I invoke the Good Genii that Surround Miss Pooles Villa to shine upon
my journey thro the Petworth road which by your fortunate advice I mean
to take but whether I come on Wednesday or Thursday That Day shall
be marked on my calendar with a Star of the first magnitude

Eartham will be my first temple & altar My wife is like a flame of many
colours of precious jewels whenever she hears it named Excuse my haste &
recieve my hearty Love & Respect

I am dear Sir
Your Sincere
William Blake

My fingers Emit sparks of fire with Expectation of my future labours

[To] M^r [Thomas] Butts, G^t. Marlborough Street
near Oxford Street, London

[Postmark: Sep 23 1800]

Dear Friend of My Angels

We are safe arrived at our Cottage without accident or hindrance tho it
was between Eleven & Twelve OClock at night before we could get home,
owing to the necessary shifting of our boxes & portfolios from one Chaise
to another. We had Seven different Chaises & as many different drivers. All

upon the road was chearfulness & welcome tho our luggage was very heavy there was no grumbling at all. We traveld thro a most beautiful country on a most glorious day. Our Cottage is more beautiful than I thought it & also more convenient. for tho Small it is well proportiond & if I should ever build a Palace it would be only My Cottage Enlarged. Please to tell Mrs Butts that we have dedicated a Chamber for her Service & that it has a very fine view of the Sea. Mr Hayley recievd me with his usual brotherly affection. My Wife & Sister are both very well & courting Neptune for an Embrace, whose terrors this morning made them afraid but whose mildness is often Equal to his terrors. The Villagers of Felpham are not meer Rustics they are polite & modest. Meat is cheaper than in London but the sweet air & the voices of winds trees & birds & the odours of the happy ground makes it a dwelling for immortals. Work will go on here with God speed—. A roller & two harrows lie before my window. I met a plow on my first going out at my gate the first morning after my arrival & the Plowboy said to the Plowman. "Father The Gate is Open"—I have begun to Work & find that I can work with greater pleasure than ever. Hope soon to give you a proof that Felpham is propitious to the Arts.

God bless you. I shall wish for you on Tuesday Evening as usual. Pray give My & My wife & sisters love & respects to Mrs Butts, accept them yourself & believe me for ever

Your affectionate & obliged Friend
WILLIAM BLAKE

My Sister will be in town in a week & bring with her your account & whatever else I can finish.　　Direct to Me

　　Blake: Felpham near Chichester.

Sussex

[To] M^r [Thomas] Butts, Great Marlborough Street

Felpham Octr 2^d 1800

Friend of Religion & Order

I thank you for your very beautiful & encouraging Verses which I account a Crown of Laurels & I also thank you for your reprehension of follies by me fosterd. Your prediction will I hope be fulfilled in me. & in future I am the determined advocate of Religion & Humility the two bands of Society. Having been so full of the Business of Settling the sticks & feathers of my nest. I have not got any forwarder with the three Marys or with any other of your commissions but hope, now I have commenced a new life of industry to do credit to that new life by Improved Works: Recieve from me a return of verses such as Felpham produces by me tho not such as she produces by her Eldest Son. however such as they are. I cannot resist the temptation to send them to you

To my Friend Butts I write
My first Vision of Light
On the yellow sands sitting
The Sun was Emitting
His Glorious beams   5
From Heavens high Streams
Over Sea over Land
My Eyes did Expand
Into regions of air
Away from all Care   10
Into regions of fire
Remote from Desire
The Light of the Morning
Heavens Mountains adorning
In particles bright   15
The jewels of Light
Distinct shone & clear—
Amazd & in fear
I each particle gazed,
Astonishd Amazed   20
For each was a Man
Human formd. Swift I ran
For they beckond to me
Remote by the Sea
Saying. Each grain of Sand   25
Every Stone on the Land
Each rock & each hill
Each fountain & rill
Each herb & each tree
Mountain hill Earth & Sea   30
Cloud Meteor & Star
Are Men Seen Afar
I stood in the Streams
Of Heavens bright beams
And Saw Felpham sweet   35
Beneath my bright feet
In soft Female charms
And in her fair arms
My Shadow I knew
And my wifes shadow too   40
And My Sister & Friend.
We like Infants descend
In our Shadows on Earth
Like a weak mortal birth
My Eyes more & more   45
Like a Sea without shore

Continue Expanding
The Heavens commanding
Till the Jewels of Light
Heavenly Men beaming bright   50
Appeard as One Man
Who Complacent began
My limbs to infold
In his beams of bright gold
Like dross purgd away   55
All my mire & my clay
Soft consumd in delight
In his bosom Sun bright
I remaind. Soft he smild
And I heard his voice Mild   60
Saying This is My Fold
O thou Ram hornd with gold
Who awakest from Sleep
On the Sides of the Deep
On the Mountains around   65
The roarings resound
Of the lion & wolf
The loud Sea & deep gulf.
These are guards of My Fold
O thou Ram hornd with gold   70
And the voice faded mild
I remaind as a Child
All I ever had known
Before me bright Shone
I saw you & your wife   75
By the fountains of Life
Such the Vision to me
Appeard on the Sea

Mrs Butts will I hope Excuse my not having finishd the Portrait. I wait for less hurried moments. Our Cottage looks more & more beautiful. And tho the weather is wet, the Air is very Mild. much Milder than it was in London when we came away. Chichester is a very handsome City Seven miles from us we can get most Conveniences there. The Country is not so destitute of accomodations to our wants as I expected it would be We have had but little time for viewing the Country but what we have seen is Most Beautiful & the People are Genuine Saxons handsomer than the people about London. Mrs Butts will Excuse the following lines

To Mrs Butts

Wife of the Friend of those I most revere.
Recieve this tribute from a Harp sincere
Go on in Virtuous Seed sowing on Mold
Of Human Vegetation & Behold
Your Harvest Springing to Eternal life   5
Parent of Youthful Minds & happy Wife
                    W B—
        I am for Ever Yours

                    WILLIAM BLAKE

[To] Mr Butts, Great Marlborough Street, London

September 11. 1801 [See below]

My Dear Sir
    I hope you will continue to excuse my want of steady perseverance by
which want I am still so much your debtor & you so much my Credit-er but
such as I can be I will: I can be grateful & I can soon Send you some of your
designs which I have nearly completed. In the mean time by my Sisters
hands I transmit to Mrs Butts an attempt at your likeness which I hope
She who is the best judge will think like Time flies faster, (as seems to me),
here than in London I labour incessantly & accomplish not one half of what
I intend. because my Abstract folly hurries me often away while I am at
work, carrying me over Mountains & Valleys which are not Real in a Land
of Abstraction where Spectres of the Dead wander. This I endeavour to
prevent & with my whole might Chain my feet to the world of Duty & Reality. but in vain! the faster I bind the better is the Ballast for I so far from
being bound down take the world with me in my flights & often it seems
lighter than a ball of wool rolled by the wind Bacon & Newton would prescribe ways of making the world heavier to me & Pitt would prescribe distress
for a medicinal potion. but as none on Earth can give me Mental Distress, & I
know that all Distress inflicted by Heaven is a Mercy. a Fig for all Corporeal
Such Distress is My mock & scorn. Alas wretched happy ineffectual
labourer of times moments that I am! who shall deliver me from this Spirit
of Abstraction & Improvidence. Such my Dear Sir Is the truth of my state.
& I tell it you in palliation of my seeming neglect of your most pleasant orders.
but I have not neglected them & yet a Year is rolled over & only now I
approach the prospect of sending you some which you may expect soon. I
should have sent them by My Sister but as the Coach goes three times a
week to London & they will arrive as safe as with her. I shall have an opportunity of inclosing several together which are not yet completed. I thank
you again & again for your generous forbearance. of which I have need—&
now I must express my wishes to see you at Felpham & to shew you M^r

Hayleys Library. which is still unfinishd but is in a finishing way & looks well. I ought also to mention my Extreme disappointment at Mr Johnsons forgetfulness, who appointd to call on you but did Not. He is also a happy Abstract known by all his Friends as the most innocent forgetter of his own Interests. He is nephew to <the late> Mr Cowper the Poet you would like him much   I continue painting Miniatures & Improve more & more as all my friends tell me. but my Principal labour at this time is Engraving Plates for Cowpers Life a Work of Magnitude which Mr Hayley is now Labouring with all his matchless industry & which will be a most valuable acquisition to Literature not only on account of Mr Hayleys composition but also as it will contain Letters of Cowper to his friends Perhaps or rather Certainly the very best letters that ever were published

My wife joins with me in Love to You & Mrs Butts hoping that her joy is now increased & yours also in an increase of family & of health & happiness

I remain Dear Sir
Ever Yours Sincerely
WILLIAM BLAKE—

Felpham Cottage
of Cottages the prettiest
September 11. 1801

Next time I have the happiness to see you I am determined to paint another Portrait of you from Life in my best manner for Memory will not do in such minute operations. for I have now discoverd that without Nature before the painters Eye he can never produce any thing in the walks of Natural Painting Historical Designing is one thing & Portrait Painting another & they are as Distinct as any two Arts can be Happy would that Man be who could unite them

P.S. Please to Remember our best respects to Mr Birch & tell him that Felpham Men are the mildest of the human race if it is the will of Providence they shall be the wisest We hope that he will next Summer joke us face to face—God bless you all

To Mr Flaxman, Sculptor, Buckingham Street, Fitzroy Square, London

Oct 19 1801

Dear Flaxman,

I rejoice to hear that your Great Work is accomplish'd. Peace opens the way to greater still. The Kingdoms of this World are now become the Kingdoms of God & his Christ, & we shall reign with him for ever & ever. The Reign of Literature & the Arts Commences. Blessed are those who are found studious of Literature & Humane & polite accomplishments. Such have their lamps burning & such shall shine as the stars.

Mr Thomas, your friend to whom you was so kind as to make honourable mention of me, has been at Felpham & did me the favor to call on me. I have promis'd him to send my designs for Comus when I have done them, directed to you.

Now I hope to see the Great Works of Art, as they are so near to Felpham, Paris being scarce further off than London. But I hope that France & England will henceforth be as One Country and their Arts One, & that you will Ere long be erecting Monuments In Paris—Emblems of Peace.

My wife joins with me in love to You & Mrs Flaxman.

I remain, Yours Sincerely
WILLIAM BLAKE

[Postscript in Hayley's hand]

I have just seen Weller—all yr Friends in the south are willing to await yr Leisure for Works of Marble, but Weller says it would soothe & comfort the good sister of the upright Mr. D. to see a little sketch from yr Hand. adio.

[To] Mr Butts, Great Marlborough Street, Oxford Street, London

Felpham Jany 10. 1802

Dear Sir

Your very kind & affectionate Letter & the many kind things you have said in it: calld upon me for an immediate answer. but it found My Wife & Myself so Ill & My wife so very ill that till now I have not been able to do this duty. The Ague & Rheumatism have been almost her constant Enemies which she has combated in vain ever since we have been here, & her sickness is always my sorrow of course But what you tell me about your sight afflicted me not a little; & that about your health in another part of your letter makes me intreat you to take due care of both it is a part of our duty to God & man to take due care of his Gifts & tho we ought not think *more* highly of ourselves, yet we ought to think *As* highly of ourselves as immortals ought to think

When I came down here I was more sanguine than I am at present but it was because I was ignorant of many things which have since occurred & chiefly the unhealthiness of the place Yet I do not repent of coming, on a thousand accounts. & Mr H I doubt not will do ultimately all that both he & I wish that is to lift me out of difficulty. but this is no easy matter to a man who having Spiritual Enemies of such formidable magnitude cannot expect to want natural hidden ones

Your approbation of my pictures is a Multitude to Me & I doubt not that all your kind wishes in my behalf shall in due time be fulfilled. Your kind offer of pecuniary assistance I can only thank you for at present because I have enough to serve my present purpose here. our expenses are small & our income from our incessant labour fully adequate to them at present. I am now engaged in Engraving 6 small plates for a New Edition of Mr Hayleys Triumphs of Temper. from drawings by Maria Flaxman sister to my friend the Sculptor and it seems that other things will follow in course if I do but Copy these well. but Patience! if Great things do not turn out it is because such things depend on the Spiritual & not on the Natural World & if it was fit for me I doubt not that I should be Employd in Greater things & when it is proper my Talents shall be properly exercised in Public. as I hope they are now in private. for till then. I leave no stone unturnd & no path unexplord that tends to improvement in my beloved Arts. One thing of real consequence I have accomplishd by coming into the country. which is to me consolation enough, namely. I have recollected all my scatterd thoughts on Art & resumed my primitive & original ways of Execution in both painting & Engraving. which in the confusion of London I had very much lost & obliterated from my mind. But whatever becomes of my labours I would rather that they should be preservd in your Green House (not as you mistakenly call it dung hill). than in the cold gallery of fashion.—The Sun may yet shine & then they will be brought into open air.

But you have so generously & openly desired that I will divide my griefs with you that I cannot hide what it is now become my duty to explain—My unhappiness has arisen from a source which if explord too narrowly might hurt my pecuniary circumstances. As my dependence is on Engraving at present & particularly on the Engravings I have in hand for Mr H. & I find on all hands great objections to my doing any thing but the meer drudgery of business & intimations that if I do not confine myself to this I shall not live. this has always pursud me. You will understand by this the source of all my uneasiness This from Johnson & Fuseli brought me down here & this from M^r H will bring me back again for that I cannot live without doing my duty to lay up treasures in heaven is Certain & Determined & to this I have long made up my mind & why this should be made an objection to Me while Drunkenness Lewdness Gluttony & even Idleness itself does not hurt other men let Satan himself Explain—The Thing I have most at Heart! more than life or all that seems to make life comfortable without. Is the Interest of True Religion & Science & whenever any thing appears to affect that Interest. (Especially if I myself omit any duty to my [self] <Station> as a Soldier of Christ) It gives me the greatest of torments, I am not ashamed afraid or averse to tell You what Ought to be Told. That I am under the direction of Messengers from Heaven Daily & Nightly but the nature of such things is not as some suppose. without trouble or care. Temptations are on the right hand & left behind the sea of time & space roars & follows swiftly he who keeps not right onward is lost & if our footsteps slide in clay how can we do otherwise than fear & tremble. but I should not have troubled You with this account of my spiritual state unless it had been necessary in explaining the actual cause of my uneasiness into which you are so kind as to Enquire for I never obtrude such things on others unless questiond & then I never disguise the truth—But if we fear to do the dictates of our Angels & tremble at the Tasks set before us. if we refuse to do Spiritual Acts.

because of Natural Fears of Natural Desires! Who can describe the dismal torments of such a state!—I too well remember the Threats I heard!—If you who are organised by Divine Providence for Spiritual communion. Refuse & bury your Talent in the Earth even tho you should want Natural Bread. Sorrow & Desperation pursues you thro life! & after death shame & confusion of face to eternity—Every one in Eternity will leave you aghast at the Man who was crownd with glory & honour by his brethren & betrayd their cause to their enemies. You will be calld the base Judas who betrayd his Friend!—Such words would make any Stout man tremble & how then could I be at ease? But I am now no longer in That State & now go on again with my Task Fearless. and tho my path is difficult. I have no fear of stumbling while I keep it

My wife desires her kindest Love to Mrs Butts & I have permitted her to send it to you also. we often wish that we could unite again in Society & hope that the time is not distant when we shall do so. being determind not to remain another winter here but to return to London

> I hear a voice you cannot hear that says I must not stay
> I see a hand you cannot see that beckons me away

Naked we came here naked of Natural things & naked we shall return. but while clothd with the Divine Mercy we are richly clothd in Spiritual & suffer all the rest gladly Pray give my Love to Mrs Butts & your family I am Yours Sincerely

WILLIAM BLAKE

P.S. Your Obliging proposal of Exhibiting my two Pictures likewise calls for my thanks I will finish the other & then we shall judge of the matter with certainty

[To] Mr Butts, G^r Marlborough Street

Felpham Novr. 22: 1802

Dear Sir

My Brother tells me that he fears you are offended with me. I fear so too because there appears some reason why you might be so. But when you have heard me out you will not be so

I have now given two years to the intense study of those parts of the art which relate to light & shade & colour & am Convincd that either my understanding is incapable of comprehending the beauties of Colouring or the Pictures which I painted for You Are Equal in Every part of the Art & superior in One to any thing that has been done since the age of Rafael.—<All> S^r J Reynolds's discourses <to the Royal Academy> will shew. that the Venetian finesse in Art can never be united with the Majesty of Colouring necessary to Historical beauty. & in a letter to the Revd Mr Gilpin author of a work on Picturesque Scenery he says Thus "It may be worth consideration whether the epithet Picturesque is not applicable to the excellencies of the inferior Schools rather than to the higher. The works of Michael Angelo Rafael &ᵉ appear to me to have nothing of it: whereas Ruben & the Venetian Painters may almost be said to have Nothing Else. —Perhaps Picturesque is somewhat synonymous to the word Taste which we should think improperly applied to Homer or Milton but very well to Prior or Pope. I suspect that the application of these words are to Excellencies of an inferior order & which are incompatible with the Grand Style You are certainly right in saying that Variety of Tints & Forms is Picturesque: but it must be rememberd on the other hand. that the reverse of this—(*uniformity of Colour & a long continuation of lines*) produces Grandeur"———So Says Sⁱʳ Joshua and So say I for I have now proved that the parts of the art which I neglected to display in those little pictures & drawings which I had the pleasure & profit to do for you are incompatible with the designs—There is nothing in the Art which our Painters do. that I can confess myself ignorant of I also Know & Understand & can assuredly affirm that the works I have done for You are Equal to Carrache or Rafael (and I and now Seven years older than Rafael was when he died) I say they are Equal to Carrache or Rafael or Else I am Blind Stupid Ignorant and Incapable in two years Study to understand those things which a Boarding School Miss can comprehend in a fortnight. Be assured My dear Friend that there is not one touch in those Drawings & Pictures but what came from my Head & my Heart in Unison. That I am Proud of being their Author and Grateful to you my Employer. & that I look upon you as the Chief of my Friends whom I would endeavour to please because you among all men have enabled me to produce these things. I would not send you a Drawing or a Picture till I had again reconsiderd my notions of Art & had put myself back as if I was a learner I have proved that I am Right & shall now Go on with the Vigor I was in my Childhood famous for

But I do not pretend to be Perfect. but if my Works have faults Caracche Corregios & Rafaels have faults also. let me observe that the yellow leather flesh of old men the ill drawn & ugly young women & above all the dawbed black & yellow shadows that are found in most fine ay & the finest pictures. I altogether reject as ruinous to Effect tho Connoisseurs may think otherwise.

Let me also notice that Carraches Pictures are not like Correggios nor Correggios like Rafaels & if neither of them was to be encouraged till he did like any of the others he must die without Encouragement My Pictures are unlike any of these Painters & I would have them to be so I think the manner I adopt More Perfect than any other no doubt They thought the same of theirs

You will be tempted to think that As I improved The Pictures &ᵉ that I did for you are not what I would now wish them to be. On this I beg to say That they are What I intended them & that I know I never shall do better for if I was to do them over again they would lose as much as they gaind because they were done in the heat of My Spirits

But You will Justly enquire why I have not written All this time to you? I answer I have been very Unhappy & could not think of troubling you about it or any of my real Friends (I have written many letters to you which I burnd & did not send) & why I have not before now finishd the Miniature I promissd to Mrs Butts? I answer I have not till now in any degree pleased myself & now I must intreat you to Excuse faults for Portrait Painting is the direct contrary to Designing & Historical Painting in every respect—If you have not Nature before you for Every Touch you cannot Paint Portrait. & if you have Nature before you at all you cannot Paint History it was Michall Angelos opinion & is Mine. Pray Give My Wife's love with mine to Mrs Butts assure her that it cannot be long before I have the pleasure of Painting from you in Person & then that She may Expect a likeness but now I have done All I could & know she will forgive any failure in consideration of the Endeavour.

And now let me finish with assuring you that Tho I have been very unhappy I am so no longer I am again Emerged into the light of Day I still & shall to Eternity Embrace Christianity and Adore him who is the Express image of God but I have traveld thro Perils & Darkness not unlike a Champion I have Conquerd and shall still Go on Conquering Nothing can withstand the fury of my Course among the Stars of God & in the Abysses of the Accuser My Enthusiasm is still what it was only Enlarged and confirmd

I now Send Two Pictures & hope you will approve of them I have inclosed the Account of Money recievd & Work done which I ought long ago to have sent you pray forgive Errors in omissions of this kind I am incapable of many attentions which it is my Duty to observe towards you thro multitude of employment & thro hope of soon seeing you again I often omit to Enquire of you But pray let me now hear how you do & of the welfare of your family

Accept my Sincere love & respect

I remain Yours Sincerely

WILL^m BLAKE

A Piece of Sea Weed Serves for a Barometer [i]t gets wet & dry as the weather gets so

[To Thomas Butts, 22 November 1802]

Dear Sir

After I had finishd my Letter I found that I had not said half what I intended to say & in particular I wish to ask you what subject you choose to be painted on the remaining Canvas which I brought down with me (for there were three) and to tell you that several of the Drawings were in great forwardness you will see by the Inclosed Account that the remaining Number of Drawings which you gave me orders for is Eighteen I will finish these with all possible Expedition if indeed I have not tired you or as it is politely calld Bored you too much already or if you would rather cry out Enough Off Off! tell me in a Letter of forgiveness if you were offended & of accustomd friendship if you were not. But I will bore you more with

some Verses which My Wife desires me to Copy out & send you with her
kind love & Respect they were Composed <above> a twelve-month ago [*in
a*] <while> Walk<ing> from Felpham to Lavant to meet my Sister

With happiness stretchd across the hills
In a cloud that dewy sweetness distills
With a blue sky spread over with wings
And a mild sun that mounts & sings
With trees & fields full of Fairy elves   5
And little devils who fight for themselves
Remembring the Verses that Hayley sung   t
When my heart knockd against the root of my tongue
With Angels planted in Hawthorn bowers
And God himself in the passing hours   10
With Silver Angels across my way
And Golden Demons that none can stay
With my Father hovering upon the wind
And my Brother Robert just behind
And my Brother John the evil one   15
In a black cloud making his mone
Tho dead they appear upon my path
Notwithstanding my terrible wrath
They beg they intreat they drop their tears
Filld full of hopes filld full of fears   20
With a thousand Angels upon the Wind
Pouring disconsolate from behind
To drive them off & before my way
A frowning Thistle implores my stay
What to others a trifle appears   25
Fills me full of smiles or tears
For double the vision my Eyes do see
And a double vision is always with me
With my inward Eye 'tis an old Man grey
With my outward a Thistle across my way   30
"If thou goest back the thistle said
Thou art to endless woe betrayd
For here does Theotormon lower
And here is Enitharmons bower
And Los the terrible thus hath sworn   35
Because thou backward dost return
Poverty Envy old age & fear
Shall bring thy Wife upon a bier
And Butts shall give what Fuseli gave
A dark black Rock & a gloomy Cave."   40

I struck the Thistle with my foot
And broke him up from his delving root
"Must the duties of life each other cross"

"Must every joy be dung & dross"
'Must my dear Butts feel cold neglect"   45
"Because I give Hayley his due respect'
"Must Flaxman look upon me as wild"
"And all my friends be with doubts beguild'
"Must my Wife live in my Sisters bane"
"Or my sister survive on my Loves pain'   50
"The curses of Los the terrible shade"
"And his dismal terrors make me afraid"

So I spoke & struck in my wrath
The old man weltering upon my path
Then Los appeard in all his power   55
In the Sun he appeard descending before
My face in fierce flames in my double sight
Twas outward a Sun: inward Los in his might

"My hands are labourd day & night"
"And Ease comes never in my sight"   60
"My Wife has no indulgence given"
"Except what comes to her from heaven"
"We eat little we drink less"
"This Earth breeds not our happiness"
"Another Sun feeds our lifes streams"   65
"We are not warmed with thy beams"
"Thou measurest not the Time to me"
"Nor yet the Space that I do see"
"My Mind is not with thy light arrayd"
"Thy terrors shall not make me afraid"   70

When I had my Defiance given
The Sun stood trembling in heaven
The Moon that glowd remote below
Became leprous & white as snow
And every Soul of men on the Earth   75
Felt affliction & sorrow & sickness & dearth
Los flamd in my path & the Sun was hot
With the bows of my Mind & the Arrows of Thought
My bowstring fierce with Ardour breathes
My arrows glow in their golden sheaves   80
My brothers & father march before
The heavens drop with human gore

Now I a fourfold vision see
And a fourfold vision is given to me
Tis fourfold in my supreme delight   85
And three fold in soft Beulahs night
And twofold Always. May God us keep
From Single vision & Newtons sleep

I also inclose you some Ballads by Mr Hayley with prints to them by Your H^{ble}. Servt. I should have sent them before now but could not get any thing done for You to please myself for I do assure you that I have truly studied the two little pictures I now send & do not repent of the time I have spent upon them

God bless you

Yours
W B

P.S. I have taken the liberty to trouble you with a letter to my Brother which you will be so kind as to send or give him & oblige yours W B

[To James Blake]

Felpham Jany 30–1803.

Dear Brother

Your Letter mentioning Mr Butts's account of my Ague surprized me because I have no Ague but had a Cold this Winter. You know that it is my way to make the best of everything. I never make myself nor my friends uneasy if I can help it. My Wife has had Agues & Rheumatisms almost ever since she has been here, but our time is almost out that we took the Cottage for. I did not mention our Sickness to you & should not to Mr Butts but for a determination which we have lately made namely To leave This Place—because I am now certain of what I have long doubted Viz [that H] is jealous as Stothard was & will be no further My friend than he is compelld by circumstances. The truth is As a Poet he is frightend at me & as a Painter his views & mine are opposite he thinks to turn me into a Portrait Painter as he did Poor Romney, but this he nor all the devils in hell will never do. I must own that seeing H. like S. Envious (& that he is I am now certain) made me very uneasy, but it is over & I now defy the worst & fear not while I am true to myself which I will be. This is the uneasiness I spoke of to Mr Butts but I did not tell him so plain & wish you to keep it a secret & to burn this letter because it speaks so plain I told Mr Butts that I did not wish to Explore too much the cause of our determination to leave Felpham because of pecuniary connexions between H. & me—Be not then uneasy on any account & tell my Sister not to be uneasy for I am fully Employ'd & Well Paid I have made it so much H's interest to employ me that he can no longer treat me with indifference & now it is in my power to stay or return or remove to any other place that I choose, because I am getting before hand in money matters The Profits arising from Publications are immense & I now have it in my power to commence publication with many very formidable works, which I have finishd & ready A Book price half a guinea may be got out at the Expense of Ten pounds & its almost certain profits are 500 G. I am only sorry that I did not know the methods of publishing years ago & this is one of the numerous benefits I have obtain by coming here for I should never have known the nature of Publication unless I had known H & his connexions & his method of managing. It now <would> be folly not to venture publishing. I am now Engraving Six little plates for a little work of M^r H's for which I am to have 10 G<uineas> each & the certain profits of that work are a fortune such as would make me independent supposing that I could substantiate such a one of my own & I mean to try many But I again say as I said before We are very Happy sitting at tea by a wood fire in our Cottage the wind singing above our roof & the sea roaring at a distance but if sickness comes all is unpleasant

But my letter to Mr Butts appears to me not to be so explicit as that to you for I told you that I should come to London in the Spring to commence Publisher & he <has> offerd me every assistance in his power <without knowing my intention> But since I wrote yours we have made the resolution of which we informd him viz to leave Felpham entirely. I also told you what I was about & that I was not ignorant of what was doing in London in works of art. But I did not mention Illness because I hoped to get better (for I was really very ill when I wrote to him the last time) & was not then perswaded as I am now that the air tho warm is unhealthy

However this I know will set you at Ease. I am now so full of work that I have had no time to go on with the Ballads, & my prospects of more & more work continually are certain. My Heads of Cowper for M^r H's life of Cowper have pleasd his Relations exceedingly & in Particular Lady Hesketh & Lord Cowper <to please> Lady H was a doubtful chance who almost adord her Cousin the poet & thought him all perfection & she writes that she is quite satisfied with the portraits & charmd by the great Head in particular tho she never could bear the original Picture

But I ought to mention to you that our present idea is. To take a house in some village further from the Sea Perhaps Lavant. & in or near the road to London for the sake of convenience—I also ought to inform you that I read your letter to M^r H & that he is very afraid of losing me & also very afraid that my Friends in London should have a bad opinion of the reception he has given to me But My Wife has undertaken to Print the whole number of the Plates for Cowpers work which she does to admiration & being under my own eye the prints are as fine as the French prints & please every one. in short I have Got every thing so under my thumb that it is more profitable that things should be as they are than any other way, tho not so agreeable because we wish naturally for friendship in preference to interest.—The Publishers are already indebted to My Wife Twenty Guineas for work deliverd This is a small specimen of how we go on. then fear nothing & let my Sister fear nothing because it appears to me that I am now too old & have had too much experience to be any longer imposed upon only illness makes all uncomfortable & this we must prevent by every means in our power

I send with this 5 Copies of N4 of the Ballads for Mrs Flaxman & Five more two of which you will be so good as to give to Mrs Chetwynd if she should call or send for them. These Ballads are likely to be Profitable for we have Sold all that we have had time to print. Evans the Bookseller in Pallmall says they go off very well & why should we repent of having done

them it is doing Nothing that is to be repented of & not doing such things
as these

Pray remember us both to Mr Hall when you see him

I write in great haste & with a head full of botheration about various projected works & particularly. a work now Proposed to the Public at the End of
Cowpers Life. which will very likely be of great consequence it is Cowpers
Milton the same that Fuselis Milton Gallery was painted for,, & if we succeed
in our intentions the prints to this work will be very profitable to me & not
only profitable but honourable at any rate The Project pleases Lord Cowpers family. & I am now labouring in my thoughts. Designs for this & other
works equally creditable These are works to be boasted of & therefore I
cannot feel depress'd tho I know that as far as Designing & Poetry are
concernd I am Envied in many Quarters. but I will cram the Dogs for I
know that the Public are my friends & love my works & will embrace them
whenever they see them My only Difficulty is to produce fast enough.

I go on Merrily with my Greek & Latin; am very sorry that I did not begin
to learn languages early in life as I find it very Easy. am now learning my
Hebrew. יאבג I read Greek as fluently as an Oxford scholar & the Testament is my chief master. astonishing indeed is the English Translation it is
almost word for word & if the Hebrew Bible is as well translated which I
do not doubt it is we need not doubt of its having been translated as well
as written by the Holy Ghost

　　my wife joins me in Love to you both

　　　　　　　　　　　　　　　　　I am Sincerely yours
　　　　　　　　　　　　　　　　　　　W Blake

[To] Mr Butts, Gr^t Marlborough Street

Felpham. April 25. 1803

My Dear Sir

I write in haste having recievd a pressing Letter from my Brother. I intended to have sent the Picture of the Riposo which is nearly finishd much
to my satisfaction but not quite you shall have it soon. I now send the 4
Numbers for Mr Birch with best Respects to him <The Reason the Ballads
have been suspended is the pressure of other business but they will go on
again soon>

Accept of my thanks for your kind & heartening Letter You have Faith in
the Endeavours of Me your weak brother & fellow Disciple. how great must
be your faith in our Divine Master. You are to me a Lesson of Humility
while you Exalt me by such distinguishing commendations. I know that you
see certain merits in me which by Gods Grace shall be made fully apparent
& perfect in Eternity. in the mean time I must not bury the Talents in the
Earth but do my endeavour to live to the Glory of our Lord & Saviour &
I am also grateful to the kind hand that endeavours to lift me out of
despondency even if it lifts me too high—

And now My Dear Sir Congratulate me on my return to London with the full approbation of Mr Hayley & with Promise—But Alas!

Now I may say to you what perhaps I should not dare to say to any one else. That I can alone carry on my visionary studies in London unannoyd & that I may converse with my friends in Eternity. See Visions, Dream Dreams, & prophecy & speak Parables unobserv'd & at liberty from the Doubts of other Mortals. perhaps Doubts proceeding from Kindness. but Doubts are always pernicious Especially when we Doubt our Friends Christ is very decided on this Point. "He who is Not With Me is Against Me" There is no Medium or Middle state & if a Man is the Enemy of my Spiritual Life while he pretends to be the Friend of my Corporeal. he is a Real Enemy—but the Man may be the friend of my Spiritual Life while he seems the Enemy of my Corporeal but Not Vice Versa

What is very pleasant. Every one who hears of my going to London again Applauds it as the only course for the interest of all concernd in My Works. Observing that I ought not to be away from the opportunities London affords of seeing fine Pictures and the various improvements in Works of Art going on in London

But none can know the Spiritual Acts of my three years Slumber on the banks of the Ocean unless he has seen them in the Spirit or unless he should read My long Poem descriptive of those Acts for I have in these three years composed an immense number of verses on One Grand Theme Similar to Homers Iliad or Miltons Paradise Lost the Persons & Machinery intirely new to the Inhabitants of Earth (some of the Persons Excepted) I have written this Poem from immediate Dictation twelve or sometimes twenty or thirty lines at a time without Premeditation & even against my Will. the Time it has taken in writing was thus renderd Non Existent. & an immense Poem Exists which seems to be the Labour of a long Life all producd without Labour or Study. I mention this to shew you what I think the Grand Reason of my being brought down here

I have a thousand & ten thousand things to say to you. My heart is full of futurity. I percieve that the sore travel which has been given me these three years leads to Glory & Honour. I rejoice & I tremble "I am fearfully & wonderfully made". I had been reading the cxxxix Psalm a little before your Letter arrived. I take your advice. I see the face of my Heavenly Father he lays his Hand upon my Head & gives a blessing to all my works why should I be troubled why should my heart & flesh cry out. I will go on in the Strength of the Lord through Hell will I sing forth his Praises. that the Dragons of the Deep may praise him & that those who dwell in darkness & on the Sea coasts may be gatherd into his Kingdom. Excuse my perhaps too great Enthusiasm. Please to accept of & give our Loves to Mrs Butts & your amiable Family. & believe me to be be——

Ever Yours Affectionately
WILL. BLAKE.

[To] Mr Butts, G^r Marlborough St, London

Felpham August 16. 1803

Dear Sir

I send 7 Drawings which I hope will please you. this I believe about balances our account—Our return to London draws on apace. our Expectation of meeting again with you is one of our greatest pleasures. Pray tell me how your Eyes do. I never sit down to work but I think of you & feel anxious for the sight of that friend whose Eyes have done me so much good—I omitted (very unaccountably) to copy out in my last Letter that passage in my rough sketch which related to your kindness in offering to Exhibit my 2 last Pictures in the Gallery in Berners Street it was in these Words. "I sincerely thank you for your kind offer of Exhibiting my 2 Pictures. the trouble you take on my account I trust will be recompensed to you by him who Seeth in Secret. if you should find it convenient to do so it will be gratefully rememberd by me among the other numerous kindnesses I have recievd from you"—

I go on with the remaining Subjects which you gave me commission to Execute for you but shall not be able to send any more before my return tho perhaps I may bring some with me finishd. I am at Present in a Bustle to defend myself against a very unwarrantable warrant from a Justice of Peace in Chichester. which was taken out against me by a Private in Captⁿ Leathes's troop of 1st or Royal Dragoons for an assault & Seditious words. The wretched Man has terribly Perjurd himself as has his Comrade for as to Sedition not one Word relating to the King or Government was spoken by either him or me. His Enmity arises from my having turned him out of my Garden into which he was invited as an assistant by a Gardener at work therein, without my knowledge that he was so invited. I desired him as politely as was possible to go out of the Garden, he made me an impertinent answer I insisted on his leaving the Garden he refused I still persisted in desiring his departure he then threatend to knock out my Eyes with many abominable imprecations & with some contempt for my Person it affronted my foolish Pride I therefore took him by the Elbows & pushed him before me till I had got him out. there I intended to have left him. but he turning about put himself into a Posture of Defiance threatening & swearing at me. I perhaps foolishly & perhaps not, stepped out at the Gate & putting aside his blows took him again by the Elbows & keeping his back to me pushed him forwards down the road about fifty yards he all the while endeavouring to turn round & strike me & raging & cursing which drew out several neighbours. at length when I had got him to where he was Quarterd. which was very quickly done. we were met at the Gate by the Master of the house. The Fox Inn. (who is the proprietor of my Cottage) & his wife & Daughter. & the Mans Comrade. & several other people My Landlord compelld the Soldiers to go in doors after many abusive threats against me & my wife from the two Soldiers but not one word of threat on account of Sedition was utterd at that time. This method of Revenge was Plann'd between them after they had got together into the Stable. This is the whole outline. I have for witnesses. The Gardener who is Hostler at the Fox & who Evidences that to his knowledge no word of the remotest tendency to Government or Sedition was utterd,— Our next door Neighbour a Millers wife who saw me turn him before me down the road & saw & heard all that happend at the Gate of the Inn who Evidences that no Expression of threatening on account of Sedition was utterd in the heat of their fury by either of the Dragoons. this was the womans own remark & does high honour to her good sense as she observes that whenever a quarrel happens the offence is always repeated. The Landlord of the Inn & His Wife & daughter will Evidence the Same & will evidently prove the Comrade perjurd who swore that he heard me <while> at the Gate utter Seditious words & D— the K— without which perjury I could not have been committed & I had no witness with me before the Justices who could combat his assertion as the Gardener remain in my Garden all the while & he was the only person I thought necessary to take with me. I have been before a Bench of Justices at Chichester this morning. but they as the Lawyer who wrote down the Accusation told me in private are compelld by the Military to suffer a prosecution to be enterd into altho they must know & it is manifest that the whole is a Fabricated Perjury. I have been forced to find Bail. Mr Hayley was kind enough to come forwards & Mr Seagrave Printer at Chichester. Mr H. in 100£ & Mr S. in 50£ & myself am bound in 100£ for my appearance at the Quarter Sessions which is after Michaelmass. So I shall have the Satisfaction to see my friends in Town before this Contemptible business comes on I say Contemptible for it must be manifest to every one that the whole accusation is a wilful Perjury. Thus you see my dear Friend that I cannot leave this place without some adventure. it has struck a consternation thro all the Villages round. Every Man is now afraid of speaking to or looking at a Soldier. for the peaceable Villagers have always been forward in expressing their kindness for us & they express their sorrow at our departure as soon as they hear of it Every one here is my Evidence for Peace & Good Neighbourhood & yet such is the present state of things this foolish accusation must be tried in Public. Well I am content I murmur not & doubt not that I shall recieve Justice & am only sorry for the trouble & expense. I have heard that my Accuser is a disgraced Sergeant his name is John Scholfield. perhaps it will be in your power to learn somewhat about the Man I am very ignorant of what I am requesting of you. I only suggest what I know you will be kind enough to Excuse if you can learn nothing about him & what I as well know if it is possible you will be kind enough to do in this matter

Dear Sir This perhaps was sufferd to Clear up some doubts & to give opportunity to those whom I doubted to clear themselves of all imputation. If a Man offends me ignorantly & not designedly surely I ought to consider him with favour & affection. Perhaps the simplicity of myself is the origin of all offences committed against me. If I have found this I shall have learned a most valuable thing well worth three years perseverance. I have found it! It is certain! that a too passive manner. inconsistent with my active physiognomy had done me much mischief I must now express to you my conviction that all is come from the spiritual World for Good & not for Evil.

Give me your advice in my perilous adventure. burn what I have peevishly written about any friend. I have been very much degraded & injuriously treated. but if it all arise from my own fault I ought to blame myself

O why was I born with a different face
Why was I not born like the rest of my race
When I look each one starts! when I speak I offend
Then I'm silent & passive & lose every Friend

Then my verse I dishonour. My pictures despise   5
My person degrade & my temper chastise
And the pen is my terror. the pencil my shame
All my Talents I bury, and dead is my Fame

I am either too low or too highly prizd
When Elate I am Envy'd, When Meek I'm despis'd   10

This is but too just a Picture of my Present state I pray God to keep you & all men from it & to deliver me in his own good time. Pray write to me & tell me how you & your family Enjoy health. My much terrified Wife joins me in love to you & Mrs Butts & all your family. I again take the liberty to beg of you to cause the Enclosd Letter to be deliverd to my Brother & remain Sincerely & Affectionately Yours

WILLIAM BLAKE

Blake's Memorandum in Refutation of the Information and Complaint of John Scolfield, a private Soldier, &c.

[August 1803]

The Soldier has been heard to say repeatedly, that he did not know how the Quarrel began, which he would not say if such seditious words were spoken.—

Mrs. Haynes Evidences, that she saw me turn him down the Road, & all the while we were at the Stable Door, and that not one word of charge against me was uttered, either relating to Sedition or any thing else; all he did was swearing and threatening.—

Mr. Hosier heard him say that he would be revenged, and would have me hanged if he could! He spoke this the Day after my turning him out of the Garden. Hosier says he is ready to give Evidence of this, if necessary.—

The Soldier's Comrade swore before the Magistrates, while I was present, that he heard me utter seditious words, at the Stable Door, and in particular, said, that he heard me D—n the K—g. Now I have all the Persons who were present at the Stable Door to witness that no Word relating to Seditious

Subjects was uttered, either by one party or the other, and they are ready, on their Oaths, to say that I did not utter such Words.—

Mrs. Haynes says very sensibly, that she never heard People quarrel, but they always charged each other with the Offence, and repeated it to those around, therefore as the Soldier charged not me with Seditious Words at that Time, neither did his Comrade, the whole Charge must have been fabricated in the Stable afterwards.—

If we prove the Comrade perjured who swore that he heard me D—n the K—g, I believe the whole Charge falls to the Ground.

Mr. Cosens, owner of the Mill at Felpham, was passing by in the Road, and saw me and the Soldier and William standing near each other; he heard nothing, but says we certainly were not quarrelling.—

The whole Distance that William could be at any Time of the Conversation between me and the Soldier (supposing such Conversation to have existed) is only 12 Yards, & W— says that he was backwards and forwards in the Garden. It was a still Day, there was no Wind stirring.

William says on his Oath, that the first Words that he heard me speak to the Soldier were ordering him out of the Garden; the truth is, I did not speak to the Soldier till then, & my ordering him out of the Garden was occasioned by his [P 2] saying something that I thought insulting.

The Time that I & the Soldier were together in the Garden, was not sufficient for me to have uttered the Things that he alledged.

The Soldier said to Mrs. Grinder, that it would be right to have my House searched, as I might have plans of the Country which I intended to send to the Enemy; he called me a Military Painter; I suppose mistaking the Words Miniature Painter, which he might have heard me called. I think that this proves, his having come into the Garden, with some bad Intention, or at least with a prejudiced Mind.

It is necessary to learn the Names of all that were present at the Stable Door, that we may not have any Witnesses brought against us, that were not there.

All the Persons present at the Stable Door were, Mrs. Grinder and her Daughter, all the Time; Mrs. Haynes & her Daughter all the Time; Mr. Grinder, part of the Time; Mr. Hayley's Gardener part of the Time.—Mrs. Haynes was present from my turning him out at my Gate, all the rest of the Time—What passed in the Garden, there is no Person but William & the Soldier, & myself can know.

There was not any body in Grinder's Tap-room, but an Old Man, named Jones, who (Mrs. Grinder says) did not come out—He is the same Man who lately hurt his Hand, & wears it in a sling—

The Soldier after he and his Comrade came together into the Tap-room, threatened to knock William's Eyes out (this was his often repeated Threat to me and to my Wife) because W— refused to go with him to Chichester, and swear against me. William said that he would not take a false Oath, for that he heard me say nothing of the Kind (i.e. Sedition) Mr. Grinder then reproved the Soldier for threatening William, and Mr. Grinder said, that

W— should not go, because of those Threats, especially as he was sure that no Seditious Words were Spoken.—

[P 3] William's timidity in giving his Evidence before the Magistrates, and his fear of uttering a Falsehood upon Oath, proves him to be an honest Man, & is to me an host of Strength. I am certain that if I had not turned the Soldier out of my Garden, I never should have been free from his Impertinence & Intrusion.

Mr. Hayley's Gardener came past at the Time of the Contention at the Stable Door, & going to the Comrade said to him, Is your Comrade drunk? —a Proof that he thought the Soldier abusive, & in an Intoxication of Mind.

If such a Perjury as this can take effect, any Villain in future may come & drag me and my Wife out of our House, & beat us in the Garden, or use us as he please, or is able, & afterwards go and swear our Lives away.

Is it not in the Power of any Thief who enters a Man's Dwelling, & robs him, or misuses his Wife or Children, to go & swear as this Man has sworn.

To: William Hayley

[Manuscript lost]

23 October 1804

Dear Sir

I received your kind letter with the note to Mr. Payne, and have had the cash from him. I should have returned my thanks immediately on receipt of it, but hoped to be able to send, before now, proofs of the two plates, the *Head* of R[omney] and the *Shipwreck,* which you shall soon see in a much more perfect state. I write immediately because you wish I should do so, to satisfy you that I have received your kind favour.

I take the extreme pleasure of expressing my joy at our good Lady of Lavant's continued recovery: but with a mixture of sincere sorrow on account of the beloved Councillor. My wife returns her heartfelt thanks for your kind inquiry concerning her health. She is surprisingly recovered. Electricity is the wonderful cause; the swelling of her legs and knees is entirely reduced. She is very near as free from rheumatism as she was five years ago, and we have the greatest confidence in her perfect recovery.

The pleasure of seeing another poem from your hands has truly set me longing (my wife says I ought to have said us) with desire and curiosity; but, however, "Christmas is a-coming."

Our good and kind friend Hawkins is not yet in town—hope soon to have the pleasure of seeing him, with the courage of conscious industry, worthy of his former kindness to me. For now! O Glory! and O Delight! I have entirely reduced that spectrous Fiend to his station, whose annoyance has been the ruin of my labours for the last passed twenty years of my life. He is the enemy of conjugal love and is the Jupiter of the Greeks, an iron-hearted tyrant, the ruiner of ancient Greece. I speak with perfect confidence and certainty of the fact which has passed upon me. Nebuchadnezzar had seven times passed over him; I have had twenty; thank God I was not altogether a beast as he was; but I was a slave bound in a mill among beasts and devils; these beasts and these devils are now, together with myself, become children of light and liberty, and my feet and my wife's feet are free from fetters. O lovely Felpham, parent of Immortal Friendship, to thee I am eternally indebted for my three years' rest from perturbation and the strength I now enjoy. Suddenly, on the day after visiting the Truchsessian Gallery of pictures, I was again enlightened with the light I enjoyed in my youth, and which has for exactly twenty years been closed from me as by a door and by window-shutters. Consequently I can, with confidence, promise you ocular demonstration of my altered state on the plates I am now engraving after Romney, whose spiritual aid has not a little conduced to my restoration to the light of Art. O the distress I have undergone, and my poor wife with me: incessantly labouring and incessantly spoiling what I had done well. Every one of my friends was astonished at my faults, and could not assign a reason; they knew my industry and abstinence from every pleasure for the sake of study, and yet—and yet—and yet there wanted the proofs of industry in my works. I thank God with entire confidence that it shall be so no longer —he is become my servant who domineered over me, he is even as a brother who was my enemy. Dear Sir, excuse my enthusiasm or rather madness, for I am really drunk with intellectual vision whenever I take a pencil or graver into my hand, even as I used to be in my youth, and as I have not been for twenty dark, but very profitable years. I thank God that I courageously pursued my course through darkness. In a short time I shall make my assertion good that I am become suddenly as I was at first, by producing the *Head of Romney* and the *Shipwreck* quite another thing from what you or I ever expected them to be. In short, I am now satisfied and proud of my work, which I have not been for the above long period.

If our excellent and manly friend Meyer is yet with you, please to make my wife's and my own most respectful and affectionate compliments to him, also to our kind friend at Lavant.

I remain, with my wife's joint affection,

Your sincere and obliged servant,
WILL BLAKE

To William Hayley Esqre Felpham near Chichester Sussex

Sth Molton St 4 Decr. 1804

Dear Sir

I have omitted so long to thank you for your kind & admirable Present in hopes to send Proofs of my plates but can no longer wait for them but must express my own & my wifes high gratification in the perusal of your elegant & pathetic Poem. To say that Venusia is as beautiful as Serena is only expressing private opinion which will vary in each individual, but to say that she is Your Daughter & is like You to say "tis a Girl. promising Boys hereafter" & to say God bless her for she is a peerless Jewel for a Prince to wear & that we are both highly delighted is what I could not longer omit to say. — Proofs of my Plates will wait on you in a few days. in the mean while I conclude this hasty scrawl with sincere thanks for your kind proposal in your Last letter. I have not yet been able to meet Phillips - Wilkes was not out when I calld nor any more of Washington. But I have mentiond your Proposal to our Noble Flaxman whose high & generous Spirit relinquishing the whole to me was in some measure to be Expected. But that he has reasons for not being able to furnish any designs You will readily believe he says his Engagements are so multiform that he should not be able to do them Justice. but that he will overlook & advise & do all that he can to make my designs (should they ever be attempted) What he Can. & I know his *What he Can* will be full as much as he pretends so that I should not fear to produce Somewhat in this way that must be satisfactory the only danger will be that I shall put my Name to his Designs but if it should fall out so he has Enough & to Spare & the World will know his at once & I shall glory in the Discovery. for Friendship with such a one is better than Fame! — I was about to have written to you to express my wish that two so unequal labourers might not be yoked to the same Plow & to desire you if you could to get Flaxman to do the whole because I thought it would be (to say the best of myself) like putting John Milton with John Bunyan but being at Flaxmans taking his advice about our Engravings he mentiond his having recievd a Letter from you on the same Day I recievd mine & said somewhat, I cannot tell what, that made me think you had open'd your Proposal to him— I thought at any rate it would not be prema- ture to tell him what you had said about the Designs for Edward the first. & he advised it to be done as above related

I will soon speak with Phillips about it if you will favor me with a line of direction how to proceed,—Hope in a few days to send Proofs of Plates which I must say are far beyond Any thing I have ever done. For O happi- ness never enough to be grateful for! I have lost my Confusion of Thought while at work & am as much myself when I take the Pencil or Graver into my hand as I used to be in my Youth I have indeed fought thro a Hell of terrors & horrors (which none could know but myself.) in a Divided Exis- tence now no longer Divided. nor at war with myself I shall travel on in the Strength of the Lord God as Poor Pilgrim says

My wife joins me in Love to You & to our Dear Friend & Friends at Lavant & in all Sussex

I remain Dear Sir Your Sincere & obliged
WILL BLAKE

To the Editor of the Monthly Magazine.

[In the *Monthly Magazine*, XXI (July 1, 1806) 520–521, undated]

SIR,

My indignation was exceedingly moved at reading a criticism in Bell's Weekly Messenger (25th May) on the picture of Count Ugolino, by Mr. Fuseli, in the Royal Academy exhibition; and your Magazine being as extensive in its circulation as that Paper, as it also must from its nature be more permanent, I take the advantageous opportunity to counteract the widely-diffused malice which has for many years, under the pretence of admiration of the arts, been assiduously sown and planted among the English public against true art, such as it existed in the days of Michael Angelo and Raphael. Under pretence of fair criticism and candour, the most wretched taste ever produced has been upheld for many, very many years: but now, I say, now its end is come. Such an artist as Fuseli is invulnerable, he needs not my defence; but I should be ashamed not to set my hand and shoulder, and whole strength, against those wretches who, under pretence of criticism, use the dagger and the poison.

My criticism on this picture is as follows:

Mr. Fuseli's Count Ugolino is the father of sons of feeling and dignity, who would not sit looking in their parent's face in the moment of his agony, but would rather retire and die in secret, while they suffer him to indulge his passionate and innocent grief, his innocent and venerable madness, and insanity, and fury, and whatever paltry cold hearted critics cannot, because they dare not, look upon. Fuseli's Count Ugolino is a man of wonder and admiration, of resentment against man and devil, and of humiliation before God; prayer and parental affection fills the figure from head to foot. The child in his arms, whether boy or girl signifies not, (but the critic must be a fool who has not read Dante, and who does not know a boy from a girl); I say, the child is as beautifully drawn as it is coloured—in both, inimitable! and the effect of the whole is truly sublime, on account of that very colouring which our critic calls black and heavy. The German flute colour, which was used by the Flemings, (they call it burnt bone), has possessed the eye of certain connoisseurs, that they cannot see appropriate colouring, and are blind to the gloom of a real terror.

The taste of English amateurs has been too much formed upon pictures imported from Flanders and Holland; consequently our countrymen are easily brow-beat on the subject of painting; and hence it is so common to hear a man say, "I am no judge of pictures:" but, O Englishmen! know that every man ought to be a judge of pictures, and every man is so who has not been connoisseured out of his senses.

A gentleman who visited me the other day, said, "I am very much surprised at the dislike that some connoisseurs shew on viewing the pictures of Mr. Fuseli; but the truth is, he is a hundred years beyond the present generation."

Though I am startled at such an assertion, I hope the contemporary taste will shorten the hundred years into as many hours; for I am sure that any person consulting his own eyes must prefer what is so supereminent; and I am as sure that any person consulting his own reputation, or the reputation of his country, will refrain from disgracing either by such ill-judged criticisms in future.

Yours,

WM. BLAKE.

[To] Richard Phillips Esqʳ N 6 Bridge Street, Black Friars

17 Sᵗʰ Molton Sᵗ Oct 14 [1807]

Sir,

A circumstance has occurred which has again raised my Indignation

I read in the Oracle & True Briton of Octʳ 13, 1807—that a Mʳ Blair a Surgeon has *with the Cold fury of Robespierre* caused the Police to sieze upon the Person & Goods or Property of an Astrologer & to commit him to Prison. The Man who can Read the Stars. often is opressed by their Influence, no less than the Newtonian who reads Not & cannot Read is opressed by his own Reasonings & Experiments. We are all subject to Error: Who shall say <except the Natural Religionists> that we are not all subject to Crime

My desire is that you would Enquire into this Affair & that you would publish this in your Monthly Magazine I do not pay the postage of this Letter because—you as Sheriff are bound to attend to it.

WILLIAM BLAKE

[Endorsed by Phillips (returning the letter to Blake): "W. B. Recᵈ: Octʳ. 27ᵗʰ. 1807 with Mr P.'s Comps."]

[To] George Cumberland

19 Decʳ 1808

Dear Cumberland

I am very much obliged by your kind ardour in my cause & should immediately Engage in reviving my former pursuits of printing if I had not now so long been turned out of the old channel into a new one that it is impossible for me to return to it without destroying my present course New Vanities or rather new pleasures occupy my thoughts New profits seem to arise before me so tempting that I have already involved myself in engagements that preclude all possibility of promising any thing. I have however the satisfaction to inform you that I have Myself begun to print an account of my various Inventions in Art <for> which I have procured a Publisher & am determind to pursue the plan of publishing what I may get printed without disarranging my time which in future must alone be devoted to Designing & Painting when I have got my Work printed I will send it you first of any body in the mean time believe me to be

Your Sincere friend
WILL BLAKE

[To] George Cumberland Esqre Culver Street Bristol

N 3 Fountain Court Strand 12 April 1827

Dear Cumberland

I have been very near the Gates of Death & have returned very weak & an Old Man feeble & tottering, but not in Spirit & Life not in The Real Man The Imagination which Liveth for Ever. In that I am stronger & stronger as this Foolish Body decays. I thank you for the Pains you have taken with Poor Job. I know too well that a great majority of Englishmen are fond of The Indefinite which they Measure by Newtons Doctrine of the Fluxions of an Atom. A Thing that does not Exist. These are Politicians & think that Republican Art is Inimical to their Atom. For a Line or Lineament is not formed by Chance a Line is a Line in its Minutest Subdivision[s] Strait or Crooked It is Itself & Not Intermeasurable with or by any Thing Else Such is Job but since the French Revolution Englishmen are all Intermeasurable One by Another Certainly a happy state of Agreement to which I for One do not Agree. God keep me from the Divinity of Yes & No too The Yea Nay Creeping Jesus from supposing Up & Down to be the same Thing as all Experimentalists must suppose

You are desirous I know to dispose of some of my Works & to make <them> Please. I am obliged to you & to all who do so But having none remaining of all that I had Printed I cannot Print more Except at a great loss for at the time I printed those things I had a whole House to range in now I am shut up in a Corner therefore am forced to ask a Price for them that I scarce expect to get from a Stranger. I am now Printing a Set of the Songs of Innocence & Experience for a Friend at Ten Guineas which I cannot do under Six Months consistent with my other Work, so that I have little hope of doing any more of such things. the Last Work I produced is a Poem Entitled Jerusalem the Emanation of the Giant Albion, but find that to Print it will Cost my Time the amount of Twenty Guineas One I have Finishd It contains 100 Plates but it is not likely that I shall get a Customer for it

As you wish me to send you a list with the Prices of these things they are as follows

	£	s	d
America	6.	6.	o
Europe	6.	6.	o
Visions &c	5.	5.	o
Thel	3.	3.	o
Songs of Inn. & Exp.	10.	10.	o
Urizen	6.	6.	o

The Little Card I will do as soon as Possible but when you Consider that I have been reduced to a Skeleton from which I am slowly recovering you will I hope have Patience with me.

Flaxman is Gone & we must All soon follow every one to his Own Eternal House Leaving the Delusive Goddess Nature & her Laws to get into Freedom from all Law of the Members into The Mind in which every one is King & Priest in his own House God Send it so on Earth as it is in Heaven

I am Dear Sir Yours Affectionately

WILLIAM BLAKE

Textual Notes

BY DAVID V. ERDMAN

The acceptance of Blake's poetry as he printed it has been a very long time coming. No English poet has had such absolute control over the formal appearance of his own work, lettering, illustrating, printing, and finishing it in color with his own hands and usually with a particular customer in mind; yet few have had such ill fortune with their work's subsequent publication. Blake's nineteenth-century editors were poets or poetasters with their own ideas of poetic diction and structure. Rossetti thought nothing of rounding out stanzas, remaking lines and titles, dressing Blake's naked beauty in Victorian garb. Swinburne guessed his way through difficult passages or made the implicit explicit—as when he "improved" the lyric called "Soft Snow" by changing "in a snowy day / I askd" to "on a sunny day / I wooed". Ellis and Yeats substituted, for example, "shadowy tears" for "shuddering fears", and the latter thought it better to "throw the dust against the wind" than "the sand"—and so on.

Rigorous editorial standards were finally applied, to the shorter poems, by the librarian John Sampson in 1905, who manfully cleared away the rubbish and many of the misreadings of "all editions" but had only indirect access to the manuscripts; and to the prophetic books in 1926, by Professors Sloss and Wallis. Sir Geoffrey Keynes's text of the poetry and prose, in successively revised editions from 1925 to 1957 and in volumes with and without "all the variant readings", established a still more accurate and more thorough text; and in recent years under his guidance the Blake Trust has been issuing superb facsimile volumes. Blake's designs (and words) have, as he wished, remained unchanged "above Times troubled fountains"—and the Public is at last getting to see them.

The goal of the present edition is a text as close as possible to Blake's own, even in punctuation, and with his final or preferred readings separated from earlier or deleted or alternative readings or arrangements. For the works Blake etched and printed himself, but sometimes partially effaced and sometimes rearranged, this is a matter of precise transcription, recovery of deletions, and recognition of Blake's own scribal errors, but also of taking into account the nature and limitations of his methods of production. For the few works that survive only in conventional typography the editor's task is chiefly to correct, of course within brackets, printer's errors that range from the patent to the hypothetical. For the many poems surviving only in manuscript it is a matter of retracing as exactly as possible the successive stages of composition and revision and rearrangement, especially when no final or perfect draft is plainly discernible.

All the original manuscripts and one or more copies of each of the etched and printed works have been freshly examined, and intensive effort has been applied to the restoration of deleted and altered passages of all kinds.

THE PUNCTUATION

The hazards of the present editorial choice of Blake's own punctuation are minimal with respect to the lyric poems, of short lines and firm stanzas, for here an editor's patching could mislead the reader more than omitted stopping. But the "long resounding" lines of Blake's epics and prophecies confront us with a problem to which there is no true parallel. When Blake omits nearly all punctuation, as he does in most manuscript pages and intermittently in etched ones, so much effort is required merely to follow the prose sense, the syntax, of some passages that all of us are grateful for the "bold attempt made" by Sir Geoffrey Keynes, with the help of Max Plowman, "to supply punctuation, with the admitted risk of sometimes conveying a meaning not intended by Blake" (Keynes 1957, p xiii).

Unhappily, to supply punctuation means also to remove or change some of the punctuation found. It means moving Blake's question marks to the ends of clauses, imposing a modern consistency on his semicolons and periods, adding apostrophes where his possessives are truly ambiguous in number. Blake is not steady about punctuation, but when he does attend to it he does so in the eighteenth-century rhetorical fashion: a dramatic passage is studded with what the journalist aptly calls shriek-marks; a solemn passage is retarded by blockades of colons, or a slighter pausing is suggested by small dots after members of a series of nouns or adjectives (where we would expect commas). Often the dot is placed in some caesural point in the line but not according to the grammar of clauses or phrases. Good advice to the reader would be to study some of these careful passages (many occur in *Milton*) and attend to Blake's differentiation of the "terrific" parts from the "mild & gentle" and the "prosaic" (see *Jerusalem*, Plate 3) even where he has not troubled to supply any mechanical guidance for the "true Orator" who was called upon to "chaunt" his "heroic Verse". Punctuation calculated to measure out the syntax of rational statement will almost inevitably divert both editor and reader from the oratorical variety and musical impetus of the poet's authentic voice, only to impose the bondage of "a Monotonous Cadence" from which he strove to be free.

In print it is impossible to copy Blake exactly: his colons and shriek-marks grade into each other; he compounds a comma with a question mark; his commas with unmistakable tails thin down to unmistakable periods. Moreover, one printing from his etched plate may be more lightly inked than another and miss out some apostrophes or reduce some commas to periods. In Blake the practical difference between comma and period is almost unappreciable; I have I am afraid wobbled in the transcription, inclining especially in prose passages to read commas or periods according to usual expectation (in *Island in the Moon*, for example). In some texts a few marks have been inserted, within square brackets. Only one kind of silent insertion has been practised, where brackets would be awkward: Blake nearly always supplied the apostrophe in the possessive of Los ("Los's", otherwise subject to confusion with "Loss"), and I have done so even where he did not. The aim, in short, has been to produce a text which will mediate between the reader and the manuscript or Illuminated Printing without introducing a wholly different pointing system.

POEMS FROM MANUSCRIPT

The poetical works that were never printed by or for Blake but survive in manuscript range from incomplete fragments and abandoned drafts (*Tiriel* being the most extensive of these) to perfected lyrics that awaited only a place to be put among his illuminated works (for example, some of the lyrics and ballads in "The Pickering Manuscript", a group of poems that was in a sense published by being written out fair for some unknown friend or patron). Standing in a special category is the much revised and amplified *Vala* or *The Four Zoas*, which remained a "work in progress" eternally, though prepared at one state as an elegantly inscribed illuminated manuscript—which it might have remained if it had found a purchaser.

One of the most striking things about Blake's working manuscripts is his numbering and renumbering of lines and stanzas as a poem grows at both ends and at every point and as the sequences of words, lines, and stanzas are rearranged. Sometimes no final arrangement is indicated; sometimes the indications are clear but difficult to accept, as when deletion marks cut too much away and call for substitutions which were not written (or have been lost). The present text represents a considerable advance in the recovery of erased words and lines and hence a significant advance in the reconstruction of manuscript drafts (especially of the lyrics and satiric verses in the Notebook). Recovery of complete series of several of Blake's numberings and renumberings and full attention to his guide lines and other indications of arrangement and deletion and restoration have made this possible.

In the handling of manuscript poems our aim has been to present what can be found to have been Blake's latest intention as to text, while being as explicit as possible in the notes as to his first and intermediate intentions. When ambiguities of intention have been more or less arbitrarily resolved for the final text, attention is called to the difficulty. Deleted stanzas, for example, the first stanza of "Never pain to tell thy love", have in a few instances been restored to make a complete poem—with the fact of deletion indicated.

VARIANT READINGS

Deleted or variant readings of the text selected as final are given in the following Textual Notes. The annotation of inessentials is somewhat less exhaustive for the manuscript poems than for the Illuminated canon—and is largely omitted for the prose texts. Such manuscript details as mended letters, slips of the pen, and trivial, passing revisions and deletions are not noted or are summarized to assist the reader to focus upon significant changes or variants. In the prose essays and marginalia and letters, substantive deletions and insertions are included in square and angle brackets respectively within the body of the text while minor variants or illegible deletions are silently passed over. Deleted words are retained in the final text of a poem only when Blake supplied no alternative replacements.

ABBREVIATIONS AND SYMBOLS

WORKS CITED IN THE NOTES

Bateson	F. W. Bateson (ed), *Selected Poems of William Blake* (New York: The Macmillan Co 1957)
Bloom	Harold Bloom, *Blake's Apocalypse* (Garden City, NY: Doubleday & Co, Inc 1963)
Bronowski	J. Bronowski, *William Blake: A Man Without a Mask* (Harmondsworth, Eng: Penguin Books, Inc [Pelican] 1954)
Damon	S. Foster Damon, *William Blake: His Philosophy and Symbols* (New York: Houghton Mifflin Co 1924) [But consult his forthcoming *Blake Dictionary* (Brown University Press).]
Erdman	David V. Erdman, *Blake: Prophet Against Empire* (Princeton University Press 1954)
Fisher	Peter F. Fisher, *The Valley of Vision* (University of Toronto Press 1961)
Frye	Northrop Frye, *Fearful Symmetry* (Princeton University Press 1947)
Frye "Notes"	Northrop Frye, "Notes for a Commentary on *Milton*," *The Divine Vision*, ed Vivian de Sola Pinto (London: Gollancz 1957)
Gleckner	Robert F. Gleckner, *The Piper and the Bard* (Wayne State University Press 1959)
Keynes	Geoffrey Keynes, *The Complete Writings of William Blake* (London: The Nonesuch Press; New York: Random House 1957)

Lowery   Margaret Ruth Lowery, *Windows of the Morning* (Yale University Press 1940)

Margoliouth   H. M. Margoliouth (ed), *William Blake's* Vala: *Blake's Numbered Text* (Oxford: Clarendon Press 1956)

Murry   J. M. Murry, *William Blake* (London: Jonathan Cape Inc 1933; reprint forthcoming)

Percival   Milton Percival, *William Blake's Circle of Destiny* (Columbia University Press 1938)

Sampson   John Sampson (ed), *The Poetical Works of William Blake* (Clarendon Press 1905)

Sloss and   D. J. Sloss and J. P. R. Wallis, *The Prophetic Writings of William*
Wallis   *Blake* (Clarendon Press 1926) 2 vols

SYMBOLS USED IN TEXT AND NOTES

[*thus*]   Italics within square brackets indicate words or letters deleted or erased or written over.

[thus]   Roman type within square brackets comprises matter supplied by the editor.

<thus>   Angle brackets enclose letters or words written to replace deletions, or as additions—but not including words written immediately following and in the same ink as a canceled word.

I. THE WORKS IN ILLUMINATED PRINTING

There is much to be said for the conclusion, urged by Northrop Frye in his *Fearful Symmetry*, that those writings which Blake illustrated and issued in the form of relief etchings which he called Illuminated Printing "were intended to form an exclusive and definitive canon". Yet "exclusive" and "definitive" both need qualification. The disarray of the extant early tractates may signify that the author did not wish to preserve them as units, while it would be a serious mistake on the other hand to assume that Blake intended to exclude the lyrics of "The Pickering Manuscript" since he did not illustrate them or to abandon *The Four Zoas* because he never etched it. Etching, however, did establish a text that was definitive in the sense of fixed. Once he had applied words to copper and etched surrounding surfaces away, Blake could not alter a letter except by laborious mending; he could scratch away words and even lines but could not easily add new ones. He called his plates "stereotypes" because on each he had made a whole page of text and illustration into a single solid type for printing (and subsequent coloring).

Blake was understandably reluctant to cancel whole plates, but that does not mean he regarded the making of a set of plates as the definitive completion of his poem; few of his "canonical" works lack indications of the addition or removal of one or more plates. With a more ductile medium he might well have forged a more perfect and more truly definitive canon. Yet he managed to make a virtue of the patchwork effects of his patching: a gallery of plates does not trap the observer as might a serpentine closed circle of "fair copy". Windows are left for the imagination, which may also leap from words to illustrations and back as one series supplements the other. Blake sometimes composed in units of one or two plates; if he had done so more often his shifting about of plates might have left fewer derailed paragraphs in *Milton* and *Jerusalem*—but he might then have done even more shifting. Perhaps if he had been able to make it so, each new copy of each of his works might have been in text as well as coloring a new edition.

He accepted the monolithic character of his pages, but he employed every remaining means to keep his poems in motion—varying the color of his inks and his translucent and opaque tints and washes, and varying the sequence of his plates. It may not have been his particular consideration to make each copy of his *Songs* or of each of his

Prophecies a unique work of art, although in effect that is what he did, but he was obviously pleased to make every plate of every work a vehicle of fresh vision each time he touched it.

~&

THERE is NO Natural Religion [a, b]

ALL RELIGIONS are ONE

The titles and 26 (once 27) paragraphs of the axioms here grouped into three series were color-printed from tiny etched plates (averaging about 2×2½ inches). Each paragraph is on a separate plate, except that one plate holds both "Principle 7th" and the paragraph that follows. Blake may have begun with the "a" series and then evolved the "b" series as a contrary way of saying the same thing; the third series has a different theme. But in no known copies (13 sets consisting of from 8 to 14 plates) is the grouping of axioms complete or consistent. The titles, for example, are found with the wrong groups of axioms. The most satisfactory editorial arrangement seems to be that of Keynes, which is followed here, although that of Sloss and Wallis, placing the sentence beginning "Therefore" at the end of the first series, is almost as attractive.

Date: 1788—from the internal evidence of themes and style along with the virtual certainty that these early experiments with etched copper represent what is meant by "W Blakes Original Stereotype . . . 1788" in the inscription on the last of his stereotypes, *The Ghost of Abel,* of 1822.

The Author . . . Blake] *lettered in reverse.* The other pages all seem to have been written in backhand on the copper, to print correctly, and not to have been applied by Blake's later method of transfer.

~&

THE BOOK of THEL

The *Census* describes 15 copies, without textual variation except for the deletion noted below. The title is on Plate ii.

Date: 1789–91. Despite the date "1789" on the title page, *Thel* may overlap *The Marriage of Heaven and Hell* (in date of etching) and *Visions of the Daughters of Albion* (in date of composition). Sloss and Wallis (II 267) suggest "a slightly later date" for "Thel's Motto" and Plate 6 (the conclusion). A changed style of script in these two plates shows them to have been etched no earlier than 1791—Plate 6 presumably replacing an earlier version, the Motto perhaps an afterthought.

1:1 Mne Seraphim] *sic, without question* As Keynes says, "the apparently meaningless syllable was certainly intentional, probably being a corruption of the mystical name, Bne Seraphim . . .".

6:19–20 deleted in two copies.

~&

SONGS Of INNOCENCE and Of EXPERIENCE

Twenty-one copies of *Songs of Innocence* and 27 of the combined grouping under the general title are known to exist. The *Songs of Experience,* though advertised separately in Blake's Prospectus of 1793, appear not to have been issued except in combination or to complement earlier copies of *Songs of Innocence.* The latter he continued to issue separately, feeling perhaps that they could stand alone but that the songs of Experience required to be heard as counterpoint in the progression of contraries.

Ms drafts of three Innocence songs (in *An Island in the Moon*) and of 18 Experience songs (in the Notebook) are analyzed for all variants, in the following notes. All etched copies are identical in text, except for Blake's tampering with line 12 of "The Tyger" in one copy and changing "sung" to "sang" in "The Clod & the Pebble" in another. In no two copies of *Innocence*, however, are the plates containing the songs arranged in exactly the same order. In copies of the combined volume, Blake after 19 differing arrangements (in what order we are not sure, since the dating of many copies is conjectural) settled down to that adopted in the present edition. In seven of the last eight copies printed he followed this sequence; yet since two of these printings were made not before 1815 and five not before 1825–26, i.e., in Blake's closing years, this "final" order may represent only a final weariness. For when he took pains to write out instructions as to "The Order in which the Songs . . . ought to be paged & placed" —an order followed in one copy, on 1818 paper, though the list is checked over twice as if for two bindings—Blake contrived yet one more unique arrangement.

It is suggested that the reader experiment, as Blake did, to find what different tensions and resonances are produced by different juxtapositions.

Dates: 1784–1805, approximately. Three songs appear in the ms of *An Island* (about Dec 1784). The earliest copies of *Songs of Innocence* are complete and bear the etched date "1789" but may not have been issued that soon. The backward slant of the roman lettering and the tilt of some lines suggest direct mirror-writing on the copper—except for "The Voice of the Ancient Bard," which is in the italic lettering of *Thel* and may be an early try at the method of transfer which Blake used for all subsequent lettering in relief.

Four of the *Songs of Experience* first appeared among the *Songs of Innocence*: "The Little Girl Lost" and "The Little Girl Found", "The School Boy", and "The Voice of the Ancient Bard". Thus even while making his "1789" collection Blake was accumulating contrary songs, including perhaps some not fit even temporarily for Innocence. Of the 18 songs of Experience in Blake's Notebook (in entries made between 1790 and late 1792) 12 seem fair copies of earlier drafts (though subsequently revised or expanded) and only six were unmistakably begun and composed in the Notebook, i.e., within these dates: 'The Lilly", "The Tyger", "The Human Abstract", "A Little Boy Lost", "The Chimney Sweeper", and "The Fly" (in that order).

"A Divine Image" (given here following the *Songs* proper) turned up only posthumously but must have been etched before (and been replaced by) "The Human Abstract".

Before the end of 1792 Blake had written among the Notebook poems a satiric "Motto to the Songs of Innocence & of Experience" (see above, p 490); yet he advertised the two groups as separate booklets on October 10 1793, and his combined title page is etched "1794".

Songs not in the Notebook group and hence possibly of late composition are the "Introduction", "Ah! Sun-flower", and "A Little Girl Lost". "To Tirzah" does not appear in five copies, and in style of lettering and in content it seems to belong to 1803 or later. (One cannot go by the dates given by Geoffrey Keynes and Edwin Wolf in their *William Blake's Illuminated Books: a Census* [New York 1953]; many of these are contradictory as well as conjectural.)

In the notes that follow, second or third readings implied but not given are to be understood as identical to the readings of the final text.

SONGS of INNOCENCE:

The Chimney Sweeper

3 weep &c] *to be understood as* 'weep (for "sweep")

The Little Boy lost

Ms draft in *An Island in the Moon*, Chap 11 (see p 454), is presented as a song by Quid the Cynic. In revision for *Songs of Innocence* the anapests were removed—and the mockery.

Laughing Song

An early ms version, not in Blake's hand, was written in a copy of *Poetical Sketches* that belonged to Mrs Flaxman, now in the Alexander Turnbull Library in Wellington, New Zealand. It varies from "Laughing Song" in the following particulars:

Title] Song 2nd by a Young Shepherd *ms rdg*
Lines 1–2 were lines 5–6 in the ms; lines 3–6 were 1–4.
1 green woods laugh] greenwood laughs *ms rdg*
3 air does] trees do *ms rdg*
7 Mary and Susan and Emily] Edessa, & Lyca, & Emilie *ms rdg*

HOLY THURSDAY

The ms draft in *An Island in the Moon*, Chap 11 (see text p 453), is presented as a song by Mr Obtuse Angle, the Mathematician, which is meant to enliven a dull party but fails.

Night

44 Grase] Only occurrence of the word "graze" in any spelling throughout Blake.

Nurse's Song

Ms draft in *An Island in the Moon*, Chap 11 (see text), shifts the son's reciter from Mrs Sigtagatist's Grandmother to Mrs Nannicantipot's mother to, finally, a Nurse.

*

SONGS of EXPERIENCE:

With the two exceptions indicated, all variant readings given are from Blake's ms Notebook.

EARTH'S Answer

Follows "Introduction" immediately in all copies. The Notebook draft (p 111 reversed) shows Blake arriving at the final text through precise improvements in wording:

Title] The Earths Answer *1st ms rdg*
3 light fled] eyes fled *1st ms rdg del*; orbs dead *2nd ms rdg del*
7 Starry] *1st ms rdg*, del, then reinserted above the line
10 I hear . . . men] *1st ms rdg, changed to* I hear the ancient father of me; *then* ancient father *del*
11 Selfish] Cruel *1st ms rdg del*
12 selfish] wintry *1st ms rdg del*
14 Chain'd] Closd *1st ms rdg del*
11–15 Stanza heavily del, then 16–20 written in adjacent column as replacement; final restoration of 11–15 not indicated in the Notebook (a caution against considering all Notebook deletions as final decisions: see "Never pain to tell thy love")
16 joy] delight *1st ms rdg del*
18–19 sower / Sow by night] sower sow / His seed by night *1st ms rdg* (revised to final rdg)
22 freeze] close *1st ms rdg del*
24–25] Thou my bane
Hast my love with bondage bound *1st ms rdg* (revised to final rdg)

The CLOD & the PEBBLE

Ms draft in Notebook (p 115 reversed) is identical except for lack of punctuation, and mistake of "anothers" for "another" in line 10.

5 sang] *mended from* sung (in 1825 or later when Blake was retracing the text in color in copy Z–see Blake Trust facsimile, 1955; a possibly accidental yet genuine correction by an older Blake)

HOLY THURSDAY

Ms draft in Notebook (p 103 reversed) is almost identical but less limber.

7 so many children]   so great a number *ms rdg*
8 It is]   Tis *ms rdg*
12 It is]   Tis *ms rdg*
13, 14 where-e'er]   whereeer *ms rdg*

The Little Girl Lost

This and the next poem first appeared among the *Songs of Innocence* (1789).

THE Chimney Sweeper

Ms draft in Notebook (pp 106 & 103 reversed) is almost identical.

2 weep weep] *i.e.,* sweep sweep   4 to the church]   to Church *ms p 106*
6 winters snow]   winter wind *1st ms rdg*
12 make up a heaven of]   wrap themselves up in *1st ms rdg del*

NURSES Song

Ms draft in Notebook (p 109 reversed) is identical except for:

Title] *not in ms*
3 days of my youth]   desires of youth *1st ms rdg del*; days of youth *2nd ms rdg*

The SICK ROSE

Ms draft in Notebook (p 107 reversed) is closely related to "The wild flowers song" begun just above it on the page, in the same ink.

5 Has]   Hath *ms rdg*
7 And his]   O *1st ms rdg del*; And his *2nd ms rdg*; And her *3rd ms rdg*
8 Does thy]   Doth *1st ms rdg del*

THE FLY

Ms draft in Notebook (p 101 reversed) began with three tetrameter lines and a half:

> Woe alas my guilty hand
> Brushd across thy summer joy
> All thy gilded painted pride
> Shatterd fled

These were deleted and a new beginning was made in dimeter quatrains, close to the final version except for a deleted second stanza:

> The cut worm
> Forgives the plow
> And dies in peace
> And so do thou

(Compare Proverb 6 in the *Marriage*)

Title] *not in ms*
2 summers]   summer *ms rdg*
3 thoughtless]   guilty *1st ms rdg del*
4 Has]   Hath *ms rdg*

Lines 13–16 originally followed 17–20 and were more positive in mode:
13 If thought]   Thought *1st ms rdg del*
15 And]   But *1st ms rdg del*

The Angel

Ms draft in Notebook (p 103 reversed) does not capitalize "Dream", "Queen", or "Angel". Lines 15–16 appear also as concluding lines in the ms "Infant Sorrow" (see p 720 and p 460).

15 For]   But *1st ms rdg del*

The Tyger

There are two ms drafts in Notebook (pp 109–108 reversed), the first much revised, with title and stanza 5 added in revision; the second a fair copy (crossed out after transfer to copper) of stanzas 1, 3, 5, and 6—with stanza 2 written alongside though not marked for insertion.

3 or]   or *1st ms rdg del*; & *2nd ms rdg*
4 Could]   Could *1st ms rdg del*; Dare *2nd ms rdg del*
5 In what]   In what *1st ms rdg del* (but deletion line erased); Burnt in *2nd ms rdg del*
6 Burnt the]   Burnt the *1st ms rdg del*; The Cruel *2nd ms rdg del*
7 On . . . aspire]   Could heart descend or wings aspire *2nd ms rdg* (*1st ms rdg,* not del, is the final rdg)
12 & what]   Altered in ink to "formd thy" in a late copy (P); given as "forged thy" in B. H. Malkin, *A Father's Memoirs of his Child* (London 1806), perhaps on Blake's authority, for the line seems to have troubled him.
After line 12 several starts were made on a 4th stanza, first:
> Could fetch it from the furnace deep
> And in [*thy*] <the> horrid ribs dare steep
then:
> In the well of sanguine woe
then:
> In what clay & in what mould
> Were thy eyes of fury rolld
Then all these were deleted and stanza 4 was written in almost its final form, but it was experimented with thus:
13 What . . . what]   What . . . what *1st ms rdg del*; Where . . . where *2nd ms rdg*
15 dread grasp]   the arm *1st ms rdg*; the arm *2nd ms rdg*; the grasp *3rd ms rdg*; the clasp *4th ms rdg*; dread grasp *5th ms rdg*
16 Dare]   Could *1st ms rdg del*   clasp]   clasp *1st ms rdg del*; grasp *2nd ms rdg del*
Lines 17–20 were written as follows, then numbered for rearrangement of lines and for insertion as 5th stanza:
> 5
> 3 And [*is*] [<did> he laugh] <dare he [*smile*] [<laugh>]> his work to see
> [What the [*shoulder*] <ankle> what the knee]
> 4 [*Did*] <Dare> he who made the lamb make thee
> 1 When the stars threw down their spears
> 2 And waterd heaven with their tears
22 In the]   In thee *1st ms rdg*
23 or eye]   & eye *1st and 2nd ms rdgs*
24 frame]   form *1st ms rdg del*

My Pretty ROSE TREE

Ms draft in Notebook (p 115 reversed) was the first Song of Experience copied into it; a fair copy, but soon revised:

Title] *not in ms*
6 To . . . night]   In the silent of the night *1st ms rdg del;* To tend it by day & by night *2nd ms rdg*
7 turnd away with jealousy:]   was turned from me *1st ms rdg del;* was filld with Jealousy *2nd ms rdg* (revised to final rdg).

THE LILLY

Ms draft in Notebook (p 109 reversed) lacks title and indeed can hardly be subsumed under the later title:

The [*rose puts envious*] <[*lustful*] <modest> rose> puts forth a thorn
The [*coward*] <humble> sheep a threatning horn
While the lilly white shall in love delight
[*And the lion increase freedom & peace*]
[*The prist loves war & the soldier peace*]
Nor a thorn nor a threat stain her beauty bright

The GARDEN of LOVE

Ms draft in Notebook (p 115 reversed) is a hastily written copy, identical in final readings except that it lacks title and "chapel" is spelled "chapeld" and "gowns" "gounds".

2 And saw]   And [*a*] <I> saw *ms rdg*
3 built]   *mended in ms from* build
5 gates . . . were]   gate . . . was *1st ms rdg del*

The Little Vagabond

Ms draft in Notebook (p 105 reversed) is in pencil, though the bowdlerizing revisions of lines 4 and 16 are in ink.

Title]   A pretty Vagabond *1st ms rdg* (revised to final rdg)
3 where]   when *mended to* where *ms rdg*   use'd]   usd *ms rdg*
4]   Such usage in heaven makes all go to hell *1st ms rdg del;* The poor parsons with wind like a blown bladder swell *2nd ms rdg*
13 rejoicing]   that joys for *1st ms rdg del*
16]   But shake hands & kiss him & thered be no more hell *1st ms rdg del;* But kiss him & give him both [*food*] drink & apparel *2nd ms rdg*

LONDON

Ms draft in Notebook (p 109 reversed) began as fair copy with title and three stanzas; later revised and given a 4th stanza, which was thrice revised.

1, 2 charter'd]   dirty *ms rdg*
3 mark]   see *1st ms rdg del*
6 Infants cry of fear]   voice of every child *1st ms rdg del*
7 ban] meaning prohibition or curse (or both); compare "Bow-street's ban" in *Don Juan* XI 19; Bateson, p 126, is mistaken in thinking the first meaning anachronistic.
8 mind-forg'd manacles]   german forged links *1st ms rdg* (revised to final rdg)
9 How]   But most *1st ms rdg* (del to give "most" to 4th stanza)
10] Blackens oer the churches walls *1st ms rdg del*
13–16]:

But most the midnight harlots curse
From every dismal street I hear
Weaves around the marriage hearse
And blasts the new born infants tear *1st ms rdg del*

But most [*from every*] <thro wintry> street <s> I hear
How the midnight harlots curse
Blasts the new born infants tear
And [*hangs*] <smites> with plagues the marriage hearse *2nd ms rdg del*

But most the shrieks of youth I hear *3rd ms rdg del*

But most thro midnight &c
How the youthful *4th ms rdg*

The Human Abstract

The ms draft in Notebook (p 107 reversed) is related to an earlier ms lyric, "I heard an Angel singing" (p 114 reversed), given here under "Songs and Ballads".

Title] The human Image *ms rdg*
1 Pity] Mercy *1st ms rdg del*
2 we did not make somebody] there was nobody *1st ms rdg del*
8 baits] nets *1st ms rdg del*
24 There grows one] Till they sought *1st ms rdg del*
Here follow two lines derived from the Notebook draft of "The Lilly" (see above):
They said this mystery never shall cease
The prest [*loves*] <promotes> war & the soldier peace
Also four lines in the adjacent column, though separated by another poem, probably belong to this one, if "There" means "in the human brain":
There souls of men are bought & sold
[*There*] <And> [*cradled*] <milk fed> infancy [*is sold*] for gold
And youth [*s*] to slaughter houses led
And [*maidens*] <beauty> for a bit of bread

INFANT SORROW

Ms draft in Notebook (p 113 reversed) is identical in these two stanzas, but it continues for seven more stanzas, heavily revised, with an alternative development on p 111 reversed. On p 113 the original draft before revisions was probably a fair copy from some earlier ms (except where lines 13–14 were canceled and replaced at once by extension of the stanza at the other end, lines 17–18):

(*continuation*)

And I grew day after day
Till upon the ground I stray   10
And I grew night after night
Seeking only for delight

[*But upon the netty ground*]
[*No delight was to be found*]
And I saw before me shine
Clusters of the wandring vine   15
And beyond a mirtle tree
Stretchd its blossoms out to me

But a Priest with holy look
In his hand a holy book   20
Pronouncd curses on his head
Who the fruit or blossoms shed

I beheld the Priest by night
He embracd my mirtle bright
I beheld the Priest by day   25
Where beneath my vine he lay

Like a serpent in the night
He embracd my mirtle bright
Like a serpent in the day
Underneath my vine he lay   30

So I smote him & his gore
Staind the roots my mirtle bore
But the time of youth is fled
And grey hairs are on my head   *1st ms rdg*

Extensive revisions, in a different ink, effected two major transformations. First Blake changed the singular "Priest" and associated pronouns and "serpent" to plural, "many a Priest" and "Priests" with plural pronouns and "serpents": the Priests embraced the youth's blossoms and he "smote them"; during this revision the sixth and seventh stanzas (lines 23–30) were consolidated. Meanwhile on p 111 (see p 769 below) Blake had begun some stanzas of a youth bound beneath a mirtle—an impulse combining some of the "Infant Sorrow" material with motifs from "Earths Answer" (on the same page) and leading finally to the separate poem "To my Mirtle" on p 106 (see p 770). At first an effort was made to fit the bound youth into the tale of the priest-cursed infant. Lines 31–34 (the concluding stanza) were repeated on p 111. But then Blake turned from the motifs of p 111—in which "the priest" laughs at the "simplicity" of wedlock (youth bound to mirtle tree)—to pluralize the priest and serpent of p 113. Not content with the result, he then bypassed the priests and serpents of stanza six–seven (lines 27–34 as numbered below) and, drawing again upon "Earths Answer", from which he deleted the cruel "father of men", he put "my father" in the place of the "priest" of p 111 and "many a priest" of p 113 (line 23). He changed line 26 to introduce the bondage motif, "And bound me in a mirtle shade"; this, in effect, canceled the remainder of p 113 and led to the stanzas which he numbered 1, 2, 3 on p 111 and the concluding quatrain.

The indicated fusion was not carried further ("their hands" in revised line 24 should have been changed back to "his hand"); at some point all the verses on p 113 except the first two stanzas were struck out by canceling lines; the title "Infant Sorrow" was inserted, over the two stanzas to be etched as a Song of Experience. At the post-adolescent end of the progression, "To my Mirtle" emerged, on p 106, as a poem of three couplets.

Editorial rescue work can salvage from the transitional drafts of pp 113 and 111 a compact cycle-poem (compare "The Mental Traveller") from infancy to grey hairs. Keynes (pp 889–890) presents Max Plowman's "fair copy" of the fusion of the two pages before removal of the "Infant Sorrow" stanzas—though the resultant poem should probably not bear that title. Plowman had noticed the catch-word function of the phrase "in a mirtle shade", but his reconstruction of the sequence of the writing on page 111 was unsound, and, like Keynes, I treated the phrase as a title (see p 460, fixed in the present format). Until this fourth printing I had neglected the possibility that the catch-word idea might be in itself valid. Donald K. Moore has helped me to arrive at the present interpretation of these Notebook pages, and he is preparing an article on the subject.

A variant of the Plowman "fair copy" would consist of the two unchanged "Infant Sorrow" stanzas, followed by the inserted third stanza as revised (lines 9–12 below), followed by the penultimate version of lines 23–26 and the final revisions of bypassed stanzas on p 113 (lines 31–35 ff).

For the details of p 111 see below, p 769. The process of revision of p 113 (after the first two stanzas) may be shown in composite form:

When I saw that rage was vain
And to su[c]<l>k would nothing gain   10

[I began to so] [<Seeking many an artful wile>] <Turning many
    a trick o[r] wil[e]>
I began to soothe & s[p]<m>ile

And I [grew] [<smild>] <soothd> day after day
Till upon the ground I stray
And I [grew] <smild> night after night   15
Seeking only for delight

[But upon the nettly ground]
[No delight was to be found]
And I saw before me shine
Clusters of the wandring vine   20
[And beyond a mirtle tree] <And many a lovely flower & tree>
Stretchd [its] <their> blossoms out to me

[But a] [<But many a>] [Priest] <My father then> with holy look
In [his] [<their>] hand<s> a holy book
Pronouncd curses on [his] <my> head   25
[Who the fruit or blossoms shed] <And bound me in a mirtle shade>

[I beheld the Priest<s> by night]
[[He] <They> embracd [my mirtle] <the blossoms> bright]
[I beheld the Priest<s> by day]
[Where beneath my] <Underneath the> vine<s> [he] <they> lay   30

[3] [Like [a] <to> serpent<s> in the night]
[4] [[He] <They> embracd my [mirtle] <blossoms> bright]
[1] Like [a] <to> [serpent<s> in the] <holy men by> day
[2] Underneath [my] <the> vine<s> [he] <they> lay

So I smote [him] <them> & [his] <their> gore   35
etc

A POISON TREE

Ms draft in Notebook (p 114 reversed) is identical except for punctuation and:
Title]   Christian Forbearance *ms rdg*

A Little BOY Lost

Ms draft in Notebook (p 106 reversed).

Title] *not in ms*
5 And ... how can I]   Then ... I can not *1st ms rdg del*
6 Or]   Nor *1st ms rdg del*
7 you like the litle bird]   myself so does the bird *1st ms rdg del*
Line 10 is followed in ms by two deleted lines:
    The mother followd weeping loud
    O that I such a fiend should bear
11 He]   Then *1st ms rdg del*
Lines 13–16 were written in the adjacent column.
19–20]   They bound his little ivory limbs
    In a cruel Iron chain *1st ms rdg del*
19 They]   And *2nd ms rdg del*
21 And ... place]   They ... fire *1st ms rdg del*
24 Are such things]   Such things are *1st ms rdg* (revised to final rdg)

To Tirzah

A late addition to the *Songs*, not found in copies A–E. The style of lettering points to a date later than 1802, though this upsets the traditional (but highly conjectural) dating of copies F, I–O, which contain this poem yet are assigned dates of 1795, 1796–98, and 1799–1801 in the Keynes and Wolf *Census*. Keynes himself has steadily, in his editions, assigned a date of "about 1801".

Actually the first copy of *Songs* that contains "To Tirzah" and has any firm evidence of date is copy P (on paper watermarked BUTTANSHAW 1802), followed by Q (with watermark dates of 1802 and 1804).

The School Boy

First appeared among *Songs of Innocence;* was not for some time transferred to *Songs of Experience.*

The Voice of the Ancient Bard

Began among *Songs of Innocence;* was shifted to *Songs of Experience* in some early copies yet appears occasionally in *Innocence* in copies as late as 1815.

A DIVINE IMAGE

This poem, illustrated by a youthful blacksmith hammering a human-faced sun on his anvil, was etched by Blake but never published by him (hence not strictly *in* the canon). The few extant prints seem to have been made from the plate after his death. The poem is an "Experience" reversal of the third stanza of "The Divine Image" in *Songs of Innocence*. It was evidently etched for *Songs of Experience* (the plate size is right) but replaced by "The Human Abstract", a subtler contrary. The style of lettering is transitional between that of *Songs of Innocence* and that of *Songs of Experience* or between the styles of the early and late portions of *Thel* and of *The Marriage of Heaven and Hell*. None of the published *Songs of Experience* is quite so simply and symmetrically antithetical to its counterpart in *Innocence*.

Date: 1790–91 (hitherto misdated ca 1794).

FOR CHILDREN: THE GATES of PARADISE

(first version)

Engraved on 18 plates, a first state with erased imprint; a second state with title reading "Published by W Blake Nᵒ 13 Hercules Buildings Lambeth and J. John St. Pauls Church Yard" and with some variant of "Published 17 May 1793 by W Blake Lambeth" on each plate except No 13. The only textual variant is on Plate 13 (see note).

The 17 emblem drawings are a selection from 56 drawings in Blake's Notebook; the inscriptions are simplifications of inscriptions penciled beneath the Notebook drawings (some recovered only by infrared photography).

After drawing these emblems, Blake twice rearranged them (by numbering) in the Notebook; the engraved sequence represents a fourth arrangement, maintained in the reissue of 1818, "For the Sexes".

The ms inscriptions are given here, identified by Notebook page; for later variants see "For the Sexes".

Frontispiece] What is Man that thou shouldst/magnify him & that thou shouldst set/thine heart upon him/ Job N 68

1] I found him beneath/a tree in the Garden N 63

2] O that the Everlasting has not fixd/His canon gainst Self slaughter/Shakespeare N *95*

3] Rest Rest perturbd Spirit/Shakespeare N *93*

4] Thou hast set thy heart as the/heart of God–/Ezekiel N *94*

5] [*Forthwith upright*] he rears from off the pool/His mighty stature/Milton N *91*

6] At length for hatching ripe he breaks the shell/Dryden N *69*

7] Ah luckless babe born under cruel star
And in dead parents baleful ashes bred
That little weenest now what sorrows are
Left thee for portion of thy livelihed/Spenser N *19*

8] My son My son N *34*

9] N *40, without inscription*

10] Possibly N *58*, without inscription   11] Aged Ignorance N *52*

12] N *59, without inscription*

13 & Hope]   or Hope *1st state;* What we hope we see N *61*

14] Thus the traveller hasteth in/the Evening N *15*

15] Deaths door N *71*

16] I have said to corruption thou art/my father. to the worm thou art/my mother & my sister/Job N *45*

❧

THE *MARRIAGE* of HEAVEN and HELL

On 27 plates, including title page and "A Song of Liberty"; known in nine complete copies; without textual variation except the deletions noted below. Added as frontispiece in copy B is the engraving inscribed "Our End is come / Published June 5 1793 by W Blake Lambeth". Copies in the collection of Sir Geoffrey Keynes and in the Morgan Library and the Rosenwald Collection were collated.

Date: Begun in 1790 (see Plate 3) and completed in 1792–93 (from evidence of historical allusions in the "Song of Liberty"). Plates 4, 7–10, 14–20, 25–27 have a later style of lettering than the rest.

Between the introductory poem and the "Song," the text falls into six "chapters" (Plates 3–4, 5–10, 11–13, 14–15, 16–20, 21–24) each consisting of an argument followed by an imaginative illustration, as noted by Max Plowman in 1927. The pictorial headings which mark these sections are indicated in the present text by ornamental rules.

3:1 thirty-three years]   Blake wrote "1790" in the margin, in the Butts copy. It was 33 years after 1757, the date announced by Swedenborg for the new dispensation (and the year of Blake's birth).

6: he who dwells]   *mended in the copper from* the Devil who dwells

Plate 7 uses the later style of lettering, and it may be more than mere coincidence that on this very plate Blake writes, metaphorically and somewhat cryptically, of his etching process (his own reflection or shadow being the Devil he sees in the mirror-like surface of his plate, which is the "flat sided steep" to be etched by his "corroding fires").

The most easily distinguishable component of the new lettering is a leftward pointing serif on the *g*, maintained consistently until after Nov. 1802 and then as suddenly and thoroughly abandoned in favor of the conventional rightward serif. After 1802, in texts or inscriptions from the middle period being re-etched or retouched by hand, Blake carefully adds the conventional serif, usually without effacing the leftward one, so that curious two-horned *g's* abound in works reissued in his last two decades.

20: Opposition is true Friendship.]   *del by pigment in six copies*

25:6 And weep]   And weep and bow thy reverend locks *1st rdg*, found in a separate issue of *A Story of Liberty* (so-called "Copy L").

❧

VISIONS of the Daughters of Albion

On 11 plates, including frontispiece and title page; known in 17 complete copies. The text does not vary, but the frontispiece is sometimes put at the end.

～

AMERICA *a* PROPHECY

On 18 plates, including title page and frontispiece; known in 15 copies (one posthumously printed). Proofs exist of three canceled plates (a, b, c) of an earlier version and a fragment (d) which may be a remnant of a still different version. These are in the Rosenwald Collection.

Dated "1793" and announced for sale in Blake's prospectus of that October; but perhaps the final version was completed later. The final plates seem very different in spirit and quality of drawing from the canceled ones, yet the latter can hardly have been written before 1792. The earliest copy is on paper of 1794; the "harp-shattering" lines (19–20) on Plate 2 suggest 1794 or 1795 as date of etching.

1: PRELUDIUM]   Title added (by use of a separate small plate); lacking in two copies.

2:18–21   Lines omitted from all copies except the earliest and two latest, by the expedient of covering the lower portion of the plate before printing.

3:4 Franklin . . . Hancock]   Hancock, Paine. & Warren. Gates, Franklin *Canceled Plate a*

3:10 work-bruis'd,]   work bruised. *Canceled Plate a*

3:11 and]   & *Canceled Plate a*

3:14 wrathful]   fiery *Canceled Plate a*

3:16 red]   fierce *Canceled Plate a*

16: FINIS]   *del* in at least one copy (the Fitzwilliam)

[Canceled Plates of *America*]

Plate a is identical in text to Plate 3, with variants noted above. Plate b is a variant of Plate 4 in the illustrations, but quite different in text. Plate c must have come between Plates 8 and 9 (or earlier versions of those plates); it describes the arming of the King whose "hollow voice" utters the lament and alarm of Plate 9 (described on Plate 10 as the weeping of "the Angel voice").

c:1 Then Albions Angel rose]   Words marked for deletion, to be replaced by words written in top margin (but now cut away).

c:2–3   Lines numbered in pencil "6" and "7"; a penciled arrow above line 2 was evidently meant to bring in four new lines written in the top margin (now cut away).

c:5 river:]   Followed by guide line meant to bring in words written in side margin, now all cut away except: "all in [   ] ?wild [   ] look [   ] and [   ] And L[   ]"

c:5 damp mists]   with flames *1st rdg del;* hoar frosts *2nd rdg del*

c:6 aged]   shining *1st rdg del*

c:7 cold]   gleam *1st rdg del*

c:8 on]   to *1st rdg del*

c:9 chill & heavy]   glow the fires *1st rdg del;* till by the freeze *2nd rdg del*

c:11 ancie[nt]]   eternal *1st rdg del* (the "nt" of "ancient" has been cut away)

c:13 clouds]   flames *1st rdg del*

c:15 clangors]   ardors *1st rdg del*

c:17 mustering]   glowing *1st rdg del*

c:19 holds]   fires *1st rdg del*

c:21–23   Bracketed matter deleted but not replaced.

c:25 a frowning . . . King]   Over the frowning shadow, like a King *1st rdg*

c:27–28 A marginal insertion between these lines was almost entirely cut away.

c:31 America] the red Demon *1st rdg del*
Plate d is found, the text covered over by pigment, in two copies of the gathering of colored prints called "A Large Book of Designs", No 8, in the Rosenwald copy, numbered "9" by Blake. It was printed from the bottom half of a plate of the same width and style of lettering as *America*.

❧

EUROPE a PROPHECY

On 16 plates, including title, frontispiece (also issued separately), and two full-page designs representing death by famine and death by pestilence (the latter inscribed, upon a door in the picture, "LORD [H]AVE MERC[Y] ON US"). Two complete copies known; ten copies lacking prefatory poem; variant proofs of Plates 14 and 15. Copies and proof pages in the British Museum, the Paul Mellon Collection, and the Morgan Library were collated.

1:6 travel] *for* travail (perhaps—Blake never distinguished the two words)
Lines 3:9 to 4:14 are all treated by Keynes as the speech of Los, but three speakers may be distinguished: Los (3:9–14), the envious sons of Urizen (4:3–9), and Enitharmon (4:10–14).
9:6 Shadows] A large initial "S" (distinctively colored in the Mellon copy) marks the beginning of the "dream" of history.
12:35–36 Blake had room to write these two short lines as one if he had chosen to do so.
13:9 Then] Extra indention marks the end of the "dream".
14:32 for All were forth at sport] *mended in the copper from* and all went forth to sport (On one proof an ink correction was made without the "for", according to Keynes.)
14:32–37 Lines deleted by erasure in one proof.
14:35 gate.] gate, and the angel trumpet blew! *1st rdg* (In an intermediate state of the plate the last five words of the first reading are deleted but line 32 is not changed—proof in Morgan Library.)
15:1 of Enitharmon;] of Enitharmon, before the Trumpet blew *1st rdg* (proof copy)

❧

THE SONG of LOS

On eight plates, including frontispiece, title page, and two full-page designs; known in five copies, without textual variant.

❧

THE [FIRST] BOOK of URIZEN

On 28 plates, including title page and ten full-page designs; known in seven copies, containing from 24 to 28 plates; plus some scattered plates. I have examined all but copy E.
Blake evidently committed this work to copper in haste, then deleted and mended words and lines (mostly in the paper, not the copper) and added and removed plates. There is only one possible arrangement of the text, since it is organized into numbered chapters—except that Plate 8, duplicating the numbers of Plate 10, was probably meant to replace it. Yet Plate 2 is out of order in copy E, 15 follows 18 in A, and 8 follows rather than precedes 10 in copies B, E, and F.
The ten pictorial plates are in different positions in each copy. Most of them more or less obviously relate to one or more passages in the text, however, and if we assume that the further the pictures have shifted away from their simplest textual referents the later the publication, we obtain the sequence of copies C B F D E A G,

with A the climactic exemplar of the original series (it is not later than 1800 if the provenance is correct) and G (watermark date 1818) following at a distance. For instance, the picture of Urizen in manacles, appropriate to the text of Plate 13 (or 8 or 10), follows 13 in C and precedes it in B; in the more sophisticated A it is moved to the front, as a portent of the end in the beginning. Copy G imitates the majority of the earlier copies, with a few slight movements further away from juxtaposition of picture and text but without the expression of dramatic intensities found in A.

Other evidence supports this hypothetic sequence. Copy C, lacking the added Plates 7–8, may be the earliest copy; A and G, in which "First" is deleted in titles and colophon, are probably (G certainly) the latest. Retouched letters in D and A are in the style of Blake's middle period (1791–1802). Copy B may be the first to contain Plates 7–8, since it contains an attempt to cope with the intrusion of two Fourth Chapters which is abandoned as futile. Seven leaves of B and one of D have the only dated watermark ("1794") except G.

It should be noted that the page format and lettering of 7–8 differ markedly from those of the other pages but are like those of *Ahania* and *Los*, the second and third "BOOKS" of the series, dated "1795". Although Blake did not entitle these second and third books of Urizen, he must have considered them so for some time. In Copy B the numeral in the heading "1 Urizen" is emphasized by retouching; this numeral and "First" are deleted only in copies A and G (and even in these not thoroughly). (The *Census* lettering of copies does not claim to indicate their order of publication, except for G.)

(N.B. Arrangement of plates is confirmed by Blake's folio numbering in B D G; erased numbers in A give a less sophisticated order than that of the binding; no numbers are visible in C F, [E not collated].)

Title]   FIRST *del* (in copy G, by erasure)

2: Preludium title]   FIRST *del* (in A G, by erasure). The numeral "1" is also erased in 7 of the 9 running heads ("1 URIZEN") in A and in 6 of the 8 in G.

3:11 In his]   Like *1st rdg del* (by erasure and inked replacement in G; an interesting sign of late attention to the text, for in syntax and image an obvious flaw is thus removed)

Heading: Chap: II]   erased in copy B

3:44 Shrill . . . Eternity]   Line del by scoring in ink, in A—a logical step toward removal of Plate 4; yet Plate 4 is not lacking in A, while in those copies that do lack it, this deletion is not indicated. To erase 3:44 yet keep Plate 4 makes no sense.

Plate 4 is lacking in copies D E F G; yet in these the deletions that would mend the breach, 3:44 and 5:1–2, are not indicated. Retention of Plate 4 in A casts doubt on the deduction, above, that A is later than F D E.

4:30, 49   The first of these redundant lines is erased in copy C, the second in A.

Heading: Chap: III.] *erased to* Chap: II *in* B (so that the first of the two "Chap: IV" headings, i.e. that brought in on the new Plate 8, could be changed to III; but the change was not made)

5:1–2   Lines del by scoring in ink, in copy A (logical, if Plate 4 had been removed)

5:16 On Urizens self-begotten armies]   Lines erased in A, consistent with mending in 5:22 (obviously A was the most carefully proofread copy)

5:20, 21, 29 He]   they *1st rdg del* (in all copies changed to "he" by erasure of "t" and "y"; mended to capital "He" in copy A)

5:22, 23 He]   They *1st rdg del* (erased and replaced in all copies, capitalized because beginning of line)

Note: "armies" in line 16 was the antecedent of "they" in these lines; perhaps the change from "they" to "he" implies an intent to delete line 16 in all copies. The "living creations" of 5:1 are perhaps equivalent to the "armies" (hence tentative deletion of 5:1–2?). The change transfers the work of creation from a crew of "sins" or "armies" to the single god, Urizen, and renders the word "combining" in 5:21 meaningless. The capitalized pronoun in copy A may only accidentally have theological implications.

6:8 is followed by two lines deleted from the copper; almost legible in copy B.

Plates 7 and 8 are lacking in copy C. In script and style of etching these added plates differ from the others. In the use of colons following section numbers, for instance, they resemble *Ahania* and the *Book of Los*. Before their insertion the text ran smoothly from Plate 6 to 10.

Plate 8 was evidently designed to replace 10, the omission of the refrain words "first Age" having been at first overlooked. In copies B E F the new plate follows the old (with lines 10:42–43 being marked for erasure in two of these). But the present, and better, order is followed in A D G.

Plate 15 follows Plate 18 in copy A—probably a binder's error, for the leaf has no folio number.

25:18 And the Web is a Female in embrio]   Line erased in copy A and covered by tendril.

❧

THE BOOK of AHANIA

Frontispiece, title page, and four plates of text, in ordinary intaglio etching instead of Blake's usual relief etching. Extant in only one copy in the Rosenwald Collection (lacking frontispiece [i]) and a few scattered prints of Plates i, 1, 3, 4.

❧

THE BOOK of LOS

Frontispiece, title page, and three plates of text, in ordinary intaglio etching, as *Ahania*. Extant in one copy (in the British Museum) plus a separate print of Plate 4.

❧

MILTON a Poem in 2 Books

Title page, 42 plates of text, 8 full-page designs: total 51 plates; in four copies, no one of which is complete.

The page numbering established by Keynes (and followed here to avoid confusion of reference) is slightly inconsistent in its inclusion of one of the pictorial plates (No 16), but it represents the arrangement of copy D, the latest and most nearly complete copy. (In that copy the other seven pictorial plates follow the plates here numbered 9, 14, 29, 33, 37, 39, and 40.)

Copies A and B, on paper watermarked 1808, consist of 45 plates each; copy C, on the same paper, contains five additional pages of text (here numbered 3, 4, 10, 18, 32); copy D, on paper of 1815, contains these and another addition (5). But both C and D lack the Preface (1).

Dates of composition and etching: The title page, dated "1804", announces a work in "12 Books"; yet "Finis" is etched at the conclusion of Book Two. (Compare the deleted announcement of 28 chapters in the "1804" title page of *Jerusalem*.) In letters of April and July 1803 Blake declares that he has in the previous "three years composed an immense number of verses" descriptive of his "Spiritual Acts" during those years—an account that fits *Milton* better than *Vala* or *Jerusalem*—and that these verses, "perfectly completed into a Grand Poem", only await divine assistance to "be progressively Printed & Ornamented with Prints & given to the Public". Possibly the "1804" titles mark a division of the Grand Poem into two, a large epic and a small. Yet probably only the title pages, if even they, were etched at that time. After his "1795" prophecies Blake may not have resumed his Illuminated Printing until after his 1809 Exhibition of paintings. In a letter of December 1808 he explains that he has "long been turned out of" his "former pursuits of printing" (he has been asked what etched books he has for sale) and that he will be preoccupied with painting and designing for some time to come. In the *Descriptive Catalogue* (section V) he repeats the hope for divine aid to "publish" what he has "written" and seems to refer to *Jerusalem* or *The Four Zoas* or both, a "voluminous" work. The first epic he began to print and ornament, however, was the smaller and more economically designed *Milton* (on exact halves of the plates of *Jerusalem* but inscribed so compactly as to contain nearly as many words per page). Only *Milton* fits his description of "a Poem . . . which I will soon Publish" in the ms "Public Address" of 1810 or later (see p 561). His confident wording implies that the work was nearly finished, and the etching of all but three of the extant plates appears to have been done over a fairly short period: I suggest the years 1809–10. Although the paper of copies A and B is watermarked 1808, he cannot have used it in that year (considering his December statement) nor until the Exhibition was launched in the following spring.

When he etched *Milton* he was content to write "Finis" on the 45th plate and in his first two copies to reduce the "12 Books" of his title page to "2". Later, perhaps as he saw *Jerusalem* shaping into 100 plates, he went on to make *Milton* an even 50. Most of the plates added in copies C and D appear to be filled with matter previously by-passed but to have been etched in the same period as the rest of the work. Two exceptions are extra pages 10 and 32, in a much lighter, freer style of lettering (with extra page 3 leaning in this direction). These I suspect to have been etched later than the rest, with copies C and D both completed near the time of printing of D (on 1815 paper). And in these late copies Blake, though keeping to two Books, was proud to commemorate his original plan; not only did he let the numeral print clearly "12", he used careful stipple work to strengthen the shadow emphasizing each digit.

What relation the extant *Milton* bears to the poem first described in 1803 we cannot tell. Many passages appear to be of relatively late composition (Plates 6 and 4, for example); at least two, the Preface and Plate 19 (see note) belong in allusions and tone to the 1807–9 period. Yet the first added plate (3) is a refurbished passage from the *Book of Urizen* of 1794; the last added plate (5) reads like a remnant of a version in which *Milton* had some of the character of such historical prophecies as *America*; and two other added plates (10 and 16) seem early in relation to the main body of the poem. For an exemplification of the accretive growth of the work, see the note on 2:26.

Title 2 Books *A B*]   12 Books *C D*
Plate 1 (Preface) lacking in C D.
    2:21 What] *mended from* That (the mending tentative in A but complete in C D)
    2:26 Blake first intended Plate 7 to follow (syntactical link: Classes are created by hammer and woven by looms); then Plate 6 was inserted (Classes are created and woven, from London to Dover, in immense labours), with a new link to 7 (regulated by hammers and woven by looms). Thus stand copies A B. Then Plate 3 was inserted, borrowing the original link, "woven by Enitharmons Looms", which was then deleted from 6:35–7:1 (see below). After Plate 3 Blake then inserted another new page, Plate 4 (syntactical link between 4 and 6: Blake's neighborhood resounded with engraving of animals [for the Hayley ballads], displaying naked beauty and song, from Golgonooza in immense labours, ever building ever falling). Finally he brought in Plate 5—an earlier and perhaps rejected passage also dealing with the creation of the classes. The links now are difficult but can be found. If we recognize Palamabron with fiery harrow (5:1) as a Felpham variant of Blake-Los busy etching, his "returning From breathing fields" can be taken as loosely in apposition to the "Mocking" and "Displaying" in 4:27–28. And near the end of Plate 5, if we make a long parenthesis of "Charles . . . Living Proportion", we may read: "Creating the Three Classes . . . From Golgonooza . . .".

To recover the narrative sequence from these accretions, Northrop Frye suggests reading the plates in the order 2, 7, 4, 6, 3, 8 (skipping 5). This is a useful suggestion—but does not represent (as Frye supposes) "the order of the 'C' copy". In that copy Blake's numbering of folios gives the present order: 2, 3, 4, 6, 7, 8. (Pages 2 and 3 are reversed by a binder's mistake, but the *Census* is simply wrong in reporting an order of 2, 7, 3, 6, 4, 8.)

Plate 3 added in copies C D.

Plate 4 added in C D.

Plate 5 added in D.

6:12 Theotorm]   Doubtless an error for "Theotormon"

6:35 Hammer. *C D*]   Hammers and Woven *A B*

7:1 is preceded in A B by a line deleted in C D:

        By Enitharmons Looms & Spun beneath the Spindle of Tirzah

7:3 womb: follow]   Deleted between these two words are two half lines, partly legible in copy D. *Conjectural reading:* the Reprobate are the first / ?Who [   ] by for the ?glorification [   ]

7:28 he he]   Presumably an intentional repetition; yet the similar duplication of "with with" in 15:27 is plainly a scribal error.

Plate 10 added in C D.

10:1 Enitharmon]   Not misspelled "Enitharman" despite Keynes.

10:7 Infinite]   Followed by one deleted word and line. *Conjectural reading:* until / The Space becomes ?Serpent-formed & the Womb ?Englobes (Compare *Jerusalem* 1:2)

Plate 16 is a full-page design (Milton striving with Urizen) *inscribed:* To Annihilate the Self-hood of Deceit & False Forgiveness

Plate 18 added in C D.

19:58–59 Hand . . . Hyle & Coban: / Scofield]   Allusions to the *Examiner* (in which editorials were signed with a printer's hand), Hayley, Cromek (perhaps), and Scofield; the first and third require a date of 1807 or later.

22:35 most dismal to our eyes]   Referring either to the "left Foot black" or to the "Shadowy Female"; the punctuation, being rhetorical, does not dispel the ambiguity.

22:56–62   A difficult passage. There is a dot after "Witnesses" which I take to be intrusive. It is "the two Witnesses' Faith" which appears to "the Churches" as obedience to "the death of the Cross". The colon at the end of line 57 introduces the Churches' cries, quoted as lines 58–62.

23:5 Awake]   *mended from* awake

24:57   Inserted in a stanza break, perhaps having been omitted by an accident of transcription.

24:64 blare by the . . . clarion] *i.e.* blare [lulld by] the . . . clarion

25:53 To]   The *in all copies* (a mistake noted by Margoliouth; among other signs of carelessness in the inscription of this plate note omitted word in line 38)

26:3   I have omitted an intrusive period after "dance".

Plate 27 precedes Plates 25–26 in copies A B.

27:3–41 Repeated with a few changes from *Four Zoas IX* 136:16 – 137:4.

27:60 Poetry . . . Surgery]   Line del in copper in C D; compare similar deletions in *Jerusalem* Plates 3 and 73.

28:9   It is apparently the infant Spectre who is "wretched" and "unform'd" for doubts—not "Others" or "Cabinets".

Plate 30 is preceded by a full-page design labeled "William".

30: *inscription in reverse:*   How wide the Gulf & Unpassable! between Simplicity & Insipidity / Contraries are Positives / A Negation is not a Contrary

31:56 eyes: listening the Rose]   Keynes moves the colon to follow "listening" and it may belong there; yet with the punctuation found on the plate the meaning is that the Rose, even in her sleep, hears the call of spring and prepares her sudden majestic entrance.

Plate 32 added in C D; placed after 33 in C.

32:15 כרבים]   *error for* כרבים (i.e. Kerabim)

Plate 34 is preceded by a full-page design labeled "Robert".

36:32 Enter my Cottage]   Ololon, Blake, and "Blakes Cottage at Felpham" are shown in the illustration.

37:9 Rahab]   Rahah *on the plate, but a mistake*

37:31 Assasinations] *mended from* assasinations
39:55 Calling] *mended from* calling
40:30 can be annihilated] can be ann be annihilated *all copies*
Plate 42. On the back of a drawing for this page is the *inscription:* Father &
Mother I return from flames of fire tried & pure & white (An error: the drawing that
bears this inscription is not related to *Milton*.)

JERUSALEM

Fontispiece, title page, 94 plates of text, 4 full-page designs: total 100 plates;
known in five complete copies printed by Blake and three posthumously printed. As
listed in the Keynes-Wolf *Census* (and in demonstrably chronological order) these are:
copy A (British Museum) with watermark dates of 1818–19–20; copy C (collection
of the late Frank Rinder—Blake Trust facsimile 1952) with the same dates of paper;
copy D (Harvard University Library) with watermark 1820; copy E (Paul Mellon
collection—Blake Trust color facsimile 1951) with watermark 1820; copy F (Pierpont
Morgan Library) with watermark dates of 1824, 1826; copies H, I, J posthumously
printed.

These copies and several single plates have been newly collated for the present edition—with the result that many of the deleted passages have been recovered, partly
with the aid of photographic enlargement. (A 6th copy, G, not located since 1921, has
never been described. Copy B, of 25 plates, i.e. the first chapter only, is apparently
contemporaneous with A and C, the watermark date being 1818.)

The arrangement of plates does not vary except in Chapter 2, where the present text
follows that of copies A, C, and F, the text familiar in the Rinder facsimile. The
alternative pagination, of copies D and E, is given in square brackets; that arrangement is familiar in the texts of Geoffrey Keynes. For some years a mistaken report of
the foliation of copy F supported a belief that there had been three Blakean arrangements of *Jerusalem*, with the corollary that the order of copies D and E represented
that in "the majority of the copies". At one point (Keynes, p 918) a typographical
error described this order as "constant except in one copy".

"Inconstant" might be a better description of either arrangement. After two copies
in the same order, Blake printed two in a variant order (Keynes's "standard") and then
returned to the first. Evidently he found both sequences attractive but considered
neither definitive. (See comment above on the variety of arrangements of *Songs of
Innocence and of Experience*.)

Date: See textual note on *Milton*, above. *Jerusalem* was etched and in present form
largely composed after *Milton*, though their "1804" title pages suggest some overlapping. Some pages were written and perhaps a few were etched, the Preface for instance, during the enthusiasm of the post-Felpham years. After his 1809 Exhibition,
Blake may have turned to his two epics simultaneously, but he first completed and
etched *Milton;* the final text of *Jerusalem* can hardly have been completed before 1815.
Most of the etching was probably done in 1815–20, but the deletion-marked pages
such as the Preface may survive from an earlier etching. Proof copies of Plates 28,
40 [45], and 56 were made on paper dated 1802. The fact that *Jerusalem* shows
much more variation from plate to plate than *Milton*, however, almost certainly
signifies a much longer span of composition and production. True, it was Blake's
conscious aim to achieve breadth and variety of graphic and verbal effects befitting an
epic, but time as well as stylistic choice seems to have caused some of the differences
among the plates.

For a detailed survey of these matters see my "Suppressed and Altered Passages in
Blake's *Jerusalem*" in *Studies in Bibliography* 1964.

Blake's scribal errors, here corrected without annotation, are: 5:3 "incohererent"
for "incoherent"; 16:51 "the the" for "the"; 38:37 "of of"; for "of"; 40:37 "con-

joinining" for "conjoining"; 64:31 "frownining" for "frowning"; 65:62 "him from him his" for "him from his"; 94:23 "Chastitity" for "Chastity".

In the present text all restored deletions are printed in italics, within brackets.

Title (Plate 2)]   In XXVIII Chapters *del before* etching (beneath the "on" of "Albion")

1804 . . . Molton S^t.]   *incised* (hence potentially added at any time)

Plate 1. Entire text deleted, both by incised lines emphasizing the texture and mortar-lines of the stonework and by solid inking of the plate. Text incised and so not very legible even in posthumous copies. But before the lines were cut across the text, Blake pulled a proof on which he outlined the lettering by pen and ink (see facsimile bound as frontispiece to the Blake Trust edition of the Rinder copy).

1:7 Albion behold Pitying]   *del by scratching the copper* (a somewhat conjectural reading)

3: SHEEP   GOATS]   *incised* (hence possibly a late addition)

7:65 Image   *del* (but retouched into legibility in copies B D)

8:40–41   Full stops seem required at each line end. It is the Spectre who must "labour obedient" for Los *because* Hand and Co "labour mightily" in negation.

Plate 10 is an added plate, made to fit between 9 and 11.

10:47 Righteous]   *mended from* righteous

11:3 anvils;]   I insert semicolon in place of comma, for the "Los. compelled" clause must end here.

14:34]   *Followed by colophon:* End of the 1st Chap: *del*

21:37 Childrens]   *mended from* childrens

22:10 Hatred]   *mended from* Ratred

23:7 But thou! O wretched Father!]   Jerusalem now speaks.

24:58 Dead . . . Alive]   *mended from* dead . . . alive

24:60   Followed by a line deleted almost without trace; compare 47:1.

Plate 26, engraved in white line, portrays "HAND" in flames and with nails in his extended palms, turned toward "JERUSALEM", who lifts her hands in amazement. The rhymed lines are incised in outline alongside the figures.

27:15 Willans]   *mended* (perhaps from "Williams")

Plate 28 exists in an early state (in a proof page in the Morgan Library); extensive changes were made in the picture, but not the text, before final printing. Female and male figures embracing in the center of a large flower were re-engraved from a position in which they could be assumed to be copulating to one in which they could not. Perhaps illustrating Jerusalem-Vala's attempt "to melt his [Albion's] Giant beauty, on the moony river" (19:47).

Plates 29–46 are found in two arrangements. The sequence followed here is that of copies A C F; numbers within brackets indicate the sequence of copies D E.

29:47 involve]   Possibly a mistake for "involves"; yet the construction "behold the cloud involve me" would not be unBlakean.

31:18 States . . . Systems]   These two words, in an unevenly deleted line, are somewhat conjectural.

32:34 Conjectural (and incomplete) restoration of deeply gouged deletion.

33:1 Line added (by engraving) after the etching of the plate.

33:10 blue]   *mended from* pale (in all copies, but restored to "pale" in A; a proof exists of the unmended plate)

35:6   Line crowded into a paragraph break, before etching, but indented to go with second paragraph.

35:10   Line crowded into paragraph break, before etching.

37:32–35   (reverse writing, on scroll):

> Each Man is in his Spectre's power
> Untill the arrival of that hour,
> When his Humanity awake
> And cast his Spectre into the Lake

These lines are close to the final draft in the Notebook (p 12—originally p 8) except for an unfinished 2nd stanza. A rearrangement of the 1st stanza lines was tried by numbering them 4, 3, 1, 2, but the numbers were canceled. Here is the Notebook text:

> [4] [*This world*] <Each Man> is the [*the*] <his> Spectres power
> [3] Untill the arrival of that hour
> [1] [*Untill*] <When> [*the*] <his> Humanity awake
> [2] And cast [*the*] <his own> Spectre into the Lake
>
> And there to Eternity aspire
> The selfhood in a flame of fire
> Till then the Lamb of God

40:40   Line lacking in proof (Morgan Library); added to plate by engraving.

42:47 fiend] *etched* friend; emendation suggested by W. H. Stevenson

43:28 rocks] *etched* locks, *but see line* 2; emendation suggested by Joanne Witke

43:83 trembling] *mended from* Albion slept (though "slept" is conjectural)

47:1   Blake probably did not delete this line because of its redundancy with the plate's concluding line (for a similar refrain enclosing a plate, see *America* 9) but to accommodate some rearrangement of plates subsequently abandoned.

49:35 Void] ground *rdg on plate*, error in copying *Milton* 5:22

Plate 51, a full-page illustration, was inscribed "Vala   Hyle   Skofield" when issued as a separate print. Monogram WB in lower left corner (for use with separate print) is visible in copy A and posthumous copies.

Plate 52. The 7 stanzas beginning "I saw a Monk . . ." are an almost exact transcription of stanzas numbered 1 to 7 in a much longer draft in Blake's Notebook (p 12—originally p 8). In order of composition these seven were originally stanzas 1, 2, 3, 4, 15, 16, and 14. (For another poem, of nine stanzas, drawn from the same Notebook draft, see "The Grey Monk" in the Pickering Manuscript, below.)

1 Charlemaine]   Constantine *1st ms rdg del*   3 as we]   where he *ms rdg*

5–8   A variant stanza was written beside this in the ms:
> Gibbon plied his lash of steel
> Voltaire turnd his wracking wheel
> Charlemaine & his barons bold
> Stood by & mocked in iron & gold

Another variant ms stanza was written in the margin:
> The Wheel of Voltaire whirld on high
> Gibbon aloud his lash does ply
> Charlemaine & his Clouds of War
> Muster around the Polar Star

(The final line 7 was composed after these variant stanzas were rejected.)

7 The Schools . . . rolld]   Charlemaine & his barons bold *1st ms rdg del*

9 Thou . . . afar]   Seditious Monk said Charlemaine *1st ms rdg del*

10 In vain . . . War]   The Glory of War thou condemnst in vain *1st ms rdg del*

11 your . . . you]   thy . . . thou *ms rdg*   shall] shalt *ms rdg*

17–20 When Satan . . . mercys Lord]   *ms stanza* "5" (*variant:* Mercys), *replacing:*
> Untill the Tyrant himself relent
> The Tyrant who first the black bow bent
> Slaughter shall heap the bloody plain
> Resistance & war is the Tyrants gain

21 Titus! Constantine!]   O Charlemaine O *1st ms rdg del*

23 Grecian Mocks]   mocks & scorn *1st ms rdg del*

25 For a Tear]   For the tear *1st ms rdg del;* A tear *2nd ms rdg*

27 of a Martyrs]   for anothers *1st ms rdg del;* of the Martyrs *2nd ms rdg*

25–28   Variant ms stanza, abandoned but not deleted:
> But The Tear of Love & forgiveness sweet
> And submission to death beneath his feet
> The Tear shall melt the sword of steel
> And every wound it has made shall heal

(The "feet" in the second line are the Tyrant's.)

The following stanza, numbered "8", was begun, alongside stanza 7:

a Grecian Scoff is a wracking wheel

The Roman pride is a sword of steel

[*Vict*] Glory & Victory a [*?Ron*] [*?Trojan*] [<*plaited*>] phallic Whip

("Ron" a start on "Roman"? These lines first a variant of stanza 2?)

53:8, 24 Each line added within a paragraph break, before etching

55:20 Conclave] *etched* Concave, clearly wrong for the context

56:37 earth-Worms] *mended by pen from* earth-Worm *in Morgan copy*

Plate 57. In the illustration are the names "York   London   Jerusalem".

58:3 Street] *possibly a mistake for* Streets

60:55 Not: but] *Keynes emends to* Nought but (yet compare 93:20 and 96:16; perhaps the intended opposition is "Art thou alive! or art thou Not:")

69:1 combined] *mended to* conjoined (restored in the Mellon copy by pen)

72:53   *Mirror writing:* Women the comforters of Men become the Tormenters & Punishers

73:37, 42 Deletions covered by vines in most copies; legible in posthumous copies, under magnification.

Plate 76 is a full-page illustration, with the names "Albion" and "Jesus" incised beneath its two figures. "Albion" is deleted in copies D E; "Jesus" in copies C D E F.

Plate 77, in the bottom corners, has an incised but deleted inscription in two divided lines of about ten words, the first line reading "The Real Selfhood   in the".

77:1–4 I give you . . . wall] Four lines from Blake's Notebook (p 46 reversed)

77:1 give] have given *1st ms rdg del*

Plate 81. The mirror writing in the inscription reads:

In Heaven the only Art of Living

Is Forgetting & Forgiving

Especially to the Female

But if you on Earth Forgive

You shall not find where to Live

81:15–16   Since these two lines appear below the illustration, they may be considered as its caption; but they also serve as part of the text. (Keynes prints them as such but in a note says they are not part of the text.)

Plate 82 shows many signs of haste. The deletion in lines 47–48 should perhaps be respected as a successful revision, but that in lines 67–68 leaves an awkward gap.

82:43 his hands . . . & his feet] *written* his hands . . . & his hands

83:30 Affection] *mended from* affection

83:87 Awake]   Whether given an exclamation point or not, this word seems to hang in mid-air. Plate 83 (different in technique, lettering, content) obviously did not originally follow. Part of the Daughters' song of building appears to be lost.

85:11 Myriads] *mended from* myriads

89:2 endure]   The plural subject of this verb must be the "double" nay "Twelvefold" Hermaphroditic form.

90:58 And] *mended from* and

90:67 thunder's]   I have inserted the apostrophe called for by the syntax and context; it is the thunder of Los that utters Plate 91.

91:1   Preceded by a deleted line which I can partly decipher as "Forgiveness of Enemies ?can [   ] only [   ] God [   ]"

Plate 92 includes an illustration inscribed "Jerusalem". A deleted line follows 93:1.

94:27   Line probably added during a rewriting of the page. (Examination of Plate 95 reveals that the text of Plate 94 was first etched in the top half of 95 and was probably identical to the re-etched version except for this line.)

Plate 96 is etched on what was once the lower left quarter of a large plate on which Blake had etched a commercial manifesto for "MOORE & Co's Manufactory & Warehouse, of Carpeting and Hosiery Chiswell Street. MOOR-FIELDS" in 1797 or 1798. (This broadside is reproduced in G. Keynes, *Blake's Engravings: The Separate Plates* [Dublin 1956], Plate 10, but there conjecturally dated 1790.)

98:11 Sexual Threefold] *mended from* Sexual Twofold (The plate bears other signs of hasty writing.)

98:34 regenerations] *mended from* regenations

98:45 the Covenant of] *mended from* thy Covenant (thy Covenant restored in the Morgan copy by pen)

98:48 Sacrifices] The terminal "s" almost hidden by the decorative border—but not a true deletion.

Plate 99 bears traces of an earlier use of the copper for some architectural and vaguely scenic design, not identified.

❧

FOR THE SEXES: THE GATES of PARADISE

A reissue of "For Children" of 1793, with altered title, amplified inscriptions, and four new pages of text (including the Prologue on the title page); 21 plates, extant in five complete and seven incomplete copies.

These plates, in line engraving rather than the relief etching of most of Blake's Illuminated Printing, were easily retouched from issue to issue, the later copies being more and more highly finished. The revision of text was fairly easy also, and variant earlier and later versions of some lines in the Prologue and "Keys" are noted.

Date: The new title page is undated, though Blake leaves the "1793" imprint at the foot of the frontispiece and 16 plates of emblems. As late as "Novr 22nd 1806" when "Henry Fuseli" was inscribing a gift copy "To Harriet Jane Moore", it was still the version "For Children" (copy now in the Mellon Collection). The only known copy (now lost) with the earliest version "For the Sexes" was on undated paper; the single copy in a second state (with the later wording only in line 5 of the Prologue) is on 1818 paper; the third state occurs on paper of 1825; a final state is darker. It might be unwise to date the earliest "Sexes" version as late as 1818, though it was certainly a good deal later than 1806. (The script of the captions, though modified to the post-1802 style, shows remnants of the 1793 style; that of the new verses does not.)

[Prologue]

5 Finger] fingers *1st state*
7 And the Dead Corpse from] And in the midst of *1st & 2nd states*
8 Buried] Hid it *1st & 2nd states*

THE KEYS of the GATES

15 We stood] I stood *1st & 2nd states*

❧

ON HOMERS POETRY

ON VIRGIL

Etched on a single plate; known in six copies, on unwatermarked paper. The date of about 1820 is conjectural.

❧

THE GHOST of ABEL

Two plates of Illuminated Printing; known in four copies, two on paper dated 1820 and 1821: but the colophon date is 1822.

28 The Voice of Abels Blood] A picture caption, but also a stage direction: we hear the Voice as "The Curtain falls".

29 Stereotype] Single plate or "type" of metal, etched or engraved, from which Blake printed. Blake's original examples of Illuminated Printing appear to be the "No Natural Religion" tractates; this colophon gives them the date of 1788.

[THE LAOCOÖN]

These inscriptions are engraved in lettering of varying shape and size and angle. There is no right way to read them—except all at once. Some phrases relate to specific parts of the central picture—though it is not quite clear whether the definition of "Satans Wife" belongs with the Lilith label on the "Good" snake, since Lilith was the wife of Adam—but this may be a Blakean reconstruction. The rest of the text can be read in more or less coherent thematic sequence, as attempted here. The Sloss and Wallis edition presents a topical grouping; the Keynes a mechanical one, down the center and then around from left to right. Each will work, as each different arrangement of *Songs of Innocence and of Experience* will work, with differing effects.

Goddess, Nature.] *i.e.* "whose goddess is Nature"

II. [PROPHETIC WORKS, UNENGRAVED]

TIRIEL

From the unique ms in the British Museum, in Blake's hand, on 8 foolscap leaves (8ᵛ blank), in a cover inscribed by Blake "Tiriel / MS. by Mr Blake". Written about 1789, the ms is a fair copy, with a few false starts or mended words, up through section 8, line 4. The remaining lines are a heavily revised first draft, perhaps of later date; deletions of whole lines in the earlier part may have been made when the conclusion was being drafted. Never etched or printed by Blake.

The following notes do not include all minor deletions.

1:1 *A following half-line, del:* But dark were his once piercing eyes
1:6 father] aged father *1st rdg*
1:8 arms] aged arms *1st rdg*
1:19 shrinking] living *1st rdg del;* ?shriecking *2nd rdg del*
2:10 *Next line del:* The aged father & mother saw him as they sat at play
2:25 *Next line del, after stanza break:* O venerable O most piteous O most woeful day
2:26 *Next line del:* But I can kneel down at your door. I am a harmless man
2:40 Next, a two-line stanza, del:
    The aged Tiriel could not speak his heart was full of grief
    He strove against his rising passions. but still he could not speak
2:43 *Next line del:* Fearing to tell them who he was. because of the weakness of Har
3:6 Next, a two-line stanza, del:
    Tiriel could scarce dissemble more & his tongue could scarce refrain
    But still he feard that Har & Heva would die of joy & grief.
3:24 *Next line del:* God bless my benefactors. for I cannot tarry longer
3:26 Next, a three-line stanza, del:
    Then Mnetha led him to the door & gave to him his staff
    And Har & Heva stood & watchd him till he enterd the wood
    And then they went & wept to Mnetha but they soon forgot their tears
3:32 seeks] runs *1st rdg del*
4:15 *Written in margin, with a del half-line:* Seven years of sorrow then the curse of Zazel

4:38 running] *inserted above the line* 4:48 mean] must *1st rdg del*
4:63 why . . . Tiriel] you see and know your father *1st rdg del*
4:71 flesh] limbs *1st rdg del*. Then followed ten lines del:

> Then Ijim said Lotho. Clithyma. Makuth fetch your father
> Why do you stand confounded thus. Heuxos why art thou silent
>
> O noble Ijim thou hast brought our father to [*the gates*] <our eyes>
> That we may tremble & repent before thy mighty knees
> O we are but the slaves of Fortune. & that most cruel man
> Desires our deaths. O Ijim [*tis one whose aged tongue*]
> [*Decieve the noble & xxxx*] if the eloquent voice of Tiriel
> Hath workd our ruin we submit nor strive against stern fate
>
> He spoke & kneeld upon his knee. Then Ijim on the pavement
> Set aged Tiriel. in deep thought whether these things were so

4:74 like] torn like *1st rdg del* 4:76 false as] false & [*as*] *ms*
4:79 secret] *preceded by* gloom *del*
5:5 To raise his] Display thy *1st rdg, del* earth] world *1st rdg del*
5:22 sun] slee[p] *1st rdg, del before completion of word*
5:24 Hela] *mended from* Hili (as also in 5:26, 6:1, 3, 6). The first vowel is
conjectural but is not "e". The name becomes firmly "Hela" by 6:16.
5:30 stretchd . . . all] & all the children in their silent beds *1st rdg del*
5:31 guilty] ghastly *1st rdg del* 6:14 slave] child *1st rdg del*
6:41 heavens] (*a late revision*) air *1st rdg del* 6:49 fail] *mended from* fall
7:7 Some . . . began] They fled away & hid themselves but some stood still &
thus scoffing begun *1st rdg*
7:8 cunning] cunning wretch *1st rdg* 7:17 woes] life *1st rdg del*
8:4 The rest of the ms is written with a different pen and in more hurried script;
some time may have elapsed before Blake returned to finish the work.
8:8 *A following half-line del:* Thy God of love thy heaven of joy
8:9 Here 12 lines were deleted, the 8th of which reappears in "Thel's Motto" in the
illuminated *Book of Thel*.

> Dost thou not see that men cannot be formed all alike
> Some nostrild wide breathing out blood. Some close shut up
> In silent deceit. poisons inhaling from the morning rose
> With daggers hid beneath their lips & poison in their tongue
> Or eyed with little sparks of Hell or with infernal brands   5
> Flinging flames of discontent & plagues of dark despair
> Or those whose mouths are graves whose teeth the gates of eternal death
> Can wisdom be put in a silver rod or love in a golden bowl
> Is the son of a king warmed without wool or does he cry with a voice
> Of thunder does he look upon the sun & laugh or stretch   10
> His little hands into the depths of the sea, to bring forth
> The deadly cunning of the [*scaly tribe*] <flatterer> & spread it to the morning

8:10–11 Lines inserted to replace the 12-line cancel.
8:19–20 Marginal insertion; "&c" must refer to a passage written elsewhere, not
now located.
8:21 drone] foolish crawling drone *1st rdg*
8:22 *Next line del:* Hypocrisy the idiots wisdom & the wise mans folly

❧

THE FRENCH REVOLUTION

Extant only in one set of page proofs ([A]², B–C⁴), now in the Huntington Library. The work was never published, and probably never extended beyond the first Book. Blake may have corrected galley proofs; there are relatively few printer's errors, and the punctuation seems Blakean. For example, in lines 10–11, 29–30, 35–36 we find his use of commas to compel enjambement. The colon after "hopes" in line 49 is probably the printer's misreading of Blake's exclamation mark. And the printer obviously had no help from the ms or from the author's proofreading in the matter of quotation marks. (To avoid chaos, I have inserted them at the beginnings of lines 70, 74, 75, the end of line 78, beginning of line 89, end of 104, middles of 171 and 179, ends of 174, 197, middles of 220, 221, 225, 249, 252, ends of 237, 240, and 261. The punctuation is otherwise unchanged.) See Preface, p xxiv, re lines 105-109.

I have emended the following spellings which I judge to be printer's errors: line 46 "Eeternally", line 76 "were" for "wear", line 83 "antientest" (compare lines 82, 93, etc), line 101 "cloud" for "loud", line 122 "Neckar". As for the spelling of "Seyes" for "Sieyes" in lines 163 and 201, I suspect the mistake was Blake's and insert the *i* within brackets. I have accepted as his the spelling "beastial" in line 216. The hyphen in "war-living" (line 283) may have been meant for a dash.

Correct catchwords appear at the foot of each page through 15.

~❦~

THE FOUR ZOAS

The manuscript, in the British Museum, consists of 132 pages on 70 large sheets (about 16½×12½ inches) and two small sheets and a fragment. Drawings intended as illumination occur on 84 pages. The small sheets are dealt with in the notes to pp 7, 105, and 106 and (pp 141-42) in an Appendix. Of the large sheets, 68 consist of drawing paper, mostly with watermark J Whatman 1794, supplied to Blake in 1796 for his drawings and engravings for Young's *Night Thoughts* (only the first part of which was published, in June 1797); 47 of these have working proofs for the *Night Thoughts* on one side; the other two large sheets have parts of Blake's early engraving *Edward and Elenor* on one side. For a detailed if sometimes confusing account of the ms with a reproduction of all the pages in half-tone plates, see *Vala or the Four Zoas*, edited by G. E. Bentley, Jr (Clarendon Press 1963).

In pages 1, 3-18, 23-42, begun on clean sheets of paper, we can see that Blake's initial aim was a manuscript in fine copperplate script. Revisions at first made neatly over erasures or in the wide paragraph breaks maintain this objective with a modified yet still elegant engraver's hand. Further revisions and additions, however, squeezed between lines and spilling into margins, are in Blake's usual plain hand, as is all the text inscribed on the blank spaces of the proof pages.

Possibly a complete *Vala* in copperplate hand was produced but lay unsold and open to revision which gradually reduced it to a working ms. On the other hand, it may be that the aim to keep each page in copperplate perfection was sustained through a decade or more of labor over the text and drawings, a descent to ordinary hand on any given page occurring only when that page became too cluttered with revisions to be saved as perfect. (By this definition, pages 14-18, 26, 33, 40 are unspoiled, and pages 24, 29, 38, 41 have changes suggested in pencil that could still be perfected by careful erasure and inking: contrariwise, the minor but effacing revisions on pages 19, 27, 29, 31, 37, 39 may mean that Blake was giving up.) (See note on p 40, below-p 750.)

After Blake's death the ms was in loose sheets, but stitch-marks show he had once sewed together into one group all the sheets with elegant script and into another group those sheets containing pages 43-84 and 111-112, all in his usual hand. Possibly he thought of one group as finished, the other as preliminary, and any existing sheets not stitched as rejects (for example, Night VIIb, replaced by that time by VIIa).

At various stages of revision Blake counted his lines in each Night, sometimes by 100s, sometimes by 50s or 10s, and only pages 19-22, 87-90, and 111-116 lack numbering of any sort. But all Nights contain additions made after the latest counting.

Date: ca 1796-1807? The "1797" in the title may mark the beginning of a first fair copy, while pages 141-142 represent a fragment of a preliminary draft. The work is named "the Book of Vala" in an early, erased stratum of page 3; Bentley (p 177) suggests that it may have been "originally organized in 'Books' as a continuation of" *The First Book of Urizen*, noting that borrowings from *Urizen* occur in Nights IV and V and that these Nights are called "the Four Book" and "Book the Fifth" on pp 56 and 57. Also to be noted is the use of "Book" for "Night" in VIIb, p 95. (But H. M. Margoliouth, *Vala: Blake's Numbered Text* [Clarendon Press, 1956], p 121, argues that the use of "Book" is a sign of "very late" indifference—or "a deliberate, but abandoned, idea of giving up the 'Nights'".)

It has been tempting to suppose that successive layers of copperplate, modified copperplate, and usual hand represent successive and datable stages in the growth of the ms. On this supposition all the pages in usual hand should be later than those in copperplate—and all the latter should have fairly finished drawings. But the drawings vary in finish throughout. And on certain copperplate pages a distinctly late style appears in the script, marked by the g which Blake adopted after Nov. 1802. On pages 8 and 10 this style appears in modified copperplate hand in revisions made before clutter had set in; on page 12 the basic layer of text itself is in fine copperplate hand of this late character—and so is the chapter heading of "Night the Sixth" on page 67. (It should be added that I have found no distinguishing marks of a pre-1803 script in any part of the ms, all the other g's being of the dateless, sans-serif variety. The rule of g may of course be less invariable than I have supposed. At any rate it is safer to conclude that the copperplate pages range in inception from 1797 to 1803 than to put them all in the later period.)

Bentley has found that the sheet on which pages 48–49 were written (at the beginning of Night IV) bears evidence of prior use as a backing-sheet when Blake printed Hayley's first Ballad in May 1802, but his argument (p 195) that sheets marred or defective in some such way as this were the last ones Blake would use should upset his assumption that none of the pages following 49 were inscribed before that date. As for the date of stitching of either of the groups described above, the second group includes the sheet with the May 1802 impressions and so cannot have been stitched earlier than that; that neither group can have been stitched earlier than 1803 should be the deduction from the graphic evidence of late g's in the first strata of pages in both groups (12 and 67). To suppose the other, unpierced pages not to have been *written* before 1803 would shake all present assumptions.

Even if an 1803 date for the copying out of "Night the Sixth" is accepted, its composition may have been much earlier. On the other hand the date of 1804 or later which has been accepted for Night VIII on the basis of allusions to the renewal of war and of strikingly different symbolism or idiom from the the main body of the poem (see Margoliouth, p 174) may need correction to "much later". The writing of VIII, at least, and the very late change of the poem's title to "The Four Zoas" (a pencil revision on the main title page not extended to the chaper headings) as well as a good deal of mending and revising, especially in Night I, must have occurred after Blake had begun if not completed *Milton* and *Jerusalem*. Bentley's contention (p 165) that several passages were borrowed from *Jerusalem*, rather than the other way round, is not convincing in respect to passages in *Jerusalem* 22 and 67–68, but the connections of *Vala*, 1, 21, 99 and *Jerusalem* 34[38] may go in both directions.

It should be recognized, however, that many apparently late additions to *Vala* turn out to have been salvaged from the erasure of early layers on the same or other pages. Since few of these erased early strata have been deciphered, we cannot be certain how much of the late material is actually new. (See the textual notes on pages 4, 6, 7, 72, 99.)

Readers should be cautioned against falling back on the all too hypothetical chronological groupings of Nights and parts of Nights presented in Erdman, pp 270–271 (on the basis of secondhand evidence and an ignorance of the complexities of the ms). Nevertheless certain salient historical allusions or sources remain, despite uncertainty as to how long after the event Blake wrote: negotiations conducted between Britain and France, in 1796 and 1797 (but again in 1800 and 1801); the Netherlands expedition of 1799; Napoleon's coup d'état a few weeks later; the Peace of Amiens; its rupture. Readers should also be cautioned against inaccuracies and special pleading in Bentley's criticism of these groupings (pp 168–170)—and of course also against exaggerations in my subsequent critique of the Bentley volume (in an article in *The Library* for 1964).

Bentley's warning that a second or third addition on one page may have no chronological relation with a second or third addition on another is well taken—but frequently ignored by all of us. His assumption that the original copperplate writing on all pages represents a single draft may or may not prove to be sound; yet his transcript obscures the evidence by treating the erased copperplate layer as nonexistent (when he cannot read it) and the first added layer as original.

Margoliouth's attempt to isolate a "Vala" text by selecting Blake's "fair copy of each Night before erasures, deletions, additions, and changes of order" depends heavily on the assumption that all these deduced fair copies (excluding VIII and the first part of IX) somehow constitute a homogeneous text. He is able to sort out pretty successfully those lines which were in the ms when Blake counted and numbered his lines by fifties, but not to convince us that all the counting took place at one time. The result is useful, however, and only misleading if taken as a really early state of the text or as constituting a uniform layer, so to speak.

The complexities of the ms, in short, continue to defy analysis and all assertions about meaningful physical groupings or chronologically definable layers of composition or inscription must be understood to rest on partial and ambiguous evidence.

The text given here is simply that of the latest readings, with deletions occasionally retained (in italics within square brackets) when their omission would leave gaps; when Blake replaced a deleted reading and then deleted the replacement, the earlier reading has been restored. The textual notes contain all the erased or deleted readings thus far deciphered (sometimes differing from or going beyond the Bentley transcript thanks largely to the use of infrared photography and strong magnification). Night VIIb, supplanted by VIIa but not discarded, is printed as an appendix to the text. The early fragment, pages 141–142, is given at the end of the textual notes.

The attempt to indicate Blake's occasional spacing between clauses has unfortunately resulted in some inaccurately long spaces in the present printing.

1: *title*]   VALA / OR / The Death and Judgement of the [*Eternal*] <Ancient> Man / a DREAM / of Nine Nights / by William Blake 1797 *1st rdg*

3: *inscription* VI]   5 *1st rdg*, an error corrected, not necessarily by Blake

Night the First

3:1–3 The Song . . . Battle]   Syntax and heavy inking mark these lines as a subtitle. Blake had first made several tries at a six-line introductory stanza, with erasure on erasure. Words visible at the line ends of the first version are: (1) . . . [wr]ath bo[ok] of Vala"; (3) "Round"; (6) "Dream". A second, partly erased, version reads, with revisions:

> This is the [*Dirge*] <Song> of [*Eno*] <Enitharmon> which shook the heavens with wrath
> And thus beginneth the Book of Vala which Whosoever reads
> If with his Intellect he comprehend the terrible Sentence
> The heavens [*shall*] quake, the earth [*shall move*] [*moves*] <was moved> & [*shudder*] [*shudders*] <shudderd> & the mountains
> With all their woods, the streams & valleys: [*wail*] <waild> in dismal fear
> [*To hear*] <Hearing> the [*Sound*] <march> of Long resounding strong heroic verse
> Marshalld in order for the day of intellectual battle

These lines were numbered 1 2 3 6 7 4 5; later the stanza was reduced to its final 3 lines by another numbering; finally 2–3 ("Hearing . . . Battle") were crossed out and rewritten over the erased lines below 1.

Lines 4–11 are written over nine erased lines.

3:8 no Individual Knoweth nor]   Individual Man knoweth not *1st rdg*

PAGE 4

Lines 1–16, 19–28 are written over erasures. Traces of 19 original lines (in copperplate hand) can be discerned and a few words can be read: (1) ". . . ?oft"; (2) "?Saying . . . of . . . for . . . of Eternal Life"; (3) "?Song of . . ."; (4) "?I ?see . . . of . . . ?Self . . . about"; (6) "Rejoicing ?so ?amongst . . ."; (7) "The . . . ?faded ?slept . . ."; (8) "Till ?far ?dismal . . . ?four . . . all . . ."; (9) ". . . a pleasing"; (10) "?Enion . . . of ?slavery"; (12) ". . . ?cloud"; (13) "?Where . . . the . . ."; (18) ". . . Enion"; (19) ". . . the light of day". (Bentley reads 19 and 20 but supposes them to belong to the second layer of palimpsest.)

This first stratum was erased and covered by 21 lines in modified copperplate hand; finally a third state was created by the erasure and replacement of the last 12 of these lines by 13 new lines (in the same hand) and the revision of a few words in the first 9. Six of the erased second-stratum lines were repeated elsewhere and can be verified completely: 10–13 ("Arise O Enion . . . for Lo! I have calmd my seas") are identical to 129:24–27, there crowded into a stanza break. Lines 20–21 ("All Love is lost . . . Duty instead of Liberty") reappear as lines 20–21 of the third stratum. Of erased lines 14–19 in the second stratum little can be made out: (14) "?The ?warfare . . . ?shy"; (16) "?He ?fell . . . hid in ?horrible ?caverns of mountains"; (18) ". . . ?chariot"; (19) "To . . . of . . . ?come".

Revisions from second to third state are indicated below:

Line 5 was inserted in ink over partly erased pencil loops covering erased first stratum ink. Two remnant loops I mistook for deleting strokes (see previous printings). N.B.: This correction has involved a renumbering of the lines of page 4.

7 Enion O Enion]   Enion [*come forth*] <O Enion> *latest revision;* this change and "O Pity Me" in line 9 are additions in a different pen.

8 We are . . . We]   I am . . . I *1st rdg del*

9 Jerusalem in Silent Contrition O Pity Me]   thee Enion in Jealous Despair *1st rdg del*

10 also . . . Enion]   where we may remain for ever alone *1st rdg del*

11 hast] *mended from ink* has *over pencil* hast   sweet Jerusalem] *ink over pencil* [*Enitharmon*] <Jerusalem>   17 Thy]   His *1st rdg del*

PAGE 5

First stratum entirely erased and replaced, but the last two lines were probably identical to the two lines "Arise O Enion . . . rejoice" found in the second stratum of page 4 and emerging as 129:24–25.

1 Eden]   Beulah *1st rdg del*

7 tabernacle for Jerusalem]   tabernacle [*of delight*] <for Enitharmon> *1st rdg*

9 then . . . innocent]   and . . . holy *1st rdg del*

14 In torment]   So saying *1st rdg del*   16 gnawing]   dismal *1st rdg del*

24 trembling]   ?bright *1st rdg del* (Bentley: "?dread")

28 dread]   sweet *1st rdg del*   Repentance & Contrition]   false woven bliss *1st rdg;* self woven sorrow *2d rdg del* (Bentley transcript confuses sequence of changes.) Two inserted, then deleted, lines follow:

He spurnd Enion with his foot he sprang aloft in Clouds

[*Alighting down from*] Alighting in his drunken joy in a far distant Grove

34 Dreams]   wanderings *1st rdg del*   42 pity & help]   help *1st rdg del*

43 Gate of the Tongue]   Gate of Auricular [*power*] <nerves> *1st rdg*

Ten deleted lines follow:

What have I done! said Enion accursed wretch! What deed.

Is this a deed of Love I know what I have done. I know

Too late now to repent. [*?Alone ?posessed by*] <Love is changd to> deadly [*Fears*] <Hate>

A life is blotted out & I alone remain possessd with Fears

I see the [*remembrance*] <Shadow> of the dead within my [*eyes*]   5 <Soul> wandering

In darkness & solitude forming Seas of [*Trouble*] <Doubt> & rocks of
    [*sorrow*] <Repentance>
Already are my Eyes reverted. all that I behold
Within my Soul has lost its splendor & a brooding Fear
Shadows me oer & drives me outward to a world of woe
So waild she trembling before her own Created Phantasm   10

In line 4 "A life" is probably a slip for "All life".

There follows a penciled insert, and a deleted line it would replace:

    <Who animating times on times by the Force of her sweet song>
    [*But standing on the Rocks her woven shadow glowing bright*]

But both are replaced by 6:1–5, a double insertion on that page.

PAGE 6

Of an erased first stratum of 12 copperplate lines, the first two can be recovered:
    When wilt thou smile on Tharmas O thou bringer of golden day
    Arise. O Enion arise! for Lo! I have Calmd my seas
These continue from the original concluding lines of page 5 and are identical, except
in punctuation, to 129:26–27, their intermediate occurrence being in the second stratum
of p 4 (see above).

Line 3 of the erased stratum, "His woe f . . . the crystal sky", concludes like 130:14
but begins differently. Other fragmentary recoveries are: (4) "In . . . ?faded in ?his
cave"; (7) "?Luvah . . . Rock"; (8) ". . . Enion . . . the ?Oaks"; (9) ". . . ?Chil-
dren"; (12) ". . . lovely".

Variants between the second and final text of the page follow:

1 her shining]   her silken *1st rdg del*

7 fury]   joy *1st rdg del*

After line 8 follow 30 deleted lines:

    Searching for glory wishing that the heavens had eyes to See
    And courting that the Earth would ope her Eyelids & behold
    Such wondrous beauty repining in the midst of all his glory
    That nought but Enion could be found to praise adore & love
    Three days in self admiring raptures on the rocks he flamd   5
    And three dark nights repind the solitude. but the third morn
    Astonishd he found Enion hidden in the darksom Cave

    She spoke What am I wherefore was I put forth on these rocks
    Among the Clouds to tremble in the wind in solitude
    Where is the voice that lately woke the desart Where the Face   10
    That wept among the clouds & where the voice that shall reply
    No other living thing is here. The Sea the Earth. the Heaven
    And Enion desolate where art thou Tharmas O return

    Three days she waild & three dark nights sitting among the Rocks
    While the bright spectre hid himself among the ?backing clouds   15
    Then sleep fell on her eyelids in a Chasm of the Valley
    The Sixteenth morn the Spectre stood before her manifest

    The Spectre thus spoke. <Who art thou Diminutive husk & shell
      Broke from my bonds I scorn my prison I scorn & yet I love>
                 Art thou not my slave & shalt thou dare
    To smite me with thy tongue beware lest I sting also thee,   20
    <If thou hast sinnd & art polluted know that I am pure
    And unpolluted & will bring to rigid strict account
    All thy past deeds> hear what I tell thee! mark it well! remember!
    This world is [*Mine*] <Thine> in which thou dwellest that within
      thy soul

That dark & dismal infinite where Thought roams up & down   25
Is [thine] <Mine> & there thou goest when with one Sting of my
    tongue
Envenomd thou rollst inwards to the place [of death & hell] <[where]
    <whence> I emergd>
She trembling answerd Wherefore was I born & what am I
A sorrow & a fear a living torment & naked Victim
I thought to weave a Covering [from his] <for my> Sins from wrath   30
    of Tharmas

PAGE 7 (& 143)
    Page 7 is a thicket of erased and deleted original and additional lines; the undeleted
portion is duplicated on p 143 (on a small notebook leaf) and is there revised further.
We take these revisions as Blake's latest and incorporate them into the text of p 7.

1–2 Opening . . . soard]   *p 143 replacement for the following four lines in p 7:*
    Thus they contended all the day among the Caves of Tharmas
    Twisting in fearful forms & howling <howling harsh shrieking>
    <Howling> harsh shrieking, mingling their bodies join in burning anguish
    Mingling his [horrible] <[terrible]> brightness with her tender limbs; then
    high she soar'd
(Erasure of "terrible", not noted in Bentley, returns the text to "horrible", only lined
through—or to the whole change made in p 143: "horrible [brightness] <darkness>.)
(Above "join in burning anguish" on p 7 there is a pencil erasure: "?mingle in
Terrible".)
3 nature]   Beulah *1st rdg del p 7*   The line is left incomplete on p 7; "Shrieking
. . . that . . . shudder'd at" are deleted but not replaced.
4 beast]   [?Spirit] <Spectre> *p 7;* serpent *1st rdg del p 143*   darkly wav-
ing]   lovely changing *p 7; 1st rdg del p 143*
5 metals]   poisons *p 7; 1st rdg del p 143*
6 rocky features]   scaly armour *p 7; 1st rdg p 143 del*   softning]   soften-
ing *p 7*
7 wonder]   monster *p 7; 1st rdg p 143 del*   wandring]   wandering *p 7*
8–9 With female . . . wonder]   replacing three deleted lines p 7:

    With [?Spirit] <Spectre> voice incessant wailing; in incessant thirst
    Beauty all blushing with desire mocking her fell despair

    Wandering desolate, a wonder abhorr'd by Gods & Men

    The top layer of deleted text on p 7 follows:

    [Examining the sins of Tharmas I [have] <soon> found my own
    O slay me not thou art his Wrath embodied in Deceit]
    I thought Tharmas a Sinner & murderd his Emanations
    <His secret loves & Graces Ah me wretched What have I done>
    [But] <For> now I find that all those Emanations were my Childrens   5
    Souls
    <And I have murderd them with Cruelty above atonement>
    Those that remain have fled from my cruelty into the desarts
    [Among wild beasts to roam] And thou the delusive tempter <to these
    deeds> sittest before me
    [But where is] <[Thou art not]><And art thou> Tharmas all thy
    soft delusive beauty cannot
    Tempt me to murder [honest love] <my own soul> & wipe my   10
    tears & smile
    In this thy world [for ah! how] <not mine tho> dark I feel my world
    within

    The Spectre said Thou sinful Woman. was it thy Desire
    That I should hide thee with my power & delight thee with my beauty

And now thou darkness in my presence. never from my sight
Shalt thou depart to weep in secret. In my jealous wings
I evermore will hold thee when thou goest out or comest in
Tis thou hast darkend all My World O Woman lovely bane

Under lines 1–5 of this passage are three erased lines in Blake's usual hand, the last word of the 1st line being "threatening". Partly under these but beginning in the top margin is a pencil passage of six lines, the 1st three legible (but short, as if only beginnings of lines):

When Tharmas shook his billowy hair
Two forms of horror howld beneath ?it
A male & female witherd

Perhaps of the same vintage is a block of six pencil lines written sideways in the right margin beside the original ink text lines 4–10; the left ends of these lines are invisible:

Pourd from fibrous veiny pipes
Enio[ns] Blood from torrent floods melting [*away*]
. . . chalk white rocks
spread from heaven to heaven
. . . ?monsters howld ?with ?Urizen ?around
. . . living joy fills ?albion

Earliest deletion on p 7 must have been erasure of the 1st six lines in copperplate hand (under lines 7–18 in Bentley's numbering). All six were apparently moved to p 5 for the modified copperplate addition there of lines 9–14 and 25. At least the 4th line is identical to 5:12 except for punctuation:

And said Return O Wanderer when the day of clouds is o'er;

and the 5th is a variant of 5:13–14:

So saying he . . . ?fell . . . into the restless sea

and the 3rd is like 5:11 in beginning with a *T*, ending with "sighs", and having (perhaps) "Destiny" in its center. The last word of the 1st could be "head", that of 5:9; the 2nd is illegible but its configuration does not jar with that of 5:10. The 6th erased line is identical to 5:25, so far as can be made out:

Round rolld ?the . . . globe self balanc'd

10–14] These lines, on p 143, derive from a deleted passage on p 8; see below.

10–11 For Enion . . . vast] *p* 143, inserted in a stanza break as one line running into the margin, where paper is torn; the *x* of "vortex" is missing; "vast", written above it, must have been followed by several words; cf. the "vast deep of immensity" in Night VI or the "vast black ocean" of Night VII.

14 To wander . . . woman]   Undeleted portion of the remaining lines on p 143, which consist of:

[*Shining across the ocean* / *Enion brooded groaning the golden rocks vegetate the V*] [?Vast *or* ?Vortex *paper cut away*]

[*to*] Infolding the bright woman [*from the desolating winds* / & *thus her voice* &]

PAGE 8

2 little Infants wept] *del in pencil*, with insertion below the line of three writings and erasings of "Then forms of horror howld"; deleting line then erased.

5 like richest summer shining]   like summer shines *1st rdg*

6 bright] *replaced by* fierce *above the line*; then "fierce" and the line deleting "bright" were erased

7] Thirteen deleted lines follow:

But those in Great Eternity Met in the Council of God
As One Man hovering over Gilead & Hermon
<He is the Good Shepherd He is the Lord & Master
To Create Man Morning by Morning to Give gifts at Noon day>

Enion brooded, oer the rocks, the rough rocks [?*vegetating*] <groaning   5
    vegetate>
<Such power was given to the Solitary wanderer.>
The barked Oak, the long limbd Beech; the Ches'nut tree; the Pine.
The Pear tree mild, the frowning Walnut, the sharp Crab, & Apple
    sweet,
The rough bark opens; twittering peep forth little beaks & wings
The Nightingale, the Goldfinch, Robin, Lark, Linnet & Thrush   10
The Goat leap'd from the craggy [*Rock*] <cliff>, the Sheep awoke
    from the mould
Upon its green stalk rose the Corn, waving innumerable
Infolding the bright Infants from the desolating winds

The inserted lines 3–4 derive from an erased passage in ⼞ 99, which probably derives from *Jerusalem* 34[38]:23–25; see also p 21.

The revision of line 5 would seem to have been made after and because of the insertion of 6; a date after 1805 is suggested by the letter g in "vegetate", which is in Blake's late style.

PAGE 9

1–2 And . . . mountains]   Lines inked over erasures, but first written in pencil in top margin.

The first of three erased copperplate lines preceding line 4 may read, at the end, ". . . embracd for Shame & Fear" (compare line 25); the second ends ". . . love".

Line 7 is penciled over an erased ink line,
    Till they had ?drawn the Spectre quite away from Enion
—which reappears slightly varied in 109:25–26 in Night VIII, suggesting that the "Spectrous Life" revisions of p 7 were made during the writing of VIII.

Line 8, first ending "her spectrous life in dark despair", may have been started as a replacement of 6; it was written after and above the marginal block 9–11, 14–18 which was first marked to go after 6 but then, when 7 was inserted, marked to follow 7.

9 Eno]   *written in pencil over* Ona

10 Seven thousand years]   twenty years *1st rdg del*

11 in Every year]   in the [*twenty*] <Every> years *ms rdg*   made windows into Eden]   gave visions ?toward heaven *1st rdg del*

19 Eno]   *written in pencil over* Ona

25 they kiss'd not nor embrac'd for shame & fear] They ?kissd ?not for ?shame <they> embracd not *penciled above the line*

Above 26 is a long pencil insertion running into the margin, erased and consisting of three perhaps unconnected fragments, in different strengths of pencil. The first continues the revision started in pencil above 25: "Nor kissd nor em[braced]"; the second reads "hand in hand [*in a*] Sultry paradise"; of the third only the last two words are certain: "?these ?Lovers ?swum the deep".

Below 33, in the margin but guided in, is the heading "Night the Second", but "End of The First Night" comes on p 18 and, after additions, on p 19. What we now treat as Night II was probably once headed "Night the Third"; both before and after that it was headed "First", but "End of the Second Night" is clearly marked on p 36, and "Night the Third" begins properly on p 37.

34 But . . . Tharmas]   crowded in margin, after and perhaps to replace an inserted but deleted line reading:
    Nine years they view the turning spheres [*of ?Beulah*] <reading> the Visions of Beulah
(Keynes read "living" for "turning"; Bentley mistakes the long *h* of "Enitharmon" from the line below as a *g* beginning the 6th word and reads "?gleaming" and misreads "reading" as "leading", failing to see that the *r* is written large to cover the word "of"; it is a lower case *r* writ large.)

35 fierce]   bright *1st rdg del*

37 our . . . mourn]   thy . . . weep *1st rdg del*

PAGE 10

1 frowning]   ?smiling *1st rdg del*
2 Dark]   Bright *1st rdg del*
3 let them]   how they *1st rdg del*
9 Song . . . Song]   ?Dirge . . . ?Dirge *1st rdg del*
10 Fallen]   Eternal *1st rdg del*
11 woke & flew]   wake & fly *1st rdg (ink) del*; woke & flew *erased pencil* above line, preceding ink revision of line itself (sequence of and readings of revisions confused in both Keynes and Bentley)

14–15 are additions within a stanza break, 14 later than 15. (And the g's in 14 are in Blake's late serifed style.)
The last seven words of 15 are over an erasure almost legible.
In 16 "voice" is over a word ending in *d*.
17 Enitharmon darken'd in]   Vala darkend in her *1st rdg*
18 Enitharmon a terror]   Enitharmon a Cloud *2nd rdg;* Vala lightning *1st rdg del*
20 as Vala]   O Vala *1st rdg*
22 over a deleted line almost legible.
24 followed by deleted passage (evidently replaced by 22):

> If thou drivst all the [*Males*] <Females> away from [*Vala*] <Luvah> I will drive all
> The Males away from thee

PAGE 11

4 He answer'd, darkning more with]   Los answer'd, darkning with foul *1st rdg*
5 tho]   thou *1st rdg del*
6 Fallen]   Eternal *1st rdg del*
10 Fallen]   Eternal *1st rdg del*

In the margin are nine lines marked to follow 11 but then deleted:

> Refusing to behold the Divine image which all behold
> And live thereby. he is sunk down into a deadly sleep
> But we immortal in our own strength survive by stern debate
> Till we have drawn the Lamb of God into a mortal form
> And that he must be born is certain for One must be All   5
> And comprehend within himself all things both small & great
> We therefore for whose sake all things aspire to be & live
> Will so recieve the Divine Image that amongst the Reprobate
> He may be devoted to Destruction from his mothers womb

20 is followed by this inserted and then deleted line:

> Threaten not me O visionary thine the punishment!

24 rebellious]   free *1st rdg del*

PAGE 12

A page requiring further study; some lines that seem to be original copperplate may not be; oddly enough "muttering" in 7 and "golden" in 34 have late-style g's. The erased line under 3 may end with legible words; and some of the added lines may derive from deleted ones. Inserted line 6, in pencil, has its first word inked over—in the same copperplate hand as "muttering" and "golden". (See below.)

1–3 derive from erased pencil drafts beneath 18–24; in these, line 1 appears unchanged, but "the Spirits" and "an orb of blood!" are found in the 2nd pencil draft, not the first—where the clarions are plainly Luvah's: "A groan was xxxx xxxxly The warlike Clarions / Of Luvah ceasd xxxxx xxxx ?shudderd xxxx ?Orb".

6 the other]   Keynes and Bentley read "the Man", misled by an uncrossed *t*. Not only is "the one must have murderd the Man" unidiomatic, but it is also a misconstruction of the text: the Eternal Man is weak but not under threat of murder; it is Los and Vala or Enitharmon, within him, who seek to murder each other: she sings a Dirge/Song of Death; he smites her and refuses to die; she in turn cries for help from Urizen; "And the one must have murderd the other if he had not descended".

9 he eye'd the Prince]   he Urizen eye'd *1st rdg*

10–31 are marginal additions in two blocks, the first consisting of 10–17, 30–31, but with a guide line after 17 leading in the block 18–29. Keynes and Bentley ignore the line, though Bentley notes it yet keeps 30–31 as if 18–19. Keynes copes with the bad transition this leaves to 32 ff by arbitrarily moving 24 down to a position between 29 and 32.

27–28 are crowded in as a single line running into the margin, but scansion indicates the division required

35 Rejoicing in the Victory . . . blood]   Bentley (p 168) makes much of the fact that this is an "addition written over an erased pencil line", jumping to the conclusion that "it is clear that the original passage had nothing to do with either victory or war": but the full context, at every stage of the ms, is of deadly strife between male and female, a Dirge or Song of Death, and a Urizenic victory. I now (Aug 1965) find that the erased copperplate line under 3 begins "Rejoicing in" and ends "rejoicing in victory & blood" and that the erased pencil line under 35 ends with "blood".

Erasures in the gap after 9 include a two-line variant of 23 (". . . I am God from Eternity to Eternity / Obey thy Lord . . ."). In the adjacent right margin are six erased line segments, ". . . hands Pity not Vala / ?Pity ?not Luvah / . . . / . . . / & these / . . .", apparently a draft for 14–16.

Below 34 is an erased pencil line beginning "A" and ending "of Enitharmon"; in the adjacent margin is a second line in four segments, the first, conjecturally, "Luvah said".

44 nervous]   bloody *inserted but erased rdg*   Both "fleshly" and "nervous" are written over erasures.

PAGE 13

4 But]   The ?shades of *1st rdg del*

Lines 4–10 are inserted, partly in a stanza break and partly in the margin; Bentley treats 8–10 as a late addition to this addition—apparently on the basis of imagery ("Luvah robes of blood").

9 Luvahs]   Luvah *ms rdg*

11–12 first read:

    The purple night the crimson morning & the golden day ?descended

    ?While the clear changing atmosphere display'd green fields among

(But "While" may be "Where".)

Above 16 are two erased pencil segments with a blank between:

    But monstrous delusion ?invaded   wrath ?enterd his world of love

Above 19 is an erased pencil line running into the right margin:

    In beauty love & scorn ?the ?earthbound bride & bridegroom ?sulk

20 thousand thousand spirits]   orbits high *marginal rdg erased;* demons by the thousands out of a golden cloud xxxx xxx *2nd marginal rdg erased;* whole line del, then del erased

24 Bright Souls]   ?Elements *penciled above but erased*

PAGE 14

7 Ephraim . . . to Zion]   The Mountain . . . to the Mountain *1st rdg del,* but the revisions and lines of deletion are in faint pencil and may have been erased

14 Men]   *mended from* men

16 Valleys]   *mended from* valleys

17 dark]   ?weak *1st rdg del*

20 Let us plat a]   Let ?us light *1st rdg erased,* as if Blake thought first to have the Cities call for fires (see *Song of Los* 6:20)

22 Children]   *mended from* children

PAGE 15

8 Human]   *mended from* human   10 Siez'd]   ?he ?was siezd *1st rdg erased*

11 Horse]   *mended from* horse   12 Mighty]   Eternal *1st rdg erased*

17 By night nor]   To ?light ?the *1st rdg erased*

20 Thou]   *mended from* thou *or* then

PAGE 17

1 Enion]   And Enion *1st rdg*
4] over erased line: "Why . . . . . & . . ."
7 waving]   the waving *1st rdg*
8 howl]   howls *1st rdg*
9 summers]   the summers *1st rdg*

PAGE 18

3 but he knows not that]   he knows not that the *1st rdg*
15 *followed by* End of The First Night

Pages 19–22 are bound out of order; the conjectural arrangement 21–22, 19–20 made by Keynes and Bentley seems acceptable

PAGE 21

4 One] *mended from* one (the second "one" being overlooked)
7 the Mountain of Snowdon]   Mount Gilead *1st rdg del*
9 Albion He]   Shiloh he *1st rdg mended*
13 Beulah] *mended from* beulah
15 Conways Vale]   Beth Peor *1st rdg del*
31 O] *mended from* o

PAGE 22

7 Atlantic]   deep *1st rdg del*
11 oer]   round *1st rdg del*

PAGE 19

1 is]   will soon *1st rdg del*
2 are]   will be *1st rdg del*
3 led   let *ms*   the indefinite]   all nations *1st rdg del*
8 High Snowdon]   Mount Gilead *1st rdg del*
15 followed by "End of The First Night"; the further addition on the verso, page 20, is in pencil and may have been finally rejected by Blake; serpentine spirals drawn in crayon, apparently over the writing, may mean deletion.

PAGE 20

"No satisfactory position in the text has been devised for this page", says Bentley (p 20). See preceding note.
4 Beulah]   Eternity *1st rdg del*
8 Gates] *mended from* gates
15 consuming]   tending *1st rdg del*

Night the [Second]

PAGE 23

title]   Night the [*Third*] <[*First*]> <[*First*]> *ms*, never written "Second", though the "End of the Second Night" is declared on p 36. This would have been Third when the Second began on p 9, q.v. It was evidently twice tried and rejected as First.
3 Albion]   The Man *1st rdg del*
4 Porches]   Ears *1st rdg del*
6] line crossed in pencil for deletion, and replacement written in the right margin, then deleting lines and replacement thoroughly erased. The line leaves traces: "?Remember ?O ?Urizen / Cxxmmm xxxg xxdxding / xxxvns"
7–8] ink over pencil, within a stanza break. Blake first wrote and erased a different text for 8, ending "of fallen man"; his next pencil text was followed verbatim in ink.
10 Exulting at the voice that calld him from the Feast of envy *1st & final rdg*]   Indignant at the voice that calld him from the Feast of love *2nd rdg*   "Exulting" and "envy" were lined through in pencil, and "Indignant" and "love" written in pencil in the left and right margins; then these words and the deleting lines were erased.

PAGE 24

4 followed by erased pencil:

Above him he xxx Jerusalem ?in ?the bloody ?Heaven as xxx xxx his eyes

5 great Work master] written over erasure of two words, the first of which ends in *d* and may be identical to the erased word under "Urizen" in line 9; it cannot have been "God", it can have been "lord" (5) and "the lord" (9); it did not apparently begin with a capital.

PAGE 25

2] A pencil line, followed by erased pencil lines in right margin.

6–33] An insertion beginning in a stanza break and continuing in the right margin (obviously fair copy from a working draft).

11] Blake first wrote "Fled" at the end of this line, then deleted it and began his new line with this word.

33 is not properly spliced back to the original passage; a linking line, with a verb for the "While" clause, must have been dropped in transcribing from working notes.

35] Antecedent of "they" is the human leopards, tygers (and horses) of lines 1–5, line 34 having orginally followed 5.

PAGE 26

5 Valas King] Luvahs Lord *1st rdg erased*

13 Till] But *revision, erased while wet* Dragon] *mended from* de [for demon?]

PAGE 27

9 O Lamb] I ?die *1st rdg erased*

10–12] written over two erased lines, the first perhaps beginning "Albion"

14 was love but] am love & *1st rdg* (above this line is an erased insertion beginning "And Urizen who"; it may have been identical to 15 in its first or its revised form)

17 delusion] terror *1st rdg del*

PAGE 28

2] written over erased pencil, beginning under "from" with a word that may be "Los"

11–24] marginal insertion

11 Man] *mended from* Men

18 darksom] dismal *1st rdg del*

26 pyramid] globe *mended to* Globe *1st rdg del*

29 center] center *1st rdg del;* basement *2nd rdg del* (the deletion of "center" was a strong ink stroke not easily erased)

31 Sons] *mended from* sons

PAGE 29

1 Fallen] Eternal *1st rdg erased;* Fallen *2nd rdg;* Ancient *3rd rdg pencil erased*

2 Cubes] Globes *1st rdg del*

PAGE 30

5 condensing] together *1st rdg erased*

16 wondrous] golden *1st rdg del* Central Domes] ?halls of *1st rdg erased*

19 are] *mended from* were (or perhaps vice versa) Mountains] *mended from* mountains

23 White] bright *1st rdg erased*

33 please] *mended from* pleasd

34 misty] cloudy *1st rdg del*

43 returnd] descended *1st rdg del*

PAGE 31

9–10 are written in margin at this place, though not marked to go in; put after 16 by Keynes and Bentley

PAGE 32

3–4 deleted but then marked "To come in"

7 But]   For *1st rdg del*

8 sorrow & care]   songs & joy *1st rdg erased*

12 Cubed . . . window square]   Circled . . . infinite orb *1st rdg del*. The second reading is erased; yet it is supported by the reference back to "Cubes" and "window" in 33:4–5. If ears are porches, mouth, nose, and eyes had better be doors and windows; yet the concept of micro-macrocosm is better expressed in "infinite orb immoveable", with its matching of the oxymoron in "primum mobile". If Blake hesitated to choose either reading, an editor hesitates to reject either.

12 walls & cielings]   arches all *1st rdg del*

14 is written over an erased line ending "?within"

16 Sorrowing . . . to sow]   Then . . . forth to sow *1st rdg*

PAGE 33

4 Cubes]   *mended from* cubes; orbs *1st rdg del*

6 World]   *mended from* world

8 Heaven walled round]   *over erasure;* intermediate draft, above the line, reads: [*the ?heavens <?were> walld*]

9 comforted saw]   *over erasure;* draft above line is possibly identical. The erased words may have been "in comfort saw": an *i* dot and an *f* are in the right places.

11–15 written over four revised and erased lines, traces of which are: "And ?Luvah   lding fly / R   rejoicing & triumph / S   falling / A   walkd of the Mundane Egg".

17 Body]   The *B* curiously mended, perhaps merely from *b*   Abyss]   *mended from* abyss

18 sorrow & care]   songs & joy *1st rdg erased;* below the line the erased phrase "eternal ?fear X 1" is marked to lead in a section now missing, as Bentley notes.

19–21 are at the bottom of the page but marked "2 X"

22 is headed "3"

23 number weight]   weight & measure *1st rdg del*

25 unornamented pillar]   ornamented pillar square *1st rdg*

28 strength]   pow[er] *1st rdg del*

29 season]   spring *1st rdg del*

32 right angled]   their *1st rdg del*

33 Scalene]   & oblong *1st rdg del*

36 hard subdued]   fructifying *1st rdg del*

PAGE 34

Erased pencil lines under 2–4 and in right margin:
Laughing & mocking Luvah ?breaking [word from an unrelated layer of ms?] in the woes of Vala [Bentley's "womb of Vala"]

But soon [*for them*] ?he ?formd the lovely limbs of [*Enion*] Enitharmon   xxx & to lamentation of Enion ?answer for fear

Below 3 are two layers of erased pencil, the first ending "for vindication of Urizens world", the second beginning "Thy name is familiar".

9 For]   Now *1st rdg del*

15 Elemental]   *mended from* elemental

Beneath 16–17 are about 11 erased pencil lines, the first beginning "X[*And oft*] <thus> she wails", the next two like 16–17 ("And Los said. Lo the Lilly . . . / Reproach thee & the . . ."), but the rest apparently different from final text.

23–24 Secure . . . fury] words inserted above the single line beginning "Enitharmon" and ending "infolds"; spacing and meter suggest the proper distribution.

94 reviving]   delighted *2nd rdg erased*

Erased pencil above 97 and in margin: "?From ?Ahanias ?woe all xxxx xxxx only wrath & Envy follows in xxxx their fxxxds / Urizen saxx xxxd axwxxx".

99 Enion] *written over* she
100 Thus Enion]   And oft *1st rdg del;* And thus *2nd rdg del*

PAGE 36
15 *written over* End of the Second Night *erased*
18 Spectrous]   terrible *1st rdg del*

Night the Third

PAGE 37
title]   "Third" is written over one or two erasures, possibly in the sequence:
[*Third*] <[*Fourth*]> <Third> (Bentley considers a single erasure, "First" or "Third").
Perhaps at one time Night II began on p 7, II was Third, III was Fourth.
3 Me]   thy Wife, that *1st rdg del*
4 I Embrace . . . wet My . . . my]   Embraces . . . wets her . . . her *1st rdg*
10 Thou sitst in harmony for God hath set thee over all *1st rdg del*

PAGE 38
NB: Some penciled revisions in Ahania's speech (which runs from 38:15 through
42:17) adapt it for use in *Jerusalem* 43:33-82 as a speech by two "fugitives". Changes
(e.g. of pronouns to plural) that only disrupt the text cannot have been intended for
The Four Zoas and are here noted but not adopted. Insertion of the name "Albion",
however, does suit Blake's latest intentions for this poem, as we know from its revised
title.
2 Ahania]   shadow *penciled above; both rdgs del*
7 but . . . Decree]   & all my Kingly power *1st rdg del*
8 Vala shall]   ?That Vala ?may *1st rdg;* But Vala shall *2nd rdg* (the "But" now
redundant)

PAGE 39
1 Leave . . . Light]   replacing two deleted lines:
       Raise then thy radiant eyes to him raise thy obedient hands
       And comforts shall descend from heaven into thy darkning clouds
14 Ancient]   Eternal *1st rdg erased*
15 Darkning]   Eternal *1st rdg erased;* Fallen *2nd rdg erased*
17 thee . . . thy]   the . . . with *1st rdg*
18 and 40:1 are lightly lined through in pencil; excluded from *Jerusalem.*

PAGE 40
1 In]   Of *1st rdg del*   2 Man]   *mended from* man
3 Shadow]   *mended from* shadow
10 I . . . my heart . . . me]   We . . . our hearts . . . us *pencil revision* for J
11 I]   We *xxxxxx pencil revision,* erased or faintly written
12 written in stanza break, over erased line identical to unrevised 10

PAGE 41
2-3 *ms rdg:* that shadowy Spirit of the [*Eternal*] <Fallen> One <Albion> / Luvah,
descended . . . ; [*the Eternal Man*] arose <In terror> <Albion rose>   *The wish to*
change "the One" to "Albion", carried out elsewhere on the page, was halted here
by the awkward juxtaposition of "Albion / Luvah" that would result; the earlier
reading is not deleted, and Keynes is right to call "Albion" an alternate reading.
4 Awful]   Eternal *1st rdg;* Fallen *2nd rdg erased*
5-9] Ahania, speaking parenthetically to Urizen, as in 18; bracket, in margin seems
to mean: Exclude these lines from *Jerusalem.*
6 Eyes]   *mended from* eyes
10 I]   We *pencil rdg*   Albion]   the Eternal *1st rdg;* the Falln One,
2nd rdg
12 Love]   *mended from* love
13 mighty Albion]   Eternal Man *1st rdg;* Ancient Man *2nd rdg, not del*
15 Albion]   Man *1st rdg del*
17 the Fallen Man]   the Eternal Man *1st rdg;* Albion *pencil, partly erased*

PAGE 42

The last of the pages in copperplate hand on new paper; Bentley notes that "The modified copperplate hand strangely turns into the most beautiful copperplate hand at the end of the tenth line"; but the modified hand is over original copperplate, erased.

7–8 were first written in pencil in the margin, then in ink in a stanza break.

9 &] they *penciled above but erased*

10 I saw that] the Spirits *1st rdg erased;* I saw that *penciled above and erased,* then inked in line

Beside 11–12 in the margin is the material for two lines that might have been meant to follow "now the Human Blood foamd high" but were never fitted in:

> Albion closd the Western Gate & / shut America out by the Atlantic / for a Curse and hidden horror / and an altar of victims to Sin / & Repentance

17] In the following stanza break and in the margin is this pencil draft of lines the "fugitives" speak in *Jerusalem:* Whether this is Jerusalem or Babylon we know not All is confusion All is tumult & we alone escaped *Beneath this* is an erased pencil draft:

> ?Then labour ended love for Vala
> Our hearts sick we on his Rock
> We fled from ?Jerusalem ?after ?the Merciful Lord & Saviour

18 From] for *ms rdg, a slip*

PAGE 44

2 shuddering] darkning *1st rdg del*

7 roared] reared *1st rdg mended* (sulphureous *written* uir *or* iur *in haste*)

18 Struggling to utter the voice] To take the limbs of Man *1st rdg erased,* a mistaken skipping of a line in transcription

PAGE 45

27 his voice of Thunder rolld] the voice of Tharmas rolld *1st rdg*

PAGE 46

5 Hope] Joy *1st rdg del*

PAGE 47

Night The Fourth

7 *written over erased line:*

> H d s Tharmas ?rolling ?his thundring ?seas p d thee [or ?them]

9 How . . . fled] And Tharmas said All my hope I thought <Enion> for ever gone *1st rdg*

16 beneath] upon *1st rdg del* 22 over] *for* over me?

PAGE 48

13 Eternal] Anci[ent] *1st rdg del* 21 solemn] dismal *1st rdg erased*

This page bears, as Bentley discovered, "a faint impression of mirror-printing: 'Ballad the First', &c." from p 9 of *Ballads Relating to Animals* by William Hayley, for which Blake made engravings dated 1 June 1802. Bentley (p 162) deduces that the sheet was used as backing when Blake printed the Ballad and only later used as ms paper. His further deduction or assertion that "There is no evidence to suggest that any of the succeeding pages [of *The Four Zoas*] were transcribed *before* page 48" is contradicted by his own argument (on pp 194–195 on "Anomalous pages [i.e. leaves]") to the effect that such imperfect leaves as this would have been avoided by Blake until he reached the end of his supply of perfect leaves. The discovery, in short, helps date pages 47–48, but it also seems to mark them as a late insertion. (Bentley does not count 47–48 among the anomalies. His categories consist of odd-sized leaves; "makeshift" leaves made of two overlapping pieces of paper but otherwise of good size and good enough to have been used for *Night Thoughts* proofs—for all the leaves under discussion are proofs made in 1796, with one possible exception, and available for ms use any time thereafter; three sheets that were once folded together horizontally; one with a small patch in the inner margin. In another group Bentley counts as "very late" a sheet cut into two leaves bearing Blake's 1793 engraving of *Edward and Elenor* on one side. Yet leaf 47–48 is described (p 48 n) as having vertical "creases . . . as if [from] a great weight" "made after the *Night Thoughts* engraving was printed, but after [sc. before?] the *Vala* writing . . .". Presumably the creases were made by the weight of the press and before ms use, or the whole argument collapses; elsewhere Bentley is fairly confident that the writing "appears to be *on top of* the printing" (p 162 n 1); he apparently also means us to connect the "creases" with the process which made "a regular indentation . . . where Blake's copperplate repeatedly pressed the paper". These creases & indentation surely qualify the leaf for inclusion among such "anomalous" leaves as the three once folded; the transferred printing would seem to put it rather further along the scale toward the very imperfect end.

Another kind of evidence that a succeeding page was transcribed *before* pages 47–48 is the striking fact that p 57, the title of Night The Fifth, is so early it first read "Book" (erased and written "Night"), while no such early wording occurs on the title of "Night The Fourth" on p 47.

PAGE 49
 8 griding]   dismal *1st rdg erased*
 24 seeing]   answers *1st rdg del*

PAGE 50
 2 abhorrence]   *followed by* eternal *del*
 5 dread]   great *1st rdg del*
 11] written over an apparently nonvariant draft of 12

PAGE 51
 4 dreary]   dismal *1st rdg del*
 23 Vala] *mended from* Valan   The six occurrences of such mending are on pages of rapid fair-copying; the mending is current and does not represent a change of name but a slip; perhaps from the influence of other names of emanations, Enion, Enitharmon. See 59:5, 19; 63:13; 83:12.
 24 Urizen]   U *mended from* L (for Luvah)

PAGE 52
 10 Trumpets Horns & Clarions] *mended from* trumpets horns & clarions

PAGE 53
 15 Ladles huge]   ?lables *1st rdg del*, error of rapid transcription

PAGE 54
 6 heated]   pourd *1st rdg del*
 20] *followed by deletion:* Round the branches of his heart

PAGE 55 (FIRST PORTION)
 10–15] added at bottom of page, over erased closing "End of The Fourth Night". Text originally continued with "In terrors Los . . . Abyss" (16–31, moved below); but this block was bracketed to go at the end of p 56. After line 9 is inserted the instruction: "The Council of God &ᶜ as below. to immensity 31 lines"; at the end of p 56, before the new colophon, is written: "In terrors &ᶜ <to Abyss> as 31 lines above".

PAGE 56
 11–16] over six erased lines:
     ?And ?in ?five days of Great Eternity
     The   Eternal Death
     Then ?Jesus
     Then all   [Co]ntr[ac]tion
     Then all the Space of Empyrean ?playd in   Song
     Witherd ?from ?silent ?compassion after ?countless ?woe
 13 Albion]   Man *1st rdg del*
 23 Starry Wheels]   Deep beneath *1st rdg del*

27] written over erased: "The End of the Fourth Book"; followed by instruction: "In terrors &ᵉ <to Abyss> as 31 lines above".

At bottom of page is this erased pencil:

Christs Crucifix shall be made an excuse for Executing Criminals

PAGE 55 (SECOND PORTION)

18 with noises]   in noises *1st rdg*, error of copying from *Book of Urizen*

23] *followed by instruction* Bring in here the Globe of Blood as in the B of Urizen (a reference to *Urizen* 18; Blake in pp 54-55 has been adapting *Urizen* chapters IV-V)

24 fro] *mended from* from

PAGE 56 (SECOND PORTION)

colophon] End of the Fourth [*Book*] Night

PAGE 57

Night The Fifth

title]   [*Book*] <Night> The Fifth
(I argue above that the correction of "Book" to "Night" seems evidence of early draft; it may, however, be only a careless slip in a relatively late stage of the work; Blake in these pages is writing rapid fair copy from presumably heavily revised sheets; if he had already begun to write *Milton*, in Books, such a slip would be easy.) (Note that the colophon on p 56, written first of the several for Night IV, reads simply "Night".)

5 dreary]   dismal *1st rdg del*

7 shrunk]   *written* shrink (symptom of rapid copying)

14 Nadir]   *written* Nader (or just an undotted *i*)

PAGE 58

9 & fro &]   *written* & fro & &

21 new born]   youthful *1st rdg del*

23 Urizen cast]   When Urizen cast *2nd but canceled rdg*

25 Discord began then]   Discord began & *1st rdg;* Then Discord began & *2nd rdg*   firmament *is misspelled* firmaent

An erasure of 5 lines circled in ink begins under 24-25:

> The demons ?howld round his Chariot ?raging ?Luvah Emp[tied]
> In clouds of   ?tent   Abyss
> Was Luvah   he stood ?glowing in the dark flame
> Around the Abyss [d]efiantly <?shout[ing]> xxxxx all his Demons
> Of hope & fear then sing the same song around the glowing bed

In the left margin of the 3rd and 4th lines Blake wrote "This to be before".

PAGE 59

5 Vala]   *mended from* Valan; so also in line 19

21 round red Orc]   of the deep *1st rdg del*

PAGE 60

2 Extinction]   *mended from* extinction

20 griding]   dismal *1st rdg del*

29 accursed]   dismal *1st rdg del*

PAGE 61

14 lament]   rejoice *1st rdg del*

24 a fiery]   with fiery *1st rdg*

PAGE 62

6 strength in]   strength rejoice *1st rdg*, skipping by mistake

PAGE 63

    10 Golgonooza]   G *mended from* g
    12 deadly]   dismal *1st rdg erased*
    14 dreary]   dismal *1st rdg erased*
    18 Tho]   *mended from* Uri (for Urizen, beginning next line)

PAGE 64

    5 in the noon]   with the noon *1st rdg*
    9 to]   *mended from* into
    22 Saying O]   Saying S *1st rdg*
    24 & said]   Saying *1st rdg del*

PAGE 65

    colophon: Night]   Book *1st rdg erased*

PAGE 67

Night the Sixth

    17 Woman]   W *mended from* w
    18 current]   river *1st rdg del*

PAGE 68

    1]   Then Urizen raisd his spear. but they reard up a wall of rocks *1st rdg;* the two clauses were then numbered "2" and "1" to reverse their order, and the conjunctions changed.

PAGE 69

    13 Live]   *mended*
    17 End]   Cease *1st rdg del*
    30 dreary]   dismal *1st rdg erased*

PAGE 70 (FIRST PORTION)

    10]   In the margin is a rhymed couplet in crayon, not marked for entry:
        Till thou dost injure / the distrest
        Thou shalt never have peace / within thy breast
    17]   Followed by 3 deleted lines, the first replacing the second:
        Not so closd up the Prince of Light now darkend wandring among
        <For> Urizen beheld the terrors of the Abyss wandring among
        The Ruind Spirits once his Children & the Children of Luvah
    37   Some ?as columns of fire & of water . . . in length *1st rdg*
    38 length]   breadth *1st rdg del*
    45 ff]   In the following rearrangement of lines on pages 70–71 I follow Keynes's interpretation of the series of bracketings on those pages; the textual fit hardly allows an alternative.

PAGE 71

    3 his]   their *1st rdg del*
    16 iron . . . rain]   eternal . . . snow *1st rdg del*
    26 clay]   slime *1st rdg del*
    36 his]   *mended from* him
    37 gloomy]   dismal *1st rdg del*

PAGE 72

2–9 are written over an erasure of 7½ lines which prove to be identical to the last lines on this page and the first on the next (72:34–39; 73:1–2), where they make a better textual fit. The general pace of the writing, everywhere on these pages, is rapid fair copy. The erased lines would not have fitted where they were first written; the new lines were not freshly created; the best explanation is that Blake inadvertently began copying the wrong passage, noticed his error in the middle of the 8th line, and rectified it at once.

(The erased passage begins "O what a world is here" and ends "Upon the green plains".)

PAGE 73

4 destruction]   confusion *1st rdg del*

15 bosoms]   bowels *1st rdg del*   This line is an insertion in a stanza break; its introduction of mountain riches prepares for the change in the next line.

16 So . . . iron]   So Saying he began to form of gold silver & [*brass*] iron *1st rdg*; then "Saying" was deleted and "dig" was inserted above "form" but without deletion of the latter word. The reason for removing "Saying" must have been to gain an extra metrical foot; the intention must therefore have been to retain both "dig" and "form". Of the possible alternative readings, "to dig & form" or "to dig, forming", I have adopted the latter as more characteristic.

27 feet] *mended from* foot

36 bursts] *mended from* burstings

PAGE 74

20 Snows]   ?Enion *1st rdg del*, a slip

28 Urizen]   U *written over* O (a slip?)

PAGE 75

3 by]   with *1st rdg del*   6 Shadow] *mended from* Shade

11–12 are written over erased lines which prove to be identical to 13–14; evidently a slip in copying

20 shores]   deeps *1st rdg del*   31 gorgd] *mended from* gord

PAGE 77

Night the Seventh [a]

5–17 draw upon 98:18–20; 99:1–21 (or at least a reverse direction seems improbable). More narrowly, 8–16, dealing with beasts in the plural (lions, tygers, bulls) seems to derive from 98:18–20, where they were first Bull, Lion, Tyger, but revised to Lions, Tygers.

Of the two "Nights the Seventh" this is most probably the later, meant at one time to replace the other (VIIb). This one was stitched when the other was not (see *Four Zoas* headnote, above); but the overlap of matter is not great and Blake never destroyed the earlier Night.

19] inserted in a stanza break

PAGE 78

13 rangd his Books around]   ranged his rocks a[round] Book around *1st rdg*

16 an]   his *1st rdg del*

Upside down in the left margin are written "B Blake / Catharine Blake / 76", erased. The combined ages of William (Bill) and Catharine would have been 76 in 1797–98.

PAGE 80

1 Read . . . tones] written over erasure; 2–8 are evidently an amplification, crowded between lines and continuing in the margin, yet possibly only another accidental slip in copying.

3 you]   be *ms rdg, perhaps for* ye

27 Then Orc cried]   Orc answerd *1st rdg*

44 And Orc began]   So saying he began *1st rdg*

47 affection]   wisdom *1st rdg del*

PAGE 81

7 watching cold]   cold watching *1st rdg*; "Urizen" ends in a wiggle that may include an s, perhaps for "Urizen's cold"

15 Men]   M *mended from* m

17]   Two deleted lines follow:
       She Secret joyd to see She fed herself on his Despair
       She said I am avengd for all my sufferings of old

28 the spring]   early spring *1st rdg*

PAGE 82
24 Tree]   T *mended from* t
26 in tears]   in vain *1st rdg*
33 face lightnings]   face [*thy sons*] <& his> lightnings *1st rdg*
34 Orc]   O *mended from* o
36 Sweet]   *written over* woe

PAGE 84
13 manhood was divided for the]   *written over erasure,* the first word possibly "pathway", the last "goary"
36–40]   *inserted from margin, with guide line*
36 brutish]   *moved here* from the head of the next line, where it was written but deleted while wet
39 thee not]   *between these words* is a deleted passage:
> & till
> I have thee in my arms & am again united to Los
> To be one body & One spirit with him

—perhaps deleted to avoid interference with the more effective "till" clause of 41. (Keynes puts 41–42 before the marginal insertion, which is to miss the need for this deletion as well as to overlook the guide.)

PAGE 85
2 Embracing]   E *mended from* e
15 broke]   *mended from* burst
19–20]   guided in from margin; 21 is written over a long erased line that may have been a first try
21 dark]   sweet *1st rdg del*
22 terrified]   smild & *1st rdg,* the "&" not del
24 boughs . . . fibre]   branches . . . stem *1st rdg del*
26–27]   *written over erasure:* End of the Seventh Night
33 Consummating]   ?labouring *1st rdg del*
34 That]   Thy *1st rdg del*
37–38]   *over erased:* The End of the Seventh Night
(The first "End" would have been after 25, the second after 31, for 31 ff are in a smaller sharper pen.)
41–42]   *written in margin without guide line*
43 If we]   If once we *1st rdg*

PAGE 87
2 But]   Then *1st rdg del*
3 Wondering . . . opend]   *over erasure,* after addition and erasure of words in left margin perhaps reading "Will live" or "With Love"
4–6]   insertion written as one line with strokes after a "destroy" and "performd"—but the second seems partly erased, and perhaps 4–5 should be a single line:
> That body he created but in vain for Los performd Wonders of labour
7 They . . . high]   Builded Golgonooza Los labouring inspird builded pillars high *1st rdg*
11 Urthonas world]   ?Urizens world *1st rdg*
14 beheld]   gatherd *1st rdg erased*
29 of bitter Contrition]   many Tears *1st rdg del*
35 to]   the to *1st rdg* (for ?thee to)
36–39]   in margin but guided in; Blake evidently was groping for some word preferable to "Counterpart"; in the 2nd line he even left a gap to fill in after "Counter"; in the 1st, after deleting the whole word, he underlined "Coun" as if to try again. Meanwhile (apparently) he had written and deleted "Vegetative" or "Vegetating" above "Counterpart"; though he rejected it, the only reading Blake left us with which to fill the gap, and make sense in context, is "Vegetating Counterpart" or "Counterpart, Vegetating miraculous": Spectres, without one, "ravin".
48 ancient injuries]   former injuries *1st rdg del*

PAGE 88

The only writing on this page, the engraved side of one of the leaves made by cutting in half a print of *Edward & Elenor* 1793, is the following prose aphorism:

The Christian Religion teaches that No Man is Indifferent to you but that every one is Either Your friend or your enemy. he must necessarily be either the one [*of*] or the other And that he will be equally profitable both ways if you treat him as he deserves

Page 89 contains the other half of the *Edward & Elenor* engraving.

PAGE 90

2 sat] ?stood *1st rdg erased*
3 where . . . tree] *over deletion beginning* which
5 refuge] sweet *1st rdg del*
10 labour] pleasure *1st rdg del*
12 Sacrifice] life & love *1st rdg del*
16 Lovely terrible] Lovely *1st rdg del*
22 forms sublime] sweet forms *1st rdg*
25] *followed by a deleted line:*

To hew the cavernd rocks of Dranthon into forms of beauty
28 forth delighted upon] forth upon *1st rdg*
47 fathers] *preceded by* second *del*
58 Urizen[s] Shadow] Urizen [*Spectre*] <Shadow> *ms*

PAGE 99

Night the Eighth

1 Met in] which is called *1st rdg del*
2 as] Met as *1st rdg*
4 Fallen] Eternal *1st rdg erased*
4–9 *written over five erased lines:*

[a] He is
[b] He is the Good Shepherd He is the Lord & Master
[c] He is the Shep[herd of] Albion he is all in all
[d] In Eden in the Garden of God & in heavenly Jerusalem
[e] To create Man Morning by Morning to give gifts at Noon Day

Of these lines, and unerased lines 1–3, four were moved to Night I p 8:8–11, i.e. 1, 2, *b, e* (after the revision of 1 & 2); they were later erased on p 8, and a new page, 21, was added to Night I beginning with seven lines using some of the material of 1, 2, *d*, and possibly *a* (if *a* contains the definition of Jesus as "the Christ"); three lines appear also in *Jerusalem* 34[38]:23–25, consisting of *b c d*, unchanged (unless my reading "Shepherd of Albion" is mistaken), and these follow, after one unfamiliar line, five lines which are almost identical to lines 2–6 of page 21, Night I. We should expect line *a* to contain in some form the material occurring in the same position in p 21 and *J* 34. (Here and below, *Jerusalem* is abbreviated *J*.)

They Call Jesus the Christ & they in him & he in them
Live in Perfect harmony in Eden the land of life
—thus p 21:5–6, changed to the first person in *Jerusalem:*

We call Jesus the Christ and he in us and we in him
(with the second line identical, and a third reading:

Giving receiving and forgiving each others trespasses
—followed immediately by *b c d*.) The last word in *a* could be "recompense" (see *J* 4:20, a related passage), the penultimate word "seeketh" (not "seeking"), and a largely conjectural reconstruction of the whole line that would not do violence to the graphic evidence is:

"He is Calld the Christ who forgiveth & seeketh no recompense".

Evidence that the deletion and revision on p 99 (and hence the changes on p 8 and insertion of p 21) were not made before *Jerusalem* was in progress would be the appearance there of erased lines *c d* verbatim; but of course the passage may have been saved on a separate sheet now lost. Note that *J* 34[38] inspires—or draws on—unique parts of all three pages in *Four Zoas,* as well as on common parts.

9 over head]   followed by deleted passage including five lines in margin:

> but other wings
> They had which clothd their bodies like a garment of soft down
> Silvery white shining upon the dark blue sky in silence
> Their wings touchd the heavens their fair feet hoverd above
> The swelling tides they bent over the dead corse like an arch
> Pointed at top in highest heavens of precious stones & pearl

15–16 Then Los said I behold . . . thro the broken Gates / Of thy]   Then Los beheld . . . thro the broken Gates / Of Enitharmons *1st rdg;* Then first Los beheld &c *2nd rdg*

17 I see]   inserted above the line

18 Awe]   *mended from* al (a false start?)

24 Enitharmon]   *followed by del:*

> which joins to Urizens temple
> Which is the Synagogue of Satan

25 stood]   stood at the Gate *1st rdg*

PAGE 100 (FIRST PORTION)

Between lines 1 and 2 a marginal note, "Los stood &c", with guide lines calling for an insertion from another page, may refer to the preceding words in 99:25 (though no insertion here could work); they more probably refer to 90:2 before revision: "Los stood in Golgonooza in the Gate of Luban"; insertion of all but the first and last two lines of p 90 would work quite well at this point; one would need merely to change the phrase "Into his hands" that begins 100:2 into "In his hands" in the antepenultimate line of p 90. The thematic material of 90, amplified with marginal additions, seems all an amplification backward from the "Looms in Lubans Gate" in 100:2.

In short, Blake wrote the two pages 87 and 90 as a sequence, considered using the second page as a second page for Night VIII (i.e. inserting it on p 100), but then chose to tighten the sequence (with additions at bottom of 87 and top of 90) and insert it (unquestionably a late addition) at the end of VII. This bit of masonry, which cements VII(a) closely to VIII, seems to indicate a time when Blake considered VIIb as abandoned (or moved). It should be noted that 90:1 is probably an addition, the text originally starting within the platemark, and that 99:26–27 are an addition, which must be treated parenthetically, made to round out the tale when the idea of bringing in the "Los stood . . . in the Gate of Luban" passage had been abandoned; hence too the deletion of "at the Gate" in 99:25.

11–13 Astonishd . . . saw]   Astonishd Comforted Delighted the daughters of Beulah saw *1st rdg del*

23 single]   One fold *1st rdg del*

25]   followed by nine lines marked for transfer to p 101

PAGE 101 (FIRST PORTION)

16 Upon the mighty Fiend]   On the immortal fiend *1st rdg del*

20 brooding]   *mended from* broods

27 among the Stars]   his hurtling hand *1st rdg del*

28 His hurtling hand]   Among the Stars *1st rdg del*

29]   followed by instructions to transfer lines from 100 and beginning of 101:

> But Urizen his mighty rage comes in here: to quenchless rage

PAGE 100 (SECOND PORTION)

26 But]   But ?thus *1st rdg del*

27 round]   from *1st rdg del*

PAGE 101 (SECOND PORTION)

31 repelld]   Keynes and Bentley read "expelld" (Bentley with query) but the *r* is just like that in "rage" in the next line, and the *e* cannot possibly be an *x,* a wide

and double letter in Blake's hand. (Nor would "expelld" make sense or fit Blake's usage.)

33–37]   written in margin without guide line; I follow Keynes in reading them as an addition to the transferred passage, belonging here.

34 hermaphrodite]   male *1st rdg del*

PAGE 102

7 torment] *mended from* torments
21 avert] *mended from* invert
26 words] *mended from* world

PAGE 103

8 these terrors]   the human form *1st rdg del*
14 If]   followed by deletion, perhaps "that we"; Bentley queries "?thou ?art".
15 if] *followed by* that *del*

PAGE 104 (FIRST PORTION)

10]   followed by marginal direction "We behold with wonder &ᶜ"

PAGE 113 (FIRST PORTION)

1 We . . . wonder]   Daughter of Beulah describe *1st rdg del*
2 Beelzeboul] *mended from* Baalzebole
3] followed by two deleted lines:
            The hard dentant hammers are lulld by the flute lula lula
            The bellowing furnaces blare by the long sounding Clarion
6 into wedges]   into bars *1st rdg*
14 Arnon]   the Moon *1st rdg del*
16 Satan]   Satan recieves *1st rdg*
24 Benithon] *followed by* it is *del*
25 its Islands & its Margins]   the Islands & the Margins of this Lake *1st rdg*
30 from]   to *1st rdg del*
31 thou O]   All *1st rdg del*

PAGE 104 (SECOND PORTION)

16 Begun Already]   Already *1st rdg*
21 Heavd like]   Heaving lik *1st rdg del*   24 Son] *mended from* Sons
37 Give his vegetated body]   rend the Veil of Mystery *1st rdg del*, followed by a deleted line:
            And then Call Urizen & Luvah & Tharmas & Urthona

PAGE 105 (and 145)

1–30 The Lamb . . . victims]   Identical on p 105 to earlier draft on p 145 (ms fragment), except as here noted
1 Satan]   Urizen *p 145* (the whole line a pencil addition on *p 145*)
2 shadows of torments]   Shadows of torment *p 145* (the plural perhaps a slip of the pen; not a firm *s*)
3 Amalek]   Entuthon that *1st rdg p 145 del*
4 for]   that *1st rdg p 145 del*
5 Urizen]   He *1st rdg p 145 del*
10 amidst them beamd]   around them stood *p 145*, *1st rdg p 105*
11–27] *not in p 145, marginal insertions p 105*
24 there was hidden within]   therefore they were calld / The daughters & *1st rdg del*, to allow further addition
27 namd]   calld *1st rdg del*
28 Amalek] *inserted p 105*   Stones]   Stones *p 145*; Stems *1st rdg p 105 del*
35 Away]   I have *1st rdg del, a slip*
43] followed by deleted line:
            To see the boy spring into heaven sounding from my sight
44 heat]   pre (*for "prepare"*) *1st rdg del*
50 task]   Bentley reads "lash" but there is merely an uncrossed *t*; the line reappears in *J* 68:6; the context does not allow "lash".

PAGE 106 (FIRST PORTION)
1–6 were transcribed verbatim from 145:13–17, 19
5] followed in 145 by a line deleted and not transferred:
    In which is Tirzah untranslucent an opake covering
6] followed in 145 by ten lines deleted and not transferred:
    And Rahab stripd off Luvahs robes from off the lamb of God
    Then first she saw his glory & her harlot form appeard
    In all its turpitude beneath the divine light & of Luvahs robes
    She made herself a Mantle
    Also the Vegetated bodies which Enitharmon wove in her looms   5
    Opend within the heart & in the loins & in the brain
    To Beulah & the dead in Beulah descended thro their gates
    And some were woven one fold some two fold & some threefold
    In head or heart or reins according to the fittest order
    Of most mournful pity & compassion to the spectrous dead   10
7 Jerusalem] She 1st rdg del
9 Urizen &] followed by build del
12 of] in 1st rdg del
16] followed by instruction: But when Rahab &c turn back 3 leaves

PAGE 113 (SECOND PORTION)
38 But] And 1st rdg del
38–43] over six erased lines
42 among] above 1st rdg del

PAGE 115 (p 114 has engraving without text)
1 are] were 1st rdg del
7 are our] were their 1st rdg del
10 our] their 1st rdg del
12 his brethren] Los 1st rdg del
19 Me] Los 1st rdg del
23 Rahab] Mortals 1st rdg del
32 Palamabron] Rintrah & Palamabron 1st rdg

PAGE 116
6] followed by instructions: Darkness & sorrow &c turn over leaf

PAGE 106 (SECOND PORTION)
18 Religion] followed by del: was [?tormented] <darkend> (reading in p 145:32
was "tormented")
19 felt] preceded by He del
29 thro] over 1st rdg del
39 the Spectre] Urthona 1st rdg del
42 wild] mended from wide

PAGE 107
3 his] written hos
5 Covers] 1st written at end of 4 but del
15] followed by 18 del (a slip in copying?)
17 repentant forgets] ²forgets ¹repentant ms

PAGE 108
1 on high] begun above del

PAGE 110
24 flaming] dismal 1st rdg del
29] written above 8 deleted lines:
    But Rahab [built] <hewd> a Sepulcher in the Rock of Eternity
    And placing in the Sepulcher the body which she had taken
    From the divine Lamb wept over the Sepulcher weaving

Her web of Religion around the Sepulcher times after times beside
    Jerusalems Gate
But as she wove behold the bottom of the Sepulcher   5
Rent & a door was opend thro the bottom of the Sepulcher
Into Eternity And as she wove she heard a Voice behind her calling her
She turnd & saw the Divine Vision & her
(Lines 2–3 are written over erased "The End of the Eighth Night".)
32 despair]   fear *1st rdg del*

PAGE III

12 Enitharmon . . . the Heavens]   Enion . . . Heaven *pencil*

PAGE 117

Night the Ninth

1–13] written over almost identical pencil, over erased ink lines (about 11); the endings of these can be somewhat made out: the 2nd ends "?curst the heavens", the 11th "was Ended"; these do not reappear elsewhere in the poem; apparently this passage was erased without being transferred.

PAGE 118

15 asterial]   eternal *1st rdg del*
17 sounds]   *followed by del:* Awake ye dead & come / To Judgment.
39–40] written over two erased lines, a third visible in part

PAGE 119

1–14] *written over erased title:* Vala / Night the Ninth / Being / The Last Judgment
17 Began to Enter the Holy City]   Began to draw near to the Earth *1st rdg del*
18 whirring] *a doubtful reading*
24 Beyond]   Without *1st rdg del*   41 witherd]   narrow *1st rdg del*

PAGE 120

30–31] added in pencil; after "Person" is a mark *o*
42 energy Enslavd]   honest energy *1st rdg*

PAGE 121

4 futurity]   the past *1st rdg*   6 towers]   high towers *1st rdg*
7 garden] *mended from* gardens (or possibly the other way around)
14 sword] *preceded by* plow *del*
18 unto] *ms perhaps reads* into, *but without* dot and with pen-scratch
19, 20, 21, 22 futurity]   remembrance *1st rdg del*
43 words]   voice *1st rdg del*

PAGE 122

7 to]   of *1st rdg del*   32 Eyes] *mended from* eyes

PAGE 123

14 dark]   black *1st rdg del*
16 calls]   cries *1st rdg del*
34 a throne & a]   as a throne & as a *1st rdg*
35 twenty four] over a "twenty four" that may have been mended
36 by]   of *1st rdg del*

PAGE 124

5 Redeemd Man]   Fallen man *1st rdg*
25 ardor.] followed by deletion:
                      he rose up from the Rock
    The Fallen Man wondring beheld.

PAGE 125

2 forth]   out *1st rdg del*

PAGE 126

3 Regenerate Man]   Ancient Man *1st rdg*   7O] & *1st rdg del*
11 Imagination]   Thought *1st rdg del*

PAGE 127
5 thine he]   thine when he *1st rdg*

PAGE 129
24–27 transferred from p 4 and crowded into a stanza break

PAGE 130
29 wet]   with *1st rdg del*

PAGE 132
14 a whirlwind]   Then a whirlwind *1st rdg*
19 By]   With *1st rdg del*
25 down]   of *1st rdg del*

PAGE 133
8 They]   And *1st rdg del*
9 Generative]   Vegetative *1st rdg del*
15 Science]   Nature *1st rdg del*

PAGE 135
39 Odors]   *mended from* odors

PAGE 136
8 gaping]   silent *1st rdg del*
12 Birth]   death *1st rdg del*
22 shoals]   Bentley reads "shouts"; but the line is repeated in *Milton* 27 and cf above p 122:31.
25 and Racks & Saws]   the nets and racks & ?Pins *1st rdg*
27 whips]   whipt *ms* (cf *Milton* 27:36)   sports] *mended from* sport
35 Nettle]   *mended from* nettle

PAGE 138
21 And]   Then *1st rdg del*
25 behold]   *written* beholds

❧

[Alternate Version of Night VII]
Night the Seventh [b]

PAGE 91 (FIRST PORTION)
Almost certainly the earlier of the two Nights Seven, the text of pp 91–97 was written down in that order but then rearranged by a note on p 91 that "This Night begins at line 153 the following comes in at the End" and a note on p 95 after its 14th line: "Beginning of the [*Book*] <Seventh Night>" plus a note at the end of p 98: "Then follows Thus in the Caverns of the Grave &ᵉ as it stands now in the beginning of Night the Seventh".

PAGE 95 (SECOND PORTION)
15 Roots]   tree *1st rdg overwritten*
16 brooded]   brooded dismal *1st rdg*
17 his warriors]   the Shadowy female *1st rdg del*
24]   followed by deleted line:
     The shadowy voice answered O urizen Prince of Light
(NB: Here and in line 32 "Urizen" is written over a different name, possibly "Luvah" or "Satan" though no *h* or *t* is visible.)

PAGE 96

18 temple] followed by the beginning of a line immediately deleted: "Urizen namd it Pande" (i.e. Pandemonium)

19 stature] forehead 1st rdg del

25 for] mended from of

PAGE 97

7 sands] roads 1st rdg del

10 all] [till] all ms

21 night or day] day by day 1st rdg

PAGE 98

19 Lion] Lions 1st rdg

20 Tyger] Tygers 1st rdg

31] followed by pencil direction "Then I heard the Earthquake &c" referring to a lost passage—or to some revision of 91:6 ff. Next follows the inked, and earlier, direction to bring in ". . . Thus in the Caverns of the Grave &ᵉ as it stands now . . .", i.e. pp 91ff.

PAGE 91 (second portion, i.e. text after title)

1 Thus] Now in ms, but revised when quoted on p 98

11 affection] love 1st rdg del

21 [triumphant] fury] Erasure not replaced. One wonders at what date Blake decided that even the triumphant aspect of embattled Orc must be called in doubt. The erasure is evidently a political or moral one.

30 clouds] steeds 1st rdg del (a clue to Blake's transpositions)

PAGE 92

10 clothe] Now clothe 1st rdg

12 they . . . blood They . . . helmet] the two clauses written in reverse order, then numbered "2" and "1"; yet see Jerusalem 65:7

PAGE 93

17 in hammerd steel] in darkness are 1st rdg del

19 Morn] mended, perhaps from morn

23 drinking] Bentley reads ?dropping

Two lines in the left margin, the first in pencil and the second in ink, seem not part of the text but aphoristic comment upon it:

Unorganizd Innocence, An Impossibility
Innocence dwells with Wisdom but never with Ignorance

26 Power] mended from for (a jump to "form" three words farther on)

PAGE 94

17 form of Orc which] form which 1st rdg

27 wrathful then] then furious 1st rdg del

55 rage against] anguish for 1st rdg del

PAGE 95 (FIRST PORTION)

8 Patience for] Patience of 1st rdg

PAGE 141

Fragments on a slip of note paper, not used anywhere in the final text:

Beneath the veil of [?Enion] <Vala> rose Tharmas from dewy tears
The [ancient] <eternal> man bowd his bright head & Urizen prince of light
[Astonish lookd from his bright Portals calling thus to Luvah
O Luvah in the ——————————————————]
Astonishd lookd from his bright portals. Luvah king of Love
Awakend Vala. Ariston ran forth with bright ?Onana
And dark Urthona rouzd his shady bride from her deep den

5

<[*Awaking from his stony slumber*]>
Pitying they viewd the new born demon. for they could not love
[*After their sin*] ————————————————————————— 10
Male formd the demon mild athletic force his shoulders spread
And his bright feet firm as a brazen altar. but. the parts
To love devoted. female, all astonishd stood the hosts
Of heaven, while Tharmas with wingd speed flew to the sandy shore
   <[*ocean*]>
He rested on the desart wild & on the raging sea   15
He stood & stretchd his wings &ᵉ————

With printless feet scorning the concave of the joyful sky
Female her form bright as the summer but the parts of love
Male & her brow radiant as day. darted a lovely scorn
Tharmas beheld from his high rocks & ———— ————

PAGE 142   (Notes not used in final text):
The ocean calm the clouds fold round & fiery flames of love
Inwrap the immortal limbs struggling in terrific joy
Not long thunders lightnings swift rendings & blasting winds
Sweep oer. the struggling copulation. in fell writhing pangs
They lie in twisting agonies beneath the covring heavens   5

The womb impressd Enion fled & hid in verdant mountains
Yet here his heavenly orbs &ᵉ

From Enion pours the seed of life & death in all her limbs
Frozen in the womb of Tharmas rush the rivers of Enions pain
Trembling he lay swelld with the deluge stifling in the anguish   10

III. POETICAL SKETCHES

Source: 72-page octavo pamphlet printed for Blake in 1783, with a few corrections and revisions made by Blake in some of the 22 extant copies reported. No ms is known.

A prefatory "Advertisement" (p ii) reads: "The following Sketches were the production of untutored youth, commenced in his twelfth, and occasionally resumed by the author till his twentieth year; since which time, his talents having been wholly directed to the attainment of excellence in his profession, he has been deprived of the leisure requisite to such a revisal of these sheets, as might have rendered them less unfit to meet the public eye.

"Conscious of the irregularities and defects to be found in almost every page, his friends have still believed that they possessed a poetic originality, which merited some respite from oblivion. These their opinions remain, however, to be now reproved or confirmed by a less partial public."

Blake's corrections have been adopted, as noted; other corrections are made within square brackets. The original punctuation has been retained, though it may be less Blake's than the unknown printer's.

TO SUMMER

15 youths] *printed* youth (evidently in error)

TO WINTER

11 and his hand] *printed* and in his hand (corrected by Blake in some copies)

TO THE EVENING STAR

2 while] *printed* whilst (revised by Blake in one copy)

FAIR ELENOR

6 cheek] *printed* cheeks (corrected by Blake in some copies)
61 behold] I am *1st rdg* (revised by Blake in some copies)

SONG "Love and harmony combine"

16 his] *printed* her (corrected by Blake in one copy)

MAD SONG

4 infold] *printed* unfold (altered by Blake in one copy)
7 birds] *printed* beds (corrected by Blake in some copies)

GWIN, KING OF NORWAY

9–12; 63–64   Lack of quotation marks enclosing these lines may indicate that the printer had no help from ms. Blake almost never used quotation marks.

AN IMITATION OF SPEN[S]ER

title] *printed* SPENCER (uncorrected by Blake)
13 leesing] Adjective based on Spenser's substantive leasing or lesing, a falsehood
14 other] *printed* others (revised by Blake in some copies)
15 eares] *printed* cares (corrected by Blake in one copy)
41 see] *Sic* in parallel construction with "hear" in line 40 (misconstrued by Keynes and altered to "sees")
44 warrior maid,] *printed* warrior, maid *but corrected by Blake*

BLIND-MAN'S BUFF

64 impose,] *printed* impose. *but corrected by Blake,* who also inserted the ";" in line 65.

~❧~

KING EDWARD THE THIRD

1: Scene . . . Nobles] *printed* . . . Nobles before it *but revised by Blake*
3:10 eer] *printed* ere   3:218 Exit] *printed* Exeunt
3:236 his] *printed* her (corrected by Blake in some copies; compare 291–93)
3:292 him] *printed* them (corrected by Blake in some copies)
4:45 a new song] *i.e.* the song of Scene [6]
4:48 another about all us that are to die] *i.e.* the "War Song" printed as a separate Sketch further on

~❧~

A WAR SONG TO ENGLISHMEN

Intended for the second War Song of the Chandos minstrel in "King Edward the Third" (see preceding note).

SAMSON

? warfare] *"probably a misprint for* wayfare"*—Keynes*

~❧~

[Further Sketches]

[In a Manuscript Fragment]
"then She bore Pale desire . . ."

This and the following fragment are on seven pages of an unsigned ms of 4 leaves (19.2 × 12.2 cm) in Blake's hand, probably of the early 1780s. (For description and line-for-line transcription, see "A Blake Manuscript in the Berg Collection", *Bulletin of The New York Public Library* LXII 191–201.) The first word is not indented or capitalized and was obviously not originally the beginning of the ms.

1:6 weak arm.] *followed by deletion:* Now day arose. the Golden Sun his mighty Race began Refreshing. the Cold earth. with beaming. Joy.

1:14 observing] *mended from* observd and

1:15 as well as this.] *followed by almost illegible deletion:* for all she [   ] fear and [   ]

2:26 Adoration] *followed by deletion:* Nor Could Refrain but Cry'd O this is the bles't time when Pride shall hold the Sway. N (*for* "Now"?)

3:37 Rankest Draught] *followed by deleted clause:* and Death is in the Pot

4:54 She brings . . . how to know.]   She teacheth knowledge how to know *1st rdg del and replaced by insert from p 7*

4:75 She bore honour . . . Pride.] *inserted from p 7*

5:81 bore]   brought forth *1st rdg del*

5:92 & Policy doth . . . the World]   & Emulation [*Suspition Mixt*] *1st rdg;* & Policy doth dwell with her. by Whom She had a Son Called Suspition *2nd rdg* (both rdgs evidently to be replaced by final rdg inserted from p 7)

"Woe cried the muse . . ."

A complete unit in the ms, though possibly intended as part of a larger work.

6:3 her Notes]   her ?Chauntant Notes *1st rdg* (the deleted word hardly legible)

6:6 string]   note *1st rdg del*   awful]   Shadowy *1st rdg del*

6:8 how soon]   hark how *1st rdg*

6:15 listning]   trembling *1st rdg del*

6:17 lake swift as . . . Bud]   ruffling lake while ?living clay cold corpse Corse *1st rdg* (apparently a series of false starts). The line "swift as the Nightly Blast that Blights the Infant Bud" is not marked for insert here—but is written exactly opposite the deleted passage, on p. 7.

~❧~

IV. [AN ISLAND IN THE MOON]

Original ms in Fitzwilliam Museum, Cambridge, England, obviously copied from an earlier draft, the most frequent revision being a second thought replacing a word just writen down; later changes are "Human" to "Huming" (i.e. humming), "Arse" to "ass", and "turd" to "tansey". Insignificant mendings not reported here. The name "Sigtagatist" was first written "Sistagatist" in most places, but mended.

Date: December 1784, from internal evidence.

P 1 endeavouring to conceal his]   endeavoured to conceal the *1st rdg*
the older]   This slip suggests that two of the "philosophers" are brothers. If Quid, the older, is William Blake, as is generally supposed, then Suction may be his younger brother, Robert.

P 3 Mʳˢ Sigtagatist]   & the three Philosophers com[in]g Quid the Cynic, Sipsop the Pythagorean & Suction the Epicurean enterd the room *1st rdg del*   ass]
ass *1st rdg del;* *Arse *2nd rdg del*

P 8 John Lookye Gent]   "Gent" written over deleted "Gentleman"   said Scopprell]
followed by deletion: "its a book about"

"Phebe drest like beauties Queen"

9:4 lambkins]   *mended from* lambs do

"This frog he would a wooing ride"

11:5 Sing cock]   This frog *1st rdg del*

"Hail Matrimony made of Love"

12:18 panteth]   *mended from* panted

"To be or not to be"

12:19, 20 chimneys . . . windows]   windows . . . chi *1st rdg del*

"This city & this country . . ."

13:6 jet]   *mended from* git

"Upon a holy thursday . . ."

14:8   And all in order sit waiting the chief chanters commands *1st rdg del*
14:9–10 Then like a mighty wind . . . / . . . seats of heavn among] *This couplet was first deleted and replaced by:*
      When the whole multitude of innocents their voices raise
      Like angels on the throne of heavn raising the voice of praise
which was in turn deleted for a new beginning:
      Let Cherubim & Seraphim now raise their voices high
which was deleted and replaced by the original couplet.
(For the final draft, slightly modified, see "Holy Thursday" in *Songs of Innocence.*)

"When the tongues of children . . ."

14:1 When the tongues]   The voice *1st rdg del;* The tongues *2nd rdg*
14:2 laughing is heard on]   laughing upon *1st rdg*
14:5 home . . . down]   home children the sun is down *1st rdg*
15:10 go to sleep]   *1st rdg;* sleep till its dark *2nd rdg*
15:11 The flocks are at play & we cant go away *1st rdg del*
(For the final draft see "Nurse's Song" in *Songs of Innocence.*)

"O father father . . ."

(For the final draft see "The Little Boy lost" in *Songs of Innocence.*)

"O I say you Joe"

15:6 tansey]   turd *1st rdg del*
15:10 He has given me a black eye]   To hit me with the bat *1st rdg del*
15:12 Any more than a[ny bird the] <dog or a> cat

"Theres Doctor Clash"

16:5] *two deleted lines follow:*
[*If*] <How> many Blackamoors
Coud sing with their thick lips

❧

V. [SONGS AND BALLADS]

[Written in a copy of *Poetical Sketches*]

Three poems writen in an unknown hand on the fly leaves of a copy of *Poetical Sketches* (1783) which was presented to someone with the inscription "from Mrs. Flaxman May 15 1784" and is now in the Alexander Turnbull Library, Wellington, New Zealand. One of the poems, "Song 2nd by A Young Shepherd", is a variant of the "Laughing Song" of *Songs of Innocence* (and is cited above in the notes to that poem). Now collated with photographs published by D. F. McKenzie in *Turnbull Library Record*, I, no 3 (1968) 4–8.

[From Blake's Notebook]

Most of the lyrics in Blake's Notebook (the "Rossetti Notebook", now in the British Museum, used from before 1787 until as late as 1818 for drawings, verses, prose) were published in *Songs of Experience*. The ms variants of these are given above in the textual notes to the *Songs*. The present section begins with contemporaneous lyrics (up through "The Fairy") which were in effect rejected from that publication. These are arranged not as they happen to occur in the Notebook but by closeness of theme or imagery, so that clusters of poems that seem to have suggested each other or to have derived from a common inspiration may be read together. Following these are a scattering of later lyrics, given in approximate order of composition, dating from perhaps 1800 to 1808. For other Notebook poems, see "Satiric Verses and Epigrams".

Location in the Notebook is indicated by page number following the abbreviation N. Pages used upside down and in reverse order are indicated by the abbreviation "rev". As now bound and numbered, pages 1–14 are out of order; their original order (when used by Blake) was 5, 6, 9, 10, 13, 14, 11, 12, 7, 8, 1, 2, 3, 4.

*

"Never pain to tell thy love"   N 115 rev

The poem developed out of the first four lines, and these were then deleted line by line. Editors are in agreement that the poem cannot stand without its first stanza—as Blake would surely have discovered if he had chosen to transfer it to copper. (Lines deleted in ms were restored in such poems as "Earth Answer" [third stanza].)

1 pain]   seek *1st rdg del*
12 O was no deny]   He took her with a sigh *1st rdg del*

*

"I feard the fury of my wind"   N 113 rev

1 fury]   roughness *1st rdg del*   4 And]   But *1st rdg del*

*

"I saw a chapel all of gold"   N 113 rev

8 Down . . . tore)   Till he broke the pearly door *1st rdg del*

*

"I laid me down upon a bank"   N 115 rev

*

A cradle song   N 114 rev

Line 3 was written first, followed by 4, 1, and 2; after much revision these were rearranged by numbering in the present order.

2 Dreaming oer]   Thou shalt taste *1st rdg del*

4 Little sorrows sit & weep]   Thou wilt every secret keep *1st rdg del;* Canst thou any secret keep *2nd rdg changed to* Thou canst any secret keep, *then del*

An abortive 2nd stanza was begun but deleted: "Yet a little while the moon / Silent"

Lines 5–8 were written as the 4th stanza, then numbered "2" when all stanzas were numbered in the final sequence.

8 Little pretty infant wiles]   Such as burning youth beguiles *1st rdg del*

9 feel]   touch *1st rdg del;* stroke *2nd rdg del*

10 steal]   broke *1st rdg del*

17 From . . . eye]   O the cunning wiles that creep *1st rdg del*

19 Infant . . . infant]   Female . . . female *1st rdg del*

*

"I askéd a thief . . ."   N 114 rev

Punctuation and line and stanza divisions follow the fair copy in Princeton University Library inscribed "W Blake / Lambeth / 1796", the text of which is identical to final rdg in the Notebook (in which lines 5–6 were written as one and line 9 did not begin a new stanza).

1 to steal]   if he'd steal *1st rdg*

2 He turned]   And he turnd *1st rdg del*

4 Holy]   And holy *1st rdg del*

7 He]   And he *1st rdg del*

8 And]   And he *1st rdg del*

9 said]   spoke *1st rdg del*

11 And twixt earnest & game *1st rdg;* . . . joke *2nd rdg, del*

12 He enjoyd the dame *1st rdg*

*

in a mirtle shade   N 111 rev

Strictly interpreted, the ms does not authorize the treatment of these lines as a separate poem—as I have come to realize while making corrections for the fourth printing. True, Blake's first thought may have been to make a new poem that would combine the theme of binding from "Earths Answer" (drafted just above on the same page) and the mirtle and blossoms of the expanding poem on p 113 from which he would excerpt "Infant Sorrow" (see pp 719–721). But by the time he inserted the words "in a mirtle shade"—an apparent title but really only the concluding words of the revised fifth stanza on p 113—Blake plainly meant these newer stanzas to serve as a replacement of the sixth and following stanzas on p 113.

On p 111 Blake began with two lines,

> To a lovely mirtle bound
> Blossoms showring all around

following them with what would be the first two lines of the second stanza; then he canceled this couplet and added his next, borrowing the same rhyme words. In the next column he wrote a new first stanza and a third and fourth, numbering these stanzas 1, 2, and 3 for the final arrangement (here treated as a separate poem) and making the link to p 113 with "in a mirtle shade". The poem was, of course, shorn of its first stanzas when they were taken from p 113 for "Infant Sorrow", and the two columns were lined through vertically just as the first two were. But then, or meanwhile, a truly separate poem, "To my Mirtle", was developed five pages later in the Notebook.

11 my father saw]   the priest beheld *1st rdg del*

*

To my Mirtle   N 106 rev

Salvaging unused lines from the "Infant Sorrow" drafts of pp 113 and 111 (see above), Blake first wrote down the "O how sick" couplet but then erased it before the ink was dry. He then copied from p 111 the first stanza written beneath the words "in a mirtle shade" (see above). He canceled its second couplet, perhaps not before continuing with two more couplets from p 111 on the "bound-ground" rhyme:

> To a lovely mirtle bound
> Blossoms showring all around
> Like to dung upon the ground
> Underneath my mirtle bound

He then canceled, selected, and rearranged lines to make the present poem, all that remains not lined through in the Notebook, and he gave it a title. (A similar process of reduction takes place with the "Fayette" lines. See below pp 779–780.)

*

[To go] on 1 Plate

Five poems are grouped here in accordance with Blake's penciled memorandum, on p 101 reversed (see text p 673). "Thou hast a lap full of seed" is included conjecturally: it seems to be the only current poem that would fit the title "Experiment". No plate is extant containing these five poems; indeed none of these poems is lined through vertically to indicate transfer to a plate, except the "lap full" poem.

"O lapwing . . ."   N 113 rev

An answer to the parson   N 103 rev

[Experiment]   N 111 rev

5 Shall I]   Oft Ive *1st rdg del*
6 turn]   turnd *1st rdg del*
7 For]   But *1st rdg del*
9 tearing]   pulling *1st rdg del*

Riches   N 103 rev

1 countless]   we *1st rdg del*; count *2nd rdg del*; weal *3rd rdg del* (the poet wavering between "wealth" and "countless")
3 indolent]   idle man *1st rdg del*
4 secret]   cunning *1st rdg del*

"If you trap the moment . . ."   N 105 rev

1 trap]   catch *1st rdg del*
4 You can]   Youll *1st rdg*

*

Eternity   N 105 rev

1 binds]   Previous editors have wavered between "bends" and "binds", but the dot on the *i* is visible in strong light (the whole poem is in pencil)   to himself]   himself to *1st rdg*

3 who kisses]   who just kisses *1st rdg*
4 eternity's]   an eternal *1st rdg del*

*

"I heard an Angel singing"   N 114 rev

Second attempt at an "Experience" counterpart to "The Divine Image"; written after *A Divine Image* (which see); very faintly lined through vertically and abandoned for a quite different version, "The Human Abstract", which became a Song of Experience.

3 Pity Peace]   Pity & Peace *1st rdg*
15 At his curse]   Thus he sang & *1st rdg del*
17 Down]   And down *1st rdg*
19–20 And . . . Peace]
    And Mercy & Pity & Peace descended
    The Farmers were ruind & harvest was ended *1st rdg del*

    And Mercy Pity & Peace
    Joyd at their increase
    With Povertys Increase
    Are   *2nd rdg del*

    And by distress increase
    Mercy Pity Peace   *3rd rdg del*

    By Misery to increase
    Mercy Pity Peace   *4th rdg del*

*

"Silent Silent Night"   N 113 rev

*

To Nobodaddy   N 109 rev

Lined through vertically, as if after copying, but not extant elsewhere. Title crowded in after composition; first written without the "To".

2 Father]   Man *1st rdg del*
Lines 9–10 were an afterthought, crowded in as one line.
10 females loud]   feminine *1st rdg del*

*

"Are not the joys of morning sweeter"   N 109 rev

Lined through vertically, but not extant elsewhere.

*

"How came pride in Man"   N 107 rev

Heavily deleted, and unfinished. Visually, the poem that immediately follows, "The Human Abstract" (see *Songs of Experience*), looks like a continuation of the same poem, the title being inserted later.

*

[*How to know Love from Deceit*]   N 107–106 rev

Blake may only tentatively have considered these two stanzas, written on separate pages, as one poem; he added the title after composition and later deleted it.

3 Lawless]   Always *1st rdg del*
5 confind]   inclind *1st rdg del*
6 Lawful . . . refind]   Modest prudish & confind *1st rdg del*   & refind]   &
confind *2nd rdg del*
7 To every thing but]   Never is to *1st rdg del*
8 And . . . mind]   And chains & fetters every mind *1st rdg del*

*

The wild flowers song   N 109, 107 rev

The 2nd and 3rd stanzas were written first; the introductory stanza and explanatory title were written two pages later. Previous misreading of "fond" as "found" in line 5, 1st rdg, has obscured the original Innocence theme.

3 flower]   thistle *1st rdg del*
5 slept]   was fond *1st rdg del*   earth] dark *1st rdg, del on p 107*

*

Soft Snow   N 107 rev

Lined through vertically, but not extant elsewhere.
4 And . . . crime]   Ah that sweet love should be thought a crime *1st rdg del*

*

Merlins prophecy   N 106 rev

*

"Why should I care for the men of thames"   N 113 rev

Trace of an erased title, beginning with "T"—perhaps "Thames"; text is lined through vertically—perhaps when "charterd" was taken over to the "London" poem.

7 The Ohio shall . . . me]   I spurnd his waters away from me *1st rdg del*
8 go]   long *1st rdg del*

*

Day   N 105 rev

Crossed out with a heavy vertical line, but not found elsewhere.

1 Sun]   day *1st rdg del*
4 bosom]   ancles *1st rdg del*

*

"The sword sung on the barren heath"   N 105 rev

*

"Abstinence sows sand all over"   N 105 rev

2 flaming hair]   *mended* (over what was probably only a bad scribble for the same two words)

*

"In a wife I would desire"   N 105 rev

*

Lacedemonian Instruction   N 103 rev

*

"An old maid early eer I knew"   N 100 rev

The two stanzas were written in reverse order but then numbered 2, 1.

*

Several Questions Answerd   N 99 rev

Five poems, which Blake grouped first in the order 4, 2, 3, 1, 5, then numbered to go in the present order—though the fourth ("The Question answerd") was intermediately numbered 3.

The first quatrain is repeated from p 105, where it was titled "Eternity". The other verses are copied from pp 103 and 107, with the variants indicated below:

10 These are Beautys sweetest dress]   Line added, on p 103, after cancellation of an introductory question: "Which are beauties sweetest dress". The poem began as question and answer, was changed to pure answer.

11 in women]   of women *1st rdg p 103*

17 that————]   that place *1st rdg p 107;* that man *2nd rdg p 107.*   (Was the long dash put in to avoid writing "palace"? See "London" line 12.)

18 Youll]   Twill *1st rdg del, p 99*

*

The Fairy   N 105 rev

Title]   The Marriage Ring *1st rdg del*

7 step]   tread *1st rdg del*
15 But]   And *1st rdg del*
18–20 Hes my butterfly
And a marriage ring
Is a foolish thing *1st rdg*

Hes my butterfly
& Ive pulld out the Sting
And a marriage ring
Is a childs play thing *2nd rdg*

The sequence can be made out because the first changes were made in pale ink, the later in dark ink. The title change was made in pale ink and indicates the striking change of emphasis in the revisions of 18–20. In the first draft the tenor is that the fairy's belief in the power of the ring is shown by my act of catching him: the fact that he's my fly proves the ring foolish. The second reading is ambiguous, with emphasis swinging toward the speaker: I have pulled out the sting of the superstition and rendered the ring powerless. In the final version (given in the text, above) the change from "&" to "For" renders the act undated, or predated: *Because* I have (already) destroyed the beguiling power of marriage, I can capture the fairy, without binding him. He can remain a winged joy, my butterfly.

*

The Kid   N 105 rev

&c] *written over a capital* D
No further trace of the poem is found.

*

"My Spectre around me night & day"   N 3, 2 (originally 13, 12)

Lines 1–32 on p 3, the rest on p 2
3 My]   I *1st rdg del*
The first stanza is followed by two deleted stanzas, the first numbered "2", the
second "4" then "5":

2

[*Her*] <Thy> weeping [*she*] <thou> shall neer give oer
I sin against [*her*] <thee> more & more
And never will from sin be free
Till she forgives & comes to me

[4] [<5>]

Thou hast parted from my side
Once thou wast a virgin bride
Never shalt thou a [*lover*] <true love> find
My Spectre follows thee Behind

Two stanzas to replace these, subsequently deleted also, were written alongside:

[2]

[[*To*] *In a dark cold winter night*]
<*A deep winter* [*night*] *dark & cold*>
[*Within my* [*loves*] *Heart*]
Within my heart thou didst unfold
A Fathomless & boundless deep
There we wander, there we weep

[3] [<4>]

1 When my Love did first begin
2 Thou didst call that Love a Sin
3 Secret trembling night & day
4 Driving all my Loves away

Perhaps the numbering of lines was intended to restore lines 3 and 4, which had been
heavily canceled.
Later these stanzas were lined through and levied upon for the final second stanza,
written last on p 2 but at once numbered "2".
Stanza 3 was written fourth, then meant as second (after deletion of the 2nd and
3rd), then numbered 5, then 6, and finally 3.
13–16 Dost . . . tears]   This stanza was written alongside stanza 3 and numbered "3" (when that was 2), then "6"; then it was canceled, but then numbered "4"
and inscribed "To come in".
13 Dost]   Didst *1st rdg del*
19, 22 tombs] *mended from* tomb (The "Loves" first lay in a single "tomb".)
These and the remaining stanzas went through several renumberings but without
change of relative position.
26 Crown . . . head] *written over a long line* (the first word of which was
"Pity" or "Pitying")
32 as I forgive]   & I forgive *1st rdg*

33–56   These stanzas on p 2 were numbered (and perhaps written) only after those on p 3 had been reduced to the final eight given in our text.

In stanza 11 a reversal of person from second to first is made during or immediately after composition (in the same ink and pen):

41 Till I]   Till thou *1st rdg*
42 root]   dig *1st rdg del*   Infernal] *mended from* infernal
43 I shall]   Thou shalt *1st rdg del*
45 And]   *written over* ?I

53–56   This stanza, numbered 14, is in pencil; so are the following four, the first two of which are numbered 1 and 2 as if to begin a new poem. I have so treated them.

[Postscript]

Here too there is a shift of pronouns, with the accusation now directed back to "Thou".

1 my Sins Thou]   thy Sins I *1st rdg*
2 Hast . . . own]   Have I no sins of my own *1st rdg*
3 my Sins thou]   thy Sins I *1st rdg*
4 thy]   my *1st rdg del*

*

"Mock on Mock on Voltaire Rousseau"   N 7 (originally 9)

7 blind]   *written over* mo (for "mock")   mocking] *mended from* mockers

*

Morning   N 12 (originally 8)

*

"Terror in the house does roar"   N 12 (originally 8)

*

The Birds   N 14 (originally 6)

*

"I will tell you what Joseph of Arimathea"   N 52

*

"Why was Cupid a Boy"   N 56

9 And]   Then *1st rdg del*
10 the Cupid Girls]   surely a Womans *1st rdg del*
11 cant interpret the thing]   never learns so much *1st rdg del*

*

"Now Art has lost its mental Charms"   N 79

1 Now]   When *1st rdg del*
8 War]   Armies *1st rdg del*
12 thee . . . the Ungrateful]   thy works . . . Britains *1st rdg del*
13 Isle]   Shore *1st rdg del*
14 smile]   roar *1st rdg del*

*

TO THE QUEEN

Dedication of the edition of Blair's *Grave* illustrated by Blake's drawings (engraved by Louis Schiavonetti) and published by R. H. Cromek, 1808.

*

[From Blake's Notebook]

"The Caverns of the Grave Ive seen"   N 87

```
 1 Caverns]    Visions 1st rdg del
 3 But]    Shed 1st rdg del
 5 What]    Egr (for Egremonts) 1st rdg del
 6 dauntless]    dare to 1st rdg del
 7 Can]    dare 1st rdg del
 8 flames]    waves 1st rdg del
11 Noble]    worthy 1st rdg del
15 unchangd]    shall still 1st rdg del
```

*

"I rose up at the dawn of day"   N 89

```
10 Friends &]    Friendship 1st rdg del
13–20 marginal insertion
17 For my]    For all that my 1st rdg
23 So as]    So as sure as 1st rdg
24 for]    of 1st rdg del
```

*

[A Separate Manuscript]

"A fairy skipd upon my knee"

A leaf in the Rosenwald Collection; on the back is a drawing of The Infant Hercules.

1 skipd]   *written above and partly on top of* leapt 1st rdg

*

[With Blake's Illustrations to Gray's *Poems*]

"Around the Springs of Gray my wild root weaves"

*

To Mrs Ann Flaxman

These two poems are inscribed in Blake's volume of watercolor illustrations to Gray's *Poems,* conjectured to have been given to Mrs. Flaxman in 1800.

～

[The Pickering Manuscript]

A collection made for some friend or patron: fair copies of 10 poems inscribed by Blake on 11 leaves, paginated by him 1–22; owned by B. M. Pickering in 1866; freshly collated through the courtesy of the present owner, Mrs Landon K. Thorne.

Date: The poems appear to belong to the late Felpham period; Sampson (p 267) argues a date of about 1803 (*Mary* was obviously written before that August) and observes that they "have a certain unity of their own"—but this might be due to selection rather than to composition within a brief period. They are all ballads, ranging from the lyrical to the gnomic.

*

The Golden Net

The draft in the Notebook (p 14, originally p 6) obviously precedes this version, and I treat its variants as abandoned (though not lined through). Yet its added opening line, "Beneath the white thorn lovely May", and its elimination of the "Whither young Man" line may represent revisions made *after* the Pickering fair copy.

3-4   Lines added during revision of N.
5-13   In their original sequence; but at one time Blake numbered these lines 3,4,5,6,1,2,7,8,9; at one time he canceled lines 11-14.
6 iron wire]   sweet desire *1st rdg del* N
7 tears & sighs]   sighs & tears *1st rdg* N
11-14   Lines canceled in N; replaced in adjacent column by:
Wings they had [& *when they chose*] <that soft inclose>
<Round their body when they chose>
They would let them down at will
Or make translucent *also canceled*
20 on]   by N
21 Over]   Oer N
23 Burning]   flame *1st rdg del* N; flaming *final rdg* N
24 Iron Wire]   sweet desire *1st rdg del* N
26 O when will the]   When O when will *1st rdg* N

*

The Mental Traveller

A neat copy but not exactly "fair copy"; parts or all of the following lines are written over extensive erasures: 57, 84, 89-90.

84 roams the Lion Wolf & Boar]   Keynes silently emends to "roam", but the singular verb may not be a mistake: the female flees "like the . . . Stag", the male "pursues her" as Lion Wolf & Boar "Till he becomes a . . . Babe", all metamorphoses of one person.
96 Every]   *mended from* every

*

Mary

Compare verses in the letter of 16 August 1803 (below), where Blake *applies* the sixth stanza to "my Present state" and hence must be writing after its composition.

6 Golden]   *mended from* golden
22 Envious]   *mended from* envious

*

The Crystal Cabinet

8 lovely]   *written over erasure*

*

The Grey Monk

Derived from a much longer draft in the Notebook (p 12) from which the 7 stanzas in *Jerusalem* 52 were later taken. In the following tally of variants (excluding differences of capitalization) N represents the Notebook draft. Stanzas 2 and 8 are variants of stanzas 3 and 7 of *Jerusalem*. Originally the 8th page in the Notebook, this poem immediately preceded "Mock on . . .".

2 die]   will die N
4 the Stony Bed]   her stony bed N
11–12   Identical to final rdg N, developed from a deleted line: "From his dry tongue these accents flow" (N)
15 the writing I wrote]   that All I wrote N
16 lovd]   love N
19 I mockd]   [*But*] I mockd N
20 mocks]   mocks at N
22 marched]   is marched N
23 armd]   armed N
24 avenge]   revenge N
29 a Tear]   the tear N
31 of the Martyrs]   for anothers *1st rdg del* N
33 found the Bed]   sought the bed N
36]   And usurpd the tyrants throne & bed *1st rdg del* N

*

Auguries of Innocence

A fair copy but a hasty one, with much mending of letters, especially initial capitals in lines 119–124. It is conceivable that Blake, at greater leisure, might have rearranged the lines (as was his wont) in a less desultory sequence. Following the lead of John Sampson (p 287), who printed the text in ms order followed by a "revised version for those who may prefer to read the poem as a whole, instead of as a number of disconnected proverb-couplets", and assisted by the specific suggestions of Jack Grant (in correspondence), I have presented a thematically grouped rearrangement, after the ms transcript. I concede that Blake may have wished each reader to cope with this "Riddle" by himself.

126 see not Thro]   see With *1st ms rdg*

*

Long John Brown & Little Mary Bell

The words "Long" and "Little" were added to the title as an afterthought. These words were also added in the first stanza, depriving Mary of the adjective "Pretty" and John of "Young" (though not—an oversight perhaps—in lines 8 and 9).

❧

VI. [SATIRIC VERSES AND EPIGRAMS]

[From Blake's Notebook]

The abbreviation N (Notebook) indicates pages written in right-side up; "N rev" indicates pages written in when reversed.

*

Motto to the Songs of Innocence & of Experience   N 101 rev

*

"Let the Brothels of Paris be opened'"   N 99 rev

These four stanzas and the three "Fayette" stanzas that follow are generically related but constitute in effect separate poems, the first canceled in favor of the second,
but the second also abandoned in the sense that it was left in the Notebook and given no
title.

3 Physicians]   Pestilence *1st rdg del*
8 [*So*] Every . . . slaughtering]   Followed by another quatrain written as three
lines and immediately deleted:
>   Damn praying & singing
>   Unless they will bring in
>   The blood of ten thousand by fighting or swinging
9 a great & solemn Oath]   a great Oath *1st rdg*
16 Famine]   *word del but not replaced*
18 And . . . robe]   followed by a deleted couplet:
>   But the bloodthirsty people across the water
>   Will not submit to the gibbet & halter
20 And . . . suckers . . . around] replacing a canceled line:
>   There is just such a tree at Java found
Stanza 4 ("The King awoke") was written as the 2nd stanza, followed by stanza 2
and the first couplet of 3 (the Oath business). Blake then numbered twelve of these
lines to make the "King" stanza the 3rd and the "Oath" couplet followed by the
"quartering/slaughtering" couplet the 2nd, thus temporarily abandoning the "Nobodaddy" couplet. But then he added lines 11–12 (the "hell/bell" couplet) and numbered
his four stanzas in the order printed above, then or later adding the fifth stanza.
Finally he canceled stanzas 2 and 3 with vertical lines and also drew lines through his
stanza and line numbers, apparently meaning to cancel this whole portion of the
work in favor of the Fayette stanzas that were added below.

*

"Who will exchange his own fire side"   N 99–98 rev

Below the last stanza of the preceding poem, and perhaps originally as a continuation of it although now separated by a horizontal line, Blake wrote and then deleted
the following:
>   Fayette Fayette thourt bought & sold
>   For well I see thy tears
>   Of Pity are exchangd for those
>   Of selfish slavish fears
Perhaps before deleting this stanza (just possibly before writing it) he wrote three
stanzas in the adjacent column, guided by a line to precede it—or replace it:

>   Fayette beside King Lewis stood
>   He saw him sign his hand
>   And soon he saw the famine rage
>   About the fruitful land

>   Fayette beheld the Queen to smile
>   And wink her lovely eye
>   And soon he saw the pestilence
>   From street to street to fly

[1] Fayette beheld the King & Queen
     In tears & iron bound
     But mute Fayette wept tear for tear
     And guarded them around

At some point the first two of these stanzas were firmly crossed out and the third numbered "1"; later that number was lined through, perhaps when the stanza was recopied on p 98.

At the top of p 98 Blake began afresh, abandoning everything on p 99 that he did not repeat here:

     [*Fayette beside his banner stood*]
     [*His captains false around*]
     [*Thourt bought & sold*]

[3] Who will exchange his own fire side
     For the steps of anothers door
     Who will exchange his wheaten loaf
     For the links of a dungeon floor

Though only the numeral "3" of this stanza is deleted, the whole stanza is rewritten farther down the page.

But first Blake tried two lines of a variant, immediately canceled, and then four lines, later numbered "2" and later still crossed out:

     [*Who will exchange his own hearts blood*]
     [*For the drops of a harlots eye*]

2   Will the mother exchange her new born babe
     For the dog at the wintry door
     Yet thou dost exchange thy pitying tears
     For the links of a dungeon floor

Before this stanza was deleted and before deletion of the numbers "1" and "3" alongside earlier stanzas, Blake had his first version of a three-stanza poem of Fayette and King and Queen. But he went on to write a new first stanza:

                    I
     Fayette Fayette thourt bought & sold
     And sold is thy happy morrow
     Thou gavest the tears of Pity away
     In exchange for the tears of sorrow

Before crossing this out Blake wrote "2" beside the first line, then "1" on top of that. But then leaving a ¾ inch space he began afresh, inscribing the three stanzas printed in our text—first the Fayette stanza, then the "fire side" stanza, then the "wintry seas" stanza. He then renumbered them "2", "3", "1"; then changed the "3" to "1" and vice versa, producing the sequence we have used.

While superficially the ms gives the appearance of a great many stanzas, sufficient to compose another Chattertonian ballad like "Gwin, King of Norway", it can be seen that with the Fayette stanzas Blake almost at once was aiming at a three-stanza triptich, a tableau poem of three mute figures like the three in the frontispiece of *Visions of the Daughters of Albion*—or the three *Accusers* (see Inscriptions). Most of his energy on these two manuscript pages, once the Fayette-King-Queen idea has grown out of the "Brothels" poem, is expended on arranging and rearranging a few simple rhetorical questions around the central frozen image of a moment of betrayal located at the storm center of the French Revolution.

2 stone]   steps *1st rdg del*
6 curses]   tears *1st rdg del*
10 & Pity]   Or Pity *1st rdg*

*

"When Klopstock England defied"   N 5 (originally 1) (pencil)

Date: ca 1797–99, for Blake would leave Lambeth in 1800. Klopstock had been declaring to English visitors that their language was incapable of the epic grandeur of hexameters, and he had spoken with scorn of English writers' coarseness of tone traceable to Swift. Blake defiantly glories in his English tone in the present satire. When he "sat down to write" it was evidently the "strong heroic verse" of *Vala*: compare "terrible Blake" and the "oath that made heavn quake" (lines 2 and 5) with the "terrible Sentence" and heaven quaking of the opening lines of *Vala*.

2 Uprose]   Up *mended from* Wi
10 himself]   self *is an insertion above the line*
13–14 *added in margin*
15 intripled]   ninefold *1st rdg del*   16 churn]   burn *1st rdg del*
17 And]   They *1st rdg del*   round] *mended from* around
29 From pity then]   Then after *1st rdg del*
30 removed]   *inserted above the line*
31 rose up from]   sat down to *1st rdg del*
31–32 written in margin to replace the following two lines, canceled with two slanting strokes:

     If thus Blake could Shite
     What Klopstock did write

*

On the Virginity of the Virgin Mary & Johanna Southcott
                            N 6 (originally 2)

2 swear it so]   tell you so *1st rdg*

*

"You dont believe . . ."   N 21

8 Nature] *first written with lower-case* n
11   After "said" Blake first wrote "Rich", showing that he had in mind Jesus' advice to the rich man.

*

"If it is True . . ."   N 33

10 that they might make]   to make *1st rdg*   (Blake evidently preferred to avoid a hexameter. Two extra feet in the line seemed better than one.)

*

"I am no Homers Hero you all know"   N 31

*

"The Angel that presided . . ."   N 32

2 formd of Joy & Mirth]   thou art formd for Mirth *1st rdg*
3 King] *mended from* Thing (but not very clear)

*

"Some Men created for destruction come"   N 36

3 Be they as Vile . . . can]   Friend Caiaphas is one do what he can *1st rdg del*
4 Theyll]   He'll *1st rdg del*

– 781 –

*

"If I eer Grow to Mans Estate"   N 39

*

From Cratetos   N 64

*

"If Men will act like a maid . . ."   N 65

5 fie fie]   O no *1st rdg del*   you shant]   neer shall *1st rdg del*
6 In spite]   For now *1st rdg del*

*

"Anger & Wrath my bosom rends"   N 23

*

An Epitaph   N 37

*

Another   N 37

*

Another   N 37

*

"He is a Cock would"   N 29

1–2   *1st rdg:*
He is a Cock wont
And would be a Crow if he could

*

"And his legs carried it . . ."   N 22

These lines seem to begin in medias res. Written as a fair copy, then emended, they are probably only part of an earlier draft. Insertion of the name Stewhard (Stothard) in line 8 identifies the speaker; "my Soul" in line 6 is Stewhard's. The "Man of Men" is Screwmuch (Cromek), whose death in March 1812 compels a later date for the poem than Keynes's "about 1808–1811". Rose (Billy's Lawyer) died in 1804; Schiavonetti (Assassinetti) in June 1810. Stothard's anticipated death did not come till 1834.

8 So Stewhards Soul]   he would bear my soul *1st rdg del*
14 Stewhards]   all my *1st rdg del*
15–30 *marginal addition*
16 trembling for the affront]   Deadly the affront *1st rdg del*
25 Jack Hemps Parson]   my Parson *1st rdg*   Who was the parson of Jack Hemp (Flaxman) and of Stothard—or of either in some sense?
41 laughing]   mocking *1st rdg del*
42 Recievd the Contents]   what one writes on the back of a note when it is paid, i.e. a promissory note.
43–44   *1st rdg:*
But I have writ with tears of aqua fortis
His Epitaph so sorrowful my thought is

46 our friend]   your friend *1st rdg*

51 Here lies Stewhard the Friend of All &c]   Here Blake is putting into Stewhard's mouth the three "Epitaphs" just above, which perhaps should be considered part
of the present poem, changing "John Thompson" and "John Trot" to Tom Stewhard.   Friend of]   Lord of *1st rdg del*

*

"Was I angry with Hayley who usd me so ill"   N 23

2 followed by deleted line, the last word unfinished:
       Or angry with Boydell or Bowyer or Ba[sire]
5 Macklin or Boydel or Bowyer]   Boydell or Bowyer or Basire *1st rdg del*
6 *written over erased line:*
       Mirths all your sufferings convey sir

*

Blakes apology for his Catalogue   N 62–63, 65

First and much revised draft on pp 62 and 63; title on p 62; fair copy, without title,
on p 65; Keynes, pp 595–596, separates out the first draft (with one mistake, the including of "with joy" in line 4), gives a composite of first and revised drafts on
pp 554–555, and the fair copy on pp 555–556, but without all Blake's renumbering of
lines for rearrangement.

Here we give the fair copy, with only a selection of earlier readings in the notes:

2 Bartolloze]   feather Pillows *1st rdg del*
8]   How many Thousand Connoisseurs ran raving *1st rdg*
10 Cries]   Says *1st rdg*
11–12 added first on p 63 (as direct statement)
11 Some say] *added in fair copy*
12 that] *added in fair copy*   nose]   toes *1st rdg del*
17 looking quite]   Tom Cooke proves *1st rdg del;* Looking up *2nd rdg*
Skumference]   Circumference *1st rdg del*
20   The following del lines in the revised 1st draft were evidently meant as
a paraphrase of the *Examiner's* attack:
       who cries all art is a fraud & Genius a trick
       And Blake is an unfortunate Lunatic
The title was then crowded in above this addition, "Blakes apology" being his defense
against the *Examiner.*

*

"Cosway Frazer & Baldwin . . ."   N 37

7 tother]   one *1st rdg del*
8 Virtuous]   Righteous *1st rdg del*

*

"My title as [a] Genius . . ."   N 38

1 as a genius]   as an [Artist] <Genius> *ms rdg*

*

To H   N 25

Apparently to Robert Hunt, who criticized Fuseli in *The Examiner.*

*

"P—— loved me not . . ."　　N 34

Plausibly identified in Keynes as "Phillips", the publisher.

*

"The Sussex Men are Noted Fools"　　N 24

3 H—— the painter] interpreted as "Haines" by Keynes, only a plausible guess

*

"Of H s birth . . ."　　N 27

The biographical evidence is clear that H and H——y in this and the following verses stand for Hayley.

*

On H——ys Friendship　　N 35

4　　A peck of poisons not a peck of salt *1st rdg*

*

To H——　　N 37

*

On H—— the Pick thank　　N 41

*

Imitation of Pope . . .　　N 37

*

William Cowper Esqre　　N 50

This poem, now truncated, began as an "Epitaph for William Cowper Esqre". "Epitaph for" was deleted, as were the first four lines beginning "Here lies the Man". The second line appears to end "Hayley & History" or "Hayley & Victory". The whole passage seems to have named Hayley as a callous friend of Cowper, confounded by Cowper's death and by the bookseller Johnson's commission to write his biography. Blake's thorough erasure of these four lines does not necessarily indicate a change of heart toward Hayley, for what Blake wrote in with a heavy pen to cover the erasure was the four-line outburst (next following) which names *Fuseli* as the only humane man "that eer I knew".

3 movd] *mended from* moved
4 provd] *mended from* proved
9 atrocious]　　most wicked

*

"The only Man that eer I knew"　　N 50

4 dear Christian Friends]　　sweet Christians *1st rdg del*

*

"Madman I have been calld . . ."   N 25

*

To F——   N 26

Flaxman, of course, to whom the following poem must initially be addressed.

*

"Hes a Blockhead . . ."   N 26

2 tries]   seeks *1st rdg del*

*

To Nancy F——   N 27

Mrs Anna Flaxman, wife of John Flaxman.

*

To F——   N 35

*

"S—— in Childhood . . ."   N 27

Thomas Stothard; see "Stewhard" lines above.

*

"He has observd the Golden Rule"   N 30

Written over portions of four erased lines which consist of two variants of the couplet which becomes the center of the six lines "To S————d" that follow at the bottom of the page, but here given a title later absorbed into the poem:

The Golden Rule.

?I ?sport ?with ?Fortune ?merry ?Blithe & gay
Like to the Lion sporting with his prey

With Fortune sporting Merry Blithe & gay
Like to the Lion sporting with his prey
a Sparrow

The first erased words may have been "He sports"; the second erased couplet is in the form of a prepositional phrase which might modify "He" in the Golden Rule couplet; but in the final version, below, the blithe and the golden persons take opposite voices in a dialogue.

*

To S   d   N 30

To Stothard. Combining the erased and unerased couplets at the top of the page. First written *of* Stothard.

1 You all your Youth]   He all his Youth *1st rdg*
2 youre]   hes *1st rdg del*   golden]   *written over* old *or* olden
5 Take you]   He has *1st rdg del;* Make thou *2nd rdg del*   you may wear]   he may wear *1st rdg del;* thou maist wear *2nd rdg*
6 your Share]   his share *1st rdg;* thy share *2nd rdg*

*

On S——   N 36

On Stothard.

2 Whose]   His *1st rdg del*
4 By . . . get Fat]   On . . . feed Fat *1st rdg del*
In his *Descriptive Catalogue*, p 33, Blake adapted the second couplet to a proverb
suitable for prose quotation, by removing the rhyme:
>The fox, the owl, the spider, and the mole
>By sweet reserve and modesty get fat.

*

"old acquaintance . . ."   N 24

1 old acquaintance well renew]   ?Look xxx xxxxx Flaxman & Stothard do *1st
rdg del*   The first three words are badly erased, but the meaning may be guessed:
Look how scurvilly my Calibans behave. And possibly Blake meant to retain the first
two words in his new line: "Look how (or what) old acquaintance we'll renew".

*

On F—— & S——   N 34

Flaxman & Stothard. First written "To F—— & S——".

1 them . . . them]   *mended from* thee . . . thee
2 they know neither themselves]   thou knowst neither thyself *1st rdg*
4 Fool . . . Knave]   *mended from* knave . . . Fool
In his *Descriptive Catalogue*, p 34, Blake adapted the first couplet to a proverb
suitable for prose quotation, by removing the rhyme:
>I found them blind: I taught them how to see;
>And, now, they know me not, nor yet themselves.

*

Mr Stothard to Mr Cromek   N 31

First written "Mr Cromek to Mr Stothard", but it can hardly have worked that way.
4 Backbiting]   Calumny *1st rdg del*

*

"Cro—— loves artists as . . ."   N 29

2 He loves the Art]   Cr—— loves Art *1st rdg*

*

"A Petty sneaking Knave I knew"   N 29

*

Cromek Speaks   N 41

The second couplet is an afterthought.

2 his judgment is so very Cool]   I know he always judges Cool *1st rdg*
4 Amiable state]   Because we know *1st rdg del*

*

English Encouragement of Art   N 41

Blake first wrote a "straight" version of his interpretation of Cromek's ideas. He then inserted the subtitle "Cromeks opinions put into Rhyme" and tampered with the words in a punning burlesque of the speaker's pronunciation and thoughts. I follow Keynes in separating the two versions; but Keynes adds as part of the first reading the four lines I treat as the second stanza of the following poem. That poem uses some of the same ideas and images but within a different frame. (Yet the whole second poem is still Cromekian and a kind of postscript to the first.)

It is too bad to lose from either reading the second and intermediate reading of "great multitud", namely "great Madjority".

[First reading]

3 multitud]   Madjority *2nd rdg del*   (Deleted because the final reading makes a different statement)

[Final reading]

2 Menny wouver] *Cromekian for* maneuver
4 Jenous] *Cromekian for* Genius (and "Je nous"?)   ham] *Cromekian for* them   [Compare "Pant" and "Panted" in the third item following.]

*

"When you look at a picture . . ."   N 41

4 Jenny suck awa'] *for* Je ne sais quois

*

"The Cunning sures & the Aim at yours"   N 40

*

"All Pictures thats Panted . . ."   N 40

Blake is inconsistent in his burlesque, mixing "Panted", "Painted", and "Pant", but we are hardly faced by mere misspellings. Note the rhyme "Thought/Groat".

*

"You say their Pictures . . ."   N 42

4 To be Flogd . . . Fool]   To learn to admire the works of a Fool *1st rdg del*

*

"The Errors of a Wise Man . . ."   N 42

*

"Great things are done . . ."   N 43

*

"If you play a Game of Chance . . ."   N 47

*

"No real Style of Colouring . . ."   N 21

4 All has taken Wing]   tis quite another Thing *1st rdg del*

*

"Can there be any thing more mean"   N 26

3–4 what / That Man]   that / Which he *1st rdg del*
5 Reynolds Lectures Exactly so]   This Reynolds Lectures plainly shew *1st rdg*

*

"Sir Joshua Praises Michael Angelo"   N 28

The ms is a welter of revisions, hardly worth reporting here. Line 3 originally began
"Printing his praises", an allusion to the printed Discourses.

*

"Sir Jo[s]hua praised Rubens . . ."   N 29

6 As Crooked limbs & louzy heads of hair]   Like a filthy infectious head of hair
1st rdg del; A Crooked Stick & louzy head of hair *2nd rdg del*

*

Florentine Ingratitude   N 32

6   Followed by four lines several times revised and finally deleted:
      They said Thus Learning <& Politeness> from England [<& *Polite-*
      ness>] *was sent* <we fetch>
      [[*I*] <*We*> *thought Michael Angelo did never*] <For No good Artist will
      or Can> [*Paint*] Sketch
      And tis English Politeness as fair as [*your*] <*my*> Aunt
      To [*say*] [*write*] speak [*Michael Angelo*] <Any other word> & [*mean*]
      <Act> Rembrandt
13   Is This Politeness or is it Cant *1st rdg del*

*

A Pitiful Case   N 33

Pitiful]   *mended from* Pitiable

7 did howl &]   was heard to *1st rdg del*

*

To the Royal Academy   N 33

6 for it is fit]   & you will know *1st rdg del*
7–8 *1st rdg del:*
      That Sir Joshua never wishd to speak
      Of Michael Angelo
7 meer common]   either sense or *1st rdg del*

*

"The Cripple every step . . ."   N 39

4 Pain him & Modest Doubt]   Keynes read "Pain in Modest Doubt", and it is too
bad to lose that curious phrase from the Blake canon.
Line 4 first read:
      His pains are more than others theres no doubt

*

"I Rubens am a Statesman & a Saint"   N 38

1 I Rubens am . . . &]   Rubens had been . . . or *1st rdg*
2 *1st rdg del:*
  He mixd them both & so he Learnd to Paint

*

To English Connoisseurs   N 38

*

"Swelld limbs . . ."   N 38

*

A Pretty Epigram for the Entertainment . . .   N 38

To——— *1st title del*   Major Testament of ——— *2nd title del*   A Pretty
Epigram [*To*] for those who have Given high Prices for Bad Pictures and Never
a *3rd title del*
final title for the]   for those *1st rdg*   have Paid]   pay *1st rdg del*

*

"These are the Idiots chiefest arts"   N 38

Lines 1–2 were written as 5–6 and then numbered to come first. An original first
line, "Let it be told", was deleted.

*

"Rafael Sublime Majestic . . ."   N 39

2 Executive Power]   Execution *1st rdg del*
5 Laborious]   wobly pretentious *1st rdg;* high labourd pretentious *2nd rdg del*

*

On the Great Encouragement . . .   N 40

Given] *mended from* ?giving
2 Sword or]   Button *1st rdg del;*   Cutlass]   Bauble *1st rdg del;* Buckle
2nd rdg del   a dagger or]   a Bead or a *1st rdg del*
3 Taught]   wise *1st rdg del;* Learned *2nd rdg del*   spends]   gives *1st rdg
del*
4 *1st rdg:*
  For a Smear or a Squall that is not Picture nor Tune

*

"Give pensions to the Learned Pig"   N 40

*

"When I see a Rubens . . ."   N 43

3 question thus]   say to myself *1st rdg del*
6 O pray]   we pray *1st rdg*
7 than be]   than let *1st rdg*

*

"Delicate Hands & Heads . . ."   N 46

Blake's "Book of Moonlight" has never been found.

*

"I askd my Dear Friend Orator Prigg"   N 60

At the end the ms reads "&c / to come in Barry a Poem", an indication that these verses are but a patch made for a poem (now lost, or never finished) on the rebellious Academician James Barry.

6 puffing his cheeks he replied]   smild like a Cherub & said *1st rdg del*
10 smile like a Cherub & say]   nod wink & smile & reply *1st rdg*

*

"O dear Mother outline . . ."   N 61

A variant of the preceding stanzas, perhaps meant to replace them, perhaps to follow them, in "Barry a Poem".

1–2   Then Reynolds said O woman most sage
        O dear Mother outline be not in a Rage *1st rdg*
3 mispunctuated in Keynes; the sense would require: "And what is the second—to Please & Engage?"

*

To Venetian Artists   N 61

Lines 1–2 are an insertion written on p 60 and followed by the link "Perhaps this little Fable &c".
8 one Generalizing Tone]   heres two for one *1st rdg*; what a brilliant tone *2nd rdg del*
9–10   *a marginal insertion*
11 Snap. Snap! he has]   He snapd & *1st rdg del;* Then he snapd & *2nd rdg del*
14 Those who taste colouring]   Ive tasted shadow & *1st rdg del*

*

"Great Men & Fools . . ."   N 63 rev

*

"Some people admire . . ."   N 70

*

"Her whole Life is an Epigram . . ."   N 101 rev

*

"When a Man has Married . . ."   N 4 (originally 14)

*

"Grown old in Love . . ."   N 54

*

"The Hebrew Nation . . ."   N 39

*

To God   N 73

*

"Since all the Riches . . ."   N 73

1 World]   Earth *1st rdg del*
4 Worldly]   Worldly *1st rdg del;* Earthly *2nd rdg del*

*

"To Chloes breast young Cupid . . ."   N 78

*

"Nail his neck to the Cross . . ."   N 79

*

"A Woman Scaly . . ."   N 93

*

The Washer Womans Song   N 43

❧

VII. THE EVERLASTING GOSPEL

Nine widely scattered entries in Blake's Notebook, three sections in a separate scrap of paper, and one cue line indicating a lost section are treated by Keynes as a single but unfinished poem, with "Supplementary Passages" (on the separate scrap). A table of all 13 sections, lettered *a* to *m* for convenience, follows:

Sections in Blake's Notebook (N)

a (opposing Visions of Christ) N 33
b (Was Jesus Gentle) N 100–101
c (Was Jesus Humble) N 98
d (Was Jesus Humble, revised) N 52–54 (headed "The Everlasting Gospel" and concluded with the total "78 lines" and a catch line to cue in section *e*)
e (Was Jesus Chaste) N 48–52 (concluded with the total "94 lines")
f (This Jesus will not do) N 54 (a couplet written marginally near the end of section *d*)
g (Seeing this False Christ) N 52 (a couplet written below *e* and followed by a catch phrase "What are those &c" [*m*])
h (Did Jesus teach doubt) N 48 (two couplets written sideways in pencil in the margin of *e*, probably but not necessarily related to a pencil note along the top of the page: "This was spoke by My Spectre to Voltaire Bacon &c"—the note a comment on, not a part of, the poem: by juxtaposition a comment on *e* but logically related to *h*; yet the "&c" may be a cue to a lost passage to be brought in)
i (Virgin Pure) N 120 (fourth page of a small fold of paper sewed in at the end of the Notebook—a scrap salvaged from the inner margins of a sheet printed for the fourth Hayley Ballad of 1802)

Sections not attached to the Notebook

j (Covenant of Jehovah) Prose paragraph (in pencil on page 1 of a folded leaf of 1818 note paper in the Rosenbach Foundation library; stitch-marks show that the sheet was once bound into some book, probably a notebook of its size, 9.6×16.3 cm, but not the Rossetti Notebook as has been conjectured)

k (If Moral Virtue) 14 lines (in ink, on page 4 of the same leaf, but marked "This to come first" and numbered "1")

l (What can this Gospel) 43 lines (in ink, on pages 2, 3, and the top of 4 of the same leaf, with inserted section number "2")

m (What are those) ? (section alluded to in *g* and presumably now lost, though just possibly, as Keynes suggests, an intended revision of lines 11 ff. of section *k*)

It is the present editor's conclusion that the order of composition was: *j, l, k, i, (m), a* (with some doubt), *e, g, h*(?), *b, c, d, f* (except that the lost *m*, if a variant of *k*, may have preceded *i*), and that the poet's intention may have been to reduce the poem to the sequence *d e b*, with *a* as a personal Epilogue. The other sections are given in full in the following notes, which attempt to reconstruct the sequence of composition. For a more extensive account see "Uprose Terrible Blake", in *From Sensibility to Romanticism: Essays Presented to Frederick A. Pottle,* Oxford University Press, New York 1965.

I take it that Blake began with the following prose paragraph in the vein of the Laocoön inscriptions:

[j]

PAGE 1 [PENCIL]

There is not one Moral Virtue that Jesus Inculcated but Plato & Cicero did Inculcate before him what then did Christ Inculcate. Forgiveness of Sins This alone is the Gospel & this is the Life & Immortality brought to light by Jesus. Even the Covenant of Jehovah, which is This If you forgive one another your Trespassas so shall Jehovah forgive you That he himself may dwell among you but if you Avenge you Murder the Divine Image & he cannot dwell among you [by his] because you Murder him he arises Again & you deny that he is Arisen & are blind to Spirit

Then he moved into ironic rhetorical questions in rhymed couplets:

[l]

PAGE 2 [INK]

> What can this Gospel of Jesus be
> What Life & Immortality
> What was [It] <it> that he brought to Light
> That Plato & Cicero did not write

Written in margin and guided in:

>   <The Heathen Deities wrote them all   5
>   These Moral Virtues great & small
>   What is the Accusation of Sin
>   But Moral Virtues deadly Gin>

PAGE 2 [CONTINUED]

> The Moral Virtues in their Pride
> Did [ove[r]] <oer> the World triumphant ride   10
> In Wars & Sacrifice for Sin
> And Souls to Hell ran trooping in
> The Accuser Holy God of All
> This Pharisaic Worldly Ball
> Amidst them in his Glory Beams   15
> Upon the Rivers & the Streams
> Then Jesus rose & said to [men] <Me>
> Thy Sins are all forgiven thee
> Loud Pilate Howld loud Caiphas Yelld
> When they the Gospel Light beheld   20
> [Jerusalem he said to me]

PAGE 3

  It was when Jesus said to Me
  Thy Sins are all forgiven thee
  The Christian trumpets loud proclaim
  Thro all the World in Jesus name   25
  Mutual forgiveness of each Vice
  And oped the Gates of Paradise
  The Moral Virtues in Great fear
  Formed the Cross & Nails & Spear
  And the Accuser standing by   30
  Cried out Crucify Crucify
  Our Moral Virtues neer can be
  Nor Warlike pomp & Majesty
  For Moral Virtues all begin
  In the Accusations of Sin   35
Marginal insertion
  <And [*Moral*] <all the Heroic> Virtues [*all*] <End>
  In destroying the Sinners Friend>
PAGE 3 CONTINUED
  Am I not Lucifer the Great
  And you my daughters in Great State
  The fruit of my Myster[i]ous Tree   40
  Of Good & Evil & Misery
PAGE 4

  And Death & Hell which now begin
  On every one who Forgives Sin

Note that the change of "men" to "Me" changed theory into drama. As the poem grows in later sections, the dramatic becomes increasingly dominant. But in the 1818 fragment the drama remains the static threefold scene: Christ and Lucifer arguing their opposite views before "Me" (Every man, or Blake). In a quickly deleted passage (the last line, p 2) Jesus was going to speak to Blake about Jerusalem, but the poem soon took other bearings. On the rest of p 4 Blake turned the initial prose paragraph into rhyme, and numbered and labeled this as his opening stanza:

[k]

PAGE 4 CONTINUED

  1 This to come first
  If Moral Virtue was Christianity
  Christs Pretensions were all Vanity
  And Caiphas & Pilate Men
  [*Of Moral*] <Praise Worthy> & the Lions Den
  And not the Sheepfold Allegories   5
  Of God & Heaven & their Glories
  The Moral Christian is the Cause
  Of the Unbeliever & his Laws
Two lines guided in from bottom of page:
  The Roman Virtues Warlike Fame
  Take Jesus & Jehovahs Name.   10
Stanza continued:
  For what is Antichrist but those
  Who against Sinners Heaven close
  With Iron bars in Virtuous State
  And Rhadamanthus at the Gate

Blake, still feeling his way but gaining momentum, began his next section (unless something intermediate is lost) on the fourth page of a folded piece of paper salvaged from the title page of one of the unsold Hayley Ballads of 1802 (on the first three pages of which he had written a notice of "Blakes Chaucer" in 1809). This folio scrap of paper is now bound into the Notebook but may not have been when it was written on:

[i]

NOTEBOOK PAGE 120:

Was Jesus Born of a Virgin Pure
With narrow Soul & looks demure
If he intended to take on Sin
The Mother should an Harlot been
Just such a one as Magdalen   5
With seven devils in her Pen
<Or were Jew Virgins still more Curst And more sucking
  devils nurst>
Or what was it which he took on
That he might bring Salvation   10
A Body subject to be Tempted
From neither pain nor grief Exempted
Or such a body as might not feel
The passions that with Sinners deal
Yes but they say he never fell   15
Ask Caiaphas for he can tell
He mockd the Sabbath & he mockd
The Sabbaths God & he unlockd
The Evil spirits from their Shrines
And turnd Fishermen to Divines   20

Inserted from bottom and margin of page, 6 lines crowded into 4:

[End(ed)] <Oerturnd> the Tent of Secret Sins & its Golden
cords & Pins Tis the Bloody Shrine of War
Pinnd around from Star to Star
Halls of Justice hating Vice Where the Devil Combs his Lice

These lines were first marked to go in after the "Ask Caiaphas" line but then moved to the present position. The original passage continues without stanza break:

He turnd the devils into Swine
That he might tempt the Jews to Dine
Since which a Pig has got a look
That for a Jew may be mistook   30
Obey your Parents what says he
Woman what have I to do with thee
No Earthly Parents I confess
I am doing my Fathers Business
He scornd [his] <Earths> Parents scornd [his] <Earths> God   35
And mockd the one & the others Rod
His Seventy Disciples sent
Against Religion & Government
They by the Sword of Justice fell
And him their Cruel Murderer tell   40
He left his Fathers trade to roam
A wandring Vagrant without Home
And thus he others labour stole
That he might live above Controll
The Publicans & Harlots he   45
Selected for his Company
And from the Adulteress turnd away
Gods righteous Law that lost its Prey

Keynes puts lines 17–48 into quotation marks, and perhaps Blake meant to quote Caiaphas on Jesus—but the informing voice is soon the Devil of Blake's "Memorable Fancy" of *The Marriage of Heaven and Hell*. There is more Blake than Caiaphas in the inserted lines on the "Bloody Shrine of War"; he is still feeling for the right form and tone.

Next, or concomitantly, he wrote another scrap, now lost, *m*.

Then, past the preliminaries, he turned to his main Notebook, by 1818 crammed with the drawings and essays and epigrams and songs of 30 years. Leafing forward from the front, Blake was not skipping any blanks of great size when he inscribed section *a* on page 33, though there were slightly larger spaces on 27, 28, and 30. Perhaps his first intention was a six-line stanza; the next eight lines are amplification, somewhat crowded in. After p 33 he might have used 44–45, but the next opening was ampler, with two open pages (48–49) and large blanks on 50–51 and smaller on 52–54. (As the poem took shape, Blake clustered his sections close together; if one argues for a late date for *j k l*, as truly "supplementary", one must account for their being written outside the Notebook when there was ample room for them on pp 44–45 and elsewhere. The same point applies to *i*, unless one argues improbably that the leaf was sewed into the Notebook before *i* was written on it.)

On 48–52 he wrote section *e*, rapidly, having found the poem's Socratic rhetorical pattern. The section concluded at first with lines 93–94, on p 52, and Blake counted up and inscribed his total as "94 lines", later adding 95–96 in an adjacent column. Immediately below this total he wrote 2½ lines, with an etcetera, meaning to bring in a passage from somewhere else (an indication that *m* was written before the Notebook entries:

[g]

PAGE 54

> Seeing this False Christ In fury & Passion
> I made my Voice heard all over the Nation
> What are those &ᵉ

We cannot reconstruct the "&ᵉ" (though it may possibly have been a variant of lines 11–14 of *k*: ". . . what is Antichrist but those . . ."). Nor can we be quite sure whether Blake next wrote *h*, *c*, or *b*, each working out the successful formula of *e* in application to another Moral Virtue: Humility (*c*), Gentility (*b*), and the philosophical "doubt" of Voltaire and company who "are constantly talking of the Virtues of the Human Heart" (*Jerusalem* 52):

[h]

PAGE 48

> Did Jesus teach doubt or did he
> Give any lessons of Philosophy
> Charge Visionaries with decieving
> Or call Men wise for not Believing

A related impulse, also in pencil, was the scribbling across the top of *e* on this page, "This was spoke [or *spoken*, if the trailing off of the stroke intends an *n*] by My Spectre to Voltaire Bacon &ᵉ"—the etcetera again signifying a lost passage to be brought in, perhaps.

There is some evidence that Blake wrote the Gentility section (*b*, on pages 100–101, the first large open space after *e*) before the Humility (*c*, in a narrow column on p 98). The spacing of the ms lines of *a*, *e*, *b* (and also *i*) is about 4 to 4½ to an inch, regardless of crowding, while *c* and its revision *d* are spaced about 5½ to 6 lines an inch.

As the handwriting shrinks, the mending, revision, and rearrangement of lines increase. The revised Humility section, *d*, amplified from 51 lines to "78 lines"—as Blake counted, going on with marginal insertions to make it 106—was fitted into the relatively narrow space on pp 52–54 following *e*. But then he decided to put *e* (Chastity) after *d* (Humility), cuing at the end of the latter section: "Was Jesus Chaste or did he &c", and writing a title for the poem in at the head of *d*: "The Everlasting Gospel". At about this point (in the book if not in time) he wrote a wry comment on this poem of true Christ which his devilish or Spectre voice was uttering:

[f]

PAGE 54

> I am sure This Jesus will not do
> Either for Englishman or Jew

And then he stopped. He did not mark the "Gentility" passage to come in, nor did he count its lines. The position of his title does not leave room for *a* to stand as Introduction. It remains for editorial judgment whether to consider "The Everlasting Gospel" as consisting of the Humility and Chastity sections alone, or whether to bring in the Gentility, perhaps anti-climactically, and the summary (*a*), at the end if anywhere: *d e b, a*. It does seem plain that the other segments must be thought of as abandoned rather than "additional" or "supplementary".

The variant readings of the included sections follow:

[d]

"Was Jesus Humble or did he"

Lines not in the first Humility section (*c*) are : 3–4, 21–24, 26–27, 31–58, 69–70, 85–106. Lines 12–17 were first written in the order 12 15 16 13 14 17.

25 betrays]   hates *1st rdg del* (also rdg on p 98)
29 For . . . honest triumphant Pride]   But . . . triumphant honest pride *rdg on p 98*
30 the cause that]   the Reason *rdg on p 98*
41 Bacon &]   Sir Isaac *1st rdg del*
58 Caiaphas hand]   *written over erasure, perhaps* the guilty
59 Antichrist]   the Antichrist *1st rdg* (also 1st rdg on p 98)
67–68   were in reverse order on p 98
73 If thou humblest thyself thou humblest me]   Why dost thou humble thyself to me *1st rdg on p 98, del*
84   followed by del couplet revised in lines 97–98:
> [All Corporeal lifes *a*] <This Corporeal <All> lifes> a fiction
> And is made up of Contradiction
87 I]   *written a*

[e]

"Was Jesus Chaste or did he"

10 sound of Jesus breath]   words of Jesus breath *1st rdg*
28 Devil]   God *1st rdg del*, the deletion and addition made in pencil, but firmly (as I previously failed to observe)
63 shame]   crime *1st rdg del*
85 Crying Crucify]   Crying Ive found hi[m] *1st rdg*
86 Who]   You *1st rdg del*
92 his glittring]   The antecedent is "the shadowy Man" of line 81.
95–96   were written in the next column and guided to come in.

[b]

"Was Jesus gentle or did he"

56 And put it off on the Cross & Tomb]   And on the Cross he Seald its doom *1st rdg del*

❧

VIII. [BLAKE'S EXHIBITION AND CATALOGUE OF 1809]

The Advertisement of the Exhibition, a single leaf printed on both sides, survives in only one copy, in the Bodleian Library, with the ms additions here enclosed in angle brackets.

The Advertisement of the Catalogue survives in a single copy.

[Advertisement of the Exhibition]

PAGE 1 Blake's quotation from the "Welch Triades" is traced by S. Foster Damon (see his *Dictionary* under WELSH) to No. LXXXV in the *Myvyrian Archailogy* (London 1801–7)— in which case "quotation" is the wrong term: Blake's first stanza is a free adaptation, his second an original addition.

❧

[The Catalogue]

This Catalogue of descriptive commentary on sixteen paintings ("Inventions") which Blake exhibited at his brother James's shop in Golden Square was included in the half-crown price of admission. It is the only work Blake actually published in printed form (if it is true that *Poetical Sketches* was printed for him by friends and never sold). It is alluded to, by the subtitle, in Blake's letter of 19 Dec 1808 to Cumberland as "an account of my various Inventions in Art, for which I have procured a Publisher" (i.e. the printer, D. N. Shury).

Address inserted in Blake's hand, in Huntington Library copy.

PAGE 64 want of idea] idea of want *printer's error* corrected by Blake by pen (Keynes, p 585)

❧

IX. [DESCRIPTIONS OF THE LAST JUDGMENT]

[The Design of The Last Judgment]

A letter of 1808 to Ozias Humphry, extant in three drafts, here consolidated by treating as deletions all words not in the final and briefest draft. For the separate drafts see *The Letters of William Blake*, ed. Geoffrey Keynes, London 1956, items 88, 89.

Adam & Eve kneeling in humiliation] So shown in the Petworth painting (in our illustration); "but Blake later changed his mind," notes Damon; "in the Rosenwald version [in Damon's illustration] they are standing . . ." (*Blake Dictionary*, under HUMILITY).

❧

[A Vision of The Last Judgment]

From Blake's Notebook, pages 68–72, 76–82, 84–87, 90–93. Deleted passages and insertions are indicated in the text, but insignificant deletions and mendings are ignored. The sequence of passages is not always certainly indicated by position or content; that worked out by Keynes is followed here.

Blake obviously contemplated holding another exhibition like the one of 1809, with another printed catalogue; he must have written these "Additions" "For the Year 1810" before convinced of the failure of the first exhibition.

PAGE 85 (SECOND PORTION) as a Female Will] Here Keynes adds "& Queens [of England *del.*]" from mistaking the position of a deleted passage that was written in the margin as an appendage to the sentence that follows.

❧

X. [BLAKE'S CHAUCER: PROSPECTUSES]

The two printed Prospectuses are in the British Museum.

The Notebook draft (pages 117–119) of the Second Prospectus is here combined with the printed text, since they are identical in the central portion. Matter found only in the draft is treated as deleted; words found only in the printed text are treated as insertions. (Both portions derive largely from *A Descriptive Catalogue.*)

❧

XI. [PUBLIC ADDRESS]

Untitled essay, referred to as "this Public Address" on p 56, written in scattered pages of Blake's Notebook. The inclusion of "Chaucers Canterbury Pilgrims" as a second title rests on the conjecture that "it may well belong to this essay, of which the engraving of *The Canterbury Pilgrims* is the ostensible subject", as Keynes observes. "It seems probable . . . that Blake was anticipating an announcement of the publication which he intended to work up from the raw materials" of these Notebook paragraphs. Keynes has made the first satisfactory attempt to weld these fragments into a unity, and his arrangement is followed with a few minor exceptions.

Date: 1809–10. If Blake had published these "Anecdotes of Artists" as he hopefully announces on p 56, it would have been in the spring of 1810 when he meant his Chaucer engraving to be finished; some of the notes were probably written in 1809, as the dated reminiscences reveal: the "little prints which I engraved after [Stothard] five & twenty years ago" (p 52) were issued in late 1784; the "thirty years" of the next paragraph probably refers to the beginning of Blake's efforts to find employment, in the fall of 1779. The second paragraph on p 67, however, must have been written after a dated memorandum which it skirts: "23 May 1810 found the Word Golden".

PAGE 52 a Poem concerning my Three years Herculean Labours at Felpham which I will soon Publish] A description which fits *Milton* better than *Vala* or *Jerusalem*
PAGE 62 end of paragraph] For the verses which Keynes prints here, see "Blakes apology for his Catalogue" (p 496) and textual notes (p 783).
PAGE 23 That Painted as well as Sculptured Monuments . . . the Lips of Pasch himself.] Elaborately deleted by rows of loops and strokes that turn into actual words, somewhat as follows:

  eeeeeeeeeeeeee WwwwwWThomas James Robert
  Cllllnnn AOOJlmm All Alls Hands british alls wwwndj Bluuu
  Laurelllo Affffsw Alllllll Hannalitoe WW BMillljjj Horses
  Ollllee W Hyyyiss Well saiithl Blake John Thomas f

Pasch himself was Count Pasch van Krienen, a Dutchman living in the Aegean, who in 1771 was commissioned captain of a Russian man-of-war and in 1773 published an account of inscriptions and sculptures on what he claimed were the sepulchers of

Germanico, Demos, Elpis, Lisaundro, Omero, Aristion, Promachida, Antenor, Efthinos, Efdigenos, Danae: *Breve Descrizione Dell' Arcipelago . . . Con un ragguaglio esatto di tutte le Antichita . . . e Specialmente DEL SEPOLCRO D'OMERO e d'altri celebri personaggi.* In Livorno 1773. (British Museum 10125.C.17.) I find no mention of painted sculptures in the book, however. Did Pasch visit London? Did Blake obtain this information from the lips of the Savant himself—and then discover his falsehood and so delete the paragraph? In the *Gentleman's Magazine* for August 1795, p 680, is a review of *The pretended Tomb of Homer . . . with Illustrations and Notes,* by C. Heyne, beginning: "Nothing more strongly marks the little progress made in literature by the modern Goths than the pretended discovery of the tomb of Homer, with *his skeleton, sitting, and a marble inkstand, a pen, a marble stylus, and a sharp stone, like a knife, before him,* in the island of Ios, or Nios, just where Paulus Silentiarius, in the time of Justinian, had, in an epigram, placed it. Count Pasch, of Krinen, captain of a Russian man of war, who discovered the *town* of Ephesus *entire under ground,* had made the discovery; . . .". The book itself, which I have not seen, may treat the matter soberly.

❦

XII. THE MARGINALIA

Most of the Lavater *Aphorisms* cited are given in full, but excerpts from the other works annotated have been trimmed to the bare minimum necessary to show the immediate context of Blake's remarks. Titles given below are somewhat simplified.

Annotations to *Aphorisms on Man,* Translated [by J. H. Fuseli] from the Original Manuscript of the Rev. John Casper Lavater, Citizen of Zuric. London: Printed for J. Johnson, St. Paul's Church-Yard. 1788 [1789]

The copy with Blake's annotations (and Samual Palmer's signature) is in the Huntington Library (HM 57431). The frontispiece, an engraving signed "Blake sc[ulpsit]", announces the book's purpose as a manual of self-discovery: ΓΝΩΘΕ ΣΕΑΤΤΟΝ. Though the prefatory Advertisement is dated May 1788, the book was not published till 1789. Blake obtained his copy unbound and made his notes so rapidly that the ink was blotted off on adjacent leaves, heaped out of proper order. A few afterthoughts were written in pencil: those on Nos. 287 and 384 probably by Blake; an "Admirable!" on No. 20 and "No fumbler Kisses" on No. 503 by two different writers, probably friends to whom Blake showed his marked copy as instructed in No. 643.

Someone, not certainly Blake himself, made the six substantive corrections called for by the page of Errata—correcting "command" to "commands", "whom" to "who", "subtleness" to "sullenness", "wise" to "rife" (not noticing that the listed word is another mistake for "ripe", the word called for), and inserting an article—but ignored the eight corrections of punctuation and spelling indicated.

On the title page Blake wrote and underlined his signature, *"Willm Blake",* beneath the printed "Lavater", and then enclosed the two names in an outline of a heart. He also inscribed plain "Will. Blake" at the top of page 1.

❦

Annotations to *A Treatise concerning Heaven and Hell, and of the Wonderful Things therein, as Heard and Seen,* by Emanuel Swedenborg. Translated [by William Cookworthy and Thomas Hartley] from the Original Latin. Second Edition. London: Printed by R. Hindmarsh, No. 32, Clerkenwell-Close; London, 1784

The copy with Blake's annotations (following someone else's) is in the Houghton Library, Harvard College Library.

513. †See N 73 Worlds in Universe.] A reference to No. 73 in another Swedenborg pamphlet, of which the first English translation was that of J. Clowes, Manchester, 1787: *Of the Earths in the Universe and of their Inhabitants.* The use of "Worlds" instead of "Earths" seems to imply a different translation, perhaps of much later date, but no such edition has been traced.

Annotations to *The Wisdom of Angels, concerning Divine Love and Divine Wisdom,* by Emanuel Swedenborg. Translated [by N. Tucker] from the Original Latin. London, 1788

The copy with Blake's annotations is in the British Museum. The penciled paragraphs on the flyleaf have been badly rubbed or erased, possibly not intentionally; the words supplied within brackets are highly conjectural.

Annotations to *The Wisdom of Angels concerning the Divine Providence,* by Emanuel Swedenborg. Translated [by N. Tucker] from the Latin. London, 1790

The copy with Blake's annotations is in the collection of Sir Geoffrey Keynes.

Annotations to *An Apology for the Bible, in a Series of Letters, addressed to Thomas Paine, Author of a Book entitled, The Age of Reason, Part the Second, being an Investigation of True and Fabulous Theology.* By R. Watson, D.D. F.R.S. Lord Bishop of Landaff, and Regius Professor of Divinity in the University of Cambridge. Eighth Edition. London: Printed for T. Evans, in Paternoster Row. 1797

The copy with Blake's annotations is in the Huntington Library (HM 110260).

Annotations to *Essays Moral, Economical and Political,* by Francis Bacon. London, 1798

The copy with Blake's annotations is in the collection of Sir Geoffrey Keynes.

In the quoted excerpts Bacon's colons and semicolons are treated as full stops.

PAGE i Per WILLIAM BLAKE] A curious phrase—until one sees it on many Italian title pages; one might say that this is Blake being Florentine.

PAGE 82 Bacons Reformer Villain] A caret in the note, between "Bacons" and "Villain", points to the word "Reformer", in the line above, indicating its repetition here. (Suggestion of Sir Geoffrey Keynes.)

~❦~

Annotations to *A Translation of the Inferno in English verse, with Historical Notes, and the Life of Dante.* By Henry Boyd. 2 vols. Dublin, 1785

The copy with Blake's annotations is in the collection of Sir Geoffrey Keynes, who first located the volume in 1956. Blake's comments are confined to two of Boyd's "Historical Notes", in Volume I. In the translation of the *Inferno* someone (not Blake) corrected two printer's errors (on page 207 changing "wandring son" to "wandrings on" and on page 326 changing "louban" to "Soul an") and a translator's error (on page 193 changing "His" to "Her"). Blake added the Italian above the English text on page 189: *Nel mezzo del cummin de nostra vita.*

~❦~

Annotations to Volume I of *The Works of Sir Joshua Reynolds, Knight; Late President of the Royal Academy:* . . . *(with his last corrections and additions,) and An Account of the Life and Writings of the Author,* By Edmond Malone. The second edition corrected. 3 vols. London, 1798

The copy with Blake's annotations is in the British Museum; with it are unmarked copies of Volumes 2 and 3 in the same (modern) binding.

This volume contains Malone's Account and the first eight of Reynolds' fifteen Discourses. The Discourses were not unknown to Blake, but this may have been his first opportunity to read them all. The first had been delivered at the opening of the Royal Academy, January 2, 1769, the others at the nearly annual distribution of prizes to students, from 1769 to 1790. In 1779, the year Blake entered the Academy schools, there was no discourse, but he may possibly have heard one or both of the Ninth and Tenth Discourses given in 1780. Each Discourse was currently printed for limited circulation; a collection of the first seven was published in 1778, but the next (and complete) English edition was Malone's first, in 1797.

Blake's notes were written first in pencil and later, with erasures and additions, in ink. Differences (here noted for the first time) between pencil and ink versions are treated as deletions and additions. Notes in pencil only, but unerased, are not distinguished from notes which are identical in pencil and ink; notes in ink only are treated as additions. Words partly trimmed away in binding but still legible are treated as complete.

Date: ca 1798–1809. The assumption that these marginalia are all of one kind written all at one time has resulted in the usual dating of them circa 1808, from the close relation of some of them to satires in Blake's Notebook made before and perhaps while he was writing his "Public Address" of 1809. But as early as November 22, 1802, he invoked the authority of "All Sir J Reynoldss discourses" in a letter to Thomas Butts, emphasizing particularly Reynolds' admission of incompatibility between "Venetian finesse" and "the Majesty of Colouring" necessary to historical painting (Blake's kind)—an admission Blake pounces on in Discourse IV (see marginalia on pp 89, 90, 94, and especially 97).

Keynes (p 908) speaks of "the notes on the other volumes" as "being in the *Note-*

Book with other epigrams, etc., relating to events which took place about the year 1808". This derives from a note in Sampson's edition of Blake (p 318) referring to verse epigrams, not prose notes, and inspired by Sampson's discovery that two Notebook satires on page 33 constitute Blake's response to the concluding words of Reynolds' fifteenth and last Discourse (1790, in Vol 2): "I should desire that the last words which I should pronounce in this Academy . . . might be the name of Michael Angelo."

❧

Annotations to *Observations on the Deranged Manifestations of the Mind, or Insanity,* by J. G. Spurzheim. London, 1817

The copy with Blake's annotations has not been located since the transcription by Ellis and Yeats, which is relied upon here (with removal of uncharacteristic punctuation).

❧

Annotations to *Siris: A Chain of Philosophical Reflexions and Inquiries Concerning the Virtues of Tar Water, And divers other Subjects connected together and arising from one another.* By G[eorge] [Berkeley] L[ord] B[ishop] O[f] C[loyne]. Dublin, 1744

The copy with Blake's annotations is in the collection of Lord Rothschild.

❧

Annotations to Volume I of *Poems: including Lyrical Ballads . . . ,* by William Wordsworth. 2 vols. London, 1815

The copy with Blake's marginalia is in the Cornell University Library. Blake's notes in pencil were inked over, probably by H. Crabb Robinson, who owned the volume. Robinson's list, on the fly leaf, of pages containing "notes written by Blake in pencil" includes "4" (a page now lacking annotation).

PAGE 44 Michael Angelos Sonnet vol 2 p. 179] Blake is citing Wordsworth's translation; he quotes it in his inscription in William Upcott's album, q.v.

PAGE 375 opinions of a Portrait or Landscape Painter] The "Landscape Painter" comes out in Wordsworth's contempt for poetry that "does not contain a single new image of external nature" or evidence "that the eye of the Poet had been steadily fixed upon his object" (paragraph 20) as well as in his faulting Macpherson for using imagery inappropriate to the actual "Morven before his eyes" (p 364). The Preface, from p 1 on, assumes "memory" to be the supplier of "materials" for the production of poetry.

❧

Annotations to the Preface to *The Excursion, being a portion of The Recluse, A Poem,* by William Wordsworth. London, 1814

Blake's transcript and comment on Wordsworth's Preface and the lines quoted there from "the first Book of the Recluse" are in Dr Williams's Library, London.

Blake made few mistakes in copying—"unpleasant" for "unpleasing" (a word he never used), "Whensoeer" for "whencesoe'er" (neither a Blakean word), and two wrong prepositions—but he simplified punctuation and insisted on his own spellings:

perceive, mixd, subdud, tho, askd, unalarmd, scoopd, composd, meer (for mere), chaunt (for chant), calld, inflamd, inspirest (for inspir'st), starlike (for star-like), and probably chear for cheer (though Blake actually wrote "cheear"). He capitalized rather heavily: Wordsworth's "good and evil of our mortal state" became "Good & Evil of our Mortal State", and Blake insisted on capitalizing Law Supreme, Earth, Heaven, and "Worlds To which the Heaven of Heavens is but a Veil", also "darkest Pit" and "Song"; but he resisted several of Wordsworth's capitals, turning "prophetic Spirit! that inspir'st / The human Soul of universal earth" to "Prophetic Spirit that inspirest / The Human soul of Universal Earth". Similar reversals were: "illumination,—may my Life" to "Illumination may my life" and "My Heart . . . thy unfailing love" to "My heart . . . thy unfailing Love".

❧

Annotations to *The Lord's Prayer, Newly Translated . . . with Critical and Explanatory Notes,* by Robert John Thornton, M.D. of Trinity College, Cambridge, and Member of the Royal London College of Physicians. [London] 1827

The copy with Blake's annotations is in the Huntington Library (HM 113086). Blake did no underlining in this book. In the excerpts copied here the italics and large and small capitals are as in the original. They seem to constitute part of the book's provocation.

❧

Annotation to Cellini(?)

The volume containing this note has not been located; it was quoted by Edwin J. Ellis, *The Real Blake,* London 1907, p 420, as found "in the margin of a copy of Cennini's book on fresco painting that Linnell lent to Blake". From Gilchrist's *Life of Blake,* Chapter 39, Ellis would have known that John Linnell "gave to Blake" "the first copy of Cennino Cennini's book seen in England". But there is simply nothing in that book that could have inspired a remark about the Pope and the Virgin. What Blake, according to Linnell, found in it was that "he had been using the same materials and methods in painting as Cennini describes—particularly the carpenter's glue". The book is devoted to materials and methods throughout.

But Ellis was notoriously inaccurate. Knowing of the Cennini book and confusing a tractate by Cellini with a tractate by Cennini, he can easily have attributed the marginal note to the wrong work. (Dates of Cellini editions available are given above; there was no English translation.)

On Nature's incapacity to bear, see Blake's assertion that "This World is too poor to produce one Seed" (Annotation to Reynolds, p 157). Harold Bloom suggests that the allegory of "Faith, Hope, and Charity" signified the vegetable glass of Nature to Blake because St Paul speaks of seeing through a glass, darkly, in the verse of I Corinthians preceding that naming Faith, Hope, Charity.

❧

XIII. [INSCRIPTIONS AND NOTES ON OR FOR PICTURES]

Inscriptions that are simply descriptive or wholly derivative from the traditional or individual but non-Blakean text of the picture are not included here.

Albion rose . . .

Date: "WB inv[enit] 1780" is Blake's claim to have drawn the picture or its original at that time. The engraving, with caption, must belong to the late 1790s (or later); "Albion" is a man only in *Milton* and revised *Four Zoas* and after; earlier a land (personified once in *Poetical Sketches* as woman, one in *America,* vaguely, as "sick"); there is no Dance of Death before *Milton.* The lettering is difficult to date.

*

"When the senses are shaken"

PAGE 56] Reference to page 56 in *Poetical Sketches,* i.e. lines 2–3 of the *Prologue . . . for . . . King Edward the Fourth.*

*

[List of Subjects for The History of England]

See Prospectus of October 1793 (below, "Miscellaneous Prose")
Note that the three titles after "8" and two after "15" were afterthoughts. The items after "15" were renumbered and rearranged to accommodate "17" and "18", but then these topics, though not their numbers, were deleted.

:5 The Ancient Britons]   Blake deleted "5" to make this "The frontispiece", then changed his mind and deleted that phrase.

*

[List of Subjects from] Exodus VII

Notebook p 116]   This page was the back cover of the Notebook and these pencil notes were completely rubbed away; they have not hitherto been noticed.

*

[Legends in a Small Book of Designs]
[Legend in a Large Book of Designs]

Inscriptions beneath color-printed pages from the illuminated works, as indicated; the "books" into which they were gathered are now dispersed. See the Keynes-Wolf, *Census.*

*

Chaucers Canterbury Pilgrims

Inscribed also are the names of the pilgrims and the identification of the Tabarde Inn.

*

[Descriptions of Illustrations to Milton's *L'Allegro* and *Il Penseroso*]

Transcribed from facsimile plates in *Blake, the Mystic Genius,* by Adrian van Sinderen, Syracuse University Press 1949. The originals are now in the Morgan Library.

*

Genesis [Chapter Titles in Blake's Illustrated Manuscript]

Eleven leaves, forming the beginning of an illustrated ms copy of Genesis, are in the Huntington Library. Two are title pages; nine contain the text of Genesis through IV:15, with Blake's own chapter titles, given here.

"The text follows the standard King James version, with only incidental differences in punctuation and word order. When the word 'ground' occurs in the text . . . Blake consistently adds the word 'Adamah,' usually in brackets. In IV:15, Blake amplifies the original text from 'And the Lord put a mark on Cain' to 'And the Lord set a mark upon Cain's forehead' ". *Catalogue of William Blake's Drawings and Paintings in the Huntington Library*, 1957, pp 40–42.

*

[On Blake's Illustrations to Dante]

Inscriptions in the unfinished pencil and watercolor drawings illustrating Dante's *Commedia*; see collotype facsimiles in Albert S. Roe, *Blake's Illustrations to the Divine Comedy*, Princeton University Press 1953.

*

[On Blake's Epitome of Hervey's Meditations among the Tombs]

Inscriptions in the pen and water-color drawing in the Tate Gallery; No 39 in Martin Butlin, *William Blake . . . a catalogue of the works . . . in the Tate Gallery*, London 1957.

❧

XIV. [MISCELLANEOUS PROSE]

[Prospectus]

Etched by Blake; now known only in the transcript in the Gilchrist *Life of Blake*, 1863, II 263–264. It is of course overpunctuated.

*

[On the Back of a Drawing]

Cited in Mona Wilson, *Life of Blake*, London, 1948, p 103, but without the location.

*

[Memoranda from the Notebook]

PAGE 59

From Bells Weekly Messenger

The paragraph from Salisbury occurs in the *Messenger's* 8th page, under the heading SUMMER ASSIZES. In the Notebook Blake copied it beside and below his emblematic drawing of Ugolino in prison.

In his comment Blake refers to two prints he engraved, from paintings by Morland, i.e. Le Cave. The deleted word is confusing, though legible enough, because he began by writing about "two Prints" but concluded by turning the focus on those two (paintings) he engraved from.

*

PAGE 101 REVERSED   A list of songs to be etched on one plate. See above, pp 460–461.

PAGE 88   The first selection in Bysshe is under the heading "Enjoyment", the second under "Oak".

Blake's mistakes in copying are "every" for "either" in line 7 of Behn; "For" for "Far" in line 9 of Dryden (unless he used the 3rd edition which has that variant); and—possibly these are revisions rather than mistakes: "bear/tear" for "bend/rend" in lines 3–4 and "lowring" for "towring" in line 9 (but this may be an uncrossed *t*).

*

[Blake's Autograph in the Album of William Upcott]

The Album is in the Berg Collection of The New York Public Library. My brief account of the album appeared in the Library's *Bulletin* for November 1960.

Some slight deletions and corrections have been omitted.

*

For other miscellaneous prose see scattered inscriptions in the ms of the *Four Zoas*, given in notes on pp 753, 757, 763.

∽

XV. [LETTERS, A SELECTION]

Reproductions may be seen in *Letters from William Blake to Thomas Butts 1800–1803, Printed in Facsimile*, ed. Geoffrey Keynes, Oxford University Press 1926. The originals of this group are in the collection of Kerrison Preston.

For all the letters see Keynes, 1957, but better still Keynes's edition of the Blake *Letters*, 1956, which includes receipts and accounts and letters to Blake.

Full text of the letter to Hayley of 4 Dec 1804 was recently published by George M. Harper, from the original in the Library of Congress; see *Studies in Philology* LXI 573–585.

[To Thomas Butts, 22 November 1802]

Lines 7 and 8 of the "Verses" were written in the margin and then marked for insertion with this note: "These 2 lines were omitted in transcribing & ought to come in at X"

Commentary

BY HAROLD BLOOM

I. THE WORKS IN ILLUMINATED PRINTING

THERE is NO NATURAL RELIGION

[a]

The most useful commentary on Blake's early tractates remains that of Murry (pp 12–28), despite his mystical presuppositions. As Blake's first attacks on Deism, the tractates are perhaps only tentative presentations of some of Blake's principles, but they are a very full statement of his convictions on the primacy of poetic imagination over all metaphysical and moral systems.

"There is No Natural Religion", according to Blake, because no man reasoning from fallen nature can come to see that "the real man, the imagination" and God are the same. Religion must be "revealed" in the sense that Revelation means the consuming of natural appearance by a more imaginative vision.

This first tractate argues from human desire and perception to their origin in the "Poetic or Prophetic character", but for which the "Philosophic & Experimental" faculties would be mired "at the ratio". Ratio, in Blake's use, means an abstract image or ghost of an object, which in the aggregate makes up the universe of death which is the natural experience of most men. The freshness of life depends upon the Poetic character, for even the immediacy of nature is the gift of imagination.

[b]

This second tractate against Deism identifies the ratio with the orthodox notion of right reason, and also with the natural Selfhood of man. The image of the mill in Proposition IV is the first appearance of one of Blake's prime negative emblems, to be developed later in the *Marriage* and as the dark Satanic mills of *Milton*. The "complicated wheels" of natural cycle here will serve to grind down creation in *Milton*.

Propositions V–VII are very compressed in their phrasing. The possessed are bounded, and "the bounded is loathed by its possessor". More! is a mistaken cry, for only the unbounded infinite can satisfy a fully human desire. To see the infinite in all things is to see God because it is to see as God sees, which Blake believes is the only way to see God. But to see as God sees, man must himself be infinite, a state to be attained only by the individual utterly possessed by the Poetic Character.

ALL RELIGIONS are ONE

Frye (p 28) interprets the title as meaning "that the material world provides a universal language of images and that each man's imagination speaks that language with his own accent. Religions are grammars of this language". This third tractate identifies the Poetic character with "the true man" who is the source of religion, and whose inwardness the orthodox name the soul. The attack on dualism, made on behalf of this mature man's integral humanity, anticipates the rejection of dualism in the *Marriage*.

∾

THE BOOK of THEL

Thel's name is from the Greek for "will" or "wish". The name, like so many in Blake, is ironic, for Thel's pathetic fate is the consequence of her weakness in will, and her failure to carry her pastoral innocence into the world of experience is a failure of desire.

THEL'S *Motto*

Blake's source here is presumably Ecclesiastes 12. The second part of the motto is quoted from Tiriel's death speech. Knowledge of experience must be sought of the Mole, even as wisdom and love must be put into the organs of generation.

PLATE 1

"Mne Seraphim" is, one suspects, a mistake for "the Seraphim" which, as Thel is one of the ungenerated, is all the context demands. Blake may first have intended her as a daughter of Mnetha, guardian of the vales of Har in *Tiriel,* and then simplified to "the Seraphim". The "river of Adona" is probably derived from *Paradise Lost* I 450–452, and may be an allusion to Spenser's Gardens of Adonis, an excellent analogue to the unborn world of the vales of Har.

As the youngest daughter of the Seraphim, tending the flocks of the sun, Thel is most acutely conscious that time and decay haunt even the realm of pre-existence. The echo, in line 14, of Genesis 3:8, suggests that Thel's land is one with the Garden of Eden. Thel has a choice between being born or dying into the vegetative cycle of her prison paradise.

PLATE 3

The appearance of Luvah here is the first entrance of any of the Zoas into Blake's work. Here he is the regent of the cycle of innocent sexuality.

PLATES 4,5

The worm is emblematic both of generation and of death, and epitomizes the necessary paradox of Thel's decision to be born, and subsequent flight from that decision. The clod of Clay replies for the worm because it stands at both poles of the worm's cycle, the Adamic flesh and the grave. The puzzlement of the clay, on Plate 5, is a gently satiric compounding of natural innocence and ignorance.

PLATE 6

The symbolism of the eternal gates is derived from *The Odyssey*, Book XIII, where the Cave of the Naiades is described as having two entrances, a northern one for men and a southern for gods. Blake may be aware of Porphyry's commentary on this Homeric cave, but Thel's descent into experience is *not* a neo-Platonic allegory of the soul's descent into matter, but rather a mythmaking closer to the double gates and their double-natured porter in Spenser's Gardens of Adonis (Book III, canto VI of *The Faerie Queene*). In *Milton* 26:16–18 Blake's porter is identified as Los; Spenser's porter is "Old Genius". The northern gate is the passage from lower innocence to experience, and so a gate for men, because this passage is necessary for human existence. The southern gate is the passage from experience to a higher, imaginatively organized innocence, and so more akin to the gate of the gods. Thel flees back through the northern gate, and so returns to the unorganized innocence or ignorance of the lower paradise.

The poem's most pungent irony comes in the lament that rises from the grave plot, for it first protests the strength of four senses, and then the weakness of the fifth sense, of touch and sexuality. Even in experience, Thel would have found no fulfillment. Yet her flight home heralds a darker fate; dwelt in too long, the vales of Har reduce their inhabitants to the state of the Har and Heva of *Tiriel*.

❦

THE *MARRIAGE* of HEAVEN and HELL

The Marriage of Heaven and Hell is both an intellectual satire and a prophecy of imminent apocalypse, although an element of irony severely qualifies the prophecy. Here Blake consciously comes to maturity, casts off outworn influences, and defiantly promises the world his Bible of Hell, the canon of his engraved poems.

The *kind* of satire Blake writes here has an affinity with *A Tale of a Tub* although Blake and Swift are far apart in every belief. Rabelais is the intellectual satirist closest in his vision to the *Marriage*, although his work is very different from it in form. The form of the *Marriage* is Blake's invention, and still a unique one in literature.

PLATE 2

The Argument.

This introductory poem is an oblique statement of Blake's concept of contraries, expounded later in the work, and also a satiric epitome of Blake's dialectical division of the cultural leaders of mankind into "Devils" and "Angels", respectively to be the "Reprobate" and the "Elect" of the later poem *Milton*. The cyclic irony of the Argument prepares the reader for the complex ironies that are to come.

Rintrah, later to figure in *Europe* and *Milton*, opens the poem on a note of menace. Rintrah is an angry Elijah or John the Baptist; a prophetic spirit who prepares the way before a redeemer, in this case Blake himself, who is implicitly compared to Jesus on Plate 3. As a voice crying in the wilderness, Blake typifies the artist rejected by society because his warning truth is too uncomfortable to be borne. Historically, Rintrah is the spirit of unrest and impending war in 1792, symbolizing the time of troubles brought on by French revolution and English reaction, and is sometimes ironically identified with Pitt.

The ultimate source of the Argument, and to a lesser extent of the entire *Marriage*, is in the Book of Isaiah, particularly chapters 34 and 35 (cited by Blake on Plate 3), and chapter 63 (referred to by Blake on the same plate). Isaiah 34 summons all nations to give warning of God's indignation, and prophesies "a great slaughter in the land of Idumea" which is Edom. In 1790 Edom is France, in Blake's contemporary application of the prophecy, and Blake warns of the impending counterrevolution in England. Isaiah 35 is in deliberate contrast to 34, and gives a vision of salvation in a restored Israel, as against the desolation of Edom. With these prophecies Blake compounds Isaiah 63, where the savior comes out from Edom, a fulfillment of Isaac's prophecy in Genesis 27:40. Blake's oblique and brilliant strategy is to make Jacob or Israel representative of Pitt's England, and Edom of revolutionary France, and so to indicate that his contemporary time of troubles is parallel to Isaiah's. An apocalypse is therefore at hand, with war in France to be followed, depending on English choice, either by a rebirth in England or a day of judgment that will mean an end to the world. The dominion of Edom means, in Blake's terms, that the red figure coming menacingly out of France, the "Devil" called Orc in Blake's *America* and later poems, is truly a savior, however awful he may appear to the "Angels" of Pitt's England. In the Argument this man of Edom appears as the "just man" who now "rages in the wilds", while the "Angels" are represented in "the villain" who has usurped the just man's place. A final point of irony in the Argument is that this usurpation is presented as being natural, as being part of an organic cycle. Hence the present tense in lines 6–8; the roses and thorns are simultaneous, as are the song of honey bees and the barrenness of the heath. The cryptic lines 9–13 contain an ironic reference (noted by Damon, p 316) to Exodus 17:1–8. The Mosaic miracle, performed for those of little faith, merely prepares for the usurpation of just man by villain. The reference to "red clay" in line 13 is to the literal Hebrew meaning of Adam, and also to the new Adam who comes out of Edom.

PLATE 3

"Swedenborg is the Angel"

Emanuel Swedenborg (1688–1772) began as a scientific researcher, experienced what he took to be visions (ca 1743), and began a new career as a religious writer. His followers, the New Jerusalem Church, became, for Blake, only another orthodoxy, and Swedenborg's own later writings affirm predestination and eternal punishment, doctrines abhorrent to Blake. Blake's annotations (ca 1788) to Swedenborg's *Wisdom of Angels Concerning Divine Love and Divine Wisdom* show that at one time he felt some affinity (although with reservations) to the Swedish seer, but the feeling did not survive his reading in 1790 of Swedenborg's *Divine Providence*. Among Blake's comments on *Divine Love* were "Good & Evil are here both Good & the two contraries Married" and "Heaven & Hell are born together." One can surmise that the initial impetus for Blake's writing of the *Marriage* came from his outraged reaction to *Divine Providence*. This blended with his concern at counterrevolution, and his resort to Isaiah may have reminded him of another prophecy, Swedenborg's on the *Last Judgment*, which "was commenced in the beginning of the year 1757", when Blake happened to be born. So it came about that Blake, at the Christological age of thirty-three, revived the Eternal Hell of imaginative desire within himself and rose from nature's tomb, leaving Swedenborg sitting there, with *Divine Providence* the castoff clothing of death. In that revival, the law of Blake's dialectic is formulated and given eternal statement, as a concept of contraries, born together and forever opposed in a mutual immanence.

PLATE 4

The voice of the Devil

This section is ironic in its title, as the "diabolical" nature of Blake's attack upon Christian dualism is dependent upon its being seen through "angelic" or orthodox eyes.

PLATES 5 and 6

Milton and the Devil's Party

This is one of the most frequently misread passages in Blake. Blake offers an aesthetic criticism of *Paradise Lost*, not a reading of Milton's intentions. If, with C. S. Lewis, one believes that Milton's intentions (surmised from Lewis' own Anglican orthodoxy) are precisely realized in the poem, then Blake must seem irrelevant or misguided. But Blake is not alone in his reading, both in his own time and in ours. What Blake traces is the declining movement of creative energy in *Paradise Lost* from the active of the early books to the passive of the poem's conclusion, where all initiatives not a withdrawn God's own are implicitly condemned. More simply, Blake posits a split in Milton between the moral philosopher or theologian and the poet. From this split ensues what Blake claims is a falsification *in the poem* of the relation between human desire and the idea of holiness. Milton's Satan overly embodies human desire, and Milton's Messiah is too exclusively the representation of a minimal and constraining kind of reason. Satan, in the Book of Job, is a moral accuser who torments man with the trial of physical pain. In *Paradise Lost* the wrathful fire of the Messiah is instrumental in creating Hell as a moral punishment involving physical torment. It follows then, for Blake, that "in the Book of Job Miltons Messiah is call'd Satan". In declaring for the Devil's party, and also insisting that Milton was unknowingly of it, Blake is not inverting conventional categories of moral good and evil (as Milton's Satan does on Mount Niphates). Instead, he is insisting that poetic imagination and the energy of human desire are near allied, and that for a poet as *poet* the ordinary moral categories are contained within a more limited context than the larger world of poetry makes available to him. Blake deliberately complicates this point by his ironic vocabulary, with its persuasive redefinitions of such orthodox counters as Angels, Devils, Heaven and Hell. The Gospel reference is probably to John 14:16–17, so that Blake is interpreting "the Spirit of Truth" as Desire.

A Memorable Fancy

This, and the following sections of the same title, are parodies of Swedenborg's "memorable relations", literalistic reports of what Swedenborg claimed to have experienced in the Eternal world of his visions. This first Memorable Fancy is partly Blake's reply to Milton's account in Book II, *Paradise Lost,* of the Devils' activities in Hell during Satan's absence. To Milton, the Devils are lost in wandering mazes; to Blake, they are amid the enjoyments of Genius, for the fires of Hell are active and creative energies. The mighty Devil writing with corroding fires is Blake himself, at work engraving the *Marriage* on the rock of the fallen human mind. The couplet he etches as motto to Hell's proverbs is an allusion to Chatterton's "The Dethe of Syr Charles Bawdin", lines 133–136:

> How dydd I knowe thatt ev'ry darte,
> That cutte the airie waie,
> Myghte nott fynde passage toe my harte,
> And close myne eyes for aie?

Proverbs of Hell

There is an attempt at full analysis of these Proverbs in Bloom (pp 83–88). The rhetoric of the Proverbs is antinomian, but their argument is not, and depends upon a dialectical definition of an Act, as set forth in Blake's annotations on Lavater (see p 590). The sixth Proverb is repeated in the notebook version of "The Fly". The fifty-third is repeated in Orc's defiance of "Albion's Angel" in *America,* 8:14.

PLATE 11

This section serves as a coda to the Proverbs of Hell, and explains how the priests or Angels came into existence to oppose the poets or Devils. The process is one of codifying poetry into scripture, and now calls forth its contrary in Blake's Bible of Hell, or poems restoring orthodox scriptures into their primal imaginative forms.

PLATES 12 and 13

A Memorable Fancy

This is Blake's equivalent of the banquet scene so often found in the tradition of intellectual satire, but Blake makes of the dialogue a unique kind of apocalyptic humor. In his annotations (1798) on Watson's *Apology for the Bible* Blake spoke his ultimate words on prophecy: "Every honest man is a Prophet; he utters his opinion both of private & public matters. Thus: If you go on So, the result is So". To compare that with the implicit definitions of prophecy given by Blake's Isaiah and Ezekiel here is to realize again that if any figure in modern literature stands with the Hebrew prophets, it is Blake.

PLATE 14

This, and Plate 16, seem to me the central (and most powerfully expressed) sections of the *Marriage.* Here, on Plate 14, Blake relates his apocalyptic vision to his actual work as poet and engraver. The "ancient tradition" of the world's destruction by fire after six thousand years is perhaps no more ancient than some of the early Church Fathers, interpreting together the six days of Creation and 2 Peter 3:8. The cherub and his flaming sword are in Genesis 3:24, but Blake may already be assimilating that passage to Ezekiel 28:11–16, the prophecy against "the anointed cherub that covereth", to be identified with Satan in Blake's *Milton* 9:30–35. One risks redundance in observing again how far this passage (and everything else in Blake) is from mysticism of any kind. It is Blake's work *as a creative artist* that will expunge the notion of dualism, and cleanse the doors of perception, the infinitely expandable senses of man.

PLATE 15

A Memorable Fancy

This six-chambered "Printing house in Hell" is an allegory of artistic creation, and begins "by an improvement of sensual enjoyment", as prophesied on the preceding plate. The Dragon Man, a phallic emblem, clears away the mental rubbish that impedes our sense of touch, while the Dragons enlarge our other senses. The Viper of restraint and custom folds round our fallen state, while others seek to conceal its reality by the adornments of wealth. The Eagle of imagination (see Proverb of Hell 54) defeats the Viper by making our potential infinite, while "Eagle like men" create their works "in the immense cliffs" of our temporal ruin, even as the Devil Blake cut the motto to the Proverbs into the rock. In the fourth chamber the metals of fallen appearance, introduced by the Vipers of restraint, are melted down into materia poetica, the living waters of life, by the raging Lions who are the flaming archetypes of all imaginative conception. The fifth chamber is like Yeats's "golden smithies" in "Byzantium", where "Unnam'd forms" break the flood of spirit, and cast the metals into a sixth chamber, where the class of men next to be named "the Prolific" complete the creative process.

PLATES 16 and 17

The necessary opposition between Prolific and Devourer, as set forth here, is the complement to the apocalyptic thrust of Plate 14. The Giants, our repressed energies, are the Prolific; their bonds, which refer back to Milton's fetters on Plate 6, are imposed by the Devouring, who are described by aid of the forty-ninth Proverb of Hell. Unlike the statement of contraries by the antinomian "voice of the Devil" section, this passage emphasizes the necessity for the Devourer's existence as the bounding outline of the Prolific. The Devourer, manifested independently of the Prolific, will later become "the Spectre" in Blake's symbolism.

PLATES 17–20

A Memorable Fancy

The stable here is that of the birth of Jesus, serving as ironic antechamber to the church. The vault is where Jesus was buried, but the Angel and Blake go *through* the vault rather than out of it again as Jesus did in the Resurrection. The mill is emblematic of rationalistic reduction, as it was in the early tractates, and as it will be in *Milton*. The philosophic errors of rationalistic speculation are suggested by the winding mazes of the cavern, and the abyss is all of the natural world. In a fine irony, Blake is more attached to natural reality than the Angel (the oak's twisted root as against the fungus) as together they experience the orthodox illusion of Hell. Frightened away, the Angel abandons Blake to a vision of creativity. Blake's contrary "metaphysics" subsequently expose theology in a frightening vision of intellectual cannibalism. The "seven houses of brick" are the seven churches in Asia to which the Revelation of St John the Divine is addressed.

PLATE 22

Paracelsus (Theophrastus Bombastus von Hohenheim, 1493–1541) was an alchemist and medical pioneer whose occult writings were probably of small interest to Blake, who uses him here with Behmen to deprecate Swedenborg. Jacob Behmen (Böhme, 1575–1624) was a theosophist whose influence on Blake has been somewhat exaggerated by various scholars. He counts for very little to Blake, in comparison with "Dante or Shakespear", and even less with Milton or the Bible. This passage insists that the alchemists and theosophists are more imaginative than Swedenborg, but they themselves are only candles in sunshine when compared to the poets.

PLATES 22–24

A Memorable Fancy

This section is in illustration of the proverb that concludes the *Marriage*: "One Law for the Lion & Ox is Oppression". This proverb echoes a tortured question of the dying Tiriel (*Tiriel* 8:9) and precludes the irony of Bromion's very different use of the same question in *Visions* 4:22.

The fire-cloud opposition of Devil and Angel marks them as the rising contraries, Orc and Urizen respectively. In "The worship of God" definition, "the greatest men" clearly refers to great artists, and not political figures of any kind whatsoever. "The Bible of Hell" is the impending sequence of Blake's engraved poems.

PLATE 25

A Song of Liberty

This prose poem is distinct from the *Marriage*, but Blake associated the two works. As a revolutionary prophecy, it preludes both *America* and *Visions* in its symbolism. The groan of Enitharmon, as she will come to be called, is a herald of revolution, for she is in labor with Orc, the "new born terror" of *America* and later poems. The eighth verse refers to the legend of lost Atlantis, adumbrated by Blake in *America*. The "starry king" is Urizen, who hurls the infant Orc "thro' the starry night" as Messiah expelled Satan from heaven in *Paradise Lost*. Orc sinks into the waves of the fallen world, but only as the sun does, to be reborn in constant cycle. The sea, being emblematic both of fallen nature and the chaotic tyranny of political orders founded on the doctrine of the Fall, flees away from the fire of Orc. In verse 15 Urizen ("the jealous king") and his host fall as well, "for this history has been adopted by both parties", as the *Marriage* put it (Plate 5). They fall "on Urthona's dens", to the lowest levels of creativity. This is Urthona's first appearance in Blake. Later he will be the eternal form of whom Los is the temporal manifestation, and therefore representative of the imaginative faculty when it is detached from the wholeness of man. The name (as Damon notes, p 326) is possibly a play on "Earth-owner", the earth being Urthona's element.

From verse 18 on Urizen is identified with Jehovah and Moses, while Orc becomes a rebel against the Mosaic law, stamping it to dust. He loosens the horses of instruction from their Urizenic dens, ending the strife of negations between lion and wolf. The Chorus identifies the priests of Urizen with those of Odin, whose emblem is the raven. The final line appears again in *America* (8:13) and *Visions* (8:10). Its emphasis is on the individuality of all life, and the consequent unholiness of all codes of conformity.

As a political allegory, *A Song of Liberty* has probable reference to the rout of Brunswick's army at Valmy by the forces of the new French Republic (see Erdman, pp 176–179). The triumphant tone of the *Song* and its rhetorical immediacy fit the celebration of a contemporary revolutionary success.

❧

VISIONS of the Daughters of Albion

This hymn to free love is further along into Blake's mythic universe than *The Book of Thel*, but less involved in personal myth than *America* and subsequent poems. Fisher (p 207) characterizes it, briefly and well, as the poem in which "Blake explores the failure of the fallen understanding to cope with the organization of desire". Several scholars have interpreted *Visions* as a neo-Platonic fantasy on the legend of Persephone, a legend which in no way fits the actual events of the poem. They have been misled by Blake's irony in naming the Urizenic rapist Bromion, since "Bromios" is a title of Dionysus or Bacchus. The name, in *Visions*, is palpably ironic, as there is nothing Dionysiac about the Deistic and Puritanical Bromion. He is "bromios" only in the literal meaning of that word, for he is perpetually "roaring" and thundering his outrageous (and thoroughly conventional) morality.

The starting point of Blake's *Visions* may well have been Ossian's *Oithona*, in much the same sense that Swedenborg provided a starting point for Blake's *Marriage*. Frye (p 238) suggests that "Blake may have been protesting against" *Oithona*, where the heroine prefers death to the dishonor of rape. In any case, the names in Blake's *Visions* have an Ossianic ring to them. Theotormon is evidently tormented by his conception of God, hence his name.

The Title: The reference is evidently to what the Daughters see, since they serve as a lamenting chorus throughout.

The Motto: This clearly establishes the primacy of vision over the limited awareness of the natural heart. In reference to Theotormon and Bromion, the motto is pathetic; in reference to Oothoon, it is ironic, for she progresses in the poem to a point where her heart's knowledge expands to include all that her vision has experienced.

The Argument

Spoken by Oothoon, this is a guide to the poem until her ravishment by Bromion, though it differs in tone from the seventeen lines of intense action it summarizes. The tone of the Argument is deliberately flat, and may suggest the state of emotional exhaustion but continued moral defiance in which the poem finally leaves Oothoon. The first three lines of the Argument make clear that Oothoon's initial hesitations were due to sexual inexperience, not to a flaw in her love for Theotormon. Leutha, in whose vale she hides, appears in *Europe* as a mocking sexual temptress, and in *Milton* 9:28–30 as the emanation of a Satan whose social disguise is a benevolent mildness, but whose nature is a secret jealousy. To hide in Leutha's vale is to evade sexual reality, and to pluck Leutha's flower and rise up from her vale is to attempt to give oneself to that reality. The "terrible thunders" of the roaring Bromion intervene, to ruin the voluntary aspect of that attempt.

Visions

The Daughters of Albion are Blake's version of the Hesperides, daughters of Atlas, for Albion "is the Atlas of the Greeks". The Atlantic (with which Theotormon is identified) and the Urizenic storm clouds above it (identified with Bromion) separate the Daughters from their sister Oothoon, whose flight toward Theotormon is a movement of unification toward her sisters as well. The faint but indubitable political allegory is elucidated by Erdman (pp 219–223). The myth of Atlantis is associated throughout the poem with the legend of the Hesperides, most strongly in the symbolism of Oothoon's act of plucking the "bright Marygold" as an offering to Theotormon. Like the Golden Apples of the Hesperides, the Marygold is sacred to the sun, and is also an emblem of the unfallen world. By carrying this emblem toward her desired union with Theotormon, Oothoon expresses a wish to carry over Innocence into Experience.

The reactions of Oothoon, Bromion, and Theotormon to the rape are very complex, and have been the principal obstacles to the proper understanding of the poem. Bromion is brutal but not stupid, and the Urizenic twistings of his morality are ironically instructive. He is both a debased Puritan, and a very sophisticated Deist, a combination essential to Blake's polemical purpose. His sadistic pride in the rape is tempered both by a bad conscience, and by a revulsion from the sexual awakening he has brought about in his victim. Theotormon's simpler conflict is between the torments of jealousy and continued love, with a masochistic element also entering the rhetoric of his reaction. The vision of Oothoon and Bromion as being bound, back to back, is not reality, but Theotormon's wish fulfillment, just as the caves of the binding scene represent the windings of his own fallen consciousness. Oothoon's reaction is the most subtle and complex of the three. The crucial passage is Plate 2, lines 11–19, which is one of the most frequently misread in Blake. Oothoon *begins* by seeming to accept the morality of her ravisher and her lover, but the acceptance is belied by the psychic actuality of her reaction to her new state. She cannot weep because she is not moved to do so, though she attempts to simulate despair. But the writhing of her limbs indicates instead that her sexual desire has been aroused, and that it only remains for Theotormon truly to fulfill her. His failure prompts the substitute gratification (for both of them) of her masochistic and momentary submission to a Promethean punishment. Lines 18–19 constitute one of Blake's most outrageous ironies. From that nadir on, Oothoon moves forward into the full rhetorical power of her new freedom.

Damon (p 330) notes that Bromion's speech (4:13–24) is answered in *Milton* 28:15–18. Line 22 of Bromion's speech echoes (and reverses) the last line of the *Marriage*, and recalls also *Tiriel* 8:9.

Urizen appears, by name, for the first time in Blake's poetry, on Plate 5, line 3. His name is probably based on the Greek for "to draw with a compass", and echoes the sound (and meaning) of "horizon", based on the same Greek root.

Lines 8–9 on Plate 5 are employed again, with variations, in *The Four Zoas* II 35:3–4. Lines 39–40 are echoed more closely in *The Four Zoas* VIII 108:11–12. Oothoon's final affirmation, in lines 9–10, Plate 8, is repeated in Enitharmon's song, *The Four Zoas* II 34:78–79. See also the final line of *A Song of Liberty*, and Orc in *America*, Plate 8, line 13.

~&

AMERICA *a* PROPHECY

Blake's *America* is at once a political allegory based on the American Revolution, an introduction to one poet's mythic world, and a moral prophecy in the tradition of the Hebrew prophets. For the political allegory, see Erdman, pp 53–60 and pp 234–241.

PRELUDIUM

1:1–10   This opening scene suggests the world of Northern mythology. The shadowy and nameless female is an early form of Vala. Red Orc (from the Latin "Orcus" for Hell) is the imprisoned spirit of organic life. At "fourteen suns", puberty, halfway through the lunar cycle, he is ready to revolt. Politically, the fourteen suns refer to the years 1762–1776.

1:11 – 2:17   Orc portrays his aspirations by references to political symbols of revolt (for their authenticity, see Erdman, p 239 n 32). The silence of the shadowy female identifies her with nature, barren when not possessed by man. Orc's rape is intended to give her a voice, and succeeds, and yet is felt by nature as torment and "eternal death", Blake's ironical term for generative life.

2:18–21   For a probable biographical interpretation of these lines, see Erdman, p 264.

A PROPHECY

3:1   This is repeated as the last line of *Africa*, in *The Song of Los*.

3:14–15   This is the King of England, a dragon form even as Pharaoh is identified with a dragon by Ezekiel.

4:7–11   Orc rises as a Devil to oppose the King as Angel, in a vocabulary drawn from the *Marriage*. For line 11, see *Paradise Lost* I 62–63.

5:1   The Stone of night suggests the pillows of Jacob in Genesis 28:11, and the tablets of the Law.

6:1–15   In Orc's great oration, we can hear what Erdman terms "Blake's poetic paraphrase of the Declaration of Independence". Lines 1–2 recapitulate the opening of the *Marriage*, while throughout the speech there are echoes of Oothoon's chants. Orc's final lines are repeated in Blake's first attempt at Apocalypse, Night IX of *The Four Zoas*.

7:1–7   One of Blake's most ironic speeches, since it is the Angel who is actually "serpent-form'd", being the dragon of death.

8:1–17　　Orc identifies Urizen with the Jehovah of Exodus, as he was in *A Song of Liberty*. Redeemed man (lines 15–16) is identified with the walkers in the furnace of Daniel 3:25. In lines 16–17, redeemed man is associated with the image of Nebuchadnezzar's dream (Daniel 2:31–35), with the subtle and crucial difference that Orc's man is one stage nearer to salvation than Nebuchadnezzar's image is, for the feet of iron and clay are feet of brass, the thighs of brass are of silver, and the silver breast is golden, like the head.

9:1–27　　This Angelic reply attempts to arouse the king's governors against Orc, but Washington and the other rebels have already turned themselves defiantly toward the eastern world of Urizen's England (line 11). The mother of Orc is Enitharmon, but Blake does not name her in this speech, and Albion's Angel appears to identify Orc's mother with the shadowy female of the Preludium. Either way, Orc is a child of nature who has rebelled against her restraints.

10:1–12　　Damon (pp 336–337) gives the fullest account of Blake's possible sources for this version of the Atlantis legend. Whatever the sources, Blake's use of the legend differs in emphasis from any other I know. Britain and America are separated by the Atlantic, fallen form of Atlas, whom Blake took as another version of his Albion. Now, in vision, the summits of Atlantis rise up again for Blake, as a consequence of the American Revolution and the mythic revolt of Orc. The archetypes of Eternity are revealed in an ancient palace, built by Ariston, king of beauty and "best" of the Greeks. Yet, whatever his merits, his bride or emanation was a stolen one, which may be Blake's suggestion that the archetype of Atlantis itself was stolen from a British-Hebrew original. This use of Ariston is probably derived from Herodotus (Book VI, 61–66). Ariston occurs again in Blake in *Africa*, in the *Song of Los*.

11:1 – 14:16　　This is the central action of *America*, and is properly a political one. The Angels become Devils and follow Boston in repudiating the covenant of Urizen. Governor Bernard was recalled from Massachusetts in 1769, but Blake identifies him with British colonial rule in general.

　　Against the rebel Americans, Albion's Angel sends the enormous plagues of the Book of Revelation, for he claims to be the scourge of God.

14:17 – 16:23　　This reversal of the plagues onto England's shores is treated fully by Erdman (pp 53–60), who traces this apocalyptic visitation upon England to the precedent of the Great Pestilence in 1348, which followed English aggressions against France. Among the consequences are mass desertions among the British troops (15:3–5), the sickening and madness of the ruling circles (15:6–10), and the exposure of the Angelic timeserving laureate for the reptile he is (15:16–18). More fundamental even is the rout of the priests (15:19–22), which liberates females from the tyranny of marital restraints (Erdman, pp 58–59). As the flames of desire advance, Urizen-Jehovah is revealed (16:3–12) in all his leprous impotence, to prevail only for the twelve years more until France joins the Revolution (16:14–15). In the poem's final lines, thrones shake in France, Spain, and Italy, and the flames of desire advance to consume the five fallen senses, so as to restore men to their unfallen potential.

❧

EUROPE a PROPHECY

　　This is the subtlest and most difficult of Blake's poems, outside of the three epics, and perhaps the most rewarding as a poem. For its historical allegory, see Erdman, pp 185–186 and 193–207, and for an account of its prophetic framework, Erdman, pp 245–249. For an attempt at a comprehensive critical reading, see Bloom, pp 146–161.

　　The broad political allegory of *Europe* traces the process by which England entered into war with France in 1793, following the execution of Louis XVI. As myth, *Europe* is a more imaginatively audacious version of *America*, taking the non-historical events of that poem and placing them in a more revelatory perspective. *Europe* precedes Blake's epics in trying to give a vision of all the Christian centuries, the seventh Eye of God or Orc cycle in Blake's symbolism.

PLATE iii

This charming introductory plate provides an absolute tonal contrast both to the Preludium and the poem proper. In a light vein, Blake repeats the central truth of the *Marriage:* human sensual limitations are willful, and keep us from the eternal world. The fifth sensuous window, sexual touch, is open to us, but the perverse pleasures of inhibition keep us from reality.

PRELUDIUM

1:1 – 2:18   This Preludium, following the situation of the one to *America,* is a prophecy of the Apocalypse. It begins with the same "nameless shadowy female" of the earlier poem, but now she has a voice, with which she laments the mortality of her beloved, brought forth and then destroyed in cycle after cycle. Orc is a Tammuz, and this lament echoes the ones for that dying vegetative god in Ezekiel 8:14 and *Paradise Lost* I 446–457. Enitharmon, Queen of Heaven, presides over these cycles, unaware that the coming eighth birth of Orc, as Jesus, will be the final one.

A PROPHECY

3:1–4   This is a parody of the first stanza of the Hymn in Milton's "On the Morning of Christ's Nativity". For Blake's very complex allusiveness here, see Erdman, pp 245–247.

3:11–12   Another ironic allusion to Milton's poem, here to stanza VI.

4:1–14   This is all part of a song of Los, with the sons of Urizen dramatically depicted in it as uttering lines 3–9. Erdman (p 246 n 5) reads it differently, assigning lines 3–9 to the sons of Urizen directly, and lines 1–14 to Enitharmon. This is very possible, but loses the complex irony of Los's dramatic self-deception and his misunderstanding of the new birth. See Bloom, p 150.

6:1 – 8:12   This is the song of triumph of the Female Will, with its cult of chastity (6:5) and its alliance with the dream of a remote heaven (6:6–7). Enitharmon sends her sons, the primal artists, to instruct the human race in her deceptions. Rintrah and Palamabron ought respectively to prophesy and civilize, but instead their functions are subverted by their emanations, Ocalythron, a goddess of jealousy, and Elynittria, a goddess of chastity.

9:1–5   This is the nightmare of the eighteen Christian centuries, the passage serving as a transition from mythic origins to contemporary history.

9:6–16   We are taken back both to the close of *America* and *A Song of Liberty*. The council here historically is the one that collapsed in 1783, after the climax of the American War (Erdman, pp 194–195). In literary terms, this passage alludes to the defeated host of Satan in *Paradise Lost* I. Even as that host built Pandemonium for their comfort, so Albion's Angels now seek out a giant temple for further deliberations.

10:1–15   This is the beginning of Blake's use of the Druids in his symbolism. There is a full commentary on this element in Blake in Fisher, pp 32–53 and 63–66. The temple here may be the famous serpentine one at Avebury. Albion's Angels are about to sacrifice humans in a war against Orc, and so Blake sees them as priests of Druidic natural religion. Historically, they are George III, Pitt, and the cabinet that tried three times to go to war, in 1787, 1790, 1791, while mythically they represent all fallen mankind, warring against their own salvation. Verulam, the home of Bacon, and the title he took, is the entrance into the temple, for Blake insists upon associating the experimental and empirical approach to nature with Druidism. The Zodiac, fixed order of Urizen's star world, serves as the pillars of the temple.

10:16-23   For this anticipation of contemporary phenomenology, see Bloom, pp 155-156.

10:24-31   The southern porch is the temple's intellectual quarter, for Blake identifies the serpentine temple with natural man. The Stone of Night, a Jacob's Pillow and Decalogue in *America*, is here also the fallen human skull, in a parody of Plato's Cave.

11:1-5   The brazen Book is the Bible of Heaven, the orthodox reading of the Bible as opposed to Blake's reading in his Bible of Hell, or canon of engraved poems. The copies of the brazen Book are the legal and doctrinal codes of kingdoms and churches.

12:1-20   Here the youth of England are compelled to hear their doom proclaimed by Albion's Angel, in a ban against the thought-creating fires of Orc. Erdman (pp 197-198) is able to identify this with precision as the particular ban ushering in a period of reaction in 1792. Lines 14-20 are identified by Erdman (pp 199-200) as the downfall of Chancellor Thurlow, handled by Blake as an omen of the ultimate downfall of all Albion's Angels.

12:21-31   This passage, particularly in Enitharmon's triumph, parallels the lyric "London" in *Songs of Experience*.

12:32 – 13:8   For the historical allegory here, involving Pitt's three attempts to lead England into war, see Erdman, pp 195-196. Mythically, Rintrah, the "red limb'd Angel" of 13:1, makes three attempts to bring about an apocalyptic situation, but only the fourth attempt, by Newton, is a success. The use of Newton here is clearly a satiric stroke on Blake's part. Newton, who himself wrote a commentary on Revelation, blows the trumpet of Apocalypse because his achievement fully revealed the cosmos of Deism. Newton's "enormous blast" is his explanation of the universe, which exposes the Angelic hosts as so many dying leaves of autumn.

13:9 – 14:36   Enitharmon summons her children, for history has now reached its climax. Ethinthus is an emanation associated with the waters' rejection of the earthworm, and so is a spirit of exclusive female materiality. Manatha-Vorcyon has all the emblems of inspiration, but being dominated by Ethinthus, he is reduced to a "soft delusion". Leutha, previously encountered in *Visions,* is frequently used by Blake as a symbol of hypocrisy in sexual matters. Antamon, who ought to represent the graphic arts, is merely a sensualist under Leutha's sway. The seven churches (14:20) are an ironic reference to the seven churches in Asia, to whom John the Divine addressed Revelation. Sotha, who ought to be the spirit of music, and his emanation, are merely intended by Enitharmon as seducers of Orc. This obscure paean of Female triumph ends with Orc's rejection of his mother (like the rejection by Jesus of Mary) and Enitharmon subsequently weeps.

14:37 – 15:11   This is the Europe of early 1793, on the eve of war between England and France, taken by Blake to be the wars of Edom, preceding a Last Judgment. In 14:37 – 15:2 the light of the morning appears in France, as the French finally follow the Americans in revolution. The coming vintage will be of blood, and the rising of Los is an ambiguous one, involving the serpentine thunder of the Druidic Urizen. Yet the prophetic cry of Los shakes nature, and the strife of blood may be a liberation. This passage is illustrated on Plate 10 of *America*, which is reproduced in this volume.

~⌐

THE SONG of LOS

Of Blake's revolutionary prophecies, this is the weakest, because of the merely pedestrian *Africa* section that begins it. Yet *Asia*, its second part, is a remarkable and very effective poem in its own right. The purpose of *The Song of Los* is to give the background for the action of *America* and *Europe,* and also for the *Urizen-Ahania-Los* sequence of poems. By doing so, *The Song of Los* connects the two series, binding together myth and history, particularly in *Africa,* which precedes *America* in historical action, ending as it does with the first line of *America.*

AFRICA

3:2   The four harps are the four principal continents.

3:11   Rintrah, the oldest son of Los, is here only an agent of Urizen. Later in Blake he will tend always to be a spirit of angry prophecy.

3:18–19   Palamabron is made the giver of Hermetic doctrine, which Blake associates, rather unfavorably, with less esoteric Greek modes of thought.

3:20   The sons of Har would include all men, on the basis of his role in *Tiriel.*

3:22–24   Blake clearly associates the Gospel with his own *Visions* poem, though to make Theotormon the patron of Christianity implies that faith's nearness to the springs of jealous torment and repressed desire.

3:28–31   These lines are based very loosely upon *Europe.* Antamon is a spirit of graphic art, but associated with Leutha, a spirit of sexual hypocrisy, and is credited with the "loose Bible" of Mahomet, which presumably means only that the Koran is a poor reflection of the Bible. The Northern mythology of Odin, with its warlike emphasis, is given by Sotha, a spirit of music, whose vagrant emanation, Diralada, figured in *Europe* as Thiralatha. Blake attempted to clarify these dark matters in *Milton,* Plate 27.

4:1–21   This very rapid sketch of European intellectual history traces the main stages in Blake's myth of decline, from the loss of Eternity (lines 1–4) to the emergence of natural man (5–12), to the growth of abstraction and empiricism in metaphysics with its culmination in Newton and Locke (13–17) until the final manifestation of natural religion in Rousseau and Voltaire, which comes to cover the whole earth (18–21).

ASIA

6:1 – 7:40   Throughout *Asia,* one can feel Blake's poetic relief, as he ceases to catalogue disaster, and turns instead to admonition and prophecy. *Asia* follows the action of *Europe* in Blake's chronological sequence, as Orc enters again, creating thought with his fires of desire. The angry cry of the spider-kings of Asia (6:9 – 7:8) is ostensibly a Malthusian defense of their own tyranny, but it functions satirically, revealing the kings for what they are. Roused by them, Urizen flies from Europe to Judea, but Orc's pillar of fire triumphs over the pillar of cloud, and the presages of Apocalypse begin to manifest themselves.

～∾

THE [FIRST] BOOK of URIZEN

This poem is primarily an intellectual satire, directed at accounts of cosmic and human genesis in the Bible, Plato, and Milton, and is only secondarily a serious reworking of those accounts in its own right. Urizen, as his name's possible origin in the Greek *ourizein* would indicate, is the power in the fallen psyche that marks boundaries, defines the horizon, separates and divides, and in general limits and reduces. Yet, in Eternity, Urizen was the entire intellect of Man. The poem's central irony is its constant implicit contrast between what Urizen is and what he was.

PLATE 2   Preludium   The primeval Priest is Urizen himself. His place is in the north, following Isaiah 14:13 and *Paradise Lost* V 689 ff.

3:13–17   Urizen is a demonic parody of the Jehovah of Genesis and *Paradise Lost*, as befits the principal being in Blake's "Bible of Hell", promised by Blake at the conclusion of the *Marriage*. In these lines, Blake satirizes the creation by contraction in *Paradise Lost* VII 168–173.

3:27–35   The secret preparations of Satan in *Paradise Lost* VI 520 ff are suggested here, together with the depiction of Jehovah as a mountain god throughout the Bible. That Urizen should be both the orthodox God and the genuine Satan is almost the central point of Blake's satire in this poem, a point that he develops from Plates 5–6 of the *Marriage*.

3:36–39   These globes will later be the hearts of natural Selfhoods in the fallen world. They are associated with the Newtonian vision of space.

4:7   Urizen's idea of his holiness is an implicit denial of Blake's passionate belief that everything that lives is holy.

4:9   The fear of futurity is also Urizen's invention, for it had no place in the eternal world before him. In a sense, he has changed a state of perpetual becoming into a state of being, and in the process has isolated the moment of his own existence.

4:10–13   There is a generic echo here of Milton's Satan on Mount Niphates, despairing of the hateful siege of contraries, and choosing evil as his good.

4:16–23   This complex passage combines Satan's journey through Chaos, especially *Paradise Lost* II 927–942 ("Natures wide womb" coming from Milton) and God's creation of the firmament in Genesis 1:6–7, for to Blake these are the same event.

4:24–40   Urizen as lawgiver parodies Jehovah's gift of the Decalogue, with the Stone of night replacing the Rock of Sinai. The insistence on uniformity carries on from Tiriel and Bromion.

4:41–49   The rage of the other Eternals is the ironic cause of the Fall, in a parody of the Divine Wrath creating the flames of eternal fury in *Paradise Lost*.

5:19–37   There is a deliberately distorted reflection here, and elsewhere in the poem, of the labors of Plato's Demiourgos in the *Timaeus*. More direct is the ironic reference to Milton's War in Heaven, *Paradise Lost* VI 639–674.

5:38 ff   Los (whose name may be derived from the Chaucerian "loos", a word for poetic fame) is at this point a desperate satire upon the impossibility of being a poet in a thoroughly fallen age. If the Eternal intellect has become deranged, then the imagination must be disordered also.

10:1 – 13:19   The changes of Urizen appear again in *The Four Zoas* IV 54:1–55:9 and in *Milton* 5:10–27. They represent Blake's ironic equivalent of the seven days of Creation, and of the seven times that shall pass over Nebuchadnezzar as prophesied in his dream of the Fall (Daniel 4:32). As Urizen sleeps through his changes, Los labors to organize some definite outline for him, including the desperate invention of clock-time (10:15–18). This Los is as much a satirical figure as Urizen is, and his botching efforts result in the grotesqueness of our fallen body, facing west toward its death (13:12–17).

13:20 – 15:13   This reunion of Los and Urizen is again satirically intended, being an allegory of the fate of poetic imagination, forced by despair to merge itself into a blend of formless nature and the minimal order it has made from that nature.

18:1 – 20:25   Pity, as in "The Human Abstract" of Experience, is a divisive element for Blake, being allied as it is to the fear and selfish possessiveness of the natural heart. Here, Pity is a satiric equivalent of Christian *agapé*, the charity of God that led to the creation of Adam and Eve. Los, by this equivocal Pity for Urizen, becomes the Urizenic death he beholds, and is divided in two. The result is a fallen Los or Adam, and Enitharmon or Eve, whose name indicates her role as the mother of "numberless" fallen descendants. Horrified by this separate female form, the unfallen Eternals complete the

Fall by fastening down the woof of Science as a tent over the fallen, thus giving an objective existence to the order of nature. Within this tent, Los as a diminished perception resulting in time, and Enitharmon as a materialized perception of space unite, after a "natural" courtship of mutual torments, so as to generate time's serpent, Orc. His appearance in fallen nature seems a manifestation of Orcus or Hell to the Eternals, who close down Eternity for their self-protection.

The subsequent story of jealousy, attempted sacrifice, and the arousing of a dead God to life is a very complex satire upon the fundamental myth preserved in the tales of Oedipus and Laius, and of Abraham and Isaac.

20:26 – 25:22   This sequence, of Urizen exploring his dens, is Blake's presentation of how fallen reason attempts to deal with the phenomenal world. In 20:33–41, Blake combines suggestions from Proverbs 8:27, *Paradise Lost* VII 225 ff, and the *Timaeus* to show us Urizen as cosmic architect. The fundamental pattern of Urizen's explorations is set by Satan's journey through Chaos in *Paradise Lost* II. Horrified by his own world, Urizen resorts to the cursing of a Tiriel. His four principal sons are the elements, of whom Fuzon is the most crucial, his name suggesting the fire of nature. Urizen's tears of pity form the Net of Religion, embryo of the Female Will.

25:23 – 28:23   Here Urizen's children fall, the "Cities" being Urizen's creations. The children's senses shrink in a parody of the seven days of creation, until they invent their own death. The saving remnant of thirty cities in Egypt, clearly based on *Tiriel* 5, takes us from Blake's Genesis into his Exodus, for Egypt is the land of spiritual death from which mankind led by Fuzon must flee, and is identified with the chaos of "the salt ocean rolled englob'd". "The pendulous earth" of 28:21 is from *Paradise Lost* IV 1000.

～◆～

THE BOOK of AHANIA

This very beautiful poem is generally neglected, or treated as a mere continuation of *The Book of Urizen*. Though its action carries on from *Urizen*, it is an altogether different kind of work, with a very individual tone, quite unlike anything in *Urizen*. Though there are some elements of intellectual satire in *Ahania*, the poem is primarily a lament, implicitly for Fuzon in the first four chapters, and explicitly by Ahania for Urizen and herself in the fifth.

2:1–29   Erdman (pp 289–290) makes a probable identification of Fuzon with Robespierre in the historical allegory. In the moral allegory, Fuzon is a Promethean version of Moses, and suffers a fate like that of Prometheus or Christ, with elements of the disasters of Balder and Absalom as well.

Line 12 alludes to Genesis 1:2. Fuzon's resort to his father's kind of creation, a globe, as a weapon, is a subtle indication of his limitations as a revolutionary. His revolt is a sexual one, directed against the cold loins of his father, and it fails because it only confirms Urizen in his hatred of generative life.

2:30–43   Ahania's name appears to be founded on Athena's, another wisdom goddess, though Ahania has a more direct relation to Satan's daughter and beloved, Sin (line 34 and *Paradise Lost* II 757–761) whose birth was parallel to that of Athena. Urizen's rejection of Ahania is an ambiguous one, and is responsible for the moon-goddess of various mythologies. Where Ahania, in Eternity, incarnated Urizen's delight in his own activity, the pleasure of intellect, here she has become an opposing principle, as far as he is concerned. Damon (p 360) suggested Plato's *Philebus* as a source for Blake's *Ahania*, and this seems very likely, but it ought to be noted that Blake satirizes and opposes Plato's insistence that wisdom contrasts with and is superior to every kind of pleasure.

2:44 – 3:46   The phallic beam of Fuzon becomes the pillar of fire of Exodus, until Los reunites it to the energy of nature.

In his solipsistic broodings, Urizen creates the black bow, to figure later in Blake, particularly as Satan's black bow in *Jerusalem* 52. After the self-delusion of 3:38, Fuzon suffers the fate of Balder. The death-giving rock becomes "Mount Sinai, in Arabia" (Galatians 4:25), which Paul identified with the bondage of Jerusalem, and her children. Galatians 4:26 ff, it ought to be noted, probably suggested the Jerusalem who is Albion's emanation in Blake's major poem.

3:47–4:44 This crucifixion of Fuzon on the Tree of Mystery (from "The Human Abstract") associates him with Christ, but even more directly with the brazen serpent Moses raised in the wilderness, since Fuzon becomes a serpent in a forty-year transformation based on the Israelites' wanderings. With the new cycle of revolt beginning in Asia (see *The Song of Los*), the career of Fuzon is over.

4:45–5:47 Ahania's lament recalls Oothoon's in *Visions*, as well as The Song of Solomon, the lyric fragment "Thou hast a lap full of seed" in Blake's Notebook, and "Earth's Answer" in *Songs of Experience*. It is also counterpointed against the triumphant song of Wisdom, Jehovah's Ahania, in Proverbs 8.

❧

THE BOOK of LOS

This poem intersects the action of *The Book of Urizen* in the midst of Chapter IV. Like *Urizen*, it is essentially an intellectual satire, but it lacks the grotesque power of *Urizen*. Nevertheless its theme is central to Blake, and it defines the dilemma of Los, which the rest of Blake's poetry exists to resolve.

3:1–26 Eno, like Enion in *The Four Zoas*, is evidently the mother of generative existence, now reduced to guiding the chariot of Leutha, the sexual temptress whose prison paradise of mock-chastity Oothoon had to escape in *Visions*. Eno's lament is an ironic fable in which the four prime Blakean sins of Covet, Envy, Wrath, and Wantonness enter the world through a failure of the imagination, as contraries fall to the status of negations through the imputing of impurities.

3:27–4:42 Los, an active and perceptive being, is compelled to be a passive watchman of Urizen. Unable to bear this role, his creative impulse destroys Urizen's provisional world (4:15 ff), but with this stay against chaos gone, Los himself falls into the abyss. As Los falls, his involuntary motion divides time and space, and then leads to a contemplation which changes the nature of the fall.

4:43–5:57 The first creation of Los is the Polypus, organic life without demarcations. In 5:2–5, Los becomes the creative principle in the God of Genesis 1, and Blake parodies His separation of darkness and light, leading to the emergence of light in 5:10 ff. There is a further parody, of Exodus 33:23, in 5:12–15. Terrified by this serpentine vision of Urizen, Los is yet inspired by it to the task of bending Urizen into a more definite form. Los thus takes on the task of Demiourgos from Urizen, and his work, in Blake's view, is mistaken and absurd. He creates our fallen world, with its dead sun, and finally the "Human Illusion" or Adamic man, with the four rivers of Eden becoming the four fallen senses. The poem's final line is Blake's ironic summation of wholly natural existence.

❧

MILTON

Blake's *Milton* is a foreshortened or "brief" epic, on the possible model of Milton's *Paradise Regained*. Like *Paradise Regained*, Blake's poem has a clear thematic relation to the Book of Job. Though Blake originally planned *Milton* as an epic in twelve books, perhaps to replace *The Four Zoas*, there is little evidence that a full earlier version of the poem ever existed. There is, however, much internal evidence that the present poem is reduced or modified from what would have been a very different kind of poem. Erdman (p 394) speculates that the earlier version "constituted a visionary account of the English Revolution". Whatever its initial form, the extant *Milton* has surprisingly little historical allegory as compared to Blake's other major poems.

Unlike the Book of Job and *Paradise Regained,* works presenting their theodicy through dramatic dialogues, *Milton* centers itself on the consciousness of the poet himself. The struggle is clearly an internal one, between those qualities in Blake that would compel him to surrender his prophetic function, and everything in him that desires to follow Milton's heroic dedication as a poet. Blake is the Job of his own poem, and confronts a tempting Satan, whom he overcomes only by following Milton's example. Milton, in the poem, is shown as casting off his own selfhood, and moving toward a visionary emancipation that Blake desires as his own. It is important to note that Blake does not give us a pattern in which Milton merely assumes Blake's own position. Blake's poem is a genuinely purgatorial one. He wants to be an incarnation of the Poetical Character, as Milton was before him, and for this he needs Milton's aid, or rather the aid of what was most radical and imaginative in Milton. What belonged to religious convention and "moral virtue" in the historical Milton is of no help to Blake, nor was it to Milton himself, in Blake's view.

The difficulties of Blake's *Milton* are in its poetic structure, rather than in its use of personal myth. As poetic myth, *Milton* is considerably less complex than *The Four Zoas* or *Jerusalem.* But, like *Jerusalem, Milton* confronts its reader with problems of continuity, and of sudden changes in perspective. The principal problem is the relationship of the Bard's Song (2:25 – 13:44) to the rest of the poem. Commentary on this relationship is given below. The general problem of transitions is also dealt with below, each time the poem's context or narrative shifts.

The motto is from *Paradise Lost* I 26.

PLATE 1, Preface.   The distinction between the Classics and the Bible here is clearly Miltonic in its origin. Milton's Jesus, in *Paradise Regained* IV 331–364, exalts the Hebrew Scriptures over Greek literature, and even asserts "that rather *Greece* from us these Arts deriv'd; / Ill imitated". Blake's literary polemic is directed primarily against the English Augustans, as usual, for their having set up the Classics rather than the Sublime of the Bible as models for emulation. The Daughters of Albion have replaced the Daughters of Beulah, with the result that even pre-Augustans like Shakespeare and Milton failed to attain their full imaginative potential.

"And did those feet in ancient time"

The Dedicatory Quatrains: This poem, out of its context and retitled *Jerusalem,* is famous as a hymn. The "dark Satanic Mills" of line 8 are primarily those mentioned on Plate 4 of the poem, rather than the actual mills of British industry. The "Chariot of fire" of line 12 probably has direct reference to Gray's vision of Milton in *The Progress of Poesy.*

The epigraph: This is a reproof of Moses to Joshua, who would have silenced an "unauthorized" outburst of prophesying. As epigraph, it establishes that the poem's Milton is to become like the prophetic Moses, rather than the Moses who gave the law. In the poem, Moses is redeemed as Palamabron.

Book the First

2:1–15 The Invocation: Blake calls on the Daughters of Inspiration or Hebraic Muses for aid, as Milton called on a Hebraized Urania. But Blake both admonishes and invokes his Muses, as is proper for a poem in which the hero goes into the deep to redeem his Emanation, and in which the Emanation herself must cast off all traces of the Female Will. For, though the realms of Beulah "delight", they present "delusions". So Blake emphasizes *"my* hand", *"my* right arm", and *"my* brain", (italics added) and makes it clear that the Muses merely perform a ministry, provide a means for the unfallen imagination ("Eternal Great Humanity Divine") to plant his paradise of poetry in an individual creator's mind. The "Spectres of the Dead" (line 9) are natural forms unredeemed by imagination, until they are made, by the poem, in the image of the Divine Humanity. The "False Tongue" is the fallen Tharmas, become the Covering Cherub or accuser of sin, for the sense of taste in Eden becomes the serpent's lying tongue in Beulah. The invocation ends with the sacrifice of Jesus, who was born into "Death Eternal", our life, in the ironically named "heavens of Albion", the world of natural experience, as ironically termed "heavens beneath Beulah".

2:16-24   The "one hundred years" of line 17 represents an approximation, Milton having died in 1674. The "intricate mazes" recall the mazes of argument in which the fallen angels of *Paradise Lost* II 561 are trapped. The "Sixfold Emanation" may refer to Milton's three wives and three daughters or even to Milton's literary works, or to the English society he sought to create. Seeing the torment of what ought to be the total form of his love, Milton resolves at last to descend, to be reborn into the natural world. The specific cause of his resolution is his hearing of the Bard's Song, which begins as cosmic history and then turns to a crucial episode in Blake's own life.

2:26   The three classes of men are the Reprobate, the Redeemed, and the Elect. The classes are expounded in 25:31-37, and go back to the division in the *Marriage* between the Devils (Reprobate) and the Angels (Elect). The Redeemed are a battleground on which Reprobate and Elect meet, for the Redeemed can be won to either class. In Blake's *Milton*, Milton is Reprobate, Satan Elect, and Blake himself Redeemed.

3:6-40   This passage recapitulates *The Book of Urizen, The Book of Los,* and Night IV of *The Four Zoas.*

3:41 - 4:5   In this greatly condensed presentation of his central myth, Blake accomplishes a radical simplification which is not inconsistent with the myth of the Fall in *The Four Zoas.* From the Bard's perspective (it is after all his song) all the human faculties first appeared in the fallen world through the agency of Los, for all three classes of mankind are created by the imagination. So Rintrah the Reprobate prophet, Palamabron the Redeemed poet, and Satan the Elect accuser are all children of Los and Enitharmon, of the mental forms conditioning fallen reality. Satan is "the Miller of Eternity" because his mills of reductive intellect attempt to grind down creation, and so destroy the minute particulars that constitute the human. By being incarnated, Satan takes on definite form, and so error is consolidated for a casting-out in the Apocalypse, though Satan resists, "Refusing Form in vain". The Great Harvest will reveal Satan as Urizen, "Prince of the Starry Wheels". Damon (p 405) notes the brilliant shift in Blake's imagery from Night IX of *The Four Zoas* where Urizen was plowman in the apocalyptic harvest. Here, in *Milton,* the Zodiac of Urizen as sky god becomes the plow of the Reprobate prophet Rintrah, while the harrow of the divine purpose is given to Palamabron, the Redeemed poet who in the moral allegory represents everything in Moses that was free of the Law, and everything in Blake that can surmount nervous fear. The Mills of Satan, grinding on in our temporal existence, are at one with the tyrannical star world of nature, the Mundane Shell formed by Urizen as a stay against the chaos of fallen Tharmas. Here, in the natural dimension, the Three Classes of fallen mankind take their sexual and threefold texture; threefold because Tharmas, the Zoa of unity, is lost. If Innocence, realm of Tharmas, could be restored, the Fourfold Human would exist again.

4:6-14   This speech of Los to Satan introduces the difficult theme of the quarrel between Satan and Palamabron, which on the biographical level would appear to have been a falling out at Felpham between the Elect Hayley-Satan and the Redeemed (or rather, redeemable) Blake-Palamabron. The Rintrah of the quarrel was evidently Blake's deceased brother Robert, surviving as Blake's visionary conscience. The best account of this quarrel remains Frye, pp 327-332, but Hayley's case is presented ably in Morchard Bishop's *Blake's Hayley* (London 1951), Chapters XVII-XIX.

Satan is "Newton's Pantocrator", because his mills grind out mental visions of a fallen world of fixed spatial and temporal dimensions. "Pantocrator" is Newton's own coinage, combining pantograph, an instrument for making copies, and cosmocrator, St

Paul's word for the "rulers of the darkness of this world", in the passage Blake used as epigraph for *The Four Zoas*. Or it may simply mean "universal ruler". The "Harrow of Shaddai", of the Almighty, belongs to Palamabron-Blake and has been usurped by Satan-Hayley, the false artist, with his "Deist" belief in "a scheme of Human conduct invisible & incomprehensible". The wrath of Los is the cleansing anger of imaginative conscience, provoked by Elect usurpation.

4:21–28   For the London geography and its relevance here, see Erdman, p 368. Blake refers to his London residence after his return from Felpham; "Calvarys foot" is the former site of the gallows at Tyburn, and the Cherubim here are the young soldiers of England. "Cherubim", presumably on the model of the Covering Cherub of Genesis and Ezekiel, who is the blocking agent keeping man from paradise. The precious stones adorning them may come from the prophecy against the Covering Cherub in Ezekiel 28:13–16. Damon, p 406, refers to a passage in Böhme's *Aurora*, but like every other attempt to link Böhme and Blake this seems to me unnecessarily remote.

4:26   is strikingly close to Blake's wording in a letter to Butts, April 25, 1803, where the Corporeal Friend who is a Spiritual Enemy is Hayley.

4:27–28   is a complex irony; the British troops or Cherubim, as they march on the reviewing grounds, display a human beauty that mocks the "Druidical Mathematical Proportion" to which their drillmasters would reduce them.

5:1–4   Like 4:21, this is one of the sudden shifts in perspective that crowd the early plates of the poem. 4:21 ff was a vision of the corporeal London as seen from Blake's position in the city; in 5:1–4 his memory returns to Felpham, and the dark incident where he so disconcerted Hayley that "Satan fainted beneath the artillery". The "artillery" here consists of the shafts of flame thrown off by the harrow of poetry, flame too intense for the unimaginative Satan-Hayley to bear, for he has not sacrificed self as Christ did in his sacrifice.

5:5–14   Another radical shift in perspective; this is the antithesis to 5:3–4, directly preceding. Instead of Christ's sacrifice, we are given a vision of the cruel and deceptive beauty of the Daughters of Albion, whose temptations Milton and all men must overcome. The Daughters, in their illusory Heavens of Beulah (the delights of natural sexuality when these are mistaken for an imaginative finality) take up the Satanic elect. The Elect cannot be redeemed, as the other two classes can, for the Redeemed and the Reprobate are the Two Contraries, but the Elect are the Reasoning Negative, or negation in the *Marriage's* vocabulary. So the Elect can only be saved by being "Created continually", that is, re-created through the artist's labors, at the same time that they are created continually in a darker sense, in the cruelties of Moral Law.

5:15–37   Here Blake works in the mode of his most pungent irony, for the pity of the Daughters is sadistic. They lament the sense limitations of fallen man, but the lament becomes a mockery of human aspiration to rise above the Udanadan, or lake of sorrow, Blake's emblem for the watery illusions of materiality.

5:38–7:3   This sequence depends for its power and excitement on Blake's daring in manipulating his perspectives. The reader's immediate problem is to keep up with the apparent shifts in continuity. In 5:38 the Daughters create the Three Classes through their singing; in 5:39–42 we are given a relevant historical instance of the Three Classes in operation. Milton is the Reprobate; Cromwell, being "ready" for redemption, the Redeemed; Kings Charles and James are Elect, but call out for the Reprobate prophet to grant them the re-creation of Atonement. James has created the "night of prosperity and wantonness", perhaps by involuntarily preparing the way for a mercantile ascendancy. Now, he repents, seeking the purifying fires of the city of Los, which may appear in the corporeal London as apocalyptic "heaps of smoking ruins". A presage of that salvation is then given in 5:43–44, where the arrows of fire that subdued Satan are assigned to Elynittria, the emanation of Palamabron, a reference expanded on Plates 11–12. Elynittria, Catherine Blake in the biographical allegory, was introduced in *Europe*. The next transition, moving out from this defeat of Satan, takes place in 6:1 ff, as the saving work of Los in his City is manifested to us. The symbolism of Plate 6, like so much else in *Milton*, is largely derived from *Europe*, and opposes the postlapsarian world of European history to the activity of Los. The climax to this opposition is attained in the last transition in this dazzling sequence, the transition in 6:32 through 7:3, where the triumph of Los over (and in) history is to have shaped the Three Classes of men.

7:4–30   Here the poem's more strictly narrative sequence begins again, as we return to the struggle of Blake and Hayley, Palamabron and Satan, Contrary and Negation. The "incomparable mildness" of line 4 demonstrates a fine bitterness on Blake's part, for he felt he had suffered much from Hayley's smugly infuriating mildness. The formulaic repetition of "Mark well my words! they are of your eternal salvation" throughout the Bard's Song is an effective intimation of how crucial Blake felt the whole episode to be to his poetic life. The Harrow of the Almighty *is* epic poetry, for by it Palamabron-Blake could harrow the natural world so as to compel a revelation. When, constrained by the threat of ingratitude, Blake yielded to Hayley and became a kind of obedient decorator, while Hayley set up as major poet, the vehicle of inspiration and its guiding spirits were severely upset (lines 17–19). Unable to bear this self-betrayal longer, Palamabron-Blake summons Los the Poetic Genius and Satan-Hayley to a judgment.

7:31–40   The wind of Beulah is Blake's version of the Romantic "correspondent breeze" (as Wordsworth termed it). As an inspiring force it roots up nature, which suggests the analogue of Shelley's West Wind. The Gnomes, who take Palamabron's side, are the product of a primordial perception of a presence in the natural world that requires redemption, which only the poet can bring to them.

7:41–47   The raging of the horses and maddening of the Harrow is an allegory of balked and mishandled inspiration. This first judgment of Los is curiously rendered; it is difficult to see its full relevance to a situation for which Los shares the responsibility, as he admits in 8:19.

8:1–22   This very complex movement of the poem has a wryly humorous element, as in lines 4–10, but essentially plays on the pathos of Blake's condition as an artist of genius under the patronage of an officious poetaster. Damon's remark (p 407) that "Hayley finds the work he has given Blake quite disrupted with Blake's own ideas" is an accurate reduction of lines 4–10 to biographical allegory. The Mills of Satan ring with the drunken dancing of Blake's exuberant visions, and the repentant Los mourns his part in not keeping poetaster and poet at their proper stations. His apt moral takes us back to the equivocal aspects of "pity" in "The Human Abstract" and *The Book of Urizen*.

8:23–45   This is perhaps the most obscure passage in the Bard's Song, and probably relies too much on biographical allegory for us to recover its full sense. Thulloh is presumably a friend to both Palamabron and Satan, or perhaps "the natural sympathy between Blake and Hayley" as Damon (p 407) surmised. Lines 23–26 may reflect the actual day following a climactic quarrel between the two men. After their significance as actors in *Visions of the Daughters of Albion*, one would expect Theotormon and Bromion to take the side of societal convention, but the references to Michael and his struggle with Satan give Blake's myth of personal travail an apocalyptic dimension, for which see Revelation 12:7 ff. Most crucial is the entrance of Rintrah into the quarrel, which makes it an episode in the chronicle of British prophecy and its tribulations.

8:46–9:12   This extraordinary passage is one of the triumphs of Blake's condensed and intricate style in *Milton*. The Assembly compels Satan to reveal himself for what he is, but only after the heavenly Elect have made a fearful mistake in judgment. The "Two Witnesses", Rintrah and Palamabron, constitute a very subtle reference to Revelation 11:3. For a detailed analysis of the reference, see Frye, p 334, and again Frye, "Notes", pp 130–131. Still more subtle is the nature of the judgment of Eden; it goes against the prophetic anger of Rintrah, that is, against Blake's own poetic vocation. On the level of biographical allegory, this seems to be Blake's bitter revelation of his terrible sense of isolation in the argument with Hayley. But Palamabron-Blake is saved by Satan-Hayley's own loss of temper, which reveals the Miller of Eternity as what he is, the

Covering Cherub and false tongue of the Accuser of Sin. "Satan is among the Reprobate" in 9:12 is one of Blake's most ferocious ironies, for Satan goes over to Rintrah only by a momentary fury of involuntary self-revelation, in which his usual cunning mildness is set aside and his deathly hatred of poetic genius is made clear.

9:13–35   This is the actual epiphany of Satan. Urizen is recalled throughout, as is the Covering Cherub of Ezekiel 28:14–16.

9:36–52   The Assembly of Eden learns its error, but responds to the crisis only with lament. The separation between Palamabron and Rintrah, pity and wrath, is a division in Blake's own psyche, attributable to the principle of Satan within his own self. The result is a further slaying of Albion, the full humanity of man.

10:1–21   The identity of Satan as Urizen is revealed at last to Los and Enitharmon, who take necessary measures against their old enemy. But whereas Los vows not to succumb to Urizenic religion, Enitharmon's customary failure of nerve deepens the Fall through the creation of a further "Female Space", here the unredeemed land called Canaan, to signify the England that Milton must hallow into an Israel.

The reappearance of Elynittria and Ocalythron (for whom, see the commentary on *Europe*) in this context is an indirect condemnation by Los of Palamabron and Rintrah, for their emanations have become rampaging female wills. Poet and prophet are both responsible for the fall of their created worlds into Jealousy. This is the background for 10:21, where Los laments that Satan has been triumphant in his divisions.

11:1–14   Eon is an alternative name for an emanation. Here, the struggle between Satan and Palamabron has expanded into its cosmic form of the struggle between Urizen and Los. The Thames is both a river of Beulah and of the generative land of England, rocky or fallen Albion; the same mythic formulation appears in Spenser, where the Thames, by being married to the Medway, becomes an image of concord, of the world Blake called Beulah. Lines 6–14 are an epitome of the fallen state of a kind frequently encountered in *The Four Zoas*.

11:15–27   Here we are offered Eden's justification for its verdict against Palamabron. The necessity of the dialectic of the Three Classes compels the existence of natural evil in this world; this is theodicy, but not Blake's theodicy.

11:28 – 13:7   This begins the last movement of the Bard's Song, which is entirely devoted to Leutha's lament and its consequences. Leutha is Satan's emanation, and appeared previously, in *Europe*, as a sexual temptress, and earlier, in *Visions of the Daughters of Albion*, as the guardian of Oothoon's prison-paradise of untried sexuality. In 12:39, there is an allusion to *Paradise Lost* II 760, which establishes that Leutha is Blake's version of Milton's Sin, Satan's daughter and mistress. Unlike Milton's Sin, Leutha is a Magdalen, and seeks to redeem both Satan and herself. Most directly, she symbolizes the world of torment that the Satanic element in each of us makes for ourselves.

There may be a very subtle political allegory in the Great Assembly, the epiphany of Satan and the repentance of Leutha, for which see Erdman, pp 396–397, but unlike the political allegory of *The Four Zoas*, which so frequently reinforces the moral allegory, it does seem unintegrated with the main significance of *Milton*. The torments of external warfare in Europe are crucial to *The Four Zoas* as they were to *The Prelude*, but they recede in the purgatorial *Milton*, where Blake's subject is so directly his own imaginative crisis as caused by contending forces within his own self. The fundamental Jobean trial of *Milton* concerns Blake's ability to sustain his poetic vocation.

The lament of Leutha offers a basically psychological explanation of Hayley-Satan's attempt to usurp the civilizing harrow of Blake-Palamabron's art. Satan's imaginative powers, at once his muse and the final form of his art, abandoned him for Palamabron, only to be repulsed by the jealous possessiveness of Palamabron's emanation. In horror at her own jealousy, Leutha mars the masculine or active forming powers of Satan, leaving him only the receptive feminine perceptions that ensue in "admiration join'd with envy". What results is the Satanic Hayley, a parody of the Augustan virtuoso, whose attempt to move from the patronizing of genius to usurping its function results in the disaster already recounted in the poem. The added element in Leutha's account is that her appearance enraged the "living creatures" of the Harrow, for her illusory rainbow was seen by them as a parody of the bow of Elynittria, mistress of the arrows of desire. The catastrophe is now graphically termed "a Hell of our own making" in the very dramatic line 12:23. The fierce Harrow now becomes Revelation's emblem of the Fall of a third of heaven, in the brilliant image of 12:25–27, where the flaming discharges from the Harrow are at once shooting stars and fires raging through the stubble of the heavenly fields. After this Fall, the dark fires of *Paradise Lost*, Book I, come into play, and Leutha as Sin forms the Covering Cherub or "Serpent of precious stones & gold" from them. The second half of line 12:30 may be an oblique reference to Aaron's breastplate, which for Blake was another form of the Covering Cherub. As a revolt against Satan, the refusal of the Gnomes to labor is an indication of the final integrity of fallen nature. After the Fall, confronting Palamabron and his emanation is too much for Satan. Like Urizen in *The Book of Ahania*, Satan drives his emanation from him and so confirms his fallen state. Too late repentant, Leutha yields herself to the Divine Pity.

13:8–44   Here the identification of Leutha and Satan becomes complete, as together they are "the Spectre of Luvah" or selfhood of the natural, passional man. In reaction to Leutha's revelations, the now undeceived Assembly moves to meet the situation of the Fall, in ways already familiar to us from *The Four Zoas*. The fallen space of Enitharmon, our world, receives the providential time span of the six thousand years of fallen history, and the Seven Eyes of God and Two Limits are applied to the inchoate world.

What is new to Blake's myth in these closing lines of the Bard's Song is the moving reconciliation of emanations in lines 36 ff. But, though brought to the poet's bed, Leutha cannot be freed from the nightmare of history. Like Milton's Sin, she first brings Death into the world, and then the various sinister incarnations of the Female Will. Her distorted dreams of genesis have their consequences both in Blake's work (Lambeth) and in the mental labyrinths of the university cities. Oothoon, who stands here and elsewhere in Blake for the organized innocence of free love, and who will receive her reward in the final lines of *Milton*, is the guardian of Satan's forsaken emanation, and with her appearance as a charming emblem of the liberation that is to come, the Bard ends his awesome song.

13:45 – 14:9   The reaction to the Bard's Song is one of Blake's supreme ironies in *Milton*. It is clear that the Assembly of Eden in the poem do not represent the Reprobate but rather are a higher version of the Redeemed, which is to say that they themselves require redemption. Many of them are unable to accept the Bard's Song, because of its harsh revelation that Pity and Love are not necessarily good. The Bard relies for his authority on the Poetic Genius within him, a declaration that causes a troubled murmuring in the heavens, for it raises the doubtful theme of how the generative world is to be saved, if at all. From that doubtfulness, the Bard takes refuge in Milton's bosom, for of the heavenly Redeemed, Milton, greatest of English poet-prophets, is uniquely able to grasp the meaning of the Bard's Song.

14:10–32   Milton's Declaration   This is one of the poem's crucial moments of choice. Milton chooses incarnation again (finally to merge with Blake), which means that from the standpoint of the eternal world Milton goes to "Eternal Death". In line 14, a line of immense reverberation, Milton denies his own election as one of the Puritan saints. Though he had attempted to change the epic from the theme of warfare to that of heroic martyrdom, particularly in the invocation to Book IX of *Paradise Lost*, Milton now discovers that England has not learned this lesson from him, for with the other nations it still follows after the older epic "Gods of Priam" in brute warfare. Milton's impulse in descending is apocalyptic (lines 17–28), an attempt not to hasten the Last Judgment, but to prepare himself for it. He discovers that he is prematurely in Eternity (line 28), and that he has not cast off his own Selfhood. The crucial moment in this, his speech of dedication, comes in line 20; he knows now that he must descend to the sepulcher, our fallen world, if he is to see the morning of the Resurrection break. He is thus a renewal of the archetype of the watchers at the sepulcher of Jesus. Blake, one suspects, intends us to remember the opening of the *Marriage,* where the poet, at the Christological age, rose in the body to proclaim the gospel of Hell.

The climax of Milton's speech (lines 28–32) is his recognition that his prophetic legacy or emanation is endangered. As Satan-Hayley appears to triumph, it becomes clear that those in Eternity who could be deluded by him must dwell with the Classical Muses, whom Milton had repudiated, and not with the Hebraic Daughters of Beulah. So Milton declares that he, an Eternal still plagued by Selfhood, is himself Satan-Hayley unless he can undergo the purgation of descent. In the moving conclusion to his speech, he undoes the errors of *Paradise Lost,* and goes to claim the Hells of fallen reality as the creative furnaces of the prophet's art.

14:33–42   The world of Beulah intervenes between the Eternity Milton abandons and the generative world of mortality he seeks to re-enter. The hermaphroditic Shadow is the mortal garment, which Milton enters and so takes on instead of the robe of the covenant. It is shadow rather than reality, and hermaphroditic because solipsistic, at once a male subject and a female object, confused in the self-regarding brooding of our deathly life. As a twenty-seven-fold, the shadow's total form is all historical error in spiritual matters, for the twenty-seven entities are the Churches of delusion. Opposed to the deathly cycle of the Churches are the Seven Angels or Eyes of God, who impose an order upon history, and who lament Milton's reabsorption into the nightmare of material events.

15:1–20   Milton, though he has chosen deliberately to enter illusion, is enabled by the Seven Angels to retain a sense of his spiritual body, which walks in Eden though its possessor is a sleepwalker in Beulah and then in Generation. The Eighth Image Divine is attached to the Seven as an emblem of apocalypse, and suggests that Milton's redemptive aspect is allied to Jesus.

Milton's descent associates him with the Polypus, Ovidian emblem of the Material world, or the natural existence proper. As Milton moves through the Shadow, he seems a comet, whose downward course suggests the fall of his Satan in his own epic.

15:21–35   The Vortex   The vortex is the eddy or whirlpool of eternal consciousness, whose center is the object eternal consciousness intends. Since center and circumference are not separate in eternal vision, the perceiver is at once at the apex of his vision, and yet able to regard it from a distance. But when Milton passes into Beulah, he leaves eternity for time, and moves to the apex of his own vision. He is thus objectified, and the eternal circumference of his vision rolls up behind him. The eddy of perception is solidified into the globed universe of Newtonian observation. What survives of eternal vision depends upon the temporal perceiver's imagination, for he can still encompass his vortex and see the object world in its human dimension (line 27), as "one infinite plane" (32). See Frye, p 350, and Bloom, pp 325–326.

15:36–46   This is Blake's most brilliant application of his vortex image. As Milton emerges into time and space, he first sees the fallen giant Man. He enters the heart of Albion, again passing through an apex of vision ("what was underneath soon seemd above", line 42) and discovers that fallen Urizen ("cloudy heaven") and fallen Tharmas ("stormy seas") now dominate that heart, reducing it to ruin. As Milton falls into time and space, the vortex he has just breached rolls behind him and forms a descending globe. So Milton, in highest irony, appears to the world, in his return, much as his falling Satan did.

15:47–50   Milton enters Blake by the foot because by doing so he alters Blake's *stance,* from Palamabron to Rintrah, from civilizing poet to redeeming prophet. The union between Milton and Blake is temporal and provisional; hence by the *left* foot. But the first result of such union is negative; Milton is still burdened by the Spectre, and the black cloud may well be Puritan doctrine, as Damon, p 413, surmised.

15:51 – 17:8   The Three Heavens of Beulah refer to the threefold or sexual vision which is the highest that Beulah or redeemed nature can afford. Milton now learns, through his union with Blake, that his wives and daughters could have brought him to such vision, and still can, if he will rescue them from Ulro by sacrificing his Selfhood. The close association between Beulah and Ulro here, one of the most difficult points in Blake's symbolism, appears as the theme of "The Crystal Cabinet", as is well expounded by Frye, p 234.

17:9–30   Rahab is to Milton here as Leutha was to Satan, chief of his emanations. The other wives and daughters are the daughters of the sonless Zelophehad (Numbers 26:33). Milton, in his old age, was sonless, and left his legacy to the Female Will or the sensuous tyranny of the fallen natural world. The daughters of Zelophehad prevailed on Moses to legalize female inheritance, which Blake interpreted as a yielding to the Female Will. Rahab presides then over Milton's five fallen senses, and the legend of Milton dictating to his womenfolk is transformed into an extraordinary stony vision of a Mosaic Milton, the Rock Sinai, dictating law to six lesser masses of stone. Hor is the mountain-top where Aaron died (Numbers 20:22 ff); Peor is a Moabite mountain (Numbers 23:28); Bashan is a high region, rather than a mountain; Abarim is a mountain range in Moab (Numbers 27:12); Lebanon is of course another mountain range, with Hermon its highest peak. By placing all these in Midian, Blake associates Milton's desert wanderings during his return with the similar wanderings of Moses, and of Christ in the Temptation. The lands mentioned in line 20 are united by their opposition to the Israelites. Milton wanders in the Mundane Shell which is Urizen's fallen world, the twenty-seven Heavens and Hells of the natural religions. The twenty-seven-fold opaqueness ends "where the lark mounts", in a deliberate anticipation of the beautiful myth Blake creates on Plates 35–36 of this poem. Milton, as a traveller from Eternity, is passing outward to Satan's seat, toward his great struggle with Urizen on Plate 19 of the poem.

17:31 – 18:50   Milton's return is misunderstood by the spirits of the fallen world. Los and Enitharmon, with very different reactions, see Milton's arrival as a descent of Satan, coming to visit fresh afflictions on the Job-like Albion. The Shadowy Female, bride of Orc, and so the material environment of natural man, declares her intention of entrapping the new prophet, by drawing him into the divisions of Rahab and Tirzah. Rahab is the image of the visible church, and Tirzah of the necessity of natural limitation; between them they form the barrier the new prophet must pass.

Orc makes yet another appeal for the Shadowy Female to reassume the role of Vala, his emanation, but the appeal is disregarded. Nevertheless, he is attended in his afflictions by Oothoon and the now repentant Leutha, who is a presage of a redeemed Babylon. The struggle between man and nature goes on, until it can be subsumed by the greater struggle Milton is about to inaugurate.

18:51 – 19:14   This magnificent sequence is close to the center of the poem's complexities of meaning. The contest of Urizen with Milton will go on, in one form or another, until the poem's conclusion.

Urizen begins by turning the clay under Milton's feet to a purgatorial marble, but this is insufficient to stop the prophet's advance, and Urizen therefore is compelled to a direct wrestling match, reminiscent of the wrestling at Peniel between Jehovah and Jacob. But Milton, as the New Israel, seeks no Urizenic blessing; his high purpose is to remake Urizen-Jehovah in the image of man, by using the red clay that formed Adam, as an agent of humanization.

The Arnon River divides the cross-Jordan lands of the Israelites from Moab. Blake may be employing the association between the Arnon and the Red Sea in Numbers 21:14. The Arnon is a river of error, and like the Red Sea, its crossing symbolizes a movement toward life, from Moab to Canaan, from Urizen to a redeemed Luvah who is Christ. In *Jerusalem* 89:25, and on Plate 38 of this poem, the Arnon is a river of possessive love, the jealousy of the Selfhood.

Mahanaim (from Genesis 32:2) is the place of Jacob's wrestling with Jehovah. Succoth may be a complex reference here, combining 1 Kings 7:46 and Genesis 33:17.

Beth Peor (Deuteronomy 34:6) is the burial place of Moses. A radical simplification of the passage's meaning might be ventured in these terms: Urizen is seeking to baptize Milton into the moral law, lest a new Incarnation come into the fullness of prophetic vision. Milton seeks to mold Urizen into a New Adam, utilizing the materials with which Christ gave vision to the blind man (Frye, "Notes", p 134). Since Urizen is a Deist conception of Jehovah, Milton is seeking to re-form a contemporary vision of God. The clay is of Succoth, because Milton wishes to bring about a festival of human harvest (Genesis 33:17) in which the Divinity will be proper to a new Temple (1 Kings 7:46) of restored Man.

19:15–26   This is a comprehensive vision of the fallen world, the Urizenic Mundane Shell, which Milton strives to clear away. The geography of it is repeated from *The Four Zoas.*

19:27 – 20:6   If Milton were to be enticed across the river, to a symbolic Canaan, he would give up his quest for a New Israel of awakened Albion. Watching the struggle between the life-giving Milton and death-giving Urizen, and fearing Milton's triumph, Rahab and Tirzah attempt the essentially political temptation to which the historical Milton once yielded. Rahab here is the tendency within the prophet toward founding yet another church; Tirzah is the parallel tendency toward ascetic restrictiveness. For Blake, the historical Milton erred by serving Cromwell's imperfect revolution, whose goddesses were Rahab and Tirzah in different guises, Hermaphroditic emblems of religion-hid-in-war, and sadism-hid-in-natural possessiveness. The reference to Entuthon, the forest of error, and the hermaphrodite symbolism both attest to the solipsistic vision of Ulro.

The song of temptation (19:36 – 20:6) opens with a reference to Ephraim as a synonym for the northern kingdom of Israel (whose capital was at Tirzah, and whose main tribe was Ephraim) for the northern kingdom stands for the lost tribes and spiritual bondage. The Amalekites are traditional enemies of the Promise, and are associated here with the Urizenic chain of jealousy binding Orc the natural man, which Milton has descended to unbind in accordance with ancient prophecy. The remainder of the passage deals with contemporary Europe, visualized as being a ghost world, in Rephaim's Vale (see 2 Samuel 5:18–25, where Rephaim, meaning perhaps giant shades, is the place of assembly for the Philistines before David smites them). In this ghostly Europe, the best emanations lament, and humanity is crucified by natural religion and puritanical restrictiveness. The symbolism of *Jerusalem* is introduced to give a culminating effect of tyranny, with the figures of Hand, Hyle, Coban, Scofield, and Reuben, the first four being sons of Albion and the last a son of his biblical prototype, Jacob. Hand, Hyle, and Coban are the triple Accuser of man in *Jerusalem.* Hand is the Spectre of Urizen or fallen mind; Hyle is fallen matter, and Coban is an emblem of political tyranny. Scofield (the actual soldier who accused Blake of treason) is a new Adam of the Urizenic kind, a soldier who stands before the gate of every Reuben, the ordinary, unstable man among Jacob's sons. In 19:58 ff, Hand has become the rock of the Law, and Hyle and Coban, the Law's surroundings in Sinai and Horeb. Tirzah's triumph is to have separated the sexes still further (19:60 – 20:2) and given them the illusive vision of the triple heavens of Beulah as a final goal. The song ends with a further invitation into the bondage of the earthly kingdom, where Milton would be a King of Canaan, like Cromwell, and reign in Hazor (burned by Joshua in Joshua 11:10–13), a city of destruction.

20:7–14   Throughout the remainder of the poem, Milton's Reprobate, prophetic, Human portion is in the domain of Eternity; his Elect portion, belonging to the past, is frozen into the rock of the Law; his redemptive aspect battles on, re-forming Urizen.

20:15–24   In this difficult passage, the Elect portion or Spectre of Milton surges over ("redounding") from Blake's left foot, where the two poets were joined. Since only the Reprobate in Milton has joined Blake, his "Spectrous body", or everything Miltonic that Blake rejected in the *Marriage,* is free to seek a place at the tomb of the Law, the abode of the Covering Cherub on Sinai in Horeb.

20:25–42   In a return to "The Fly", Blake gives an epitome of the entire poem. The descent of Milton begins to awaken Albion, a stirring which inaugurates a statement of the poem's theme, the necessity of casting off everything in the self that is not human. As even a fly is a Minute Particular of creation, capable of opening within to the eternal contraries, so man is urged all the more to open his internal gates to reality, to "seek not thy heavenly father then beyond the skies". Beyond the skies is Chaos, the Ulro of a Newtonian universe, and the proper realm of the giants Og and Anak, menaces to the quest for the Promised Land (see Numbers 21 and Joshua 11:21). The "brain and heart and loins" of man can either constitute a Urizenic Web of Mystery or Seat of Satan, or can open into the City of Art, in the sexual potential of fallen man. So Milton, falling into our hearts in his imaginative return, can remind us of our ability to turn inward to find salvation.

20:43–21:3   Like the Eternals in The Book of Urizen, the Eternals here are treated with an evident irony, for they resent Milton's quest. The Shadowy Eighth is the Eternal Milton and also an emblem of Christ; the Watchers are the Seven Eyes. Forced out of Eden, the Eight descend into the generative world through the head, heart, and loins of Los, and become guards against the Ulro. Pondering this descent, Los fears the departure of his sons Rintrah and Palamabron, his own powers of cleansing wrath and genuine or civilizing pity, for the descent of the Eight is a sign that apocalypse may be at hand. The mention of Reuben and Gad is a reference to Joshua 22, where those tribes build an altar to God, which is mistaken by the other tribes as a transgression. Blake therefore implies that the threatened departure of Rintrah and Palamabron is only provisional, a seeming abandonment of Los. Misunderstanding, Los weeps, gazing into the black water of fallen history, the blood of Albion, which in Jerusalem 4:10 will be spoken of as accumulating against a judgment. In this moment of despair, Los is saved by a poetic recollection, the old prophecy of Milton's liberation of Orc. The descent of Los to Udan-Adan, a world of illusive appearances, is a deliberate reduction of the imagination to the poverty of night, for in the Satanic state Los encounters, either the Shadow of restrained desire or the Spectral censor is always awake. By descending to view things at their worst, Los prepares himself for his apotheosis on Plate 22.

21:4–14   This great declaration reverberates throughout the poem, for by it Blake and Milton have become one poet. Blake is henceforth both Reprobate and Redeemed, prophet and poet, and so enjoys a greater power of vision. The entrance of Milton is by the foot, for that is the body part associated with Urthona, and the unity of Milton and Blake is through the Los in each. Where the imagination, in Eternity, found its true place in the earth of Eden, the auricular nerves of strong Urthona, it now dwells in Ulro beneath Beulah. But these nether regions have been opened to the sight of Eternity, by the vast breach Milton's descent has made in the heart of the ruined Albion. Though Blake is not aware, at the moment of union, that he has received Milton's power, he is granted the vision of the natural world as a redeemable bright sandal, on the left or time-bound foot. In an act of acceptance and prophetic will, Blake binds the sandal on for the forward walk of the ensuing poem.

21:15–22:3   In this beautiful transition, the mental awakening of Blake and of Milton receives its complement in the resolution to descend of Ololon, the aggregate of Milton's sixfold emanation. Ololon is the river of life in Eden, akin to the "pure river" of Revelation 22:1. Since the eternal form of his emanations constitutes Milton's potential achievement, rather than his actual ones, it is useful to identify Ololon as "history-as-it-should-have-been" (see Erdman, p 394 and p 401). In that sense, Ololon is like the "cancelled cycles" of Shelley's Prometheus Unbound IV, and her reunion with Milton is indeed a "marriage of prophecy and history". The lamentation of Ololon (she is both sixfold and single, and so is alternately "they" and "she") is an outcry of lost human potential, but more than "the crying of women to the gods" is involved (see Fisher, p 248, for the probable source of Ololon's name). It is the lament of everything unawakened that now desires the message of "Milton the Awakener". All of Eden that failed to understand the Bard's Song now understands that Reprobate message.

The resolve of Ololon brings into Milton's world what the historical Milton failed to give, the vision of a redeemed woman, the bride of the Great Marriage of biblical tradition (see Frye, pp 351–352). That the appearance of Jesus to a world in torment is associated with the descent of Ololon links her in turn to the bride, "new Jerusalem", of Revelation 21:2.

22:4–25   In response to Ololon, Blake now moves to his second union, with Los, an act that completes the transformation of Los as begun in *The Four Zoas*. After becoming one with Milton, Blake could see Generation in its redemptive aspect. After his integration with Los, the Ulro can be redeemed, for Los binds on the poet's sandals in the satanic Udan-Adan, the nadir of vision. The terror of both Los and Blake is an anticipatory dread of the violent transformation an apocalyptic renewal necessarily involves. After their union, the terrors of Los become "fury & strength" in Blake. The whole process is Wordsworthian, as feeling comes in aid of feeling, and diversity of strength attends the poet-prophet. Immensely moving as the speech of Los (lines 19–25) is, it denies the pathos of loss, as if Blake were determined to avoid a central Wordsworthian theme. The Los of this speech is almost Urthona again, or at least knows what Urthona knows.

22:26–23:30   Here Blake is distinct from Palamabron, as he could not be in the Bard's Song. The point is surely a deliberate one, showing that Blake has progressed from being a son of Los to Los himself. With Los, Blake is going to the "supreme abode" of art, Golgonooza, but finds the Gate barred by wrath and pity, Rintrah and Palamabron, prophetic and civilizing functions that cannot yet understand the favorable turn in their battle. To them, Milton is a "Shadow terrible", like his own Lucifer, who will unchain the natural energies of Orc so prematurely as to unloose the enemies of vision upon the sleeping Albion. From the vegetating left foot of Milton, the sons of Los behold a cloud of Puritanical thought darkening Europe. Most simply, the sons blame "Miltons Religion" for the "Deism" of Blake's age. Deism now means not only the beliefs of Voltaire and Rousseau, but the decline of the visionary Swedenborg into his own variety of dogmatic orthodoxy and predestinarianism. Against these the sons set the enthusiasm of the Methodist Revival, whose activities are a presage of the apocalyptic advent. Whitefield and Wes[t]ley, forms of Rintrah and Palamabron respectively, are the two "Witnesses" of Revelation 11:8, Elijah and Moses, and the Great City is at once London and Sodom or Egypt, city of tyrannical bondage. Signs of apocalypse crowd upon us, from the rising of natural man in America to the wars of revolution in Europe. The Covering Cherub, advancing from the East, is the terror of continental warfare. To the sons, Milton's return is another aspect of this war; he is part of the Urizenic Puritanical order, one with the Triple Accuser or sons of Albion, and covered by the garment of religious warfare, woven by Gwendolen and Conwenna, oldest and youngest of the Daughters of Albion, or aggregate Female Will. Correct as they are about the historical Milton, the sons of Los are now mistaken, and their father rejects their proposal to imprison the returned poet in the lowest regions of the imaginative conception of man. By a curious irony, Blake conceives of the physiological laws of existence as a dungeon formed by the imagination, a foundation for all that we build upon in our conceptions of the self.

23:31–24:43   Los warns against "fury premature", like the religious violence of the Protestant reformers. There is some element here of self-chastisement on Blake's part, of the gathering conviction that even for the prophet a mode of patience is necessary. To quench the Sun of Salah in Udan Adan would be to gratify prematurely a lust for completion like that of Tamar (see Genesis 39) who was compelled by Judah to postpone her rightful claim to his son Salah (or Shelah). What Los fears is the imaginative waste of history repeating itself again, as the generations of his sons, like the tribes of Israel, have been lost to him. The other Zoas being gone, he is left alone "the Watchman of Eternity", with his four principal sons to take the place of his brethren. In his unhappy remembrances, Los reviews the falling away of the Gentile nations, the loss of Joseph, and the subsequent captivity in Egypt of the Chosen. If Rintrah and Palamabron follow all these, they will become ruins of Ulro. Against such a falling off, Los opposes the resurrection of Lazarus, a type of the raising of Albion. The Covering Cherub subsumes this miracle of Jesus and is now described in the symbolism of the Churches or false cycles of belief pretending to found themselves on Jesus. The warning of Los to his sons culminates in the fear of a reduction to the merely natural level of the Polypus. Against this fate, the visionary places of Bowlahoola and Allamanda exist, for beyond them the human cannot fall into disorganization. The complex speech climaxes in the insistence that Milton is a portent of apocalypse.

24:44–67   This grotesque passage has its equivalents and possible sources in Spenser and Milton, though to know that neither excuses nor saves it. Anthropomorphic myth has its difficulties, and Blake was not the poet to evade them.

24:68–76   This fine recovery is most memorable for lines 72–73, one of Blake's great commonplaces.

25:1–65   We are moving toward the great vision of Generation becoming the world of Los, which will end the first book of *Milton*. This vision is introduced by the Wine-press of warfare in Blake's own time, for these wars herald the Last Vintage, just as the recovery of nature through the vision of Los is also a herald of the End.

The Wine-press, as Blake grimly stresses, is most dreadful in the central cities, like the London of the *Songs*, where human thought is crushed. The song at the Vintage, and response of Los to the suppliant souls, indicate again the necessity for patience and the putting aside of premature judgment.

The speech of Los to the Labourers of the Vintage emphasizes the Three Classes of the Bard's Song as apocalyptic categories. Among the creations of the Elect are the Greek and Northern mythologies, which are overcome now by the biblical image of "the Supper of the Lamb & his Bride", and the Blakean image of the "awaking of Albion".

25:66 – 26:12   Certainly one of the great chants in Blake, this is also one of the rare appearances in his most mature work of a celebration of the natural world, though the celebration is deliberately and severely qualified by lines 26:11–12.

Here, in the climactic passages of Book I, the world of Generation is recovered for the prophetic vision, by being re-seen as a creation of Los, and no longer of Urizen. This is the redemption of Experience, as Book II of *Milton* will center on the redemption of Innocence. This chant then, and all that follows it down to the end of Book I, celebrates a prodigious enterprise of the poet's eye, unlike anything earlier in Blake's poetry, and having no parallel in *Jerusalem*, where it would be out of place.

The star world of Experience, no longer seen as Urizenic in its movements, is in harmony with the now calm Ocean of Tharmas. The triumphant triple repetition of "These are the Sons [or Children] of Los" confirms the new parentage of the phenomenal world; the Fly of Experience is redeemed from death to a dance of life; and most remarkable of all, the wind appears, uniquely in Blake's poetry, as a benevolent force of inspiration, unlike the destructive, nature-uprooting wind of Beulah. Together, the mundane is seen as "the Visions of Eternity", even as Wordsworth saw such visions in the Simplon Pass. But all this is seeing "as it were the hem" of the garments of Eternity, as Blake reminds us we are beholding such rapture "with our vegetable eyes".

26:13–22   Like the two Gates in *Thel* 6:1, these Gates presumably stem from Homer's Cave of the Nymphs, and Blake's use of them may involve something of the symbolism in Porphyry's commentary on the matter. But, as in *Thel*, Blake's use of the Gates is Spenserian (as in the Gardens of Adonis) and not esoteric; no profound immersion in the bathos of the occultist is necessary to understand Blake here, or anywhere else. Damon (p 421) usefully associates the southern descent to the body with Urizen, and the northern ascent from the body with Urthona. Being born involves achieving the mundane incarnation of which Urizen is the designer; dying places one in the realm of the imagination. Los bends his sustaining force against the east, because that is Luvah's quarter now vacated, and the consequently unruly passions (idealized in Beulah as the Three Heavens or sexual state) might interfere with the regularity of birth and death on which the fallen system is founded. Since a revelation is at hand, the work of Los and his sons must now be to preserve nature and man against the Last Judgment.

26:23–46   This expositional sequence of passages has no particular poetic value, and yet forms the necessary base from which the greatness of Plate 29 rises. Allamanda (whose name suggests the alimentary canal as Bowlahoola suggests the bowels) is the cultivated land around the City of Los, and is a place of humanized labor or visionary commerce, with a function in society akin to the one the alimentary canal has in the body. Luban, encountered previously in *The Four Zoas*, is the principal gate into the City, and is properly identified with the saving function of individual vision. Cathedron is also familiar from *The Four Zoas*, as the place where mortal garments are woven. Blake emphasizes that while the coverings are benevolent and natural, they are not the product of natural but of spiritual power. Plate 26 ends with a denial of all natural causation, an extravagance even for Blake, but justified in this apocalyptic context. The use of "ratio" in a reductive sense in line 46 carries us back all the way to the early illuminated tracts, and is another instance of the deliberate and radical unity of Blake's work.

27:1–41   Most of this is from *The Four Zoas*, Night IX, though expanded and differently arranged. The changes are noted in Damon, p 420. See my commentary on *The Four Zoas* IX 136:13–137:1.
    The function of the vision of the Wine-Press, in this context, Plate 27, is both to afford a contrast to the saving work of Los (hence the "But" that begins Plate 27, and the "But" that begins line 42) and to give apocalyptic significance to the warfare of Blake's age. The powerful metaphor of lines 8–10, in which "War on Earth" is at once Wine-Press and the "Printing-Press Of Los", is an epitome of the direction of the entire passage. What Blake-Los, *in this poem*, does with the Wine-Press, is to turn the image of warfare against itself, so as to turn the wheel of Revelation against the wheel of natural bloodletting. Blake anticipates the demonic reversal of this image in the blank verse poem of *Jerusalem* 77, where the wheel of warfare reappears as "the Wheel of Religion", going "against the current of Creation".

27:42 – 29:65, the end of Book I   This is a continuous chant celebrating the world of Los and his Sons, and maintains an extraordinary tone of exaltation, climaxing in Plate 29, one of Blake's greatest poetic achievements. Lines 29:4–24 seem to me almost without equal in Blake, since they are only expositional and yet have the rapturous eloquence of the greatest of Blake's dramatic passages, including *Milton* 40:28–41, and *Jerusalem* 91:1–31.

27:42–63   These purely expositional passages, deliberately prosaic, have no surprises, but are illuminating deductions from Blake's lifelong attempt to create a grammar of the imagination. Allamanda, the visionary commerce of the Eternal City of Man, is the product of human labor; it is cultivated land reclaimed from the forests of error. On one level, this means that the human nervous system is itself a human creation; Blake insists that all human functions must have conscious sources. The Twenty-seven Heavens of Beulah are the moon-phased Churches of human illusion, mistaken religious doctrines throughout fallen history. These are projected from Ulro, the place of the vegetated False Tongue that was unfallen Tharmas. The ambiguous "it is the Sense of Touch" refers both to Allamanda and the False Tongue, for Allamanda is what Los seeks to make out of the fallen sense of Touch. Against the humanizing labors of Los and his Sons we find in the same place, the human body, the negating labors of the perverted Sons of the Zoas, like Theotormon. The Mills of these self-tormenting beings exist to reduce nature to chaos, and the human to nature. In lines 55–63 the conflict between the opposing Sons is shown in its consequences in the world of Time and Space. The Four Zoas appear here each in his characteristic art: Poetry for Tharmas, Painting for Luvah, Music for Urthona, Architecture for Urizen. In the mundane world, initially created by Urizen the Architect, only Architecture abides in the guise of Science or the unity of fallen knowledge. Through this Providence, the three other Zoas operate in our world but in disguised formulations. The pastoral vision of Tharmas appears as Religion's vision of Paradise, the imaginative harmonies of Urthona survive in the structure of Law, and the visual art of Luvah continues in medicine's attempts to preserve the human form. Surprising as Blake's identifications initially may seem, they carry considerable insight into human intricacies. Line 63 divides up all knowledge into its founding units, the nervous and digestive systems of man.

28:1–43   Here the sons of Los seem to be both the guiding principles of the creative arts and the general spirit behind all saving human labor. The near quotation in line 3 from Theseus in *A Midsummer Night's Dream*, Act V, Scene I, reverses something of Shakespeare's meaning, as Damon notes, pp 421–422. The sons of Los are mostly those who appeared in *Europe*, but there they were seen in their fallen aspect, and not as apocalyptic laborers. Antamon is the spirit of design, in the artist's sense of bounding outline; in *Europe* he represented the collapse of outline into a gross sensuality. Theotormon, in his Urizenic guise an embodiment of masochistic fear, is as a Son of Los a spirit of mutuality, as is Sotha, who also has musical associations, and who declines into a spirit of War in the mundane dimension. Ozoth stands for a broader artist's vision than Antamon, and presumably for self-limiting vision in natural decay.

The work of the Sons of Los here, on Plate 28, is to save the Human Abstract by making it into the Divine Image, to redeem nature into human particulars. So Antamon draws particular images, and the Daughters clothe the spectres so as to create the more human forms that even nature, properly apprehended, can provide.

The symbolism of the sevens and eights in the work of Theotormon, Sotha, and Ozoth, presumably has some relation to the Seven Eyes of God or Angels who attend Milton, and to the Eighth Eye, Jesus, who sometimes appears in their company as a direct sign of apocalypse. See Frye, "Notes", pp 126–127 n 1.

28:44–29:3   In *Europe*, 14:22, Enitharmon, counseling Oothoon to "woman's secrecy", insisted that "Between two moments bliss is ripe", rather than *in* a moment of fulfillment. Here, that sinister statement is reversed, for in the world of vision opened by Los the aperture between two moments is guarded by the benevolence of a Daughter of Beulah. The whole of this passage is a saving vision of time, even as the concluding passages, from 29:4 to the close of Book I, constitute a saving vision of space. The poet's work conquers the Eternity that teases us out of thought, for imaginative time triumphs over clock time by denying its categories.

29:4–26   The sky is a tent on the analogue of the tents of Israel in the Wandering; like those tents it is moved each time the divinely led imagination of man chooses to move it. The universe, and the last judgment upon it, are seen by each man according to the position that he holds, for the celestial regions are the creations of human vision. Each loss of a man diminishes the heavens, quite literally, for the appearances of Newtonian vision are delusions of Ulro, solipsistic consequences of abstract reasoning, and not to be seen through any instrument whatsoever. For all space is visionary as is all time, except for the irreducible particulars of the red globule of man's blood and the pulsation of the human artery. To reduce to smaller than those human particulars, we must open into Eternity, from the center of our own being. The particulars themselves, like the digestive and nervous systems, are creations of Los, invisible suns within us that give forth the pure flame of life.

29:27–End of the First Book   Most of this is eloquent recapitulation, necessary to fill out the vision of the redemption of the world of Experience. The Four Senses are to be related to the Zoas, the Optic being Urizen's, the Nostrils Luvah's, the Ears Urthona's, and the closed Nerves of the Tongue Tharmas'. The fifth sense, as before, is the lost sense of touch, having been unified in Eternity by Tharmas as taste and touch together.

The error of Urizen's mundane creation is summarized in lines 32–34; the limits of Opacity and Translucence, Contraction and Expansion, are set in the natural world of Luvah, 35–39. The work of Los is epitomized in 40–46, after which a grand summation of themes and images is attempted. Blake allows himself the bitter and effective irony of line 49, where the virtues undoubtedly urged upon him by Hayley receive a definitive statement.

In the final passage of Book I, the war of vision against Satan's Watch-Fiends is seen in its darker aspects, for the greater emphasis falls on the multiple forms of the adversary, the Female Will in its many guises of Rahab, Tirzah, and the Daughters of Zelophehad. The identity of Blake's situation and biblical tribulation is again suggested, for Blake's Vale of Surrey is one with Horeb, desert of moral virtue, ensuing in Rephaim, or the shades of a death-in-life. In the final sweep of vision here, the waters of the earth rise to wash the black Woof of death woven by Tirzah's restrictive doctrines, and the gore of suffering humanity is "woven" into the great veil of covering nature, the oceans from the Atlantic to the South Sea. All of Ocean together is now the Erythrean, the Red Sea of affliction over which the vision of Los must help us to pass. The Elohim are one of the Seven Eyes as gods of creation, and so all of Nature, seen through the eyes of Blake-Los, can be considered a necessary part of the bloody progression toward revelation. With this deliberately equivocal declaration, the precarious recovery of Experience is completed.

MILTON
Book the Second

30:1 – 31:7 The Vision of Beulah This is Blake's most extended treatment of the state of Beulah or organized Innocence. The most extensive commentaries on Blake's Beulah are in Percival, pp 52–59, Frye, pp 227–235, and, in much more general terms, in my *The Visionary Company* (New York 1961), pp 15–27.

As Book II of *Milton* concerns the self-purgation of Milton and of Ololon, and the recovery of Innocence by their reunion in the Great Marriage, it is appropriate, indeed inevitable, that the Book open with an account of the lower paradise of Beulah, for the redemption of that state from its ambiguities will be central to the Book's theme.

Beulah is both static and less than fully human, though it is a vision of the earthly paradise, or nature in its best and most imaginative aspect. There can be no progression through contraries in it, and progression is necessary to human existence, whether to the fallen human in Generation or the primordial or restored human in Eden. The paradox of Beulah is therefore that it is both a higher and lower state than Generation or Experience. The dangerous similarity of the lower level or gate of Beulah to Ulro is always in Blake's mind, and hovers throughout this long description which opens Book II of the poem.

In 30:10–12 the maternal aspect of Beulah is emphasized, but Blake is careful to indicate that Beulah appears as the loving Mother Nature only to its own inhabitants; to the Sons of Eden it is only a moonlit rest from the "great Wars of Eternity", the imaginative struggles of creation. The proper inhabitants of Beulah are the Emanations, as befits a sexual state-of-being. One of Blake's subtlest references, in 30:24–25, is to the caduceus, the winged staff of Hermes, for which see Percival, pp 53–54. George Sandys, in his commentary on *Metamorphoses* II, appears to be Blake's source.

31:8–27 The descent of Ololon to Beulah is associated with the apocalyptic coming of the Lord, for Ololon is the totality of Milton's achievement, and the function of the poet is to bring about the time of Revelation. Europe's expectation of the Judgment, as manifested in a universal lament, is felt even by the Four Elements, for they are the residue of the Zoas. In their totality as the world of matter they are Satan and Rahab, respectively intellectual and spiritual solipsism as these are derived from a vision of reality as matter alone. Individually the Elements are Fairies-Air-Urizen, Nymphs-Water-Tharmas, Gnomes-Earth-Urthona, and Genii-Fire-Luvah. These are of Generation alone, and can be saved only by Creation, by the artist's vision. Without being newly created through the Mental War of the Eternals, they are doomed to the Corporeal strife of Blake's day, the wars of revolution and reaction, the wars of the natural man howling as a threat to the European conception of the heavens. The "All Beulah weeps" is an appropriate conclusion to this elemental recital of woes.

31:28–63   The Lamentation of Beulah   This great chant has no real parallel elsewhere in Blake, for Blake wrote this kind of poetry only when the context of his work absolutely demanded it, and neither his earlier works set in the state of Innocence nor his vision of that state restored in *The Four Zoas*, Night IX, called for an expression of the full glory of Beulah as seen from the standpoint of Generation. The earlier visions of Beulah were from within that state, though it can be argued that the ironies of Experience flickered throughout.

From Generation, any song of Beulah must be a Song of Spring, like the Song of Solomon, even as from Eden the songs of Beulah would seem to betoken the Autumn of the body, while Generation would seem the start of fresh, natural life, the Spring of the fallen year. The "Thou" addressed in lines 28 and 46 of this chant is the generative man, and so the subtle paradox, on which the entire chant depends, is that it is a lamentation which we, men of Generation, hear as a rejoicing Song of Spring. The inhabitants of Beulah are lamenting the descent of Ololon from Eden through Beulah to Generation; they see this as a fall. But their weeping is as Spring rain to us, for any song of the Earthly Paradise must seem happy when heard from the experiential world.

The chant takes the Nightingale's song as the foremost in nature, perhaps honoring Milton in so doing, since the invocation to Book III of *Paradise Lost* contains the poet's comparison of his nocturnal labors in composing his poem to the nightingale's singing. More central to the chant are the two emblematic identifications, of the Lark's song, and of the wild thyme's attributes, as messengers of Los, signs that the creating vision is at hand. As such they recur in 35:48 – 36:12 and in 42:29–30, the poem's conclusion.

Og (Numbers 21:33–35) and Anak (Numbers 13:33) are giant figures who opposed the Israelites, and are called the arches of Albion's Tomb in *Jerusalem* 49:54–59. Here Blake uses them ironically, for they guard the Center of individual vision though they have an impulse to destroy it, just as Og and the Anakites sought to destroy the Israelites, but nurtured their resolution instead, refining the Israelites through the struggle of contraries.

Even as the close of Book I was a redemption of Generation, so this chant is the first expression in the poem of the redemption of Beulah. Book I showed us the consequences of Milton's decision to descend; Book II has now begun to show us what follows from Ololon's answering decision.

32:1–7   The sudden transition here is thematically appropriate, for Ololon is descending through Beulah on a quest for the newly generated Milton. Left behind in Eden is Milton's Eternal Form, watched over by the Seven Angels. In a startling use of his manuscript poem, "My Spectre around me", Blake now sums up his brief epic's major conflict. The Heavens of Eden are built on cruelty because they have an element of exclusiveness. Milton's natural part or Spectre is pursuing Ololon through the Ulro, quite vainly, but the reward for his quest is that she is now descending to him. Lines 6–7 may reflect Blake's bitterness at his detractors, but primarily they anticipate the great declaration of Milton on Plate 41, particularly 41:12–24.

32:8–9   We do not know how much Hebrew Blake had, yet it is clear that his Hillel here has nothing to do with the famous rabbi, but rather has some relation to the *Helel* or day-star of Isaiah 14:12, first translated in the Vulgate as Lucifer. The confusion of Helel and Hillel, in this context, is an ancient one, but it is difficult to see why Blake repeats it unless he definitely wishes us to recall Isaiah 14:12, as a Hebraic (or Babylonian) analogue to the myth of Phaethon. Lucifer is one of Blake's Seven Eyes of God or Angels of the Presence; the "Hillel" reference presumably reinforces the confession of fallen history that takes up the rest of Plate 32.

32:10–43   Essentially this is doctrinal recapitulation of Blake's own central story, but he phrases it with extraordinary vigor, and it is certainly his most memorable presentation of the myth of "States". In his *Vision of the Last Judgment* Blake wrote of States that "when distant they appear as One Man but as you approach they appear Multitudes of Nations". The Seven Eyes, which are both historical cycles and stages within individual life, are not Individuals but Combinations thereof, multitudes awaiting the Judgment. They know themselves therefore to be impermanent and fallen; as Druids (line 11) they founded natural religion based on warfare and human sacrifice, under the dominion of Albion's Spectre. They proceed to the story of the two Limits of Satan and Adam, the twenty-seven Churches and other familiar matter, but with the radical innovation of the new State of Eternal Annihilation of Self, about to be created in the regenerated Milton. The best commentary on this state remains that of Murry, *passim*. Line 29 is rhetorically curious for Blake, yet very moving in its context.

The sequence reaches its climax with the identity of Imagination and "the Human Existence" in line 32. The brilliant condensation of 32:34 ought to be pondered by anyone who has been baffled by Blake's attitude toward sexual love; divided from Imagination it becomes a State, and States must yield to progression, and not attempt permanence in their own right. The judgments that follow, on the Memory and the Reason, are characteristic, but more tempered now by tolerance than ever before. The plate ends with one of the central images of *Milton*, probably suggested to Blake by his own earlier use of it in the *Marriage*, where Swedenborg's writings were the linen clothes folded up, castoff garments of Natural Religion. Milton has announced his resolve to descend by taking off the robe of the promise on Plate 14. Here, at the close of Plate 32, the Regenerate see in the castoff clothes of the body of death the destruction of the natural destiny woven for them by the Female Will.

33:1–24   Ultimately this plate stems from Isaiah 62, with its crucial fourth verse. The speaker of Plate 33 is the unfallen Man-God, and he addresses what will become Rahab-Tirzah-Vala, the aggregate Female Will, ironically called "Virgin Babylon". This outcry against jealousy, the dark secret love of natural possessiveness, is carried over from the Notebook poems and *Visions*.

34:1–23   This difficult descent of Ololon is best explained in Frye, "Notes", pp 136–137: "Her journey differs from Milton's in that she traverses the created rather than the creating states, or the four emanation worlds". In order, these are Beulah, Alla (a place of sleep in *Jerusalem* 89:58), Al-Ulro, and Or-Ulro (these do not occur elsewhere in Blake's work). Since these four states reflect the four eternal ones, it would seem that Alla has the same relation to Beulah that Beulah has to Eden. This means that Alla would be a state of unconditioned dreaming, a fantasy world. The two lower states are emanations of our world, which means that even Generation can only create and love a form of Ulro, Al-Ulro. Beneath this is the "creation" of Ulro, the monstrosity of Or-Ulro. As visions, Blake assigns these four states to the Head, Heart, Loins, and digestive system respectively, following the generic structure of the Zoas.

Ololon, with great courage, seeks out the Or-Ulro, which is described by allusion to Thel's vision at the end of her *Book*. Since her quest is for Milton, she must follow the track of his course "To where the Contraries of Beulah War beneath Negations Banner". As these Contraries are equally true in that context, such war leads to no progression, and so exalts only the barren cause of Negation.

34:24 – 35:33   This vision of our life, of Blake's historical moment and ours, is developed from the similar vision in Night VIII of *The Four Zoas*, especially 113:8–15. Lines 34:32–39 are repeated from *Milton* 19:15–21, so as to remind us of our situation. Powerful as this sequence on Plates 34–35 is, it is essentially a consolidation of symbolism presented earlier in the poem, including the reappearance of the daughters of Zelophehad. It may be noted that the "War & Hunting" of Eden are of course "Mental Fight", and that their function as the "Two Fountains of the River of Life" is renewed in the apocalyptic "Moment" of 35:48–53. The exaltation of work done in the generative world in 35:18–25 is very moving. Without "passing the Polypus", or mass of natural life, the new Jerusalem of Golgonooza cannot be seen. When sexual incarnation is accepted, as it has been by Milton, the poetic or Four-fold vision becomes possible, and the City of Art is seen.

The "they" of 35:29–31 is Ololon, for she is at once single and six-fold, even as Milton is at once sleeping in Eden, wrestling with Urizen in the mundane world, and seeking Ololon without pause.

35:34–41   This beautiful passage is deliberately poised before the Moment of salvation. Ololon's descent through the earthly paradise to the fallen earth of time and space has opened a wide road from Ulro to Eden, a way of salvation, directly contrary to the way of destruction opened by Sin and Death in *Paradise Lost*. The glory of Ololon's multitudes is the special radiance of the Divine coming again as the Human.

35:42 – 36:12   This sequence, at once one of Blake's triumphs of invention and a central statement of his beliefs, is organized around the Messengers of Los, the Lark and the Wild Thyme, both of them introduced earlier in the poem. The saving Moment exists in each day, but Blake particularizes a Moment in his Felpham garden on Plate 36. Nevertheless, the wonderful description down to 36:12 is concerned with each day, and not a particular day of Blake's experience.

The whole of this sequence finds a clear parallel in Wordsworth's account of "spots of time" in The *Prelude*, for like Wordsworth Blake is concerned with renovation, and a renovation initially dependent upon mundane experience. The distinction, as always between Blake and Wordsworth, comes in Blake's insistence on a vision that surmounts the context of nature, for Golgonooza is vital to the passage, and cannot be apprehended naturally.

It is important to remember that the Moment is that of Ololon's actual arrival in our world, a pulsation of the artery in which Blake's work as poet is done. The Moment is hidden from the merely Satanic vision of empiricism, even though it is a moment within the context of space and time. Its two streams stem from the pure river of water of life in Revelation 22:1. One flows through the poet's act of creation on to a restored earthly paradise and then on to Eden or finality. The reference to "Los's western Wall" may be to the human body as a limit of the Fall. The other stream at first appears to be lost, since it flows through the abyss of space and the organized delusions of the Twenty-seven Churches, only to end in Satans Seat, or mere waste and error, but beyond that Seat it flows again into Golgonooza and is reunited to its sister stream. This is one of Blake's most hopeful declarations, for it insists that nothing is lost from the poet's Moment, a statement directly contrary to Shelley's in *The Defence of Poetry*, where the mind in creation is confronted by the necessity of loss.

The Wild Thyme is the messenger of Los from Generation to Eden, a destructive demon only to the dweller in Ulro. As a purple flower on Luvah's rock of sacrifice, the Wild Thyme recalls the traditional pastoral emblem for the death of a young man or god. But the tomb here is empty; Luvah, being Christ, is risen, and Ololon awaits the risen man.

The Larks fly backward in time through the Heavens of the Twenty-seven Churches into which the Seven Eyes are divided, for Luther or Protestantism is the most recent of the Churches. As a reminder of the creative power of Los, the Lark prevents the deathly slumber of any of the Seven Eyes. The Twenty-eighth Lark, like the sometime-mentioned Eighth Eye, is a direct emblem of apocalypse in the here and now, and hence the final Lark or "mighty Angel" who meets Ololon as she descends into Blake's garden to herald the revelation that is to climax the poem.

36:13 – 37:3   Ololon here is represented again as being both the plural "They" of 36:14, the mighty Hosts of emanations voluntarily descending from their selfish separate existences in Eden, and the "One Female . . . a Virgin of twelve years" who will give herself to Milton in the Great Marriage. Confronting her in his garden, Blake hails her as a Daughter of Inspiration or true Muse, who can bring to a culmination the poet-prophet's three-year epic labor, and comfort the exhausted wife of the poet. Ololon has taken on herself the guilt of having driven Milton from Eternity, by her act of separate existence there, though this can be termed an "act" only in an ironic sense.

37:4 – 38:8   In this sequence, Milton's Shadow is identified with everything in the fallen world that blocks imaginative redemption. Blake concentrates here most of his negative symbols in a powerful catalogue of dread. All of them are united in an attempt to usurp the truth; taken together they represent the imposture of organized religion down through the ages. The fullest commentary on this sequence is in Damon, pp 426–427, and, more indirectly, in Frye, "Notes", *passim*.

Milton's Shadow consists of the errors of vision in his work, and the consequent influence of those errors on English culture. Yet Milton's errors form only a small part of the Shadow, which in its most comprehensive form appears as the Covering Cherub, guardian of the truth become a demonic agent. Within the Shadow or Cherub are Satan and Rahab, and many lesser forms of error. The Wicker Man of Scandinavia, a "Druidic" figure possibly derived from Caesar's *Commentaries* (see Damon, p 426), burns his victims in the stars, the symbols of the tyranny of the Sons of Albion.

The Milton who descends into Blake's garden to confront Ololon is at once both "a Cloud & Human Form", a Shadow of error and the true individuality who must be separated from it. In Milton, Blake beholds the gods of the heathen, and draws their list, with fine irony, from Milton's own catalogue in *Paradise Lost* I 374–521. As demonic beings, they are involved in the star world, and so Og and Sihon, enemies of Israel, are found in the constellations Orion and Ophiucus respectively. Orion is visualized by Blake as a giant constellation, embracing the whole of the southern sky, in the form of a twenty-seven fold serpent. Blake may have chosen Orion because of the story in which that hunter perpetually pursues, as a suitor, the Pleiades, who always elude him. Such a pursuit is suggestive of Blake's concept of the Female Will. Ophiucus, on Blake's *Laocoön* plate, is associated with the serpent-knowledge of Good and Evil, the "cloven fiction" of fallen morality. Here, in *Milton*, Ophiucus stands for the twenty-one constellations of the northern sky.

The list of gods from 37:20 ff follows the list in *Paradise Lost* very closely. Even the hermaphroditic symbolism is drawn from the same Miltonic passage, especially from I 421–431.

The Twenty-seven Churches, which follow, are named for their founders. Adam through Lamech are drawn from Genesis 5; Noah through Terah from Genesis 11 and Luke 3:36; Abraham through Luther comprise Blake's version of the seven Churches of the Jews and the Christians. The first group is called Hermaphroditic because associated with the shadow world of the Ulro, where the worshiper and his god are merely images of one another. "Hermaphroditic" is Blake's word for what we tend to call "solipsistic". The second group is called the Female-Males, because here the god worshiped is external to the worshiper, the result being a nature religion of the Tirzah variety, in which the male is pent-up within the womb of nature, and so under the dominion of the female. In the third group, the Male-Females, the god worshiped is external also, yet here the religion is more ostensibly a male one, but is ruled over by a female deity, Rahab, the claim to exclusive salvation and the warfare carried out to enforce that claim. 37:43 identifies Rahab with the Whore of Babylon in Revelation.

The attack on Newton in 37:44–46 is relevant because Blake thought that the mental vision encouraged by Newtonian speculation allowed men to put up with their place in the Covering Cherub of war and societal exploitation. This is amplified in 37:47–49.

Together Sihon and Og compose the Mundane Shell or spectral universe, at once star world and our earth of tyranny and mystery. The Forty-eight constellations are at once the "Cities of the Levites", and so the priest-dominated cities of our world, and "the Heads of the Great Polypus", or the natural intelligences of the fallen world. Because we are moving toward apocalypse, Blake allows himself to interpolate 37:55–59, where the Fires of Los rage in the Caves of Urthona, and thus human creative energy survives in the depths of the Mundane Shell. To descend to these depths is indeed a necessity, for the human experience must include even the forest of night and error.

Out of this dark pronouncement Blake draws the strength to attain the climactic vision of his poem, which begins in the descent of the puritanically attired Milton into the Felpham garden where Ololon and Blake await him.

38:9–27   In this sequence we have the epiphany of Satan, no longer in the particular manifestation of a "mild" Satan-Hayley, but now revealed as what he is, the beast from the sea, the blood-dimmed tide that precedes salvation. His twenty-seven folds are beautiful, for the Churches gather to themselves much of the beauty of this world. For all his sinister splendor, Satan is a thunderer who lacks courage. Yet he has strength insofar as he exists within each man's Spectre. That is part of the meaning of Blake's crying out "I also stood in Satans bosom", for Satan is the ruin in every man. This ruin is spiritual, as the quotation from St Paul implies (2 Corinthians 5:1). What Blake sees in Satan's bosom is the landscape of Ulro, and finally the manifestation of the Whore of Babylon in the communion cup and other mysteries of the Church.

38:28 – 39:2   This is the contest of Milton and Satan, carrying on from the wrestling between Milton and Urizen. Milton refuses to found another sect and thus become only another in the oppressive cycle of the Churches. He chooses instead the difficult way of casting out his Spectre, of annihilating his Selfhood. The selfish virtues of the natural heart culminate in the self's fear of death, but Milton has come to teach us to despise death. Satan's rebuttal is mere bluster, and is interestingly akin to the vainglory of Shelley's Jupiter as he ineffectually confronts Demogorgon in *Prometheus Unbound*.

39:3–31   This is Satan's defeat, as the Seven Angels absurdly claimed by him sound instead the trumpets that usher in the Apocalypse. In his catastrophe Satan achieves a final demonic parody of the truth, very like his appearance at the opening of *Paradise Lost* II.

39:32–61   The struggle of England to awaken here may be based on Milton's vision of an awakening Albion in *Areopagitica*. Though Albion fails to rise here, since Apocalypse is only being heralded, his struggles are rewarded by the sleep of Beulah, as contrasted to his former, deeper sleep in the Night of Beulah. Los keeps watch beneath the moon of Beulah, but the antagonist Urizen begins now to falter in his striving with Milton's Spirit, a contest which has been going on all through the poem. The final lines of Plate 39 are Blake's attempt to explain and justify one of his poem's difficulties, the simultaneous presence of the same figure in different states and places.

40:1–27   Here, in the confrontation between Milton and Ololon, Blake brings together the poet and his creation, man and what is worthy to be loved. Ololon rejects natural religion and the Female Will, naming a formidable list of the Enlightened whom Blake took to be the high priests of Deism, "this impossible absurdity", as she yields to the inspired man or Poetic Genius. Once rejected, Rahab is forced to appear as her true self, the Whore of Babylon in John's vision of Revelation. Beneath this demonic epiphany there is shown the parody of Israel, the nations of fallen nature.

40:28 – 41:28   The terrible majesty of this supreme declaration is independent of even Blake's complexities. One may note the imagery of taking off false garments, which is prevalent throughout the poem. It ought also to be noted that the idiot Questioner is primarily the Spectre, the enemy within every man, rather than just Blake's enemies. One must also warn against misunderstanding 41:25. Blake is certainly not repudiating sexuality. Ololon is to cease to be a virgin; clearly "the Sexual Garments" refer to what is called Female Love in "My Spectre around me . . .". Ololon accepts Human Love, the opposite to the "dark secret love" or Female Love of the "Sexual" state. This would not be worth dwelling upon, were it not that this misinterpretation of Blake is still a prevalent one.

41:29 – 42:15   The sexual fears of Ololon in Eden are now revealed and purged. She awakens to the understanding that she and Milton are truly Contraries, who must war the wars of life, the creative struggles of Eden. In 41:37 – 42:1 she realizes that she must enter her own Vortex, as Milton did his, and so reform her vision. Blake's writing is deliberately dramatic here, and in consequence difficult. Since Ololon becomes "a Double Six-fold Wonder", the shriek of the departing virginal or Female Will portion of her is a shriek of terror at what it takes to be eternal death. But for the purged and humanized half this is a shriek of birth. The Ololon of Female Love joins Milton's rejected Shadow in the depths of the chaotic sea, the watery world of the Ulro. But the Ololon who has chosen Human Love appears as the Dove sent to Noah on that sea. This latter Ololon re-descends to Blake's vale as "a Moony Ark" of salvation, thus heralding the appearance of Jesus in the Starry Eight, folded in the Garment that is at once redemption and imaginative expression, a garment woven in the warfare of six thousand years of fallen history.

42:16 – 43   Here, in the poem's final vision, Blake comes back to himself, triumphantly answering the perplexities of the Bard's Song. The Four Zoas and their trumpets momentarily impel Blake toward his own Last Judgment, but he revives, to await a mortal destiny, following Milton in the belief that body and soul must die together, and be resurrected together. In the assured closing passages, Blake gathers together many of his poem's emblems: the Lark and the Wild Thyme as messengers of Los; the rising of Los and Enitharmon as a wind of possible inspiration; the labors of Rintrah and Palamabron. To these he adds the Oothoon of *Visions*, weeping with joy over the Human Harvest she was denied in that poem. Los is now altogether transformed from the erring creature of the early Nights of *The Four Zoas*. Like Amos and the other prophets, he "listens to the Cry of the Poor Man", and his prophetic anger is bent over London as a cloud of menace, a demand for social justice that threatens destruction if denied. In the closing lines, the Mills of Satan have vanished, and the greatness of the Apocalypse is imminent. It is difficult not to hear the single line of the final plate as a prophetic battle cry, ringing with challenge and with the confidence of the poet-prophet who has been tried severely, and has triumphed over his trials.

↜

JERUSALEM

Structure: The immediate theme of *Jerusalem* is "war and peace", or better yet "peace without vengeance" (Erdman, p 427). What makes *Jerusalem* so very complex is that most of the poem internalizes this theme, so that the terrors of war and vengeance refer primarily to a struggle within Blake's own psyche. What conditions that psyche, as Blake-Los wars against his own Spectre, is the poet's awareness of the later stages of the European conflict against Napoleon, and the subsequent problems of peace in a world dominated by Reaction. For a commentary on these aspects of *Jerusalem*, see Erdman, pp 427–449.

The structure of Jerusalem raises many problems, which the poem's critics (this one included) have not been able to solve. Yet the problem may be only that the poem has not had enough accurate and close readers as yet; in time it may seem no more and no less difficult in structure than *The Faerie Queene* or *The Prelude*, works curiously and wonderfully put together but each on a basis not so discursive as it may first appear.

It is possible that Blake's model for *Jerusalem* was the Book of Ezekiel, in the same general sense that *Paradise Lost* was the model for *The Four Zoas*, and *Paradise Regained* for *Milton*. The Book of Ezekiel, unlike those of the other prophets, has a highly methodical arrangement, being divided into two parts of twenty-four chapters each. Part I is disaster: Jerusalem is besieged, it falls, and the State falls with it. Part II is the painful recovery, in which the people slowly come to regeneration. Looking more closely at each part—the first is subdivided into roughly these divisions: Ezekiel's vision of the Chariot, and his taking up the role of prophet; prophecies of the nation's destruction; the wrongdoings of Jerusalem and the punishment that will ensue; the same as to Judah; finally the prophecy that the State must fall. Part II seems to be in three sections: prophecies on the downfall of the heathen nations; prophecies of the redemption of Judah and Israel; a vision of the restoring of Jerusalem, including provisions for a rebuilt Temple. The structure of Blake's *Jerusalem* has many similarities to this, though not of course to the same degree or in the same way that the Revelation of John bases itself on Ezekiel.

Blake's *Jerusalem* is divided into four equal chapters, each of which depends for its progression on a dialectical struggle of contraries. In Chapter 1 these are Albion and Los, with Albion incarnating the acceptance of chaos and destruction, and Los opposing such acceptance in the name of prophecy and creation. The conflict of forces here is akin to that in the opening quarter of Ezekiel, with Los-Blake in the role of Ezekiel and the English people or Albion in the role of the Jews or Israel. In Blake's second chapter Los works to create an image of salvation from the mere repetition of Albion's natural history. This is Blake's equivalent of Ezekiel's evolving prophecy of the State's destruction for lack of good works. In his third chapter Blake opposes "Deism", the end product of Albion's history, and the vision of a savior, the Blakean Jesus. The parallel is the next movement in Ezekiel, the prophetic denunciation of Ammon, Moab, Edom, Philistia, Tyre, Sidon, and Egypt, which is the prototype for Blake's attack on Mystery and Nature; indeed Blake's Covering Cherub is borrowed from Ezekiel's denunciation of Tyre. Blake's fourth chapter opposes error and truth directly, out of which confrontation comes a prophecy of the Last Judgment; Ezekiel's closing chapters are visions of redemption, and of a City and Temple worthy of that redemption. This general parallel between *Jerusalem* and Ezekiel cannot be taken too far; Blake for instance directly follows Ezekiel and Revelation when he describes Golgonooza, but the description is in the first chapter of his poem, rather than the last. Yet the broad pattern of resemblance exists, and it accounts, I think, for much of Blake's structural procedure in *Jerusalem*. Like Ezekiel, Blake has a strong taste for intellectual symbolism; indeed his central symbolism of the Four Zoas goes back to Ezekiel through Revelation. Yet one senses a stronger link still between Blake and Ezekiel. Ezekiel was the first prophet to put aside the tradition of collective guilt and to insist upon an individual prophetic stance for salvation. His holy remnant is a community, but he always insists upon them as individuals. This emphasis upon personal responsibility heightens Ezekiel's sense of prophetic solitude, and makes him all the more exemplary for Blake. The personal struggle of *Jerusalem*, between the Los in Blake and the Spectre in Blake, is more in the lonely tradition of Ezekiel than in that of the other prophets.

1:1–3   This repeats Ololon's outcry toward the close of *Milton*, 41:37 – 42:1.

PLATE 3   Blake founds this defense of his metric on Milton's introductory remarks to *Paradise Lost*.

Chap: 1

4:1–2   Eternal Death here is Generation, Eternal Life is Eden.

4:3–5   This is probably based on Milton's habit of composing at night, as set forth in the invocations of *Paradise Lost*.

4:33–34   There may be a memory here of Spenser's marriage of the Thames and the Medway.

5:25–33   The Sons of Albion, with three exceptions, have names derived from men involved in Blake's trial for alleged seditious utterances. Kwantok (Quantock), Peachey, and Brereton were judges at the trial. Scofield and Kox are the troopers (Schofield and Cock) who falsely accused Blake; Kotope, Bowen, Hutton, and Slayd presumably had some connection with the case. The first three of the sons, "Hand & Hyle & Coban" are purely invented figures. Hand is evidently based historically on the brothers Hunt, whose magazine had attacked Blake as an insane artist. Hyle as a name suggests both the much-maligned Hayley (who helped mightily in getting Blake acquitted) and a Greek word for "matter", while Coban suggests both Caliban and Francis Bacon of Verulam, whom Blake despised.

More vital than their dubious origins are the functions of these demonic beings. Only four of them matter in *Jerusalem;* the rest fill out a symbolic pattern for Blake. They are at once a Urizenic Zodiac and a sinister jury, before which man is tried and condemned. Hand, Hyle, and Coban are a Triple Accuser, in another pattern that seemed archetypal to Blake, embracing the accusers of Socrates, of Bunyan's Faithful, and perhaps the accusing "comforters" of Job. Hand sometimes represents the three, or all twelve brothers together, and is an equivalent of Satan or the Spectre of Urizen. Scofield is the new

Adam, the typical Englishman of Blake's day. In a broad sense Hand represents fallen reason, Hyle fallen nature, and Coban fallen society, with Scofield the product of their workings.

5:40–45   These sinister representatives of the Female Will are given names drawn from the histories of Britain by Geoffrey of Monmouth and Milton. Only Cambel and Gwendolen have individual importance in the poem; Cambel is the emanation of Hyle and Gwendolen of Hand. For useful speculation on the specific origins of their names, see Damon, p 437.

5:66 – 7:7   Until now, no detailed commentary on the poem has been necessary, for its essential oppositions are familiar to us from *The Four Zoas* and *Milton*. From this point on, an involved conflict peculiar to this poem commences, the struggle of Los against the Spectre of Urthona, his own brother and other self. The earlier form of this struggle in Blake came in Night VIIa in *The Four Zoas*, but there Los was not yet what he became in *Milton*, a figure identical with the awakened imagination in Blake. Even as a central struggle throughout *Milton* took place between Urizen and Milton, so a central struggle in *Jerusalem* is between the Spectre of Urthona and Los, both of them being viewed as impulses *within Blake*. The Spectre of Urthona is now everything in Blake's psyche that wishes to join Albion in his fall, while Los is everything in Blake that goes on writing poems and painting pictures. Blake's psychic cartography is difficult here, and has been elucidated best in Frye, pp 292–299.

The Spectre of Urthona hates Albion and Los (6:6–7) because Los compels him to work for Albion's salvation, when there is not the slightest sign that Albion wants to be saved. Yet Los cannot work without the Spectre of Urthona, for no artistic form can be achieved without the instrumental will of the ordinary ego, with all its stupified jealousies, prides, and fears. The Spectre of Urthona is the involuntary servant of Los, a Caliban to his Prospero, but this Caliban and Prospero are components of the one self, the will and the imagination of each single man.

There is every reason to feel the terrible poignance of a poet's autobiography in 6:8 – 7:7. The Spectre of Urthona wishes to eat and drink, but all Los gives him is song. Still, Los is terrified though finally indomitable, and he has cause for his terror.

7:8–50   Clearly this transcends autobiography, for what confronts Los here is a precise equivalent to the torments visited by the Furies upon Shelley's Prometheus. The anguish here is Blake's, but it is more than the anguish of the unheeded prophet. Primarily, his Spectre wants Los to despair, and protests his refusal to despair. There is more than enough cause; the Triple Accuser is loose in England, and the dictates of that Augustan trinity—reason, nature, and society—serve to confirm the fallen condition of Albion. Coban's son is Nimrod, the tyrant who hunts mankind (for Blake's source, see *Paradise Lost* XII 24 ff) which means that society will be displaced completely by the organized murder of warfare. Kox, Scofield's companion, is the Noah of the "indefinite" world presided over by the starry wheels, so that all of us are seen as a soldiery run amok. The most dreadful implication is in the appearance of Scofield as the new Adam made of the red loam of Edom, for the prophecy of the red man from Edom as savior (Isaiah 63:1–6) is being subverted. The wars of Revolution have produced a brutal Accuser, rather than an image of salvation. Knowing all this, the Spectre of Urthona sums up the tormented situation by the myth of Luvah in the furnaces of affliction, which on one level signifies the debasement of Christianity into natural religion, and on another the martyrdom of France by England. Out of that religion of vengeance Satan, the Spectre of Albion, will emerge as the regent of "a Law of Sin".

7:51 – 8:20   This moving passage heralds a movement in Blake dialectically counter to that in *Milton;* there he had to change from the Pity of Palamabron to the cleansing Wrath of Rintrah. Now, he requires the reverse, for Wrath unchecked would deliver him over to the Spectre here. There is no contradiction here; the theme of *Milton* was poetic incarnation and a theodicy achieved through the imagination. *Jerusalem* begins with all this achieved; its personal theme is the problem of attaining apocalyptic forgiveness through the anti-apocalyptic virtues of patience and pity. The "Religion of Generation" was founded by Urizen to destroy Jerusalem, the Christian Liberty created by the art and love of the whole man, unfallen Albion. But by the work of Blake's poem, this dark religion can be turned inside out, and be transformed into "holy Generation, Image of regeneration". Experience and fallen sexuality are to be redeemed by "mutual forgiveness between Enemies", a more-than-Christian hope.

Hand's manifestation (7:71 – 8:6) is best interpreted by Erdman, pp 422-425. Hand, based on the Hunt brothers' *Examiner,* represents the perversion by Satan of the written word, and so the negation of Blake's work as poet-prophet. What Los-Blake needs to avoid is the "indignant self-righteousness" of Hand, into which the Spectre of Urthona-Blake has fallen. The moral heroism reaches its height in 8:13-19, where Blake demonstrates a total awareness of his grim situation.

8:21-29   Shinar is another name for Babylon, which to Blake is what Europe is fast becoming. London Stone is the hidden center of London and the world, and may be regarded as the foundation stone upon which Golgonooza must be built. It is possible (though with much twisting) to find Hebrew roots in the name Golgonooza which would make it mean "the hidden hub" or center, but the more obvious New Golgotha suggests the same, with no twisting. Golgotha means the place of the skull, or of the wheel or hub, and by many traditions was the navel of the universe. On "London Stone", see Erdman, p 429. Blake stands on the ruin "Of old Jerusalem, of Druid Britain, of Rome, and of modern British freedom", and works at his poem, menaced not only by all his enemies, but more seriously by the Spectre within himself.

8:30 – 9:31   The particular greatness of *Jerusalem* as a poem is in the dramatic and humanistic power of this kind of declaration. The "Chastity" of 8:32 is the Spectre's pretence of moral innocence, its self-righteousness. In a complex way, a passage like this is Blake's equivalent of Wordsworth's "Resolution and Independence", for Blake also is achieving the resolution of inner doubt and despair through seeing his inward struggle as an essential part of the poetic process, rather than just a merely personal psychic torment.

In the negating labors of Hand, Blake sees the deformation of the human image, and fights against this corporeal war by writing and engraving his poem. Lines 9:29-31 might well be *Jerusalem's* motto; they deliberately repeat Palamabron's call to a judgment between Satan and himself (*Milton* 8:46-48)

9:32 – 10:6   For Blake's use of Erin, see Erdman, pp 446-447. Symbolically, "the Spaces of Erin" are a barrier for Albion against the flood of chaos, against a space and time not taken up into a saving vision. Behind this symbolism lay contemporary political fact, or rather the hope that the struggle for Irish emancipation might kindle a more intense struggle for liberty in England.

10:7-21   This is Blake's apologia for his poem's complexities. A systematic vision of all existence is necessary for the poet in an age where the reasoning power has been corrupted. That the vision may be partial Blake admits, but this is the price of creation in a bad time.

10:22 – 11:7   The Children of Los are his creative acts, which the Spectre is willing to surrender, for the temporal will in itself has no impulse toward creation. The Spectre's reply attacks Los where he (and Blake) are most vulnerable, in their sensitivity to the dark, possessive love, or jealousy of their emanative portions. The god of the Spectre is Urizen, for the Spectre is the sickness unto death, the despair of the self at its own meaningless and repetitive existence. There is an echo of Milton's Satan despairing atop Mount Niphates in 10:56 ff, and perhaps a touch of Spenser's Despair as well. Line 11:5 is Blake's definition of his poetic purpose. The "Dead" of 11:6 are those who live in the experiential world.

11:8 – 12:24   The creations of Los join him here in his battle against the sons and daughters of Albion. Scofield, the New Adam of war, takes the place of Reuben, oldest of the sons of Israel. Reuben is the natural man in *Jerusalem,* while Hand is his Spectre. The association with the mandrake here is based on Genesis 30:14, and is best elucidated by Frye, p 369. The mandrake is a symbol of the vegetated or natural man. Scofield is an unnatural distortion of the already fallen natural, and his growth threatens to undermine the foundations of our spiritual freedom.

In the lament of the Labourers of Los, there are two themes, the second sounded by Los himself. The first is the replacement of Jerusalem by Vala as the emanation of Albion. Even as Jerusalem represented Albion's liberty from all limitation, so Vala represents his natural bondage. The lament of Los centers on his consciousness that his Spectre's accusations are true, for Enitharmon continues to divide from him. For an account of this fresh division, see Bloom, p 378.

12:25-44   This vision of the continual building up of Golgonooza introduces a chant on the complementary themes of the City of Art and the world of fallen Albion surrounding its walls. What Blake gives in this introductory passage is a more humanistic version of Herbert's "The Church Floore". Ethinthus appeared in *Europe* as a daughter of Enitharmon who denied the earth-worm's love, and enjoyed instead the dark secret love that kills. Buried at Tyburn-Golgotha, the Druid *omphalos*, she is now to be transfigured, for the New City ends the cycle of denial and frustration.

Lambeth is praised because Blake's myth was first tentatively formed there, to help accomplish the overcoming of self, and inspire the "builders in hope". With the poignant reminder that Jerusalem herself is outside the City, Blake passes into his account of its walls.

12:45 - 13:29   Blake follows Ezekiel and Revelation in broad outline here, but the complex detail is mostly his own. For tables of correspondences that illuminate this sequence, see Damon, p 433, and Frye, pp 277-278.

The general pattern of symbolism here depends on the image of two sets of wheels whirling counter to one another. One set belongs to the living creatures or Zoas of Ezekiel's vision, the other to the zodiac of Albion's sons. In 13:13-14, we are told that the wheels of Los and his brethren are a divine parody of the natural wheels, a divine analogy drawn from nature which works to subvert nature. For all their fantastic properties, the walls of the City are sometimes humanized, particularly in 12:57-60.

The four points here clearly belong to mental rather than corporeal space, and define the position of the unfallen Albion. The Western Gate is closed because of the fall of Tharmas, so as to symbolize our inability to find our way back to Eden directly through the body. The most crucial aspect of all the gates is their terror for us; though this is the City of salvation through art, Blake cannot give us an altogether human image for his city, any more than Ezekiel or Yeats could. So the eastern gate toward Eden is frozen solid, signifying the limitations even of art in giving us an entrance into the eternal world. The "sevens" are derived from the imagery of the Revelation of John. Their presence in the Eastern Gate of Luvah associates them with the Savior, but the association is a complex one. Death exists because the way to Eden is blocked, and disease because the Beulah of love and fulfillment is stonified, and only Christ-as-Luvah can end death and disease. But the way to the fallen states through Luvah is not blocked; there we find the seven enormities of religion-hid-in-war, and the ambiguous forms of Generation.

The final complexity of this whole sequence, once its associations are worked out by reference to *The Four Zoas*, is Blake's insistence on fourfoldness, following Ezekiel. That each Zoa or Gate should open four ways into the four different states of being is essential to Blake's pattern, but it forces his reader into a kind of cartography which is not in itself imaginative. Ezekiel and the poet of Revelation force their readers into similar mental acrobatics, and perhaps this kind of vision demands a foray into the "mystical mathematics of the City of Heaven".

13:30 - 14:15   This comprehensive catalogue of dread is the negation of vision, and is the grimmest passage of this kind in Blake. Most simply, it is his description of Ulro, and resembles the underworlds and hells of Virgil, Dante, and Milton. The Salamandrine men of 13:43 are presumably all of us, dwelling in our useless heat of anger. As this is unredeemed nature, the Twenty-seven Churches of natural religion are an inevitable part of the vision. Yet all of this eternally exists "to those who enter into them" like Los. For all its horror, the world of nature is indestructible until the Last Judgment.

The summary of terrors reaches its height in 14:1 ff where the major symbols of the Fall in *The Four Zoas* are brought together, ending with the lovely, but sinister because separated, emanations.

14:16–34　　Against nature and its torments Los sets his own creations in this extraordinary passage, which in effect attempts to describe a poem's state-of-being. Lines 26–28 are a sad admission that art shares something of the limitations of the Fall. Line 29 echoes Ephesians 3:18. In 31–34, Jerusalem has all but vanished from sight; the function of Los and his creations is to restore her before it is too late.

15:1 – 16:27　　This is Blake's own "awful Vision" of his England, or his personal part in the more comprehensive vision Los has of the world of Albion. The Divine Man Albion and his Emanation, Jerusalem, have been displaced by Satan and Vala. The Polypus of vegetating life is no longer Orc, organic energy in revolt against societal limitations, but now has become the sons of Albion, whose fibres of hatred vegetate over the whole earth, imposing limitations everywhere. As a man in whom Los is dominant, Blake declares himself a prophet in 15:8, able to comprehend all time in one mental vision, an act raising him from a Bard of Experience to a Four-fold seer. Yet the age is a fearful antagonist for the prophet. The reductive mental modes of Bacon and Newton have been "sheathd in dismal steel"; the Enlightenment has ensued in warfare. These "iron scourges" are essentially mental, and torment not only Albion but Blake as well, who is bleakly conscious of the serpentine windings of reasonings in his system to end systems, bruising the minute articulations of poetic expression.

The wheels of Ezekiel's vision and of the Sons of Albion are opposed again in 15:14–20, with Locke and Newton supplying the instruments to create the delusions of materiality. As the Sons of Los work on against nature, the natural man suffers in the cycle of fallen history, from Noah to Abram. The flight of Abram to become Abraham is part of the work of Los, another stage on the difficult way toward salvation.

The Valley of the Son of Hinnom is named by Jeremiah (7:31–32) as the place where children were burned in sacrifice. This is the origin of the name Gehenna as a hell. Albion lives now in a world where the children are sacrificed to Moloch the war god, and against that world Los sets his furnaces. In the passage 16:1–27, Blake gives us a counterpoint between the labors of the sons of Los and the Creation of Albion which groans to be delivered by Los.

16:28–60　　The work of the Furnaces of Los here is to transfer the setting of the Bible to Britain. Though there is considerable imaginative cause for Blake's imitation of Numbers 2, the result is a little disconcerting, and the most devoted of readers might wish that Blake had been neither so strict nor so explicit in working out his analogies.

16:61–69　　This fine recovery is dependent on the merciless listing that precedes it. The counties of Britain can become the regions of the Israelite tribes because all of history depends upon Los's creation for its energies. The use of archetypes here is directly contrary to Plato's use of his forms.

17:1–47　　Los sends the Spectre of Urthona to labor against nature in the four elements, yet Los himself works by indirection, fearing the beauty, however delusive, of the generative world. He masks himself in the hideousness of the Spectre, producing the fine irony of lines 13–15, where death flees life for fear of its life. The personal allegory here is self-deprecatory, for Blake accuses himself of lacking openness, which is obviously true enough. A more profound allegory involved is the necessity of the imagination seeking the disguise of the will when it seeks to overcome nature, or to cause nature to reveal itself.

The remainder of this sequence deals with Blake's poignant attempt to clarify his rejection of Female Love. The Spectre, utterly divided from Los, would be merely a negation, for an isolated will is helpless other than to destroy. But Enitharmon separated completely from Los becomes a contrary. Though this is essential if Los is to function as he must, he has grown weary of his isolation. The poet in Blake longs for an object-world that would come close and be a beloved companion, but only on terms other than "a pretence of love to destroy love".

17:48–63   This recapitulates the birth of Enitharmon from *The Book of Urizen*, and expresses a very direct sense of mental torment, remarkably disciplined considering its intensity. There is an implication here that poetic creation, which ought to be only gain, has become primarily loss, as far as the creator is most directly concerned. The anguish compels and justifies the violent outbreak of lines 59–63, which ends a movement of the poem. Erdman (p 383 and p 442 n) interprets this biographically, as one of Blake's "fantasies of fighting back" at his accusers. Skofield may be a representative of the negative aspect of the two-faced symbol Bath, the poisonous potential of the physical body. Or he may be a spiritual rather than a physical enemy, an agent of the Church that claims authority over an English poet. The Accuser is deliberately ambiguous, straddling the cloven fiction of body and soul, but Blake-Los seeks to compel error to appear without its wily ambiguities. But the Accuser and the brutalized natural man alike are warned by the prophet that their hatred serves a purpose contrary to what they intend. Harsh as the passage is, it is a fitting climax to the epiphany of Los in the first chapter of *Jerusalem*.

The poem now begins a new movement, setting forth the history and condition of the Man whom Los works to save. For the rest of its length, the first chapter of the poem is concerned with the relations between Albion, Jerusalem, and Vala.

18:1–10   The imaginative man can choose either to expand his circumference or his center, but the spectral Sons of Albion succeed in contracting both in a masterwork of Urizenic solipsism. Most simply, they achieve both a cosmology and a psychology of doubt and despair, and then turn themselves accusingly on Jerusalem. Jerusalem may best be understood as a more humanistic version of Milton's Christian Liberty, the freedom of the redeemed man from every institutionalized restraint on his spiritual freedom. For Blake, Jerusalem is the beloved creation or potential creation of the fully imaginative man. She is therefore what Wordsworth calls our sense of "something evermore about to be", our "possible sublimity". At the least, she is every artist's imaginative freedom to seek his own Word, but in the apocalypse or world of altogether fulfilled desire she is both City and Woman, where one lives and what one loves, when both are as they ought to be. To cast her out is the necessary aim of the Sons of Albion, for if she is reunited to man, their reign ends.

18:11–43   Here the ascetic's horror at mere sexuality, utterly alien to Blake, is assigned by him to the Accusers, who are interested only in war as a mode of sexual gratification. They come and go from Albion's bosom not as wheels radiating from the true Wheel, but as reflections sent forth by a reflection, the fallen Albion, a mere appearance in the great Deep of mundane reality.

18:44 – 19:39   Lines 19:1–14, except for line 8, are repeated from *The Four Zoas* IX 119:32 – 120:3.

These are the phenomenal effects of Albion's disaster, which as 18:44 intimates is in the first place a sexual malady. The natural world, "exil'd from his breast", is now separated from him. The whole of this passage should be compared with the opening speech of Prometheus in Shelley's lyrical drama. The Eon of 19:16 is another name for the Emanation, Jerusalem. The "dark incessant sky" of 19:22 deliberately recalls the "black incessant Sky" of *The Four Zoas* IX 119:12. Line 19:38 repeats *Milton* 39:52.

19:40–47   Havilah is a golden land surrounded by a river of paradise in Genesis 2:11, but also a son of Cush and so brother to the murderous Nimrod in Genesis 10:6–10. Vala thus has paradisal beauty as "the Lilly of Havilah", but she is a sister to Nimrod, and her assimilating "in one" with Jerusalem is a destruction of Albion's liberty.

20:1 – 24:60   This long sequence is a unit, and an effective one, though one may wonder if Blake ought not to have condensed it. He had worked out the core of this myth in *The Four Zoas* VII 83:7–22 with great economy. Here he seems burdened by the necessity of demonstrating the tragic consequences when the forgiveness of sins does not take place.

Albion is associated with Job in 21:4, and the briefest way of understanding the whole sequence is to consider Albion as a Job who fails to surmount his trials, and whose sons are sacrificed to the gods of war and nature (21:38–49). The religion of Vala (22:1–11) is a demonic version of Christianity, but it draws on the darker aspects of the sacrifice of Jesus and the warlike character of Jehovah. In Skofield's vision (he being the New Adam) Jehovah is Nimrod, and the prophetic Valley of Vision is given over to war. Lines 22:1, 10–12, 14–15, 20–24 are repeated from *The Four Zoas* I 4:6–9, 19–20, 28–32, as a brilliant and deliberate parody of the dialogue between Tharmas and Enion. 23:24–25 is repeated from the similar symbolic event in *The Four Zoas* I 15:5 ff.

24:61 – 25:16   Albion's despair culminates in his acceptance of the veil of Vala as reality, which means that he is reconciled to his own fallen existence. This, to Blake, is the supreme calamity, and is the fit sequel to the grim history of religion Albion has recited on Plate 24. The Atlantic drowns out Atlantis, and the Erythrean, the Red Sea of blood and error, rises so that its depths are revealed. The blood-dimmed tide is loosed, and the lamenting voice of Innocence is raised on Plate 25. The Luvah of 25:6 is very much suffering France, and the mythic Zoa of Love, and a type of the suffering Saviour. The overt reference to Matthew 10:29 is legitimate in this context, but Blake ends the first chapter of his poem in a more individual strain, by a reference to his own doctrine of States, already adumbrated in *Milton*. The closing words deliberately return us, full circle, to the opening words of the poem proper, on Plate 4.

PLATE 27   As Chapter 1 set forth the contraries of Los and the Albion who sleeps in Ulro, it was fittingly addressed to the public, to sheep and goats alike. The second chapter of the poem records the struggles of Los to transform sight into vision, and events into prophecy. It is directed to the Jews as the people of the Bible, urging them to fulfill their role in events by accepting what Blake, agreeing with Christian orthodoxy, regarded as their prophetic destiny. Behind the statements in Plate 27 are traditions that have bemused many of Blake's commentators and will no doubt go on bemusing many others. Blake was a poet, a revolutionary moralist, and a profound rebel against social, religious, political, and psychological conventions. He was not an antiquarian, a mystic, an occultist or theosophist, and not much of a scholar of any writings beyond the Bible and other poetry insofar as it resembled the Bible. His references to esoteric traditions are few, and tend to be superficial when they are not mocking. Here, on Plate 27, they are cursory, and are brought in to support convictions very much Blake's own, convictions quite contrary to the traditions called on for their support. The "Learned" are undoubtedly such zealots as Jacob Bryant and Edward Davies, but what they took, absurdly, for a literal truth of identification between Britain and Israel, Blake takes as an imaginative truth. All religions are one, and there is no natural religion. It follows that Druidism, the impostures of historical and institutional Judaism and Christianity, and Deism must be one, and that all true religion must be one also. In the same way, the cabalistic tradition of the Adam Kadmon or Divine Man must be one with Blake's myth of Albion, though in fact the actual cabalists would have been outraged at the humanistic "impieties" of Blake's myth, for their God was altogether transcendent.

The fine lyric in marching quatrains is a relief after Blake's deliberate blurring of distinctions in his prefatory remarks. It is one of Blake's most personal poems, and is an autobiographical epitome of the whole of *Jerusalem*. The places named in the four opening stanzas were associated by Blake with his own childhood (see Erdman, p 437). Lines 25 ff appear to refer to an excavation in 1811 near Paddington, which uncovered bones of Tyburn victims, conceivably those of the regicides. For this and other historical associations relevant here, see Erdman, p 438. The historical reference of the stanzas starting with line 45 is certainly to the later stages of the Napoleonic wars.

Chap: 2.

28:1–27   Blake opens with a Urizenic Albion, burdened by a consciousness of sin, who solidifies nature into the solid rocks of the reductive Ulro vision. On this metaphysical foundation of certainty, Albion seeks to build a world of Moral Virtue, the pride of the self alienated from other selves. The deadly tree of line 15 is like the Tree of Mystery in the *Book of Ahania* and *The Four Zoas* VII 29 ff. In the twelve Altars of Albion, Blake returns to a symbol from *Milton* 37:20 ff.

29:1–25   This is the Spectre of Urizen or Satan, who must be distinguished from the Spectre of Urthona. In *Jerusalem,* Satan is Albion's Spectre, while the Spectre of Urthona is the shadow-self alternately of Los or Blake. Crucial to Plate 29 is Blake's insistence that Albion's Spectre, Satan, is the God of this world, worshiped under the divine names of Jesus and Jehovah. The "Deism" of this speech of the Spectre is closer to historical Deism than is usual in Blake, though the element of caricature remains present.

29:26–34   Vala now appears as the demonic parody of Jerusalem, and a fit mistress for a solipsistic brooder, properly "reflecting back to Albion in Sexual Reasoning Hermaphroditic". Though she is clothed "in colours of autumn ripeness", this is a false harvest of "life abstracted", withdrawn from its unitary fullness, and it mingles darkness with false light on the "furrowd field" of Albion's creation. Like the light of nature in Wordsworth's "Intimations" ode and Shelley's "The Triumph of Life", it is a light that obscures the Divine Vision, and causes life and joy to fade.

29:35 – 30:16   Much of this dramatic dialogue is simply a lie, as is appropriate for Vala. Albion's declaration of passion is a mirror image of the accusations against Israel made by the prophets. Yet its final lines show regret for all that is lost.

30:17–42   This defiance of the Female Will marks the beginning of the attempt of Los, in this chapter, to make time work against the Accuser. There may be an echo of 1 Corinthians 11:8–9 in lines 27–28. Merlin is Blake's name for Reuben's imaginative portion, even as Hand is Reuben's Spectre, enrooting himself into Bashan, the land of Og (see Numbers 32:33).

30:43 – 32:42   For the symbolism of these plates, see Damon, p 449 and Bloom, pp 393–394. Very briefly, Los sends Reuben over Jordan in order to organize the senses of fallen man, thus setting a limit to contraction. There is of course a very grim humor in this myth; Reuben flees back continually because fallen mankind cannot bear to confront the grim reality they have become. Each time Reuben is sent back by Los, another sense is realized in the fallen world. Though mankind seek to reject Reuben as the image of reality, his presence works upon them anyway: they "became what they beheld". While Los carries on this process, the doctrine of States is instituted by Divine mercy, setting the Two Limits of Satan and Adam. 30:45 combines references to 1 Kings 7:46 and Joshua 15:6. 31:5 refers us to Daniel 3:25, and makes us realize again that Los is "the form of the fourth . . . like the Son of God".

From this evidence of the Divine Will the Sons and Daughters of Albion flee in terror, yet their limits are now fixed also.

The passage, 32:25–42, summarizes the principal myth of fall in *The Four Zoas.* It also introduces the figure of Brittania, the unified form of Jerusalem and Vala when restored together.

32:43–56   This is one of Blake's moments of affirmation, in which a poetry of statement is raised to its heights through the support of the larger context the Blakean kind of epic affords. Of all Blake's poetic gifts, this is perhaps the easiest to underestimate.

33:1 – 35:23   This sequence is at once the culmination of Albion's despair, and the answering resolution of Los and Blake. The "Eight thousand years" of 33:7 is possibly a mistake for "Six thousand," as Blake elsewhere sets that as the term of fallen history.

On Plate 33 Los surmounts his own wrath against Albion, but Albion flees him never-theless, always followed by "the Eternal Vision" of Jesus. From 34:28 on, this is scaled down to Blake's share of vision, as he gives us the voice of the spiritual form of London. He hears the voice from his own residence in the city, and goes on to a more extensive myth of the role of the British cities in the restoration of Albion. Verulam, the title given to Francis Bacon, and a Roman townsite, is to be redeemed like Canterbury, York, and Edinburgh into genuine holiness, as part of a great humanization outlined in 34:44–54. Canterbury and York are chosen as the crucial cities of the Church of England, and Edinburgh, of Scotland.

The Gate of Los, particularized in London, can be seen only through the emana-tions, that is, through the work of art or of love. In his despair, Albion desires to flee through the gate in the wrong direction, so as to be ground down into the Eternal Death of cyclic natural life by the Mills of Satan. The depth of Albion's despair is sounded in the poignant lines 35:22–23.

35:24 – 36:44   This begins a sequence that lasts through Plate 41, in which the cities of Britain fail to rescue Albion despite their concerted effort to bear him back through the Gate of Los to Eden. The indubitable historical allegory is expounded in Erdman, pp 439–444, and much symbolic detail is provided in Damon, pp 450–452.

The "four" of 36:4 are the cities already mentioned, while the "Porch of sixteen pillars" occurs again in 48:7 as the sixteen books of the Bible Blake judged to be most inspired. The arrival of the twenty-four other cathedral cities presents the difficulty of 36:22–23, which Damon (p 451) interprets as the procession "of the Body". Since Albion has passed through the Gate into Ulro, he may suffer the fate of Milton's Satan at the opening of *Paradise Lost*. 36:31–39 is a brilliant description of the fate of Milton's rebel.

36:45–61   For the rest of this listing, see 41:1–24. Lines 48–51 form an instructive and charming miniature myth of salvation, based on the transfer of the see of Selsey to Chichester in 1075, caused by coast erosion. Line 51 is one of Blake's smaller triumphs. Very moving also is Blake's roughly humorous tribute to his mother tongue in 58–60.

37:1–22   This historical Bath, whose major importance comes on Plate 40, is identi-fied by Erdman (p 440) as Richard Warner, the best-known man of letters in that city, who in 1804 published a sermon, *War Inconsistent with Christianity*. Damon (p 451) identifies Bath in the moral allegory with the duality of the physical body. Either the Erdman or the Damon interpretation is perfectly consonant with 37:3, on different and quite intentional levels of meaning.

The flight of Jerusalem to the protection of Blake's imagination is conveyed in the brilliant symbolism of lines 15–22, where Oothoon's palace is Blake's own poetry.

37:23 – 38:11   This failure of nerve on the part of the Cities is best expounded in Erdman, pp 441–442, who rightly terms it "satiric or at least critical" and compares the reasoning of the Cities to the circular quietism of Theotormon in *Visions*. Very remarkable is Blake's comparison (37:27–30) of this anguished quietism of his con-temporaries to the catharsis tragedy performs upon its spectators. Blake, like Shelley, D. H. Lawrence, and others in his line of vision, repudiates tragic art for reasons as profound as they are disputable. The Zoas, now present as the human faculties in 38:1–5, are seen at their very worst, as Blake sets forth a contemporary world in which the best lack all conviction, and in which all best things are thus confused to ill. The satiric conclusion (38:6–11) surveys the fallen world, only to ensue in the conviction that the Cities will perish in Druid sacrifice whether they act or remain passive. By refusing to enter into their Spectres, they deny any instrumentality by which the situation could be bettered, and so resort to a pathetically misplaced prayer.

38:12–79   This powerful dramatic speech is heroic but mistaken, as Los and the Cities he persuades must discover, for what Los urges is the doing of the wrong deed for the right reason. Los's speech is both an expression of Blake's prophetic but in-effectual anger, and a defense of the Blakean theory of art. It is also a palpable indica-tion of Blake's spiritual loneliness, his longing for support in his almost-hopeless fight. A particular expression of this loneliness comes in lines 37–38, with the reference to Oshea and Caleb fighting in the valleys of Peor. This is very probably an allusion to a quarrel between Blake and a close friend, Fuseli I would guess, or less likely Flaxman, but an artist in any case. Oshea and Caleb (see Numbers 14:6–38 and 26:65) were the only Israelites who left Egypt and survived to enter the Promised Land with their descendants. There is no account of their fighting one another in the Bible. Eloquently but very indirectly Blake is telling us that he and another old survivor of the generation that endured Egyptian tyranny now battle one another in the valley of the tomb of Moral Virtue, where Moses was buried. The harshness of Los's world is epitomized by "the terrible Family Contentions of those who love each other".

Balaam (38:39) was the heathen enchanter who prophesied the greatness of Israel, but then attempted to corrupt the Israelites (Numbers 22:3 – 24:25 and 31:8, 16). In Revelation 2:14 he appears as a tempter to idolatry, which is probably the meaning of his Armies here.

38:80 – 39:20   The Cities, urged on by Los, attempt to become the Cherubs of Ezekiel's vision, but their "kindest violence" does not prevail against the Starry Wheels of Albion, for the re-entry into Eden from Ulro is not to be won through the Will, but only through the constant process of imaginative work until the day of Divine Power, of apocalypse, comes.

39:21–44   The Cities, vegetating in the Ulro after their failure, see even the barrier provided by individual vision, Erin, given over to false Religion. They resign their powers to Los, thus confirming his role as Elijah, the Spirit of Prophecy. The Cities suffer the fate of those who confronted Reuben when he crossed Jordan; they too fall utterly into the state of nature. With their emanations lost to them, they become fit subjects for Bath's elegy.

40:1 – 41:28   The speech of Bath (40:3–32) is one of Blake's poorest dramatic efforts, perhaps his poorest, if we read it as a straightforward lament not designed to show Bath's inadequacy or ambiguous impulses. Yet it is not straightforward, and is designed to show "the futility of speaking out", as Erdman (p 443) puts it. It is deliberately a weak speech, because it is meant to fail, since only the secret, creative work of Los can save the nation, and that only in the fullness of time.

Bath's references to the sleep of Africa may be sad reflections on the earlier inability of the Africans to end the slave trade, or they may refer to the Egyptian bondage of the Israelites. But Bath has small right to his weak moralizings, whether we take him as Richard Warner or the ambiguous duality of the fallen body. Oxford, to whom he yields his office, is even more inadequate, and the treatment Blake gives him on Plate 41 is certainly satirical. The historical Oxford appears to have been an Edward Marsh of Wadham, according to Gilchrist's identification of "Edward, the bard of Oxford", mentioned by Blake in a letter to Hayley, January 27, 1804. Oxford's feeble contribution (41:10–15) cannot move Albion, and Blake ends this sequence of the Cities with the bitter reflection that these cathedral sites have become the worst enemies of Jerusalem, for they continue to be temples dedicated to the "Religion of Generation", Deism.

42:1–81   As lines 3–4 show by their allusion to *Urizen* VIII 3, Albion is now wholly given over to Urizen. But his threats against Los do not appall the prophet, who affirms that he is Urthona, the Fourth man whom Daniel saw in the furnaces. The speech of Los is one of Blake's most eloquent defenses of the artist's task, particularly in lines 25–28. Against him, Albion sends Hand and Hyle, to capture him as they have "the Twenty-four rebellious ingratitudes", the cathedral Cities. But the stance of the prophet (55–56) is too resolute for the spirits of false reason and corrupted nature to harm him. In this, he is the contrary of the other Friends of Albion, the Cities, who now "repent of their human kindness" and utter a demonic lament, while Los continues his saving labors, the setting of limits to the Fall.

43:1–83   Albion, in this arrangement of the poem having just attempted to destroy Los, is now wholly given over to the Accuser, to the worship of Satan-Urizen. The Divine Vision is now seen only in the light of a setting sun, and the appropriately named Reactor, Satan, has captured Jerusalem by taking Ephratah, where David searched out a habitation for the ark of God (Psalms 132:1–8). From this disaster only the Spectre of Urthona and Enitharmon escape, presumably bearing with them their metaphysical attributes of fallen time and space respectively.

The great sequence 33–82 is repeated from *The Four Zoas* III 39:15 – 42:19, with a few changes and omissions as noted by Damon, p 447. By appropriating this scene for *Jerusalem*, Blake gives it a better context for its picture of a nerveless Job who chooses Satan for his God.

44:1 – 45:1   In 44:1–15, this is essentially a moving autobiographical summary, with Blake granting his own Spectre of Urthona the fine compliment of 44:15. From 44:16 on, we are again with the prophet Los, vehemently delivering his protests at social and economic tyranny, and subtly distinguishing between the inadequacies of the "sexual" vision of Beulah, and the vision of a restored Humanity in which sexual union attains ultimate completion.

45:2–38   One of the poem's great passages, properly interpreted on many different levels: see Margoliouth, *William Blake* (London 1951), p 157, Erdman, pp 433–434, and Bloom, pp 398–401. Erdman remarks that the "Diogenes-like search" of Los is "the central *action* of the whole poem and is shown beginning in the frontispiece". If action be only an outward event, this is certainly true, though in a wider sense the struggles between Los and the Spectre of Urthona, Los and Albion, and Los and the whole crew of Satanic Accusers, form the epic "action" of the poem. Yet this passage is one of the centers of the poem, and contains the core of Blake's prophetic answer to the idiot questionings of despair, as Schorer and Erdman observe. Los, in his search, hopes to find external tempters who have hid themselves within Albion, but what he finds is that the Minute Particulars have been murdered. The Accusers are brickmakers, like the Israelites in their Egyptian bondage, and Heber and Terah, ancestors of Israel through Abraham, are also the ancestors of Albion. The pyramid is both an emblem of tyranny and the tomb of the natural man. Coming down to London, Los-Blake finds the same reductive and generalizing tyranny at work, and is moved to the crisis of lines 29–38, in which he both transcends his own desire for vengeance against the Satanic accusers, and resolves to complete his prophetic role by persuading the Sons of Albion against vengeance. Within the poem's myth, this means converting the natural man, despite his spectral condition. In terms of the poem's relation to its own contemporary world, this meant seeking a just peace with France. Its contemporary application for mid-twentieth-century America is perhaps too obvious to be labored.

45:39 – 46:2   This sequence, particularly in Vala's reply to Jerusalem, is founded on the account of the Fall in the first three Nights of *The Four Zoas*.

46:3 – 48:12   The general power of this sequence is founded to an unusual degree upon Blake's careful preparation for it. Difficult as it is, all of it should by this point be familiar to the poem's reader, and Blake introduces no new symbols. A clarified continuity in passages like these is Blake's justification for his procedure, since without the grammar of his personal symbolism he could not say so extraordinarily much in so few lines. The collapse of man's hope in the nightmare of history is the theme of this sequence, and the context Blake has developed allows him to make so large a statement with appropriate authority.

48:13–52   The lament of Beulah for "the terrible Separation" of Albion and Jerusalem is a ritual preparation for the oration of Erin that concludes the second chapter. In answer to the lament, Enion reappears, and in the Atlantic wastes, Vale of Rephaim or shades, which is the fallen form of lost Atlantis, she extends a saving Moment of Time until it includes all of fallen history. After rescuing fallen Space by a similar act of vision, she waits in mourning for Albion's revival. She is the earth itself, mother of generative life, when seen by the poet's vision and separated from her demonic parody, Tirzah. Through her work, Los is able again to see the finger of God touch the seventh and last furnace or cycle of history. Until that cycle is completed, Jerusalem will be preserved in the Spaces of Erin, the bulwark formed by each creative act against the chaotic sea.

48:53 – 50:17   This speech of Erin is a fully matured version of Oothoon's laments against the willful limitation of human sensory powers. The center of the speech is in 49:52–60, where the tomb of the Law is associated with the struggle of Blake's Milton to humanize Urizen. For a good commentary upon the difficult notion of "Divine Analogy" as Blake uses it, here and elsewhere in *Jerusalem*, see Frye, pp 384–388 and 394–401. For the political significance of Erin's speech, see Erdman, pp 444–447.

50:18–30   The prayer of the Daughters of Beulah here is founded on Ephesians 4:26, which might well be taken as the motto for the entire poem.

PLATE 52   The third chapter of the poem marches remorselessly toward a confrontation of "Deism" and Blake's vision of Jesus, and is appropriately addressed to the Deists. There is not much accuracy, one fears, in Blake's indictment of historical Deism, and indeed by "the Deists" he does not mean Toland, Collins, Tindal and the other controversialists who argued for a religion of Nature against the Anglican orthodoxy of *their* day. Blake means the orthodoxy of *his* day, a Church of England that had covertly assimilated many Deist attitudes. Primarily, he means Rahab, the Eternal State Religion, the organized violence carried out in the names of Jesus and Jehovah. Blake's defense of "a Monk or a Methodist" here certainly does not mean that he was in full sympathy with either figure, but only that he was resolved to defend Enthusiasm or even superstition against every "enlightened" attack, for Enthusiasm was an analogy of his own imaginative stance.

Chap. 3

53:1–29   The Vehicular Form is the outward circumference of an individual energy; Los is therefore the earthly form of what was Urthona. The creation of Los, his City of Art, is always being built, and always is in process of decaying, for Los has no static form.

54:1–32   Albion, confirmed in his Fall, now turns his hatred to his Sons, for they are assimilated to Luvah, the natural affections Albion has come to hate. Albion's Spectre is associated with Arthur or British kingship, both here and in Blake's *Descriptive Catalogue*. The association broadens to kingship in general in *Jerusalem* 64:15–17.

The Druid Rocks round Canaan, the Promised Land, in lines 25–26, are either kings or peoples opposing the Israelites.

55:1–69   This is a familiar symbolism from Blake's earlier attempts at epic. The saving remnant of Eternity elect the Seven Eyes of God, with a voice greater than the voice that gave the Law on Sinai, or the voice that commanded the Covering Cherub to block off Havilah or the Garden of Eden. The allusion in line 27 to the Song of Deborah (Judges 5) suggests a similar mingling of human and divine forces in combat. Shiloh, the emanation of France as Jerusalem is of Albion, figured in Night I of *The Four Zoas* as a ruined place of the Redeemer. Here also the reference is primarily to Genesis 49: 10, usually interpreted by Christians as an early prophecy of Christ, though there may also be a reference to Joshua 18:1, where Shiloh is the place of the Tabernacle.

The great passage lines 36–46 is both a serene acceptance of the necessity for natural experience, and an exalted affirmation that the poet's vision transcends the context of nature. The defense of Blake's art, and demonstration of unity between his ethic and aesthetic, are carried out with great economy and pungency in lines 60–65.

56:1–43   Los comes forth as the messenger of the Seven Eyes and of the Eighth that is Apocalypse, provoking the Daughters of Albion to a savage irony. Chapter 3 transfers the role of adversary from the Sons to the Daughters of Albion, with a consequent increase in the ferocity of spiritual combat.

Most likely, 3–25 is a complexly sardonic song of Los, in which he sometimes takes on the dramatic character of the Daughters for grimly satirical reasons. The Daughters reply in lines 26–28, after which Los answers with a mocking imitation of their feminine speech rhythms in lines 29–37. The Daughters respond again in lines 39–40, after which Los ends this extraordinary exchange with lines 42–43, in which I take "the Church Paul" to be the twenty-fourth Church, in Blake's cycle, the first after Jesus, or the first Church of the Seventh Eye, to be followed by "Constantine, Charlemaine, Luther" (see *Milton* 37:35–43) and that twenty-eighth Church identical with the apocalyptic Eighth Eye. Damon however (p 456) takes "the Church Paul" to be the actual St Paul's in London, which would give the passage a very different sense. In Los's vision the "Three Women around The Cross" in the Church of Paul would be Rahab, Tirzah, and Vala.

57:1–18   The Cities are deluged by the sea of materiality, and speak from the deeps with a courage they have assumed belatedly. Their bitter aphorisms are rhetorical questions, which is very nearly Blake's entire point here. Rosamonds Bower (line 7) was an underground tunnel in Oxfordshire, perhaps built by Henry II for his mistress Rosamond Clifford. Though sought by the Divine Vision, Albion flees, usurping the Plow of Nations, even as Satan usurped the Harrow of Palamabron in *Milton*, and with as dreadful results. Only the Seven Eyes, or Los among the fallen, can plow up mundane reality, and the Zoas refuse Albion's authority. Albion becomes material to be plowed up, yet this is providential, for the plowing separates him from his Spectre, and everything in him that can be saved comes to rest on the Rock of Ages. He reaches his Vortex in 17–18, and remains at it until Plate 95, when he will at last be redeemed by vision.

58:1 – 59:55   This sequence begins as a countermovement against redemption, but the work of Los enters again at 58:16, to turn the strife of Contraries toward progression. Following his earlier suggestions that both Los and Urizen created the Mundane Shell, Blake now sets the two creators against one another in a further extension of the poem's central struggle.

Lines 59:10–21 go back to *Milton* 17:15–25 and 34:32–39. After this rapid mapping of the fallen world, Blake returns to his symbol of Cathedron, from *The Four Zoas*, to show the Daughters of Los or of Beulah at their constant labor of maintaining the basis of all physical life, even of Rahab and Tirzah.

60:1–69   This plate begins a new movement of Chapter 3. Plates 60 through 62 trace the crisis of Albion's emanation, as she confronts her own despair. In Plates 63 through 75, Blake creates the most elaborate of his fantasias depicting the cruel triumph of the Female Will, as it refuses to join Jerusalem in repentance and seeks to perpetuate the nightmare of Blake's age, and our own.

The terror of Los, at the start of Plate 60, is due to the inevitable identity of Albion's Spectre and Luvah, for the natural man has become Satanic in Blake's age. Orc is at the close of his cycle, and has assimilated to Urizen.

The Song of the Lamb (lines 10–37) is an attempt to rouse Jerusalem from her excessive self-condemnations, and so to give back to the spiritual liberty of mankind something of her legitimate pride. The Mizraim of line 18, from Genesis 10:6, is another name for Egypt.

The inability of Jerusalem fully to respond is clearly not due to inadequate understanding on her part, but to weariness, a delusion she cannot escape.

61:1 – 62:1   The Divine Voice offers Jerusalem the shock of this extraordinary comfort, Blake's application of the sexual ethics of his *Visions of the Daughters of Albion* to the story of the Virgin Birth. The major theme of *Jerusalem*, the necessity of mutual forgiveness, thus receives the highest kind of sanction.

The names in 61:31–33 are those of the four rivers of Paradise. Line 61:52 approximates the third line of the magnificent Epilogue to Blake's *The Gates of Paradise*.

62:2–42   This is the ordeal of English Liberty, unable to see its deliverance, possessing faith but no hope. The genealogy of the Maternal Line (lines 9–12) is Blake's own invention, so as to trace the birth of the truth even from the "feminine delusion". The names are either drawn from the age before the Flood, or from Canaanite women. Cainah is Blake's own derivation from Cain; Ada, Zillah, and Naamah are of the house of Lamech; Shuah and Tamar were Judah's wives, and were Canaanites, like the whore Rahab. Blake's listing of Mary as a daughter of the heathen is again of his own devising.

In line 14, Jerusalem becomes the Magdalen of John 20:1-18. Line 16 alludes to Job 19:26, and line 18 is directly from John 11:25. The torturous pilgrimage of Jerusalem repeats that of the Israelites through the desert, with a characteristic modification of biblical symbols in line 28.

63:1 – 64:5   For the probable historical allegory here, see Erdman, p 431. The slaughter of the Human Unity (Tharmas) by Luvah is part of the central myth of *The Four Zoas*. For the "Looking-Glass of Enitharmon" (63:38) see Damon, p 458.

64:6 – 67:1   This is the epiphany of Vala as the total form of the Daughters of Albion in their evil-doings. The "Caves of Machpelah" (64:38) are the sepulchers of the Patriarchs and their wives. Central in this sequence is the Druid sacrifice of Luvah and the wars of nature following from the sacrifice. Lines 65:6-55 are repeated from *The Four Zoas* VII [b] 92:9-53, with a few additions.

The "Giant dance" (Blake may have thought that the literal meaning of Stonehenge) is a dance into madness by the Sons of Albion, and is a large metaphor for the deathly autointoxication of spectral reason. It produces the ironic self-victimization of 65:72-79. Despite this madness, the strength of Albion's Sons continues, and enables them to build the "Babel-Stonehenge" of natural religion, with its two Covering Cherubs, Voltaire and Rousseau, once upholders of the truth, but now intellectual oppressors in their own turn. Their natural and reasonable morality is blamed by Blake for the self-betrayal of the Revolution, and for Luvah-France now being exposed to English "reasonable" vengeance.

For the remarkable passage 66:16-34, see Frye, p 398 and Bloom, p 411. Combined here are references to Aztec sacrifice, the slaying by Jael of Sisera, and the soldiers' mocking of Jesus, as well as situations in "The Mental Traveller" and *Milton* (Urizen's attempt to subdue Milton). In this passage, Jesus becomes another Luvah, another ritual substitute for the sick-unto-death Albion. The effect of this sacrifice is a further derangement of the natural world, and yet another "shrinking together" of human sense perception.

67:2-43   From this disordered nature comes the revelation of the Shadowy Female, Rahab and Tirzah in one, presiding over the wars of mankind "till the Great Polypus of Generation covered the Earth". Blake puts the head of this creature in Verulam, because the philosophy of nature stems from Francis Bacon of Verulam.

67:44 – 68:9   With a few additions, including the mention of Skofield, this passage is taken from *The Four Zoas* VIII 105:30-53.

68:10-70   Skofield, the Adam of Rahab-Tirzah's world, has just been identified as the Spectre of Joseph. Man in such a world is bound down by his five senses, and sacrificed to everything beneath him in the order of being. In reaction to this sacrifice, the Warriors who worship a goddess of battles sing a hymn of masochistic surrender. Uzzah (line 51) was slain by God for laying hands on the Ark in 1 Chronicles 13:10. Here he becomes the type of all warriors who die to satisfy the cruel delight of the Daughters of Albion.

The reference to "the City of Rehob in Hamath" (line 55) is one of Blake's subtlest uses of biblical material, as that is the first city mentioned in the land of Canaan, when Moses sends men to spy out the land (Numbers 13:21). The Daughters bring the Israelite spies from Egypt, to raise jealousy in the Kings of Canaan. Meribah Kadesh (line 61) is the place in the wilderness where the people murmured against Moses, and he caused water to come from the rock. In Ezekiel, this becomes the ideal southern limit of the land of Israel, even as Rehob in Hamath is the northern limit. Blake may be indicating the Daughters' dominance over the entire land, since for him Canaan is England. He may also be aware that the literal meaning of Meribah is "strife".

The whole of this sequence culminates in line 63, Blake's clearest identification of war as a mode of substitute sexual gratification, as indeed the greatest of sexual perversions.

69:1–44   In this general decay of life, the warriors are reduced to the vegetative world at its lowest level. In contrast to the law of generosity by which Beulah or nature at its highest should work, even that state is now corrupted by Rahab and her Moral Law of jealousy. The extraordinary passage, lines 38–44, is based on Milton's vision of heavenly love in *Paradise Lost* VIII 620–629. The Holy of Holies in the Temple, a sacred center, is a Female Mystery that Jesus comes into the world to rend, for in Eden all is holy.

69:45–70:16   Hand, in Jerusalem's eclipse, here becomes revealed as the Triple Accuser, influenced by what Blake took to be the intellectual uniformity of "Bacon & Newton & Locke".

70:17–31   Rahab hides deep within the Accuser, refusing to come forth. Blake's description of her activity here is very close to the action of "The Crystal Cabinet".

70:32–71:63   This is Blake's last survey of the world of the Sons of Albion, preparatory to the revelation of Rahab as the Whore of Babylon. For a general commentary on this listing, see Damon, p 460. After this fearful survey, Los gives up his attempts to rouse Albion directly (71:56–63), lest he contribute to a final catastrophe for fallen mankind. This appears to be a poignant outward surrender of Blake's immediate prophetic role, and perhaps a defense of the poem's elaborate and hidden symbolism.

72:1–52   This carries on from 16:28–60, but in a more organized form, as Damon (p 460) points out, since Ireland is closer to salvation than England, in Blake's view, for political reasons akin to those that caused Blake to create his Erin symbol earlier in the poem.

The quietists and mystics, with some contemporary Methodist aid, are given the gentle task of guarding the safe Gate toward Beulah, which indicates the definite but limited place Blake granted them in the spiritual life.

73:1–45   Here the opposition is sharpened between the creation of Los and the "World of Opakeness". For "Peleg & Joktan" in line 28, see Genesis 10:25. The Limits beyond which nature cannot fall are attributed by Blake to the mercy of Los and Jesus, now necessarily identified, while to Voltaire is credited the negating vision of Deism, which makes of these Limits a sign of Divine restrictiveness of mankind. The opposition between imagination and nature leads to the contrary creation of two groupings of prominent figures in history, the kings and nobles "Created by Rahab & Tirzah in Ulro", and the patriarchs, prophets, philosophers, and poets created by Los.

73:46–74:57   Lines 48–49 are reworked from *Milton* 26:31–32. Throughout this sequence, Blake sees presages of the time of troubles that must precede the opening stages of a revelation. London becomes Babylon, genuine art is displaced by impostures (74:24–26) and Hyle, emblem of natural morality, becomes Gog, Ezekiel's and Revelation's symbol of the enemy of God's kingdom. Reuben, Albion's unstable son, sleeps on the Stone of Night, and is coveted by the Daughters of Albion for their own sadistic ends. They cut his Fibres, but this release from the natural does not prevail, as Reuben is vegetated again in Bashan, a land of petrification. Reuben's brothers suffer similar fates, with the highly favored sons of Rachel ironically ending in the Land of Cabul, a land "good for nothing" (1 Kings 9:13).

Even here, amid these disasters, Blake sees Erin or the saving vision arise from the now terrible Zoas, as Dinah, the daughter of Jacob for whom Jacob's sons slaughtered in Shechem. The New Erin is "beautiful but terrible", associated as she is with bloodshed, but the vision that will contend with Antichrist must have its own qualities of terrible beauty.

75:1–27   This is at last the revelation of Rahab as Babylon the Great, the scarlet whore of John's vision. Bath appears on the scene as the equivocal body of man, accompanied by the imagination of Merlin, but also by the tyranny of Bladud (who founded the city) and of Arthur. For Bladud's special significance here, see Damon, p 461.

Plate 75 is a consolidation of negative symbols. Bath bears the Cup of Rahab, a healer become a destroyer, in a demonic parody based upon Revelation 17:4. The twenty-seven Heavens and their Churches are now revealed in the "strong delusive light of Time & Space". Against this totally revealed error, Blake sets the breaking through of Jesus from Eternity into Time, in order to prevent the twenty-seven Churches from becoming an "Eternal Circle", an endless cycle of tyranny in time.

PLATE 77   Blake's fourth and final chapter of his major poem is intended to be definitive of his Christianity and so is directed, with prophetic irony, to all who call themselves Christians. Essentially this address concerns Christian Liberty, Blake's Jerusalem, "the liberty both of body & mind to exercise the Divine Arts of Imagination".

The introductory blank-verse poem echoes King Lear's speech when he is awakened from his madness, Act IV, Scene VII, lines 45–48. Lear's wheel of fire is made one here with the Satanic starry wheels.

Chapter 4

78:1 – 80:5   Even as Albion, in Chapter 3, turned against his Sons, their Spectres have now turned against him, but they cannot destroy him, for as the end of time approaches Los grows more powerful. The image of 78:4 is drawn from Isaiah 30:14. Rebuffed by Los, the Spectre Sons attack Erin, while making Rahab the queen of a universal Deism.

The despair of Jerusalem, more desperate than ever before, dominates this sequence. She is "disorganized", and almost invisible and inaudible. In her lament, she sees herself as dissolving "among the towers of Heshbon" (79:3, for which see Numbers 21:25), while all the places of salvation have fallen into the earth. The land of Albion has shrunk to the narrow island of Britain as viewed by the empirical eye, and the universal society of nations has broken up. The very identity of Canaan and Britain, upon which the poem is founded, has been abrogated, and Thames and Jordan no longer mingle. Finding that she is now no more than "a narrow doleful form in the dark land of Cabul", good for nothing but sorrow, she is moved to a desperate questioning of Vala.

80:5–31   Without warning, Blake gives us a lamenting reply by Vala, rather than the triumphant sadism we would expect, for Vala now senses the coming end, as will the Daughters of Albion after her. This speech is a confession of guilt for the fall of Albion, but also an attempt to shift that guilt to Luvah, whose return she still expects, as she has taken up the role of a nature goddess awaiting the annual revival of her lover, Luvah as the dying god of the vegetation cycle. In this densely and deliberately ambiguous speech, she is dramatically portrayed as being insanely confused, for she repents of Albion's death yet fears to see him live again, lest he revenge himself upon Luvah, and she prays to Jesus *not* to revive the dead, in contradiction of his inevitable function.

80:32–82   The Spindle of Necessity, which belongs to Tirzah, the mother of our mortality, turns on, and the wars of nature continue. Over these slaughters and sacrifices the indefinite form of Rahab hovers, but that she has been forced to take definite form, just once, at the end of Chapter 3, now creates a fearfulness among her own priestesses, the Daughters of Albion. This fearfulness leads to the fall of Hand and Hyle, as the Satanic camp begins inevitably to devour itself. As Hand sleeps, secure in his reasonable self-satisfaction, his emanation Cambel asserts herself by taking a separate form, and then further naturalizing her unwary lover. Gwendolen, lusting after Hyle, seeks to possess him utterly by preparing him for rebirth as her own progeny. As an allegory, this is very rich, and undoubtedly represents Blake's reading of the intellectual crisis of his own age. The world made by rational empiricism becomes a womb in which that vision is imprisoned, to be born again into spiritual second childhood.

80:83 – 82:79   The plot of Gwendolen and Cambel is one of Blake's most complex inventions. The fullest comments upon it are in Frye, p 402, and Bloom, pp 420–421. The Seventh Eye approaches its climax, and the Daughters wish to be certain that any new birth is enslaved to them from the start, for they have labored long to subdue men to their will. Fearing the fates of Jerusalem and the now anguished Vala, Gwendolen instructs her sisters in the falsehood she creates of a plot against them by Los and Enitharmon. Her falsehood is prophetic against her, and Hyle is reborn as the winding worm of Generation, foretelling Gwendolen's destruction. Cambel, a fiercer emanation, does not fear the infant Hyle, and forms Hand as a similar natural portent, only to encounter the sorrow of having borne deformity.

82:80 – 83:84   Beholding the repentance of Gwendolen and her other sisters, and the defeat of Cambel, Los is comforted at his work, and for the first time declares that he can recover his eternal form as Urthona when and where he will. Los's comfort is due to his observing a genuine change of heart in the camp of the enemy, which is a presage of the greater change to come.

Yet with the comfort comes an exhausted sense of being condemned to labor on in the harsh, generative world. Though Los is now more certain than before that Albion can be saved, his own labors must become more rather than less strenuous (83:1–3), so that he fears he may forget Eternity altogether. Few lines even in Blake are as personally poignant as 83:53. What sustains Los is courage, and a greater sense of the coming integration with his Spectre of Urthona.

The "Dogs of Leutha" (83:82), mentioned earlier in 45:15–16, appear to refer both to the London Isle of Dogs on the Thames, and to a Blakean variation on the myth of Actaeon, for which see Damon, p 463.

83:85 – 84:30   This Song of the Daughters of Albion demonstrates genuine repentance but great mental disorder on their part. They are in Babylon on Euphrates, once one of the rivers of Paradise, and their lament echoes Psalm 137, for it contrasts the lovely land they have lost with their current terrible abode. They see the London of Blake's illustration to the "London" in *Songs of Experience*, and they hear the voice of Reuben, now driven out as a perpetual wanderer. The song climaxes with the coming of Hand in the thick darkness, a more terrible Hand, who has developed from the winding worm of mortality into a dreadful combination of Molech and Chemosh, devourers of infant life. In their terror, the Daughters attempt both to appease Hand, and to call upon Los for aid. In a failure of nerve, they forget their repentance, and assimilate again with Rahab.

84:31 – 85:21   This is an even more difficult mythic event, involving Blake's complex notion of "Divine Analogy". The Daughters consciously hide in a Falsehood, but Los will see to it that this Falsehood will be turned inside out, so that an allegory of the truth can be made from it. Canaan is the Promised Land, which becomes Beulah when married by Jehovah. Though the Daughters' religion of moon worship is a false one, it is an inverted analogue of the limited but genuine truth of Beulah. Los places Reuben, all of natural mankind, in this now "Divine Analogy", and so begins a saving cycle of history, where there had been only a repetitive cycle of nature.

Out of this achievement, there rises the marvelous passage, 85:14–21, the first genuinely peaceful one in the poem.

85:22 – 86:32   This song of Los is built around Revelation 21:2, which is echoed in 86:19.

86:33 – 88:48   This is Los's own crisis with his emanation, largely based on the account of Los, Enitharmon, and Enion in Night I of *The Four Zoas*. What is new, and very different, is the mature insistence upon sovereignty by Los in 88:1–15. The reference to "Sussex shore" in 88:23 is undoubtedly to the Blakes' residence at Felpham, when for a while Blake seemed separated from his creative achievement. The rejoicing of the Spectre of Urthona (88:34–43) is a sign of how far he still is from genuine integration with Los. He is justified in rejoicing, for he symbolizes the pride of the fallen will in its own strength and independence.

88:49 – 89:62   This is the revelation of the Antichrist or Covering Cherub, the sign that the Apocalypse is about to take place. It comes at the verge of disaster, as Jerusalem takes the Cup of poison from Vala's hand, in demonic parody of the communion ceremony (88:56). The four instruments of the Crucifixion (89:1) do not liberate mankind from natural torment, for the Hermaphroditic or solipsistic doctrine of the Churches subverts Christ's sacrifice, and transforms it into the "Wine-press of Love & Wrath", the spiritualized natural warfare sanctioned by the Churches. The discipline of the Churches follows the forms Blake's Jesus sought to overthrow: Pharisees, Scribes, Presbytery, High Priest, Priest, and Sadducees, though it is not easy to know from this odd list precisely what Blake thought the Pharisees and Sadducees to be.

The Covering Cherub is fitly a consolidation of Blake's negative symbols, including Aaron's Zodiacal breastplate; a demonic opposite of the Resurrection (89:13); a perverted reflection of Eden; Egypt on the Gihon, that is, on a paradisal river fallen into the slavish Nile; the Sea of Rephaim, presumably the Red Sea with its shades of drowned Egyptians; the Minute Particulars in Egyptian bondage; Pharaoh; Leviathan as "the Dragon of the River" (Ezekiel 29:3).

The Cherub (who is serpentine, and winged) reflects a series of sinister biblical emblems. The Pison, first river in Paradise, has become the Arnon, river of Jealousy and possessiveness. The Fish-pools of Heshbon are compared to the eyes of the beloved in Song of Solomon 7:4. Rabbath contained the iron bedstead of the last of the giants, Og of Bashan (Deuteronomy 3:11), Hiddekel and Euphrates are the last of the rivers of Paradise (Genesis 2:14). The wings of the Cherub are eyeless (89:41) in contradistinction to the many-eyed wings of the Zoas, Ezekiel's Cherubim. The whole of this catalogue of dread is summed up in 89:62.

90:1–68 This is essentially a "doctrinal" sequence, in preparation for the dramatic eloquence of Plate 91. The Masculine and the Sublime are the expression of the Zoas in action and in art respectively, the Feminine and the Pathos being the same for the emanations. None of these are "Universal Characteristics" or "Attributes", which belong to the composite Human alone. As Los proclaims this truth, the Sons of Albion are compelled to reveal their Druidic-Deistic faith for what it is (lines 58–68).

91:1 – 92:27 This is Los's triumph, and contains what may well be Blake's supreme dramatic speech, 91:1–30, a speech deliberately recalling many of the crucial declarations of Blake's poetic career. This speech is addressed to the Spectre of Urthona, and precedes Los's final struggle with, and triumph over him.

Among the major echoes of Blake's earlier work in Los's speech, the most important are: "A Poison Tree" in lines 1–2, and the Satan-Palamabron struggle from Milton in the same lines; the fifth Memorable Fancy of the Marriage in lines 7–10; 9–10 also echo the opening address of Chapter 4, "To the Christians". Lines 11–14 ultimately derive from the complaint of Urizen-Jehovah to the Archbishop in The French Revolution, and more immediately from Blake's Milton in his resolve to descend. Line 17 reflects Blake's vision of Eden throughout his poetry. Most characteristic is the mingled moral and aesthetic emphasis on the necessity of organizing the Minute Particulars of vision, as against merely accumulating them into the disorganized aggregate of the Moral Law. Perhaps the most remarkable dramatic aspect of Los's speech is that it demonstrates an absolute prophetic assurance, a humanistic truth thoroughly mastered, and yet is cried aloud, weeping, in the "horrible darkness" directly preceding an apocalyptic dawn.

In the final conflict with the Spectre of Urthona (91:32–57) Blake rejects all occultism, a point his myriads of esoteric interpreters have chosen not to understand. The Smaragdine Table of Hermes is the fundamental text in occult tradition, and is a brief statement of the correspondence of the suprasensual "above" and the sensual "below". Here it is an incantation of the Spectre to trap Los in the "below", and therefore only another "rational" mode of demonstration.

With the Spectre of Urthona finally subdued, Los is able to understand the meaning of English history as an analogue of the greater union of nations and men to come (92:1–6) and to withstand a last, terrified protest of the Female Will in his emanation (92:7–27).

93:1–27   Enitharmon's lament here refers back to the Bard's Song in *Milton* and for a final time in this poem attempts to proclaim a demonic unity of biblical and British symbolism. Line 8 refers to Genesis 30:14–16.

In Los's positive appeal to his Sons, the "Waking Death" of line 18 is the Spectre of Urthona. The whole passage (18–26) follows the pattern of Matthew 24:3–15.

94:1 – 96:2   This awakening of Albion and subsequent restoration of the Zoas to their proper work grants Blake the legitimate self-praise of 95:19–20, and the extraordinary joy of 95:21–22, lines so moving to Blake himself that he repeats them in 96: 1–2.

96:3–43   Line 16 is at once one of Blake's simplest, and most sublimely reverberating, and the entire passage is perhaps Blake's most humanistic statement of his imaginative faith.

97:1 – 98:27   The Bow takes us back to the prefatory stanzas to *Milton*, and represents a fully realized poetic art.

98:28 – 99:5   The Covenant of Priam (98:46) is at once the Classical vision of virtue as belonging foremost to the warrior, and the poetic art founded upon that vision.

Though the epic's final lines (99:1–5) depict a cycle, this is not the generative alternation of Innocence and Experience, but the creative rhythm of Eden and Beulah, perpetually returning upon one another.

❧

II. [PROPHETIC WORKS, UNENGRAVED]

TIRIEL

This harsh and compelling poem is the first by Blake to use his characteristic line, the septenarius or fourteener. This seven-beat line may have been suggested to Blake by ballads in Percy, or Elizabethan poetry, or possibly even by certain passages in the King James Bible.

Tiriel's name has been traced to a source in the occult writer Cornelius Agrippa, but this is very remote and contributes nothing to a reading of the poem. I suspect that the name plays upon the first syllable of "tyrant" and compounds this with the Hebrew name for the Almighty. Tiriel's struggle is to maintain himself as an almighty tyrant despite his bodily decay, and his failure to learn until too late the limitations of his self-proclaimed holiness is as much a failure in a conception of divinity as it is in one of political authority.

Erdman (pp 122–124) suggests that Tiriel's madness is based on the living example of George III, and such an element of historical symbolism does fit very well into the total thematic significance of the poem, as do the echoes of Lear's madness.

Critics have noted that Tiriel is an early version of Urizen, and like Urizen he may on one level of meaning represent Blake's satiric vision of the Jehovah of deistic orthodoxy, irascible and insanely rationalistic.

I

The poem's opening episode implies that Tiriel's own death is approaching, as his dying wife is the "fire" (line 29) of his existence. Her fading leads him to hysterical denunciations of his children, who have rebelled against his domestic tyranny. "Sons of the Curse" in line 9 suggest that Tiriel now regards himself as the Curse or the Law incarnate. The reference to "the western plains" in line 2 marks the onset of Blake's directional symbolism, in which the west stands for man's body, with its potential either for sensual salvation or natural decay. The names Myratana, Heuxos, and Yuva seem to have no special significance, but Zazel may be a modification of the Hebrew Azazel ("scapegoat").

2

Confronted by approaching extinction, Tiriel retreats to his conception of an earthly paradise, the vales of Har. As Har means "mountain" in Hebrew, the very phrase "vales of Har" is an irony, possibly in deliberate contrast to the prophetic cry that "every valley shall be exalted". Blake's vales of Har were to be transformed later into the lower level or limit of the state-of-being he called Beulah or Innocence. Here, in *Tiriel*, this state is exposed only in its aspect of natural ignorance, of perpetual infants aging into idiocy in the persons of Har and Heva, the Adam and Eve of this barren paradise. They are guarded by Mnetha, tutelary genius of their state. Her name is evidently founded on an amalgam of Athena and Mnemosyne, Urizenic wisdom and memory as mother of the Classical muses. Damon (p 307) allegorizes Har and Heva as eighteenth-century poetry and painting, but that seems too narrow an interpretation. Har is natural man, the isolated selfhood that can avoid death only as Swift's Struldbruggs avoid it. He can also be compared to Tennyson's Tithonus and Eliot's Gerontion, for they also age without being reborn in the imagination. Har was the creator of Tiriel, even as man entrapped in a state of nature invents Urizen as his god.

3

This pathetic encounter confronts Tiriel with the realization that his quest either to preserve his tyrannical self or to find some meaningful escape from it cannot be fulfilled in the natural paradise. He goes forth into the wilderness again, still unable to see that he must purge his conception of his own self.

4

Frye (p 243) indicates Isaiah 13:21 as the likely source of the name "Ijim". The Ijim are satyrs or wild men who will dance in the ruins of the fallen tyranny, Babylon. Blake's Ijim is a self-brutalized wanderer in a deathly nature, who is unable to believe that the change in Tiriel has taken place. The animistic superstitions of Ijim are a popular support for the negative holiness of a Tiriel, and do not cease even after the god they worship has begun to die.

In line 76 Matha may be a name for matter (Damon, p 308), while Orcus, a Latin name for hell, is certainly a source for the name of Blake's Orc.

5

The curses of Tiriel are probably an oblique satire on the cursing Jehovah of tradition. The heavy clouds are Urizenic, and the ruin that comes from them can be related to the consequences of the Fall upon the human consciousness. Tiriel's five daughters are his senses, since his realm is the body. Hela, goddess of hell in Northern mythology, is ironically named, for she is Tiriel's sense of touch, his sexuality. Tiriel's thirty sons are probably representative of his past creations; his reduction of them is repeated in Urizen's dispersal of the thirty cities in *The Book of Urizen* IX 94 ff.

6 and 7

The aged tyrant reveals his augmented senility by his decision to seek out the vale of Har again, despite his earlier experience there. Blind but not helpless, his curse transforms his daughter into a Medusa, and blights his last source of life. The encounter with the outcast Zazel enforces upon Tiriel the ironic lesson of having inherited the fate he invented for another.

8

Tiriel's self-revulsion here is born of his understanding that it has come too late. The question in line 9 is answered in the last line of *The Marriage of Heaven and Hell*, and reasserted in a rhetorical question by the Urizenic Bromion in *Visions of the Daughters of Albion*.

❧

THE FRENCH REVOLUTION

This is Blake's most direct historical and political poem, and is his major attempt at popular poetry. The imagery throughout is characteristic of him, but the narrative form is not, and the systematic avoidance of his emergent mythology results in the inhibition of his real gifts as a poet. Yet the poem is a successful experiment, although Blake did not care to repeat it. Its exact relation to the events of the actual Revolution is set forth most fully and accurately by Erdman (pp 148–159), who notes Blake's "considerable liberties . . . with the sequence and relationship of events". Blake presents the Assembly as being more important than it was, and sets the scene in Paris rather than Versailles. His radical simplification and condensation of events into one crucial day is a step toward mythology, as is his vision of pre-Revolutionary history as a tyrannous slumber of five thousand years. Mythological also is his mingling of historical and fictive personages, the latter class including the dukes of Burgundy and of Bourbon. More profoundly mythopoeic is the close relation throughout the poem between the failing world of nature and its portents of apocalypse, and the decaying world of society and its signs of rebellion. This relation is carried through the poem by an extraordinary profusion (for Blake) of epic similes, of which line 9 is a particularly fine example. The central images of the poem are cloud and fire, cloud representing the old order and its failure of vision, while the fire that delights in its own form and is for growth and not consuming serves as a sublime image for the Promethean revolution that impends. The general atmosphere of the poem is akin to that of the closing chapters of Revelation, as befits a vision of the time of troubles that shall precede the end of nature and its cycles.

The meter of the poem is unique in Blake, being an anapestic variant of his more characteristic fourteener.

❧

THE FOUR ZOAS

Title: The ultimate source for Blake's myth of the four Zoas is in the first chapter, the Book of the Prophet Ezekiel. Ezekiel's vision, opening his book, is of a fiery cloud or northern whirlwind, in the midst of which appears "the likeness of four living creatures". Together, "they had the likeness of a man", and serve to introduce Ezekiel's vision of God's glory. That vision is renewed in the Revelation of St John the Divine, chapter 4, where the four living creatures of Ezekiel are translated by the Greek "Zoa". Taking this plural form as an English singular, Blake formed the plural "Zoas" for the four living creatures who together make up Albion, the man of his myth.

Epigraph: Read in its context, this verse of Ephesians explains the necessity for putting on the whole armor of God, and so states for Blake the necessity of preparing for the mental strife of his epic poem. His subject will not be the contention of flesh-and-blood beings, but the struggle between the fallen faculties of man. These psychic forces now rule the darkness of our world, but once constituted the heavenly man. Since his epic is to tell of the fall of "the Ancient Man" into the sleep of death, Blake will begin by considering "spiritual wickedness in high places", as this spirit caused our fall from our full humanity.

Earlier Title: *Vala*   Her name is presumably founded on the word "veil", since in one aspect she represents the veil of illusion interposed by the phenomenal world between man and reality.

Night the First

3:1   The Aged Mother is Eno, whose lament opened *The Book of Los*.

3:6–10   Blake's marginal references, to John 17:21–23 and 1:14 (from which he quotes), are intended to establish the relevance of Albion and the Zoas myth to a vision of Christianity. See my note to 133:1–30. The first reference is to the prayer of Jesus for his apostles, "that they all may be one; as thou, Father, art in me, and I in thee". The poem aspires to a state where all the Zoas may be one in Albion, who when integrated will embody the oneness of man and God. The second reference, by juxtaposition to "the Universal Man", identifies Albion as Blake's Word made flesh.

3:9 – 4:3   Los and Urthona   Los is the fourth one in the same sense as "the form of the fourth" walking in the fire, in Daniel 3:25. Like that fourth one, Los the Poetic Genius is the image of salvation. Perhaps the name "Urthona" is a play upon "fourth one".

Urthona, the unfallen Los, possessed the earth of the eternal world. In a remarkable metaphor, that "Earth of Eden" is identified with the human sense of hearing, in which Urthona, primal power of perception-creation, propagated his Emanations, the total forms of what he imagined and loved. "Fairies of Albion" before the Fall, these became the Heathen gods of fallen history. Urthona is thus the creator of all mythology.

4:3   Daughter of Beulah, the invocation   This is Blake's form of the epic invocation to the Muse. His muse is not a Classical daughter of Memory, but a Hebraic daughter of Divine Inspiration. Beulah is the "new name" spoken by God in Isaiah 62:2–4, and applied to Zion as the land that "shall be married" by its Lord.

4:5 – 5:28   Tharmas and Enion   Tharmas is the "Parent power" because his function in the eternal world is to hold the other Zoas together in the unity of Albion. His fall, manifested as a "darkning in the West", shatters that unity into a chaotic flood. A hint for the symbolism of this flood was provided for Blake by Isaiah 59:19 – 60:5, but the general pattern is given by the chaos in which Genesis begins.

As parent power, Tharmas embodied human potential, the capacity to transform desire into actuality. His particular emanation is the total form or image of that capacity, Enion the earth mother, whose unfallen function is best exemplified by the loving motherhood of nature in the less ironic of the *Songs of Innocence*.

The opening lament of Tharmas reveals a gradually increasing sense of loss, a growing realization that the forms of Eternity are dissolving. The "Living" of line 4:7 are the three other Zoas, more illusively active in the decline of their parent power. Jerusalem, introduced in line 4:8, is the emanation of Albion. By so naming her, Blake again follows the tradition of the Hebrew prophets with their idealizing personifications of "the city of the Lord". As Albion is a unity of human and divine life, his emanative portion is the glory and joy of such life, particularly the apocalyptic liberty it confers as its greatest gift. As the glory of Tharmas darkens, that liberty becomes hidden in a labyrinth of deceptive "natural" virtues and forms.

Behind the situation at the opening of Night I is the revolt against Albion and subsequent mutual strife, of the Zoas Luvah and Urizen, and the culpable falling away from Eternal existence of Albion himself. The flight of the emanations to Tharmas has incurred the jealousy of Enion, and that first manifestation of selfish possessiveness begins the ruin of Innocence and fall of Tharmas, which is the principal subject of Night I. While one must be wary of overly explicit or reductive allegorizings of the Zoas and their actions, the pattern of meaning here is instructive toward a reader's control of the poem's total meaning. As the faculties of integral man divide against him, and against one another, the residual components of their healthier state flee to the refuge of Tharmas, for he is the guardian of the unsundered Innocence they seek to repossess. But his apparent possession, momentary as it is, of the glory of unitary man and of the fourth or saving component of that man, is itself the cause of his own ordeal of jealousy. The body or outward form of his own realm turns against him, unable to see him as he was. And indeed, by seeking to become more than Innocence, he has become something less; he too, in his terror, seeks to appropriate for himself. His selfish virtue of possessive pity for a glory not altogether his own begins the process of disorganization of his realm. The torment of Enion's jealousy is the earth's passion at first encountering division, and the effect of such passion is to divide further as love yields to reproach, harmony to analysis, and a self-destructive masochism brings the remnants of an earthly paradise into ruin.

Separated from Enion, Tharmas sees her experience a "death" different from the kind she had known in Eden, where emanative forms had sacrificed themselves that the creative process might continue afresh. Now her separation condemns Tharmas to the state of chaos in which Genesis begins. As he sinks down into the sea of time and space he becomes one with "the circle of Destiny", the phenomenal world of mere repetition. His Spectre (5:15), the dark double or shadow self left to him when his created world withdraws, is the suicidal impulse toward chaos even as his former role was the sum of impulses toward unity. As this spectre and Enion's shadowy self fall together, they assume the status held by their probable prototypes, the sea god Thaumas (whose name means "a wonder") and the shore goddess Eione, in Hesiod's *Theogony*. Thaumas is another Old Man of the Sea, father of Iris, the rainbow who betokens an end to flood. As goddess of the shore, the watery waste of Newtonian nature, Blake's Enion weaves chaotic Tharmas into the cycle of "nine days & nights" which complete the first fall, and which constitute on another level the nine nightmares that together form the poem. The terror of Enion at her own creation (5:27) is founded on her consciousness that the physical ruin of Tharmas was caused by her withdrawal, which rendered him indefinite.

5:29-43   Beulah and Ulro, and their spaces   Percival (pp 83-84) traces what he takes to be the influence of Swedenborg on Blake's "spaces", but Blake's is an original description of a relation between feelings and outer appearances, very much akin to a phenomenological approach. In the repose of Beulah, the actions of its daughters are benevolent, and their spaces are temporary realities that do not insist on their own permanence. These are manifested in the provisional metaphysics, and beliefs, through which most artists pass in their development; able to abandon such positions, in turn, after each has served its purpose. In the crisis of Man's fall, Beulah becomes Ulro, a development shown in condensed form in "The Crystal Cabinet". Terrified at the Circle of Destiny, with its remorseless movement toward the negative unity of death, Blake's Muses create Ulro as a space where the Circle can be confined. Ulro may be derived from "unrule" or "unruly"; it is in any case a chaotic state of consciousness, characterized by the kind of solipsistic brooding Urizen exhibits throughout the poem. By naturalizing the Spectre (as contrasted with the work of Los, in *Jerusalem*, who seeks to humanize it), the Daughters give death a vegetative form, and so perpetuate what they seek to avoid. In their terror, they close the Gate of the Tongue against Tharmas, and so close off his way back to their paradise. Immensely rich in its meaning, this symbolism includes (as Frye notes, p 282) a reference to the General Epistle of James (3:5-8) where the fallen tongue "is an unruly evil" (perhaps this "unruly" suggested Ulro, with which the Spectre of Tharmas is identical). Unfallen Tharmas is taste and touch combined in the full sexuality of Beulah; fallen Tharmas cannot taste, and his touch is diffused into a watery embrace. The fall of the tongue in "To Tirzah" is part of the same complex, as is the appearance of "Tharmas the Vegetated Tongue" in *Jerusalem*, for which see the comment on *Jerusalem* 14:2-9.

8:1 - 10:8   Los and Enitharmon, as Enion's children   In *The Book of Urizen*, Enitharmon was created from Los as Eve was from Adam. Here they are born together, children of the contentious embrace of the Spectre of Tharmas and the shadowy Enion, and so their inheritance is strife. This change in Blake's myth is necessary, for Urthona, like Albion, must fall not in his proper person but through the more culpable falls of Tharmas, Luvah, and Urizen. Los appears in the fallen world, together with Urthona's emanation, as one of the lost children of Experience. Their rejection of Enion rehumanizes her, but her castoff share in the Spectre becomes their own. Enion is thus first saved by maternal grief, and then driven by it to the abyss of non-existence. As mythic pattern, this is clear enough. She has given birth to mortal forms, but in that generation she has traced the image of regeneration. Though they will function (for a time) as the temporal and spatial limitations that circumscribe the fallen consciousness, they will at last transform time into a medium of prophecy and space into the prophet's creation. But they begin as servants of the Spectre; wills toward death. The remarkable passage 9:9–18 shows their creation as providential; the imaginative act in Beulah that balances the negative creation of the Ulro.

10:9 – 11:2   Enitharmon's Song of Death   The function of this brief chant is to place the fall of Tharmas against the larger background of Albion's fall. Luvah's usurpation of Urizen's chariot of the sun is founded on the story of Phaethon at the opening of Book II of Ovid's *Metamorphoses*. In Blake's poem, this usurpation most simply represents an aggression of man's emotional life against his intellect, but more crucially it relates man's fall to a displacement of the universal sexuality implicit in his unsundered being, by an idea of sex, an abstraction in place of the reality.

11:20 – 12:35   The descent of Urizen   The strife of Los and Enitharmon, as a new Adam and Eve, calls down Urizen as god of their new world, to offer them dominion over Luvah and Vala, a rule of repression over the sinful heart. The reference to Urizen as a prince of light is both an ironic glance at the Enlightenment, and an allusion to Urizen's new role as the Satan of orthodox tradition.

12:36 – 16:20   The marriage feast, and its song   The marriage of Los and Enitharmon is necessarily a disaster, for it confirms Urizen's triumph, and symbolizes an acceptance of the fallen state, with the full burden of dualism, the negating strife of Spectre and Emanation (cf Percival, p 150). The bread and wine of this feast are the body and blood of fallen Albion, but the symbolism is demonic in this context, for the feast is an acceptance of mortality. Opposed to it is the vision of Luvah as the Christ (13:8–9). The nuptial song, with its grim and overwhelming eloquence, sets mortal warfare and the limits of the fallen body against the implied intellectual warfare and infinite potential of the eternal world. That it is given a biblical context, with the Hebrew hills rejecting mercy for bloodshed, marks its wars as being also religious ones. Mount Ephraim represents the Northern Kingdom of Israel, centered on Tirzah; Mount Zion, the Southern Kingdom of Judah, centered on Jerusalem. Orc makes his first entrance into the poem as the "fierce Terror" of 16:9, followed by the first appearance of the Spectre of Urthona at 16:11, for together these are the dark forces of Experience. The demons of the deep (Ulro) seek strife between Orc and the Spectre of Urthona, lest those beings combine against Urizen, as they will later in the poem. The Spectre of Urthona, a more crucial figure in *Jerusalem* than here, is Blake's version of the ego, the timid and hysterical selfhood whose fears cripple Urthona in most creative personalities.

16:21 – 18:7   Enion's Lamentation   This combines the assumptions of Innocence and the facts of Experience, with the inevitable embittered bewilderment.

18:11–15   Damon (p 368) calls the Palm tree a symbol of martyrdom, and the Oak one of stubborn error. They stand at the boundary between Beulah and Generation, but as symbols they belong to the latter state. The Rock of Ages, the fallen Albion's couch, marks the limit of Contraction, or furthest reach of the Fall.

21:1–15   The Eternals in Council   As the Zoas together constitute Albion, and he the sum of reality, Blake makes it difficult to account for this saving remnant. The most searching attempt to puzzle out this matter is in Percival, pp 45–46.

The Shiloh reference of 21:9 is probably to Genesis 49:10 rather than to Joshua 18:1, for the Shiloh of Genesis is a type of the Savior, in Christian interpretation.

Blake alternated Gilead and Snowdon in 21:7, and Beth Peor and Conways Vale in 21:15. The Gilead reference is probably to the "fearful and afraid" of Judges 7:3, rather than to the Hill of Witness in Genesis 31. Erdman (p 288 n 9) speculates that both the Snowdon and Conways Vale references are to the flight of Thelwall and other radicals to Wales in 1797, which would link up to the situation of Judges 7. Beth Peor is the burial place of Moses (Deuteronomy 34:6), and for Blake would have an intimate connection with "the Wars of Death".

21:23   For the North as Urizen's realm, where he rallies his forces before the heavenly revolt, Blake followed *Paradise Lost* V 689 and Isaiah 14:13.

22:4–5   For Anak, see Numbers 13:33. For Sihon, Numbers 21:21 ff. For Og, Numbers 21:33–35. In *Milton*, these enemies of the Israelites are all workers in Satan's cause.

19:9–15   The Seven Eyes of God   The divine remnant of the Eternals, having safeguarded what is unfallen by drawing up Eternity's tent, complete their provision for the fallen by electing the Seven Eyes. This symbolism is founded on Zechariah 4:10 and Revelation 4:5 and 5:6, and is developed in Night VIII of the poem, and again in *Milton* 13:14–27, and *Jerusalem* 55:31–38. The best account of this symbolism is in Damon, p 389. For a fuller comment see p 881 of this edition.

19:13   Mount Ephraim   Ephraim is a prophetic name for the Northern Kingdom, Israel, and its capital Tirzah. Ephraim is also the place where Jesus journeyed after the raising of Lazarus (John 11:54). Albion, wandering in the kingdom of Tirzah, is followed by Jesus, who will turn the old Ephraim of mortality into the new one of resurrection.

20:1–15   The Reversed Wheels   The opposition between Enitharmon and the Daughters of Beulah emerges in their conflicting attitudes toward Jerusalem, the bereft Emanation of the fallen Man. The wheels and their living creatures are derived from the chariot and cherubim in Ezekiel, chapter 1, but are a demonic parody of their original. Urizen and Luvah, each attempting to swallow up the other, cause the chariot or divine body to reverse its true motion, which ought to be upward and inward, toward a center of vision. Instead, the wheels go downwards and outwards, into Newtonian time and space. The wars of Urizen and Luvah are thus contrasted to the creative strife they ought to have been. The fullest discussion of Blake's directional symbolism is in Percival, pp 46–89.

Night the [Second]

This Night deals with the fall of Luvah, even as the first concerned the fall of Tharmas. Where Tharmas falls into the watery abyss of chaos, Luvah is cast into the furnaces of affliction, for the delighted fire of passion in Eternity becomes a torment in the world of space and time, just as the water of life becomes the sea of death.

23:1–8   This passage, in an earlier form, served as the opening of *Vala*, commencing with the present third line. Man, wearily reposing on the "Couch of Death" that is his fallen existence, now loses his desire for regeneration, and considers his selfhood as reality. The "sickning Spheres" (line 3) or reversed wheels of the Zoas, combined with Enion's lament for lost Innocence, afflict Albion's "Porches" or senses. Unwilling to bear affliction, he turns to Urizen as regent, and abdicates the mutable struggle of Generation. Though he knows the guilt of both head and heart against his integrity, he chooses to cast out all further desire. Blake intends the choice to have historical as well as psychological reference for his reader.

23:9 – 25:39   Urizen as Workmaster   Urizen's task is to preserve Generation even though its genius, Luvah, has been banished by man. The task proves impossible, but Urizen's effort is dismally heroic, like that of Milton's fallen angels in the building of Pandemonium, or of Plato's demiurge in his struggle to model a world on an eternal pattern. Urizen still stands in the human brain, his rightful place, but his light is "sickening", like Hyperion's in Book I of Keats's epic fragment. And like Keats's sun god, Urizen suffers a failure of nerve as he beholds futurity (23:15). His title as Work master (24:5) may derive from Bacon's reference to God as "that great work-master", *Advancement of Learning* II, a parallel first noted by B. Blackstone, *English Blake* (Cambridge University Press, 1949), p 220. As designer of the Mundane Shell, Urizen most closely resembles Milton's creating God in *Paradise Lost,* Book VII. The singing Bands of Heaven in 24:9 suggest the "celestial quires" of *Paradise Lost* VII 253–260, and the golden compasses of 24:12 are cetainly derived from lines 225–226 of the same book of that poem. Proverb of Hell 44 reappears in 25:3, to provide a "diabolic" contrary to these Miltonic allusions.

The passages from 25:7 through 26:3 are an eloquent summary of the effects of Urizen's creation. These effects are epitomized in the gnomic power of 25:6, which precedes and prophesies against the account of Urizen's world.

25:7   Tyburn is the place of the gallows; there is savage irony in juxtaposing it with Oxford, where imagination is strangled in the Druid Temples of the State Church.

25:9   The reference, as in earlier passages in Blake similar to this, is to the legend of lost Atlantis.

25:14   The Lambeth reference here is against the Church's palace.

25:17–18   Damon (p 370) usefully suggests that the reference here is to the episode of Sabrina's drowning in Geoffrey of Monmouth's *History of the Kings of Britain,* II, IV.

25:21 ff   The symbolism of the sons of Jacob becomes more prominent in *Jerusalem.* Here it is enough to know that Reuben represents the natural man of Urizen's world, while Levi is the archetypal embodiment of priestcraft in that world. They sleep on mountain-tops because of the long imaginative tradition that identifies mountains with fallen gods or heroes, as with Mount Atlas. The Daughters of Albion, whose names are derived from Geoffrey of Monmouth, also figure more largely in *Jerusalem.* In the aggregate, they display the emotions of Ulro, and are opposed to the Daughters of Beulah. Nimrod, first hunter of men, is a traditional type of tyranny. The Stonehenge reference in 25:33 is developed in *Jerusalem* 65:56 ff; for here it is enough to know that Blake's "Druidism" is the primordial religion of human sacrifice, and therefore equivalent to all natural religion whatsoever, the "Druidism" of the English State Church being its addiction to aggressive war.

25:40 ff   Luvah in the furnaces of Urizen   The "Furnaces of affliction" are suggested by Isaiah 48:10, where God declares that the transgressing Israel will be refined in such a furnace. So Luvah must begin his regeneration, and since Blake assigns the furnace to Urizen, the meaning includes the necessity for re-thinking the conceptual basis for man's emotional life. But Urizen is hardly a disinterested refiner, as opposed to Los, in this poem and in *Jerusalem.* Urizen's furnace is an intellectual system trapping the natural or fallen body within its limits, and so imprisoning Luvah or natural energy in a cycle of martyrdom, like the children of Israel in the iron furnace of Egypt (hence the "iron power" of Urizen in 25:43). The crucial passage 25:40 – 26:3 is repeated in *Jerusalem* 7:30–37, and in both places demonstrates Urizen's fearful reaction to the first manifestation of a mystery or dying-god religion. Luvah has become a Tammuz or Adonis, and Vala the nature goddess to whom he is sacrificed. Urizen's vision of this transformation accounts for the growing sense of unease that will lead, in Night the Third, to his rejection of his own female principle, Ahania, and his consequent downfall.

26:4 – 28:2   Lament of Luvah   As 28:2 makes clear, the whole of this moving lament is an example of dramatic self-delusion on Luvah's part. In his sufferings, he identifies his lost function with the whole of reality, and produces a doctrine which is excellent D. H. Lawrence, but not at all representative of Blake. His passion against what he chooses to call "that Human delusion", the unfallen Albion, is simply a madness, an attempt at "reasoning from the loins", which is no more congenial to Blake than is the error Lawrence called "sex in the head."

Luvah's fantastic account of Vala's evolution is a natural history of natural religion, and therefore a masterpiece of imaginative error. The great goddess of nature begins as the earth worm of mortality, at once the starting point and the dreaded close of natural cycle. Nurtured by the possessive sexual love of that cycle, she becomes the serpent of jealousy, and then a fearsome Dragon whose function is like Job's Leviathan, to serve as an emblem of the tyranny of nature. When she is absorbed into the great deep, she becomes one with the chaotic illusion that blocks man from his paradise. From that chaos she emerges as one of the "little weeping Infants" of Experience, where Luvah teaches her the labyrinthine ways of that state, until she becomes its divinity and withdraws herself from her tormented lover. But the destructive impulse of all mystery-religion consumes Vala as well as Luvah, until at last the passionate energy of nature is subdued to Urizen's purposes (28:3–10) and mystery-religion is subsumed by the restrictive morality of the Jehovah-priestcraft.

28:10 Bulls of Luvah Blake identifies Luvah with the ox or bull of Ezekiel's and John's visions. Similarly, Urizen is the lion, Tharmas the eagle, and Urthona the man.

28:11–21 This is Blake at very nearly his bitterest, as he contrasts those who see "these visions" of man's fall away from his true image, and those who selfishly busy themselves in their families, or deny vision and turn to commerce, or else follow Urizen most closely by accepting a fallen universe as a final reality to be measured out by "science".

28:25 ff Urizen as cosmic Architect As Urizen directs the building of the Mundane Shell, he is not yet altogether fallen, which accounts both for his still genuinely divine power as a creator, and also for his dismay at the woe of his brethren (28:22). It is vital to remember that the Urizen of Night II is Blake's *partial* vision of the Jehovah of Genesis and of *Paradise Lost* VII. Though Blake does not consider the mundane creation as more than the second stage in a three-stage fall, he adopts a dialectical attitude and regards it as an act of mercy, for many of its aspects are clearly preferable to the chaoses that both precede and follow it. In Blake's myth the fall of Tharmas is equivalent to the chaos in which Genesis begins. Blake dissents from Genesis by insisting that Eternity preceded the first chaos (cf his *Vision of the Last Judgment*). The fall of Luvah provides the molten, passionate energy that Urizen can mold into the mundane creation. Urizen's own fall, in Night III, is the equivalent of Noah's flood, and ruins his cosmos, leaving Los (as Urthona's remnant) to do the work of rebuilding under the rule of the now chaotic Tharmas (in Night IV). It is in this stage that fallen man as we know him is created. Therefore the Jehovah in Genesis and *Paradise Lost* who creates the physical world is Urizen, but the Jehovah in the same works who creates Adam is Los under the dominion of Tharmas, or a flawed but still active imagination being directed by an unorganized potential for greater life. The other two faculties of man are more thoroughly suspect, which helps explain Blake's stubborn insistence on the saving role of imagination.

The best account of Urizen's Mundane Shell is in Percival (pp 59–68). Fundamentally, Blake's description of its making is deliberate parody of *Paradise Lost* VII and Plato's *Timaeus*. Built at the level of the stars, the Shell stretches from Beulah to Tyburn in Blake's England, and so becomes a vision of heaven for the Ulro. As such, it contains a consistent astrological symbolism, clearly charted by Percival (pp 152–161). It also features many details identifying it with ancient Egypt, which is Blake's choice as the ultimate home for Druidism or the original religion of fallen man. The kingdom of Tiriel, in that poem, is probably Egypt, and so the paradise of Har is presumably in Abyssinia. The fall of Tiriel's realm is an earlier version of the ruin of Urizen's world in Night III.

28:26 The pyramid, aside from its Egyptian associations, is an excellent image for a constricted or Urizenic conception.

28:32   The "strong scales" are the zodiacal sign Libra, which follows Leo (Urizen as lion, and as prince of the house of the sun). At Libra, the heavens are balanced, and day and night are equal, which means the Mundane Shell is at its greatest moment. Cf Percival, pp 155–156.

29:4   An echo of *Paradise Lost* VII 241.

29:16 – 30:2   A deliberate echo of Blake's own *Africa*, line 33, in *The Song of Los*.

30:10   The bitter irony of this line ought not to be missed.

30:13   Margoliouth, p 103, thinks this "suggests a reference to the practice of human sacrifice at the foundation of a building", which is very possible. There is certainly a reference also to a sacrifice of some of the eternal world's lost beauty, which Vala embodied.

30:23 ff   This "Semblance" is Ahania, Urizen's emanation.

33:16–18   The golden chain is from *Paradise Lost* II 1051. For the chain's symbolism in Blake, see Percival, p 61.

34:57–92   Song of Enitharmon   This is Blake's hymn of the triumphant Female Will, and presents a vision like Enitharmon's in *Europe*. Here the young Enitharmon, in a lyric of frightening eloquence, aspires toward the dominion of a delusive heaven that she manifests in *Europe*.

35:1 – 36:13   Song of Enion   Possibly Blake's most poignant *Song of Experience*, this biblical lyric echoes Zechariah 8:17 in its second line, and Job 28:12–13 in its very powerful lines, 35:11–13. Dramatically fitting as this is for Enion, at this point in the poem, it is difficult not to think of Blake himself in lines 35:11–15.

Night the Third

The fall of Urizen is caused by a failure of intellectual desire, and by the intellect's revulsion from its own desires. Ahania resembles the Wisdom of Proverbs 8:22–36, daily the delight of God. She is Urizen's source of renewal, the wise passivity in which he must take pleasure or else lose the active role of mental energy that is his life. Essentially Night III attempts a perfecting of the material used in *The Book of Ahania*, 37:13 ff. The fears of Urizen follow the pattern of Pharaoh's in Exodus 1, and Herod's in Matthew 2, and of Zeus in the Promethean myth. The Prophetic boy is Orc, and the dark Ocean Tharmas, his foster parent.

39:6   The wine presses of Luvah are another form of his furnaces of affliction. In the context of temporal warfare, the wine press symbolizes enslaved energy, and the blood of Luvah streaming from it is a parody of the life-giving blood of Albion in the feasts of Eternity.

39:15 – 42:19   With variants (fully analyzed by Margoliouth, pp 110–111) this passage is repeated in *Jerusalem* 43:33–82. As another account of the Fall, it presents a brilliant and clear image of how an idea of the Holy was conceived, an idea that raised the mistaken Urizen to a spurious divinity and now condemns him to ruin. Lines 40:29–34 echo Psalm 143, which cannot have been one of Blake's favorites. 40:15 is a striking anticipation of the fourth stanza of Shelley's "Ode to the West Wind".

41:13–16   In this passage Albion is seen as a kind of Job, and Luvah as an afflicting Satan. The reaction of Albion, in the following lines, accounts for the role of Orc in the Lambeth books and in this poem.

42:17 and insertion (p 751)   These extraordinary lines sum up the fall of Luvah and raise a question that Urizen will not tolerate. Line 17 reverberates gently against line 13, and gives a complete image of the fall of nature into the serpent of time and space, and the further transformation of the serpent into the blocking or Covering Cherub, separating the emotional life from its full gratification. The question "Whether this is Jerusalem or Babylon" makes explicit Ahania's doubt of the fundamentals of Urizen's created world, an artifice of Jerusalem but a realization of Babylon. To her revealing evocation he reacts only with the murderous wrath of a Tiriel.

42:21 ff   Urizen's delusion is necessarily an intellectual error. Unable to tolerate a home truth, he persuades himself that casting off Ahania is a rejection of death by life. But as Ahania is his own best creation, his only principle of delight, and all he can love, he merely rejects life itself. Even Urizen cannot sustain a cerebration that takes no pleasure in itself, and so he too must fall. The process begins with the flight of his sons or lesser imaginative achievements, and goes on to the collapse of the Mundane Shell.

44:19 ff   With the revolt of the Zoas thus completed in universal ruin, chaos comes again under the sway of the spectre or remnant of Tharmas, who is now one with "the affrighted Ocean". With his reappearance, the tone of Night III modulates to a terrible pathos. Tharmas, once the impulse toward integration, is now so disorganized that he cannot maintain any attitude or desire for more than a moment.

45:13   Entuthon Benithon   Blake uses this name for the wilderness aspect of the Ulro. Erdman suggests that it combines the sound values of "tooth" and "bone".

Night The Fourth

The central events in Night IV are the entrance of the Spectre of Urthona, and the setting of limits to the ruin of Urizen by the enforced labor of Los. These events are complementary, for the labor of Los cannot become apocalyptic until he and the Spectre of Urthona cease to be separate from one another. Together they make up the ego of fallen man, Los as the active and the Spectre as the passive component. Fallen Tharmas approximates the id, Orc the libido, and the spectral Urizen the superego, if an attempt to translate Blake's psychic cartography into Freud's seems worth the making.

47:2   Los and Enitharmon, last seen in Urizen's world, have been carried down to Tharmas in its ruin.

48:1   The use of the Notebook epigram identifies the *fall* of Innocence with sexual repression.

48:4-10   Tharmas is now in despair, or in a hope unwilling to be fed. Conscious that love and rage have become one emotion in him, he knows that only a return of Enion will heal him, but refuses to know that such a return is possible only in apocalypse. His instinct toward life is as antithetical as his emotions. Though he prefers a created universe to the chaotic deluge, he will be content with a world of death and decay, renewed by Los but perpetually to be destroyed by himself. He is insane, as befits instinctual will in our fallen universe. Yet, even in his madness, he is not deceived; "some little semblance" is all of Enion he can recover through so equivocal a renewal of earth.

48:11-20   Los, as this passage evidences, is at this point scarcely healthier than Tharmas. As in *The Book of Urizen* and *The Book of Los* he is as yet only a primitive imagination, and even more mistaken than Tharmas. Line 12 is derived from Job 38:11, where the voice of God from the whirlwind boasts that he alone had contained the Deluge. Los too is claiming the godhood and so repeating the error of his teacher, Urizen. The irony of his speech is in its final line, for the shadow of Urthona is soon to rise as the Spectre.

48:25   The fiery hair of the poet is a prevalent image in the Age of Sensibility.

48:28   The Architect divine is merely Urizen, and Enitharmon's devotion to him has its sinister quality.

49:11-14   The Spectre of Urthona is possibly Blake's most original invention, for he has only much more generalized forms in other poets and mythographers. The best commentary on him is in Frye, pp 292-299. Each man's Spectre of Urthona is that part in him that begins by fearing old age, poverty, sickness, loneliness, and then expands to an omnipresent anxiety, a nameless dread of death-in-life, of time as an oppressive burden daily increasing in weight. The Spectre of Urthona haunts Romantic poetry; his struggles with Los are the staple of Blake's *Jerusalem*, and his presence is strong in the later books of *The Prelude* and in *The Excursion*. In Shelley he is the First Spirit of "The Two Spirits: an Allegory", the Ruin that shadows Love in *Prometheus Unbound*, the charioteer of "The Triumph of Life". Perhaps his most vivid manifestations, outside of Blake, are in John Clare's "Secret Love", Coleridge's "Dejection: an Ode", and Wordsworth's "Resolution and Independence". The Spectre is irresolute and dependent, colored dismally blue in a parody of the color of imagination, shod and armored in iron as befits a self-crippled and time-obsessed will. He is a cripple (like Thor and Vulcan, similar residues of Urthona) but his strength within any artist is a subtle and persistent reality.

49:27–29   The Spectre's consciousness of alteration and decay in Tharmas and himself echoes that of Satan in his speech to Beelzebub, *Paradise Lost* I 84 ff.

51:7–8   Cf Erdman, pp 280–281, where these lines are read as Blake's allegory of his personal situation.

51:28–31   A survival of the pastoral vision of Innocence, once incarnate in Tharmas.

54:1 ff   Damon (p 397) notes this and subsequent passages as repetitions of *The Book of Urizen* and *The Book of Ahania*. This one repeats *Urizen*, Chap: IV b.

56:1   A direct quotation from John 11:21. 56:2–3 is from John 11:22. The reply of Jesus (John 11:23) is repeated in 56:18. Albion is thus a Lazarus who will be raised after his "vegetated" sleep of death.

56:8   The "Shadow of wings" may be derived from the commentary by Sandys on Ovid's *Metamorphosis* II where the wings of Mercury's rod, the caduceus, are held to symbolize the mind's activity in calming the masculine and feminine serpents twined beneath it. Cf Percival, pp 53–54.

56:14–16   The Polypus, in this context a mass of undifferentiated organic life, may also be Ovidian in origin. Here it provides the quasi-chaotic material upon which Jesus imposes the saving limits of Opacity (Satan, or fallen Urizen) and Contraction (Adam, or fallen Albion).

56:23 ff   The Starry Wheels are the reversed wheels of Urizen, identified with the Zodiac. "Eternal Death" means our mundane life, or death as viewed by the Eternals. The "Seventh furnace", like the Seventh Eye of God, is an emblem of salvation. The reference is to Daniel 3:19, where the fiery furnace is heated "seven times more than it was wont to be heated".

55 (continued):   Here the Fall is completed, and the poetic imagination collapses into its unnecessary limitations. Blake's irony is palpable, for the terror of Los is founded on a misunderstanding of the pattern of salvation.

Night The Fifth

The single theme of Night V is the establishing of the Orc cycle, the torment of man's passions in the world of Generation. As narrative, Night V moves from the dance of Los that confirms his fall to Urizen's determination to explore his dens, an exploration that will prompt him to found a religion of concealment.

57:1–17   The dance of Los   Carried down into the world of Tharmas by Urizen's fall, Los and Enitharmon are at first still the children of Eternity. The star world has collapsed, but even in that artifice Los and Enitharmon represented the potential of a higher state of existence. Now, in the welter of nature as we know it, they suffer the pangs of naturalization. Los stonifies as Urizen did; his anvil of creativity is cold, and the furnaces of his molding energies are out. He is not yet bound to time, but with

Enitharmon he shrinks into fixed space. He is in danger of becoming a Deist imagination, wholly absorbed into a vegetative or generative context.

57:18 ff   The birth and binding of Orc follow the pattern of *The Book of Urizen*, with the crucial change that now Orc is seen as a reborn Luvah, one of a cycle of such rebirths that will come to a saving climax in the birth of Jesus.

59:5   The black bow is evidently a reference to cannon or muskets, for which see Erdman, p 300 and pp 390–391. Therefore, Vala has become the goddess of self-destructive warfare in Blake's time, even as Luvah-Orc has become a dying god whose manifestation is the Napoleonic wars. The association of mystery-religion, war, and a repressed or perverted sexuality is a constant one throughout Blake's work.

59:11–16   These lines are used again, in rearranged form, in *Jerusalem* 40. The changes and rearrangement are fully noted in Margoliouth, p 123. Here they describe the fall of Urthona, and the appearance in the post-Deluge world of his Spectre, and of Enitharmon.

59:21 ff   For the most part, the story of the jealousy of Los, and his subsequent binding of Orc, follows the pattern set by *The Book of Urizen*. One major difference is in 60:3–5, where Golgonooza, the New Jerusalem which is a city of art, and its principal gate, Luban, are first mentioned by Blake. Golgonooza as a name may have reference to Golconda, or to Golgotha or New Golgotha. Luban is sometimes an alternate name for Mount Ararat, where Noah's ark came to rest; this is appropriate for a gate of salvation. Cf Sloss and Wallis, I, p 25 n. The Lake of Udan Adan is the watery illusion of our present world.

61:10   Storgous Appetite   "Storgous" is derived by Blake from a Greek word for parental love. Blake later uses that word, Storge, as another name for the river Arnon, which one must cross on the passage from the natural to the imaginative body. Storgous appetite is therefore the possessive paternal love manifested in some of the *Songs of Innocence*, and must be left behind if the poet is to free himself from the context of nature.

63:11   Dranthon   Evidently Blake intended to develop this road as a symbol of repentant nature, judging by this reference, and the later, deleted line in Night VII, where Los began "to hew the cavern'd rocks of Dranthon into forms of beauty".

63:24 – 65:12   Lament of Urizen   This piercing and self-deceiving ululation represents Urizen's resolve to function in a completely fallen world, and is ironically akin to Satan's meditation on Mount Niphates in *Paradise Lost* IV. The lament is uttered in the "dens of Urthona" or fallen world as shaped by Los. Urizen and his host fell into those dens in *A Song of Liberty* 16, where Urizen's fall is associated with the fall of Milton's Satan.

Erdman, pp 343–444, finds historical allegory in this lament, connecting it to the madness of George III early in 1801. The value of this identification comes in the reading of Night VI, where Urizen's exploration of his dens becomes, on the historical level, a survey of the horrors of George's kingdom.

On the level of a more internalized allegory, Urizen's sorrow is very like the dangerous nostalgia of Milton's Satan, and demonstrates the inadequacy of an "enlightened" intellect, however powerful, when struggling to overcome the disabilities of a fallen nature. The errors of reason, in Urizen's lament, are exposed as failures in vision. Like Satan on Niphates, Urizen accuses himself of everlasting guilt, and finds no means of recovery but a vow to negative action. To "Explore these dens" is to conduct a kind of empiric survey of our natural condition that can lead only to natural religion, in which the selfhood seeks to defend its deathly isolation against the "deep pulsation" of struggling Orc. The final line of Urizen's lament is its most ironic, for it is at once a Blakean motto and a plain statement of Urizen's resolve to protect his kind of "Thought" from a "love" he now considers hellish.

64:27   This startling echo of "The Tyger" helps confirm that poem's dramatic speaker as being Urizenic in his self-delusion.

Night the Sixth

The pattern of Night VI is provided by Satan's journey through Chaos in *Paradise Lost* II, with the important difference that Satan seeks an escape from Hell, while Urizen surveys what have become *his* dens, and then becomes god of this world. Blake is developing more fully the similar process of *The Book of Urizen* VIII.

67:5 ff   Urizen's encounter with his daughters recalls Satan's with his daughter, Sin, and son, Death, in *Paradise Lost* II. There is also about the daughters a suggestion of the three Norns and of the Daniades, while Urizen's curses recall Tiriel's and possibly Lear's. Together, the three daughters represent human nature within the limits of Urizen's world and, more directly, the fallen body. They drive Urizen back because they worship Tharmas as god of their chaos. The daughters are named in Night VII. Here, they are presented as symbolic appearances.

The first may represent the loins, as her sorrowing repetition of urn-filling and pouring suggests the self-renewing cycle of sexuality. The whore named Mystery in Revelation 17:5 (on Blake's reading) has Babylon written on her forehead; presumably Urizen's oldest daughter is Mystery or Babylon, mother of harlots.

The second, clad ironically in blue, the Virgin Mary's color, is evidently the natural heart, deceptive yet central, drawing to herself the waters of nature, once the blood of Albion.

The youngest, clad in green, is possibly the "vegetated mind", sundering the waters into the four fallen senses of man. Together, the three match the three maidens of Blake's "The Golden Net".

68:5 ff   Urizen's lamentation and curse closely follow the Lord's curse on the daughters of Zion, in the closing verses of Isaiah 3. Line 26 echoes *Visions of the Daughters of Albion*, line 23.

68:28 – 69:22   The confusions of fallen Tharmas are shown in his offer of a suicide pact, for his inducement and threat are the same.

69:23 – 71:14   In these grim passages Urizen explores the ruined South, once his quarter in the eternal world. What he encounters therefore are aberrations of the mind, manifesting themselves in the distorted forms of nature.

71:15–24   The East, now empty, was the heart of Eternity, domain of Luvah. The fall of Urizen into this vacuity imitates Satan's troubles in navigating Chaos, *Paradise Lost* II 931–940. Where Satan reacts by fighting his way on, Urizen entrenches and creates his religion.

71:35   The "iron pen" of Urizen is from Jeremiah 17:1. Blake had used it earlier in "Samson", and uses it later in *The Everlasting Gospel*.

72:13   The Vortex, developed more fully in *Milton*, is a mental system or way of looking at things. Here, a Newtonian way of observing the chaos of Urizenic space.

72:22 – 73:15   Urizen's resolution is crucial for everything that follows in the poem. As his name indicates, he is a setter of bounds, a Devourer of the Prolific. But, in this ruined world, he can find no bounds, not even an up and down (72:28–29). In his Notes on the *Illustrations to Dante*, Blake comments on a diagram of Hell's Circles that "In Equivocal Worlds Up & Down are Equivocal". This is Urizen's desperate discovery; his solution, heroic but mistaken, is in the arbitrariness of 73:14: "Here will I fix my foot & here rebuild". There is a compass image in "fix my foot", as though Blake were thinking of his own frontispiece to *Europe*, "The Ancient of Days Striking the First Circle of the Earth".

73:31 ff   The Web of Religion recapitulates *The Book of Urizen* VIII.

74:12 ff   The Four Caverns are the four ruined worlds of the Zoas, and now the four quarters of our world. Blake's directional symbolism receives a full commentary in Percival, pp 15–17. Urizen's true home is the South, but in the Fall he inhabits the

West, for he is now the setting rather than the noonday sun. Urthona is still in the North, his true place, but the North has become a solid darkness, toward which Urizen is drawn. Orc burns in the South, but his true quarter is the East of perpetual new birth. Tharmas should have his domain in the West, but has been displaced by Urizen. The East is left for him, but he wanders instead, searching for Enion.

74:30 ff   Here the world of Urthona is seen at its worst, a deadness imprisoning Orc. I suspect that lines 33-34 contain a savage judgment of Augustan poetry and art, the imagination wasted down "into the doleful vales".

75:1-24   The alliance of Tharmas and the Spectre of Urthona, against Urizen and in defense of Orc, is the first positive turn in the poem's action, and a presage of the poem's double crisis in Nights VII and VIII. Tharmas and the Spectre have been allied before, against Los, so as to force him into limiting chaos. But that was a more negative working together. Now Tharmas shows a desire for survival, to the extent that the energy of Orc seems worth protecting against the arts of Urizen. The Spectre of Urthona, though he is everything close to home that impedes the imagination from its full expression, nevertheless senses that his own existence is threatened by the limiting quest of Urizen. In the stricter terms of Blake's myth, the birth of Orc is the first appearance of Luvah in the postlapsarian world. With this appearance, all the Zoas are present again, though each is self-divided and flawed. However dimly, the Spectre of Urthona and Tharmas now long for apocalypse, and instinctively they associate Orc with that hope.

Erdman (p 347) relates the Spectre of Urthona's appearance here to that of Spenser's Talus. Lines 75:19-22, as Erdman notes, are repeated (with changes) from a canceled plate of *America*, where the fifty-two armies represented the militia of the fifty-two counties of England and Wales. Here the fifty-two armies are Urthona's, and may therefore represent the weeks as divisions of fallen time (cf. Damon, p 378). The four sons of Urizen also standing against him may be the elements, as Damon suggests.

75:25-34   To Urizen's vision, Tharmas is disorganized space, and the Spectre of Urthona is disordered time. Opposing them, Urizen like a giant Spider first takes refuge in his Web of Religion, and then vibrates it against his adversaries. The Web is the fallen world as seen through the natural veil of Mystery. As finite vision, the Web menaces Tharmas; as predestined time, it menaces the Spectre. At the opening of Night VII Tharmas and the Spectre will flee from the Web for fear of being absorbed into it.

Night the Seventh [a]

The two sections of Night VII are alternate ways of preparing for the blackness of Night VIII and the liberation of Night IX. I find it difficult to believe that VII [a] is not the later in composition, but in this belief I am guided only by what I take to be internal evidence. Whichever was later, our understanding of the poem's total design can only benefit by a study of both versions. I do not think it accurate (or fair to the poem) to read Nights VII [a] and VII [b] as being an intentional sequence, in that order. VII [a] in at least some respects is an imaginative advance on VII [b].

77:1-4   The Spectre of Urthona and Tharmas flee from Urizen's Web because it shows them what they most fear: the will's loss of control over actuality when the actual is viewed through the veil of religious mystery. In that vision of confinement, the loss of potential in Tharmas is magnified, and the Spectre's dread of individual death is assimilated into a pattern of fate.

77:5-19   This brilliant passage is an epitome of Urizen's ruined world, with energies balked and exasperated by enforced passivity. Urizen's horses ought to be drawing the chariot of the unfallen mind; his lions and tygers, reduced to wrath, ought to be at the work of creation. The apocalyptic plow and harrow, and the bulls of Luvah, emblems of divine renewal, are lost in a prolific chaos lacking outline. But, even in confronting this sublime waste, Urizen is envious of Orc, with the murderous envy of age for youth, restraint for desire.

77:20 ff   Orc's situation here is the same as in the Preludium to *America*.

78:1–15   The Tree of Mystery and its growth refer back to *The Book of Ahania* III and ultimately to *Paradise Lost* IX 1101–1110 and to the Mystery of Revelation 17:5. The envy of Urizen blights Los also, for in this newly emergent and ruined world Los has not yet achieved a genuine identity apart from Urizen. The entanglement of the book of iron in the stems of Mystery suggests an association of war and religion.

78:17–41   Urizen confronting the bound Orc suggests Zeus defied by the tortured Prometheus, and also the probing Satan of *Paradise Regained,* seeking certainty as to Christ's identity. Like Zeus, Urizen seeks an alliance with a dangerous rebel; like Satan, he needs to know if his adversary is a savior, in this case a reappearance of Luvah. The crucial question is in line 41, which twists Urizen's true fear, that Orc's torments may be an atonement for the other fallen Eternals.

79:25–37   The three daughters of Urizen, whom he cursed while exploring his dens, arise now as involuntary nourishers of the bound Orc. As they represent the confined physical powers of man, their bread is an emblem of frustration, and is properly associated with the fruit of Mystery in Night VIII.

80:1–26   Urizen's sermon is one of Blake's fiercest ironies, mounting in Blake's concealed prophetic anger until the climax of lines 9–21, at once an attack upon Malthus and upon all eighteenth-century versions of social benevolence. These lines look back to "The Human Abstract", and beyond that to the prophetic passion for social justice in Amos and his successors. In Blake's own historical context they are a visionary parody of a speech by Pitt in Parliament in November 1800, in which that Urizenic minister insisted that any increase in the consumption of bread by the poor was to be avoided. See the discussion in Erdman, pp 341–342.

80:27–42   This speech of dramatic self-revelation establishes Orc's identity as Luvah reborn into time, and indicates also the process by which restrained desire becomes a shadow of itself, and comes to govern the unwilling. The Promethean Orc suffers the fate of Phaethon, and the stolen light becomes a fire for consuming, not for growth. The ironic "triumph . . . the Godlike State" brought about by the joint plot of Luvah and Urizen against the wholeness of Man, is now seen as the source of "the Orc cycle", the organic aging of passion into restraint. The cycle's emblem is the "Serpent body" organized by Orc in the passage that follows. For the political allegory of the Serpent here, see Erdman, p 348.

80:46   This parody of the communion ritual identifies Orc's cycle with a religion of Mystery, an identification confirmed in 81:4.

81:23 – 82:14   Los laments the consequences of cyclic decay both in Enitharmon's outer form and in her wavering affections toward him. He apprehends, for the first time in a fully fallen world, the separateness from him of a Female Will.

82:15 – 83:33   This scene of temptation, "beneath the Tree of Mystery", is founded on the temptation of Eve by Satan in *Paradise Lost,* Book IX. The Shadow of Enitharmon is the residue of Enitharmon in a world utterly reduced to the level of physical nature; from being the numberless emanation or interior paramour of the poet's vision, she has become the numbered and measured form of fallen space. In more personal terms, she is the demonic parody of any poet's muse, and her love entraps the poet in a world of dearth. Her tempter, the Spectre of Urthona, is in this passage at his most "insane brutish deformd", the imagination trapped in a temporal will, unable to extricate itself from a crippling fear of futurity.

The Shadow's account of Albion's fall introduces a new element into the myth, when Urizen is spoken of as a son of Albion by Vala. Sonship is highly equivocal here; Urizen is "First born of Generation", which means that his first manifestation as an entirely separate being was due to Albion's embrace of Vala. That embrace, a fall through pity, was a forsaking of the activity of Eden for the passivity of Beulah; a movement of decay, from the inner to the outer world. By choosing the repose of Vala over the imaginative liberty that is Jerusalem, Albion begets the separation of Urizen that was so powerfully described at the opening of *The Book of Urizen*. As Beulah, with its relationship of male lover and beloved female, falls into Generation, where subject and object are separated into hostility, Albion beholds Vala as "a double form", male and female, subject and object absorbed into one another, an emblem of the "hermaphroditic" state of Ulro. Lamenting this dark vision, the Shadow of Enitharmon embraces the Spectre in the hope that he will punish Vala, and submit that temptress to the power of Orc.

84:1–42   The genuine difficulties of this finely complex speech are psychological rather than mythic. The Spectre knows that he is only a slave embracing a "lovely Delusion", but his desperation is absolute. He secretly dreads the possible consequences of a marriage of time and space, ruined creator and flawed creation, but he knows of no alternative. Fearing death, laboring under a nostalgia for the visionary past, he embraces the fallen world at its darkest, in the gamble that he views futurity through the Shadow of Enitharmon. But the coupling brings forth the "wonder horrible" of 85:7, to be revealed in Night VIII as a new and more dangerous form of Vala.

85:26–31   This is a central passage in the poem, for it heralds a contrary union to that of the Shadow of Enitharmon and the Spectre of Urthona. The Spectre's impulse toward Los is the first presage in the poem of an apocalyptic hope. Together now, and despite Enitharmon's flight from them, Los and the Spectre behold the Center opened, which means that a vision contrary to that of the vortex is now available. Eternity opens from the center outwards, as man ceases to see from the dwarfing end of vision. And together, Los and the Spectre labor to build the new Golgotha that is Blake's city of art. Though the building takes place in a largely ruined world, the twofold limit of Satan (opacity) and Adam (contraction) has been set, beyond which that world cannot fall.

87:13   The Limit of Translucence, where Los stands in doubt and trembling before succumbing to Enitharmon and the fruit of Mystery, is *the* point of crisis in the fallen world, for at this point the visionary either overcomes the limitations of nature, or else sinks back, exhausted with his failed effort. In Night V, the Limit of Translucence is associated with Luban and Luban appears to be a principal gate into Blake's New Jerusalem. The Limit of Translucence is the upper limit of Beulah, and from it the way leads either up and in to Eden, or down and out to Ulro, where Los now follows it. For a commentary on this difficult point in Blake's symbolism see Frye, pp 389–392, and pp 448–449 n 56.

87:15–29   Enitharmon, like Eve, has tasted first of the fruit, but her entreaty that Los eat is altogether unlike Eve's temptation of Adam. Enitharmon has learned the lesson of Romans 7:7–9, which Blake echoes here, in lines 17–18. But Los, to their mutual despair, learns the same lesson, and is condemned to the living death of the six thousand years of fallen human history.

87:30–39   The saving myth of *"Counterparts"* is the Spectre's consolation for Los, a gift from the day-laboring self to the afflicted imagination. The Spectre and Los can be saved because they are counterparts, and together they can form a creative will, an organizing form in the chaos of time. The labor of Los and his Spectre can effect counterparts for others, and this is Blake's statement of the purposes of his own art.

87:40–52   The reply of Los is to agree, and to extend the consolation to Enitharmon by invoking the greatest of counterparts, the redeeming Lamb of God or reborn Luvah, but this is a consolation that Enitharmon will not accept.

90:1–14   This eloquent and complex passage is the first in the poem that shows us a Los who is a mature visionary poet. His desire in lines 8–10 is that of Blake himself, and the fabrication of "embodied semblances" is the work of *The Four Zoas*. The vow "To form a world . . . To comfort Orc in his dire sufferings" is a poet's resolve to create a poem that will comfort the natural man by liberating him from his fallen condition. The consequence of the resolve is first seen in lines 13–14, where the fires of Urthona are rekindled, and in the following speech of Enitharmon (lines 15–24) where she is able, for a saving moment, to share the hopes of Los.

90:25–67 The labors of Los follow one pattern: to prepare for apocalypse by transforming fallen or Urizenic war into the intellectual combats of the eternal world. So he harvests the flames of Orc, gathering up again the energies of natural man so as to shape them for mental fight. To do this, he takes a stance (lines 32–34) and draws a circle of imagination that is the contrary to the sinister work of Urizen as the Ancient of Days, when he marked out the circles of fallen nature. The firm outline of imaginative creation is drawn (line 35), and then colored by Enitharmon, who in one temporal context may be Catherine Blake, helping her husband at his work.

Out of the ranks of war, Los rescues Rintrah and Palamabron first, tutelary spirits respectively of Hebrew prophecy or the "science of wrath" and of Greek wisdom or the "science of pity". In the general revival of hope, even the sickened instinct that is Tharmas can begin to expect the return of his lost potential, Enion. Finally, even Urizen is separated from his Spectrous form which survives however (line 60) to play a dark role in Night VIII. Thiriel, Urizen's oldest son, and the prime element of air, becomes the providential breath of compassion, Palamabron, while the renovated Urizen becomes the angry prophet who heralds revelation. This version of Night VII concludes with the moving realization of Los that the restored Urizen is once again his brother, and no longer his enemy.

Night the Eighth

In Night VIII Blake explores the prelude to apocalypse, the great winter of the world in 1804, when Albion seemed doomed to a final ruin, uneasily stirring in his sleep of death. The historical background of Night VIII is sketched in Erdman, pp 369–374. Blake's principal purpose in Night VIII is to integrate his contemporary political, social, and religious context, which he chooses to call Deism or Natural Religion, into the mythic structure of his poem. He accomplishes this integration by opposing a regenerated Los, who gathers up the scattered power of Urthona and Tharmas, to a culmination of error in a Satan of warfare and in Rahab, who is the Female Will incarnate, the mystery of State Religion hid in war, and so the final product of Urizen's delusions.

99:1–10 The saving remnant of Eternity, or Council of God, appeared earlier in Blake as the Eternals of *The Book of Urizen* and in Night I, when they assembled on Gilead or Snowdon. Meeting in the Human Form Divine of Jesus, they act now to assure that the sleeping Albion will contract no further past his Adamic limits. Hermon, a sacred mountain, is associated in Psalms 133:3 with a dwelling together in unity, and with eternal life.

99:11–14 The reference here is 2 Kings 4:35, the resurrection of the Shunammite's son.

99:15 – 100:25 The extraordinary transformation undergone by Los and Enitharmon, from the cruel children of the poem's start to these compassionate workers for salvation, is an epitome of the entire poem's progress. Cathedron (the name may play upon Catherine, or cathedral, or both) is set up in Luban, a gate of mercy in the city of art. Cathedron is based on the inversion of a demonic industrial image into an artifice of salvation, its looms being the natural means of generation, but so viewed as to be an emblem of overcoming the existent cycle *through* an apotheosis of cycle, or space becoming the mercy of a more human form. The furnaces of Los are a similar reversal of imagery, for they are now a creative emblem of time's swiftness as Eternity approaches.

101:1–29, 100 continued, 101:30–37 Urizen's bafflement is a skillful irony on Blake's part, for nothing in Urizen's theory of vision can account for the identity of Orc, Luvah, and the Lamb of God which he now beholds. The precious stones of the serpentine Orc identify him also with the Covering Cherub, or nature as a barrier to man's desires. Uveth, Urizen's third daughter, repeats her function from Night VI, and is associated also with the nameless female of the Preludium to *America*.

Urizen's armament is related to the artillery of Milton's Satan, *Paradise Lost* VI 484–766, and to British munitions of 1804 by Erdman, pp 369–371. Urizen's battle takes the unintended turn of compelling error to appear in its ultimate form: Satan or the selfhood proper. Frye, p 125, gives the best account of this Satan's hermaphroditic state, in which the male and female contraries of Experience are compounded into the self-absorbed state of Ulro or solipsism, for which the hermaphrodite is an apt emblem. The ultimate social form of such solipsism is the war of England against France, which prompts Blake to the apocalyptic yearnings of Night VIII.

101:39–40   These lines clearly and movingly refer to Blake's own works of art, and their prophetic mission "against the stirring battle". That mission's necessity is demonstrated in the passage following (down to 102:13) which stresses the inner ravages of war and "Secret religion".

102:14 – 103:31   Urizen's epiphany as war-god is followed here by a lament of Vala for the dying-god aspect of Luvah, at once her son and lover. The lament of Vala is self-deluding, for in 103:3 she identifies Orc as Luvah's slayer and not as his reborn form. Her lust for vengeance, the sadistic cruelty of the fallen heart, becomes another root of Urizenic religion, and so intensifies mystery that the furious Urizen is tangled still further in his own net. The process is another instance of the times drawing near their end.

103:32 – 104:10   In dialectical recoil from the religion of Vala and Urizen, the poem moves to its work of salvation, the forming of "a Universal female form", Jerusalem, the emanation of Albion, who is the contrary of Vala.

113:1–37   This brilliant but overly condensed passage is in the style of *Jerusalem*. The Spindles of Tirzah and Rahab perform the work of inscrutable fate or necessity, and are thus contrary to the Looms of Enitharmon and the Forges of Los. The Mills of Satan and Beelzeboul grind down creation and accuse mankind of powerlessness to affect its fate. The Arnon River, boundary between Israel and Moab, is like the Red Sea, a passage from spiritual death into life (see Numbers 21:14 for Blake's source). Og and Sihon, who aid Satan, were giant kings who opposed the Israelites in their wanderings. Associated with them here are Entuthon Benithon and Udan Adan, forest of error and lake of Urizenic delusion. Rahab, the whore of Joshua 2, is again Blake's version of the Whore of Babylon in Revelations. For commentary on Blake's Rahab, see Frye, pp 299–303, and Bloom, pp 259–261. In this passage, she is the Druid priestess, who with her flint knife attempts to destroy the Lamb of God.

105:1–30   This is a full epiphany of Rahab, associating her with the accusation of sin against the Lamb of God. "The heights of Amalek" may contain a reference to Numbers 24:20, where Amalek is spoken of as the first of the nations, but which shall perish forever in the judgment. The Synagogue of Satan is from Revelation 3:9. In line 7 the reference is to Isaiah 53:12 as fulfilled in Mark 15:28. Vala in lines 13–15, like Rahab, derives from the woman of Revelation 17:3–6. The twelve forms of the judging Sanhedrim are a foreboding of the Sons of Albion in *Jerusalem*.

105:31–53   Blake used this song again in *Jerusalem* 67:44 – 68:9, where it is sung by Tirzah. The song's theme is jealous and murderous possessiveness masking itself as maternal benevolence. The river Kanah and the tribal region of Manasseh were in the Northern Kingdom of Israel, of which Tirzah was the capital. The symbolism here is akin to that of "To Tirzah", the late addition to *Songs of Experience*. Ebal is a mount of cursing in Deuteronomy 27:13. For Noah, Malah, Hoglah, Milcah, and Tirzah Blake drew on the texts, Numbers 26:33 and 27:8, where these five daughters of Zelophehad cause Moses to legislate for a separate female inheritance. For Blake, they become the five fallen senses, seeking to appropriate the human reality for themselves. Shechem in 105:52 is the mountain city, rather than Dinah's lover in Genesis.

105:55   There may be an allusion here to the cruel text of Judges 20:6.

106:14   There is an identity suggested here between Los and Joseph of Arimathea, as Damon (p 386) notes.

113 continued:45 – 116:2   Though it is weighed down by a catalogue of names (the generations of Los) and by a reference to the difficult myth of Satan and Palamabron (fully developed in the Bard's Song of *Milton*) this remains a great and climactic passage. It testifies to a dramatically matured Los, the patient apocalyptic worker of Jerusalem. Of the catalogue of names (115:1–10), omitting those occurring previously, Ananton never occurs again. Ozoth is a guardian of vision in *Milton* 28:29–39. Ohana, Mydon, Ellayol, Natho, Gon, and Harhath are not mentioned elsewhere, but presumably have a similar function. Only Ochim, of the remaining male names, has no other mention, but he is flanked by fallen beings, and so is presumably one himself. Of the daughters first mentioned here, Elythiria is named by Damon as the element of Air, and Enanto of Earth (p 388). Moab and Midian are drawn from Numbers 25; Adah and Zillah are wives of Lamech, Genesis 4:19. Naamah, in Genesis 4:22, is Tubal Cain's sister. Caina is Blake's own invention; Tamar figures in Genesis 38. For a good attempt at interpreting the function of this catalogue, see Damon, pp 387–388. *Jerusalem* 62:8–12 is another version of the female part of the catalogue.

For the Satan-Palamabron episode, see the comment on *Milton*, p 824. In 115:42–50, Blake gives his first listing of the Seven Eyes of God, employed later in *Milton* 13:14–27, and in *Jerusalem* 55:31–33. For a commentary on them see Frye, pp 360–371. The biblical sources may be: Lucifer, Isaiah 14:12; Molech, 1 Kings 11:7; Elohim, the early chapters of Genesis; Shaddai, parts of Genesis and most of Job; Pachad, the "fear" of Genesis 31:53.

106:18 – 107:20   In this magnificent sequence, Urizen degenerates into his final form before the Last Judgment, and becomes a supine Satanic figure, like those of Milton (*Paradise Lost* X 511–515) and Dante. His pity for the Shadowy Female is the culminating mental error of Deism, representing its exaltation of the supposed virtues of the natural heart. In this, his ultimate fall, Urizen becomes absorbed into "the indefinite lust" of the degenerated Orc. On the level of psychic cartography, the superego has been reduced to chaos, and societal and cultural restraint has succumbed to all the forces it sought to contain. For a historical reading, see Erdman, p 373.

107:21–38   Here the effects of Urizen's petrification are felt by Tharmas and Urthona-Los. Lines 31–32 are crucial, for they show Los prepared against the coming crisis.

108:1 – 110:28   These chants of Ahania and Enion are further presages of the approaching end, for the outcast wanderers of the poem's beginning return now, to sum up the situation and, Cassandra-like, to prophesy against it. Ahania's chant is fundamentally a lament, for her visions cannot take man out of a fallen world, as the mind's eye is confined within the circumference the mind's weariness has established. But Enion's voice pierces beyond despair, for the lost delight of instinctual unity still knows its own potential. Her chant gathers together the scattered emblems of human unity, and sees the possibility of an event that will transform natural repetition into human renewal.

109:21 contains a reference to Matthew 25:6.

111:1–24, end of the Eighth Night   The triumph of Rahab brings the close of the Eighth Night down to Blake's own moment in time. Here Rahab is the English State Church who offers up the children of English liberty on the altar of the war god into whom Urizen has degenerated. She is also the Whore of Revelation, but temporizes in her iniquity as she considers the fates of Enion and Ahania. Her wavering, as "She commund with Orc in secret", is Blake's very subtle allegorization of the rise of Deism in England, and its spiritual infiltration of the State Church. The critical elements in Deism unite with Orc against Mystery, but the constructive elements in Deism form another Mystery from the ashes of Revealed religion. Babylon comes again in a new Infancy, a demonic Second Coming of the Yeatsian kind. This manifestation of Antichrist is, to Blake, a portent of the desired end, and the Last Judgment comes close upon it.

Night the Ninth Being The Last Judgment

The Ninth Night is the most poetically successful section of *The Four Zoas*, and taken by itself is one of Blake's most remarkable achievements. It is the longest of the Nights, and the simplest to follow as far as narrative continuity is concerned. For apocalyptic pattern, Blake drew detailed hints from Revelation and general ones from *Northern Antiquities* II Fable 32, "Of the Twilight of the Gods", but the design of the Ninth Night is very much his own.

117:1–9   The mortal terror of Los causes him to attack the universe of death at its vital centers, the sun that was once Urizen and the moon that was Luvah. The crucified body of the cosmic man is not to be restored directly by so natural an impulse (hence "fibrous Strength" in line 7 and "dark roots" in line 8) but the process of judgment has begun, for the Los of this instinctual action is still imaginative man.

117:14   See Revelation 6:14.

117:19–23   See Revelation 6:9–10.

117:24–118:6   This fiercely pathetic passage is one of Blake's great vitalizings of a conceptual allegory, here the overthrow of the notions of what Frye (p 298) calls "yardstick space" and "clock-time".

119:17   The Holy City here is Golgonooza, but the City of Art is now the expanded center of an awakened universe. The whole passage, lines 16–23, seems a likely source for Yeats's "Byzantium".

119:26   The rock of Albion's nightmare is in Urizen's abandoned realm, the South, where Orc was tormented in Nights VI and VII.

119:33–120:3   This passage, with variations, appears again as *Jerusalem* 19:1–14.

120:28   See Psalms 148:7.

120:49–51   The "line of blood" is the "line of scarlet thread" of Joshua 2:18, taken by orthodox tradition as a sign of Christ's sacrifice, which made of Rahab a type of the Church. Here, the Rahab of the churches is redeemed of her error, the claim to exclusiveness of salvation. Line 50 links the passage to the second line of "To Spring", which opened Blake's first work.

121:33–39   The revival and subsequent "death" of Ahania is one of the genuinely difficult moments in Night IX. For somewhat varying interpretations see Damon, p 392; Frye, p 307; Margoliouth, p 148; Bloom, p 271. As Ahania was cast out because Urizen feared his own affections, her premature reunion with him may represent the self-deception of the mind (Blake's included) in an apocalyptic age; the awakened mind becomes too joyful at being able to take pleasure in itself again, and this too-easy gratification cannot survive the intensities of what must be a complex struggle of self-integration. The passage following, 122:12–15, associates Ahania's fate with the exemplary pattern of self-sacrifice practised by the emanations in the state of Eden.

122:18   See Revelation 21:2–10.

123:20   See Revelation 1:7.

123:27–28   See Luke 21:27, and Revelation 1:7.

123:34–35   See Revelation 4:2–4.

123:38   Margoliouth (p 148) takes "Life's" as a plural, and so an equivalent of the Zoas, which ruins the fine ethical force of this passage. The "four Wonders" and "Four Starry Universes" are the Zoas (as based on Revelation 4:6) but perhaps Blake's point in line 38 is that the Zoas, in Eternity, are definitive of Life, hence the possessive in "Life's".

124:1–5   This is one of the deliberate crises in Blake's vision, and must have some reference to the lessons learned from an age of political revolution.

124:6–29   This brilliant fantasia of Urizen-as-Plowman begins the work of restoration. Apocalypse in its positive sense of re-creation begins in the human mind, where the repentant Urizen has reclaimed his proper station. The physical universe had become a hell, and must therefore be plowed up by the mind. The ultimate source of 124:17–22 is Isaiah 2:4, but the authentic passion against war is very much Blake's own. The "dens of death" of line 21 are the dens of Urthona or the Ulro, the underground world that must be reclaimed first before the Generation of Luvah and the Beulah of Tharmas can be redeemed.

124:30–125:21   The plowing is followed here by the sowing of what will be the final human harvest. Probably Blake's ultimate source is Matthew 13:3–8.

125:22–35   Urizen's first work being done, he is allowed a momentary rest, which means that Ahania can be and is revived. Line 25 echoes Revelation 14:15. Line 26 identifies Ahania with the harvest goddess.

125:36–39   The revived Albion attempts to enter the condition of fire, Eden, but he must remain in the Millenium of Beulah, for the end is not yet.

126:1–129:11   The restoration of Luvah and Vala   As Orc, the natural man, is now consumed, his eternal forms of Luvah and Vala now reappear, the children of Experience or Generation. They return to their rightful "place of seed", and so generative sexuality is raised to a more fulfilled level. 126:9–17 is a fine summary of the entire poem. 126:34 is an echo of Aeneid VII 808–809, presumably by way of Pope's Essay on Criticism 172–173. What follows is an exaltation of the experiential world, climaxing in the great pastoral chant of 128:4–16. There are significant echoes of The Book of Thel throughout this passage, particularly in 126:18–26 and 127:7–27. The redeemed Vala is the triumphant contrary to poor Thel, for Vala encounters a state of Generation seen through the power of a humanized mind.

129:12–131:19   The restoration of Tharmas and Enion   The next step in Apocalypse is the recovery of Beulah or Innocence, the instinctual realm of Tharmas the Shepherd. Tharmas has become the Old Man of the Sea, a voice of Chaos, in which form the revived Vala first sees and hears him. In his repentance he calms his seas (129:27) and so Enion is able to return. 129:34 probably echoes Song of Solomon 2:14, though "clefts of the rock" is a widely recurrent phrase in the Bible. The children of 130:4 and following are the return into Blake's poetry of the lost children of the Songs of Innocence.

131:22–132:1   The harvest is now ready, and Urizen moves to be the joyful reaper. His cry of "Times are Ended" echoes Revelation 10:6, and his role fulfills Revelation 14:14–16. The restored human affections perceive the great light of a mental clearing, as the clouds that were Urizen's vanish or are absorbed into the seas of Tharmas, and then depart with the floods, for Tharmas too has been reintegrated.

132:2–17   Urizen dismantles his star world in order to perform his work as harvester. I do not find any particular astrological references in this passage, but see Margoliouth, p 151, and the general discussion of astrological symbolism in Percival, pp 145–161. The rising of Enion is the special joy attendant upon the resurrection of the body, in Blake's large sense of the body as being all of the soul that sense can perceive. Enion's "gentle light" is the pleasure of the body at recognizing its own restored integrity.

132:18–39   This marvelous passage centers on the humanization of nature, for "Tharmas humanizing" means that all instinctual life wakens into a human awareness. The "Golden Moth" of line 21 may be a butterfly, as in the association of moth, butterfly, and a last judgment in "Auguries of Innocence". The difficult line 39 associates the transcended natural world with the tomb of Jesus, and identifies Jesus with Los, who now becomes Urthona again.

133:1–30   The head of Albion was at the zenith, the South, domain of Urizen, and now the place of festival in the apocalypse. The shuddering at the feast is caused by the still separate existence of the emanations, for eternal existence has not yet been re-achieved. The speech of the Eternal is a summary of Blake's epic theme of fall and redemption. The marginal reference to Ephesians 3:10 is not without irony. The text is: "To the intent that now unto the principalities and powers in heavenly places might be known by the church the manifold wisdom of God", and Blake's motto to *The Four Zoas* is Ephesians 6:12: "For we wrestle not against flesh and blood, but against principalities, against powers, against the rulers of the darkness of this world, against spiritual wickedness in high places". For Blake the English State Church is the antagonist, and the lesson it must learn is "That Man subsists by Brotherhood & Universal Love", else the apocalypse will mean not renovation but destruction.

The Beulah reference in line 30 is appropriate, since Eden has not yet been regained, and Beulah is the garden of the South.

133:31 – 135:33   The Winnowing   The apocalyptic process of threshing and winnowing is Blake's invention, and has no precedent in Revelation. Margoliouth (p 152) suggests the preaching of John the Baptist as source (Matthew 3:12). 134:1, in a striking variation, is used by Yeats as an epigraph to his Crossways group of lyrics. The Mystery Tharmas condemns is again the Harlot of Revelation 17, or "Religion hid in war", as Blake most suggestively named Rahab. 134:18–23 are repeated from *America*, the lines taking on a new power in this larger context. The "New Song" of 134:31 echoes Revelation 5:9. Sotha, in *Africa*, is associated with a code of war; the African is now presumably free of the code. From 135:4 on, this becomes one of Blake's most exuberant and moving passages.

135:34 – 137:4   The Vintage   The source for the wine presses of Luvah is Revelation 14:17–19. The passage is complex, for the vintage is at once a Dionysiac orgy of rebirth, the European war of Blake's age, and the self-immolation of the natural man. 136:3 is reworked in *Milton* 27. There, as here, war is associated with sado-masochistic perversion, and with the naturalizing of imaginative energy.

137:5–17   The restored Urthona is still the crippled smith of several mythic traditions, for his imaginative powers are not wholly healed. But he is supported by Tharmas the shepherd, who is again the human integral, our instinct for wholeness. The work of the emanations is to weave the eternal garments for the exhausted sons and daughters of Luvah, who are now made into the passions of Eden in 137:18–43.

137:34 – 138:19   We are back now in the residue of Blake's contemporary world, suffering the final afflictions of natural tyranny, which culminate in the Ulro-terror of 138:11–15. Between the last "Winter in the night of Time" in 138:19, and the new Sun of line 20, the world turns inside out, and reality at last appears.

138:20 to the end   Blake's vision here attains one of its triumphs. The "Science" of the last line is the total knowledge attainable by an organized imaginative consciousness through the experience of the liberating perspective of art. The entire passage emphasizes an expansion of perception and closes on the appropriate figure of the absolute artist Urthona having replaced the temporal prophet Los. If there is a personal reference, Blake may have been hinting that he hoped to put the prophetic burden aside with the completion of his epic. But as *The Four Zoas* was never properly completed in the Blakean sense, the burden of the valley of vision was transferred to *Milton* and *Jerusalem*.

[Alternate Version of Night VII]

Night the Seventh [b]

95:15 – 96:18   The Triumph of Urizen   Whatever the precise historical background may be here (see Erdman, pp 298–302 and Margoliouth, p 140, for conflicting views) any useful reading of Urizen's triumph as Work Master must start with "the Babylonian England of 1799", in Erdman's phrase. As with Night VII [a], Blake is preoccupied by a vision of Experience, the life of bondage in the fallen world of dehumanized men. But here the vision is sometimes involved as much in history as in personal myth; a passage like 95:15–17 is a direct attack on Blake's England.

95:20   There is evidently an ironic identification here of Urizen with the God of Psalm 104.

95:31 – 96:18   Urizen's Temple is dedicated to the selfish virtues of the natural heart, symbolized here by the sun of Los, which became the heart of Urizen in *The Book of Urizen*. The association between temple prostitution and a religion of chastity is one of Blake's pervasive ironies.

96:19–27   The Los of this passage is certainly evolving away from the primitive war bard of earlier Nights, but he is not yet the Los of Night VII [a], which is one of many indications that VII [a] might be later in composition than VII [b]. For an opposing view, see Margoliouth, p 144.

96:28 – 97:17   The chaotic desperation of Tharmas here is a powerful expression of justified but confused rage, the rage of innocence and unity at a torturing division that evades understanding. Tharmas continues to seek the "Crystal form" of his unfallen reality, as embodied in his lost emanation, Enion. But his only way of questing is to threaten a still more dreadful chaos than is already existent.

97:28 – 98:6   In this Urizenic world of ruin, where Los is only an inchoate rhapsode, though no longer destructive, and Tharmas a self-contradictory turbulence, Enitharmon is a fearful mother of warfare, whose better impulses are drowned out by her fear. One of Blake's most ironic biblical allusions is made in 98:2–6, with reference to Isaiah 21:8–12. 97:34 may contain a grim allusion to Psalm 37:31.

98:7–31   The trees and beasts of a Urizenic universe also learn "the selfish virtues of the natural heart", and participate in the warfare that is nature's own strife. The Prester Serpent is probably a reference to the priest-tyrant, Prester John, a good representative of the Urizenic Archpriest who inculcates the seven deadly virtues that are the "seven Diseases of Man". The religion of war is culminated in the tormenting vibrations of Urizen's Web, a veil of delusion that constitutes any religiously apprehended reality.

91 (SECOND PORTION)   This account of Orc's uprising is recapitulated from the Preludium to *America*. But the shadowy daughter of Urthona there has become a sinister Vortex figure, a whirlpool of illusion that threatens to draw in and drown human existence. In lines 14–15 she is identified as Vala, and is classed with the Harlot of Revelation.

The rising of Orc as "the glorious King" (line 30) is related by Erdman (pp 290–300) to the British campaign against revolutionary France in 1799. Margoliouth (p 140) regards the war against Orc as an allegory of war as such, or of the general European War of 1792–1802. Either way, the historical allegory leads up to the brilliant lines (92:12–15) in which the Roman soldiers at the Crucifixion are seen as identical with the members of the British Parliament in the autumn of 1799, "voting the crucifixion of Luvah at home and abroad", as Erdman (p 300) puts it. In a larger context, this torment of the natural man is evident throughout the "death of Six thousand years" of fallen human history.

The passage 91:11 – 93:19 is repeated in *Jerusalem* 65:6–55, with changes as analyzed by Margoliouth, pp 140–141. This passage, climaxing in the song of "the demons of the deep", gives a vision of industrial tyranny (see Erdman, pp 312–313) and of war's destructiveness, allying them under the image of Vala as Urizen's harlot, nature depraved by repression into the aberrations of domestic exploitation and foreign aggression.

93:24–32   The consequence is the perversion of Orc into Mystery's Serpent, at once the assimilation of revolt to tyranny and the passing of revived human desire into the frustrations of State Religion. Erdman, p 291, traces the historical allegory here of the rise of Napoleon. Wounded nature, or Vala as torn by Orc, is the residue of Blake's Europe in the winter of 1799–1800, as a century turns over in its torment.

93:36 – 94:36   The despair of Tharmas here is the anguish of betrayed Innocence, for Blake's myth moves toward its deliberate nadir in Night VIII. Seeing the rent Vala, Tharmas desperately hopes this is a form of his lost Enion, but is again condemned to despair.

94:37 – 95:14   What Vala sees are the emblems of a Urizenic world moving toward a consolidation of error. She explores Urizen's completely realized dens, and the clouds given off by her journeyings rise as "doubt", in the special Blakean sense of self-contradiction, or the denial of creative vision. Against this killing doubt the daughters of Beulah, Blake's muses, protect the imaginative life by naming the aggregate form of error as Satan, the death wish, or selfhood incarnate.

III. POETICAL SKETCHES

Blake's early poems, as collected in *Poetical Sketches*, are the culminating works of the literary period that can be said to begin with the death of Pope in 1744 and conveniently to end with the first major poems of Blake and Wordsworth in 1789. This period, usefully named the "age of sensibility" or of "the sublime", shows a development toward a new kind of lyric poem, frequently a transformed version of the "great ode" of Cowley and Dryden, and sometimes a more radical invention, an English attempt to duplicate the Hebrew prophetic poem. *Poetical Sketches* can be viewed as a workshop of Blake's developing imaginative ambitions, as he both follows the poets of sensibility in their imitations of Spenser, Shakespeare, and Milton, and goes beyond them in venturing more strenuously on the Hebraic sublime. Sensibility is a heightened mode of consciousness, and Blake follows his age in seeking a new *inwardness* in these early poems, which shadow forth the most original aspect of his later mythology, the psychological doctrine of coexistent "states-of-being", each with its distinctive imagery, and each productive of distinct imaginative forms. Perhaps the unique freshness of *Poetical Sketches* can be epitomized by noting Blake's first achievements in the greatest of his projects: to give definite form to the strong workings of imagination that produced the cloudy sublime images of the earlier poets of sensibility. In the best poems of Blake's youth the sublime feelings of poets like Gray and Collins find a radiant adequacy of visionary outline, the clarity of the rising prophet increasingly certain of his vocation.

The Poems to the Seasons: In this fourfold invocation to the human seasons, the young Blake transvalues the customary mode of personification, and anticipates the humanizing addresses to natural phenomena of Wordsworth and his followers, as abstract personifications merge into the figures of a new myth.

TO SPRING

This is, in a sense, Blake's first song of Innocence, and hails as bridegroom for the "love-sick land" of England a figure who will appear finally as Tharmas, the shepherd of the unsundered pastoral state of human childhood. There is a generic echo of the imagery of returning Spring in the Song of Songs, and perhaps of Thomson's *Seasons*. The haunting phrase, "the clear windows of the morning", is deliberately recalled and assimilated to the "window" of Joshua 2:18 in *The Four Zoas*, Night IX, 1.

TO SUMMER

This youth with "ruddy limbs and flourishing hair" is the ancestor of Blake's Orc, rebel against outworn conventions. Like the "rich haired youth of Morn" of William Collins' "Ode on the Poetical Character", Blake's Summer is associated with the sun and with a poetical revival, "laurel wreaths against the sultry heat". Summer also suggests "the ruddy limbs and flaming hair" of a later fragment by Blake. See p 465.

TO AUTUMN

Lowery (pp 85–86) noted the echo of Milton's conclusion to *Lycidas* in the closing lines of this poem. Unique among Blake's seasons, Autumn is allowed to sing his own song, and one might indulge fancy by finding in this a hint of the figure of Los, the mature Poetic Genius of Blake's cosmos. The speaker of the opening lines of *To Autumn* is the earth; the Miltonic conclusion is a promise of the "golden load" of Blake's lyricism still to come.

TO WINTER

Here the speaker of the poem is an individual, for the first time in this series. The season disregards his address, and is then spoken of in the third person, again for the first time in Blake's grouping. Frye (p 182) finds a premonition of Urizen, the limiter of man's desires, in Winter. Some of the poem's imagistic details come from Thomson's *Winter*, as Lowery notes (pp 152–155). Mount Hecla is an Icelandic volcano, so that the poem's conclusion acquires a particular menace in its final image of the demonic being, pent in its destructive home. Blake may be remembering "Hecla flaming through a waste of snow" in Thomson's *Winter*, line 888.

TO THE EVENING STAR

Lowery (pp 100–102) notes the influence of Spenser's "Epithalamion", lines 285–295. The poem suggests the pastoral vision of Blake's state of Innocence.

TO MORNING

This enigmatic little poem seems ironic in its echoes of Spenser's "Epithalamion" and Psalms 6, and hints at Blake's later embodiments of the Female Will. The virgin huntress Diana is assimilated here to Aurora, even as Apollo and Cupid are compounded in Blake's "How sweet I roam'd from field to field".

FAIR ELENOR

This Gothic exercise is evidently derived from several ballads in Percy's *Reliques*. Damon (p 255) notes the similarity of lines 34–36 to Psalm 91:5–6.

SONG "How sweet I roam'd . . ."

The tradition is that Blake was not yet fourteen when he wrote this song. It is a clear anticipation of the symbolism of a later poem, "The Golden Net", and can be called his first Song of Experience. The prince of love is identified with or assumes the role of the sun god, and his entrapping deceptions are made one with the natural world.

MAD SONG

This is the best and most Blakean poem in *Poetical Sketches*, and is essentially an intellectual satire. The Elizabethan "mad song" and its imitations are Blake's starting point, but his radical innovation is to make the song a satire upon both its willfully deranged singer and the mental world that singer seeks to escape. The singer's heaven is the self-paved vault of materialist concepts of space; his earth is conditioned by a self-torturing and mechanical concept of time, which he seeks to escape by crowding after night. There is a first appearance of Blake's grim satiric humor in the twisted use of the word "comforts" in line 22.

TO THE MUSES

A gentler satire than the "Mad Song", this subtly defiant and confident "lament" employs the diction of Augustan minor poetry (itself debased from Milton) to mock that poetry's lack of inspiration. The burden is the same as Gray's "Stanzas to Mr. Bentley" or the close of Collins' "Ode on the Poetical Character", but the tone is very different from the plangency of the poets of sensibility. The poem seems to echo Milton's "Comus", lines 98 f. and Psalms 19:4–5.

GWIN, KING OF NORWAY

Though not an effective poem, this ballad is interesting as Blake's first handling of the theme of political and social revolt. Lowery (pp 165–167 and 177–183) traces the influence of *Hardyknute* in Percy's *Reliques,* and also of Ossian and of Chatterton's "Godred Crovan". Erdman (pp 19–20) points out possible references to the revolutionary situation in America. One may note the curiously inconclusive final stanzas as being characteristic of Blake's later poems of rebellion.

AN IMITATION OF SPEN[S]ER

This is clearly a conscious experiment, and not just an unsuccessful attempt to write Spenserian stanzas. The second stanza is another expression of Blake's lasting dislike of Augustan poetry.

❧

KING EDWARD THE THIRD

There is a full study of this fragment by Erdman (pp 60-80), who demonstrates Blake's ironic intent in seeming to praise an English invasion of France as a crusade for "Liberty". The implied satire may be directed partly at Thomson's "Liberty", where liberty is a somewhat commercial virtue, as it is in the second scene of Blake's play. The main theme of the play, in Erdman's interpretation, is the impending harvest of bloodshed and plagues that will be the necessary consequence of Edward's imperialistic campaign. Blake's irony is most evident in the excessively brutal war song that ends the fragment.

❧

PROLOGUE, INTENDED FOR . . . KING EDWARD THE FOURTH

This spirited fragment makes explicit the moral judgments of Blake's *King Edward the Third.* Its topical reference, as Erdman notes (p 15), is to the American War.

PROLOGUE TO KING JOHN

Blake's experiments in cadenced prose, presumably after Ossian (though the biblical element is already heard), led to his later successes with the fourteener, but are not very impressive in their own right. Erdman (p 14) indicates the relation of this piece to other English protests against the waging of the American War.

A WAR SONG TO ENGLISHMEN

This apparently bloodthirsty paean is replete with deliberate confusions, and is clearly ironic in its intent. The unresolved contradiction between the "Angel of Fate" in the first stanza and "a holy God" in the second; the absurd emotional confusion throughout the second stanza; the hyperbole throughout; all these testify to Blake's talent for parody, and presage aspects of a later poem like *The Book of Urizen.*

THE COUCH OF DEATH

Erdman (p 75) reads this as a coda to the *Edward the Third* fragment, showing victims of the Black Death, suffering for the sins of their rulers. The influences of Chatterton and of biblical diction are again evident.

CONTEMPLATION

This rather inconclusive prose poem is vaguely Miltonic or biblical, and seems to reject the pastoral escape offered by Contemplation. The attitude expressed as to mortality is hardly characteristic of Blake.

SAMSON.

The sense of proportion and command of drama in this piece redeem it from its grandiloquence, and largely justify its sustained Miltonic imitation. The "iron pens" of the invocation, derived from Job 19:24 and Jeremiah 17:1, appear later in Blake as the iron pen or pens of Urizen in *The Four Zoas* VI 71:35, 41, and as the very different Iron pen of Jesus in page 52, line 13, of *The Everlasting Gospel*.

❧

[Further Sketches]

"then She bore Pale desire . . ."

This prose fragment has in it many elements that found more lucid expression in Blake's later poetry. It is so slapdash that it suggests the most rapid kind of composition, and needs to be read as only a curiosity, granting us a privileged entry into its young creator's flow of consciousness. Erdman (pp 48–50) reads it "as a document of response to the American Revolution", which on one of its many bewildering levels it may well be.

"Woe cried the muse . . ."

This fragment of cadenced prose is an overwrought instance of Sensibility run wild, and another example of the youthful Blake playfully experimenting in that borderland where the sublime joins the morbid.

Index of
Titles and First Lines

Page numbers that are preceded by "t" "c" refer to Textual Notes and Commentary respectively. Variant titles or first lines that appear in the Textual Notes only will have "t" references only.